Everyman, I will go with thee,
and be thy guide

THE EVERYMAN
LIBRARY

The Everyman Library was founded by J. M. Dent in 1906. He chose the name Everyman because he wanted to make available the best books ever written in every field to the greatest number of people at the cheapest possible price. He began with Boswell's 'Life of Johnson'; his one-thousandth title was Aristotle's 'Metaphysics', by which time sales exceeded forty million.

Today Everyman paperbacks remain true to J. M. Dent's aims and high standards, with a wide range of titles at affordable prices in editions which address the needs of today's readers. Each new text is reset to give a clear, elegant page and to incorporate the latest thinking and scholarship. Each book carries the pilgrim logo, the character in 'Everyman', a medieval morality play, a proud link between Everyman past and present.

Charles Dickens

DOMBEY AND SON

Edited by
VALERIE PURTON

Series Editor
MICHAEL SLATER
University of London

with illustrations by
H. K. BROWNE (Phiz)

EVERYMAN
J. M. DENT · LONDON
CHARLES E. TUTTLE
VERMONT

Introduction and other critical apparatus
© J. M. Dent 1997

Dombey and Son first published
in Everyman in 1907
This text first published in Everyman in 1997

J. M. Dent
Orion Publishing Group
Orion House,
5 Upper St Martin's Lane, London WC2H 9EA
and
Charles E. Tuttle Co. Inc.
28 South Main Street, Rutland,
Vermont 05701, USA

Typeset in Sabon by CentraCet Limited, Cambridge
Printed in Great Britain by
The Guernsey Press Co. Ltd, Guernsey, C.I.

British Library Cataloguing-in-Publication Data
is available upon request.

ISBN 0 460 87684 8

CONTENTS

ILLUSTRATIONS

NOTE ON THE AUTHOR, EDITOR
AND SERIES EDITOR

CHARLES DICKENS was born at Portsea, Portsmouth, on 7 February 1812. In 1817 the Dickens family settled in Chatham. These years, 1817–22, were the happiest of Dickens's early life. They came to an end when his father, John Dickens, was recalled to London and the family began its slow slide towards bankruptcy. In February 1824, John Dickens was imprisoned for debt in the Marshalsea and the twelve-year-old Charles was sent to work in a run-down warehouse off the Strand, labelling and packaging bottles of boot blacking. His sense of humiliation and thwarted ambition was acute, and the experience (which may have lasted a year) proved traumatic. His father was discharged from prison later in 1824, under the Insolvent Debtors' Act, and some months later Charles was removed from the warehouse and sent to school. In 1827 he was articled as a solicitor's clerk in Gray's Inn. He learned shorthand, became a reporter at Doctors' Commons and later a skilled reporter of Parliamentary debates. In the years from 1833 to 1836 he wrote a number of short stories and sketches which were published in various journals and collected in *Sketches by Boz* (1836), accompanied by illustrations by George Cruikshank. In April of the same year he married Catherine Hogarth, daughter of a newspaper editor. *Pickwick Papers*, begun in that year as a monthly instalment publication, soon became a great popular success. It was followed by *Oliver Twist* in 1837, *Nicholas Nickleby* in 1838–9 and (in his weekly periodical *Master Humphrey's Clock*) *The Old Curiosity Shop* and *Barnaby Rudge*, 1841. He made a triumphant tour of the United States in 1842 and in the same year published a critical account of his experience there in *American Notes*.

A Christmas Carol was published in 1843 and inaugurated the highly successful series of Christmas Books in the 1840s. *Martin Chuzzlewit* appeared in 1843–4 and *Dombey and Son* in 1846–8. *David Copperfield* was completed in 1850, the year in which he founded his own weekly magazine *Household Words*, a characteristically vivacious and imaginative family miscellany, which carried the serialised *Hard Times* in 1854. In that novel, as in its predecessor *Bleak House* (1852–3) and its successor *Little Dorrit* (1855–7), Dickens anatomised and satirised the social and political condition of England. In 1858 he and his wife formally separated and he moved to his new home at Gad's Hill in Kent. In the same year he began his career as a professional public reader of his work, a strenuous enterprise that proved highly lucrative as well as seriously harmful to his health. *A Tale of Two Cities* appeared in 1859 and *Great Expectations* in 1860–1, both serialised in Dickens's successor to *Household Words*, *All the Year Round*. His last novel to be completed in the old twenty-number monthly format was *Our Mutual Friend* (1864–5). In the winter of 1867–8 he toured the United States with his readings. In 1870 he began *The Mystery of Edwin Drood*, but had completed only half of it when he suffered a stroke at Gad's Hill and died on 9 June.

VALERIE PURTON was educated at Cambridge University and then studied and taught at the Universities of Alberta and East Anglia. She teaches for the Open University and for Anglia Polytechnic University at City College, Norwich. She is the author of *A Coleridge Chronology* and, with Christopher Sturman, of *Poems by Two Brothers* (on poetry by Tennyson's father and uncle), and of articles on Dickens in journals such as *ARIEL* and *The Dickensian*.

MICHAEL SLATER is Professor of Victorian Literature at Birkbeck College, University of London, and a former Editor of *The Dickensian*. He is the author of *Dickens and Women* (1983) and has published a number of other books and articles relating to Dickens, as well as editions of *The Christmas Books* and *Nicholas Nickleby*. He is also Editor of the *Dent Uniform Edition of Dickens' Journalism*, of which two volumes have been published: *Sketches by Boz and Other Early Papers 1833–9* (1994) and *'The Amusements of the People' and Other Papers: Reports, Essays and Reviews 1834–51* (1996).

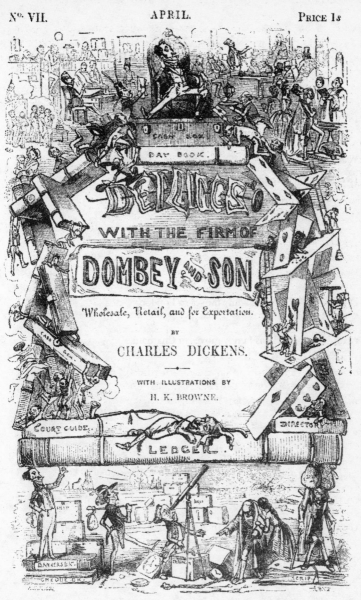

No. VII.   APRIL.   PRICE 1s

DEALINGS WITH THE FIRM OF DOMBEY AND SON

Wholesale, Retail, and for Exportation.

BY

CHARLES DICKENS.

WITH ILLUSTRATIONS BY
H. K. BROWNE.

LONDON: BRADBURY & EVANS, WHITEFRIARS.

AGENTS:—J. MENZIES, EDINBURGH; J. MACLEOD, GLASGOW; J. M'GLASHAN, DUBLIN.

CHRONOLOGY OF DICKENS'S LIFE

Year	Age	Life
1812		Born in Portsea, Portsmouth, 7 February
1815	3	Dickens family moves to London
1817	5	Dickens family moves to Chatham
1822	10	Dickens family (now 6 children) moves to London
1824	12	Works at Warren's Blacking. John Dickens (father) in Marshalsea Debtors Prison for a few months

CHRONOLOGY OF HIS TIMES

Year	Literary Context	Historical Events
1812	Byron, *Childe Harold* I & II	1811–20 Regency of George, Prince of Wales 1812–14 War with America
1813	Austen, *Pride and Prejudice* Southey becomes Poet Laureate	
1814	Austen, *Mansfield Park* Scott, *Waverley* Wordsworth, *The Excursion*	
1815		Battle of Waterloo
1816	Austen, *Emma*	Spa Fields Riots
1817	Keats, *Poems* Austen dies	
1818	Mary Shelley, *Frankenstein*	
1819	Byron, *Don Juan* I & II Eliot born Whitman born	Peterloo Massacre The Six Acts
1820	Keats, *Lamia . . . and other Poems* Flaubert born	Accession of George IV Cato Street Conspiracy
1821	Keats dies De Quincey, *Confessions . . . Opium Eater*	Greek War of Liberation Napoleon dies
1822	Byron, *Vision of Judgement* Shelley dies	Suicide of Castlereagh
1823	Grimm Brothers, *German Popular Stories* (illus. G. Cruikshank)	Agricultural unrest
1824	Byron dies	

Year	Age	Life
1825	13	Starts school at Wellington House Academy
1827	15	Becomes junior clerk in solicitor's office
1829	17	Becomes a freelance reporter at Doctors' Commons
1830	18	Acquires British Museum Reader's Card
1831	19	Falls in love with Maria Beadnell. Appointed Parliamentary reporter
1833	21	First story written and published, 'A Dinner at Poplar Walk'
1834	22	Joins reporting staff of the *Morning Chronicle*
1835	23	Engaged to Catherine Hogarth
1836	24	*Sketches by Boz* published. Marries Catherine. *Pickwick Papers* begun. Resigns from the *Morning Chronicle*
1837	25	*Pickwick Papers* completed. Mary Hogarth (sister-in-law) dies. Becomes editor of *Bentley's Miscellany*
1838	26	*Oliver Twist* [dates given for publication of the novels refer to completion of their serialisation]
1839	27	*Nicholas Nickleby*
1840	28	Dickens begins *Master Humphrey's Clock*
1841	29	*The Old Curiosity Shop*; *Barnaby Rudge*
1842	30	Visits America (Jan.–Jun.). *American Notes*

Year	Literary Context	Historical Events
1825	Hazlitt, *Spirit of the Age*	Stockton–Darlington railway opens
1826	Disraeli, *Vivian Gray*	
1827	Blake dies	University of London founded
1828	Meredith born D. G. Rossetti born	Catholic Emancipation Act
1829	Jerrold, *Black-ey'd Susan*	
1830	Tennyson, *Poems Chiefly Lyrical*	Accession of William IV July Revolution in France Wellington's ministry falls
1831		First cholera epidemic
1832	Carroll born Walter Scott dies	First Reform Bill
1833	Carlyle, *Sartor Resartus* Newman, *Tracts for the Times*	Abolition of slavery throughout British Empire State funding of schools begins
1834	Bulwer-Lytton, *Last Days of Pompeii* Coleridge and Lamb die	Tolpuddle Martyrs New Poor Law
1837	Carlyle, *The French Revolution* Lockhart, *Life of Scott*	Accession of Victoria
1838		Anti-Corn Law League Chartist petitions published London–Birmingham railway opens
1839	Carlyle, *Chartism*	First Factory Inspectors' Report
1840	Hardy born	Penny postage introduced
1841	Carlyle, *Heroes and Hero-Worship*	Peel becomes Prime Minister
1842	Tennyson, *Poems* Browning, *Dramatic Lyrics* Macaulay, *Lays of Ancient Rome*	Chartist riots Report on Sanitary Conditions of Labouring Population

Year	Age	Life
1843	31	*A Christmas Carol*
1844	32	Dickens and family stay in Genoa. *Martin Chuzzlewit*; *The Chimes*
1845	33	Dickens family returns from Italy. *The Cricket on the Hearth*
1846	34	Dickens family reside in Lausanne, Switzerland (June–Nov.). *Pictures from Italy*. Brief editorship of *Daily News*. *The Battle of Life*
1847	35	Dickens family, having moved to Paris in Nov. 1846, continued to reside there until March. Sets up Urania Cottage with Miss Burdett-Coutts.
1848	36	*Dombey and Son*; *The Haunted Man*
1850	38	Begins his weekly miscellany, *Household Words*. *David Copperfield*
1851	39	John Dickens dies
1853	41	*Bleak House*. Tours Italy and Switzerland with Wilkie Collins

Year	Literary Context	Historical Events
1843	Carlyle, *Past and Present* Ruskin, *Modern Painters* I Wordsworth made Poet Laureate	
1844	Disraeli, *Coningsby* Elizabeth Barrett, *Poems*	Rochdale Pioneers found Co-operative Store
1845	Disraeli, *Sybil*	Railway speculation Newman joins Catholic Church
1846		Repeal of Corn Laws
1847	Emily Brontë, *Wuthering Heights* Charlotte Brontë, *Jane Eyre* Tennyson, *The Princess*	
1848	Emily Brontë dies Thackeray, *Vanity Fair*	European Revolutions Chartist movement collapses after mass meeting in London Cholera epidemic Pre-Raphaelite Brotherhood founded
1849	Thackeray, *Pendennis* Ruskin, *Seven Lamps of Architecture*	
1850	Tennyson, *In Memoriam* Wordsworth dies Wordsworth, *The Prelude* Kingsley, *Alton Locke*	Pope appoints Catholic bishops to England
1851	Ruskin, *The Stones of Venice* Melville, *Moby-Dick*	Great Exhibition Gold discovered in New South Wales J. M. W. Turner dies
1852	Stowe, *Uncle Tom's Cabin* Thackeray, *Henry Esmond*	Napoleon III becomes Emperor of France Duke of Wellington dies
1853	Charlotte Brontë, *Villette*	Indian Civil Service open to competition

Year	Literary Context	Historical Events
1854	Thoreau, *Walden*	Crimean War begins Newspaper Stamp Duty abolished Palmerston's premiership begins
1855	Browning, *Men and Women* Gaskell, *North and South* Kingsley, *Westward Ho!* Charlotte Brontë dies	
1856	Elizabeth Barrett Browning, *Aurora Leigh* Wilde and Shaw born	End of Crimean War
1857	Trollope, *Barchester Towers* Flaubert, *Madame Bovary*	Indian Mutiny
1858	Eliot, *Scenes of Clerical Life*	Indian Viceroyalty established
1859	Tennyson, *Idylls of the King* Darwin, *Origin of Species* Mill, *On Liberty* Smiles, *Self-Help*	Rise of Fenianism in Ireland
1860	Collins, *The Woman in White* Eliot, *The Mill on the Floss*	
1861	Reade, *The Cloister and the Hearth*	Death of Prince Consort American Civil War begins
1862	Mill, *Utilitarianism*	
1863	Kingsley, *Water Babies* Eliot, *Romola* Thackeray dies	Gettysburg Address Slavery abolished in USA
1864	Newman, *Apologia Pro Vita Sua*	
1865	Carroll, *Alice's Adventures in Wonderland* Arnold, *Essays in Criticism*	President Lincoln assassinated Palmerston dies American Civil War ends
1866	Swinburne, *Poems and Ballads* Dostoyevsky, *Crime and Punishment*	First Barnardo Home Atlantic Cable laid
1867	Marx, *Das Kapital*	Disraeli's Reform Bill
1868	Browning, *The Ring and the Book* Collins, *The Moonstone*	Gladstone becomes Prime Minister

Year   *Age*   *Life*

Year	Literary Context	Historical Events
1869	Arnold, *Culture and Anarchy* Blackmore, *Lorna Doone*	Suez Canal opens Mill advocates emancipation of women
1870	D. G. Rossetti, *Poems*	Education Act: free public education in Board Schools Franco-Prussian War Fall of Napoleon III

SERIES EDITOR'S PREFACE

The Everyman Dickens is intended to be the most complete edition of Dickens's works so far published. It will be the first paperback edition to provide thorough and coherent coverage of all his shorter fiction as well as his extensive non-fictional writings. In addition to the fifteen novels and the five *Christmas Books*, the Everyman Dickens will include all the Christmas stories from *Household Words* and *All the Year Round*, all other short fiction, the two travel books and all Dickens's writings for children. Four volumes in the series will present the first-ever annotated edition of *Sketches by Boz*, *The Uncommercial Traveller* and other journalism, a substantial amount of which has been out of print for many years. Each volume will contain all the earliest illustrations to the work or works featured in it, kindly supplied by The Dickens House, and all Dickens's prefaces.

Every volume will be edited by a specialist in Victorian literature who has a particular interest in the work he or she is dealing with. Where appropriate, explanatory notes will be supplemented by a historical appendix giving more general background information on the text in question.

Throughout the series references to Dickens's published letters will be given as either 'Pilgrim' or 'Nonesuch'. 'Pilgrim' means *The Pilgrim Edition of the Letters of Charles Dickens*, eds M. House, G. Storey, K. Tillotson *et al.* (1965–in progress), and 'Nonesuch' means *The Letters of Charles Dickens*, ed. W. Dexter, 3 vols (1938), part of the Nonesuch Press Edition of Dickens's Works.

MICHAEL SLATER

INTRODUCTION

DOMBEY AND SON is generally regarded as the first novel of
Dickens's maturity. If *Martin Chuzzlewit*, finished two years earlier,
is a transitional novel, then that transition – from, at one extreme,
the picaresque improvisation of *The Pickwick Papers* to, at the
other, the grand design of *Our Mutual Friend* – has been made in
Dombey. It is also the novel in which Dickens's social concerns
develop, as Kathleen Tillotson noted, so that 'a pervasive unease
about contemporary society takes the place of an intermittent
concern about specific social wrongs' (*Novels of the 1840s* [1954],
p. 157). That 'pervasive unease' is revealed not only in Dickens's
overt attack on the workings of capitalist society, exemplified in his
surtitle, 'Dealings with the Firm of Dombey', but also in his
treatment of the underlying value system which produced such a
society: the 'separate spheres' of public and private, head and heart,
embodied in the figures of Mr Dombey and Florence. Today's
readers are bound to see this in terms of gender: Dickens's critique
is ultimately directed towards the dominance of male values over
female ones. For readers approaching the millennium, Miss Tox's
words (in the original ending to Chapter 16) have proved both
serious and prophetic: 'To think ... that Dombey and Son should
be a Daughter after all!' In the novel's title itself, then, meaning is
concealed yet revealed.

'No other novel', says Peter Ackroyd, 'is so intimately bound up
with the circumstances and texture of Dickens's life at the time of
its writing' (*Dickens* [1993], p. 106). A brief account of how the
novel was produced and received, and of its significance in the life
of its author, may suggest some broad avenues to re-reading.

For *Dombey*, Dickens planned not only the overall structure
(including for the first time making an immediate decision on the
title), but also the whole writing process. After a two-year break
following the qualified commercial success of *Chuzzlewit*, he was
more than ready to begin another major work. John Forster records
that as early as March 1846 Dickens had talked of producing a
'new book in shilling numbers', which 'was to do with Pride what

its predecessor had done with Selfishness' (*The Life of Charles Dickens*, Book VI, Chapter 2). This approach, with its hint of a caricatured Humour figure at the centre, suggests the influence of Ben Jonson, and Dickens had indeed acted in *Every Man in His Humour* in the autumn of 1845. The original idea was as structured as were the author's geographical movements during its execution: Lausanne, Paris, London; a three-act structure that moved from sin through suffering to repentance. Yet against the fixity of this design there is the fluidity of contemporaneity, as the novel followed the rapid development of English society in the 1840s.

Dickens's early and late novels, as has often been noted, chart the move from the separated parochial England of the eighteenth century to the complexly interconnected society of the nineteenth century. *Dombey and Son* stands at the midpoint, pulled by conflicting forces: carefully planned though it is, it remains a deeply ambiguous work. It is the first great novel of that supreme agent for interconnection, the railway, and is both written and set in the years of the Railway Boom. Specific railway lines and journeys can be traced (as indeed they can in Hardy's *Jude the Obscure*, forty years later, which charts another epoch of social and spiritual transformation). Staggs's Gardens is demolished in the redevelopment of the Camden Town slums as a result of the extension of the Great Eastern Railway. Major Bagstock and Mr Dombey go by train to Birmingham, on the line from Euston opened in 1838. Carker ignores the railway timetable and is killed by the 4 a.m. express racing through Paddock Wood in Kent. When the omniscient narrator calls, in Chapter 47, for a 'good spirit' to take the roofs off the hidden dens of vice and poverty in the city, therefore, he has already provided one answer – the railway itself, a great destroyer certainly, but also a great cleanser. Such ambiguity about a central image suggests a deeper ambiguity in the novel's conception, which seems to be linked to its place in Dickens's own life.

Dombey and Son proved to be a watershed in Dickens's career in two important ways. It was during its composition that he conceived the idea of the Public Readings, which were to occupy – and probably shorten – the final years of his life. It was also during its composition that he wrote the autobiographical fragment which he sent to Forster, and in which he confronted for the first time the blacking factory episode in his childhood. *Dombey and Son* obviously gave him access to his own experience much more directly than the earlier works, and this, I would argue, is largely because of his intense identification with all three central figures. Here, more painfully than anywhere else, Dickens confronts and tries to reconcile the divisions in his own nature. There is from the beginning a protectiveness in his attitude towards Mr Dombey, the character whose personality and value system the plot itself ruthlessly exposes and destroys. Forster notes his 'nervous dread of caricature in the face of his merchant-hero' (*op.cit.*, Book VI, Chapter 2). The projected Humour figure becomes a potentially tragic one. This cold, hard, prosperous man is one of several characters (Bounderby and Headstone are others) upon whom, in the later novels, Dickens rings fantastic changes on his own life story and whom he makes bear the guilt for his own ever-increasing success. At the same time, Mr Dombey allows him to explore his simultaneous awareness of failure and isolation. Dickens's own passionate 'marriage' to his audience is transformed in Dombey into the nightmare opposite he dreaded: the coldness of rejection by the public. There is a poignant anticipation in Dombey's response to Edith's rebellion of events in Dickens's own private life eleven years later: 'Do you know who I am, madam? Do you know what I represent? . . . People to say that Mr Dombey – Mr Dombey! – was separated from his wife! . . . You're absurd!' (p. 633).

Early in the novel Dombey is shown projecting his own vulnerability on to his baby son: '. . . he wiped blinding tears from his eyes as he [paced up and down his room] . . . and often said . . . "Poor little fellow!" . . . he pitied himself through the child' (p. 20). It is in exploring this psychological identification of adult with child, in creating the inner life of Little Paul and in setting himself the strangely modernist task of presenting the child's dying exclusively through the child's eyes, that Dickens seems to have been enabled to make a connection between his own adult and child selves – a connection which bypasses the easy route of sentimentality. F. R. Leavis has shown how sharply observed is Paul's assertive, Dombey-like and not at all idealised character (*Dickens the Novelist* [1970], p. 15). Indeed, Dickens's original plan was to keep Paul alive until he was nine and to show him too 'using' Florence (see Appendix, p. 889 below). While composing the Mrs Pipchin chapters, he wrote earnestly to Forster, seeming to conceive the idea of autobiography in the act of writing:

> I hope you will like Mrs Pipchin's establishment. It is from the life, and I was there – I don't suppose I was eight years old. . . . Shall I leave you my life in MS., when I die? There are some things in it that would touch you very much. . . . [Forster, *op. cit.*, Book VI, Chapter 2]

Thus he approaches circuitously the most painful part of his childhood: he had, as he must have been aware, moved into lodgings at the house of Mrs Roylance, Mrs Pipchin's original, not at eight years old, but at twelve, when his father had been sent to the Marshalsea Prison and he himself had just begun work at Warren's Blacking. It was only after regaining access to his own childhood through the writing of *Dombey and Son* that Dickens could begin the novel more generally recognised as triumphantly autobiographical, *David Copperfield*.

Paul is close to his creator not only in being, as Dickens has been, a sickly child kept indoors, but also in his love for his elder sister. Florence owes a great deal to Dickens's sister Fanny, who protected Charles as Florence does Paul. However, in real life it was Charles, not Fanny, who was neglected. It was Fanny who seemed destined for a glittering career (as a singer), while Charles wasted his life in the factory. When Fanny was presented with the Royal Academy Silver Medal, Dickens wrote in the autobiographical fragment he showed to Forster:

> ... the tears ran down my face. I felt as if my heart were rent. I prayed, when I went to bed that night, to be lifted out of the humiliation and neglect in which I was. I never had suffered so much before. [Forster, *op. cit.*, Book I, Chapter 2]

Dickens penned these words while tracing the neglect of the fictional Florence and while watching Fanny herself die of consumption: in fiction he reverses the fates of the sickly boy and the beautiful girl. Florence's immolation thus achieves a particular intensity, while her characterisation remains necessarily vague. Her experience, as well as Paul's and Mr Dombey's, is filled with the surreal intensity of her creator's remembered life; it is this triple identification which is new and rare and which gives the book its particular power.

Florence also touches on Dickens's immediate concern in embodying a link which fascinated and roused him, and his age, between the innocent heroine and the 'Fallen Woman'. During the writing of the second half of the novel, Dickens was working with Miss Angela Burdett-Coutts on Urania Cottage, her 'Home for Fallen Women'. The very name 'Urania' marks his instinct to dissolve the rigid opposition between Madonna and Magdalen which characterised Victorian culture. 'Urania' is an epithet for Venus, but also means 'celestial': thus Dickens establishes a link between the gutter and the heavens. In *Dombey*, there is a powerful example of this collapsing of opposites. In the elopement scene in

Chapter 47, Florence literally steps in as surrogate for Edith. She accepts from her father the label Edith has earned, experiences physically the violence he feels towards his wife, and takes upon herself Edith's punishment, being effectively thrown out on the streets. Dickens sets up in his plot a rigid moral structure, which he then collapses in this ambiguous double figure of Woman as both innocent and guilty, child and temptress, daughter and lover.

Another opposition which blurs in the novel is that between author and reader. The whole novel enacts with its readers the 'melting' process which is its theme, and it was from *Dombey* that Dickens first conceived the idea of direct interaction with readers through Public Readings. The early numbers, as usual, were tried out on an audience of friends, and Dickens shortly afterwards wrote bashfully to Forster:

> I was thinking the other day that in these days of lecturings and readings a great deal of money might possibly be made (if it were not infra dig) by one's having readings of one's own books. [Forster, *op. cit.*, Book v, Chapter 5]

Perhaps social insecurity, perhaps prompted by the revived memories of the blacking factory, contributed to his embarrassment.

Fearing Forster's disapproval, he tries to pass this off as a joke: 'What do you say? Will you step to Dean Street . . . ? Or shall I take St James'?' It is appropriate then that the first reading of a major novel should have been 'The Story of Little Dombey', performed in St Martin's Hall in London on 10 June 1858, after six weeks in which Dickens had read abridgements of the Christmas Books. 'It is our greatest triumph everywhere,' he reported on the first tour of the provinces. Interaction with the audience closed both the traditional gap between author and reader, and the distinction between fact and fiction:

> If you saw the mothers, and fathers, and sisters, and brothers in mourning who invariably come to 'Little Dombey', and if you studied the wonderful expression of comfort and reliance with which they hang about me, as if I had been with them, all kindness and delicacy, at their own little death-bed, you would think it one of the strangest things in the world. [Pilgrim VIII, 676]

Until recently, *Dombey and Son* seemed a difficult book to read because of its apparently uncritical presentation of the Victorian heroine. Julian Moynahan found Florence unbearable: 'Remove her pall of quasi-religious mystery and Dombey's daughter is at best a sentimentalist lacking decent self-respect, at worst a masochist' (J. Gross and G. Pearson [eds], *Dickens and the Twentieth Century* [1962], p. 130). Moynahan's defensive brusqueness throughout the essay suggests a powerful response to the novel followed by an abrupt rejection of that response – very similar, in fact, to Mr Dombey's response to Florence. Moynahan also reads the novel in the light of later realist texts and ignores the theatrical mode through which Dickens habitually presents the human psyche. Florence is profitably read in terms, not of Thackeray's Amelia or George Eliot's Mirah, but of the great sentimental heroines whom Dickens encountered in his reading of Fielding and Goldsmith, but more importantly whom he saw in the popular plays of Mrs Inchbald, of Sheridan and of Victorian melodrama – who, in their turn, descend from Jacobean tragedy. (The obvious link with *King Lear* has been well discussed and is not quite to my purpose here, since Cordelia is in many ways a strong rival rather than a complement to her father's masculinity.) Florence has highly respectable literary ancestors, notably Perdita in Shakespeare's *A Winter's Tale* and Belvidera in Otway's *Venice Preserved*. Both reveal that sentimental/erotic 'melting' was not the prerogative of the Victorians. Here is the 'family reunion' in *A Winter's Tale* – an earlier configuration of jealous father, persecuted mother, ill-fated son and cruelly rejected daughter: '... their joy waded in tears. There was a casting up of eyes, holding up of hands, with countenances of such distraction ... [they] did – I would fain say bleed tears' (Act v, Sc. 2). In Otway's *Venice Preserved*, Belvidera's power over her father anticipates Florence's final victory:

> Fall at his feet, cling round his reverent knees,
> Speak to him with thy eyes, and with thy tears
> Melt his hard heart, and wake dead nature in him,
> Crush him in thy arms and torture him with thy softness.
>
> [Act IV, Sc. 4, ll. 532–5]

The unmistakable eroticism of such language invites a psychoanalytical reading – and this approach has become a popular one too for *Dombey and Son*. Beneath the configurations of tableaux like father striking daughter, or father kneeling to daughter, psychoanalytical reading suggests a power quite different from that of the realist novel – the power of fairy-tale to break our deepest taboos by transforming and thus disguising our deepest fantasies. The whole novel can be read in this way as being about the desire to return to what Jacques Lacan calls the 'Imaginary' stage of unlimited contact with the maternal breast – about the most primitive desire of all, in fact, the desire to be nurtured. It begins as a very literal drama about breast feeding and Paul's desperate need for nourishment ('Can't something temporary be done with a teapot?' is Mr Chick's immortal contribution). Motherhood and the maternal are then explored, from Polly Toodle's warm fecundity to Mrs Skewton's unnatural sterility. The last words of the latter to Edith are a reminder of that primal relationship: 'For I nursed you' (p. 563). The image of the breast is used as a conventional metaphor for love and virtue: 'And did that breast of Florence – Florence, so ingenuous and true ... hold any other secret?' (p. 241).

When Mr Dombey rejects Florence's love after Paul's death, the connotations become more complex: Dombey is refusing to be nurtured, but he is also guilty of something analogous to sexual aggression: 'Florence strove against the cruel wound in her breast, and tried to think of him whose hand had made it only with hope' (p. 311).

In the climactic scene after Edith's departure, the breast becomes literal once again. Florence's father physically abuses her by striking her and she, the victim rather than the assailant, feels shame: 'Then she knew – in a moment, for she shunned it instantly, that on her breast there was the darkening mark of an angry hand' (p. 654).

In the reconciliation scene, Dombey at last submits and allows himself to be nurtured at the breast he had spurned: 'Upon the breast that he had bruised, against the heart that he had almost broken, she laid his face, now covered with his hands, and said, sobbing: "Papa, love, I am a mother"' (p. 810). Femaleness thus overcomes and absorbs into itself the energies of masculinity. The official narrative voice acclaims this as a triumph, but the novel as a whole reads much more ambivalently.

Even if one does not 'buy into' a full psychoanalytical reading, it is obvious by any reading that Dombey and Son is centrally concerned with the rigid separation of male and female values in society. The energy of the narrative comes from the tension between the public values of a male-dominated mercantile society represented by Mr Dombey and the private values of love and female submissiveness represented by Florence. The whole book is therefore structured on the separation of two sets of value terms: hard, cold, male, linearity, money, the railway, on the one hand, and soft, warm, female, boundlessness, love, the sea, on the other. Mid-Victorian society is presented as privileging the first set of (masculine) values over the second. Polly Toodle is one of three transforming female figures in the novel (the third being Harriet Carker) who show how this hierarchy can be reversed. She teaches this to Florence by rewriting the narrative of her mother's death:

> '[She] died, never to be seen again by any one on earth, and was buried in the ground where the trees grow.'
> 'The cold ground?' said the child, shuddering again.
> 'No! the warm ground,' returned Polly, seizing her advantage, 'where the ugly little seeds turn into beautiful flowers, and into grass, and corn, and I don't know what all besides. Where good people turn into bright angels, and fly away to Heaven!' [p. 26]

After a long process of suffering, this reversal of values, in which the spiritual triumphs over the material, is made permanent and Dombey's Firm (and his firmness) are dissolved in Florence's tears.

There is, however, a paradox at the heart of such a resolution. Florence prevails, not by rewriting society's concept of femaleness but by writing it more strongly. She is more, not less, of a Victorian heroine by the end. Michael Slater puts this clearly in *Dickens and Women* (1983):

> Here is Dickens apparently preoccupied with women as the insulted and injured of mid-Victorian England yet voicing no general condemnation of prevailing patriarchal beliefs and attitudes; rather, he seems to see the social and sexual trials of his heroines as a sort of tragic nurture which serves to bring them to their full 'womanly' (or spiritually superior) potential. [p. 244]

The whole enterprise, in fact, lends itself to a deconstructive reading.

Dickens's early novels are characteristically structured by the setting up of rigid, unbending oppositions. *Oliver Twist* is predicated on what Steven Connor calls the 'unnegotiable antagonism' of good and evil (Introduction to Everyman *Oliver Twist* [1994], p. xxvii). *Martin Chuzzlewit* schematically divides the selfish from the generous. The later novels, too, are marked by strenuous efforts at separation. Dickens's world in *Dombey* begins confused and becomes more black and white as the novel progresses; the 'community of good' identifies itself and moves away from the community of evil. Thus Sol Gills, Walter, then Captain Cuttle, Mr Toots, Susan Nipper, eventually Polly Toodle and Miss Tox are gathered in a community loosely based on the Wooden Midshipman, with Florence as presiding deity. Rob the Grinder has his chance there, but opts instead for Mr Carker. Mrs MacStinger makes an attack, but is repulsed. Meanwhile, Carker, Major Bagstock and Mrs Skewton fawn on Mr Dombey. And yet these binary oppositions cannot hold: they collapse because one of the opposing terms, 'boundlessness', encompasses the others. The whole principle of rigid separation goes against the very 'boundlessness' which the novel is at pains to propound, via the central image of the sea. Dickens makes distinctions while preaching against making distinctions.

The conclusion as we have it officially perpetuates the polarisation of values, simply reversing the hierarchy so that female values are made to triumph over male. The underlying ambiguity of this resolution is evident, however, in two final paragraphs which Dickens cancelled at proof stage, having overwritten by seven lines: these were obviously intended to recall and to balance the conclusion to Chapter 16:

> And look upon us, angels of young children, with regards not quite estranged, when the swift river bears us to the ocean!

The Number plan explicitly reminds Dickens to 'End with the sea – carrying through what the waves were always saying, and the invisible country far away!' Accordingly, Chapter 62 originally ended:

> Never from the mighty sea may voices rise too late, to come between us and the unseen region on the other shore! Better, far better, that they whispered of that region in our childish ears, and the swift river hurried us away!

There are many negatives and self-contradictions in this passage. The 'voices' (of the waves) are said to 'come between' the living and the dead: however, the previous paragraph (and the whole novel) has shown that in fact their function is to collapse such distinctions, to help us to reach 'that blessed shore'. The last sentence strikes a particularly negative note and threatens to negate the earlier hope suggested by Paul's death: its implication can only be that Paul, had he lived, might have been one of those for whom the 'voices rise too late'. In its uncertainty and self-contradiction, this original conclusion reveals an alternative reading which the official narrative voice of the novel has strenuously suppressed: that Florence and the all-embracing love she represents have more to do with death than with life. Life is connected with the railway, with the new Staggs's Gardens, with the bustle of the City. The sea is connected with a whole series of deathbeds, all presided over by Florence, the siren who soothes people into accepting 'easeful death'. When Moynahan talks of Florence's 'pall of quasi-religious mystery', he is being wilfully unfair to Dickens's seriously held belief in the value of Christian meekness, but he does pick up the link between that sort of love and death: to go 'back to the womb' of boundless maternal love is to die. Thus meaning dissolves into ambiguity.

Even in the self-denyingly economical ending as we have it, there is ambiguity. 'What is money after all?' Paul had asked. Mr Dombey is shown to have found an answer by moving from the rigidity of monetary transaction to the openness of a love which knows no exchange rates. Yet his metaphors move with him: in his passion for his granddaughter, he 'hoards her in his heart'. Meanwhile, the mercantile values grow again, implausibly, in, of all people, Sol Gills: 'The whisper is that Mr Gills's money has begun to turn itself, and that it is turning itself over and over pretty briskly' (p. 839).

In the end, it is not the qualities themselves, but their rigid separation, the separation of the channelled 'male' energy represented by the railway and of the open 'female' energy represented by the sea, that seems to turn both sorts of energy into death: the railway destroys Carker, the sea carries off Paul. Away from the main narrative there are many recognitions of the need to collapse such rigid distinctions. These explorations are to be found, surprisingly, in exactly those sentimental and melodramatic parts which have traditionally been dismissed as unfortunate lapses of style. The Wooden Midshipman (himself as hard and unfeeling as any Dombey) presides over several fruitful variations on the theme of maleness. Sol Gills is mild and gentle and protected by others from knowledge of the hard truths of life; Captain Cuttle (a hard name and wearer of a 'hard glazed hat') tends Florence with 'womanly tenderness'; Mr Toots combines a deep voice with an impossibly flimsy name and a propensity for bursting into tears; Mr Toodle, though rough and gruff, leaves all important matters to Polly. In the same way, the 'comic grotesque' mode allows exploration of femaleness too. Polly Toodle is decisive and (as Mr Dombey discovers to his surprise) both maternal and the controller of her family's affairs. Susan Nipper shows her love through bouts of comic aggression. Negatively, Mrs Skewton invests her capital (her daughter's beauty) with all the acumen of the men on the Stock Exchange, while Mrs Pipchin is an ogre and a bully.

If the sentimental scenes suggest ways of dissolving the male/ female distinction through comedy, it is in the melodrama, until recently so summarily dismissed, that society's values are most radically attacked. Between the antipodes of Mr Dombey and Florence stand Carker and Edith. The latter combines adult sexuality, conveyed through the stylised eroticism of the melodramatic code, with 'masculine' pride and aggression. This is the result, it is made clear, of 'commodification', of being treated as a beautiful, marketable object. The former, equally committed to success in society's market, is 'soft', feline, accommodating, sexually enthralled by Edith, a parasite who thrives on Mr Dombey's hard masculinity. Whereas the sentimental scenes show how gender distinctions may be healthily dissolved, the melodramatic scenes show the emotional perversions which may result from an unhealthily 'commodified' society.

However, despite its social criticism, *Dombey and Son* is not ultimately, like *Bleak House*, a 'social novel': it has instead an intensity which comes from the unremitting focus on a central relationship. 'Tension between hero and heroine mounts highest in *Dombey and Son*,' says Alexander Welsh (*The City of Dickens* [1971], p. 188), and by that he does not mean what Lord Jeffery called fondly the 'little loves of Walter and Florence', but the passion between father and daughter. This is emphasised by Dickens at every stage and in a strange way is reminiscent of the relationship in a novel Dickens admired, Mary Shelley's *Frankenstein*, where another unwanted progeny demands its rights to a father's love. The flight across the world by Victor and the Monster has the same uncertainty about who is hunter and who victim, and the tale is read by feminist critics today as also dealing with the way in which female values could be rejected and thereby made monstrous in the nineteenth century (see, for example, Sandra Gilbert and Susan Gubar, *The Madwoman in the Attic* [1979], pp. 240–1).

There are many ways of reading *Dombey and Son*, depending on the preoccupations of each generation to encounter it. I have tried to suggest some of the ways in which it might be read as we enter the twenty-first century. What cannot be denied is its huge power, which comes, as this Introduction has tried to show, from the combined effect of many codes of writing and from the transformations made by the author upon his own life and upon the cultural norms of his time – as well as from the strong presence, during the writing, of its first readers. Today the novel challenges us to revise our preconceptions about Dickens and his Victorianism: far from being clichéd or stereotyped in its presentation of sexuality, it sheds light, in its kaleidoscopic displacements and disguisings, into the darkest places of our imagination.

VALERIE PURTON

NOTE ON THE TEXT AND ILLUSTRATIONS

The complete manuscript of *Dombey and Son*, with the plans for each number, is in the Forster Collection at the Victoria and Albert Museum in London. The novel appeared in nineteen monthly parts from October 1846 until April 1848, Numbers 1 to 3 being written in Switzerland, Numbers 4 to 6 in Paris and Numbers 7 to 19, including a final double number, in London.

The full title on the monthly-part wrappers was: 'Dealings with the Firm of Dombey and Son: Wholesale, Retail and for Exportation'. After the first edition in 1848, there followed the Cheap Edition in 1858, the Library Edition in 1859 and the Charles Dickens Edition in 1867. The present edition is based on that of 1867, the last to be published in Dickens's lifetime that contains his own revisions. The original Everyman Edition of 1907 modernised the 1867 edition with regard to certain spellings, e.g. 'Harrowgate' becomes 'Harrogate', and by no longer capitalising such words as 'papa', 'mama' and 'uncle', and this policy has been continued by the present editor. Some obvious misprints have been silently corrected.

Dickens 'overwrote' the first number by some six printed pages; he therefore had to cancel many passages in Chapters 1 to 3 at proof stage. For a detailed account of the textual history of the novel, including these and other unpublished passages, see the Clarendon Edition of *Dombey and Son*, ed. Alan Horsman (Oxford, 1974).

Dombey and Son was illustrated by Hablot K. Browne (Phiz). In the first volume edition, there were thirty-eight illustrations, a frontispiece (centring on Florence and Paul) and a vignette title page (showing Captain Cuttle and Rob the Grinder). For further discussions of the illustrations, see Forster's *Life*, Book VI, Chapter 2; Alan Horsman in the Clarendon Edition, pp. 865–71; Michael Steig in *Dickens and Phiz* (1978); John Butt and Kathleen Tillotson in *Dickens at Work* (1957); and Q. D. Leavis in *Dickens the Novelist* (1970) by F. R. and Q. D. Leavis.

The story is dedicated
with great esteem to
The Marchioness of Normanby[1]

PREFACES

PREFACE TO THE FIRST EDITION

I cannot forego my usual opportunity of saying farewell to my readers in this greeting-place, though I have only to acknowledge the unbounded warmth and earnestness of their sympathy in every stage of the journey we have just concluded.

If any of them have felt a sorrow in one of the principal incidents on which this fiction turns,[1] I hope it may be a sorrow of that sort which endears the sharers in it, one to another. This is not unselfish in me. I may claim to have felt it, at least as much as anybody else; and I would fain be remembered kindly for my part in the experience.

DEVONSHIRE TERRACE,
Twenty-Fourth March, 1848.

PREFACE TO THE FIRST CHEAP EDITION (1858)

I make so bold as to believe that the faculty (or the habit) of closely and carefully observing the characters of men is a rare one. I have not even found, within my experience, that the faculty (or the habit) of closely and carefully observing so much as the faces of men, is a general one by any means. The two commonest mistakes in judgment that I suppose to arise from the former default, are, the confounding of shyness with arrogance, and the not understanding that an obstinate nature exists in a perpetual struggle with itself.

Mr Dombey undergoes no violent internal change,[1] either in this book, or in life. A sense of his injustice is within him all along. The more he represses it, the more unjust he necessarily is. Internal shame and external circumstances may bring the contest to the surface in a week, or a day; but it has been a contest for years, and is only fought out then, after a long balance of victory.

It is ten years since I dismissed Mr Dombey. I have not been impatient to offer this critical remark upon him, and I offer it with some confidence.

I began this book by the lake of Geneva, and went on with it for some months in France.[2] The association between the writing and the place of writing is so curiously strong in my mind, that at this day, although I know every stair in the little Midshipman's house, and could swear to every pew in the church in which Florence was married, or to every young gentleman's bedstead in Doctor Blimber's establishment, I yet confusedly imagine Captain Cuttle as secluding himself from Mrs Mac Stinger among the mountains of Switzerland. Similarly, when I am reminded by any chance of what it was that the waves were always saying, I wander in my fancy for a whole winter night about the streets of Paris – as I really did, with a heavy heart, on the night when my little friend and I parted company for ever.[*]

London, April, 1858.

[*] The Preface to the Cheap Edition was reprinted, with the following minor variants, in the Library Edition (1859) and as the 'Author's Preface' to the Charles Dickens Edition (1867):

p.xli 1858: closely and carefully 1867: correctly
p.xli 1858: arrogance 1867: arrogance – a very common mistake indeed
p.xli 1858: internal 1867: OMITTED
p.xli 1858: life 1867: real life
p.xli 1858: the surface 1867: a close
p.xli 1858: then, 1859/1867: OMITTED
p.xli 1858: It . . . years 1859: Years have elapsed
p.xli 1858: It is ten years . . . confidence 1867: OMITTED
p.xlii 1858: France 1867: France, before pursuing it in England
p.xlii 1858: know 1867: know, in my fancy,
p.xlii 1858/59 and MS of 67: I . . . fancy 1867: my remembrance wanders
p.xlii 1858: really 1867: restlessly
p.xlii 1858: when 1867: when I had written the chapter in which
p.xlii 1858: for ever 1867: OMITTED
p.xlii 1858: London . . . 1858 1859/1867: OMITTED

DOMBEY AND SON

CHAPTER I

Dombey and Son

Dombey sat in the corner of the darkened room in the great arm-chair by the bedside, and Son lay tucked up warm in a little basket bedstead, carefully disposed on a low settee immediately in front of the fire and close to it, as if his constitution were analogous to that of a muffin, and it was essential to toast him brown while he was very new.

Dombey was about eight-and-forty years of age. Son about eight-and-forty minutes. Dombey was rather bald, rather red, and though a handsome well-made man, too stern and pompous in appearance, to be prepossessing. Son was very bald, and very red, and though (of course) an undeniably fine infant, somewhat crushed and spotty in his general effect, as yet. On the brow of Dombey, Time and his brother Care had set some marks, as on a tree that was to come down in good time – remorseless twins they are for striding through their human forests, notching as they go – while the countenance of Son was crossed and recrossed with a thousand little creases, which the same deceitful Time would take delight in smoothing out and wearing away with the flat part of his scythe, as a preparation of the surface for his deeper operations.

Dombey, exulting in the long-looked-for event, jingled and jingled the heavy gold watch-chain that depended from below his trim blue coat, whereof the buttons sparkled phosphorescently in the feeble rays of the distant fire. Son, with his little fists curled up and clenched, seemed, in his feeble way, to be squaring at existence for having come upon him so unexpectedly.

'The house will once again, Mrs Dombey,' said Mr Dombey, 'be not only in name but in fact Dombey and Son; Dom-bey and Son!'

The words had such a softening influence, that he appended a term of endearment to Mrs Dombey's name (though not without some hesitation, as being a man but little used to that form of address): and said, 'Mrs Dombey, my – my dear.'

A transient flush of faint surprise overspread the sick lady's face as she raised her eyes towards him.

'He will be christened Paul, my – Mrs Dombey – of course.'

She feebly echoed, 'Of course,' or rather expressed it by the motion of her lips, and closed her eyes again.

'His father's name, Mrs Dombey, and his grandfather's! I wish his grandfather were alive this day!' And again he said 'Dom-bey and Son,' in exactly the same tone as before.

Those three words conveyed the one idea of Mr Dombey's life. The earth was made for Dombey and Son to trade in, and the sun and moon were made to give them light. Rivers and seas were formed to float their ships; rainbows gave them promise of fair weather; winds blew for or against their enterprises; stars and planets circled in their orbits, to preserve inviolate a system of which they were the centre. Common abbreviations took new meanings in his eyes, and had sole reference to them: A. D. had no concern with anno Domini, but stood for anno Dombei – and Son.

He had risen, as his father had before him, in the course of life and death, from Son to Dombey, and for nearly twenty years had been the sole representative of the firm. Of those years he had been married, ten – married, as some said, to a lady with no heart to give him; whose happiness was in the past, and who was content to bind her broken spirit to the dutiful and meek endurance of the present. Such idle talk was little likely to reach the ears of Mr Dombey, whom it nearly concerned; and probably no one in the world would have received it with such utter incredulity as he, if it had reached him. Dombey and Son had often dealt in hides, but never in hearts. They left that fancy ware to boys and girls, and boarding-schools and books. Mr Dombey would have reasoned: That a matrimonial alliance with himself *must*, in the nature of things, be gratifying and honourable to any woman of common sense. That the hope of giving birth to a new partner in such a house, could not fail to awaken a glorious and stirring ambition in the breast of the least ambitious of her sex. That Mrs Dombey had entered on that social contract of matrimony: almost necessarily part of a genteel and wealthy station, even without reference to the perpetuation of family firms: with her eyes fully open to these advantages. That Mrs Dombey had had daily practical knowledge of his position in society. That Mrs Dombey had always sat at the head of his table, and done the honours of his house in a remarkably lady-like and becoming manner. That Mrs Dombey must have been happy. That she couldn't help it.

Or, at all events, with one drawback. Yes. That he would have allowed. With only one; but that one certainly involving much. They had been married ten years, and until this present day on which Mr Dombey sat jingling and jingling his heavy gold watch-chain in the great arm-chair by the side of the bed, had had no issue.

To speak of; none worth mentioning. There had been a girl some six years before, and the child, who had stolen into the chamber unobserved, was now crouching timidly, in a corner whence she could see her mother's face. But what was a girl to Dombey and Son! In the capital of the House's name and dignity, such a child was merely a piece of base coin that couldn't be invested – a bad Boy – nothing more.

Mr Dombey's cup of satisfaction was so full at this moment, however, that he felt he could afford a drop or two of its contents, even to sprinkle on the dust in the by-path of his little daughter.

So he said, 'Florence, you may go and look at your pretty brother, if you like, I dare say. Don't touch him!'

The child glanced keenly at the blue coat and stiff white cravat, which, with a pair of creaking boots and a very loud ticking watch, embodied her idea of a father; but her eyes returned to her mother's face immediately, and she neither moved nor answered.

Next moment, the lady had opened her eyes and seen the child; and the child had run towards her; and, standing on tiptoe, the better to hide her face in her embrace, had clung about her with a desperate affection very much at variance with her years.

'Oh Lord bless me!' said Mr Dombey, rising testily. 'A very ill-advised and feverish proceeding this, I am sure. I had better ask Doctor Peps if he'll have the goodness to step up stairs again perhaps. I'll go down. I'll go down. I needn't beg you,' he added, pausing for a moment at the settee before the fire, 'to take particular care of this young gentleman, Mrs—'

'Blockitt, Sir?' suggested the nurse, a simpering piece of faded gentility, who did not presume to state her name as a fact, but merely offered it as a mild suggestion.

'Of this young gentleman, Mrs Blockitt.'

'No, Sir, indeed. I remember when Miss Florence was born—'

'Ay, ay, ay,' said Mr Dombey, bending over the basket bedstead, and slightly bending his brows at the same time. 'Miss Florence was all very well, but this is another matter. This young gentleman has to accomplish a destiny. A destiny, little fellow!' As he thus apostrophised the infant he raised one of his hands to his lips, and kissed it; then, seeming to fear that the action involved some compromise of his dignity, went, awkwardly enough, away.

Doctor Parker Peps, one of the Court Physicians, and a man of immense reputation for assisting at the increase of great families, was walking up and down the drawing-room with his hands behind him, to the unspeakable admiration of the family Surgeon, who had regularly puffed[1] the case for the last six weeks, among all his patients, friends, and acquaintances, as one to which he was in hourly expectation day and night of being summoned, in conjunction with Doctor Parker Peps.

'Well, Sir,' said Doctor Parker Peps, in a round, deep sonorous voice, muffled for the occasion, like the knocker,[2] 'do you find that your dear lady is at all roused by your visit?'

'Stimulated as it were?' said the family practitioner faintly: bowing at the same time to the Doctor, as much as to say, 'Excuse my putting in a word, but this is a valuable connexion.'

Mr Dombey was quite discomfited by the question. He had thought so little of the patient, that he was not in a condition to answer it. He said that it would be a satisfaction to him, if Doctor Parker Peps would walk up stairs again.

'Good! We must not disguise from you, Sir,' said Doctor Parker Peps, 'that there is a want of power in Her Grace the Duchess – I beg your pardon; I confound names: I should say, in your amiable lady. That there is a certain degree of languor, and a general absence of elasticity, which we would rather – not—'

'See,' interposed the family practitioner with another inclination of the head.

'Quite so,' said Doctor Parker Peps, 'which we would rather not see. It would appear that the system of Lady Cankaby – excuse me: I should say of Mrs Dombey: I confuse the names of cases—'

'So very numerous,' murmured the family practitioner – 'can't be expected I'm sure – quite wonderful if otherwise – Doctor Parker Peps's West End practice—'

'Thank you,' said the Doctor, 'quite so. It would appear, I was observing, that the system of our patient has sustained a shock, from which it can only hope to rally by a great and strong—'

'And vigorous,' murmured the family practitioner.

'Quite so,' assented the Doctor – 'and vigorous effort. Mr Pilkins here, who from his position of medical adviser in this family – no one better qualified to fill that position, I am sure.'

'Oh!' murmured the family practitioner. ' "Praise from Sir Hubert Stanley!" '[3]

'You are good enough,' returned Doctor Parker Peps, 'to say so. Mr Pilkins who, from his position, is best acquainted with the patient's constitution in its normal state (an acquaintance very valuable to us in forming our opinions on these occasions), is of opinion, with me, that Nature must be called upon to make a vigorous effort in this instance; and that if our interesting friend the Countess of Dombey – I *beg* your pardon; Mrs Dombey – should not be—'

'Able,' said the family practitioner.

'To make that effort successfully,' said Doctor Parker Peps, 'then a crisis might arise, which we should both sincerely deplore.'

With that, they stood for a few seconds looking at the ground. Then, on the motion – made in dumb show – of Doctor Parker Peps, they went up stairs; the family practitioner opening the room door for that distinguished professional, and following him out, with most obsequious politeness.

To record of Mr Dombey that he was not in his way affected by this intelligence, would be to do him an injustice. He was not a man of whom it could properly be said that he was ever startled or shocked; but he certainly had a sense within him, that if his wife should sicken and decay, he would be very sorry, and that he would find a something gone from among his plate and furniture, and other household possessions, which was well worth the having, and could not be lost without sincere regret. Though it would be a cool, business-like, gentlemanly, self-possessed regret, no doubt.

His meditations on the subject were soon interrupted, first by the rustling of garments on the staircase, and then by the sudden whisking into the room of a lady rather past the middle age than otherwise, but dressed in a very juvenile manner, particularly as to the tightness of her bodice, who, running up to him with a kind of screw in her face and carriage, expressive of suppressed emotion, flung her arms round his neck, and said in a choking voice,

'My dear Paul! He's quite a Dombey!'

'Well, well!' returned her brother – for Mr Dombey was her brother – 'I think he *is* like the family. Don't agitate yourself, Louisa.'

'It's very foolish of me,' said Louisa, sitting down, and taking out her pocket-handkerchief, 'but he's – he's such a perfect Dombey! *I* never saw anything like it in my life!'

'But what is this about Fanny, herself?' said Mr Dombey. 'How is Fanny?'

'My dear Paul,' returned Louisa, 'it's nothing whatever. Take my word, it's nothing whatever. There is exhaustion, certainly, but nothing like what I underwent myself, either with George or Frederick. An effort is necessary. That's all. If dear Fanny were a Dombey! – But I dare say she'll make it; I have no doubt she'll

make it. Knowing it to be required of her, as a duty, of course she'll
make it. My dear Paul, it's very weak and silly of me, I know, to be
so trembly and shaky from head to foot; but I am so very queer
that I must ask you for a glass of wine and a morsel of that cake. I
thought I should have fallen out of the staircase window, as I came
down from seeing dear Fanny, and that tiddy ickle sing.' These last
words originated in a sudden vivid reminiscence of the baby.

They were succeeded by a gentle tap at the door.

'Mrs Chick,' said a very bland female voice outside, 'how are you
now, my dear friend?'

'My dear Paul,' said Louisa in a low voice, as she rose from her
seat, 'it's Miss Tox. The kindest creature! I never could have got
here without her! Miss Tox, my brother Mr Dombey. Paul, my
dear, my very particular friend Miss Tox.'

The lady thus specially presented, was a long lean figure, wearing
such a faded air that she seemed not to have been made in what
linen-drapers call 'fast colours' originally, and to have, by little and
little, washed out. But for this she might have been described as the
very pink of general propitiation and politeness. From a long habit
of listening admiringly to everything that was said in her presence,
and looking at the speakers as if she were mentally engaged in
taking off impressions of their images upon her soul, never to part
with the same but with life, her head had quite settled on one side.
Her hands had contracted a spasmodic habit of raising themselves
of their own accord as in involuntary admiration. Her eyes were
liable to a similar affection. She had the softest voice that ever was
heard; and her nose, stupendously aquiline, had a little knob in the
very centre or key-stone of the bridge, whence it tended downwards
towards her face, as in an invincible determination never to turn up
at anything.

Miss Tox's dress, though perfectly genteel and good, had a
certain character of angularity and scantiness. She was accustomed
to wear odd weedy little flowers in her bonnets and caps. Strange
grasses were sometimes perceived in her hair; and it was observed
by the curious, of all her collars, frills, tuckers, wristbands, and
other gossamer articles – indeed of everything she wore which had
two ends to it intended to unite – that the two ends were never on
good terms, and wouldn't quite meet without a struggle. She had
furry articles for winter wear, as tippets, boas, and muffs, which
stood up on end in a rampant manner, and were not at all sleek.
She was much given to the carrying about of small bags with snaps
to them, that went off like little pistols when they were shut up; and

when full-dressed, she wore round her neck the barrenest of lockets, representing a fishy old eye, with no approach to speculation[4] in it. These and other appearances of a similar nature, had served to propagate the opinion, that Miss Tox was a lady of what is called a limited independence, which she turned to the best account. Possibly her mincing gait encouraged the belief, and suggested that her clipping a step of ordinary compass into two or three, originated in her habit of making the most of everything.

'I am sure,' said Miss Tox, with a prodigious curtsey, 'that to have the honour of being presented to Mr Dombey is a distinction which I have long sought, but very little expected at the present moment. My dear Mrs Chick – may I say Louisa!'

Mrs Chick took Miss Tox's hand in hers, rested the foot of her wine glass upon it, repressed a tear, and said in a low voice 'Bless you!'

'My dear Louisa then,' said Miss Tox, 'my sweet friend, how are you now?'

'Better,' Mrs Chick returned. 'Take some wine. You have been almost as anxious as I have been, and must want it, I am sure.'

Mr Dombey of course officiated.

'Miss Tox, Paul,' pursued Mrs Chick, still retaining her hand, 'knowing how much I have been interested in the anticipation of the event of to-day, has been working at a little gift for Fanny, which I promised to present. It is only a pin-cushion for the toilette table, Paul, but I do say, and will say, and must say, that Miss Tox has very prettily adapted the sentiment to the occasion. I call "Welcome little Dombey" Poetry, myself!'

'Is that the device?' inquired her brother.

'That is the device,' returned Louisa.

'But do me the justice to remember, my dear Louisa,' said Miss Tox in a tone of low and earnest entreaty, 'that nothing but the – I have some difficulty in expressing myself – the dubiousness of the result would have induced me to take so great a liberty: "Welcome, Master Dombey," would have been much more congenial to my feelings, as I am sure you know. But the uncertainty attendant on angelic strangers will, I hope, excuse what must otherwise appear an unwarrantable familiarity.' Miss Tox made a graceful bend as she spoke, in favour of Mr Dombey, which that gentleman graciously acknowledged. Even the sort of recognition of Dombey and Son, conveyed in the foregoing conversation, was so palatable to him, that his sister, Mrs Chick – though he affected to consider her a weak good-natured person – had perhaps more influence over him than anybody else.

'Well!' said Mrs Chick, with a sweet smile, 'after this, I forgive Fanny everything!'

It was a declaration in a Christian spirit, and Mrs Chick felt that it did her good. Not that she had anything particular to forgive in her sister-in-law, nor indeed anything at all, except her having married her brother – in itself a species of audacity – and her having, in the course of events, given birth to a girl instead of a boy: which, as Mrs Chick had frequently observed, was not quite what she had expected of her, and was not a pleasant return for all the attention and distinction she had met with.

Mr Dombey being hastily summoned out of the room at this moment, the two ladies were left alone together. Miss Tox immediately became spasmodic.[5]

'I knew you would admire my brother. I told you so beforehand, my dear,' said Louisa.

Miss Tox's hands and eyes expressed how much.

'And as to his property, my dear!'

'Ah!' said Miss Tox, with deep feeling.

'Im–mense!'

'But his deportment, my dear Louisa!' said Miss Tox. 'His presence! His dignity! No portrait that I have ever seen of any one has been half so replete with those qualities. Something so stately, you know: so uncompromising: so very wide across the chest: so upright! A pecuniary Duke of York,[6] my love, and nothing short of it!' said Miss Tox. 'That's what I should designate him.'

'Why, my dear Paul!' exclaimed his sister, as he returned, 'you look quite pale! There's nothing the matter?'

'I am sorry to say, Louisa, that they tell me that Fanny—'

'Now, my dear Paul,' returned his sister rising, 'don't believe it. If you have any reliance on my experience, Paul, you may rest assured that there is nothing wanting but an effort on Fanny's part. And that effort,' she continued, taking off her bonnet, and adjusting her cap and gloves, in a business-like manner, 'she must be encouraged, and really, if necessary, urged to make. Now, my dear Paul, come up stairs with me.'

Mr Dombey, who, besides being generally influenced by his sister for the reason already mentioned, had really faith in her as an experienced and bustling matron, acquiesced: and followed her, at once, to the sick chamber.

The lady lay upon her bed as he had left her, clasping her little daughter to her breast. The child clung close about her, with the same intensity as before, and never raised her head, or moved her soft cheek from her mother's face, or looked on those who stood around, or spoke, or moved, or shed a tear.

'Restless without the little girl,' the Doctor whispered Mr Dombey. 'We found it best to have her in again.'

There was such a solemn stillness round the bed; and the two medical attendants seemed to look on the impassive form with so much compassion and so little hope, that Mrs Chick was for the moment diverted from her purpose. But presently summoning courage, and what she called presence of mind, she sat down by the bedside, and said in the low precise tone of one who endeavours to awaken a sleeper:

'Fanny! Fanny!'

There was no sound in answer but the loud ticking of Mr Dombey's watch and Doctor Parker Peps's watch, which seemed in the silence to be running a race.

'Fanny, my dear,' said Mrs Chick, with assumed lightness, 'here's Mr Dombey come to see you. Won't you speak to him? They want to lay your little boy – the baby, Fanny, you know; you have hardly seen him yet, I think – in bed; but they can't till you rouse yourself a little. Don't you think it's time you roused yourself a little? Eh?'

She bent her ear to the bed, and listened: at the same time looking round at the bystanders, and holding up her finger.

'Eh?' she repeated, 'what was it you said, Fanny? I didn't hear you.'

No word or sound in answer. Mr Dombey's watch and Dr Parker Peps's watch seemed to be racing faster.

'Now, really, Fanny, my dear,' said the sister-in-law, altering her position, and speaking less confidently, and more earnestly, in spite of herself, 'I shall have to be quite cross with you, if you don't rouse yourself. It's necessary for you to make an effort, and perhaps a very great and painful effort which you are not disposed to make; but this is a world of effort you know, Fanny, and we must never yield, when so much depends upon us. Come! Try! I must really scold you if you don't!'

The race in the ensuing pause was fierce and furious. The watches seemed to jostle, and to trip each other up.

'Fanny!' said Louisa, glancing round, with a gathering alarm. 'Only look at me. Only open your eyes to show me that you hear and understand me; will you? Good Heaven, gentlemen, what is to be done!'

The two medical attendants exchanged a look across the bed; and the Physician, stooping down, whispered in the child's ear. Not having understood the purport of his whisper, the little creature turned her perfectly colourless face, and deep dark eyes towards him; but without loosening her hold in the least.

The whisper was repeated.

'Mama!' said the child.

The little voice, familiar and dearly loved, awakened some show of consciousness, even at that ebb. For a moment, the closed eyelids trembled, and the nostril quivered, and the faintest shadow of a smile was seen.

'Mama!' cried the child sobbing aloud. 'Oh dear Mama! oh dear Mama!'

The Doctor gently brushed the scattered ringlets of the child, aside from the face and mouth of the mother. Alas how calm they lay there; how little breath there was to stir them!

Thus, clinging fast to that slight spar within her arms, the mother drifted out upon the dark and unknown sea that rolls round all the world.

CHAPTER 2

In which Timely Provision is made for an Emergency that will sometimes arise in the best regulated Families

'I shall never cease to congratulate myself,' said Mrs Chick, 'on having said, when I little thought what was in store for us, – really as if I was inspired by something, – that I forgave poor dear Fanny everything. Whatever happens, that must always be a comfort to me!'

Mrs Chick made this impressive observation in the drawing-room, after having descended thither from the inspection of the mantua-makers,[1] up stairs, who were busy on the family mourning. She delivered it for the behoof of Mr Chick, who was a stout bald gentleman, with a very large face, and his hands continually in his pockets, and who had a tendency in his nature to whistle and hum tunes, which, sensible of the indecorum of such sounds in a house of grief, he was at some pains to repress at present.

'Don't you over-exert yourself, Loo,' said Mr Chick, 'or you'll be laid up with spasms, I see. Right tol loor rul! Bless my soul, I forgot! We're here one day and gone the next!'

Mrs Chick contented herself with a glance of reproof, and then proceeded with the thread of her discourse.

'I am sure,' she said, 'I hope this heart-rending occurrence will be a warning to all of us, to accustom ourselves to rouse ourselves, and to make efforts in time where they're required of us. There's a moral in everything, if we would only avail ourselves of it. It will be our own faults if we lose sight of this one.'

Mr Chick invaded the grave silence which ensued on this remark with the singularly inappropriate air of 'A cobbler there was';[2] and checking himself, in some confusion, observed, that it was undoubtedly our own faults if we didn't improve such melancholy occasions as the present.

'Which might be better improved, I should think, Mr C.,' retorted his helpmate, after a short pause, 'than by the introduction, either of the college hornpipe,[3] or the equally unmeaning and unfeeling remark of rump-te-iddity, bow-wow-wow!' – which Mr Chick had indeed indulged in, under his breath, and which Mrs Chick repeated in a tone of withering scorn.

'Merely habit, my dear,' pleaded Mr Chick.

'Nonsense! Habit!' returned his wife. 'If you're a rational being, don't make such ridiculous excuses. Habit! If I was to get a habit (as you call it) of walking on the ceiling, like the flies, I should hear enough of it, I dare say.'

It appeared so probable that such a habit might be attended with some degree of notoriety, that Mr Chick didn't venture to dispute the position.

'How's the baby, Loo?' asked Mr Chick: to change the subject.

'What baby do you mean?' answered Mrs Chick. 'I am sure the morning I have had, with that dining-room down stairs one mass of babies, no one in their senses would believe.'

'One mass of babies!' repeated Mr Chick, staring with an alarmed expression about him.

'It would have occurred to most men,' said Mrs Chick, 'that poor dear Fanny being no more, it becomes necessary to provide a nurse.'

'Oh! Ah!' said Mr Chick. 'Toor-rul – such is life, I mean. I hope you are suited, my dear.'

'Indeed I am not,' said Mrs Chick; 'nor likely to be, so far as I can see. Meanwhile, of course, the child is—'

'Going to the very Deuce,'[4] said Mr Chick, thoughtfully, 'to be sure.'

Admonished, however, that he had committed himself, by the indignation expressed in Mrs Chick's countenance at the idea of a Dombey going there; and thinking to atone for his misconduct by a bright suggestion, he added:

'Couldn't something temporary be done with a teapot?'

If he had meant to bring the subject prematurely to a close he could not have done it more effectually. After looking at him for some moments in silent resignation, Mrs Chick walked majestically to the window and peeped through the blind, attracted by the sound of wheels. Mr Chick, finding that his destiny was, for the time, against him, said no more, and walked off. But it was not always thus with Mr Chick. He was often in the ascendant himself, and at those times punished Louisa roundly. In their matrimonial bickerings they were, upon the whole, a well-matched, fairly-balanced, give-and-take couple. It would have been, generally speaking, very difficult to have betted on the winner. Often when Mr Chick seemed beaten, he would suddenly make a start, turn the tables, clatter them about the ears of Mrs Chick, and carry all before him. Being liable himself to similar unlooked-for checks from Mrs Chick, their little contests usually possessed a character of uncertainty that was very animating.

Miss Tox had arrived on the wheels just now alluded to, and came running into the room in a breathless condition.

'My dear Louisa,' said Miss Tox, 'is the vacancy still unsupplied?'

'You good soul, yes,' said Mrs Chick.

'Then, my dear Louisa,' returned Miss Tox, 'I hope and believe – but in one moment, my dear, I'll introduce the party.'

Running down stairs again as fast as she had run up, Miss Tox got the party out of the hackney-coach, and soon returned with it under convoy.

It then appeared that she had used the word, not in its legal or business acceptation, when it merely expresses an individual, but as a noun of multitude, or signifying many: for Miss Tox escorted a plump rosy-cheeked wholesome apple-faced young woman, with an infant in her arms; a younger woman not so plump, but apple-faced also, who led a plump and apple-faced child in each hand; another plump and also apple-faced boy who walked by himself; and finally, a plump and apple-faced man, who carried in his arms another plump and apple-faced boy, whom he stood down on the floor, and admonished, in a husky whisper, to 'kitch hold of his brother Johnny.'

'My dear Louisa,' said Miss Tox, 'knowing your great anxiety,

Miss Tox introduces 'the party'

and wishing to relieve it, I posted off myself to the Queen Char-lotte's Royal Married Females,[5] which you had forgot, and put the question, Was there anybody there that they thought would suit? No, they said there was not. When they gave me that answer, I do assure you, my dear, I was almost driven to despair on your account. But it did so happen, that one of the Royal Married Females, hearing the inquiry, reminded the matron of another who had gone to her own home, and who, she said, would in all likelihood be most satisfactory. The moment I heard this, and had it corroborated by the matron – excellent references and unimpeach-able character – I got the address, my dear, and posted off again.'

'Like the dear good Tox, you are!' said Louisa.

'Not at all,' returned Miss Tox. 'Don't say so. Arriving at the house (the cleanest place, my dear! You might eat your dinner off the floor), I found the whole family sitting at table; and feeling that no account of them could be half so comfortable to you and Mr Dombey as the sight of them all together, I brought them all away. This gentleman,' said Miss Tox, pointing out the apple-faced man, 'is the father. Will you have the goodness to come a little forward, Sir?'

The apple-faced man having sheepishly complied with this request, stood chuckling and grinning in a front row.

'This is his wife, of course,' said Miss Tox, singling out the young woman with the baby. 'How do you do, Polly?'

'I'm pretty well, I thank you, ma'am,' said Polly.

By way of bringing her out dexterously, Miss Tox had made the inquiry as in condescension to an old acquaintance whom she hadn't seen for a fortnight or so.

'I'm glad to hear it,' said Miss Tox. 'The other young woman is her unmarried sister who lives with them, and would take care of her children. Her name's Jemima. How do you do, Jemima?'

'I'm pretty well, I thank you, ma'am,' returned Jemima.

'I'm very glad indeed to hear it,' said Miss Tox. 'I hope you'll keep so. Five children. Youngest six weeks. The fine little boy with the blister on his nose is the eldest. The blister, I believe,' said Miss Tox, looking round upon the family, 'is not constitutional, but accidental?'

The apple-faced man was understood to growl, 'Flat iron.'

'I beg your pardon, Sir,' said Miss Tox, 'did you? – '

'Flat iron,' he repeated.

'Oh yes,' said Miss Tox. 'Yes! quite true. I forgot. The little creature, in his mother's absence, smelt a warm flat iron. You're quite right, Sir. You were going to have the goodness to inform me, when we arrived at the door, that you were by trade a—'

'Stoker,' said the man.

'A choker!' said Miss Tox, quite aghast.

'Stoker,' said the man. 'Steam ingine.'

'Oh-h! Yes!' returned Miss Tox, looking thoughtfully at him, and seeming still to have but a very imperfect understanding of his meaning.

'And how do you like it, Sir?'

'Which, mum?' said the man.

'That,' replied Miss Tox. 'Your trade.'

'Oh! Pretty well, mum. The ashes sometimes gets in here;' touching his chest: 'and makes a man speak gruff, as at the present time. But it *is* ashes, mum, not crustiness.'

Miss Tox seemed to be so little enlightened by this reply, as to find a difficulty in pursuing the subject. But Mrs Chick relieved her, by entering into a close private examination of Polly, her children, her marriage certificate, testimonials, and so forth. Polly coming out unscathed from this ordeal, Mrs Chick withdrew with her report to her brother's room, and as an emphatic comment on it, and corroboration of it, carried the two rosiest little Toodles with her, Toodle being the family name of the apple-faced family.

Mr Dombey had remained in his own apartment since the death of his wife, absorbed in visions of the youth, education, and destination of his baby son. Something lay at the bottom of his cool heart, colder and heavier than its ordinary load; but it was more a sense of the child's loss than his own, awakening within him an almost angry sorrow. That the life and progress on which he built such hopes, should be endangered in the outset by so mean a want; that Dombey and Son should be tottering for a nurse, was a sore humiliation. And yet in his pride and jealousy, he viewed with so much bitterness the thought of being dependent for the very first step towards the accomplishment of his soul's desire, on a hired serving-woman who would be to the child, for the time, all that even his alliance could have made his own wife, that in every new rejection of a candidate he felt a secret pleasure. The time had now come, however, when he could no longer be divided between these two sets of feelings. The less so, as there seemed to be no flaw in the title of Polly Toodle after his sister had set it forth, with many commendations on the indefatigable friendship of Miss Tox.

'These children look healthy,' said Mr Dombey. 'But to think of their some day claiming a sort of relationship to Paul! Take them away, Louisa! Let me see this woman and her husband.'

Mrs Chick bore off the tender pair of Toodles, and presently returned with that tougher couple whose presence her brother had commanded.

'My good woman,' said Mr Dombey, turning round in his easy chair, as one piece, and not as a man with limbs and joints, 'I understand you are poor, and wish to earn money by nursing the little boy, my son, who has been so prematurely deprived of what can never be replaced. I have no objection to your adding to the comforts of your family by that means. So far as I can tell, you seem to be a deserving object. But I must impose one or two conditions on you, before you enter my house in that capacity. While you are here, I must stipulate that you are always known as – say as Richards – an ordinary name, and convenient. Have you any objection to be known as Richards? You had better consult your husband.'

As the husband did nothing but chuckle and grin, and continually draw his right hand across his mouth, moistening the palm, Mrs Toodle, after nudging him twice or thrice in vain, dropped a curtsey and replied 'that perhaps if she was to be called out of her name, it would be considered in the wages.'

'Oh, of course,' said Mr Dombey. 'I desire to make it a question of wages, altogether. Now, Richards, if you nurse my bereaved child, I wish you to remember this always. You will receive a liberal stipend in return for the discharge of certain duties, in the perform-ance of which, I wish you to see as little of your family as possible. When those duties cease to be required and rendered, and the stipend ceases to be paid, there is an end of all relations between us. Do you understand me?'

Mrs Toodle seemed doubtful about it; and as to Toodle himself, he had evidently no doubt whatever, that he was all abroad.[6]

'You have children of your own,' said Mr Dombey. 'It is not at all in this bargain that you need become attached to my child, or that my child need become attached to you. I don't expect or desire anything of the kind. Quite the reverse. When you go away from here, you will have concluded what is a mere matter of bargain and sale, hiring and letting: and will stay away. The child will cease to remember you; and you will cease, if you please, to remember the child.'

Mrs Toodle, with a little more colour in her cheeks than she had had before, said 'she hoped she knew her place.'

'I hope you do, Richards,' said Mr Dombey. 'I have no doubt you know it very well. Indeed it is so plain and obvious that it could hardly be otherwise. Louisa, my dear, arrange with Richards about money, and let her have it when and how she pleases. Mr what's-your-name, a word with you, if you please!'

Thus arrested on the threshold as he was following his wife out of the room, Toodle returned and confronted Mr Dombey alone. He was a strong, loose, round-shouldered, shuffling, shaggy fellow, on whom his clothes sat negligently: with a good deal of hair and whisker, deepened in its natural tint, perhaps by smoke and coal-dust: hard knotty hands: and a square forehead, as coarse in grain as the bark of an oak. A thorough contrast in all respects to Mr Dombey, who was one of those close-shaved close-cut moneyed gentlemen who are glossy and crisp like new bank-notes, and who seem to be artificially braced and tightened as by the stimulating action of golden shower-baths.

'You have a son, I believe?' said Mr Dombey.

'Four on 'em, Sir. Four hims and a her. All alive!'

'Why, it's as much as you can afford to keep them!' said Mr Dombey.

'I couldn't hardly afford but one thing in the world less, Sir.'

'What is that?'

'To lose 'em, Sir.'

'Can you read?' asked Mr Dombey.

'Why, not partick'ler, Sir.'

'Write?'

'With chalk, Sir?'

'With anything?'

'I could make shift to chalk a little bit, I think, if I was put to it,' said Toodle after some reflection.

'And yet,' said Mr Dombey, 'you are two or three and thirty, I suppose?'

'Thereabouts, I suppose, Sir,' answered Toodle, after more reflection.

'Then why don't you learn?' asked Mr Dombey.

'So I'm a going to, Sir. One of my little boys is a going to learn me, when he's old enough, and been to school himself.'

'Well!' said Mr Dombey, after looking at him attentively, and with no great favour, as he stood gazing round the room (principally round the ceiling) and still drawing his hand across and across his mouth. 'You heard what I said to your wife just now?'

'Polly heerd it,' said Toodle, jerking his hat over his shoulder in the direction of the door, with an air of perfect confidence in his better half. 'It's all right.'

'As you appear to leave everything to her,' said Mr Dombey, frustrated in his intention of impressing his views still more distinctly on the husband, as the stronger character, 'I suppose it is of no use my saying anything to you.'

'Not a bit,' said Toodle. 'Polly heerd it. *She's* awake, Sir.'

'I won't detain you any longer then,' returned Mr Dombey disappointed. 'Where have you worked all your life?'

'Mostly underground, Sir, 'till I got married. I come to the level then. I'm a going on one of these here railroads when they comes into full play.'[7]

As the last straw breaks the laden camel's back, this piece of underground information crushed the sinking spirits of Mr Dombey. He motioned his child's foster-father to the door, who departed by no means unwillingly: and then turning the key, paced up and down the room in solitary wretchedness. For all his starched, impenetrable dignity and composure, he wiped blinding tears from his eyes as he did so; and often said, with an emotion of which he would not, for the world, have had a witness, 'Poor little fellow!'

It may have been characteristic of Mr Dombey's pride, that he pitied himself through the child. Not poor me. Not poor widower, confiding by constraint in the wife of an ignorant Hind[8] who has been working 'mostly underground' all his life, and yet at whose door Death had never knocked, and at whose poor table four sons daily sit – but poor little fellow!

Those words being on his lips, it occurred to him – and it is an instance of the strong attraction with which his hopes and fears and all his thoughts were tending to one centre – that a great temptation was being placed in this woman's way. Her infant was a boy too. Now, would it be possible for her to change them?

Though he was soon satisfied that he had dismissed the idea as romantic and unlikely – though possible, there was no denying – he could not help pursuing it so far as to entertain within himself a picture of what his condition would be, if he should discover such an imposture when he was grown old. Whether a man so situated, would be able to pluck away the result of so many years of usage, confidence, and belief, from the impostor, and endow a stranger with it?

As his unusual emotion subsided, these misgivings gradually melted away, though so much of their shadow remained behind, that he was constant in his resolution to look closely after Richards himself, without appearing to do so. Being now in an easier frame of mind, he regarded the woman's station as rather an advantageous circumstance than otherwise, by placing, in itself, a broad distance between her and the child, and rendering their separation easy and natural.

Meanwhile terms were ratified and agreed upon between Mrs Chick and Richards, with the assistance of Miss Tox; and Richards being with much ceremony invested with the Dombey baby, as if it were an Order,[9] resigned her own, with many tears and kisses, to Jemima. Glasses of wine were then produced, to sustain the drooping spirits of the family.

'You'll take a glass yourself, Sir, won't you?' said Miss Tox, as Toodle appeared.

'Thankee, mum,' said Toodle, 'since you *are* suppressing.'[10]

'And you're very glad to leave your dear good wife in such a comfortable home, ain't you, Sir?' said Miss Tox, nodding and winking at him stealthily.

'No, mum,' said Toodle. 'Here's wishing of her back agin.'

Polly cried more than ever at this. So Mrs Chick, who had her matronly apprehensions that this indulgence in grief might be prejudicial to the little Dombey ('acid, indeed,' she whispered Miss Tox), hastened to the rescue.

'Your little child will thrive charmingly with your sister Jemima, Richards,' said Mrs Chick; 'and you have only to make an effort – this is a world of effort, you know, Richards – to be very happy indeed. You have been already measured for your mourning, haven't you, Richards?'

'Ye–es, ma'am,' sobbed Polly.

'And it'll fit beautifully, I know,' said Mrs Chick, 'for the same young person has made me many dresses. The very best materials, too!'

'Lor, you'll be so smart,' said Miss Tox, 'that your husband won't know you; will you, Sir?'

'I should know her,' said Toodle, gruffly, 'anyhows and anywheres.'

Toodle was evidently not to be bought over.

'As to living, Richards, you know,' pursued Mrs Chick, 'why the very best of everything will be at your disposal. You will order your little dinner every day; and anything you take a fancy to, I'm sure will be as readily provided as if you were a lady.'

'Yes, to be sure!' said Miss Tox, keeping up the ball with great sympathy. 'And as to porter![11] – quite unlimited, will it not, Louisa?'

'Oh, certainly!' returned Mrs Chick in the same tone. 'With a little abstinence, you know, my dear, in point of vegetables.'

'And pickles, perhaps,' suggested Miss Tox.

'With such exceptions,' said Louisa, 'she'll consult her choice entirely, and be under no restraint at all, my love.'

'And then, of course, you know,' said Miss Tox, 'however fond she is of her own dear little child – and I'm sure, Louisa, *you* don't blame her for being fond of it?'

'Oh no!' cried Mrs Chick, benignantly.

'Still,' resumed Miss Tox, 'she naturally must be interested in her young charge, and must consider it a privilege to see a little cherub closely connected with the superior classes, gradually unfolding itself from day to day at one common fountain. Is it not so, Louisa?'

'Most undoubtedly!' said Mrs Chick. 'You see, my love, she's already quite contented and comfortable, and means to say good-bye to her sister Jemima and her little pets, and her good honest husband, with a light heart and a smile; don't she, my dear!'

'Oh yes!' cried Miss Tox. 'To be sure she does!'

Notwithstanding which, however, poor Polly embraced them all round in great distress, and finally ran away to avoid any more particular leave-taking between herself and the children. But the stratagem hardly succeeded as well as it deserved; for the smallest boy but one divining her intent, immediately began swarming up stairs after her – if that word of doubtful etymology be admissible – on his arms and legs; while the eldest (known in the family by the name of Biler,[12] in remembrance of the steam engine) beat a demoniacal tattoo with his boots, expressive of grief; in which he was joined by the rest of the family.

A quantity of oranges and halfpence thrust indiscriminately on each young Toodle, checked the first violence of their regret, and the family were speedily transported to their own home, by means of the hackney-coach[13] kept in waiting for that purpose. The children, under the guardianship of Jemima, blocked up the window, and dropped out oranges and halfpence all the way along. Mr Toodle himself preferred to ride behind among the spikes,[14] as being the mode of conveyance to which he was best accustomed.

CHAPTER 3

In which Mr Dombey, as a Man and a Father, is seen at the head of the Home-Department

The funeral of the deceased lady having been 'performed' to the entire satisfaction of the undertaker, as well as of the neighbourhood at large, which is generally disposed to be captious on such a point, and is prone to take offence at any omissions or shortcomings in the ceremonies, the various members of Mr Dombey's household subsided into their several places in the domestic system. That small world, like the great one out of doors, had the capacity of easily forgetting its dead; and when the cook had said she was a quiet-tempered lady, and the housekeeper had said it was the common lot, and the butler had said who'd have thought it, and the housemaid had said she couldn't hardly believe it, and the footman had said it seemed exactly like a dream, they had quite worn the subject out, and began to think their mourning was wearing rusty too.

On Richards, who was established upstairs in a state of honourable captivity, the dawn of her new life seemed to break cold and grey. Mr Dombey's house was a large one, on the shady side of a tall, dark, dreadfully genteel street in the region between Portland Place and Bryanstone Square.[1] It was a corner house, with great wide areas containing cellars frowned upon by barred windows, and leered at by crooked-eyed doors leading to dustbins. It was a house of dismal state, with a circular back to it, containing a whole suit of drawing-rooms looking upon a gravelled yard, where two gaunt trees, with blackened trunks and branches, rattled rather than rustled, their leaves were so smoke-dried. The summer sun was never on the street, but in the morning about breakfast-time, when it came with the water-carts[2] and the old-clothes men, and the people with geraniums, and the umbrella-mender, and the man who trilled the little bell of the Dutch clock[3] as he went along. It was soon gone again to return no more that day; and the bands of music and the straggling Punch's shows[4] going after it, left it a prey to the most dismal of organs, and white mice; with now and then a porcupine[5] to vary the entertainments; until the butlers whose families were dining out, began to stand at the house-doors in the twilight, and the lamplighter[6] made his nightly failure in attempting to brighten up the street with gas.

It was as blank a house inside as outside. When the funeral was over, Mr Dombey ordered the furniture to be covered up – perhaps to preserve it for the son with whom his plans were all associated – and the rooms to be ungarnished, saving such as he retained for himself on the ground floor. Accordingly, mysterious shapes were made of tables and chairs, heaped together in the middle of rooms, and covered over with great winding-sheets. Bell-handles, window-blinds, and looking-glasses, being papered up in journals, daily and weekly, obtruded fragmentary accounts of deaths and dreadful murders. Every chandelier or lustre, muffled in holland,[7] looked like a monstrous tear depending from the ceiling's eye. Odours, as from vaults and damp places, came out of the chimneys. The dead and buried lady was awful in a picture-frame of ghastly bandages. Every gust of wind that rose, brought eddying round the corner from the neighbouring mews, some fragments of the straw[8] that had been strewn before the house when she was ill, mildewed remains of which were still cleaving to the neighbourhood; and these, being always drawn by some invisible attraction to the threshold of the dirty house to let immediately opposite, addressed a dismal eloquence to Mr Dombey's windows.

The apartments which Mr Dombey reserved for his own inhabiting, were attainable from the hall, and consisted of a sitting-room; a library, which was in fact a dressing-room, so that the smell of hot-pressed paper, vellum, morocco, and Russia leather,[9] contended in it with the smell of divers pairs of boots and a kind of conservatory or little glass breakfast-room beyond, commanding a prospect of the trees before-mentioned, and generally speaking, of a few prowling cats. These three rooms opened upon one another. In the morning, when Mr Dombey was at his breakfast in one or other of the two first-mentioned of them, as well as in the afternoon when he came home to dinner, a bell was rung for Richards to repair to this glass chamber, and there walk to and fro with her young charge. From the glimpses she caught of Mr Dombey at these times, sitting in the dark distance, looking out towards the infant from among the dark heavy furniture – the house had been inhabited for years by his father, and in many of its appointments was old-fashioned and grim – she began to entertain ideas of him in his solitary state, as if he were a lone prisoner in a cell, or a strange apparition that was not to be accosted or understood.

Little Paul Dombey's foster-mother had led this life herself, and had carried little Paul through it for some weeks; and had returned up stairs one day from a melancholy saunter through the dreary rooms of state (she never went out without Mrs Chick, who called on fine mornings, usually accompanied by Miss Tox, to take her and baby for an airing – or in other words, to march them gravely up and down the pavement, like a walking funeral); when, as she was sitting in her own room, the door was slowly and quietly opened, and a dark-eyed little girl looked in.

'It's Miss Florence come home from her aunt's, no doubt,' thought Richards, who had never seen the child before. 'Hope I see you well, Miss.'

'Is that my brother?' asked the child, pointing to the baby.

'Yes, my pretty,' answered Richards. 'Come and kiss him.'

But the child, instead of advancing, looked her earnestly in the face, and said:

'What have you done with my mama?'

'Lord bless the little creeter!' cried Richards, 'what a sad question! I done? Nothing, Miss.'

'What have *they* done with my mama?' inquired the child.

'I never saw such a melting thing in all my life!' said Richards, who naturally substituted for this child one of her own, inquiring for herself in like circumstances. 'Come nearer here, my dear Miss! Don't be afraid of me.'

'I am not afraid of you,' said the child, drawing nearer. 'But I want to know what they have done with my mama.'

'My darling,' said Richards, 'you wear that pretty black frock in remembrance of your mama.'

'I can remember my mama,' returned the child, with tears springing to her eyes, 'in any frock.'

'But people put on black, to remember people when they're gone.'

'Where gone?' asked the child.

'Come and sit down by me,' said Richards, 'and I'll tell you a story.'

With a quick perception that it was intended to relate to what she had asked, little Florence laid aside the bonnet she had held in her hand until now, and sat down on a stool at the nurse's feet, looking up into her face.

'Once upon a time,' said Richards, 'there was a lady – a very good lady, and her little daughter dearly loved her.'

'A very good lady and her little daughter dearly loved her,' repeated the child.

'Who, when God thought it right that it should be so, was taken ill and died.'

The child shuddered.

'Died, never to be seen again by any one on earth, and was buried in the ground where the trees grow.'

'The cold ground?' said the child, shuddering again.

'No! The warm ground,' returned Polly, seizing her advantage, 'where the ugly little seeds turn into beautiful flowers, and into grass, and corn, and I don't know what all besides. Where good people turn into bright angels, and fly away to Heaven!'

The child, who had drooped her head, raised it again, and sat looking at her intently.

'So; let me see,' said Polly, not a little flurried between this earnest scrutiny, her desire to comfort the child, her sudden success, and her very slight confidence in her own powers. 'So, when this lady died, wherever they took her, or wherever they put her, she went to GOD! and she prayed to Him, this lady did,' said Polly, affecting herself beyond measure; being heartily in earnest, 'to teach her little daughter to be sure of that in her heart: and to know that she was happy there and loved her still: and to hope and try – Oh, all her life – to meet her there one day, never, never, never to part any more.'

'It was my mama!' exclaimed the child, springing up, and clasping her round the neck.

'And the child's heart,' said Polly, drawing her to her breast; 'the little daughter's heart was so full of the truth of this, that even when she heard it from a strange nurse that couldn't tell it right, but was a poor mother herself and that was all, she found a comfort in it – didn't feel so lonely – sobbed and cried upon her bosom – took kindly to the baby lying in her lap and – there, there, there!' said Polly, smoothing the child's curls and dropping tears upon them. 'There, poor dear!'

'Oh well, Miss Floy! And won't your pa be angry neither!' cried a quick voice at the door, proceeding from a short, brown, womanly girl of fourteen, with a little snub nose, and black eyes like jet beads. 'When it was 'tickerlerly given out that you wasn't to go and worrit the wet nurse.'

'She don't worry me,' was the surprised rejoinder of Polly. 'I am very fond of children.'

'Oh! but begging your pardon, Mrs Richards, that don't matter, you know,' returned the black-eyed girl, who was so desperately sharp and biting that she seemed to make one's eyes water. 'I may be very fond of pennywinkles,[10] Mrs Richards, but it don't follow that I'm to have 'em for tea.'

'Well, it don't matter,' said Polly.

'Oh, thank'ee Mrs Richards, don't it!' returned the sharp girl. 'Remembering, however, if you'll be so good, that Miss Floy's under my charge, and Master Paul's under your'n.'

'But still we needn't quarrel,' said Polly.

'Oh no, Mrs Richards,' rejoined Spitfire. 'Not at all, I don't wish it, we needn't stand upon that footing, Miss Floy being a permanency, Master Paul a temporary.'[11] Spitfire made use of none but comma pauses; shooting out whatever she had to say in one sentence, and in one breath, if possible.

'Miss Florence has just come home, hasn't she?' asked Polly.

'Yes, Mrs Richards, just come, and here, Miss Floy, before you've been in the house a quarter of an hour, you go a smearing your wet face against the expensive mourning that Mrs Richards is a wearing for your ma!' With this remonstrance, young Spitfire, whose real name was Susan Nipper, detached the child from her new friend by a wrench – as if she were a tooth. But she seemed to do it, more in the excessively sharp exercise of her official functions, than with any deliberate unkindness.

'She'll be quite happy, now she has come home again,' said Polly, nodding to her with an encouraging smile upon her wholesome face, 'and will be so pleased to see her dear papa to-night.'

'Lork, Mrs Richards!' cried Miss Nipper, taking up her words with a jerk. 'Don't. See her dear papa indeed! I should like to see her do it!'

'Won't she then?' asked Polly.

'Lork, Mrs Richards, no, her pa's a deal too wrapped up in somebody else, and before there was a somebody else to be wrapped up in she never was a favourite, girls are thrown away in this house, Mrs Richards, I assure you.'

The child looked quickly from one nurse to the other, as if she understood and felt what was said.

'You surprise me!' cried Polly. 'Hasn't Mr Dombey seen her since—'

'No,' interrupted Susan Nipper. 'Not once since, and he hadn't hardly set his eyes upon her before that for months and months, and I don't think he'd have known her for his own child if he had met her in the streets, or would know her for his own child if he was to meet her in the streets to-morrow, Mrs Richards, as to *me*,' said Spitfire, with a giggle, 'I doubt if he's aweer of my existence.'

'Pretty dear!' said Richards; meaning, not Miss Nipper, but the little Florence.

'Oh! there's a Tartar[12] within a hundred miles of where we're now in conversation, I can tell you, Mrs Richards, present company always excepted too,' said Susan Nipper; 'wish you good morning, Mrs Richards, now Miss Floy, you come along with me, and don't go hanging back like a naughty wicked child that judgments is no example to, don't.'

In spite of being thus adjured, and in spite also of some hauling on the part of Susan Nipper, tending towards the dislocation of her right shoulder, little Florence broke away, and kissed her new friend affectionately.

'Good-bye!' said the child. 'God bless you! I shall come to see you again soon, and you'll come to see me? Susan will let us. Won't you, Susan?'

Spitfire seemed to be in the main a good-natured little body, although a disciple of that school of trainers of the young idea[13] which holds that childhood, like money, must be shaken and rattled and jostled about a good deal to keep it bright. For, being thus appealed to with some endearing gestures and caresses, she folded her small arms and shook her head, and conveyed a relenting expression into her very-wide-open black eyes.

'It ain't right of you to ask it, Miss Floy, for you know I can't refuse you, but Mrs Richards and me will see what can be done, if Mrs Richards likes, I may wish, you see, to take a voyage to Chaney,[14] Mrs Richards, but I mayn't know how to leave the London Docks.'

Richards assented to the proposition.

'This house ain't so exactly ringing with merry-making,' said Miss Nipper, 'that one need be lonelier than one must be. Your Toxes and your Chickses may draw out my two front double teeth, Mrs Richards, but that's no reason why I need offer 'em the whole set.'

This proposition was also assented to by Richards, as an obvious one.

'So I'm agreeable, I'm sure,' said Susan Nipper, 'to live friendly, Mrs Richards, while Master Paul continues a permanency, if the means can be planned out without going openly against orders, but goodness gracious ME, Miss Floy, you haven't got your things off yet, you naughty child, you haven't, come along!'

With these words, Susan Nipper, in a transport of coercion, made a charge at her young ward, and swept her out of the room.

The child, in her grief and neglect, was so gentle, so quiet, and uncomplaining; was possessed of so much affection that no one seemed to care to have, and so much sorrowful intelligence that no one seemed to mind or think about the wounding of; that Polly's heart was sore when she was left alone again. In the simple passage that had taken place between herself and the motherless little girl, her own motherly heart had been touched no less than the child's; and she felt, as the child did, that there was something of confidence and interest between them from that moment.

Notwithstanding Mr Toodle's great reliance on Polly, she was perhaps in point of artificial accomplishments very little his superior. But she was a good plain sample of a nature that is ever, in the mass, better, truer, higher, nobler, quicker to feel, and much more constant to retain, all tenderness and pity, self-denial and devotion, than the nature of men. And, perhaps, unlearned as she was, she could have brought a dawning knowledge home to Mr Dombey at that early day, which would not then have struck him in the end like lightning.

But this is from the purpose. Polly only thought, at that time, of improving on her successful propitiation of Miss Nipper, and devising some means of having little Florence beside her, lawfully, and without rebellion. An opening happened to present itself that very night.

She had been rung down into the glass room as usual, and had walked about and about it a long time, with the baby in her arms, when, to her great surprise and dismay, Mr Dombey came out, suddenly, and stopped before her.

'Good evening, Richards.'

Just the same austere, stiff gentleman, as he had appeared to her on that first day. Such a hard-looking gentleman, that she involuntarily dropped her eyes and her curtsey at the same time.

'How is Master Paul, Richards?'

'Quite thriving, Sir, and well.'

'He looks so,' said Mr Dombey, glancing with great interest at the tiny face she uncovered for his observation, and yet affecting to be half careless of it. 'They give you everything you want, I hope?'

'Oh yes, thank you, Sir.'

She suddenly appended such an obvious hesitation to this reply, however, that Mr Dombey, who had turned away, stopped, and turned round again, inquiringly.

'I believe nothing is so good for making children lively and cheerful, Sir, as seeing other children playing about 'em,' observed Polly, taking courage.

'I think I mentioned to you, Richards, when you came here,' said

Mr Dombey, with a frown, 'that I wished you to see as little of your family as possible. You can continue your walk if you please.'

With that, he disappeared into his inner room; and Polly had the satisfaction of feeling that he had thoroughly misunderstood her object, and that she had fallen into disgrace without the least advancement of her purpose.

Next night, she found him walking about the conservatory when she came down. As she stopped at the door, checked by this unusual sight, and uncertain whether to advance or retreat, he called her in.

'If you really think that sort of society is good for the child,' he said sharply, as if there had been no interval since she proposed it, 'where's Miss Florence?'

'Nothing could be better than Miss Florence, Sir,' said Polly eagerly, 'but I understood from her little maid that they were not to—'

Mr Dombey rang the bell, and walked till it was answered.

'Tell them always to let Miss Florence be with Richards when she chooses, and go out with her, and so forth. Tell them to let the children be together, when Richards wishes it.'

The iron was now hot, and Richards, striking on it boldly – it was a good cause and she was bold in it, though instinctively afraid of Mr Dombey – requested that Miss Florence might be sent down then and there, to make friends with her little brother.

She feigned to be dandling the child as the servant retired on this errand, but she thought that she saw Mr Dombey's colour changed; that the expression of his face quite altered; that he turned, hurriedly, as if to gainsay what he had said, or she had said, or both, and was only deterred by very shame.

And she was right. The last time he had seen his slighted child, there had been that in the sad embrace between her and her dying mother, which was at once a revelation and a reproach to him. Let him be absorbed as he would in the Son on whom he built such high hopes, he could not forget that closing scene. He could not forget that he had had no part in it. That, at the bottom of its clear depths of tenderness and truth, lay those two figures clasped in each other's arms, while he stood on the bank above them, looking down, a mere spectator – not a sharer with them – quite shut out.

Unable to exclude these things from his remembrance, or to keep his mind free from such imperfect shapes of the meaning with which they were fraught, as were able to make themselves visible to him through the mist of his pride, his previous feelings of indifference towards little Florence changed into an uneasiness of an extraordinary kind. He almost felt as if she watched and distrusted him. As if she held the clue to something secret in his breast, of the nature of which he was hardly informed himself. As if she had an innate knowledge of one jarring and discordant string within him, and her very breath could sound it.

His feeling about the child had been negative from her birth. He had never conceived an aversion to her: it had not been worth his while or in his humour. She had never been a positively disagreeable object to him. But now he was ill at ease about her. She troubled his peace. He would have preferred to put her idea aside altogether, if he had known how. Perhaps – who shall decide on such mysteries! – he was afraid that he might come to hate her.

When little Florence timidly presented herself, Mr Dombey stopped in his pacing up and down and looked towards her. Had he looked with greater interest and with a father's eye, he might have read in her keen glance the impulses and fears that made her waver; the passionate desire to run clinging to him, crying, as she hid her face in his embrace, 'Oh father, try to love me! there's no one else!' the dread of a repulse; the fear of being too bold, and of offending him; the pitiable need in which she stood of some assurance and encouragement; and how her overcharged young heart was wandering to find some natural resting-place, for its sorrow and affection.

But he saw nothing of this. He saw her pause irresolutely at the door and look towards him; and he saw no more.

'Come in,' he said, 'come in: what is the child afraid of?'

She came in; and after glancing round her for a moment with an uncertain air, stood pressing her small hands hard together, close within the door.

'Come here, Florence,' said her father, coldly. 'Do you know who I am?'

'Yes, papa.'

'Have you nothing to say to me?'

The tears that stood in her eyes as she raised them quickly to his face, were frozen by the expression it wore. She looked down again, and put out her trembling hand.

Mr Dombey took it loosely in his own, and stood looking down upon her for a moment, as if he knew as little as the child what to say or do.

'There! Be a good girl,' he said, patting her on the head, and regarding her as it were by stealth with a disturbed and doubtful look. 'Go to Richards! Go!'

The Dombey family

His little daughter hesitated for another instant as though she would have clung about him still, or had some lingering hope that he might raise her in his arms and kiss her. She looked up in his face once more. He thought how like her expression was then, to what it had been when she looked round at the doctor – that night – and instinctively dropped her hand and turned away.

It was not difficult to perceive that Florence was at a great disadvantage in her father's presence. It was not only a constraint upon the child's mind, but even upon the natural grace and freedom of her actions. Still Polly persevered with all the better heart for seeing this; and, judging of Mr Dombey by herself, had great confidence in the mute appeal of poor little Florence's mourning dress. 'It's hard indeed,' thought Polly, 'if he takes only to one little motherless child, when he has another, and that a girl, before his eyes.'

So, Polly kept her before his eyes, as long as she could, and managed so well with little Paul, as to make it very plain that he was all the livelier for his sister's company. When it was time to withdraw upstairs again, she would have sent Florence into the inner room to say good-night to her father, but the child was timid and drew back: and when she urged her again, said, spreading her hands before her eyes, as if to shut out her own unworthiness, 'Oh, no, no! He don't want me. He don't want me!'

The little altercation between them had attracted the notice of Mr Dombey, who inquired from the table where he was sitting at his wine, what the matter was.

'Miss Florence was afraid of interrupting, Sir, if she came in to say good-night,' said Richards.

'It doesn't matter,' returned Mr Dombey. 'You can let her come and go without regarding me.'

The child shrunk as she listened – and was gone before her humble friend looked round again.

However, Polly triumphed not a little in the success of her well-intentioned scheme, and in the address[15] with which she had brought it to bear: whereof she made a full disclosure to Spitfire when she was once more safely intrenched upstairs. Miss Nipper received that proof of her confidence, as well as the prospect of their free association for the future, rather coldly, and was anything but enthusiastic in her demonstrations of joy.

'I thought you would have been pleased,' said Polly.

'Oh yes, Mrs Richards, I'm very well pleased, thank you,'

returned Susan, who had suddenly become so very upright that she seemed to have put an additional bone in her stays.[16]

'You don't show it,' said Polly.

'Oh! Being only a permanency I couldn't be expected to show it like a temporary,' said Susan Nipper. 'Temporaries carries it all before 'em here, I find, but though there's a excellent party-wall[17] between this house and the next, I mayn't exactly like to go to it, Mrs Richards, notwithstanding!'

CHAPTER 4

In which some more First Appearances are made on the Stage of these Adventures

Though the offices of Dombey and Son were within the liberties of the City of London, and within hearing of Bow Bells,[1] when their clashing voices were not drowned by the uproar in the streets, yet were there hints of adventurous and romantic story to be observed in some of the adjacent objects. Gog and Magog[2] held their state within ten minutes' walk; the Royal Exchange was close at hand; the Bank of England, with its vaults of gold and silver 'down among the dead men' underground, was their magnificent neighbour. Just round the corner stood the rich East India House,[3] teeming with suggestions of precious stuffs and stones, tigers, elephants, how-dahs, hookahs, umbrellas, palm trees, palanquins, and gorgeous princes of a brown complexion sitting on carpets, with their slippers very much turned up at the toes. Anywhere in the immediate vicinity there might be seen pictures of ships speeding away full sail to all parts of the world; outfitting warehouses ready to pack off anybody anywhere, fully equipped in half an hour; and little timber midshipmen[4] in obsolete naval uniforms, eternally employed outside the shop doors of nautical instrument-makers in taking observations of the hackney coaches.

Sole master and proprietor of one of these effigies – of that which might be called, familiarly, the woodenest – of that which thrust itself out above the pavement, right leg foremost, with a suavity the least endurable, and had the shoe buckles and flapped waistcoat the least reconcilable to human reason, and bore at its right eye the most offensively disproportionate piece of machinery – sole master and proprietor of that midshipman[5] and proud of him too, an

elderly gentleman in a Welsh wig[6] had paid house-rent, taxes, and
dues, for more years than many a full-grown midshipman of flesh
and blood has numbered in his life; and midshipmen who have
attained a pretty green old age, have not been wanting in the
English navy.

The stock-in-trade of this old gentleman comprised chronometers, barometers, telescopes, compasses, charts, maps, sextants,
quadrants, and specimens of every kind of instrument used in the
working of a ship's course, or the keeping of a ship's reckoning, or
the prosecuting of a ship's discoveries. Objects in brass and glass
were in his drawers and on his shelves, which none but the initiated
could have found the top of, or guessed the use of, or having once
examined, could have ever got back again into their mahogany
nests without assistance. Everything was jammed into the tightest
cases, fitted into the narrowest corners, fenced up behind the most
impertinent cushions, and screwed into the acutest angles, to
prevent its philosophical composure from being disturbed by the
rolling of the sea. Such extraordinary precautions were taken in
every instance to save room, and keep the thing compact; and so
much practical navigation was fitted, and cushioned, and screwed
into every box (whether the box was a mere slab, as some were, or
something between a cocked hat and a starfish, as others were, and
those quite mild and modest boxes as compared with others); that
the shop itself, partaking of the general infection, seemed almost to
become a snug, sea-going, ship-shape concern, wanting only good
sea-room, in the event of an unexpected launch, to work its way
securely to any desert island in the world.

Many minor incidents in the household life of the Ships' Instrument-maker who was proud of his little midshipman, assisted and
bore out this fancy. His acquaintance lying chiefly among ship-
chandlers and so forth, he had always plenty of the veritable ships'
biscuit on his table. It was familiar with dried meats and tongues,
possessing an extraordinary flavour of rope yarn. Pickles were
produced upon it, in great wholesale jars, with 'dealer in all kinds
of Ships' Provisions' on the label; spirits were set forth in case
bottles with no throats. Old prints of ships with alphabetical
references to their various mysteries, hung in frames upon the walls;
the Tartar Frigate under weigh, was on the plates; outlandish shells,
seaweeds, and mosses, decorated the chimneypiece; the little wain-
scotted back parlour was lighted by a sky-light, like a cabin.

Here he lived too, in skipper-like state, all alone with his nephew
Walter: a boy of fourteen who looked quite enough like a midship-

man, to carry out the prevailing idea. But there it ended, for Solomon Gills himself (more generally called old Sol) was far from having a maritime appearance. To say nothing of his Welsh wig, which was as plain and stubborn a Welsh wig as ever was worn, and in which he looked like anything but a Rover, he was a slow, quiet-spoken, thoughtful old fellow, with eyes as red as if they had been small suns looking at you through a fog; and a newly-awakened manner, such as he might have acquired by having stared for three or four days successively through every optical instrument in his shop, and suddenly come back to the world again, to find it green. The only change ever known in his outward man, was from a complete suit of coffee-colour cut very square, and ornamented with glaring buttons, to the same suit of coffee-colour minus the inexpressibles[7] which were then of a pale nankeen.[8] He wore a very precise shirt-frill, and carried a pair of first-rate spectacles on his forehead, and a tremendous chronometer in his fob, rather than doubt which precious possession, he would have believed in a conspiracy against it on the part of all the clocks and watches in the City, and even of the very Sun itself. Such as he was, such he had been in the shop and parlour behind the little midshipman, for years upon years; going regularly aloft to bed every night in a howling garret remote from the lodgers, where, when gentlemen of England who lived below at ease had little or no idea of the state of the weather, it often blew great guns.

It is half-past five o'clock, and an autumn afternoon, when the reader and Solomon Gills become acquainted. Solomon Gills is in the act of seeing what time it is by the unimpeachable chronometer. The usual daily clearance has been making in the City for an hour or more; and the human tide is still rolling westward. 'The streets have thinned,' as Mr Gills says, 'very much.' It threatens to be wet to-night. All the weather-glasses in the shop are in low spirits, and the rain already shines upon the cocked hat of the wooden midshipman.

'Where's Walter, I wonder!' said Solomon Gills, after he had carefully put up the chronometer again. 'Here's dinner been ready, half an hour, and no Walter!'

Turning round upon his stool behind the counter, Mr Gills looked out among the instruments in the window, to see if his nephew might be crossing the road. No. He was not among the bobbing umbrellas, and he certainly was not the newspaper boy in the oilskin cap who was slowly working his way along the piece of brass outside, writing his name over Mr Gills' name with his forefinger.

'If I didn't know he was too fond of me to make a run of it, and go and enter himself aboard ship against my wishes, I should begin to be fidgetty,' said Mr Gills, tapping two or three weather-glasses with his knuckles. 'I really should. All in the Downs, eh! Lots of moisture! Well! it's wanted.'

'I believe,' said Mr Gills, blowing the dust off the glass top of a compass case, 'that you don't point more direct and due to the back parlour than the boy's inclination does after all. And the parlour couldn't bear straighter either. Due north. Not the twentieth part of a point either way.'

'Halloa, Uncle Sol!'

'Halloa, my boy!' cried the Instrument-maker, turning briskly round. 'What! you are here, are you?'

A cheerful-looking, merry boy, fresh with running home in the rain; fair-faced, bright-eyed, and curly-haired.

'Well, uncle, how have you got on without me all day? Is dinner ready? I'm so hungry.'

'As to getting on,' said Solomon good-naturedly, 'it would be odd if I couldn't get on without a young dog like you a great deal better than with you. As to dinner being ready, it's been ready this half hour and waiting for you. As to being hungry, *I* am!'

'Come along then, uncle!' cried the boy. 'Hurrah for the admiral!'9

'Confound the admiral!' returned Solomon Gills. 'You mean the Lord Mayor.'

'No I don't!' cried the boy. 'Hurrah for the admiral! Hurrah for the admiral! For–ward!'

At this word of command, the Welsh wig and its wearer were borne without resistance into the back parlour, as at the head of a boarding party of five hundred men; and Uncle Sol and his nephew were speedily engaged on a fried sole with a prospect of steak to follow.

'The Lord Mayor, Wally,' said Solomon, 'for ever! No more admirals. The Lord Mayor's *your* admiral.'

'Oh, is he though!' said the boy, shaking his head. 'Why, the Sword Bearer's better than him. He draws *his* sword sometimes.'

'And a pretty figure he cuts with it for his pains,' returned the uncle. 'Listen to me, Wally, listen to me. Look on the mantel-shelf.'

'Why, who has cocked my silver mug up there, on a nail?' exclaimed the boy.

'I have,' said his uncle. 'No more mugs now. We must begin to drink out of glasses to-day, Walter. We are men of business. We belong to the City. We started in life this morning.'

'Well, uncle,' said the boy, 'I'll drink out of anything you like, so long as I can drink to you. Here's to you, Uncle Sol, and Hurrah for the—'

'Lord Mayor,' interrupted the old man.

'For the Lord Mayor, Sheriffs, Common Council, and Livery,'[10] said the boy. 'Long life to 'em!'

The uncle nodded his head with great satisfaction. 'And now,' he said, 'let's hear something about the firm.'

'Oh! there's not much to be told about the Firm, uncle,' said the boy, plying his knife and fork. 'It's a precious dark set of offices, and in the room where I sit, there's a high fender, and an iron safe, and some cards about ships that are going to sail, and an almanack, and some desks and stools, and an inkbottle, and some books, and some boxes, and a lot of cobwebs, and in one of 'em, just over my head, a shrivelled-up bluebottle that looks as if it had hung there ever so long.'

'Nothing else?' said the uncle.

'No, nothing else, except an old bird-cage (I wonder how *that* ever came there!) and a coal-scuttle.'

'No bankers' books, or cheque books, or bills, or such tokens of wealth rolling in from day to day?' said old Sol, looking wistfully at his nephew out of the fog that always seemed to hang about him, and laying an unctuous emphasis upon the words.

'Oh yes, plenty of that, I suppose,' returned his nephew carelessly; 'but all that sort of thing's in Mr Carker's room, or Mr Morfin's, or Mr Dombey's.'

'Has Mr Dombey been there to-day?' inquired the Uncle.

'Oh yes! In and out all day.'

'He didn't take any notice of you, I suppose?'

'Yes he did. He walked up to my seat – I wish he wasn't so solemn and stiff, uncle – and said, "Oh! you are the son of Mr Gills the Ships' Instrument-maker." "Nephew, Sir," I said. "I said nephew, boy," said he. But I could take my oath he said son, uncle.'

'You're mistaken I dare say. It's no matter.'

'No, it's no matter, but he needn't have been so sharp, I thought. There was no harm in it though he did say son. Then he told me that you had spoken to him about me, and that he had found me employment in the House accordingly, and that I was expected to be attentive and punctual, and then he went away. I thought he didn't seem to like me much.'

'You mean, I suppose,' observed the Instrument-maker, 'that you didn't seem to like him much.'

'Well, uncle,' returned the boy, laughing. 'Perhaps so; I never thought of that.'

Solomon looked a little graver as he finished his dinner, and glanced from time to time at the boy's bright face. When dinner was done, and the cloth was cleared away (the entertainment had been brought from a neighbouring eating-house), he lighted a candle, and went down below into a little cellar, while his nephew, standing on the mouldy staircase, dutifully held the light. After a moment's groping here and there, he presently returned with a very ancient-looking bottle, covered with dust and dirt.

'Why, Uncle Sol!' said the boy, 'what are you about! that's the wonderful Madeira! – there's only one more bottle!'

Uncle Sol nodded his head, implying that he knew very well what he was about; and having drawn the cork in solemn silence, filled two glasses and set the bottle and a third clean glass on the table.

'You shall drink the other bottle, Wally,' he said, 'when you come to good fortune; when you are a thriving, respected, happy man; when the start in life you have made to-day shall have brought you, as I pray Heaven it may! – to a smooth part of the course you have to run, my child. My love to you!'

Some of the fog that hung about old Sol seemed to have got into his throat; for he spoke huskily. His hand shook too, as he clinked his glass against his nephew's. But having once got the wine to his lips, he tossed it off like a man, and smacked them afterwards.

'Dear uncle,' said the boy, affecting to make light of it, while the tears stood in his eyes, 'for the honour you have done me, et cetera, et cetera. I shall now beg to propose Mr Solomon Gills with three times three and one cheer more. Hurrah! and you'll return thanks, uncle, when we drink the last bottle together; won't you?'

They clinked their glasses again; and Walter, who was hoarding his wine, took a sip of it, and held the glass up to his eye with as critical an air as he could possibly assume.

His uncle sat looking at him for some time in silence. When their eyes at last met, he began at once to pursue the theme that had occupied his thoughts, aloud, as if he had been speaking all the while.

'You see, Walter,' he said, 'in truth this business is merely a habit with me. I am so accustomed to the habit that I could hardly live if I relinquished it: but there's nothing doing, nothing doing. When that uniform was worn,' pointing out towards the little midshipman, 'then indeed, fortunes were to be made and were made. But competition, competition – new invention, new invention – alteration, alteration – the world's gone past me. I hardly know where I am myself; much less where my customers are.'

'Never mind 'em, uncle!'

'Since you came home from weekly boarding-school at Peckham, for instance – and that's ten days,' said Solomon, 'I don't remember more than one person that has come into the shop.'

'Two, uncle, don't you recollect? There was the man who came to ask for change for a sovereign—'[11]

'That's the one,' said Solomon.

'Why, uncle! don't you call the woman anybody, who came to ask the way to Mile-End Turnpike?'[12]

'Oh! it's true,' said Solomon, 'I forgot her. Two persons.'

'To be sure, they didn't buy anything,' cried the boy.

'No. They didn't buy anything,' said Solomon, quietly.

'Nor want anything,' cried the boy.

'No. If they had, they'd have gone to another shop,' said Solomon, in the same tone.

'But there were two of 'em, uncle,' cried the boy, as if that were a great triumph. 'You said only one.'

'Well, Wally,' resumed the old man, after a short pause; 'not being like the Savages who came on Robinson Crusoe's Island,[13] we can't live on a man who asks for change for a sovereign, and a woman who inquires the way to Mile-End Turnpike. As I said just now, the world has gone past me. I don't blame it; but I no longer understand it. Tradesmen are not the same as they used to be, apprentices are not the same, business is not the same, business commodities are not the same. Seven-eighths of my stock is old-fashioned. I am an old-fashioned man in an old-fashioned shop, in a street that is not the same as I remember it. I have fallen behind the time, and am too old to catch it again. Even the noise it makes a long way ahead, confuses me.'

Walter was going to speak, but his uncle held up his hand.

'Therefore, Wally – therefore it is that I am anxious you should be early in the busy world, and on the world's track. I am only the ghost of this business – its substance vanished long ago; and when I die, its ghost will be laid. As it is clearly no inheritance for you then, I have thought it best to use for your advantage, almost the only fragment of the old connexion that stands by me, through long habit. Some people suppose me to be wealthy. I wish for your sake they were right. But whatever I leave behind me, or whatever I can give you, you in such a house as Dombey's are in the road to use well and make the most of. Be diligent, try to like it, my dear boy, work for a steady independence, and be happy!'

'I'll do everything I can, uncle, to deserve your affection. Indeed I will,' said the boy, earnestly.

'I know it,' said Solomon. 'I am sure of it,' and he applied himself to a second glass of the old Madeira, with increased relish. 'As to the Sea,' he pursued, 'that's well enough in fiction, Wally, but it won't do in fact: it won't do at all. It's natural enough that you should think about it, associating it with all these familiar things; but it won't do, it won't do.'

Solomon Gills rubbed his hands with an air of stealthy enjoyment, as he talked of the sea, though; and looked on the seafaring objects about him with inexpressible complacency.

'Think of this wine for instance,' said old Sol, 'which has been to the East Indies and back, I'm not able to say how often, and has been once round the world. Think of the pitch-dark nights, the roaring winds, and rolling seas: '

'The thunder, lightning, rain, hail, storm of all kinds,' said the boy.

'To be sure,' said Solomon, – 'that this wine has passed through. Think what a straining and creaking of timbers and masts: what a whistling and howling of the gale through ropes and rigging:'

'What a clambering aloft of men, vying with each other who shall lie out first upon the yards[14] to furl the icy sails, while the ship rolls and pitches, like mad!' cried his nephew.

'Exactly so,' said Solomon: 'has gone on, over the old cask that held this wine. Why, when the Charming Sally went down in the —'

'In the Baltic Sea, in the dead of night; five-and-twenty minutes past twelve when the captain's watch stopped in his pocket; he lying dead against the main-mast – on the fourteenth of February, seventeen forty-nine!' cried Walter, with great animation.

'Ay, to be sure!' cried old Sol, 'quite right! Then, there were five hundred casks of such wine aboard; and all hands (except the first mate, first lieutenant, two seamen, and a lady, in a leaky boat) going to work to stave the casks, got drunk and died drunk, singing "Rule Britannia," when she settled and went down, and ending with one awful scream in chorus.'

'But when the George the Second drove ashore, uncle, on the coast of Cornwall, in a dismal gale, two hours before daybreak, on the fourth of March, 'seventy-one, she had near two hundred horses aboard; and the horses breaking loose down below, early in the gale, and tearing to and fro, and trampling each other to death, made such noises, and set up such human cries, that the crew believing the ship to be full of devils, some of the best men, losing heart and head, went overboard in despair, and only two were left alive, at last, to tell the tale.'

'And when,' said old Sol, 'when the Polyphemus—'

'Private West India Trader, burden three hundred and fifty tons, Captain, John Brown of Deptford. Owners, Wiggs and Co.,' cried Walter.

'The same,' said Sol; 'when she took fire, four days' sail with a fair wind out of Jamaica Harbour, in the night—'

'There were two brothers on board,' interposed his nephew, speaking very fast and loud, 'and there not being room for both of them in the only boat that wasn't swamped, neither of them would consent to go, until the elder took the younger by the waist and flung him in. And then the younger rising in the boat, cried out, "Dear Edward, think of your promised wife at home. I'm only a boy. No one waits at home for me. Leap down into my place!" and flung himself into the sea!'

The kindling eye and heightened colour of the boy, who had risen from his seat in the earnestness of what he said and felt, seemed to remind old Sol of something he had forgotten, or that his encircling mist had hitherto shut out. Instead of proceeding with any more anecdotes, as he had evidently intended but a moment before, he gave a short dry cough, and said, 'Well! suppose we change the subject.'

The truth was, that the simple-minded uncle in his secret attraction towards the marvellous and adventurous – of which he was, in some sort, a distant relation, by his trade – had greatly encouraged the same attraction in the nephew; and that everything that had ever been put before the boy to deter him from a life of adventure, had had the usual unaccountable effect of sharpening his taste for it. This is invariable. It would seem as if there never was a book written, or a story told, expressly with the object of keeping boys on shore, which did not lure and charm them to the ocean, as a matter of course.

But an addition to the little party now made its appearance, in the shape of a gentleman in a wide suit of blue, with a hook instead of a hand attached to his right wrist; very bushy black eyebrows; and a thick stick in his left hand, covered all over (like his nose) with knobs. He wore a loose black silk handkerchief round his neck, and such a very large coarse shirtcollar, that it looked like a small sail. He was evidently the person for whom the spare wine-glass was intended, and evidently knew it; for having taken off his rough outer coat, and hung up, on a particular peg behind the door, such a hard glazed hat as a sympathetic person's head might ache at the sight of, and which left a red rim round his own forehead as if he had been wearing a tight basin, he brought a chair to where the clean glass was, and sat himself down behind it. He was usually addressed as Captain, this visitor; and had been a pilot, or a skipper, or a privateers-man,[15] or all three perhaps; and was a very salt-looking man indeed.

His face, remarkable for a brown solidity, brightened as he shook hands with uncle and nephew; but he seemed to be of a laconic disposition, and merely said:

'How goes it?'

'All well,' said Mr Gills, pushing the bottle towards him.

He took it up, and having surveyed and smelt it, said with extraordinary expression:

'*The?*'

'*The,*' returned the Instrument-Maker.

Upon that he whistled as he filled his glass, and seemed to think they were making holiday indeed.

'Wal'r!' he said, arranging his hair (which was thin) with his hook, and then pointing it at the Instrument-maker, 'Look at him! Love! Honour! And Obey!'[16] Overhaul your catechism till you find that passage, and when found turn the leaf down. Success, my boy!'

He was so perfectly satisfied both with his quotation and his reference to it, that he could not help repeating the words again in a low voice, and saying he had forgotten 'em these forty year.

'But I never wanted two or three words in my life that I didn't know where to lay my hand upon 'em, Gills,' he observed. 'It comes of not wasting language as some do.'

The reflection perhaps reminded him that he had better, like young Norval's father, 'increase his store.'[17] At any rate he became silent, and remained so, until old Sol went out into the shop to light it up, when he turned to Walter, and said, without any introductory remark:

'I suppose he could make a clock if he tried?'

'I shouldn't wonder, Captain Cuttle,' returned the boy.

'And it would go!' said Captain Cuttle, making a species of serpent in the air with his hook. 'Lord, how that clock would go!'

For a moment or two he seemed quite lost in contemplating the pace of this ideal timepiece, and sat looking at the boy as if his face were the dial.

'But he's chockfull of science,' he observed, waving his hook towards the stock-in-trade. 'Look'ye here! Here's a collection of 'em. Earth, air, or water. It's all one. Only say where you'll have it. Up in a balloon? There you are. Down in a bell? There you are. D'ye want to put the North Star in a pair of scales and weigh it? He'll do it for you.'

It may be gathered from these remarks that Captain Cuttle's reverence for the stock of instruments was profound, and that his philosophy knew little or no distinction between trading in it and inventing it.

'Ah!' he said, with a sigh, 'it's a fine thing to understand 'em. And yet it's a fine thing not to understand 'em. I hardly know which is best. It's so comfortable to sit here and feel that you might be weighed, measured, magnified, electrified, polarized, played the very devil with: and never know how.'

Nothing short of the wonderful Madeira, combined with the occasion (which rendered it desirable to improve and expand Walter's mind), could have ever loosened his tongue to the extent of giving utterance to this prodigious oration. He seemed quite amazed himself at the manner in which it opened up to view the sources of the taciturn delight he had had in eating Sunday dinners in that parlour for ten years. Becoming a sadder and a wiser man, he mused and held his peace.

'Come!' cried the subject of his admiration, returning. 'Before you have your glass of grog,[18] Ned, we must finish the bottle.'

'Stand by!' said Ned, filling his glass. 'Give the boy some more.'

'No more, thank'e, uncle!'

'Yes, yes,' said Sol, 'a little more. We'll finish the bottle, to the House, Ned – Walter's house. Why it may be his house one of these days, in part. Who knows? Sir Richard Whittington[19] married his master's daughter.'

'"Turn again Whittington, Lord Mayor of London, and when you are old you will never depart from it,"'[20] interposed the Captain. 'Wal'r! Overhaul the book, my lad.'

'And although Mr Dombey hasn't a daughter,' Sol began.

'Yes, yes, he has, uncle,' said the boy, reddening and laughing.

'Has he?' cried the old man. 'Indeed I think he has too.'

'Oh! I know he has,' said the boy. 'Some of 'em were talking about it in the office to-day. And they do say, uncle and Captain Cuttle,' lowering his voice, 'that he's taken a dislike to her, and that she's left, unnoticed, among the servants, and that his mind's so set all the while upon having his son in the House, that although he's only a baby now, he is going to have balances struck oftener than formerly, and the books kept closer than they used to be, and has even been seen (when he thought he wasn't) walking in the Docks, looking at his ships and property and all that, as if he was exulting like, over what he and his son will possess together. That's what they say. Of course I don't know.'

'He knows all about her already, you see,' said the Instrument-maker.

'Nonsense, uncle,' cried the boy, still reddening and laughing, boy-like. 'How can I help hearing what they tell me?'

'The Son's a little in our way at present, I'm afraid, Ned,' said the old man, humouring the joke.

'Very much,' said the Captain.

'Nevertheless, we'll drink him,' pursued Sol. 'So, here's to Dombey and Son.'

'Oh, very well, uncle,' said the boy merrily. 'Since you have introduced the mention of her, and have connected me with her, and have said that I know all about her, I shall make bold to amend the toast. So here's to Dombey – and Son – and Daughter!'

CHAPTER 5

Paul's Progress and Christening

Little Paul, suffering no contamination from the blood of the Toodles, grew stouter and stronger every day. Every day, too, he was more and more ardently cherished by Miss Tox, whose devotion was so far appreciated by Mr Dombey that he began to regard her as a woman of great natural good sense, whose feelings did her credit and deserved encouragement. He was so lavish of this condescension, that he not only bowed to her, in a particular manner, on several occasions, but even entrusted such stately recognitions of her to his sister as 'pray tell your friend, Louisa, that she is very good,' or 'mention to Miss Tox, Louisa, that I am obliged to her'; specialities which made a deep impression on the lady thus distinguished.

Miss Tox was often in the habit of assuring Mrs Chick, that 'nothing could exceed her interest in all connected with the development of that sweet child'; and an observer of Miss Tox's proceedings might have inferred so much without declaratory confirmation. She would preside over the innocent repasts of the young heir, with ineffable satisfaction, almost with an air of joint proprietorship with Richards in the entertainment. At the little ceremonies of the bath and toilette, she assisted with enthusiasm. The administration of infantine doses of physic[1] awakened all the active sympathy of her character; and being on one occasion secreted in a cupboard (whither she had fled in modesty), when Mr Dombey was introduced into the nursery by his sister, to behold his son, in the course of preparation for bed, taking a short walk uphill over Richards's gown, in a short and airy linen jacket, Miss Tox was so transported beyond the ignorant present as to be unable to refrain from crying out, 'Is he not beautiful, Mr Dombey! Is he not a Cupid, Sir!' and then almost sinking behind the closet door with confusion and blushes.

'Louisa,' said Mr Dombey, one day, to his sister, 'I really think I must present your friend with some little token, on the occasion of Paul's christening. She has exerted herself so warmly in the child's behalf from the first, and seems to understand her position so thoroughly (a very rare merit in this world, I am sorry to say), that it would really be agreeable to me to notice her.'

Let it be no detraction from the merits of Miss Tox, to hint that in Mr Dombey's eyes, as in some others that occasionally see the light, they only achieved that mighty piece of knowledge, the understanding of their own position, who showed a fitting reverence for his. It was not so much their merit that they knew themselves, as that they knew him, and bowed low before him.

'My dear Paul,' returned his sister, 'you do Miss Tox but justice, as a man of your penetration was sure, I knew, to do. I believe if there are three words in the English language for which she has a respect amounting almost to veneration, those words are, Dombey and Son.'

'Well,' said Mr Dombey, 'I believe it. It does Miss Tox credit.'

'And as to anything in the shape of a token, my dear Paul,' pursued his sister, 'all I can say is that anything you give Miss Tox will be hoarded and prized, I am sure, like a relic. But there *is* a way, my dear Paul, of showing your sense of Miss Tox's friendliness in a still more flattering and acceptable manner, if you should be so inclined.'

'How is that?' asked Mr Dombey.

'Godfathers, of course,' continued Mrs Chick, 'are important in point of connexion and influence.'

'I don't know why they should be, to my son,' said Mr Dombey, coldly.

'Very true, my dear Paul,' retorted Mrs Chick, with an extraordinary show of animation, to cover the suddenness of her conversion; 'and spoken like yourself. I might have expected nothing else from you. I might have known that such would have been your opinion. Perhaps;' here Mrs Chick flattered again, as not quite comfortably feeling her way; 'perhaps that is a reason why you might have the less objection to allowing Miss Tox to be godmother to the dear thing, if it were only as deputy and proxy for some one else. That it would be received as a great honour and distinction, Paul, I need not say.'

'Louisa,' said Mr Dombey, after a short pause, 'it is not to be supposed—'

'Certainly not,' cried Mrs Chick, hastening to anticipate a refusal, 'I never thought it was.'

Mr Dombey looked at her impatiently.

'Don't flurry me, my dear Paul,' said his sister; 'for that destroys me. I am far from strong. I have not been quite myself, since poor dear Fanny departed.'

Mr Dombey glanced at the pocket-handkerchief which his sister applied to her eyes, and resumed:

'It is not to be supposed, I say—'

'And I say,' murmured Mrs Chick, 'that I never thought it was.'

'Good Heavens, Louisa!' said Mr Dombey.

'No, my dear Paul,' she remonstrated with tearful dignity, 'I must really be allowed to speak. I am not so clever, or so reasoning, or so eloquent, or so anything, as you are. I know that very well. So much the worse for me. But if they were the last words I had to utter – and last words should be very solemn to you and me, Paul, after poor dear Fanny – I should still say I never thought it was. And what is more,' added Mrs Chick with increased dignity, as if she had withheld her crushing argument until now, 'I never did think it was.'

Mr Dombey walked to the window and back again.

'It is not to be supposed, Louisa,' he said (Mrs Chick had nailed her colours to the mast[2] and repeated 'I know it isn't,' but he took no notice of it), 'but that there are many persons who, supposing that I recognised any claim at all in such a case, have a claim upon me superior to Miss Tox's. But I do not. I recognise no such thing.

Paul and myself will be able, when the time comes, to hold our own
– the house, in other words, will be able to hold its own, and
maintain its own, and hand down its own of itself, and without any
such commonplace aids. The kinds of foreign help which people
usually seek for their children, I can afford to despise; being above
it, I hope. So that Paul's infancy and childhood pass away well, and
I see him becoming qualified without waste of time for the career
on which he is destined to enter, I am satisfied. He will make what
powerful friends he pleases in after-life, when he is actively maintaining – and extending, if that is possible – the dignity and credit
of the Firm. Until then, I am enough for him, perhaps, and all in
all. I have no wish that people should step in between us. I would
much rather show my sense of the obliging conduct of a deserving
person like your friend. Therefore let it be so; and your husband
and myself will do well enough for the other sponsors,[3] I dare say.'

In the course of these remarks, delivered with great majesty and
grandeur, Mr Dombey had truly revealed the secret feelings of his
breast. An indescribable distrust of anybody stepping in between
himself and his son; a haughty dread of having any rival or partner
in the boy's respect and deference; a sharp misgiving, recently
acquired, that he was not infallible in his power of bending and
binding human wills; as sharp a jealousy of any second check or
cross; these were, at that time, the master-keys of his soul. In all his
life, he had never made a friend. His cold and distant nature had
neither sought one, nor found one. And now when that nature
concentrated its whole force so strongly on a partial scheme of
parental interest and ambition, it seemed as if its icy current, instead
of being released by this influence, and running clear and free, had
thawed for but an instant to admit its burden, and then frozen with
it into one unyielding block.

Elevated thus to the godmothership of little Paul, in virtue of her
insignificance, Miss Tox was from that hour chosen and appointed
to office; and Mr Dombey further signified his pleasure that the
ceremony, already long delayed, should take place without further
postponement. His sister, who had been far from anticipating so
signal a success, withdrew as soon as she could, to communicate it
to her best of friends; and Mr Dombey was left alone in his library.

There was anything but solitude in the nursery; for there, Mrs
Chick and Miss Tox were enjoying a social evening, so much to the
disgust of Miss Susan Nipper, that that young lady embraced every
opportunity of making wry faces behind the door. Her feelings were
so much excited on the occasion, that she found it indispensable to

afford them this relief, even without having the comfort of any audience or sympathy whatever. As the knight-errants of old relieved their minds by carving their mistress's names in deserts, and wildernesses, and other savage places where there was no probability of there ever being anybody to read them, so did Miss Susan Nipper curl her snub nose into drawers and wardrobes, put away winks of disparagement in cupboards, shed derisive squints into stone pitchers, and contradict and call names out in the passage.

The two interlopers, however, blissfully unconscious of the young lady's sentiments, saw little Paul safe through all the stages of undressing, airy exercise, supper and bed; and then sat down to tea before the fire. The two children now lay, through the good offices of Polly, in one room; and it was not until the ladies were established at their tea-table that happening to look towards the little beds, they thought of Florence.

'How sound she sleeps!' said Miss Tox.

'Why, you know, my dear, she takes a great deal of exercise in the course of the day,' returned Mrs Chick, 'playing about little Paul so much.'

'She is a curious child,' said Miss Tox.

'My dear,' retorted Mrs Chick, in a low voice: 'Her mama, all over!'

'Indeed!' said Miss Tox. 'Ah dear me!'

A tone of most extraordinary compassion Miss Tox said it in, though she had no distinct idea why, except that it was expected of her.

'Florence will never, never, never, be a Dombey,' said Mrs Chick, 'not if she lives to be a thousand years old.'

Miss Tox elevated her eyebrows, and was again full of commiseration.

'I quite fret and worry myself about her,' said Mrs Chick with a sigh of modest merit. 'I really don't see what is to become of her when she grows older, or what position she is to take. She don't gain on her papa in the least. How can one expect she should, when she is so very unlike a Dombey?'

Miss Tox looked as if she saw no way out of such a cogent argument as that, at all.

'And the child, you see,' said Mrs Chick, in deep confidence, 'has poor Fanny's nature. She'll never make an effort in after-life, I'll venture to say. Never! She'll never wind and twine herself about her papa's heart like—'

'Like the ivy?' suggested Miss Tox.

'Like the ivy,' Mrs Chick assented. 'Never! She'll never glide and nestle into the bosom of her papa's affections like – the —'

'Startled fawn?' suggested Miss Tox.

'Like the startled fawn,' said Mrs Chick. 'Never! Poor Fanny! Yet, how I loved her!'

'You must not distress yourself, my dear,' said Miss Tox, in a soothing voice. 'Now really! You have too much feeling.'

'We have all our faults,' said Mrs Chick, weeping and shaking her head. 'I dare say we have. I never was blind to hers. I never said I was. Far from it. Yet how I loved her!'

What a satisfaction it was to Mrs Chick – a commonplace piece of folly enough, compared with whom her sister-in-law had been a very angel of womanly intelligence and gentleness – to patronise and be tender to the memory of that lady: in exact pursuance of her conduct to her in her lifetime: and to thoroughly believe herself, and take herself in, and make herself uncommonly comfortable on the strength of her toleration! What a mighty pleasant virtue toleration should be when we are right, to be so very pleasant when we are wrong, and quite unable to demonstrate how we come to be invested with the privilege of exercising it!

Mrs Chick was yet drying her eyes and shaking her head, when Richards made bold to caution her that Miss Florence was awake and sitting in her bed. She had risen, as the nurse said, and the lashes of her eyes were wet with tears. But no one saw them glistening save Polly. No one else leant over her, and whispered soothing words to her, or was near enough to hear the flutter of her beating heart.

'Oh! dear nurse!' said the child, looking earnestly up in her face, 'let me lie by my brother!'

'Why, my pet?' said Richards.

'Oh! I think he loves me,' cried the child wildly. 'Let me lie by him. Pray do!'

Mrs Chick interposed with some motherly words about going to sleep like a dear, but Florence repeated her supplication, with a frightened look, and in a voice broken by sobs and tears.

'I'll not wake him,' she said, covering her face and hanging down her head. 'I'll only touch him with my hand, and go to sleep. Oh, pray, pray, let me lie by my brother to-night, for I believe he's fond of me!'

Richards took her without a word, and carrying her to the little bed in which the infant was sleeping, laid her down by his side. She crept as near him as she could without disturbing his rest; and stretching out one arm so that it timidly embraced his neck, and hiding her face on the other, over which her damp and scattered hair fell loose, lay motionless.

'Poor little thing,' said Miss Tox; 'she has been dreaming, I dare say.'

This trivial incident had so interrupted the current of conversation, that it was difficult of resumption; and Mrs Chick moreover had been so affected by the contemplation of her own tolerant nature, that she was not in spirits. The two friends accordingly soon made an end of their tea, and a servant was dispatched to fetch a hackney cabriolet[4] for Miss Tox. Miss Tox had great experience in hackney cabs, and her starting in one was generally a work of time, as she was systematic in the preparatory arrangements.

'Have the goodness, if you please, Towlinson,' said Miss Tox, 'first of all, to carry out a pen and ink and take his number legibly.'

'Yes, Miss,' said Towlinson.

'Then, if you please, Towlinson,' said Miss Tox, 'have the goodness to turn the cushion. Which,' said Miss Tox apart to Mrs Chick, 'is generally damp, my dear.'

'Yes, Miss,' said Towlinson.

'I'll trouble you also, if you please,' said Miss Tox, 'with this card and this shilling. He's to drive to the card, and is to understand that he will not on any account have more than the shilling.'

'No, Miss,' said Towlinson.

'And – I'm sorry to give you so much trouble, Towlinson,' – said Miss Tox, looking at him pensively.

'Not at all, Miss,' said Towlinson.

'Mention to the man, then, if you please, Towlinson,' said Miss Tox, 'that the lady's uncle is a magistrate, and that if he gives her any of his impertinence he will be punished terribly. You can pretend to say that, if you please, Towlinson, in a friendly way, and because you know it was done to another man, who died.'

'Certainly, Miss,' said Towlinson.

'And now good night to my sweet, sweet, sweet, godson,' said Miss Tox, with a soft shower of kisses at each repetition of the adjective; 'and Louisa, my dear friend, promise me to take a little something warm before you go to bed, and not to distress yourself!'

It was with extreme difficulty that Nipper, the black-eyed, who looked on steadfastly, contained herself at this crisis, and until the subsequent departure of Mrs Chick. But the nursery being at length free of visitors, she made herself some recompense for her late restraint.

'You might keep me in a strait-waistcoat for six weeks,' said Nipper, 'and when I got it off I'd only be more aggravated, who ever heard the like of them two Griffins,[5] Mrs Richards?'

'And then to talk of having been dreaming, poor dear!' said Polly.

'Oh, you beauties!' cried Susan Nipper, affecting to salute the door by which the ladies had departed. 'Never be a Dombey won't she? It's to be hoped she won't, we don't want any more such, one's enough.'

'Don't wake the children, Susan dear,' said Polly.

'I'm very much beholden to you, Mrs Richards,' said Susan, who was not by any means discriminating in her wrath, 'and really feel it as a honour to receive your commands, being a black slave and a mulotter.[6] Mrs Richards, if there's any other orders you can give me, pray mention 'em.'

'Nonsense; orders,' said Polly.

'Oh! bless your heart, Mrs Richards,' cried Susan, 'temporaries always orders permanencies here, didn't you know that, why wherever was you born, Mrs Richards? But wherever you was born, Mrs Richards,' pursued Spitfire, shaking her head resolutely, 'and whenever, and however (which is best known to yourself), you may bear in mind, please, that it's one thing to give orders, and quite another thing to take 'em. A person may tell a person to dive off a bridge head foremost into five-and-forty feet of water, Mrs Richards, but a person may be very far from diving.'

'There now,' said Polly, 'you're angry because you're a good little thing, and fond of Miss Florence; and yet you turn round on me, because there's nobody else.'

'It's very easy for some to keep their tempers, and be soft-spoken, Mrs Richards,' returned Susan, slightly mollified, 'when their child's made as much of as a prince, and is petted and patted till it wishes its friends further, but when a sweet young pretty innocent, that never ought to have a cross word spoken to or of it, is run down, the case is very different indeed. My goodness gracious me, Miss Floy, you naughty, sinful child, if you don't shut your eyes this minute, I'll call in them hobgoblins that lives in the cock-loft to come and eat you up alive!'

Here Miss Nipper made a horrible lowing, supposed to issue from a conscientious goblin of the bull species, impatient to discharge the severe duty of his position. Having further composed her young charge by covering her head with the bedclothes, and making three or four angry dabs at the pillow, she folded her arms, and screwed up her mouth, and sat looking at the fire for the rest of the evening.

Though little Paul was said, in nursery phrase, 'to take a deal of notice for his age,' he took as little notice of all this as of the preparations for his christening on the next day but one; which nevertheless went on about him, as to his personal apparel, and that of his sister and the two nurses, with great activity. Neither did he, on the arrival of the appointed morning, show any sense of its importance; being, on the contrary, unusually inclined to sleep, and unusually inclined to take it ill in his attendants that they dressed him to go out.

It happened to be an iron-grey autumnal day, with a shrewd east wind blowing – a day in keeping with the proceedings. Mr Dombey represented in himself the wind, the shade, and the autumn of the christening. He stood in his library to receive the company, as hard and cold as the weather; and when he looked out through the glass room, at the trees in the little garden, their brown and yellow leaves came fluttering down, as if he blighted them.

Ugh! They were black, cold rooms; and seemed to be in mourning, like the inmates of the house. The books, precisely matched as to size, and drawn up in line, like soldiers, looked in their cold, hard, slippery uniforms, as if they had but one idea among them, and that was a freezer. The bookcase, glazed and locked, repudiated all familiarities. Mr Pitt in bronze on the top, with no trace of his celestial origin[7] about him, guarded the unattainable treasure like an enchanted Moor.[8] A dusty urn at each high corner, dug up from an ancient tomb, preached desolation and decay, as from two pulpits; and the chimney-glass, reflecting Mr Dombey and his portrait at one blow, seemed fraught with melancholy meditations.

The stiff and stark fire-irons appeared to claim a nearer relationship than anything else there to Mr Dombey, with his buttoned coat, his white cravat, his heavy gold watch-chain, and his creaking boots. But this was before the arrival of Mr and Mrs Chick, his lawful relatives, who soon presented themselves.

'My dear Paul,' Mrs Chick murmured, as she embraced him, 'the beginning, I hope, of many joyful days!'

'Thank you, Louisa,' said Mr Dombey, grimly. 'How do you do, Mr John?'

'How do you do, Sir?' said Chick.

He gave Mr Dombey his hand, as if he feared it might electrify him. Mr Dombey took it as if it were a fish, or seaweed, or some such clammy substance, and immediately returned it to him with exalted politeness.

'Perhaps, Louisa,' said Mr Dombey, slightly turning his head in his cravat, as if it were a socket, 'you would have preferred a fire?'

'Oh, my dear Paul, no,' said Mrs Chick, who had much ado to keep her teeth from chattering; 'not for me.'

'Mr John,' said Mr Dombey, 'you are not sensible of any chill?'

Mr John, who had already got both his hands in his pockets over the wrists, and was on the very threshold of that same canine chorus which had given Mrs Chick so much offence on a former occasion, protested that he was perfectly comfortable.

He added in a low voice, 'With my tiddle tol toor rul' – when he was providentially stopped by Towlinson, who announced:

'Miss Tox!'

And enter that fair enslaver, with a blue nose and indescribably frosty face, referable to her being very thinly clad in a maze of fluttering odds and ends, to do honour to the ceremony.

'How do you do, Miss Tox?' said Mr Dombey.

Miss Tox, in the midst of her spreading gauzes, went down altogether like an opera-glass shutting-up; she curtseyed so low, in acknowledgment of Mr Dombey's advancing a step or two to meet her. 'I can never forget this occasion, Sir,' said Miss Tox, softly. ''Tis impossible. My dear Louisa, I can hardly believe the evidence of my senses.'

If Miss Tox could believe the evidence of one of her senses, it was a very cold day. That was quite clear. She took an early opportunity of promoting the circulation in the tip of her nose by secretly chafing it with her pocket-handkerchief, lest, by its very low temperature, it should disagreeably astonish the baby when she came to kiss it.

The baby soon appeared, carried in great glory by Richards; while Florence, in custody of that active young constable, Susan Nipper, brought up the rear. Though the whole nursery party were dressed by this time in lighter mourning[9] than at first, there was enough in the appearance of the bereaved children, to make the day no brighter. The baby too – it might have been Miss Tox's nose – began to cry. Thereby, as it happened, preventing Mr Chick from the awkward fulfilment of a very honest purpose he had; which was, to make much of Florence. For this gentleman, insensible to the superior claims of a perfect Dombey (perhaps on account of having the honour to be united to a Dombey himself, and being familiar with excellence), really liked her, and showed that he liked

The Christening Party

her, and was about to show it in his own way now, when Paul cried, and his helpmate stopped him short.

'Now Florence, child!' said her aunt, briskly, 'what are you doing, love? Show yourself to him. Engage his attention, my dear!'

The atmosphere became or might have become colder and colder, when Mr Dombey stood frigidly watching his little daughter, who, clapping her hands, and standing on tip-toe before the throne of his son and heir, lured him to bend down from his high estate, and look at her. Some honest act of Richards's may have aided the effect, but he did look down, and held his peace. As his sister hid behind her nurse, he followed her with his eyes; and when she peeped out with a merry cry to him, he sprang up and crowed lustily – laughing outright when she ran in upon him; and seeming to fondle her curls with his tiny hands, while she smothered him with kisses.

Was Mr Dombey pleased to see this? He testified no pleasure by the relaxation of a nerve; but outward tokens of any kind of feeling were unusual with him. If any sunbeam stole into the room to light the children at their play, it never reached his face. He looked on so fixedly and coldly, that the warm light vanished even from the laughing eyes of little Florence, when, at last, they happened to meet his.

It was a dull, grey, autumn day indeed, and in a minute's pause and silence that took place, the leaves fell sorrowfully.

'Mr John,' said Mr Dombey, referring to his watch, and assuming his hat and gloves. 'Take my sister, if you please: my arm to-day is Miss Tox's. You had better go first with Master Paul, Richards. Be very careful.'

In Mr Dombey's carriage, Dombey and Son, Miss Tox, Mrs Chick, Richards, and Florence. In a little carriage following it, Susan Nipper and the owner Mr Chick. Susan looking out of window, without intermission, as a relief from the embarrassment of confronting the large face of that gentleman, and thinking whenever anything rattled that he was putting up in paper an appropriate pecuniary compliment for herself.

Once upon the road to church, Mr Dombey clapped his hands for the amusement of his son. At which instance of parental enthusiasm Miss Tox was enchanted. But exclusive of this incident, the chief difference between the christening party and a party in a mourning coach, consisted in the colours of the carriage and horses.

Arrived at the church steps, they were received by a portentous beadle.[10] Mr Dombey dismounting first to help the ladies out, and standing near him at the church door, looked like another beadle. A beadle less gorgeous but more dreadful; the beadle of private life; the beadle of our business and our bosoms.

Miss Tox's hand trembled as she slipped it through Mr Dombey's arm, and felt herself escorted up the steps, preceded by a cocked hat and a Babylonian[11] collar. It seemed for a moment like that other solemn institution, 'Wilt thou have this man, Lucretia?' 'Yes, I will.'

'Please to bring the child in quick out of the air there,' whispered the beadle, holding open the inner door of the church.

Little Paul might have asked with Hamlet 'into my grave?'[12] so chill and earthy was the place. The tall shrouded pulpit and reading desk; the dreary perspective of empty pews stretching away under the galleries, and empty benches mounting to the roof and lost in the shadow of the great grim organ; the dusty matting and cold stone slabs; the grisly free seats[13] in the aisles; and the damp corner by the bell-rope, where the black trestles used for funerals were stowed away, along with some shovels and baskets, and a coil or two of deadly-looking rope; the strange, unusual, uncomfortable smell, and the cadaverous light; were all in unison. It was a cold and dismal scene.

'There's a wedding just on, Sir,' said the beadle, 'but it'll be over directly, if you'll walk into the westry here.'

Before he turned again to lead the way, he gave Mr Dombey a bow and a half smile of recognition, importing that he (the beadle) remembered to have had the pleasure of attending on him when he buried his wife, and hoped he had enjoyed himself since.

The very wedding looked dismal as they passed in front of the altar. The bride was too old and the bridegroom too young and a superannuated beau with one eye and an eyeglass stuck in its blank companion, was giving away the lady, while the friends were shivering. In the vestry the fire was smoking; and an over-aged and over-worked and under-paid attorney's clerk, 'making a search,' was running his forefinger down the parchment pages of an immense register (one of a long series of similar volumes) gorged with burials. Over the fireplace was a ground-plan of the vaults underneath the church; and Mr Chick, skimming the literary portion of it aloud, by way of enlivening the company, read the reference to Mrs Dombey's tomb in full before he could stop himself.

After another cold interval, a wheezy little pew-opener[14] afflicted with an asthma, appropriate to the churchyard, if not to the church, summoned them to the font. Here they waited some little time while the marriage party enrolled themselves; and meanwhile the wheezy little pew-opener – partly in consequence of her infirmity, and partly that the marriage party might not forget her – went about the building coughing like a grampus.[15]

Presently the clerk (the only cheerful-looking object there, and *he* was an undertaker) came up with a jug of warm water, and said something, as he poured it into the font, about taking the chill off; which millions of gallons boiling hot could not have done for the occasion. Then the clergyman, an amiable and mild-looking young curate, but obviously afraid of the baby, appeared like the principal character in a ghost-story, 'a tall figure all in white'; at sight of whom Paul rent the air with his cries, and never left off again till he was taken out black in the face.

Even when that event had happened, to the great relief of everybody, he was heard under the portico, during the rest of the ceremony, now fainter, now louder, now hushed, now bursting forth again with an irrepressible sense of his wrongs. This so distracted the attention of the two ladies, that Mrs Chick was constantly deploying into the centre aisle, to send out messages by the pew-opener, while Miss Tox kept her Prayer-book open at the Gunpowder Plot,[16] and occasionally read responses from that service.

During the whole of these proceedings, Mr Dombey remained as impassive and gentlemanly as ever, and perhaps assisted in making it so cold, that the young curate smoked at the mouth as he read. The only time that he unbent his visage in the least, was when the clergyman, in delivering (very unaffectedly and simply) the closing exhortation, relative to the future examination of the child by the sponsors, happened to rest his eye on Mr Chick; and then Mr Dombey might have been seen to express by a majestic look, that he would like to catch him at it.

It might have been well for Mr Dombey, if he had thought of his own dignity a little less; and had thought of the great origin and purpose of the ceremony in which he took so formal and so stiff a part, a little more. His arrogance contrasted strangely with its history.[17]

When it was all over, he again gave his arm to Miss Tox, and conducted her to the vestry, where he informed the clergyman how much pleasure it would have given him to have solicited the honour of his company at dinner, but for the unfortunate state of his household affairs. The register signed, and the fees paid, and the pew-opener (whose cough was very bad again) remembered, and the beadle gratified, and the sexton[18] (who was accidentally on the door-steps, looking with great interest at the weather) not forgotten, they got into the carriage again, and drove home in the same bleak fellowship.

There they found Mr Pitt turning up his nose at a cold collation, set forth in a cold pomp of glass and silver, and looking more like a dead dinner lying in state than a social refreshment. On their arrival Miss Tox produced a mug for her godson, and Mr Chick a knife and fork and spoon in a case. Mr Dombey also produced a bracelet for Miss Tox; and, on the receipt of this token, Miss Tox was tenderly affected.

'Mr John,' said Mr Dombey, 'will you take the bottom of the table, if you please? What have you got there, Mr John?'

'I have got a cold fillet of veal here, Sir,' replied Mr Chick, rubbing his numbed hands hard together. 'What have *you* got there, Sir?'

'This,' returned Mr Dombey, 'is some cold preparation of calf's head, I think. I see cold fowls – ham – patties – salad – lobster. Miss Tox will do me the honour of taking some wine? Champagne to Miss Tox.'

There was a toothache in everything. The wine was so bitter cold that it forced a little scream from Miss Tox, which she had great difficulty in turning into a 'Hem!' The veal had come from such an airy pantry, that the first taste of it had struck a sensation as of cold lead to Mr Chick's extremities. Mr Dombey alone remained unmoved. He might have been hung up for sale at a Russian fair as a specimen of a frozen gentleman.

The prevailing influence was too much even for his sister. She made no effort at flattery or small talk, and directed all her efforts to looking as warm as she could.

'Well, Sir,' said Mr Chick, making a desperate plunge, after a long silence, and filling a glass of sherry; 'I shall drink this, if you'll allow me, Sir, to little Paul.'

'Bless him!' murmured Miss Tox, taking a sip of wine.

'Dear little Dombey!' murmured Mrs Chick.

'Mr John,' said Mr Dombey, with severe gravity, 'my son would feel and express himself obliged to you, I have no doubt, if he could appreciate the favour you have done him. He will prove, in time to come, I trust, equal to any responsibility that the obliging disposition of his relations and friends, in private, or the onerous nature of our position, in public, may impose upon him.'

The tone in which this was said admitting of nothing more, Mr Chick relapsed into low spirits and silence. Not so Miss Tox, who, having listened to Mr Dombey with even a more emphatic attention than usual, and with a more expressive tendency of her head to one side, now leant across the table, and said to Mrs Chick softly:

'Louisa!'

'My dear,' said Mrs Chick.

'Onerous nature of our position in public may – I have forgotten the exact term.'

'Expose him to,' said Mrs Chick.

'Pardon me, my dear,' returned Miss Tox, 'I think not. It was more rounded and flowing. Obliging disposition of relations and friends in private, or onerous nature of position in public – may – impose upon him!'

'Impose upon him, to be sure,' said Mrs Chick.

Miss Tox struck her delicate hands together lightly, in triumph; and added, casting up her eyes, 'eloquence indeed!'

Mr Dombey, in the meanwhile, had issued orders for the attendance of Richards, who now entered curtseying, but without the baby; Paul being asleep after the fatigues of the morning. Mr Dombey, having delivered a glass of wine to this vassal, addressed her in the following words: Miss Tox previously settling her head on one side, and making other little arrangements for engraving them on her heart.

'During the six months or so, Richards, which have seen you an inmate of this house, you have done your duty. Desiring to connect some little service to you with this occasion, I considered how I could best effect that object, and I also advised with my sister, Mrs —'

'Chick,' interposed the gentleman of that name.

'Oh, hush, if you *please!*' said Miss Tox.

'I was about to say to you, Richards,' resumed Mr Dombey, with an appalling glance at Mr John, 'that I was further assisted in my decision, by the recollection of a conversation I held with your husband in this room, on the occasion of your being hired, when he disclosed to me the melancholy fact that your family, himself at the head, were sunk and steeped in ignorance.'

Richards quailed under the magnificence of the reproof.

'I am far from being friendly,' pursued Mr Dombey, 'to what is called by persons of levelling sentiments, general education. But it is necessary that the inferior classes should continue to be taught to know their position, and to conduct themselves properly. So far I approve of schools. Having the power of nominating a child on the foundation of an ancient establishment, called (from a worshipful company) the Charitable Grinders;[19] where not only is a wholesome education bestowed upon the scholars, but where a dress and badge is likewise provided for them; I have (first communicating, through Mrs Chick, with your family) nominated your eldest son to an existing vacancy; and he has this day, I am informed, assumed the habit. The number of her son, I believe,' said Mr Dombey, turning to his sister and speaking of the child as if he were a hackney-coach, 'is one hundred and forty-seven. Louisa, you can tell her.'

'One hundred and forty-seven,' said Mrs Chick. 'The dress, Richards, is a nice, warm, blue baize tailed coat and cap, turned up with orange-coloured binding; red worsted stockings and very strong leather small-clothes.[20] One might wear the articles one's-self,' said Mrs Chick, with enthusiasm, 'and be grateful.'

'There, Richards!' said Miss Tox. 'Now, indeed, you may be proud. The Charitable Grinders!'

'I am sure I am very much obliged, Sir,' returned Richards faintly, 'and take it very kind that you should remember my little ones.' At the same time a vision of Biler as a Charitable Grinder, with his very small legs encased in the serviceable clothing described by Mrs Chick, swam before Richards's eyes, and made them water.

'I am very glad to see you have so much feeling, Richards,' said Miss Tox.

'It makes one almost hope, it really does,' said Mrs Chick, who prided herself on taking trustful views of human nature, 'that there may yet be some faint spark of gratitude and right feeling in the world.'

Richards deferred to these compliments by curtseying and murmuring her thanks; but finding it quite impossible to recover her spirits from the disorder into which they had been thrown by the image of her son in his precocious nether garments, she gradually approached the door and was heartily relieved to escape by it.

Such temporary indications of a partial thaw that had appeared with her, vanished with her; and the frost set in again, as cold and hard as ever. Mr Chick was twice heard to hum a tune at the bottom of the table, but on both occasions it was a fragment of the Dead March in Saul.[21] The party seemed to get colder and colder, and to be gradually resolving itself into a congealed and solid state, like the collation round which it was assembled. At length Mrs Chick looked at Miss Tox, and Miss Tox returned the look, and they both rose and said it was really time to go. Mr Dombey receiving this announcement with perfect equanimity, they took leave of that gentleman, and presently departed under the protection of Mr Chick; who, when they had turned their backs upon the house and left its master in his usual solitary state, put his hands in his pockets, threw himself back in the carriage, and whistled 'With a hey ho chevy!'[22] through; conveying into his face as he did so, an expression of such gloomy and terrible defiance, that Mrs Chick dared not protest, or in any way molest him.

Richards, though she had little Paul on her lap, could not forget her own first-born. She felt it was ungrateful; but the influence of the day fell even on the Charitable Grinders, and she could hardly help regarding his pewter badge, number one hundred and forty-seven, as, somehow, a part of its formality and sternness. She spoke, too, in the nursery, of his 'blessed legs,' and was again troubled by his spectre in uniform.

'I don't know what I wouldn't give,' said Polly, 'to see the poor little dear before he gets used to 'em.'

'Why, then, I tell you what, Mrs Richards,' retorted Nipper, who had been admitted to her confidence, 'see him and make your mind easy.'

'Mr Dombey wouldn't like it,' said Polly.

'Oh, wouldn't he, Mrs Richards!' retorted Nipper, 'he'd like it very much, I think, when he was asked.'

'You wouldn't ask him, I suppose, at all?' said Polly.

'No, Mrs Richards, quite contrairy,' returned Susan, 'and them two inspectors Tox and Chick, not intending to be on duty to-morrow, as I heard 'em say, me and Miss Floy will go along with you to-morrow morning, and welcome, Mrs Richards, if you like, for we may as well walk there, as up and down a street, and better too.'

Polly rejected the idea pretty stoutly at first; but by little and little she began to entertain it, as she entertained more and more distinctly the forbidden pictures of her children, and her own home. At length, arguing that there could be no great harm in calling for a moment at the door, she yielded to the Nipper proposition.

The matter being settled thus, little Paul began to cry most piteously, as if he had a foreboding that no good would come of it.

'What's the matter with the child?' asked Susan.

'He's cold, I think,' said Polly, walking with him to and fro, and hushing him.

It was a bleak autumnal afternoon indeed; and as she walked, and hushed, and, glancing through the dreary windows, pressed the little fellow closer to her breast, the withered leaves came showering down.

CHAPTER 6

Paul's Second Deprivation

Polly was beset by so many misgivings in the morning, that but for the incessant promptings of her black-eyed companion, she would have abandoned all thoughts of the expedition, and formally petitioned for leave to see number one hundred and forty-seven, under the awful shadow of Mr Dombey's roof. But Susan, who was personally disposed in favour of the excursion, and who (like Tony Lumpkin),[1] if she could bear the disappointments of other people with tolerable fortitude, could not abide to disappoint herself, threw so many ingenious doubts in the way of this second thought, and stimulated the original intention with so many ingenious arguments, that almost as soon as Mr Dombey's stately back was turned, and that gentleman was pursuing his daily road towards the City, his unconscious son was on his way to Staggs's Gardens.[2]

This euphonious locality was situated in a suburb, known by the inhabitants of Staggs's Gardens by the name of Camberling Town; a designation which the Strangers' Map of London, as printed (with a view to pleasant and commodious reference) on pocket-handkerchiefs, condenses, with some show of reason, into Camden Town. Hither the two nurses bent their steps, accompanied by their charges; Richards carrying Paul, of course, and Susan leading little Florence by the hand, and giving her such jerks and pokes from time to time, as she considered it wholesome to administer.

The first shock of a great earthquake had, just at that period rent the whole neighbourhood to its centre. Traces of its course were visible on every side. Houses were knocked down; streets broken through and stopped; deep pits and trenches dug in the ground; enormous heaps of earth and clay thrown up; buildings that were undermined and shaking, propped by great beams of wood. Here, a chaos of carts, overthrown and jumbled together, lay topsy-turvy at the bottom of a steep unnatural hill; there, confused treasures of iron soaked and rusted in something that had accidentally become a pond. Everywhere were bridges that led nowhere; thoroughfares that were wholly impassable; Babel towers of chimneys, wanting half their height; temporary wooden houses and enclosures, in the most unlikely situations; carcases of ragged tenements, and fragments of unfinished walls and arches, and piles of scaffolding, and wildernesses of bricks and giant forms of cranes, and tripods straddling above nothing. There were a hundred thousand shapes and substances of incompleteness, wildly mingled out of their places, upside down, burrowing in the earth, aspiring in the air, mouldering in the water, and unintelligible as any dream. Hot springs and fiery eruptions, the usual attendants upon earthquakes, lent their contributions of confusion to the scene. Boiling water hissed and heaved within dilapidated walls; whence, also, the glare and roar of flames came issuing forth; and mounds of ashes blocked up rights of way, and wholly changed the law and custom of the neighbourhood.

In short, the yet unfinished and unopened Railroad[3] was in progress; and, from the very core of all this dire disorder, trailed smoothly away, upon its mighty course of civilisation and improvement.

But as yet, the neighbourhood was shy to own the Railroad. One or two bold speculators had projected streets; and one had built a little, but had stopped among the mud and ashes to consider farther of it. A bran-new Tavern, redolent of fresh mortar and size, and fronting nothing at all, had taken for its sign The Railway Arms; but that might be rash enterprise – and then it hoped to sell drink to the workmen. So, the Excavators' House of Call had sprung up from a beer-shop; and the old-established Ham and Beef Shop had become the Railway Eating House, with a roast leg of pork daily, through interested motives of a similar immediate and popular description. Lodging-house keepers were favourable in like manner; and for the like reasons were not to be trusted. The general belief was very slow. There were frowzy fields, and cow-houses, and dunghills, and dustheaps, and ditches, and gardens, and summer-houses, and carpet-beating grounds, at the very door of the Railway. Little tumuli of oyster shells in the oyster season, and of lobster shells in the lobster season, and of broken crockery and faded cabbage leaves in all seasons, encroached upon its high places. Posts, and rails, and old cautions to trespassers, and backs of mean houses, and patches of wretched vegetation, stared it out of countenance. Nothing was better for it, or thought of being so. If the miserable waste ground lying near it could have laughed, it would have laughed it to scorn, like many of the miserable neighbours.

Staggs's Gardens was uncommonly incredulous. It was a little row of houses, with little squalid patches of ground before them, fenced off with old doors, barrel staves, scraps of tarpaulin, and dead bushes; with bottomless tin kettles and exhausted iron fenders, thrust into the gaps. Here, the Staggs's Gardeners trained scarlet beans, kept fowls and rabbits, erected rotten summer-houses (one was an old boat), dried clothes, and smoked pipes. Some were of opinion that Staggs's Gardens derived its name from a deceased capitalist, one Mr Staggs,[4] who had built it for his delectation. Others, who had a natural taste for the country, held that it dated from those rural times when the antlered herd, under the familiar denomination of Staggses, had resorted to its shady precincts. Be this as it may, Staggs's Gardens was regarded by its population as a sacred grove not to be withered by railroads; and so confident were they generally of its long outliving any such ridiculous inventions, that the master chimney-sweeper at the corner, who was understood to take the lead in the local politics of the Gardens, had publicly declared that on the occasion of the Railroad opening, if ever it did open, two of his boys should ascend the flues of his dwelling, with instructions to hail the failure with derisive jeers from the chimney-pots.

To this unhallowed spot, the very name of which had hitherto been carefully concealed from Mr Dombey by his sister, was little Paul now borne by Fate and Richards.

'That's my house, Susan,' said Polly, pointing it out.

'Is it, indeed, Mrs Richards?' said Susan, condescendingly.

'And there's my sister Jemima at the door, I do declare!' cried Polly, 'with my own sweet precious baby in her arms!'

The sight added such an extensive pair of wings to Polly's impatience, that she set off down the Gardens at a run, and bouncing on Jemima, changed babies with her in a twinkling; to the utter astonishment of that young damsel, on whom the heir of the Dombeys seemed to have fallen from the clouds.

'Why, Polly!' cried Jemima. 'You! what a turn you *have* given me! who'd have thought it! come along in, Polly! How well you do look to be sure! The children will go half wild to see you, Polly, that they will.'

That they did, if one might judge from the noise they made, and the way in which they dashed at Polly and dragged her to a low chair in the chimney corner, where her own honest apple face became immediately the centre of a bunch of smaller pippins, all laying their rosy cheeks close to it, and all evidently the growth of the same tree. As to Polly, she was full as noisy and vehement as the children; and it was not until she was quite out of breath, and her hair was hanging all about her flushed face, and her new christening attire was very much dishevelled, that any pause took place in the confusion. Even then, the smallest Toodle but one remained in her lap, holding on tight with both arms round her neck; while the smallest Toodle but two mounted on the back of the chair, and made desperate efforts, with one leg in the air, to kiss her round the corner.

'Look! there's a pretty little lady come to see you,' said Polly; 'and see how quiet she is! what a beautiful little lady, ain't she?'

This reference to Florence, who had been standing by the door not unobservant of what passed, directed the attention of the younger branches towards her; and had likewise the happy effect of leading to the formal recognition of Miss Nipper, who was not quite free from a misgiving that she had been already slighted.

'Oh do come in and sit down a minute, Susan, please,' said Polly. 'This is my sister Jemima, this is. Jemima, I don't know what I should ever do with myself, if it wasn't for Susan Nipper; I shouldn't be here now but for her.'

'Oh do sit down, Miss Nipper, if you please,' quoth Jemima.

Susan took the extreme corner of a chair, with a stately and ceremonious aspect.

'I never was so glad to see anybody in all my life; now really I never was, Miss Nipper,' said Jemima.

Susan relaxing, took a little more of the chair, and smiled graciously.

'Do untie your bonnet-strings, and make yourself at home, Miss Nipper, please,' entreated Jemima. 'I am afraid it's a poorer place than you're used to; but you'll make allowances, I'm sure.'

The black-eyed was so softened by this deferential behaviour, that she caught up little Miss Toodle who was running past, and took her to Banbury Cross[5] immediately.

'But where's my pretty boy?' said Polly. 'My poor fellow? I came all this way to see him in his new clothes.'

'Ah what a pity!' cried Jemima. 'He'll break his heart, when he hears his mother has been here. He's at school, Polly.'

'Gone already!'

'Yes. He went for the first time yesterday, for fear he should lose any learning. But it's half-holiday, Polly: if you could only stop till he comes home – you and Miss Nipper, leastways,' said Jemima, mindful in good time of the dignity of the black-eyed.

'And how does he look, Jemima, bless him!' faltered Polly.

'Well, really he don't look so bad as you'd suppose,' returned Jemima.

'Ah!' said Polly, with emotion, 'I knew his legs must be too short.'

'His legs *is* short,' returned Jemima; 'especially behind, but they'll get longer, Polly, every day.'

It was a slow, prospective kind of consolation; but the cheerfulness and good nature with which it was administered, gave it a value it did not intrinsically possess. After a moment's silence, Polly asked, in a more sprightly manner:

'And where's Father, Jemima dear?' – for by that patriarchal appellation, Mr Toodle was generally known in the family.

'There again!' said Jemima. 'What a pity! Father took his dinner with him this morning, and isn't coming home till night. But he's always talking of you, Polly, and telling the children about you; and is the peaceablest, patientest, best-temperedst soul in the world, as he always was and will be!'

'Thankee, Jemima,' cried the simple Polly; delighted by the speech, and disappointed by the absence.

'Oh you needn't thank me, Polly,' said her sister, giving her a sound kiss upon the cheek, and then dancing little Paul cheerfully. 'I say the same of you sometimes, and think it too.'

In spite of the double disappointment, it was impossible to regard in the light of a failure a visit which was greeted with such a reception; so the sisters talked hopefully about family matters, and about Biler, and about all his brothers and sisters: while the black-eyed, having performed several journeys to Banbury Cross and back, took sharp note of the furniture, the Dutch clock, the cupboard, the castle on the mantel-piece with red and green windows in it, susceptible of illumination by a candle-end within; and the pair of small black velvet kittens, each with a lady's reticule in its mouth; regarded by the Staggs's Gardeners as prodigies of imitative art. The conversation soon becoming general lest the black-eyed should go off at score[6] and turn sarcastic, that young lady related to Jemima a summary of everything she knew concerning Mr Dombey, his prospects, family, pursuits, and character. Also an exact inventory of her personal wardrobe, and some account of her principal relations and friends. Having relieved her mind of these disclosures, she partook of shrimps and porter, and evinced a disposition to swear eternal friendship.

Little Florence herself was not behindhand in improving the

occasion: for, being conducted forth by the young Toodles to inspect some toad-stools and other curiosities of the Gardens, she entered with them, heart and soul, on the formation of a temporary breakwater across a small green pool that had collected in a corner. She was still busily engaged in that labour, when sought and found by Susan; who, such was her sense of duty, even under the humanizing influence of shrimps, delivered a moral address to her (punctuated with thumps) on her degenerate nature, while washing her face and hands; and predicted that she would bring the grey hairs of her family in general, with sorrow to the grave. After some delay, occasioned by a pretty long confidential interview above stairs on pecuniary subjects, between Polly and Jemima, an interchange of babies was again effected – for Polly had all this time retained her own child, and Jemima little Paul – and the visitors took leave.

But first the young Toodles, victims of a pious fraud, were deluded into repairing in a body to a chandler's shop[7] in the neighbourhood, for the ostensible purpose of spending a penny; and when the coast was quite clear, Polly fled: Jemima calling after her that if they could only go round towards the City Road on their way back, they would be sure to meet little Biler coming from school.

'Do you think that we might make time to go a little round in that direction, Susan?' inquired Polly, when they halted to take breath.

'Why not, Mrs Richards?' returned Susan.

'It's getting on towards our dinner-time you know,' said Polly.

But lunch had rendered her companion more than indifferent to this grave consideration, so she allowed no weight to it, and they resolved to go 'a little round.'

Now it happened that poor Biler's life had been, since yesterday morning, rendered weary by the costume of the Charitable Grinders. The youth of the streets could not endure it. No young vagabond could be brought to bear its contemplation for a moment, without throwing himself upon the unoffending wearer, and doing him a mischief. His social existence had been more like that of an early Christian, than an innocent child of the nineteenth century. He had been stoned in the streets. He had been overthrown into gutters; bespattered with mud; violently flattened against posts. Entire strangers to his person had lifted his yellow cap off his head and cast it to the winds. His legs had not only undergone verbal criticisms and revilings, but had been handled and pinched. That very morning, he had received a perfectly unsolicited black eye on his way to the Grinders' establishment, and had been punished for it by the master: a superannuated old Grinder of savage disposition, who had been appointed schoolmaster because he didn't know anything, and wasn't fit for anything, and for whose cruel cane all chubby little boys had a perfect fascination.

Thus it fell out that Biler, on his way home, sought unfrequented paths; and slunk along by narrow passages and back streets, to avoid his tormentors. Being compelled to emerge into the main road, his ill fortune brought him at last where a small party of boys, headed by a ferocious young butcher, were lying in wait for any means of pleasurable excitement that might happen. These, finding a Charitable Grinder in the midst of them – unaccountably delivered over, as it were, into their hands – set up a general yell and rushed upon him.

But it so fell out likewise, that, at the same time, Polly, looking hopelessly along the road before her, after a good hour's walk, had said it was no use going any further, when suddenly she saw this sight. She no sooner saw it than, uttering a hasty exclamation, and giving Master Dombey to the black-eyed, she started to the rescue of her unhappy little son.

Surprises, like misfortunes, rarely come alone. The astonished Susan Nipper and her two young charges were rescued by the bystanders from under the very wheels of a passing carriage before they knew what had happened; and at that moment (it was market-day) a thundering alarm of 'Mad Bull' was raised.

With a wild confusion before her, of people running up and down, and shouting, and wheels running over them, and boys fighting, and mad bulls coming up, and the nurse in the midst of all these dangers being torn to pieces, Florence screamed and ran. She ran till she was exhausted, urging Susan to do the same; and then, stopping and wringing her hands as she remembered they had left the other nurse behind, found, with a sensation of terror not to be described, that she was quite alone.

'Susan! Susan!' cried Florence, clapping her hands in the very ecstasy of her alarm. 'Oh, where are they? where are they?'

'Where are they?' said an old woman, coming hobbling across as fast as she could from the opposite side of the way. 'Why did you run away from 'em?'

'I was frightened,' answered Florence. 'I didn't know what I did. I thought they were with me. Where are they?'

The old woman took her by the wrist, and said, 'I'll show you.'

Polly rescues the Charitable Grinder

She was a very ugly old woman, with red rims round her eyes, and a mouth that mumbled and chattered of itself when she was not speaking. She was miserably dressed, and carried some skins over her arm. She seemed to have followed Florence some little way at all events, for she had lost her breath; and this made her uglier still, as she stood trying to regain it: working her shrivelled yellow face and throat into all sorts of contortions.

Florence was afraid of her, and looked, hesitating, up the street, of which she had almost reached the bottom. It was a solitary place – more a back road than a street – and there was no one in it but herself and the old woman.

'You needn't be frightened now,' said the old woman, still holding her tight. 'Come along with me.'

'I – I don't know you. What's your name?' asked Florence.

'Mrs Brown,' said the old woman. 'Good Mrs Brown.'

'Are they near here?' asked Florence, beginning to be led away.

'Susan an't far off,' said Good Mrs Brown; 'and the others are close to her.'

'Is anybody hurt?' cried Florence.

'Not a bit of it,' said Good Mrs Brown.

The child shed tears of delight on hearing this, and accompanied the old woman willingly; though she could not help glancing at her face as they went along – particularly at that industrious mouth – and wondering whether Bad Mrs Brown, if there were such a person, was at all like her.

They had not gone far, but had gone by some very uncomfortable places, such as brick-fields and tile-yards, when the old woman turned down a dirty lane, where the mud lay in deep black ruts in the middle of the road. She stopped before a shabby little house, as closely shut up as a house that was full of cracks and crevices could be. Opening the door with a key she took out of her bonnet, she pushed the child before her into a back room, where there was a great heap of rags of different colours lying on the floor; a heap of bones, and a heap of sifted dust or cinders; but there was no furniture at all, and the walls and ceiling were quite black.

The child became so terrified that she was stricken speechless, and looked as though about to swoon.

'Now don't be a young mule,' said Good Mrs Brown, reviving her with a shake. 'I'm not a going to hurt you. Sit upon the rags.'

Florence obeyed her, holding out her folded hands, in mute supplication.

'I'm not a going to keep you, even, above an hour,' said Mrs Brown. 'D'ye understand what I say?'

The child answered with great difficulty, 'Yes.'

'Then,' said Good Mrs Brown, taking her own seat on the bones, 'don't vex me. If you don't, I tell you I won't hurt you. But if you do, I'll kill you. I could have you killed at any time – even if you was in your own bed at home. Now let's know who you are, and what you are, and all about it.'

The old woman's threats and promises; the dread of giving her offence; and the habit, unusual to a child, but almost natural to Florence now, of being quiet, and repressing what she felt, and feared, and hoped; enabled her to do this bidding, and to tell her little history, or what she knew of it. Mrs Brown listened attentively, until she had finished.

'So your name's Dombey, eh?' said Mrs Brown.

'Yes, ma'am.'

'I want that pretty frock, Miss Dombey,' said Good Mrs Brown, 'and that little bonnet, and a petticoat or two, and anything else you can spare. Come! Take 'em off.'

Florence obeyed, as fast as her trembling hands would allow; keeping, all the while, a frightened eye on Mrs Brown. When she had divested herself of all the articles of apparel mentioned by that lady, Mrs B. examined them at leisure, and seemed tolerably well satisfied with their quality and value.

'Humph!' she said, running her eyes over the child's slight figure, 'I don't see anything else – except the shoes. I must have the shoes, Miss Dombey.'

Poor little Florence took them off with equal alacrity, only too glad to have any more means of conciliation about her. The old woman then produced some wretched substitutes from the bottom of the heap of rags, which she turned up for that purpose; together with a girl's cloak, quite worn out and very old; and the crushed remains of a bonnet that had probably been picked up from some ditch or dunghill. In this dainty raiment, she instructed Florence to dress herself; and as such preparation seemed a prelude to her release the child complied with increased readiness, if possible.

In hurriedly putting on the bonnet, if that may be called a bonnet which was more like a pad to carry loads on, she caught it in her hair which grew luxuriantly, and could not immediately disentangle it. Good Mrs Brown whipped out a large pair of scissors, and fell into an unaccountable state of excitement.

'Why couldn't you let me be,' said Mrs Brown, 'when I was contented? You little fool!'

'I beg your pardon. I don't know what I have done,' panted Florence. 'I couldn't help it.'

'Couldn't help it!' cried Mrs Brown. 'How do you expect I can help it? Why, Lord!' said the old woman, ruffling her curls with a furious pleasure, 'anybody but me would have had 'em off first of all.'

Florence was so relieved to find that it was only her hair and not her head which Mrs Brown coveted, that she offered no resistance or entreaty, and merely raised her mild eyes towards the face of that good soul.

'If I hadn't once had a gal of my own – beyond seas now – that was proud of her hair,' said Mrs Brown, 'I'd have had every lock of it. She's far away, she's far away! Oho! Oho!'

Mrs Brown's was not a melodious cry, but, accompanied with a wild tossing up of her lean arms, it was full of passionate grief, and thrilled to the heart of Florence, whom it frightened more than ever. It had its part, perhaps, in saving her curls; for Mrs Brown, after hovering about her with the scissors for some moments, like a new kind of butterfly, bade her hide them under the bonnet and let no trace of them escape to tempt her. Having accomplished this victory over herself, Mrs Brown resumed her seat on the bones, and smoked a very short black pipe, mowing and mumbling all the time, as if she were eating the stem.

When the pipe was smoked out, she gave the child a rabbit-skin to carry, that she might appear the more like her ordinary companion, and told her that she was now going to lead her to a public street whence she could inquire her way to her friends. But she cautioned her, with threats of summary and deadly vengeance in case of disobedience, not to talk to strangers, nor to repair to her own home (which may have been too near for Mrs Brown's convenience), but to her father's office in the City; also to wait at the street corner where she would be left, until the clock struck three. These directions Mrs Brown enforced with assurances that there would be potent eyes and ears in her employment cognizant of all she did; and these directions Florence promised faithfully and earnestly to observe.

At length, Mrs Brown, issuing forth, conducted her changed and ragged little friend through a labyrinth of narrow streets and lanes and alleys, which emerged, after a long time, upon a stable yard, with a gateway at the end, whence the roar of a great thoroughfare made itself audible. Pointing out this gateway, and informing Florence that when the clocks struck three she was to go to the left, Mrs Brown, after making a parting grasp at her hair which seemed involuntary and quite beyond her own control, told her she knew what to do, and bade her go and do it: remembering that she was watched.

With a lighter heart, but still sore afraid, Florence felt herself released, and tripped off to the corner. When she reached it, she looked back and saw the head of Good Mrs Brown peeping out of the low wooden passage, where she had issued her parting injunctions; likewise the fist of Good Mrs Brown shaking towards her. But though she often looked back afterwards – every minute, at least, in her nervous recollection of the old woman – she could not see her again.

Florence remained there, looking at the bustle in the street, and more and more bewildered by it; and in the meanwhile the clocks appeared to have made up their minds never to strike three any more. At last the steeples rang out three o'clock; there was one close by, so she couldn't be mistaken; and – after often looking over her shoulder, and often going a little way, and as often coming back again, lest the all-powerful spies of Mrs Brown should take offence – she hurried off, as fast as she could in her slipshod shoes, holding the rabbit-skin tight in her hand.

All she knew of her father's offices was that they belonged to Dombey and Son, and that that was a great power belonging to the City. So she could only ask the way to Dombey and Son's in the City; and as she generally made inquiry of children – being afraid to ask grown people – she got very little satisfaction indeed. But by dint of asking her way to the City after a while, and dropping the rest of her inquiry for the present, she really did advance, by slow degrees, towards the heart of that great region which is governed by the terrible Lord Mayor.

Tired of walking, repulsed and pushed about, stunned by the noise and confusion, anxious for her brother and the nurses, terrified by what she had undergone, and the prospect of encountering her angry father in such an altered state; perplexed and frightened alike by what had passed, and what was passing, and what was yet before her; Florence went upon her weary way with tearful eyes, and once or twice could not help stopping to ease her bursting heart by crying bitterly. But few people noticed her at those times, in the garb she wore: or if they did, believed that she was tutored to excite compassion, and passed on. Florence, too, called to her aid all the firmness and self-reliance of a character that her sad experience had prematurely formed and tried: and keeping the end she had in view steadily before her, steadily pursued it.

It was full two hours later in the afternoon than when she had started on this strange adventure, when, escaping from the clash and clangour of a narrow street full of carts and waggons, she peeped into a kind of wharf or landing-place upon the river-side, where there were a great many packages, casks, and boxes, strewn about; a large pair of wooden scales; and a little wooden house on wheels, outside of which, looking at the neighbouring masts and boats, a stout man stood whistling, with his pen behind his ear, and his hands in his pockets, as if his day's work were nearly done.

'Now then!' said this man, happening to turn round. 'We haven't got anything for you, little girl. Be off!'

'If you please, is this the City?' asked the trembling daughter of the Dombeys.

'Ah! It's the City. You know that well enough, I dare say. Be off! We haven't got anything for you.'

'I don't want anything, thank you,' was the timid answer 'Except to know the way to Dombey and Son's.'

The man, who had been strolling carelessly towards her, seemed surprised by this reply, and looking attentively in her face, rejoined:

'Why, what can *you* want with Dombey and Son's?'

'To know the way there, if you please.'

The man looked at her yet more curiously, and rubbed the back of his head so hard in his wonderment that he knocked his own hat off.

'Joe!' he called to another man – a labourer – as he picked it up and put it on again.

'Joe it is!' said Joe.

'Where's that young spark of Dombey's who's been watching the shipment of them goods?'

'Just gone, by t'other gate,' said Joe.

'Call him back a minute.'

Joe ran up an archway, bawling as he went, and very soon returned with a blithe-looking boy.

'You're Dombey's jockey,[8] an't you?' said the first man.

'I'm in Dombey's House, Mr Clark,' returned the boy.

'Look'ye here, then,' said Mr Clark.

Obedient to the indication of Mr Clark's hand, the boy approached towards Florence, wondering, as well he might, what he had to do with her. But she, who had heard what passed, and who, besides the relief of so suddenly considering herself safe at her journey's end, felt reassured beyond all measure by his lively youthful face and manner, ran eagerly up to him, leaving one of the slipshod shoes upon the ground and caught his hand in both of hers.

'I am lost, if you please!' said Florence.

'Lost!' cried the boy.

'Yes, I was lost this morning, a long way from here – and I have had my clothes taken away, since – and I am not dressed in my own now – and my name is Florence Dombey, my little brother's only sister – and, oh dear, dear, take care of me, if you please!' sobbed Florence, giving full vent to the childish feelings she had so long suppressed, and bursting into tears. At the same time her miserable bonnet falling off, her hair came tumbling down about her face: moving to speechless admiration and commiseration, young Walter, nephew of Solomon Gills, Ships' Instrument-maker in general.

Mr Clark stood wrapt in amazement: observing under his breath, *I* never saw such a start on *this* wharf before. Walter picked up the shoe, and put it on the little foot as the Prince in the story might have fitted Cinderella's slipper on. He hung the rabbit-skin over his left arm; gave the right to Florence; and felt, not to say like Richard Whittington[9] – that is a tame comparison – but like Saint George of England, with the dragon lying dead before him.

'Don't cry, Miss Dombey,' said Walter, in a transport of enthusiasm. 'What a wonderful thing for me that I am here! You are as safe now as if you were guarded by a whole boat's crew of picked men from a man-of-war. Oh, don't cry.'

'I won't cry any more,' said Florence. 'I am only crying for joy.'

'Crying for joy!' thought Walter, 'and I'm the cause of it! Come along, Miss Dombey. There's the other shoe off now! Take mine, Miss Dombey.'

'No, no, no,' said Florence, checking him in the act of impetuously pulling off his own. 'These do better. These do very well.'

'Why, to be sure,' said Walter, glancing at her foot, 'mine are a mile too large. What am I thinking about! You never could walk in *mine!* Come along, Miss Dombey. Let me see the villain who will dare molest you now.'

So Walter, looking immensely fierce, led off Florence, looking very happy; and they went arm-in-arm along the streets, perfectly indifferent to any astonishment that their appearance might or did excite by the way.

It was growing dark and foggy, and beginning to rain too, but they cared nothing for this: being both wholly absorbed in the late adventures of Florence, which she related with the innocent good faith and confidence of her years, while Walter listened as if, far from the mud and grease of Thames Street, they were rambling alone among the broad leaves and tall trees of some desert island in the tropics – as he very likely fancied, for the time, they were.

'Have we far to go?' asked Florence at last, lifting up her eyes to her companion's face.

'Ah! By-the-bye,' said Walter, stopping, 'let me see; where are we? Oh! I know. But the offices are shut up now, Miss Dombey. There's nobody there. Mr Dombey has gone home long ago. I suppose we must go home too? or, stay. Suppose I take you to my uncle's, where I live – it's very near here – and go to your house in a coach to tell them you are safe, and bring you back some clothes. Won't that be best?'

'I think so,' answered Florence. 'Don't you? What do you think?'

As they stood deliberating in the street, a man passed them, who glanced quickly at Walter as he went by, as if he recognised him; but seeming to correct that first impression, he passed on without stopping.

'Why, I think it's Mr Carker,' said Walter. 'Carker in our House. Not Carker our manager, Miss Dombey – the other Carker; the junior – Halloa! Mr Carker!'

'Is that Walter Gay?' said the other, stopping and returning. 'I couldn't believe it, with such a strange companion.'

As he stood near a lamp, listening with surprise to Walter's hurried explanation, he presented a remarkable contrast to the two youthful figures arm-in-arm before him. He was not old, but his hair was white; his body was bent, or bowed as if by the weight of some great trouble: and there were deep lines in his worn and melancholy face. The fire of his eyes, the expression of his features, the very voice in which he spoke, were all subdued and quenched, as if the spirit within him lay in ashes. He was respectably, though very plainly dressed, in black; but his clothes, moulded to the general character of his figure, seemed to shrink and abase themselves upon him, and to join in the sorrowful solicitation which the whole man from head to foot expressed, to be left unnoticed, and alone in his humility.

And yet his interest in youth and hopefulness was not extinguished with the other embers of his soul, for he watched the boy's earnest countenance as he spoke with unusual sympathy, though with an inexplicable show of trouble and compassion, which escaped into his looks, however hard he strove to hold it prisoner. When Walter, in conclusion, put to him the question he had put to Florence, he still stood glancing at him with the same expression, as if he had read some fate upon his face, mournfully at variance with its present brightness.

'What do you advise, Mr Carker?' said Walter, smiling. 'You always give me good advice, you know, when you *do* speak to me. That's not often, though.'

'I think your own idea is the best,' he answered: looking from Florence to Walter, and back again.

'Mr Carker,' said Walter, brightening with a generous thought, 'Come! Here's a chance for you. Go you to Mr Dombey's, and be the messenger of good news. It may do you some good, Sir. I'll remain at home. You shall go.'

'I!' returned the other.

'Yes. Why not, Mr Carker?' said the boy.

He merely shook him by the hand in answer; he seemed in a manner ashamed and afraid even to do that; and bidding him good night, and advising him to make haste, turned away.

'Come, Miss Dombey,' said Walter, looking after him as they turned away also, 'we'll go to my uncle's as quick as we can. Did you ever hear Mr Dombey speak of Mr Carker the junior, Miss Florence?'

'No,' returned the child, mildly, 'I don't often hear papa speak.'

'Ah! true! more shame for him,' thought Walter. After a minute's pause, during which he had been looking down upon the gentle patient little face moving on at his side, he bestirred himself with his accustomed boyish animation and restlessness to change the subject; and one of the unfortunate shoes coming off again opportunely, proposed to carry Florence to his uncle's in his arms. Florence, though very tired, laughingly declined the proposal, lest he should let her fall; and as they were already near the wooden midshipman, and as Walter went on to cite various precedents, from shipwrecks and other moving accidents, where younger boys than he had triumphantly rescued and carried off older girls than Florence, they were still in full conversation about it when they arrived at the instrument-maker's door.

'Holloa, Uncle Sol!' cried Walter, bursting into the shop and speaking incoherently and out of breath, from that time forth, for the rest of the evening. 'Here's a wonderful adventure! Here's Mr Dombey's daughter lost in the streets, and robbed of her clothes by an old witch of a woman – found by me – brought home to our parlour to rest – look here!'

'Good Heaven!' said Uncle Sol, starting back against his favourite compass-case. 'It can't be! Well, I—'

'No, nor anybody else,' said Walter, anticipating the rest. 'Nobody would, nobody could, you know. Here! just help me lift the little sofa near the fire, will you, Uncle Sol – take care of the plates – cut some dinner for her, will you, uncle – throw those shoes under the grate. Miss Florence – put your feet on the fender to dry – how damp they are – here's an adventure, uncle, eh? – God bless my soul, how hot I am!'

Solomon Gills was quite as hot, by sympathy, and in excessive bewilderment. He patted Florence's head, pressed her to eat, pressed her to drink, rubbed the soles of her feet with his pocket-handkerchief heated at the fire, followed his locomotive nephew with his eyes, and ears, and had no clear perception of anything except that he was being constantly knocked against and tumbled over by that excited young gentleman, as he darted about the room attempting to accomplish twenty things at once, and doing nothing at all.

'Here, wait a minute, uncle,' he continued, catching up a candle, 'till I run upstairs, and get another jacket on, and then I'll be off. I say, uncle, isn't this an adventure?'

'My dear boy,' said Solomon, who, with his spectacles on his forehead and the great chronometer in his pocket, was incessantly oscillating between Florence on the sofa and his nephew in all parts of the parlour, 'it's the most extraordinary—'

'No, but do, uncle, please – do, Miss Florence – dinner, you know, uncle.'

'Yes, yes, yes,' cried Solomon, cutting instantly into a leg of mutton, as if he were catering for a giant. 'I'll take care of her, Wally! I understand. Pretty dear! Famished, of course. You go and get ready. Lord bless me! Sir Richard Whittington thrice Lord Mayor of London.'

Walter was not very long in mounting to his lofty garret and descending from it, but in the meantime Florence, overcome by fatigue, had sunk into a doze before the fire. The short interval of quiet, though only a few minutes in duration, enabled Solomon Gills so far to collect his wits as to make some little arrangements for her comfort, and to darken the room, and to screen her from the blaze. Thus, when the boy returned, she was sleeping peacefully.

'That's capital!' he whispered, giving Solomon such a hug that it squeezed a new expression into his face. 'Now I'm off. I'll just take

a crust of bread with me, for I'm very hungry – and – don't wake
her, Uncle Sol.'

'No, no,' said Solomon. 'Pretty child.'

'Pretty, indeed!' cried Walter. 'I never saw such a face, Uncle Sol.
Now I'm off.'

'That's right,' said Solomon, greatly relieved.

'I say, Uncle Sol,' cried Walter, putting his face in at the door.

'Here he is again,' said Solomon.

'How does she look now?'

'Quite happy,' said Solomon.

'That's famous! now I'm off.'

'I hope you are,' said Solomon to himself.

'I say, Uncle Sol,' cried Walter, reappearing at the door.

'Here he is again!' said Solomon.

'We met Mr Carker the junior in the street, queerer than ever. He
bade me good-bye, but came behind us here – there's an odd thing!
– for when we reached the shop door, I looked round, and saw him
going quietly away, like a servant who had seen me home, or a
faithful dog. How does she look now, uncle?'

'Pretty much the same as before, Wally,' replied Uncle Sol.

'That's right. Now I *am* off!'

And this time he really was: and Solomon Gills, with no appetite
for dinner, sat on the opposite side of the fire, watching Florence in
her slumber, building a great many airy castles of the most fantastic
architecture; and looking, in the dim shade, and in the close vicinity
of all the instruments, like a magician disguised in a Welsh wig and
a suit of coffee colour, who held the child in an enchanted sleep.

In the meantime, Walter proceeded towards Mr Dombey's house
at a pace seldom achieved by a hack horse from the stand; and yet
with his head out of window every two or three minutes, in
impatient remonstrance with the driver. Arriving at his journey's
end, he leaped out, and breathlessly announcing his errand to the
servant, followed him straight into the library, where there was a
great confusion of tongues, and where Mr Dombey, his sister, and
Miss Tox, Richards, and Nipper, were all congregated together.

'Oh! I beg your pardon, sir,' said Walter, rushing up to him, 'but
I'm happy to say it's all right, sir. Miss Dombey's found!'

The boy with his open face, and flowing hair, and sparkling eyes,
panting with pleasure and excitement, was wonderfully opposed to
Mr Dombey, as he sat confronting him in his library chair.

'I told you, Louisa, that she would certainly be found,' said Mr
Dombey, looking slightly over his shoulder at that lady, who wept

in company with Miss Tox. 'Let the servants know that no further steps are necessary. This boy who brings the information, is young Gay, from the office. How was my daughter found, Sir? I know how she was lost.' Here he looked majestically at Richards. 'But how was she found? Who found her?'

'Why, I believe *I* found Miss Dombey, Sir,' said Walter modestly; 'at least I don't know that I can claim the merit of having exactly found her, Sir, but I was the fortunate instrument of—'

'What do you mean, Sir,' interrupted Mr Dombey, regarding the boy's evident pride and pleasure in his share of the transaction with an instinctive dislike, 'by not having exactly found my daughter, and by being a fortunate instrument? Be plain and coherent, if you please.'

It was quite out of Walter's power to be coherent, but he rendered himself as explanatory as he could, in his breathless state, and stated why he had come alone.

'You hear this, girl?' said Mr Dombey sternly to the black-eyed. 'Take what is necessary, and return immediately with this young man to fetch Miss Florence home. Gay, you will be rewarded to-morrow.'

'Oh! thank you, Sir,' said Walter. 'You are very kind. I'm sure I was not thinking of any reward, Sir.'

'You are a boy,' said Mr Dombey, suddenly and almost fiercely; 'and what you think of, or affect to think of, is of little consequence. You have done well, Sir. Don't undo it. Louisa, please to give the lad some wine.'

Mr Dombey's glance followed Walter Gay with sharp disfavour, as he left the room under the pilotage of Mrs Chick; and it may be that his mind's eye followed him with no greater relish, as he rode back to his uncle's with Miss Susan Nipper. There they found that Florence, much refreshed by sleep, had dined, and greatly improved the acquaintance of Solomon Gills, with whom she was on terms of perfect confidence and ease. The black-eyed (who had cried so much that she might now be called the red-eyed, and who was very silent and depressed) caught her in her arms without a word of contradiction or reproach, and made a very hysterical meeting of it. Then converting the parlour, for the nonce, into a private tiring room, she dressed her, with great care, in proper clothes; and presently led her forth, as like a Dombey as her natural disqualifications admitted of her being made.

'Good night!' said Florence, running up to Solomon. 'You have been very good to me.'

Old Sol was quite delighted, and kissed her like her grandfather.

'Good night, Walter! Good-bye!' said Florence.

'Good-bye!' said Walter, giving both his hands.

'I'll never forget you,' pursued Florence. 'No! indeed I never will. Good-bye, Walter!'

In the innocence of her grateful heart, the child lifted up her face to his. Walter, bending down his own, raised it again, all red and burning; and looked at Uncle Sol, quite sheepishly.

'Where's Walter?' 'Good night, Walter!' 'Goodbye, Walter!' 'Shake hands once more, Walter!' This was still Florence's cry, after she was shut up with her little maid, in the coach. And when the coach at length moved off, Walter on the door-step gaily returned the waving of her handkerchief, while the wooden midshipman behind him seemed, like himself, intent upon that coach alone, excluding all the other passing coaches from his observation.

In good time Mr Dombey's mansion was gained again, and again there was a noise of tongues in the library. Again, too, the coach was ordered to wait – 'for Mrs Richards,' one of Susan's fellow-servants ominously whispered, as she passed with Florence.

The entrance of the lost child made a slight sensation, but not much. Mr Dombey, who had never found her, kissed her once upon the forehead, and cautioned her not to run away again, or wander anywhere with treacherous attendants. Mrs Chick stopped in her lamentations on the corruption of human nature, even when beckoned to the paths of virtue by a Charitable Grinder; and received her with a welcome something short of the reception due to none but perfect Dombeys. Miss Tox regulated her feelings by the models before her. Richards, the culprit Richards, alone poured out her heart in broken words of welcome, and bowed herself over the little wandering head as if she really loved it.

'Ah, Richards!' said Mrs Chick, with a sigh. 'It would have been much more satisfactory to those who wish to think well of their fellow-creatures, and much more becoming in you, if you had shown some proper feeling, in time, for the little child that is now going to be prematurely deprived of its natural nourishment.'

'Cut off,' said Miss Tox, in a plaintive whisper, 'from one common fountain!'

'If it was *my* ungrateful case,' said Mrs Chick, solemnly, 'and I had *your* reflections, Richards, I should feel as if the Charitable Grinders' dress would blight my child, and the education choke him.'

For the matter of that – but Mrs Chick didn't know it – he had been pretty well blighted by the dress already; and as to the education, even its retributive effect might be produced in time, for it was a storm of sobs and blows.

'Louisa!' said Mr Dombey. 'It is not necessary to prolong these observations. The woman is discharged and paid. You leave this house, Richards, for taking my son – my son,' said Mr Dombey, emphatically repeating these two words, 'into haunts and into society which are not to be thought of without a shudder. As to the accident which befell Miss Florence this morning, I regard that as, in one great sense, a happy and fortunate circumstance; inasmuch as, but for that occurrence, I never could have known – and from your own lips too – of what you had been guilty. I think, Louisa, the other nurse, the young person,' here Miss Nipper sobbed aloud, 'being so much younger, and necessarily influenced by Paul's nurse, may remain. Have the goodness to direct that this woman's coach is paid to' – Mr Dombey stopped and winced – 'to Staggs's Gardens.'

Polly moved towards the door, with Florence holding to her dress, and crying to her in the most pathetic manner not to go away. It was a dagger in the haughty father's heart, an arrow in his brain, to see how the flesh and blood he could not disown, clung to this obscure stranger, and he sitting by. Not that he cared to whom his daughter turned, or from whom turned away. The swift sharp agony struck through him, as he thought of what his son might do.

His son cried lustily that night, at all events. Sooth to say, poor Paul had better reason for his tears than sons of that age often have, for he had lost his second mother – his first, so far as he knew – by a stroke as sudden as that natural affliction which had darkened the beginning of his life. At the same blow, his sister too, who cried herself to sleep so mournfully, had lost as good and true a friend. But that is quite beside the question. Let us waste no words about it.

CHAPTER 7

A Bird's-eye glimpse of Miss Tox's Dwelling-place: also of the State of Miss Tox's Affections

Miss Tox inhabited a dark little house that had been squeezed, at some remote period of English History, into a fashionable neighbourhood at the west end of the town, where it stood in the shade like a poor relation of the great street round the corner, coldly looked down upon by mighty mansions. It was not exactly in a court, and it was not exactly in a yard; but it was in the dullest of No-Thoroughfares, rendered anxious and haggard by distant double knocks. The name of this retirement, where grass grew between the chinks in the stone pavement, was Princess's Place;[1] and in Princess's Place was Princess's Chapel, with a tinkling bell, where sometimes as many as five-and-twenty people attended service on a Sunday. The Princess's Arms was also there, and much resorted to by splendid footmen. A sedan chair was kept inside the railing before the Princess's Arms, but it had never come out within the memory of man; and on fine mornings, the top of every rail (there were eight-and-forty, as Miss Tox had often counted) was decorated with a pewter-pot.

There was another private house besides Miss Tox's in Princess's Place: not to mention an immense pair of gates, with an immense pair of lion-headed knockers on them, which were never opened by any chance, and were supposed to constitute a disused entrance to somebody's stables. Indeed, there was a smack of stabling in the air of Princess's Place; and Miss Tox's bedroom (which was at the back) commanded a vista of Mews, where hostlers, at whatever sort of work engaged, were continually accompanying themselves with effervescent noises; and where the domestic and confidential garments of coachmen and their wives and families, usually hung, like Macbeth's banners,[2] on the outward walls.

At this other private house in Princess's Place, tenanted by a retired butler who had married a housekeeper, apartments were let Furnished, to a single gentleman: to wit, a wooden-featured, blue-faced Major, with his eyes starting out of his head, in whom Miss Tox recognised, as she herself expressed it, 'something so truly military'; and between whom and herself, an occasional interchange of newspapers and pamphlets, and such Platonic dalliance, was effected through the medium of a dark servant of the Major's, whom Miss Tox was quite content to classify as a 'native,' without connecting him with any geographical idea whatever.

Perhaps there never was a smaller entry and staircase, than the entry and staircase of Miss Tox's house. Perhaps, taken altogether, from top to bottom, it was the most inconvenient little house in England, and the crookedest; but then, Miss Tox said, what a situation! There was very little daylight to be got there in the winter: no sun at the best of times: air was out of the question, and traffic

was walled out. Still Miss Tox said, think of the situation! So said
the blue-faced Major, whose eyes were starting out of his head:
who gloried in Princess's Place: and who delighted to turn the
conversation at his club, whenever he could, to something connected with some of the great people in the great street round the
corner, that he might have the satisfaction of saying they were his
neighbours.

The dingy tenement inhabited by Miss Tox was her own; having
been devised and bequeathed to her by the deceased owner of the
fishy eye in the locket, of whom a miniature portrait, with a
powdered head and a pigtail, balanced the kettle-holder on opposite
sides of the parlour fireplace. The greater part of the furniture was
of the powdered-head and pig-tail period: comprising a plate-
warmer, always languishing and sprawling its four attenuated bow
legs in somebody's way; and an obsolete harpsichord, illuminated
round the maker's name with a painted garland of sweet peas.

Although Major Bagstock had arrived at what is called in polite
literature, the grand meridian of life, and was proceeding on his
journey down-hill with hardly any throat, and a very rigid pair of
jaw-bones, and long-flapped elephantine ears, and his eyes and
complexion in the state of artificial excitement already mentioned,
he was mightily proud of awakening an interest in Miss Tox, and
tickled his vanity with the fiction that she was a splendid woman,
who had her eye on him. This he had several times hinted at the
club: in connexion with little jocularities, of which old Joe Bagstock,
old Joey Bagstock, old J. Bagstock, old Josh Bagstock, or so forth,
was the perpetual theme: it being, as it were, the Major's stronghold
and donjon-keep of light humour, to be on the most familiar terms
with his own name.

'Joey B., Sir,' the major would say, with a flourish of his walking-
stick, 'is worth a dozen of you. If you had a few more of the
Bagstock breed among you, Sir, you'd be none the worse for it. Old
Joe, Sir, needn't look far for a wife, even now, if he was on the
look-out; but he's hard-hearted, Sir, is Joe – he's tough, Sir, tough,
and de-vilish sly!' After such a declaration wheezing sounds would
be heard; and the Major's blue would deepen into purple, while his
eyes strained and started convulsively.

Notwithstanding his very liberal laudation of himself, however,
the Major was selfish. It may be doubted whether there ever was a
more entirely selfish person at heart; or at stomach is perhaps a
better expression, seeing that he was more decidedly endowed with
that latter organ than with the former. He had no idea of being

overlooked or slighted by anybody; least of all, had he the remotest comprehension of being overlooked and slighted by Miss Tox.

And yet, Miss Tox, as it appeared, forgot him – gradually forgot him. She began to forget him soon after her discovery of the Toodle family. She continued to forget him up to the time of the christening. She went on forgetting him with compound interest after that. Something or somebody had superseded him as a source of interest.

'Good morning, ma'am,' said the Major, meeting Miss Tox in Princess's Place, some weeks after the changes chronicled in the last chapter.

'Good morning, Sir,' said Miss Tox; very coldly.

'Joe Bagstock, ma'am,' observed the Major, with his usual gallantry, 'has not had the happiness of bowing to you at your window, for a considerable period. Joe has been hardly used, ma'am. His sun has been behind a cloud.'

Miss Tox inclined her head; but very coldly indeed.

'Joe's luminary has been out of town, ma'am, perhaps,' inquired the Major.

'I? out of town? oh no, I have not been out of town,' said Miss Tox. 'I have been much engaged lately. My time is nearly all devoted to some very intimate friends. I am afraid I have none to spare, even now. Good morning, Sir!'

As Miss Tox, with her most fascinating step and carriage, disappeared from Princess's Place, the Major stood looking after her with a bluer face than ever: muttering and growling some not at all complimentary remarks.

'Why, damme, Sir,' said the Major, rolling his lobster eyes round and round Princess's Place, and apostrophizing its fragrant air, 'six months ago, the woman loved the ground Josh Bagstock walked on. What's the meaning of it?'

The Major decided, after some consideration, that it meant man-traps; that it meant plotting and snaring; that Miss Tox was digging pitfalls. 'But you won't catch Joe, ma'am,' said the Major. 'He's tough, ma'am, tough, is J. B. Tough, and de-vilish sly!' over which reflection he chuckled for the rest of the day.

But still, when that day and many other days were gone and past, it seemed that Miss Tox took no heed whatever of the Major, and thought nothing at all about him. She had been wont, once upon a time, to look out at one of her little dark windows by accident, and blushingly return the Major's greeting; but now, she never gave the Major a chance, and cared nothing at all whether he looked over the way or not. Other changes had come to pass too. The Major, standing in the shade of his own apartments, could make out that an air of greater smartness had recently come over Miss Tox's house; that a new cage with gilded wires had been provided for the ancient little canary bird; that divers ornaments, cut out of coloured cardboards and paper, seemed to decorate the chimneypiece and tables; that a plant or two had suddenly sprung up in the windows; that Miss Tox occasionally practised on the harpsichord, whose garland of sweet peas was always displayed ostentatiously, crowned with the Copenhagen and Bird Waltzes in a Music Book of Miss Tox's own copying.[3]

Over and above all this, Miss Tox had long been dressed with uncommon care and elegance in slight mourning. But this helped the Major out of his difficulty; and he determined within himself that she had come into a small legacy, and grown proud.

It was on the very next day after he had eased his mind by arriving at this decision, that the Major, sitting at his breakfast, saw an apparition so tremendous and wonderful in Miss Tox's little drawing-room, that he remained for some time rooted to his chair; then, rushing into the next room, returned with a double-barrelled opera-glass, through which he surveyed it intently for some minutes.

'It's a baby, Sir,' said the Major, shutting up the glass again, 'for fifty thousand pounds!'

The Major couldn't forget it. He could do nothing but whistle, and stare to that extent, that his eyes compared with what they now became, had been in former times quite cavernous and sunken. Day after day, two, three, four times a week, this baby reappeared. The Major continued to stare and whistle. To all other intents and purposes he was alone in Princess's Place. Miss Tox had ceased to mind what he did. He might have been black as well as blue, and it would have been of no consequence to her.

The perseverance with which she walked out of Princess's Place to fetch this baby and its nurse, and walked back with them, and walked home with them again, and continually mounted guard over them; and the perseverance with which she nursed it herself, and fed it, and played with it, and froze its young blood[4] with airs upon the harpsichord; was extraordinary. At about this same period, too, she was seized with a passion for looking at a certain bracelet; also with a passion for looking at the moon, of which she would take long observations from her chamber window. But whatever she looked at; sun, moon, stars, or bracelet; she looked no more at the Major. And the Major whistled, and stared, and wondered, and dodged about his room, and could make nothing of it.

'You'll quite win my brother Paul's heart, and that's the truth, my dear,' said Mrs Chick, one day.

Miss Tox turned pale.

'He grows more like Paul every day,' said Mrs Chick.

Miss Tox returned no other reply than by taking the little Paul in her arms, and making his cockade[5] perfectly flat and limp with her caresses.

'His mother, my dear,' said Miss Tox, 'whose acquaintance I was to have made through you, does he at all resemble her?'

'Not at all,' returned Louisa.

'She was – she was pretty, I believe?' faltered Miss Tox.

'Why, poor dear Fanny was interesting,' said Mrs Chick, after some judicial consideration. 'Certainly interesting. She had not that air of commanding superiority which one would somehow expect, almost as a matter of course, to find in my brother's wife; nor had she that strength and vigour of mind which such a man requires.'

Miss Tox heaved a deep sigh.

'But she was pleasing:' said Mrs Chick: 'extremely so. And she meant! – oh, dear, how well poor Fanny meant!'

'You Angel!' cried Miss Tox to little Paul. 'You picture of your own papa!'

If the Major could have known how many hopes and ventures, what a multitude of plans and speculations, rested on that baby head; and could have seen them hovering, in all their heterogeneous confusion and disorder, round the puckered cap of the unconscious little Paul; he might have stared indeed. Then would he have recognised, among the crowd, some few ambitious motes and beams belonging to Miss Tox; then would he perhaps have understood the nature of that lady's faltering investment in the Dombey Firm.

If the child himself could have awakened in the night, and seen, gathered about his cradle-curtains, faint reflections of the dreams that other people had of him, they might have scared him, with good reason. But he slumbered on, alike unconscious of the kind intentions of Miss Tox, the wonder of the Major, the early sorrows of his sister, and the stern visions of his father; and innocent that any spot of earth contained a Dombey or a Son.

CHAPTER 8

Paul's further Progress, Growth, and Character

Beneath the watching and attentive eyes of Time – so far another Major – Paul's slumbers gradually changed. More and more light broke in upon them; distincter and distincter dreams disturbed them; an accumulating crowd of objects and impressions swarmed about his rest; and so he passed from babyhood to childhood, and became a talking, walking, wondering Dombey.

On the downfall and banishment of Richards, the nursery may be said to have been put into commission: as a Public Department is sometimes, when no individual Atlas can be found to support it. The Commissioners were, of course, Mrs Chick and Miss Tox: who devoted themselves to their duties with such astonishing ardour that Major Bagstock had every day some new reminder of his being forsaken, while Mr Chick, bereft of domestic supervision, cast himself upon the gay world, dined at clubs and coffee-houses, smelt of smoke on three distinct occasions, went to the play by himself, and in short, loosened (as Mrs Chick once told him) every social bond, and moral obligation.

Yet, in spite of his early promise, all this vigilance and care could not make little Paul a thriving boy. Naturally delicate, perhaps, he pined and wasted after the dismissal of his nurse, and, for a long time, seemed but to wait his opportunity of gliding through their hands, and seeking his lost mother. This dangerous ground in his steeple-chase towards manhood passed, he still found it very rough riding, and was grievously beset by all the obstacles in his course. Every tooth was a break-neck fence, and every pimple in the measles a stone wall to him. He was down in every fit of the hooping-cough, and rolled upon and crushed by a whole field of small diseases, that came trooping on each other's heels to prevent his getting up again. Some bird of prey got into his throat instead of the thrush;[1] and the very chickens[2] turning ferocious – if they have anything to do with that infant malady to which they lend their name – worried him like tiger-cats.

The chill of Paul's christening had struck home, perhaps to some sensitive part of his nature, which could not recover itself in the cold shade of his father; but he was an unfortunate child from that day. Mrs Wickam often said she never see a dear so put upon.

Mrs Wickam was a waiter's wife – which would seem equivalent to being any other man's widow – whose application for an

engagement in Mr Dombey's service had been favourably considered, on account of the apparent impossibility of her having any
followers, or any one to follow; and who, from within a day or two
of Paul's sharp weaning, had been engaged as his nurse. Mrs
Wickam was a meek woman, of a fair complexion, with her
eyebrows always elevated, and her head always drooping, who was
always ready to pity herself, or to be pitied, or to pity anybody else;
and who had a surprising natural gift of viewing all subjects in an
utterly forlorn and pitiable light, and bringing dreadful precedents
to bear upon them, and deriving the greatest consolation from the
exercise of that talent.

It is hardly necessary to observe, that no touch of this quality
ever reached the magnificent knowledge of Mr Dombey. It would
have been remarkable, indeed, if any had; when no one in the house
– not even Mrs Chick or Miss Tox – dared ever whisper to him that
there had, on any one occasion, been the least reason for uneasiness
in reference to little Paul. He had settled, within himself, that the
child must necessarily pass through a certain routine of minor
maladies, and that the sooner he did so the better. If he could have
bought him off, or provided a substitute, as in the case of an
unlucky drawing for the militia, he would have been glad to do so
on liberal terms. But as this was not feasible, he merely wondered,
in his haughty manner, now and then, what Nature meant by it;
and comforted himself with the reflection that there was another
milestone passed upon the road, and that the great end of the
journey lay so much the nearer. For the feeling uppermost in his
mind, now and constantly intensifying, and increasing in it as Paul
grew older, was impatience. Impatience for the time to come, when
his visions of their united consequence and grandeur would be
triumphantly realized.

Some philosophers[3] tell us that selfishness is at the root of our
best loves and affections. Mr Dombey's young child was, from the
beginning, so distinctly important to him as a part of his own
greatness, or (which is the same thing) of the greatness of Dombey
and Son, that there is no doubt his parental affection might have
been easily traced, like many a goodly superstructure of fair fame,
to a very low foundation. But he loved his son with all the love he
had. If there were a warm place in his frosty heart, his son occupied
it; if its very hard surface could receive the impression of any image,
the image of that son was there; though not so much as an infant,
or as a boy, but as a grown man – the 'Son' of the Firm. Therefore
he was impatient to advance into the future, and to hurry over the

intervening passages of his history. Therefore he had little or no anxiety about them, in spite of his love; feeling as if the boy had a charmed life, and *must* become the man with whom he held such constant communication in his thoughts, and for whom he planned and projected, as for an existing reality, every day.

Thus Paul grew to be nearly five years old. He was a pretty little fellow; though there was something wan and wistful in his small face, that gave occasion to many significant shakes of Mrs Wickam's head, and many long-drawn inspirations of Mrs Wickam's breath. His temper gave abundant promise of being imperious in after-life; and he had as hopeful an apprehension of his own importance, and the rightful subservience of all other things and persons to it, as heart could desire. He was childish and sportive enough at times, and not of a sullen disposition; but he had a strange, old-fashioned, thoughtful way, at other times, of sitting brooding in his miniature armchair, when he looked (and talked) like one of those terrible little Beings in the Fairy tales,[4] who, at a hundred and fifty or two hundred years of age, fantastically represent the children for whom they have been substituted. He would frequently be stricken with this precocious mood upstairs in the nursery; and would sometimes lapse into it suddenly, exclaiming that he was tired: even while playing with Florence, or driving Miss Tox in single harness. But at no time did he fall into it so surely, as when, his little chair being carried down into his father's room, he sat there with him after dinner, by the fire. They were the strangest pair at such a time that ever firelight shone upon. Mr Dombey so erect and solemn, gazing at the blaze; his little image, with an old, old face, peering into the red perspective with the fixed and rapt attention of a sage. Mr Dombey entertaining complicated worldly schemes and plans; the little image entertaining Heaven knows what wild fancies, half-formed thoughts, and wandering speculations. Mr Dombey stiff with starch and arrogance; the little image by inheritance, and in unconscious imitation. The two so very much alike, and yet so monstrously contrasted.

On one of these occasions, when they had both been perfectly quiet for a long time, and Mr Dombey only knew that the child was awake by occasionally glancing at his eye, where the bright fire was sparkling like a jewel, little Paul broke silence thus:

'Papa! what's money?'

The abrupt question had such immediate reference to the subject of Mr Dombey's thoughts, that Mr Dombey was quite disconcerted.

'What is money, Paul?' he answered. 'Money?'

'Yes,' said the child, laying his hands upon the elbows of his little chair, and turning the old face up towards Mr Dombey's; 'what is money?'

Mr Dombey was in a difficulty. He would have liked to give him some explanation involving the terms circulating-medium, currency, depreciation of currency, paper, bullion, rates of exchange, value of precious metals in the market, and so forth; but looking down at the little chair, and seeing what a long way down it was, he answered: 'Gold, and silver, and copper. Guineas, shillings, half-pence. You know what they are?'

'Oh yes, I know what they are,' said Paul. 'I don't mean that, papa. I mean what's money after all?'

Heaven and Earth, how old his face was as he turned it up again towards his father's!

'What is money after all!' said Mr Dombey, backing his chair a little, that he might the better gaze in sheer amazement at the presumptuous atom that propounded such an inquiry.

'I mean, papa, what can it do?' returned Paul, folding his arms (they were hardly long enough to fold), and looking at the fire, and up at him, and at the fire, and up at him again.

Mr Dombey drew his chair back to its former place, and patted him on the head. 'You'll know better by-and-by, my man,' he said. 'Money, Paul, can do anything.' He took hold of the little hand, and beat it softly against one of his own, as he said so.

But Paul got his hand free as soon as he could; and rubbing it gently to and fro on the elbow of his chair, as if his wit were in the palm, and he were sharpening it – and looking at the fire again, as though the fire had been his adviser and prompter – repeated, after a short pause:

'Anything, papa?'

'Yes. Anything – almost,' said Mr Dombey.

'Anything means everything, don't it, papa?' asked his son: not observing, or possibly not understanding, the qualification.

'It includes it: yes,' said Mr Dombey.

'Why didn't money save me my mama?' returned the child. 'It isn't cruel, is it?'

'Cruel!' said Mr Dombey, settling his neckcloth, and seeming to resent the idea. 'No. A good thing can't be cruel.'

'If it's a good thing, and can do anything,' said the little fellow, thoughtfully, as he looked back at the fire, 'I wonder why it didn't save me my mama.'

He didn't ask the question of his father this time. Perhaps he had seen, with a child's quickness, that it had already made his father uncomfortable. But he repeated the thought aloud, as if it were quite an old one to him, and had troubled him very much; and sat with his chin resting on his hand, still cogitating and looking for an explanation in the fire.

Mr Dombey having recovered from his surprise, not to say his alarm (for it was the very first occasion on which the child had ever broached the subject of his mother to him, though he had had him sitting by his side, in this same manner, evening after evening), expounded to him how that money, though a very potent spirit, never to be disparaged on any account whatever, could not keep people alive whose time was come to die; and how that we must all die, unfortunately, even in the City, though we were never so rich. But how that money caused us to be honoured, feared, respected, courted, and admired, and made us powerful and glorious in the eyes of all men; and how that it could, very often, even keep off death, for a long time together. How, for example, it had secured to his mama the services of Mr Pilkins, by which he, Paul, had often profited himself; likewise of the great Doctor Parker Peps, whom he had never known. And how it could do all, that could be done. This, with more to the same purpose, Mr Dombey instilled into the mind of his son, who listened attentively, and seemed to understand the greater part of what was said to him.

'It can't make me strong and quite well, either, papa; can it?' asked Paul, after a short silence; rubbing his tiny hands.

'Why, you *are* strong and quite well,' returned Mr Dombey. 'Are you not?'

Oh! the age of the face that was turned up again, with an expression, half of melancholy, half of slyness, on it!

'You are as strong and well as such little people usually are? Eh?' said Mr Dombey.

'Florence is older than I am, but I'm not as strong and well as Florence, I know,' returned the child; 'but I believe that when Florence was as little as me, she could play a great deal longer at a time without tiring herself. I am so tired sometimes,' said little Paul, warming his hands, and looking in between the bars of the grate, as if some ghostly puppet-show were performing there, 'and my bones ache so (Wickam says it's my bones), that I don't know what to do.'

'Aye! But that's at night,' said Mr Dombey, drawing his own chair closer to his son's, and laying his hand gently on his back; 'little people should be tired at night, for then they sleep well.'

'Oh, it's not at night, papa,' returned the child, 'it's in the day; and I lie down in Florence's lap, and she sings to me. At night I dream about such cu-ri-ous things!'

And he went on, warming his hands again, and thinking about them, like an old man or a young goblin.

Mr Dombey was so astonished, and so uncomfortable, and so perfectly at a loss how to pursue the conversation, that he could only sit looking at his son by the light of the fire, with his hand resting on his back, as if it were detained there by some magnetic attraction. Once he advanced his other hand, and turned the contemplative face towards his own for a moment. But it sought the fire again as soon as he released it; and remained, addressed towards the flickering blaze, until the nurse appeared, to summon him to bed.

'I want Florence to come for me,' said Paul.

'Won't you come with your poor nurse Wickam, Master Paul?' inquired that attendant, with great pathos.

'No, I won't,' replied Paul, composing himself in his armchair again, like the master of the house.

Invoking a blessing upon his innocence, Mrs Wickam withdrew, and presently Florence appeared in her stead. The child immediately started up with sudden readiness and animation, and raised towards his father in bidding him good night, a countenance so much brighter, so much younger, and so much more childlike altogether, that Mr Dombey, while he felt greatly re-assured by the change, was quite amazed at it.

After they had left the room together, he thought he heard a soft voice singing; and remembering that Paul had said his sister sung to him, he had the curiosity to open the door and listen, and look after them. She was toiling up the great, wide, vacant staircase, with him in her arms; his head was lying on her shoulder, one of his arms thrown negligently round her neck. So they went, toiling up; she singing all the way, and Paul sometimes crooning out a feeble accompaniment. Mr Dombey looked after them until they reached the top of the staircase – not without halting to rest by the way – and passed out of his sight; and then he still stood gazing upwards, until the dull rays of the moon, glimmering in a melancholy manner through the dim skylight, sent him back to his own room.

Mrs Chick and Miss Tox were convoked in council at dinner next day; and when the cloth was removed, Mr Dombey opened the proceedings by requiring to be informed, without any gloss or reservation, whether there was anything the matter with Paul, and what Mr Pilkins said about him.

'For the child is hardly,' said Mr Dombey, 'as stout as I could wish.'

'With your usual happy discrimination, my dear Paul,' returned Mrs Chick, 'you have hit the point at once. Our darling is *not* altogether as stout as we could wish. The fact is, that his mind is too much for him. His soul is a great deal too large for his frame. I am sure the way in which that dear child talks!' said Mrs Chick, shaking her head; 'no one would believe. His expressions, Lucretia, only yesterday upon the subject of Funerals!—'

'I am afraid,' said Mr Dombey, interrupting her testily, 'that some of those persons upstairs suggest improper subjects to the child. He was speaking to me last night about his – about his Bones,' said Mr Dombey, laying an irritated stress upon the word. 'What on earth has anybody to do with the – with the – Bones of my son? He is not a living skeleton, I suppose.'

'Very far from it,' said Mrs Chick, with unspeakable expression.

'I hope so,' returned her brother. 'Funerals again! who talks to the child of funerals? We are not undertakers, or mutes, or grave-diggers, I believe.'

'Very far from it,' interposed Mrs Chick, with the same profound expression as before.

'Then who puts such things into his head?' said Mr Dombey. 'Really I was quite dismayed and shocked last night. Who puts such things into his head, Louisa?'

'My dear Paul,' said Mrs Chick, after a moment's silence, 'it is of no use inquiring. I do not think, I will tell you candidly, that Wickam is a person of very cheerful spirit, or what one would call a—'

'A daughter of Momus,'[5] Miss Tox softly suggested.

'Exactly so,' said Mrs Chick; 'but she is exceedingly attentive and useful, and not at all presumptuous; indeed I never saw a more biddable woman. If the dear child,' pursued Mrs Chick, in the tone of one who was summing up what had been previously quite agreed upon, instead of saying it all for the first time, 'is a little weakened by that last attack, and is not in quite such vigorous health as we could wish; and if he has some temporary weakness in his system, and does occasionally seem about to lose, for the moment, the use of his—'

Mrs Chick was afraid to say limbs, after Mr Dombey's recent

objection to bones, and therefore waited for a suggestion from Miss Tox, who, true to her office, hazarded 'members.'

'Members!' repeated Mr Dombey.

'I think the medical gentleman mentioned legs this morning, my dear Louisa, did he not?' said Miss Tox.

'Why, of course he did, my love,' retorted Mrs Chick, mildly reproachful. 'How can you ask me? You heard him. I say, if our dear Paul should lose, for the moment, the use of his legs, these are casualties common to many children at his time of life, and not to be prevented by any care or caution. The sooner you understand that, Paul, and admit that, the better.'

'Surely you must know, Louisa,' observed Mr Dombey, 'that I don't question your natural devotion to, and regard for, the future head of my house. Mr Pilkins saw Paul this morning, I believe?' said Mr Dombey.

'Yes; he did,' returned his sister. 'Miss Tox and myself were present, Miss Tox and myself are always present. We make a point of it. Mr Pilkins has seen him for some days past, and a very clever man I believe him to be. He says it is nothing to speak of; which I can confirm, if that is any consolation; but he recommended, to-day, sea-air. Very wisely, Paul, I feel convinced.'

'Sea-air,' repeated Mr Dombey, looking at his sister.

'There is nothing to be made uneasy by, in that,' said Mrs Chick. 'My George and Frederick were both ordered sea-air, when they were about his age; and I have been ordered it myself a great many times. I quite agree with you, Paul, that perhaps topics may be incautiously mentioned upstairs before him, which it would be as well for his little mind not to expatiate upon; but I really don't see how that is to be helped in the case of a child of his quickness. If he were a common child, there would be nothing in it. I must say I think, with Miss Tox, that a short absence from this house, the air of Brighton, and the bodily and mental training of so judicious a person as Mrs Pipchin[6] for instance—'

'Who is Mrs Pipchin, Louisa?' asked Mr Dombey; aghast at this familiar introduction of a name he had never heard before.

'Mrs Pipchin, my dear Paul,' returned his sister, 'is an elderly lady – Miss Tox knows her whole history – who has for some time devoted all the energies of her mind, with the greatest success, to the study and treatment of infancy, and who has been extremely well connected. Her husband broke his heart in – how did you say her husband broke his heart, my dear? I forget the precise circumstances.'

'In pumping water out of the Peruvian Mines,'[7] replied Miss Tox.

'Not being a Pumper himself, of course,' said Mrs Chick, glancing at her brother; and it really did seem necessary to offer the explanation, for Miss Tox had spoken of him as if he had died at the handle; 'but having invested money in the speculation, which failed. I believe that Mrs Pipchin's management of children is quite astonishing. I have heard it commended in private circles ever since I was – dear me – how high!' Mrs Chick's eye wandered about the bookcase near the bust of Mr Pitt, which was about ten feet from the ground.

'Perhaps I should say of Mrs Pipchin, my dear Sir,' observed Miss Tox, with an ingenuous blush, 'having been so pointedly referred to, that the encomium which has been passed upon her by your sweet sister is well merited. Many ladies and gentlemen, now grown up to be interesting members of society, have been indebted to her care. The humble individual who addresses you was once under her charge. I believe juvenile nobility itself is no stranger to her establishment.'

'Do I understand that this respectable matron keeps an establishment, Miss Tox?' inquired Mr Dombey, condescendingly.

'Why, I really don't know,' rejoined that lady, 'whether I am justified in calling it so. It is not a Preparatory School by any means. Should I express my meaning,' said Miss Tox, with peculiar sweetness, 'if I designated it an infantine Boarding-House of a very select description?'

'On an exceedingly limited and particular scale,' suggested Mrs Chick, with a glance at her brother.

'Oh! Exclusion itself!' said Miss Tox.

There was something in this. Mrs Pipchin's husband having broken his heart of the Peruvian mines was good. It had a rich sound. Besides, Mr Dombey was in a state almost amounting to consternation at the idea of Paul remaining where he was one hour after his removal had been recommended by the medical practitioner. It was a stoppage and delay upon the road the child must traverse, slowly at the best, before the goal was reached. Their recommendation of Mrs Pipchin had great weight with him; for he knew that they were jealous of any interference with their charge, and he never for a moment took it into account that they might be solicitous to divide a responsibility, of which he had, as shown just now, his own established views. Broke his heart of the Peruvian mines, mused Mr Dombey. Well, a very respectable way of doing it.

'Supposing we should decide, on to-morrow's inquiries, to send Paul down to Brighton to this lady, who would go with him?' inquired Mr Dombey, after some reflection.

'I don't think you could send the child anywhere at present without Florence, my dear Paul,' returned his sister, hesitating. 'It's quite an infatuation with him. He's very young, you know, and has his fancies.'

Mr Dombey turned his head away, and going slowly to the bookcase, and unlocking it, brought back a book to read.

'Anybody else, Louisa?' he said, without looking up, and turning over the leaves.

'Wickam, of course. Wickam would be quite sufficient, I should say,' returned his sister. 'Paul being in such hands as Mrs Pipchin's, you could hardly send anybody who would be a further check upon her. You would go down yourself once a-week at least, of course.'

'Of course,' said Mr Dombey; and sat looking at one page for an hour afterwards, without reading one word.

This celebrated Mrs Pipchin was a marvellous ill-favoured, ill-conditioned old lady, of a stooping figure, with a mottled face, like bad marble, a hook nose, and a hard grey eye, that looked as if it might have been hammered at on an anvil without sustaining any injury. Forty years at least had elapsed since the Peruvian mines had been the death of Mr Pipchin; but his relict still wore black bombazeen,[8] of such a lustreless, deep, dead, sombre shade, that gas itself couldn't light her up after dark, and her presence was a quencher to any number of candles. She was generally spoken of as 'a great manager' of children; and the secret of her management was, to give them everything that they didn't like, and nothing that they did – which was found to sweeten their dispositions very much. She was such a bitter old lady, that one was tempted to believe there had been some mistake in the application of the Peruvian machinery, and that all her waters of gladness and milk of human kindness, had been pumped out dry, instead of the mines.

The Castle of this ogress and child-queller was in a steep by-street at Brighton; where the soil was more than usually chalky, flinty, and sterile, and the houses were more than usually brittle and thin; where the small front-gardens had the unaccountable property of producing nothing but marigolds, whatever was sown in them; and where snails were constantly discovered holding on to the street doors, and other public places they were not expected to ornament, with the tenacity of cupping-glasses.[9] In the winter-time the air couldn't be got out of the Castle, and in the summer-time it couldn't be got in. There was such a continual reverberation of wind in it, that it sounded like a great shell, which the inhabitants were obliged to hold to their ears night and day, whether they liked it or no. It was not, naturally, a fresh-smelling house; and in the window of the front parlour, which was never opened, Mrs Pipchin kept a collection of plants in pots, which imparted an earthy flavour of their own to the establishment. However choice examples of their kind, too, these plants were of a kind peculiarly adapted to the embowerment of Mrs Pipchin. There were half-a-dozen specimens of the cactus, writhing round bits of lath, like hairy serpents; another specimen shooting out broad claws, like a green lobster; several creeping vegetables, possessed of sticky and adhesive leaves; and one uncomfortable flower-pot hanging to the ceiling, which appeared to have boiled over, and tickling people underneath with its long green ends, reminded them of spiders – in which Mrs Pipchin's dwelling was uncommonly prolific, though perhaps it challenged competition still more proudly, in the season, in point of earwigs.

Mrs Pipchin's scale of charges being high, however, to all who could afford to pay, and Mrs Pipchin very seldom sweetening the equable acidity of her nature in favour of anybody, she was held to be an old lady of remarkable firmness, who was quite scientific in her knowledge of the childish character. On this reputation, and on the broken heart of Mr Pipchin, she had contrived, taking one year with another, to eke out a tolerably sufficient living since her husband's demise. Within three days after Mrs Chick's first allusion to her, this excellent old lady had the satisfaction of anticipating a handsome addition to her current receipts, from the pocket of Mr Dombey; and of receiving Florence and her little brother Paul, as inmates of the Castle.

Mrs Chick and Miss Tox, who had brought them down on the previous night (which they all passed at an Hotel), had just driven away from the door, on their journey home again; and Mrs Pipchin, with her back to the fire, stood, reviewing the new-comers, like an old soldier. Mrs Pipchin's middle-aged niece, her good-natured and devoted slave, but possessing a gaunt and iron-bound aspect, and much afflicted with boils on her nose, was divesting Master Bitherstone of the clean collar he had worn on parade. Miss Pankey, the only other little boarder at present, had that moment been walked off to the Castle Dungeon (an empty apartment at the back, devoted to correctional purposes), for having sniffed thrice, in the presence of visitors.

'Well, Sir,' said Mrs Pipchin to Paul, 'how do you think you shall like me?'

'I don't think I shall like you at all,' replied Paul. 'I want to go away. This isn't my house.'

'No. It's mine,' retorted Mrs Pipchin.

'It's a very nasty one,' said Paul.

'There's a worse place in it than this though,' said Mrs Pipchin, 'where we shut up our bad boys.'

'Has *he* ever been in it?' asked Paul: pointing out Master Bitherstone.

Mrs Pipchin nodded assent; and Paul had enough to do, for the rest of that day, in surveying Master Bitherstone from head to foot, and watching all the workings of his countenance, with the interest attaching to a boy of mysterious and terrible experiences.

At one o'clock there was a dinner, chiefly of the farinaceous and vegetable kind, when Miss Pankey (a mild little blue-eyed morsel of a child, who was shampooed every morning, and seemed in danger of being rubbed away, altogether) was led in from captivity by the ogress herself, and instructed that nobody who sniffed before visitors ever went to Heaven. When this great truth had been thoroughly impressed upon her, she was regaled with rice; and subsequently repeated the form of grace established in the Castle, in which there was a special clause, thanking Mrs Pipchin for a good dinner. Mrs Pipchin's niece, Berinthia, took cold pork. Mrs Pipchin, whose constitution required warm nourishment, made a special repast of mutton-chops, which were brought in hot and hot, between two plates, and smelt very nice.

As it rained after dinner, and they couldn't go out walking on the beach, and Mrs Pipchin's constitution required rest after chops, they went away with Berry (otherwise Berinthia) to the Dungeon; an empty room looking out upon a chalk wall and a water-butt, and made ghastly by a ragged fireplace without any stove in it. Enlivened by company, however, this was the best place after all; for Berry played with them there, and seemed to enjoy a game at romps as much as they did; until Mrs Pipchin knocking angrily at the wall, like the Cock Lane Ghost[10] revived, they left off, and Berry told them stories in a whisper until twilight.

For tea there was plenty of milk and water, and bread and butter, with a little black tea-pot for Mrs Pipchin and Berry, and buttered toast unlimited for Mrs Pipchin, which was brought in, hot and hot, like the chops. Though Mrs Pipchin got very greasy, outside, over this dish, it didn't seem to lubricate her internally, at all; for she was as fierce as ever, and the hard grey eye knew no softening.

After tea, Berry brought out a little workbox, with the Royal Pavilion on the lid, and fell to working busily; while Mrs Pipchin, having put on her spectacles and opened a great volume bound in green baize, began to nod. And whenever Mrs Pipchin caught herself falling forward into the fire, and woke up, she filliped Master Bitherstone on the nose for nodding too.

At last it was the children's bedtime, and after prayers they went to bed. As little Miss Pankey was afraid of sleeping alone in the dark, Mrs Pipchin always made a point of driving her up stairs herself, like a sheep; and it was cheerful to hear Miss Pankey moaning long afterwards, in the least eligible chamber, and Mrs Pipchin now and then going in to shake her. At about half-past nine o'clock the odour of a warm sweet-bread (Mrs Pipchin's constitution wouldn't go to sleep without sweet-bread) diversified the prevailing fragrance of the house, which Mrs Wickam said was 'a smell of building'; and slumber fell upon the Castle shortly after.

The breakfast next morning was like the tea over night, except that Mrs Pipchin took her roll instead of toast, and seemed a little more irate when it was over. Master Bitherstone read aloud to the rest a pedigree from Genesis[11] (judiciously selected by Mrs Pipchin), getting over the names with the ease and clearness of a person tumbling up the treadmill. That done, Miss Pankey was borne away to be shampoo'd; and Master Bitherstone to have something else done to him with salt water, from which he always returned very blue and dejected. Paul and Florence went out in the meantime on the beach with Wickam – who was constantly in tears – and at about noon Mrs Pipchin presided over some Early Readings. It being a part of Mrs Pipchin's system not to encourage a child's mind to develop and expand itself like a young flower, but to open it by force like an oyster, the moral of these lessons was usually of a violent and stunning character: the hero – a naughty boy – seldom, in the mildest catastrophe, being finished off by anything less than a lion, or a bear.[12]

Such was life at Mrs Pipchin's. On Saturday Mr Dombey came down; and Florence and Paul would go to his Hotel, and have tea. They passed the whole of Sunday with him, and generally rode out before dinner; and on these occasions Mr Dombey seemed to grow, like Falstaff's assailants,[13] and instead of being one man in buckram, to become a dozen. Sunday evening was the most melancholy evening in the week; for Mrs Pipchin always made a point of being particularly cross on Sunday nights. Miss Pankey was generally brought back from an aunt's at Rottingdean, in deep distress; and Master Bitherstone, whose relatives were all in India, and who was required to sit, between the services, in an erect position with his head against the parlour wall, neither moving hand nor foot, suffered so acutely in his young spirits that he once asked Florence, on a Sunday night, if she could give him any idea of the way back to Bengal.

But it was generally said that Mrs Pipchin was a woman of system with children; and no doubt she was. Certainly the wild ones went home tame enough, after sojourning for a few months beneath her hospitable roof. It was generally said, too, that it was highly creditable of Mrs Pipchin to have devoted herself to this way of life, and to have made such a sacrifice of her feelings, and such a resolute stand against her troubles, when Mr Pipchin broke his heart in the Peruvian mines.

At this exemplary old lady, Paul would sit staring in his little armchair by the fire, for any length of time. He never seemed to know what weariness was, when he was looking fixedly at Mrs Pipchin. He was not fond of her; he was not afraid of her; but in those old, old moods of his, she seemed to have a grotesque attraction for him. There he would sit, looking at her, and warming his hands, and looking at her, until he sometimes quite confounded Mrs Pipchin, Ogress as she was. Once she asked him, when they were alone, what he was thinking about.

'You,' said Paul, without the least reserve.

'And what are you thinking about me?' asked Mrs Pipchin.

'I'm thinking how old you must be,' said Paul.

'You mustn't say such things as that, young gentleman,' returned the dame. 'That'll never do.'

'Why not?' asked Paul.

'Because it's not polite,' said Mrs Pipchin, snappishly.

'Not polite?' said Paul.

'No.'

'It's not polite,' said Paul, innocently, 'to eat all the mutton-chops and toast, Wickam says.'

'Wickam,' retorted Mrs Pipchin, colouring, 'is a wicked, impudent, bold-faced hussy.'

'What's that?' inquired Paul.

'Never you mind, Sir,' retorted Mrs Pipchin. 'Remember the story of the little boy that was gored to death by a mad bull for asking questions.'

'If the bull was mad,' said Paul, 'how did he know that the boy had asked questions? Nobody can go and whisper secrets to a mad bull. I don't believe that story.'

'You don't believe it, Sir?' repeated Mrs Pipchin, amazed.

'No,' said Paul.

'Not if it should happen to have been a tame bull, you little Infidel?' said Mrs Pipchin.

As Paul had not considered the subject in that light, and had founded his conclusions on the alleged lunacy of the bull, he allowed himself to be put down for the present. But he sat turning it over in his mind, with such an obvious intention of fixing Mrs Pipchin presently, that even that hardy old lady deemed it prudent to retreat until he should have forgotten the subject.

From that time, Mrs Pipchin appeared to have something of the same odd kind of attraction towards Paul, as Paul had towards her. She would make him move his chair to her side of the fire, instead of sitting opposite; and there he would remain in a nook between Mrs Pipchin and the fender, with all the light of his little face absorbed into the black bombazeen drapery, studying every line and wrinkle of her countenance, and peering at the hard grey eye, until Mrs Pipchin was sometimes fain to shut it on pretence of dozing. Mrs Pipchin had an old black cat, who generally lay coiled upon the centre foot of the fender, purring egotistically, and winking at the fire until the contracted pupils of his eyes were like two notes of admiration.[14] The good old lady might have been – not to record it disrespectfully – a witch, and Paul and the cat her two familiars as they all sat by the fire together. It would have been quite in keeping with the appearance of the party if they had all sprung up the chimney in a high wind one night, and never been heard of any more.

This, however, never came to pass. The cat, and Paul, and Mrs Pipchin, were constantly to be found in their usual places after dark; and Paul, eschewing the companionship of Master Bitherstone, went on studying Mrs Pipchin, and the cat, and the fire, night after night, as if they were a book of necromancy, in three volumes.

Mrs Wickam put her own construction on Paul's eccentricities: and being confirmed in her low spirits by a perplexed view of chimneys from the room where she was accustomed to sit, and by the noise of the wind, and by the general dulness (gashliness[15] was Mrs Wickam's strong expression) of her present life, deduced the most dismal reflections from the foregoing premises. It was a part of Mrs Pipchin's policy to prevent her own 'young hussy' – that

Paul and Mrs Pipchin

was Mrs Pipchin's generic name for female servant – from communicating with Mrs Wickam: to which end she devoted much of her time to concealing herself behind doors, and springing out on that devoted maiden, whenever she made an approach towards Mrs Wickam's apartment. But Berry was free to hold what converse she could in that quarter consistently with the discharge of the multifarious duties at which she toiled incessantly from morning to night; and to Berry Mrs Wickam unburdened her mind.

'What a pretty fellow he is when he's asleep!' said Berry, stopping to look at Paul in bed, one night when she took up Mrs Wickam's supper.

'Ah!' sighed Mrs Wickam. 'He need be.'

'Why, he's not ugly when he's awake,' observed Berry.

'No, ma'am. Oh, no. No more was my uncle's Betsey Jane,' said Mrs Wickam.

Berry looked as if she would like to trace the connexion of ideas between Paul Dombey and Mrs Wickam's uncle's Betsey Jane.

'My uncle's wife,' Mrs Wickam went on to say, 'died just like his mama. My uncle's child took on just as Master Paul do. My uncle's child made people's blood run cold, sometimes, she did!'

'How?' asked Berry.

'I wouldn't have sat up all night alone with Betsey Jane!' said Mrs Wickam, 'not if you'd have put Wickam into business next morning for himself. I couldn't have done it, Miss Berry.'

Miss Berry naturally asked why not? But Mrs Wickam, agreeably to the usage of some ladies in her condition, pursued her own branch of the subject without any compunction.

'Betsey Jane,' said Mrs Wickam, 'was as sweet a child as I could wish to see. I couldn't wish to see a sweeter. Everything that a child could have in the way of illnesses, Betsey Jane had come through. The Cramps was as common to her,' said Mrs Wickam, 'as biles[16] is to yourself, Miss Berry.' Miss Berry involuntarily wrinkled her nose.

'But Betsey Jane,' said Mrs Wickam, lowering her voice, and looking round the room, and towards Paul in bed, 'had been minded, in her cradle, by her departed mother. I couldn't say how, nor I couldn't say when, nor I couldn't say whether the dear child knew it or not, but Betsey Jane had been watched by her mother, Miss Berry! You may say nonsense! I an't offended, Miss. I hope you may be able to think in your own conscience that it *is* nonsense; you'll find your spirits all the better for it in this – you'll excuse my being so free – in this burying-ground of a place; which is wearing of me down. Master Paul's a little restless in his sleep. Pat his back, if you please.'

'Of course you think,' said Berry, gently doing what she was asked, 'that *he* has been nursed by his mother, too?'

'Betsey Jane,' returned Mrs Wickam in her most solemn tones, 'was put upon as that child has been put upon, and changed as that child has changed. I have seen her sit, often and often, think, think, thinking, like him. I have seen her look, often and often, old, old, old, like him. I have heard her, many a time, talk just like him. I consider that child and Betsey Jane on the same footing entirely, Miss Berry.'

'Is your uncle's child alive?' asked Berry.

'Yes, Miss, she is alive,' returned Mrs Wickam with an air of triumph, for it was evident Miss Berry expected the reverse; 'and is married to a silver-chaser. Oh yes, Miss, SHE is alive,' said Mrs Wickam, laying strong stress on her nominative case.

It being clear that somebody was dead, Mrs Pipchin's niece inquired who it was.

'I wouldn't wish to make you uneasy,' returned Mrs Wickam, pursuing her supper. 'Don't ask me.'

This was the surest way of being asked again. Miss Berry repeated her question, therefore; and after some resistance, and reluctance, Mrs Wickam laid down her knife, and again glancing round the room and at Paul in bed, replied:

'She took fancies to people; whimsical fancies, some of them; others, affections that one might expect to see – only stronger than common. They all died.'

This was so very unexpected and awful to Mrs Pipchin's niece, that she sat upright on the hard edge of the bedstead, breathing short, and surveying her informant with looks of undisguised alarm.

Mrs Wickam shook her left forefinger stealthily towards the bed where Florence lay; then turned it upside down, and made several emphatic points at the floor; immediately below which was the parlour in which Mrs Pipchin habitually consumed the toast.

'Remember my words, Miss Berry,' said Mrs Wickam, 'and be thankful that Master Paul is not too fond of you. I am, that he's not too fond of me, I assure you; though there isn't much to live for – you'll excuse my being so free – in this jail of a house!'

Miss Berry's emotion might have led to her patting Paul too hard on the back, or might have produced a cessation of that soothing monotony, but he turned in his bed just now, and, presently awaking, sat up in it with his hair hot and wet from the effects of some childish dream, and asked for Florence.

She was out of her own bed at the first sound of his voice and bending over his pillow immediately, sang him to sleep again. Mrs Wickam shaking her head, and letting fall several tears, pointed out the little group to Berry, and turned her eyes up to the ceiling.

'Good night, Miss!' said Wickam, softly. 'Good night! Your aunt is an old lady, Miss Berry, and it's what you must have looked for, often.'

This consolatory farewell, Mrs Wickam accompanied with a look of heartfelt anguish; and being left alone with the two children again, and becoming conscious that the wind was blowing mournfully, she indulged in melancholy – that cheapest and most accessible of luxuries – until she was overpowered by slumber.

Although the niece of Mrs Pipchin did not expect to find that exemplary dragon prostrate on the hearth-rug when she went downstairs, she was relieved to find her unusually fractious and severe, and with every present appearance of intending to live a long time to be a comfort to all who knew her. Nor had she any symptoms of declining, in the course of the ensuing week, when the constitutional viands still continued to disappear in regular succession, notwithstanding that Paul studied her as attentively as ever, and occupied his usual seat between the black skirts and the fender, with unwavering constancy.

But as Paul himself was no stronger at the expiration of that time than he had been on his first arrival, though he looked much healthier in the face, a little carriage was got for him, in which he could lie at his ease, with an alphabet and other elementary works of reference, and be wheeled down to the sea-side. Consistent in his odd tastes, the child set aside a ruddy-faced lad who was proposed as the drawer of this carriage, and selected, instead, his grandfather – a weazen, old, crab-faced man, in a suit of battered oilskin, who had got tough and stringy from long pickling in salt water, and who smelt like a weedy sea-beach when the tide is out. With this notable attendant to pull him along, and Florence always walking by his side, and the despondent Wickam bringing up the rear, he went down to the margin of the ocean every day; and there he would sit or lie in his carriage for hours together: never so distressed as by the company of children – Florence alone excepted, always.

'Go away, if you please,' he would say to any child who came to bear him company. 'Thank you, but I don't want you.'

Some small voice, near his ear, would ask him how he was, perhaps.

'I am very well, I thank you,' he would answer. 'But you had better go and play, if you please.'

Then he would turn his head, and watch the child away, and say to Florence, 'We don't want any others, do we? Kiss me, Floy.'

He had even a dislike, at such times, to the company of Wickam, and was well pleased when she strolled away, as she generally did, to pick up shells and acquaintances. His favourite spot was quite a lonely one, far away from most loungers; and with Florence sitting by his side at work, or reading to him, or talking to him, and the wind blowing on his face, and the water coming up among the wheels of his bed, he wanted nothing more.

'Floy,' he said one day, 'where's India, where that boy's friends live?'

'Oh, it's a long, long distance off,' said Florence, raising her eyes from her work.

'Weeks off?' asked Paul.

'Yes, dear. Many weeks' journey, night and day.'

'If you were in India, Floy,' said Paul, after being silent for a minute, 'I should – what is that mama did? I forget.'

'Loved me!' answered Florence.

'No, no. Don't I love you now, Floy? What is it? – Died. If you were in India, I should die, Floy.'

She hurriedly put her work aside, and laid her head down on his pillow, caressing him. And so would she, she said, if he were there. He would be better soon.

'Oh! I am a great deal better now!' he answered. 'I don't mean that. I mean that I should die of being so sorry and so lonely, Floy!'

Another time, in the same place, he fell asleep, and slept quietly for a long time. Awaking suddenly, he listened, started up, and sat listening.

Florence asked him what he thought he heard.

'I want to know what it says,' he answered, looking steadily in her face. 'The sea, Floy, what is it that it keeps on saying?'

She told him that it was only the noise of the rolling waves.

'Yes, yes,' he said. 'But I know that they are always saying something. Always the same thing. What place is over there?' He rose up, looking eagerly at the horizon.

She told him that there was another country opposite, but he said he didn't mean that: he meant farther away – farther away!

Very often afterwards, in the midst of their talk, he would break off, to try to understand what it was that the waves were always saying; and would rise up in his couch to look towards that invisible region, far away.

CHAPTER 9

In which the Wooden Midshipman gets into Trouble

That spice of romance and love of the marvellous, of which there was a pretty strong infusion in the nature of young Walter Gay, and which the guardianship of his uncle, old Solomon Gills, had not very much weakened by the waters of stern practical experience, was the occasion of his attaching an uncommon and delightful interest to the adventure of Florence with Good Mrs Brown. He pampered and cherished it in his memory, especially that part of it with which he had been associated: until it became the spoiled child of his fancy, and took its own way, and did what it liked with it.

The recollection of those incidents, and his own share in them, may have been made the more captivating, perhaps, by the weekly dreamings of old Sol and Captain Cuttle on Sundays. Hardly a Sunday passed, without mysterious references being made by one or other of those worthy chums to Richard Whittington; and the latter gentleman had even gone so far as to purchase a ballad[1] of considerable antiquity, that had long fluttered among many others, chiefly expressive of maritime sentiments, on a dead wall in the Commercial Road: which poetical performance set forth the courtship and nuptials of a promising young coal-whipper[2] with a certain 'lovely Peg,'[3] the accomplished daughter of the master and part-owner of a Newcastle collier.[4] In this stirring legend, Captain Cuttle descried a profound metaphysical bearing on the case of Walter and Florence; and it excited him so much, that on very festive occasions, as birthdays and a few other non-Dominical[5] holidays, he would roar through the whole song in the little back parlour; making an amazing shake on the word Pe–e–eg, with which every verse concluded, in compliment to the heroine of the piece.

But a frank, free-spirited, open-hearted boy, is not much given to analysing the nature of his own feelings, however strong their hold upon him: and Walter would have found it difficult to decide this point. He had a great affection for the wharf where he had encountered Florence, and for the streets (albeit not enchanting in themselves) by which they had come home. The shoes that had so often tumbled off by the way, he preserved in his own room; and, sitting in the little back parlour of an evening, he had drawn a whole gallery of fancy portraits of Good Mrs Brown. It may be that he became a little smarter in his dress after that memorable occasion; and he certainly liked in his leisure time to walk towards that quarter of the town where Mr Dombey's house was situated, on the vague chance of passing little Florence in the street. But the sentiment of all this was as boyish and innocent as could be. Florence was very pretty, and it is pleasant to admire a pretty face. Florence was defenceless and weak, and it was a proud thought that he had been able to render her any protection and assistance. Florence was the most grateful little creature in the world, and it was delightful to see her bright gratitude beaming in her face. Florence was neglected and coldly looked upon, and his breast was full of youthful interest for the slighted child in her dull, stately home.

Thus it came about that, perhaps some half-a-dozen times in the course of the year, Walter pulled off his hat to Florence in the street, and Florence would stop to shake hands. Mrs Wickam (who, with a characteristic alteration of his name, invariably spoke of him as 'Young Graves') was so well used to this, knowing the story of their acquaintance, that she took no heed of it at all. Miss Nipper, on the other hand, rather looked out for these occasions: her sensitive young heart being secretly propitiated by Walter's good looks, and inclining to the belief that its sentiments were responded to.

In this way, Walter, so far from forgetting or losing sight of his acquaintance with Florence, only remembered it better and better. As to its adventurous beginning, and all those little circumstances which gave it a distinctive character and relish, he took them into account, more as a pleasant story very agreeable to his imagination, and not to be dismissed from it, than as a part of any matter of fact with which *he* was concerned. They set off Florence very much, to his fancy; but not himself. Sometimes he thought (and then he walked very fast) what a grand thing it would have been for him to have been going to sea on the day after that first meeting, and to have gone, and to have done wonders there, and to have stopped away a long time, and to have come back an Admiral of all the colours of the dolphin,[6] or at least a Post-Captain[7] with epaulettes of insupportable brightness, and have married Florence (then a beautiful young woman) in spite of Mr Dombey's teeth, cravat, and watch-chain, and borne her away to the blue shores of somewhere or other, triumphantly. But these flights of fancy seldom burnished the brass plate of Dombey and Son's offices into a tablet of golden hope, or shed a brilliant lustre on their dirty sky-lights; and when the Captain and Uncle Sol talked about Richard Whittington and masters' daughters, Walter felt that he understood his true position at Dombey and Son's, much better than they did.

So it was that he went on doing what he had to do from day to day, in a cheerful, pains-taking, merry spirit; and saw through the sanguine complexion of Uncle Sol and Captain Cuttle; and yet entertained a thousand indistinct and visionary fancies of his own, to which theirs were work-a-day probabilities. Such was his condition at the Pipchin period, when he looked a little older than of yore, but not much; and was the same light-footed, light-hearted, light-headed lad, as when he charged into the parlour at the head of Uncle Sol and the imaginary boarders, and lighted him to bring up *the* Madeira.

'Uncle Sol,' said Walter, 'I don't think you're well. You haven't eaten any breakfast. I shall bring a doctor to you, if you go on like this.'

'He can't give me what I want, my boy,' said Uncle Sol. 'At least he is in good practice if he can – and then he wouldn't.'

'What is it, uncle? Customers?'

'Aye,' returned Solomon, with a sigh. 'Customers would do.'

'Confound it, uncle!' said Walter, putting down his breakfast cup with a clatter, and striking his hand on the table: 'when I see the people going up and down the street in shoals all day, and passing and re-passing the shop every minute, by scores, I feel half tempted to rush out, collar somebody, bring him in, and make him buy fifty pounds' worth of instruments for ready money. What are you looking in at the door for? –' continued Walter, apostrophizing an old gentleman with a powdered head (inaudibly to him of course), who was staring at a ship's telescope with all his might and main. '*That's* no use. I could do that. Come in and buy it!'

The old gentleman, however, having satiated his curiosity, walked calmly away.

'There he goes!' said Walter. 'That's the way with 'em all. But, uncle – I say, Uncle Sol' – for the old man was meditating, and had not responded to his first appeal. 'Don't be cast down. Don't be out of spirits, uncle. When orders *do* come, they'll come in such a crowd, you won't be able to execute 'em.'

'I shall be past executing 'em, whenever they come, my boy,' returned Solomon Gills. 'They'll never come to this shop again, till I am out of it.'

'I say, uncle! You mustn't really, you know!' urged Walter. 'Don't!'

Old Sol endeavoured to assume a cheery look, and smiled across the little table at him as pleasantly as he could.

'There's nothing more than usual the matter; is there, uncle?' said Walter, leaning his elbows on the tea-tray, and bending over, to speak the more confidentially and kindly. 'Be open with me, uncle, if there is, and tell me all about it.'

'No, no, no,' returned old Sol. 'More than usual? No, no. What should there be the matter more than usual?'

Walter answered with an incredulous shake of his head. 'That's what I want to know,' he said, 'and you ask *me!* I'll tell you what, uncle, when I see you like this, I am quite sorry that I live with you.'

Old Sol opened his eyes involuntarily.

'Yes. Though nobody ever was happier than I am and always have been with you, I am quite sorry that I live with you, when I see you with anything on your mind.'

'I am a little dull at such times, I know,' observed Solomon, meekly rubbing his hands.

'What I mean, Uncle Sol,' pursued Walter, bending over a little more to pat him on the shoulder, 'is, that then I feel you ought to have, sitting here and pouring out the tea instead of me, a nice little dumpling of a wife, you know, – a comfortable, capital, cosy old lady, who was just a match for you, and knew how to manage you, and keep you in good heart. Here am I, as loving a nephew as ever was (I am sure I ought to be!) but I am only a nephew, and I can't be such a companion to you when you're low and out of sorts as she would have made herself, years ago, though I'm sure I'd give any money if I could cheer you up. And so I say, when I see you with anything on your mind, that I feel quite sorry you haven't got somebody better about you than a blundering young rough-and-tough boy like me, who has got the will to console you, uncle, but hasn't got the way – hasn't got the way,' repeated Walter, reaching over further yet, to shake his uncle by the hand.

'Wally, my dear boy,' said Solomon, 'if the cosy little old lady had taken her place in this parlour five and forty years ago, I never could have been fonder of her than I am of you.'

'*I* know that, Uncle Sol,' returned Walter. 'Lord bless you, I know that. But you wouldn't have had the whole weight of any uncomfortable secrets if she had been with you, because she would have known how to relieve you of 'em, and I don't.'

'Yes, yes, you do,' returned the instrument-maker.

'Well then, what's the matter, Uncle Sol?' said Walter, coaxingly. 'Come! What's the matter?'

Solomon Gills persisted that there was nothing the matter; and maintained it so resolutely, that his nephew had no resource but to make a very indifferent imitation of believing him.

'All I can say is, Uncle Sol, that if there is—'

'But there isn't,' said Solomon.

'Very well,' said Walter. 'Then I've no more to say; and that's lucky, for my time's up for going to business. I shall look in by-and-by when I'm out, to see how you get on, uncle. And mind, uncle! I'll never believe you again, and never tell you anything more about Mr Carker the Junior, if I find out that you have been deceiving me!'

Solomon Gills laughingly defied him to find out anything of the kind; and Walter, revolving in his thoughts all sorts of impracticable ways of making fortunes and placing the wooden midshipman in a position of independence, betook himself to the offices of Dombey and Son with a heavier countenance than he usually carried there.

There lived in those days, round the corner – in Bishopsgate Street Without[8] – one Brogley, sworn broker and appraiser,[9] who kept a shop where every description of secondhand furniture was exhibited in the most uncomfortable aspect, and under circumstances and in combinations the most completely foreign to its purpose. Dozens of chairs hooked on to washing-stands, which with difficulty poised themselves on the shoulders of sideboards, which in their turn stood upon the wrong side of dining-tables, gymnastic with their legs upward on the tops of other dining-tables, were among its most reasonable arrangements. A banquet array of dish-covers, wine-glasses, and decanters was generally to be seen, spread forth upon the bosom of a four-post bedstead, for the entertainment of such genial company as half-a-dozen pokers, and a hall lamp. A set of window curtains with no windows belonging to them, would be seen gracefully draping a barricade of chests of drawers, loaded with little jars from chemists' shops; while a homeless hearthrug severed from its natural companion the fireside, braved the shrewd east wind in its adversity, and trembled in melancholy accord with the shrill complainings of a cabinet piano, wasting away, a string a day, and faintly resounding to the noises of the street in its jangling and distracted brain. Of motionless clocks that never stirred a finger, and seemed as incapable of being successfully wound up, as the pecuniary affairs of their former owners, there was always great choice in Mr Brogley's shop; and various looking-glasses, accidentally placed at compound interest of reflection and refraction, presented to the eye an eternal perspective of bankruptcy and ruin.

Mr Brogley himself was a moist-eyed, pink-complexioned, crisp-haired man, of a bulky figure and an easy temper – for that class of Caius Marius[10] who sits upon the ruins of other people's Carthages, can keep up his spirits well enough. He had looked in at Solomon's shop sometimes to ask a question about articles in Solomon's way of business; and Walter knew him sufficiently to give him good day when they met in the street, but as that was the extent of the broker's acquaintance with Solomon Gills also, Walter was not a little surprised when he came back in the course of the forenoon, agreeably to his promise, to find Mr Brogley sitting in the back parlour with his hands in his pockets, and his hat hanging up behind the door.

'Well, Uncle Sol!' said Walter. The old man was sitting ruefully on the opposite side of the table, with his spectacles over his eyes, for a wonder, instead of on his forehead. 'How are you now?'

Solomon shook his head, and waved one hand towards the broker, as introducing him.

'Is there anything the matter?' asked Walter, with a catching in his breath.

'No, no. There's nothing the matter,' said Mr Brogley. 'Don't let it put you out of the way.'

Walter looked from the broker to his uncle in mute amazement.

'The fact is,' said Mr Brogley, 'there's a little payment on a bond debt – three hundred and seventy odd, over due: and I'm in possession.'

'In possession!' cried Walter, looking round at the shop.

'Ah!' said Mr Brogley, in confidential assent, and nodding his head as if he would urge the advisability of their all being comfortable together. 'It's an execution. That's what it is. Don't let it put you out of the way. I come myself, because of keeping it quiet and sociable. You know me. It's quite private.'

'Uncle Sol!' faltered Walter.

'Wally, my boy,' returned his uncle. 'It's the first time. Such a calamity never happened to me before. I'm an old man to begin.' Pushing up his spectacles again (for they were useless any longer to conceal his emotion), he covered his face with his hand, and sobbed aloud, and his tears fell down upon his coffee-coloured waistcoat.

'Uncle Sol! Pray! oh don't!' exclaimed Walter, who really felt a thrill of terror in seeing the old man weep. 'For God's sake don't do that. Mr Brogley, what shall I do?'

'*I* should recommend you looking up a friend or so,' said Mr Brogley, 'and talking it over.'

'To be sure!' cried Walter, catching at anything. 'Certainly! Thankee. Captain Cuttle's the man, uncle. Wait till I run to Captain Cuttle. Keep your eye upon my uncle, will you, Mr Brogley, and make him as comfortable as you can while I am gone? Don't despair, Uncle Sol. Try and keep a good heart, there's a dear fellow!'

Saying this with great fervour, and disregarding the old man's broken remonstrances, Walter dashed out of the shop again as hard as he could go; and, having hurried round to the office to excuse himself on the plea of his uncle's sudden illness, set off, full speed, for Captain Cuttle's residence.

Everything seemed altered as he ran along the streets. There were the usual entanglement and noise of carts, drays, omnibuses, waggons, and foot passengers, but the misfortune that had fallen on the wooden midshipman made it strange and new. Houses and shops were different from what they used to be, and bore Mr Brogley's warrant on their fronts in large characters. The broker seemed to have got hold of the very churches; for their spires rose into the sky with an unwonted air. Even the sky itself was changed, and had an execution in it plainly.

Captain Cuttle lived on the brink of a little canal near the India Docks, where there was a swivel bridge which opened now and then to let some wandering monster of a ship come roaming up the street like a stranded leviathan.[11] The gradual change from land to water, on the approach to Captain Cuttle's lodgings, was curious. It began with the erection of flag staffs, as appurtenances to public-houses; then came slopsellers' shops, with Guernsey shirts, sou'wester hats,[12] and canvas pantaloons, at once the tightest and the loosest of their order, hanging up outside. These were succeeded by anchor and chain-cable forges, where sledge-hammers were dinging upon iron all day long. Then came rows of houses, with little vane-surmounted masts uprearing themselves from among the scarlet beans. Then, ditches. Then, pollard willows. Then, more ditches. Then, unaccountable patches of dirty water, hardly to be descried, for the ships that covered them. Then, the air was perfumed with chips;[13] and all other trades were swallowed up in mast, oar, and block making,[14] and boat building. Then, the ground grew marshy and unsettled. Then, there was nothing to be smelt but rum and sugar. Then, Captain Cuttle's lodgings – at once a first floor and a top story, in Brig Place – were close before you.

The Captain was one of those timber-looking men, suits of oak as well as hearts,[15] whom it is almost impossible for the liveliest imagination to separate from any part of their dress, however insignificant. Accordingly, when Walter knocked at the door, and the Captain instantly poked his head out of one of his little front windows, and hailed him, with the hard glazed hat already on it, and the shirt-collar like a sail, and the wide suit of blue, all standing as usual, Walter was as fully persuaded that he was always in that state, as if the Captain had been a bird and those had been his feathers.

'Wal'r, my lad!' said Captain Cuttle. 'Stand by and knock again. Hard! It's washing day.'

Walter, in his impatience, gave a prodigious thump with the knocker.

'Hard it is!' said Captain Cuttle, and immediately drew in his head, as if he expected a squall.

Nor was he mistaken: for a widow lady, with her sleeves rolled up to her shoulders, and her arms frothy with soap-suds and smoking with hot water, replied to the summons with startling rapidity. Before she looked at Walter she looked at the knocker, and then, measuring him with her eyes from head to foot, said she wondered he had left any of it.

'Captain Cuttle's at home, I know,' said Walter with a conciliatory smile.

'Is he?' replied the widow lady. 'In-deed!'

'He has just been speaking to me,' said Walter, in breathless explanation.

'Has he?' replied the widow lady. 'Then p'raps you'll give him Mrs MacStinger's respects, and say that the next time he lowers himself and his lodgings by talking out of winder she'll thank him to come down and open the door too.' Mrs MacStinger spoke loud, and listened for any observations that might be offered from the first floor.

'I'll mention it,' said Walter, 'if you'll have the goodness to let me in, ma'am.'

For he was repelled by a wooden fortification extending across the doorway, and put there to prevent the little MacStingers in their moments of recreation from tumbling down the steps.

'A boy that can knock my door down,' said Mrs MacStinger contemptuously, 'can get over that, I should hope!' But Walter, taking this as a permission to enter, and getting over it, Mrs MacStinger immediately demanded whether an Englishwoman's house was her castle[16] or not; and whether she was to be broke in upon by 'raff.' On these subjects her thirst for information was still very importunate, when Walter, having made his way up the little staircase through an artificial fog occasioned by the washing, which covered the banisters with a clammy perspiration, entered Captain Cuttle's room, and found that gentleman in ambush behind the door.

'Never owed her a penny, Wal'r,' said Captain Cuttle, in a low voice, and with visible marks of trepidation on his countenance. 'Done her a world of good turns, and the children too. Vixen at times, though. Whew!'

'I should go away, Captain Cuttle,' said Walter.

'Dursn't do it, Wal'r,' returned the Captain. 'She'd find me out, wherever I went. Sit down. How's Gills?'

The Captain was dining (in his hat) off cold loin of mutton, porter, and some smoking hot potatoes, which he had cooked himself, and took out of a little saucepan before the fire as he wanted them. He unscrewed his hook at dinner-time, and screwed a knife into its wooden socket instead, with which he had already begun to peel one of these potatoes for Walter. His rooms were very small, and strongly impregnated with tobacco-smoke, but snug enough: everything being stowed away, as if there were an earthquake regularly every half-hour.

'How's Gills?' inquired the Captain.

Walter, who had by this time recovered his breath, and lost his spirits – or such temporary spirits as his rapid journey had given him – looked at his questioner for a moment, said 'Oh, Captain Cuttle!' and burst into tears.

No words can describe the Captain's consternation at this sight. Mrs MacStinger faded into nothing before it. He dropped the potato and the fork – and would have dropped the knife too if he could – and sat gazing at the boy, as if he expected to hear next moment that a gulf had opened in the City, which had swallowed up his old friend, coffee-coloured suit, buttons, chronometer, spectacles, and all.

But when Walter told him what was really the matter, Captain Cuttle, after a moment's reflection, started up into full activity. He emptied out of a little tin canister on the top shelf of the cupboard, his whole stock of ready money (amounting to thirteen pounds and half-a-crown), which he transferred to one of the pockets of his square blue coat; further enriched that depository with the contents of his plate chest, consisting of two withered atomies[17] of teaspoons, and an obsolete pair of knock-kneed sugar-tongs; pulled up his immense double-cased silver watch from the depths in which it reposed, to assure himself that that valuable was sound and whole; re-attached the hook to his right wrist; and seizing the stick covered over with knobs, bade Walter come along.

Remembering, however, in the midst of his virtuous excitement, that Mrs MacStinger might be lying in wait below, Captain Cuttle hesitated at last, not without glancing at the window, as if he had some thoughts of escaping by that unusual means of egress, rather than encounter his terrible enemy. He decided, however, in favour of stratagem.

'Wal'r,' said the Captain, with a timid wink, 'go afore, my lad. Sing out, "good-bye, Captain Cuttle," when you're in the passage, and shut the door. Then wait at the corner of the street 'till you see me.'

These directions were not issued without a previous knowledge of the enemy's tactics, for when Walter got downstairs, Mrs MacStinger glided out of the little back kitchen, like an avenging spirit. But not gliding out upon the Captain, as she had expected, she merely made a further allusion to the knocker, and glided in again.

Some five minutes elapsed before Captain Cuttle could summon courage to attempt his escape; for Walter waited so long at the street corner, looking back at the house, before there were any symptoms of the hard glazed hat. At length the Captain burst out of the door with the suddenness of an explosion, and coming towards him at a great pace, and never once looking over his shoulder, pretended, as soon as they were well out of the street, to whistle a tune.

'Uncle much hove down, Wal'r?' inquired the Captain, as they were walking along.

'I am afraid so. If you had seen him this morning, you would never have forgotten it.'

'Walk fast, Wal'r, my lad,' returned the Captain, mending his pace; 'and walk the same all the days of your life.[18] Overhaul the catechism for that advice, and keep it!'

The Captain was too busy with his own thoughts of Solomon Gills, mingled perhaps with some reflections on his late escape from

Mrs MacStinger, to offer any further quotations on the way for Walter's moral improvement. They interchanged no other word until they arrived at old Sol's door, where the unfortunate wooden midshipman, with his instrument at his eye, seemed to be surveying the whole horizon in search of some friend to help him out of his difficulty.

'Gills!' said the Captain, hurrying into the back parlour, and taking him by the hand quite tenderly. 'Lay your head well to the wind, and we'll fight through it. All you've got to do,' said the Captain, with the solemnity of a man who was delivering himself of one of the most precious practical tenets ever discovered by human wisdom, 'is to lay your head well to the wind, and we'll fight through it!'

Old Sol returned the pressure of his hand, and thanked him.

Captain Cuttle, then, with a gravity suitable to the nature of the occasion, put down upon the table the two teaspoons and the sugar-tongs, the silver watch, and the ready money; and asked Mr Brogley, the broker, what the damage was.

'Come! What do you make of it?' said Captain Cuttle.

'Why, Lord help you!' returned the broker; 'you don't suppose that property's of any use, do you?'

'Why not?' inquired the Captain.

'Why? The amount's three hundred and seventy, odd,' replied the broker.

'Never mind,' returned the Captain, though he was evidently dismayed by the figures: 'all's fish that comes to your net, I suppose?'

'Certainly,' said Mr Brogley. 'But sprats an't whales, you know.'

The philosophy of this observation seemed to strike the Captain. He ruminated for a minute; eyeing the broker, meanwhile, as a deep genius; and then called the instrument-maker aside.

'Gills,' said Captain Cuttle, 'what's the bearings of this business? Who's the creditor?'

'Hush!' returned the old man. 'Come away. Don't speak before Wally. It's a matter of security for Wally's father – an old bond. I've paid a good deal of it, Ned, but the times are so bad with me that I can't do more just now. I've foreseen it, but I couldn't help it. Not a word before Wally, for all the world.'

'You've got *some* money, haven't you?' whispered the Captain.

'Yes, yes – oh yes – I've got some,' returned old Sol, first putting his hands into his empty pockets, and then squeezing his Welsh wig between them, as if he thought he might wring some gold out of it;

Captain Cuttle consoles his friend

'but I – the little I have got, isn't convertible, Ned; it can't be got at. I have been trying to do something with it for Wally, and I'm old fashioned, and behind the time. It's here and there, and – and, in short, it's as good as nowhere,' said the old man, looking in bewilderment about him.

He had so much the air of a half-witted person who had been hiding his money in a variety of places, and had forgotten where, that the Captain followed his eyes, not without a faint hope that he might remember some few hundred pounds concealed up the chimney, or down in the cellar. But Solomon Gills knew better than that.

'I'm behind the time altogether, my dear Ned,' said Sol, in resigned despair, 'a long way. It's no use my lagging on so far behind it. The stock had better be sold – it's worth more than this debt – and I had better go and die somewhere, on the balance. I haven't any energy left. I don't understand things. This had better be the end of it. Let 'em sell the stock and take *him* down,' said the old man, pointing feebly to the wooden midshipman, 'and let us both be broken up together.'

'And what d'ye mean to do with Wal'r?' said the Captain. 'There, there! Sit ye down, Gills, sit ye down, and let me think o' this. If I warn't a man on a small annuity, that was large enough till to-day, I hadn't need to think of it. But you only lay your head well to the wind,' said the Captain, again administering that unanswerable piece of consolation, 'and you're all right!'

Old Sol thanked him from his heart, and went and laid it against the back parlour fireplace instead.

Captain Cuttle walked up and down the shop for some time, cogitating profoundly, and bringing his bushy black eyebrows to bear so heavily on his nose, like clouds settling on a mountain, that Walter was afraid to offer any interruption to the current of his reflections. Mr Brogley, who was averse to being any constraint upon the party, and who had an ingenious cast of mind, went, softly whistling, among the stock; rattling weatherglasses, shaking compasses as if they were physic, catching up keys with loadstones, looking through telescopes, endeavouring to make himself acquainted with the use of the globes, setting parallel rulers astride on to his nose, and amusing himself with other philosophical transactions.

'Wal'r?' said the Captain at last. 'I've got it.'

'Have you, Captain Cuttle?' cried Walter, with great animation.

'Come this way, my lad,' said the Captain. 'The stock's one

security. I'm another. Your governor's the man to advance the money.'

'Mr Dombey!' faltered Walter.

The Captain nodded gravely. 'Look at him,' he said. 'Look at Gills. If they was to sell off these things now, he'd die of it. You know he would. We mustn't leave a stone unturned – and there's a stone for you.'

'A stone! – Mr Dombey!' faltered Walter.

'You run round to the office, first of all, and see if he's there,' said Captain Cuttle, clapping him on the back. 'Quick!'

Walter felt he must not dispute the command – a glance at his uncle would have determined him if he had felt otherwise – and disappeared to execute it. He soon returned, out of breath, to say that Mr Dombey was not there. It was Saturday, and he had gone to Brighton.

'I tell you what, Wal'r!' said the Captain, who seemed to have prepared himself for this contingency in his absence. 'We'll go to Brighton. I'll back you, my boy. I'll back you, Wal'r. We'll go to Brighton by the afternoon's coach.'

If the application must be made to Mr Dombey at all, which was awful to think of, Walter felt that he would rather prefer it alone and unassisted, than backed by the personal influence of Captain Cuttle, to which he hardly thought Mr Dombey would attach much weight. But as the Captain appeared to be of quite another opinion, and was bent upon it, and as his friendship was too zealous and serious to be trifled with by one so much younger than himself, he forbore to hint the least objection. Cuttle, therefore, taking a hurried leave of Solomon Gills, and returning the ready money, the teaspoons, the sugar-tongs, and the silver watch, to his pocket – with a view, as Walter thought, with horror, to making a gorgeous impression on Mr Dombey – bore him off to the coach-office, without a minute's delay, and repeatedly assured him, on the road, that he would stick by him to the last.

CHAPTER 10

*Containing the Sequel of the
Midshipman's Disaster*

Major Bagstock, after long and frequent observation of Paul, across Princess's Place, through his double-barrelled opera-glass; and after receiving many minute reports, daily, weekly, and monthly, on that subject, from the native who kept himself in constant communication with Miss Tox's maid for that purpose; came to the conclusion that Dombey, Sir, was a man to be known, and that J. B. was the boy to make his acquaintance.

Miss Tox, however, maintaining her reserved behaviour, and frigidly declining to understand the Major whenever he called (which he often did) on any little fishing excursion connected with this project, the Major, in spite of his constitutional toughness and slyness, was fain to leave the accomplishment of his desire in some measure to chance, 'which,' as he was used to observe with chuckles at his club, 'has been fifty to one in favour of Joey B., Sir, ever since his elder brother died of Yellow Jack[1] in the West Indies.'

It was some time coming to his aid in the present instance, but it befriended him at last. When the dark servant, with full particulars, reported Miss Tox absent on Brighton service, the Major was suddenly touched with affectionate reminiscences of his friend Bill Bitherstone of Bengal, who had written to ask him, if he ever went that way, to bestow a call upon his only son. But when the same dark servant reported Paul at Mrs Pipchin's, and the Major, referring to the letter favoured by Master Bitherstone on his arrival in England – to which he had never had the least idea of paying any attention – saw the opening that presented itself, he was made so rabid by the gout, with which he happened to be then laid up, that he threw a footstool at the dark servant in return for his intelligence, and swore he would be the death of the rascal before he had done with him: which the dark servant was more than half disposed to believe.

At length the Major being released from his fit, went one Saturday growling down to Brighton, with the native behind him; apostrophizing Miss Tox all the way, and gloating over the prospect of carrying by storm the distinguished friend to whom she attached so much mystery, and for whom she had deserted him.

'Would you, ma'am, would you!' said the Major, straining with vindictiveness, and swelling every already swollen vein in his head.

'Would you give Joey B. the go-by,[2] ma'am? Not yet, ma'am, not yet! Damme, not yet, Sir. Joe is awake, ma'am. Bagstock is alive, Sir. J. B. knows a move or two, ma'am. Josh has his weather-eye open, Sir. You'll find him tough, ma'am. Tough, Sir, tough is Joseph. Tough, and de-vilish sly!'

And very tough indeed Master Bitherstone found him, when he took that young gentleman out for a walk. But the Major, with his complexion like a Stilton cheese, and his eyes like a prawn's, went roving about, perfectly indifferent to Master Bitherstone's amusement, and dragging Master Bitherstone along, while he looked about him high and low, for Mr Dombey and his children.

In good time the Major, previously instructed by Mrs Pipchin, spied out Paul and Florence, and bore down upon them; there being a stately gentleman (Mr Dombey, doubtless) in their company. Charging with Master Bitherstone into the very heart of the little squadron, it fell out, of course, that Master Bitherstone spoke to his fellow-sufferers. Upon that the Major stopped to notice and admire them; remembered with amazement that he had seen and spoken to them at his friend Miss Tox's in Princess's Place; opined that Paul was a devilish fine fellow, and his own little friend; inquired if he remembered Joey B. the Major; and finally, with a sudden recollection of the conventionalities of life, turned and apologised to Mr Dombey.

'But my little friend here, Sir,' said the Major, 'makes a boy of me again. An old soldier, Sir – Major Bagstock, at your service – is not ashamed to confess it.' Here the Major lifted his hat. 'Damme Sir,' cried the Major with sudden warmth. 'I envy you.' Then he recollected himself, and added, 'Excuse my freedom.'

Mr Dombey begged he wouldn't mention it.

'An old campaigner, Sir,' said the Major, 'a smoke-dried, sun-burnt, used-up, invalided old dog of a Major, Sir, was not afraid of being condemned for his whim by a man like Mr Dombey. I have the honour of addressing Mr Dombey, I believe?'

'I am the present unworthy representative of that name, Major,' returned Mr Dombey.

'By G—, Sir,' said the Major, 'it's a great name. It's a name, Sir,' said the Major firmly, as if he defied Mr Dombey to contradict him, and would feel it his painful duty to bully him if he did, 'that is known and honoured in the British possessions abroad. It is a name, Sir, that a man is proud to recognise. There is nothing adulatory in Joseph Bagstock, Sir. His Royal Highness the Duke of York[3] observed on more than one occasion, "there is no adulation in Joey. He is a plain old soldier is Joe. He is tough to a fault is Joseph:" but it's a great name, Sir. By the Lord, it's a great name!' said the Major, solemnly.

'You are good enough to rate it higher than it deserves, perhaps, Major,' returned Mr Dombey.

'No, Sir,' said the Major. 'My little friend here, Sir, will certify for Joseph Bagstock that he is a thoroughgoing, downright, plain-spoken, old Trump, Sir, and nothing more. That boy, Sir,' said the Major in a lower tone, 'will live in history. That boy, Sir, is not a common production. Take care of him, Mr Dombey.'

Mr Dombey seemed to intimate that he would endeavour to do so.

'Here is a boy here, Sir,' pursued the Major, confidentially, and giving him a thrust with his cane. 'Son of Bitherstone of Bengal. Bill Bitherstone formerly of ours.[4] That boy's father and myself, Sir, were sworn friends. Wherever you went, Sir, you heard of nothing but Bill Bitherstone and Joe Bagstock. Am I blind to that boy's defects? By no means. He's a fool, Sir.'

Mr Dombey glanced at the libelled Master Bitherstone, of whom he knew at least as much as the Major did, and said, in quite a complacent manner, 'Really?'

'That is what he is, Sir,' said the Major. 'He's a fool. Joe Bagstock never minces matters. The son of my old friend Bill Bitherstone, of Bengal, is a born fool, Sir.' Here the Major laughed till he was almost black. 'My little friend is destined for a public school,[5] I presume, Mr Dombey?' said the Major when he had recovered.

'I am not quite decided,' returned Mr Dombey. 'I think not. He is delicate.'

'If he's delicate, Sir,' said the Major, 'you are right. None but the tough fellows could live through it, Sir, at Sandhurst.[6] We put each other to the torture there, Sir. We roasted the new fellows at a slow fire, and hung 'em out of a three pair of stairs window, with their heads downwards. Joseph Bagstock, Sir, was held out of the window by the heels of his boots, for thirteen minutes by the college clock.'

The Major might have appealed to his countenance in corroboration of this story. It certainly looked as if he had hung out a little too long.

'But it made us what we were, Sir,' said the Major, settling his shirt frill. 'We were iron, Sir, and it forged us. Are you remaining here, Mr Dombey?'

'I generally come down once a week, Major,' returned that gentleman. 'I stay at the Bedford.'

'I shall have the honour of calling at the Bedford, Sir, if you'll permit me,' said the Major. 'Joey B., Sir, is not in general a calling man, but Mr Dombey's is not a common name. I am much indebted to my little friend, Sir, for the honour of this introduction.'

Mr Dombey made a very gracious reply; and Major Bagstock, having patted Paul on the head, and said of Florence that her eyes would play the Devil with the youngsters before long – 'and the oldsters too, Sir, if you come to that,' added the Major, chuckling very much – stirred up Master Bitherstone with his walking-stick, and departed with that young gentleman, at a kind of half-trot; rolling his head and coughing with great dignity, as he staggered away, with his legs very wide asunder.

In fulfilment of his promise, the Major afterwards called on Mr Dombey; and Mr Dombey, having referred to the army list, afterwards called on the Major. Then the Major called at Mr Dombey's house in town; and came down again, in the same coach as Mr Dombey. In short, Mr Dombey and the Major got on uncommonly well together, and uncommonly fast: and Mr Dombey observed of the Major, to his sister, that besides being quite a military man he was really something more, as he had a very admirable idea of the importance of things unconnected with his own profession.

At length Mr Dombey, bringing down Miss Tox and Mrs Chick to see the children, and finding the Major again at Brighton, invited him to dinner at the Bedford, and complimented Miss Tox highly, beforehand, on her neighbour and acquaintance. Notwithstanding the palpitation of the heart which these allusions occasioned her, they were anything but disagreeable to Miss Tox, as they enabled her to be extremely interesting, and to manifest an occasional incoherence and distraction which she was not at all unwilling to display. The Major gave her abundant opportunities of exhibiting this emotion: being profuse in his complaints, at dinner, of her desertion of him and Princess's Place: and as he appeared to derive great enjoyment from making them, they all got on very well.

None the worse on account of the Major taking charge of the whole conversation, and showing as great an appetite in that respect as in regard of the various dainties on the table, among which he may be almost said to have wallowed: greatly to the aggravation of his inflammatory tendencies. Mr Dombey's habitual silence and reserve yielding readily to this usurpation, the Major felt that he was coming out and shining: and in the flow of spirits thus engendered, rang such an infinite number of new changes on his own name that he quite astonished himself. In a word, they were all very well pleased. The Major was considered to possess an inexhaustible fund of conversation; and when he took a late farewell, after a long rubber, Mr Dombey again complimented the blushing Miss Tox on her neighbour and acquaintance.

But all the way home to his own hotel, the Major incessantly said to himself, and of himself, 'Sly, Sir – sly, Sir – de-vil-ish sly!' And when he got there, sat down in a chair, and fell into a silent fit of laughter, with which he was sometimes seized, and which was always particularly awful. It held him so long on this occasion that the dark servant, who stood watching him at a distance, but dared not for his life approach, twice or thrice gave him over for lost. His whole form, but especially his face and head, dilated beyond all former experience; and presented to the dark man's view, nothing but a heavy mass of indigo. At length he burst into a violent paroxysm of coughing, and when that was a little better burst into such ejaculations as the following:

'Would you, ma'am, would you? Mrs Dombey, eh, ma'am? I think not, ma'am. Not while Joe B. can put a spoke in your wheel, ma'am. J. B.'s even with you now, ma'am. He isn't altogether bowled out, yet, Sir, isn't Bagstock. She's deep, Sir, deep, but Josh is deeper. Wide awake is old Joe – broad awake, and staring, Sir!' There was no doubt of this last assertion being true, and to a very fearful extent; as it continued to be during the greater part of that night, which the Major chiefly passed in similar exclamations, diversified with fits of coughing and choking that startled the whole house.

It was on the day after this occasion (being Sunday) when, as Mr Dombey, Mrs Chick, and Miss Tox were sitting at breakfast, still eulogising the Major, Florence came running in: her face suffused with a bright colour, and her eyes sparkling joyfully: and cried,

'Papa! papa! Here's Walter! and he won't come in.'

'Who?' cried Mr Dombey. 'What does she mean? What is this?'

'Walter, papa!' said Florence timidly; sensible of having approached the presence with too much familiarity. 'Who found me when I was lost.'

'Does she mean young Gay, Louisa?' inquired Mr Dombey, knitting his brows. 'Really, this child's manners have become very boisterous. She cannot mean young Gay, I think. See what it is, will you?'

Mrs Chick hurried into the passage, and returned with the information that it was young Gay, accompanied by a very strange-looking person; and that young Gay said he would not take the liberty of coming in, hearing Mr Dombey was at breakfast, but would wait until Mr Dombey should signify that he might approach.

'Tell the boy to come in now,' said Mr Dombey. 'Now, Gay, what is the matter? Who sent you down here? Was there nobody else to come?'

'I beg your pardon, Sir,' returned Walter. 'I have not been sent. I have been so bold as to come on my own account, which I hope you'll pardon when I mention the cause.'

But Mr Dombey, without attending to what he said, was looking impatiently on either side of him (as if he were a pillar in his way) at some object behind.

'What's that?' said Mr Dombey. 'Who is that? I think you have made some mistake in the door, Sir.'

'Oh, I'm very sorry to intrude with any one, Sir,' cried Walter, hastily, 'but this is – this is Captain Cuttle, Sir.'

'Wal'r, my lad,' observed the Captain in a deep voice: 'stand by!'

At the same time the Captain, coming a little further in, brought out his wide suit of blue, his conspicuous shirt-collar, and his knobby nose in full relief, and stood bowing to Mr Dombey, and waving his hook politely to the ladies, with the hard glazed hat in his one hand, and a red equator round his head which it had newly imprinted there.

Mr Dombey regarded this phenomenon with amazement and indignation, and seemed by his looks to appeal to Mrs Chick and Miss Tox against it. Little Paul, who had come in after Florence, backed towards Miss Tox as the Captain waved his hook, and stood on the defensive.

'Now, Gay,' said Mr Dombey. 'What have you got to say to me?'

Again the Captain observed, as a general opening of the conversation that could not fail to propitiate all parties, 'Wal'r, stand by!'

'I am afraid, Sir,' began Walter, trembling, and looking down at the ground, 'that I take a very great liberty in coming – indeed, I am sure I do. I should hardly have had the courage to ask to see you, Sir, even after coming down, I am afraid, if I had not overtaken Miss Dombey, and—'

'Well!' said Mr Dombey, following his eyes as he glanced at the attentive Florence, and frowning unconsciously as she encouraged him with a smile. 'Go on, if you please.'

'Aye, aye,' observed the Captain, considering it incumbent on him, as a point of good breeding, to support Mr Dombey. 'Well said! Go on, Wal'r.'

Captain Cuttle ought to have been withered by the look which Mr Dombey bestowed upon him in acknowledgment of his patronage. But quite innocent of this, he closed one eye in reply, and gave Mr Dombey to understand by certain significant motions of his hook, that Walter was a little bashful at first, and might be expected to come out shortly.

'It is entirely a private and personal matter, that has brought me here, Sir,' continued Walter, faltering, 'and Captain Cuttle—'

'Here!' interposed the Captain, as an assurance that he was at hand, and might be relied upon.

'Who is a very old friend of my poor uncle's, and a most excellent man, Sir,' pursued Walter, raising his eyes with a look of entreaty in the Captain's behalf, 'was so good as to offer to come with me, which I could hardly refuse.'

'No, no, no,' observed the Captain complacently. 'Of course not. No call for refusing. Go on, Wal'r.'

'And therefore, Sir,' said Walter, venturing to meet Mr Dombey's eye, and proceeding with better courage in the very desperation of the case, now that there was no avoiding it, 'therefore I have come, with him, Sir, to say that my poor old uncle is in very great affliction and distress. That, through the gradual loss of his business, and not being able to make a payment, the apprehension of which has weighed very heavily upon his mind, months and months, as indeed I know, Sir, he has an execution in his house, and is in danger of losing all he has, and breaking his heart. And that if you would, in your kindness, and in your old knowledge of him as a respectable man, do anything to help him out of his difficulty, Sir, we never could thank you enough for it.'

Walter's eyes filled with tears as he spoke; and so did those of Florence. Her father saw them glistening, though he appeared to look at Walter only.

'It is a very large sum, Sir,' said Walter. 'More than three hundred pounds. My uncle is quite beaten down by his misfortune, it lies so heavy on him; and is quite unable to do anything for his own relief. He doesn't even know yet, that I have come to speak to you. You would wish me to say, Sir,' added Walter, after a moment's hesitation, 'exactly what it is I want. I really don't know, Sir. There is my uncle's stock, on which I believe I may say, confidently, there are no other demands, and there is Captain Cuttle, who would wish to be security too. I – I hardly like to mention,' said Walter, 'such earnings as mine; but if you would allow them – accumulate – payment – advance – uncle – frugal, honourable, old man.' Walter trailed off, through these broken sentences, into silence; and stood, with downcast head, before his employer.

Considering this a favourable moment for the display of the valuables, Captain Cuttle advanced to the table; and clearing a space among the breakfast-cups at Mr Dombey's elbow, produced the silver watch, the ready money, the teaspoons, and the sugar-tongs; and piling them up into a heap that they might look as precious as possible, delivered himself of these words:

'Half a loaf's better than no bread, and the same remark holds good with crumbs. There's a few. Annuity of one hundred pound prannum[7] also ready to be made over. If there is a man chock full of science in the world, it's old Sol Gills. If there is a lad of promise – one flowing,' added the Captain, in one of his happy quotations, 'with milk and honey[8] – it's his nevy!'

The Captain then withdrew to his former place, where he stood arranging his scattered locks with the air of a man who had given the finishing touch to a difficult performance.

When Walter ceased to speak, Mr Dombey's eyes were attracted to little Paul, who, seeing his sister hanging down her head and silently weeping in her commiseration for the distress she had heard described, went over to her, and tried to comfort her: looking at Walter and his father as he did so, with a very expressive face. After the momentary distraction of Captain Cuttle's address, which he regarded with lofty indifference, Mr Dombey again turned his eyes upon his son, and sat steadily regarding the child, for some moments, in silence.

'What was this debt contracted for?' asked Mr Dombey at length. 'Who is the creditor?'

'He don't know,' replied the Captain, putting his hand on Walter's shoulder. 'I do. It came of helping a man that's dead now, and that's cost my friend Gills many a hundred pound already. More particulars in private, if agreeable.'

'People who have enough to do to hold their own way,' said Mr Dombey, unobservant of the Captain's mysterious signs behind Walter, and still looking at his son, 'had better be content with their own obligations and difficulties, and not increase them by engaging for other men. It is an act of dishonesty and presumption, too,' said Mr Dombey, sternly; 'great presumption; for the wealthy could do no more. Paul, come here!'

The child obeyed: and Mr Dombey took him on his knee.

'If you had money now—' said Mr Dombey. 'Look at me!'

Paul, whose eyes had wandered to his sister, and to Walter, looked his father in the face.

'If you had money now,' said Mr Dombey; 'as much money as young Gay has talked about; what would you do?'

'Give it to his old uncle,' returned Paul.

'Lend it to his old uncle, eh?' retorted Mr Dombey. 'Well! When you are old enough, you know, you will share my money, and we shall use it together.'

'Dombey and Son,' interrupted Paul, who had been tutored early in the phrase.

'Dombey and Son,' repeated his father. 'Would you like to begin to be Dombey and Son, now, and lend this money to young Gay's uncle?'

'Oh! if you please, papa!' said Paul: 'and so would Florence.'

'Girls,' said Mr Dombey, 'have nothing to do with Dombey and Son. Would *you* like it?'

'Yes, papa, yes!'

'Then you shall do it,' returned his father. 'And you see, Paul,' he added, dropping his voice, 'how powerful money is, and how anxious people are to get it. Young Gay comes all this way to beg for money, and you, who are so grand and great, having got it, are going to let him have it, as a great favour and obligation.'

Paul turned up the old face for a moment, in which there was a sharp understanding of the reference conveyed in these words: but it was a young and childish face immediately afterwards: when he slipped down from his father's knee, and ran to tell Florence not to cry any more, for he was going to let young Gay have the money.

Mr Dombey then turned to a side-table, and wrote a note and sealed it. During the interval, Paul and Florence whispered to Walter, and Captain Cuttle beamed on the three, with such aspiring and ineffably presumptuous thoughts as Mr Dombey never could have believed in. The note being finished, Mr Dombey turned round to his former place, and held it out to Walter.

'Give that,' he said, 'the first thing to-morrow morning, to Mr Carker. He will immediately take care that one of my people releases your uncle from his present position, by paying the amount at issue; and that such arrangements are made for its repayment as may be consistent with your uncle's circumstances. You will consider that this is done for you by Master Paul.'

Walter in the emotion of holding in his hand the means of

releasing his good uncle from his trouble, would have endeavoured to express something of his gratitude and joy. But Mr Dombey stopped him short.

'You will consider that it is done,' he repeated, 'by Master Paul. I have explained that to him, and he understands it. I wish no more to be said.'

As he motioned towards the door, Walter could only bow his head and retire. Miss Tox, seeing that the Captain appeared about to do the same, interposed.

'My dear Sir,' she said, addressing Mr Dombey, at whose munificence both she and Mrs Chick were shedding tears copiously; 'I think you have overlooked something. Pardon me, Mr Dombey, I think, in the nobility of your character, and its exalted scope, you have omitted a matter of detail.'

'Indeed, Miss Tox!' said Mr Dombey.

'The gentleman with the – Instrument,' pursued Miss Tox, glancing at Captain Cuttle, 'has left upon the table, at your elbow—'

'Good Heaven!' said Mr Dombey, sweeping the Captain's property from him, as if it were so much crumb indeed. 'Take these things away. I am obliged to you, Miss Tox; it is your usual discretion. Have the goodness to take these things away, Sir!'

Captain Cuttle felt he had no alternative but to comply. But he was so much struck by the magnanimity of Mr Dombey, in refusing treasures lying heaped up to his hand, that when he had deposited the teaspoons and sugar-tongs in one pocket, and the ready money in another, and had lowered the great watch down slowly into its proper vault, he could not refrain from seizing that gentleman's right hand in his own solitary left, and while he held it open with his powerful fingers, bringing the hook down upon its palm in a transport of admiration. At this touch of warm feeling and cold iron, Mr Dombey shivered all over.

Captain Cuttle then kissed his hook to the ladies several times, with great elegance and gallantry; and having taken a particular leave of Paul and Florence, accompanied Walter out of the room. Florence was running after them in the earnestness of her heart, to send some message to old Sol, when Mr Dombey called her back, and bade her stay where she was.

'Will you *never* be a Dombey, my dear child!' said Mrs Chick, with pathetic reproachfulness.

'Dear aunt,' said Florence. 'Don't be angry with me. I am so thankful to papa!'

She would have run and thrown her arms about his neck if she had dared; but as she did not dare, she glanced with thankful eyes towards him, as he sat musing; sometimes bestowing an uneasy glance on her, but, for the most part, watching Paul, who walked about the room with the new-blown dignity of having let young Gay have the money.

And young Gay – Walter – what of him?

He was overjoyed to purge the old man's hearth from bailiffs and brokers, and to hurry back to his uncle with the good tidings. He was overjoyed to have it all arranged and settled next day before noon; and to sit down at evening in the little back parlour with old Sol and Captain Cuttle; and to see the instrument-maker already reviving, and hopeful for the future, and feeling that the wooden midshipman was his own again. But without the least impeachment of his gratitude to Mr Dombey, it must be confessed that Walter was humbled and cast down. It is when our budding hopes are nipped beyond recovery by some rough wind, that we are the most disposed to picture to ourselves what flowers they might have borne, if they had flourished; and now, when Walter found himself cut off from that great Dombey height, by the depth of a new and terrible tumble, and felt that all his old wild fancies had been scattered to the winds in the fall, he began to suspect that they might have led him on to harmless visions of aspiring to Florence in the remote distance of time.

The Captain viewed the subject in quite a different light. He appeared to entertain a belief that the interview at which he had assisted was so very satisfactory and encouraging, as to be only a step or two removed from a regular betrothal of Florence to Walter; and that the late transaction had immensely forwarded, if not thoroughly established, the Whittingtonian hopes. Stimulated by this conviction, and by the improvement in the spirits of his old friend, and by his own consequent gaiety, he even attempted, in favouring them with the ballad of 'Lovely Peg' for the third time in one evening, to make an extemporaneous substitution of the name 'Florence'; but finding this difficult, on account of the word Peg invariably rhyming to leg (in which personal beauty the original was described as having excelled all competitors), he hit upon the happy thought of changing it to Fle–e–eg; which he accordingly did, with an archness almost supernatural, and a voice quite vociferous, notwithstanding that the time was close at hand when he must seek the abode of the dreadful Mrs MacStinger.

CHAPTER 11

Paul's Introduction to a new Scene

Mrs Pipchin's constitution was made of such hard metal, in spite of its liability to the fleshly weaknesses of standing in need of repose after chops, and of requiring to be coaxed to sleep by the soporific agency of sweet-breads,[1] that it utterly set at naught the predictions of Mrs Wickam, and showed no symptoms of decline. Yet, as Paul's rapt interest in the old lady continued unabated, Mrs Wickam would not budge an inch from the position she had taken up. Fortifying and entrenching herself on the strong ground of her uncle's Betsey Jane, she advised Miss Berry, as a friend, to prepare herself for the worst; and forewarned her that her aunt might, at any time, be expected to go off suddenly, like a powder-mill.

Poor Berry took it all in good part, and drudged and slaved away as usual; perfectly convinced that Mrs Pipchin was one of the most meritorious persons in the world, and making every day innumerable sacrifices of herself upon the altar of that noble old woman. But all these immolations of Berry were somehow carried to the credit of Mrs Pipchin by Mrs Pipchin's friends and admirers; and were made to harmonise with, and carry out, that melancholy fact of the deceased Mr Pipchin having broken his heart in the Peruvian mines.

For example, there was an honest grocer and general dealer in the retail line of business, between whom and Mrs Pipchin there was a small memorandum book, with a greasy red cover, perpetually in question, and concerning which divers secret councils and conferences were continually being held between the parties to the register, on the mat in the passage, and with closed doors in the parlour. Nor were there wanting dark hints from Master Bitherstone (whose temper had been made revengeful by the solar heats of India acting on his blood), of balances unsettled, and of a failure, on one occasion within his memory, in the supply of moist sugar at teatime. This grocer being a bachelor, and not a man who looked upon the surface for beauty, had once made honourable offers for the hand of Berry, which Mrs Pipchin had, with contumely and scorn, rejected. Everybody said how laudable this was in Mrs Pipchin, relict of a man who had died of the Peruvian mines; and what a staunch, high, independent spirit the old lady had. But nobody said anything about poor Berry, who cried for six weeks (being soundly rated by her good aunt all the time), and lapsed into a state of hopeless spinsterhood.

'Berry's very fond of you, ain't she?' Paul once asked Mrs Pipchin when they were sitting by the fire with the cat.

'Yes,' said Mrs Pipchin.

'Why?' asked Paul.

'Why?' returned the disconcerted old lady. 'How can you ask such things, Sir! why are you fond of your sister Florence?'

'Because she's very good,' said Paul. 'There's nobody like Florence.'

'Well!' retorted Mrs Pipchin, shortly, 'and there's nobody like me, I suppose.'

'Ain't there really though?' asked Paul, leaning forward in his chair, and looking at her very hard.

'No,' said the old lady.

'I am glad of that,' observed Paul, rubbing his hands thoughtfully. 'That's a very good thing.'

Mrs Pipchin didn't dare to ask him why, lest she should receive some perfectly annihilating answer. But as a compensation to her wounded feelings, she harassed Master Bitherstone to that extent until bedtime, that he began that very night to make arrangements for an overland return to India, by secreting from his supper a quarter of a round of bread and a fragment of moist Dutch cheese, as the beginning of a stock of provision to support him on the voyage.

Mrs Pipchin had kept watch and ward over little Paul and his sister for nearly twelve months. They had been home twice, but only for a few days; and had been constant in their weekly visits to Mr Dombey at the hotel. By little and little Paul had grown stronger, and had become able to dispense with his carriage; though he still looked thin and delicate; and still remained the same old, quiet, dreamy child that he had been when first consigned to Mrs Pipchin's care. One Saturday afternoon, at dusk, great consternation was occasioned in the castle by the unlooked-for announcement of Mr Dombey as a visitor to Mrs Pipchin. The population of the parlour was immediately swept upstairs as on the wings of a whirlwind, and after much slamming of bedroom doors, and trampling overhead, and some knocking about of Master Bitherstone by Mrs Pipchin, as a relief to the perturbation of her spirits, the black bombazeen garments of the worthy old lady darkened the audience-chamber where Mr Dombey was contemplating the vacant armchair of his son and heir.

'Mrs Pipchin,' said Mr Dombey, 'how do you do?'

'Thank you, Sir,' said Mrs Pipchin, 'I am pretty well, considering.'

Mrs Pipchin always used that form of words. It meant, consider-ing her virtues, sacrifices, and so forth.

'I can't expect, Sir, to be very well,' said Mrs Pipchin, taking a chair and fetching her breath; 'but such health as I have, I am grateful for.'

Mr Dombey inclined his head with the satisfied air of a patron, who felt that this was the sort of thing for which he paid so much a quarter. After a moment's silence he went on to say:

'Mrs Pipchin, I have taken the liberty of calling, to consult you in reference to my son. I have had it in my mind to do so for some time past; but have deferred it from time to time, in order that his health might be thoroughly re-established. You have no misgivings on that subject, Mrs Pipchin?'

'Brighton has proved very beneficial, Sir,' returned Mrs Pipchin. 'Very beneficial, indeed.'

'I purpose,' said Mr Dombey, 'his remaining at Brighton.'

Mrs Pipchin rubbed her hands, and bent her grey eyes on the fire.

'But,' pursued Mr Dombey, stretching out his forefinger, 'but possibly that he should now make a change, and lead a different kind of life here. In short, Mrs Pipchin, that is the object of my visit. My son is getting on, Mrs Pipchin. Really he is getting on.'

There was something melancholy in the triumphant air with which Mr Dombey said this. It showed how long Paul's childish life had been to him, and how his hopes were set upon a later stage of his existence. Pity may appear a strange word to connect with any one so haughty and so cold, and yet he seemed a worthy subject for it at that moment.

'Six years old!' said Mr Dombey, settling his neckcloth – perhaps to hide an irrepressible smile that rather seemed to strike upon the surface of his face and glance away, as finding no resting-place, than to play there for an instant. 'Dear me, six will be changed to sixteen, before we have time to look about us.'

'Ten years,' croaked the unsympathetic Pipchin, with a frosty glistening of her hard grey eye, and a dreary shaking of her bent head, 'is a long time.'

'It depends on circumstances,' returned Mr Dombey; 'at all events, Mrs Pipchin, my son is six years old, and there is no doubt, I fear, that in his studies he is behind many children of his age – or his youth,' said Mr Dombey, quickly answering what he mistrusted was a shrewd twinkle of the frosty eye, 'his youth is a more appropriate expression. Now, Mrs Pipchin, instead of being behind his peers, my son ought to be before them; far before them. There is an eminence ready for him to mount upon. There is nothing of chance or doubt in the course before my son. His way in life was clear and prepared, and marked out before he existed. The education of such a young gentleman must not be delayed. It must not be left imperfect. It must be very steadily and seriously undertaken, Mrs Pipchin.'

'Well, Sir,' said Mrs Pipchin, 'I can say nothing to the contrary.'

'I was quite sure, Mrs Pipchin,' returned Mr Dombey, approvingly, 'that a person of your good sense could not, and would not.'

'There is a great deal of nonsense – and worse – talked about young people not being pressed too hard at first, and being tempted on, and all the rest of it, Sir,' said Mrs Pipchin, impatiently rubbing her hooked nose. 'It never was thought of in my time, and it has no business to be thought of now. My opinion is "keep 'em at it."'

'My good madam,' returned Mr Dombey, 'you have not acquired your reputation undeservedly; and I beg you to believe, Mrs Pipchin, that I am more than satisfied with your excellent system of management, and shall have the greatest pleasure in commending it whenever my poor commendation' – Mr Dombey's loftiness when he affected to disparage his own importance, passed all bounds – 'can be of any service. I have been thinking of Doctor Blimber's, Mrs Pipchin.'

'My neighbour, Sir?' said Mrs Pipchin. 'I believe the Doctor's is an excellent establishment. I've heard that it's very strictly conducted, and there is nothing but learning going on from morning to night.'

'And it's very expensive,' added Mr Dombey.

'And it's very expensive, Sir,' returned Mrs Pipchin, catching at the fact, as if in omitting that, she had omitted one of its leading merits.

'I have had some communication with the Doctor, Mrs Pipchin,' said Mr Dombey, hitching his chair anxiously a little nearer to the fire, 'and he does not consider Paul at all too young for his purpose. He mentioned several instances of boys in Greek at about the same age. If I have any little uneasiness in my own mind, Mrs Pipchin, on the subject of this change, it is not on that head. My son not having known a mother has gradually concentrated much – too much – of his childish affection on his sister. Whether their separation—' Mr Dombey said no more, but sat silent.

'Hoity-toity!' exclaimed Mrs Pipchin, shaking out her black

bombazeen skirts, and plucking up all the ogress within her. 'If she don't like it, Mr Dombey, she must be taught to lump it.' The good lady apologised immediately afterwards for using so common a figure of speech, but said (and truly) that that was the way *she* reasoned with 'em.

Mr Dombey waited until Mrs Pipchin had done bridling and shaking her head, and frowning down a legion of Bitherstones and Pankeys; and then said quietly, but correctively, 'He, my good madam, he.'

Mrs Pipchin's system would have applied very much the same mode of cure to any uneasiness on the part of Paul, too; but as the hard grey eye was sharp enough to see that the recipe, however Mr Dombey might admit its efficacy in the case of the daughter, was not a sovereign remedy for the son, she argued the point; and contended that change, and new society, and the different form of life he would lead at Doctor Blimber's, and the studies he would have to master, would very soon prove sufficient alienations. As this chimed in with Mr Dombey's own hope and belief, it gave that gentleman a still higher opinion of Mrs Pipchin's understanding: and as Mrs Pipchin, at the same time, bewailed the loss of her dear little friend (which was not an overwhelming shock to her, as she had long expected it, and had not looked, in the beginning, for his remaining with her longer than three months), he formed an equally good opinion of Mrs Pipchin's disinterestedness. It was plain that he had given the subject anxious consideration, for he had formed a plan, which he announced to the ogress, of sending Paul to the Doctor's as a weekly boarder for the first half year, during which time Florence would remain at the castle, that she might receive her brother there, on Saturdays. This would wean him by degrees, Mr Dombey said; probably with a recollection of his not having been weaned by degrees on a former occasion.

Mr Dombey finished the interview by expressing his hope that Mrs Pipchin would still remain in office as general superintendent and overseer of his son, pending his studies at Brighton; and having kissed Paul, and shaken hands with Florence, and beheld Master Bitherstone in his collar of state, and made Miss Pankey cry by patting her on the head (in which region she was uncommonly tender, on account of a habit Mrs Pipchin had of sounding it with her knuckles, like a cask), he withdrew to his hotel and dinner: resolved that Paul, now that he was getting so old and well, should begin a vigorous course of education forthwith, to qualify him for the position in which he was to shine; and that Doctor Blimber should take him in hand immediately.

Whenever a young gentleman was taken in hand by Doctor Blimber, he might consider himself sure of a pretty tight squeeze. The Doctor only undertook the charge of ten young gentlemen, but he had, always ready, a supply of learning for a hundred, on the lowest estimate; and it was at once the business and delight of his life to gorge the unhappy ten with it.

In fact, Doctor Blimber's establishment was a great hot-house, in which there was a forcing apparatus incessantly at work. All the boys blew before their time. Mental green peas were produced at Christmas, and intellectual asparagus all the year round. Mathematical gooseberries (very sour ones too) were common at untimely seasons, and from mere sprouts of bushes, under Doctor Blimber's cultivation. Every description of Greek and Latin vegetable was got off the driest twigs of boys, under the frostiest circumstances. Nature was of no consequence at all. No matter what a young gentleman was intended to bear, Doctor Blimber made him bear to pattern, somehow or other.

This was all very pleasant and ingenious, but the system of forcing was attended with its usual disadvantages. There was not the right taste about the premature productions, and they didn't keep well. Moreover, one young gentleman, with a swollen nose and an excessively large head (the oldest of the ten who had 'gone through' everything), suddenly left off blowing one day, and remained in the establishment a mere stalk. And people did say that the Doctor had rather overdone it with young Toots, and that when he began to have whiskers he left off having brains.

There young Toots was, at any rate; possessed of the gruffest of voices and the shrillest of minds; sticking ornamental pins into his shirt, and keeping a ring in his waistcoat pocket to put on his little finger by stealth, when the pupils went out walking; constantly falling in love by sight with nurserymaids, who had no idea of his existence; and looking at the gas-lighted world over the little iron bars in the left-hand corner window of the front three pairs of stairs, after bedtime, like a greatly overgrown cherub who had sat up aloft much too long.[2]

The Doctor was a portly gentleman in a suit of black, with strings at his knees, and stockings below them. He had a bald head, highly polished; a deep voice; and a chin so very double, that it was a wonder how he ever managed to shave into the creases. He had likewise a pair of little eyes that were always half shut up, and a mouth that was always half expanded into a grin, as if he had, that moment, posed a boy,[3] and were waiting to convict him from his own lips. Insomuch, that when the Doctor put his right hand into the breast of his coat, and with his other hand behind him, and a scarcely perceptible wag of his head, made the commonest observation to a nervous stranger, it was like a sentiment from the sphynx, and settled his business.

The Doctor's was a mighty fine house, fronting the sea. Not a joyful style of house within, but quite the contrary. Sad-coloured curtains, whose proportions were spare and lean, hid themselves despondently behind the windows. The tables and chairs were put away in rows, like figures in a sum: fires were so rarely lighted in the rooms of ceremony, that they felt like wells, and a visitor represented the bucket; the dining-room seemed the last place in the world where any eating or drinking was likely to occur; there was no sound through all the house but the ticking of a great clock in the hall, which made itself audible in the very garrets: and sometimes a dull crying of young gentlemen at their lessons, like the murmurings of an assemblage of melancholy pigeons.

Miss Blimber, too, although a slim and graceful maid, did no soft violence to the gravity of the house. There was no light nonsense about Miss Blimber. She kept her hair short and crisp, and wore spectacles. She was dry and sandy with working in the graves of deceased languages. None of your live languages for Miss Blimber. They must be dead – stone dead – and then Miss Blimber dug them up like a Ghoul.

Mrs Blimber, her mama, was not learned herself, but she pretended to be, and that did quite as well. She said at evening parties, that if she could have known Cicero,[4] she thought she could have died contented. It was the steady joy of her life to see the Doctor's young gentlemen go out walking, unlike all other young gentlemen, in the largest possible shirt-collars, and the stiffest possible cravats. It was so classical, she said.

As to Mr Feeder, B.A., Doctor Blimber's assistant, he was a kind of human barrel-organ, with a little list of tunes at which he was continually working, over and over again, without any variation. He might have been fitted up with a change of barrels, perhaps, in early life, if his destiny had been favourable; but it had not been; and he had only one, with which, in a monotonous round, it was his occupation to bewilder the young ideas of Doctor Blimber's young gentlemen. The young gentlemen were prematurely full of carking anxieties. They knew no rest from the pursuit of stony-

hearted verbs, savage noun-substantives, inflexible syntactic passages, and ghosts of exercises that appeared to them in their dreams.
Under the forcing system, a young gentleman usually took leave of
his spirits in three weeks. He had all the cares of the world on his
head in three months. He conceived bitter sentiments against his
parents or guardians in four; he was an old misanthrope, in five;
envied Curtius[6] that blessed refuge in the earth, in six; and at the
end of the first twelvemonth had arrived at the conclusion, from
which he never afterwards departed, that all the fancies of the
poets, and lessons of the sages, were a mere collection of words and
grammar, and had no other meaning in the world.

But he went on blow, blow, blowing, in the Doctor's hot-house,
all the time; and the Doctor's glory and reputation were great, when
he took his wintry growth home to his relations and friends.

Upon the Doctor's doorsteps one day, Paul stood with a fluttering
heart, and with his small right hand in his father's. His other hand
was locked in that of Florence. How tight the tiny pressure of that
one; and how loose and cold the other!

Mrs Pipchin hovered behind the victim, with her sable plumage
and her hooked beak, like a bird of ill omen. She was out of breath
– for Mr Dombey, full of great thoughts, had walked fast – and she
croaked hoarsely as she waited for the opening of the door.

'Now, Paul,' said Mr Dombey, exultingly. 'This is the way indeed
to be Dombey and Son, and have money. You are almost a man
already.'

'Almost,' returned the child.

Even his childish agitation could not master the sly and quaint
yet touching look, with which he accompanied the reply.

It brought a vague expression of dissatisfaction into Mr Dombey's face; but the door being opened, it was quickly gone.

'Doctor Blimber is at home, I believe?' said Mr Dombey.

The man said yes; and as they passed in, looked at Paul as if he
were a little mouse, and the house were a trap. He was a weak-eyed
young man, with the first faint streaks or early dawn of a grin on
his countenance. It was mere imbecility; but Mrs Pipchin took it
into her head that it was impudence, and made a snap at him
directly.

'How dare you laugh behind the gentleman's back?' said Mrs
Pipchin. 'And what do you take me for?'

'I ain't a laughing at nobody, and I'm sure I don't take you for
nothing, ma'am,' returned the young man, in consternation.

'A pack of idle dogs!' said Mrs Pipchin, 'only fit to be turnspits.[6]

Go and tell your master that Mr Dombey's here or it'll be worse for you!'

The weak-eyed young man went, very meekly, to discharge himself of this commission; and soon came back to invite them to the Doctor's study.

'You're laughing again, Sir,' said Mrs Pipchin, when it came to her turn, bringing up the rear, to pass him in the hall.

'I *ain't*,' returned the young man, grievously oppressed, 'I never see such a thing as this!'

'What is the matter, Mrs Pipchin?' said Mr Dombey, looking round. 'Softly! Pray!'

Mrs Pipchin, in her deference, merely muttered at the young man as she passed on, and said, 'Oh! he was a precious fellow' – leaving the young man, who was all meekness and incapacity, affected even to tears by the incident. But Mrs Pipchin had a way of falling foul of all meek people; and her friends said who could wonder at it, after the Peruvian mines!

The Doctor was sitting in his portentous study, with a globe at each knee, books all round him, Homer[7] over the door, and Minerva[8] on the mantel-shelf. 'And how do you do, Sir?' he said to Mr Dombey; 'and how is my little friend?' Grave as an organ was the Doctor's speech; and when he ceased, the great clock in the hall seemed (to Paul at least) to take him up, and to go on saying, 'how, is, my, lit, tle, friend? how, is, my, lit, tle, friend?' over and over and over again.

The little friend being something too small to be seen at all from where the Doctor sat, over the books on his table, the Doctor made several futile attempts to get a view of him round the legs; which Mr Dombey perceiving, relieved the Doctor from his embarrassment by taking Paul up in his arms, and sitting him on another little table, over against the Doctor, in the middle of the room.

'Ha!' said the Doctor, leaning back in his chair with his hand in his breast. 'Now I see my little friend. How do you do, my little friend?'

The clock in the hall wouldn't subscribe to this alteration in the form of words, but continued to repeat 'how, is, my, lit, tle, friend? how, is, my, lit, tle, friend?'

'Very well, I thank you, Sir,' returned Paul, answering the clock quite as much as the Doctor.

'Ha!' said Doctor Blimber. 'Shall we make a man of him?'

'Do you hear, Paul?' added Mr Dombey; Paul being silent.

'Shall we make a man of him?' repeated the Doctor.

'I had rather be a child,' replied Paul.

'Indeed!' said the Doctor. 'Why?'

The child sat on the table looking at him, with a curious expression of suppressed emotion in his face, and beating one hand proudly on his knee as if he had the rising tears beneath it, and crushed them. But his other hand strayed a little way the while, a little farther – farther from him yet – until it lighted on the neck of Florence. 'This is why,' it seemed to say, and then the steady look was broken up and gone; the working lip was loosened; and the tears came streaming forth.

'Mrs Pipchin,' said his father, in a querulous manner, 'I am really very sorry to see this.'

'Come away from him, do, Miss Dombey,' quoth the matron.

'Never mind,' said the Doctor, blandly nodding his head, to keep Mrs Pipchin back. 'Ne-ver mind; we shall substitute new cares and new impressions, Mr Dombey, very shortly. You would still wish my little friend to acquire—'

'Everything, if you please, Doctor,' returned Mr Dombey, firmly.

'Yes,' said the Doctor, who, with his half-shut eyes, and his usual smile, seemed to survey Paul with the sort of interest that might attach to some choice little animal he was going to stuff. 'Yes, exactly. Ha! We shall impart a great variety of information to our little friend, and bring him quickly forward, I dare say. I dare say. Quite a virgin soil, I believe you said, Mr Dombey?'

'Except some ordinary preparation at home, and from this lady,' replied Mr Dombey, introducing Mrs Pipchin, who instantly communicated a rigidity to her whole muscular system, and snorted defiance beforehand, in case the Doctor should disparage her; 'except so far, Paul has, as yet, applied himself to no studies at all.'

Doctor Blimber inclined his head, in gentle tolerance of such insignificant poaching as Mrs Pipchin's, and said he was glad to hear it. It was much more satisfactory, he observed, rubbing his hands, to begin at the foundation. And again he leered at Paul, as if he would have liked to tackle him with the Greek alphabet on the spot.

'That circumstance, indeed, Doctor Blimber,' pursued Mr Dombey, glancing at his little son, 'and the interview I have already had the pleasure of holding with you, renders any further explanation, and consequently, any further intrusion on your valuable time, so unnecessary, that—'

'Now, Miss Dombey!' said the acid Pipchin.

'Permit me,' said the Doctor, 'one moment. Allow me to present

Mrs Blimber and my daughter, who will be associated with the domestic life of our young Pilgrim to Parnassus.[9] Mrs Blimber,' for the lady, who had perhaps been in waiting, opportunely entered, followed by her daughter, that fair Sexton in spectacles, 'Mr Dombey. My daughter Cornelia, Mr Dombey. Mr Dombey, my love,' pursued the Doctor, turning to his wife, 'is so confiding as to – do you see our little friend?'

Mrs Blimber, in an excess of politeness, of which Mr Dombey was the object, apparently did not, for she was backing against the little friend, and very much endangering his position on the table. But, on this hint, she turned to admire his classical and intellectual lineaments, and turning again to Mr Dombey, said, with a sigh, that she envied his dear son.

'Like a bee, Sir,' said Mrs Blimber, with uplifted eyes, 'about to plunge into a garden of the choicest flowers, and sip the sweets for the first time. Virgil, Horace, Ovid, Terence, Plautus, Cicero.[10] What a world of honey have we here. It may appear remarkable, Mr Dombey, in one who is a wife – the wife of such a husband—'

'Hush, hush,' said Doctor Blimber. 'Fie for shame.'

'Mr Dombey will forgive the partiality of a wife,' said Mrs Blimber, with an engaging smile.

Mr Dombey answered 'Not at all': applying those words, it is to be presumed, to the partiality, and not to the forgiveness.

'—And it may seem remarkable in one who is a mother also,' resumed Mrs Blimber.

'And such a mother,' observed Mr Dombey, bowing with some confused idea of being complimentary to Cornelia.

'But really,' pursued Mrs Blimber, 'I think if I could have known Cicero, and been his friend, and talked with him in his retirement at Tusculum[11] (beautiful Tusculum!), I could have died contented.'

A learned enthusiasm is so very contagious, that Mr Dombey half believed this was exactly his case; and even Mrs Pipchin, who was not, as we have seen, of an accommodating disposition generally, gave utterance to a little sound between a groan and a sigh, as if she would have said that nobody but Cicero could have proved a lasting consolation under that failure of the Peruvian mines, but that he indeed would have been a very Davy-lamp[12] of refuge.

Cornelia looked at Mr Dombey through her spectacles, as if she would have liked to crack a few quotations with him from the authority in question. But this design, if she entertained it, was frustrated by a knock at the room-door.

'Who is that?' said the Doctor. 'Oh! Come in, Toots; come in.

Mr Dombey, Sir.' Toots bowed. 'Quite a coincidence!' said Doctor Blimber. 'Here we have the beginning and the end. Alpha and Omega. Our head boy, Mr Dombey.'

The Doctor might have called him their head and shoulders boy, for he was at least that much taller than any of the rest.

He blushed very much at finding himself among strangers, and chuckled aloud.

'An addition to our little Portico,[13] Toots,' said the Doctor; 'Mr Dombey's son.'

Young Toots blushed again: and finding, from a solemn silence which prevailed, that he was expected to say something, said to Paul, 'How are you?' in a voice so deep, and a manner so sheepish, that if a lamb had roared it couldn't have been more surprising.

'Ask Mr Feeder, if you please, Toots,' said the Doctor, 'to prepare a few introductory volumes for Mr Dombey's son, and to allot him a convenient seat for study. My dear, I believe Mr Dombey has not seen the dormitories.'

'If Mr Dombey will walk upstairs,' said Mrs Blimber, 'I shall be more than proud to show him the dominions of the drowsy god.'[14]

With that, Mrs Blimber, who was a lady of great suavity, and a wiry figure, and who wore a cap composed of sky-blue materials, proceeded upstairs with Mr Dombey and Cornelia; Mrs Pipchin following, and looking out sharp for her enemy the footman.

While they were gone, Paul sat upon the table, holding Florence by the hand, and glancing timidly from the Doctor round and round the room, while the Doctor, leaning back in his chair, with his hand in his breast as usual, held a book from him at arm's length, and read. There was something very awful in this manner of reading. It was such a determined, unimpassioned, inflexible, cold-blooded way of going to work. It left the Doctor's countenance exposed to view; and when the Doctor smiled auspiciously at his author, or knit his brows, or shook his head and made wry faces at him, as much as to say, 'Don't tell me, Sir; I know better,' it was terrific.

Toots, too, had no business to be outside the door, ostentatiously examining the wheels in his watch, and counting his half-crowns. But that didn't last long; for Doctor Blimber, happening to change the position of his tight plump legs, as if he were going to get up, Toots swiftly vanished, and appeared no more.

Mr Dombey and his conductress were soon heard coming downstairs again, talking all the way; and presently they re-entered the Doctor's study.

'I hope, Mr Dombey,' said the Doctor, laying down his book, 'that the arrangements meet your approval.'

'They are excellent, Sir,' said Mr Dombey.

'Very fair, indeed,' said Mrs Pipchin, in a low voice; never disposed to give too much encouragement.

'Mrs Pipchin,' said Mr Dombey, wheeling round, 'will, with your permission, Doctor and Mrs Blimber, visit Paul now and then.'

'Whenever Mrs Pipchin pleases,' observed the Doctor.

'Always happy to see her,' said Mrs Blimber.

'I think,' said Mr Dombey, 'I have given all the trouble I need, and may take my leave. Paul, my child,' he went close to him, as he sat upon the table. 'Good-bye.'

'Good-bye, Papa.'

The limp and careless little hand that Mr Dombey took in his, was singularly out of keeping with the wistful face. But he had no part in its sorrowful expression. It was not addressed to him. No, no. To Florence – all to Florence.

If Mr Dombey in his insolence of wealth, had ever made an enemy, hard to appease and cruelly vindictive in his hate, even such an enemy might have received the pang that wrung his proud heart then, as compensation for his injury.

He bent down over his boy, and kissed him. If his sight were dimmed as he did so, by something that for a moment blurred the little face, and made it indistinct to him, his mental vision may have been, for that short time, the clearer perhaps.

'I shall see you soon, Paul. You are free on Saturdays and Sundays, you know.'

'Yes, papa,' returned Paul: looking at his sister. 'On Saturdays and Sundays.'

'And you'll try and learn a great deal here, and be a clever man,' said Mr Dombey; 'won't you?'

'I'll try,' returned the child wearily.

'And you'll soon be grown up now!' said Mr Dombey.

'Oh! very soon!' replied the child. Once more the old, old look passed rapidly across his features like a strange light. It fell on Mrs Pipchin, and extinguished itself in her black dress. That excellent ogress stepped forward to take leave and to bear off Florence, which she had long been thirsting to do. The move on her part roused Mr Dombey, whose eyes were fixed on Paul. After patting him on the head, and pressing his small hand again, he took leave of Doctor Blimber, Mrs Blimber, and Miss Blimber, with his usual polite frigidity, and walked out of the study.

Despite his entreaty that they would not think of stirring, Doctor Blimber, Mrs Blimber, and Miss Blimber all pressed forward to attend him to the hall; and thus Mrs Pipchin got into a state of entanglement with Miss Blimber and the Doctor, and was crowded out of the study before she could clutch Florence. To which happy accident Paul stood afterwards indebted for the dear remembrance, that Florence ran back to throw her arms round his neck, and that hers was the last face in the doorway: turned towards him with a smile of encouragement, the brighter for the tears through which it beamed.

It made his childish bosom heave and swell when it was gone; and sent the globes, the books, blind Homer and Minerva, swimming round the room. But they stopped, all of a sudden; and then he heard the loud clock in the hall still gravely inquiring 'how, is, my, lit, tle, friend? how, is, my, lit, tle, friend?' as it had done before.

He sat, with folded hands, upon his pedestal, silently listening. But he might have answered 'weary, weary! very lonely, very sad!' And there, with an aching void in his young heart, and all outside so cold, and bare, and strange, Paul sat as if he had taken life unfurnished, and the upholsterer were never coming.

CHAPTER 12

Paul's Education

After the lapse of some minutes, which appeared an immense time to little Paul Dombey on the table, Doctor Blimber came back. The Doctor's walk was stately, and calculated to impress the juvenile mind with solemn feelings. It was a sort of march; but when the Doctor put out his right foot, he gravely turned upon his axis, with a semi-circular sweep towards the left; and when he put out his left foot, he turned in the same manner towards the right. So that he seemed, at every stride he took, to look about him as though he were saying, 'Can anybody have the goodness to indicate any subject, in any direction, on which I am uninformed? I rather think not.'

Mrs Blimber and Miss Blimber came back in the Doctor's company; and the Doctor, lifting his new pupil off the table, delivered him over to Miss Blimber.

'Cornelia,' said the Doctor, 'Dombey will be your charge at first. Bring him on, Cornelia, bring him on.'

Miss Blimber received her young ward from the Doctor's hands; and Paul, feeling that the spectacles were surveying him, cast down his eyes. 'How old are you, Dombey?' said Miss Blimber.

'Six,' answered Paul, wondering, as he stole a glance at the young lady, why her hair didn't grow long like Florence's, and why she was like a boy.

'How much do you know of your Latin Grammar, Dombey?' said Miss Blimber.

'None of it,' answered Paul. Feeling that the answer was a shock to Miss Blimber's sensibility, he looked up at the three faces that were looking down at him, and said:

'I hav'n't been well. I have been a weak child. I couldn't learn a Latin Grammar when I was out, every day, with old Glubb. I wish you'd tell old Glubb to come and see me, if you please.'

'What a dreadful low name!' said Mrs Blimber. 'Unclassical to a degree! Who is the monster, child?'

'What monster?' inquired Paul.

'Glubb,' said Mrs Blimber, with a great disrelish.

'He's a no more a monster than you are,' returned Paul.

'What!' cried the Doctor, in a terrible voice. 'Aye, aye, aye? Aha! What's that?'

Paul was dreadfully frightened; but still he made a stand for the absent Glubb, though he did it trembling.

'He's a very nice old man, ma'am,' he said. 'He used to draw my couch. He knows all about the deep sea, and the fish that are in it, and the great monsters that come and lie on rocks in the sun, and dive into the water again when they're startled, blowing and splashing so, that they can be heard for miles. There are some creatures,' said Paul, warming with his subject, 'I don't know how many yards long, and I forget their names, but Florence knows, that pretend to be in distress; and when a man goes near them, out of compassion, they open their great jaws, and attack him. But all he has got to do,' said Paul, boldly tendering this information to the very Doctor himself, 'is to keep on turning as he runs away, and then, as they turn slowly, because they are so long, and can't bend, he's sure to beat them. And though old Glubb don't know why the sea should make me think of my mama that's dead, or what it is that it is always saying – always saying! he knows a great deal about it. And I wish,' the child concluded with a sudden falling of his countenance, and failing in his animation, as he looked like one forlorn, upon the three strange faces, 'that you'd let old Glubb come here to see me, for I know him very well, and he knows me.'

'Ha!' said the Doctor, shaking his head: 'this is bad, but study will do much.'

Mrs Blimber opined, with something like a shiver, that he was an unaccountable child; and, allowing for the difference of visage, looked at him pretty much as Mrs Pipchin had been used to do.

'Take him round the house, Cornelia,' said the Doctor, 'and familiarise him with his new sphere. Go with that young lady, Dombey.'

Dombey obeyed; giving his hand to the abstruse Cornelia, and looking at her sideways, with timid curiosity, as they went away together. For her spectacles, by reason of the glistening of the glasses, made her so mysterious, that he didn't know where she was looking, and was not indeed quite sure that she had any eyes at all behind them.

Cornelia took him first to the schoolroom, which was situated at the back of the hall, and was approached through two baize doors, which deadened and muffled the young gentlemen's voices. Here, there were eight young gentlemen in various stages of mental prostration, all very hard at work, and very grave indeed. Toots, as an old hand, had a desk to himself in one corner: and a magnificent man, of immense age, he looked, in Paul's young eyes, behind it.

Mr Feeder, B.A., who sat at another little desk, had his Virgil stop[1] on, and was slowly grinding that tune to four young gentlemen. Of the remaining four, two, who grasped their foreheads convulsively, were engaged in solving mathematical problems; one with his face like a dirty window, from much crying, was endeavouring to flounder through a hopeless number of lines before dinner; and one sat looking at his task in stony stupefaction and despair – which it seemed had been his condition ever since breakfast time.

The appearance of a new boy did not create the sensation that might have been expected. Mr Feeder, B.A. (who was in the habit of shaving his head for coolness, and had nothing but little bristles on it), gave him a bony hand, and told him he was glad to see him – which Paul would have been very glad to have told *him*, if he could have done so with the least sincerity. Then Paul, instructed by Cornelia, shook hands with the four young gentlemen at Mr Feeder's desk; then with the two young gentlemen at work on the problems, who were very feverish; then with the gentleman at work against time, who was very inky; and lastly with the young gentleman in a state of stupefaction, who was flabby and quite cold.

Paul having been already introduced to Toots, that pupil merely chuckled and breathed hard, as his custom was, and pursued the occupation in which he was engaged. It was not a severe one; for on account of his having 'gone through' so much (in more senses than one), and also of his having, as before hinted, left off blowing in his prime, Toots now had licence to pursue his own course of study: which was chiefly to write long letters to himself from persons of distinction, addressed 'P. Toots, Esquire, Brighton, Sussex,' and to preserve them in his desk with great care.

These ceremonies passed, Cornelia led Paul upstairs to the top of the house; which was rather a slow journey, on account of Paul being obliged to land both feet on every stair, before he mounted another. But they reached their journey's end at last; and there, in a front room, looking over the wild sea, Cornelia showed him a nice little bed with white hangings, close to the window, on which there was already beautifully written on a card in round text – down strokes very thick, and up strokes very fine – DOMBEY; while two other little bedsteads in the same room were announced through like means, as respectively appertaining unto BRIGGS and TOZER.

Just as they got downstairs again into the hall, Paul saw the weak-eyed young man who had given that mortal offence to Mrs Pipchin, suddenly seize a very large drumstick, and fly at a gong that was hanging up, as if he had gone mad, or wanted vengeance. Instead of receiving warning, however, or being instantly taken into custody, the young man left off unchecked, after having made a dreadful noise. Then Cornelia Blimber said to Dombey that dinner would be ready in a quarter of an hour, and perhaps he had better go into the school-room among his 'friends.'

So Dombey, deferentially passing the great clock which was still as anxious as ever to know how he found himself, opened the school-room door a very little way, and strayed in like a lost boy; shutting it after him with some difficulty. His friends were all dispersed about the room except the stony friend, who remained immoveable. Mr Feeder was stretching himself in his grey gown, as if, regardless of expense, he were resolved to pull the sleeves off.

'Heigh ho hum!' cried Mr Feeder, shaking himself like a cart-horse. 'Oh dear me, dear me! Ya-a-a-ah!'

Paul was quite alarmed by Mr Feeder's yawning; it was done on such a great scale, and he was so terribly in earnest. All the boys too (Toots excepted) seemed knocked up[2] and were getting ready for dinner – some newly tying their neck-cloths, which were very stiff indeed; and others washing their hands or brushing their hair, in an adjoining ante-chamber – as if they didn't think they should enjoy it at all.

Young Toots, who was ready beforehand, and had therefore nothing to do, and had leisure to bestow upon Paul, said, with heavy good nature:

'Sit down, Dombey.'

'Thank you, Sir,' said Paul.

His endeavouring to hoist himself on to a very high window-seat, and his slipping down again, appeared to prepare Toots's mind for the reception of a discovery.

'You're a very small chap,' said Mr Toots.

'Yes, Sir, I'm small,' returned Paul. 'Thank you, Sir.'

For Toots had lifted him into the seat, and done it kindly too.

'Who's your tailor?' inquired Toots, after looking at him for some moments.

'It's a woman that has made my clothes as yet,' said Paul. 'My sister's dressmaker.'

'My tailor's Burgess and Co.,' said Toots. 'Fash'nable. But very dear.'

Paul had wit enough to shake his head, as if he would have said it was easy to see *that*; and indeed he thought so.

'Your father's regularly rich, ain't he?' inquired Mr Toots.

'Yes, Sir,' said Paul. 'He's Dombey and Son.'

'And which?' demanded Toots.

'And Son, Sir,' replied Paul.

Mr Toots made one or two attempts, in a low voice, to fix the firm in his mind; but not quite succeeding, said he would get Paul to mention the name again to-morrow morning, as it was rather important. And indeed he purposed nothing less than writing himself a private and confidential letter from Dombey and Son immediately.

By this time the other pupils (always excepting the stony boy) gathered round. They were polite, but pale; and spoke low; and they were so depressed in their spirits, that in comparison with the general tone of that company, Master Bitherstone was a perfect Miller, or complete Jest Book.[3] And yet he had a sense of injury upon him, too, had Bitherstone.

'You sleep in my room, don't you?' asked a solemn young gentleman, whose shirt-collar curled up the lobes of his ears.

'Master Briggs?' inquired Paul.

'Tozer,' said the young gentleman.

Paul answered yes; and Tozer, pointing out the stony pupil, said that was Briggs. Paul had already felt certain that it must be either Briggs or Tozer, though he didn't know why.

'Is yours a strong constitution?' inquired Tozer.

Paul said he thought not. Tozer replied that *he* thought not also judging from Paul's looks, and that it was a pity, for it need be. He then asked Paul if he were going to begin with Cornelia; and on Paul saying 'yes,' all the young gentlemen (Briggs excepted) gave a low groan.

It was drowned in the tintinnabulation of the gong, which sounding again with great fury, there was a general move towards the dining-room; still excepting Briggs the stony boy, who remained where he was, and as he was; and on its way to whom Paul presently encountered a round of bread, genteelly served on a plate and napkin, and with a silver fork lying crosswise on the top of it.

Doctor Blimber was already in his place in the dining-room, at the top of the table, with Miss Blimber and Mrs Blimber on either side of him. Mr Feeder in a black coat was at the bottom. Paul's chair was next to Miss Blimber; but it being found, when he sat in it, that his eyebrows were not much above the level of the table-cloth, some books were brought in from the Doctor's study, on which he was elevated, and on which he always sat from that time – carrying them in and out himself on after occasions, like a little elephant and castle.[4]

Grace having been said by the Doctor, dinner began. There was some nice soup; also roast meat, boiled meat, vegetables, pie, and cheese. Every young gentleman had a massive silver fork, and a napkin; and all the arrangements were stately and handsome. In particular, there was a butler in a blue coat and bright buttons, who gave quite a winey flavour to the table beer; he poured it out so superbly.

Nobody spoke, unless spoken to, except Doctor Blimber, Mrs Blimber, and Miss Blimber, who conversed occasionally. Whenever a young gentleman was not actually engaged with his knife and fork or spoon, his eye, with an irresistible attraction, sought the eye of Doctor Blimber, Mrs Blimber, or Miss Blimber, and modestly rested there. Toots appeared to be the only exception to this rule. He sat next Mr Feeder on Paul's side of the table, and frequently looked behind and before the intervening boys to catch a glimpse of Paul.

Only once during dinner was there any conversation that included the young gentlemen. It happened at the epoch of the cheese, when the Doctor, having taken a glass of port wine, and hemmed twice or thrice, said:

'It is remarkable, Mr Feeder, that the Romans —'

At the mention of this terrible people, their implacable enemies, every young gentleman fastened his gaze upon the Doctor, with an assumption of the deepest interest. One of the number who happened to be drinking, and who caught the doctor's eye glaring at him through the side of his tumbler, left off so hastily that he was convulsed for some moments, and in the sequel ruined Doctor Blimber's point.

'It is remarkable, Mr Feeder,' said the Doctor, beginning again slowly, 'that the Romans, in those gorgeous and profuse entertainments of which we read in the days of the Emperors, when luxury had attained a height unknown before or since, and when whole provinces were ravaged to supply the splendid means of one Imperial Banquet —'

Here the offender, who had been swelling and straining, and waiting in vain for a full stop, broke out violently.

'Johnson,' said Mr Feeder, in a low reproachful voice, 'take some water.'

The Doctor, looking very stern, made a pause until the water was brought, and then resumed:

'And when, Mr Feeder —'

But Mr Feeder, who saw that Johnson must break out again, and who knew that the Doctor would never come to a period[5] before the young gentlemen until he had finished all he meant to say, couldn't keep his eye off Johnson; and thus was caught in the fact of not looking at the Doctor, who consequently stopped.

'I beg your pardon, Sir,' said Mr Feeder, reddening. 'I beg your pardon, Doctor Blimber.'

'And when,' said the Doctor, raising his voice, 'when, Sir, as we read, and have no reason to doubt — incredible as it may appear to the vulgar of our time — the brother of Vitellius[6] prepared for him a feast, in which were served, of fish, two thousand dishes —'

'Take some water, Johnson — dishes, Sir,' said Mr Feeder.

'Of various sorts of fowl, five thousand dishes.'

'Or try a crust of bread,' said Mr Feeder.

'And one dish,' pursued Doctor Blimber, raising his voice still higher as he looked all round the table, 'called, from its enormous dimensions, the Shield of Minerva, and made, among other costly ingredients, of the brains of pheasants —'

'Ow, ow, ow!' (from Johnson).

'Woodcocks—'

'Ow, ow, ow!'

'The sounds[7] of the fish called scari—'

'You'll burst some vessel in your head,' said Mr Feeder. 'You had better let it come.'

'And the spawn of the lamprey, brought from the Carpathian Sea,' pursued the Doctor, in his severest voice; 'when we read of costly entertainments such as these, and still remember, that we have a Titus—'

'What would be your mother's feelings if you died of apoplexy!' said Mr Feeder.

'A Domitian—'

'And you're blue, you know,' said Mr Feeder.

'A Nero, a Tiberius, a Caligula, a Heliogabalus,[8] and many more,' pursued the Doctor; 'it is, Mr Feeder – if you are doing me the honour to attend – remarkable: VERY – remarkable, Sir—'

But Johnson, unable to suppress it any longer, burst at that moment into such an overwhelming fit of coughing, that although both his immediate neighbours thumped him on the back, and Mr Feeder himself held a glass of water to his lips, and the butler walked him up and down several times between his own chair and the sideboard, like a sentry, it was full five minutes before he was moderately composed, and then there was a profound silence.

'Gentlemen,' said Doctor Blimber, 'rise for Grace! Cornelia, lift Dombey down' – nothing of whom but his scalp was accordingly seen above the table-cloth. 'Johnson will repeat to me to-morrow morning before breakfast, without book, and from the Greek Testament, the first chapter of the Epistle of Saint Paul to the Ephesians. We will resume our studies, Mr Feeder, in half-an-hour.'

The young gentlemen bowed and withdrew. Mr Feeder did likewise. During the half-hour, the young gentlemen, broken into pairs, loitered arm-in-arm up and down a small piece of ground behind the house, or endeavoured to kindle a spark of animation in the breast of Briggs. But nothing happened so vulgar as play. Punctually at the appointed time, the gong was sounded, and the studies, under the joint auspices of Doctor Blimber and Mr Feeder, were resumed.

As the Olympic game of lounging up and down had been cut shorter than usual that day, on Johnson's account, they all went out for a walk before tea. Even Briggs (though he hadn't begun yet) partook of this dissipation; in the enjoyment of which he looked

Doctor Blimber's Young Gentlemen as they appeared when enjoying themselves

over the cliff two or three times darkly. Doctor Blimber accompanied them; and Paul had the honour of being taken in tow by the Doctor himself: a distinguished state of things, in which he looked very little and feeble.

Tea was served in a style no less polite than the dinner; and after tea, the young gentlemen rising and bowing as before, withdrew to fetch up the unfinished tasks of that day, or to get up the already looming tasks of to-morrow. In the meantime Mr Feeder withdrew to his own room; and Paul sat in a corner wondering whether Florence was thinking of him, and what they were all about at Mrs Pipchin's.

Mr Toots, who had been detained by an important letter from the Duke of Wellington, found Paul out after a time; and having looked at him for a long while, as before, inquired if he was fond of waistcoats.

Paul said 'Yes, Sir.'

'So am I,' said Toots.

No word more spake Toots that night; but he stood looking at Paul as if he liked him; and as there was company in that, and Paul was not inclined to talk, it answered his purpose better than conversation.

At eight o'clock or so, the gong sounded again for prayers in the dining-room, where the butler afterwards presided over a side-table, on which bread and cheese and beer were spread for such young gentlemen as desired to partake of those refreshments. The ceremonies concluded by the Doctor's saying, 'Gentlemen, we will resume our studies at seven to-morrow'; and then, for the first time, Paul saw Cornelia Blimber's eye, and saw that it was upon him. When the Doctor had said these words, 'Gentlemen, we will resume our studies at seven to-morrow,' the pupils bowed again, and went to bed.

In the confidence of their own room upstairs, Briggs said his head ached ready to split, and that he should wish himself dead if it wasn't for his mother, and a blackbird he had at home. Tozer didn't say much, but he sighed a good deal, and told Paul to look out, for his turn would come to-morrow. After uttering those prophetic words, he undressed himself moodily, and got into bed. Briggs was in his bed too, and Paul in his bed too, before the weak-eyed young man appeared to take away the candle, when he wished them good night and pleasant dreams. But his benevolent wishes were in vain, as far as Briggs and Tozer were concerned: for Paul, who lay awake for a long while, and often woke afterwards, found that Briggs was ridden by his lesson as a nightmare: and that Tozer, whose mind was affected in his sleep by similar causes, in a minor degree, talked unknown tongues, or scraps of Greek and Latin – it was all one to Paul – which, in the silence of night, had an inexpressibly wicked and guilty effect.

Paul had sunk into a sweet sleep, and dreamed that he was walking hand in hand with Florence through beautiful gardens, when they came to a large sunflower which suddenly expanded itself into a gong, and began to sound. Opening his eyes, he found that it was a dark, windy morning, with a drizzling rain: and that the real gong was giving dreadful note of preparation,⁹ down in the hall.

So he got up directly, and found Briggs with hardly any eyes, for nightmare and grief had made his face puffy, putting his boots on: while Tozer stood shivering and rubbing his shoulders in a very bad humour. Poor Paul couldn't dress himself easily, not being used to it, and asked them if they would have the goodness to tie some strings for him; but as Briggs merely said 'Bother!' and Tozer, 'Oh yes!' he went down when he was otherwise ready, to the next story, where he saw a pretty young woman in leather gloves, cleaning a stove. The young woman seemed surprised at his appearance, and asked him where his mother was. When Paul told her she was dead, she took her gloves off, and did what he wanted; and furthermore rubbed his hands to warm them; and gave him a kiss; and told him whenever he wanted anything of that sort – meaning in the dressing way – to ask for 'Melia; which Paul, thanking her very much, said he certainly would. He then proceeded softly on his journey downstairs, towards the room in which the young gentlemen resumed their studies, when, passing by a door that stood ajar, a voice from within cried, 'Is that Dombey?' On Paul replying, 'Yes, ma'am': for he knew the voice to be Miss Blimber's: Miss Blimber said, 'Come in, Dombey.' And in he went.

Miss Blimber presented exactly the appearance she had presented yesterday, except that she wore a shawl. Her little light curls were as crisp as ever, and she had already her spectacles on, which made Paul wonder whether she went to bed in them. She had a cool little sitting-room of her own up there, with some books in it, and no fire. But Miss Blimber was never cold, and never sleepy.

'Now, Dombey,' said Miss Blimber, 'I am going out for a constitutional.'

Paul wondered what that was, and why she didn't send the footman out to get it in such unfavourable weather. But he made no observation on the subject: his attention being devoted to a little pile of new books on which Miss Blimber appeared to have been recently engaged.

'These are yours, Dombey,' said Miss Blimber.

'All of 'em, ma'am?' said Paul.

'Yes,' returned Miss Blimber; 'and Mr Feeder will look you out some more very soon, if you are as studious as I expect you will be, Dombey.'

'Thank you, ma'am,' said Paul.

'I am going out for a constitutional,' resumed Miss Blimber; 'and while I am gone, that is to say in the interval between this and breakfast, Dombey, I wish you to read over what I have marked in these books, and to tell me if you quite understand what you have got to learn. Don't lose time, Dombey, for you have none to spare, but take them downstairs, and begin directly.'

'Yes, ma'am,' answered Paul.

There were so many of them, that although Paul put one hand under the bottom book and his other hand and his chin on the top book, and hugged them all closely, the middle book slipped out before he reached the door, and then they all tumbled down on the floor. Miss Blimber said, 'Oh, Dombey, Dombey, this is really very careless!' and piled them up afresh for him; and this time, by dint of balancing them with great nicety, Paul got out of the room, and down a few stairs before two of them escaped again. But he held the rest so tight, that he only left one more on the first floor, and one in the passage; and when he had got the main body down into the schoolroom, he set off upstairs again to collect the stragglers. Having at last amassed the whole library, and climbed into his place, he fell to work, encouraged by a remark from Tozer to the effect that he 'was in for it now'; which was the only interruption he received till breakfast time. At that meal, for which he had no appetite, everything was quite as solemn and genteel as at the others; and when it was finished, he followed Miss Blimber upstairs.

'Now, Dombey,' said Miss Blimber. 'How have you got on with those books?'

They comprised a little English, and a deal of Latin – names of things, declensions of articles and substantives, exercises thereon, and preliminary rules – a trifle of orthography, a glance at ancient history, a wink or two at modern ditto, a few tables, two or three weights and measures, and a little general information. When poor Paul had spelt out number two, he found he had no idea of number one; fragments whereof afterwards obtruded themselves into number three, which slided into number four, which grafted itself on to number two. So that whether twenty Romuluses made a Remus, or hic hæc hoc was troy weight, or a verb always agreed with an ancient Briton, or three times four was Taurus a bull[10] were open questions with him.

'Oh, Dombey, Dombey!' said Miss Blimber, 'this is very shocking.'

'If you please,' said Paul, 'I think if I might sometimes talk a little to old Glubb, I should be able to do better.'

'Nonsense, Dombey,' said Miss Blimber. 'I couldn't hear of it. This is not the place for Glubbs of any kind. You must take the books down, I suppose, Dombey, one by one, and perfect yourself in the day's instalment of subject A; before you turn at all to subject B. And now take away the top book, if you please, Dombey, and return when you are master of the theme.'

Miss Blimber expressed her opinions on the subject of Paul's uninstructed state with a gloomy delight, as if she had expected this result, and were glad to find that they must be in constant communication. Paul withdrew with the top task, as he was told, and laboured away at it, down below; sometimes remembering every word of it, and sometimes forgetting it all, and everything else besides: until at last he ventured upstairs again to repeat the lesson, when it was nearly all driven out of his head before he began, by Miss Blimber's shutting up the book, and saying, 'Go on, Dombey!' a proceeding so suggestive of the knowledge inside of her, that Paul looked upon the young lady with consternation, as a kind of learned Guy Faux, or artificial Bogle,[11] stuffed full of scholastic straw.

He acquitted himself very well, nevertheless; and Miss Blimber commending him as giving promise of getting on fast, immediately provided him with subject B; from which he passed to C, and even D before dinner. It was hard work, resuming his studies, soon after dinner; and he felt giddy and confused and drowsy and dull. But all the other young gentlemen had similar sensations, and were obliged to resume their studies too, if there were any comfort in that. It was a wonder that the great clock in the hall, instead of being constant to its first inquiry, never said, 'Gentlemen, we will now resume our studies,' for that phrase was often enough repeated in its neighbourhood. The studies went round like a mighty wheel, and the young gentlemen were always stretched upon it.

After tea there were exercises again, and preparations for next day by candle-light. And in due course there was bed; where, but for that resumption of the studies which took place in dreams, were rest and sweet forgetfulness.

Oh Saturdays! Oh happy Saturdays, when Florence always came at noon, and never would, in any weather, stay away, though Mrs Pipchin snarled and growled, and worried her bitterly. Those Saturdays were Sabbaths[12] for at least two little Christians among all the Jews, and did the holy Sabbath work of strengthening and knitting up a brother's and a sister's love.

Not even Sunday nights – the heavy Sunday nights, whose shadow darkened the first waking burst of light on Sunday mornings – could mar those precious Saturdays. Whether it was the great sea-shore, where they sat, and strolled together; or whether it was only Mrs Pipchin's dull back room, in which she sang to him so softly, with his drowsy head upon her arm; Paul never cared. It was Florence. That was all he thought of. So, on Sunday nights, when the Doctor's dark door stood agape to swallow him up for another week, the time was come for taking leave of Florence; no one else.

Mrs Wickam had been drafted home to the house in town, and Miss Nipper, now a smart young woman, had come down. To many a single combat with Mrs Pipchin, did Miss Nipper gallantly devote herself; and if ever Mrs Pipchin in all her life had found her match, she had found it now. Miss Nipper threw away the scabbard[13] the first morning she arose in Mrs Pipchin's house. She asked and gave no quarter. She said it must be war, and war it was; and Mrs Pipchin lived from that time in the midst of surprises, harassings, and defiances, and skirmishing attacks that came bouncing in upon her from the passage, even in unguarded moments of chops, and carried desolation to her very toast.

Miss Nipper had returned one Sunday night with Florence, from walking back with Paul to the Doctor's, when Florence took from her bosom a little piece of paper, on which she had pencilled down some words.

'See here, Susan,' she said. 'These are the names of the little books that Paul brings home to do those long exercises with, when he is so tired. I copied them last night while he was writing.'

'Don't shew 'em to me, Miss Floy, if you please,' returned Nipper, 'I'd as soon see Mrs Pipchin.'

'I want you to buy them for me, Susan, if you will, to-morrow morning. I have money enough,' said Florence.

'Why, goodness gracious me, Miss Floy,' returned Miss Nipper, 'how can you talk like that, when you have books upon books already, and masterses and missesses a teaching of you everything continual, though my belief is that your pa, Miss Dombey, never would have learnt you nothing, never would have thought of it, unless you'd asked him – when he couldn't well refuse; but giving consent when asked, and offering when unasked, Miss, is quite two things: I may not have my objections to a young man's keeping company with me, and when he puts the question, may say "yes," but that's not saying "would you be so kind as like me."'

'But you can buy me the books, Susan; and you will, when you know I want them.'

'Well, Miss, and why do you want 'em?' replied Nipper; adding, in a lower voice, 'If it was to fling at Mrs Pipchin's head, I'd buy a cart-load.'

'I think I could perhaps give Paul some help, Susan, if I had these books,' said Florence, 'and make the coming week a little easier to him. At least I want to try. So buy them for me, dear, and I will never forget how kind it was of you to do it!'

It must have been a harder heart than Susan Nipper's that could have rejected the little purse Florence held out with these words, or the gentle look of entreaty with which she seconded her petition. Susan put the purse in her pocket without reply, and trotted out at once upon her errand.

The books were not easy to procure: and the answer at several shops was, either that they were just out of them, or that they never kept them, or that they had had a great many last month, or that they expected a great many next week. But Susan was not easily baffled in such an enterprise; and having entrapped a white-haired youth, in a black calico apron, from a library where she was known, to accompany her in her quest, she led him such a life in going up and down, that he exerted himself to the utmost, if it were only to get rid of her; and finally enabled her to return home in triumph.

With these treasures then, after her own daily lessons were over, Florence sat down at night to track Paul's footsteps through the thorny ways of learning; and being possessed of a naturally quick and sound capacity, and taught by that most wonderful of masters, love, it was not long before she gained upon Paul's heels, and caught and passed him.

Not a word of this was breathed to Mrs Pipchin: but many a night when they were all in bed, and when Miss Nipper, with her hair in papers and herself asleep in some uncomfortable attitude, reposed unconscious by her side; and when the chinking ashes in the grate were cold and grey; and when the candles were burnt down and guttering out; – Florence tried so hard to be a substitute for one small Dombey, that her fortitude and perseverance might have almost won her a free right to bear the name herself.

And high was her reward, when one Saturday evening, as little Paul was sitting down as usual to 'resume his studies,' she sat down by his side, and showed him all that was so rough, made smooth, and all that was so dark, made clear and plain, before him. It was nothing but a startled look in Paul's wan face – a flush – a smile – and then a close embrace – but God knows how her heart leapt up at this rich payment for her trouble.

'Oh, Floy!' cried her brother, 'how I love you! How I love you, Floy!'

'And I you, dear!'

'Oh! I am sure of that, Floy.'

He said no more about it, but all that evening sat close by her, very quiet; and in the night he called out from his little room within hers, three or four times, that he loved her.

Regularly, after that, Florence was prepared to sit down with Paul on Saturday night, and patiently assist him through so much as they could anticipate together, of his next week's work. The cheering thought that he was labouring on where Florence had just toiled before him, would, of itself, have been a stimulant to Paul in the perpetual resumption of his studies; but coupled with the actual lightening of his load, consequent on this assistance, it saved him, possibly, from sinking underneath the burden which the fair Cornelia Blimber piled upon his back.

It was not that Miss Blimber meant to be too hard upon him, or that Doctor Blimber meant to bear too heavily on the young gentlemen in general. Cornelia merely held the faith in which she had been bred; and the Doctor, in some partial confusion of his ideas, regarded the young gentlemen as if they were all Doctors, and were born grown up. Comforted by the applause of the young gentlemen's nearest relations, and urged on by their blind vanity and ill-considered haste, it would have been strange if Doctor Blimber had discovered his mistake, or trimmed his swelling sails to any other tack.

Thus in the case of Paul. When Doctor Blimber said he made great progress, and was naturally clever, Mr Dombey was more bent than ever on his being forced and crammed. In the case of Briggs, when Doctor Blimber reported that he did not make great progress yet, and was not naturally clever, Briggs senior was inexorable in the same purpose. In short, however high and false the temperature at which the Doctor kept his hothouse, the owners

Paul's exercises

of the plants were always ready to lend a helping hand at the bellows, and to stir the fire.

Such spirits as he had in the outset, Paul soon lost of course. But he retained all that was strange, and old, and thoughtful in his character: and under circumstances so favourable to the development of those tendencies, became even more strange, and old, and thoughtful, than before.

The only difference was, that he kept his character to himself. He grew more thoughtful and reserved, every day; and had no such curiosity in any living member of the Doctor's household, as he had had in Mrs Pipchin. He loved to be alone; and in those short intervals when he was not occupied with his books, liked nothing so well as wandering about the house by himself, or sitting on the stairs, listening to the great clock in the hall. He was intimate with all the paper-hanging in the house; saw things that no one else saw in the patterns; found out miniature tigers and lions running up the bedroom walls, and squinting faces leering in the squares and diamonds of the floor-cloth.

The solitary child lived on, surrounded by this arabesque work of his musing fancy, and no one understood him. Mrs Blimber thought him 'odd,' and sometimes the servants said among themselves that little Dombey 'moped'; but that was all.

Unless young Toots had some idea on the subject, to the expression of which he was wholly unequal. Ideas, like ghosts (according to the common notion of ghosts), must be spoken to a little before they will explain themselves; and Toots had long left off asking any questions of his own mind. Some mist there may have been, issuing from that leaden casket, his cranium, which, if it could have taken shape and form, would have become a genie; but it could not; and it only so far followed the example of the smoke in the Arabian story,[14] as to roll out in a thick cloud, and there hang and hover. But it left a little figure visible upon a lonely shore, and Toots was always staring at it.

'How are you?' he would say to Paul, fifty times a day.

'Quite well, Sir, thank you,' Paul would answer.

'Shake hands,' would be Toots's next advance.

Which Paul, of course, would immediately do. Mr Toots generally said again, after a long interval of staring and hard breathing, 'How are you?' To which Paul again replied, 'Quite well, Sir, thank you.'

One evening Mr Toots was sitting at his desk, oppressed by correspondence, when a great purpose seemed to flash upon him.

He laid down his pen, and went off to seek Paul, whom he found at last, after a long search, looking through the window of his little bedroom.

'I say!' cried Toots, speaking the moment he entered the room, lest he should forget it; 'what do you think about?'

'Oh! I think about a great many things,' replied Paul.

'Do you, though?' said Toots, appearing to consider that fact in itself surprising.

'If you had to die,' said Paul, looking up into his face—

Mr Toots started, and seemed much disturbed.

'—Don't you think you would rather die on a moonlight night when the sky was quite clear, and the wind blowing, as it did last night?'

Mr Toots said, looking doubtfully at Paul, and shaking his head, that he didn't know about that.

'Not blowing, at least,' said Paul, 'but sounding in the air like the sea sounds in the shells. It was a beautiful night. When I had listened to the water for a long time, I got up and looked out. There was a boat over there, in the full light of the moon; a boat with a sail.'

The child looked at him so steadfastly, and spoke so earnestly, that Mr Toots, feeling himself called upon to say something about this boat, said, 'Smugglers.' But with an impartial remembrance of there being two sides to every question, he added, 'or Preventive.'[15]

'A boat with a sail,' repeated Paul, 'in the full light of the moon. The sail like an arm, all silver. It went away into the distance, and what do you think it seemed to do as it moved with the waves?'

'Pitch,' said Mr Toots.

'It seemed to beckon,' said the child, 'to beckon me to come! – There she is! There she is!'

Toots was almost beside himself with dismay at this sudden exclamation, after what had gone before, and cried 'Who?'

'My sister Florence!' cried Paul, 'looking up here, and waving her hand. She sees me – she sees me! Good night, dear, good night, good night.'

His quick transition to a state of unbounded pleasure, as he stood at his window, kissing and clapping his hands: and the way in which the light retreated from his features as she passed out of his view, and left a patient melancholy on the little face: were too remarkable wholly to escape even Toots's notice.

Their interview being interrupted at this moment by a visit from Mrs Pipchin, who usually brought her black skirts to bear upon

Paul just before dusk, once or twice a week, Toots had no opportunity of improving the occasion; but it left so marked an impression on his mind that he twice returned, after having exchanged the usual salutations, to ask Mrs Pipchin how she did. This the irascible old lady conceived to be a deeply-devised and long-meditated insult, originating in the diabolical invention of the weak-eyed young man downstairs, against whom she accordingly lodged a formal complaint with Doctor Blimber that very night; who mentioned to the young man that if he ever did it again, he should be obliged to part with him.

The evenings being longer now, Paul stole up to his window every evening to look out for Florence. She always passed and repassed at a certain time, until she saw him; and their mutual recognition was a gleam of sunshine in Paul's daily life. Often after dark, one other figure walked alone before the Doctor's house. He rarely joined them on the Saturday now. He could not bear it. He would rather come unrecognised, and look up at the windows where his son was qualifying for a man; and wait, and watch, and plan, and hope.

Oh! could he but have seen, or seen as others did, the slight spare boy above, watching the waves and clouds at twilight, with his earnest eyes, and breasting the window of his solitary cage when birds flew by, as if he would have emulated them, and soared away!

CHAPTER 13

Shipping Intelligence and Office Business

Mr Dombey's offices were in a court where there was an old-established stall of choice fruit at the corner: where perambulating merchants, of both sexes, offered for sale at any time between the hours of ten and five, slippers, pocket-books, sponges, dogs' collars, and Windsor soap, and sometimes a pointer or an oil-painting.

The pointer always came that way, with a view to the Stock Exchange, where a sporting taste (originating generally in bets of new hats) is much in vogue. The other commodities were addressed to the general public; but they were never offered by the vendors to Mr Dombey. When he appeared, the dealers in those wares fell off respectfully. The principal slipper and dogs' collar man – who considered himself a public character, and whose portrait was screwed on to an artist's door in Cheapside – threw up his forefinger to the brim of his hat as Mr Dombey went by. The ticket-porter,[1] if he were not absent on a job, always ran officiously before to open Mr Dombey's office door as wide as possible, and hold it open, with his hat off, while he entered.

The clerks within were not a whit behindhand in their demonstrations of respect. A solemn hush prevailed, as Mr Dombey passed through the outer office. The wit of the Counting-House became in a moment as mute, as the row of leathern fire-buckets hanging up behind him. Such vapid and flat daylight as filtered through the ground-glass windows and skylights, leaving a black sediment upon the panes, showed the books and papers, and the figures bending over them, enveloped in a studious gloom, and as much abstracted in appearance, from the world without, as if they were assembled at the bottom of the sea; while a mouldy little strong room in the obscure perspective, where a shady lamp was always burning, might have represented the cavern of some ocean-monster, looking on with a red eye at these mysteries of the deep.

When Perch the messenger, whose place was on a little bracket like a timepiece, saw Mr Dombey come in – or rather when he felt that he was coming, for he had usually an instinctive sense of his approach – he hurried into Mr Dombey's room, stirred the fire, quarried fresh coals from the bowels of the coal-box, hung the newspaper to air[2] upon the fender, put the chair ready, and the screen in its place, and was round upon his heel on the instant of Mr Dombey's entrance, to take his great-coat and hat, and hang them up. Then Perch took the newspaper, and gave it a turn or two in his hands before the fire, and laid it, deferentially, at Mr Dombey's elbow. And so little objection had Perch to doing deferential in the last degree, that if he might have laid himself at Mr Dombey's feet, or might have called him by some such title as used to be bestowed upon the Caliph Haroun Alraschid,[3] he would have been all the better pleased.

As this honour would have been an innovation and an experiment, Perch was fain to content himself by expressing as well as he could, in his manner, You are the light of my Eyes. You are the Breath of my Soul. You are the commander of the Faithful Perch! With this imperfect happiness to cheer him, he would shut the door softly, walk away on tiptoe, and leave his great chief to be stared at, through a dome-shaped window in the leads, by ugly chimney-pots and backs of houses, and especially by the bold window of a hair-cutting saloon on a first floor, where a waxen effigy, bald as a

Mussulman[4] in the morning, and covered after eleven o'clock in the day, with luxuriant hair and whiskers in the latest Christian fashion, showed him the wrong side of its head for ever.

Between Mr Dombey and the common world, as it was accessible through the medium of the outer office – to which Mr Dombey's presence in his own room may be said to have struck like damp, or cold air – there were two degrees of descent. Mr Carker in his own office was the first step; Mr Morfin, in *his* own office, was the second. Each of these gentlemen occupied a little chamber like a bath-room, opening from the passage outside Mr Dombey's door. Mr Carker, as Grand Vizier, inhabited the room that was nearest to the Sultan. Mr Morfin, as an officer of inferior state, inhabited the room that was nearest to the clerks.

The gentleman last mentioned was a cheerful-looking, hazel-eyed elderly bachelor: gravely attired, as to his upper man, in black; and as to his legs, in pepper and salt colour. His dark hair was just touched here and there with specks of grey, as though the tread of Time had splashed it; and his whiskers were already white. He had a mighty respect for Mr Dombey, and rendered him due homage; but as he was of a genial temper himself, and never wholly at his ease in that stately presence, he was disquieted by no jealousy of the many conferences enjoyed by Mr Carker, and felt a secret satisfaction in having duties to discharge, which rarely exposed him to be singled out for such distinction. He was a great musical amateur in his way – after business; and had a paternal affection for his violoncello, which was once in every week transported from Islington, his place of abode, to a certain club-room hard by the Bank, where quartettes of the most tormenting and excruciating nature were executed every Wednesday evening by a private party.

Mr Carker was a gentleman thirty-eight or forty years old, of a florid complexion, and with two unbroken rows of glistening teeth, whose regularity and whiteness were quite distressing. It was impossible to escape the observation of them, for he showed them whenever he spoke; and bore so wide a smile upon his countenance (a smile, however, very rarely, indeed, extending beyond his mouth), that there was something in it like the snarl of a cat. He affected a stiff white cravat, after the example of his principal, and was always closely buttoned up and tightly dressed. His manner towards Mr Dombey was deeply conceived and perfectly expressed. He was familiar with him, in the very extremity of his sense of the distance between them. 'Mr Dombey, to a man in your position from a man in mine, there is no show of subservience compatible with the transaction of business between us, that I should think sufficient. I frankly tell you, Sir, I give it up altogether. I feel that I could not satisfy my own mind; and Heaven knows, Mr Dombey, you can afford to dispense with the endeavour.' If he had carried these words about with him, printed on a placard, and had constantly offered it to Mr Dombey's perusal on the breast of his coat, he could not have been more explicit than he was.

This was Carker the Manager. Mr Carker the Junior, Walter's friend, was his brother; two or three years older than he, but widely removed in station. The younger brother's post was on the top of the official ladder; the elder brother's at the bottom. The elder brother never gained a stave[5] or raised his foot to mount one. Young men passed above his head, and rose and rose; but he was always at the bottom. He was quite resigned to occupy that low condition: never complained of it: and certainly never hoped to escape from it.

'How do you do this morning?' said Mr Carker the Manager, entering Mr Dombey's room soon after his arrival one day: with a bundle of papers in his hand.

'How do you do, Carker?' said Mr Dombey, rising from his chair, and standing with his back to the fire. 'Have you anything there for me?'

'I don't know that I need trouble you,' returned Carker, turning over the papers in his hand. 'You have a committee to-day at three, you know.'

'And one at three, three-quarters,' added Mr Dombey.

'Catch you forgetting anything!' exclaimed Carker, still turning over his papers. 'If Mr Paul inherits your memory, he'll be a troublesome customer in the house. One of you is enough.'

'You have an accurate memory of your own,' said Mr Dombey.

'Oh! I!' returned the manager. 'It's the only capital of a man like me.'

Mr Dombey did not look less pompous or at all displeased, as he stood leaning against the chimneypiece, surveying his (of course unconscious) clerk, from head to foot. The stiffness and nicety of Mr Carker's dress, and a certain arrogance of manner, either natural to him or imitated from a pattern not far off, gave great additional effect to his humility. He seemed a man who would contend against the power that vanquished him, if he could, but who was utterly borne down by the greatness and superiority of Mr Dombey.

'Is Morfin here?' asked Mr Dombey after a short pause, during which Mr Carker had been fluttering his papers, and muttering little abstracts of their contents to himself.

'Morfin's here,' he answered, looking up with his widest and most sudden smile; 'humming musical recollections – of his last night's quartette party, I suppose – through the walls between us and driving me half mad. I wish he'd make a bonfire of his violoncello, and burn his music-books in it.'

'You respect nobody, Carker, I think,' said Mr Dombey.

'No?' inquired Carker, with another wide and most feline show of his teeth. 'Well! Not many people, I believe. I wouldn't answer perhaps,' he murmured, as if he were only thinking it, 'for more than one.'

A dangerous quality, if real; and a not less dangerous one, if feigned. But Mr Dombey hardly seemed to think so, as he still stood with his back to the fire, drawn up to his full height, and looking at his head-clerk with a dignified composure, in which there seemed to lurk a stronger latent sense of power than usual.

'Talking of Morfin,' resumed Mr Carker, taking out one paper from the rest, 'he reports a junior dead in the agency at Barbados, and proposes to reserve a passage in the Son and Heir – she'll sail in a month or so – for the successor. You don't care who goes, I suppose? We have nobody of that sort here.'

Mr Dombey shook his head with supreme indifference.

'It's no very precious appointment,' observed Mr Carker, taking up a pen, with which to endorse a memorandum on the back of the paper. 'I hope he may bestow it on some orphan nephew of a musical friend. It may perhaps stop *his* fiddle-playing, if he has a gift that way. Who's that? Come in!'

'I beg your pardon, Mr Carker. I didn't know you were here, Sir,' answered Walter, appearing with some letters in his hand, unopened, and newly arrived. 'Mr Carker the Junior, Sir—'

At the mention of this name, Mr Carker the Manager was, or affected to be, touched to the quick with shame and humiliation. He cast his eyes full on Mr Dombey with an altered and apologetic look, abased them on the ground, and remained for a moment without speaking.

'I thought, Sir,' he said suddenly and angrily, turning on Walter, 'that you had been before requested not to drag Mr Carker the Junior into your conversation.'

'I beg your pardon,' returned Walter. 'I was only going to say that Mr Carker the Junior had told me he believed you were gone out, or I should not have knocked at the door when you were engaged with Mr Dombey. These are letters for Mr Dombey, Sir.'

'Very well, Sir,' returned Mr Carker the Manager, plucking them sharply from his hand. 'Go about your business.'

But in taking them with so little ceremony, Mr Carker dropped one on the floor, and did not see what he had done; neither did Mr Dombey observe the letter lying near his feet. Walter hesitated for a moment, thinking that one or other of them would notice it; but finding that neither did, he stopped, came back, picked it up, and laid it himself on Mr Dombey's desk. The letters were post-letters,' and it happened that the one in question was Mrs Pipchin's regular report, directed as usual – for Mrs Pipchin was but an indifferent penwoman – by Florence. Mr Dombey, having his attention silently called to this letter by Walter, started, and looked fiercely at him, as if he believed that he had purposely selected it from all the rest.

'You can leave the room, Sir!' said Mr Dombey, haughtily.

He crushed the letter in his hand; and having watched Walter out at the door, put it in his pocket without breaking the seal.

'You want somebody to send to the West Indies, you were saying,' observed Mr Dombey, hurriedly.

'Yes,' replied Carker.

'Send young Gay.'

'Good, very good indeed. Nothing easier,' said Mr Carker, without any show of surprise, and taking up the pen to re-endorse the letter, as coolly as he had done before. '"Send young Gay."'

'Call him back,' said Mr Dombey.

Mr Carker was quick to do so, and Walter was quick to return.

'Gay,' said Mr Dombey, turning a little to look at him over his shoulder. 'Here is a—'

'An opening,' said Mr Carker, with his mouth stretched to the utmost.

'In the West Indies. At Barbados. I am going to send you,' said Mr Dombey, scorning to embellish the bare truth, 'to fill a junior situation in the counting-house at Barbados. Let your uncle know from me, that I have chosen you to go to the West Indies.'

Walter's breath was so completely taken away by his astonishment, that he could hardly find enough for the repetition of the words 'West Indies.'

'Somebody must go,' said Mr Dombey, 'and you are young and healthy, and your uncle's circumstances are not good. Tell your uncle that you are appointed. You will not go yet. There will be an interval of a month – or two perhaps.'

'Shall I remain there, Sir?' inquired Walter.

'Will you remain there, Sir!' repeated Mr Dombey, turning a little more round towards him. 'What do you mean? What does he mean, Carker?'

'Live there, Sir,' faltered Walter.

'Certainly,' returned Mr Dombey.

Walter bowed.

'That's all,' said Mr Dombey, resuming his letters. 'You will explain to him in good time about the usual outfit and so forth, Carker, of course. He needn't wait, Carker.'

'You needn't wait, Gay,' observed Mr Carker: bare to the gums.

'Unless,' said Mr Dombey, stopping in his reading without looking off the letter, and seeming to listen. 'Unless he has anything to say.'

'No, Sir,' returned Walter, agitated and confused, and almost stunned, as an infinite variety of pictures presented themselves to his mind; among which Captain Cuttle, in his glazed hat, transfixed with astonishment at Mrs MacStinger's, and his uncle bemoaning his loss in the little back parlour, held prominent places. 'I hardly know – I – I am much obliged, Sir.'

'He needn't wait, Carker,' said Mr Dombey.

And as Mr Carker again echoed the words, and also collected his papers as if he were going away too, Walter felt that his lingering any longer would be an unpardonable intrusion – especially as he had nothing to say – and therefore walked out quite confounded.

Going along the passage, with the mingled consciousness and helplessness of a dream, he heard Mr Dombey's door shut again, as Mr Carker came out: and immediately afterwards that gentleman called to him.

'Bring your friend Mr Carker the Junior to my room, Sir, if you please.'

Walter went to the outer office and apprised Mr Carker the Junior of his errand, who accordingly came out from behind a partition where he sat alone in one corner, and returned with him to the room of Mr Carker the Manager.

That gentleman was standing with his back to the fire, and his hands under his coat-tails, looking over his white cravat as unpromisingly as Mr Dombey himself could have looked. He received them without any change in his attitude or softening of his harsh and black expression: merely signing to Walter to close the door.

'John Carker,' said the Manager, when this was done, turning suddenly upon his brother, with his two rows of teeth bristling as if he would have bitten him, 'what is the league between you and this young man, in virtue of which I am haunted and hunted by the mention of your name? Is it not enough for you, John Carker, that I am your near relation, and can't detach myself from that—'

'Say disgrace, James,' interposed the other in a low voice, finding that he stammered for a word. 'You mean it, and have reason, say disgrace.'

'From that disgrace,' assented his brother with keen emphasis, 'but is the fact to be blurted out and trumpeted, and proclaimed continually in the presence of the very House! In moments of confidence too? Do you think your name is calculated to harmonise in this place with trust and confidence, John Carker?'

'No,' returned the other. 'No, James. God knows I have no such thought.'

'What is your thought, then?' said his brother, 'and why do you thrust yourself in my way? Haven't you injured me enough already?'

'I have never injured you, James, wilfully.'

'You are my brother,' said the Manager. 'That's injury enough.'

'I wish I could undo it, James.'

'I wish you could and would.'

During this conversation, Walter had looked from one brother to the other, with pain and amazement. He who was the Senior in years, and Junior in the house, stood, with his eyes cast upon the ground, and his head bowed, humbly listening to the reproaches of the other. Though these were rendered very bitter by the tone and look with which they were accompanied, and by the presence of Walter whom they so much surprised and shocked, he entered no other protest against them than by slightly raising his right hand in a deprecatory manner, as if he would have said, 'Spare me!' So, had they been blows, and he a brave man, under strong constraint, and weakened by bodily suffering, he might have stood before the executioner.

Generous and quick in all his emotions, and regarding himself as the innocent occasion of these taunts Walter now struck in, with all the earnestness he felt.

'Mr Carker,' he said, addressing himself to the Manager. 'Indeed, indeed, this is my fault solely. In a kind of heedlessness, for which I cannot blame myself enough, I have, I have no doubt, mentioned Mr Carker the Junior much oftener than was necessary; and have allowed his name sometimes to slip through my lips, when it was against your express wish. But it has been my own mistake, Sir. We have never exchanged one word upon the subject – very few, indeed, on any subject. And it has not been,' added Walter, after a moment's pause, 'all heedlessness on my part, Sir; for I have felt an interest in Mr Carker ever since I have been here, and have hardly been able to help speaking of him sometimes, when I have thought of him so much!'

Walter said this from his soul, and with the very breath of honour. For he looked upon the bowed head, and the downcast eyes, and upraised hand, and thought, 'I have felt it; and why should I not avow it in behalf of this unfriended, broken man!'

'In truth, you have avoided me, Mr Carker,' said Walter, with the tears rising to his eyes; so true was his compassion. 'I know it, to my disappointment and regret. When I first came here, and ever since, I am sure I have tried to be as much your friend, as one of my age could presume to be; but it has been of no use.'

'And observe,' said the Manager, taking him up quickly, 'it will be of still less use, Gay, if you persist in forcing Mr John Carker's name on people's attention. That is not the way to befriend Mr John Carker. Ask him if he thinks it is.'

'It is no service to me,' said the brother. 'It only leads to such a conversation as the present, which I need not say I could have well spared. No one can be a better friend to me:' he spoke here very distinctly, as if he would impress it upon Walter: 'than in forgetting me, and leaving me to go my way, unquestioned and unnoticed.'

'Your memory not being retentive, Gay, of what you are told by others,' said Mr Carker the Manager, warming himself with great and increased satisfaction, 'I thought it well that you should be told this from the best authority,' nodding towards his brother. 'You are not likely to forget it now, I hope. That's all; Gay. You can go.'

Walter passed out of the door, and was about to close it after him, when, hearing the voice of the brothers again, and also the mention of his own name, he stood irresolutely, with his hand upon the lock, and the door ajar, uncertain whether to return or go away. In this position he could not help overhearing what followed.

'Think of me more leniently, if you can, James,' said John Carker, 'when I tell you I have had – how could I help having, with my history, written here' – striking himself upon the breast – 'my whole heart awakened by my observation of that boy, Walter Gay. I saw in him when he first came here, almost my other self.'

'Your other self!' repeated the Manager, disdainfully.

'Not as I am, but as I was when I first came here too; as sanguine, giddy, youthful, inexperienced; flushed with the same restless and adventurous fancies; and full of the same qualities, fraught with the same capacity of leading on to good or evil.'

'I hope not,' said his brother, with some hidden and sarcastic meaning in his tone.

'You strike me sharply; and your hand is steady, and your thrust is very deep,' returned the other, speaking (or so Walter thought) as if some cruel weapon actually stabbed him as he spoke. 'I imagined all this when he was a boy. I believed it. It was a truth to me. I saw him lightly walking on the edge of an unseen gulf where so many others walk with equal gaiety, and from which—'

'The old excuse,' interrupted his brother, as he stirred the fire. 'So many. Go on. Say, so many fall.'

'From which ONE traveller fell,' returned the other, 'who set forward, on his way, a boy like him, and missed his footing more and more, and slipped a little and a little lower, and went on stumbling still, until he fell headlong and found himself below a shattered man. Think what I suffered, when I watched that boy.'

'You have only yourself to thank for it,' returned the brother.

'Only myself,' he assented with a sigh. '*I* don't seek to divide the blame or shame.'

'You *have* divided the shame,' James Carker muttered through his teeth. And through so many and such close teeth, he could mutter well.

'Ah, James,' returned his brother, speaking for the first time in an accent of reproach, and seeming, by the sound of his voice, to have covered his face with his hands, 'I have been, since then, a useful foil to you. You have trodden on me freely in your climbing up. Don't spurn me with your heel!'

A silence ensued. After a time, Mr Carker the Manager was heard rustling among his papers, as if he had resolved to bring the interview to a conclusion. At the same time his brother withdrew nearer to the door.

'That's all,' he said. 'I watched him with such trembling and such fear, as was some little punishment to me, until he passed the place where I first fell; and then, though I had been his father, I believe I never could have thanked God more devoutly. I didn't dare to warn him, and advise him; but if I had seen direct cause, I would have shown him my example. I was afraid to be seen speaking with him, lest it should be thought I did him harm, and tempted him to evil, and corrupted him: or lest I really should. There may be such contagion in me; I don't know. Piece out my history, in connexion with young Walter Gay, and what he has made me feel; and think of me more leniently, James, if you can.'

With these words he came out to where Walter was standing. He turned a little paler when he saw him there, and paler yet when Walter caught him by the hand, and said in a whisper:

'Mr Carker, pray let me thank you! Let me say how much I feel for you! How sorry I am, to have been the unhappy cause of all this! How I almost look upon you now as my protector and guardian! How very, very much, I feel obliged to you and pity you!' said Walter, squeezing both his hands, and hardly knowing, in his agitation, what he did or said.

Mr Morfin's room being close at hand and empty, and the door wide open, they moved thither by one accord: the passage being seldom free from some one passing to or fro. When they were there, and Walter saw in Mr Carker's face some traces of the emotion within, he almost felt as if he had never seen the face before; it was so greatly changed.

'Walter,' he said, laying his hand on his shoulder. 'I am far removed from you, and may I ever be. Do you know what I am?'

'What you are!' appeared to hang on Walter's lips, as he regarded him attentively.

'It was begun,' said Carker, 'before my twenty-first birthday – led up to, long before, but not begun till near that time. I had robbed them when I came of age. I robbed them afterwards. Before my twenty-second birthday, it was all found out; and then, Walter, from all men's society, I died.'

Again his last few words hung trembling upon Walter's lips, but he could neither utter them, nor any of his own.

'The House was very good to me. May Heaven reward the old man for his forbearance! This one, too, his son, who was then newly in the firm, where I had held great trust! I was called into that room which is now his – I have never entered it since – and came out, what you know me. For many years I sat in my present seat, alone as now, but then a known and recognised example to the rest. They were all merciful to me, and I lived. Time has altered that part of my poor expiation; and I think, except the three heads of the House, there is no one here who knows my story rightly. Before the little boy grows up, and has it told to him, my corner may be vacant. I would rather that it might be so! This is the only change to me since that day, when I left all youth, and hope, and good men's company, behind me in that room. God bless you,

Walter! Keep you, and all dear to you, in honesty, or strike them dead!'

Some recollection of his trembling from head to foot, as if with excessive cold, and of his bursting into tears, was all that Walter could add to this, when he tried to recall exactly what had passed between them.

When Walter saw him next, he was bending over his desk in his old silent, drooping, humbled way. Then, observing him at his work, and feeling how resolved he evidently was that no further intercourse should arise between them, and thinking again and again on all he had seen and heard that morning in so short a time, in connexion with the history of both the Carkers, Walter could hardly believe that he was under orders for the West Indies, and would soon be lost to Uncle Sol, and Captain Cuttle, and to glimpses few and far between of Florence Dombey – no, he meant Paul – and to all he loved, and liked, and looked for, in his daily life.

But it was true, and the news had already penetrated to the outer office; for while he sat with a heavy heart, pondering on these things, and resting his head upon his arm, Perch the messenger, descending from his mahogany bracket, and jogging his elbow, begged his pardon, but wished to say in his ear, Did he think he could arrange to send home to England a jar of preserved Ginger, cheap, for Mrs Perch's own eating, in the course of her recovery from her next confinement?

CHAPTER 14

Paul grows more and more Old-fashioned, and goes Home for the Holidays

When the Midsummer vacation approached, no indecent manifestations of joy were exhibited by the leaden-eyed young gentlemen assembled at Doctor Blimber's. Any such violent expression as 'breaking up,' would have been quite inapplicable to that polite establishment. The young gentlemen oozed away, semi-annually, to their own homes; but they never broke up. They would have scorned the action.

Tozer, who was constantly galled and tormented by a starched white cambric neckerchief, which he wore at the express desire of

Mrs Tozer, his parent, who, designing him for the Church, was of opinion that he couldn't be in that forward state of preparation too soon – Tozer said, indeed, that choosing between two evils, he thought he would rather stay where he was, than go home. However inconsistent this declaration might appear with that passage in Tozer's Essay on the subject, wherein he had observed 'that the thoughts of home and all its recollections awakened in his mind the most pleasing emotions of anticipation and delight,' and had also likened himself to a Roman General, flushed with a recent victory over the Iceni, or laden with Carthaginian spoil, advancing within a few hours' march of the Capitol, pre-supposed, for the purposes of the simile, to be the dwelling-place of Mrs Tozer, still it was very sincerely made. For it seemed that Tozer had a dreadful uncle, who not only volunteered examinations of him, in the holidays, on abstruse points, but twisted innocent events and things, and wrenched them to the same fell purpose. So that if this uncle took him to the Play, or, on a similar pretence of kindness, carried him to see a Giant, or a Dwarf, or a Conjurer, or anything, Tozer knew he had read up some classical allusion to the subject beforehand, and was thrown into a state of mortal apprehension: not foreseeing where he might break out, or what authority he might not quote against him.

As to Briggs, *his* father made no show of artifice about it. He never would leave him alone. So numerous and severe were the mental trials of that unfortunate youth in vacation time, that the friends of the family (then resident near Bayswater, London) seldom approached the ornamental piece of water in Kensington Gardens, without a vague expectation of seeing Master Briggs's hat floating on the surface, and an unfinished exercise lying on the bank. Briggs, therefore, was not at all sanguine on the subject of holidays; and these two sharers of little Paul's bedroom were so fair a sample of the young gentlemen in general, that the most elastic among them contemplated the arrival of those festive periods with genteel resignation.

It was far otherwise with little Paul. The end of these first holidays was to witness his separation from Florence, but who ever looked forward to the end of the holidays whose beginning was not yet come! Not Paul, assuredly. As the happy time drew near, the lions and tigers climbing up the bedroom walls, became quite tame and frolicsome. The grim sly faces in the squares and diamonds of the floor-cloth, relaxed and peeped out at him with less wicked eyes. The grave old clock had more of personal interest in the tone of its formal inquiry; and the restless sea went rolling on all night, to the sounding of a melancholy strain – yet it was pleasant too – that rose and fell with the waves, and rocked him, as it were, to sleep.

Mr Feeder, B.A., seemed to think that he, too, would enjoy the holidays very much. Mr Toots projected a life of holidays from that time forth; for, as he regularly informed Paul every day, it was his 'last half' at Doctor Blimber's, and he was going to begin to come into his property directly.

It was perfectly understood between Paul and Mr Toots, that they were intimate friends, notwithstanding their distance in point of years and station. As the vacation approached and Mr Toots breathed harder and stared oftener in Paul's society, than he had done before, Paul knew that he meant he was sorry they were going to lose sight of each other, and felt very much obliged to him for his patronage and good opinion.

It was even understood by Doctor Blimber, Mrs Blimber, and Miss Blimber, as well as by the young gentlemen in general, that Toots had somehow constituted himself protector and guardian of Dombey, and the circumstance became so notorious, even to Mrs Pipchin, that the good old creature cherished feelings of bitterness and jealousy against Toots; and, in the sanctuary of her own home, repeatedly denounced him as a 'chuckle-headed noodle.' Whereas the innocent Toots had no more idea of awakening Mrs Pipchin's wrath, than he had of any other definite possibility or proposition. On the contrary, he was disposed to consider her rather a remarkable character, with many points of interest about her. For this reason he smiled on her with so much urbanity, and asked her how she did, so often, in the course of her visits to little Paul, that at last she one night told him plainly, she wasn't used to it, whatever he might think; and she could not, and she would not bear it, either from himself or any other puppy then existing: at which unexpected acknowledgment of his civilities, Mr Toots was so alarmed that he secreted himself in a retired spot until she had gone. Nor did he ever again face the doughty Mrs Pipchin, under Doctor Blimber's roof.

They were within two or three weeks of the holidays, when, one day, Cornelia Blimber called Paul into her room, and said, 'Dombey, I am going to send home your analysis.'

'Thank you, ma'am,' returned Paul.

'You know what I mean, do you, Dombey?' inquired Miss Blimber, looking hard at him through the spectacles.

'No, ma'am,' said Paul.

'Dombey, Dombey,' said Miss Blimber, 'I begin to be afraid you are a sad boy. When you don't know the meaning of an expression, why don't you seek for information?'

'Mrs Pipchin told me I wasn't to ask questions,' returned Paul.

'I must beg you not to mention Mrs Pipchin to me, on any account, Dombey,' returned Miss Blimber. 'I couldn't think of allowing it. The course of study here, is very far removed from anything of that sort. A repetition of such allusions would make it necessary for me to request to hear, without a mistake, before breakfast-time to-morrow morning, from *Verbum personale* down to *simillima cygno*.'[1]

'I didn't mean, ma'am—' began little Paul.

'I must trouble you not to tell me that you didn't mean, if you please, Dombey,' said Miss Blimber, who preserved an awful politeness in her admonitions. 'That is a line of argument I couldn't dream of permitting.'

Paul felt it safest to say nothing at all, so he only looked at Miss Blimber's spectacles. Miss Blimber having shaken her head at him gravely, referred to a paper lying before her.

'"Analysis of the character of P. Dombey." If my recollection serves me,' said Miss Blimber breaking off, 'the word analysis as opposed to synthesis, is thus defined by Walker.[2] "The resolution of an object, whether of the senses or of the intellect, into its first elements." As opposed to synthesis, you observe. *Now* you know what analysis is, Dombey.'

Dombey didn't seem to be absolutely blinded by the light let in upon his intellect, but he made Miss Blimber a little bow.

'"Analysis,"' resumed Miss Blimber, casting her eye over the paper, '"of the character of P. Dombey. I find that the natural capacity of Dombey is extremely good; and that his general disposition to study may be stated in an equal ratio. Thus, taking eight as our standard and highest number, I find these qualities in Dombey stated each at six three-fourths!"'

Miss Blimber paused to see how Paul received this news. Being undecided whether six three-fourths meant six pounds fifteen, or sixpence three farthings, or six foot three, or three quarters past six, or six somethings that he hadn't learnt yet, with three unknown something elses over, Paul rubbed his hands and looked straight at Miss Blimber. It happened to answer as well as anything else he could have done; and Cornelia proceeded.

'"Violence two. Selfishness two. Inclination to low company, as evinced in the case of a person named Glubb, originally seven, but since reduced. Gentlemanly demeanour four, and improving with advancing years." Now what I particularly wish to call your attention to, Dombey, is the general observation at the close of this analysis.'

Paul set himself to follow it with great care.

'"It may be generally observed of Dombey,"' said Miss Blimber, reading in a loud voice, and at every second word directing her spectacles towards the little figure before her: '"that his abilities and inclinations are good, and that he has made as much progress as under the circumstances could have been expected. But it is to be lamented of this young gentleman that he is singular (what is usually termed old-fashioned) in his character and conduct, and that, without presenting anything in either which distinctly calls for reprobation, he is often very unlike other young gentlemen of his age and social position." Now, Dombey,' said Miss Blimber, laying down the paper, 'do you understand that?'

'I think I do, ma'am,' said Paul.

'This analysis, you see, Dombey,' Miss Blimber continued, 'is going to be sent home to your respected parent. It will naturally be very painful to him to find that you are singular in your character and conduct. It is naturally painful to us; for we can't like you, you know, Dombey, as well as we could wish.'

She touched the child upon a tender point. He had secretly become more and more solicitous from day to day, as the time of his departure drew more near, that all the house should like him. From some hidden reason, very imperfectly understood by himself – if understood at all – he felt a gradually increasing impulse of affection, towards almost everything and everybody in the place. He could not bear to think that they would be quite indifferent to him when he was gone. He wanted them to remember him kindly; and he had made it his business even to conciliate a great hoarse shaggy dog, chained up at the back of the house, who had previously been the terror of his life: that even he might miss him when he was no longer there.

Little thinking that in this, he only showed again the difference between himself and his compeers, poor tiny Paul set it forth to Miss Blimber as well as he could, and begged her, in despite of the official analysis, to have the goodness to try and like him. To Mrs Blimber, who had joined them, he preferred the same petition: and when that lady could not forbear, even in his presence, from giving utterance to her often-repeated opinion, that he was an odd child, Paul told her that he was sure she was quite right; that he thought it must be his bones, but he didn't know; and that he hoped she would overlook it, for he was fond of them all.

'Not so fond,' said Paul, with a mixture of timidity and perfect frankness, which was one of the most peculiar and most engaging qualities of the child, 'not so fond as I am of Florence, of course; that could never be. You couldn't expect that, could you, ma'am?'

'Oh! the old-fashioned little soul!' cried Mrs Blimber, in a whisper.

'But I like everybody here very much,' pursued Paul, 'and I should grieve to go away, and think that any one was glad that I was gone, or didn't care.'

Mrs Blimber was now quite sure that Paul was the oddest child in the world; and when she told the Doctor what had passed, the Doctor did not controvert his wife's opinion. But he said, as he had said before, when Paul first came, that study would do much; and he also said, as he had said on that occasion, 'Bring him on, Cornelia! Bring him on!'

Cornelia had always brought him on as vigorously as she could; and Paul had had a hard life of it. But over and above the getting through his tasks, he had long had another purpose always present to him, and to which he still held fast. It was, to be a gentle, useful, quiet little fellow, always striving to secure the love and attachment of the rest; and though he was yet often to be seen at his old post on the stairs, or watching the waves and clouds from his solitary window, he was oftener found, too, among the other boys, modestly rendering them some little voluntary service. Thus it came to pass, that even among those rigid and absorbed young anchorites, who mortified themselves beneath the roof of Doctor Blimber, Paul was an object of general interest; a fragile little plaything that they all liked, and that no one would have thought of treating roughly. But he could not change his nature, or re-write the analysis; and so they all agreed that Dombey was old-fashioned.

There were some immunities, however, attaching to the character enjoyed by no one else. They could have better spared a newer-fashioned child, and that alone was much. When the others only bowed to Doctor Blimber and family on retiring for the night, Paul would stretch out his morsel of a hand, and boldly shake the Doctor's; also Mrs Blimber's; also Cornelia's. If anybody was to be begged off from impending punishment, Paul was always the delegate. The weak-eyed young man himself had once consulted him, in reference to a little breakage of glass and china. And it was darkly rumoured that the butler, regarding him with favour such as that stern man had never shown before to mortal boy, had sometimes mingled porter with his table-beer[3] to make him strong.

Over and above these extensive privileges, Paul had free right of entry to Mr Feeder's room, from which apartment he had twice led Mr Toots into the open air in a state of faintness, consequent on an unsuccessful attempt to smoke a very blunt cigar: one of a bundle which that young gentleman had covertly purchased on the shingle from a most desperate smuggler, who had acknowledged, in confidence, that two hundred pounds was the price set upon his head, dead or alive, by the Custom House. It was a snug room, Mr Feeder's, with his bed in another little room inside of it, and a flute, which Mr Feeder couldn't play yet, but was going to make a point of learning, he said, hanging up over the fireplace. There were some books in it, too, and a fishing-rod; for Mr Feeder said he should certainly make a point of learning to fish, when he could find time. Mr Feeder had amassed, with similar intentions, a beautiful little curly secondhand key-bugle, a chess-board and men, a Spanish Grammar, a set of sketching materials, and a pair of boxing-gloves. The art of self-defence Mr Feeder said he should undoubtedly make a point of learning, as he considered it the duty of every man to do; for it might lead to the protection of a female in distress.

But Mr Feeder's great possession was a large green jar of snuff, which Mr Toots had brought down as a present, at the close of the last vacation; and for which he had paid a high price, as having been the genuine property of the Prince Regent. Neither Mr Toots nor Mr Feeder could partake of this or any other snuff, even in the most stinted and moderate degree, without being seized with convulsions of sneezing. Nevertheless it was their great delight to moisten a box-full with cold tea, stir it up on a piece of parchment with a paper-knife, and devote themselves to its consumption then and there. In the course of which cramming of their noses, they endured surprising torments with the constancy of martyrs: and, drinking table-beer at intervals, felt all the glories of dissipation.

To little Paul sitting silent in their company, and by the side of his chief patron, Mr Toots, there was a dread charm in these reckless occasions: and when Mr Feeder spoke of the dark mysteries of London, and told Mr Toots that he was going to observe it himself closely in all its ramifications in the approaching holidays, and for that purpose had made arrangements to board with two old maiden ladies at Peckham,[4] Paul regarded him as if he were the hero of some book of travels or wild adventure, and was almost afraid of such a slashing[5] person.

Going into this room one evening, when the holidays were very near, Paul found Mr Feeder filling up the blanks in some printed letters, while some others, already filled up and strewn before him, were being folded and sealed by Mr Toots. Mr Feeder said, 'Aha, Dombey, there you are, are you?' – for they were always kind to him, and glad to see him – and then said, tossing one of the letters towards him, 'And *there* you are, too, Dombey. That's yours.'

'Mine, Sir?' said Paul.

'Your invitation,' returned Mr Feeder.

Paul, looking at it, found, in copper-plate print, with the exception of his own name and the date, which were in Mr Feeder's Penmanship, that Doctor and Mrs Blimber requested the pleasure of Mr P. Dombey's company at an early party on Wednesday Evening the Seventeenth Instant; and that the hour was half-past seven o'clock; and that the object was Quadrilles.[6] Mr Toots also showed him, by holding up a companion sheet of paper, that Doctor and Mrs Blimber requested the pleasure of Mr Toots's company at an early party on Wednesday Evening the Seventeenth Instant, when the hour was half-past seven o'clock, and when the object was Quadrilles. He also found on glancing at the table where Mr Feeder sat, that the pleasure of Mr Briggs's company, and of Mr Tozer's company, and of every young gentleman's company, was requested by Doctor and Mrs Blimber on the same genteel occasion.

Mr Feeder then told him, to his great joy, that his sister was invited, and that it was a half-yearly event, and that, as the holidays began that day, he could go away with his sister after the party, if he liked, which Paul interrupted him to say he *would* like, very much. Mr Feeder then gave him to understand that he would be expected to inform Doctor and Mrs Blimber, in superfine small-hand, that Mr P. Dombey would be happy to have the honour of waiting on them, in accordance with their polite invitation. Lastly, Mr Feeder said, he had better not refer to the festive occasion, in the hearing of Doctor and Mrs Blimber; as these preliminaries, and the whole of the arrangements, were conducted on principles of classicality and high breeding; and that Doctor and Mrs Blimber on the one hand, and the young gentlemen on the other, were supposed, in their scholastic capacities, not to have the least idea of what was in the wind.

Paul thanked Mr Feeder for these hints, and pocketing his invitation, sat down on a stool by the side of Mr Toots as usual. But Paul's head, which had long been ailing more or less, and was sometimes very heavy and painful, felt so uneasy that night, that he was obliged to support it on his hand. And yet it dropped so, that by little and little it sunk on Mr Toots's knees, and rested there, as if it had no care to be ever lifted up again.

That was no reason why he should be deaf; but he must have been, he thought, for, by and by, he heard Mr Feeder calling in his ear, and gently shaking him to rouse his attention. And when he raised his head, quite scared, and looked about him, he found that Doctor Blimber had come into the room; and that the window was open, and that his forehead was wet with sprinkled water; though how all this had been done without his knowledge, was very curious indeed.

'Ah! Come, come! That's well! How is my little friend now?' said Doctor Blimber, encouragingly.

'Oh, quite well, thank you, Sir,' said Paul.

But there seemed to be something the matter with the floor, for he couldn't stand upon it steadily; and with the walls too, for they were inclined to turn round and round, and could only be stopped by being looked at very hard indeed. Mr Toots's head had the appearance of being at once bigger and farther off than was quite natural: and when he took Paul in his arms, to carry him upstairs, Paul observed with astonishment that the door was in quite a different place from that in which he had expected to find it, and almost thought, at first, that Mr Toots was going to walk straight up the chimney.

It was very kind of Mr Toots to carry him to the top of the house so tenderly; and Paul told him that it was. But Mr Toots said he would do a great deal more than that, if he could; and indeed he did more as it was: for he helped Paul to undress, and helped him to bed, in the kindest manner possible, and then sat down by the bedside and chuckled very much; while Mr Feeder, B.A., leaning over the bottom of the bedstead, set all the little bristles on his head bolt upright with his bony hands, and then made believe to spar at Paul with great science, on account of his being all right again, which was so uncommonly facetious, and kind too in Mr Feeder, that Paul, not being able to make up his mind whether it was best to laugh or cry at him, did both at once.

How Mr Toots melted away, and Mr Feeder changed into Mrs Pipchin, Paul never thought of asking, neither was he at all curious to know; but when he saw Mrs Pipchin standing at the bottom of the bed, instead of Mr Feeder, he cried out, 'Mrs Pipchin, don't tell Florence!'

'Don't tell Florence what, my little Paul?' said Mrs Pipchin, coming round to the bedside, and sitting down in the chair.

'About me,' said Paul.

'No, no,' said Mrs Pipchin.

'What do you think I mean to do when I grow up, Mrs Pipchin?' inquired Paul, turning his face towards her on his pillow, and resting his chin wistfully on his folded hands.

Mrs Pipchin couldn't guess.

'I mean,' said Paul, 'to put my money all together in one Bank, never try to get any more, go away into the country with my darling Florence, have a beautiful garden, fields, and woods, and live there with her all my life!'

'Indeed!' cried Mrs Pipchin.

'Yes,' said Paul. 'That's what I mean to do, when I—' He stopped, and pondered for a moment.

Mrs Pipchin's grey eye scanned his thoughtful face.

'If I grow up,' said Paul. Then he went on immediately to tell Mrs Pipchin all about the party, about Florence's invitation, about the pride he would have in the admiration that would be felt for her by all the boys, about their being so kind to him and fond of him, about his being so fond of them, and about his being so glad of it. Then he told Mrs Pipchin about the analysis, and about his being certainly old-fashioned, and took Mrs Pipchin's opinion on that point, and whether she knew why it was, and what it meant. Mrs Pipchin denied the fact altogether, as the shortest way of getting out of the difficulty; but Paul was far from satisfied with that reply, and looked so searchingly at Mrs Pipchin for a truer answer, that she was obliged to get up and look out of the window to avoid his eyes.

There was a certain calm Apothecary[7] who attended at the establishment when any of the young gentlemen were ill, and somehow *he* got into the room and appeared at the bedside, with Mrs Blimber. How they came there, or how long they had been there, Paul didn't know; but when he saw them, he sat up in bed, and answered all the Apothecary's questions at full length, and whispered to him that Florence was not to know anything about it, if he pleased, and that he had set his mind upon her coming to the party. He was very chatty with the Apothecary, and they parted excellent friends. Lying down again with his eyes shut, he heard the Apothecary say, out of the room and quite a long way off – or he dreamed it – that there was a want of vital power (what was that, Paul wondered!) and great constitutional weakness. That as the little fellow had set his heart on parting with his school-mates on the seventeenth, it would be better to indulge the fancy if he grew no worse. That he was glad to hear from Mrs Pipchin, that the little fellow would go to his friends in London on the eighteenth. That he would write to Mr Dombey, when he should have gained a better knowledge of the case, and before that day. That there was no immediate cause for – what? Paul lost that word. And that the little fellow had a fine mind, but was an old-fashioned boy.

What old fashion could that be, Paul wondered with a palpitating heart, that was so visibly expressed in him; so plainly seen by so many people!

He could neither make it out, nor trouble himself long with the effort. Mrs Pipchin was again beside him, if she had ever been away (he thought she had gone out with the Doctor, but it was all a dream perhaps), and presently a bottle and glass got into her hands magically, and she poured out the contents for him. After that, he had some real good jelly, which Mrs Blimber brought to him herself; and then he was so well, that Mrs Pipchin went home, at his urgent solicitation, and Briggs and Tozer came to bed. Poor Briggs grumbled terribly about his own analysis, which could hardly have discomposed him more if it had been a chemical process; but he was very good to Paul, and so was Tozer, and so were all the rest, for they every one looked in before going to bed, and said, 'How are you now, Dombey?' 'Cheer up, little Dombey!' and so forth. After Briggs had got into bed, he lay awake for a long time, still bemoaning his analysis, and saying he knew it was all wrong, and they couldn't have analysed a murderer worse, and how would Doctor Blimber like it if his pocket-money depended on it? It was very easy, Briggs said, to make a galley-slave of a boy all the half-year, and then score him up idle; and to crib two dinners a-week out of his board, and then score him up greedy: but that wasn't going to be submitted to, he believed, was it? Oh! Ah!

Before the weak-eyed young man performed on the gong next morning, he came upstairs to Paul and told him he was to lie still, which Paul very gladly did. Mrs Pipchin reappeared a little before the Apothecary, and a little after the good young woman whom Paul had seen cleaning the stove, on that first morning (how long ago it seemed now!) had brought him his breakfast. There was another consultation a long way off, or else Paul dreamed it again; and then the Apothecary, coming back with Doctor and Mrs Blimber, said:

'Yes, I think, Doctor Blimber, we may release this young gentleman from his books just now; the vacation being so very near at hand.'

'By all means,' said Doctor Blimber. 'My love, you will inform Cornelia, if you please.'

'Assuredly,' said Mrs Blimber.

The Apothecary bending down, looked closely into Paul's eyes, and felt his head, and his pulse, and his heart, with so much interest and care, that Paul said, 'Thank you, Sir.'

'Our little friend,' observed Doctor Blimber, 'has never complained.'

'Oh no!' replied the Apothecary. 'He was not likely to complain.'

'You find him greatly better?' said Doctor Blimber.

'Oh! he is greatly better, Sir,' returned the Apothecary.

Paul had begun to speculate, in his own odd way, on the subject that might occupy the Apothecary's mind just at that moment; so musingly had he answered the two questions of Doctor Blimber. But the Apothecary happening to meet his little patient's eyes, as the latter set off on that mental expedition, and coming instantly out of his abstraction with a cheerful smile, Paul smiled in return and abandoned it.

He lay in bed all that day, dozing and dreaming, and looking at Mr Toots: but got up on the next, and went downstairs. Lo and behold, there was something the matter with the great clock; and a workman on a pair of steps had taken its face off, and was poking instruments into the works by the light of a candle! This was a great event for Paul, who sat down on the bottom stair, and watched the operation attentively: now and then glancing at the clock face, leaning all askew, against the wall hard by, and feeling a little confused by a suspicion that it was ogling him.

The workman on the steps was very civil; and as he said, when he observed Paul, 'How do you do, Sir?' Paul got into conversation with him, and told him he hadn't been quite well lately. The ice being thus broken, Paul asked him a multitude of questions about chimes and clocks: as, whether people watched up in the lonely church steeples by night to make them strike, and how the bells were rung when people died, and whether those were different bells from wedding bells, or only sounded dismal in the fancies of the living. Finding that his new acquaintance was not very well informed on the subject of the Curfew Bell[8] of ancient days, Paul gave him an account of that institution; and also asked him, as a practical man, what he thought about King Alfred's idea[9] of measuring time by the burning of candles; to which the workman

replied, that he thought it would be the ruin of the clock trade if it
was to come up again. In fine,[10] Paul looked on, until the clock had
quite recovered its familiar aspect, and resumed its sedate inquiry:
when the workman, putting away his tools in a long basket bade
him good day, and went away. Though not before he had whispered
something, on the door-mat, to the footman, in which there was
the phrase 'old-fashioned' – for Paul heard it.

What could that old fashion be, that seemed to make the people
sorry! What could it be!

Having nothing to learn now, he thought of this frequently;
though not so often as he might have done, if he had had fewer
things to think of. But he had a great many; and was always
thinking, all day long.

First, there was Florence coming to the party. Florence would see
that the boys were fond of him; and that would make her happy.
This was his great theme. Let Florence once be sure that they were
gentle and good to him, and that he had become a little favourite
among them, and then she would always think of the time he had
passed there, without being very sorry. Florence might be all the
happier too for that, perhaps, when he came back.

When he came back! Fifty times a day, his noiseless little feet
went up the stairs to his own room, as he collected every book and
scrap, and trifle that belonged to him, and put them all together
there, down to the minutest thing, for taking home! There was no
shade of coming back on little Paul; no preparation for it, or other
reference to it, grew out of anything he thought or did, except this
slight one in connexion with his sister. On the contrary, he had to
think of everything familiar to him, in his contemplative moods and
in his wanderings about the house, as being to be parted with; and
hence the many things he had to think of, all day long.

He had to peep into those rooms upstairs, and think how solitary
they would be when he was gone, and wonder through how many
silent days, weeks, months, and years, they would continue just as
grave and undisturbed. He had to think – would any other child
(old-fashioned, like himself) stray there at any time, to whom the
same grotesque distortions of pattern and furniture would manifest
themselves; and would anybody tell that boy of little Dombey, who
had been there once?

He had to think of a portrait on the stairs, which always looked
earnestly after him as he went away, eyeing it over his shoulder:
and which, when he passed it in the company of any one, still
seemed to gaze at him, and not at his companion. He had much to

think of, in association with a print that hung up in another place, where, in the centre of a wondering group, one figure that he knew, a figure with a light about its head – benignant, mild, and merciful – stood pointing upward.[11]

At his own bedroom window, there were crowds of thoughts that mixed with these, and came on, one upon another, like the rolling waves. Where those wild birds lived, that were always hovering out at sea in troubled weather; where the clouds rose and first began; whence the wind issued on its rushing flight, and where it stopped; whether the spot where he and Florence had so often sat, and watched, and talked about these things, could ever be exactly as it used to be without them; whether it could ever be the same to Florence, if he were in some distant place, and she were sitting there alone.

He had to think, too, of Mr Toots, and Mr Feeder, B.A.; of all the boys; and of Doctor Blimber, Mrs Blimber, and Miss Blimber; of home, and of his aunt and Miss Tox; of his father, Dombey and Son, Walter with the poor old uncle who had got the money he wanted, and that gruff-voiced Captain with the iron hand. Besides all this, he had a number of little visits to pay, in the course of the day; to the schoolroom, to Doctor Blimber's study, to Mrs Blimber's private apartment, to Miss Blimber's, and to the dog. For he was free of the whole house now, to range it as he chose; and, in his desire to part with everybody on affectionate terms, he attended, in his way, to them all. Sometimes he found places in books for Briggs, who was always losing them; sometimes he looked up words in dictionaries for other young gentlemen who were in extremity; sometimes he held skeins of silk for Mrs Blimber to wind; sometimes he put Cornelia's desk to rights; sometimes he would even creep into the Doctor's study, and, sitting on the carpet near his learned feet, turn the globes softly, and go round the world, or take a flight among the far-off stars.

In those days immediately before the holidays, in short, when the other young gentlemen were labouring for dear life through a general resumption[12] of the studies of the whole half-year, Paul was such a privileged pupil as had never been seen in that house before. He could hardly believe it himself; but his liberty lasted from hour to hour, and from day to day; and little Dombey was caressed by every one. Doctor Blimber was so particular about him, that he requested Johnson to retire from the dinner-table one day, for having thoughtlessly spoken to him as 'poor little Dombey'; which Paul thought rather hard and severe, though he had flushed at the moment, and wondered why Johnson should pity him. It was the more questionable justice, Paul thought, in the Doctor, from his having certainly overheard that great authority give his assent on the previous evening, to the proposition (stated by Mrs Blimber) that poor dear little Dombey was more old-fashioned than ever. And now it was that Paul began to think it must surely be old-fashioned to be very thin, and light, and easily tired, and soon disposed to lie down anywhere and rest; for he couldn't help feeling that these were more and more his habits every day.

At last the party-day arrived; and Doctor Blimber said at breakfast, 'Gentlemen, we will resume our studies on the twenty-fifth of next month.' Mr Toots immediately threw off his allegiance, and put on his ring and mentioning the Doctor in casual conversation shortly afterwards, spoke of him as 'Blimber!' This act of freedom inspired the older pupils with admiration and envy; but the younger spirits were appalled, and seemed to marvel that no beam fell down and crushed him.

Not the least allusion was made to the ceremonies of the evening, either at breakfast or at dinner; but there was a bustle in the house all day, and in the course of his perambulations, Paul made acquaintance with various strange benches and candlesticks, and met a harp in a green great-coat[13] standing on the landing outside the drawing-room door. There was something queer, too, about Mrs Blimber's head at dinner-time, as if she had screwed her hair up too tight; and though Miss Blimber showed a graceful bunch of plaited hair on each temple, she seemed to have her own little curls in paper underneath, and in a play-bill[14] too: for Paul read 'Theatre Royal' over one of her sparkling spectacles, and 'Brighton' over the other.

There was a grand array of white waistcoats and cravats in the young gentlemen's bedrooms as evening approached; and such a smell of singed hair, that Doctor Blimber sent up the footman with his compliments, and wished to know if the house was on fire. But it was only the hairdresser curling the young gentlemen, and over-heating his tongs in the ardour of business.

When Paul was dressed – which was very soon done, for he felt unwell and drowsy, and was not able to stand about it very long – he went down into the drawing-room; where he found Doctor Blimber pacing up and down the room full dressed, but with a dignified and unconcerned demeanour, as if he thought it barely possible that one or two people might drop in by and by. Shortly afterwards, Mrs Blimber appeared, looking lovely, Paul thought;

and attired in such a number of skirts that it was quite an excursion to walk round her. Miss Blimber came down soon after her mama; a little squeezed in appearance, but very charming.

Mr Toots and Mr Feeder were the next arrivals. Each of these gentlemen brought his hat in his hand, as if he lived somewhere else; and when they were announced by the butler, Doctor Blimber said, 'Aye, aye, aye! God bless my soul!' and seemed extremely glad to see them. Mr Toots was one blaze of jewellery and buttons: and he felt the circumstance so strongly, that when he had shaken hands with the Doctor, and had bowed to Mrs Blimber and Miss Blimber, he took Paul aside, and said, 'What do you think of this, Dombey!'

But notwithstanding this modest confidence in himself, Mr Toots appeared to be involved in a good deal of uncertainty whether, on the whole, it was judicious to button the bottom button of his waistcoat, and whether, on a calm revision of all the circumstances, it was best to wear his wristbands turned up or turned down. Observing that Mr Feeder's were turned up, Mr Toots turned his up; but the wristbands of the next arrival being turned down, Mr Toots turned his down. The differences in point of waistcoat buttoning, not only at the bottom, but at the top too, became so numerous and complicated as the arrivals thickened, that Mr Toots was continually fingering that article of dress, as if he were performing on some instrument; and appeared to find the incessant execution it demanded, quite bewildering.

All the young gentlemen, tightly cravatted, curled, and pumped,[15] and with their best hats in their hands, having been at different times announced and introduced, Mr Baps, the dancing-master, came, accompanied by Mrs Baps, to whom Mrs Blimber was extremely kind and condescending. Mr Baps was a very grave gentleman, with a slow and measured manner of speaking, and before he had stood under the lamp five minutes, he began to talk to Toots (who had been silently comparing pumps with him) about what you were to do with your raw materials when they came into your ports in return for your drain of gold. Mr Toots, to whom the question seemed perplexing, suggested 'Cook 'em.' But Mr Baps did not appear to think that would do.

Paul now slipped away from the cushioned corner of a sofa, which had been his post of observation, and went downstairs into the tea-room to be ready for Florence, whom he had not seen for nearly a fortnight, as he had remained at Doctor Blimber's on the previous Saturday and Sunday, lest he should take cold. Presently she came: looking so beautiful in her simple ball dress, with her fresh flowers in her hand, and when she knelt down on the ground to take Paul round the neck and kiss him (for there was no one there, but his friend and another young woman waiting to serve out the tea), he could hardly make up his mind to let her go again, or to take away her bright and loving eyes from his face.

'But what is the matter, Floy?' asked Paul, almost sure that he saw a tear there.

'Nothing, darling; nothing,' returned Florence.

Paul touched her cheek gently with his finger – and it *was* a tear! 'Why, Floy!' said he.

'We'll go home together, and I'll nurse you, love,' said Florence.

'Nurse me!' echoed Paul.

Paul couldn't understand what that had to do with it, nor why the two young women looked on so seriously, nor why Florence turned away her face for a moment, and then turned it back, lighted up again with smiles.

'Floy,' said Paul, holding a ringlet of her dark hair in his hand. 'Tell me, dear. Do *you* think I have grown old-fashioned?'

His sister laughed, and fondled him, and told him 'No.'

'Because I know they say so,' returned Paul, 'and I want to know what they mean, Floy.'

But a loud double knock coming at the door, and Florence hurrying to the table, there was no more said between them. Paul wondered again when he saw his friend whisper to Florence, as if she were comforting her; but a new arrival put that out of his head speedily.

It was Sir Barnet Skettles, Lady Skettles, and Master Skettles. Master Skettles was to be a new boy after the vacation, and Fame had been busy, in Mr Feeder's room, with his father, who was in the House of Commons, and of whom Mr Feeder had said that when he *did* catch the Speaker's eye (which he had been expected to do for three or four years), it was anticipated that he would rather touch up the Radicals.[16]

'And what room is this now, for instance?' said Lady Skettles to Paul's friend, 'Melia.

'Doctor Blimber's study, ma'am,' was the reply.

Lady Skettles took a panoramic survey of it through her glass, and said to Sir Barnet Skettles, with a nod of approval, 'Very good.' Sir Barnet assented, but Master Skettles looked suspicious and doubtful.

'And this little creature, now,' said Lady Skettles, turning to Paul. 'Is he one of the—'

'Young gentlemen, ma'am; yes, ma'am,' said Paul's friend.

'And what is your name, my pale child?' said Lady Skettles.

'Dombey,' answered Paul.

Sir Barnet Skettles immediately interposed, and said that he had had the honour of meeting Paul's father at a public dinner, and that he hoped he was very well. Then Paul heard him say to Lady Skettles, 'City – very rich – most respectable – Doctor mentioned it.' And then he said to Paul, 'Will you tell your good papa that Sir Barnet Skettles rejoiced to hear that he was very well, and sent him his best compliments?'

'Yes, Sir,' answered Paul.

'That is my brave boy,' said Sir Barnet Skettles. 'Barnet,' to Master Skettles, who was revenging himself for the studies to come, on the plum-cake, 'this is a young gentleman you ought to know. This is a young gentleman you *may* know, Barnet,' said Sir Barnet Skettles, with an emphasis on the permission.

'What eyes! What hair! What a lovely face!' exclaimed Lady Skettles softly, as she looked at Florence through her glass.

'My sister,' said Paul, presenting her.

The satisfaction of the Skettleses was now complete. And as Lady Skettles had conceived, at first sight, a liking for Paul, they all went up stairs together: Sir Barnet Skettles taking care of Florence, and young Barnet following.

Young Barnet did not remain long in the background after they had reached the drawing-room, for Dr Blimber had him out in no time, dancing with Florence. He did not appear to Paul to be particularly happy, or particularly anything but sulky, or to care much what he was about; but as Paul heard Lady Skettles say to Mrs Blimber, while she beat time with her fan, that her dear boy was evidently smitten to death by that angel of a child, Miss Dombey, it would seem that Skettles Junior was in a state of bliss, without showing it.

Little Paul thought it a singular coincidence that nobody had occupied his place among the pillows; and that when he came into the room again, they should all make way for him to go back to it, remembering it was his. Nobody stood before him either, when they observed that he liked to see Florence dancing, but they left the space in front quite clear, so that he might follow her with his eyes. They were so kind, too, even the strangers, of whom there were soon a great many, that they came and spoke to him every now and then, and asked him how he was, and if his head ached, and whether he was tired. He was very much obliged to them for all their kindness and attention, and reclining propped up in his corner, with Mrs Blimber and Lady Skettles on the same sofa, and Florence coming and sitting by his side as soon as every dance was ended, he looked on very happily indeed.

Florence would have sat by him all night, and would not have danced at all of her own accord, but Paul made her, by telling her how much it pleased him. And he told her the truth, too; for his small heart swelled, and his face glowed, when he saw how much they all admired her, and how she was the beautiful little rosebud of the room.

From his nest among the pillows, Paul could see and hear almost everything that passed, as if the whole were being done for his amusement. Among other little incidents that he observed, he observed Mr Baps the dancing-master get into conversation with Sir Barnet Skettles, and very soon asked him, as he had asked Mr Toots, what you were to do with your raw materials, when they came into your ports in return for your drain of gold – which was such a mystery to Paul that he was quite desirous to know what ought to be done with them.

Sir Barnet Skettles had much to say upon the question, and said it; but it did not appear to solve the question, for Mr Baps retorted, Yes, but supposing Russia stepped in with her tallows; which struck Sir Barnet almost dumb, for he could only shake his head after that, and say, Why then you must fall back upon your cottons, he supposed.

Sir Barnet Skettles looked after Mr Baps when he went to cheer up Mrs Baps (who, being quite deserted, was pretending to look over the music-book of the gentleman who played the harp), as if he thought him a remarkable kind of man; and shortly afterwards he said so in those words to Doctor Blimber, and inquired if he might take the liberty of asking who he was, and whether he had ever been in the Board of Trade. Doctor Blimber answered no, he believed not; and that in fact he was a Professor of —

'Of something connected with statistics, I'll swear?' observed Sir Barnet Skettles.

'Why no, Sir Barnet,' replied Doctor Blimber, rubbing his chin. 'No, not exactly.'

'Figures of some sort, I would venture a bet,' said Sir Barnet Skettles.

'Why yes,' said Doctor Blimber, 'yes, but not of that sort. Mr Baps is a very worthy sort of man, Sir Barnet, and – in fact he's our professor of dancing.'

Paul was amazed to see that this piece of information quite altered Sir Barnet Skettles' opinion of Mr Baps, and that Sir Barnet flew into a perfect rage, and glowered at Mr Baps over on the other side of the room. He even went so far as to D[17] Mr Baps to Lady Skettles, in telling her what had happened, and to say that it was like his most con-sum-mate and con-foun-ded impudence.

There was another thing that Paul observed. Mr Feeder, after imbibing several custard-cups of negus,[18] began to enjoy himself. The dancing in general was ceremonious, and the music rather solemn – a little like church music in fact – but after the custard-cups, Mr Feeder told Mr Toots that he was going to throw a little spirit into the thing. After that, Mr Feeder not only began to dance as if he meant dancing and nothing else, but secretly to stimulate the music to perform wild tunes. Further, he became particular in his attentions to the ladies; and dancing with Miss Blimber, whispered to her – whispered to her! – though not so softly but that Paul heard him say this remarkable poetry,

> 'Had I a heart for falsehood framed,
> I ne'er could injure You!'[19]

This, Paul heard him repeat to four young ladies in succession. Well might Mr Feeder say to Mr Toots, that he was afraid he should be the worse for it to-morrow!

Mrs Blimber was a little alarmed by this – comparatively speaking – profligate behaviour; and especially by the alteration in the character of the music, which, beginning to comprehend low melodies that were popular in the streets, might not unnaturally be supposed to give offence to Lady Skettles. But Lady Skettles was so very kind as to beg Mrs Blimber not to mention it; and to receive her explanation that Mr Feeder's spirits sometimes betrayed him into excesses on these occasions, with the greatest courtesy and politeness; observing, that he seemed a very nice sort of person for his situation, and that she particularly liked the unassuming style of his hair – which (as already hinted) was about a quarter of an inch long.

Once, when there was a pause in the dancing, Lady Skettles told Paul that he seemed very fond of music. Paul replied, that he was; and if she was too, she ought to hear his sister, Florence, sing. Lady Skettles presently discovered that she was dying with anxiety to have that gratification; and though Florence was at first very much frightened at being asked to sing before so many people, and begged earnestly to be excused, yet, on Paul calling her to him, and saying,

'Do, Floy! Please! For me, my dear!' she went straight to the piano, and began. When they all drew a little away, that Paul might see her; and when he saw her sitting there all alone, so young, and good, and beautiful, and kind to him; and heard her thrilling voice, so natural and sweet, and such a golden link between him and all his life's love and happiness, rising out of the silence; he turned his face away, and hid his tears. Not, as he told them when they spoke to him, not that the music was too plaintive or too sorrowful, but it was so dear to him.

They all loved Florence! How could they help it! Paul had known beforehand that they must and would; and sitting in his cushioned corner, with calmly folded hands, and one leg loosely doubled under him, few would have thought what triumph and delight expanded his childish bosom while he watched her, or what a sweet tranquillity he felt. Lavish encomiums on 'Dombey's sister' reached his ears from all the boys: admiration of the self-possessed and modest little beauty was on every lip: reports of her intelligence and accomplishments floated past him, constantly; and, as if borne upon the air of the summer night, there was a half-intelligible sentiment diffused around, referring to Florence and himself, and breathing sympathy for both, that soothed and touched him.

He did not know why. For all that the child observed, and felt, and thought, that night – the present and the absent; what was then and what had been – were blended like the colours in the rainbow, or in the plumage of rich birds when the sun is shining on them, or in the softening sky when the same sun is setting. The many things he had had to think of lately, passed before him in the music; not as claiming his attention over again, or as likely evermore to occupy it, but as peacefully disposed of and gone. A solitary window, gazed through years ago, looked out upon an ocean, miles and miles away; upon its waters, fancies, busy with him only yesterday, were hushed and lulled to rest like broken waves. The same mysterious murmur he had wondered at, when lying on his couch upon the beach, he thought he still heard sounding through his sister's song, and through the hum of voices, and the tread of feet, and having some part in the faces flitting by, and even in the heavy gentleness of Mr Toots, who frequently came up to shake him by the hand. Through the universal kindness he still thought he heard it, speaking to him; and even his old-fashioned reputation seemed to be allied to it, he knew not how. Thus little Paul sat musing, listening, looking on, and dreaming; and was very happy.

Until the time arrived for taking leave: and then, indeed, there was a sensation in the party. Sir Barnet Skettles brought up Skettles Junior to shake hands with him, and asked him if he would remember to tell his good papa, with his best compliments, that he, Sir Barnet Skettles, had said he hoped the two young gentlemen would become intimately acquainted. Lady Skettles kissed him, and parted his hair upon his brow, and held him in her arms; and even Mrs Baps – poor Mrs Baps! Paul was glad of that – came over from beside the music-book of the gentleman who played the harp, and took leave of him quite as heartily as anybody in the room.

'Good-bye, Doctor Blimber,' said Paul, stretching out his hand.

'Good-bye, my little friend,' returned the Doctor.

'I'm very much obliged to you, Sir,' said Paul, looking innocently up into his awful face. 'Ask them to take care of Diogenes[20] if you please.'

Diogenes was the dog: who had never in his life received a friend into his confidence, before Paul. The Doctor promised that every attention should be paid to Diogenes in Paul's absence, and Paul having again thanked him, and shaken hands with him, bade adieu to Mrs Blimber and Cornelia with such heartfelt earnestness that Mrs Blimber forgot from that moment to mention Cicero to Lady Skettles, though she had fully intended it all the evening. Cornelia, taking both Paul's hands in hers, said, 'Dombey, Dombey, you have always been my favourite pupil. God bless you!' And it showed, Paul thought, how easily one might do injustice to a person; for Miss Blimber meant it – though she *was* a Forcer.

A buzz then went round among the young gentlemen, of 'Dombey's going!' 'Little Dombey's going!' and there was a general move after Paul and Florence down the staircase and into the hall, in which the whole Blimber family were included. Such a circumstance, Mr Feeder said aloud, as had never happened in the case of any former young gentleman within his experience; but it would be difficult to say if this were sober fact or custard-cups. The servants, with the butler at their head, had all an interest in seeing Little Dombey go; and even the weak-eyed young man, taking out his books and trunks to the coach that was to carry him and Florence to Mrs Pipchin's for the night, melted visibly.

Not even the influence of the softer passion on the young gentlemen – and they all, to a boy, doted on Florence – could restrain them from taking quite a noisy leave of Paul; waving hats after him, pressing downstairs to shake hands with him, crying individually 'Dombey, don't forget me!' and indulging in many such ebullitions of feeling, uncommon among those young Chesterfields.[21] Paul

Paul goes home for the holidays

whispered Florence, as she wrapped him up before the door was opened, Did she hear them? Would she ever forget it? Was she glad to know it? And a lively delight was in his eyes as he spoke to her.

Once, for a last look, he turned and gazed upon the faces thus addressed to him, surprised to see how shining and how bright and numerous they were, and how they were all piled and heaped up, as faces are at crowded theatres. They swam before him as he looked, like faces in an agitated glass; and next moment he was in the dark coach outside, holding close to Florence. From that time, whenever he thought of Doctor Blimber's, it came back as he had seen it in this last view; and it never seemed to be a real place again, but always a dream, full of eyes.

This was not quite the last of Doctor Blimber's, however. There was something else. There was Mr Toots. Who, unexpectedly letting down one of the coach-windows, and looking in, said, with a most egregious chuckle, 'Is Dombey there?' and immediately put it up again, without waiting for an answer. Nor was this quite the last of Mr Toots, even; for before the coachman could drive off, he as suddenly let down the other window, and looking in with a precisely similar chuckle, said in a precisely similar tone of voice, 'Is Dombey there?' and disappeared precisely as before.

How Florence laughed! Paul often remembered it, and laughed himself whenever he did so.

But there was much, soon afterwards – next day, and after that – which Paul could only recollect confusedly. As, why they stayed at Mrs Pipchin's days and nights, instead of going home; why he lay in bed, with Florence sitting by his side; whether that had been his father in the room, or only a tall shadow on the wall; whether he had heard his doctor say, of some one, that if they had removed him before the occasion on which he had built up fancies, strong in proportion to his own weakness, it was very possible he might have pined away.

He could not even remember whether he had often said to Florence, 'Oh Floy, take me home, and never leave me!' but he thought he had. He fancied sometimes he had heard himself repeating, 'Take me home, Floy! take me home!'

But he could remember, when he got home, and was carried up the well-remembered stairs, that there had been the rumbling of a coach for many hours together, while he lay upon the seat, with Florence still beside him, and old Mrs Pipchin sitting opposite. He remembered his old bed too, when they laid him down in it: his aunt, Miss Tox, and Susan: but there was something else, and recent too, that still perplexed him.

'I want to speak to Florence, if you please,' he said. 'To Florence by herself, for a moment!'

She bent down over him, and the others stood away.

'Floy, my pet, wasn't that papa in the hall, when they brought me from the coach?'

'Yes, dear.'

'He didn't cry, and go into his room, Floy, did he, when he saw me coming in?'

Florence shook her head, and pressed her lips against his cheek.

'I'm very glad he didn't cry,' said little Paul. 'I thought he did. Don't tell them that I asked.'

CHAPTER 15

Amazing Artfulness of Captain Cuttle, and a new Pursuit for Walter Gay

Walter could not, for several days, decide what to do in the Barbados business; and even cherished some faint hope that Mr Dombey might not have meant what he had said, or that he might change his mind, and tell him he was not to go. But as nothing occurred to give this idea (which was sufficiently improbable in itself) any touch of confirmation, and as time was slipping by, and he had none to lose, he felt that he must act, without hesitating any longer.

Walter's chief difficulty was, how to break the change in his affairs to Uncle Sol, to whom he was sensible it would be a terrible blow. He had the greater difficulty in dashing Uncle Sol's spirits with such an astounding piece of intelligence, because they had lately recovered very much, and the old man had become so cheerful, that the little back parlour was itself again. Uncle Sol had paid the first appointed portion of the debt to Mr Dombey, and was hopeful of working his way through the rest; and to cast him down afresh, when he had sprung up so manfully from his troubles, was a very distressing necessity.

Yet it would never do to run away from him. He must know of it beforehand: and how to tell him was the point. As to the question of going or not going, Walter did not consider that he had any power of choice in the matter. Mr Dombey had truly told him that he was young, and that his uncle's circumstances were not good; and Mr Dombey had plainly expressed, in the glance with which he had accompanied that reminder, that if he declined to go he might stay at home if he chose, but not in his counting-house. His uncle and he lay under a great obligation to Mr Dombey, which was of Walter's own soliciting. He might have begun in secret to despair of ever winning that gentleman's favour, and might have thought that he was now and then disposed to put a slight upon him, which was hardly just. But what would have been duty without that, was still duty with it – or Walter thought so – and duty must be done.

When Mr Dombey had looked at him, and told him he was young, and that his uncle's circumstances were not good, there had been an expression of disdain in his face; a contemptuous and disparaging assumption that he would be quite content to live idly on a reduced old man, which stung the boy's generous soul. Determined to assure Mr Dombey, in so far as it was possible to give him the assurance without expressing it in words, that indeed he mistook his nature, Walter had been anxious to show even more cheerfulness and activity after the West Indian interview than he had shown before: if that were possible, in one of his quick and zealous disposition. He was too young and inexperienced to think, that possibly this very quality in him was not agreeable to Mr Dombey, and that it was no stepping-stone to his good opinion to be elastic and hopeful of pleasing under the shadow of his powerful displeasure, whether it were right or wrong. But it may have been – it may have been – that the great man thought himself defied in this new exposition of an honest spirit, and purposed to bring it down.

'Well! at last and at least, Uncle Sol must be told,' thought Walter, with a sigh. And as Walter was apprehensive that his voice might perhaps quaver a little, and that his countenance might not be quite as hopeful as he could wish it to be, if he told the old man himself, and saw the first effects of his communication on his wrinkled face, he resolved to avail himself of the services of that powerful mediator, Captain Cuttle. Sunday coming round, he set off therefore, after breakfast, once more to beat up Captain Cuttle's quarters.[1]

It was not unpleasant to remember, on the way thither, that Mrs MacStinger resorted to a great distance every Sunday morning, to attend the ministry of the Reverend Melchisedech Howler, who, having been one day discharged from the West India Docks on a false suspicion (got up expressly against him by the general enemy)[2] of screwing gimlets into puncheons,[3] and applying his lips to the orifice, had announced the destruction of the world for that day two years, at ten in the morning, and opened a front parlour for the reception of ladies and gentlemen of the Ranting persuasion,[4] upon whom, on the first occasion of their assemblage, the admonitions of the Reverend Melchisedech had produced so powerful an effect, that, in their rapturous performance of a sacred jig, which closed the service, the whole flock broke through into a kitchen below, and disabled a mangle belonging to one of the fold.

This the Captain, in a moment of uncommon conviviality, had confided to Walter and his uncle, between the repetitions of lovely Peg, on the night when Brogley the broker was paid out. The Captain himself was punctual in his attendance at a church in his own neighbourhood, which hoisted the Union Jack every Sunday morning; and where he was good enough – the lawful beadle being infirm – to keep an eye upon the boys, over whom he exercised great power, in virtue of his mysterious hook. Knowing the regularity of the Captain's habits, Walter made all the haste he could, that he might anticipate his going out; and he made such good speed, that he had the pleasure, on turning into Brig Place, to behold the broad blue coat and waistcoat hanging out of the Captain's open window, to air in the sun.

It appeared incredible that the coat and waistcoat could be seen by mortal eyes without the Captain: but he certainly was not in them, otherwise his legs – the houses in Brig Place not being lofty – would have obstructed the street door, which was perfectly clear. Quite wondering at this discovery, Walter gave a single knock.

'Stinger,' he distinctly heard the Captain say, up in his room, as if that were no business of his. Therefore Walter gave two knocks.

'Cuttle,' he heard the Captain say upon that; and immediately afterwards the Captain, in his clean shirt and braces, with his neckerchief hanging loosely round his throat like a coil of rope, and his glazed hat on, appeared at the window, leaning out over the broad blue coat and waistcoat.

'Wal'r!' cried the captain, looking down upon him in amazement.

'Ay, ay, Captain Cuttle,' returned Walter, 'only me.'

'What's the matter, my lad?' inquired the Captain, with great concern. 'Gill an't been and sprung nothing again?'

'No, no,' said Walter. 'My uncle's all right, Captain Cuttle.'

The Captain expressed his gratification, and said he would come down below and open the door, which he did.

'Though you're early, Wal'r,' said the Captain, eyeing him still doubtfully, when they got upstairs.

'Why, the fact is, Captain Cuttle,' said Walter, sitting down, 'I was afraid you would have gone out, and I want to benefit by your friendly counsel.'

'So you shall,' said the Captain; 'what'll you take?'

'I want to take your opinion, Captain Cuttle,' returned Walter, smiling. 'That's the only thing for me.'

'Come on then,' said the Captain. 'With a will, my lad!'

Walter related to him what had happened; and the difficulty in which he felt respecting his uncle, and the relief it would be to him if Captain Cuttle, in his kindness, would help him to smooth it away; Captain Cuttle's infinite consternation and astonishment at the prospect unfolded to him, gradually swallowing that gentleman up, until it left his face quite vacant, and the suit of blue, the glazed hat, and the hook, apparently without an owner.

'You see, Captain Cuttle,' pursued Walter, 'for myself, I am young, as Mr Dombey said, and not to be considered. I am to fight my way through the world, I know; but there are two points I was thinking, as I came along, that I should be very particular about, in respect to my uncle. I don't mean to say that I deserve to be the pride and delight of his life – you believe me, I know – but I am. Now, don't you think I am?'

The Captain seemed to make an endeavour to rise from the depths of his astonishment, and get back to his face; but the effort being ineffectual, the glazed hat merely nodded with a mute, unutterable meaning.

'If I live and have my health,' said Walter, 'and I am not afraid of that, still, when I leave England I can hardly hope to see my uncle again. He is old, Captain Cuttle; and besides, his life is a life of custom—'

'Steady, Wal'r! Of a want of custom!' said the Captain, suddenly reappearing.

'Too true,' returned Walter, shaking his head; 'but I meant a life of habit, Captain Cuttle – that sort of custom. And if (as you very truly said, I am sure) he would have died the sooner for the loss of the stock, and all those objects to which he has been accustomed for so many years, don't you think he might die a little sooner for the loss of—'

'Of his Nevy,' interposed the Captain. 'Right!'

'Well then,' said Walter, trying to speak gaily, 'we must do our best to make him believe that the separation is but a temporary one, after all; but as I know better, or dread that I know better, Captain Cuttle, and as I have so many reasons for regarding him with affection, and duty, and honour, I am afraid I should make but a very poor hand at that, if I tried to persuade him of it. That's my great reason for wishing you to break it out to him; and that's the first point.'

'Keep her off a point or so!' observed the Captain, in a contemplative voice.

'What did you say, Captain Cuttle?' inquired Walter.

'Stand by!' returned the Captain thoughtfully.

Walter paused to ascertain if the Captain had any particular information to add to this, but as he said no more, went on.

'Now, the second point, Captain Cuttle. I am sorry to say, I am not a favourite with Mr Dombey. I have always tried to do my best, and I have always done it; but he does not like me. He can't help his likings and dislikings, perhaps. I say nothing of that. I only say that I am certain he does not like me. He does not send me to this post as a good one; he disdains to represent it as being better than it is; and I doubt very much if it will ever lead me to advancement in the House – whether it does not, on the contrary, dispose of me for ever, and put me out of the way. Now, we must say nothing of this to my uncle, Captain Cuttle, but must make it out to be as favourable and promising as we can; and when I tell you what it really is, I only do so, that in case any means should ever arise of lending me a hand, so far off, I may have one friend at home who knows my real situation.'

'Wal'r, my boy,' replied the Captain, 'in the Proverbs of Solomon⁵ you will find the following words, "May we never want a friend in need, nor a bottle to give him!" When found, make a note of.'

Here the Captain stretched out his hand to Walter, with an air of downright good faith that spoke volumes; at the same time repeating (for he felt proud of the accuracy and pointed application of his quotation), 'When found, make a note of.'

'Captain Cuttle,' said Walter, taking the immense fist extended to him by the Captain in both his hands, which it completely filled, 'next to my Uncle Sol, I love you. There is no one on earth in whom I can more safely trust, I am sure. As to the mere going away, Captain Cuttle, I don't care for that; why should I care for that! If I were free to seek my own fortune – if I were free to go as a common sailor – if I were free to venture on my own account to the farthest end of the world – I would gladly go! I would have gladly gone, years ago, and taken my chance of what might come of it. But it

was against my uncle's wishes, and against the plans he had formed
for me; and there was an end of that. But what I feel, Captain
Cuttle, is that we have been a little mistaken all along, and that, so
far as any improvement in my prospects is concerned, I am no
better off now than I was when I first entered Dombey's House –
perhaps a little worse, for the House may have been kindly inclined
towards me then, and it certainly is not now.'

'Turn again, Whittington,' muttered the disconsolate Captain,
after looking at Walter for some time.

'Aye,' replied Walter, laughing, 'and turn a great many times,
too, Captain Cuttle, I'm afraid, before such fortune as his ever turns
up again. Not that I complain,' he added, in his lively, animated,
energetic way. 'I have nothing to complain of. I am provided for. I
can live. When I leave my uncle, I leave him to you; and I can leave
him to no one better, Captain Cuttle. I haven't told you all this
because I despair, not I; it's to convince you that I can't pick and
choose in Dombey's House, and that where I am sent, there I must
go, and what I am offered, that I must take. It's better for my uncle
that I should be sent away; for Mr Dombey is a valuable friend to
him, as he proved himself, you know when, Captain Cuttle; and I
am persuaded he won't be less valuable when he hasn't me there,
every day, to awaken his dislike. So hurrah for the West Indies,
Captain Cuttle! How does that tune go that the sailors sing?

> 'For the Port of Barbados,' Boys!
>> Cheerily!
> Leaving old England behind us, Boys!
>> Cheerily!'

Here the Captain roared in chorus –

> 'Oh cheerily, cheerily!
>> Oh cheer—i—ly!'

The last line reaching the quick ears of an ardent skipper not
quite sober, who lodged opposite, and who instantly sprung out of
bed, threw up his window, and joined in, across the street, at the
top of his voice, produced a fine effect. When it was impossible to
sustain the concluding note any longer, the skipper bellowed forth
a terrific 'ahoy!' intended in part as a friendly greeting, and in part
to show that he was not at all breathed. That done, he shut down
his window, and went to bed again.

'And now, Captain Cuttle,' said Walter, handing him the blue
coat and waistcoat, and bustling very much, 'if you'll come and

break the news to Uncle Sol (which he ought to have known, days upon days ago, by rights), I'll leave you at the door, you know, and walk about until the afternoon.'

The Captain, however, scarcely appeared to relish the commission, or to be by any means confident of his powers of executing it. He had arranged the future life and adventures of Walter so very differently, and so entirely to his own satisfaction; he had felicitated himself so often on the sagacity and foresight displayed in that arrangement, and had found it so complete and perfect in all its parts; that to suffer it to go to pieces all at once, and even to assist in breaking it up, required a great effort of his resolution. The Captain, too, found it difficult to unload his old ideas upon the subject, and to take a perfectly new cargo on board, with that rapidity which the circumstances required, or without jumbling and confounding the two. Consequently, instead of putting on his coat and waistcoat with anything like the impetuosity that could alone have kept pace with Walter's mood, he declined to invest himself with those garments at all at present; and informed Walter that on such a serious matter, he must be allowed to 'bite his nails a bit.'

'It's an old habit of mine, Wal'r,' said the Captain, 'any time these fifty year. When you see Ned Cuttle bite his nails, Wal'r, then you may know that Ned Cuttle's aground.'

Thereupon the Captain put his iron hook between his teeth, as if it were a hand; and with an air of wisdom and profundity that was the very concentration and sublimation of all philosophical reflection and grave inquiry, applied himself to the consideration of the subject in its various branches.

'There's a friend of mine,' murmured the Captain, in an absent manner, 'but he's at present coasting round to Whitby, that would deliver such an opinion on this subject, or any other that could be named, as would give Parliament six and beat 'em. Been knocked overboard, that man,' said the Captain, 'twice, and none the worse for it. Was beat in his apprenticeship, for three weeks (off and on), about the head with a ring-bolt. And yet a clearer-minded man don't walk.'

In spite of his respect for Captain Cuttle, Walter could not help inwardly rejoicing at the absence of this sage, and devoutly hoping that his limpid intellect might not be brought to bear on his difficulties until they were quite settled.

'If you was to take and show that man the buoy at the Nore,'[7] said Captain Cuttle in the same tone, 'and ask him his opinion of it, Wal'r, he'd give you an opinion that was no more like that buoy

Profound cogitation of Captain Cuttle

than your uncle's buttons are. There ain't a man that walks –
certainly not on *two* legs – that can come near him. Not near him!'

'What's his name, Captain Cuttle?' inquired Walter, determined
to be interested in the Captain's friend.

'His name's Bunsby,' said the Captain. 'But Lord, it might be
anything for the matter of that, with such a mind as his!'

The exact idea which the Captain attached to this concluding
piece of praise, he did not further elucidate; neither did Walter seek
to draw it forth. For on his beginning to review, with the vivacity
natural to himself and to his situation, the leading points in his own
affairs, he soon discovered that the Captain had relapsed into his
former profound state of mind; and that while he eyed him
steadfastly from beneath his bushy eyebrows, he evidently neither
saw nor heard him, but remained immersed in cogitation.

In fact, Captain Cuttle was labouring with such great designs,
that far from being aground, he soon got off into the deepest of
water, and could find no bottom to his penetration. By degrees it
became perfectly plain to the Captain that there was some mistake
here; that it was undoubtedly much more likely to be Walter's
mistake than his; that if there were really any West India scheme
afoot, it was a very different one from what Walter, who was young
and rash, supposed; and could only be some new device for making
his fortune with unusual celerity. 'Or if there should be any little
hitch between 'em,' thought the Captain, meaning between Walter
and Mr Dombey, 'it only wants a word in season from a friend of
both parties, to set it right and smooth, and make all taut again.'
Captain Cuttle's deduction from these considerations was, that as
he already enjoyed the pleasure of knowing Mr Dombey, from
having spent a very agreeable half-hour in his company at Brighton
(on the morning when they borrowed the money); and that, as a
couple of men of the world, who understood each other, and were
mutually disposed to make things comfortable, could easily arrange
any little difficulty of this sort, and come at the real facts; the
friendly thing for him to do would be, without saying anything
about it to Walter at present, just to step up to Mr Dombey's house
– say to the servant 'Would ye be so good, my lad, as report Cap'en
Cuttle here?' – meet Mr Dombey in a confidential spirit – hook him
by the button-hole – talk it over – make it all right – and come
away triumphant!

As these reflections presented themselves to the Captain's mind,
and by slow degrees assumed this shape and form, his visage cleared
like a doubtful morning when it gives place to a bright noon. His

eyebrows, which had been in the highest degree portentous, smoothed their rugged bristling aspect, and became serene; his eyes, which had been nearly closed in the severity of his mental exercise, opened freely; a smile which had been at first but three specks – one at the right-hand corner of his mouth, and one at the corner of each eye – gradually overspread his whole face, and rippling up into his forehead, lifted the glazed hat: as if that too had been aground with Captain Cuttle, and were now, like him, happily afloat again.

Finally the Captain left off biting his nails, and said, 'Now, Wal'r, my boy, you may help me on with them slops.' By which the Captain meant his coat and waistcoat.

Walter little imagined why the Captain was so particular in the arrangement of his cravat, as to twist the pendent ends into a sort of pigtail, and pass them through a massive gold ring with a picture of a tomb upon it, and a neat iron railing, and a tree, in memory of some deceased friend. Nor why the Captain pulled up his shirt-collar to the utmost limits allowed by the Irish linen below, and by so doing decorated himself with a complete pair of blinkers; nor why he changed his shoes, and put on an unparalleled pair of ankle-jacks,[8] which he only wore on extraordinary occasions. The Captain being at length attired to his own complete satisfaction, and having glanced at himself from head to foot in a shaving-glass which he removed from a nail for that purpose, took up his knotted stick, and said he was ready.

The Captain's walk was more complacent than usual when they got out into the street; but this Walter supposed to be the effect of the ankle-jacks, and took little heed of. Before they had gone very far, they encountered a woman selling flowers; when the Captain stopping short, as if struck by a happy idea, made a purchase of the largest bundle in her basket: a most glorious nosegay, fan-shaped, some two feet and a half round, and composed of all the jolliest-looking flowers that blow.

Armed with this little token which he designed for Mr Dombey, Captain Cuttle walked on with Walter until they reached the Instrument-maker's door, before which they both paused.

'You're going in?' said Walter.

'Yes,' returned the Captain, who felt that Walter must be got rid of before he proceeded any further, and that he had better time his projected visit somewhat later in the day.

'And you won't forget anything?'

'No,' returned the Captain.

'I'll go upon my walk at once,' said Walter, 'and then I shall be out of the way, Captain Cuttle.'

'Take a good long 'un, my lad!' replied the Captain, calling after him. Walter waved his hand in assent, and went his way.

His way was nowhere in particular; but he thought he would go out into the fields, where he could reflect upon the unknown life before him, and resting under some tree ponder quietly. He knew no better fields than those near Hampstead, and no better means of getting at them than by passing Mr Dombey's house.

It was as stately and as dark as ever, when he went by and glanced up at its frowning front. The blinds were all pulled down, but the upper windows stood wide open, and the pleasant air stirring those curtains and waving them to and fro, was the only sign of animation in the whole exterior. Walter walked softly as he passed, and was glad when he had left the house a door or two behind.

He looked back then; with the interest he had always felt for the place since the adventure of the lost child, years ago; and looked especially at those upper windows. While he was thus engaged, a chariot drove to the door, and a portly gentleman in black, with a heavy watch-chain, alighted, and went in. When he afterwards remembered this gentleman and his equipage together, Walter had no doubt he was a physician; and then he wondered who was ill; but the discovery did not occur to him until he had walked some distance, thinking listlessly of other things.

Though still, of what the house had suggested to him; for Walter pleased himself with thinking that perhaps the time might come, when the beautiful child who was his old friend and had always been so grateful to him and so glad to see him since, might interest her brother in his behalf and influence his fortunes for the better. He liked to imagine this – more, at that moment, for the pleasure of imagining her continued remembrance of him, than for any worldly profit he might gain: but another and more sober fancy whispered to him that if he were alive then, he would be beyond the sea and forgotten; she married, rich, proud, happy. There was no more reason why she should remember him with any interest in such an altered state of things, than any plaything she ever had. No, not so much.

Yet Walter so idealised the pretty child whom he had found wandering in the rough streets, and so identified her with her innocent gratitude of that night and the simplicity and truth of its expression, that he blushed for himself as a libeller when he argued that she could ever grow proud. On the other hand, his meditations were of that fantastic order that it seemed hardly less libellous in him to imagine her grown a woman: to think of her as anything but the same artless, gentle, winning little creature, that she had been in the days of Good Mrs Brown. In a word, Walter found out that to reason with himself about Florence at all, was to become very unreasonable indeed; and that he could do no better than preserve her image in his mind as something precious, unattainable, unchangeable, and indefinite – indefinite in all but its power of giving him pleasure, and restraining him like an angel's hand from anything unworthy.

It was a long stroll in the fields that Walter took that day, listening to the birds, and the Sunday bells, and the softened murmur of the town – breathing sweet scents; glancing sometimes at the dim horizon beyond which his voyage and his place of destination lay; then looking round on the green English grass and the home landscape. But he hardly once thought, even of going away, distinctly; and seemed to put off reflection idly, from hour to hour, and from minute to minute, while he yet went on reflecting all the time.

Walter had left the fields behind him, and was plodding homeward in the same abstracted mood, when he heard a shout from a man, and then a woman's voice calling to him loudly by name. Turning quickly in his surprise, he saw that a hackney-coach, going in the contrary direction, had stopped at no great distance; that the coachman was looking back from his box and making signals to him with his whip; and that a young woman inside was leaning out of the window, and beckoning with immense energy. Running up to this coach, he found that the young woman was Miss Nipper, and that Miss Nipper was in such a flutter as to be almost beside herself.

'Staggs's Gardens, Mr Walter!' said Miss Nipper: 'if you please, oh do!'

'Eh?' cried Walter; 'what is the matter?'

'Oh, Mr Walter, Staggs's Gardens, if you please!' said Susan.

'There!' cried the coachman, appealing to Walter, with a sort of exulting despair; 'that's the way the young lady's been a goin' on for up'ards of a mortal hour, and me continivally backing out of no thoroughfares, where she *would* drive up. I've had a many fares in this coach, first and last, but never such a fare as her.'

'Do you want to go to Staggs's Gardens, Susan?' inquired Walter.

'Ah! *She* wants to go there! WHERE IS IT?' growled the coachman.

'I don't know where it is!' exclaimed Susan, wildly. 'Mr Walter, I was there once myself, along with Miss Floy and our poor darling Master Paul, on the very day when you found Miss Floy in the City, for we lost her coming home, Mrs Richards and me, and a mad bull, and Mrs Richards's eldest, and though I went there afterwards, I can't remember where it is, I think it's sunk into the ground. Oh, Mr Walter, don't desert me, Staggs's Gardens, if you please! Miss Floy's darling – all our darlings – little, meek, meek Master Paul! Oh Mr Walter!'

'Good God!' cried Walter. 'Is he very ill?'

'The pretty flower!' cried Susan, wringing her hands, 'has took the fancy that he'd like to see his old nurse, and I've come to bring her to his bedside, Mrs Staggs, of Polly Toodle's Gardens, some one pray!'

Greatly moved by what he heard, and catching Susan's earnestness immediately, Walter, now that he understood the nature of her errand, dashed into it with such ardour that the coachman had enough to do to follow closely as he ran before, inquiring here and there and everywhere, the way to Staggs's Gardens.

There was no such place as Staggs's Gardens.[9] It had vanished from the earth. Where the old rotten summer-houses once had stood, palaces now reared their heads, and granite columns of gigantic girth opened a vista to the railway world beyond. The miserable waste ground, where the refuse-matter had been heaped of yore, was swallowed up and gone; and in its frowsy stead were tiers of warehouses, crammed with rich goods and costly merchandise. The old by-streets now swarmed with passengers and vehicles of every kind: the new streets that had stopped disheartened in the mud and waggon-ruts, formed towns within themselves, originating wholesome comforts and conveniences belonging to themselves, and never tried nor thought of until they sprung into existence. Bridges that had led to nothing, led to villas, gardens, churches, healthy public walks. The carcasses of houses, and beginnings of new thoroughfares, had started off upon the line at steam's own speed, and shot away into the country in a monster train.

As to the neighbourhood which had hesitated to acknowledge the railroad in its straggling days, that had grown wise and penitent, as any Christian might in such a case, and now boasted of its powerful and prosperous relation. There were railway patterns in its drapers' shops, and railway journals in the windows of its newsmen. There were railway hotels, office-houses, lodging-houses, boarding-houses; railway plans, maps, views, wrappers, bottles, sandwich-boxes, and time-tables; railway hackney-coach and cab-stands; railway omnibuses, railway streets and buildings, railway hangers-on and parasites, and flatterers out of all calculation. There was even railway time[10] observed in clocks, as if the sun itself had given in. Among the vanquished was the master chimney-sweeper, whilom[11] incredulous at Staggs's Gardens, who now lived in a stuccoed house three stories high, and gave himself out, with golden flourishes upon a varnished board, as contractor for the cleansing of railway chimneys by machinery.

To and from the heart of this great change, all day and night, throbbing currents rushed and returned incessantly like its life's blood. Crowds of people and mountains of goods, departing and arriving scores upon scores of times in every four-and-twenty hours, produced a fermentation in the place that was always in action. The very houses seemed disposed to pack up and take trips. Wonderful Members of Parliament, who, little more than twenty years before, had made themselves merry with the wild railroad theories of engineers, and given them the liveliest rubs in cross-examination, went down into the north with their watches in their hands, and sent on messages before by the electric telegraph,[12] to say that they were coming. Night and day the conquering engines rumbled at their distant work, or, advancing smoothly to their journey's end, and gliding like tame dragons into the allotted corners grooved out to the inch for their reception, stood bubbling and trembling there, making the walls quake, as if they were dilating with the secret knowledge of great powers yet unsuspected in them, and strong purposes not yet achieved.

But Staggs's Gardens had been cut up root and branch. Oh woe the day when 'not a rood of English ground'[13] – laid out in Staggs's Gardens – is secure!

At last, after much fruitless inquiry, Walter, followed by the coach and Susan, found a man who had once resided in that vanished land, and who was no other than the master sweep before referred to, grown stout, and knocking a double knock at his own door. He knowed Toodle, he said, well. Belonged to the Railroad, didn't he?

'Yes, Sir, yes!' cried Susan Nipper from the coach window.

Where did he live now? hastily inquired Walter.

He lived in the Company's own Buildings, second turning to the right, down the yard, cross over, and take the second on the right again. It was number eleven; they couldn't mistake it; but if they did, they had only to ask for Toodle, Engine Fireman, and any one would show them which was his house. At this unexpected stroke of success, Susan Nipper dismounted from the coach with all speed, took Walter's arm, and set off at a breathless pace on foot; leaving the coach there to await their return.

'Has the little boy been long ill, Susan?' inquired Walter, as they hurried on.

'Ailing for a deal of time, but no one knew how much,' said Susan; adding, with excessive sharpness, 'Oh, them Blimbers!'

'Blimbers?' echoed Walter.

'I couldn't forgive myself at such a time as this, Mr Walter,' said Susan, 'and when there's so much serious distress to think about, if I rested hard on any one, especially on them that little darling Paul speaks well of, but I *may* wish that the family was set to work in a stony soil to make new roads, and that Miss Blimber went in front, and had the pickaxe!'

Miss Nipper then took breath, and went on faster than before, as if this extraordinary aspiration had relieved her. Walter, who had by this time no breath of his own to spare, hurried along without asking any more questions; and they soon, in their impatience, burst in at a little door and came into a clean parlour full of children.

'Where's Mrs Richards?' exclaimed Susan Nipper, looking round. 'Oh Mrs Richards, Mrs Richards, come along with me, my dear creetur!'

'Why, if it an't Susan!' cried Polly, rising with her honest face and motherly figure from among the group, in great surprise.

'Yes, Mrs Richards, it's me,' said Susan, 'and I wish it wasn't, though I may not seem to flatter when I say so, but little Master Paul is very ill, and told his pa to-day that he would like to see the face of his old nurse, and him and Miss Floy hope you'll come along with me — and Mr Walter, Mrs Richards — forgetting what is past, and do a kindness to the sweet dear that is withering away. Oh, Mrs Richards, withering away!' Susan Nipper crying, Polly shed tears to see her, and to hear what she had said; and all the children gathered round (including numbers of new babies); and Mr Toodle, who had just come home from Birmingham, and was eating his dinner out of a basin, laid down his knife and fork, and put on his wife's bonnet and shawl for her, which were hanging up behind the door; then tapped her on the back; and said, with more fatherly feeling than eloquence, 'Polly! cut away!'

So they got back to the coach, long before the coachman expected them; and Walter, putting Susan and Mrs Richards inside, took his seat on the box himself that there might be no more mistakes, and deposited them safely in the hall of Mr Dombey's house – where, by the bye, he saw a mighty nosegay lying, which reminded him of the one Captain Cuttle had purchased in his company that morning. He would have lingered to know more of the young invalid, or waited any length of time to see if he could render the least service; but, painfully sensible that such conduct would be looked upon by Mr Dombey as presumptuous and forward, he turned slowly, sadly, anxiously, away.

He had not gone five minutes' walk from the door, when a man came running after him, and begged him to return. Walter retraced his steps as quickly as he could, and entered the gloomy house with a sorrowful foreboding.

CHAPTER 16

What the Waves were always saying

Paul had never risen from his little bed. He lay there, listening to the noises in the street, quite tranquilly; not caring much how the time went, but watching it and watching everything about him with observing eyes.

When the sunbeams struck into his room through the rustling blinds, and quivered on the opposite wall like golden water, he knew that evening was coming on, and that the sky was red and beautiful. As the reflection died away, and a gloom went creeping up the wall, he watched it deepen, deepen, deepen, into night. Then he thought how the long streets were dotted with lamps, and how the peaceful stars were shining overhead. His fancy had a strange tendency to wander to the river, which he knew was flowing through the great city; and now he thought how black it was, and how deep it would look, reflecting the hosts of stars – and more than all, how steadily it rolled away to meet the sea.

As it grew later in the night, and footsteps in the street became so rare that he could hear them coming, count them as they passed, and lose them in the hollow distance, he would lie and watch the many-coloured ring about the candle, and wait patiently for day. His only trouble was, the swift and rapid river. He felt forced, sometimes, to try to stop it – to stem it with his childish hands – or choke its way with sand – and when he saw it coming on, resistless, he cried out! But a word from Florence, who was always at his side, restored him to himself; and leaning his poor head upon her breast, he told Floy of his dream, and smiled.

When day began to dawn again, he watched for the sun; and when its cheerful light began to sparkle in the room, he pictured to himself – pictured! he saw – the high church towers rising up into the morning sky, the town reviving, waking, starting into life once more, the river glistening as it rolled (but rolling fast as ever), and the country bright with dew. Familiar sounds and cries came by degrees into the street below; the servants in the house were roused and busy; faces looked in at the door, and voices asked his attendants softly how he was. Paul always answered for himself, 'I am better. I am a great deal better, thank you! Tell papa so!'

By little and little, he got tired of the bustle of the day, the noise of carriages and carts, and people passing and repassing; and would fall asleep, or be troubled with a restless and uneasy sense again – the child could hardly tell whether this were in his sleeping or his waking moments – of that rushing river. 'Why, will it never stop, Floy?' he would sometimes ask her. 'It is bearing me away, I think!'

But Floy could always soothe and reassure him; and it was his daily delight to make her lay her head down on his pillow, and take some rest.

'You are always watching me, Floy. Let me watch *you*, now!' They would prop him up with cushions in a corner of his bed, and there he would recline the while she lay beside him: bending forward oftentimes to kiss her, and whispering to those who were near that she was tired, and how she had sat up so many nights beside him.

Thus, the flush of the day, in its heat and light, would gradually decline; and again the golden water would be dancing on the wall.

He was visited by as many as three grave doctors – they used to assemble downstairs, and come up together – and the room was so quiet, and Paul was so observant of them (though he never asked of anybody what they said), that he even knew the difference in the sound of their watches. But his interest centred in Sir Parker Peps, who always took his seat on the side of the bed. For Paul had heard them say long ago, that that gentleman had been with his mama when she clasped Florence in her arms, and died. And he could not forget it, now. He liked him for it. He was not afraid.

The people round him changed as unaccountably as on that first night at Doctor Blimber's – except Florence; Florence never changed – and what had been Sir Parker Peps, was now his father, sitting with his head upon his hand. Old Mrs Pipchin dozing in an easy chair, often changed to Miss Tox, or his aunt; and Paul was quite content to shut his eyes again, and see what happened next without emotion. But this figure with its head upon its hand returned so often, and remained so long, and sat so still and solemn, never speaking, never being spoken to, and rarely lifting up its face, that Paul began to wonder languidly if it were real; and in the night-time saw it sitting there, with fear.

'Floy!' he said. 'What *is* that?'

'Where, dearest?'

'There! at the bottom of the bed.'

'There's nothing there, except papa!'

The figure lifted up its head, and rose, and coming to the bedside, said: 'My own boy! Don't you know me?'

Paul looked it in the face, and thought, was this his father? But the face so altered to his thinking, thrilled while he gazed as if it were in pain; and before he could reach out both his hands to take it between them, and draw it towards him, the figure turned away quickly from the little bed, and went out at the door.

Paul looked at Florence with a fluttering heart, but he knew what she was going to say, and stopped her with his face against her lips. The next time he observed the figure sitting at the bottom of the bed, he called to it.

'Don't be so sorry for me, dear papa! Indeed I am quite happy!'

His father coming and bending down to him – which he did quickly, and without first pausing by the bedside – Paul held him round the neck, and repeated those words to him several times, and very earnestly; and Paul never saw him in his room again at any time, whether it were day or night, but he called out, 'Don't be so sorry for me! Indeed I am quite happy!' This was the beginning of his always saying in the morning that he was a great deal better, and that they were to tell his father so.

How many times the golden water danced upon the wall; how many nights the dark, dark river rolled towards the sea in spite of him; Paul never counted, never sought to know. If their kindness, or his sense of it, could have increased, they were more kind, and he more grateful every day; but whether they were many days or few, appeared of little moment now, to the gentle boy.

One night he had been thinking of his mother, and her picture in the drawing-room downstairs, and thought she must have loved sweet Florence better than his father did, to have held her in her arms when she felt that she was dying – for even he, her brother, who had such dear love for her, could have no greater wish than that. The train of thought suggested to him to inquire if he had ever seen his mother; for he could not remember whether they had told him, yes or no, the river running very fast, and confusing his mind.

'Floy, did I ever see mama?'

'No, darling, why?'

'Did I ever see any kind face, like mama's, looking at me when I was a baby, Floy?'

He asked, incredulously, as if he had some vision of a face before him.

'Oh yes, dear!'

'Whose, Floy?'

'Your old nurse's. Often.'

'And where is my old nurse?' said Paul. 'Is she dead too? Floy, are we *all* dead, except you?'

There was a hurry in the room, for an instant – longer, perhaps; but it seemed no more – then all was still again; and Florence, with her face quite colourless, but smiling, held his head upon her arm. Her arm trembled very much.

'Show me that old nurse, Floy, if you please!'

'She is not here, darling. She shall come to-morrow.'

'Thank you, Floy!'

Paul closed his eyes with those words, and fell asleep. When he awoke, the sun was high, and the broad day was clear and warm. He lay a little, looking at the windows, which were open, and the curtains rustling in the air, and waving to and fro: then he said, 'Floy, is it to-morrow? Is she come?'

Some one seemed to go in quest of her. Perhaps it was Susan. Paul thought he heard her telling him when he had closed his eyes again, that she would soon be back; but he did not open them to see. She kept her word – perhaps she had never been away – but the next thing that happened was a noise of footsteps on the stairs, and then Paul woke – woke mind and body – and sat upright in his bed. He saw them now about him. There was no grey mist before them, as there had been sometimes in the night. He knew them every one, and called them by their names.

'And who is this? Is this my old nurse?' said the child, regarding with a radiant smile, a figure coming in.

Yes, yes. No other stranger would have shed those tears at sight of him, and called him her dear boy, her pretty boy, her own poor blighted child. No other woman would have stooped down by his bed, and taken up his wasted hand, and put it to her lips and breast, as one who had some right to fondle it. No other woman would have so forgotten everybody there but him and Floy, and been so full of tenderness and pity.

'Floy! this is a kind good face!' said Paul. 'I am glad to see it again. Don't go away, old nurse! Stay here.'

His senses were all quickened, and he heard a name he knew.

'Who was that, who said "Walter"?' he asked, looking round. 'Some one said Walter. Is he here? I should like to see him very much.'

Nobody replied directly; but his father soon said to Susan, 'Call him back, then: let him come up!' After a short pause of expectation, during which he looked with smiling interest and wonder, on his nurse, and saw that she had not forgotten Floy, Walter was brought into the room. His open face and manner, and his cheerful eyes, had always made him a favourite with Paul; and when Paul saw him, he stretched out his hand, and said 'Good-bye!'

'Good-bye, my child!' said Mrs Pipchin, hurrying to his bed's head. 'Not good-bye?'

For an instant, Paul looked at her with the wistful face with which he had so often gazed upon her in his corner by the fire. 'Ah yes,' he said placidly, 'good-bye! Walter dear, goodbye!' – turning his head to where he stood, and putting out his hand again. 'Where is papa?'

He felt his father's breath upon his cheek, before the words had parted from his lips.

'Remember Walter, dear papa,' he whispered, looking in his face. 'Remember Walter. I was fond of Walter!' The feeble hand waved in the air, as if it cried 'good-bye!' to Walter once again.

'Now lay me down,' he said, 'and, Floy, come close to me, and let me see you!'

Sister and brother wound their arms around each other, and the golden light came streaming in, and fell upon them, locked together.

'How fast the river runs, between its green banks and the rushes, Floy! But it's very near the sea. I hear the waves! They always said so!'

Presently he told her that the motion of the boat upon the stream was lulling him to rest. How green the banks were now, how bright the flowers growing on them, and how tall the rushes! Now the boat was out at sea, but gliding smoothly on. And now there was a shore before him. Who stood on the bank! —

He put his hands together, as he had been used to do at his

prayers. He did not remove his arms to do it; but they saw him fold them so, behind her neck.

'Mama is like you, Floy. I know her by the face! But tell them that the print upon the stairs at school is not divine enough. The light about the head is shining on me as I go!'

The golden ripple on the wall came back again, and nothing else stirred in the room. The old, old fashion! The fashion that came in with our first garments, and will last unchanged until our race has run its course, and the wide firmament is rolled up like a scroll. The old, old fashion – Death!

Oh thank GOD, all who see it, for that older fashion yet, of Immortality! And look upon us, angels of young children, with regards not quite estranged, when the swift river bears us to the ocean![1]

CHAPTER 17

Captain Cuttle does a little Business
for the young people

Captain Cuttle, in the exercise of that surprising talent for deep-laid and unfathomable scheming, with which (as is not unusual in men of transparent simplicity) he sincerely believed himself to be endowed by nature, had gone to Mr Dombey's house on the eventful Sunday, winking all the way as a vent for his superfluous sagacity, and had presented himself in the full lustre of the ankle-jacks before the eyes of Towlinson. Hearing from that individual, to his great concern, of the impending calamity, Captain Cuttle, in his delicacy, sheered off again confounded; merely handing in the nosegay as a small mark of his solicitude, and leaving his respectful compliments for the family in general, which he accompanied with an expression of his hope that they would lay their heads well to the wind under existing circumstances, and a friendly intimation that he would 'look up again' to-morrow.

The Captain's compliments were never heard of any more. The Captain's nosegay, after lying in the hall all night, was swept into the dust-bin next morning; and the Captain's sly arrangement, involved in one catastrophe with greater hopes and loftier designs, was crushed to pieces. So, when an avalanche bears down a mountain – forest, twigs and bushes suffer with the trees, and all perish together.

When Walter returned home on the Sunday evening from his long walk, and its memorable close, he was too much occupied at first by the tidings he had to give them, and by the emotions naturally awakened in his breast by the scene through which he had passed, to observe either that his uncle was evidently unacquainted with the intelligence the Captain had undertaken to impart, or that the Captain made signals with his hook, warning him to avoid the subject. Not that the Captain's signals were calculated to have proved very comprehensible, however attentively observed; for, like those Chinese sages who are said in their conferences to write certain learned words in the air that are wholly impossible of pronunciation, the Captain made such waves and flourishes as nobody without a previous knowledge of his mystery, would have been at all likely to understand.

Captain Cuttle, however, becoming cognisant of what had happened, relinquished these attempts, as he perceived the slender chance that now existed of his being able to obtain a little easy chat with Mr Dombey before the period of Walter's departure. But in admitting to himself, with a disappointed and crestfallen countenance, that Sol Gills must be told, and that Walter must go – taking the case for the present as he found it, and not having it enlightened or improved beforehand by the knowing management of a friend – the Captain still felt an unabated confidence that he, Ned Cuttle, was the man for Mr Dombey; and that, to set Walter's fortunes quite square, nothing was wanted but that they two should come together. For the Captain never could forget how well he and Mr Dombey had got on at Brighton; with what nicety each of them had put in a word when it was wanted; how exactly they had taken one another's measure; nor how Ned Cuttle had pointed out that resource in the first extremity, and had brought the interview to the desired termination. On all these grounds the Captain soothed himself with thinking that though Ned Cuttle was forced by the pressure of events to 'stand by' almost useless for the present, Ned would fetch up with a wet sail in good time, and carry all before him.

Under the influence of this good-natured delusion, Captain Cuttle even went so far as to revolve in his own bosom, while he sat looking at Walter and listening with a tear on his shirt-collar to what he related, whether it might not be at once genteel and politic to give Mr Dombey a verbal invitation, whenever they should meet, to come and cut his mutton in Brig Place on some day of his own naming, and enter on the question of his young friend's prospects over a social glass. But the uncertain temper of Mrs MacStinger, and the possibility of her setting up her rest in the passage during such an entertainment, and there delivering some homily of an uncomplimentary nature, operated as a check on the Captain's hospitable thoughts, and rendered him timid of giving them encouragement.

One fact was quite clear to the Captain, as Walter, sitting thoughtfully over his untasted dinner, dwelt on all that had happened; namely, that however Walter's modesty might stand in the way of his perceiving it himself, he was, as one might say, a member of Mr Dombey's family. He had been, in his own person, connected with the incident he so pathetically described; he had been by name remembered and commended in close association with it; and his fortunes must have a particular interest in his employer's eyes. If the Captain had any lurking doubt whatever of his own conclusions, he had not the least doubt that they were good conclusions for the peace of mind of the Instrument-maker. Therefore he availed himself of so favourable a moment for breaking the West Indian Intelligence to his old friend, as a piece of extraordinary preferment; declaring that for his part he would freely give a hundred thousand pounds (if he had it) for Walter's gain in the long-run, and that he had no doubt such an investment would yield a handsome premium.

Solomon Gills was at first stunned by the communication, which fell upon the little back parlour like a thunderbolt, and tore up the hearth savagely. But the Captain flashed such golden prospects before his dim sight: hinted so mysteriously at Whittingtonian consequences; laid such emphasis on what Walter had just now told them: and appealed to it so confidently as a corroboration of his predictions, and a great advance towards the realisation of the romantic legend of Lovely Peg: that he bewildered the old man. Walter, for his part, feigned to be so full of hope and ardour, and so sure of coming home again soon, and backed up the Captain with such expressive shakings of his head and rubbings of his hands, that Solomon, looking first at him and then at Captain Cuttle, began to think he ought to be transported with joy.

'But I'm behind the time, you understand,' he observed in apology, passing his hand nervously down the whole row of bright buttons on his coat, and then up again, as if they were beads and he were telling them twice over: 'and I would rather have my dear boy here. It's an old-fashioned notion, I dare say. He was always fond of the sea. He's' – and he looked wistfully at Walter – 'he's glad to go.'

'Uncle Sol!' cried Walter, quickly, 'if you say that, I *won't* go. No, Captain Cuttle, I won't. If my uncle thinks I could be glad to leave him, though I was going to be made Governor of all the Islands in the West Indies, that's enough. I'm a fixture.'

'Wal'r, my lad,' said the Captain. 'Steady! Sol Gills, take an observation of your nevy.'

Following with his eyes the majestic action of the Captain's hook, the old man looked at Walter.

'Here is a certain craft,' said the Captain, with a magnificent sense of the allegory into which he was soaring, 'a-going to put out on a certain voyage. What name is wrote upon that craft indelibly? Is it The Gay? or,' said the Captain, raising his voice as much as to say, observe the point of this, 'is it The Gills?'

'Ned,' said the old man, drawing Walter to his side, and taking his arm tenderly through his, 'I know. I know. Of course I know that Wally considers me more than himself always. That's in my mind. When I say he is glad to go, I mean I hope he is. Eh? look you, Ned, and you too, Wally, my dear, this is new and unexpected to me; and I'm afraid my being behind the time, and poor, is at the bottom of it. Is it really good fortune for him, do you tell me, now?' said the old man, looking anxiously from one to the other. 'Really and truly? Is it? I can reconcile myself to almost anything that advances Wally, but I won't have Wally putting himself at any disadvantage for me, or keeping anything from me. You, Ned Cuttle!' said the old man, fastening on the Captain, to the manifest confusion of that diplomatist; 'are you dealing plainly by your old friend? Speak out, Ned Cuttle. Is there anything behind? Ought he to go? How do you know it first, and why?'

As it was a contest of affection and self-denial, Walter struck in with infinite effect, to the Captain's relief; and between them they tolerably reconciled old Sol Gills, by continued talking, to the project; or rather so confused him, that nothing, not even the pain of separation, was distinctly clear to his mind.

He had not much time to balance the matter; for on the very next day, Walter received from Mr Carker the Manager, the necessary credentials for his passage and outfit, together with the information that the Son and Heir would sail in a fortnight, or within a day or two afterwards at latest. In the hurry of preparation: which Walter purposely enhanced as much as possible: the old man lost what little self-possession he ever had; and so the time of departure drew on rapidly.

The Captain, who did not fail to make himself acquainted with all that passed, through inquiries of Walter from day to day, found the time still tending on towards his going away, without any occasion offering itself, or seeming likely to offer itself, for a better understanding of his position. It was after much consideration of this fact, and much pondering over such an unfortunate combination of circumstances, that a bright idea occurred to the Captain. Suppose he made a call on Mr Carker, and tried to find out from *him* how the land really lay!

Captain Cuttle liked this idea very much. It came upon him in a moment of inspiration, as he was smoking an early pipe in Brig Place after breakfast; and it was worthy of the tobacco. It would quiet his conscience, which was an honest one, and was made a little uneasy by what Walter had confided to him, and what Sol Gills had said; and it would be a deep, shrewd act of friendship. He would sound Mr Carker carefully, and say much or little, just as he read that gentleman's character, and discovered that they got on well together or the reverse.

Accordingly without the fear of Walter before his eyes (who he knew was at home packing), Captain Cuttle again assumed his ankle-jacks and mourning brooch, and issued forth on this second expedition. He purchased no propitiatory nosegay on the present occasion, as he was going to a place of business; but he put a small sunflower in his button-hole to give himself an agreeable relish of the country; and with this, and the knobby stick, and the glazed hat, bore down upon the offices of Dombey and Son.

After taking a glass of warm rum-and-water at a tavern close by, to collect his thoughts, the Captain made a rush down the court, lest its good effects should evaporate, and appeared suddenly to Mr Perch.

'Matey,' said the Captain, in persuasive accents. 'One of your Governors is named Carker.'

Mr Perch admitted it; but gave him to understand, as in official duty bound, that all his Governors were engaged, and never expected to be disengaged any more.

'Look'ee here, mate,' said the Captain in his ear; 'my name's Cap'en Cuttle.'

The Captain would have hooked Perch gently to him, but Mr Perch eluded the attempt; not so much in design, as in starting at the sudden thought that such a weapon unexpectedly exhibited to

Mrs Perch might, in her then condition, be destructive to that lady's hopes.

'If you'll be so good as just report Cap'en Cuttle here, when you get a chance,' said the Captain, 'I'll wait.'

Saying which, the Captain took his seat on Mr Perch's bracket, and drawing out his handkerchief from the crown of the glazed hat, which he jammed between his knees (without injury to its shape, for nothing human could bend it), rubbed his head well all over, and appeared refreshed. He subsequently arranged his hair with his hook, and sat looking round the office, contemplating the clerks with a serene respect.

The Captain's equanimity was so impenetrable, and he was altogether so mysterious a being, that Perch the messenger was daunted.

'What name was it you said?' asked Mr Perch, bending down over him as he sat on the bracket.

'Cap'en,' in a deep hoarse whisper.

'Yes,' said Mr Perch, keeping time with his head.

'Cuttle.'

'Oh!' said Mr Perch, in the same tone, for he caught it, and couldn't help it; the Captain, in his diplomacy, was so impressive. 'I'll see if he's disengaged now. I don't know. Perhaps he may be for a minute.'

'Aye, aye, my lad, I won't detain him longer than a minute,' said the Captain, nodding with all the weighty importance that he felt within him. Perch, soon returning, said, 'Will Captain Cuttle walk this way?'

Mr Carker the Manager, standing on the hearth-rug before the empty fireplace, which was ornamented with a castellated sheet of brown paper, looked at the Captain as he came in, with no very special encouragement.

'Mr Carker?' said Captain Cuttle.

'I believe so,' said Mr Carker, showing all his teeth.

The Captain liked his answering with a smile; it looked pleasant. 'You see,' began the Captain, rolling his eyes slowly round the little room, and taking in as much of it as his shirt-collar permitted; 'I'm a seafaring man myself, Mr Carker, and Wal'r, as is on your books here, is a'most a son of mine.'

'Walter Gay?' said Mr Carker, showing all his teeth again.

'Wal'r Gay it is,' replied the Captain, 'right!' The Captain's manner expressed a warm approval of Mr Carker's quickness of perception. 'I'm a intimate friend of his and his uncle's. Perhaps,' said the Captain, 'you may have heard your head Governor mention my name? – Captain Cuttle.'

'No!' said Mr Carker, with a still wider demonstration than before.

'Well,' resumed the Captain, 'I've the pleasure of his acquaintance. I waited upon him down on the Sussex coast there, with my young friend Wal'r, when – in short, when there was a little accommodation wanted.' The Captain nodded his head in a manner that was at once comfortable, easy, and expressive. 'You remember, I dare say?'

'I think,' said Mr Carker, 'I had the honour of arranging the business.'

'To be sure!' returned the Captain. 'Right again! you had. Now I've took the liberty of coming here—'

'Won't you sit down?' said Mr Carker, smiling.

'Thank'ee,' returned the Captain, availing himself of the offer. 'A man does get more way upon himself, perhaps, in his conversation, when he sits down. Won't you take a cheer[1] yourself?'

'No thank you,' said the Manager, standing, perhaps from the force of winter habit, with his back against the chimney-piece, and looking down upon the Captain with an eye in every tooth and gum. 'You have taken the liberty, you were going to say – though it's none—'

'Thank'ee kindly, my lad,' returned the Captain: 'of coming here, on account of my friend Wal'r. Sol Gills, his uncle, is a man of science, and in science he may be considered a clipper;[2] but he ain't what I should altogether call a able seaman – not a man of practice. Walter is as trim a lad as ever stepped; but he's a little down by the head[3] in one respect, and that is modesty. Now what I should wish to put to you,' said the Captain, lowering his voice, and speaking in a kind of confidential growl, 'in a friendly way, entirely between you and me, and for my own private reckoning, 'till your head Governor has wore round a bit,[4] and I can come alongside of him, is this. – Is everything right and comfortable here, and is Wal'r out'ard bound with a pretty fair wind?'

'What do you think now, Captain Cuttle?' returned Carker, gathering up his skirts and settling himself in his position. '*You* are a practical man; what do you think?'

The acuteness and significance of the Captain's eye as he cocked it in reply, no words short of those unutterable Chinese words before referred to could describe.

'Come!' said the Captain, unspeakably encouraged, 'what do you say? Am I right or wrong?'

So much had the Captain expressed in his eye, emboldened and incited by Mr Carker's smiling urbanity, that he felt himself in as fair a condition to put the question, as if he had expressed his sentiments with the utmost elaboration.

'Right,' said Mr Carker, 'I have no doubt.'

'Out'ard bound with fair weather, then, I say,' cried Captain Cuttle.

Mr Carker smiled assent.

'Wind right astern, and plenty of it,' pursued the Captain.

Mr Carker smiled assent again.

'Aye, aye!' said Captain Cuttle, greatly relieved and pleased. 'I know'd how she headed, well enough; I told Wal'r so. Thank'ee, thank'ee.'

'Gay has brilliant prospects,' observed Mr Carker, stretching his mouth wider yet: 'all the world before him.'

'All the world and his wife too, as the saying is,' returned the delighted Captain.

At the word 'wife' (which he had uttered without design), the Captain stopped, cocked his eye again, and putting the glazed hat on the top of the knobby stick, gave it a twirl, and looked sideways at his always smiling friend.

'I'd bet a gill of old Jamaica,' said the Captain, eyeing him attentively, 'that I know what you're smiling at.'

Mr Carker took his cue, and smiled the more.

'It goes no farther?' said the Captain, making a poke at the door with the knobby stick to assure himself that it was shut.

'Not an inch,' said Mr Carker.

'You're a thinking of a capital F perhaps?' said the Captain.

Mr Carker didn't deny it.

'Anything about a L,' said the Captain, 'or a O?'

Mr Carker still smiled.

'Am I right again?' inquired the Captain in a whisper, with a scarlet circle on his forehead swelling in his triumphant joy.

Mr Carker, in reply, still smiling, and now nodding assent, Captain Cuttle rose and squeezed him by the hand, assuring him, warmly, that they were on the same tack, and that as for him (Cuttle) he had laid his course that way all along. 'He know'd her first,' said the Captain, with all the secrecy and gravity that the subject demanded, 'in an uncommon manner – *you* remember his finding her in the street when she was a'most a babby – he has liked her ever since, and she him, as much as two such youngsters can. We've always said, Sol Gills and me, that they was cut out for each other.'

A cat, or a monkey, or a hyena, or a death's-head, could not have shown the Captain more teeth at one time, than Mr Carker showed him at this period of their interview.

'There's a general in-draught that way,' observed the happy Captain. 'Wind and water sets in that direction, you see. Look at his being present t'other day!'

'Most favourable to his hopes,' said Mr Carker.

'Look at his being towed along in the wake of that day!' pursued the Captain. 'Why, what can cut him adrift now?'

'Nothing,' replied Mr Carker.

'You're right again,' returned the Captain, giving his hand another squeeze. 'Nothing it is. So! steady! There's a son gone: pretty little creetur. Ain't there?'

'Yes, there's a son gone,' said the acquiescent Carker.

'Pass the word, and there's another ready for you,' quoth the Captain. 'Nevy of a scientific uncle! Nevy of Sol Gills! Wal'r! Wal'r, as is already in your business! And' – said the Captain, rising gradually to a quotation he was preparing for a final burst, 'who – comes from Sol Gills's daily, *to* your business, and your buzzums.'[5]

The Captain's complacency as he gently jogged Mr Carker with his elbow, on concluding each of the foregoing short sentences, could be surpassed by nothing but the exultation with which he fell back and eyed him when he had finished this brilliant display of eloquence and sagacity; his great blue waistcoat heaving with the throes of such a masterpiece, and his nose in a state of violent inflammation from the same cause.

'Am I right?' said the Captain.

'Captain Cuttle,' said Mr Carker, bending down at the knees, for a moment, in an odd manner, as if he were falling together to hug the whole of himself at once, 'your views in reference to Walter Gay are thoroughly and accurately right. I understand that we speak together in confidence.'

'Honour!' interposed the Captain. 'Not a word.'

'To him or any one?' pursued the Manager.

Captain Cuttle frowned and shook his head.

'But merely for your own satisfaction and guidance – and guidance, of course,' repeated Mr Carker, 'with a view to your future proceedings.'

'Thank'ee kindly, I am sure,' said the Captain, listening with great attention.

'I have no hesitation in saying, that's the fact. You have hit the probabilities exactly.'

'And with regard to your head Governor,' said the Captain, 'why, an interview had better come about nat'ral between us. There's time enough.'

Mr Carker, with his mouth from ear to ear, repeated, 'Time enough.' Not articulating the words, but bowing his head affably, and forming them with his tongue and lips.

'And as I know now – it's what I always said – that Wal'r's in a way to make his fortune,' said the Captain.

'To make his fortune,' Mr Carker repeated, in the same dumb manner.

'And as Wal'r's going on this little voyage is, as I may say, in his day's work, and a part of his general expectations here,' said the Captain.

'Of his general expectations here,' assented Mr Carker, dumbly as before.

'Why, so long as I know that,' pursued the Captain, 'there's no hurry, and my mind's at ease.'

Mr Carker still blandly assenting in the same voiceless manner, Captain Cuttle was strongly confirmed in his opinion that he was one of the most agreeable men he had ever met, and that even Mr Dombey might improve himself on such a model. With great heartiness, therefore, the Captain once again extended his enormous hand (not unlike an old block in colour), and gave him a grip that left upon his smoother flesh a proof impression of the chinks and crevices with which the Captain's palm was liberally tattooed.

'Farewell!' said the Captain. 'I an't a man of many words, but I take it very kind of you to be so friendly, and above-board. You'll excuse me if I've been at all intruding, will you?' said the Captain.

'Not at all,' returned the other.

'Thank'ee. My berth an't very roomy,' said the Captain, turning back again, 'but it's tolerably snug; and if you was to find yourself near Brig Place, number nine, at any time – will you make a note of it? – and would come upstairs, without minding what was said by the person at the door, I should be proud to see you.'

With that hospitable invitation, the Captain said 'Good day!' and walked out and shut the door; leaving Mr Carker still reclining against the chimney-piece. In whose sly look and watchful manner; in whose false mouth, stretched but not laughing; in whose spotless cravat and very whiskers, even in whose silent passing of his soft hand over his white linen and his smooth face; there was something desperately cat-like.

The unconscious Captain walked out in a state of self-glorification that imparted quite a new cut to the broad blue suit. 'Stand by, Ned!' said the Captain to himself. 'You've done a little business for the youngsters to-day, my lad!'

In his exultation, and in his familiarity, present and prospective, with the House, the Captain, when he reached the outer office, could not refrain from rallying Mr Perch a little, and asking him whether he thought everybody was still engaged. But not to be bitter on a man who had done his duty, the Captain whispered in his ear, that if he felt disposed for a glass of rum-and-water, and would follow, he would be happy to bestow the same upon him.

Before leaving the premises, the Captain, somewhat to the astonishment of the clerks, looked round from a central point of view, and took a general survey of the office as part and parcel of a project in which his young friend was nearly interested. The strong-room excited his special admiration; but, that he might not appear too particular, he limited himself to an approving glance, and, with a graceful recognition of the clerks as a body, that was full of politeness and patronage, passed out into the court. Being promptly joined by Mr Perch, he conveyed that gentleman to the tavern, and fulfilled his pledge – hastily, for Perch's time was precious.

'I'll give you for a toast,' said the Captain, 'Wal'r!'

'Who?' submitted Mr Perch.

'Wal'r!' repeated the Captain, in a voice of thunder.

Mr Perch, who seemed to remember having heard in infancy that there was once a poet of that name,[6] made no objection; but he was much astonished at the Captain's coming into the City to propose a poet; indeed, if he had proposed to put a poet's statue up – say Shakespeare's for example – in a civic thoroughfare, he could hardly have done a greater outrage to Mr Perch's experience. On the whole, he was such a mysterious and incomprehensible character, that Mr Perch decided not to mention him to Mrs Perch at all, in case of giving rise to any disagreeable consequences.

Mysterious and incomprehensible, the Captain, with that lively sense upon him of having done a little business for the youngsters, remained all day, even to his most intimate friends; and but that Walter attributed his winks and grins, and other such pantomimic reliefs of himself, to his satisfaction in the success of their innocent deception upon old Sol Gills, he would assuredly have betrayed himself before night. As it was, however, he kept his own secret; and went home late from the Instrument-maker's house, wearing the glazed hat so much on one side, and carrying such a beaming expression in his eyes, that Mrs MacStinger (who might have been brought up at Doctor Blimber's, she was such a Roman matron)[7] fortified herself, at the first glimpse of him, behind the open street door, and refused to come out to the contemplation of her blessed infants, until he was securely lodged in his own room.

CHAPTER 18

Father and Daughter

There is a hush through Mr Dombey's house. Servants gliding up and downstairs rustle, but make no sound of footsteps. They talk together constantly, and sit long at meals, making much of their meat and drink, and enjoying themselves after a grim unholy fashion. Mrs Wickam, with her eyes suffused with tears, relates melancholy anecdotes; and tells them how she always said at Mrs Pipchin's that it would be so, and takes more table-ale than usual, and is very sorry but sociable. Cook's state of mind is similar. She promises a little fry for supper, and struggles about equally against her feelings and the onions. Towlinson begins to think there's a fate in it, and wants to know if anybody can tell him of any good that ever came of living in a corner house. It seems to all of them as having happened a long time ago; though yet the child lies, calm and beautiful, upon his little bed.

After dark there come some visitors – noiseless visitors, with shoes of felt – who have been there before; and with them comes that bed of rest which is so strange a one for infant sleepers. All this time, the bereaved father has not been seen even by his attendant; for he sits in an inner corner of his own dark room when any one is there, and never seems to move at other times except to pace it to and fro. But in the morning it is whispered among the household that he was heard to go upstairs in the dead night, and that he stayed there – in the room – until the sun was shining.

At the offices in the City, the ground-glass windows are made more dim by shutters; and while the lighted lamps upon the desks are half extinguished by the day that wanders in, the day is half extinguished by the lamps, and unusual gloom prevails. There is not much business done. The clerks are indisposed to work; and they make assignations to eat chops in the afternoon, and go up the river. Perch, the messenger, stays long upon his errands; and finds himself in bars of public-houses, invited thither by friends, and holding forth on the uncertainty of human affairs. He goes home to Ball's Pond earlier in the evening than usual, and treats Mrs Perch to a veal cutlet and Scotch ale. Mr Carker the Manager treats no one; neither is he treated; but alone in his own room he shows his teeth all day; and it would seem that there is something gone from Mr Carker's path – some obstacle removed – which clears his way before him.

Now the rosy children living opposite to Mr Dombey's house, peep from their nursery windows down into the street; for there are four black horses at his door, with feathers on their heads; and feathers tremble on the carriage that they draw; and these, and an array of men with scarves and staves, attract a crowd. A juggler who was going to twirl the basin, puts his loose coat on again over his fine dress; and his trudging wife, one-sided with her heavy baby in her arms, loiters to see the company come out. But closer to her dingy breast she presses her baby, when the burden that is so easily carried is borne forth; and the youngest of the rosy children at the high window opposite, needs no restraining hand to check her in her glee, when, pointing with her dimpled finger, she looks into her nurse's face, and asks 'What's that?'

And now, among the knot of servants dressed in mourning, and the weeping women, Mr Dombey passes through the hall to the other carriage that is waiting to receive him. He is not 'brought down,' these observers think, by sorrow and distress of mind. His walk is as erect, his bearing is as stiff as ever it has been. He hides his face behind no handkerchief, and looks before him. But that his face is something sunk and rigid, and is pale, it bears the same expression as of old. He takes his place within the carriage, and three other gentlemen follow. Then the grand funeral moves slowly down the street. The feathers are yet nodding in the distance, when the juggler has the basin spinning on a cane, and has the same crowd to admire it. But the juggler's wife is less alert than usual with the money-box, for a child's burial has set her thinking that perhaps the baby underneath her shabby shawl may not grow up to be a man, and wear a sky-blue fillet[1] round his head, and salmon-coloured worsted drawers,[2] and tumble in the mud.

The feathers wind their gloomy way along the streets, and come within the sound of a church bell. In this same church, the pretty boy received all that will soon be left of him on earth – a name. All of him that is dead, they lay there, near the perishable substance of his mother. It is well. Their ashes lie where Florence in her walks – oh lonely, lonely walks! – may pass them any day.

The service over, and the clergyman withdrawn, Mr Dombey looks round, demanding in a low voice, whether the person who has been requested to attend to receive instructions for the tablet, is there?

Some one comes forward, and says 'Yes.'

Mr Dombey intimates where he would have it placed; and shows him, with his hand upon the wall, the shape and size; and how it is to follow the memorial to the mother. Then, with his pencil, he writes out the inscription, and gives it to him: adding, 'I wish to have it done at once.'

'It shall be done immediately, Sir.'

'There is really nothing to inscribe but name and age, you see.'

The man bows, glancing at the paper, but appears to hesitate. Mr Dombey not observing his hesitation, turns away, and leads towards the porch.

'I beg your pardon, Sir;' a touch falls gently on his mourning cloak; 'but as you wish it done immediately, and it may be put in hand when I get back—'

'Well?'

'Will you be so good as to read it over again? I think there's a mistake.'

'Where?'

The statuary[3] gives him back the paper, and points out, with his pocket rule, the words, 'beloved and only child.'

'It should be, "son," I think, Sir?'

'You are right. Of course. Make the correction.'

The father, with a hastier step, pursues his way to the coach. When the other three, who follow closely, take their seats, his face is hidden for the first time – shaded by his cloak. Nor do they see it any more that day. He alights first, and passes immediately into his own room. The other mourners (who are only Mr Chick, and two of the medical attendants) proceed up stairs to the drawing-room, to be received by Mrs Chick and Miss Tox. And what the face is, in the shut-up chamber underneath: or what the thoughts are: what the heart is, what the contest or the suffering: no one knows.

The chief thing that they know below stairs, in the kitchen, is that 'it seems like Sunday.' They can hardly persuade themselves but that there is something unbecoming, if not wicked, in the conduct of the people out of doors, who pursue their ordinary occupations, and wear their every-day attire. It is quite a novelty to have the blinds up, and the shutters open: and they make themselves dismally comfortable over bottles of wine, which are freely broached as on a festival. They are much inclined to moralise. Mr Towlinson proposes with a sigh, 'Amendment[4] to us all!' for which, as Cook says with another sigh, 'There's room enough, God knows.' In the evening, Mrs Chick and Miss Tox take to needlework again. In the evening also, Mr Towlinson goes out to take the air, accompanied by the housemaid, who has not yet tried her mourning bonnet. They are very tender to each other at dusky street-corners, and Towlinson has visions of leading an altered and blameless existence as a serious greengrocer in Oxford Market.[5]

There is sounder sleep and deeper rest in Mr Dombey's house to-night, than there has been for many nights. The morning sun awakens the old household, settled down once more in their old ways. The rosy children opposite run past with hoops. There is a splendid wedding in the church. The juggler's wife is active with the money-box in another quarter of the town. The mason sings and whistles as he chips out P-A-U-L in the marble slab before him.

And can it be that in a world so full and busy, the loss of one weak creature makes a void in any heart, so wide and deep that nothing but the width and depth of vast eternity can fill it up! Florence, in her innocent affliction, might have answered, 'Oh my brother, oh my dearly loved and loving brother! Only friend and companion of my slighted childhood! Could any less idea shed the light already dawning on your early grave, or give birth to the softened sorrow that is springing into life beneath this rain of tears!'

'My dear child,' said Mrs Chick, who held it as a duty incumbent on her, to improve the occasion, 'when you are as old as I am—'

'Which will be the prime of life,' observed Miss Tox.

'You will then,' pursued Mrs Chick, gently squeezing Miss Tox's hand in acknowledgment of her friendly remark, 'you will then know that all grief is unavailing, and that it is our duty to submit.'

'I will try, dear aunt. I do try,' answered Florence, sobbing.

'I am glad to hear it,' said Mrs Chick, 'because, my love, as our dear Miss Tox – of whose sound sense and excellent judgment, there cannot possibly be two opinions—'

'My dear Louisa, I shall really be proud, soon,' said Miss Tox.

—'will tell you, and confirm by her experience,' pursued Mrs Chick, 'we are called upon on all occasions to make an effort. It is required of us. If any – my dear,' turning to Miss Tox, 'I want a word. Mis – Mis—'

'Demeanour?' suggested Miss Tox.

'No, no, no,' said Mrs Chick. 'How can you! Goodness me, it's on the end of my tongue. Mis—'

'Placed affection?' suggested Miss Tox, timidly.

'Good gracious, Lucretia!' returned Mrs Chick. 'How very monstrous! Misanthrope, is the word I want. The idea! Misplaced affection! I say, if any misanthrope were to put, in my presence, the question, "Why were we born?" I should reply, "To make an effort."'

'Very good indeed,' said Miss Tox, much impressed by the originality of the sentiment. 'Very good.'

'Unhappily,' pursued Mrs Chick, 'we have a warning under our own eyes. We have but too much reason to suppose, my dear child, that if an effort had been made in time, in this family, a train of the most trying and distressing circumstances might have been avoided. Nothing shall ever persuade me,' observed the good matron, with a resolute air, 'but that if that effort had been made by poor dear Fanny, the poor dear darling child would at least have had a stronger constitution.'

Mrs Chick abandoned herself to her feelings for half a moment; but, as a practical illustration of her doctrine, brought herself up short, in the middle of a sob, and went on again.

'Therefore, Florence, pray let us see that you have some strength of mind, and do not selfishly aggravate the distress in which your poor papa is plunged.'

'Dear aunt!' said Florence, kneeling quickly down before her, that she might the better and more earnestly look into her face. 'Tell me more about papa. Pray tell me about him! Is he quite heartbroken?'

Miss Tox was of a tender nature, and there was something in this appeal that moved her very much. Whether she saw it in a succession, on the part of the neglected child, to the affectionate concern so often expressed by her dead brother – or a love that sought to twine itself about the heart that had loved him, and that could not bear to be shut out from sympathy with such a sorrow, in such sad community of love and grief – or whether she only recognised the earnest and devoted spirit which, although discarded and repulsed, was wrung with tenderness long unreturned, and in the waste and solitude of this bereavement cried to him to seek a comfort in it, and to give some, by some small response – whatever may have been her understanding of it, it moved Miss Tox. For the moment she forgot the majesty of Mrs Chick, and, patting Florence hastily on the cheek, turned aside and suffered the tears to gush from her eyes, without waiting for a lead from that wise matron.

Mrs Chick herself lost, for a moment, the presence of mind on which she so much prided herself; and remained mute, looking on the beautiful young face that had so long, so steadily, and patiently, been turned towards the little bed. But recovering her voice – which was synonymous with her presence of mind, indeed they were one and the same thing – she replied with dignity:

'Florence, my dear child, your poor papa is peculiar at times; and to question me about him, is to question me upon a subject which I really do not pretend to understand. I believe I have as much influence with your papa as anybody has. Still, all I can say is, that he has said very little to me; and that I have only seen him once or twice for a minute at a time, and indeed have hardly seen him then, for his room has been dark. I have said to your papa, "Paul!" – that is the exact expression I used – "Paul! why do you not take something stimulating?" Your papa's reply has always been, "Louisa, have the goodness to leave me. I want nothing. I am better by myself." If I was to be put upon my oath to-morrow, Lucretia, before a magistrate,' said Mrs Chick, 'I have no doubt I could venture to swear to those identical words.'

Miss Tox expressed her admiration by saying, 'My Louisa is ever methodical!'

'In short, Florence,' resumed her aunt, 'literally nothing has passed between your poor papa and myself, until to-day; when I mentioned to your papa that Sir Barnet and Lady Skettles had written exceedingly kind notes – our sweet boy! Lady Skettles loved him like a – where's my pocket handkerchief?'

Miss Tox produced one,

'Exceedingly kind notes, proposing that you should visit them for change of scene. Mentioning to your papa that I thought Miss Tox and myself might now go home (in which he quite agreed), I inquired if he had any objection to your accepting this invitation. He said, "No, Louisa, not the least!"'

Florence raised her tearful eyes.

'At the same time, if you would prefer staying here, Florence, to paying this visit at present, or to going home with me—'

'I should much prefer it, aunt,' was the faint rejoinder.

'Why then, child,' said Mrs Chick, 'you can. It's a strange choice, I must say. But you always *were* strange. Anybody else at your time

of life, and after what has passed – my dear Miss Tox, I have lost
my pocket-handkerchief again – would be glad to leave here, one
would suppose.'

'I should not like to feel,' said Florence, 'as if the house was
avoided. I should not like to think that the – his – the rooms up
stairs were quite empty and dreary, aunt. I would rather stay here,
for the present. Oh my brother! oh my brother!'

It was a natural emotion, not to be suppressed; and it would
make way even between the fingers of the hands with which she
covered up her face. The overcharged and heavy-laden breast must
sometimes have that vent, or the poor wounded solitary heart
within it would have fluttered like a bird with broken wings, and
sunk down in the dust.

'Well, child!' said Mrs Chick, after a pause. 'I wouldn't on any
account say anything unkind to you, and that I'm sure you know.
You will remain here, then, and do exactly as you like. No one will
interfere with you, Florence, or wish to interfere with you, I'm
sure.'

Florence shook her head in sad assent.

'I had no sooner begun to advise your poor papa that he really
ought to seek some distraction and restoration in a temporary
change,' said Mrs Chick, 'than he told me he had already formed
the intention of going into the country for a short time. I'm sure I
hope he'll go very soon. He can't go too soon. But I suppose there
are some arrangements connected with his private papers and so
forth, consequent on the affliction that has tried us all so much – I
can't think what's become of mine: Lucretia, lend me yours, my
dear – that may occupy him for one or two evenings in his own
room. Your papa's a Dombey, child, if ever there was one,' said
Mrs Chick, drying both her eyes at once with great care on opposite
corners of Miss Tox's handkerchief. 'He'll make an effort. There's
no fear of him.'

'Is there nothing, aunt,' said Florence, trembling, 'I might do
to –'

'Lord, my dear child,' interposed Mrs Chick, hastily, 'what are
you talking about? If your papa said to Me – I have given you his
exact words, "Louisa, I want nothing; I am better by myself" –
what do you think he'd say to you? You mustn't show yourself to
him, child. Don't dream of such a thing.'

'Aunt,' said Florence, 'I will go and lie down on my bed.'

Mrs Chick approved of this resolution, and dismissed her with a
kiss. But Miss Tox, on a faint pretence of looking for the mislaid

handkerchief, went upstairs after her; and tried in a few stolen minutes to comfort her, in spite of great discouragement from Susan Nipper. For Miss Nipper, in her burning zeal, disparaged Miss Tox as a crocodile; yet her sympathy seemed genuine, and had at least the vantage-ground of disinterestedness – there was little favour to be won by it.

And was there no one nearer and dearer than Susan, to uphold the striving heart in its anguish? Was there no other neck to clasp; no other face to turn to? no one else to say a soothing word to such deep sorrow? Was Florence so alone in the bleak world that nothing else remained to her? Nothing. Stricken motherless and brotherless at once – for in the loss of little Paul, that first and greatest loss fell heavily upon her – this was the only help she had. Oh, who can tell how much she needed help at first!

At first, when the house subsided into its accustomed course, and they had all gone away, except the servants, and her father shut up in his own rooms, Florence could do nothing but weep, and wander up and down, and sometimes, in a sudden pang of desolate remembrance, fly to her own chamber, wring her hands, lay her face down on her bed, and know no consolation: nothing but the bitterness and cruelty of grief. This commonly ensued upon the recognition of some spot or object very tenderly associated with him; and it made the miserable house, at first, a place of agony.

But it is not in the nature of pure love to burn so fiercely and unkindly long. The flame that in its grosser composition has the taint of earth, may prey upon the breast that gives it shelter; but the sacred fire from heaven is as gentle in the heart, as when it rested on the heads of the assembled twelve, and showed each man his brother, brightened and unhurt.[6] The image conjured up, there soon returned the placid face, the softened voice, the loving looks, the quiet trustfulness and peace; and Florence, though she wept still, wept more tranquilly, and courted the remembrance.

It was not very long before the golden water, dancing on the wall, in the old place, at the old serene time, had her calm eye fixed upon it as it ebbed away. It was not very long before that room again knew her, often; sitting there alone, as patient and as mild as when she had watched beside the little bed. When any sharp sense of its being empty smote upon her, she could kneel beside it, and pray God – it was the pouring out of her full heart – to let one angel love her and remember her.

It was not very long before, in the midst of the dismal house so wide and dreary, her low voice in the twilight, slowly and stopping sometimes, touched the old air to which he had so often listened, with his drooping head upon her arm. And after that, and when it was quite dark, a little strain of music trembled in the room: so softly played and sung, that it was more like the mournful recollection of what she had done at his request on that last night, than the reality repeated. But it was repeated, often – very often, in the shadowy solitude; and broken murmurs of the strain still trembled on the keys, when the sweet voice was hushed in tears.

Thus she gained heart to look upon the work with which her fingers had been busy by his side on the sea-shore; and thus it was not very long before she took to it again – with something of a human love for it, as if it had been sentient and had known him; and, sitting in a window, near her mother's picture, in the unused room so long deserted, wore away the thoughtful hours.

Why did the dark eyes turn so often from this work to where the rosy children lived? They were not immediately suggestive of her loss; for they were all girls: four little sisters. But they were motherless like her – and had a father.

It was easy to know when he had gone out and was expected home, for the elder child was always dressed and waiting for him at the drawing-room window, or in the balcony; and when he appeared, her expectant face lighted up with joy, while the others at the high window, and always on the watch too, clapped their hands, and drummed them on the sill, and called to him. The elder child would come down to the hall, and put her hand in his, and lead him up the stairs; and Florence would see her afterwards sitting by his side, or on his knee, or hanging coaxingly about his neck and talking to him: and though they were always gay together, he would often watch her face as if he thought her like her mother that was dead. Florence would sometimes look no more at this, and bursting into tears would hide behind the curtain as if she were frightened, or would hurry from the window. Yet she could not help returning; and her work would soon fall unheeded from her hands again.

It was the house that had been empty, years ago. It had remained so for a long time. At last, and while she had been away from home, this family had taken it; and it was repaired and newly painted; and there were birds and flowers about it and it looked very different from its old self. But she never thought of the house. The children and their father were all in all.

When he had dined, she could see them, through the open windows, go down with their governess or nurse, and cluster round the table; and in the still summer weather, the sound of their childish voices and clear laughter would come ringing across the street, into the drooping air of the room in which she sat. Then they would climb and clamber upstairs with him, and romp about him on the sofa, or group themselves at his knee, a very nosegay of little faces, while he seemed to tell them some story. Or they would come running out into the balcony; and then Florence would hide herself quickly, lest it should check them in their joy, to see her in her black dress, sitting there alone.

The elder child remained with her father when the rest had gone away, and made his tea for him – happy little housekeeper she was then! – and sat conversing with him, sometimes at the window, sometimes in the room, until the candles came. He made her his companion, though she was some years younger than Florence; and she could be as staid and pleasantly demure, with her little book or work-box, as a woman. When they had candles, Florence from her own dark room was not afraid to look again. But when the time came for the child to say 'Good night, papa,' and go to bed, Florence would sob and tremble as she raised her face to him, and could look no more.

Though still she would turn, again and again, before going to bed herself, from the simple air that had lulled him to rest so often, long ago, and from the other low soft broken strain of music, back to that house. But that she ever thought of it, or watched it, was a secret which she kept within her own young breast.

And did that breast of Florence – Florence, so ingenuous and true – so worthy of the love that he had borne her, and had whispered in his last faint words – whose guileless heart was mirrored in the beauty of her face, and breathed in every accent of her gentle voice – did that young breast hold any other secret? Yes. One more.

When no one in the house was stirring, and the lights were all extinguished, she would softly leave her own room, and with noiseless feet descend the staircase, and approach her father's door. Against it, scarcely breathing, she would rest her face and head, and press her lips, in the yearning of her love. She crouched upon the cold stone floor outside it, every night, to listen even for his breath; and in her one absorbing wish to be allowed to show him some affection, to be a consolation to him, to win him over to the endurance of some tenderness from her, his solitary child, she would have knelt down at his feet, if she had dared, in humble supplication.

No one knew it. No one thought of it. The door was ever closed, and he shut up within. He went out once or twice, and it was said in the house that he was very soon going on his country journey; but he lived in those rooms, and lived alone, and never saw her, or inquired for her. Perhaps he did not even know that she was in the house.

One day, about a week after the funeral, Florence was sitting at her work, when Susan appeared, with a face half laughing and half crying, to announce a visitor.

'A visitor! To me, Susan!' said Florence, looking up in astonishment.

'Well, it *is* a wonder, ain't it now, Miss Floy?' said Susan; 'but I wish you had a many visitors, I do, indeed, for you'd be all the better for it, and it's my opinion that the sooner you and me goes even to them old Skettleses, Miss, the better for both, I may not wish to live in crowds, Miss Floy, but still I'm not a oyster.'[7]

To do Miss Nipper justice, she spoke more for her young mistress than herself; and her face showed it.

'But the visitor, Susan,' said Florence.

Susan, with an hysterical explosion that was as much a laugh as a sob, and as much a sob as a laugh, answered,

'Mr Toots!'

The smile that appeared on Florence's face passed from it in a moment, and her eyes filled with tears. But at any rate it was a smile, and that gave great satisfaction to Miss Nipper.

'My own feelings exactly, Miss Floy,' said Susan, putting her apron to her eyes, and shaking her head. 'Immediately I see that Innocent in the Hall, Miss Floy, I burst out laughing first, and then I choked.'

Susan Nipper involuntarily proceeded to do the like again on the spot. In the meantime Mr Toots, who had come up stairs after her, all unconscious of the effect he produced, announced himself with his knuckles on the door, and walked in very briskly.

'How d'ye do, Miss Dombey?' said Mr Toots. 'I'm very well, I thank you; how are you?'

Mr Toots – than whom there were few better fellows in the world, though there may have been one or two brighter spirits – had laboriously invented this long burst of discourse with the view of relieving the feelings both of Florence and himself. But finding that he had run through his property, as it were, in an injudicious manner, by squandering the whole before taking a chair, or before Florence had uttered a word, or before he had well got in at the door, he deemed it advisable to begin again.

'How d'ye do, Miss Dombey?' said Mr Toots. 'I'm very well, I thank you; how are you?'

Florence gave him her hand, and said she was very well.

'I'm very well indeed,' said Mr Toots, taking a chair. 'Very well indeed, I am. I don't remember,' said Mr Toots, after reflecting a little, 'that I was ever better, thank you.'

'It's very kind of you to come,' said Florence, taking up her work. 'I am very glad to see you.'

Mr Toots responded with a chuckle. Thinking that might be too lively, he corrected it with a sigh. Thinking that might be too melancholy, he corrected it with a chuckle. Not thoroughly pleasing himself with either mode of reply, he breathed hard.

'You were very kind to my dear brother,' said Florence, obeying her own natural impulse to relieve him by saying so. 'He often talked to me about you.'

'Oh, it's of no consequence,' said Mr Toots hastily. 'Warm, ain't it?'

'It is beautiful weather,' replied Florence.

'It agrees with *me!*' said Mr Toots. 'I don't think I ever was so well as I find myself at present, I'm obliged to you.'

After stating this curious and unexpected fact, Mr Toots fell into a deep well of silence.

'You have left Dr Blimber's, I think?' said Florence, trying to help him out.

'I should hope so,' returned Mr Toots. And tumbled in again.

He remained at the bottom, apparently drowned, for at least ten minutes. At the expiration of that period, he suddenly floated, and said,

'Well! Good morning, Miss Dombey.'

'Are you going?' asked Florence, rising.

'I don't know, though. No, not just at present,' said Mr Toots, sitting down again, most unexpectedly. 'The fact is – I say, Miss Dombey!'

'Don't be afraid to speak to me,' said Florence, with a quiet smile, 'I should be very glad if you would talk about my brother.'

'Would you, though?' retorted Mr Toots, with sympathy in every fibre of his otherwise expressionless face. 'Poor Dombey! I'm sure I never thought that Burgess and Co. – fashionable tailors (but very dear), that we used to talk about – would make this suit of clothes for such a purpose.' Mr Toots was dressed in mourning. 'Poor Dombey! I say! Miss Dombey!' blubbered Toots.

'Yes,' said Florence.

'There's a friend he took to very much at last. I thought you'd like to have him, perhaps, as a sort of keepsake. You remember his remembering Diogenes?'

'Oh yes! oh yes!' cried Florence.

'Poor Dombey! So do I,' said Mr Toots.

Mr Toots, seeing Florence in tears, had great difficulty in getting beyond this point, and had nearly tumbled into the well again. But a chuckle saved him on the brink.

'I say,' he proceeded, 'Miss Dombey! I could have had him stolen for ten shillings, if they hadn't given him up: and I would: but they were glad to get rid of him, I think. If you'd like to have him, he's at the door. I brought him on purpose for you. He ain't a lady's dog, you know,' said Mr Toots, 'but you won't mind that, will you?'

In fact Diogenes was at that moment, as they presently ascertained from looking down into the street, staring through the window of a hackney cabriolet,[8] into which, for conveyance to that spot, he had been ensnared, on a false pretence of rats among the straw. Sooth to say, he was as unlike a lady's dog as dog might be; and in his gruff anxiety to get out, presented an appearance sufficiently unpromising, as he gave short yelps out of one side of his mouth, and overbalancing himself by the intensity of every one of those efforts, tumbled down into the straw, and then sprung panting up again, putting out his tongue, as if he had come express to a Dispensary to be examined for his health.

But though Diogenes was as ridiculous a dog as one would meet with on a summer's day;[9] a blundering, ill-favoured, clumsy, bullet-headed dog, continually acting on a wrong idea that there was an enemy in the neighbourhood, whom it was meritorious to bark at; and though he was far from good-tempered, and certainly was not clever, and had hair all over his eyes, and a comic nose, and an inconsistent tail, and a gruff voice; he was dearer to Florence, in virtue of that parting remembrance of him, and that request that he might be taken care of, than the most valuable and beautiful of his kind. So dear, indeed, was this same ugly Diogenes, and so welcome to her, that she took the jewelled hand of Mr Toots and kissed it in her gratitude. And when Diogenes, released, came tearing up the stairs and bouncing into the room (such a business as there was first, to get him out of the cabriolet!), dived under all the furniture, and wound a long iron chain, that dangled from his neck, round legs of chairs and tables, and then tugged at it until his eyes became unnaturally visible, in consequence of their nearly starting out of his head; and when he growled at Mr Toots, who affected familiarity; and went pell-mell at Towlinson, morally convinced that he was the enemy whom he had barked at round the corner all his life and had never seen yet; Florence was as pleased with him as if he had been a miracle of discretion.

Mr Toots was so overjoyed by the success of his present, and was so delighted to see Florence bending down over Diogenes, smoothing his coarse back with her little delicate hand – Diogenes graciously allowing it from the first moment of their acquaintance – that he felt it difficult to take leave, and would, no doubt, have been a much longer time in making up his mind to do so, if he had not been assisted by Diogenes himself, who suddenly took it into his head to bay Mr Toots, and to make short runs at him with his mouth open. Not exactly seeing his way to the end of these demonstrations, and sensible that they placed the pantaloons constructed by the art of Burgess and Co. in jeopardy, Mr Toots, with chuckles, lapsed out at the door: by which, after looking in again two or three times, without any object at all, and being on each occasion greeted with a fresh run from Diogenes, he finally took himself off and got away.

'Come, then, Di! Dear Di! Make friends with your new mistress. Let us love each other, Di!' said Florence, fondling his shaggy head. And Di, the rough and gruff, as if his hairy hide were pervious to the tear that dropped upon it, and his dog's heart melted as it fell, put his nose up to her face, and swore fidelity.

Diogenes the man[10] did not speak plainer to Alexander the Great than Diogenes the dog spoke to Florence. He subscribed to the offer of his little mistress cheerfully, and devoted himself to her service. A banquet was immediately provided for him in a corner; and when he had eaten and drunk his fill, he went to the window where Florence was sitting, looking on, rose up on his hind legs, with his awkward fore paws on her shoulders, licked her face and hands, nestled his great head against her heart, and wagged his tail till he was tired. Finally, Diogenes coiled himself up at her feet and went to sleep.

Although Miss Nipper was nervous in regard of dogs, and felt it necessary to come into the room with her skirts carefully collected about her, as if she were crossing a brook on stepping-stones; also to utter little screams and stand up on chairs when Diogenes stretched himself: she was in her own manner affected by the kindness of Mr Toots, and could not see Florence so alive to the attachment and society of this rude friend of little Paul's, without

Poor Paul's friend

some mental comments thereupon that brought the water to her eyes. Mr Dombey, as a part of her reflections, may have been, in the association of ideas, connected with the dog; but, at any rate, after observing Diogenes and his mistress all the evening, and after exerting herself with much good-will to provide Diogenes a bed in an ante-chamber outside his mistress's door, she said hurriedly to Florence, before leaving her for the night:

'Your pa's going off, Miss Floy, to-morrow morning.'

'To-morrow morning, Susan?'

'Yes, Miss; that's the orders. Early.'

'Do you know,' asked Florence, without looking at her, 'where papa is going, Susan?'

'Not exactly, Miss. He's going to meet that precious Major first, and I must say if I was acquainted with any Major myself (which Heavens forbid), it shouldn't be a blue one!'

'Hush, Susan!' urged Florence gently.

'Well, Miss Floy,' returned Miss Nipper, who was full of burning indignation, and minded her stops even less than usual. 'I can't help it, blue he is, and while I was a Christian, although humble, I would have natural-coloured friends, or none.'

It appeared from what she added and had gleaned downstairs, that Mrs Chick had proposed the Major for Mr Dombey's companion, and that Mr Dombey, after some hesitation, had invited him.

'Talk of *him* being a change, indeed!' observed Miss Nipper to herself with boundless contempt. 'If he's a change give me a constancy.'

'Good night, Susan,' said Florence.

'Good night, my darling dear Miss Floy.'

Her tone of commiseration smote the chord so often roughly touched, but never listened to while she or any one looked on. Florence left alone, laid her head upon her hand, and pressing the other over her swelling heart, held free communication with her sorrows.

It was a wet night; and the melancholy rain fell pattering and dropping with a wearied sound. A sluggish wind was blowing, and went moaning round the house, as if it were in pain or grief. A shrill noise quivered through the trees. While she sat weeping, it grew late, and dreary midnight tolled out from the steeples.

Florence was little more than a child in years – not yet fourteen – and the loneliness and gloom of such an hour in the great house where Death had lately made its own tremendous devastation, might have set an older fancy brooding on vague terrors. But her innocent imagination was too full of one theme to admit them. Nothing wandered in her thoughts but love – a wandering love, indeed, and cast away – but turning always to her father.

There was nothing in the dropping of the rain, the moaning of the wind, the shuddering of the trees, the striking of the solemn clocks, that shook this one thought, or diminished its interest. Her recollections of the dear dead boy – and they were never absent – were itself; the same thing. And oh, to be shut out: to be so lost: never to have looked into her father's face or touched him since that hour!

She could not go to bed, poor child, and never had gone yet, since then, without making her nightly pilgrimage to his door. It would have been a strange sad sight, to see her now, stealing lightly down the stairs through the thick gloom, and stopping at it with a beating heart, and blinded eyes, and hair that fell down loosely and unthought of; and touching it outside with her wet cheek. But the night covered it, and no one knew.

The moment that she touched the door on this night, Florence found that it was open. For the first time it stood open, though by but a hair's breadth: and there was a light within. The first impulse of the timid child – and she yielded to it – was to retire swiftly. Her next, to go back, and to enter; and this second impulse held her in irresolution on the staircase.

In its standing open, even by so much as that chink, there seemed to be hope. There was encouragement in seeing a ray of light from within, stealing through the dark stern doorway, and falling in a thread upon the marble floor. She turned back, hardly knowing what she did, but urged on by the love within her, and the trial they had undergone together, but not shared: and with her hands a little raised and trembling, glided in.

Her father sat at his old table in the middle room. He had been arranging some papers, and destroying others, and the latter lay in fragile ruins before him. The rain dripped heavily upon the glass panes in the outer room, where he had so often watched poor Paul, a baby; and the low complainings of the wind were heard without.

But not by him. He sat with his eyes fixed on the table, so immersed in thought, that a far heavier tread than the light foot of his child could make, might have failed to rouse him. His face was turned towards her. By the waning lamp, and at that haggard hour, it looked worn and dejected; and in the utter loneliness surrounding him, there was an appeal to Florence that struck home.

'Papa! papa! speak to me, dear papa!'

He started at her voice, and leaped up from his seat. She was close before him, with extended arms, but he fell back.

'What is the matter?' he said, sternly. 'Why do you come here? What has frightened you?'

If anything had frightened her, it was the face he turned upon her. The glowing love within the breast of his young daughter froze before it, and she stood and looked at him as if stricken into stone.

There was not one touch of tenderness or pity in it. There was not one gleam of interest, parental recognition, or relenting in it. There was a change in it, but not of that kind. The old indifference and cold constraint had given place to something: what, she never thought and did not dare to think, and yet she felt it in its force, and knew it well without a name: that as it looked upon her, seemed to cast a shadow on her head.

Did he see before him the successful rival of his son, in health and life? Did he look upon his own successful rival in that son's affection? Did a mad jealousy and withered pride, poison sweet remembrances that should have endeared and made her precious to him? Could it be possible that it was gall to him to look upon her in her beauty and her promise: thinking of his infant boy!

Florence had no such thoughts. But love is quick to know when it is spurned and hopeless: and hope died out of hers, as she stood looking in her father's face.

'I ask you, Florence, are you frightened? Is there anything the matter, that you come here?'

'I came, papa—'

'Against my wishes. Why?'

She saw he knew why: it was written broadly on his face: and dropped her head upon her hands with one prolonged low cry.

Let him remember it in that room, years to come. It has faded from the air, before he breaks the silence. It may pass as quickly from his brain, as he believes, but it is there. Let him remember it in that room, years to come!

He took her by the arm. His hand was cold, and loose, and scarcely closed upon her.

'You are tired, I dare say,' he said, taking up the light, and leading her towards the door, 'and want rest. We all want rest. Go, Florence. You have been dreaming.'

The dream she had had, was over then, God help her! and she felt that it could never more come back.

'I will remain here to light you up the stairs. The whole house is yours above there,' said her father, slowly. 'You are its mistress now. Good night!'

Still covering her face, she sobbed, and answered 'Good night, dear papa,' and silently ascended. Once she looked back as if she would have returned to him, but for fear. It was a momentary thought, too hopeless to encourage; and her father stood there with the light – hard, unresponsive, motionless – until the fluttering dress of his fair child was lost in the darkness.

Let him remember it in that room, years to come. The rain that falls upon the roof: the wind that mourns outside the door: may have foreknowledge in their melancholy sound. Let him remember it in that room, years to come!

The last time he had watched her, from the same place, winding up those stairs, she had had her brother in her arms. It did not move his heart towards her now, it steeled it: but he went into his room, and locked his door, and sat down in his chair, and cried for his lost boy.

Diogenes was broad awake upon his post, and waiting for his little mistress.

'Oh, Di! Oh, dear Di! Love me for his sake!'

Diogenes already loved her for her own, and didn't care how much he showed it. So he made himself vastly ridiculous by performing a variety of uncouth bounces in the ante-chamber, and concluded, when poor Florence was at last asleep, and dreaming of the rosy children opposite, by scratching open her bedroom door: rolling up his bed into a pillow: lying down on the boards, at the full length of his tether, with his head towards her: and looking lazily at her, upside down, out of the tops of his eyes, until from winking and winking he fell asleep himself, and dreamed, with gruff barks, of his enemy.

CHAPTER 19

Walter goes away

The Wooden Midshipman at the Instrument-maker's door, like the hard-hearted little midshipman he was, remained supremely indifferent to Walter's going away, even when the very last day of his sojourn in the back parlour was on the decline. With his quadrant at his round black knob of an eye, and his figure in its old attitude of indomitable alacrity, the midshipman displayed his elfin small-clothes to the best advantage, and, absorbed in scientific pursuits, had no sympathy with worldly concerns. He was so far the creature of circumstances, that a dry day covered him with dust, and a misty day peppered him with little bits of soot, and a wet day brightened up his tarnished uniform for the moment, and a very hot day blistered him; but otherwise he was a callous, obdurate, conceited midshipman, intent on his own discoveries, and caring as little for what went on about him, terrestrially, as Archimedes at the taking of Syracuse.[1]

Such a midshipman he seemed to be, at least, in the then position of domestic affairs. Walter eyed him kindly many a time in passing in and out; and poor old Sol, when Walter was not there, would come and lean against the doorpost, resting his weary wig as near the shoe-buckles of the guardian genius of his trade and shop as he could. But no fierce idol with a mouth from ear to ear, and a murderous visage made of parrot's feathers, was ever more indifferent to the appeals of its savage votaries, than was the midshipman to these marks of attachment.

Walter's heart felt heavy as he looked round his old bedroom, up among the parapets and chimney-pots, and thought that one more night already darkening would close his acquaintance with it, perhaps for ever. Dismantled of his little stock of books and pictures, it looked coldly and reproachfully on him for his desertion, and had already a foreshadowing upon it of its coming strangeness. 'A few hours more,' thought Walter, 'and no dream I ever had here when I was a school-boy will be so little mine as this old room. The dream may come back in my sleep, and I may return waking to this place, it may be: but the dream at least will serve no other master, and the room may have a score, and every one of them may change, neglect, misuse it.'

But his uncle was not to be left alone in the little back parlour, where he was then sitting by himself; for Captain Cuttle, considerate in his roughness, stayed away against his will, purposely that they should have some talk together unobserved: so Walter, newly returned home from his last day's bustle, descended briskly, to bear him company.

'Uncle,' he said gaily, laying his hand upon the old man's shoulder, 'what shall I send you home from Barbados?'

'Hope, my dear Wally. Hope that we shall meet again, on this side of the grave. Send me as much of that as you can.'

'So I will, uncle: I have enough and to spare, and I'll not be chary of it! And as to lively turtles, and limes for Captain Cuttle's punch, and preserves for you on Sundays, and all that sort of thing, why I'll send you ship-loads, uncle: when I'm rich enough.'

Old Sol wiped his spectacles, and faintly smiled.

'That's right, uncle!' cried Walter, merrily, and clapping him half a dozen times more upon the shoulder. 'You cheer up me! I'll cheer up you! We'll be as gay as larks to-morrow morning, uncle, and we'll fly as high! As to my anticipations, they are singing out of sight now.'

'Wally, my dear boy,' returned the old man, 'I'll do my best, I'll do my best.'

'And *your* best, uncle,' said Walter, with his pleasant laugh, 'is the best best that I know. You'll not forget what you're to send *me*, uncle?'

'No, Wally, no,' replied the old man; 'everything I hear about Miss Dombey, now that she is left alone, poor lamb, I'll write. I fear it won't be much though, Wally.'

'Why, I'll tell you what, uncle,' said Walter, after a moment's hesitation, 'I have just been up there.'

'Ay, ay, ay?' murmured the old man, raising his eyebrows, and his spectacles with them.

'Not to see *her*,' said Walter, 'though I could have seen her, I dare say, if I had asked, Mr Dombey being out of town: but to say a parting word to Susan. I thought I might venture to do that, you know, under the circumstances, and remembering when I saw Miss Dombey last.'

'Yes, my boy, yes,' replied his uncle, rousing himself from a temporary abstraction.

'So I saw her,' pursued Walter, 'Susan, I mean: and I told her I was off and away to-morrow. And I said, uncle, that you had always had an interest in Miss Dombey since that night when she was here, and always wished her well and happy, and always would be proud and glad to serve her in the least: I thought I might say that, you know, under the circumstances. Don't you think so?'

'Yes, my boy, yes,' replied his uncle, in the same tone as before.

'And I added,' pursued Walter, 'that if she – Susan, I mean – could ever let you know, either through herself, or Mrs Richards, or anybody else who might be coming this way, that Miss Dombey *was* well and happy, you would take it very kindly, and would write so much to me, and I should take it very kindly too. There! Upon my word, uncle,' said Walter, 'I scarcely slept all last night through thinking of doing this; and could not make up my mind when I was out, whether to do it or not; and yet I am sure it is the true feeling of my heart, and I should have been quite miserable afterwards if I had not relieved it.'

His honest voice and manner corroborated what he said, and quite established its ingenuousness.

'So, if you ever see her, uncle,' said Walter, 'I mean Miss Dombey now – and perhaps you may, who knows! – tell her how much I felt for her; how much I used to think of her when I was here; how I spoke of her, with the tears in my eyes, uncle, on this last night before I went away. Tell her that I said I never could forget her gentle manner, or her beautiful face, or her sweet kind disposition that was better than all. And as I didn't take them from a woman's feet, or a young lady's: only a little innocent child's,' said Walter: 'tell her, if you don't mind, uncle, that I kept those shoes – she'll remember how often they fell off, that night – and took them away with me as a remembrance!'

They were at that very moment going out at the door in one of Walter's trunks. A porter carrying off his baggage on a truck for shipment at the docks on board the Son and Heir, had got possession of them; and wheeled them away under the very eye of the insensible Midshipman before their owner had well finished speaking.

But that ancient mariner might have been excused his insensibility to the treasure as it rolled away. For, under his eye at the same moment, accurately within his range of observation, coming full into the sphere of his startled and intensely wide-awake look-out, were Florence and Susan Nipper: Florence looking up into his face half timidly, and receiving the whole shock of his wooden ogling!

More than this, they passed into the shop, and passed in at the parlour door before they were observed by anybody but the Midshipman. And Walter, having his back to the door, would have known nothing of their apparition even then, but for seeing his uncle spring out of his own chair, and nearly tumble over another.

'Why, uncle!' exclaimed Walter. 'What's the matter?'

Old Solomon replied, 'Miss Dombey!'

'Is it possible?' cried Walter, looking round and starting up in his turn. 'Here!'

Why, it was so possible and so actual, that, while the words were on his lips, Florence hurried past him; took Uncle Sol's snuff-coloured lappels, one in each hand; kissed him on the cheek; and turning, gave her hand to Walter with a simple truth and earnestness that was her own, and no one else's in the world!

The Wooden Midshipman on the look out

'Going away, Walter!' said Florence.

'Yes, Miss Dombey,' he replied, but not so hopefully as he endeavoured: 'I have a voyage before me.'

'And your uncle,' said Florence, looking back at Solomon. 'He is sorry you are going, I am sure. Ah! I see he is! Dear Walter, I am very sorry too.'

'Goodness knows,' exclaimed Miss Nipper, 'there's a many we could spare instead, if numbers is a object, Mrs Pipchin as a overseer would come cheap at her weight in gold, and if a knowledge of black slavery should be required, them Blimbers is the very people for the sitiwation.'

With that Miss Nipper untied her bonnet strings, and after looking vacantly for some moments into a little black teapot that was set forth with the usual homely service on the table, shook her head and a tin canister, and began unasked to make the tea.

In the meantime Florence had turned again to the Instrument-maker, who was as full of admiration as surprise. 'So grown!' said old Sol. 'So improved! And yet not altered! Just the same!'

'Indeed!' said Florence.

'Ye—yes,' returned old Sol, rubbing his hands slowly, and considering the matter half aloud, as something pensive in the bright eyes looking at him arrested his attention. 'Yes, that expression was in the younger face, too!'

'You remember me,' said Florence with a smile, 'and what a little creature I was then?'

'My dear young lady,' returned the Instrument-maker, 'how could I forget you, often as I have thought of you and heard of you since! At the very moment, indeed, when you came in, Wally was talking about you to me, and leaving messages for you, and—'

'Was he?' said Florence. 'Thank you, Walter! Oh thank you, Walter! I was afraid you might be going away and hardly thinking of me;' and again she gave him her little hand so freely and so faithfully that Walter held it for some moments in his own, and could not bear to let it go.

Yet Walter did not hold it as he might have held it once, nor did its touch awaken those old day-dreams of his boyhood that had floated past him sometimes even lately, and confused him with their indistinct and broken shapes. The purity and innocence of her endearing manner, and its perfect trustfulness, and the undisguised regard for him that lay so deeply seated in her constant eyes, and glowed upon her fair face through the smile that shaded – for alas! it was a smile too sad to brighten – it, were not of their romantic race. They brought back to his thoughts the early deathbed he had seen her tending, and the love the child had borne her; and on the wings of such remembrances she seemed to rise up, far above his idle fancies, into clearer and serener air.

'I – I am afraid I must call you Walter's uncle, Sir,' said Florence to the old man, 'if you'll let me.'

'My dear young lady,' cried old Sol. 'Let you! Good gracious!'

'We always knew you by that name, and talked of you,' said Florence, glancing round, and sighing gently. 'The nice old parlour! Just the same! How well I recollect it!'

Old Sol looked first at her, then at his nephew, and then rubbed his hands, and rubbed his spectacles, and said below his breath, 'Ah! time, time, time!'

There was a short silence: during which Susan Nipper skilfully impounded two extra cups and saucers from the cupboard, and awaited the drawing of the tea with a thoughtful air.

'I want to tell Walter's uncle,' said Florence, laying her hand timidly upon the old man's as it rested on the table, to bespeak his attention, 'something that I am anxious about. He is going to be left alone, and if he will allow me – not to take Walter's place, for that I couldn't do, but to be his true friend and help him if I ever can while Walter is away, I shall be very much obliged to him indeed. Will you? May I, Walter's uncle?'

The Instrument-maker, without speaking, put her hand to his lips, and Susan Nipper, leaning back with her arms crossed, in the chair of presidency into which she had voted herself, bit one end of her bonnet strings, and heaved a gentle sigh as she looked up at the skylight.

'You will let me come to see you,' said Florence, 'when I can; and you will tell me everything about yourself and Walter; and you will have no secrets from Susan when she comes and I do not, but will confide in us, and trust us, and rely upon us. And you'll try to let us be a comfort to you? Will you, Walter's uncle?'

The sweet face looking into his, the gentle pleading eyes, the soft voice, and the light touch on his arm made the more winning by a child's respect and honour for his age, that gave to all an air of graceful doubt and modest hesitation – these, and her natural earnestness, so overcame the poor old Instrument-maker, that he only answered:

'Wally! say a word for me, my dear. I'm very grateful.'

'No, Walter,' returned Florence with her quiet smile. 'Say nothing for him, if you please. I understand him very well, and we must learn to talk together without you, dear Walter.'

The regretful tone in which she said these latter words, touched Walter more than all the rest.

'Miss Florence,' he replied, with an effort to recover the cheerful manner he had preserved while talking with his uncle, 'I know no more than my uncle, what to say in acknowledgment of such kindness, I am sure. But what could I say, after all, if I had the power of talking for an hour, except that it is like you?'

Susan Nipper began upon a new part of her bonnet string, and nodded at the skylight, in approval of the sentiment expressed.

'Oh! but, Walter,' said Florence, 'there is something that I wish to say to you before you go away, and you must call me Florence, if you please, and not speak like a stranger.'

'Like a stranger!' returned Walter. 'No. I couldn't speak so. I am sure, at least, I couldn't feel like one.'

'Aye, but that is not enough, and is not what I mean. For, Walter,' added Florence, bursting into tears, 'he liked you very much, and said before he died that he was fond of you, and said "Remember Walter!" and if you'll be a brother to me, Walter, now that he is gone and I have none on earth, I'll be your sister all my life, and think of you like one wherever we may be! This is what I wished to say, dear Walter, but I cannot say it as I would, because my heart is full.'

And in its fulness and its sweet simplicity, she held out both her hands to him. Walter taking them, stooped down and touched the tearful face that neither shrunk nor turned away, nor reddened as he did so, but looked up at him with confidence and truth. In that one moment, every shadow of doubt or agitation passed away from Walter's soul. It seemed to him that he responded to her innocent appeal, beside the dead child's bed: and, in the solemn presence he had seen there, pledged himself to cherish and protect her very image, in his banishment, with brotherly regard; to garner up her simple faith, inviolate and hold himself degraded if he breathed upon it any thought that was not in her own breast when she gave it to him.

Susan Nipper, who had bitten both her bonnet strings at once, and imparted a great deal of private emotion to the skylight, during this transaction, now changed the subject by inquiring who took milk and who took sugar; and being enlightened on these points, poured out the tea. They all four gathered socially about the little table, and took tea under that young lady's active superintendence;

and the presence of Florence in the back parlour, brightened the Tartar frigate on the wall.

Half an hour ago Walter, for his life, would have hardly called her by her name. But he could do so now when she entreated him. He could think of her being there, without a lurking misgiving that it would have been better if she had not come. He could calmly think how beautiful she was, how full of promise, what a home some happy man would find in such a heart one day. He could reflect upon his own place in that heart, with pride; and with a brave determination, if not to deserve it – he still thought that far above him – never to deserve it less.

Some fairy influence must surely have hovered round the hands of Susan Nipper when she made the tea, engendering the tranquil air that reigned in the back parlour during its discussion. Some counter-influence must surely have hovered round the hands of Uncle Sol's chronometer, and moved them faster than the Tartar frigate ever went before the wind. Be this as it may, the visitors had a coach in waiting at a quiet corner not far off; and the chronometer, on being incidentally referred to, gave such a positive opinion that it had been waiting a long time, that it was impossible to doubt the fact, especially when stated on such unimpeachable authority. If Uncle Sol had been going to be hanged by his own time, he never would have allowed that the chronometer was too fast, by the least fraction of a second.

Florence at parting recapitulated to the old man all that she had said before, and bound him to their compact. Uncle Sol attended her lovingly to the legs of the Wooden Midshipman and there resigned her to Walter, who was ready to escort her and Susan Nipper to the coach.

'Walter,' said Florence by the way, 'I have been afraid to ask you before your uncle. Do you think you will be absent very long?'

'Indeed,' said Walter, 'I don't know. I fear so. Mr Dombey signified as much, I thought, when he appointed me.'

'Is it a favour, Walter?' inquired Florence, after a moment's hesitation, and looking anxiously in his face.

'The appointment?' returned Walter.

'Yes.'

Walter would have given anything to have answered in the affirmative, but his face answered before his lips could, and Florence was too attentive to it not to understand its reply.

'I am afraid you have scarcely been a favourite with papa,' she said, timidly.

'There is no reason,' replied Walter, smiling, 'why I should be.'

'No reason, Walter!'

'There *was* no reason,' said Walter, understanding what she meant. 'There are many people employed in the house. Between Mr Dombey and a young man like me, there's a wide space of separation. If I do my duty, I do what I ought, and do no more than all the rest.'

Had Florence any misgiving of which she was hardly conscious: any misgiving that had sprung into an indistinct and undefined existence since that recent night when she had gone down to her father's room: that Walter's accidental interest in her, and early knowledge of her, might have involved him in that powerful displeasure and dislike? Had Walter any such idea, or any sudden thought that it was in her mind at that moment? Neither of them hinted at it. Neither of them spoke at all, for some short time. Susan, walking on the other side of Walter, eyed them both sharply; and certainly Miss Nipper's thoughts travelled in that direction, and very confidently too.

'You may come back very soon,' said Florence, 'perhaps, Walter.'

'I *may* come back,' said Walter, 'an old man, and find you an old lady. But I hope for better things.'

'Papa,' said Florence, after a moment, 'will – will recover from his grief, and – speak more freely to me one day, perhaps; and if he should, I will tell him how much I wish to see you back again, and ask him to recall you for my sake.'

There was a touching modulation in these words about her father, that Walter understood too well.

The coach being close at hand, he would have left her without speaking, for now he felt what parting was; but Florence held his hand when she was seated, and then he found there was a little packet in her own.

'Walter,' she said, looking full upon him with her affectionate eyes, 'like you, I hope for better things. I will pray for them, and believe that they will arrive. I made this little gift for Paul. Pray take it with my love, and do not look at it until you are gone away. And now, God bless you, Walter! never forget me. You are my brother, dear!'

He was glad that Susan Nipper came between them, or he might have left her with a sorrowful remembrance of him. He was glad too that she did not look out of the coach again, but waved the little hand to him instead, as long as he could see it.

In spite of her request, he could not help opening the packet that night when he went to bed. It was a little purse: and there was money in it.

Bright rose the sun next morning, from his absence in strange countries, and up rose Walter with it to receive the Captain, who was already at the door: having turned out earlier than was necessary, in order to get under weigh while Mrs MacStinger was yet slumbering. The Captain pretended to be in tip-top spirits, and brought a very smoky tongue in one of the pockets of the broad blue coat for breakfast.

'And Wal'r,' said the Captain, when they took their seats at table, 'if your uncle's the man I think him, he'll bring out the last bottle of *the* Madeira on the present occasion.'

'No, no, Ned,' returned the old man. 'No! That shall be opened when Walter comes home again.'

'Well said!' cried the Captain. 'Hear him!'

'There it lies,' said Sol Gills, 'down in the little cellar, covered with dirt and cobwebs. There may be dirt and cobwebs over you and me perhaps, Ned, before it sees the light.'

'Hear him!' cried the Captain. 'Good morality! Wal'r, my lad. Train up a fig-tree in the way it should go, and when you are old sit under the shade on it.[2] Overhaul the – Well,' said the Captain on second thoughts, 'I an't quite certain where that's to be found, but when found, make a note of. Sol Gills, heave a-head again!'

'But there, or somewhere, it shall lie, Ned, until Wally comes back to claim it,' said the old man. 'That's all I meant to say.'

'And well said too,' returned the Captain; 'and if we three don't crack that bottle in company, I'll give you two leave to drink my allowance!'

Notwithstanding the Captain's excessive joviality, he made but a poor hand at the smoky tongue, though he tried very hard, when anybody looked at him, to appear as if he were eating with a vast appetite. He was terribly afraid, likewise, of being left alone with either uncle or nephew; appearing to consider that his only chance of safety as to keeping up appearances, was in there being always three together. This terror on the part of the Captain, reduced him to such ingenious evasions as running to the door, when Solomon went to put his coat on, under pretence of having seen an extraordinary hackney-coach pass: and darting out into the road when Walter went upstairs to take leave of the lodgers, on a feint of smelling fire in a neighbouring chimney. These artifices Captain Cuttle deemed inscrutable by any uninspired observer.

Walter was coming down from his parting expedition upstairs, and was crossing the shop to go back to the little parlour, when he saw a faded face he knew, looking in at the door, and darted towards it.

'Mr Carker!' cried Walter, pressing the hand of John Carker the Junior. 'Pray come in! This is kind of you, to be here so early to say good-bye to me. You knew how glad it would make me to shake hands with you, once, before going away. I cannot say how glad I am to have this opportunity. Pray come in.'

'It is not likely that we may ever meet again, Walter,' returned the other, gently resisting his invitation, 'and I am glad of this opportunity too. I may venture to speak to you, and to take you by the hand, on the eve of separation. I shall not have to resist your frank approaches, Walter, any more.'

There was a melancholy in his smile as he said it, that showed he had found some company and friendship for his thoughts even in that.

'Ah, Mr Carker!' returned Walter. 'Why did you resist them? You could have done me nothing but good, I am very sure.'

He shook his head. 'If there were any good,' he said, 'I could do on this earth, I would do it, Walter, for you. The sight of you from day to day, has been at once happiness and remorse to me. But the pleasure has outweighed the pain. I know that, now, by knowing what I lose.'

'Come in, Mr Carker, and make acquaintance with my good old uncle,' urged Walter. 'I have often talked to him about you, and he will be glad to tell you all he hears from me. I have not,' said Walter, noticing his hesitation, and speaking with embarrassment himself: 'I have not told him anything about our last conversation, Mr Carker; not even him, believe me.'

The grey Junior pressed his hand, and tears rose in his eyes.

'If I ever make acquaintance with him, Walter,' he returned, 'it will be that I may hear tidings of you. Rely on my not wronging your forbearance and consideration. It would be to wrong it, not to tell him all the truth, before I sought a word of confidence from him. But I have no friend or acquaintance except you: and even for your sake, am little likely to make any.'

'I wish,' said Walter, 'you had suffered me to be your friend indeed. I always wished it, Mr Carker, as you know; but never half so much as now, when we are going to part.'

'It is enough,' replied the other, 'that you have been the friend of my own breast, and that when I have avoided you most, my heart inclined the most towards you, and was fullest of you. Walter, good-bye!'

'Good-bye, Mr Carker. Heaven be with you, Sir!' cried Walter, with emotion.

'If,' said the other, retaining his hand while he spoke; 'if when you come back, you miss me from my old corner, and should hear from any one where I am lying, come and look upon my grave. Think that I might have been as honest and as happy as you! And let *me* think, when I know my time is coming on, that some one like my former self may stand there, for a moment, and remember me with pity and forgiveness! Walter, good-bye!'

His figure crept like a shadow down the bright, sun-lighted street, so cheerful yet so solemn in the early summer morning; and slowly passed away.

The relentless chronometer at last announced that Walter must turn his back upon the Wooden Midshipman: and away they went, himself, his uncle, and the Captain, in a hackney-coach to a wharf, where they were to take steam-boat for some Reach down the river, the name of which, as the Captain gave it out, was a hopeless mystery to the ears of landsmen. Arrived at this Reach (whither the ship had repaired by last night's tide), they were boarded by various excited watermen[3] and among others by a dirty Cyclops[4] of the Captain's acquaintance, who, with his one eye, had made the Captain out some mile and a half off, and had been exchanging unintelligible roars with him ever since. Becoming the lawful prize of this personage, who was frightfully hoarse and constitutionally in want of shaving, they were all three put aboard the Son and Heir. And the Son and Heir was in a pretty state of confusion, with sails lying all bedraggled on the wet decks, loose ropes tripping people up, men in red shirts running barefoot to and fro, casks blockading every foot of space, and, in the thickest of the fray, a black cook in a black caboose[5] up to his eyes in vegetables and blinded with smoke.

The Captain immediately drew Walter into a corner, and with a great effort, that made his face very red, pulled up the silver watch, which was so big, and so tight in his pocket, that it came out like a bung.

'Wal'r,' said the Captain, handing it over, and shaking him heartily by the hand, 'a parting gift, my lad. Put it back half an hour every morning, and about another quarter towards the arter-noon, and it's a watch that'll do you credit.'

'Captain Cuttle! I couldn't think of it!' cried Walter, detaining him, for he was running away. 'Pray take it back. I have one already.'

'Then, Wal'r,' said the Captain, suddenly diving into one of his pockets and bringing up the two teaspoons and the sugar-tongs, with which he had armed himself to meet such an objection, 'take this here trifle of plate, instead.'

'No, no, I couldn't indeed!' cried Walter, 'a thousand thanks! Don't throw them away, Captain Cuttle!' for the Captain was about to jerk them overboard. 'They'll be of much more use to you than me. Give me your stick. I have often thought that I should like to have it. There! Goodbye, Captain Cuttle! Take care of my uncle! Uncle Sol, God bless you!'

They were over the side in the confusion, before Walter caught another glimpse of either; and when he ran up to the stern, and looked after them, he saw his uncle hanging down his head in the boat, and Captain Cuttle rapping him on the back with the great silver watch (it must have been very painful), and gesticulating hopefully with the teaspoons and sugar-tongs. Catching sight of Walter, Captain Cuttle dropped the property into the bottom of the boat with perfect unconcern, being evidently oblivious of its existence, and pulling off the glazed hat hailed him lustily. The glazed hat made quite a show in the sun with its glistening, and the Captain continued to wave it until he could be seen no longer. Then the confusion on board, which had been rapidly increasing, reached its height; two or three other boats went away with a cheer; the sails shone bright and full above, as Walter watched them spread their surface to the favourable breeze; the water flew in sparkles from the prow; and off upon her voyage went the Son and Heir, as hopefully and trippingly as many another son and heir, gone down, had started on his way before her.

Day after day, old Sol and Captain Cuttle kept her reckoning in the little back parlour and worked out her course, with the chart spread before them on the round table. At night, when old Sol climbed upstairs, so lonely, to the attic where it sometimes blew great guns, he looked up at the stars and listened to the wind, and kept a longer watch than would have fallen to his lot on board the ship. The last bottle of the old Madeira, which had had its cruising days, and known its dangers of the deep, lay silently beneath its dust and cobwebs, in the meanwhile, undisturbed.

CHAPTER 20

Mr Dombey goes upon a Journey

'Mr Dombey, Sir,' said Major Bagstock, 'Joey B. is not in general a man of sentiment, for Joseph is tough. But Joe has his feelings, Sir, and when they *are* awakened – Damme, Mr Dombey,' cried the Major with sudden ferocity, 'this is weakness, and I won't submit to it!'

Major Bagstock delivered himself of these expressions on receiving Mr Dombey as his guest at the head of his own staircase in Princess's Place. Mr Dombey had come to breakfast with the Major, previous to their setting forth on their trip; and the ill-starred Native had already undergone a world of misery arising out of the muffins, while, in connexion with the general question of boiled eggs, life was a burden to him.

'It is not for an old soldier of the Bagstock breed,' observed the Major, relapsing into a mild state, 'to deliver himself up, a prey to his own emotions; but – damme, Sir,' cried the Major, in another spasm of ferocity, 'I condole with you!'

The Major's purple visage deepened in its hue, and the Major's lobster eyes stood out in bolder relief, as he shook Mr Dombey by the hand, imparting to that peaceful action as defiant a character as if it had been the prelude to his immediately boxing Mr Dombey for a thousand pound a side and the championship of England. With a rotatory motion of his head, and a wheeze very like the cough of a horse, the Major then conducted his visitor to the sitting-room, and there welcomed him (having now composed his feelings) with the freedom and frankness of a travelling companion.

'Dombey,' said the Major, 'I'm glad to see you. I'm proud to see you. There are not many men in Europe to whom J. Bagstock would say that – for Josh is blunt, Sir: it's his nature – but Joey B. is proud to see you, Dombey.'

'Major,' returned Mr Dombey, 'you are very obliging.'

'No, Sir,' said the Major, 'Devil a bit!¹ That's not my character. If that had been Joe's character, Joe might have been by this time, Lieutenant-General Sir Joseph Bagstock, K.C.B.,² and might have received you in very different quarters. You don't know old Joe yet, I find. But this occasion, being special, is a source of pride to me. By the Lord, Sir,' said the Major resolutely, 'it's an honour to me!'

Mr Dombey, in his estimation of himself and his money, felt that this was very true, and therefore did not dispute the point. But the

instinctive recognition of such a truth by the Major, and his plain
avowal of it, were very agreeable. It was a confirmation to Mr
Dombey, if he had required any, of his not being mistaken in the
Major. It was an assurance to him that his power extended beyond
his own immediate sphere; and that the Major, as an officer and a
gentleman, had a no less becoming sense of it, than the beadle of
the Royal Exchange.

And if it were ever consolatory to know this, or the like of this, it
was consolatory then, when the impotence of his will, the instability
of his hopes, the feebleness of wealth, had been so direfully
impressed upon him. What could it do, his boy had asked him.
Sometimes, thinking of the baby question, he could hardly forbear
inquiring, himself, what *could* it do indeed: what had it done?

But these were lonely thoughts, bred late at night in the sullen
despondency and gloom of his retirement, and pride easily found
its reassurance in many testimonies to the truth, as unimpeachable
and precious as the Major's. Mr Dombey, in his friendlessness,
inclined to the Major. It cannot be said that he warmed towards
him, but he thawed a little. The Major had had some part – and
not too much – in the days by the seaside. He was a man of the
world, and knew some great people. He talked much, and told
stories; and Mr Dombey was disposed to regard him as a choice
spirit who shone in society, and who had not that poisonous
ingredient of poverty with which choice spirits in general are too
much adulterated. His station was undeniable. Altogether the Major
was a creditable companion, well accustomed to a life of leisure,
and to such places as that they were about to visit, and having an
air of gentlemanly ease about him that mixed well enough with his
own City character, and did not compete with it at all. If Mr
Dombey had any lingering idea that the Major, as a man accustomed, in the way of his calling, to make light of the ruthless hand
that had lately crushed his hopes, might unconsciously impart some
useful philosophy to him, and scare away his weak regrets, he hid
it from himself, and left it lying at the bottom of his pride,
unexamined.

'Where is my scoundrel?' said the Major, looking wrathfully
round the room.

The Native, who had no particular name, but answered to any
vituperative epithet, presented himself instantly at the door and
ventured to come no nearer.

'You villain!' said the choleric Major, 'where's the breakfast?'

The dark servant disappeared in search of it, and was quickly heard reascending the stairs in such a tremulous state, that the plates and dishes on the tray he carried, trembling sympathetically as he came, rattled again, all the way up.

'Dombey,' said the Major, glancing at the Native as he arranged the table, and encouraging him with an awful shake of his fist when he upset a spoon, 'here is a devilled[3] grill, a savoury pie, a dish of kidneys, and so forth. Pray sit down. Old Joe can give you nothing but camp fare, you see.'

'Very excellent fare, Major,' replied his guest; and not in mere politeness either; for the Major always took the best possible care of himself, and indeed ate rather more of rich meats than was good for him, insomuch that his Imperial complexion was mainly referred by the faculty to that circumstance.

'You have been looking over the way, Sir,' observed the Major. 'Have you seen our friend?'

'You mean Miss Tox,' retorted Mr Dombey. 'No.'

'Charming woman, Sir,' said the Major, with a fat laugh rising in his short throat, and nearly suffocating him.

'Miss Tox is a very good sort of person, I believe,' replied Mr Dombey.

The haughty coldness of the reply seemed to afford Major Bagstock infinite delight. He swelled and swelled, exceedingly: and even laid down his knife and fork for a moment, to rub his hands.

'Old Joe, Sir,' said the Major, 'was a bit of a favourite in that quarter once. But Joe has had his day. J. Bagstock is extinguished – outrivalled – floored, Sir. I tell you what, Dombey.' The Major paused in his eating, and looked mysteriously indignant. 'That's a de-vilish ambitious woman, Sir.'

Mr Dombey said 'Indeed?' with frigid indifference mingled perhaps with some contemptuous incredulity as to Miss Tox having the presumption to harbour such a superior quality.

'That woman, Sir,' said the Major, 'is, in her way, a Lucifer. Joey B. has had his day, Sir, but he keeps his eyes. He sees, does Joe. His Royal Highness the late Duke of York observed of Joey, at a levee,[4] that he saw.'

The Major accompanied this with such a look, and, between eating, drinking, hot tea, devilled grill, muffins, and meaning, was altogether so swollen and inflamed about the head, that even Mr Dombey showed some anxiety for him.

'That ridiculous old spectacle, Sir,' pursued the Major, 'aspires. She aspires sky-high, Sir. Matrimonially, Dombey.'

'I am sorry for her,' said Mr Dombey.

'Don't say that, Dombey,' returned the Major in a warning voice.

'Why should I not, Major?' said Mr Dombey.

The Major gave no answer but the horse's cough, and went on eating vigorously.

'She has taken an interest in your household,' said the Major, stopping short again, 'and has been a frequent visitor at your house for some time now.'

'Yes,' replied Mr Dombey with great stateliness, 'Miss Tox was originally received there, at the time of Mrs Dombey's death, as a friend of my sister's; and being a well-behaved person, and showing a liking for the poor infant, she was permitted – I may say encouraged – to repeat her visits with my sister, and gradually to occupy a kind of footing of familiarity in the family. I have,' said Mr Dombey, in the tone of a man who was making a great and valuable concession, 'I have a respect for Miss Tox. She has been so obliging as to render many little services in my house: trifling and insignificant services perhaps, Major, but not to be disparaged on that account: and I hope I have had the good fortune to be enabled to acknowledge them by such attention and notice as it has been in my power to bestow. I hold myself indebted to Miss Tox, Major,' added Mr Dombey, with a slight wave of his hand, 'for the pleasure of your acquaintance.'

'Dombey,' said the Major, warmly: 'no! No, Sir! Joseph Bagstock can never permit that assertion to pass uncontradicted. Your knowledge of old Joe, Sir, such as he is, and old Joe's knowledge of you, Sir, had its origin in a noble fellow, Sir – in a great creature, Sir. Dombey!' said the Major, with a struggle which it was not very difficult to parade, his whole life being a struggle against all kinds of apoplectic symptoms, 'we knew each other through your boy.'

Mr Dombey seemed touched, as it is not improbable the Major designed he should be, by this allusion. He looked down and sighed: and the Major, rousing himself fiercely, again said, in reference to the state of mind into which he felt himself in danger of falling, that this was weakness, and nothing should induce him to submit to it.

'Our friend had a remote connexion with that event,' said the Major, 'and all the credit that belongs to her, J. B. is willing to give her, Sir. Notwithstanding which, ma'am,' he added, raising his eyes from his plate, and casting them across Princess's Place, to where Miss Tox was at that moment visible at her window watering her flowers, 'you're a scheming jade, ma'am, and your ambition is a piece of monstrous impudence. If it only made yourself ridiculous, ma'am,' said the Major, rolling his head at the unconscious Miss

Tox, while his starting eyes appeared to make a leap towards her, 'you might do that to your heart's content, ma'am, without any objection, I assure you, on the part of Bagstock.' Here the Major laughed frightfully up in the tips of his ears and in the veins of his head. 'But when, ma'am,' said the Major, 'you compromise other people, and generous, unsuspicious people too, as a repayment for their condescension, you stir the blood of old Joe in his body.'

'Major,' said Mr Dombey, reddening. 'I hope you do not hint at anything so absurd on the part of Miss Tox as—'

'Dombey,' returned the Major, 'I hint at nothing. But Joey B. has lived in the world, Sir: lived in the world with his eyes open, Sir, and his ears cocked: and Joe tells you, Dombey, that there's a devilish artful and ambitious woman over the way.'

Mr Dombey involuntarily glanced over the way; and an angry glance he sent in that direction, too.

'That's all on such a subject that shall pass the lips of Joseph Bagstock,' said the Major firmly. 'Joe is not a tale-bearer, but there are times when he must speak, when he *will* speak! – confound your arts, ma'am,' cried the Major, again apostrophising his fair neighbour, with great ire, – 'when the provocation is too strong to admit of his remaining silent.'

The emotion of this outbreak threw the Major into a paroxysm of horse's coughs, which held him for a long time. On recovering he added:

'And now, Dombey, as you have invited Joe – old Joe, who has no other merit, Sir, but that he is tough and hearty – to be your guest and guide at Leamington, command him in any way you please, and he is wholly yours. I don't know, Sir,' said the Major, wagging his double chin with a jocose air, 'what it is you people see in Joe to make you hold him in such great request, all of you; but this I know, Sir, that if he wasn't pretty tough, and obstinate in his refusals, you'd kill him among you with your invitations and so forth, in double-quick time.'

Mr Dombey, in a few words, expressed his sense of the preference he received over those other distinguished members of society who were clamouring for the possession of Major Bagstock. But the Major cut him short by giving him to understand that he followed his own inclinations, and that they had risen up in a body and said with one accord, 'J. B., Dombey is the man for you to choose as a friend.'

The Major being by this time in a state of repletion, with essence of savoury pie oozing out at the corners of his eyes, and devilled grill and kidneys tightening his cravat: and the time moreover approaching for the departure of the railway train to Birmingham, by which they were to leave town: the Native got him into his great-coat with immense difficulty, and buttoned him up until his face looked staring and gasping, over the top of that garment, as if he were in a barrel. The Native then handed him separately, and with a decent interval between each supply, his wash-leather gloves, his thick stick, and his hat; which latter article the Major wore with a rakish air on one side of his head, by way of toning down his remarkable visage. The Native had previously packed, in all possible and impossible parts of Mr Dombey's chariot, which was in waiting, an unusual quantity of carpet-bags and small portman-teaus, no less apoplectic in appearance than the Major himself: and having filled his own pockets with Seltzer water,[5] East India sherry, sandwiches, shawls, telescopes, maps, and newspapers, any or all of which light baggage the Major might require at any instant of the journey, he announced that everything was ready. To complete the equipment of this unfortunate foreigner (currently believed to be a prince in his own country), when he took his seat in the rumble[6] by the side of Mr Towlinson, a pile of the Major's cloaks and great-coats was hurled upon him by the landlord, who aimed at him from the pavement with those great missiles like a Titan,[7] and so covered him up, that he proceeded, in a living tomb, to the railroad station.

But before the carriage moved away, and while the Native was in the act of sepulture, Miss Tox appearing at her window waved a lily-white handkerchief. Mr Dombey received this parting salutation very coldly – very coldly even for him – and honouring her with the slightest possible inclination of his head, leaned back in the carriage with a very discontented look. His marked behaviour seemed to afford the Major (who was all politeness in his recognition of Miss Tox) unbounded satisfaction; and he sat for a long time afterwards, leering, and choking, like an over-fed Mephistopheles.

During the bustle of preparation at the railway,[8] Mr Dombey and the Major walked up and down the platform side by side; the former taciturn and gloomy, and the latter entertaining him, or entertaining himself, with a variety of anecdotes and reminiscences, in most of which Joe Bagstock was the principal performer. Neither of the two observed that in the course of these walks, they attracted the attention of a working man who was standing near the engine, and who touched his hat every time they passed; for Mr Dombey habitually looked over the vulgar herd, not at them; and the Major was looking, at the time, into the core of one of his stories. At length, however, this man stepped before them as they turned round, and pulling his hat off, and keeping it off, ducked his head to Mr Dombey.

'Beg your pardon, Sir,' said the man, 'but I hope you're a doin' pretty well, Sir.'

He was dressed in a canvas suit abundantly besmeared with coal-dust and oil, and had cinders in his whiskers, and a smell of half-slaked ashes all over him. He was not a bad-looking fellow, nor even what could be fairly called a dirty-looking fellow, in spite of this; and, in short, he was Mr Toodle, professionally clothed.

'I shall have the honour of stokin' of you down,[9] Sir,' said Mr Toodle. 'Beg your pardon, Sir. I hope you find yourself a coming round!'

Mr Dombey looked at him, in return for his tone of interest, as if a man like that would make his very eyesight dirty.

''Scuse the liberty, Sir,' said Toodle, seeing he was not clearly remembered, 'but my wife Polly, as was called Richards in your family—'

A change in Mr Dombey's face, which seemed to express recollection of him, and so it did, but it expressed in a much stronger degree an angry sense of humiliation, stopped Mr Toodle short.

'Your wife wants money, I suppose,' said Mr Dombey, putting his hand in his pocket, and speaking (but that he always did) haughtily.

'No thank'ee, Sir,' returned Toodle, 'I can't say she does. *I* don't.'

Mr Dombey was stopped short now in his turn: and awkwardly: with his hand in his pocket.

'No, Sir,' said Toodle, turning his oilskin cap round and round; 'we're a doin' pretty well, Sir; we haven't no cause to complain in the worldly way, Sir. We've had four more since then, Sir, but we rubs on.'[10]

Mr Dombey would have rubbed on to his own carriage, though in so doing he had rubbed the stoker underneath the wheels; but his attention was arrested by something in connexion with the cap still going slowly round and round in the man's hand.

'We lost one babby,' observed Toodle, 'there's no denyin'.'

'Lately,' added Mr Dombey, looking at the cap.

'No, Sir, up'ard of three years ago, but all the rest is hearty. And in the matter o' readin', Sir,' said Toodle, ducking again, as if to remind Mr Dombey of what had passed between them on that subject long ago, 'them boys o' mine, they learned me, among 'em, arter all. They've made a wery tolerable scholar of me, Sir, them boys.'

'Come, Major,' said Mr Dombey.

'Beg your pardon, Sir,' resumed Toodle, taking a step before them and deferentially stopping them again, still cap in hand: 'I wouldn't have troubled you with such a pint except as a way of gettin' in the name of my son Biler – christened Robin, – him as you was so good as to make a Charitable Grinder on.'

'Well, man,' said Mr Dombey in his severest manner, 'What about him?'

'Why, Sir,' returned Toodle, shaking his head with a face of great anxiety and distress, 'I'm forced to say, Sir, that he's gone wrong.'

'He has gone wrong, has he?' said Mr Dombey, with a hard kind of satisfaction.

'He has fell into bad company, you see, genelmen,' pursued the father, looking wistfully at both, and evidently taking the Major into the conversation with the hope of having his sympathy. 'He has got into bad ways. God send he may come to again, genelmen, but he's on the wrong track now! You could hardly be off hearing of it somehow, Sir,' said Toodle, again addressing Mr Dombey individually; 'and it's better I should out and say my boy's gone rather wrong. Polly's dreadful down about it, genelmen,' said Toodle with the same dejected look, and another appeal to the Major.

'A son of this man's whom I caused to be educated, Major,' said Mr Dombey, giving him his arm. 'The usual return!'

'Take advice from plain old Joe, and never educate that sort of people, Sir,' returned the Major. 'Damme, Sir, it never does! It always fails!'

The simple father was beginning to submit that he hoped his son, the quondam[11] Grinder, huffed and cuffed and flogged and badged, and taught, as parrots are, by a brute jobbed into[12] his place of schoolmaster with as much fitness for it as a hound, might not have been educated on quite a right plan in some undiscovered respect, when Mr Dombey angrily repeating 'The usual return!' led the Major away. And the Major being heavy to hoist into Mr Dombey's carriage, elevated in mid-air, and having to stop and swear that he would flay the Native alive, and break every bone in his skin, and visit other physical torments upon him, every time he couldn't get his foot on the step, and fell back on that dark exile, had barely time before they started to repeat hoarsely that it would never do:

that it always failed: and that if he were to educate 'his own vagabond,' he would certainly be hanged.

Mr Dombey assented bitterly; but there was something more in his bitterness, and in his moody way of falling back in the carriage, and looking with knitted brows at the changing objects without, than the failure of that noble educational system administered by the Grinders' Company. He had seen upon the man's rough cap a piece of new crape,[13] and he had assured himself, from his manner and his answers, that he wore it for his son.

So! from high to low, at home or abroad, from Florence in his great house to the coarse churl who was feeding the fire then smoking before them, every one set up some claim or other to a share in his dead boy, and was a bidder against him! Could he ever forget how that woman had wept over his pillow, and called him her own child! or how he, waking from his sleep, had asked for her, and had raised himself in his bed and brightened when she came in!

To think of this presumptuous raker among coals and ashes going on before there, with his sign of mourning! To think that he dared to enter, even by a common show like that, into the trial and disappointment of a proud gentleman's secret heart! To think that this lost child, who was to have divided with him his riches, and his projects, and his power, and allied with whom he was to have shut out all the world as with a double door of gold, should have let in such a herd to insult him with their knowledge of his defeated hopes, and their boasts of claiming community of feeling with himself, so far removed: if not of having crept into the place wherein he would have lorded it, alone!

He found no pleasure or relief in the journey. Tortured by these thoughts he carried monotony with him, through the rushing landscape, and hurried headlong, not through a rich and varied country, but a wilderness of blighted plans and gnawing jealousies. The very speed at which the train was whirled along mocked the swift course of the young life that had been borne away so steadily and so inexorably to its fore-doomed end. The power that forced itself upon its iron way – its own – defiant of all paths and roads, piercing through the heart of every obstacle, and dragging living creatures of all classes, ages, and degrees behind it, was a type of the triumphant monster, Death.

Away, with a shriek, and a roar, and a rattle, from the town, burrowing among the dwellings of men and making the streets hum, flashing out into the meadows for a moment, mining in through the damp earth, booming on in darkness and heavy air, bursting out again into the sunny day so bright and wide; away, with a shriek, and a roar, and a rattle, through the fields, through the woods, through the corn, through the hay, through the chalk, through the mould, through the clay, through the rock, among objects close at hand and almost in the grasp, ever flying from the traveller, and a deceitful distance ever moving slowly within him: like as in the track of the remorseless monster, Death!

Through the hollow, on the height, by the heath, by the orchard, by the park, by the garden, over the canal, across the river, where the sheep are feeding, where the mill is going, where the barge is floating, where the dead are lying, where the factory is smoking, where the stream is running, where the village clusters, where the great cathedral rises, where the bleak moor lies, and the wild breeze smooths or ruffles it at its inconstant will; away, with a shriek, and a roar, and a rattle, and no trace to leave behind but dust and vapour: like as in the track of the remorseless monster, Death!

Breasting the wind and light, the shower and sunshine, away, and still away, it rolls and roars, fierce and rapid, smooth and certain, and great works and massive bridges crossing up above, fall like a beam of shadow an inch broad, upon the eye, and then are lost. Away, and still away, onward and onward ever: glimpses of cottage-homes, of houses, mansions, rich estates, of husbandry and handicraft, of people, of old road and paths that look deserted, small, and insignificant as they are left behind: and so they do, and what else is there but such glimpses, in the track of the indomitable monster, Death!

Away, with a shriek, and a roar, and a rattle, plunging down into the earth again, and working on in such a storm of energy and perseverance, that amidst the darkness and whirlwind the motion seems reversed, and to tend furiously backward, until a ray of light upon the wet wall shows its surface flying past like a fierce stream. Away once more into the day, and through the day, with a shrill yell of exultation, roaring, rattling, tearing on, spurning everything with its dark breath, sometimes pausing for a minute where a crowd of faces are, that in a minute more are not; sometimes lapping water greedily, and before the spout at which it drinks has ceased to drip upon the ground, shrieking, roaring, rattling through the purple distance!

Louder and louder yet, it shrieks and cries as it comes tearing on resistless to the goal: and now its way, still like the way of Death, is strewn with ashes thickly. Everything around is blackened. There are dark pools of water, muddy lanes, and miserable habitations far below. There are jagged walls and falling houses close at hand, and through the battered roofs and broken windows, wretched rooms are seen, where want and fever hide themselves in many wretched shapes, while smoke and crowded gables, and distorted chimneys, and deformity of brick and mortar penning up deformity of mind and body, choke the murky distance. As Mr Dombey looks out of his carriage window, it is never in his thoughts that the monster who has brought him there has let the light of day in on these things: not made or caused them. It was the journey's fitting end, and might have been the end of everything; it was so ruinous and dreary.

So, pursuing the one course of thought, he had the one relentless monster still before him. All things looked black, and cold, and deadly upon him, and he on them. He found a likeness to his misfortune everywhere. There was a remorseless triumph going on about him, and it galled and stung him in his pride and jealousy, whatever form it took: though most of all when it divided with him the love and memory of his lost boy.

There was a face – he had looked upon it, on the previous night, and it on him with eyes that read his soul, though they were dim with tears, and hidden soon behind two quivering hands – that often had attended him in fancy, on this ride. He had seen it, with the expression of last night, timidly pleading to him. It was not reproachful, but there was something of doubt, almost of hopeful incredulity in it, which, as he once more saw that fade away into a desolate certainty of his dislike, was like reproach. It was a trouble to him to think of this face of Florence.

Because he felt any new compunction towards it? No. Because the feeling it awakened in him – of which he had had some old foreshadowing in older times – was full-formed now, and spoke out plainly, moving him too much, and threatening to grow too strong for his composure. Because the face was abroad, in the expression of defeat and persecution that seemed to encircle him like the air. Because it barbed the arrow of that cruel and remorseless enemy on which his thoughts so ran, and put into its grasp a double-handed sword. Because he knew full well, in his own breast, as he stood there, tinging the scene of transition before him with the morbid colours of his own mind, and making it a ruin and a picture of decay, instead of hopeful change, and promise of better things, that life had quite as much to do with his complainings as death. One child was gone, and one child left. Why was the object of his hope removed instead of her?

The sweet, calm, gentle presence in his fancy, moved him to no reflection but that. She had been unwelcome to him from the first; she was an aggravation of his bitterness now. If his son had been his only child, and the same blow had fallen on him, it would have been heavy to bear; but infinitely lighter than now, when it might have fallen on her (whom he could have lost, or he believed it, without a pang), and had not. Her loving and innocent face rising before him, had no softening or winning influence. He rejected the angel, and took up with the tormenting spirit crouching in his bosom. Her patience, goodness, youth, devotion, love, were as so many atoms in the ashes upon which he set his heel. He saw her image in the blight and blackness all around him, not irradiating but deepening the gloom. More than once upon this journey, and now again as he stood pondering at this journey's end, tracing figures in the dust with his stick, the thought came into his mind, what was there he could interpose between himself and it?

The Major, who had been blowing and panting all the way down, like another engine, and whose eye had often wandered from his newspaper to leer at the prospect, as if there were a procession of discomfited Miss Toxes pouring out in the smoke of the train, and flying away over the fields to hide themselves in any place of refuge, aroused his friend by informing him that the post-horses were harnessed and the carriage ready.

'Dombey,' said the Major, rapping him on the arm with his cane, 'don't be thoughtful. It's a bad habit. Old Joe, Sir, wouldn't be as tough as you see him, if he had ever encouraged it. You are too great a man, Dombey, to be thoughtful. In your position, Sir, you're far above that kind of thing.'

The Major even in his friendly remonstrances, thus consulting the dignity and honour of Mr Dombey, and showing a lively sense of their importance, Mr Dombey felt more than ever disposed to defer to a gentleman possessing so much good sense and such a well-regulated mind; accordingly he made an effort to listen to the Major's stories, as they trotted along the turnpike road; and the Major, finding both the pace and the road a great deal better adapted to his conversational powers than the mode of travelling they had just relinquished, came out for his entertainment.

In this flow of spirits and conversation, only interrupted by his usual plethoric symptoms, and by intervals of lunch, and from time to time by some violent assault upon the Native, who wore a pair of ear-rings in his dark-brown ears, and on whom his European clothes sat with an outlandish impossibility of adjustment – being, of their own accord, and without any reference to the tailor's art, long where they ought to be short, short where they ought to be long, tight where they ought to be loose, and loose where they ought to be tight – and to which he imparted a new grace, whenever the Major attacked him, by shrinking into them like a shrivelled nut, or a cold monkey – in this flow of spirits and conversation, the Major continued all day: so that when evening came on, and found them trotting through the green and leafy road near Leamington, the Major's voice, what with talking and eating and chuckling and choking, appeared to be in the box under the rumble, or in some neighbouring hay-stack. Nor did the Major improve it at the Royal Hotel, where rooms and dinner had been ordered, and where he so oppressed his organs of speech by eating and drinking, that when he retired to bed he had no voice at all, except to cough with, and could only make himself intelligible to the dark servant by gasping at him.

He not only rose next morning, however, like a giant refreshed,[14] but conducted himself, at breakfast, like a giant refreshing. At this meal they arranged their daily habits. The Major was to take the responsibility of ordering everything to eat and drink; and they were to have a late breakfast together every morning, and a late dinner together every day. Mr Dombey would prefer remaining in his own room, or walking in the country by himself, on that first day of their sojourn at Leamington; but next morning he would be happy to accompany the Major to the Pump-room,[15] and about the town. So they parted until dinner-time. Mr Dombey retired to nurse his wholesome thoughts in his own way. The Major, attended by the Native carrying a camp-stool, a great-coat, and an umbrella, swaggered up and down through all the public places: looking into subscription books to find out who was there, looking up old ladies by whom he was much admired, reporting J. B. tougher than ever, and puffing his rich friend Dombey wherever he went. There never was a man who stood by a friend more staunchly than the Major, when in puffing him, he puffed himself.

It was surprising how much new conversation the Major had to let off at dinner-time, and what occasion he gave Mr Dombey to admire his social qualities. At breakfast next morning, he knew the contents of the latest newspapers received; and mentioned several subjects in connexion with them, on which his opinion had recently been sought by persons of such power and might, that they were only to be obscurely hinted at. Mr Dombey, who had been so long shut up within himself, and who had rarely, at any time, overstepped the enchanted circle within which the operations of Dombey and Son were conducted, began to think this an improvement on his solitary life, and in place of excusing himself for another day, as he had thought of doing when alone, walked out with the Major arm-in-arm.

CHAPTER 21

New Faces

The Major, more blue-faced and staring – more over-ripe, as it were, than ever – and giving vent, every now and then, to one of the horse's coughs, not so much of necessity as in a spontaneous explosion of importance, walked arm-in-arm with Mr Dombey up the sunny side of the way, with his cheeks swelling over his tight stock,[1] his legs majestically wide apart, and his great head wagging from side to side, as if he were remonstrating within himself for being such a captivating object. They had not walked many yards, before the Major encountered somebody he knew, nor many yards farther before the Major encountered somebody else he knew, but he merely shook his fingers at them as he passed, and led Mr Dombey on: pointing out the localities as they went, and enlivening the walk with any current scandal suggested by them.

In this manner the Major and Mr Dombey were walking arm-in-arm, much to their own satisfaction, when they beheld advancing towards them, a wheeled chair, in which a lady was seated, indolently steering her carriage by a kind of rudder in front, while it was propelled by some unseen power in the rear. Although the lady was not young, she was very blooming in the face – quite rosy – and her dress and attitude were perfectly juvenile. Walking by the side of the chair, and carrying her gossamer parasol with a proud and weary air, as if so great an effort must be soon abandoned and the parasol dropped, sauntered a much younger lady, very handsome, very haughty, very wilful, who tossed her head and drooped her eyelids, as though, if there were anything in all the world worth looking into, save a mirror, it certainly was not the earth or sky.

'Why, what the devil have we here, Sir!' cried the Major, stopping as this little cavalcade drew near.

'My dearest Edith!' drawled the lady in the chair, 'Major Bagstock!'

The Major no sooner heard the voice, than he relinquished Mr Dombey's arm, darted forward, took the hand of the lady in the chair and pressed it to his lips. With no less gallantry, the Major folded both his gloves upon his heart, and bowed low to the other lady. And now, the chair having stopped, the motive power became visible in the shape of a flushed page pushing behind, who seemed to have in part outgrown and in part out-pushed his strength, for when he stood upright he was tall, and wan, and thin, and his plight appeared the more forlorn from his having injured the shape of his hat, by butting at the carriage with his head to urge it forward, as is sometimes done by elephants in Oriental countries.

'Joe Bagstock,' said the Major to both ladies, 'is a proud and happy man for the rest of his life.'

'You false creature!' said the old lady in the chair, insipidly. 'Where do you come from? I can't bear you.'

'Then suffer old Joe to present a friend, ma'am,' said the Major, promptly, 'as a reason for being tolerated. Mr Dombey, Mrs Skewton.' The lady in the chair was gracious. 'Mr Dombey, Mrs Granger.' The lady with the parasol was faintly conscious of Mr Dombey's taking off his hat, and bowing low. 'I am delighted, Sir,' said the Major, 'to have this opportunity.'

The Major seemed in earnest, for he looked at all the three, and leered in his ugliest manner.

'Mrs Skewton, Dombey,' said the Major, 'makes havoc in the heart of old Josh.'

Mr Dombey signified that he didn't wonder at it.

'You perfidious goblin,' said the lady in the chair, 'have done! How long have you been here, bad man?'

'One day,' replied the Major.

'And can you be a day, or even a minute,' returned the lady, slightly settling her false curls and false eyebrows with her fan, and showing her false teeth, set off by her false complexion, 'in the garden of what's-its-name—'

'Eden, I suppose, mama,' interrupted the younger lady, scornfully.

'My dear Edith,' said the other, 'I cannot help it. I never can remember those frightful names – without having your whole Soul and Being inspired by the sight of Nature; by the perfume,' said Mrs Skewton, rustling a handkerchief that was faint and sickly with essences, 'of her artless breath, you creature!'

The discrepancy between Mrs Skewton's fresh enthusiasm of words, and forlornly faded manner, was hardly less observable

Major Bagstock is delighted to have that opportunity

than that between her age, which was about seventy, and her
dress, which would have been youthful for twenty-seven. Her
attitude in the wheeled chair (which she never varied) was one in
which she had been taken in a barouche,[2] some fifty years before,
by a then fashionable artist who had appended to his published
sketch the name of Cleopatra: in consequence of a discovery made
by the critics of the time, that it bore an exact resemblance to that
Princess as she reclined on board her galley.[3] Mrs Skewton was a
beauty then, and bucks[4] threw wine-glasses over their heads by
dozens in her honour. The beauty and the barouche had both
passed away, but she still preserved the attitude, and for this reason
expressly, maintained the wheeled chair and the butting page: there
being nothing whatever, except the attitude, to prevent her from
walking.

'Mr Dombey is devoted to Nature, I trust?' said Mrs Skewton,
settling her diamond brooch. And by the way, she chiefly lived
upon the reputation of some diamonds, and her family connexions.

'My friend Dombey, ma'am,' returned the Major, 'may be
devoted to her in secret, but a man who is paramount in the greatest
city in the universe—'

'No one can be a stranger,' said Mrs Skewton, 'to Mr Dombey's
immense influence.'

As Mr Dombey acknowledged the compliment with a bend of his
head, the younger lady glancing at him, met his eyes.

'You reside here, madam?' said Mr Dombey, addressing her.

'No, we have been to a great many places. To Harrogate and
Scarborough, and into Devonshire. We have been visiting, and
resting here and there. Mama likes change.'

'Edith of course does not,' said Mrs Skewton, with a ghastly
archness.

'I have not found that there is any change in such places,' was the
answer, delivered with supreme indifference.

'They libel me. There is only one change, Mr Dombey,' observed
Mrs Skewton, with a mincing sigh, 'for which I really care, and that
I fear I shall never be permitted to enjoy. People cannot spare one.
But seclusion and contemplation are my what's-his-name—'

'If you mean Paradise, mama, you had better say so, to render
yourself intelligible,' said the younger lady.

'My dearest Edith,' returned Mrs Skewton, 'you know that I am
wholly dependent upon you for those odious names. I assure you,
Mr Dombey, Nature intended me for an Arcadian.[5] I am thrown
away in society. Cows are my passion. What I have ever sighed for,

has been to retreat to a Swiss farm, and live entirely surrounded by cows – and china.'

This curious association of objects, suggesting a remembrance of the celebrated bull[6] who got by mistake into a crockery shop, was received with perfect gravity by Mr Dombey, who intimated his opinion that Nature was, no doubt, a very respectable institution.

'What I want,' drawled Mrs Skewton, pinching her shrivelled throat, 'is heart.' It was frightfully true in one sense, if not in that in which she used the phrase. 'What I want, is frankness, confidence, less conventionality, and freer play of soul. We are so dreadfully artificial.'

We were, indeed.

'In short,' said Mrs Skewton, 'I want Nature everywhere. It would be so extremely charming.'

'Nature is inviting us away now, mama, if you are ready,' said the younger lady, curling her handsome lip. At this hint, the wan page, who had been surveying the party over the top of the chair, vanished behind it, as if the ground had swallowed him up.

'Stop a moment, Withers!' said Mrs Skewton, as the chair began to move; calling to the page with all the languid dignity with which she had called in days of yore to a coachman with a wig, cauliflower nosegay,[7] and silk stockings. 'Where are you staying, abomination?'

The Major was staying at the Royal Hotel, with his friend Dombey.

'You may come and see us any evening when you are good,' lisped Mrs Skewton. 'If Mr Dombey will honour us, we shall be happy. Withers, go on!'

The Major again pressed to his blue lips the tips of the fingers that were disposed on the ledge of the wheeled chair with careful carelessness, after the Cleopatra model: and Mr Dombey bowed. The elder lady honoured them both with a very gracious smile and a girlish wave of her hand; the younger lady with the very slightest inclination of her head that common courtesy allowed.

The last glimpse of the wrinkled face of the mother, with that patched colour on it which the sun made infinitely more haggard and dismal than any want of colour could have been, and of the proud beauty of the daughter with her graceful figure and erect deportment, engendered such an involuntary disposition on the part of both the Major and Mr Dombey to look after them, that they both turned at the same moment. The page, nearly as much aslant as his own shadow, was toiling after the chair, uphill, like a slow battering-ram; the top of Cleopatra's bonnet was fluttering in exactly the same corner to the inch as before; and the Beauty, loitering by herself a little in advance, expressed in all her elegant form, from head to foot, the same supreme disregard of everything and everybody.

'I tell you what, Sir,' said the Major, as they resumed their walk again. 'If Joe Bagstock were a younger man, there's not a woman in the world whom he'd prefer for Mrs Bagstock to that woman. By George, Sir!' said the Major, 'she's superb!'

'Do you mean the daughter?' inquired Mr Dombey.

'Is Joey B. a turnip, Dombey,' said the Major, 'that he should mean the mother?'

'You were complimentary to the mother,' returned Mr Dombey.

'An ancient flame, Sir,' chuckled Major Bagstock. 'De-vilish ancient. I humour her.'

''She impresses me as being perfectly genteel,' said Mr Dombey.

'Genteel, Sir,' said the Major, stopping short, and staring in his companion's face. 'The Honourable Mrs Skewton, Sir, is sister to the late Lord Feenix, and aunt to the present Lord. The family are not wealthy – they're poor, indeed – and she lives upon a small jointure,[8] but if you come to blood, Sir!' The Major gave a flourish with his stick and walked on again, in despair of being able to say what you came to, if you came to that.

'You addressed the daughter, I observed,' said Mr Dombey, after a short pause, 'as Mrs Granger.'

'Edith Skewton, Sir,' returned the Major, stopping short again, and punching a mark in the ground with his cane, to represent her, 'Married (at eighteen) Granger of Ours;' whom the Major indicated by another punch. 'Granger, Sir,' said the Major, tapping the last ideal portrait, and rolling his head emphatically, 'was Colonel of Ours; a de-vilish handsome fellow, Sir, of forty-one. He died, Sir, in the second year of his marriage.' The Major ran the representative of the deceased Granger through and through the body with his walking-stick, and went on again, carrying his stick over his shoulder.

'How long is this ago?' asked Mr Dombey, making another halt.

'Edith Granger, Sir,' replied the Major, shutting one eye, putting his head on one side, passing his cane into his left hand, and smoothing his shirt-frill with his right, 'is, at this present time, not quite thirty. And damme, Sir,' said the Major, shouldering his stick once more, and walking on again, 'she's a peerless woman!'

'Was there any family?' asked Mr Dombey presently.

'Yes, Sir,' said the Major. 'There was a boy.'

Mr Dombey's eyes sought the ground, and a shade came over his face.

'Who was drowned, Sir,' pursued the Major. 'When a child of four or five years old.'

'Indeed?' said Mr Dombey, raising his head.

'By the upsetting of a boat in which his nurse had no business to have put him,' said the Major. 'That's *his* history. Edith Granger is Edith Granger still; but if tough old Joey B., Sir, were a little younger and a little richer, the name of that immortal paragon should be Bagstock.'

The Major heaved his shoulders, and his cheeks, and laughed more like an over-fed Mephistopheles than ever, as he said the words.

'Provided the lady made no objection, I suppose?' said Mr Dombey coldly.

'By Gad, Sir,' said the Major, 'the Bagstock breed are not accustomed to that sort of obstacle. Though it's true enough that Edith might have married twen-ty times, but for being proud, Sir, proud.'

Mr Dombey seemed, by his face, to think no worse of her for that.

'It's a great quality after all,' said the Major. 'By the Lord, it's a high quality! Dombey! You are proud yourself, and your friend, Old Joe, respects you for it, Sir.'

With this tribute to the character of his ally, which seemed to be wrung from him by the force of circumstances and the irresistible tendency of their conversation, the Major closed the subject, and glided into a general exposition of the extent to which he had been beloved and doated on by splendid women and brilliant creatures.

On the next day but one, Mr Dombey and the Major encountered the Honourable Mrs Skewton and her daughter in the Pump-room; on the day after, they met them again very near the place where they had met them first. After meeting them thus, three or four times in all, it became a point of mere civility to old acquaintances that the Major should go there one evening. Mr Dombey had not originally intended to pay visits, but on the Major announcing this intention, he said he would have the pleasure of accompanying him. So the Major told the Native to go round before dinner, and say, with his and Mr Dombey's compliments, that they would have the honour of visiting the ladies that same evening, if the ladies were alone. In answer to which message, the Native brought back a very small note with a very large quantity of scent about it, indited by the Honourable Mrs Skewton to Major Bagstock, and briefly saying, 'You are a shocking bear, and I have a great mind not to forgive you, but if you are very good indeed,' which was underlined, 'you may come. Compliments (in which Edith unites) to Mr Dombey.'

The Honourable Mrs Skewton and her daughter, Mrs Granger, resided, while at Leamington, in lodgings that were fashionable enough and dear enough, but rather limited in point of space and conveniences; so that the Honourable Mrs Skewton, being in bed, had her feet in the window and her head in the fireplace, while the Honourable Mrs Skewton's maid was quartered in a closet[9] within the drawing-room, so extremely small, that, to avoid developing the whole of its accommodations, she was obliged to writhe in and out of the door like a beautiful serpent. Withers, the wan page, slept out of the house immediately under the tiles at a neighbouring milk-shop; and the wheeled chair, which was the stone of that young Sisyphus,[10] passed the night in a shed belonging to the same dairy, where new-laid eggs were produced by the poultry connected with the establishment, who roosted on a broken donkey-cart, persuaded, to all appearance, that it grew there, and was a species of tree.

Mr Dombey and the Major found Mrs Skewton arranged, as Cleopatra, among the cushions of a sofa: very airily dressed; and certainly not resembling Shakespeare's Cleopatra, whom age could not wither.[11] On their way up stairs they had heard the sound of a harp, but it had ceased on their being announced, and Edith now stood beside it handsomer and haughtier than ever. It was a remarkable characteristic of this lady's beauty that it appeared to vaunt and assert itself without her aid, and against her will. She knew that she was beautiful: it was impossible that it could be otherwise: but she seemed with her own pride to defy her very self.

Whether she held cheap attractions that could only call forth admiration that was worthless to her, or whether she designed to render them more precious to admirers by this usage of them, those to whom they *were* precious seldom paused to consider.

'I hope, Mrs Granger,' said Mr Dombey, advancing a step towards her, 'we are not the cause of your ceasing to play?'

'*You?* oh no!'

'Why do you not go on then, my dearest Edith?' said Cleopatra.

'I left off as I began – of my own fancy.'

The exquisite indifference of her manner in saying this: an indifference quite removed from dulness or insensibility, for it was pointed with proud purpose: was well set off by the carelessness with which she drew her hand across the strings, and came from that part of the room.

'Do you know, Mr Dombey,' said her languishing mother, playing with a hand-screen,[12] 'that occasionally my dearest Edith and myself actually almost differ—'

'Not quite, sometimes, mama?' said Edith.

'Oh never quite, my darling! Fie, fie, it would break my heart,' returned her mother, making a faint attempt to pat her with the screen, which Edith made no movement to meet, '—about these cold conventionalities of manner that are observed in little things? Why are we not more natural? Dear me! With all those yearnings, and gushings, and impulsive throbbings that we have implanted in our souls, and which are so very charming, why are we not more natural?'

Mr Dombey said it was very true, very true.

'We could be more natural I suppose if we tried?' said Mrs Skewton.

Mr Dombey thought it possible.

'Devil a bit, ma'am,' said the Major. 'We couldn't afford it. Unless the world was peopled with J. B.'s – tough and blunt old Joes, ma'am, plain red herrings with hard roes, Sir – we couldn't afford it. It wouldn't do.'

'You naughty Infidel,' said Mrs Skewton, 'be mute.'

'Cleopatra commands,' returned the Major, kissing his hand, 'and Antony Bagstock obeys.'

'The man has no sensitiveness,' said Mrs Skewton, cruelly holding up the hand-screen so as to shut the Major out. 'No sympathy. And what do we live for *but* sympathy! What else is so extremely charming! Without that gleam of sunshine on our cold cold earth,' said Mrs Skewton, arranging her lace tucker, and complacently observing the effect of her bare lean arm, looking upward from the wrist, 'how could we possibly bear it? In short, obdurate man!' glancing at the Major, round the screen, 'I would have my world all heart, and Faith is so excessively charming, that I won't allow you to disturb it, do you hear?'

The Major replied that it was hard in Cleopatra to require the world to be all heart, and yet to appropriate to herself the hearts of all the world, which obliged Cleopatra to remind him that flattery was insupportable to her, and that if he had the boldness to address her in that strain any more, she would positively send him home.

Withers the Wan, at this period, handing round the tea, Mr Dombey again addressed himself to Edith.

'There is not much company here, it would seem?' said Mr Dombey, in his own portentous gentlemanly way.

'I believe not. We see none.'

'Why really,' observed Mrs Skewton from her couch, 'there are no people here just now with whom we care to associate.'

'They have not enough heart,' said Edith, with a smile. The very twilight of a smile: so singularly were its light and darkness blended.

'My dearest Edith rallies me, you see!' said her mother, shaking her head: which shook a little of itself sometimes, as if the palsy twinkled now and then in opposition to the diamonds. 'Wicked one!'

'You have been here before, if I am not mistaken?' said Mr Dombey. Still to Edith.

'Oh, several times. I think we have been everywhere.'

'A beautiful country!'

'I suppose it is. Everybody says so.'

'Your cousin Feenix raves about it, Edith,' interposed her mother from her couch.

The daughter slightly turned her graceful head, and raising her eyebrows by a hair's-breadth, as if her cousin Feenix were of all the mortal world the least to be regarded, turned her eyes again towards Mr Dombey.

'I hope, for the credit of my good taste, that I am tired of the neighbourhood,' she said.

'You have almost reason to be, madam,' he replied, glancing at a variety of landscape drawings, of which he had already recognised several as representing neighbouring points of view, and which were strewn abundantly about the room, 'if these beautiful productions are from your hand.'

She gave him no reply, but sat in a disdainful beauty, quite amazing.

'Have they that interest?' said Mr Dombey. 'Are they yours?'

'Yes.'

'And you play, I already know.'

'Yes.'

'And sing?'

'Yes.'

She answered all these questions, with a strange reluctance: and with that remarkable air of opposition to herself, already noticed as belonging to her beauty. Yet she was not embarrassed, but wholly self-possessed. Neither did she seem to wish to avoid the conversation, for she addressed her face, and – so far as she could – her manner also, to him; and continued to do so, when he was silent.

'You have many resources against weariness at least,' said Mr Dombey.

'Whatever their efficiency may be,' she returned, 'you know them all now. I have no more.'

'May I hope to prove them all?'[13] said Mr Dombey, with solemn gallantry, laying down a drawing he had held, and motioning towards the harp.

'Oh certainly! If you desire it!'

She rose as she spoke, and crossing by her mother's couch, and directing a stately look towards her, which was instantaneous in its duration, but inclusive (if any one had seen it) of a multitude of expressions, among which that of the twilight smile, without the smile itself, overshadowed all the rest, went out of the room.

The Major, who was quite forgiven by this time, had wheeled a little table up to Cleopatra, and was sitting down to play picquet[14] with her. Mr Dombey, not knowing the game, sat down to watch them for his edification until Edith should return.

'We are going to have some music, Mr Dombey, I hope?' said Cleopatra.

'Mrs Granger has been kind enough to promise so,' said Mr Dombey.

'Ah! That's very nice. Do you propose, Major?'

'No, ma'am,' said the Major. 'Couldn't do it.'

'You're a barbarous being,' replied the lady, 'and my hand's destroyed. You are fond of music, Mr Dombey?'

'Eminently so,' was Mr Dombey's answer.

'Yes. It's very nice,' said Cleopatra, looking at her cards. 'So much heart in it – undeveloped recollections of a previous state of existence[15] – and all that – which is so truly charming. Do you know,' simpered Cleopatra, reversing the knave of clubs, who had come into her game with his heels uppermost, 'that if anything could tempt me to put a period to my life,[16] it would be curiosity to find out what it's all about, and what it means; there are so many provoking mysteries, really, that are hidden from us. Major, you to play.'

The Major played; and Mr Dombey, looking on for his instruction, would soon have been in a state of dire confusion but that he gave no attention to the game whatever, and sat wondering instead when Edith would come back.

She came at last, and sat down to her harp, and Mr Dombey rose
and stood beside her, listening. He had little taste for music, and no
knowledge of the strain she played, but he saw her bending over it,
and perhaps he heard among the sounding strings some distant
music of his own, that tamed the monster of the iron road, and
made it less inexorable.

Cleopatra had a sharp eye, verily, at picquet. It glistened like a
bird's, and did not fix itself upon the game, but pierced the room
from end to end, and gleamed on harp, performer, listener,
everything.

When the haughty beauty had concluded, she arose, and receiving
Mr Dombey's thanks and compliments in exactly the same manner
as before, went with scarcely any pause to the piano, and began
there.

Edith Granger, any song but that! Edith Granger, you are very
handsome, and your touch upon the keys is brilliant, and your
voice is deep and rich; but not the air that his neglected daughter
sang to his dead son!

Alas, he knows it not; and if he did, what air of hers would stir
him, rigid man! Sleep, lonely Florence, sleep! Peace in thy dreams,
although the night has turned dark, and the clouds are gathering,
and threaten to discharge themselves in hail!

CHAPTER 22

A Trifle of Management by
Mr Carker the Manager

Mr Carker the Manager sat at his desk, smooth and soft as usual,
reading those letters which were reserved for him to open, backing
them occasionally with such memoranda and references as their
business purport required, and parcelling them out into little heaps
for distribution through the several departments of the House. The
post had come in heavy that morning, and Mr Carker the Manager
had a good deal to do.

The general action of a man so engaged – pausing to look over a
bundle of papers in his hand, dealing them round in various
portions, taking up another bundle and examining its contents with
knitted brows and pursed-out lips – dealing, and sorting and
pondering by turns – would easily suggest some whimsical resem-

blance to a player at cards. The face of Mr Carker the Manager was in good keeping with such a fancy. It was the face of a man who studied his play, warily: who made himself master of all the strong and weak points of the game: who registered the cards in his mind as they fell about him, knew exactly what was on them, what they missed, and what they made: who was crafty to find out what the other players held, and who never betrayed his own hand.

The letters were in various languages, but Mr Carker the Manager read them all. If there had been anything in the offices of Dombey and Son that he could *not* read, there would have been a card wanting in the pack. He read almost at a glance, and made combinations of one letter with another and one business with another as he went on, adding new matter to the heaps – much as a man would know the cards at sight, and work out their combinations in his mind after they were turned. Something too deep for a partner, and much too deep for an adversary, Mr Carker the Manager sat in the rays of the sun that came down slanting on him through the skylight, playing his game alone.

And although it is not among the instincts wild or domestic of the cat tribe to play at cards, feline from sole to crown was Mr Carker the Manager, as he basked in the strip of summer-light and warmth that shone upon his table and the ground as if they were a crooked dial-plate,[1] and himself the only figure on it. With hair and whiskers deficient in colour at all times, but feebler than common in the rich sunshine, and more like the coat of a sandy tortoise-shell cat; with long nails, nicely pared and sharpened; with a natural antipathy to any speck of dirt, which made him pause sometimes and watch the falling motes of dust, and rub them off his smooth white hand or glossy linen: Mr Carker the Manager, sly of manner, sharp of tooth, soft of foot, watchful of eye, oily of tongue, cruel of heart, nice of habit, sat with a dainty steadfastness and patience at his work, as if he were waiting at a mouse's hole.

At length the letters were disposed of, excepting one which he reserved for a particular audience. Having locked the more confidential correspondence in a drawer, Mr Carker the Manager rang his bell.

'Why do *you* answer it?' was his reception of his brother.

'The messenger is out, and I am the next,' was the submissive reply.

'You are the next?' muttered the Manager. 'Yes! Creditable to me! There!'

Pointing to the heaps of opened letters, he turned disdainfully away, in his elbow-chair, and broke the seal of that one which he held in his hand.

'I am sorry to trouble you, James,' said the brother, gathering them up, 'but—'

'Oh! you have something to say. I knew that. Well?'

Mr Carker the Manager did not raise his eyes or turn them on his brother, but kept them on his letter, though without opening it.

'Well?' he repeated sharply.

'I am uneasy about Harriet.'

'Harriet who? what Harriet? I know nobody of that name.'

'She is not well, and has changed very much of late.'

'She changed very much, a great many years ago,' replied the Manager; 'and that is all I have to say.'

'I think if you would hear me—'

'Why should I hear you, Brother John?' returned the Manager, laying a sarcastic emphasis on those two words, and throwing up his head, but not lifting his eyes. 'I tell you, Harriet Carker made her choice many years ago between her two brothers. She may repent it, but she must abide by it.'

'Don't mistake me. I do not say she *does* repent it. It would be black ingratitude in me to hint at such a thing,' returned the other. 'Though believe me, James, I am as sorry for her sacrifice as you.'

'As I?' exclaimed the Manager. 'As I?'

'As sorry for her choice – for what you call her choice – as you are angry at it,' said the Junior.

'Angry?' repeated the other, with a wide show of his teeth.

'Displeased. Whatever word you like best. You know my meaning. There is no offence in my intention.'

'There is offence in everything you do,' replied his brother, glancing at him with a sudden scowl, which in a moment gave place to a wider smile than the last. 'Carry those papers away, if you please. I am busy.'

His politeness was so much more cutting than his wrath, that the Junior went to the door. But stopping at it, and looking round, he said:

'When Harriet tried in vain to plead for me with you, on your first just indignation, and my first disgrace; and when she left you, James, to follow my broken fortunes, and devote herself, in her mistaken affection, to a ruined brother, because without her he had no one, and was lost; she was young and pretty. I think if you could see her now – if you would go and see her – she would move your admiration and compassion.'

The Manager inclined his head, and showed his teeth, as who should say, in answer to some careless small-talk, 'Dear me! Is that the case?' but said never a word.

'We thought in those days: you and I both: that she would marry young, and lead a happy and light-hearted life,' pursued the other. 'Oh if you knew how cheerfully she cast those hopes away; how cheerfully she has gone forward on the path she took, and never once looked back; you never could say again that her name was strange in your ears. Never!'

Again the Manager inclined his head, and showed his teeth, and seemed to say, 'Remarkable indeed! You quite surprise me!' And again he uttered never a word.

'May I go on?' said John Carker, mildly.

'On your way?' replied his smiling brother. 'If you will have the goodness.'

John Carker, with a sigh, was passing slowly out at the door, when his brother's voice detained him for a moment on the threshold.

'If she has gone, and goes, her own way cheerfully,' he said, throwing the still unfolded letter on his desk, and putting his hands firmly in his pockets, 'you may tell her that I go as cheerfully on mine. If she has never once looked back, you may tell her that I have, sometimes, to recall her taking part with you,[2] and that my resolution is no easier to wear away;' he smiled very sweetly here; 'than marble.'

'I tell her nothing of you. We never speak about you. Once a year, on your birthday, Harriet says always, "Let us remember James by name, and wish him happy," but we say no more.'

'Tell it then, if you please,' returned the other, 'to yourself. You can't repeat it too often, as a lesson to you to avoid the subject in speaking to me. I know no Harriet Carker. There is no such person. *You* may have a sister; make much of her. I have none.'

Mr Carker the Manager took up the letter again, and waved it with a smile of mock courtesy towards the door. Unfolding it as his brother withdrew, and looking darkly after him as he left the room, he once more turned round in his elbow-chair, and applied himself to a diligent perusal of its contents.

It was in the writing of his great chief, Mr Dombey, and dated from Leamington. Though he was a quick reader of all other letters, Mr Carker read this slowly; weighing the words as he went, and bringing every tooth in his head to bear upon them. When he had read it through once, he turned it over again, and picked out these passages. 'I find myself benefited by the change, and am not yet inclined to name any time for my return.' 'I wish, Carker, you would arrange to come down once and see me here, and let me know how things are going on, in person.' 'I omitted to speak to you about young Gay. If not gone per Son and Heir, or if Son and Heir still lying in the Docks, appoint some other young man and keep him in the City for the present. I am not decided.' 'Now that's unfortunate!' said Mr Carker the Manager, expanding his mouth, as if it were made of India-rubber: 'for he is far away.'

Still that passage, which was in a postscript, attracted his attention and his teeth, once more.

'I think,' he said, 'my good friend Captain Cuttle mentioned something about being towed along in the wake of that day. What a pity he's so far away!'

He refolded the letter, and was sitting trifling with it, standing it long-wise and broad-wise on his table, and turning it over and over on all sides – doing pretty much the same thing, perhaps, by its contents – when Mr Perch the messenger knocked softly at the door, and coming in on tiptoe, bending his body at every step as if it were the delight of his life to bow, laid some papers on the table.

'Would you please to be engaged, Sir?' asked Mr Perch, rubbing his hands, and deferentially putting his head on one side, like a man who felt he had no business to hold it up in such a presence, and would keep it as much out of the way as possible.

'Who wants me?'

'Why, Sir,' said Mr Perch, in a soft voice, 'really nobody, Sir, to speak of at present. Mr Gills the Ship's Instrument-maker, Sir, has looked in, about a little matter of payment, he says: but I mentioned to him, Sir, that you was engaged several deep; several deep.'

Mr Perch coughed once behind his hand, and waited for further orders.

'Anybody else?'

'Well, Sir,' said Mr Perch, 'I wouldn't of my own self take the liberty of mentioning, Sir, that there was anybody else; but that same young lad that was here yesterday, Sir, and last week, has been hanging about the place; and it looks, Sir,' added Mr Perch, stopping to shut the door, 'dreadful unbusiness-like to see him whistling to the sparrows down the court, and making of 'em answer him.'

'You said he wanted something to do, didn't you, Perch?' asked Mr Carker, leaning back in his chair and looking at that officer.

'Why, Sir,' said Mr Perch, coughing behind his hand again, 'his expression certainly were that he was in wants of a sitiwation,[3] and that he considered something might be done for him about the Docks, being used to fishing with a rod and line: but—' Mr Perch shook his head very dubiously indeed.

'What does he say when he comes?' asked Mr Carker.

'Indeed, Sir,' said Mr Perch, coughing another cough behind his hand, which was always his resource as an expression of humility when nothing else occurred to him, 'his observation generally air that he would humbly wish to see one of the gentlemen, and that he wants to earn a living. But you see, Sir,' added Perch, dropping his voice to a whisper, and turning, in the inviolable nature of his confidence, to give the door a thrust with his hand and knee, as if that would shut it any more when it was shut already, 'it's hardly to be bore, Sir, that a common lad like that should come a prowling here, and saying that his mother nursed our House's young gentleman, and that he hopes our House will give him a chance on that account. I am sure, Sir,' observed Mr Perch, 'that although Mrs Perch was at that time nursing as thriving a little girl, Sir, as we've ever took the liberty of adding to our family, I wouldn't have made so free as drop a hint of her being capable of imparting nourishment, not if it was never so!'

Mr Carker grinned at him like a shark, but in an absent, thoughtful manner.

'Whether,' submitted Mr Perch, after a short silence, and another cough, 'it mightn't be best for me to tell him, that if he was seen here any more he would be given into custody; and to keep to it! With respect to bodily fear,' said Mr Perch, 'I'm so timid, myself, by nature, Sir, and my nerves is so unstrung by Mrs Perch's state, that I could take my affidavit[4] easy.'

'Let me see this fellow, Perch,' said Mr Carker. 'Bring him in!'

'Yes, Sir. Begging your pardon, Sir,' said Mr Perch, hesitating at the door, 'he's rough, Sir, in appearance.'

'Never mind. If he's there, bring him in. I'll see Mr Gills directly. Ask him to wait.'

Mr Perch bowed; and shutting the door, as precisely and carefully as if he were not coming back for a week, went on his quest among the sparrows in the court. While he was gone, Mr Carker assumed his favourite attitude before the fireplace, and stood looking at the door; presenting, with his under lip tucked into the smile that showed his whole row of upper teeth, a singularly crouching appearance.

The messenger was not long in returning, followed by a pair of

heavy boots that came bumping along the passage like boxes. With
the unceremonious words 'Come along with you!' – a very unusual
form of introduction from his lips – Mr Perch then ushered into the
presence a strong-built lad of fifteen, with a round red face, a round
sleek head, round black eyes, round limbs, and round body, who,
to carry out the general rotundity of his appearance, had a round
hat in his hand, without a particle of brim to it.

Obedient to a nod from Mr Carker, Perch had no sooner
confronted the visitor with that gentleman than he withdrew. The
moment they were face to face alone, Mr Carker, without a word
of preparation, took him by the throat, and shook him until his
head seemed loose upon his shoulders.

The boy, who in the midst of his astonishment could not help
staring wildly at the gentleman with so many white teeth who was
choking him, and at the office walls, as though determined, if he
were choked, that his last look should be at the mysteries for his
intrusion into which he was paying such a severe penalty, at last
contrived to utter –

'Come, Sir! You let me alone, will you!'

'Let you alone!' said Mr Carker. 'What! I have got you, have I?'
There was no doubt of that, and tightly too. 'You dog,' said Mr
Carker, through his set jaws, 'I'll strangle you!'

Biler whimpered, would he though? oh no he wouldn't – and
what was he doing of – and why didn't he strangle somebody of his
own size and not *him*: but Biler was quelled by the extraordinary
nature of his reception, and, as his head became stationary, and he
looked the gentleman in the face, or rather in the teeth, and saw
him snarling at him, he so far forgot his manhood as to cry.

'I haven't done nothing to you, Sir,' said Biler, otherwise Rob,
otherwise Grinder, and always Toodle.

'You young scoundrel!' replied Mr Carker, slowly releasing him,
and moving back a step into his favourite position. 'What do you
mean by daring to come here?'

'I didn't mean no harm, Sir,' whimpered Bob, putting one hand
to his throat, and the knuckles of the other in his eyes. 'I'll never
come again, Sir. I only wanted work.'

'Work, young Cain⁵ that you are!' repeated Mr Carker, eyeing
him narrowly. 'An't you the idlest vagabond in London?'

The impeachment, while it much affected Mr Toodle Junior,
attached to his character so justly, that he could not say a word in
denial. He stood looking at the gentleman, therefore, with a
frightened, self-convicted, and remorseful air. As to his looking at

him, it may be observed that he was fascinated by Mr Carker, and never took his round eyes off him for an instant.

'An't you a thief?' said Mr Carker, with his hands behind him in his pockets.

'No, Sir,' pleaded Rob.

'You are!' said Mr Carker.

'I an't indeed, Sir,' whimpered Rob. 'I never did such a thing as thieve, Sir, if you'll believe me. I know I've been going wrong, Sir, ever since I took to bird-catching and walking-matching.[6] I'm sure a cove[7] might think,' said Mr Toodle Junior, with a burst of penitence, 'that singing birds was innocent company, but nobody knows what harm is in them little creeturs and what they brings you down to.'

They seemed to have brought *him* down to a velveteen[8] jacket and trousers very much the worse for wear, a particularly small red waistcoat like a gorget,[9] an interval of blue check, and the hat before mentioned.

'I an't been home twenty times since them birds got their will of me,' said Rob, 'and that's ten months. How can I go home when everybody's miserable to see me! I wonder,' said Biler, blubbering outright, and smearing his eyes with his coat-cuff, 'that I haven't been and drownded myself over and over again.'

All of which, including his expression of surprise at not having achieved this last scarce performance, the boy said, just as if the teeth of Mr Carker drew it out of him, and he had no power of concealing anything with that battery of attraction in full play.

'You're a nice young gentleman!' said Mr Carker, shaking his head at him. 'There's hemp-seed sown for *you*,[10] my fine fellow!'

'I'm sure, Sir,' returned the wretched Biler, blubbering again, and again having recourse to his coat-cuff: 'I shouldn't care, sometimes, if it was growed too. My misfortunes all began in wagging, Sir; but what could I do, exceptin' wag?'

'Excepting what?' said Mr Carker.

'Wag, Sir. Wagging from school.'

'Do you mean pretending to go there, and not going?' said Mr Carker.

'Yes, Sir, that's wagging, Sir,' returned the quondam Grinder, much affected. 'I was chivied through the streets, Sir, when I went there, and pounded when I got there. So I wagged and hid myself, and that began it.'

'And you mean to tell me,' said Mr Carker, taking him by the throat again, holding him out at arm's-length, and surveying him in silence for some moments, 'that you want a place, do you?'

'I should be thankful to be tried, Sir,' returned Toodle Junior, faintly.

Mr Carker the Manager pushed him backward into a corner – the boy submitting quietly, hardly venturing to breathe, and never once removing his eyes from his face – and rang the bell.

'Tell Mr Gills to come here.'

Mr Perch was too deferential to express surprise or recognition of the figure in the corner: and Uncle Sol appeared immediately.

'Mr Gills!' said Carker, with a smile, 'sit down. How do you do? You continue to enjoy your health, I hope?'

'Thank you, Sir,' returned Uncle Sol, taking out his pocketbook, and handing over some notes as he spoke. 'Nothing ails me in body but old age. Twenty-five, Sir.'

'You are as punctual and exact, Mr Gills,' replied the smiling Manager, taking a paper from one of his many drawers, and making an endorsement on it, while Uncle Sol looked over him, 'as one of your own chronometers. Quite right.'

'The Son and Heir has not been spoken, I find by the list, Sir,' said Uncle Sol, with a slight addition to the usual tremor in his voice.

'The Son and Heir has not been spoken,' returned Carker. 'There seems to have been tempestuous weather, Mr Gills, and she has probably been driven out of her course.'

'She is safe, I trust in Heaven!' said old Sol.

'She is safe, I trust in Heaven!' assented Mr Carker in that voiceless manner of his: which made the observant young Toodle tremble again. 'Mr Gills,' he added aloud, throwing himself back in his chair, 'you must miss your nephew very much?'

Uncle Sol, standing by him, shook his head and heaved a deep sigh.

'Mr Gills,' said Carker, with his soft hand playing round his mouth, and looking up into the Instrument-maker's face, 'it would be company to you to have a young fellow in your shop just now, and it would be obliging me if you would give one house-room for the present. No, to be sure,' he added quickly, in anticipation of what the old man was going to say, 'there's not much business doing there, I know; but you can make him clean the place out, polish up the instruments; drudge, Mr Gills. That's the lad!'

Sol Gills pulled down his spectacles from his forehead to his eyes, and looked at Toodle Junior standing upright in the corner: his head presenting the appearance (which it always did) of having been newly drawn out of a bucket of cold water; his small waistcoat rising and falling quickly in the play of his emotions; and his eyes intently fixed on Mr Carker, without the least reference to his proposed master.

'Will you give him house-room, Mr Gills?' said the Manager.

Old Sol, without being quite enthusiastic on the subject, replied that he was glad of any opportunity, however slight, to oblige Mr Carker, whose wish on such a point was a command: and that the Wooden Midshipman would consider himself happy to receive in his berth any visitor of Mr Carker's selecting.

Mr Carker bared himself to the tops and bottoms of his gums: making the watchful Toodle Junior tremble more and more: and acknowledged the Instrument-maker's politeness in his most affable manner.

'I'll dispose of him so, then, Mr Gills,' he answered, rising and shaking the old man by the hand, 'until I make up my mind what to do with him, and what he deserves. As I consider myself responsible for him, Mr Gills,' here he smiled a wide smile at Rob, who shook before it: 'I shall be glad if you'll look sharply after him, and report his behaviour to me. I'll ask a question or two of his parents as I ride home this afternoon – respectable people – to confirm some particulars in his own account of himself; and that done, Mr Gills, I'll send him round to you to-morrow morning. Good-bye!'

His smile at parting was so full of teeth, that it confused old Sol, and made him vaguely uncomfortable. He went home, thinking of raging seas, foundering ships, drowning men, an ancient bottle of Madeira never brought to light, and other dismal matter.

'Now, boy!' said Mr Carker, putting his hand on young Toodle's shoulder, and bringing him out into the middle of the room. 'You have heard me?'

Rob said, 'Yes, Sir.'

'Perhaps you understand,' pursued his patron, 'that if you ever deceive or play tricks with me, you had better have drowned yourself, indeed, once for all, before you came here?'

There was nothing in any branch of mental acquisition that Rob seemed to understand better than that.

'If you have lied to me,' said Mr Carker, 'in anything, never come in my way again. If not, you may let me find you waiting for me somewhere near your mother's house this afternoon. I shall leave this at five o'clock, and ride there on horseback. Now, give me the address.'

Rob repeated it slowly, as Mr Carker wrote it down. Rob even spelt it over a second time, letter by letter, as if he thought that the omission of a dot or scratch could lead to his destruction. Mr Carker then handed him out of the room; and Rob, keeping his round eyes fixed upon his patron to the last, vanished for the time being.

Mr Carker the Manager did a great deal of business in the course of the day, and bestowed his teeth upon a great many people. In the office, in the court, in the street, and on 'Change, they glistened and bristled to a terrible extent. Five o'clock arriving, and with it Mr Carker's bay horse, they got on horseback, and went gleaming up Cheapside.

As no one can easily ride fast, even if inclined to do so, through the press and throng of the City at that hour, and as Mr Carker was not inclined, he went leisurely along, picking his way among the carts and carriages, avoiding whenever he could the wetter and more dirty places in the over-watered road, and taking infinite pains to keep himself and his steed clean. Glancing at the passers-by while he was thus ambling on his way, he suddenly encountered the round eyes of the sleek-headed Rob intently fixed upon his face as if they had never been taken off, while the boy himself, with a pocket-handkerchief twisted up like a speckled eel and girded round his waist, made a very conspicuous demonstration of being prepared to attend upon him, at whatever pace he might think proper to go.

This attention, however flattering, being one of an unusual kind, and attracting some notice from the other passengers, Mr Carker took advantage of a clearer thoroughfare and a cleaner road, and broke into a trot. Rob immediately did the same. Mr Carker presently tried a canter; Rob was still in attendance. Then a short gallop; it was all one to the boy. Whenever Mr Carker turned his eyes to that side of the road, he still saw Toodle Junior holding his course, apparently without distress, and working himself along by the elbows after the most approved manner of professional gentlemen who get over the ground for wagers.

Ridiculous as this attendance was, it was a sign of an influence established over the boy, and therefore Mr Carker, affecting not to notice it, rode away into the neighbourhood of Mr Toodle's house. On his slackening his pace here, Rob appeared before him to point out the turnings; and when he called to a man at a neighbouring gateway to hold his horse, pending his visit to the Buildings that had succeeded Staggs's Gardens, Rob dutifully held the stirrup, while the Manager dismounted.

'Now, Sir,' said Mr Carker, taking him by the shoulder, 'come along!'

The prodigal son[11] was evidently nervous of visiting the parental abode; but Mr Carker pushing him on before, he had nothing for it but to open the right door, and suffer himself to be walked into the midst of his brothers and sisters, mustered in overwhelming force round the family tea-table. At sight of the prodigal in the grasp of a stranger, these tender relations united in a general howl, which smote upon the prodigal's breast so sharply when he saw his mother stand up among them, pale and trembling, with the baby in her arms, that he lent his own voice to the chorus.

Nothing doubting now that the stranger, if not Mr Ketch[12] in person, was one of that company, the whole of the young family wailed the louder, while its more infantine members, unable to control the transports of emotion appertaining to their time of life, threw themselves on their backs like young birds when terrified by a hawk, and kicked violently. At length, poor Polly making herself audible, said, with quivering lips, 'Oh Rob, my poor boy, what have you done at last!'

'Nothing, mother,' cried Rob, in a piteous voice, 'ask the gentleman!'

'Don't be alarmed,' said Mr Carker, 'I want to do him good.'

At this announcement, Polly, who had not cried yet, began to do so. The elder Toodles, who appeared to have been meditating a rescue, unclenched their fists. The younger Toodles clustered round their mother's gown, and peeped from under their own chubby arms at their desperado brother and his unknown friend. Everybody blessed the gentleman with the beautiful teeth, who wanted to do good.

'This fellow,' said Mr Carker to Polly, giving him a gentle shake, 'is your son, eh, ma'am?'

'Yes, Sir,' sobbed Polly, with a curtsey; 'yes, Sir.'

'A bad son, I am afraid?' said Mr Carker.

'Never a bad son to me, Sir,' returned Polly.

'To whom then?' demanded Mr Carker.

'He has been a little wild, Sir,' returned Polly, checking the baby, who was making convulsive efforts with his arms and legs to launch himself on Biler, through the ambient air, 'and has gone with wrong companions: but I hope he has seen the misery of that, Sir, and will do well again.'

Mr Carker looked at Polly, and the clean room, and the clean children, and the simple Toodle face, combined of father and mother, that was reflected and repeated everywhere about him – and seemed to have achieved the real purpose of his visit.

'Your husband, I take it, is not at home?' he said.

'No, Sir,' replied Polly. 'He's down the line at present.'

The prodigal Rob seemed very much relieved to hear it: though still in the absorption of all his faculties in his patron, he hardly took his eyes from Mr Carker's face, unless for a moment at a time to steal a sorrowful glance at his mother.

'Then,' said Mr Carker, 'I'll tell you how I have stumbled on this boy of yours, and who I am, and what I am going to do for him.'

This Mr Carker did, in his own way; saying that he at first intended to have accumulated nameless terrors on his presumptuous head, for coming to the whereabout of Dombey and Son. That he had relented, in consideration of his youth, his professed contrition, and his friends. That he was afraid he took a rash step in doing anything for the boy, and one that might expose him to the censure of the prudent; but that he did it of himself and for himself, and risked the consequences single-handed; and that his mother's past connexion with Mr Dombey's family had nothing to do with it, and that Mr Dombey had nothing to do with it, but that he, Mr Carker, was the be-all and the end-all of this business. Taking great credit to himself for his goodness, and receiving no less from all the family then present, Mr Carker signified, indirectly but still pretty plainly, that Rob's implicit fidelity, attachment, and devotion, were for evermore his due, and the least homage he could receive. And with this great truth Rob himself was so impressed, that standing gazing on his patron with tears rolling down his cheeks, he nodded his shiny head until it seemed almost as loose as it had done under the same patron's hands that morning.

Polly, who had passed Heaven knows how many sleepless nights on account of this her dissipated firstborn, and had not seen him for weeks and weeks, could have almost kneeled to Mr Carker the Manager, as to a Good Spirit – in spite of his teeth. But Mr Carker rising to depart, she only thanked him with her mother's prayers and blessings; thanks so rich when paid out of the Heart's mint, especially for any service Mr Carker had rendered, that he might have given back a large amount of change, and yet been overpaid.

As that gentleman made his way among the crowding children to the door, Rob retreated on his mother, and took her and the baby in the same repentant hug.

'I'll try hard, dear mother, now. Upon my soul I will!' said Rob.

'Oh do, my dear boy! I am sure you will, for our sakes and your own!' cried Polly, kissing him. 'But you're coming back to speak to me, when you have seen the gentleman away?'

'I don't know, mother.' Rob hesitated, and looked down. 'Father – when's he coming home?'

'Not till two o'clock to-morrow morning.'

'I'll come back, mother dear!' cried Rob. And passing through the shrill cry of his brothers and sisters in reception of this promise, he followed Mr Carker out.

'What!' said Mr Carker, who had heard this. 'You have a bad father, have you?'

'No, Sir!' returned Rob, amazed. 'There ain't a better nor a kinder father going, than mine is.'

'Why don't you want to see him then?' inquired his patron.

'There's such a difference between a father and a mother, Sir,' said Rob, after faltering for a moment. 'He couldn't hardly believe yet that I was going to do better – though I know he'd try to – but a mother – *she* always believes what's good, Sir; at least I know my mother does, God bless her!'

Mr Carker's mouth expanded, but he said no more until he was mounted on his horse, and had dismissed the man who held it, when, looking down from the saddle steadily into the attentive and watchful face of the boy, he said:

'You'll come to me to-morrow morning, and you shall be shown where that old gentleman lives; that old gentleman who was with me this morning; where you are going, as you heard me say.'

'Yes, Sir,' returned Rob.

'I have a great interest in that old gentleman, and in serving him, you serve me, boy, do you understand? Well,' he added, interrupting him, for he saw his round face brighten when he was told that: 'I see you do. I want to know all about that old gentleman, and how he goes on from day to day – for I am anxious to be of service to him – and especially who comes there to see him. Do you understand?'

Rob nodded his steadfast face, and said 'Yes, Sir,' again.

'I should like to know that he has friends who are attentive to him, and that they don't desert him – for he lives very much alone now, poor fellow; but that they are fond of him, and of his nephew who has gone abroad. There is a very young lady who may perhaps come to see him. I want particularly to know all about *her*.'

'I'll take care, Sir,' said the boy.

'And take care,' returned his patron, bending forward to advance
his grinning face closer to the boy's, and pat him on the shoulder
with the handle of his whip: 'take care you talk about affairs of
mine to nobody but me.'

'To nobody in the world, Sir,' replied Rob, shaking his head.

'Neither there,' said Mr Carker, pointing to the place they had
just left, 'nor anywhere else. I'll try how true and grateful you can
be. I'll prove you!' Making this, by his display of teeth and by the
action of his head, as much a threat as a promise, he turned from
Rob's eyes, which were nailed upon him as if he had won the boy
by a charm, body and soul, and rode away. But again becoming
conscious, after trotting a short distance, that his devoted hench-
man, girt as before, was yielding him the same attendance, to the
great amusement of sundry spectators, he reined up, and ordered
him off. To insure his obedience, he turned in the saddle and
watched him as he retired. It was curious to see that even then Rob
could not keep his eyes wholly averted from his patron's face, but,
constantly turning and turning again to look after him, involved
himself in a tempest of buffetings and jostlings from the other
passengers in the street: of which, in the pursuit of the one
paramount idea, he was perfectly heedless.

Mr Carker the Manager rode on at a foot-pace, with the easy air
of one who had performed all the business of the day in a
satisfactory manner, and got it comfortably off his mind. Complacent and affable as man could be, Mr Carker picked his way along
the streets and hummed a soft tune as he went. He seemed to purr,
he was so glad.

And in some sort, Mr Carker, in his fancy, basked upon a hearth
too. Coiled up snugly at certain feet, he was ready for a spring, or
for a tear, or for a scratch, or for a velvet touch, as the humour
took him and occasion served. Was there any bird in a cage, that
came in for a share of his regards?

'A very young lady!' thought Mr Carker the Manager, through
his song. 'Ay! when I saw her last, she was a little child. With dark
eyes and hair, I recollect, and a good face; a very good face! I dare
say she's pretty.'

More affable and pleasant yet, and humming his song until his
many teeth vibrated to it, Mr Carker picked his way along, and
turned at last into the shady street where Mr Dombey's house
stood. He had been so busy, winding webs round good faces, and
obscuring them with meshes, that he hardly thought of being at this
point of his ride, until, glancing down the cold perspective of tall

houses, he reined in his horse quickly within a few yards of the door. But to explain why Mr Carker reined in his horse quickly and what he looked at in no small surprise, a few digressive words are necessary.

Mr Toots, emancipated from the Blimber thraldom and coming into the possession of a certain portion of his worldly wealth, 'which,' as he had been wont, during his last half-year's probation, to communicate to Mr Feeder every evening as a new discovery, 'the executors couldn't keep him out of,' had applied himself, with great diligence, to the science of Life. Fired with a noble emulation to pursue a brilliant and distinguished career, Mr Toots had furnished a choice set of apartments; had established among them a sporting bower, embellished with the portraits of winning horses, in which he took no particle of interest; and a divan, which made him poorly. In this delicious abode, Mr Toots devoted himself to the cultivation of those gentle arts which refine and humanise existence, his chief instructor in which was an interesting character called the Game Chicken, who was always to be heard of at the bar of the Black Badger, wore a shaggy white great-coat in the warmest weather, and knocked Mr Toots about the head three times a week, for the small consideration of ten and six per visit.

The Game Chicken, who was quite the Apollo of Mr Toots's Pantheon,[13] had introduced to him a marker who taught billiards, a Life Guard who taught fencing, a job-master who taught riding, a Cornish gentleman who was up to anything in the athletic line, and two or three other friends connected no less intimately with the fine arts. Under whose auspices Mr Toots could hardly fail to improve apace, and under whose tuition he went to work.

But however it came about, it came to pass, even while these gentlemen had the gloss of novelty upon them, that Mr Toots felt, he didn't know how, unsettled and uneasy. There were husks in his corn, that even Game Chickens couldn't peck up; gloomy giants in his leisure, that even Game Chickens couldn't knock down. Nothing seemed to do Mr Toots so much good as incessantly leaving cards at Mr Dombey's door. No tax-gatherer in the British dominions – that wide-spread territory on which the sun never sets,[14] and where the tax-gatherer never goes to bed – was more regular and persevering in his calls than Mr Toots.

Mr Toots never went up stairs; and always performed the same ceremonies, richly dressed for the purpose, at the hall door.

'Oh! Good morning!' would be Mr Toots's first remark to the servant. 'For Mr Dombey,' would be Mr Toots's next remark, as he handed in a card. 'For Miss Dombey,' would be his next, as he handed in another.

Mr Toots would then turn round as if to go away; but the man knew him by this time, and knew he wouldn't.

'Oh, I beg your pardon,' Mr Toots would say, as if a thought had suddenly descended on him. 'Is the young woman at home?'

The man would rather think she was, but wouldn't quite know. Then he would ring a bell that rang upstairs, and would look up the staircase, and would say, yes, she *was* at home, and was coming down. Then Miss Nipper would appear, and the man would retire.

'Oh! How de do?' Mr Toots would say, with a chuckle and a blush.

Susan would thank him, and say she was very well.

'How's Diogenes going on?' would be Mr Toots's second interrogation.

Very well indeed. Miss Florence was fonder and fonder of him every day. Mr Toots was sure to hail this with a burst of chuckles, like the opening of a bottle of some effervescent beverage.

'Miss Florence is quite well, Sir,' Susan would add.

'Oh, it's of no consequence, thank'ee,' was the invariable reply of Mr Toots; and when he had said so, he always went away very fast.

Now it is certain that Mr Toots had a filmy something in his mind, which led him to conclude that if he could aspire successfully, in the fulness of time, to the hand of Florence, he would be fortunate and blest. It is certain that Mr Toots, by some remote and roundabout road, had got to that point, and that there he made a stand. His heart was wounded; he was touched; he was in love. He had made a desperate attempt, one night, and had sat up all night for the purpose, to write an acrostic on Florence, which affected him to tears in the conception. But he never proceeded in the execution further than the words 'For when I gaze,' – the flow of imagination in which he had previously written down the initial letters of the other seven lines, deserting him at that point.

Beyond devising that very artful and politic measure of leaving a card for Mr Dombey daily, the brain of Mr Toots had not worked much in reference to the subject that held his feelings prisoner. But deep consideration at length assured Mr Toots that an important step to gain, was, the conciliation of Miss Susan Nipper, preparatory to giving her some inkling of his state of mind.

A little light and playful gallantry towards this lady seemed the means to employ in that early chapter of the history, for winning her to his interests. Not being able quite to make up his mind about it, he consulted the Chicken – without taking that gentleman into his confidence; merely informing him that a friend in Yorkshire had written to him (Mr Toots) for his opinion on such a question. The Chicken replying that his opinion always was, 'Go in and win,' and further, 'When your man's before you and your work cut out, go in and do it,' Mr Toots considered this a figurative way of supporting his own view of the case, and heroically resolved to kiss Miss Nipper next day.

Upon the next day, therefore, Mr Toots, putting into requisition some of the greatest marvels that Burgess and Co. had ever turned out, went off to Mr Dombey's upon this design. But his heart failed him so much as he approached the scene of action, that, although he arrived on the ground at three o'clock in the afternoon, it was six before he knocked at the door.

Everything happened as usual, down to the point where Susan said her young mistress was well, and Mr Toots said it was of no consequence. To her amazement, Mr Toots, instead of going off like a rocket, after that observation, lingered and chuckled.

'Perhaps you'd like to walk up stairs, Sir!' said Susan.

'Well, I think I will come in!' said Mr Toots.

But instead of walking up stairs, the bold Toots made an awkward plunge at Susan when the door was shut, and embracing that fair creature, kissed her on the cheek.

'Go along with you!' cried Susan, 'or I'll tear your eyes out.'

'Just another!' said Mr Toots.

'Go along with you!' exclaimed Susan, giving him a push. 'Innocents like you, too! Who'll begin next? Go along, Sir!'

Susan was not in any serious strait, for she could hardly speak for laughing; but Diogenes, on the staircase, hearing a rustling against the wall, and a shuffling of feet, and seeing through the banisters that there was some contention going on, and foreign invasion in the house, formed a different opinion, dashed down to the rescue, and in the twinkling of an eye had Mr Toots by the leg.

Susan screamed, laughed, opened the street-door, and ran down stairs; the bold Toots tumbled staggering out into the street, with Diogenes holding on to one leg of his pantaloons, as if Burgess and Co. were his cooks, and had provided that dainty morsel for his holiday entertainment; Diogenes shaken off, rolled over and over in the dust, got up again, whirled round the giddy Toots and snapped at him: and all this turmoil, Mr Carker, reining up his horse and sitting a little at a distance, saw to his amazement, issue from the stately house of Mr Dombey.

Mr Toots becomes particular – Diogenes also

Mr Carker remained watching the discomfited Toots, when Diogenes was called in, and the door shut: and while that gentleman, taking refuge in a doorway near at hand, bound up the torn leg of his pantaloons with a costly silk handkerchief that had formed part of his expensive outfit for the adventure.

'I beg your pardon, Sir,' said Mr Carker, riding up, with his most propitiatory smile. 'I hope you are not hurt?'

'Oh no, thank you,' replied Mr Toots, raising his flushed face, 'it's of no consequence.' Mr Toots would have signified, if he could, that he liked it very much.

'If the dog's teeth have entered the leg, Sir—' began Carker, with a display of his own.

'No, thank you,' said Mr Toots, 'it's all quite right. It's very comfortable, thank you.'

'I have the pleasure of knowing Mr Dombey,' observed Carker.

'Have you though?' rejoined the blushing Toots.

'And you will allow me, perhaps, to apologise, in his absence,' said Mr Carker, taking off his hat, 'for such a misadventure and to wonder how it can possibly have happened.'

Mr Toots is so much gratified by this politeness, and the lucky chance of making friends with a friend of Mr Dombey, that he pulls out his card-case, which he never loses an opportunity of using, and hands his name and address to Mr Carker: who responds to that courtesy by giving him his own, and with that they part.

As Mr Carker picks his way so softly past the house, glancing up at the windows, and trying to make out the pensive face behind the curtain looking at the children opposite, the rough head of Diogenes comes clambering up close by it, and the dog, regardless of all soothing, barks and growls, and makes at him from that height, as if he would spring down and tear him limb from limb.

Well spoken, Di, so near your Mistress! Another, and another with your head up, your eyes flashing, and your vexed mouth worrying itself, for want of him! Another, as he picks his way along! You have a good scent, Di, – cats, boy, cats!

CHAPTER 23

Florence Solitary, and the
Midshipman Mysterious

Florence lived alone in the great dreary house, and day succeeded day, and still she lived alone; and the blank walls looked down upon her with a vacant stare, as if they had a Gorgon-like[1] mind to stare her youth and beauty into stone.

No magic dwelling-place in magic story, shut up in the heart of a thick wood, was ever more solitary and deserted to the fancy, than was her father's mansion in its grim reality, as it stood lowering on the street: always by night, when lights were shining from neighbouring windows, a blot upon its scanty brightness; always by day, a frown upon its never-smiling face.

There were not two dragon sentries keeping ward before the gate of this abode, as in magic legend are usually found on duty over the wronged innocence imprisoned; but besides a glowering visage, with its thin lips parted wickedly, that surveyed all comers from above the archway of the door, there was a monstrous fantasy of rusty iron, curling and twisting like a petrifaction of an arbour over the threshold, budding in spikes and corkscrew points, and bearing, one on either side, two ominous extinguishers, that seemed to say, 'Who enter here, leave light behind!' There were no talismanic characters engraven on the portal, but the house was now so neglected in appearance, that boys chalked the railings and the pavement – particularly round the corner where the side wall was – and drew ghosts on the stable door; and being sometimes driven off by Mr Towlinson, made portraits of him, in return, with his ears growing out horizontally from under his hat. Noise ceased to be, within the shadow of the roof. The brass band that came into the street once a week, in the morning, never brayed a note in at those windows; but all such company, down to a poor little piping organ[2] of weak intellect, with an imbecile party of automaton dancers, waltzing in and out at folding-doors, fell off from it with one accord, and shunned it as a hopeless place.

The spell upon it was more wasting than the spell that used to set enchanted houses sleeping once upon a time but left their waking freshness unimpaired.

The passive desolation of disuse was everywhere silently manifest about it. Within doors, curtains, drooping heavily, lost their old folds and shapes, and hung like cumbrous palls. Hecatombs of furniture, still piled and covered up, shrunk like imprisoned and forgotten men, and changed insensibly. Mirrors were dim as with the breath of years. Patterns of carpets faded and became perplexed and faint, like the memory of those years' trifling incidents. Boards, starting at unwonted footsteps, creaked and shook. Keys rusted in the locks of doors. Damp started on the walls, and as the stains came out, the pictures seemed to go in and secrete themselves. Mildew and mould began to lurk in closets. Fungus trees grew in corners of the cellars. Dust accumulated, nobody knew whence nor how; spiders, moths, and grubs were heard of every day. An exploratory blackbeetle now and then was found immovable upon the stairs, or in an upper room, as wondering how he got there. Rats began to squeak and scuffle in the nighttime, through dark galleries they mined behind the panelling.

The dreary magnificence of the state rooms, seen imperfectly by the doubtful light admitted through closed shutters, would have answered well enough for an enchanted abode. Such as the tarnished paws of gilded lions, stealthily put out from beneath their wrappers; the marble lineaments of busts on pedestals, fearfully revealing themselves through veils; the clocks that never told the time, or, if wound up by any chance, told it wrong, and struck unearthly numbers, which are not upon the dial; the accidental tinklings among the pendant lustres, more startling than alarm-bells; the softened sounds and laggard air that made their way among these objects, and a phantom crowd of others, shrouded and hooded, and made spectral of shape. But, besides, there was the great staircase, where the lord of the place so rarely set his foot, and by which his little child had gone up to Heaven. There were other staircases and passages where no one went for weeks together; there were two closed rooms associated with dead members of the family, and with whispered recollections of them; and to all the house but Florence, there was a gentle figure moving through the solitude and gloom, that gave to every lifeless thing a touch of present human interest and wonder.

For Florence lived alone in the deserted house, and day succeeded day, and still she lived alone, and the cold walls looked down upon her with a vacant stare, as if they had a Gorgon-like mind to stare her youth and beauty into stone.

The grass began to grow upon the roof, and in the crevices of the basement paving. A scaly crumbling vegetation sprouted round the window-sills. Fragments of mortar lost their hold upon the insides of the unused chimneys, and came dropping down. The two trees with the smoky trunks were blighted high up, and the withered branches domineered above the leaves. Through the whole building white had turned yellow, yellow nearly black; and since the time when the poor lady died, it had slowly become a dark gap in the long monotonous street.

But Florence bloomed there, like the king's fair daughter in the story. Her books, her music, and her daily teachers, were her only real companions, Susan Nipper and Diogenes excepted: of whom the former, in her attendance on the studies of her young mistress, began to grow quite learned herself, while the latter, softened possibly by the same influences, would lay his head upon the window-ledge, and placidly open and shut his eyes upon the street, all through a summer morning; sometimes pricking up his head to look with great significance after some noisy dog in a cart, who was barking his way along, and sometimes, with an exasperated and unaccountable recollection of his supposed enemy in the neighbour-hood, rushing to the door, whence, after a deafening disturbance, he would come jogging back with a ridiculous complacency that belonged to him, and lay his jaw upon the window-ledge again, with the air of a dog who had done a public service.

So Florence lived in her wilderness of a home, within the circle of her innocent pursuits and thoughts, and nothing harmed her. She could go down to her father's rooms now, and think of him, and suffer her loving heart humbly to approach him, without fear of repulse. She could look upon the objects that had surrounded him in his sorrow, and could nestle near his chair, and not dread the glance that she so well remembered. She could render him such little tokens of her duty and service, as putting everything in order for him with her own hands, binding little nosegays for his table, changing them as one by one they withered, and he did not come back, preparing something for him every day, and leaving some timid mark of her presence near his usual seat. To-day, it was a little painted stand for his watch; to-morrow she would be afraid to leave it, and would substitute some other trifle of her making not so likely to attract his eye. Waking in the night, perhaps, she would tremble at the thought of his coming home and angrily rejecting it, and would hurry down with slippered feet and quickly beating heart, and bring it away. At another time, she would only lay her face upon his desk, and leave a kiss there, and a tear.

Still no one knew of this. Unless the household found it out when she was not there – and they all held Mr Dombey's rooms in awe – it was as deep a secret in her breast as what had gone before it.

Florence stole into those rooms at twilight, early in the morning, and at times when meals were served down-stairs.[3] And although they were in every nook the better and the brighter for her care, she entered and passed out as quietly as any sunbeam, excepting that she left her light behind.

Shadowy company attended Florence up and down the echoing house, and sat with her in the dismantled rooms. As if her life were an enchanted vision, there arose out of her solitude ministering thoughts, that made it fanciful and unreal. She imagined so often what her life would have been if her father could have loved her and she had been a favourite child, that sometimes, for the moment, she almost believed it was so, and, borne on by the current of that pensive fiction, seemed to remember how they had watched her brother in his grave together; how they had freely shared his heart between them; how they were united in the dear remembrance of him; how they often spoke about him yet; and her kind father, looking at her gently, told her of their common hope and trust in God. At other times she pictured to herself her mother yet alive. And oh the happiness of falling on her neck, and clinging to her with the love and confidence of all her soul! And oh the desolation of the solitary house again, with evening coming on, and no one there!

But there was one thought, scarcely shaped out to herself, yet fervent and strong within her, that upheld Florence when she strove, and filled her true young heart, so sorely tried, with constancy of purpose. Into her mind, as into all others contending with the great affliction of our mortal nature, there had stolen solemn wonderings and hopes, arising in the dim world beyond the present life, and murmuring, like faint music, of recognition in the far-off land between her brother and her mother: of some present consciousness in both of her: some love and commiseration for her: and some knowledge of her as she went her way upon the earth. It was a soothing consolation to Florence to give shelter to these thoughts, until one day – it was soon after she had last seen her father in his own room, late at night – the fancy came upon her, that, in weeping for his alienated heart, she might stir the spirits of the dead against him. Wild, weak, childish, as it may have been to think so, and to tremble at the half-formed thought, it was the impulse of her loving nature; and from that hour Florence strove against the cruel wound in her breast, and tried to think of him whose hand had made it only with hope.

Her father did not know – she held to it from that time – how much she loved him. She was very young, and had no mother, and had never learned, by some fault or misfortune, how to express to him that she loved him. She would be patient, and would try to gain that art in time, and win him to a better knowledge of his only child.

This became the purpose of her life. The morning sun shone down upon the faded house, and found the resolution bright and fresh within the bosom of its solitary mistress. Through all the duties of the day, it animated her; for Florence hoped that the more she knew, and the more accomplished she became, the more glad he would be when he came to know and like her. Sometimes she wondered, with a swelling heart and rising tear, whether she was proficient enough in anything to surprise him when they should become companions. Sometimes she tried to think if there were any kind of knowledge that would bespeak his interest more readily than another. Always: at her books, her music, and her work: in her morning walks, and in her nightly prayers: she had her engrossing aim in view. Strange study for a child, to learn the road to a hard parent's heart!

There were many careless loungers through the street, as the summer evening deepened into night, who glanced across the road at the sombre house, and saw the youthful figure at the window, such a contrast to it, looking upward at the stars as they began to shine, who would have slept the worse if they had known on what design she mused so steadfastly. The reputation of the mansion as a haunted house, would not have been the gayer with some humble dwellers elsewhere, who were struck by its external gloom in passing and repassing on their daily avocations,[4] and so named it, if they could have read its story in the darkening face. But Florence held her sacred purpose, unsuspected and unaided: and studied only how to bring her father to the understanding that she loved him, and made no appeal against him in any wandering thought.

Thus Florence lived alone in the deserted house, and day succeeded day, and still she lived alone, and the monotonous walls looked down upon her with a stare, as if they had a Gorgon-like intent to stare her youth and beauty into stone.

Susan Nipper stood opposite to her young mistress one morning, as she folded and sealed a note she had been writing: and showed in her looks an approving knowledge of its contents.

'Better late than never, dear Miss Floy,' said Susan, 'and I do say, that even a visit to them old Skettleses will be a God-send.'

'It is very good of Sir Barnet and Lady Skettles, Susan,' returned

Florence, with a mild correction of that young lady's familiar mention of the family in question, 'to repeat their invitation so kindly.'

Miss Nipper, who was perhaps the most thoroughgoing partisan on the face of the earth, and who carried her partisanship into all matters great or small, and perpetually waged war with it against society, screwed up her lips and shook her head, as a protest against any recognition of disinterestedness in the Skettleses, and a plea in bar[5] that they would have valuable consideration for their kindness, in the company of Florence.

'They know what they're about, if ever people did,' murmured Miss Nipper, drawing in her breath, 'oh! trust them Skettleses for that!'

'I am not very anxious to go to Fulham, Susan, I confess,' said Florence thoughtfully: 'but it will be right to go. I think it will be better.'

'Much better,' interposed Susan, with another emphatic shake of her head.

'And so,' said Florence, 'though I would prefer to have gone when there was no one there, instead of in this vacation time, when it seems there are some young people staying in the house, I have thankfully said yes.'

'For which I say, Miss Floy, Oh be joyful!' returned Susan. 'Ah! h–h!'

This last ejaculation, with which Miss Nipper frequently wound up a sentence, at about that epoch of time, was supposed below the level of the hall to have a general reference to Mr Dombey, and to be expressive of a yearning in Miss Nipper to favour that gentleman with a piece of her mind. But she never explained it; and it had, in consequence, the charm of mystery, in addition to the advantage of the sharpest expression.

'How long it is before we have any news of Walter, Susan!' observed Florence, after a moment's silence.

'Long indeed, Miss Floy!' replied her maid. 'And Perch said, when he came just now to see for letters – but what signifies what *he* says!' exclaimed Susan, reddening and breaking off. 'Much *he* knows about it!'

Florence raised her eyes quickly, and a flush overspread her face.

'If I hadn't,' said Susan Nipper, evidently struggling with some latent anxiety and alarm, and looking full at her young mistress, while endeavouring to work herself into a state of resentment with the unoffending Mr Perch's image, 'if I hadn't more manliness than that insipidest of his sex, I'd never take pride in my hair again, but turn it up behind my ears, and wear coarse caps, without a bit of border, until death released me from my insignificance. I may not be a Amazon,[6] Miss Floy, and wouldn't so demean myself by such disfigurement, but anyways I'm not a giver up, I hope.'

'Give up! What?' cried Florence, with a face of terror.

'Why, nothing, Miss,' said Susan. 'Good gracious, nothing! it's only that wet curl-paper of a man Perch, that any one might almost make away with, with a touch, and really it would be a blessed event for all parties if some one *would* take pity on him, and would have the goodness!'

'Does he give up the ship, Susan?' inquired Florence, very pale.

'No, Miss,' returned Susan, 'I should like to see him make so bold as to do it to my face! No, Miss, but he goes on about some bothering ginger that Mr Walter was to send to Mrs Perch, and shakes his dismal head, and says he hopes it may be coming; anyhow, he says, it can't come now in time for the intended occasion, but may do for next, which really,' said Miss Nipper, with aggravated scorn, 'puts me out of patience with the man, for though I can bear a great deal, I am not a camel, neither am I,' added Susan, after a moment's consideration, 'if I know myself, a dromedary[7] neither.'

'What else does he say, Susan?' inquired Florence, earnestly. 'Won't you tell me?'

'As if I wouldn't tell you anything, Miss Floy, and everything!' said Susan. 'Why, Miss, he says that there begins to be a general talk about the ship, and that they have never had a ship on that voyage half so long unheard of, and that the Captain's wife was at the office yesterday, and seemed a little put out about it, but any one could say that, we knew nearly that before.'

'I must visit Walter's uncle,' said Florence, hurriedly, 'before I leave home. I will go and see him this morning. Let us walk there, directly, Susan.'

Miss Nipper having nothing to urge against the proposal, but being perfectly acquiescent, they were soon equipped, and in the streets, and on their way towards the little Midshipman.

The state of mind in which poor Walter had gone to Captain Cuttle's, on the day when Brogley the broker came into possession, and when there seemed to him to be an execution in the very steeples, was pretty much the same as that in which Florence now took her way to Uncle Sol's; with this difference, that Florence suffered the added pain of thinking that she had been, perhaps the innocent occasion of involving Walter in peril, and all to whom he was dear, herself included, in an agony of suspense. For the rest, uncertainty and danger seemed written upon everything. The weathercocks on spires and housetops were mysterious with hints of stormy wind, and pointed, like so many ghostly fingers, out to dangerous seas, where fragments of great wrecks were drifting, perhaps, and helpless men were rocked upon them into a sleep as deep as the unfathomable waters. When Florence came into the City, and passed gentlemen who were talking together, she dreaded to hear them speaking of the ship, and saying it was lost. Pictures and prints of vessels fighting with the rolling waves filled her with alarm. The smoke and clouds, though moving gently, moved too fast for her apprehensions, and made her fear there was a tempest blowing at that moment on the ocean.

Susan Nipper may or may not have been affected similarly, but having her attention much engaged in struggles with boys, whenever there was any press of people – for, between that grade of human kind and herself, there was some natural animosity that invariably broke out, whenever they came together – it would seem that she had not much leisure on the road for intellectual operations.

Arriving in good time abreast of the Wooden Midshipman on the opposite side of the way, and waiting for an opportunity to cross the street, they were a little surprised at first to see, at the Instrument-maker's door, a round-headed lad, with his chubby face addressed towards the sky, who, as they looked at him, suddenly thrust into his capacious mouth two fingers of each hand, and with the assistance of that machinery whistled, with astonishing shrillness, to some pigeons at a considerable elevation in the air.

'Mrs Richards's eldest, Miss!' said Susan, 'and the worrit of Mrs Richards's life!'

As Polly had been to tell Florence of the resuscitated prospects of her son and heir, Florence was prepared for the meeting: so, a favourable moment presenting itself they both hastened across, without any further contemplation of Mrs Richards's bane. That sporting character, unconscious of their approach, again whistled with his utmost might, and then yelled in a rapture of excitement, 'Strays! Whoo-oop! Strays!' which identification had such an effect upon the conscience-stricken pigeons,[8] that instead of going direct to some town in the North of England, as appeared to have been their original intention, they began to wheel and falter; whereupon Mrs Richards's firstborn pierced them with another whistle, and again yelled, in a voice that rose above the turmoil of the street, 'Strays! Whoo-oop! Strays!'

From this transport,' he was abruptly recalled to terrestrial objects, by a poke from Miss Nipper, which sent him into the shop.

'Is this the way you show your penitence, when Mrs Richards has been fretting for you months and months?' said Susan, following the poke. 'Where's Mr Gills?'

Rob, who smoothed his first rebellious glance at Miss Nipper when he saw Florence following, put his knuckles to his hair, in honour of the latter, and said to the former, that Mr Gills was out.

'Fetch him home,' said Miss Nipper, with authority, 'and say that my young lady's here.'

'I don't know where he's gone,' said Rob.

'Is *that* your penitence?' cried Susan, with stinging sharpness.

'Why, how can I go and fetch him when I don't know where to go?' whimpered the baited Rob. 'How can you be so unreasonable?'

'Did Mr Gills say when he should be home?' asked Florence.

'Yes, Miss,' replied Rob, with another application of his knuckles to his hair. 'He said he should be home early in the afternoon; in about a couple of hours from now, Miss.'

'Is he very anxious about his nephew?' inquired Susan.

'Yes, Miss,' returned Rob, preferring to address himself to Florence and slighting Nipper; 'I should say he was very much so. He ain't indoors, Miss, not a quarter of an hour together. He can't settle in one place five minutes. He goes about, like a – just like a stray,' said Rob, stooping to get a glimpse of the pigeons through the window, and checking himself, with his fingers half-way to his mouth, on the verge of another whistle.

'Do you know a friend of Mr Gills, called Captain Cuttle?' inquired Florence, after a moment's reflection.

'Him with a hook, Miss?' rejoined Rob, with an illustrative twist of his left hand. 'Yes, Miss. He was here the day before yesterday.'

'Has he not been here since?' asked Susan.

'No, Miss,' returned Rob, still addressing his reply to Florence.

'Perhaps Walter's uncle has gone there, Susan,' observed Florence, turning to her.

'To Captain Cuttle's, Miss?' interposed Rob; 'no, he's not gone there, Miss. Because he left particular word that if Captain Cuttle called, I should tell him how surprised he was, not to have seen him yesterday, and should make him stop till he came back.'

'Do you know where Captain Cuttle lives?' asked Florence.

Rob replied in the affirmative, and turning to a greasy parchment book on the shop desk, read the address aloud.

Florence again turned to her maid and took counsel with her in a low voice, while Rob the round-eyed, mindful of his patron's secret charge, looked on and listened. Florence proposed that they should go to Captain Cuttle's house; hear from his own lips, what he thought of the absence of any tidings of the Son and Heir; and bring him, if they could, to comfort Uncle Sol. Susan at first objected slightly, on the score of distance, but a hackney-coach being mentioned by her mistress, withdrew that opposition, and gave in her assent. There were some minutes of discussion between them before they came to this conclusion, during which the staring Rob paid close attention to both speakers, and inclined his ear to each by turns, as if he were appointed arbitrator of the arguments.

In fine, Rob was dispatched for a coach, the visitors keeping shop meanwhile; and when he brought it, they got into it, leaving word for Uncle Sol that they would be sure to call again, on their way back. Rob having stared after the coach until it was as invisible as the pigeons had now become, sat down behind the desk with a most assiduous demeanour; and in order that he might forget nothing of what had transpired, made notes of it on various small scraps of paper, with a vast expenditure of ink. There was no danger of these documents betraying anything if accidentally lost; for long before a word was dry, it became as profound a mystery to Rob, as if he had no part whatever in its production.

While he was yet busy with these labours, the hackney-coach, after encountering unheard-of difficulties from swivel-bridges, soft roads, impassable canals, caravans of casks, settlements of scarlet-beans and little wash-houses, and many such obstacles abounding in that country, stopped at the corner of Brig Place. Alighting here, Florence and Susan Nipper walked down the street, and sought out the abode of Captain Cuttle.

It happened by evil chance to be one of Mrs MacStinger's great cleaning days. On these occasions, Mrs MacStinger was knocked up by the policeman[10] at a quarter before three in the morning, and rarely succumbed before twelve o'clock next night. The chief object of this institution appeared to be, that Mrs MacStinger should move all the furniture into the back garden at early dawn, walk about the house in pattens[11] all day, and move the furniture back again after dark. These ceremonies greatly fluttered those doves the young MacStingers, who were not only unable at such times to find any resting place for the soles of their feet, but generally came in for a good deal of pecking from the maternal bird during the progress of the solemnities.

At the moment when Florence and Susan Nipper presented themselves at Mrs MacStinger's door, that worthy but redoubtable female was in the act of conveying Alexander MacStinger, aged two years and three months, along the passage for forcible deposition in a sitting posture on the street pavement; Alexander being black in the face with holding his breath after punishment, and a cool paving-stone being usually found to act as a powerful restorative in such cases.

The feelings of Mrs MacStinger, as a woman and a mother, were outraged by the look of pity for Alexander which she observed on Florence's face. Therefore, Mrs MacStinger asserting those finest emotions of our nature, in preference to weakly gratifying her curiosity, shook and buffeted Alexander both before and during the application of the paving-stone, and took no further notice of the strangers.

'I beg your pardon, ma'am,' said Florence, when the child had found his breath again, and was using it. 'Is this Captain Cuttle's house?'

'No,' said Mrs MacStinger.

'Not Number Nine?' asked Florence, hesitating.

'Who said it wasn't Number Nine?' said Mrs MacStinger.

Susan Nipper instantly struck in, and begged to inquire what Mrs MacStinger meant by that, and if she knew whom she was talking to.

Mrs MacStinger in retort, looked at her all over. 'What do you want with Captain Cuttle, I should wish to know?' said Mrs MacStinger.

'Should you? Then I'm sorry that you won't be satisfied,' returned Miss Nipper.

'Hush, Susan! If you please!' said Florence. 'Perhaps you can have the goodness to tell us where Captain Cuttle lives, ma'am, as he don't live here.'

'Who says he don't live here?' retorted the implacable Mac-Stinger. 'I said it wasn't Cap'en Cuttle's house – and it ain't his house – and forbid it, that it ever should be his house – for Cap'en Cuttle don't know how to keep a house – and don't deserve to have a house – it's *my* house – and when I let the upper floor to Cap'en Cuttle, oh I do a thankless thing, and cast pearls before swine!'[12]

Mrs MacStinger pitched her voice for the upper windows in offering these remarks, and cracked off each clause sharply by itself as if from a rifle possessing an infinity of barrels. After the last shot, the Captain's voice was heard to say, in feeble remonstrance from his own room, 'Steady below!'

'Since you want Cap'en Cuttle, there he is!' said Mrs MacStinger, with an angry motion of her hand. On Florence making bold to enter, without any more parley, and on Susan following, Mrs MacStinger recommenced her pedestrian exercise in pattens, and Alexander MacStinger (still on the paving-stone), who had stopped in his crying to attend to the conversation, began to wail again, entertaining himself during that dismal performance, which was quite mechanical, with a general survey of the prospect, terminating in the hackney-coach.

The Captain in his own apartment was sitting with his hands in his pockets and his legs drawn up under his chair, on a very small desolate island, lying about midway in an ocean of soap and water. The Captain's windows had been cleaned, the walls had been cleaned, the stove had been cleaned, and everything, the stove excepted, was wet, and shining with soft soap and sand: the smell of which dry-saltery impregnated the air. In the midst of the dreary scene, the Captain, cast away upon his island, looked round on the waste of waters with a rueful countenance, and seemed waiting for some friendly bark to come that way, and take him off.

But when the Captain, directing his forlorn visage towards the door, saw Florence appear with her maid, no words can describe his astonishment. Mrs MacStinger's eloquence having rendered all other sounds but imperfectly distinguishable, he had looked for no rarer visitor than the potboy[13] or the milkman; wherefore, when Florence appeared, and coming to the confines of the island, put her hand in his, the Captain stood up, aghast, as if he supposed her, for the moment, to be some young member of the Flying Dutchman's family.[14]

Instantly recovering his self-possession, however, the Captain's first care was to place her on dry land, which he happily accomplished, with one motion of his arm. Issuing forth, then, upon the main, Captain Cuttle took Miss Nipper round the waist, and bore her to the island also. Captain Cuttle, then, with great respect and admiration, raised the hand of Florence to his lips, and standing off a little (for the island was not large enough for three), beamed on her from the soap and water like a new description of Triton.[15]

'You are amazed to see us, I am sure,' said Florence, with a smile.

The inexpressibly gratified Captain kissed his hook in reply, and growled, as if a choice and delicate compliment were included in the words, 'Stand by! Stand by!'

'But I couldn't rest,' said Florence, 'without coming to ask you what you think about dear Walter – who is my brother now – and whether there is anything to fear, and whether you will not go and console his poor uncle every day, until we have some intelligence of him?'

At these words Captain Cuttle, as by an involuntary gesture, clapped his hand to his head, on which the hard glazed hat was not, and looked discomfited.

'Have you any fears for Walter's safety?' inquired Florence, from whose face the Captain (so enraptured he was with it) could not take his eyes: while she in her turn, looked earnestly at him, to be assured of the sincerity of his reply.

'No, Heart's-delight,'[16] said Captain Cuttle, 'I am not afeard. Wal'r is a lad as'll go through a deal o' hard weather. Wal'r is a lad as'll bring as much success to that 'ere brig as a lad is capable on. Wal'r,' said the Captain, his eyes glistening with the praise of his young friend, and his hook raised to announce a beautiful quotation, 'is what you may call a out'ard and visible sign of an in'ard and spirited grasp,[17] and when found make a note of.'

Florence, who did not quite understand this, though the Captain evidently thought it full of meaning, and highly satisfactory, mildly looked to him for something more.

'I am not afeard, my Heart's-delight,' resumed the Captain. 'There's been most uncommon bad weather in them latitudes, there's no denyin', and they have drove and drove and been beat off, may be t'other side the world. But the ship's a good ship, and the lad's a good lad; and it ain't easy, thank the Lord,' the Captain made a little bow, 'to break up hearts of oak,[18] whether they're in brigs or buzzums.[19] Here we have 'em both ways, which is bringing it up with a round turn,[20] and so I ain't a bit afeard as yet.'

'As yet?' repeated Florence.

'Not a bit,' returned the Captain, kissing his iron hand; 'and afore I begin to be, my Heart's-delight, Wal'r will have wrote home from the island, or from some port or another, and made all taut and ship-shape. And with regard to old Sol Gills,' here the Captain became solemn, 'who I'll stand by, and not desert until death do us part, and when the stormy winds do blow, do blow, do blow[21] – overhaul the Catechism,' said the Captain parenthetically, 'and there you'll find them expressions – if it would console Sol Gills to have the opinion of a seafaring man as has got a mind equal to any undertaking that he puts it alongside of, and as was all but smashed in his 'prenticeship, and of which the name is Bunsby, that 'ere man shall give him such an opinion in his own parlour as'll stun him. Ah!' said Captain Cuttle, vauntingly, 'as much as if he'd gone and knocked his head again a door!'

'Let us take this gentleman to see him, and let us hear what he says,' cried Florence. 'Will you go with us now? We have a coach here.'

Again the Captain clapped his hand to his head, on which the hard glazed hat was not, and looked discomfited. But at this instant a most remarkable phenomenon occurred. The door opening, without any note of preparation, and apparently of itself, the hard glazed hat in question skimmed into the room like a bird, and alighted heavily at the Captain's feet. The door then shut as violently as it had opened, and nothing ensued in explanation of the prodigy.

Captain Cuttle picked up his hat, and having turned it over with a look of interest and welcome, began to polish it on his sleeve. While doing so, the Captain eyed his visitors intently, and said in a low voice:

'You see I should have bore down on Sol Gills yesterday, and this morning, but she – she took it away and kep it. That's the long and short of the subject.'

'Who did, for goodness sake?' asked Susan Nipper.

'The lady of the house, my dear,' returned the Captain, in a gruff whisper, and making signals of secrecy. 'We had some words about the swabbing of these here planks, and she – in short,' said the Captain, eyeing the door, and relieving himself with a long breath, 'she stopped my liberty.'[22]

'Oh! I wish she had me to deal with!' said Susan, reddening with the energy of the wish. 'I'd stop her!'

'Would you, do you think, my dear?' rejoined the Captain, shaking his head doubtfully, but regarding the desperate courage of the fair aspirant with obvious admiration. 'I don't know. It's difficult navigation. She's very hard to carry on with, my dear. You never can tell how she'll head, you see. She's full one minute, and round[23] upon you next. And when she is a tartar,' said the Captain, with the perspiration breaking out upon his forehead—. There was nothing but a whistle emphatic enough for the conclusion of the sentence, so the Captain whistled tremulously. After which he again shook his head, and recurring to his admiration of Miss Nipper's devoted bravery, timidly repeated, 'Would you, do you think, my dear?'

Susan only replied with a bridling smile, but that was so very full of defiance, that there is no knowing how long Captain Cuttle might have stood entranced in its contemplation, if Florence in her anxiety had not again proposed their immediately resorting to the oracular Bunsby. Thus reminded of his duty, Captain Cuttle put on the glazed hat firmly, took up another knobby stick, with which he had supplied the place of that one given to Walter, and offering his arm to Florence, prepared to cut his way through the enemy.

It turned out, however, that Mrs MacStinger had already changed her course, and that she headed, as the Captain had remarked she often did, in quite a new direction. For when they got downstairs, they found that exemplary woman beating the mats on the door-steps, with Alexander, still upon the paving-stone, dimly looming through a fog of dust; and so absorbed was Mrs MacStinger in her household occupation, that when Captain Cuttle and his visitors passed, she beat the harder, and neither by word nor gesture showed any consciousness of their vicinity. The Captain was so well pleased with this easy escape – although the effect of the door-mat on him was like a copious administration of snuff, and made him sneeze until the tears ran down his face – that he could hardly believe his good fortune; but more than once, between the door and the hackney-coach, looked over his shoulder, with an obvious apprehension of Mrs MacStinger's giving chase yet.

However, they got to the corner of Brig Place without any molestation from that terrible fire-ship;[24] and the Captain mounting the coach-box[25] – for his gallantry would not allow him to ride inside with the ladies, though besought to do so – piloted the driver on his course for Captain Bunsby's vessel, which was called the Cautious Clara, and was lying hard by Ratcliffe.

Arrived at the wharf off which this great commander's ship was jammed in among some five hundred companions, whose tangled rigging looked like monstrous cobwebs half swept down, Captain Cuttle appeared at the coach-window, and invited Florence and Miss Nipper to accompany him on board; observing that Bunsby was to the last degree soft-hearted in respect of ladies, and that nothing would so much tend to bring his expansive intellect into a state of harmony as their presentation to the Cautious Clara.

Florence readily consented; and the Captain, taking her little hand in his prodigious palm, led her, with a mixed expression of patronage, paternity, pride, and ceremony, that was pleasant to see, over several very dirty decks, until, coming to the Clara, they found that cautious craft (which lay outside the tier)[26] with her gangway removed, and half a dozen feet of river interposed between herself and her nearest neighbour. It appeared, from Captain Cuttle's explanation, that the great Bunsby, like himself, was cruelly treated by his landlady, and that when her usage of him for the time being was so hard that he could bear it no longer, he set this gulf between them as a last resource.

'Clara a-hoy!' cried the Captain, putting a hand to each side of his mouth.

'A-hoy!' cried a boy, like the Captain's echo, tumbling up from below.

'Bunsby aboard?' cried the Captain, hailing the boy in a stentorian voice, as if he were half-a-mile off instead of two yards.

'Aye, aye!' cried the boy, in the same tone.

The boy then shoved out a plank to Captain Cuttle, who adjusted it carefully, and led Florence across: returning presently for Miss Nipper. So they stood upon the deck of the Cautious Clara, in whose standing rigging,[27] divers fluttering articles of dress were curing,[28] in company with a few tongues and some mackerel.

Immediately there appeared, coming slowly up above the bulk-head of the cabin, another bulk-head – human, and very large – with one stationary eye in the mahogany face, and one revolving one, on the principle of some lighthouses. This head was decorated with shaggy hair, like oakum,[29] which had no governing inclination towards the north, east, west, or south, but inclined to all four quarters of the compass, and to every point upon it. The head was followed by a perfect desert of chin, and by a shirt-collar and neckerchief, and by a dreadnought pilot-coat, and by a pair of dreadnought pilot-trousers, whereof the waistband was so very broad and high, that it became a succedaneum[30] for a waistcoat: being ornamented near the wearer's breast-bone with some massive wooden buttons, like backgammon men. As the lower portions of these pantaloons became revealed, Bunsby stood confessed; his hands in their pockets, which were of vast size; and his gaze directed, not to Captain Cuttle or the ladies, but the mast-head.

The profound appearance of this philosopher, who was bulky and strong, and on whose extremely red face an expression of taciturnity sat enthroned, not inconsistent with his character, in which that quality was proudly conspicuous, almost daunted Captain Cuttle, though on familiar terms with him. Whispering to Florence that Bunsby had never in his life expressed surprise, and was considered not to know what it meant, the Captain watched him as he eyed his mast-head, and afterwards swept the horizon; and when the revolving eye seemed to be coming round in his direction, said:

'Bunsby, my lad, how fares it?'

A deep, gruff, husky utterance, which seemed to have no connexion with Bunsby, and certainly had not the least effect upon his face, replied, 'Aye, aye, shipmet, how goes it?' At the same time Bunsby's right hand and arm, emerging from a pocket, shook the Captain's, and went back again.

'Bunsby,' said the Captain, striking home at once, 'here you are; a man of mind, and a man as can give an opinion. Here's a young lady as wants to take that opinion, in regard of my friend Wal'r; likewise my t'other friend, Sol Gills, which is a character for you to come within hail of, being a man of science, which is the mother of inwention, and knows no law.[31] Bunsby, will you wear,[32] to oblige me, and come along with us?'

The great commander, who seemed by the expression of his visage to be always on the look-out for something in the extremest distance, and to have no oracular knowledge of anything within ten miles, made no reply whatever.

'Here is a man,' said the Captain, addressing himself to his fair auditors, and indicating the commander with his outstretched hook, 'that has fell down more than any man alive; that has had more accidents happen to his own self than the Seamen's Hospital to all hands; that took as many spars and bars and bolts about the outside of his head when he was young, as you'd want a order for on Chatham-yard to build a pleasure-yacht with; and yet that got his opinions in that way, it's my belief, for there an't nothing like 'em afloat or ashore.'

The stolid commander appeared, by a very slight vibration in his elbows, to express some satisfaction in this encomium; but if his face had been as distant as his gaze was, it could hardly have enlightened the beholders less in reference to anything that was passing in his thoughts.

'Shipmet,' said Bunsby, all of a sudden, and stooping down to look out under some interposing spar, 'what'll the ladies drink?'

Captain Cuttle, whose delicacy was shocked by such an inquiry in connexion with Florence, drew the sage aside, and seeming to explain in his ear, accompanied him below; where, that he might not take offence, the Captain drank a dram himself, which Florence and Susan, glancing down the open skylight, saw the sage, with difficulty finding room for himself between his berth and a very little brass fireplace, serve out for self and friend. They soon reappeared on deck, and Captain Cuttle, triumphing in the success of his enterprise, conducted Florence back to the coach, while Bunsby followed, escorting Miss Nipper, whom he hugged upon the way (much to that young lady's indignation) with his pilot-coated arm, like a blue bear.

The Captain put his oracle inside, and gloried so much in having secured him, and having got that mind into a hackney-coach, that he could not refrain from often peeping in at Florence through the little window behind the driver, and testifying his delight in smiles, and also in taps upon his forehead, to hint to her that the brain of Bunsby was hard at it. In the meantime, Bunsby, still hugging Miss Nipper (for his friend, the Captain, had not exaggerated the softness of his heart) uniformly preserved his gravity of deportment, and showed no other consciousness of her or anything.

Uncle Sol, who had come home, received them at the door, and ushered them immediately into the little back parlour: strangely altered by the absence of Walter. On the table, and about the room, were the charts and maps on which the heavy-hearted Instrument-maker had again and again tracked the missing vessel across the sea, and on which, with a pair of compasses that he still had in his hand, he had been measuring, a minute before, how far she must have driven, to have driven here or there: and trying to demonstrate that a long time must elapse before hope was exhausted.

'Whether she can have run,' said Uncle Sol, looking wistfully over the chart; 'but no, that's almost impossible. Or whether she can have been forced by stress of weather, – but that's not reasonably likely. Or whether there is any hope she so far changed her course as – but even I can hardly hope that!' With such broken suggestions, poor old Uncle Sol roamed over the great sheet before him, and could not find a speck of hopeful probability in it large enough to set one small point of the compasses upon.

Florence saw immediately – it would have been difficult to help seeing – that there was a singular indescribable change in the old man, and that while his manner was far more restless and unsettled than usual, there was yet a curious, contradictory decision in it, that perplexed her very much. She fancied once that he spoke wildly, and at random; for on her saying she regretted not to have seen him when she had been there before that morning, he at first replied that he had been to see her, and directly afterwards seemed to wish to recall that answer.

Solemn reference is made to Mr Bunsby

'You have been to see me?' said Florence. 'To-day?'

'Yes, my dear young lady,' returned Uncle Sol, looking at her and away from her in a confused manner. 'I wished to see you with my own eyes, and to hear you with my own ears, once more before—' Then he stopped.

'Before when? Before what?' said Florence, putting her hand upon his arm.

'Did I say "before"?' replied old Sol. 'If I did, I must have meant before we should have news of my dear boy.'

'You are not well,' said Florence, tenderly. 'You have been so very anxious. I am sure you are not well.'

'I am as well,' returned the old man, shutting up his right hand, and holding it out to show her: 'as well and firm as any man at my time of life can hope to be. See! It's steady. Is its master not as capable of resolution and fortitude as many a younger man? I think so. We shall see.'

There was that in his manner more than in his words, though they remained with her too, which impressed Florence so much that she would have confided her uneasiness to Captain Cuttle at that moment, if the Captain had not seized that moment for expounding the state of circumstances on which the opinion of the sagacious Bunsby was requested, and entreating that profound authority to deliver the same.

Bunsby, whose eye continued to be addressed to somewhere about the half-way house between London and Gravesend, two or three times put out his rough right arm, as seeking to wind it for inspiration round the fair form of Miss Nipper; but that young female having withdrawn herself, in displeasure, to the opposite side of the table, the soft heart of the Commander of the Cautious Clara met with no response to its impulses. After sundry failures in this wise, the Commander, addressing himself to nobody, thus spake; or rather the voice within him said of its own accord, and quite independent of himself, as if he were possessed by a gruff spirit:

'My name's Jack Bunsby!'

'He was christened John,' cried the delighted Captain Cuttle. 'Hear him!'

'And what I says,' pursued the voice, after some deliberation, 'I stands to.'

The Captain, with Florence on his arm, nodded at the auditory,[33] and seemed to say, 'Now he's coming out. This is what I meant when I brought him.'

'Whereby,' proceeded the voice, 'why not? If so, what odds? Can any man say otherwise? No. Awast then!'

When it had pursued its train of argument to this point, the voice stopped, and rested. It then proceeded very slowly, thus:

'Do I believe that this here Son and Heir's gone down, my lads? Mayhap. Do I say so? Which? If a skipper stands out by Sen' George's Channel, making for the Downs, what's right ahead of him? The Goodwins.[34] He isn't forced to run upon the Goodwins, but he may. The bearings of this observation lays in the application on it. That an't no part of my duty. Awast then, keep a bright look-out for'ard, and good luck to you!'

The voice here went out of the back parlour and into the street, taking the Commander of the Cautious Clara with it, and accompanying him on board again with all convenient expedition where he immediately turned in, and refreshed his mind with a nap.

The students of the sage's precepts, left to their own application of his wisdom upon a principle which was the main leg of the Bunsby tripod, as it is perchance of some other oracular stools – looked upon one another in a little uncertainty; while Rob the Grinder, who had taken the innocent freedom of peering in, and listening, through the skylight in the roof, came softly down from the leads,[35] in a state of very dense confusion. Captain Cuttle, however, whose admiration of Bunsby was, if possible, enhanced by the splendid manner in which he had justified his reputation and come through this solemn reference, proceeded to explain that Bunsby meant nothing but confidence; that Bunsby had no misgivings; and that such an opinion as that man had given, coming from such a mind as his, was Hope's own anchor, with good roads[36] to cast it in. Florence endeavoured to believe that the Captain was right; but the Nipper, with her arms tight folded, shook her head in resolute denial, and had no more trust in Bunsby than in Mr Perch himself.

The philosopher seemed to have left Uncle Sol pretty much where he had found him, for he still went roaming about the watery world, compasses in hand, and discovering no rest for them. It was in pursuance of a whisper in his ear from Florence, while the old man was absorbed in this pursuit, that Captain Cuttle laid his heavy hand upon his shoulder.

'What cheer, Sol Gills?' cried the Captain, heartily.

'But so so, Ned,' returned the Instrument-maker. 'I have been remembering, all this afternoon, that on the very day when my boy entered Dombey's house and came home late to dinner, sitting just there where you stand, we talked of storm and shipwreck, and I could hardly turn him from the subject.'

But meeting the eyes of Florence, which were fixed with earnest scrutiny upon his face, the old man stopped and smiled.

'Stand by, old friend!' cried the Captain. 'Look alive! I tell you what, Sol Gills; arter I've convoyed Heart's-delight safe home,' here the Captain kissed his hook to Florence, 'I'll come back and take you in tow[37] for the rest of this blessed day. You'll come and eat your dinner along with me, Sol, somewheres or another.'

'Not to-day, Ned!' said the old man quickly, and appearing to be unaccountably startled by the proposition. 'Not to-day. I couldn't do it!'

'Why not?' returned the Captain, gazing at him in astonishment.

'I – I have so much to do. I – I mean to think of, and arrange. I couldn't do it, Ned, indeed. I must go out again, and be alone, and turn my mind to many things to-day.'

The Captain looked at the Instrument-maker, and looked at Florence, and again at the Instrument-maker. 'To-morrow, then,' he suggested at last.

'Yes, yes. To-morrow,' said the old man. 'Think of me to-morrow. Say to-morrow.'

'I shall come here early, mind, Sol Gills,' stipulated the Captain.

'Yes, yes. The first thing to-morrow morning,' said old Sol; 'and now good-bye, Ned Cuttle, and God bless you!'

Squeezing both the Captain's hands, with uncommon fervour, as he said it, the old man turned to Florence, folded hers in his own, and put them to his lips; then hurried her out to the coach with very singular precipitation. Altogether, he made such an effect on Captain Cuttle that the Captain lingered behind, and instructed Rob to be particularly gentle and attentive to his master until the morning: which injunction he strengthened with the payment of one shilling down, and the promise of another sixpence before noon next day. This kind office performed, Captain Cuttle, who considered himself the natural and lawful body-guard of Florence, mounted the box with a mighty sense of his trust, and escorted her home. At parting, he assured her that he would stand by Sol Gills, close and true; and once again inquired of Susan Nipper, unable to forget her gallant words in reference to Mrs MacStinger, 'Would you, do you think, my dear, though?'

When the desolate house had closed upon the two, the Captain's thoughts reverted to the old Instrument-maker, and he felt uncomfortable. Therefore, instead of going home, he walked up and down the street several times, and, eking out his leisure until evening, dined late at a certain angular little tavern in the City, with a public parlour like a wedge, to which glazed hats much resorted. The Captain's principal intention was to pass Sol Gills's after dark, and look in through the window: which he did. The parlour door stood open, and he could see his old friend writing busily and steadily at the table within, while the little Midshipman, already sheltered from the night dews, watched him from the counter; under which Rob the Grinder made his own bed, preparatory to shutting the shop. Reassured by the tranquillity that reigned within the precincts of the wooden mariner, the Captain headed for Brig Place, resolving to weigh anchor[38] betimes in the morning.

CHAPTER 24

The Study of a Loving Heart

Sir Barnet and Lady Skettles, very good people, resided in a pretty villa at Fulham, on the banks of the Thames; which was one of the most desirable residences in the world when a rowing-match happened to be going past, but had its little inconveniences at other times, among which may be enumerated the occasional appearance of the river in the drawing-room, and the contemporaneous disappearance of the lawn and shrubbery.

Sir Barnet Skettles expressed his personal consequence chiefly through an antique gold snuff-box, and a ponderous silk pocket-handkerchief, which he had an imposing manner of drawing out of his pocket like a banner, and using with both hands at once. Sir Barnet's object in life was constantly to extend the range of his acquaintance. Like a heavy body dropped into water – not to disparage so worthy a gentleman by the comparison – it was in the nature of things that Sir Barnet must spread an ever-widening circle about him, until there was no room left. Or, like a sound in the air, the vibration of which, according to the speculation of an ingenious modern philosopher, may go on travelling for ever through the interminable fields of space, nothing but coming to the end of his mortal tether could stop Sir Barnet Skettles in his voyage of discovery through the social system.

Sir Barnet was proud of making people acquainted with people. He liked the thing for its own sake, and it advanced his favourite object too. For example, if Sir Barnet had the good fortune to get hold of a raw recruit, or a country gentleman, and ensnared him to his hospitable villa, Sir Barnet would say to him, on the morning after his arrival, 'Now, my dear Sir, is there anybody you would like to know? Who is there you would wish to meet? Do you take any interest in writing people, or in painting or sculpturing people, or in acting people, or in anything of that sort?' Possibly the patient answered yes, and mentioned somebody, of whom Sir Barnet had no more personal knowledge than of Ptolemy the Great.[1] Sir Barnet replied, that nothing on earth was easier, as he knew him very well: immediately called on the aforesaid somebody, left his card, wrote a short note, – 'My dear Sir – penalty of your eminent position – friend at my house naturally desirous – Lady Skettles and myself participate – trust that genius being superior to ceremonies, you will do us the distinguished favour of giving us the pleasure,' etc., etc., – and so killed a brace of birds[2] with one stone, dead as door-nails.

With the snuff-box and banner in full force, Sir Barnet Skettles propounded his usual inquiry to Florence on the first morning of her visit. When Florence thanked him, and said there was no one in particular whom she desired to see, it was natural she should think with a pang, of poor lost Walter. When Sir Barnet Skettles, urging his kind offer, said, 'My dear Miss Dombey, are you sure you can remember no one whom your good papa – to whom I beg you to present the best compliments of myself and Lady Skettles when you write – might wish you to know?' it was natural, perhaps, that her poor head should droop a little, and that her voice should tremble as it softly answered in the negative.

Skettles Junior, much stiffened as to his cravat, and sobered down as to his spirits, was at home for the holidays, and appeared to feel himself aggrieved by the solicitude of his excellent mother that he should be attentive to Florence. Another and a deeper injury under which the soul of young Barnet chafed, was the company of Dr and Mrs Blimber, who had been invited on a visit to the paternal roof-tree, and of whom the young gentleman often said he would have preferred their passing the vacation at Jericho.[3]

'Is there anybody *you* can suggest now, Doctor Blimber?' said Sir Barnet Skettles, turning to that gentleman.

'You are very kind, Sir Barnet,' returned Doctor Blimber. 'Really I am not aware that there is, in particular. I like to know my fellow-men in general, Sir Barnet. What does Terence[4] say? Any one who is the parent of a son is interesting to *me*.'

'Has Mrs Blimber any wish to see any remarkable person?' asked Sir Barnet, courteously.

Mrs Blimber replied, with a sweet smile and a shake of her sky-blue cap, that if Sir Barnet could have made her known to Cicero, she would have troubled him; but such an introduction not being feasible, and she already enjoying the friendship of himself and his amiable lady, and possessing with the Doctor her husband their joint confidence in regard to their dear son – here young Barnet was observed to curl his nose – she asked no more.

Sir Barnet was fain, under these circumstances, to content himself for the time with the company assembled. Florence was glad of that; for she had a study to pursue among them, and it lay too near her heart, and was too precious and momentous, to yield to any other interest.

There were some children staying in the house. Children who were as frank and happy with fathers and with mothers as those rosy faces opposite home. Children who had no restraint upon their love, and freely showed it. Florence sought to learn their secret; sought to find out what it was she had missed; what simple art they knew, and she knew not; how she could be taught by them to show her father that she loved him, and to win his love again.

Many a day did Florence thoughtfully observe these children. On many a bright morning did she leave her bed when the glorious sun rose, and walking up and down upon the river's bank, before any one in the house was stirring, look up at the windows of their rooms, and think of them, asleep, so gently tended and affectionately thought of. Florence would feel more lonely then, than in the great house all alone; and would think sometimes that she was better there than here, and that there was greater peace in hiding herself than in mingling with others of her age, and finding how unlike them all she was. But attentive to her study, though it touched her to the quick at every little leaf she turned in the hard book, Florence remained among them, and tried with patient hope, to gain the knowledge that she wearied for.

Ah! how to gain it! how to know the charm in its beginning! There were daughters here, who rose up in the morning, and lay down to rest at night, possessed of fathers' hearts already. They had no impulse to overcome, no coldness to dread, no frown to smooth away. As the morning advanced, and the windows opened one by one, and the dew began to dry upon the flowers and grass, and youthful feet began to move upon the lawn, Florence, glancing round at the bright faces, thought what was there she could learn from these children? It was too late to learn from them; each could approach her father fearlessly, and put up her lips to meet the ready kiss, and wind her arm about the neck that bent down to caress her. *She* could not begin by being so bold. Oh! could it be that there was less and less hope as she studied more and more!

She remembered well, that even the old woman who had robbed her when a little child – whose image and whose house, and all she had said and done, were stamped upon her recollection, with the enduring sharpness of a fearful impression made at that early period of life – had spoken fondly of her daughter, and how terribly even she had cried out in the pain of hopeless separation from her child. But her own mother, she would think again, when she recalled this, had loved her well. Then, sometimes, when her thoughts reverted swiftly to the void between herself and her father, Florence would tremble, and the tears would start upon her face, as she pictured to herself her mother living on, and coming also to dislike her, because of her wanting the unknown grace that should conciliate that father naturally, and had never done so from her cradle. She knew that this imagination did wrong to her mother's memory, and had no truth in it, or base to rest upon; and yet she tried so hard to justify him, and to find the whole blame in herself, that she could not resist its passing, like a wild cloud, through the distance of her mind.

There came among the other visitors, soon after Florence, one beautiful girl, three or four years younger than she, who was an orphan child, and who was accompanied by her aunt, a grey-haired lady, who spoke much to Florence, and who greatly liked (but that they all did) to hear her sing of an evening, and would always sit near her at that time, with motherly interest. They had only been two days in the house, when Florence, being in an arbour in the garden one warm morning, musingly observant of a youthful group upon the turf, through some intervening boughs, and wreathing flowers for the head of one little creature among them who was the pet and plaything of the rest, heard this same lady and her niece, in pacing up and down a sheltered nook close by, speak of herself.

'Is Florence an orphan like me, aunt?' said the child.

'No, my love. She has no mother, but her father is living.'

'Is she in mourning for her poor mama, now?' inquired the child quickly.

'No; for her only brother.'

'Has she no other brother?'

'None.'

'No sister?'

'None.'

'I am very, very sorry!' said the little girl.

As they stopped soon afterwards to watch some boats, and had been silent in the meantime, Florence, who had risen when she heard her name, and had gathered up her flowers to go and meet them, that they might know of her being within hearing, resumed her seat and work, expecting to hear no more; but the conversation recommenced next moment.

'Florence is a favourite with every one here, and deserves to be, I am sure,' said the child, earnestly. 'Where is her papa?'

The aunt replied, after a moment's pause, that she did not know. Her tone of voice arrested Florence, who had started from her seat again; and held her fastened to the spot, with her work hastily caught up to her bosom, and her two hands saving it from being scattered on the ground.

'He is in England, I hope, aunt,' said the child.

'I believe so. Yes; I know he is, indeed.'

'Has he ever been here?'

'I believe not. No.'

'Is he coming here to see her?'

'I believe not.'

'Is he lame, or blind, or ill, aunt?' asked the child.

The flowers that Florence held to her breast began to fall when she heard those words, so wonderingly spoken. She held them closer; and her face hung down upon them.

'Kate,' said the lady, after another moment of silence, 'I will tell you the whole truth about Florence as I have heard it, and believe it to be. Tell no one else, my dear, because it may be little known here, and your doing so would give her pain.'

'I never will!' exclaimed the child.

'I know you never will,' returned the lady. 'I can trust you as myself. I fear then, Kate, that Florence's father cares little for her, very seldom sees her, never was kind to her in her life, and now quite shuns her and avoids her. She would love him dearly if he would suffer her, but he will not – though for no fault of hers; and she is greatly to be loved and pitied by all gentle hearts.'

More of the flowers that Florence held, fell scattering on the ground; those that remained were wet, but not with dew; and her face dropped upon her laden hands.

'Poor Florence! Dear, good Florence!' cried the child.

'Do you know why I have told you this, Kate?' said the lady.

'That I may be very kind to her, and take great care to try to please her. Is that the reason, aunt?'

'Partly,' said the lady, 'but not all. Though we see her so cheerful; with a pleasant smile for every one; ready to oblige us all, and bearing her part in every amusement here: she can hardly be quite happy, do you think she can, Kate?'

'I am afraid not,' said the little girl.

'And you can understand,' pursued the lady, 'why her observation of children who have parents who are fond of them, and proud of them – like many here, just now – should make her sorrowful in secret?'

'Yes, dear aunt,' said the child, 'I understand that very well. Poor Florence!'

More flowers strayed upon the ground, and those she yet held to her breast trembled as if a wintry wind were rustling them.

'My Kate,' said the lady, whose voice was serious, but very calm and sweet, and had so impressed Florence from the first moment of her hearing it, 'of all the youthful people here, you are her natural and harmless friend; you have not the innocent means, that happier children have—'

'There are none happier, aunt!' exclaimed the child, who seemed to cling about her.

'—As other children have, dear Kate, of reminding her of her misfortune. Therefore I would have you, when you try to be her little friend, try all the more for that, and feel that the bereavement you sustained – thank Heaven! before you knew its weight – gives you claim and hold upon poor Florence.'

'But I am not without a parent's love, aunt, and I never have been,' said the child, 'with you.'

'However that may be, my dear,' returned the lady, 'your misfortune is a lighter one than Florence's; for not an orphan in the wide world can be so deserted as the child who is an outcast from a living parent's love.'

The flowers were scattered on the ground like dust, the empty hands were spread upon the face; and orphaned Florence, shrinking down upon the ground, wept long and bitterly.

But true of heart and resolute in her good purpose, Florence held to it as her dying mother held by her upon the day that gave Paul life. He did not know how much she loved him. However long the time in coming, and however slow the interval, she must try to bring that knowledge to her father's heart one day or other. Meantime she must be careful in no thoughtless word, or look, or burst of feeling awakened by any chance circumstance, to complain against him, or to give occasion for these whispers to his prejudice.

Even in the response she made the orphan child, to whom she was attracted strongly, and whom she had such occasion to remember, Florence was mindful of him. If she singled her out too plainly (Florence thought) from among the rest, she would confirm – in one mind certainly: perhaps in more – the belief that he was cruel and unnatural. Her own delight was no set-off to this. What she had overheard was a reason, not for soothing herself, but for saving him; and Florence did it, in pursuance of the study of her heart.

She did so always. If a book were read aloud, and there were anything in the story that pointed at an unkind father, she was in pain for their application of it to him; not for herself. So with any trifle of an interlude that was acted, or picture that was shown, or game that was played, among them. The occasions for such tenderness towards him were so many, that her mind misgave her often, it would indeed be better to go back to the old house, and live again within the shadow of its dull walls, undisturbed. How few who saw sweet Florence, in her spring of womanhood, the modest little queen of those small revels, imagined what a load of sacred care lay heavy in her breast! How few of those who stiffened in her father's freezing atmosphere, suspected what a heap of fiery coals⁵ was piled upon his head!

Florence pursued her study patiently, and, failing to acquire the secret of the nameless grace she sought, among the youthful company who were assembled in the house, often walked out alone, in the early morning, among the children of the poor. But still she found them all too far advanced to learn from. They had won their household places long ago, and did not stand without, as she did, with a bar across the door.

There was one man whom she several times observed at work very early, and often with a girl of about her own age seated near him. He was a very poor man, who seemed to have no regular employment, but now went roaming about the banks of the river when the tide was low, looking out for bits and scraps in the mud; and now worked at the unpromising little patch of garden-ground before his cottage; and now tinkered up a miserable old boat that belonged to him; or did some job of that kind for a neighbour, as chance occurred. Whatever the man's labour, the girl was never employed; but sat, when she was with him, in a listless, moping state, and idle.

Florence had often wished to speak to this man; yet she had never taken courage to do so, as he made no movement towards her. But one morning when she happened to come upon him suddenly, from a by-path among some pollard willows which terminated in the little shelving[6] piece of stony ground that lay between his dwelling and the water, where he was bending over a fire he had made to caulk[7] the old boat which was lying bottom upwards, close by, he raised his head at the sound of her footstep, and gave her Good morning.

'Good morning,' said Florence, approaching nearer, 'you are at work early.'

'I'd be glad to be often at work earlier, Miss, if I had work to do.'

'Is it so hard to get?' asked Florence.

'*I* find it so,' replied the man.

Florence glanced to where the girl was sitting, drawn together with her elbows on her knees, and her chin on her hands, and said:

'Is that your daughter?'

He raised his head quickly, and looking towards the girl with a brightened face, nodded to her, and said 'Yes.' Florence looked towards her too, and gave her a kind salutation; the girl muttered something in return, ungraciously and sullenly.

'Is she in want of employment also?' said Florence.

The man shook his head. 'No, Miss,' he said. 'I work for both.'

'Are there only you two, then?' inquired Florence.

'Only us two,' said the man. 'Her mother has been dead these ten years. Martha!' (he lifted up his head again, and whistled to her) 'won't you say a word to the pretty young lady?'

The girl made an impatient gesture with her cowering shoulders, and turned her head another way. Ugly, misshapen, peevish, ill-conditioned, ragged, dirty – but beloved! Oh, yes! Florence had seen her father's look towards her, and she knew whose look it had no likeness to.

'I'm afraid she's worse this morning, my poor girl!' said the man, suspending his work, and contemplating his ill-favoured child, with a compassion that was the more tender for being rough.

'She is ill, then!' said Florence.

The man drew a deep sigh. 'I don't believe my Martha's had five short days' good health,' he answered, looking at her still, 'in as many long years.'

'Aye! and more than that, John,' said a neighbour, who had come down to help him with the boat.

'More than that, you say, do you?' cried the other, pushing back his battered hat, and drawing his hand across his forehead. 'Very like. It seems a long, long time.'

'And the more the time,' pursued the neighbour, 'the more you've favoured and humoured her, John, till she's got to be a burden to herself, and everybody else.'

'Not to me,' said her father, falling to his work again. 'Not to me.'

Florence could feel – who better? – how truly he spoke. She drew a little closer to him, and would have been glad to touch his rugged hand, and thank him for his goodness to the miserable object that he looked upon with eyes so different from any other man's.

'Who would favour my poor girl – to call it favouring – if I didn't?' said the father.

'Aye, aye,' cried the neighbour. 'In reason, John. But you! You rob yourself to give to her. You bind yourself hand and foot on her account. You make your life miserable along of her. And what does *she* care! You don't believe she knows it?'

The father lifted up his head again, and whistled to her. Martha made the same impatient gesture with her crouching shoulders, in reply; and he was glad and happy.

'Only for that, Miss,' said the neighbour, with a smile, in which there was more of secret sympathy than he expressed; 'only to get that, he never lets her out of his sight!'

'Because the day'll come, and has been coming a long while,' observed the other, bending low over his work, 'when to get half as much from that unfort'nate child of mine – to get the trembling of a finger, or the waving of a hair – would be to raise the dead.'

Florence softly put some money near his hand on the old boat, and left him.

And now Florence began to think, if she were to fall ill, if she were to fade like her dear brother, would he then know that she had loved him; would she then grow dear to him; would he come to her bedside, when she was weak and dim of sight, and take her into his embrace, and cancel all the past? Would he so forgive her, in that changed condition, for not having been able to lay open her childish heart to him, as to make it easy to relate with what emotions she had gone out of his room that night; what she had meant to say if she had had the courage; and how she had endeavoured, afterwards, to learn the way she never knew in infancy?

Yes, she thought if she were dying, he would relent. She thought, that if she lay, serene and not unwilling to depart, upon the bed that was curtained round with recollections of their darling boy, he would be touched home, and would say, 'Dear Florence, live for me, and we will love each other as we might have done, and be as happy as we might have been these many years!' She thought that if she heard such words from him, and had her arms clasped round him, she could answer with a smile, 'It is too late for anything but this; I never could be happier, dear father!' and so leave him, with a blessing on her lips.

The golden water she remembered on the wall, appeared to Florence, in the light of such reflections, only as a current flowing on to rest, and to a region where the dear ones, gone before, were waiting, hand in hand; and often when she looked upon the darker river rippling at her feet, she thought with awful wonder, but not terror, of that river which her brother had so often said was bearing him away.

The father and his sick daughter were yet fresh in Florence's mind, and, indeed, that incident was not a week old, when Sir Barnet and his lady going out walking in the lanes one afternoon, proposed to her to bear them company. Florence readily consenting, Lady Skettles ordered out young Barnet as a matter of course. For nothing delighted Lady Skettles so much, as beholding her eldest son with Florence on his arm.

Barnet, to say the truth, appeared to entertain an opposite sentiment on the subject, and on such occasions frequently expressed himself audibly, though indefinitely, in reference to 'a parcel of girls.' As it was not easy to ruffle her sweet temper, however, Florence generally reconciled the young gentleman to his fate after a few minutes, and they strolled on amicably: Lady Skettles and Sir Barnet following, in a state of perfect complacency and high gratification.

This was the order of procedure on the afternoon in question: and Florence had almost succeeded in overruling the present objections of Skettles Junior to his destiny, when a gentleman on horseback came riding by, looked at them earnestly as he passed, drew in his rein, wheeled round, and came riding back again, hat in hand.

The gentleman had looked particularly at Florence; and when the little party stopped, on his riding back, he bowed to her, before saluting Sir Barnet and his lady. Florence had no remembrance of having ever seen him, but she started involuntarily when he came near her, and drew back.

Mr Carker introduces himself to Florence and the Skettles family

'My horse is perfectly quiet, I assure you,' said the gentleman.

It was not that, but something in the gentleman himself – Florence could not have said what – that made her recoil as if she had been stung.

'I have the honour to address Miss Dombey, I believe?' said the gentleman, with a most persuasive smile. On Florence inclining her head, he added, 'My name is Carker. I can hardly hope to be remembered by Miss Dombey, except by name. Carker.'

Florence, sensible of a strange inclination to shiver, though the day was hot, presented him to her host and hostess; by whom he was very graciously received.

'I beg pardon,' said Mr Carker, 'a thousand times! But I am going down to-morrow morning to Mr Dombey, at Leamington, and if Miss Dombey can intrust me with any commission, need I say how *very* happy I shall be?'

Sir Barnet immediately divining that Florence would desire to write a letter to her father, proposed to return, and besought Mr Carker to come home and dine in his riding gear. Mr Carker had the misfortune to be engaged to dinner, but if Miss Dombey wished to write, nothing would delight him more than to accompany them back, and to be her faithful slave in waiting as long as she pleased. As he said this with his widest smile, and bent down close to her to pat his horse's neck, Florence meeting his eyes, saw, rather than heard him say, 'There is no news of the ship!'

Confused, frightened, shrinking from him, and not even sure that he had said those words, for he seemed to have shown them to her in some extraordinary manner through his smile, instead of uttering them, Florence faintly said that she was obliged to him, but she would not write; she had nothing to say.

'Nothing to send, Miss Dombey?' said the man of teeth.

'Nothing,' said Florence, 'but my – but my dear love – if you please.'

Disturbed as Florence was, she raised her eyes to his face with an imploring and expressive look, that plainly besought him, if he knew – which he as plainly did – that any message between her and her father was an uncommon charge, but that one most of all, to spare her. Mr Carker smiled and bowed low, and being charged by Sir Barnet with the best compliments of himself and Lady Skettles, took his leave and rode away; leaving a favourable impression upon that worthy couple. Florence was seized with such a shudder as he went, that Sir Barnet, adopting the popular superstition, supposed somebody was passing over her grave.[8] Mr Carker, turning a corner, on the instant, looked back, and bowed, and disappeared, as if he rode off to the churchyard straight, to do it.

CHAPTER 25

Strange News of Uncle Sol

Captain Cuttle, though no sluggard, did not turn out so early on the morning after he had seen Sol Gills, through the shop-window, writing in the parlour, with the Midshipman upon the counter, and Rob the Grinder making up his bed below it, but that the clocks struck six as he raised himself on his elbow, and took a survey of his little chamber. The Captain's eyes must have done severe duty, if he usually opened them as wide on awaking as he did that morning; and were but roughly rewarded for their vigilance, if he generally rubbed them half as hard. But the occasion was no common one, for Rob the Grinder had certainly never stood in the doorway of Captain Cuttle's bedroom before, and in it he stood then, panting at the Captain, with a flushed and touzled air of bed about him, that greatly heightened both his colour and expression.

'Holloa!' roared the Captain. 'What's the matter?'

Before Rob could stammer a word in answer, Captain Cuttle turned out, all in a heap, and covered the boy's mouth with his hand.

'Steady, my lad,' said the Captain, 'don't ye speak a word to me as yet!'

The Captain, looking at his visitor in great consternation, gently shouldered him into the next room, after laying this injunction upon him; and disappearing for a few moments, forthwith returned in the blue suit. Holding up his hand in token of the injunction not yet being taken off, Captain Cuttle walked up to the cupboard, and poured himself out a dram; a counterpart of which he handed to the messenger. The Captain then stood himself up in a corner, against the wall, as if to forestall the possibility of being knocked backwards by the communication that was to be made to him; and having swallowed his liquor, with his eyes fixed on the messenger, and his face as pale as his face could be, requested him to 'heave ahead.'

'Do you mean, tell you, Captain?' asked Rob, who had been greatly impressed by these precautions.

'Aye!' said the Captain.

'Well, Sir,' said Rob, 'I ain't got much to tell. But look here!'

Rob produced a bundle of keys. The Captain surveyed them, remained in his corner, and surveyed the messenger.

'And look here!' pursued Rob.

The boy produced a sealed packet, which Captain Cuttle stared at as he had stared at the keys.

'When I woke this morning, Captain,' said Rob, 'which was about a quarter after five, I found these on my pillow. The shop-door was unbolted and unlocked, and Mr Gills gone.'

'Gone!' roared the Captain.

'Flowed,[1] Sir,' returned Rob.

The Captain's voice was so tremendous, and he came out of his corner with such way on him, that Rob retreated before him into another corner: holding out the keys and packet, to prevent himself from being run down.

'"For Captain Cuttle," Sir,' cried Rob, 'is on the keys, and on the packet too. Upon my word and honour, Captain Cuttle, I don't know anything more about it. I wish I may die if I do! Here's a sitiwation for a lad that's just got a sitiwation,' cried the unfortunate Grinder, screwing his cuff into his face: 'his master bolted with his place, and him blamed for it!'

These lamentations had reference to Captain Cuttle's gaze, or rather glare, which was full of vague suspicions, threatenings, and denunciations. Taking the proffered packet from his hand, the Captain opened it and read as follows: –

'My dear Ned Cuttle. Enclosed is my will!' The Captain turned it over, with a doubtful look – 'and Testament.[2] – Where's the Testament?' said the Captain, instantly impeaching the ill-fated Grinder. 'What have you done with that, my lad?'

'*I* never see it,' whimpered Rob. 'Don't keep on suspecting an innocent lad, Captain. *I* never touched the Testament.'

Captain Cuttle shook his head, implying that somebody must be made answerable for it; and gravely proceeded: –

'Which don't break open for a year, or until you have decisive intelligence of my dear Walter, who is dear to you, Ned, too, I am sure.' The Captain paused and shook his head in some emotion; then, as a re-establishment of his dignity in this trying position, looked with exceeding sternness at the Grinder. 'If you should never hear of me, or see me more, Ned, remember an old friend as he will remember you to the last – kindly; and at least until the period I have mentioned has expired, keep a home in the old place for

Walter. There are no debts, the loan from Dombey's house is paid off, and all my keys I send with this. Keep this quiet, and make no inquiry for me; it is useless. So no more, dear Ned, from your true friend, Solomon Gills.' The Captain took a long breath, and then read these words, written below: '"The boy Rob, well recommended, as I told you, from Dombey's house. If all else should come to the hammer, take care, Ned, of the little Midshipman."'

To convey to posterity any idea of the manner in which the Captain, after turning this letter over and over, and reading it a score of times, sat down in his chair, and held a court-martial on the subject in his own mind, would require the united genius of all the great men, who, discarding their own untoward days, have determined to go down to posterity, and have never got there. At first the Captain was too much confounded and distressed to think of anything but the letter itself; and even when his thoughts began to glance upon the various attendant facts, they might, perhaps, as well have occupied themselves with their former theme, for any light reflected on them. In this state of mind, Captain Cuttle having the Grinder before the court, and no one else, found it a great relief to decide, generally, that he was an object of suspicion: which the Captain so clearly expressed in his visage, that Rob remonstrated.

'Oh, don't, Captain!' cried the Grinder. 'I wonder how you can! what have I done to be looked at, like that?'

'My lad,' said Captain Cuttle, 'don't you sing out afore you're hurt. And don't you commit yourself, whatever you do.'

'I haven't been and committed nothing, Captain!' answered Rob.

'Keep her free, then,' said the Captain, impressively, 'and ride easy.'

With a deep sense of the responsibility imposed upon him, and the necessity of thoroughly fathoming this mysterious affair, as became a man in his relations with the parties, Captain Cuttle resolved to go down and examine the premises, and to keep the Grinder with him. Considering that youth as under arrest at present, the Captain was in some doubt whether it might not be expedient to handcuff him, or tie his ankles together, or attach a weight to his legs; but not being clear as to the legality of such formalities, the Captain decided merely to hold him by the shoulder all the way, and knock him down if he made any objection.

However, he made none, and consequently got to the Instrument-maker's house without being placed under any more stringent restraint. As the shutters were not yet taken down, the Captain's first care was to have the shop opened; and when the daylight was freely admitted, he proceeded, with its aid, to further investigation.

The Captain's first care was to establish himself in a chair in the shop, as President of the solemn tribunal that was sitting within him; and to require Rob to lie down in his bed under the counter, show exactly where he discovered the keys and packet when he awoke, how he found the door when he went to try it, how he started off to Brig Place – cautiously preventing the latter imitation from being carried farther than the threshold – and so on to the end of the chapter. When all this had been done several times, the Captain shook his head and seemed to think the matter had a bad look.

Next, the Captain, with some indistinct idea of finding a body, instituted a strict search over the whole house; groping in the cellars with a lighted candle, thrusting his hook behind doors, bringing his head into violent contact with beams, and covering himself with cobwebs. Mounting up to the old man's bedroom, they found that he had not been in bed on the previous night, but had merely lain down on the coverlet, as was evident from the impression yet remaining there.

'And *I* think, Captain,' said Rob, looking round the room, 'that when Mr Gills was going in and out so often, these last few days, he was taking little things away, piecemeal, not to attract attention.'

'Aye!' said the Captain, mysteriously. 'Why so, my lad?'

'Why,' returned Rob, looking about, 'I don't see his shaving tackle. Nor his brushes, Captain. Nor no shirts. Nor yet his shoes.'

As each of these articles was mentioned, Captain Cuttle took particular notice of the corresponding department of the Grinder, lest he should appear to have been in recent use, or should prove to be in present possession thereof. But Rob had no occasion to shave, certainly was not brushed, and wore the clothes he had worn for a long time past, beyond all possibility of mistake.

'And what should you say,' said the Captain – 'not committing yourself – about his time of sheering off? Hey?'

'Why, I think, Captain,' returned Rob, 'that he must have gone pretty soon after I began to snore.'

'What o'clock was that?' said the Captain, prepared to be very particular about the exact time.

'How can I tell, Captain!' answered Rob. 'I only know that I'm a heavy sleeper at first, and a light one towards morning; and if Mr Gills had come through the shop near daybreak, though ever so much on tip-toe, I'm pretty sure I should have heard him shut the door at all events.'

On mature consideration of this evidence, Captain Cuttle began to think that the Instrument-maker must have vanished of his own accord; to which logical conclusion he was assisted by the letter addressed to himself, which, as being unquestionably in the old man's handwriting, would seem, with no great forcing, to bear the construction, that he arranged of his own will, to go, and so went. The Captain had next to consider where and why? and as there was no way whatsoever that he saw to the solution of the first difficulty, he confined his meditations to the second.

Remembering the old man's curious manner, and the farewell he had taken of him; unaccountably fervent at the time, but quite intelligible now; a terrible apprehension strengthened on the Captain, that, overpowered by his anxieties and regrets for Walter, he had been driven to commit suicide. Unequal to the wear and tear of daily life, as he had often professed himself to be, and shaken as he no doubt was by the uncertainty and deferred hope he had undergone, it seemed no violently strained misgiving, but only too probable.

Free from debt, and with no fear for his personal liberty, or the seizure of his goods, what else but such a state of madness could have hurried him away alone and secretly? As to his carrying some apparel with him, if he had really done so – and they were not even sure of that – he might have done so, the Captain argued, to prevent inquiry, to distract attention from his probable fate, or to ease the very mind that was now revolving all these possibilities. Such, reduced into plain language, and condensed within a small compass, was the final result and substance of Captain Cuttle's deliberations; which took a long time to arrive at this pass, and were, like some more public deliberations, very discursive and disorderly.

Dejected and despondent in the extreme, Captain Cuttle felt it just to release Rob from the arrest in which he had placed him, and to enlarge him, subject to a kind of honourable inspection which he still resolved to exercise; and having hired a man, from Brogley the Broker, to sit in the shop during their absence, the Captain, taking Rob with him, issued forth upon a dismal quest after the mortal remains of Solomon Gills.

Not a station-house or bone-house, or work-house in the metropolis escaped a visitation from the hard glazed hat. Along the wharves, among the shipping on the bank-side, up the river, down the river, here, there, everywhere, it went gleaming where men were thickest, like the hero's helmet in an epic battle. For a whole week the Captain read of all the found and missing people in all the newspapers and hand-bills,[4] and went forth on expeditions at all hours of the day to identify Solomon Gills, in poor little ship-boys who had fallen overboard, and in tall foreigners with dark beards who had taken poison – 'to make sure,' Captain Cuttle said, 'that it warn't him.' It is a sure thing that it never was, and that the good Captain had no other satisfaction.

Captain Cuttle at last abandoned these attempts as hopeless, and set himself to consider what was to be done next. After several new perusals of his poor friend's letter, he considered that the maintenance of 'a home in the old place for Walter' was the primary duty imposed upon him. Therefore, the Captain's decision was, that he would keep house on the premises of Solomon Gills himself, and would go into the instrument-business, and see what came of it.

But as this step involved the relinquishment of his apartments at Mrs MacStinger's, and he knew that resolute woman would never hear of his deserting them, the Captain took the desperate determination of running away.

'Now, look ye here, my lad,' said the Captain to Rob, when he had matured this notable scheme, 'to-morrow, I shan't be found in this here roadstead[5] till night – not till arter midnight p'rhaps. But you keep watch till you hear me knock, and the moment you do, turn-to, and open the door.'

'Very good, Captain,' said Rob.

'You'll continue to be rated on these here books,' pursued the Captain condescendingly, 'and I don't say but what you may get promotion, if you and me should pull together with a will. But the moment you hear me knock to-morrow night, whatever time it is, turn-to and show yourself smart with the door.'

'I'll be sure to do it, Captain,' replied Rob.

'Because you understand,' resumed the Captain, coming back again to enforce this charge upon his mind, 'there may be, for anything I can say, a chase; and I might be took while I was waiting, if you didn't show yourself smart with the door.'

Rob again assured the Captain that he would be prompt and wakeful; and the Captain having made this prudent arrangement, went home to Mrs MacStinger's for the last time.

The sense the Captain had of its being the last time, and of the awful purpose hidden beneath his blue waistcoat, inspired him with such a mortal dread of Mrs MacStinger, that the sound of that lady's foot downstairs at any time of the day, was sufficient to throw him into a fit of trembling. It fell out, too, that Mrs MacStinger was in a charming temper – mild and placid as a house-lamb; and Captain Cuttle's conscience suffered terrible twinges, when she came up to inquire if she could cook him nothing for his dinner.

'A nice small kidney-pudding now, Cap'en Cuttle,' said his landlady: 'or a sheep's heart. Don't mind my trouble.'

'No thank'ee, ma'am,' returned the Captain.

'Have a roast fowl,' said Mrs MacStinger, 'with a bit of weal stuffing and some egg sauce. Come, Cap'en Cuttle! Give yourself a little treat!'

'No thank'ee, ma'am,' returned the Captain very humbly.

'I'm sure you're out of sorts, and want to be stimulated,' said Mrs MacStinger. 'Why not have, for once in a way, a bottle of sherry wine?'

'Well, ma'am,' rejoined the Captain, 'if you'd be so good as take a glass or two, I think I would try that. Would you do me the favour, ma'am,' said the Captain, torn to pieces by his conscience, 'to accept a quarter's rent ahead?'

'And why so, Cap'en Cuttle?' retorted Mrs MacStinger – sharply, as the Captain thought.

The Captain was frightened to death. 'If you would, ma'am,' he said with submission, 'it would oblige me. I can't keep my money very well. It pays itself out. I should take it kind if you'd comply.'

'Well, Cap'en Cuttle,' said the unconscious MacStinger, rubbing her hands, 'you can do as you please. It's not for me, with my family, to refuse, no more than it is to ask.'

'And would you, ma'am,' said the Captain, taking down the tin canister in which he kept his cash, from the top shelf of the cupboard, 'be so good as offer eighteen-pence a-piece to the little family all round? If you could make it convenient, ma'am, to pass the word presently for them children to come for'ard, in a body, I should be glad to see 'em.'

These innocent MacStingers were so many daggers to the Captain's breast, when they appeared in a swarm, and tore at him with the confiding trustfulness he so little deserved. The eye of Alexander MacStinger, who had been his favourite, was insupportable to the Captain; the voice of Juliana MacStinger, who was the picture of her mother, made a coward of him.

Captain Cuttle kept up appearances, nevertheless, tolerably well, and for an hour or two was very hardly used and roughly handled by the young MacStingers: who in their childish frolics, did a little damage also to the glazed hat, by sitting in it, two at a time, as in a nest, and drumming on the inside of the crown with their shoes. At length the Captain sorrowfully dismissed them: taking leave of these cherubs with the poignant remorse and grief of a man who was going to execution.

In the silence of night, the Captain packed up his heavier property in a chest, which he locked, intending to leave it there in all probability for ever, but on the forlorn chance of one day finding a man sufficiently bold and desperate to come and ask for it. Of his lighter necessaries, the Captain made a bundle; and disposed his plate about his person, ready for flight. At the hour of midnight, when Brig Place was buried in slumber and Mrs MacStinger was lulled in sweet oblivion, with her infants around her, the guilty Captain, stealing down on tiptoe, in the dark, opened the door, closed it softly after him, and took to his heels.

Pursued by the image of Mrs MacStinger springing out of bed, and, regardless of costume, following and bringing him back; pursued also by a consciousness of his enormous crime; Captain Cuttle held on at a great pace, and allowed no grass to grow under his feet, between Brig Place and the Instrument-maker's door. It opened when he knocked – for Rob was on the watch – and when it was bolted and locked behind him, Captain Cuttle felt comparatively safe.

'Whew!' cried the Captain, looking round him. 'It's a breather!'⁶

'Nothing the matter, is there, Captain?' cried the gaping Rob.

'No, no!' said Captain Cuttle, after changing colour, and listening to a passing footstep in the street. 'But mind ye, my lad; if any lady, except either of them two as you see t'other day, ever comes and asks for Cap'en Cuttle, be sure to report no person of that name known, nor never heard of here; observe them orders, will you?'

'I'll take care, Captain,' returned Rob.

'You might say – if you liked,' hesitated the Captain, 'that you'd read in the paper that a Cap'en of that name was gone to Australia, emigrating, along with a whole ship's complement of people as had all swore never to come back no more.'

Rob nodded his understanding of these instructions; and Captain Cuttle promising to make a man of him, if he obeyed orders, dismissed him, yawning, to his bed under the counter, and went aloft to the chamber of Solomon Gills.

What the Captain suffered next day, whenever a bonnet passed, or how often he darted out of the shop to elude imaginary MacStingers, and sought safety in the attic, cannot be told. But to avoid the fatigues attendant on this means of self-preservation, the Captain curtained the glass door of communication between the shop and parlour, on the inside, fitted a key to it from the bunch that had been sent to him: and cut a small hole of espial in the wall. The advantage of this fortification is obvious. On a bonnet appearing, the Captain instantly slipped into his garrison, locked himself up, and took a secret observation of the enemy. Finding it a false alarm, the Captain instantly slipped out again. And the bonnets in the street were so very numerous, and alarms were so inseparable from their appearance, that the Captain was almost incessantly slipping in and out all day long.

Captain Cuttle found time, however, in the midst of this fatiguing service to inspect the stock; in connexion with which he had the general idea (very laborious to Rob) that too much friction could not be bestowed upon it, and that it could not be made too bright. He also ticketed a few attractive-looking articles at a venture, at prices ranging from ten shillings to fifty pounds, and exposed them in the window to the great astonishment of the public.

After effecting these improvements, Captain Cuttle, surrounded by the instruments, began to feel scientific: and looked up at the stars at night, through the skylight, when he was smoking his pipe in the little back parlour before going to bed, as if he had established a kind of property in them. As a tradesman in the City, too, he began to have an interest in the Lord Mayor, and the Sheriffs, and in Public Companies; and felt bound to read the quotations of the Funds[7] every day, though he was unable to make out, on any principle of navigation, what the figures meant, and could have very well dispensed with the fractions. Florence, the Captain waited on, with his strange news of Uncle Sol, immediately after taking possession of the Midshipman; but she was away from home. So the Captain sat himself down in his altered station of life, with no company but Rob the Grinder; and losing count of time, as men do when great changes come upon them, thought musingly of Walter, and of Solomon Gills, and even of Mrs MacStinger herself, as among the things that had been.

CHAPTER 26

Shadows of the Past and Future

'Your most obedient, Sir,' said the Major. 'Damme, Sir, a friend of my friend Dombey's is a friend of mine, and I'm glad to see you!'

'I am infinitely obliged, Carker,' explained Mr Dombey, 'to Major Bagstock, for his company and conversation. Major Bagstock has rendered me great service, Carker.'

Mr Carker the Manager, hat in hand, just arrived at Leamington, and just introduced to the Major, showed the Major his whole double range of teeth, and trusted he might take the liberty of thanking him with all his heart for having effected so great an improvement in Mr Dombey's looks and spirits.

'By Gad, Sir,' said the Major, in reply, 'there are no thanks due to me, for it's a give and take affair. A great creature like our friend Dombey, Sir,' said the Major, lowering his voice, but not lowering it so much as to render it inaudible to that gentleman, 'cannot help improving and exalting his friends. He strengthens and invigorates a man, Sir, does Dombey, in his moral nature.'

Mr Carker snapped at the expression. In his moral nature. Exactly. The very words he had been on the point of suggesting.

'But when my friend Dombey, Sir,' added the Major, 'talks to you of Major Bagstock, I must crave leave to set him and you right. He means plain Joe, Sir – Joey B. – Josh. Bagstock – Joseph – rough and tough Old J., Sir. At your service.'

Mr Carker's excessively friendly inclinations towards the Major, and Mr Carker's admiration of his roughness, toughness, and plainness, gleamed out of every tooth in Mr Carker's head.

'And now, Sir,' said the Major, 'you and Dombey have the devil's own amount of business to talk over.'

'By no means, Major,' observed Mr Dombey.

'Dombey,' said the Major, defiantly, 'I know better; a man of your mark – the Colossus[1] of commerce – is not to be interrupted. Your moments are precious. We shall meet at dinner-time. In the interval, old Joseph will be scarce. The dinner-hour is a sharp seven, Mr Carker.'

With that, the Major, greatly swollen as to his face, withdrew; but immediately putting in his head at the door again, said:

'I beg your pardon. Dombey, have you any message to 'em?'

Mr Dombey in some embarrassment, and not without a glance at

the courteous keeper of his business confidence, intrusted the Major
with his compliments.

'By the Lord, Sir,' said the Major, 'you must make it something
warmer than that, or old Joe will be far from welcome.'

'Regards then, if you will, Major,' returned Mr Dombey.

'Damme, Sir,' said the Major, shaking his shoulders and his great
cheeks jocularly: 'make it something warmer than that.'

'What you please, then, Major,' observed Mr Dombey.

'Our friend is sly, Sir, sly, Sir, de-vilish sly,' said the Major,
staring round the door at Carker. 'So is Bagstock.' But stopping in
the midst of a chuckle, and drawing himself up to his full height,
the Major solemnly exclaimed, as he struck himself on the chest,
'Dombey! I envy your feelings. God bless you!' and withdrew.

'You must have found the gentleman a great resource,' said
Carker, following him with his teeth.

'Very great indeed,' said Mr Dombey.

'He has friends here, no doubt,' pursued Carker. 'I perceive from
what he has said, that you go into society here. Do you know,'
smiling horribly, 'I am so very glad that you go into society!'

Mr Dombey acknowledged this display of interest on the part of
his second in command, by twirling his watch-chain, and slightly
moving his head.

'You were formed for society,' said Carker. 'Of all the men I
know, you are the best adapted, by nature and by position, for
society. Do you know I have been frequently amazed that you
should have held it at arm's length so long!'

'I have had my reasons, Carker. I have been alone, and indifferent
to it. But you have great social qualifications yourself, and are the
more likely to have been surprised.'

'Oh! I!' returned the other, with ready self-disparagement. 'It's
quite another matter in the case of a man like me. I don't come into
comparison with you.'

Mr Dombey put his hand to his neckcloth, settled his chin in it,
coughed, and stood looking at his faithful friend and servant for a
few moments in silence.

'I shall have the pleasure, Carker,' said Mr Dombey at length:
making as if he swallowed something a little too large for his throat:
'to present you to my – to the Major's friends. Highly agreeable
people.'

'Ladies among them, I presume?' insinuated the smooth Manager.

'They are all – that is to say, they are both – ladies,' replied Mr
Dombey.

'Only two?' smiled Carker.

'They are only two. I have confined my visits to their residence, and have made no other acquaintance here.'

'Sisters, perhaps?' quoth Carker.

'Mother and daughter,' replied Mr Dombey.

As Mr Dombey dropped his eyes, and adjusted his neckcloth again, the smiling face of Mr Carker the Manager became in a moment, and without any stage of transition, transformed into a most intent and frowning face, scanning his closely, and with an ugly sneer. As Mr Dombey raised his eyes, it changed back, no less quickly, to its old expression, and showed him every gum of which it stood possessed.

'You are very kind,' said Carker, 'I shall be delighted to know them. Speaking of daughters, I have seen Miss Dombey.'

There was a sudden rush of blood to Mr Dombey's face.

'I took the liberty of waiting on her,' said Carker, 'to inquire if she could charge me with any little commission. I am not so fortunate as to be the bearer of any but her – but her dear love.'

Wolf's face that it was then, with even the hot tongue revealing itself through the stretched mouth, as the eyes encountered Mr Dombey's!

'What business intelligence is there?' inquired the latter gentleman, after a silence, during which Mr Carker had produced some memoranda and other papers.

'There is very little,' returned Carker. 'Upon the whole we have not had our usual good fortune of late, but that is of little moment to you. At Lloyd's,[2] they give up the Son and Heir for lost. Well, she was insured, from her keel to her masthead.'

'Carker,' said Mr Dombey, taking a chair near him, 'I cannot say that young man, Gay, ever impressed me favourably—'

'Nor me,' interposed the Manager.

'But I wish,' said Mr Dombey, without heeding the interruption, 'he had never gone on board that ship. I wish he had never been sent out.'

'It is a pity you didn't say so, in good time, is it not?' retorted Carker, coolly. 'However. I think it's all for the best. I really think it's all for the best. Did I mention that there was something like a little confidence between Miss Dombey and myself?'

'No,' said Mr Dombey, sternly.

'I have no doubt,' returned Mr Carker, after an impressive pause, 'that wherever Gay is, he is much better where he is, than at home here. If I were, or could be, in your place, I should be satisfied of that. I am quite satisfied of it myself. Miss Dombey is confiding and young – perhaps hardly proud enough, for your daughter – if she have a fault. Not that that is much though, I am sure. Will you check these balances with me?'

Mr Dombey leaned back in his chair, instead of bending over the papers that were laid before him, and looked the Manager steadily in the face. The Manager, with his eyelids slightly raised, affected to be glancing at his figures, and to await the leisure of his principal. He showed that he affected this, as if from great delicacy, and with a design to spare Mr Dombey's feelings; and the latter, as he looked at him, was cognizant of his intended consideration, and felt that but for it, this confidential Carker would have said a great deal more, which he, Mr Dombey, was too proud to ask for. It was his way in business, often. Little by little, Mr Dombey's gaze relaxed, and his attention became diverted to the papers before him; but while busy with the occupation they afforded him, he frequently stopped, and looked at Mr Carker again. Whenever he did so, Mr Carker was demonstrative, as before, in his delicacy, and impressed it on his great chief more and more.

While they were thus engaged; and under the skilful culture of the Manager, angry thoughts in reference to poor Florence brooded and bred in Mr Dombey's breast, usurping the place of the cold dislike that generally reigned there; Major Bagstock, much admired by the old ladies of Leamington, and followed by the Native, carrying the usual amount of light baggage, straddled[3] along the shady side of the way, to make a morning call on Mrs Skewton. It being mid-day when the Major reached the bower of Cleopatra, he had the good fortune to find his Princess on her usual sofa, languishing over a cup of coffee, with the room so darkened and shaded for her more luxurious repose, that Withers, who was in attendance on her, loomed like a phantom page.

'What insupportable creature is this, coming in?' said Mrs Skewton. 'I cannot bear it. Go away, whoever you are!'

'You have not the heart to banish J. B., ma'am!' said the Major, halting midway, to remonstrate, with his cane over his shoulder.

'Oh it's you, is it? On second thoughts, you may enter,' observed Cleopatra.

The Major entered accordingly, and advancing to the sofa pressed her charming hand to his lips.

'Sit down,' said Cleopatra, listlessly waving her fan, 'a long way off. Don't come too near me, for I am frightfully faint and sensitive this morning, and you smell of the Sun. You are absolutely tropical.'

'By George, ma'am,' said the Major, 'the time has been when Joseph Bagstock has been grilled and blistered by the Sun; the time was, when he was forced, ma'am, into such full blow, by high hothouse heat in the West Indies, that he was known as the Flower. A man never heard of Bagstock, ma'am, in those days; he heard of the Flower – the Flower of Ours. The Flower may have faded, more or less, ma'am,' observed the Major, dropping into a much nearer chair than had been indicated by his cruel Divinity, 'but it is a tough plant yet, and constant as the evergreen.'

Here the Major, under cover of the dark room, shut up one eye, rolled his head like a Harlequin, and, in his great self-satisfaction, perhaps went nearer to the confines of apoplexy than he had ever gone before.

'Where is Mrs Granger?' inquired Cleopatra of her page.

Withers believed she was in her own room.

'Very well,' said Mrs Skewton. 'Go away, and shut the door. I am engaged.'

As Withers disappeared, Mrs Skewton turned her head languidly towards the Major, without otherwise moving, and asked him how his friend was?

'Dombey, ma'am,' returned the Major, with a facetious gurgling in his throat, 'is as well as a man in his condition *can* be. His condition is a desperate one, ma'am. He is touched, is Dombey! Touched!' cried the Major. 'He is bayonetted through the body.'

Cleopatra cast a sharp look at the Major, that contrasted forcibly with the affected drawl in which she presently said—

'Major Bagstock, although I know but little of the world, – nor can I really regret my inexperience, for I fear it is a false place, full of withering conventionalities: where Nature is but little regarded, and where the music of the heart, and the gushing of the soul and all that sort of thing, which is so truly poetical, is seldom heard, – I cannot misunderstand your meaning. There is an allusion to Edith – to my extremely dear child,' said Mrs Skewton, tracing the outline of her eyebrows with her forefinger, 'in your words, to which the tenderest of chords vibrates excessively!'

'Bluntness, ma'am,' returned the Major, 'has ever been the characteristic of the Bagstock breed. You are right. Joe admits it.'

'And that allusion,' pursued Cleopatra, 'would involve one of the most – if not positively *the* most – touching, and thrilling, and sacred emotions of which our sadly-fallen nature is susceptible, I conceive.'

The Major laid his hand upon his lips, and wafted a kiss to
Cleopatra, as if to identify the emotion in question.

'I feel that I am weak. I feel that I am wanting in that energy,
which should sustain a mama: not to say a parent: on such a
subject,' said Mrs Skewton, trimming her lips with the laced edge
of her pocket-handkerchief; 'but I can hardly approach a topic so
excessively momentous to my dearest Edith without a feeling of
faintness. Nevertheless, bad man, as you have boldly remarked
upon it, and as it has occasioned me great anguish:' Mrs Skewton
touched her left side with her fan: 'I will not shrink from my duty.'

The Major, under cover of the dimness, swelled, and swelled, and
rolled his purple face about, and winked his lobster eye, until he fell
into a fit of wheezing, which obliged him to rise and take a turn or
two about the room, before his fair friend could proceed.

'Mr Dombey,' said Mrs Skewton, when she at length resumed,
'was obliging enough, now many weeks ago, to do us the honour
of visiting us here; in company, my dear Major, with yourself. I
acknowledge – let me be open – that it is my failing to be the
creature of impulse, and to wear my heart, as it were, outside. I
know my failing full well. My enemy cannot know it better. But I
am not penitent; I would rather not be frozen by the heartless
world, and am content to bear this imputation justly.'

Mrs Skewton arranged her tucker, pinched her wiry throat to
give it a soft surface, and went on, with great complacency.

'It gave me (my dearest Edith too, I am sure) infinite pleasure to
receive Mr Dombey. As a friend of yours, my dear Major, we were
naturally disposed to be prepossessed in his favour; and I fancied
that I observed an amount of Heart in Mr Dombey, that was
excessively refreshing.'

'There is devilish little heart in Dombey now, ma'am,' said the
Major.

'Wretched man!' cried Mrs Skewton, looking at him languidly,
'pray be silent.'

'J. B. is dumb, ma'am,' said the Major.

'Mr Dombey,' pursued Cleopatra, smoothing the rosy hue upon
her cheeks, 'accordingly repeated his visit; and possibly finding
some attraction in the simplicity and primitiveness of our tastes –
for there is always a charm in nature – it is so very sweet – became
one of our little circle every evening. Little did I think of the awful
responsibility into which I plunged when I encouraged Mr Dombey
– to –'

'To beat up these quarters, ma'am,' suggested Major Bagstock.

'Coarse person!' said Mrs Skewton, 'you anticipate my meaning, though in odious language.'

Here Mrs Skewton rested her elbow on the little table at her side, and suffering her wrist to droop in what she considered a graceful and becoming manner, dangled her fan to and fro, and lazily admired her hand while speaking.

'The agony I have endured,' she said mincingly, 'as the truth has by degrees dawned upon me, has been too exceedingly terrific to dilate upon. My whole existence is bound up in my sweetest Edith; and to see her change from day to day – my beautiful pet, who has positively garnered up her heart[4] since the death of that most delightful creature, Granger – is the most affecting thing in the world.'

Mrs Skewton's world was not a very trying one if one might judge of it by the influence of its most affecting circumstance upon her; but this by the way.

'Edith,' simpered Mrs Skewton, 'who is the perfect pearl of my life, is said to resemble me. I believe we *are* alike.'

'There is one man in the world who will never admit that any one resembles you, ma'am,' said the Major: 'and that man's name is Old Joe Bagstock.'

Cleopatra made as if she would brain the flatterer with her fan, but relenting, smiled upon him and proceeded:

'If my charming girl inherits any advantages from me, wicked one!': the Major was the wicked one: 'she inherits also my foolish nature. She has great force of character – mine has been said to be immense, though I don't believe it – but once moved, she is susceptible and sensitive to the last extent. What are my feelings when I see her pining! They destroy me.'

The Major advancing his double chin, and pursing up his blue lips into a soothing expression, affected the profoundest sympathy.

'The confidence,' said Mrs Skewton, 'that has subsisted between us – the free development of soul, and openness of sentiment – is touching to think of. We have been more like sisters than mama and child.'

'J. B.'s own sentiment,' observed the Major, 'expressed by J. B. fifty thousand times!'

'Do not interrupt, rude man!' said Cleopatra. 'What are my feelings, then, when I find that there is one subject avoided by us! That there is a what's-his-name – a gulf – opened between us. That my own artless Edith is changed to me! They are of the most poignant description, of course.'

The Major left his chair, and took one nearer to the little table.

'From day to day I see this, my dear Major,' proceeded Mrs Skewton. 'From day to day I feel this. From hour to hour I reproach myself for that excess of faith and trustfulness which has led to such distressing consequences; and almost from minute to minute, I hope that Mr Dombey may explain himself, and relieve the torture I undergo, which is extremely wearing. But nothing happens, my dear Major; I am the slave of remorse – take care of the coffee-cup: you are so very awkward – my darling Edith is an altered being; and I really don't see what is to be done, or what good creature I can advise with.'

Major Bagstock, encouraged perhaps by the softened and confidential tone into which Mrs Skewton, after several times lapsing into it for a moment, seemed now to have subsided for good, stretched out his hand across the little table, and said with a leer,

'Advise with Joe, ma'am.'

'Then, you aggravating monster,' said Cleopatra, giving one hand to the Major, and tapping his knuckles with her fan, which she held in the other: 'why don't you talk to me? you know what I mean. Why don't you tell me something to the purpose?'

The Major laughed, and kissed the hand she had bestowed upon him, and laughed again immensely.

'Is there as much Heart in Mr Dombey as I gave him credit for?' languished Cleopatra tenderly. 'Do you think he is in earnest, my dear Major? Would you recommend his being spoken to, or his being left alone? Now tell me, like a dear man, what would you advise.'

'Shall we marry him to Edith Granger, ma'am?' chuckled the Major, hoarsely.

'Mysterious creature!' returned Cleopatra, bringing her fan to bear upon the Major's nose. 'How can *we* marry him?'

'Shall we marry him to Edith Granger, ma'am, I say?' chuckled the Major again.

Mrs Skewton returned no answer in words, but smiled upon the Major with so much archness and vivacity, that that gallant officer considering himself challenged, would have imprinted a kiss on her exceedingly red lips, but for her interposing the fan with a very winning and juvenile dexterity. It might have been in modesty; it might have been in apprehension of some danger to their bloom.

'Dombey, ma'am,' said the Major, 'is a great catch.'

'Oh, mercenary wretch!' cried Cleopatra, with a little shriek, 'I am shocked.'

'And Dombey, ma'am,' pursued the Major, thrusting forward his head, and distending his eyes, 'is in earnest. Joseph says it; Bagstock knows it; J. B. keeps him to the mark. Leave Dombey to himself, ma'am. Dombey is safe, ma'am. Do as you have done; do no more; and trust to J. B. for the end.'

'You really think so, my dear Major?' returned Cleopatra, who had eyed him very cautiously, and very searchingly, in spite of her listless bearing.

'Sure of it, ma'am,' rejoined the Major. 'Cleopatra the peerless, and her Antony[5] Bagstock, will often speak of this, triumphantly, when sharing the elegance and wealth of Edith Dombey's establishment. Dombey's right-hand man, ma'am,' said the Major, stopping abruptly in a chuckle, and becoming serious, 'has arrived.'

'This morning?' said Cleopatra.

'This morning, ma'am,' returned the Major. 'And Dombey's anxiety for his arrival, ma'am, is to be referred – take J. B.'s word for this; for Joe is de-vilish sly' – the Major tapped his nose, and screwed up one of his eyes tight: which did not enhance his native beauty – 'to his desire that what is in the wind should become known to him, without Dombey's telling and consulting him. For Dombey is as proud, ma'am,' said the Major, 'as Lucifer.'[6]

'A charming quality,' lisped Mrs Skewton; 'reminding one of dearest Edith.'

'Well, ma'am,' said the Major. 'I have thrown out hints already, and the right-hand man understands 'em; and I'll throw out more, before the day is done. Dombey projected this morning a ride to Warwick Castle, and to Kenilworth, to-morrow, to be preceded by a breakfast with us. I undertook the delivery of this invitation. Will you honour us so far, ma'am?' said the Major, swelling with shortness of breath and slyness, as he produced a note, addressed to the Honourable Mrs Skewton, by favour of Major Bagstock, wherein hers ever faithfully, Paul Dombey, besought her and her amiable and accomplished daughter to consent to the proposed excursion; and in a postscript unto which, the same ever faithfully Paul Dombey entreated to be recalled to the remembrance of Mrs Granger.

'Hush!' said Cleopatra, suddenly, 'Edith!'

The loving mother can scarcely be described as resuming her insipid and affected air when she made this exclamation; for she had never cast it off; nor was it likely that she ever would or could, in any other place than in the grave. But hurriedly dismissing whatever shadow of earnestness, or faint confession of a purpose, laudable or wicked, that her face, or voice, or manner, had, for the moment, betrayed, she lounged upon the couch, her most insipid and most languid self again, as Edith entered the room.

Edith, so beautiful and stately, but so cold and so repelling. Who, slightly acknowledging the presence of Major Bagstock, and directing a keen glance at her mother, drew back the curtain from a window, and sat down there, looking out.

'My dearest Edith,' said Mrs Skewton, 'where on earth have you been? I have wanted you, my love, most sadly.'

'You said you were engaged, and I stayed away,' she answered, without turning her head.

'It was cruel to Old Joe, ma'am,' said the Major in his gallantry.

'It was very cruel, I know,' she said, still looking out – and said with such calm disdain, that the Major was discomfited, and could think of nothing in reply.

'Major Bagstock, my darling Edith,' drawled her mother, 'who is generally the most useless and disagreeable creature in the world; as you know—'

'It is surely not worth while, mama,' said Edith, looking round, 'to observe these forms of speech. We are quite alone. We know each other.'

The quiet scorn that sat upon her handsome face – a scorn that evidently lighted on herself, no less than them – was so intense and deep, that her mother's simper, for the instant, though of a hardy constitution, drooped before it.

'My darling girl,' she began again.

'Not woman yet?' said Edith, with a smile.

'How very odd you are to-day, my dear! Pray let me say, my love, that Major Bagstock has brought the kindest of notes from Mr Dombey, proposing that we should breakfast with him to-morrow, and ride to Warwick and Kenilworth. Will you go, Edith?'

'Will I go!' she repeated, turning very red, and breathing quickly as she looked round at her mother.

'I knew you would, my own,' observed the latter carelessly. 'It is, as you say, quite a form[7] to ask. Here is Mr Dombey's letter, Edith.'

'Thank you. I have no desire to read it,' was her answer.

'Then perhaps I had better answer it myself,' said Mrs Skewton, 'though I had thought of asking *you* to be my secretary, darling.' As Edith made no movement and no answer, Mrs Skewton begged the Major to wheel her little table nearer, and to set open the desk it contained, and to take out pen and paper for her; all which congenial offices of gallantry the Major discharged, with much submission and devotion.

'Your regards, Edith, my dear?' said Mrs Skewton, pausing, pen in hand, at the postscript.

'What you will, mama,' she answered, without turning her head, and with supreme indifference.

Mrs Skewton wrote what she would, without seeking for any more explicit directions, and handed her letter to the Major, who receiving it as a precious charge, made a show of laying it near his heart, but was fain to put it in the pocket of his pantaloons on account of the insecurity of his waistcoat. The Major then took a very polished and chivalrous farewell of both ladies, which the elder one acknowledged in her usual manner, while the younger, sitting with her face addressed to the window, bent her head so slightly that it would have been a greater compliment to the Major to have made no sign at all, and to have left him to infer that he had not been heard or thought of.

'As to alteration in her, Sir,' mused the Major on his way back; on which expedition – the afternoon being sunny and hot – he ordered the Native and the light baggage to the front, and walked in the shadow of that expatriated prince: 'as to alteration, Sir, and pining, and so forth, that won't go down with Joseph Bagstock. None of that, Sir. It won't do here. But as to there being something of a division between 'em – or a gulf as the mother calls it – damme, Sir, that seems true enough. And it's odd enough! Well, Sir!' panted the Major, 'Edith Granger and Dombey are well matched; let 'em fight it out! Bagstock backs the winner!'

The Major, by saying these latter words aloud, in the vigour of his thoughts, caused the unhappy Native to stop, and turn round, in the belief that he was personally addressed. Exasperated to the last degree by this act of insubordination, the Major (though he was swelling with enjoyment of his own humour, at the moment of its occurrence) instantly thrust his cane among the Native's ribs, and continued to stir him up, at short intervals, all the way to the Hotel.

Nor was the Major less exasperated as he dressed for dinner, during which operation the dark servant underwent the pelting of a shower of miscellaneous objects, varying in size from a boot to a hairbrush, and including everything that came within his master's reach. For the Major plumed himself[8] on having the Native in a perfect state of drill, and visited the least departure from strict discipline with this kind of fatigue duty.[9] Add to this, that he maintained the Native about his person as a counter-irritant against the gout, and all other vexations, mental as well as bodily; and the Native would appear to have earned his pay – which was not large.

At length, the Major having disposed of all the missiles that were convenient to his hand, and having called the Native so many new names as must have given him great occasion to marvel at the resources of the English language, submitted to have his cravat put on; and being dressed, and finding himself in a brisk flow of spirits after this exercise, went downstairs to enliven 'Dombey' and his right-hand man.

Dombey was not yet in the room, but the right-hand man was there, and his dental treasures were, as usual, ready for the Major.

'Well, Sir!' said the Major. 'How have you passed the time since I had the happiness of meeting you? Have you walked at all?'

'A saunter of barely half an hour's duration,' returned Carker. 'We have been so much occupied.'

'Business, eh?' said the Major.

'A variety of little matters necessary to be gone through,' replied Carker. 'But do you know – this is quite unusual with me, educated in a distrustful school, and who am not generally disposed to be communicative,' he said, breaking off, and speaking in a charming tone of frankness – 'but I feel quite confidential with you, Major Bagstock.'

'You do me honour, Sir,' returned the Major. 'You may be.'

'Do you know, then,' pursued Carker, 'that I have not found my friend – *our* friend, I ought rather to call him—'

'Meaning Dombey, Sir?' cried the Major. 'You see me, Mr Carker, standing here! J. B.?'

He was puffy enough to see, and blue enough; and Mr Carker intimated that he had that pleasure.

'Then you see a man, Sir, who would go through fire and water to serve Dombey,' returned Major Bagstock.

Mr Carker smiled, and said he was sure of it. 'Do you know, Major,' he proceeded: 'to resume where I left off: that I have not found our friend so attentive to business to-day, as usual?'

'No?' observed the delighted Major.

'I have found him a little abstracted, and with his attention disposed to wander,' said Carker.

'By Jove, Sir,' cried the Major, 'there's a lady in the case.'

'Indeed, I begin to believe there really is,' returned Carker; 'I thought you might be jesting when you seemed to hint at it; for I know you military men—'

The Major gave the horse's cough, and shook his head and shoulders, as much as to say, 'Well! we *are* gay dogs,[10] there's no denying.' He then seized Mr Carker by the button-hole, and with starting eyes whispered in his ear, that she was a woman of extraordinary charms, Sir. That she was a young widow, Sir. That she was of a fine family, Sir. That Dombey was over head and ears in love with her, Sir, and that it would be a good match on both sides; for she had beauty, blood, and talent, and Dombey had fortune; and what more could any couple have? Hearing Mr Dombey's footsteps without, the Major cut himself short by saying, that Mr Carker would see her to-morrow morning, and would judge for himself; and between his mental excitement, and the exertion of saying all this in wheezy whispers, the Major sat gurgling in the throat and watering at the eyes, until dinner was ready.

The Major, like some other noble animals, exhibited himself to great advantage at feeding-time. On this occasion, he shone resplendent at one end of the table, supported by the milder lustre of Mr Dombey at the other; while Carker on one side lent his ray to either light, or suffered it to merge into both, as occasion arose.

During the first course or two, the Major was usually grave; for the Native, in obedience to general orders, secretly issued, collected every sauce and cruet round him, and gave him a great deal to do, in taking out the stoppers, and mixing up the contents in his plate. Besides which, the Native had private zests and flavours on a side-table, with which the Major daily scorched himself; to say nothing of strange machines out of which he spirted unknown liquids into the Major's drink. But on this occasion, Major Bagstock, even amidst these many occupations, found time to be social; and his sociality consisted in excessive slyness for the behoof of Mr Carker, and the betrayal of Mr Dombey's state of mind.

'Dombey,' said the Major, 'you don't eat; what's the matter?'

'Thank you,' returned that gentleman, 'I am doing very well; I have no great appetite to-day.'

'Why, Dombey, what's become of it?' asked the Major. 'Where's it gone? You haven't left it with your friends, I'll swear, for I can answer for their having none to-day at luncheon. I can answer for one of 'em, at least: I won't say which.'

Then the Major winked at Carker, and became so frightfully sly, that his dark attendant was obliged to pat him on the back, without orders, or he would probably have disappeared under the table.

In a later stage of the dinner: that is to say, when the Native

'Joe B is sly Sir; devilish sly'

stood at the Major's elbow ready to serve the first bottle of champagne: the Major became still slyer.

'Fill this to the brim, you scoundrel,' said the Major, holding up his glass. 'Fill Mr Carker's to the brim too. And Mr Dombey's too. By Gad, gentlemen,' said the Major, winking at his new friend, while Mr Dombey looked into his plate with a conscious air, 'we'll consecrate this glass of wine to a Divinity whom Joe is proud to know, and at a distance humbly and reverently to admire. Edith,' said the Major, 'is her name; angelic Edith!'

'To angelic Edith!' cried the smiling Carker.

'Edith, by all means,' said Mr Dombey.

The entrance of the waiters with new dishes caused the Major to be slyer yet, but in a more serious vein. 'For though among ourselves, Joe Bagstock mingles jest and earnest on this subject, Sir,' said the Major, laying his finger on his lips, and speaking half apart to Carker, 'he holds that name too sacred to be made the property of these fellows, or of any fellows. Not a word, Sir, while they are here!'

This was respectful and becoming on the Major's part, and Mr Dombey plainly felt it so. Although embarrassed in his own frigid way, by the Major's allusions, Mr Dombey had no objection to such rallying, it was clear, but rather courted it. Perhaps the Major had been pretty near the truth, when he had divined that morning that the great man who was too haughty formally to consult with, or confide in his prime minister, on such a matter, yet wished him to be fully possessed of it. Let this be how it may, he often glanced at Mr Carker while the Major plied his light artillery;[11] and seemed watchful of its effect upon him.

But the Major, having secured an attentive listener, and a smiler who had not his match in all the world – 'in short, a de-vilish intelligent and agreeable fellow,' as he often afterwards declared – was not going to let him off with a little slyness personal to Mr Dombey. Therefore, on the removal of the cloth, the Major developed himself as a choice spirit in the broader and more comprehensive range of narrating regimental stories, and cracking regimental jokes, which he did with such prodigal exuberance, that Carker was (or feigned to be) quite exhausted with laughter and admiration: while Mr Dombey looked on over his starched cravat, like the Major's proprietor, or like a stately showman who was glad to see his bear dancing[12] well.

When the Major was too hoarse with meat and drink, and the display of his social powers, to render himself intelligible any

longer, they adjourned to coffee. After which, the Major inquired
of Mr Carker the Manager, with little apparent hope of an answer
in the affirmative, if he played picquet.

'Yes, I play picquet a little,' said Mr Carker.

'Backgammon, perhaps?' observed the Major, hesitating.

'Yes, I play backgammon a little too,' replied the man of teeth.

'Carker plays at all games, I believe,' said Mr Dombey, laying
himself on a sofa like a man of wood without a hinge or a joint in
him; 'and plays them well.'

In sooth, he played the two in question, to such perfection, that
the Major was astonished, and asked him, at random, if he played
chess.

'Yes, I play chess a little,' answered Carker. 'I have sometimes
played, and won a game – it's a mere trick – without seeing the
board.'

'By Gad, Sir!' said the Major, staring, 'you are a contrast to
Dombey, who plays nothing.'

'Oh! *He!*' returned the manager. '*He* has never had occasion to
acquire such little arts. To men like me, they are sometimes useful.
As at present, Major Bagstock, when they enable me to take a hand
with you.'

It might be only the false mouth, so smooth and wide; and yet
there seemed to lurk beneath the humility and subserviency of this
short speech, a something like a snarl; and, for a moment, one
might have thought that the white teeth were prone to bite the hand
they fawned upon. But the Major thought nothing about it; and Mr
Dombey lay meditating with his eyes half shut, during the whole of
the play, which lasted until bed-time.

By that time, Mr Carker, though the winner, had mounted high
into the Major's good opinion, insomuch that when he left the
Major at his own room before going to bed, the Major as a special
attention, sent the Native – who always rested on a mattress spread
upon the ground at his master's door – along the gallery, to light
him to his room in state.

There was a faint blur on the surface of the mirror in Mr Carker's
chamber, and its reflection was, perhaps, a false one. But it showed,
that night, the image of a man, who saw, in his fancy, a crowd of
people slumbering on the ground at his feet, like the poor Native at
his master's door: who picked his way among them: looking down,
maliciously enough: but trod upon no upturned face – as yet.

CHAPTER 27

Deeper Shadows

Mr Carker the Manager rose with the lark, and went out, walking in the summer day. His meditations – and he meditated with contracted brows while he strolled along – hardly seemed to soar as high as the lark, or to mount in that direction; rather they kept close to their nest upon the earth, and looked about, among the dust and worms. But there was not a bird in the air, singing unseen, farther beyond the reach of human eye than Mr Carker's thoughts. He had his face so perfectly under control, that few could say more, in distinct terms, of its expression, than that it smiled or that it pondered. It pondered now, intently. As the lark rose higher, he sank deeper in thought. As the lark poured out her melody clearer and stronger, he fell into a graver and profounder silence. At length, when the lark came headlong down, with an accumulating stream of song, and dropped among the green wheat near him, rippling in the breath of the morning like a river, he sprang up from his reverie, and looked round with a sudden smile, as courteous and as soft as if he had had numerous observers to propitiate; nor did he relapse, after being thus awakened; but clearing his face, like one who bethought himself that it might otherwise wrinkle and tell tales, went smiling on, as if for practice.

Perhaps with an eye to first impressions, Mr Carker was very carefully and trimly dressed, that morning. Though always somewhat formal, in his dress, in imitation of the great man whom he served, he stopped short of the extent of Mr Dombey's stiffness: at once perhaps because he knew it to be ludicrous, and because in doing so he found another means of expressing his sense of the difference and distance between them. Some people quoted him indeed, in this respect, as a pointed commentary, and not a flattering one, on his icy patron – but the world is prone to misconstruction, and Mr Carker was not accountable for its bad propensity.

Clean and florid: with his light complexion, fading as it were, in the sun, and his dainty step enhancing the softness of the turf: Mr Carker the Manager strolled about meadows, and green lanes, and glided among avenues of trees, until it was time to return to breakfast. Taking a nearer way back, Mr Carker pursued it, airing his teeth, and said aloud as he did so, 'Now to see the second Mrs Dombey!'

He had strolled beyond the town, and re-entered it by a pleasant walk, where there was a deep shade of leafy trees, and where there were a few benches here and there for those who chose to rest. It not being a place of general resort at any hour, and wearing at that time of the still morning the air of being quite deserted and retired, Mr Carker had it, or thought he had it, all to himself. So, with the whim of an idle man, to whom there yet remained twenty minutes for reaching a destination easily accessible in ten, Mr Carker threaded the great boles of the trees, and went passing in and out, before this one and behind that, weaving a chain of footsteps on the dewy ground.

But he found he was mistaken in supposing there was no one in the grove, for as he softly rounded the trunk of one large tree, on which the obdurate bark was knotted and overlapped like the hide of a rhinoceros or some kindred monster of the ancient days before the Flood, he saw an unexpected figure sitting on a bench near at hand, about which, in another moment, he would have wound the chain he was making.

It was that of a lady, elegantly dressed and very handsome, whose dark proud eyes were fixed upon the ground, and in whom some passion or struggle was raging. For as she sat looking down, she held a corner of her under lip within her mouth, her bosom heaved, her nostril quivered, her head trembled, indignant tears were on her cheek, and her foot was set upon the moss as though she would have crushed it into nothing. And yet almost the self-same glance that showed him this, showed him the self-same lady rising with a scornful air of weariness and lassitude, and turning away with nothing expressed in face or figure but careless beauty and imperious disdain.

A withered and very ugly old woman, dressed not so much like a gipsy as like any of that medley race of vagabonds who tramp about the country, begging, and stealing, and tinkering, and weaving rushes, by turns, or all together, had been observing the lady, too; for, as she rose, this second figure strangely confronting the first, scrambled up from the ground – out of it, it almost appeared – and stood in the way.

'Let me tell your fortune, my pretty lady,' said the old woman, munching with her jaws, as if the Death's Head[1] beneath her yellow skin were impatient to get out.

'I can tell it for myself,' was the reply.

'Aye, aye, pretty lady; but not right. You didn't tell it right when you were sitting there. I see you! Give me a piece of silver, pretty lady, and I'll tell your fortune true. There's riches, pretty lady, in your face.'

'I know,' returned the lady, passing her with a dark smile, and a proud step. 'I knew it before.'

'What! You won't give me nothing?' cried the old woman. 'You won't give me nothing to tell your fortune, pretty lady? How much will you give me *not* to tell it, then? Give me something, or I'll call it after you!' croaked the old woman, passionately.

Mr Carker, whom the lady was about to pass close, slinking against his tree as she crossed to gain the path, advanced so as to meet her, and pulling off his hat as she went by, bade the old woman hold her peace. The lady acknowledged his interference with an inclination of the head, and went her way.

'You give me something then, or I'll call it after her!' screamed the old woman, throwing up her arms, and pressing forward against his outstretched hand. 'Or come,' she added, dropping her voice suddenly, looking at him earnestly, and seeming in a moment to forget the object of her wrath, 'give me something, or I'll call it after *you!*'

'After *me*, old lady!' returned the Manager, putting his hand in his pocket.

'Yes,' said the woman, steadfast in her scrutiny, and holding out her shrivelled hand. '*I* know!'

'What do you know?' demanded Carker, throwing her a shilling. 'Do you know who the handsome lady is?'

Munching like that sailor's wife of yore, who had chestnuts in her lap, and scowling like the witch who asked for some in vain,[2] the old woman picked the shilling up, and going backwards, like a crab, or like a heap of crabs: for her alternately expanding and contracting hands might have represented two of that species, and her creeping face, some half-a-dozen more: crouched on the veinous root of an old tree, pulled out a short black pipe from within the crown of her bonnet, lighted it with a match, and smoked in silence, looking fixedly at her questioner.

Mr Carker laughed, and turned upon his heel.

'Good!' said the old woman. 'One child dead, and one child living: one wife dead, and one wife coming. Go and meet her!'

In spite of himself, the Manager looked round again, and stopped. The old woman, who had not removed her pipe, and was munching and mumbling while she smoked, as if in conversation with an invisible familiar,[3] pointed with her finger in the direction he was going, and laughed.

'What was that you said, Beldamite?'[4] he demanded.

The woman mumbled, and chattered, and smoked, and still pointed before him; but remained silent. Muttering a farewell that was not complimentary, Mr Carker pursued his way, but as he turned out of that place, and looked over his shoulder at the root of the old tree, he could yet see the finger pointing before him, and thought he heard the woman screaming, 'Go and meet her!'

Preparations for a choice repast were completed, he found, at the hotel; and Mr Dombey, and the Major, and the breakfast, were awaiting the ladies. Individual constitution has much to do with the development of such facts, no doubt; but in this case, appetite carried it hollow[5] over the tender passion; Mr Dombey being very cool and collected, and the Major fretting and fuming in a state of violent heat and irritation. At length the door was thrown open by the Native, and, after a pause, occupied by her languishing along the gallery, a very blooming, but not very youthful lady, appeared.

'My dear Mr Dombey,' said the lady, 'I am afraid we are late, but Edith has been out already looking for a favourable point of view for a sketch, and kept me waiting for her. Falsest of Majors,' giving him her little finger, 'how do you do?'

'Mrs Skewton,' said Mr Dombey, 'let me gratify my friend Carker:' Mr Dombey unconsciously emphasised the word friend, as saying, 'no really; I do allow him to take credit for that distinction'; 'by presenting him to you. You have heard me mention Mr Carker.'

'I am charmed, I am sure,' said Mrs Skewton, graciously.

Mr Carker was charmed, of course. Would he have been more charmed on Mr Dombey's behalf, if Mrs Skewton had been (as he at first supposed her) the Edith whom they had toasted over night?

'Why, where, for Heaven's sake, is Edith?' exclaimed Mrs Skewton, looking round. 'Still at the door, giving Withers orders about the mounting of those drawings! My dear Mr Dombey, will you have the kindness—'

Mr Dombey was already gone to seek her. Next moment he returned, bearing on his arm the same elegantly dressed and very handsome lady whom Mr Carker had encountered underneath the trees.

'Carker—' began Mr Dombey. But their recognition of each other was so manifest, that Mr Dombey stopped surprised.

'I am obliged to the gentleman,' said Edith, with a stately bend, 'for sparing me some annoyance from an importunate beggar just now.'

'I am obliged to my good fortune,' said Mr Carker, bowing low, 'for the opportunity of rendering so slight a service to one whose servant I am proud to be.'

As her eye rested on him for an instant, and then lighted on the ground, he saw in its bright and searching glance a suspicion that he had not come up at the moment of his interference, but had secretly observed her sooner. As he saw that, she saw in *his* eye that her distrust was not without foundation.

'Really,' cried Mrs Skewton, who had taken this opportunity of inspecting Mr Carker through her glass, and satisfying herself (as she lisped audibly to the Major) that he was all heart; 'really now, this is one of the most enchanting coincidences that I ever heard of. The idea! My dearest Edith, there is such an obvious destiny in it, that really one might almost be induced to cross one's arms upon one's frock, and say, like those wicked Turks, there is no What's-his-name but Thingummy, and What-you-may-call-it is his prophet!'[6]

Edith deigned no revision of this extraordinary quotation from the Koran, but Mr Dombey felt it necessary to offer a few polite remarks.

'It gives me great pleasure,' said Mr Dombey, with cumbrous gallantry, 'that a gentleman so nearly connected with myself as Carker is, should have had the honour and happiness of rendering the least assistance to Mrs Granger.' Mr Dombey bowed to her. 'But it gives me some pain, and it occasions me to be really envious of Carker;' he unconsciously laid stress on these words, as sensible that they must appear to involve a very surprising proposition; 'envious of Carker, that I had not that honour and that happiness myself.' Mr Dombey bowed again. Edith, saving for a curl of her lip, was motionless.

'By the Lord, Sir,' cried the Major, bursting into speech at sight of the waiter, who was come to announce breakfast, 'it's an extraordinary thing to me that no one can have the honour and happiness of shooting all such beggars through the head without being brought to book for it. But here's an arm for Mrs Granger if she'll do J. B. the honour to accept it; and the greatest service Joe can render you, ma'am, just now, is, to lead you in to table!'

With this, the Major gave his arm to Edith; Mr Dombey led the way with Mrs Skewton; Mr Carker went last, smiling on the party.

'I am quite rejoiced, Mr Carker,' said the lady-mother, at breakfast, after another approving survey of him through her glass, 'that you have timed your visit so happily, as to go with us to-day. It is the most enchanting expedition!'

'Any expedition would be enchanting in such society,' returned Carker; 'but I believe it is, in itself, full of interest.'

'Oh!' cried Mrs Skewton, with a faded little scream of rapture, 'the Castle is charming! – associations of the Middle Ages – and all that – which is so truly exquisite. Don't you dote upon the Middle Ages, Mr Carker?'

'Very much, indeed,' said Mr Carker.

'Such charming times!' cried Cleopatra. 'So full of faith! So vigorous and forcible! So picturesque! So perfectly removed from commonplace! Oh dear! If they would only leave us a little more of the poetry of existence in these terrible days!'

Mrs Skewton was looking sharp after Mr Dombey all the time she said this, who was looking at Edith: who was listening, but who never lifted up her eyes.

'We are dreadfully real, Mr Carker,' said Mrs Skewton; 'are we not?'

Few people had less reason to complain of their reality than Cleopatra, who had as much that was false about her as could well go to the composition of anybody with a real individual existence. But Mr Carker commiserated our reality nevertheless, and agreed that we were very hardly used in that regard.

'Pictures at the Castle, quite divine!' said Cleopatra. 'I hope you dote upon pictures?'

'I assure you, Mrs Skewton,' said Mr Dombey, with solemn encouragement of his Manager, 'that Carker has a very good taste for pictures; quite a natural power of appreciating them. He is a very creditable artist himself. He will be delighted, I am sure, with Mrs Granger's taste and skill.'

'Damme, Sir!' cried Major Bagstock, 'my opinion is, that you're the admirable Carker,[7] and can do anything.'

'Oh!' smiled Carker, with humility, 'you are much too sanguine, Major Bagstock. I can do very little. But Mr Dombey is so generous in his estimation of any trivial accomplishment a man like myself may find it almost necessary to acquire, and to which, in his very different sphere, he is far superior, that—' Mr Carker shrugged his shoulders, deprecating further praise, and said no more.

All this time, Edith never raised her eyes, unless to glance towards her mother when that lady's fervent spirit shone forth in words. But as Carker ceased, she looked at Mr Dombey for a moment. For a moment only; but with a transient gleam of scornful wonder on her face, not lost on one observer, who was smiling round the board.

Mr Dombey caught the dark eyelash in its descent, and took the opportunity of arresting it.

'You have been to Warwick often, unfortunately?' said Mr Dombey.

'Several times.'

'The visit will be tedious to you, I am afraid.'

'Oh no; not at all.'

'Ah! You are like your cousin Feenix, my dearest Edith,' said Mrs Skewton. 'He has been to Warwick Castle fifty times, if he has been there once; yet if he came to Leamington to-morrow – I wish he would, dear angel! – he would make his fifty-second visit next day.'

'We are all enthusiastic, are we not, mama?' said Edith, with a cold smile.

'Too much so, for our peace, perhaps, my dear,' returned her mother; 'but we won't complain. Our own emotions are our recompense. If, as your cousin Feenix says, the sword wears out[8] the what's-its-name—'

'The scabbard, perhaps,' said Edith.

'Exactly – a little too fast, it is because it is bright and glowing, you know, my dearest love.'

Mrs Skewton heaved a gentle sigh, supposed to cast a shadow on the surface of that dagger of lath,[9] whereof her susceptible bosom was the sheath: and leaning her head on one side, in the Cleopatra manner, looked with pensive affection on her darling child.

Edith had turned her face towards Mr Dombey when he first addressed her, and had remained in that attitude, while speaking to her mother, and while her mother spoke to her, as though offering him her attention, if he had anything more to say. There was something in the manner of this simple courtesy: almost defiant, and giving it the character of being rendered on compulsion, or as a matter of traffic to which she was a reluctant party: again not lost upon that same observer who was smiling round the board. It set him thinking of her as he had first seen her, when she had believed herself to be alone among the trees.

Mr Dombey having nothing else to say, proposed – the breakfast being now finished, and the Major gorged, like any Boa Constrictor – that they should start. A barouche being in waiting, according to the orders of that gentleman, the two ladies, the Major and himself, took their seats in it; the Native and the wan page mounted the box, Mr Towlinson being left behind; and Mr Carker, on horseback, brought up the rear.

Mr Carker cantered behind the carriage, at the distance of a hundred yards or so, and watched it, during all the ride, as if he were a cat, indeed, and its four occupants, mice. Whether he looked to one side of the road, or to the other – over distant landscape, with its smooth undulations, wind-mills, corn, grass, bean-fields, wild-flowers, farm-yards, hay-ricks, and the spire among the wood – or upwards in the sunny air, where butterflies were sporting round his head, and birds were pouring out their songs – or downward, where the shadows of the branches interlaced, and made a trembling carpet on the road – or onward, where the overhanging trees formed aisles and arches, dim with the softened light that steeped through leaves – one corner of his eye was ever on the formal head of Mr Dombey, addressed towards him, and the feather in the bonnet, drooping so neglectfully and scornfully between them; much as he had seen the haughty eyelids droop; not least so, when the face met that now fronting it. Once, and once only, did his wary glance release these objects; and that was, when a leap over a low hedge, and a gallop across a field, enabled him to anticipate the carriage coming by the road, and to be standing ready, at the journey's end, to hand the ladies out. Then, and but then, he met her glance for an instant in her first surprise; but when he touched her, in alighting, with his soft white hand, it overlooked him altogether as before.

Mrs Skewton was bent on taking charge of Mr Carker herself, and showing him the beauties of the Castle. She was determined to have his arm, and the Major's too. It would do that incorrigible creature: who was the most barbarous infidel in point of poetry: good to be in such company. This chance arrangement left Mr Dombey at liberty to escort Edith: which he did, stalking before them through the apartments with a gentlemanly solemnity.

'Those darling bygone times, Mr Carker,' said Cleopatra, 'with their delicious fortresses, and their dear old dungeons, and their delightful places of torture, and their romantic vengeances, and their picturesque assaults and sieges, and everything that makes life truly charming! How dreadfully we have degenerated!'

'Yes, we have fallen off deplorably,' said Mr Carker.

The peculiarity of their conversation was, that Mrs Skewton, in spite of her ecstasies, and Mr Carker, in spite of his urbanity, were both intent on watching Mr Dombey and Edith. With all their conversational endowments, they spoke somewhat distractedly, and at random in consequence.

'We have no Faith left, positively,' said Mrs Skewton, advancing her shrivelled ear; for Mr Dombey was saying something to Edith.

'We have no Faith in the dear old Barons, who were the most delightful creatures – or in the dear old Priests, who were the most warlike of men – or even in the days of that inestimable Queen Bess,[10] upon the wall there, which were so extremely golden. Dear creature! She was all Heart! And that charming father of hers! I hope you dote on Harry the Eighth!'[11]

'I admire him very much,' said Carker.

'So bluff!' cried Mrs Skewton, 'wasn't he? So burly. So truly English. Such a picture, too, he makes, with his dear little peepy eyes, and his benevolent chin!'

'Ah, ma'am!' said Carker, stopping short; 'but if you speak of pictures, there's a composition! What gallery in the world can produce the counterpart of that?'

As the smiling gentleman thus spake, he pointed through a doorway to where Mr Dombey and Edith were standing alone in the centre of another room.

They were not interchanging a word or a look. Standing together, arm in arm, they had the appearance of being more divided than if seas had rolled between them. There was a difference even in the pride of the two, that removed them farther from each other, than if one had been the proudest and the other the humblest specimen of humanity in all creation. He, self-important, unbending, formal, austere. She, lovely and graceful in an uncommon degree, but totally regardless of herself and him and everything around, and spurning her own attractions with her haughty brow and lip, as if they were a badge or livery[12] she hated. So unmatched were they, and opposed, so forced and linked together by a chain which adverse hazard and mischance had forged: that fancy might have imagined the pictures on the walls around them, startled by the unnatural conjunction, and observant of it in their several expressions. Grim knights and warriors looked scowling on them. A churchman, with his hand upraised, denounced the mockery of such a couple coming to God's altar. Quiet waters in landscapes, with the sun reflected in their depths, asked, if better means of escape were not at hand, was there no drowning left? Ruins cried, 'Look here, and see what We are, wedded to uncongenial Time!' Animals, opposed by nature, worried one another, as a moral to them. Loves and Cupids took to flight afraid, and Martyrdom had no such torment in its painted history of suffering.

Nevertheless, Mrs Skewton was so charmed by the sight to which Mr Carker invoked her attention, that she could not refrain from saying, half aloud, how sweet, how very full of soul it was! Edith, overhearing, looked round, and flushed indignant scarlet to her hair.

'My dearest Edith knows I was admiring her!' said Cleopatra, tapping her, almost timidly, on the back with her parasol. 'Sweet pet!'

Again Mr Carker saw the strife he had witnessed so unexpectedly among the trees. Again he saw the haughty languor and indifference come over it, and hide it like a cloud.

She did not raise her eyes to him; but with a slight peremptory motion of them, seemed to bid her mother come near. Mrs Skewton thought it expedient to understand the hint, and advancing quickly, with her two cavaliers, kept near her daughter from that time.

Mr Carker now, having nothing to distract his attention, began to discourse upon the pictures and to select the best, and point them out to Mr Dombey: speaking with his usual familiar recognition of Mr Dombey's greatness, and rendering homage by adjusting his eye-glass for him, or finding out the right place in his catalogue, or holding his stick, or the like. These services did not so much originate with Mr Carker, in truth, as with Mr Dombey himself, who was apt to assert his chieftainship by saying, with subdued authority, and in an easy way – for him – 'Here, Carker, have the goodness to assist me, will you?' which the smiling gentleman always did with pleasure.

They made the tour of the pictures, the walls, crow's nest,[13] and so forth; and as they were still one little party, and the Major was rather in the shade: being sleepy during the process of digestion: Mr Carker became communicative and agreeable. At first, he addressed himself for the most part to Mrs Skewton; but as that sensitive lady was in such ecstasies with the works of art, after the first quarter of an hour, that she could do nothing but yawn (they were such perfect inspirations, she observed as a reason for that mark of rapture), he transferred his attentions to Mr Dombey. Mr Dombey said little beyond an occasional 'Very true, Carker,' or 'Indeed, Carker,' but he tacitly encouraged Carker to proceed, and inwardly approved of his behaviour very much: deeming it as well that somebody should talk, and thinking that his remarks, which were, as one might say, a branch of the parent establishment, might amuse Mrs Granger. Mr Carker, who possessed an excellent discretion, never took the liberty of addressing that lady, direct; but she seemed to listen, though she never looked at him; and once or twice, when he was emphatic in his peculiar humility, the twilight smile stole over her face, not as a light, but as a deep black shadow.

Warwick Castle being at length pretty well exhausted, and the Major very much so: to say nothing of Mrs Skewton, whose peculiar demonstrations of delight had become very frequent indeed: the carriage was again put in requisition, and they rode to several admired points of view in the neighbourhood. Mr Dombey ceremoniously observed of one of these, that a sketch, however slight, from the fair hand of Mrs Granger, would be a remembrance to him of that agreeable day: though he wanted no artificial remembrance, he was sure (here Mr Dombey made another of his bows), which he must always highly value. Withers the lean having Edith's sketch-book under his arm, was immediately called upon by Mrs Skewton to produce the same: and the carriage stopped, that Edith might make the drawing, which Mr Dombey was to put away among his treasures.

'But I am afraid I trouble you too much,' said Mr Dombey.

'By no means. Where would you wish it taken from?' she answered, turning to him with the same enforced attention as before.

Mr Dombey, with another bow, which cracked the starch in his cravat, would beg to leave that to the Artist.

'I would rather you chose for yourself,' said Edith.

'Suppose then,' said Mr Dombey, 'we say from here. It appears a good spot for the purpose, or – Carker, what do *you* think?'

There happened to be in the foreground, at some little distance, a grove of trees, not unlike that in which Mr Carker had made his chain of footsteps in the morning, and with a seat under one tree, greatly resembling, in the general character of its situation, the point where his chain had broken.

'Might I venture to suggest to Mrs Granger,' said Carker, 'that that is an interesting – almost a curious – point of view?'

She followed the direction of his riding-whip with her eyes, and raised them quickly to his face. It was the second glance they had exchanged since their introduction, and would have been exactly like the first, but that its expression was plainer.

'Will you like that?' said Edith to Mr Dombey.

'I shall be charmed,' said Mr Dombey to Edith.

Therefore the carriage was driven to the spot where Mr Dombey was to be charmed; and Edith, without moving from her seat, and opening her sketch-book with her usual proud indifference, began to sketch.

'My pencils are all pointless,' she said, stopping and turning them over.

'Pray allow me,' said Mr Dombey. 'Or Carker will do it better, as he understands these things. Carker, have the goodness to see to these pencils for Mrs Granger.'

Mr Carker rode up close to the carriage-door on Mrs Granger's side, and letting the rein fall on his horse's neck, took the pencils from her hand with a smile and a bow, and sat in the saddle leisurely mending them. Having done so, he begged to be allowed to hold them, and to hand them to her as they were required; and thus Mr Carker, with many commendations of Mrs Granger's extraordinary skill – especially in trees – remained close at her side, looking over the drawing as she made it. Mr Dombey in the meantime stood bolt upright in the carriage like a highly respectable ghost, looking on too; while Cleopatra and the Major dallied as two ancient doves might do.

'Are you satisfied with that, or shall I finish it a little more?' said Edith, showing the sketch to Mr Dombey.

Mr Dombey begged that it might not be touched; it was perfection.

'It is most extraordinary,' said Carker, bringing every one of his red gums to bear upon his praise. 'I was not prepared for anything so beautiful, and so unusual altogether.'

This might have applied to the sketcher no less than to the sketch; but Mr Carker's manner was openness itself – not as to his mouth alone, but as to his whole spirit. So it continued to be while the drawing was laid aside for Mr Dombey, and while the sketching materials were put up; then he handed in the pencils (which were received with a distant acknowledgment of his help, but without a look) and tightening his rein, fell back, and followed the carriage again.

Thinking, perhaps, as he rode, that even this trivial sketch had been made and delivered to its owner, as if it had been bargained for and bought. Thinking, perhaps, that although she had assented with such perfect readiness to his request, her haughty face, bent over the drawing, or glancing at the distant objects represented in it, had been the face of a proud woman, engaged in a sordid and miserable transaction. Thinking, perhaps, of such things: but smiling certainly, and while he seemed to look about him freely, in enjoyment of the air and exercise, keeping always that sharp corner of his eye upon the carriage.

A stroll along the haunted ruins of Kenilworth,[14] and more rides to more points of view; most of which, Mrs Skewton reminded Mr Dombey, Edith had already sketched, as he had seen in looking over her drawings: brought the day's expedition to a close. Mrs Skewton and Edith were driven to their own lodgings; Mr Carker was graciously invited by Cleopatra to return thither with Mr Dombey and the Major, in the evening, to hear some of Edith's music; and the three gentlemen repaired to their hotel to dinner.

The dinner was the counterpart of yesterday's, except that the Major was twenty-four hours more triumphant and less mysterious. Edith was toasted again. Mr Dombey was again agreeably embarrassed. And Mr Carker was full of interest and praise.

There were no other visitors at Mrs Skewton's. Edith's drawings were strewn about the room, a little more abundantly than usual perhaps; and Withers, the wan page, handed round a little stronger tea. The harp was there; the piano was there; and Edith sang and played. But even the music was played by Edith to Mr Dombey's order, as it were, in the same uncompromising way. As thus.

'Edith, my dearest love,' said Mrs Skewton, half an hour after tea, 'Mr Dombey is dying to hear you, I know.'

'Mr Dombey has life enough left to say so for himself, mama, I have no doubt.'

'I shall be immensely obliged,' said Mr Dombey.

'What do you wish?'

'Piano?' hesitated Mr Dombey.

'Whatever you please. You have only to choose.'

Accordingly, she began with the piano. It was the same with the harp; the same with her singing; the same with the selection of the pieces that she sang and played. Such frigid and constrained, yet prompt and pointed acquiescence with the wishes he imposed upon her, and on no one else, was sufficiently remarkable to penetrate through all the mysteries of picquet, and impress itself on Mr Carker's keen attention. Nor did he lose sight of the fact that Mr Dombey was evidently proud of his power, and liked to show it.

Nevertheless, Mr Carker played so well – some games with the Major, and some with Cleopatra, whose vigilance of eye in respect of Mr Dombey and Edith no lynx could have surpassed – that he even heightened his position in the lady-mother's good graces; and when on taking leave he regretted that he would be obliged to return to London next morning, Cleopatra trusted: community of feeling not being met with every day: that it was far from being the last time they would meet.

'I hope so,' said Mr Carker, with an expressive look at the couple in the distance, as he drew towards the door, following the Major. 'I think so.'

Mr Dombey, who had taken a stately leave of Edith, bent, or made some approach to a bend, over Cleopatra's couch, and said, in a low voice:

'I have requested Mrs Granger's permission to call on her to-morrow morning – for a purpose – and she has appointed twelve o'clock. May I hope to have the pleasure of finding you at home, madam, afterwards?'

Cleopatra was so much fluttered and moved, by hearing this, of course, incomprehensible speech, that she could only shut her eyes, and shake her head, and give Mr Dombey her hand; which Mr Dombey, not exactly knowing what to do with, dropped.

'Dombey, come along!' cried the Major, looking in at the door. 'Damme, Sir, old Joe has a great mind to propose an alteration in the name of the Royal Hotel, and that it should be called the Three Jolly Bachelors, in honour of ourselves and Carker.' With this the Major slapped Mr Dombey on the back, and winking over his shoulder at the ladies, with a frightful tendency of blood to the head, carried him off.

Mrs Skewton reposed on her sofa, and Edith sat apart, by her harp, in silence. The mother, trifling with her fan, looked stealthily at the daughter more than once, but the daughter, brooding gloomily with downcast eyes, was not to be disturbed.

Thus they remained for a long hour, without a word, until Mrs Skewton's maid appeared, according to custom, to prepare her gradually for night. At night, she should have been a skeleton, with dart and hour-glass,[15] rather than a woman, this attendant; for her touch was as the touch of Death. The painted object shrivelled underneath her hand; the form collapsed, the hair dropped off, the arched dark eyebrows changed to scanty tufts of grey; the pale lips shrunk, the skin became cadaverous and loose; an old, worn, yellow, nodding woman, with red eyes, alone remained in Cleopatra's place, huddled up, like a slovenly bundle, in a greasy flannel gown.

The very voice was changed, as it addressed Edith, when they were alone again.

'Why don't you tell me,' it said sharply, 'that he is coming here to-morrow by appointment?'

'Because you know it,' returned Edith, 'Mother.'

The mocking emphasis she laid on that one word!

'You know he has bought me,' she resumed. 'Or that he will, to-morrow. He has considered of his bargain; he has shown it to his friend; he is even rather proud of it; he thinks that it will suit him, and may be had sufficiently cheap; and he will buy to-morrow. God, that I have lived for this, and that I feel it!'

Compress into one handsome face the conscious self-abasement, and the burning indignation of a hundred women, strong in passion and in pride; and there it hid itself with two white shuddering arms.

'What do you mean?' returned the angry mother. 'Haven't you from a child—'

'A child!' said Edith, looking at her, 'when was I a child? What childhood did you ever leave to me? I was a woman – artful, designing, mercenary, laying snares for men – before I knew myself, or you, or even understood the base and wretched aim of every new display I learnt. You gave birth to a woman. Look upon her. She is in her pride to-night.'

And as she spoke, she struck her hand upon her beautiful bosom, as though she would have beaten down herself.

'Look at me,' she said, 'who have never known what it is to have an honest heart, and love. Look at me, taught to scheme and plot when children play; and married in my youth – an old age of design – to one for whom I had no feeling but indifference. Look at me, whom he left a widow, dying before his inheritance descended to him – a judgment on you! well deserved! – and tell me what has been my life for ten years since.'

'We have been making every effort to endeavour to secure to you a good establishment,' rejoined her mother. 'That has been your life. And now you have got it.'

'There is no slave in a market; there is no horse in a fair: so shown and offered and examined and paraded, mother, as I have been, for ten shameful years,' cried Edith, with a burning brow, and the same bitter emphasis on the one word. 'Is it not so? Have I been made the bye-word of all kinds of men? Have fools, have profligates, have boys, have dotards, dangled after me, and one by one rejected me, and fallen off, because you were too plain with all your cunning: yes, and too true, with all those false pretences: until we have almost come to be notorious? The licence of look and touch,' she said, with flashing eyes, 'have I submitted to it, in half the places of resort upon the map of England. Have I been hawked and vended here and there, until the last grain of self-respect is dead within me, and I loathe myself? Has *this* been my late childhood? I had none before. Do not tell me that I had, to-night, of all nights in my life!'

'You might have been well married,' said her mother, 'twenty times at least, Edith, if you had given encouragement enough.'

'No! Who takes me, refuse that I am, and as I well deserve to be,' she answered, raising her head, and trembling in her energy of shame and stormy pride, 'shall take me, as this man does, with no art of mine put forth to lure him. He sees me at the auction, and he thinks it well to buy me. Let him! When he came to view me – perhaps to bid – he required to see the roll of my accomplishments. I gave it to him. When he would have me show one of them, to justify his purchase to his men, I require of him to say which he demands, and I exhibit it. I will do no more. He makes the purchase of his own will, and with his own sense of its worth, and the power of his money; and I hope it may never disappoint him. *I* have not vaunted and pressed the bargain; neither have you, so far as I have been able to prevent you.'

'You talk strangely to-night, Edith, to your own mother.'

'It seems so to me; stranger to me than you,' said Edith. 'But my education was completed long ago. I am too old now, and have fallen too low, by degrees, to take a new course, and to stop yours, and to help myself. The germ of all that purifies a woman's breast, and makes it true and good, has never stirred in mine, and I have nothing else to sustain me when I despise myself.' There had been a touching sadness in her voice, but it was gone, when she went on to say, with a curled lip, 'So, as we are genteel and poor, I am content that we should be made rich by these means; all I say, is, I have kept the only purpose I have had the strength to form – I had almost said the power, with you at my side, mother – and have not tempted this man on.'

'This man! You speak,' said her mother, 'as if you hated him.'

'And you thought I loved him, did you not?' she answered, stopping on her way across the room, and looking round. 'Shall I tell you,' she continued, with her eyes fixed on her mother, 'who already knows us thoroughly, and reads us right, and before whom I have even less of self-respect or confidence than before my own inward self; being so much degraded by his knowledge of me?'

'This is an attack, I suppose,' returned her mother coldly, 'on poor, unfortunate what's-his-name – Mr Carker! Your want of self-respect and confidence, my dear, in reference to that person (who is very agreeable, it strikes me), is not likely to have much effect on your establishment. Why do you look at me so hard? Are you ill?'

Edith suddenly let fall her face, as if it had been stung, and while she pressed her hands upon it, a terrible tremble crept over her whole frame. It was quickly gone; and with her usual step, she passed out of the room.

The maid who should have been a skeleton, then reappeared, and giving one arm to her mistress, who appeared to have taken off her manner with her charms, and to have put on paralysis with her flannel gown, collected the ashes of Cleopatra, and carried them away in the other, ready for to-morrow's revivification.

CHAPTER 28

Alterations

'So the day has come at length, Susan,' said Florence to the excellent Nipper, 'when we are going back to our quiet home!'

Susan drew in her breath with an amount of expression not easily described, and further relieving her feelings with a smart cough, answered, 'Very quiet indeed, Miss Floy, no doubt. Excessive so.'

'When I was a child,' said Florence, thoughtfully, and after musing for some moments, 'did you ever see that gentleman who has taken the trouble to ride down here to speak to me, now three times – three times, I think, Susan?'

'Three times, Miss,' returned the Nipper. 'Once when you was out a walking with them Sket—'

Florence gently looked at her, and Miss Nipper checked herself.

'With Sir Barnet and his lady, I mean to say, Miss, and the young gentleman. And two evenings since then.'

'When I was a child, and when company used to come to visit papa, did you ever see that gentleman at home, Susan?' asked Florence.

'Well, Miss,' returned her maid, after considering, 'I really couldn't say I ever did. When your poor dear ma died, Miss Floy, I was very new in the family, you see, and *my* element:' the Nipper bridled, as opining that her merits had been always designedly extinguished by Mr Dombey: 'was the floor below the attics.'

'To be sure,' said Florence, still thoughtfully; 'you are not likely to have known who came to the house. I quite forgot.'

'Not, Miss, but what we talked about the family and visitors,' said Susan, 'and but what I heard much said, although the nurse before Mrs Richards *did* make unpleasant remarks when I was in company, and hint at little Pitchers,[1] but that could only be attributed, poor thing,' observed Susan, with composed forbearance, 'to habits of intoxication, for which she was required to leave, and did.'

Florence, who was seated at her chamber window, with her face resting on her hand, sat looking out, and hardly seemed to hear what Susan said, she was so lost in thought.

'At all events, Miss,' said Susan, 'I remember very well that this same gentleman, Mr Carker, was almost, if not quite, as great a gentleman with your papa then, as he is now. It used to be said in the house then, Miss, that he was at the head of all your pa's affairs in the City, and managed the whole, and that your pa minded him more than anybody, which, begging your pardon, Miss Floy, he might easy do, for he never minded anybody else. I knew that, Pitcher as I might have been.'

Susan Nipper, with an injured remembrance of the nurse before Mrs Richards, emphasised 'Pitcher' strongly.

'And that Mr Carker has not fallen off, Miss,' she pursued, 'but has stood his ground, and kept his credit with your pa, I know from what is always said among our people by that Perch, whenever he comes to the house; and though he's the weakest weed in the world, Miss Floy, and no one can have a moment's patience with the man, he knows what goes on in the City tolerable well, and says that your pa does nothing without Mr Carker, and leaves all to Mr Carker, and acts according to Mr Carker, and has Mr Carker always at his elbow, and I do believe that he believes (that washiest of Perches!) that after your pa, the Emperor of India is the child unborn to Mr Carker.'

Not a word of this was lost on Florence, who, with an awakened interest in Susan's speech, no longer gazed abstractedly on the prospect without, but looked at her, and listened with attention.

'Yes, Susan,' she said, when that young lady had concluded. 'He is in papa's confidence, and is his friend, I am sure.'

Florence's mind ran high on this theme, and had done for some days. Mr Carker, in the two visits with which he had followed up his first one, had assumed a confidence between himself and her – a right on his part to be mysterious and stealthy, in telling her that the ship was still unheard of – a kind of mildly restrained power and authority over her – that made her wonder, and caused her great uneasiness. She had no means of repelling it, or of freeing herself from the web he was gradually winding about her; for that would have required some art and knowledge of the world, opposed to such address as his; and Florence had none. True, he had said no more to her than that there was no news of the ship, and that he feared the worst; but how he came to know that she was interested in the ship, and why he had the right to signify his knowledge to her, so insidiously and darkly, troubled Florence very much.

This conduct on the part of Mr Carker, and her habit of often considering it with wonder and uneasiness, began to invest him with an uncomfortable fascination in Florence's thoughts. A more distinct remembrance of his features, voice, and manner: which she sometimes courted, as a means of reducing him to the level of a real personage, capable of exerting no greater charm over her than another: did not remove the vague impression. And yet he never frowned, or looked upon her with an air of dislike or animosity, but was always smiling and serene.

Again, Florence, in pursuit of her strong purpose with reference to her father, and her steady resolution to believe that she was herself unwittingly to blame for their so cold and distant relations, would recall to mind that this gentleman was his confidential friend, and would think, with an anxious heart, could her struggling tendency to dislike and fear him be a part of that misfortune in her, which had turned her father's love adrift, and left her so alone? She dreaded that it might be; sometimes believed it was: then she resolved that she would try to conquer this wrong feeling; persuaded herself that she was honoured and encouraged by the notice of her father's friend; and hoped that patient observation of him and trust in him would lead her bleeding feet along that stony road which ended in her father's heart.

Thus, with no one to advise her – for she could advise with no one without seeming to complain against him – gentle Florence tossed on an uneasy sea of doubt and hope; and Mr Carker, like a scaly monster of the deep, swam down below, and kept his shining eye upon her.

Florence had a new reason in all this for wishing to be at home again. Her lonely life was better suited to her course of timid hope and doubt; and she feared sometimes, that in her absence she might miss some hopeful chance of testifying her affection for her father. Heaven knows, she might have set her mind at rest, poor child! on this last point; but her slighted love was fluttering within her, and, even in her sleep, it flew away in dreams, and nestled, like a wandering bird come home, upon her father's neck.

Of Walter she thought often. Ah! how often, when the night was gloomy, and the wind was blowing round the house! But hope was strong in her breast. It is so difficult for the young and ardent, even with such experience as hers, to imagine youth and ardour quenched like a weak flame, and the bright day of life merging into night, at noon, that hope was strong yet. Her tears fell frequently for Walter's sufferings; but rarely for his supposed death, and never long.

She had written to the old Instrument-maker, but had received no answer to her note: which indeed required none. Thus matters stood with Florence on the morning when she was going home, gladly, to her old secluded life.

Doctor and Mrs Blimber, accompanied (much against his will) by their valued charge, Master Barnet, were already gone back to Brighton, where that young gentleman and his fellow-pilgrims to Parnassus were then, no doubt, in the continual resumption of their studies. The holiday time was past and over; most of the juvenile guests at the villa had taken their departure; and Florence's long visit was come to an end.

There was one guest, however, albeit not resident within the house, who had been very constant in his attention to the family, and who still remained devoted to them. This was Mr Toots, who after renewing, some weeks ago, the acquaintance he had had the happiness of forming with Skettles Junior, on the night when he burst the Blimberian bonds and soared into freedom with his ring on, called regularly every other day, and left a perfect pack of cards at the hall-door; so many indeed, that the ceremony was quite a deal[2] on the part of Mr Toots, and a hand at whist on the part of the servant.

Mr Toots, likewise, with the bold and happy idea of preventing the family from forgetting him (but there is reason to suppose that this expedient originated in the teeming brain of the Chicken), had established a six-oared cutter,[3] manned by aquatic friends of the Chicken's and steered by that illustrious character in person, who wore a bright red fireman's coat for the purpose, and concealed the perpetual black eye with which he was afflicted, beneath a green shade. Previous to the institution of this equipage, Mr Toots sounded the Chicken on a hypothetical case, as, supposing the Chicken to be enamoured of a young lady named Mary, and to have conceived the intention of starting a boat of his own, what would he call that boat? The Chicken replied, with divers strong asseverations, that he would either christen it Poll or The Chicken's Delight. Improving on this idea, Mr Toots, after deep study and the exercise of much invention, resolved to call his boat The Toots's Joy, as a delicate compliment to Florence, of which no man knowing the parties, could possibly miss the appreciation.

Stretched on a crimson cushion in his gallant bark, with his shoes in the air, Mr Toots, in the exercise of his project, had come up the river, day after day, and week after week, and had flitted to and fro, near Sir Barnet's garden, and had caused his crew to cut across and across the river at sharp angles, for his better exhibition to any lookers-out from Sir Barnet's windows, and had had such evolutions performed by The Toots's Joy as had filled all the neighbouring part of the water-side with astonishment. But whenever he saw any one in Sir Barnet's garden on the brink of the river, Mr Toots always feigned to be passing there, by a combination of coincidences of the most singular and unlikely description.

'How are you, Toots?' Sir Barnet would say, waving his hand from the lawn, while the artful Chicken steered close in shore.

'How de do, Sir Barnet?' Mr Toots would answer, 'What a surprising thing that I should see *you* here!'

Mr Toots, in his sagacity, always said this, as if, instead of that being Sir Barnet's house, it were some deserted edifice on the banks of the Nile, or Ganges.

'I never was so surprised!' Mr Toots would exclaim. – 'Is Miss Dombey there?'

Whereupon Florence would appear, perhaps.

'Oh, Diogenes is quite well, Miss Dombey,' Mr Toots would cry. 'I called to ask this morning.'

'Thank you very much!' the pleasant voice of Florence would reply.

'Won't you come ashore, Toots?' Sir Barnet would say then. 'Come! you're in no hurry. Come and see us.'

'Oh, it's of no consequence, thank you!' Mr Toots would blushingly rejoin. 'I thought Miss Dombey might like to know, that's all. Good-bye!' And poor Mr Toots, who was dying to accept the invitation, but hadn't the courage to do it, signed to the Chicken, with an aching heart, and away went the Joy, cleaving the water like an arrow.

The Joy was lying in a state of extraordinary splendour, at the garden steps, on the morning of Florence's departure. When she went downstairs to take leave, after her talk with Susan, she found Mr Toots awaiting her in the drawing-room.

'Oh, how de do, Miss Dombey?' said the stricken Toots, always dreadfully disconcerted when the desire of his heart was gained, and he was speaking to her; 'thank you, I'm very well indeed, I hope you're the same, so was Diogenes yesterday.'

'You are very kind,' said Florence.

'Thank you, it's of no consequence,' retorted Mr Toots. 'I thought perhaps you wouldn't mind, in this fine weather, coming home by water, Miss Dombey. There's plenty of room in the boat for your maid.'

'I am very much obliged to you,' said Florence, hesitating. 'I really am – but I would rather not.'

'Oh, it's of no consequence,' retorted Mr Toots. 'Good morning!'

'Won't you wait and see Lady Skettles?' asked Florence, kindly.

'Oh no, thank you,' returned Mr Toots, 'it's of no consequence at all.'

So shy was Mr Toots on such occasions, and so flurried! But Lady Skettles entering at the moment, Mr Toots was suddenly seized with a passion for asking her how she did, and hoping she was very well; nor could Mr Toots by any possibility leave off shaking hands with her, until Sir Barnet appeared: to whom he immediately clung with the tenacity of desperation.

'We are losing, to-day, Toots,' said Sir Barnet, turning towards Florence, 'the light of our house, I assure you.'

'Oh, it's of no conseq— I mean yes, to be sure,' faltered the embarrassed Toots. 'GOOD morning!'

Notwithstanding the emphatic nature of this farewell, Mr Toots, instead of going away, stood leering about him, vacantly. Florence, to relieve him, bade adieu, with many thanks, to Lady Skettles, and gave her arm to Sir Barnet.

'May I beg of you, my dear Miss Dombey,' said her host, as he conducted her to the carriage, 'to present my best compliments to your dear papa?'

It was distressing to Florence to receive the commission, for she felt as if she were imposing on Sir Barnet by allowing him to believe that a kindness rendered to her, was rendered to her father. As she could not explain, however, she bowed her head and thanked him; and again she thought that the dull home, free from such embarrassments, and such reminders of her sorrow, was her natural and best retreat.

Such of her late friends and companions as were yet remaining at the villa, came running from within, and from the garden, to say good-bye. They were all attached to her, and very earnest in taking leave of her. Even the household were sorry for her going, and the servants came nodding and curtseying round the carriage door. As Florence looked round on the kind faces, and saw among them those of Sir Barnet and his lady, and of Mr Toots, who was chuckling and staring at her from a distance, she was reminded of the night when Paul and she had come from Doctor Blimber's: and when the carriage drove away, her face was wet with tears.

Sorrowful tears, but tears of consolation, too; for all the softer memories connected with the dull old house to which she was returning made it dear to her, as they rose up. How long it seemed since she had wandered through the silent rooms: since she had last crept, softly and afraid, into those her father occupied: since she had felt the solemn but yet soothing influence of the beloved dead in every action of her daily life! This new farewell reminded her, besides, of her parting with poor Walter: of his looks and words that night: and of the gracious blending she had noticed in him, of tenderness for those he left behind, with courage and high spirit. His little history was associated with the old house too, and gave it a new claim and hold upon her heart.

Even Susan Nipper softened towards the home of so many years, as they were on their way towards it. Gloomy as it was, and rigid justice as she rendered to its gloom, she forgave it a great deal. 'I shall be glad to see it again, I don't deny, Miss,' said the Nipper. 'There ain't much in it to boast of, but I wouldn't have it burnt or pulled down, neither!'

'You'll be glad to go through the old rooms, won't you, Susan?' said Florence, smiling.

'Well, Miss,' returned the Nipper, softening more and more towards the house, as they approached it nearer, 'I won't deny but what I shall, though I shall hate 'em again, to-morrow, very likely.'

Florence felt that, for her, there was greater peace within it than elsewhere. It was better and easier to keep her secret shut up there, among the tall dark walls, than to carry it abroad into the light, and try to hide it from a crowd of happy eyes. It was better to pursue the study of her loving heart, alone, and find no new discouragements in loving hearts about her. It was easier to hope, and pray, and love on, all uncared for, yet with constancy and patience, in the tranquil sanctuary of such remembrances: although it mouldered, rusted, and decayed about her: than in a new scene, let its gaiety be what it would. She welcomed back her old enchanted dream of life, and longed for the old dark door to close upon her, once again.

Full of such thoughts, they turned into the long and sombre street. Florence was not on that side of the carriage which was nearest to her home, and as the distance lessened between them and it, she looked out of her window for the children over the way.

She was thus engaged, when an exclamation from Susan caused her to turn quickly round.

'Why, Gracious me!' cried Susan, breathless, 'where's our house!'

'Our house!' said Florence.

Susan, drawing in her head from the window, thrust it out again, drew it in again as the carriage stopped, and stared at her mistress in amazement.

There was a labyrinth of scaffolding raised all round the house from the basement to the roof. Loads of bricks and stones, and heaps of mortar, and piles of wood, blocked up half the width and length of the broad street at the side. Ladders were raised against the walls: labourers were climbing up and down; men were at work upon the steps of the scaffolding: painters and decorators were busy inside; great rolls of ornamental paper were being delivered from a cart at the door; an upholsterer's waggon also stopped the way; no furniture was to be seen through the gaping and broken windows in any of the rooms; nothing but workmen, and the implements of their several trades, swarming from the kitchens to the garrets. Inside and outside alike: bricklayers, painters, carpenters, masons: hammer, hod, brush, pickaxe, saw, and trowel: all at work together, in full chorus.

Florence descended from the coach, half doubting if it were, or could be the right house, until she recognised Towlinson, with a sun-burnt face, standing at the door to receive her.

'There is nothing the matter?' inquired Florence.

'Oh no, Miss.'

'There are great alterations going on.'

'Yes, Miss, great alterations,' said Towlinson.

Florence passed him as if she were in a dream, and hurried upstairs. The garish light was in the long-darkened drawing-room, and there were steps and platforms, and men in paper caps, in the high places. Her mother's picture was gone with the rest of the movables, and on the mark where it had been, was scrawled in chalk, 'this room in-panel. Green and gold.' The staircase was a labyrinth of posts and planks like the outside of the house, and a whole Olympus of plumbers and glaziers was reclining in various attitudes, on the skylight. Her own room was not yet touched within, but there were beams and boards raised against it without, baulking the daylight. She went up swiftly to that other bedroom, where the little bed was; and a dark giant of a man with a pipe in his mouth, and his head tied up in a pocket-handkerchief, was staring in at the window.

It was here that Susan Nipper, who had been in quest of Florence, found her, and said, would she go downstairs to her papa, who wished to speak to her.

'At home! and wishing to speak to me!' cried Florence, trembling.

Susan, who was infinitely more distraught than Florence herself, repeated her errand; and Florence, pale and agitated, hurried down again, without a moment's hesitation. She thought upon the way down, would she dare to kiss him? The longing of her heart resolved her, and she thought she would.

Her father might have heard that heart beat, when it came into his presence. One instant, and it would have beat against his breast—

But he was not alone. There were two ladies there; and Florence stopped. Striving so hard with her emotion, that if her brute friend Di had not burst in and overwhelmed her with his caresses as a welcome home – at which one of the ladies gave a little scream, and that diverted her attention from herself – she would have swooned upon the floor.

'Florence,' said her father, putting out his hand: so stiffly that it held her off: 'how do you do?'

Florence took the hand between her own, and putting it timidly to her lips, yielded to its withdrawal. It touched the door in shutting it, with quite as much endearment as it had touched her.

'What dog is that?' said Mr Dombey, displeased.

'It is a dog, papa – from Brighton.'

'Well!' said Mr Dombey; and a cloud passed over his face, for he understood her.

'He is very good-tempered,' said Florence, addressing herself with her natural grace and sweetness to the two lady strangers. 'He is only glad to see me. Pray forgive him.'

She saw in the glance they interchanged, that the lady who had screamed, and who was seated, was old; and that the other lady, who stood near her papa, was very beautiful, and of an elegant figure.

'Mrs Skewton,' said her father, turning to the first, and holding out his hand, 'this is my daughter Florence.'

'Charming, I am sure,' observed the lady, putting up her glass. 'So natural! My darling Florence, you must kiss me, if you please.'

Florence having done so, turned towards the other lady, by whom her father stood waiting.

'Edith,' said Mr Dombey, 'this is my daughter Florence. Florence, this lady will soon be your mama.'

Mr Dombey introduces his daughter Florence

Florence started, and looked up at the beautiful face in a conflict of emotions, among which the tears that name awakened, struggled for a moment with surprise, interest, admiration, and an indefinable sort of fear. Then she cried out, 'Oh, papa, may you be happy! may you be very, very happy all your life!' and then fell weeping on the lady's bosom.

There was a short silence. The beautiful lady, who at first had seemed to hesitate whether or no she should advance to Florence, held her to her breast, and pressed the hand with which she clasped her, close about her waist, as if to reassure her and comfort her. Not one word passed the lady's lips. She bent her head down over Florence, and she kissed her on the cheek, but she said no word.

'Shall we go on through the rooms,' said Mr Dombey, 'and see how our workmen are doing? Pray allow me, my dear madam.'

He said this in offering his arm to Mrs Skewton, who had been looking at Florence through her glass, as though picturing to herself what she might be made, by the infusion – from her own copious storehouse, no doubt – of a little more Heart and Nature. Florence was still sobbing on the lady's breast, and holding to her, when Mr Dombey was heard to say from the Conservatory:

'Let us ask Edith. Dear me, where is she?'

'Edith, my dear!' cried Mrs Skewton, 'where are you? Looking for Mr Dombey somewhere, I know. We are here, my love.'

The beautiful lady released her hold of Florence, and pressing her lips once more upon her face, withdrew hurriedly, and joined them. Florence remained standing in the same place: happy, sorry, joyful, and in tears, she knew not how, or how long, but all at once: when her new mama came back, and took her in her arms again.

'Florence,' said the lady, hurriedly, and looking into her face with great earnestness. 'You will not begin by hating me?'

'By hating you, mama?' cried Florence, winding her arm round her neck, and returning the look.

'Hush! Begin by thinking well of me,' said the beautiful lady. 'Begin by believing that I will try to make you happy, and that I am prepared to love you, Florence. Good-bye. We shall meet again soon. Good-bye! Don't stay here, now.'

Again she pressed her to her breast – she had spoken in a rapid manner, but firmly – and Florence saw her rejoin them in the other room.

And now Florence began to hope that she would learn from her new and beautiful mama, how to gain her father's love; and in her sleep that night, in her lost old home, her own mama smiled radiantly upon the hope, and blessed it. Dreaming Florence!

CHAPTER 29

The Opening of the Eyes of Mrs Chick

Miss Tox, all unconscious of any such rare appearances in connexion with Mr Dombey's house, as scaffoldings and ladders, and men with their heads tied up in pocket-handkerchiefs, glaring in at the windows like flying genii or strange birds, – having breakfasted one morning at about this eventful period of time, on her customary viands; to wit, one French roll rasped,[1] one egg new laid (or warranted to be), and one little pot of tea, wherein was infused one little silver scoopful of that herb on behalf of Miss Tox, and one little silver scoopful on behalf of the teapot – a flight of fancy in which good housekeepers delight; went upstairs to set forth the bird waltz on the harpsichord, to water and arrange the plants, to dust the nick-nacks, and according to her daily custom, to make her little drawing-room the garland of Princess's Place.

Miss Tox endued herself with a pair of ancient gloves, like dead leaves, in which she was accustomed to perform these avocations – hidden from human sight at other times in a table drawer – and went methodically to work; beginning with the bird waltz; passing, by a natural association of ideas, to her bird – a very high-shouldered canary, stricken in years, and much rumpled, but a piercing singer, as Princess's Place well knew; taking, next in order, the little china ornaments, paper fly-cages, and so forth; and coming round, in good time, to the plants, which generally required to be snipped here and there with a pair of scissors, for some botanical reason that was very powerful to Miss Tox.

Miss Tox was slow in coming to the plants, this morning. The weather was warm, the wind southerly; and there was a sigh of the summer-time in Princess's Place, that turned Miss Tox's thoughts upon the country. The pot-boy attached to the Princess's Arms had come out with a can and trickled water, in a flowing pattern, all over Princess's Place, and it gave the weedy ground a fresh scent – quite a growing scent, Miss Tox said. There was a tiny blink of sun peeping in from the great street round the corner, and the smoky sparrows hopped over it and back again, brightening as they passed:

or bathed in it, like a stream, and became glorified sparrows, unconnected with chimneys. Legends[2] in praise of Ginger-Beer, with pictorial representations of thirsty customers submerged in the effervescence, or stunned by the flying corks, were conspicuous in the window of the Princess's Arms. They were making late hay, somewhere out of town; and though the fragrance had a long way to come, and many counter fragrances to contend with among the dwellings of the poor (may God reward the worthy gentlemen who stickle for the Plague as part and parcel of the wisdom of our ancestors, and who do their little best to keep those dwellings miserable!),[3] yet it was wafted faintly into Princess's Place, whispering of Nature and her wholesome air, as such things will, even unto prisoners and captives, and those who are desolate and oppressed, in very spite of aldermen and knights to boot: at whose sage nod – and how they nod! – the rolling world stands still!

Miss Tox sat down upon the window-seat, and thought of her good papa deceased – Mr Tox, of the Customs Department of the public service; and of her childhood, passed at a seaport, among a considerable quantity of cold tar, and some rusticity. She fell into a softened remembrance of meadows, in old time, gleaming with buttercups, like so many inverted firmaments of golden stars; and how she had made chains of dandelion-stalks for youthful vowers of eternal constancy, dressed chiefly in nankeen; and how soon those fetters had withered and broken.

Sitting on the window-seat, and looking out upon the sparrows and the blink of sun, Miss Tox thought likewise of her good mama deceased – sister to the owner of the powdered head and pigtail – of her virtues and her rheumatism. And when a man with bulky legs, and a rough voice, and a heavy basket on his head that crushed his hat into a mere black muffin, came crying flowers down Princess's Place, making his timid little roots of daisies shudder in the vibration of every yell he gave, as though he had been an ogre, hawking little children, summer recollections were so strong upon Miss Tox, that she shook her head, and murmured she would be comparatively old before she knew it – which seemed likely.

In her pensive mood, Miss Tox's thoughts went wandering on Mr Dombey's track; probably because the Major had returned home to his lodgings opposite, and had just bowed to her from his window. What other reason could Miss Tox have for connecting Mr Dombey with her summer days and dandelion fetters? Was he more cheerful? thought Miss Tox. Was he reconciled to the decrees of fate? Would he ever marry again? and if yes, whom? What sort of person now!

A flush – it was warm weather – overspread Miss Tox's face as, while entertaining these meditations, she turned her head, and was surprised by the reflection of her thoughtful image in the chimney-glass.[4] Another flush succeeded when she saw a little carriage drive into Princess's Place, and make straight for her own door. Miss Tox arose, took up her scissors hastily, and so coming, at last, to the plants, was very busy with them when Mrs Chick entered the room.

'How is my sweetest friend!' exclaimed Miss Tox, with open arms.

A little stateliness was mingled with Miss Tox's sweetest friend's demeanour, but she kissed Miss Tox, and said, 'Lucretia, thank you, I am pretty well. I hope you are the same. Hem!'

Mrs Chick was labouring under a peculiar little monosyllabic cough; a sort of primer, or easy introduction to the art of coughing.

'You call very early, and how kind that is, my dear!' pursued Miss Tox. 'Now, have you breakfasted?'

'Thank you, Lucretia,' said Mrs Chick, 'I have. I took an early breakfast' – the good lady seemed curious on the subject of Princess's Place, and looked all round it as she spoke – 'with my brother, who has come home.'

'He is better, I trust, my love,' faltered Miss Tox.

'He is greatly better, thank you. Hem!'

'My dear Louisa must be careful of that cough,' remarked Miss Tox.

'It's nothing,' returned Mrs Chick. 'It's merely change of weather. We must expect change.'

'Of weather?' asked Miss Tox, in her simplicity.

'Of everything,' returned Mrs Chick. 'Of course we must. It's a world of change. Any one would surprise me very much, Lucretia, and would greatly alter my opinion of their understanding, if they attempted to contradict or evade what is so perfectly evident. Change!' exclaimed Mrs Chick, with severe philosophy. 'Why, my gracious me, what is there that does *not* change! even the silkworm, who I am sure might be supposed not to trouble itself about such subjects, changes into all sorts of unexpected things continually.'

'My Louisa,' said the mild Miss Tox, 'is ever happy in her illustrations.'

'You are so kind, Lucretia,' returned Mrs Chick, a little softened, 'as to say so, and to think so, I believe. I hope neither of us may have any cause to lessen our opinion of the other, Lucretia.'

'I am sure of it,' returned Miss Tox.

Mrs Chick coughed as before, and drew lines on the carpet with the ivory end of her parasol. Miss Tox, who had experience of her fair friend, and knew that under the pressure of any slight fatigue or vexation she was prone to a discursive kind of irritability, availed herself of the pause, to change the subject.

'Pardon me, my dear Louisa,' said Miss Tox, 'but have I caught sight of the manly form of Mr Chick in the carriage?'

'He is there,' said Mrs Chick, 'but pray leave him there. He has his newspaper, and would be quite contented for the next two hours. Go on with your flowers, Lucretia, and allow me to sit here and rest.'

'My Louisa knows,' observed Miss Tox, 'that between friends like ourselves, any approach to ceremony would be out of the question. Therefore—' Therefore Miss Tox finished the sentence, not in words but action; and putting on her gloves again, which she had taken off, and arming herself once more with her scissors, began to snip and clip among the leaves with microscopic industry.

'Florence has returned home also,' said Mrs Chick, after sitting silent for some time, with her head on one side, and her parasol sketching on the floor; 'and really Florence is a great deal too old now, to continue to lead that solitary life to which she has been accustomed. Of course she is. There can be no doubt about it. I should have very little respect, indeed, for anybody who could advocate a different opinion. Whatever my wishes might be, I *could not* respect them. We cannot command our feelings to such an extent as that.'

Miss Tox assented, without being particular as to the intelligibility of the proposition.

'If she's a strange girl,' said Mrs Chick, 'and if my brother Paul cannot feel perfectly comfortable in her society, after all the sad things that have happened, and all the terrible disappointments that have been undergone, then, what is the reply? That he must make an effort. That he is bound to make an effort. We have always been a family remarkable for effort. Paul is at the head of the family; almost the only representative of it left – for what am I – *I* am of no consequence—'

'My dearest love,' remonstrated Miss Tox.

Mrs Chick dried her eyes, which were, for the moment, overflowing; and proceeded:

'And consequently he is more than ever bound to make an effort. And though his having done so, comes upon me with a sort of shock – for mine is a very weak and foolish nature; which is anything but a blessing I am sure; I often wish my heart was a marble slab, or a paving-stone—'

'My sweet Louisa,' remonstrated Miss Tox again.

'Still, it is a triumph to me to know that he is so true to himself, and to his name of Dombey; although, of course, I always knew he would be. I only hope,' said Mrs Chick, after a pause, 'that she may be worthy of the name too.'

Miss Tox filled a little green watering-pot from a jug, and happening to look up when she had done so, was so surprised by the amount of expression Mrs Chick had conveyed into her face, and was bestowing upon her, that she put the little watering-pot on the table for the present, and sat down near it.

'My dear Louisa,' said Miss Tox, 'will it be the least satisfaction to you, if I venture to observe in reference to that remark, that I, as a humble individual, think your sweet niece in every way most promising?'

'What do you mean, Lucretia?' returned Mrs Chick, with increased stateliness of manner. 'To what remark of mine, my dear, do you refer?'

'Her being worthy of her name, my love,' replied Miss Tox.

'If,' said Mrs Chick, with solemn patience, 'I have not expressed myself with clearness, Lucretia, the fault of course is mine. There is, perhaps, no reason why I should express myself at all, except the intimacy that has subsisted between us, and which I very much hope, Lucretia – confidently hope – nothing will occur to disturb. Because, why should I do anything else? There is no reason; it would be absurd. But I wish to express myself clearly, Lucretia; and therefore to go back to that remark, I must beg to say that it was not intended to relate to Florence, in any way.'

'Indeed!' returned Miss Tox.

'No,' said Mrs Chick, shortly and decisively.

'Pardon me, my dear,' rejoined her meek friend; 'but I cannot have understood it. I fear I am dull.'

Mrs Chick looked round the room and over the way; at the plants, at the bird, at the watering-pot, at almost everything within view, except Miss Tox; and finally dropping her glance upon Miss Tox, for a moment, on its way to the ground, said, looking meanwhile with elevated eyebrows at the carpet:

'When I speak, Lucretia, of her being worthy of the name, I speak of my brother Paul's second wife. I believe I have already said, in effect, if not in the very words I now use, that it is his intention to marry a second wife.'

Miss Tox left her seat in a hurry, and returned to her plants; clipping among the stems and leaves, with as little favour as a barber working at so many pauper heads of hair.

'Whether she will be fully sensible of the distinction conferred upon her,' said Mrs Chick, in a lofty tone, 'is quite another question. I hope she may be. We are bound to think well of one another in this world, and I hope she may be. I have not been advised with myself. If I had been advised with, I have no doubt my advice would have been cavalierly received, and therefore it is infinitely better as it is. I much prefer it as it is.'

Miss Tox, with head bent down, still clipped among the plants. Mrs Chick, with energetic shakings of her own head from time to time, continued to hold forth, as if in defiance of somebody.

'If my brother Paul had consulted with me, which he sometimes does – or rather, sometimes used to do; for he will naturally do that no more now, and this is a circumstance which I regard as a relief from responsibility,' said Mrs Chick, hysterically, 'for I thank Heaven I am not jealous—' here Mrs Chick again shed tears: 'if my brother Paul had come to me, and had said, "Louisa, what kind of qualities would you advise me to look out for, in a wife?" I should certainly have answered, "Paul, you must have family, you must have beauty, you must have dignity, you must have connexion." Those are the words I should have used. You might have led me to the block immediately afterwards,' said Mrs Chick, as if that consequence were highly probable, 'but I should have used them. I should have said, "Paul! You to marry a second time without family! You to marry without beauty! You to marry without dignity! You to marry without connexion! There is nobody in the world, not mad, who could dream of daring to entertain such a preposterous idea!"'

Miss Tox stopped clipping; and with her head among the plants, listened attentively. Perhaps Miss Tox thought there was hope in this exordium, and the warmth of Mrs Chick.

'I should have adopted this course of argument,' pursued the discreet lady, 'because I trust I am not a fool. I make no claim to be considered a person of superior intellect – though I believe some people have been extraordinary enough to consider me so; one so little humoured as I am, would very soon be disabused of any such notion; but I trust I am not a downright fool. And to tell ME,' said Mrs Chick with ineffable disdain, 'that my brother Paul Dombey could ever contemplate the possibility of uniting himself to anybody – I don't care who' – she was more sharp and emphatic in that short clause than in any other part of her discourse – 'not possessing these requisites, would be to insult what understanding I *have* got, as much as if I was to be told that I was born and bred an elephant, which I *may* be told next,' said Mrs Chick, with resignation. 'It wouldn't surprise me at all. I expect it.'

In the moment's silence that ensued, Miss Tox's scissors gave a feeble clip or two: but Miss Tox's face was still invisible, and Miss Tox's morning gown was agitated. Mrs Chick looked sideways at her, through the intervening plants, and went on to say, in a tone of bland conviction, and as one dwelling on a point of fact that hardly required to be stated:

'Therefore, of course my brother Paul has done what was to be expected of him, and what anybody might have foreseen he would do, if he entered the marriage state again. I confess it takes me rather by surprise, however gratifying; because when Paul went out of town I had no idea at all that he would form any attachment out of town, and he certainly had no attachment when he left here. However, it seems to be extremely desirable in every point of view. I have no doubt the mother is a most genteel and elegant creature, and I have no right whatever to dispute the policy of her living with them: which is Paul's affair, not mine – and as to Paul's choice, herself, I have only seen her picture yet, but that is beautiful indeed. Her name is beautiful too,' said Mrs Chick, shaking her head with energy, and arranging herself in her chair; 'Edith is at once uncommon, as it strikes me, and distinguished. Consequently, Lucretia, I have no doubt you will be happy to hear that the marriage is to take place immediately – of course, you will:' great emphasis again: 'and that you are delighted with this change in the condition of my brother, who has shown you a great deal of pleasant attention at various times.'

Miss Tox made no verbal answer, but took up the little watering-pot with a trembling hand, and looked vacantly round as if considering what article of furniture would be improved by the contents. The room door opening at this crisis of Miss Tox's feelings, she started, laughed aloud, and fell into the arms of the person entering; happily insensible alike of Mrs Chick's indignant countenance and of the Major at his window over the way, who had his double-barrelled eye-glass in full action, and whose face and figure were dilated with Mephistophelean[5] joy.

Not so the expatriated Native, amazed supporter of Miss Tox's

The eyes of Mrs Chick are opened to Lucretia Tox

swooning form, who, coming straight upstairs, with a polite inquiry touching Miss Tox's health (in exact pursuance of the Major's malicious instructions), had accidentally arrived in the very nick of time to catch the delicate burden in his arms, and to receive the contents of the little watering-pot in his shoe; both of which circumstances, coupled with his consciousness of being closely watched by the wrathful Major, who had threatened the usual penalty in regard to every bone in his skin in case of any failure, combined to render him a moving spectacle of mental and bodily distress.

For some moments, this afflicted foreigner remained clasping Miss Tox to his heart, with an energy of action in remarkable opposition to his disconcerted face, while that poor lady trickled slowly down upon him the very last sprinklings of the little watering-pot, as if he were a delicate exotic (which indeed he was), and might be almost expected to blow while the gentle rain descended. Mrs Chick, at length recovering sufficient presence of mind to interpose, commanded him to drop Miss Tox upon the sofa and withdraw; and the exile promptly obeying, she applied herself to promote Miss Tox's recovery.

But none of that gentle concern which usually characterises the daughters of Eve in their tending of each other; none of that freemasonry in fainting, by which they are generally bound together in a mysterious bond of sisterhood; was visible in Mrs Chick's demeanour. Rather like the executioner who restores the victim to sensation previous to proceeding with the torture (or was wont to do so, in the good old times for which all true men wear perpetual mourning), did Mrs Chick administer the smelling-bottle,[6] the slapping on the hands, the dashing of cold water on the face, and other proved remedies. And when, at length, Miss Tox opened her eyes, and gradually became restored to animation and consciousness, Mrs Chick drew off as from a criminal, and reversing the precedent of the murdered king of Denmark, regarded her more in anger than in sorrow.[7]

'Lucretia!' said Mrs Chick. 'I will not attempt to disguise what I feel. My eyes are opened, all at once. I wouldn't have believed this, if a Saint had told it to me.'

'I am foolish to give way to faintness,' Miss Tox faltered. 'I shall be better presently.'

'You will be better presently, Lucretia!' repeated Mrs Chick, with exceeding scorn. 'Do you suppose I am blind? Do you imagine I am in my second childhood? No, Lucretia! I am obliged to you!'

Miss Tox directed an imploring, helpless kind of look towards her friend, and put her handkerchief before her face.

'If any one had told me this yesterday,' said Mrs Chick, with majesty, 'or even half-an-hour ago, I should have been tempted, I almost believe, to strike them to the earth. Lucretia Tox, my eyes are opened to you all at once. The scales:' here Mrs Chick cast down an imaginary pair, such as are commonly used in grocers' shops: 'have fallen from my sight.[8] The blindness of my confidence is past, Lucretia. It has been abused and played upon, and evasion is quite out of the question now, I assure you.'

'Oh! to what do you allude so cruelly, my love?' asked Miss Tox, through her tears.

'Lucretia,' said Mrs Chick, 'ask your own heart. I must entreat you not to address me by any such familiar term as you have just used, if you please. I have some self-respect left, though you may think otherwise.'

'Oh, Louisa!' cried Miss Tox. 'How can you speak to me like that?'

'How can I speak to you like that?' retorted Mrs Chick, who, in default of having any particular argument to sustain herself upon, relied principally on such repetitions for her most withering effects. 'Like that! You may well say like that, indeed!'

Miss Tox sobbed pitifully.

'The idea!' said Mrs Chick, 'of your having basked at my brother's fireside, like a serpent,[9] and wound yourself, through me, almost into his confidence, Lucretia, that you might, in secret, entertain designs upon him, and dare to aspire to contemplate the possibility of his uniting himself to *you*! Why, it is an idea,' said Mrs Chick, with sarcastic dignity, 'the absurdity of which almost relieves its treachery.'

'Pray, Louisa,' urged Miss Tox, 'do not say such dreadful things.'

'Dreadful things!' repeated Mrs Chick. 'Dreadful things! Is it not a fact, Lucretia, that you have just now been unable to command your feelings even before me, whose eyes you had so completely closed?'

'I have made no complaint,' sobbed Miss Tox. 'I have said nothing. If I have been a little overpowered by your news, Louisa, and have ever had any lingering thought that Mr Dombey was inclined to be particular towards me, surely *you* will not condemn me.'

'She is going to say,' said Mrs Chick, addressing herself to the whole of the furniture, in a comprehensive glance of resignation and appeal, 'She is going to say – I know it – that I have encouraged her!'

'I don't wish to exchange reproaches, dear Louisa,' sobbed Miss Tox. 'Nor do I wish to complain. But, in my own defence—'

'Yes,' cried Mrs Chick, looking round the room with a prophetic smile, 'that's what she's going to say. I knew it. You had better say it. Say it openly! Be open, Lucretia Tox,' said Mrs Chick, with desperate sternness, 'whatever you are.'

'In my own defence,' faltered Miss Tox, 'and only in my own defence against your unkind words, my dear Louisa, I would merely ask you if you haven't often favoured such a fancy, and even said it might happen, for anything we could tell?'

'There is a point,' said Mrs Chick, rising, not as if she were going to stop at the floor, but as if she were about to soar up, high, into her native skies, 'beyond which endurance becomes ridiculous, if not culpable. I can bear much; but not too much. What spell was on me when I came into this house this day, I don't know; but I had a presentiment – a dark presentiment,' said Mrs Chick, with a shiver, 'that something was going to happen. Well may I have had that foreboding, Lucretia, when my confidence of many years is destroyed in an instant, when my eyes are opened all at once, and when I find you revealed in your true colours. Lucretia, I have been mistaken in you. It is better for us both that this subject should end here. I wish you well, and I shall ever wish you well. But, as an individual who desires to be true to herself in her own poor position, whatever that position may be, or may not be – and as the sister of my brother – and as the sister-in-law of my brother's wife – and as a connexion by marriage of my brother's wife's mother – may I be permitted to add, as a Dombey? – I can wish you nothing else but good morning.'

These words, delivered with cutting suavity, tempered and chastened by a lofty air of moral rectitude, carried the speaker to the door. There she inclined her head in a ghostly and statue-like manner, and so withdrew to her carriage, to seek comfort and consolation in the arms of Mr Chick her lord.

Figuratively speaking, that is to say; for the arms of Mr Chick were full of his newspaper. Neither did that gentleman address his eyes towards his wife otherwise than by stealth. Neither did he offer any consolation whatever. In short, he sat reading, and humming fag ends of tunes, and sometimes glancing furtively at her without delivering himself of a word, good, bad, or indifferent.

In the meantime Mrs Chick sat swelling and bridling, and tossing her head, as if she were still repeating that solemn formula of farewell to Lucretia Tox. At length, she said aloud, 'Oh the extent to which her eyes had been opened that day!'

'To which your eyes have been opened, my dear!' repeated Mr Chick.

'Oh, don't talk to me!' said Mrs Chick. 'If you can bear to see me in this state, and not ask me what the matter is, you had better hold your tongue for ever.'

'What *is* the matter, my dear?' asked Mr Chick.

'To think,' said Mrs Chick, in a state of soliloquy, 'that she should ever have conceived the base idea of connecting herself with our family by a marriage with Paul! To think that when she was playing at horses with that dear child who is now in his grave – I never liked it at the time – she should have been hiding such a double-faced design! I wonder she was never afraid that something would happen to her. She is fortunate if nothing does.'

'I really thought, my dear,' said Mr Chick slowly, after rubbing the bridge of his nose for some time with his newspaper, 'that you had gone on the same tack yourself, all along, until this morning; and had thought it would be a convenient thing enough, if it could have been brought about.'

Mrs Chick instantly burst into tears, and told Mr Chick that if he wished to trample upon her with his boots, he had better do it.

'But with Lucretia Tox I have done,' said Mrs Chick, after abandoning herself to her feelings for some minutes, to Mr Chick's great terror. 'I can bear to resign Paul's confidence in favour of one who, I hope and trust, may be deserving of it, and with whom he has a perfect right to replace poor Fanny if he chooses; I can bear to be informed, in Paul's cool manner, of such a change in his plans, and never to be consulted until all is settled and determined; but deceit I can *not* bear, and with Lucretia Tox I have done. It is better as it is,' said Mrs Chick, piously; 'much better. It would have been a long time before I could have accommodated myself comfortably with her, after this; and I really don't know, as Paul is going to be very grand, and these are people of condition, that she would have been quite presentable, and might not have compromised myself. There's a providence in everything; everything works for the best; I have been tried to-day, but, upon the whole I don't regret it.'

In which Christian spirit, Mrs Chick dried her eyes, and smoothed her lap, and sat as became a person calm under a great wrong. Mr Chick, feeling his unworthiness no doubt, took an early opportunity of being set down at a street corner and walking away, whistling, with his shoulders very much raised, and his hands in his pockets.

While poor excommunicated Miss Tox, who, if she were a fawner and toad-eater,[10] was at least an honest and a constant one, and had ever borne a faithful friendship towards her impeacher, and had been truly absorbed and swallowed up in devotion to the magnificence of Mr Dombey – while poor excommunicated Miss Tox watered her plants with her tears, and felt that it was winter in Princess's Place.

CHAPTER 30

The Interval before the Marriage

Although the enchanted house was no more, and the working world had broken into it, and was hammering and crashing and tramping up and down stairs all day long, keeping Diogenes in an incessant paroxysm of barking, from sunrise to sunset – evidently convinced that his enemy had got the better of him at last, and was then sacking the premises in triumphant defiance – there was, at first, no other great change in the method of Florence's life. At night, when the workpeople went away, the house was dreary and deserted again; and Florence, listening to their voices echoing through the hall and staircase as they departed, pictured to herself the cheerful homes to which they were returning, and the children who were waiting for them, and was glad to think that they were merry and well pleased to go.

She welcomed back the evening silence as an old friend, but it came now with an altered face, and looked more kindly on her. Fresh hope was in it. The beautiful lady who had soothed and caressed her, in the very room in which her heart had been so wrung, was a spirit of promise to her. Soft shadows of the bright life dawning, when her father's affection should be gradually won, and all, or much should be restored, of what she had lost on the dark day when a mother's love had faded with a mother's last breath on her cheek, moved about her in the twilight and were welcome company. Peeping at the rosy children her neighbours, it was a new and precious sensation to think that they might soon speak together and know each other; when she would not fear, as of old, to show herself before them, lest they should be grieved to see her in her black dress sitting there alone!

In her thoughts of her new mother, and in the love and trust overflowing her pure heart towards her, Florence loved her own dead mother more and more. She had no fear of setting up a rival in her breast. The new flower sprang from the deep-planted and long-cherished root, she knew. Every gentle word that had fallen from the lips of the beautiful lady, sounded to Florence like an echo of the voice long hushed and silent. How could she love that memory less for living tenderness, when it was her memory of all parental tenderness and love!

Florence was, one day, sitting reading in her room, and thinking of the lady and her promised visit soon – for her book turned on a kindred subject – when, raising her eyes, she saw her standing in the doorway.

'Mama!' cried Florence, joyfully meeting her. 'Come again!'

'Not mama yet,' returned the lady, with a serious smile, as she encircled Florence's neck with her arm.

'But very soon to be,' cried Florence.

'Very soon now, Florence: very soon.'

Edith bent her head a little, so as to press the blooming cheek of Florence against her own, and for some few moments remained thus silent. There was something so very tender in her manner, that Florence was even more sensible of it than on the first occasion of their meeting.

She led Florence to a chair beside her, and sat down: Florence looking in her face, quite wondering at its beauty, and willingly leaving her hand in hers.

'Have you been alone, Florence, since I was here last?'

'Oh yes!' smiled Florence, hastily.

She hesitated and cast down her eyes; for her new mama was very earnest in her look, and the look was intently and thoughtfully fixed upon her face.

'I – I – am used to be alone,' said Florence. 'I don't mind it at all. Di and I pass whole days together, sometimes.' Florence might have said, whole weeks and months.

'Is Di your maid, love?'

'My dog, mama,' said Florence, laughing. 'Susan is my maid.'

'And these are your rooms,' said Edith, looking round. 'I was not shown these rooms the other day. We must have them improved, Florence. They shall be made the prettiest in the house.'

'If I might change them, mama,' returned Florence; 'there is one upstairs I should like much better.'

'Is this not high enough, dear girl?' asked Edith, smiling.

'The other was my brother's room,' said Florence, 'and I am very fond of it. I would have spoken to papa about it when I came home, and found the workmen here, and everything changing: but—'

Florence dropped her eyes, lest the same look should make her falter again.

'—but I was afraid it might distress him; and as you said you would be here again soon, mama, and are the mistress of everything, I determined to take courage and ask you.'

Edith sat looking at her, with her brilliant eyes intent upon her face, until Florence raising her own, she, in her turn, withdrew her gaze, and turned it on the ground. It was then that Florence thought how different this lady's beauty was, from what she had supposed. She had thought it of a proud and lofty kind; yet her manner was so subdued and gentle, that if she had been of Florence's own age and character, it scarcely could have invited confidence more.

Except when a constrained and singular reserve crept over her; and then she seemed (but Florence hardly understood this, though she could not choose but notice it, and think about it) as if she were humbled before Florence, and ill at ease. When she had said that she was not her mama yet, and when Florence had called her the mistress of everything there, this change in her was quick and startling; and now, while the eyes of Florence rested on her face, she sat as though she would have shrunk and hidden from her, rather than as one about to love and cherish her, in right of such a near connexion.

She gave Florence her ready promise, about her new room, and said she would give directions about it herself. She then asked some questions concerning poor Paul; and when they had sat in conversation for some time, told Florence she had come to take her to her own home.

'We have come to London now, my mother and I,' said Edith, 'and you shall stay with us until I am married. I wish that we should know and trust each other, Florence.'

'You are very kind to me,' said Florence, 'dear mama. How much I thank you!'

'Let me say now, for it may be the best opportunity,' continued Edith, looking round to see that they were quite alone, and speaking in a lower voice, 'that when I am married, and have gone away for some weeks, I shall be easier at heart if you will come home here.

No matter who invites you to stay elsewhere, come home here. It is better to be alone than – what I would say is,' she added, checking herself, 'that I know well you are best at home, dear Florence.'

'I will come home on the very day, mama.'

'Do so. I rely on that promise. Now, prepare to come with me, dear girl. You will find me downstairs when you are ready.'

Slowly and thoughtfully did Edith wander alone through the mansion of which she was so soon to be the lady: and little heed took she of all the elegance and splendour it began to display. The same indomitable haughtiness of soul, the same proud scorn expressed in eye and lip, the same fierce beauty, only tamed by a sense of its own little worth, and of the little worth of everything around it, went through the grand saloons and halls, that had got loose among the shady trees, and raged and rent themselves. The mimic roses on the walls and floors were set round with sharp thorns, that tore her breast; in every scrap of gold so dazzling to the eye, she saw some hateful atom of her purchase-money; the broad high mirrors showed her, at full length, a woman with a noble quality yet dwelling in her nature, who was too false to her better self, and too debased and lost, to save herself. She believed that all this was so plain, more or less, to all eyes, that she had no resource or power of self-assertion but in pride: and with this pride, which tortured her own heart night and day, she fought her fate out, braved it, and defied it.

Was this the woman whom Florence – an innocent girl, strong only in her earnestness and simple truth – could so impress and quell, that by her side she was another creature, with her tempest of passion hushed, and her very pride itself subdued? Was this the woman who now sat beside her in a carriage, with her arms entwined, and who, while she courted and entreated her to love and trust her, drew her fair head to nestle on her breast, and would have laid down life to shield it from wrong or harm?

Oh, Edith! it were well to die, indeed, at such a time! Better and happier far, perhaps, to die so, Edith, than to live on to the end!

The Honourable Mrs Skewton, who was thinking of anything rather than of such sentiments – for, like many genteel persons who have existed at various times, she set her face against death altogether, and objected to the mention of any such low and levelling upstart – had borrowed a house in Brook Street, Grosvenor Square, from a stately relative (one of the Feenix brood), who was out of town, and who did not object to lending it, in the handsomest manner, for nuptial purposes, as the loan implied his final release and acquittance from all further loans and gifts to Mrs Skewton and her daughter. It being necessary for the credit of the family to make a handsome appearance at such a time, Mrs Skewton, with the assistance of an accommodating tradesman resident in the parish of Mary-le-bone, who lent out all sorts of articles to the nobility and gentry, from a service of plate to an army of footmen, clapped into this house a silver-headed butler (who was charged extra on that account, as having the appearance of an ancient family retainer), two very tall young men in livery, and a select staff of kitchen-servants, so that a legend arose, downstairs, that Withers the page, released at once from his numerous household duties, and from the propulsion of the wheeled-chair (inconsistent with the metropolis), had been several times observed to rub his eyes and pinch his limbs, as if he misdoubted his having overslept himself at the Leamington milkman's, and being still in a celestial dream. A variety of requisites in plate and china being also conveyed to the same establishment from the same convenient source, with several miscellaneous articles, including a neat chariot and a pair of bays, Mrs Skewton cushioned herself on the principal sofa, in the Cleopatra attitude, and held her court in fair state.

'And how,' said Mrs Skewton, on the entrance of her daughter and her charge, 'is my charming Florence? You must come and kiss me, Florence, if you please, my love.'

Florence was timidly stooping to pick out a place in the white part of Mrs Skewton's face, when that lady presented her ear, and relieved her of her difficulty.

'Edith, my dear,' said Mrs Skewton, 'positively, I – stand a little more in the light, my sweetest Florence, for a moment.'

Florence blushingly complied.

'You don't remember, dearest Edith,' said her mother, 'what you were when you were about the same age as our exceedingly precious Florence, or a few years younger?'

'I have long forgotten, mother.'

'For positively, my dear,' said Mrs Skewton, 'I do think that I see a decided resemblance to what you were then, in our extremely fascinating young friend. And it shows,' said Mrs Skewton, in a lower voice, which conveyed her opinion that Florence was in a very unfinished state, 'what cultivation will do.'

'It does, indeed,' was Edith's stern reply.

Her mother eyed her sharply for a moment, and feeling herself on unsafe ground, said, as a diversion:

'My charming Florence, you must come and kiss me once more, if you please, my love.'

Florence complied, of course, and again imprinted her lips on Mrs Skewton's ear.

'And you have heard, no doubt, my darling pet,' said Mrs Skewton, detaining her hand, 'that your papa, whom we all perfectly adore and dote upon, is to be married to my dearest Edith this day week.'

'I knew it would be very soon,' returned Florence, 'but not exactly when.'

'My darling Edith,' urged her mother, gaily, 'is it possible you have not told Florence?'

'Why should I tell Florence?' she returned, so suddenly and harshly, that Florence could scarcely believe it was the same voice.

Mrs Skewton then told Florence, as another and safer diversion, that her father was coming to dinner, and that he would no doubt be charmingly surprised to see her; as he had spoken last night of dressing in the City,[1] and had known nothing of Edith's design, the execution of which, according to Mrs Skewton's expectation, would throw him into a perfect ecstasy. Florence was troubled to hear this; and her distress became so keen, as the dinner-hour approached, that if she had known how to frame an entreaty to be suffered to return home, without involving her father in her explanation, she would have hurried back on foot, bareheaded, breathless, and alone, rather than incur the risk of meeting his displeasure.

As the time drew nearer, she could hardly breathe. She dared not approach a window, lest he should see her from the street. She dared not go upstairs to hide her emotion, lest, in passing out at the door, she should meet him unexpectedly; besides which dread, she felt as though she never could come back again if she were summoned to his presence. In this conflict of fears, she was sitting by Cleopatra's couch, endeavouring to understand and to reply to the bald discourse of that lady, when she heard his foot upon the stair.

'I hear him now!' cried Florence, starting. 'He is coming!'

Cleopatra, who in her juvenility was always playfully disposed, and who in her self-engrossment did not trouble herself about the nature of this agitation, pushed Florence behind her couch, and dropped a shawl over her, preparatory to giving Mr Dombey a rapture of surprise. It was so quickly done, that in a moment Florence heard his awful step in the room.

He saluted his intended mother-in-law, and his intended bride.
The strange sound of his voice thrilled through the whole frame of
his child.

'My dear Dombey,' said Cleopatra, 'come here and tell me how
your pretty Florence is.'

'Florence is very well,' said Mr Dombey, advancing towards the
couch.

'At home?'

'At home,' said Mr Dombey.

'My dear Dombey,' returned Cleopatra, with bewitching vivacity;
'now are you sure you are not deceiving me? I don't know what my
dearest Edith will say to me when I make such a declaration, but
upon my honour I am afraid you are the falsest of men, my dear
Dombey.'

Though he had been; and had been detected on the spot, in the
most enormous falsehood that was ever said or done; he could
hardly have been more disconcerted than he was, when Mrs
Skewton plucked the shawl away, and Florence, pale and trembling,
rose before him like a ghost. He had not yet recovered his presence
of mind, when Florence had run up to him, clasped her hands round
his neck, kissed his face, and hurried out of the room. He looked
round as if to refer the matter to somebody else, but Edith had gone
after Florence, instantly.

'Now, confess, my dear Dombey,' said Mrs Skewton, giving him
her hand, 'that you never were more surprised and pleased in your
life.'

'I never was more surprised,' said Mr Dombey.

'Nor pleased, my dearest Dombey?' returned Mrs Skewton,
holding up her fan.

'I – yes, I am exceedingly glad to meet Florence here,' said Mr
Dombey. He appeared to consider gravely about it for a moment,
and then said, more decidedly, 'Yes, I really am very glad indeed to
meet Florence here.'

'You wonder how she comes here?' said Mrs Skewton, 'don't
you?'

'Edith, perhaps—' suggested Mr Dombey.

'Ah! wicked guesser!' replied Cleopatra, shaking her head. 'Ah!
cunning, cunning man! One shouldn't tell these things; your sex,
my dear Dombey, are so vain, and so apt to abuse our weaknesses;
but you know my open soul – very well; immediately.'

This was addressed to one of the very tall young men who
announced dinner.

'But Edith, my dear Dombey,' she continued in a whisper, 'when she cannot have you near her – and as I tell her, she cannot expect that always – will at least have near her something or somebody belonging to you. Well, how extremely natural that is! And in this spirit, nothing would keep her from riding off to-day to fetch our darling Florence. Well, how excessively charming that is!'

As she waited for an answer, Mr Dombey answered, 'Eminently so.'

'Bless you, my dear Dombey, for that proof of heart!' cried Cleopatra, squeezing his hand. 'But I am growing too serious! Take me downstairs, like an angel, and let us see what these people intend to give us for dinner. Bless you, dear Dombey!'

Cleopatra skipping off her couch with tolerable briskness after the last benediction, Mr Dombey took her arm in his and led her ceremoniously downstairs; one of the very tall young men on hire, whose organ of veneration[2] was imperfectly developed, thrusting his tongue into his cheek, for the entertainment of the other very tall young man on hire, as the couple turned into the dining-room.

Florence and Edith were already there, and sitting side by side. Florence would have risen when her father entered, to resign her chair to him; but Edith openly put her hand upon her arm, and Mr Dombey took an opposite place at the round table.

The conversation was almost entirely sustained by Mrs Skewton. Florence hardly dared to raise her eyes, lest they should reveal the traces of tears; far less dared to speak; and Edith never uttered one word, unless in answer to a question. Verily, Cleopatra worked hard, for the establishment that was so nearly clutched; and verily it should have been a rich one to reward her!

'And so your preparations are nearly finished at last, my dear Dombey?' said Cleopatra, when the dessert was put upon the table, and the silver-headed butler had withdrawn. 'Even the lawyers' preparations!'

'Yes, madam,' replied Mr Dombey; 'the deed of settlement, the professional gentlemen inform me, is now ready, and as I was mentioning to you, Edith has only to do us the favour to suggest her own time for its execution.'

Edith sat like a handsome statue; as cold, as silent, and as still.

'My dearest love,' said Cleopatra, 'do you hear what Mr Dombey says? Ah, my dear Dombey!' aside to that gentleman, 'how her absence,[3] as the time approaches, reminds me of the days, when that most agreeable of creatures, her papa, was in your situation!'

'I have nothing to suggest. It shall be when you please,' said Edith, scarcely looking over the table at Mr Dombey.

'To-morrow?' suggested Mr Dombey.

'If you please.'

'Or would next day,' said Mr Dombey, 'suit your engagements better?'

'I have no engagements. I am always at your disposal. Let it be when you like.'

'No engagements, my dear Edith!' remonstrated her mother, 'when you are in a most terrible state of flurry all day long, and have a thousand and one appointments with all sorts of tradespeople!'

'They are of your making,' returned Edith, turning on her with a slight contraction of her brow. 'You and Mr Dombey can arrange between you.'

'Very true indeed, my love, and most considerate of you!' said Cleopatra. 'My darling Florence, you must really come and kiss me once more, if you please, my dear!'

Singular coincidence, that these gushes of interest in Florence hurried Cleopatra away from almost every dialogue in which Edith had a share, however trifling. Florence had certainly never undergone so much embracing, and perhaps had never been, unconsciously, so useful in her life.

Mr Dombey was far from quarrelling, in his own breast, with the manner of his beautiful betrothed. He had that good reason for sympathy with haughtiness and coldness, which is found in a fellow-feeling. It flattered him to think how these deferred to him, in Edith's case, and seemed to have no will apart from his. It flattered him to picture to himself, this proud and stately woman doing the honours of his house, and chilling his guests after his own manner. The dignity of Dombey and Son would be heightened and maintained, indeed, in such hands.

So thought Mr Dombey, when he was left alone at the dining-table, and mused upon his past and future fortunes: finding no uncongeniality in an air of scant and gloomy state that pervaded the room, in colour a dark brown, with black hatchments[4] of pictures blotching the walls, and twenty-four black chairs, with almost as many nails in them as so many coffins, waiting like mutes,[5] upon the threshold of the Turkey carpet; and two exhausted negroes holding up two withered branches of candelabra on the sideboard, and a musty smell prevailing as if the ashes of ten thousand dinners were entombed in the sarcophagus below it. The owner of the house lived much abroad; the air of England seldom agreed long with a member of the Feenix family; and the room had gradually put itself into deeper and still deeper mourning for him, until it was become so funereal as to want nothing but a body in it to be quite complete.

No bad representation of the body, for the nonce, in his unbending form, if not in his attitude, Mr Dombey looked down into the cold depths of the dead sea of mahogany on which the fruit dishes and decanters lay at anchor: as if the subjects of his thoughts were rising towards the surface one by one, and plunging down again. Edith was there in all her majesty of brow and figure, and close to her came Florence, with her timid head turned to him, as it had been, for an instant, when she left the room; and Edith's eyes upon her, and Edith's hand put out protectingly. A little figure in a low arm-chair came springing next into the light, and looked upon him wonderingly, with its bright eyes and its old-young face, gleaming as in the flickering of an evening fire. Again came Florence close upon it, and absorbed his whole attention. Whether as a fore-doomed difficulty and disappointment to him; whether as a rival who had crossed him in his way, and might again; whether as his child, of whom, in his successful wooing, he could stoop to think, as claiming, at such a time, to be no more estranged; or whether as a hint to him that the mere appearance of caring for his own blood should be maintained in his new relations; he best knew. Indifferently well, perhaps, at best; for marriage company and marriage altars, and ambitious scenes – still blotted here and there with Florence – always Florence – turned up so fast, and so confusedly, that he rose, and went upstairs, to escape them.

It was quite late at night before candles were brought; for at present they made Mrs Skewton's head ache, she complained; and in the meantime Florence and Mrs Skewton talked together (Cleopatra being very anxious to keep her close to herself), or Florence touched the piano softly for Mrs Skewton's delight; to make no mention of a few occasions in the course of the evening, when that affectionate lady was impelled to solicit another kiss, and which always happened after Edith had said anything. They were not many, however, for Edith sat apart by an open window during the whole time (in spite of her mother's fears that she would take cold), and remained there until Mr Dombey took leave. He was serenely gracious to Florence when he did so; and Florence went to bed in a room within Edith's, so happy and hopeful, that she thought of her late self as if it were some other poor deserted girl who was to be pitied for her sorrow; and in her pity, sobbed herself to sleep.

The week fled fast. There were drives to milliners, dressmakers, jewellers, lawyers, florists, pastry-cooks; and Florence was always of the party. Florence was to go to the wedding. Florence was to cast off her mourning, and to wear a brilliant dress on the occasion. The milliner's intentions on the subject of this dress – the milliner was a Frenchwoman, and greatly resembled Mrs Skewton – were so chaste and elegant, that Mrs Skewton bespoke one like it for herself. The milliner said it would become her to admiration, and that all the world would take her for the young lady's sister.

The week fled faster. Edith looked at nothing and cared for nothing. Her rich dresses came home, and were tried on, and were loudly commended by Mrs Skewton and the milliners, and were put away without a word from her. Mrs Skewton made their plans for every day, and executed them. Sometimes Edith sat in the carriage when they went to make purchases; sometimes, when it was absolutely necessary, she went into the shops. But Mrs Skewton conducted the whole business whatever it happened to be; and Edith looked on as uninterested and with as much apparent indifference as if she had no concern in it. Florence might perhaps have thought she was haughty and listless, but that she was never so to her. So Florence quenched her wonder in her gratitude whenever it broke out, and soon subdued it.

The week fled faster. It had nearly winged its flight away. The last night of the week, the night before the marriage was come. In the dark room – for Mrs Skewton's head was no better yet, though she expected to recover permanently tomorrow – were that lady, Edith, and Mr Dombey. Edith was at her open window looking out into the street; Mr Dombey and Cleopatra were talking softly on the sofa. It was growing late; and Florence being fatigued, had gone to bed.

'My dear Dombey,' said Cleopatra, 'you will leave me Florence to-morrow, when you deprive me of my sweetest Edith.'

Mr Dombey said he would, with pleasure.

'To have her about me, here, while you are both at Paris, and to think that, at her age, I am assisting in the formation of her mind, my dear Dombey,' said Cleopatra, 'will be a perfect balm to me in the extremely shattered state to which I shall be reduced.'

Edith turned her head suddenly. Her listless manner was exchanged, in a moment, to one of burning interest, and, unseen in the darkness, she attended closely to their conversation.

Mr Dombey would be delighted to leave Florence in such admirable guardianship.

'My dear Dombey,' returned Cleopatra, 'a thousand thanks for your good opinion. I feared you were going, with malice afore-thought,[6] as the dreadful lawyers say – those horrid proses! – to condemn me to utter solitude.'

'Why do me so great an injustice, my dear madam?' said Mr Dombey.

'Because my charming Florence tells me so positively she must go home to-morrow,' returned Cleopatra, 'that I began to be afraid, my dearest Dombey, you were quite a Bashaw.'[7]

'I assure you, madam!' said Mr Dombey, 'I have laid no com-mands on Florence; and if I had, there are no commands like your wish.'

'My dear Dombey,' replied Cleopatra, 'what a courtier you are! Though I'll not say so, either; for courtiers have no heart, and yours pervades your charming life and character. And are you really going so early, my dear Dombey!'

Oh, indeed! it was late, and Mr Dombey feared he must.

'Is this a fact, or is it all a dream!' lisped Cleopatra. 'Can I believe, my dearest Dombey, that you are coming back tomorrow to deprive me of my sweet companion; my own Edith!'

Mr Dombey, who was accustomed to take things literally, reminded Mrs Skewton that they were to meet first at the church.

'The pang,' said Mrs Skewton, 'of consigning a child, even to you, my dear Dombey, is one of the most excruciating imaginable; and combined with a naturally delicate constitution, and the extreme stupidity of the pastry-cook who has undertaken the breakfast, is almost too much for my poor strength. But I shall rally, my dear Dombey, in the morning; do not fear for me, or be uneasy on my account. Heaven bless you! My dearest Edith!' she cried archly. 'Somebody is going, pet.'

Edith, who had turned her head again towards the window, and whose interest in their conversation had ceased, rose up in her place, but made no advance towards him, and said nothing. Mr Dombey, with a lofty gallantry adapted to his dignity and the occasion, betook his creaking boots towards her, put her hand to his lips, said, 'To-morrow morning I shall have the happiness of claiming this hand as Mrs Dombey's,' and bowed himself solemnly out.

Mrs Skewton rang for candles as soon as the house-door had closed upon him. With the candles appeared her maid, with the

juvenile dress that was to delude the world to-morrow. The dress
had savage retribution in it, as such dresses ever have, and made
her infinitely older and more hideous than her greasy flannel gown.
But Mrs Skewton tried it on with mincing satisfaction; smirked at
her cadaverous self in the glass, as she thought of its killing effect
upon the Major; and suffering her maid to take it off again, and to
prepare her for repose, tumbled into ruins like a house of painted
cards.

All this time, Edith remained at the dark window looking out
into the street. When she and her mother were at last left alone, she
moved from it for the first time that evening, and came opposite to
her. The yawning, shaking, peevish figure of the mother, with her
eyes raised to confront the proud erect form of her daughter, whose
glance of fire was bent downward upon her, had a conscious air
upon it, that no levity or temper could conceal.

'I am tired to death,' said she. 'You can't be trusted for a moment.
You are worse than a child. Child! No child would be half so
obstinate and undutiful.'

'Listen to me, mother,' returned Edith, passing these words by
with a scorn that would not descend to trifle with them. 'You must
remain alone here until I return.'

'Must remain alone here, Edith, until you return!' repeated her
mother.

'Or in that name upon which I shall call to-morrow to witness
what I do, so falsely, and so shamefully, I swear I will refuse the
hand of this man in the church. If I do not, may I fall dead upon
the pavement!'

The mother answered with a look of quick alarm, in no degree
diminished by the look she met.

'It is enough,' said Edith, steadily, 'that we are what we are. I will
have no youth and truth dragged down to my level. I will have no
guileless nature undermined, corrupted, and perverted, to amuse
the leisure of a world of mothers. You know my meaning. Florence
must go home.'

'You are an idiot, Edith,' cried her angry mother. 'Do you expect
there can ever be peace for you in that house, till she is married,
and away?'

'Ask me, or ask yourself, if I ever expect peace in that house,'
said her daughter, 'and you know the answer.'

'And am I to be told to-night, after all my pains and labour, and
when you are going, through me, to be rendered independent,' her
mother almost shrieked in her passion, while her palsied head shook

like a leaf, 'that there is corruption and contagion in me, and that I am not fit company for a girl! What are you, pray? What are you?'

'I have put the question to myself,' said Edith, ashy pale, and pointing to the window, 'more than once when I have been sitting there, and something in the faded likeness of my sex has wandered past outside; and God knows I have met with my reply. Oh mother, mother, if you had but left me to my natural heart when I too was a girl – a younger girl than Florence – how different I might have been!'

Sensible that any show of anger was useless here, her mother restrained herself, and fell a whimpering, and bewailed that she had lived too long, and that her only child had cast her off, and that duty towards parents was forgotten in these evil days, and that she had heard unnatural taunts, and cared for life no longer.

'If one is to go on living through continual scenes like this,' she whined, 'I am sure it would be much better for me to think of some means of putting an end to my existence. Oh! The idea of your being my daughter, Edith, and addressing me in such a strain!'

'Between us, mother,' returned Edith, mournfully, 'the time for mutual reproaches is past.'

'Then why do you revive it?' whimpered her mother. 'You know that you are lacerating me in the cruellest manner. You know how sensitive I am to unkindness. At such a moment, too, when I have so much to think of, and am naturally anxious to appear to the best advantage! I wonder at you, Edith. To make your mother a fright upon your wedding-day!'

Edith bent the same fixed look upon her, as she sobbed and rubbed her eyes; and said in the same low steady voice, which had neither risen nor fallen since she first addressed her, 'I have said that Florence must go home.'

'Let her go!' cried the afflicted and affrighted parent, hastily. 'I am sure I am willing she should go. What is the girl to me?'

'She is so much to me, that rather than communicate, or suffer to be communicated to her, one grain of the evil that is in my breast, mother, I would renounce you, as I would (if you gave me cause) renounce him in the church to-morrow,' replied Edith. 'Leave her alone. She shall not, while I can interpose, be tampered with and tainted by the lessons I have learned. This is no hard condition on this bitter night.'

'If you had proposed it in a filial manner, Edith,' whined her mother, 'perhaps not; very likely not. But such extremely cutting words—'

'They are past and at an end between us now,' said Edith. 'Take your own way, mother; share as you please in what you have gained; spend, enjoy, make much of it; and be as happy as you will. The object of our lives is won. Henceforth let us wear it silently. My lips are closed upon the past from this hour. I forgive you your part in to-morrow's wickedness. May God forgive my own!'

Without a tremor in her voice, or frame, and passing onward with a foot that set itself upon the neck of every soft emotion, she bade her mother good night, and repaired to her own room.

But not to rest; for there was no rest in the tumult of her agitation when alone. To and fro, and to and fro, and to and fro again, five hundred times, among the splendid preparations for her adornment on the morrow; with her dark hair shaken down, her dark eyes flashing with a raging light, her broad white bosom red with the cruel grasp of the relentless hand with which she spurned it from her, pacing up and down with an averted head, as if she would avoid the sight of her own fair person, and divorce herself from its companionship. Thus, in the dead time of the night before her bridal, Edith Granger wrestled with her unquiet spirit, tearless, friendless, silent, proud, and uncomplaining.

At length it happened that she touched the open door which led into the room where Florence lay.

She started, stopped, and looked in.

A light was burning there, and showed her Florence in her bloom of innocence and beauty, fast asleep. Edith held her breath, and felt herself drawn on towards her.

Drawn nearer, nearer, nearer yet; at last, drawn so near, that stooping down, she pressed her lips to the gentle hand that lay outside the bed, and put it softly to her neck. Its touch was like the prophet's rod[8] of old upon the rock. Her tears sprung forth beneath it, as she sunk upon her knees, and laid her aching head and streaming hair upon the pillow by its side.

Thus Edith Granger passed the night before her bridal. Thus the sun found her on her bridal morning.

CHAPTER 31

The Wedding

Dawn, with its passionless blank face, steals shivering to the church beneath which lies the dust of little Paul and his mother, and looks in at the window. It is cold and dark. Night crouches yet, upon the pavement, and broods, sombre and heavy, in nooks and corners of the building. The steeple-clock, perched up above the houses, emerging from beneath another of the countless ripples in the tide of time that regularly roll and break on the eternal shore, is greyly visible, like a stone beacon, recording how the sea flows on; but within doors, dawn, at first, can only peep at night, and see that it is there.

Hovering feebly round the church, and looking in, dawn moans and weeps for its short reign, and its tears trickle on the window-glass, and the trees against the church-wall bow their heads, and wring their many hands in sympathy. Night, growing pale before it, gradually fades out of the church, but lingers in the vaults below, and sits upon the coffins. And now comes bright day, burnishing the steeple-clock, and reddening the spire, and drying up the tears of dawn, and stifling its complaining; and the scared dawn, following the night, and chasing it from its last refuge, shrinks into the vaults itself and hides, with a frightened face, among the dead, until night returns, refreshed, to drive it out.

And now, the mice, who have been busier with the prayer-books than their proper owners, and with the hassocks, more worn by their little teeth than by human knees, hide their bright eyes in their holes, and gather close together in affright at the resounding clashing of the church-door. For the beadle, that man of power, comes early this morning with the sexton; and Mrs Miff, the wheezy little pew-opener – a mighty dry old lady, sparely dressed, with not an inch of fulness anywhere about her – is also here, and has been waiting at the church-gate half-an-hour, as her place is, for the beadle.

A vinegary face has Mrs Miff, and a mortified bonnet, and eke a thirsty soul for sixpences and shillings. Beckoning to stray people to come into pews, has given Mrs Miff an air of mystery; and there is reservation in the eye of Mrs Miff, as always knowing of a softer seat, but having her suspicions of the fee. There is no such fact as Mr Miff, nor has there been, these twenty years, and Mrs Miff would rather not allude to him. He held some bad opinions, it would seem, about free seats,[1] and though Mrs Miff hopes he may be gone upwards, she couldn't positively undertake to say so.

Busy is Mrs Miff this morning at the church-door, beating and dusting the altar-cloth, the carpet, and the cushions; and much has Mrs Miff to say, about the wedding they are going to have. Mrs Miff is told, that the new furniture and alterations in the house cost full five thousand pound if they cost a penny; and Mrs Miff has heard, upon the best authority, that the lady hasn't got a sixpence wherewithal to bless herself. Mrs Miff remembers, likewise, as if it had happened yesterday, the first wife's funeral, and then the christening, and then the other funeral; and Mrs Miff says, by-the-bye she'll soap-and-water that 'ere tablet presently, against the company arrive. Mr Sownds, the Beadle, who is sitting in the sun upon the church steps all this time (and seldom does anything else, except, in cold weather, sitting by the fire), approves of Mrs Miff's discourse, and asks if Mrs Miff has heard it said, that the lady is uncommon handsome? The information Mrs Miff has received, being of this nature, Mr Sownds the Beadle, who, though orthodox and corpulent, is still an admirer of female beauty, observes, with unction, yes, he hears she is a spanker[2] – an expression that seems somewhat forcible to Mrs Miff, or would, from any lips but those of Mr Sownds the Beadle.

In Mr Dombey's house, at this same time, there is great stir and bustle, more especially among the women: not one of whom has had a wink of sleep since four o'clock, and all of whom were full dressed before six. Mr Towlinson is an object of greater consideration than usual to the housemaid, and the cook says at breakfast-time that one wedding makes many, which the housemaid can't believe, and don't think true at all. Mr Towlinson reserves his sentiments on this question; being rendered something gloomy by the engagement of a foreigner with whiskers (Mr Towlinson is whiskerless himself), who has been hired to accompany the happy pair to Paris, and who is busy packing the new chariot. In respect of this personage, Mr Towlinson admits, presently, that he never knew of any good that ever come of foreigners; and being charged by the ladies with prejudice, says, look at Bonaparte[3] who was at the head of 'em, and see what *he* was always up to! Which the housemaid says is very true.

The pastry-cook is hard at work in the funereal room in Brook Street, and the very tall young men are busy looking on. One of the very tall young men already smells of sherry, and his eyes have a tendency to become fixed in his head, and to stare at objects without seeing them. The very tall young man is conscious of this failing in himself; and informs his comrade that it's his 'exciseman.' The very tall young man would say excitement, but his speech is hazy.

The men who play the bells have got scent of the marriage: and the marrow-bones and cleavers[4] too; and a brass band too. The first, are practising in a back settlement near Battle-bridge;[5] the second, put themselves in communication, through their chief, with Mr Towlinson, to whom they offer terms to be bought off; and the third, in the person of an artful trombone, lurks and dodges round the corner, waiting for some traitor tradesman[6] to reveal the place and hour of breakfast, for a bribe. Expectation and excitement extend further yet, and take a wider range. From Balls Pond, Mr Perch brings Mrs Perch to spend the day with Mr Dombey's servants, and accompany them, surreptitiously, to see the wedding. In Mr Toots's lodgings, Mr Toots attires himself as if he were at least the Bridegroom; determined to behold the spectacle in splendour from a secret corner of the gallery, and thither to convey the Chicken: for it is Mr Toots's desperate intent to point out Florence to the Chicken, then and there, and openly to say, 'Now, Chicken, I will not deceive you any longer; the friend I have sometimes mentioned to you is myself; Miss Dombey is the object of my passion; what are your opinions, Chicken, in this state of things, and what, on the spot, do you advise?' The so-much-to-be-astonished Chicken, in the meanwhile, dips his beak into a tankard of strong beer, in Mr Toots's kitchen, and pecks up two pounds of beefsteaks. In Princess's Place, Miss Tox is up and doing; for she too, though in sore distress, is resolved to put a shilling in the hands of Mrs Miff, and see the ceremony which has a cruel fascination for her, from some lonely corner. The quarters of the Wooden Midshipman are all alive; for Captain Cuttle, in his ankle-jacks and with a huge shirt-collar, is seated at his breakfast, listening to Rob the Grinder as he reads the marriage service to him beforehand, under orders, to the end that the Captain may perfectly understand the solemnity he is about to witness: for which purpose, the Captain gravely lays injunctions on his chaplain, from time to time, to 'put about,' or to 'overhaul that 'ere article again,' or to stick to his own duty, and leave the Amens to him, the Captain; one of which he repeats, whenever a pause is made by Rob the Grinder, with sonorous satisfaction.

Besides all this, and much more, twenty nursery-maids in Mr Dombey's street alone, have promised twenty families of little women, whose instinctive interest in nuptials dates from their cradles, that they shall go and see the marriage. Truly, Mr Sownds the Beadle has good reason to feel himself in office, as he suns his portly figure on the church steps, waiting for the marriage hour. Truly, Mrs Miff has cause to pounce on an unlucky dwarf child, with a giant baby, who peeps in at the porch, and drive her forth with indignation!

Cousin Feenix has come over from abroad, expressly to attend the marriage. Cousin Feenix was a man about town, forty years ago; but he is still so juvenile in figure and in manner, and so well got up, that strangers are amazed when they discover latent wrinkles in his lordship's face, and crows' feet in his eyes; and first observe him, not exactly certain when he walks across a room, of going quite straight to where he wants to go. But Cousin Feenix, getting up at half-past seven o'clock or so, is quite another thing from Cousin Feenix got up; and very dim, indeed, he looks, while being shaved at Long's Hotel, in Bond Street.

Mr Dombey leaves his dressing-room, amidst a general whisking away of the women on the staircase, who disperse in all directions, with a great rustling of skirts, except Mrs Perch, who, being (but that she always is) in an interesting situation, is not nimble, and is obliged to face him, and is ready to sink with confusion as she curtseys; – may Heaven avert all evil consequences from the house of Perch! Mr Dombey walks up to the drawing-room to bide his time. Gorgeous are Mr Dombey's new blue coat, fawn-coloured pantaloons, and lilac waistcoat; and a whisper goes about the house, that Mr Dombey's hair is curled.

A double knock announces the arrival of the Major, who is gorgeous too, and wears a whole geranium in his button-hole, and has his hair curled tight and crisp, as well the Native knows.

'Dombey!' says the Major, putting out both hands, 'how are you?'

'Major,' says Mr Dombey, 'how are You?'

'By Jove, Sir,' says the Major, 'Joey B. is in such case this morning, Sir,' – and here he hits himself hard upon the breast – 'in such case this morning, Sir, that, damme, Dombey, he has half a mind to make a double marriage of it, Sir, and take the mother.'

Mr Dombey smiles; but faintly, even for him; for Mr Dombey feels that he is going to be related to the mother, and that, under those circumstances, she is not to be joked about.

'Dombey,' says the Major, seeing this, 'I give you joy. I congratulate you, Dombey. By the Lord, Sir,' says the Major, 'you are more to be envied, this day, than any man in England!'

Here again Mr Dombey's assent is qualified; because he is going to confer a great distinction on a lady; and, no doubt, she is to be envied most.

'As to Edith Granger, Sir,' pursues the Major, 'there is not a woman in all Europe but might – and would, Sir, you will allow Bagstock to add – and would give her ears, and her earrings, too, to be in Edith Granger's place.'

'You are good enough to say so, Major,' says Mr Dombey.

'Dombey,' returns the Major, 'you know it. Let us have no false delicacy. You know it. Do you know it, or do you not, Dombey?' says the Major, almost in a passion.

'Oh, really, Major—'

'Damme, Sir,' retorts the Major, 'do you know that fact, or do you not? Dombey! Is old Joe your friend? Are we on that footing of unreserved intimacy, Dombey, that may justify a man – a blunt old Joseph B., Sir – in speaking out; or am I to take open order,[7] Dombey, and to keep my distance, and to stand on forms?'[8]

'My dear Major Bagstock,' says Mr Dombey, with a gratified air, 'you are quite warm.'[9]

'By Gad, Sir,' says the Major, 'I am warm. Joseph B. does not deny it, Dombey. He is warm. This is an occasion, Sir, that calls forth all the honest sympathies remaining in an old, infernal, battered, used-up, invalided, J. B. carcase. And I tell you what, Dombey – at such a time a man must blurt out what he feels, or put a muzzle on; and Joseph Bagstock tells you to your face, Dombey, as he tells his club behind your back, that he never will be muzzled when Paul Dombey is in question. Now, damme, Sir,' concludes the Major, with great firmness, 'what do you make of that?'

'Major,' says Mr Dombey, 'I assure you that I am really obliged to you. I had no idea of checking your too partial friendship.'

'Not too partial, Sir!' exclaims the choleric Major. 'Dombey, I deny it.'

'Your friendship I will say then,' pursues Mr Dombey, 'on any account. Nor can I forget, Major, on such an occasion as the present, how much I am indebted to it.'

'Dombey,' says the Major, with appropriate action, 'that is the hand of Joseph Bagstock: of plain old Joey B., Sir, if you like that better! That is the hand of which His Royal Highness the late Duke of York did me the honour to observe, Sir, to His Royal Highness the late Duke of Kent,[10] that it was the hand of Josh.: a rough and tough, and possibly an up-to-snuff,[11] old vagabond. Dombey, may the present moment be the least unhappy of our lives. God bless you!'

Now enters Mr Carker, gorgeous likewise, and smiling like a wedding-guest indeed. He can scarcely let Mr Dombey's hand go, he is so congratulatory; and he shakes the Major's hand so heartily at the same time, that his voice shakes too, in accord with his arms, as it comes sliding from between his teeth.

'The very day is auspicious,' says Mr Carker. 'The brightest and most genial weather! I hope I am not a moment late?'

'Punctual to your time, Sir,' says the Major.

'I am rejoiced, I am sure,' says Mr Carker. 'I was afraid I might be a few seconds after the appointed time, for I was delayed by a procession of waggons; and I took the liberty of riding round to Brook Street' – this to Mr Dombey – 'to leave a few poor rarities of flowers for Mrs Dombey. A man in my position, and so distinguished as to be invited here, is proud to offer some homage in acknowledgment of his vassalage: and as I have no doubt Mrs Dombey is overwhelmed with what is costly and magnificent;' with a strange glance at his patron; 'I hope the very poverty of my offering may find favour for it.'

'Mrs Dombey, that is to be,' returns Mr Dombey, condescendingly, 'will be very sensible of your attention, Carker, I am sure.'

'And if she is to be Mrs Dombey this morning, Sir,' says the Major, putting down his coffee-cup, and looking at his watch, 'it's high time we were off!'

Forth, in a barouche, ride Mr Dombey, Major Bagstock, and Mr Carker, to the church. Mr Sownds the Beadle has long risen from the steps, and is in waiting with his cocked hat[12] in his hand. Mrs Miff curtseys and proposes chairs in the vestry.[13] Mr Dombey prefers remaining in the church. As he looks up at the organ, Miss Tox in the gallery shrinks behind the fat leg of a cherub on a monument, with cheeks like a young Wind. Captain Cuttle, on the contrary, stands up and waves his hook, in token of welcome and encouragement. Mr Toots informs the Chicken, behind his hand, that the middle gentleman, he in the fawn-coloured pantaloons, is the father of his love. The Chicken hoarsely whispers Mr Toots that he's as stiff a cove as ever he see, but that it is within the resources of Science to double him up,[14] with one blow in the waistcoat.

Mr Sownds and Mrs Miff are eyeing Mr Dombey from a little distance, when the noise of approaching wheels is heard, and Mr Sownds goes out; Mrs Miff, meeting Mr Dombey's eye as it is withdrawn from the presumptuous maniac upstairs, who salutes him with so much urbanity, drops a curtsey, and informs him that she believes his 'good lady' is come. Then there is a crowding and a whispering at the door, and the good lady enters, with a haughty step.

There is no sign upon her face, of last night's suffering; there is no trace in her manner, of the woman on the bended knees reposing her wild head, in beautiful abandonment, upon the pillow of the sleeping girl. That girl, all gentle and lovely, is at her side – a striking contrast to her own disdainful and defiant figure, standing there, composed, erect, inscrutable of will, resplendent and majestic in the zenith of its charms, yet beating down, and treading on, the admiration that it challenges.

There is a pause while Mr Sownds the Beadle glides into the vestry for the clergyman and clerk. At this juncture, Mrs Skewton speaks to Mr Dombey: more distinctly and emphatically than her custom is, and moving at the same time, close to Edith.

'My dear Dombey,' said the good mama, 'I fear I must relinquish darling Florence after all, and suffer her to go home, as she herself proposed. After my loss of to-day, my dear Dombey, I feel I shall not have spirits, even for her society.'

'Had she not better stay with you?' returns the Bridegroom.

'I think not, my dear Dombey. No, I think not. I shall be better alone. Besides, my dearest Edith will be her natural and constant guardian when you return, and I had better not encroach upon her trust, perhaps. She might be jealous. Eh, dear Edith?'

The affectionate mama presses her daughter's arm, as she says this; perhaps entreating her attention earnestly.

'To be serious, my dear Dombey,' she resumes, 'I will relinquish our dear child, and not inflict my gloom upon her. We have settled that, just now. She fully understands, dear Dombey. Edith, my dear, – she fully understands.'

Again, the good mother presses her daughter's arm. Mr Dombey offers no additional remonstrance; for the clergyman and clerk appear; and Mrs Miff, and Mr Sownds the Beadle, group the party in their proper places at the altar rails.

'"Who giveth this woman to be married to this man?"'

Cousin Feenix does that. He has come from Baden-Baden[15] on purpose. 'Confound it,' Cousin Feenix says – good-natured creature, Cousin Feenix – 'when we *do* get a rich City fellow into the family, let us show him some attention; let us do something for him.'

'*I* give this woman to be married to this man,' saith Cousin Feenix therefore. Cousin Feenix, meaning to go in a straight line, but turning off sideways by reason of his wilful legs, gives the wrong woman to be married to this man, at first – to wit, a bridesmaid of some condition, distantly connected with the family, and ten years Mrs Skewton's junior – but Mrs Miff, interposing her mortified bonnet, dexterously turns him back, and runs him, as on castors, full at the 'good lady': whom Cousin Feenix giveth to be married to this man accordingly.

And will they in the sight of heaven—?

Aye, that they will: Mr Dombey says he will. And what says Edith? *She* will.

So, from that day forward, for better for worse, for richer for poorer, in sickness and in health, to love and to cherish, till death do them part, they plight their troth to one another, and are married.

In a firm, free hand, the Bride subscribes her name in the register, when they adjourn to the vestry. 'There an't a many ladies come here,' Mrs Miff says with a curtsey – to look at Mrs Miff, at such a season, is to make her mortified bonnet go down with a dip – 'writes their names like this good lady!' Mr Sownds the Beadle thinks it is a truly spanking signature, and worthy of the writer – this, however, between himself and conscience.

Florence signs too, but unapplauded, for her hand shakes. All the party sign; Cousin Feenix last; who puts his noble name into a wrong place, and enrols himself as having been born that morning.

The Major now salutes the Bride right gallantly, and carries out that branch of military tactics in reference to all the ladies: notwithstanding Mrs Skewton's being extremely hard to kiss, and squeaking shrilly in the sacred edifice. The example is followed by Cousin Feenix, and even by Mr Dombey. Lastly, Mr Carker, with his white teeth glistening, approaches Edith, more as if he meant to bite her, than to taste the sweets that linger on her lips.

There is a glow upon her proud cheek, and a flashing in her eyes, that may be meant to stay him; but it does not, for he salutes her as the rest have done, and wishes her all happiness.

'If wishes,' says he in a low voice, 'are not superfluous, applied to such a union.'

'I thank you, Sir,' she answers, with a curled lip, and a heaving bosom.

But, does Edith feel still, as on the night when she knew that Mr Dombey would return to offer his alliance, that Carker knows her thoroughly, and reads her right, and that she is more degraded by his knowledge of her, than by aught else? Is it for this reason that her haughtiness shrinks beneath his smile, like snow within the hand that grasps it firmly, and that her imperious glance droops in meeting his, and seeks the ground?

'I am proud to see,' said Mr Carker, with a servile stooping of his neck, which the revelations making by his eyes and teeth proclaim to be a lie, 'I am proud to see that my humble offering is graced by Mrs Dombey's hand, and permitted to hold so favoured a place in so joyful an occasion.'

Though she bends her head, in answer, there is something in the momentary action of her hand, as if she would crush the flowers it holds, and fling them, with contempt, upon the ground. But, she puts the hand through the arm of her new husband, who has been standing near, conversing with the Major, and is proud again, and motionless, and silent.

The carriages are once more at the church door. Mr Dombey, with his bride upon his arm, conducts her through the twenty families of little women who are on the steps, and every one of whom remembers the fashion and the colour of her every article of dress from that moment, and reproduces it on her doll, who is for ever being married. Cleopatra and Cousin Feenix enter the same carriage. The Major hands into a second carriage, Florence, and the bridesmaid who so narrowly escaped being given away by mistake, and then enters it himself, and is followed by Mr Carker. Horses prance and caper; coachmen and footmen shine in fluttering favours, flowers, and new-made liveries. Away they dash and rattle through the streets: and as they pass along, a thousand heads are turned to look at them, and a thousand sober moralists revenge themselves for not being married too, that morning, by reflecting that these people little think such happiness can't last.

Miss Tox emerges from behind the cherub's leg, when all is quiet, and comes slowly down from the gallery. Miss Tox's eyes are red, and her pocket-handkerchief is damp. She is wounded, but not exasperated, and she hopes they may be happy. She quite admits to herself the beauty of the bride, and her own comparatively feeble and faded attractions; but the stately image of Mr Dombey in his lilac waistcoat, and his fawn-coloured pantaloons, is present to her mind, and Miss Tox weeps afresh, behind her veil, on her way home to Princess's Place. Captain Cuttle, having joined in all the amens and responses, with a devout growl, feels much improved by his religious exercises; and in a peaceful frame of mind, pervades the body of the church, glazed hat in hand, and reads the tablet to the memory of little Paul. The gallant Mr Toots, attended by the faithful Chicken, leaves the building in torments of love. The Chicken is as yet unable to elaborate a scheme for winning Florence, but his first idea has gained possession of him, and he thinks the doubling up of Mr Dombey would be a move in the right direction. Mr Dombey's servants come out of their hiding-places, and prepare to rush to Brook Street, when they are delayed by symptoms of indisposition on the part of Mrs Perch, who entreats a glass of water, and becomes alarming; Mrs Perch gets better soon, however, and is borne away; and Mrs Miff, and Mr Sownds the Beadle, sit upon the steps to count what they have gained by the affair, and talk it over, while the sexton tolls a funeral.

Now, the carriages arrive at the Bride's residence, and the players on the bells begin to jingle, and the band strikes up, and Mr Punch, that model of connubial bliss, salutes his wife. Now, the people run and push, and press round in a gaping throng, while Mr Dombey, leading Mrs Dombey by the hand, advances solemnly into the Feenix Halls. Now, the rest of the wedding party alight, and enter after them. And why does Mr Carker, passing through the people to the hall-door, think of the old woman who called to him in the grove that morning? Or why does Florence, as she passes, think, with a tremble, of her childhood, when she was lost, and of the visage of Good Mrs Brown?

Now, there are more congratulations on this happiest of days, and more company, though not much; and now they leave the drawing-room, and range themselves at table in the dark-brown dining-room, which no confectioner can brighten up, let him garnish the exhausted negroes with as many flowers and love-knots as he will.

The pastry-cook has done his duty like a man, though, and a rich breakfast is set forth. Mr and Mrs Chick have joined the party, among others. Mrs Chick admires that Edith should be, by nature, such a perfect Dombey; and is affable and confidential to Mrs Skewton, whose mind is relieved of a great load, and who takes her share of the champagne. The very tall young man who suffered from excitement early, is better; but a vague sentiment of repentance has seized upon him, and he hates the other very tall young man, and wrests dishes from him by violence, and takes a grim delight in disobliging the company. The company are cool and calm, and do not outrage the black hatchments of pictures looking down upon them, by any excess of mirth. Cousin Feenix and the Major are the

Coming home from Church

gayest there; but Mr Carker has a smile for the whole table. He has an especial smile for the Bride, who very, very seldom meets it.

Cousin Feenix rises, when the company have breakfasted, and the servants have left the room; and wonderfully young he looks, with his white wristbands almost covering his hands (otherwise rather bony), and the bloom of the champagne in his cheeks.

'Upon my honour,' says Cousin Feenix, 'although it's an unusual sort of thing in a private gentleman's house, I must beg leave to call upon you to drink what is usually called a – in fact a toast.'

The Major very hoarsely indicates his approval. Mr Carker, bending his head forward over the table in the direction of Cousin Feenix, smiles and nods a great many times.

'A – in fact it's not a—' Cousin Feenix beginning again, thus, comes to a dead stop.

'Hear, hear!' says the Major, in a tone of conviction.

Mr Carker softly claps his hands, and bending forward over the table again, smiles and nods a great many more times than before, as if he were particularly struck by this last observation, and desired personally to express his sense of the good it has done him.

'It is,' says Cousin Feenix, 'an occasion in fact, when the general usages of life may be a little departed from, without impropriety; and although I never was an orator in my life, and when I was in the House of Commons, and had the honour of seconding the address, was – in fact, was laid up for a fortnight with the consciousness of failure—'

The Major and Mr Carker are so much delighted by this fragment of personal history, that Cousin Feenix laughs, and addressing them individually, goes on to say:

'And in point of fact, when I was devilish ill – still, you know, I feel that a duty devolves upon me. And when a duty devolves upon an Englishman, he is bound to get out of it, in my opinion, in the best way he can. Well! our family has had the gratification, to-day, of connecting itself, in the person of my lovely and accomplished relative, whom I now see – in point of fact, present—'

Here there is general applause.

'Present,' repeats Cousin Feenix, feeling that it is a neat point which will bear repetition, – 'with one who – that is to say, with a man, at whom the finger of scorn can never – in fact, with my honourable friend Dombey, if he will allow me to call him so.'

Cousin Feenix bows to Mr Dombey; Mr Dombey solemnly returns the bow; everybody is more or less gratified and affected by this extraordinary, and perhaps unprecedented, appeal to the feelings.

'I have not,' says Cousin Feenix, 'enjoyed those opportunities which I could have desired, of cultivating the acquaintance of my friend Dombey, and studying those qualities which do equal honour to his head, and, in point of fact, to his heart; for it has been my misfortune to be, as we used to say in my time in the House of Commons, when it was not the custom to allude to the Lords, and when the order of parliamentary proceedings was perhaps better observed than it is now – to be in – in point of fact,' says Cousin Feenix, cherishing his joke, with great slyness, and finally bringing it out with a jerk, '"in another place!"'[16]

The Major falls into convulsions, and is recovered with difficulty.

'But I know sufficient of my friend Dombey,' resumes Cousin Feenix in a graver tone, as if he had suddenly become a sadder and wiser man,[17] 'to know that he is, in point of fact, what may be emphatically called a – a merchant – a British merchant – and a – and a man. And although I have been resident abroad for some years (it would give me great pleasure to receive my friend Dombey, and everybody here, at Baden-Baden, and to have an opportunity of making 'em known to the Grand Duke), still I know enough, I flatter myself, of my lovely and accomplished relative, to know that she possesses every requisite to make a man happy, and that her marriage with my friend Dombey is one of inclination and affection on both sides.'

Many smiles and nods from Mr Carker.

'Therefore,' says Cousin Feenix, 'I congratulate the family of which I am a member, on the acquisition of my friend Dombey. I congratulate my friend Dombey on his union with my lovely and accomplished relative who possesses every requisite to make a man happy; and I take the liberty of calling on you all, in point of fact, to congratulate both my friend Dombey and my lovely and accomplished relative, on the present occasion.'

The speech of Cousin Feenix is received with great applause, and Mr Dombey returns thanks on behalf of himself and Mrs Dombey. J. B. shortly afterwards proposes Mrs Skewton. The breakfast languishes when that is done, the violated hatchments are avenged, and Edith rises to assume her travelling dress.

All the servants in the meantime, have been breakfasting below. Champagne has grown too common among them to be mentioned, and roast fowls, raised pies, and lobster-salad, have become mere drugs.[18] The very tall young man has recovered his spirits, and again alludes to the exciseman. His comrade's eye begins to emulate his own, and he, too, stares at objects without taking cognizance thereof. There is a general redness in the faces of the ladies; in the face of Mrs Perch particularly, who is joyous and beaming, and lifted so far above the cares of life, that if she were asked just now to direct a wayfarer to Ball's Pond, where her own cares lodge, she would have some difficulty in recalling the way. Mr Towlinson has proposed the happy pair; to which the silver-headed butler has responded neatly, and with emotion; for he half begins to think he *is* an old retainer of the family, and that he is bound to be affected by these changes. The whole party, and especially the ladies, are very frolicsome. Mr Dombey's cook, who generally takes the lead in society, has said, it is impossible to settle down after this, and why not go, in a party, to the play? Everybody (Mrs Perch included) has agreed to this: even the Native, who is tigerish in his drink, and who alarms the ladies (Mrs Perch particularly) by the rolling of his eyes. One of the very tall young men has even proposed a ball after the play, and it presents itself to no one (Mrs Perch included) in the light of an impossibility. Words have arisen between the housemaid and Mr Towlinson; she, on the authority of an old saw,[19] asserting marriages to be made in Heaven: he, affecting to trace the manufacture elsewhere; he, supposing that she says so, because she thinks of being married her own self: she, saying, Lord forbid, at any rate, that she should ever marry *him*. To calm these flying taunts, the silver-headed butler rises to propose the health of Mr Towlinson, whom to know is to esteem, and to esteem is to wish well settled in life with the object of his choice, wherever (here the silver-headed butler eyes the housemaid) she may be. Mr Towlinson returns thanks in a speech replete with feeling, of which the peroration turns on foreigners, regarding whom he says they may find favour, sometimes with weak and inconstant intellects that can be led away by hair, but all he hopes, is, he may never hear of no foreigner never boning[20] nothing out of no travelling chariot. The eye of Mr Towlinson is so severe and so expressive here, that the housemaid is turning hysterical, when she and all the rest, roused by the intelligence that the Bride is going away, hurry up stairs to witness her departure.

The chariot is at the door; the Bride is descending to the hall, where Mr Dombey waits for her. Florence is ready on the staircase to depart too; and Miss Nipper, who has held a middle state between the parlour and the kitchen, is prepared to accompany her. As Edith appears, Florence hastens towards her, to bid her farewell.

Is Edith cold, that she should tremble! Is there anything unnatural or unwholesome in the touch of Florence, that the beautiful form recedes and contracts, as if it could not bear it! Is there so much hurry in this going away, that Edith, with a wave of her hand, sweeps on, and is gone!

Mrs Skewton, overpowered by her feelings as a mother, sinks on her sofa in the Cleopatra attitude, when the clatter of the chariot wheels is lost, and sheds several tears. The Major, coming with the rest of the company from table, endeavours to comfort her; but she will not be comforted on any terms, and so the Major takes his leave. Cousin Feenix takes his leave, and Mr Carker takes his leave. The guests all go away. Cleopatra, left alone, feels a little giddy from her strong emotion, and falls asleep.

Giddiness prevails below stairs too. The very tall young man whose excitement came on so soon, appears to have his head glued to the table in the pantry, and cannot be detached from it. A violent revulsion has taken place in the spirits of Mrs Perch, who is low on account of Mr Perch, and tells cook that she fears he is not so much attached to his home, as he used to be, when they were only nine in family. Mr Towlinson has a singing in his ears and a large wheel going round and round inside his head. The housemaid wishes it wasn't wicked to wish that one was dead.

There is a general delusion likewise, in these lower regions, on the subject of time; everybody conceiving that it ought to be, at the earliest, ten o'clock at night, whereas it is not yet three in the afternoon. A shadowy idea of wickedness committed, haunts every individual in the party; and each one secretly thinks the other a companion in guilt, whom it would be agreeable to avoid. No man or woman has the hardihood to hint at the projected visit to the play. Any one reviving the notion of the ball, would be scouted[21] as a malignant idiot.

Mrs Skewton sleeps upstairs, two hours afterwards, and naps are not yet over in the kitchen. The hatchments in the dining-room look down on crumbs, dirty plates, spillings of wine, half-thawed ice, stale discoloured heel-taps,[22] scraps of lobster, drumsticks of fowls, and pensive jellies, gradually resolving themselves into a lukewarm gummy soup. The marriage is, by this time, almost as denuded of its show and garnish as the breakfast. Mr Dombey's servants moralise so much about it, and are so repentant over their early tea, at home, that by eight o'clock or so, they settle down into confirmed seriousness; and Mr Perch, arriving at that time from the City, fresh and jocular, with a white waistcoat and a comic song, ready to spend the evening, and prepared for any amount of dissipation, is amazed to find himself coldly received, and Mrs Perch but poorly, and to have the pleasing duty of escorting that lady home by the next omnibus.

Night closes in. Florence having rambled through the handsome house, from room to room, seeks her own chamber, where the care of Edith has surrounded her with luxuries and comforts; and divesting herself of her handsome dress, puts on her old simple mourning for dear Paul, and sits down to read, with Diogenes winking and blinking on the ground beside her. But Florence cannot read to-night. The house seems strange and new, and there are loud echoes in it. There is a shadow on her heart: she knows not why or what: but it is heavy. Florence shuts her book, and gruff Diogenes, who takes that for a signal, puts his paws upon her lap, and rubs his ears against her caressing hands. But Florence cannot see him plainly, in a little time, for there is a mist between her eyes and him, and her dead brother and dead mother shine in it like angels. Walter, too, poor wandering shipwrecked boy, oh, where is he?

The Major don't know; that's for certain; and don't care. The Major, having choked and slumbered, all the afternoon, has taken a late dinner at his club, and now sits over his pint of wine, driving a modest young man, with a fresh-coloured face, at the next table (who would give a handsome sum to be able to rise and go away, but cannot do it) to the verge of madness, by anecdotes of Bagstock, Sir, and Dombey's wedding, and Old Joe's devilish gentlemanly friend, Lord Feenix. While Cousin Feenix, who ought to be at Long's,[23] and in bed, finds himself, instead, at a gaming-table, where his wilful legs have taken him, perhaps, in his own despite.

Night, like a giant, fills the church, from pavement to roof, and holds dominion through the silent hours. Pale dawn again comes peeping through the windows; and, giving place to day, sees night withdraw into the vaults, and follows it, and drives it out, and hides among the dead. The timid mice again cower close together, when the great door clashes, and Mr Sownds and Mrs Miff, treading the circle of their daily lives, unbroken as a marriage ring, come in. Again, the cocked hat and the mortified bonnet stand in the background at the marriage hour; and again this man taketh this woman, and this woman taketh this man, on the solemn terms:

'To have and to hold, from this day forward, for better for worse, for richer for poorer, in sickness and in health, to love and to cherish, until death do them part.'

The very words that Mr Carker rides into town repeating, with his mouth stretched to the utmost, as he picks his dainty way.

CHAPTER 32

The Wooden Midshipman goes to Pieces

Honest Captain Cuttle, as the weeks flew over him in his fortified retreat, by no means abated any of his prudent provisions against surprise, because of the non-appearance of the enemy. The Captain argued that his present security was too profound and wonderful to endure much longer; he knew that when the wind stood in a fair quarter, the weathercock was seldom nailed there;[1] and he was too well acquainted with the determined and dauntless character of Mrs MacStinger, to doubt that that heroic woman had devoted herself to the task of his discovery and capture. Trembling beneath the weight of these reasons, Captain Cuttle lived a very close and retired life; seldom stirring abroad until after dark; venturing even then only into the obscurest streets; never going forth at all on Sundays; and both within and without the walls of his retreat, avoiding bonnets, as if they were worn by raging lions.

The Captain never dreamed that in the event of his being pounced upon by Mrs MacStinger, in his walks, it would be possible to offer resistance. He felt that it could not be done. He saw himself, in his mind's eye, put meekly in a hackney-coach, and carried off to his old lodgings. He foresaw that, once immured there, he was a lost man: his hat gone; Mrs MacStinger watchful of him day and night; reproaches heaped upon his head, before the infant family; himself the guilty object of suspicion and distrust; an ogre in the children's eyes, and in their mother's a detected traitor.

A violent perspiration, and a lowness of spirits always came over the Captain as this gloomy picture presented itself to his imagination. It generally did so previous to his stealing out of doors at night for air and exercise. Sensible of the risk he ran, the Captain took leave of Rob, at those times, with the solemnity which became a man who might never return: exhorting him, in the event of his (the Captain's) being lost sight of, for a time, to tread in the paths of virtue, and keep the brazen instruments well polished.

But not to throw away a chance; and to secure to himself a means, in case of the worst, of holding communication with the external world; Captain Cuttle soon conceived the happy idea of teaching Rob the Grinder some secret signal, by which that adherent might make his presence and fidelity known to his commander, in the hour of adversity. After much cogitation the Captain decided in favour of instructing him to whistle the marine melody, 'O cheerily, cheerily!' and Rob the Grinder attaining a point as near perfection in that accomplishment as a landsman could hope to reach, the Captain impressed these mysterious instructions on his mind:

'Now, my lad, stand by! If ever I'm took—'

'Took, Captain!' interposed Rob, with his round eyes wide open.

'Ah!' said Captain Cuttle darkly, 'if ever I goes away, meaning to come back to supper, and don't come within hail again twenty-four hours arter my loss, go you to Brig Place and whistle that 'ere tune near my old moorings – not as if you was a meaning of it, you understand, but as if you'd drifted there, promiscuous. If I answer in that tune, you sheer off, my lad, and come back four-and-twenty hours arterwards; if I answer in another tune, do you stand off and on,[2] and wait till I throw out further signals. Do you understand them orders, now?'

'What am I to stand off and on of, Captain?' inquired Rob. 'The horse-road?'[3]

'Here's a smart lad for you!' cried the Captain, eyeing him sternly, 'as don't know his own native alphabet! Go away a bit and come back again alternate – d'ye understand that?'

'Yes, Captain,' said Rob.

'Very good, my lad, then,' said the Captain, relenting.

That he might do it the better, Captain Cuttle sometimes condescended, of an evening after the shop was shut, to rehearse this scene: retiring into the parlour for the purpose, as into the lodgings of a supposititious MacStinger, and carefully observing the behaviour of his ally, from the hole of espial he had cut in the wall. Rob the Grinder discharged himself of his duty with so much exactness and judgment, when thus put to the proof, that the Captain presented him at divers times, with seven sixpences, in token of satisfaction; and gradually felt stealing over his spirit the resignation of a man who had made provision for the worst, and taken every reasonable precaution against an unrelenting fate.

Nevertheless, the Captain did not tempt ill-fortune, by being a whit more venturesome than before. Though he considered it a point of good breeding in himself, as a general friend of the family, to attend Mr Dombey's wedding (of which he had heard from Mr Perch), and to show that gentleman a pleasant and approving countenance from the gallery, he had repaired to the church in a hackney cabriolet with both windows up; and might have scrupled even to make that venture, in his dread of Mrs MacStinger, but that the lady's attendance on the ministry of the Reverend Melchisedech rendered it peculiarly unlikely that she would be found in communion with the Establishment.

The Captain got safe home again, and fell into the ordinary routine of his new life, without encountering any more direct alarm from the enemy, than was suggested to him by the daily bonnets in the street. But other subjects began to lay heavy on the Captain's mind. Walter's ship was still unheard of. No news came of old Sol Gills. Florence did not even know of the old man's disappearance, and Captain Cuttle had not the heart to tell her. Indeed the Captain, as his own hopes of the generous, handsome, gallant-hearted youth, whom he had loved, according to his rough manner, from a child, began to fade, and faded more and more from day to day, shrunk with instinctive pain from the thought of exchanging a word with Florence. If he had had good news to carry to her, the honest Captain would have braved the newly decorated house and splendid furniture – though these, connected with the lady he had seen at church, were awful to him – and made his way into her presence. With a dark horizon gathering around their common hopes, however, that darkened every hour, the Captain almost felt as if he were a new misfortune and affliction to her; and was scarcely less afraid of a visit from Florence, than from Mrs MacStinger herself.

It was a chill dark autumn evening, and Captain Cuttle had ordered a fire to be kindled in the little back parlour, now more than ever like the cabin of a ship. The rain fell fast, and the wind blew hard; and straying out on the housetop by that stormy bedroom of his old friend, to take an observation of the weather, the Captain's heart died within him, when he saw how wild and desolate it was. Not that he associated the weather of that time with poor Walter's destiny, or doubted that if Providence had doomed him to be lost and shipwrecked, it was over, long ago; but that beneath an outward influence, quite distinct from the subject-matter of his thoughts, the Captain's spirits sank, and his hopes turned pale, as those of wiser men had often done before him, and will often do again.

Captain Cuttle, addressing his face to the sharp wind and slanting rain, looked up at the heavy scud that was flying fast over the wilderness of house-tops, and looked for something cheery there in vain. The prospect near at hand was no better. In sundry tea-chests and other rough boxes at his feet, the pigeons of Rob the Grinder were cooing like so many dismal breezes getting up. A crazy weathercock of a midshipman, with a telescope at his eye, once visible from the street, but long bricked out, creaked and complained upon his rusty pivot as the shrill blast spun him round and round, and sported with him cruelly. Upon the Captain's coarse blue vest the cold raindrops started like steel beads; and he could hardly maintain himself aslant against the stiff Nor'-Wester that came pressing against him, importunate to topple him over the parapet, and throw him on the pavement below. If there were any Hope alive that evening, the Captain thought, as he held his hat on, it certainly kept house, and wasn't out of doors; so the Captain, shaking his head in a despondent manner, went in to look for it.

Captain Cuttle descended slowly to the little back parlour and, seated in his accustomed chair, looked for it in the fire; but it was not there, though the fire was bright. He took out his tobacco-box and pipe, and composing himself to smoke, looked for it in the red glow from the bowl, and in the wreaths of vapour that curled upward from his lips; but there was not so much as an atom of the rust of Hope's anchor in either. He tried a glass of grog; but melancholy truth was at the bottom of that well, and he couldn't finish it. He made a turn or two in the shop, and looked for Hope among the instruments; but they obstinately worked out reckonings for the missing ship, in spite of any opposition he could offer, that ended at the bottom of the lone sea.

The wind still rushing, and the rain still pattering, against the closed shutters, the Captain brought to before the Wooden Midshipman upon the counter, and thought, as he dried the little officer's uniform with his sleeve, how many years the Midshipman had seen, during which few changes – hardly any – had transpired among his ship's company; how the change had come all together, one day, as it might be; and of what a sweeping kind they were. Here was the little society of the back parlour broken up, and scattered far and wide. Here was no audience for Lovely Peg, even if there had been anybody to sing it, which there was not, for the Captain was as morally certain that nobody but he could execute that ballad, as he was that he had not the spirit, under existing circumstances, to attempt it. There was no bright face of 'Wal'r' in the house; – here the Captain transferred his sleeve for a moment from the Midshipman's uniform to his own cheek; – the familiar wig and buttons of Sol Gills were a vision of the past; Richard Whittington was knocked on the head; and every plan and project, in connexion with the Midshipman, lay drifting, without mast or rudder, on the waste of waters.

As the Captain, with a dejected face, stood revolving these thoughts, and polishing the Midshipman, partly in the tenderness of old acquaintance, and partly in the absence of his mind, a knocking at the shop-door communicated a frightful start to the frame of Rob the Grinder, seated on the counter, whose large eyes had been intently fixed on the Captain's face, and who had been debating within himself, for the five hundredth time, whether the Captain could have done a murder, that he had such an evil conscience, and was always running away.

'What's that?' said Captain Cuttle, softly.

'Somebody's knuckles, Captain,' answered Rob the Grinder.

The Captain, with an abashed and guilty air, immediately sneaked on tiptoe to the little parlour and locked himself in. Rob, opening the door, would have parleyed with the visitor on the threshold if the visitor had come in female guise; but the figure being of the male sex, and Rob's orders only applying to women, Rob held the door open and allowed it to enter: which it did very quickly, glad to get out of the driving rain.

'A job for Burgess and Co. at any rate,' said the visitor, looking over his shoulder compassionately at his own legs, which were very wet and covered with splashes. 'Oh, how-de-do, Mr Gills?'

The salutation was addressed to the Captain, now emerging from the back parlour with a most transparent and utterly futile affectation of coming out by accident.

'Thankee,' the gentleman went on to say in the same breath; 'I'm very well indeed, myself, I'm much obliged to you. My name is Toots, – *Mister* Toots.'

The Captain remembered to have seen this young gentleman at the wedding, and made him a bow. Mr Toots replied with a chuckle; and being embarrassed, as he generally was, breathed hard, shook hands with the Captain for a long time, and then falling on Rob the Grinder, in the absence of any other resource, shook hands with him in a most affectionate and cordial manner.

'I say; I should like to speak a word to you, Mr Gills, if you please,' said Toots at length, with surprising presence of mind. 'I say! Miss D. O. M. you know!'

The Captain, with responsive gravity and mystery, immediately waved his hook towards the little parlour, whither Mr Toots followed him.

'Oh! I beg your pardon though,' said Mr Toots, looking up in the Captain's face as he sat down in a chair by the fire, which the Captain placed for him; 'you don't happen to know the Chicken at all; do you, Mr Gills?'

'The Chicken?' said the Captain.

'The Game Chicken,' said Mr Toots.

The Captain shaking his head, Mr Toots explained that the man alluded to was the celebrated public character who had covered himself and his country with glory in his contest with the Nobby Shropshire One; but this piece of information did not appear to enlighten the Captain very much.

'Because he's outside: that's all,' said Mr Toots. 'But it's of no consequence; he won't get very wet, perhaps.'

'I can pass the word for him in a moment,' said the Captain.

'Well, if you *would* have the goodness to let him sit in the shop with your young man,' chuckled Mr Toots, 'I should be glad; because, you know, he's easily offended, and the damp's rather bad for his stamina. I'll call him in, Mr Gills.'

With that, Mr Toots repairing to the shop-door, sent a peculiar whistle into the night, which produced a stoical gentleman in a shaggy white great-coat and a flat-brimmed hat, with very short hair, a broken nose, and a considerable tract of bare and sterile country behind each ear.

'Sit down, Chicken,' said Mr Toots.

The compliant Chicken spat out some small pieces of straw on which he was regaling himself, and took in a fresh supply from a reserve he carried in his hand.

'There an't no drain of nothing short[4] handy, is there?' said the Chicken, generally. 'This here sluicing night is hard lines to a man as lives on his condition.'

Captain Cuttle proffered a glass of rum, which the Chicken, throwing back his head, emptied into himself, as into a cask, after proposing the brief sentiment, 'Towards us!' Mr Toots and the Captain returning then to the parlour, and taking their seats before the fire, Mr Toots began:

'Mr Gills—'

'Awast!' said the Captain. 'My name's Cuttle.'

Mr Toots looked greatly disconcerted, while the Captain proceeded gravely.

'Cap'en Cuttle is my name, and England is my nation, this here is my dwelling-place, and blessed be creation – Job,'[5] said the Captain, as an index to his authority.

'Oh! I couldn't see Mr Gills, could I?' said Mr Toots; 'because—'

A visitor of distinction

'If you could see Sol Gills, young gen'l'm'n,' said the Captain, impressively, and laying his heavy hand on Mr Toots's knee, 'old Sol, mind you – with your own eyes – as you sit there – you'd be welcomer to me, than a wind astern, to a ship becalmed. But you can't see Sol Gills. And why can't you see Sol Gills?' said the Captain, apprised by the face of Mr Toots that he was making a profound impression on that gentleman's mind. 'Because he's inwisible.'

Mr Toots in his agitation was going to reply that it was of no consequence at all. But he corrected himself, and said, 'Lor bless me!'

'That there man,' said the Captain, 'has left me in charge here by a piece of writing, but though he was a'most as good as my sworn brother, I know no more where he's gone, or why he's gone; if so be to seek his nevy, or if so be along of being not quite settled in his mind; than you do. One morning at day-break, he went over the side,' said the Captain, 'without a splash, without a ripple. I have looked for that man high and low, and never set eyes, nor ears, nor nothing else, upon him, from that hour.'

'But, good Gracious, Miss Dombey don't know—' Mr Toots began.

'Why, I ask you, as a feeling heart,' said the Captain, dropping his voice, 'why should she know? why should she be made to know, until such time as there warn't any help for it? She took to old Sol Gills, did that sweet creetur, with a kindness, with a affability, with a – what's the good of saying so? you know her.'

'I should hope so,' chuckled Mr Toots, with a conscious blush that suffused his whole countenance.

'And you come here from her?' said the Captain.

'I should think so,' chuckled Mr Toots.

'Then all I need observe, is,' said the Captain, 'that you know a angel, and are chartered *by* a angel.'

Mr Toots instantly seized the Captain's hand, and requested the favour of his friendship.

'Upon my word and honour,' said Mr Toots, earnestly, 'I should be very much obliged to you if you'd improve my acquaintance. I should like to know you, Captain, very much. I really am in want of a friend, I am. Little Dombey was my friend at old Blimber's, and would have been now, if he'd have lived. The Chicken,' said Mr Toots, in a forlorn whisper, 'is very well – admirable in his way – the sharpest man perhaps in the world; there's not a move he isn't up to, everybody says so – but I don't know – he's not everything.

So she *is* an angel, Captain. If there is an angel anywhere, it's Miss Dombey. That's what I've always said. Really though, you know,' said Mr Toots, 'I should be very much obliged to you if you'd cultivate my acquaintance.'

Captain Cuttle received this proposal in a polite manner, but still without committing himself to its acceptance; merely observing, 'Aye, aye, my lad. We shall see, we shall see'; and reminding Mr Toots of his immediate mission, by inquiring to what he was indebted for the honour of that visit.

'Why the fact is,' replied Mr Toots, 'that it's the young woman I come from. Not Miss Dombey – Susan, you know.'

The Captain nodded his head once, with a grave expression of face, indicative of his regarding that young woman with serious respect.

'And I'll tell you how it happens,' said Mr Toots. 'You know, I go and call sometimes, on Miss Dombey. I don't go there on purpose, you know, but I happen to be in the neighbourhood very often; and when I find myself there, why – why I call.'

'Nat'rally,' observed the Captain.

'Yes,' said Mr Toots. 'I called this afternoon. Upon my word and honour, I don't think it's possible to form an idea of the angel Miss Dombey was this afternoon.'

The Captain answered with a jerk of his head, implying that it might not be easy to some people, but was quite so to him.

'As I was coming out,' said Mr Toots, 'the young woman, in the most unexpected manner, took me into the pantry.'

The Captain seemed, for the moment, to object to this proceeding: and leaning back in his chair, looked at Mr Toots with a distrustful, if not threatening visage.

'Where she brought out,' said Mr Toots, 'this newspaper. She told me that she had kept it from Miss Dombey all day, on account of something that was in it, about somebody that she and Dombey used to know; and then she read the passage to me. Very well. Then she said – wait a minute; what was it she said, though!'

Mr Toots, endeavouring to concentrate his mental powers on this question, unintentionally fixed the Captain's eye, and was so much discomposed by its stern expression, that his difficulty in resuming the thread of his subject was enhanced to a painful extent.

'Oh!' said Mr Toots after long consideration. 'Oh, ah! Yes! She said that she hoped there was a bare possibility that it mightn't be true; and that as she couldn't very well come out herself, without surprising Miss Dombey, would I go down to Mr Solomon Gills the Instrument-maker's in this street, who was the party's uncle, and ask whether he believed it was true, or had heard anything else in the City. She said, if he couldn't speak to me, no doubt Captain Cuttle could. By the bye!' said Mr Toots, as the discovery flashed upon him, 'you, you know!'

The Captain glanced at the newspaper in Mr Toots's hand, and breathed short and hurriedly.

'Well,' pursued Mr Toots, 'the reason why I'm rather late is, because I went up as far as Finchley first, to get some uncommonly fine chickweed that grows there, for Miss Dombey's bird. But I came on here, directly afterwards. You've seen the paper, I suppose?'

The Captain, who had become cautious of reading the news, lest he should find himself advertised at full length by Mrs MacStinger, shook his head.

'Shall I read the passage to you?' inquired Mr Toots.

The Captain making a sign in the affirmative, Mr Toots read as follows, from the Shipping Intelligence:

'"Southampton. The barque Defiance, Henry James, Commander, arrived in this port to-day, with a cargo of sugar, coffee, and rum, reports that being becalmed on the sixth day of her passage home from Jamaica, in" – in such and such a latitude, you know,' said Mr Toots, after making a feeble dash at the figures, and tumbling over them.

'Aye!' cried the Captain, striking his clenched hand on the table. 'Heave ahead, my lad!'

' – latitude,' repeated Mr Toots, with a startled glance at the Captain, 'and longitude so-and-so, – "the look-out observed, half an hour before sunset, some fragments of a wreck, drifting at about the distance of a mile. The weather being clear, and the barque making no way, a boat was hoisted out, with orders to inspect the same, when they were found to consist of sundry large spars, and a part of the main rigging of an English brig, of about five hundred tons burden, together with a portion of the stern on which the words and letters 'Son and H—'were yet plainly legible. No vestige of any dead body was to be seen upon the floating fragments. Log of the Defiance states, that a breeze springing up in the night, the wreck was seen no more. There can be no doubt that all surmises as to the fate of the missing vessel, the Son and Heir, port of London, bound for Barbadoes, are now set at rest for ever; that she broke up in the last hurricane; and that every soul on board perished."'

Captain Cuttle, like all mankind, little knew how much hope had survived within him under discouragement, until he felt its death-shock. During the reading of the paragraph, and for a minute or two afterwards, he sat with his gaze fixed on the modest Mr Toots, like a man entranced; then, suddenly rising, and putting on his glazed hat, which, in his visitor's honour, he had laid upon the table, the Captain turned his back, and bent his head down on the little chimneypiece.

'Oh, upon my word and honour,' cried Mr Toots, whose tender heart was moved by the Captain's unexpected distress, 'this is a most wretched sort of affair this world is! Somebody's always dying, or going and doing something uncomfortable in it. I'm sure I never should have looked forward so much, to coming into my property, if I had known this. I never saw such a world. It's a great deal worse than Blimber's.'

Captain Cuttle, without altering his position, signed to Mr Toots not to mind him; and presently turned round, with his glazed hat thrust back upon his ears, and his hand composing and smoothing his brown face.

'Wal'r, my dear lad,' said the Captain, 'farewell! Wal'r, my child, my boy, and man, I loved you! He warn't my flesh and blood,' said the Captain, looking at the fire – 'I an't got none – but something of what a father feels when he loses a son, I feel in losing Wal'r. For why?' said the Captain. 'Because it an't one loss, but a round dozen. Where's that there young schoolboy with the rosy face and curly hair, that used to be as merry in this here parlour, come round every week, as a piece of music? Gone down with Wal'r. Where's that there fresh lad, that nothing couldn't tire nor put out, and that sparkled up and blushed so, when we joked him about Heart's Delight, that he was beautiful to look at? Gone down with Wal'r. Where's that there man's spirit, all afire, that wouldn't see the old man hove down for a minute, and cared nothing for itself? Gone down with Wal'r. It an't one Wal'r. There was a dozen Wal'rs that I know'd and loved, all holding round his neck when he went down, and they're a-holding round mine now!'

Mr Toots sat silent: folding and refolding the newspaper as small as possible upon his knee.

'And Sol Gills,' said the Captain, gazing at the fire, 'poor nevyless old Sol, where are *you* got to! you was left in charge of me; his last words was, "Take care of my uncle!" What came over *you*, Sol, when you went and gave the go-bye to Ned Cuttle; and what am I to put in my accounts that he's a looking down upon, respecting you! Sol Gills, Sol Gills!' said the Captain, shaking his head slowly, 'catch sight of that there newspaper, away from home, with no one as know'd Wal'r by, to say a word; and broadside to you broach, and down you pitch, head foremost!'6

Drawing a heavy sigh, the Captain turned to Mr Toots, and roused himself to a sustained consciousness of that gentleman's presence.

'My lad,' said the Captain, 'you must tell the young woman honestly that this here fatal news is too correct. They don't romance, you see, on such pints. It's entered on the ship's log, and that's the truest book as a man can write. To-morrow morning,' said the Captain, 'I'll step out and make inquiries; but they'll lead to no good. They can't do it. If you'll give me a look-in in the forenoon, you shall know what I have heerd; but tell the young woman from Cap'en Cuttle, that it's over. Over!' And the Captain, hooking off his glazed hat, pulled his handkerchief out of the crown, wiped his grizzled head despairingly, and tossed the handkerchief in again, with the indifference of deep dejection.

'Oh! I assure you,' said Mr Toots, 'really I am dreadfully sorry. Upon my word I am, though I wasn't acquainted with the party. Do you think Miss Dombey will be very much affected, Captain Gills – I mean Mr Cuttle?'

'Why, Lord love you,' returned the Captain, with something of compassion for Mr Toots's innocence. 'When she warn't no higher than that, they were as fond of one another as two young doves.'

'Were they though!' said Mr Toots, with a considerably lengthened face.

'They were made for one another,' said the Captain, mournfully; 'but what signifies that now!'

'Upon my word and honour,' cried Mr Toots, blurting out his words through a singular combination of awkward chuckles and emotion, 'I'm even more sorry than I was before. You know, Captain Gills, I – I positively adore Miss Dombey; – I – I am perfectly sore with loving her;' the burst with which this confession forced itself out of the unhappy Mr Toots, bespoke the vehemence of his feelings; 'but what would be the good of my regarding her in this manner, if I wasn't truly sorry for her feeling pain, whatever was the cause of it. Mine an't a selfish affection, you know,' said Mr Toots, in the confidence engendered by his having been a witness of the Captain's tenderness. 'It's the sort of thing with me, Captain Gills, that if I could be run over – or – or trampled upon – or – or thrown off a very high place – or anything of that sort – for

Miss Dombey's sake, it would be the most delightful thing that could happen to me.'

All this, Mr Toots said in a suppressed voice, to prevent its reaching the jealous ears of the Chicken, who objected to the softer emotions; which effort of restraint, coupled with the intensity of his feelings, made him red to the tips of his ears, and caused him to present such an affecting spectacle of disinterested love to the eyes of Captain Cuttle, that the good Captain patted him consolingly on the back and bade him cheer up.

'Thankee, Captain Gills,' said Mr Toots, 'it's kind of you, in the midst of your own troubles, to say so. I'm very much obliged to you. As I said before, I really want a friend, and should be glad to have your acquaintance. Although I am very well off,' said Mr Toots, with energy, 'you can't think what a miserable Beast I am. The hollow crowd, you know, when they see me with the Chicken, and characters of distinction like that, suppose me to be happy; but I'm wretched. I suffer for Miss Dombey, Captain Gills. I can't get through my meals; I have no pleasure in my tailor; I often cry when I'm alone. I assure you it'll be a satisfaction to me to come back to-morrow, or to come back fifty times.'

Mr Toots, with these words, shook the Captain's hand; and disguising such traces of his agitation as could be disguised on so short a notice, before the Chicken's penetrating glance, rejoined that eminent gentleman in the shop. The Chicken, who was apt to be jealous of his ascendancy, eyed Captain Cuttle with anything but favour as he took leave of Mr Toots; but followed his patron without being otherwise demonstrative of his ill-will; leaving the Captain oppressed with sorrow; and Rob the Grinder elevated with joy, on account of having had the honour of staring for nearly half an hour at the conqueror of the Nobby Shropshire One.

Long after Rob was fast asleep in his bed under the counter, the Captain sat looking at the fire; and long after there was no fire to look at, the Captain sat gazing on the rusty bars, with unavailing thoughts of Walter and old Sol crowding through his mind. Retirement to the stormy chamber at the top of the house brought no rest with it; and the Captain rose up in the morning, sorrowful and unrefreshed.

As soon as the City offices were open, the Captain issued forth to the counting-house of Dombey and Son. But there was no opening of the Midshipman's-windows that morning. Rob the Grinder, by the Captain's orders, left the shutters closed, and the house was as a house of death.

It chanced that Mr Carker was entering the office, as Captain Cuttle arrived at the door. Receiving the Manager's benison gravely and silently, Captain Cuttle made bold to accompany him into his own room.

'Well, Captain Cuttle,' said Mr Carker, taking up his usual position before the fireplace, and keeping on his hat, 'this is a bad business.'

'You have received the news as was in print yesterday, Sir?' said the Captain.

'Yes,' said Mr Carker, 'we have received it! It was accurately stated. The underwriters suffer a considerable loss. We are very sorry. No help! Such is life!'

Mr Carker pared his nails delicately with a penknife, and smiled at the Captain, who was standing by the door looking at him.

'I excessively regret poor Gay,' said Carker, 'and the crew. I understand there were some of our very best men among 'em. It always happens so. Many men with families too. A comfort to reflect that poor Gay had no family, Captain Cuttle!'

The Captain stood rubbing his chin, and looking at the Manager. The Manager glanced at the unopened letters lying on his desk, and took up the newspaper.

'Is there anything I can do for you, Captain Cuttle?' he asked, looking off it, with a smiling and expressive glance at the door.

'I wish you could set my mind at rest, Sir, on something it's uneasy about,' returned the Captain.

'Aye!' exclaimed the Manager, 'what's that? Come, Captain Cuttle, I must trouble you to be quick, if you please. I am much engaged.'

'Lookee here, Sir,' said the Captain, advancing a step. 'Afore my friend Wal'r went on this here disastrous voyage—'

'Come, come, Captain Cuttle,' interposed the smiling Manager, 'don't talk about disastrous voyages in that way. We have nothing to do with disastrous voyages here, my good fellow. You must have begun very early on your day's allowance, Captain, if you don't remember that there are hazards in all voyages whether by sea or land. You are not made uneasy by the supposition that young what's-his-name was lost in bad weather that was got up against him in these offices – are you? Fie, Captain! Sleep, and soda-water, are the best cures for such uneasiness as that.'

'My lad,' returned the Captain, slowly – 'you are a'most a lad to me, and so I don't ask your pardon for that slip of a word, – if you find any pleasure in this here sport, you an't the gentleman I took you for, and if you an't the gentleman I took you for, may be my mind has call to be uneasy. Now this is what it is, Mr Carker. – Afore that poor lad went away, according to orders, he told me that he warn't a going away for his own good, or for promotion, he know'd. It was my belief that he was wrong, and I told him so, and I come here, your head governor being absent, to ask a question or two of you in a civil way, for my own satisfaction. Them questions you answered – free. Now it'll ease my mind to know, when all is over, as it is, and when what can't be cured must be endoored – for which, as a scholar, you'll overhaul the book it's in, and thereof make a note – to know once more, in a word, that I warn't mistaken; that I warn't back'ard in my duty when I didn't tell the old man what Wal'r told me; and that the wind was truly in his sail, when he highsted of it for Barbadoes Harbour. Mr Carker,' said the Captain, in the goodness of his nature, 'when I was here last, we was very pleasant together. If I ain't been altogether so pleasant myself this morning, on account of this poor lad, and if I have chafed again any observation of yours that I might have fended off, my name is Ed'ard Cuttle, and I ask your pardon.'

'Captain Cuttle,' returned the Manager, with all possible politeness, 'I must ask you to do me a favour.'

'And what is it, Sir?' inquired the Captain.

'To have the goodness to walk off, if you please,' rejoined the Manager, stretching forth his arm, 'and to carry your jargon somewhere else.'

Every knob in the Captain's face turned white with astonishment and indignation; even the red rim on his forehead faded, like a rainbow among the gathering clouds.

'I tell you what, Captain Cuttle,' said the Manager, shaking his forefinger at him, and showing him all his teeth, but still amiably smiling, 'I was much too lenient with you when you came here before. You belong to an artful and audacious set of people. In my desire to save young what's-his-name from being kicked out of this place, neck and crop, my good Captain, I tolerated you; but for once, and only once. Now, go, my friend!'

The Captain was absolutely rooted to the ground, and speechless.

'Go,' said the good-humoured Manager, gathering up his skirts,[7] and standing astride upon the hearth-rug, 'like a sensible fellow, and let us have no turning out, or any such violent measures. If Mr Dombey were here, Captain, you might be obliged to leave in a more ignominious manner, possibly. I merely say Go!'

The Captain, laying his ponderous hand upon his chest, to assist himself in fetching a deep breath, looked at Mr Carker from head to foot, and looked round the little room, as if he did not clearly understand where he was, or in what company.

'You are deep, Captain Cuttle,' pursued Carker, with the easy and vivacious frankness of a man of the world who knew the world too well to be ruffled by any discovery of misdoing, when it did not immediately concern himself; 'but you are not quite out of sound-ings,[8] either – neither you nor your absent friend, Captain. What have you done with your absent friend, hey?'

Again the Captain laid his hand upon his chest. After drawing another deep breath, he conjured himself to 'stand by!' But in a whisper.

'You hatch nice little plots, and hold nice little councils, and make nice little appointments, and receive nice little visitors, too, Captain, hey?' said Carker, bending his brows upon him, without showing his teeth any the less: 'but it's a bold measure to come here afterwards. Not like your discretion! You conspirators, and hiders, and runners-away, should know better than that. Will you oblige me by going?'

'My lad,' gasped the Captain, in a choked and trembling voice, and with a curious action going on in the ponderous fist; 'there's a many words I could wish to say to you, but I don't rightly know where they're stowed just at present. My young friend, Wal'r, was drownded only last night, according to my reckoning, and it puts me out, you see. But you and me will come alongside o' one another again, my lad,' said the Captain, holding up his hook, 'if we live.'

'It will be anything but shrewd in you, my good fellow, if we do,' returned the Manager, with the same frankness; 'for you may rely, I give you fair warning, upon my detecting and exposing you. I don't pretend to be a more moral man than my neighbours, my good Captain; but the confidence of this house, or of any member of this house, is not to be abused and undermined while I have eyes and ears. Good day!' said Mr Carker, nodding his head.

Captain Cuttle, looking at him steadily (Mr Carker looked full as steadily at the Captain), went out of the office and left him standing astride before the fire, as calm and pleasant as if there were no more spots upon his soul than on his pure white linen, and his smooth sleek skin.

The Captain glanced, in passing through the outer counting-house, at the desk where he knew poor Walter had been used to sit, now occupied by another young boy, with a face almost as fresh and hopeful as his on the day when they tapped the famous last bottle but one of the old Madeira, in the little back parlour. The association of ideas, thus awakened, did the Captain a great deal of good; it softened him in the very height of his anger, and brought the tears into his eyes.

Arrived at the Wooden Midshipman's again, and sitting down in a corner of the dark shop, the Captain's indignation, strong as it was, could make no head against his grief. Passion seemed not only to do wrong and violence to the memory of the dead, but to be infected by death, and to droop and decline beside it. All the living knaves and liars in the world, were nothing to the honesty and truth of one dead friend.

The only thing the honest Captain made out clearly, in this state of mind, besides the loss of Walter was, that with him almost the whole world of Captain Cuttle had been drowned. If he reproached himself sometimes, and keenly too, for having ever connived at Walter's innocent deceit, he thought at least as often of the Mr Carker whom no sea could ever render up; and the Mr Dombey, whom he now began to perceive was as far beyond human recall; and the 'Heart's Delight,' with whom he must never foregather again; and the Lovely Peg, that teak-built and trim ballad, that had gone ashore upon a rock, and split into mere planks and beams of rhyme. The Captain sat in the dark shop, thinking of these things, to the entire exclusion of his own injury; and looking with as sad an eye upon the ground, as if in contemplation of their actual fragments as they floated past him.

But the Captain was not unmindful, for all that, of such decent and respectful observances in memory of poor Walter, as he felt within his power. Rousing himself, and rousing Rob the Grinder (who in the unnatural twilight was fast asleep), the Captain sallied forth with his attendant at his heels, and the door-key in his pocket, and repairing to one of those convenient slop-selling establishments of which there is abundant choice at the eastern end of London, purchased on the spot two suits of mourning – one for Rob the Grinder, which was immensely too small, and one for himself, which was immensely too large. He also provided Rob with a species of hat, greatly to be admired for its symmetry and usefulness, as well as for a happy blending of the mariner with the coal-heaver; which is usually termed a sou'wester; and which was something of a novelty in connexion with the instrument business. In their several garments, which the vendor declared to be such a miracle in point of fit as nothing but a rare combination of fortuitous circumstances ever brought about, and the fashion of which was unparalleled within the memory of the oldest inhabitant, the Captain and Grinder immediately arrayed themselves: presenting a spectacle fraught with wonder to all who beheld it.

In this altered form, the Captain received Mr Toots. 'I'm took aback, my lad, at present,' said the Captain, 'and will only confirm that there ill news. Tell the young woman to break it gentle to the young lady, and for neither of 'em never to think of me no more – 'special, mind you, that is – though I will think of them, when night comes on a hurricane and seas is mountains rowling,⁹ for which overhaul your Doctor Watts,¹⁰ brother, and when found make a note on.'

The Captain reserved, until some fitter time, the consideration of Mr Toots's offer of friendship, and thus dismissed him. Captain Cuttle's spirits were so low, in truth, that he half determined, that day, to take no further precautions against surprise from Mrs MacStinger, but to abandon himself recklessly to chance, and be indifferent to what might happen. As evening came on, he fell into a better frame of mind, however; and spoke much of Walter to Rob the Grinder, whose attention and fidelity he likewise incidentally commended. Rob did not blush to hear the Captain earnest in his praises, but sat staring at him, and affecting to snivel with sympathy, and making a feint of being virtuous, and treasuring up every word he said (like a young spy as he was) with very promising deceit.

When Rob had turned in, and was fast asleep, the Captain trimmed the candle, put on his spectacles – he had felt it appropriate to take to spectacles on entering into the Instrument Trade, though his eyes were like a hawk's – and opened the prayer-book at the Burial Service. And reading softly to himself, in the little back parlour, and stopping now and then to wipe his eyes, the Captain, in a true and simple spirit, committed Walter's body to the deep.

CHAPTER 33

Contrasts

Turn we our eyes upon two homes; not lying side by side, but wide apart, though both within easy range and reach of the great city of London.

The first is situated in the green and wooded country near

Norwood.[1] It is not a mansion; it is of no pretensions as to size; but it is beautifully arranged, and tastefully kept. The lawn, the soft, smooth slope, the flower-garden, the clumps of trees where graceful forms of ash and willow are not wanting, the conservatory, the rustic verandah with sweet-smelling creeping plants entwined about the pillars, the simple exterior of the house, the well-ordered offices, though all upon the diminutive scale proper to a mere cottage, bespeak an amount of elegant comfort within, that might serve for a palace. This indication is not without warrant; for within it is a house of refinement and luxury. Rich colours, excellently blended, meet the eye at every turn; in the furniture – its proportions admirably devised to suit the shapes and sizes of the small rooms; on the walls; upon the floors; tingeing and subduing the light that comes in through the odd glass doors and windows here and there. There are a few choice prints and pictures too; in quaint nooks and recesses there is no want of books; and there are games of skill and chance set forth on tables – fantastic chessmen, dice, backgammon, cards, and billiards.

And yet amidst this opulence of comfort, there is something in the general air that is not well. Is it that the carpets and the cushions are too soft and noiseless, so that those who move or repose among them seem to act by stealth? Is it that the prints and pictures do not commemorate great thoughts or deeds, or render nature in the poetry of landscape, hall, or hut, but are of one voluptuous cast – mere shows of form and colour – and no more? Is it that the books have all their gold outside, and that the titles of the greater part qualify them to be companions of the prints and pictures? Is it that the completeness and the beauty of the place are here and there belied by an affectation of humility, in some unimportant and inexpensive regard, which is as false as the face of the too truly painted portrait hanging yonder, or its original at breakfast in his easy chair below it? Or is it that, with the daily breath of that original and master of all here, there issues forth some subtle portion of himself, which gives a vague expression of himself to everything about him?

It is Mr Carker the Manager who sits in the easy chair. A gaudy parrot in a burnished cage upon the table tears at the wires with her beak, and goes walking, upside down, in its dome-top, shaking her house and screeching; but Mr Carker is indifferent to the bird, and looks with a musing smile at a picture on the opposite wall.

'A most extraordinary accidental likeness, certainly,' says he.

Perhaps it is a Juno;[2] perhaps a Potiphar's Wife;[3] perhaps some scornful Nymph – according as the Picture Dealers found the market, when they christened it. It is the figure of a woman, supremely handsome, who, turning away, but with her face addressed to the spectator, flashes her proud glance upon him.

It is like Edith.

With a passing gesture of his hand at the picture – what! a menace? No; yet something like it. A wave as of triumph? No; yet more like that. An insolent salute wafted from his lips? No; yet like that too – he resumes his breakfast, and calls to the chafing and imprisoned bird, who coming down into a pendant gilded hoop within the cage, like a great wedding-ring, swings in it, for his delight.

The second home is on the other side of London, near to where the busy great north road of bygone days is silent and almost deserted, except by wayfarers who toil along on foot. It is a poor, small house, barely and sparely furnished, but very clean; and there is even an attempt to decorate it, shown in the homely flowers trained about the porch and in the narrow garden. The neighbourhood in which it stands has as little of the country to recommend it, as it has of the town. It is neither of the town nor country. The former, like the giant in his travelling boots, has made a stride and passed it, and has set his brick-and-mortar heel a long way in advance; but the intermediate space between the giant's feet, as yet, is only blighted country, and not town; and, here, among a few tall chimneys belching smoke all day and night, and among the brick-fields and the lanes where turf is cut, and where the fences tumble down, and where the dusty nettles grow, and where a scrap or two of hedge may yet be seen, and where the bird-catcher still comes occasionally, though he swears every time to come no more – this second home is to be found.

She who inhabits it, is she who left the first in her devotion to an outcast brother. She withdrew from that home its redeeming spirit, and from its master's breast his solitary angel: but though his liking for her is gone, after this ungrateful slight as he considers it; and though he abandons her altogether in return, an old idea of her is not quite forgotten even by him. Let her flower-garden, in which he never sets his foot, but which is yet maintained, among all his costly alterations, as if she had quitted it but yesterday, bear witness!

Harriet Carker has changed since then, and on her beauty there has fallen a heavier shade than Time of his unassisted self can cast, all-potent as he is – the shadow of anxiety and sorrow, and the daily struggle of a poor existence. But it is beauty still; and still a gentle, quiet, and retiring beauty that must be sought out, for it cannot vaunt itself; if it could, it would be what it is, no more.

Yes. This slight, small, patient figure, neatly dressed in homely stuffs,[4] and indicating nothing but the dull, household virtues, that have so little in common with the received idea of heroism and greatness, unless, indeed, any ray of them should shine through the lives of the great ones of the earth, when it becomes a constellation and is tracked in Heaven straightway – this slight, small, patient figure, leaning on the man still young but worn and grey, is she, his sister, who, of all the world, went over to him in his shame and put her hand in his, and with a sweet composure and determination, led him hopefully upon his barren way.

'It is early, John,' she said. 'Why do you go so early?'

'Not many minutes earlier than usual, Harriet. If I have the time to spare, I should like, I think – it's a fancy – to walk once by the house where I took leave of him.'

'I wish I had ever seen or known him, John.'

'It is better as it is, my dear, remembering his fate.'

'But I could not regret it more, though I had known him. Is not your sorrow mine? And if I had, perhaps you would feel that I was a better companion to you in speaking about him, than I may seem now.'

'My dearest sister! Is there anything within the range of rejoicing or regret, in which I am not sure of your companionship?'

'I hope you think not, John, for surely there is nothing!'

'How could you be better to me, or nearer to me then, than you are in this, or anything?' said her brother. 'I feel that you did know him, Harriet, and that you shared my feelings towards him.'

She drew the hand which had been resting on his shoulder, round his neck, and answered, with some hesitation:

'No, not quite.'

'True, true!' he said; 'you think I might have done him no harm if I had allowed myself to know him better?'

'Think! I know it.'

'Designedly, Heaven knows I would not,' he replied, shaking his head mournfully; 'but his reputation was too precious to be perilled by such association. Whether you share that knowledge, or do not, my dear—'

'I do not,' she said quietly.

'It is still the truth, Harriet, and my mind is lighter when I think of him for that which made it so much heavier then.' He checked

himself in his tone of melancholy, and smiled upon her as he said
'Good-bye!'

'Good-bye, dear John! In the evening, at the old time and place, I
shall meet you as usual on your way home. Good-bye.'

The cordial face she lifted up to his to kiss him, was his home,
his life, his universe, and yet it was a portion of his punishment and
grief; for in the cloud he saw upon it – though serene and calm as
any radiant cloud at sunset – and in the constancy and devotion of
her life, and in the sacrifice she had made of ease, enjoyment, and
hope, he saw the bitter fruits of his old crime, for ever ripe and
fresh.

She stood at the door looking after him, with her hands loosely
clasped in each other, as he made his way over the frowzy and
uneven patch of ground which lay before their house, which had
once (and not long ago) been a pleasant meadow and was now a
very waste, with a disorderly crop of beginnings of mean houses,
rising out of the rubbish, as if they had been unskilfully sown there.
Whenever he looked back – as once or twice he did – her cordial
face shone like a light upon his heart; but when he plodded on his
way, and saw her not, the tears were in her eyes as she stood watching
him.

Her pensive form was not long idle at the door. There was daily
duty to discharge, and daily work to do – for such commonplace
spirits that are not heroic, often work hard with their hands – and
Harriet was soon busy with her household tasks. These discharged,
and the poor house made quite neat and orderly, she counted her
little stock of money, with an anxious face, and went out thoughtfully to buy some necessaries for their table, planning and contriv-
ing, as she went, how to save. So sordid are the lives of such low
natures, who are not only not heroic to their valets[5] and waiting-
women, but have neither valets nor waiting-women to be heroic to
withal!

While she was absent, and there was no one in the house, there
approached it by a different way from that the brother had taken, a
gentleman, a very little past his prime of life perhaps, but of a
healthy florid hue, an upright presence, and a bright clear aspect,
that was gracious and good-humoured. His eyebrows were still
black, and so was much of his hair; the sprinkling of grey observable
among the latter, graced the former very much, and showed his
broad frank brow and honest eyes to great advantage.

After knocking once at the door, and obtaining no response, this
gentleman sat down on a bench in the little porch to wait. A certain

skilful action of his fingers as he hummed some bars, and beat time on the seat beside him, seemed to denote the musician; and the extraordinary satisfaction he derived from humming something very slow and long, which had no recognisable tune, seemed to denote that he was a scientific one.

The gentleman was still twirling a theme, which seemed to go round and round and round, and in and in and in, and to involve itself like a corkscrew twirled upon a table, without getting any nearer to anything, when Harriet appeared returning. He rose up as she advanced, and stood with his head uncovered.

'You are come again, Sir!' she said, faltering.

'I take that liberty,' he answered. 'May I ask for five minutes of your leisure?'

After a moment's hesitation, she opened the door, and gave him admission to the little parlour. The gentleman sat down there, drew his chair to the table over against her, and said, in a voice that perfectly corresponded to his appearance, and with a simplicity that was very engaging:

'Miss Harriet, you cannot be proud. You signified to me, when I called t'other morning, that you were. Pardon me if I say that I looked into your face while you spoke, and that it contradicted you. I look into it again,' he added, laying his hand gently on her arm, for an instant, 'and it contradicts you more and more.'

She was somewhat confused and agitated, and could make no ready answer.

'It is the mirror of truth,' said her visitor, 'and gentleness. Excuse my trusting to it, and returning.'

His manner of saying these words, divested them entirely of the character of compliments. It was so plain, grave, unaffected, and sincere, that she bent her head, as if at once to thank him, and acknowledge his sincerity.

'The disparity between our ages,' said the gentleman, 'and the plainness of my purpose, empower me, I am glad to think, to speak my mind. That is my mind; and so you see me for the second time.'

'There is a kind of pride, Sir,' she returned, after a moment's silence, 'or what may be supposed to be pride, which is mere duty. I hope I cherish no other.'

'For yourself,' he said.

'For myself.'

'But – pardon me—' suggested the gentleman. 'For your brother John?'

'Proud of his love, I am,' said Harriet, looking full upon her visitor, and changing her manner on the instant – not that it was less composed and quiet, but that there was a deep impassioned earnestness in it that made the very tremble in her voice a part of her firmness, 'and proud of him. Sir, you who strangely know the story of his life, and repeated it to me when you were here last—'

'Merely to make my way into your confidence,' interposed the gentleman. 'For heaven's sake, don't suppose—'

'I am sure,' she said, 'you revived it, in my hearing, with a kind and good purpose. I am quite sure of it.'

'I thank you,' returned her visitor, pressing her hand hastily. 'I am much obliged to you. You do me justice, I assure you. You were going to say, that I, who know the story of John Carker's life—'

'May think it pride in me,' she continued, 'when I say that I am proud of him! I *am*. You know the time was, when I was not – when I could not be – but that is past. The humility of many years, the uncomplaining expiation, the true repentance, the terrible regret, the pain I know he has even in my affection, which he thinks has cost me dear, though Heaven knows I am happy, but for his sorrow! – oh, Sir, after what I have seen, let me conjure you, if you are in any place of power, and are ever wronged, never, for any wrong, inflict a punishment that cannot be recalled; while there is a GOD above us to work changes in the hearts He made.'

'Your brother is an altered man,' returned the gentleman, compassionately. 'I assure you I don't doubt it.'

'He was an altered man when he did wrong,' said Harriet. 'He is an altered man again, and is his true self now, believe me, Sir.'

'But we go on,' said her visitor, rubbing his forehead, in an absent manner, with his hand, and then drumming thoughtfully on the table, 'we go on in our clockwork routine, from day to day, and can't make out, or follow, these changes. They – they're a metaphysical sort of thing. We – we haven't leisure for it. We – we haven't courage. They're not taught at schools or colleges, and we don't know how to set about it. In short, we are so d——d business-like,' said the gentleman, walking to the window, and back, and sitting down again, in a state of extreme dissatisfaction and vexation.

'I am sure,' said the gentleman, rubbing his forehead again; and drumming on the table as before, 'I have good reason to believe that a jog-trot life, the same from day to day, would reconcile one to anything. One don't see anything, one don't hear anything, one don't know anything; that's the fact. We go on taking everything for granted, and so we go on, until whatever we do, good, bad, or indifferent, we do from habit. Habit is all I shall have to report, when I am called upon to plead to my conscience, on my deathbed. "Habit," says I; "I was deaf, dumb, blind, and paralytic, to a million things, from habit." "Very business-like indeed, Mr What's-your-name," says Conscience, "but it won't do here!"'

The gentleman got up and walked to the window again and back: seriously uneasy, though giving his uneasiness this peculiar expression.

'Miss Harriet,' he said, resuming his chair, 'I wish you would let me serve you. Look at me; I ought to look honest, for I know I am so, at present. Do I?'

'Yes,' she answered with a smile.

'I believe every word you have said,' he returned. 'I am full of self-reproach that I might have known this and seen this, and known you and seen you, any time these dozen years, and that I never have. I hardly know how I ever got here – creature that I am, not only of my own habit, but of other people's! But having done so, let me do something. I ask it in all honour and respect. You inspire me with both, in the highest degree. Let me do something.'

'We are contented, Sir.'

'No, no, not quite,' returned the gentleman. 'I think not quite. There are some little comforts that might smooth your life, and his. And his!' he repeated, fancying that had made some impression on her. 'I have been in the habit of thinking that there was nothing wanting to be done for him; that it was all settled and over; in short, of not thinking at all about it. I am different now. Let me do something for him. You too,' said the visitor, with careful delicacy, 'have need to watch your health closely, for his sake, and I fear it fails.'

'Whoever you may be, Sir,' answered Harriet, raising her eyes to his face, 'I am deeply grateful to you. I feel certain that in all you say, you have no object in the world but kindness to us. But years have passed since we began this life; and to take from my brother any part of what has so endeared him to me, and so proved his better resolution – any fragment of the merit of his unassisted, obscure, and forgotten reparation – would be to diminish the comfort it will be to him and me, when that time comes to each of us, of which you spoke just now. I thank you better with these tears than any words. Believe it, pray.'

The gentleman was moved, and put the hand she held out, to his lips, much as a tender father might kiss the hand of a dutiful child. But more reverently.

'If the day should ever come,' said Harriet, 'when he is restored, in part, to the position he lost—'

'Restored!' cried the gentleman, quickly. 'How can that be hoped for? In whose hands does the power of any restoration lie? It is no mistake of mine, surely, to suppose that his having gained the priceless blessing of his life, is one cause of the animosity shown to him by his brother.'

'You touch upon a subject that is never breathed between us; not even between us,' said Harriet.

'I beg your forgiveness,' said the visitor. 'I should have known it. I entreat you to forget that I have done so, inadvertently. And now, as I dare urge no more – as I am not sure that I have a right to do so – though Heaven knows, even that doubt may be habit,' said the gentleman, rubbing his head, as despondently as before, 'let me; though a stranger, yet no stranger; ask two favours.'

'What are they?' she inquired.

'The first, that if you should see cause to change your resolution, you will suffer me to be as your right hand. My name shall then be at your service: it is useless now, and always insignificant.'

'Our choice of friends,' she answered, smiling faintly, 'is not so great, that I need any time for consideration. I can promise that.'

'The second, that you will allow me sometimes, say every Monday morning, at nine o'clock – habit again – I must be business-like,' said the gentleman, with a whimsical inclination to quarrel with himself on that head, 'in walking past, to see you at the door or window. I don't ask to come in, as your brother will be gone out at that hour. I don't ask to speak to you. I merely ask to see, for the satisfaction of my own mind, that you are well, and without intrusion to remind you, by the sight of me, that you have a friend – an elderly friend, grey-haired already, and fast growing greyer – whom you may ever command.'

The cordial face looked up in his; confided in it; and promised.

'I understand, as before,' said the gentleman, rising, 'that you purpose not to mention my visit to John Carker, lest he should be at all distressed by my acquaintance with his history. I am glad of it, for it is out of the ordinary course of things, and – habit again!' said the gentleman, checking himself impatiently, 'as if there were no better course than the ordinary course!'

With that he turned to go, and walking, bareheaded, to the outside of the little porch, took leave of her with such a happy mixture of unconstrained respect and unaffected interest, as no breeding could have taught, no truth mistrusted, and nothing but a pure and single heart expressed.

Many half-forgotten emotions were awakened in the sister's mind by this visit. It was so very long since any other visitor had crossed their threshold; it was so very long since any voice of sympathy had made sad music in her ears; that the stranger's figure remained present to her, hours afterwards, when she sat at the window, plying her needle; and his words seemed newly spoken, again and again. He had touched the spring that opened her whole life; and if she lost him for a short space, it was only among the many shapes of the one great recollection of which that life was made.

Musing and working by turns; now constraining herself to be steady at her needle for a long time together, and now letting her work fall, unregarded, on her lap, and straying wheresoever her busier thoughts led, Harriet Carker found the hours glide by her, and the day steal on. The morning, which had been bright and clear, gradually became overcast; a sharp wind set in; the rain fell heavily; and a dark mist drooping over the distant town, hid it from the view.

She often looked with compassion, at such a time, upon the stragglers who came wandering into London, by the great highway hard by, and who, footsore and weary, and gazing fearfully at the huge town before them, as if foreboding that their misery there would be but as a drop of water in the sea, or as a grain of sea-sand on the shore, went shrinking on, cowering before the angry weather, and looking as if the very elements rejected them. Day after day, such travellers crept past, but always, as she thought, in one direction – always towards the town. Swallowed up in one phase or other of its immensity, towards which they seemed impelled by a desperate fascination, they never returned. Food for the hospitals, the churchyards, the prisons, the river, fever, madness, vice, and death, – they passed on to the monster, roaring in the distance, and were lost.

The chill wind was howling, and the rain was falling, and the day was darkening moodily, when Harriet, raising her eyes from the work on which she had long since been engaged with unremitting constancy, saw one of these travellers approaching.

A woman. A solitary woman of some thirty years of age; tall; well-formed; handsome; miserably dressed; the soil of many country roads in varied weather – dust, chalk, clay, gravel – clotted on her grey cloak by the streaming wet; no bonnet on her head, nothing to defend her rich black hair from the rain, but a torn handkerchief;

with the fluttering ends of which, and with her hair, the wind blinded her so that she often stopped to push them back, and look upon the way she was going.

She was in the act of doing so, when Harriet observed her. As her hands, parting on her sunburnt forehead, swept across her face, and threw aside the hindrances that encroached upon it, there was a reckless and regardless beauty in it: a dauntless and depraved indifference to more than weather: a carelessness of what was cast upon her bare head from Heaven or earth: that, coupled with her misery and loneliness, touched the heart of her fellow-woman. She thought of all that was perverted and debased within her, no less than without: of modest graces of the mind, hardened and steeled, like these attractions of the person; of the many gifts of the Creator flung to the winds like the wild hair; of all the beautiful ruin upon which the storm was beating and the night was coming.

Thinking of this, she did not turn away with a delicate indignation – too many of her own compassionate and tender sex too often do – but pitied her.

Her fallen sister came on, looking far before her, trying with her eager eyes to pierce the mist in which the city was enshrouded, and glancing, now and then, from side to side, with the bewildered and uncertain aspect of a stranger. Though her tread was bold and courageous, she was fatigued, and after a moment of irresolution, sat down upon a heap of stones; seeking no shelter from the rain, but letting it rain on her as it would.

She was now opposite the house; raising her head after resting it for a moment on both hands, her eyes met those of Harriet.

In a moment, Harriet was at the door: and the other, rising from her seat at her beck, came slowly, and with no conciliatory look towards her.

'Why do you rest in the rain?' said Harriet, gently.

'Because I have no other resting-place,' was the reply.

'But there are many places of shelter near here. This,' referring to the little porch, 'is better than where you were. You are very welcome to rest here.'

The wanderer looked at her, in doubt and surprise, but without any expression of thankfulness; and sitting down, and taking off one of her worn shoes to beat out the fragments of stone and dust that were inside, showed that her foot was cut and bleeding.

Harriet uttering an expression of pity, the traveller looked up with a contemptuous and incredulous smile.

'Why, what's a torn foot to such as me?' she said. 'And what's a torn foot in such as me, to such as you?'

'Come in and wash it,' answered Harriet, mildly, 'and let me give you something to bind it up.'

The woman caught her arm, and drawing it before her own eyes, hid them against it, and wept. Not like a woman, but like a stern man surprised into that weakness; with a violent heaving of her breast, and struggle for recovery, that showed how unusual the emotion was with her.

She submitted to be led into the house, and, evidently more in gratitude than in any care for herself, washed and bound the injured place. Harriet then put before her fragments of her own frugal dinner, and when she had eaten of them, though sparingly, besought her, before resuming her road (which she showed anxiety to do), to dry her clothes before the fire. Again, more in gratitude than with any evidence of concern in her own behalf, she sat down in front of it, and unbinding the handkerchief about her head, and letting her thick wet hair fall down below her waist, sat drying it with the palms of her hands, and looking at the blaze.

'I dare say you are thinking,' she said, lifting her head suddenly, 'that I used to be handsome, once. I believe I was – I know I was. Look here!'

She held up her hair roughly with both hands; seizing it as if she would have torn it out; then, threw it down again, and flung it back as though it were a heap of serpents.

'Are you a stranger in this place?' asked Harriet.

'A stranger!' she returned, stopping between each short reply, and looking at the fire. 'Yes. Ten or a dozen years a stranger. I have had no almanack where I have been. Ten or a dozen years. I don't know this part. It's much altered since I went away.'

'Have you been far?'

'Very far. Months upon months over the sea, and far away even then. I have been where convicts go,'[6] she added, looking full upon her entertainer. 'I have been one myself.'

'Heaven help you and forgive you!' was the gentle answer.

'Ah! Heaven help me and forgive me!' she returned, nodding her head at the fire. 'If man would help some of us a little more, God would forgive us all the sooner perhaps.'

But she was softened by the earnest manner, and the cordial face so full of mildness and so free from judgment, of her, and said, less hardily:

'We may be about the same age, you and me. If I am older, it is not above a year or two. Oh think of that!'

She opened her arms, as though the exhibition of her outward form would show the moral wretch she was; and letting them drop at her sides, hung down her head.

'There is nothing we may not hope to repair; it is never too late to amend,' said Harriet. 'You are penitent—'

'No,' she answered. 'I am not! I can't be. I am no such thing. Why should I be penitent, and all the world go free? They talk to me of my penitence. Who's penitent for the wrongs that have been done to me?'

She rose up, bound her handkerchief about her head, and turned to move away.

'Where are you going?' said Harriet.

'Yonder,' she answered, pointing with her hand. 'To London.'

'Have you any home to go to?'

'I think I have a mother. She's as much a mother, as her dwelling is a home,' she answered with a bitter laugh.

'Take this,' cried Harriet, putting money in her hand. 'Try to do well. It is very little, but for one day it may keep you from harm.'

'Are you married?' said the other, faintly, as she took it.

'No. I live here with my brother. We have not much to spare, or I would give you more.'

'Will you let me kiss you?'

Seeing no scorn or repugnance in her face, the object of her charity bent over her as she asked the question, and pressed her lips against her cheek. Once more she caught her arm, and covered her eyes with it; and then was gone.

Gone into the deepening night, and howling wind, and pelting rain; urging her way on towards the mist-enshrouded city where the blurred lights gleamed; and with her black hair, and disordered head-gear, fluttering round her reckless face.

CHAPTER 34

Another Mother and Daughter

In an ugly and dark room, an old woman, ugly and dark too, sat listening to the wind and rain, and crouching over a meagre fire. More constant to the last-named occupation than the first, she never changed her attitude, unless, when any stray drops of rain fell hissing on the smouldering embers, to raise her head with an awakened attention to the whistling and pattering outside, and gradually to let it fall again lower and lower and lower as she sunk into a brooding state of thought, in which the noises of the night were as indistinctly regarded as is the monotonous rolling of a sea by one who sits in contemplation on its shore.

There was no light in the room save that which the fire afforded. Glaring sullenly from time to time like the eye of a fierce beast half asleep, it revealed no objects that needed to be jealous of a better display. A heap of rags, a heap of bones, a wretched bed, two or three mutilated chairs or stools, the black walls and blacker ceiling, were all its winking brightness shone upon. As the old woman, with a gigantic and distorted image of herself thrown half upon the wall behind her, half upon the roof above, sat bending over the few loose bricks within which it was pent, on the damp hearth of the chimney – for there was no stove – she looked as if she were watching at some witch's altar for a favourable token; and but that the movement of her chattering jaws and trembling chin was too frequent and too fast for the slow flickering of the fire, it would have seemed an illusion wrought by the light, as it came and went, upon a face as motionless as the form to which it belonged.

If Florence could have stood within the room and looked upon the original of the shadow thrown upon the wall and roof, as it cowered thus over the fire, a glance might have sufficed to recall the figure of Good Mrs Brown; notwithstanding that her childish recollection of that terrible old woman was as grotesque and exaggerated a presentment of the truth, perhaps, as the shadow on the wall. But Florence was not there to look on; and Good Mrs Brown remained unrecognised, and sat staring at her fire, unobserved.

Attracted by a louder sputtering than usual, as the rain came hissing down the chimney in a little stream, the old woman raised her head, impatiently, to listen afresh. And this time she did not drop it again; for there was a hand upon the door, and a footstep in the room.

'Who's that?' she said, looking over her shoulder.

'One who brings you news,' was the answer, in a woman's voice.

'News? Where from?'

'From abroad.'

'From beyond seas?' cried the old woman, starting up.

'Aye, from beyond seas.'

The old woman raked the fire together, hurriedly, and going close to her visitor, who had entered, and shut the door, and who now stood in the middle of the room, put her hand upon the drenched cloak, and turned the unresisting figure, so as to have it in the full light of the fire. She did not find what she had expected, whatever that might be; for she let the cloak go again, and uttered a querulous cry of disappointment and misery.

'What is the matter?' asked her visitor.

'Oho! Oho!' cried the old woman, turning her face upward, with a terrible howl.

'What is the matter?' asked the visitor again.

'It's not my gal!' cried the old woman, tossing up her arms, and clasping her hands above her head. 'Where's my Alice? Where's my handsome daughter? They've been the death of her!'

'They've not been the death of her yet, if your name's Marwood,' said the visitor.

'Have you seen my gal, then?' cried the old woman. 'Has she wrote to me?'

'She said you couldn't read,' returned the other.

'No more I can!' exclaimed the old woman, wringing her hands.

'Have you no light here?' said the other, looking round the room.

The old woman, mumbling and shaking her head, and muttering to herself about her handsome daughter, brought a candle from a cupboard in the corner, and thrusting it into the fire with a trembling hand, lighted it with some difficulty and set it on the table. Its dirty wick burnt dimly at first, being choked in its own grease; and when the bleared eyes and failing sight of the old woman could distinguish anything by its light, her visitor was sitting with her arms folded, her eyes turned downwards, and a handkerchief she had worn upon her head lying on the table by her side.

'She sent to me by word of mouth then, my gal, Alice?' mumbled the old woman, after waiting for some moments. 'What did she say?'

'Look,' returned the visitor.

The old woman repeated the word in a scared uncertain way and, shading her eyes, looked at the speaker, round the room, and at the speaker once again.

'Alice said look again, mother;' and the speaker fixed her eyes upon her.

Again the old woman looked round the room, and at her visitor, and round the room once more. Hastily seizing the candle, and rising from her seat, she held it to the visitor's face, uttered a loud cry, set down the light, and fell upon her neck!

'It's my gal! It's my Alice! It's my handsome daughter, living and come back!' screamed the old woman, rocking herself to and fro upon the breast that coldly suffered her embrace. 'It's my gal! It's my Alice! It's my handsome daughter, living and come back!' she screamed again, dropping on the floor before her, clasping her knees, laying her head against them, and still rocking herself to and fro with every frantic demonstration of which her vitality was capable.

'Yes, mother,' returned Alice, stooping forward for a moment and kissing her, but endeavouring, even in the act, to disengage herself from her embrace. 'I am here, at last. Let go, mother; let go. Get up, and sit in your chair. What good does this do?'

'She's come back harder than she went!' cried the mother, looking up in her face, and still holding to her knees. 'She don't care for me! after all these years, and all the wretched life I've led!'

'Why, mother!' said Alice, shaking her ragged skirts to detach the old woman from them: 'there are two sides to that. There have been years for me as well as you, and there has been wretchedness for me as well as you. Get up, get up!'

Her mother rose, and cried, and wrung her hands, and stood at a little distance gazing on her. Then she took the candle again, and going round her, surveyed her from head to foot, making a low moaning all the time. Then she put the candle down, resumed her chair, and beating her hands together to a kind of weary tune, and rolling herself from side to side, continued moaning and wailing to herself.

Alice got up, took off her wet cloak, and laid it aside. That done, she sat down as before, and with her arms folded, and her eyes gazing at the fire, remained silently listening with a contemptuous face to her old mother's inarticulate complainings.

'Did you expect to see me return as youthful as I went away, mother?' she said at length, turning her eyes upon the old woman. 'Did you think a foreign life, like mine, was good for good looks? One would believe so, to hear you!'

'It an't that!' cried the mother. '*She* knows it!'

'What is it then?' returned the daughter. 'It had best be something that don't last, mother, or my way out is easier than my way in.'

'Hear that!' exclaimed the mother. 'After all these years she threatens to desert me in the moment of her coming back again!'

'I tell you, mother, for the second time, there have been years for me as well as you,' said Alice. 'Come back harder? Of course I have come back harder. What else did you expect?'

'Harder to me! To her own dear mother!' cried the old woman.

'I don't know who began to harden me, if my own dear mother didn't,' she returned, sitting with her folded arms, and knitted brows, and compressed lips as if she were bent on excluding, by force, every softer feeling from her breast. 'Listen, mother, to a word or two. If we understand each other now, we shall not fall out any more, perhaps. I went away a girl, and have come back a woman. I went away undutiful enough, and have come back no better, you may swear. But have you been very dutiful to me?'

'I!' cried the old woman. 'To my gal! A mother dutiful to her own child!'

'It sounds unnatural, don't it?' returned the daughter, looking coldly on her with her stern, regardless, hardy, beautiful face; 'but I have thought of it sometimes, in the course of *my* lone years, till I have got used to it. I have heard some talk about duty first and last; but it has always been of my duty to other people. I have wondered now and then – to pass away the time – whether no one ever owed any duty to me.'

Her mother sat mowing,[1] and mumbling, and shaking her head, but whether angrily or remorsefully, or in denial, or only in her physical infirmity, did not appear.

'There was a child called Alice Marwood,' said the daughter, with a laugh, and looking down at herself in terrible derision of herself, 'born, among poverty and neglect, and nursed in it. Nobody taught her, nobody stepped forward to help her, nobody cared for her.'

'Nobody!' echoed the mother, pointing to herself, and striking her breast.

'The only care she knew,' returned the daughter, 'was to be beaten, and stinted, and abused sometimes; and she might have done better without that. She lived in homes like this, and in the streets, with a crowd of little wretches like herself; and yet she brought good looks out of this childhood. So much the worse for her. She had better have been hunted and worried to death for ugliness.'

'Go on! go on!' exclaimed the mother.

'I am going on,' returned the daughter. 'There was a girl called Alice Marwood. She was handsome. She was taught too late, and taught all wrong. She was too well cared for, too well trained, too well helped on, too much looked after. You were very fond of her –

you were better off then. What came to that girl comes to thousands every year. It was only ruin, and she was born to it.'

'After all these years!' whined the old woman. 'My gal begins with this.'

'She'll soon have ended,' said the daughter. 'There was a criminal called Alice Marwood – a girl still, but deserted and an outcast. And she was tried, and she was sentenced. And lord, how the gentlemen in the court talked about it! and how grave the judge was on her duty, and on her having perverted the gifts of nature – as if he didn't know better than anybody there, that they had been made curses to her! – and how he preached about the strong arm of the Law – so very strong to save her, when she was an innocent and helpless little wretch; and how solemn and religious it all was. I have thought of that, many times since, to be sure!'

She folded her arms tightly on her breast, and laughed in a tone that made the howl of the old woman musical.

'So Alice Marwood was transported, mother,' she pursued, 'and was sent to learn her duty, where there was twenty times less duty, and more wickedness, and wrong, and infamy, than here. And Alice Marwood is come back a woman. Such a woman as she ought to be, after all this. In good time, there will be more solemnity, and more fine talk, and more strong arm, most likely, and there will be an end of her; but the gentlemen needn't be afraid of being thrown out of work. There's crowds of little wretches, boy and girl, growing up in any of the streets they live in, that'll keep them to it till they've made their fortunes.'

The old woman leaned her elbows on the table, and resting her face upon her two hands, made a show of being in great distress – or really was, perhaps.

'There! I have done, mother,' said the daughter, with a motion of her head, as if in dismissal of the subject. 'I have said enough. Don't let you and I talk of being dutiful, whatever we do. Your childhood was like mine, I suppose. So much the worse for both of us. I don't want to blame you, or to defend myself; why should I? That's all over long ago. But I am a woman – not a girl, now – and you and I needn't make a show of our history, like the gentlemen in the Court. *We* know all about it well enough.'

Lost and degraded as she was, there was a beauty in her, both of face and form, which, even in its worst expression, could not but be recognised as such by any one regarding her with the least attention. As she subsided into silence, and her face which had been harshly agitated, quieted down; while her dark eyes, fixed upon the

fire, exchanged the reckless light that had animated them, for one
that was softened by something like sorrow; there shone through
all her wayworn misery and fatigue, a ray of the departed radiance
of the fallen angel.

Her mother, after watching her for some time without speaking,
ventured to steal her withered hand a little nearer to her across the
table; and finding that she permitted this, to touch her face and
smooth her hair. With the feeling as it seemed, that the old woman
was at least sincere in this show of interest, Alice made no
movement to check her; so, advancing by degrees, she bound up
her daughter's hair afresh, took off her wet shoes, if they deserved
the name, spread something dry upon her shoulders, and hovered
humbly about her, muttering to herself, as she recognised her old
features and expression more and more.

'You are very poor, mother, I see,' said Alice, looking round,
when she had sat thus for some time.

'Bitter poor, my deary,' replied the old woman.

She admired her daughter, and was afraid of her. Perhaps her
admiration, such as it was, had originated long ago, when she first
found anything that was beautiful appearing in the midst of the
squalid fight of her existence. Perhaps her fear was referable, in
some sort, to the retrospect she had so lately heard. Be this as it
might, she stood, submissively and deferentially, before her child,
and inclined her head, as if in a pitiful entreaty to be spared any
further reproach.

'How have you lived?'

'By begging, my deary.'

'And pilfering, mother?'

'Sometimes, Ally – in a very small way. I am old and timid. I have
taken trifles from children now and then, my deary, but not often. I
have tramped about the country, pet, and I know what I know. I
have watched.'

'Watched?' returned the daughter, looking at her.

'I have hung about a family, my deary,' said the mother, even
more humbly and submissively than before.

'What family?'

'Hush, darling. Don't be angry with me, I did it for the love of
you. In memory of my poor gal beyond seas.' She put out her hand
deprecatingly, and drawing it back again, laid it on her lips.

'Years ago, my deary,' she pursued, glancing timidly at the
attentive and stern face opposed to her. 'I came across his little
child, by chance.'

'Whose child?'

'Not his, Alice deary; don't look at me like that; not his. How could it be his? You know he has none.'

'Whose then?' returned the daughter. 'You said his.'

'Hush, Ally; you frighten me, deary. Mr Dombey's – only Mr Dombey's. Since then, darling, I have seen them often. I have seen *him*.'

In uttering this last word, the old woman shrunk and recoiled, as if with a sudden fear that her daughter would strike her. But though the daughter's face was fixed upon her, and expressed the most vehement passion, she remained still: except that she clenched her arms tighter and tighter within each other, on her bosom, as if to restrain them by that means from doing an injury to herself, or some one else, in the blind fury of the wrath that suddenly possessed her.

'Little he thought who I was!' said the old woman, shaking her clenched hand.

'And little he cared!' muttered her daughter, between her teeth.

'But there we were,' said the old woman, 'face to face. I spoke to him, and he spoke to me. I sat and watched him as he went away down a long grove of trees: and at every step he took, I cursed him soul and body.'

'He will thrive in spite of that,' returned the daughter disdainfully.

'Aye, he is thriving,' said the mother.

She held her peace; for the face and form before her were unshaped by rage. It seemed as if the bosom would burst with the emotions that strove within it. The effort that constrained and held it pent up, was no less formidable than the rage itself: no less bespeaking the violent and dangerous character of the woman who made it. But it succeeded, and she asked, after a silence:

'Is he married?'

'No, deary,' said the mother.

'Going to be?'

'Not that I know of, deary. But his master and friend is married. Oh, we may give him joy! We may give 'em all joy! cried the old woman, hugging herself with her lean arms in her exultation. 'Nothing but joy to us will come of that marriage. Mind me!'

The daughter looked at her for an explanation.

'But you are wet and tired: hungry and thirsty,' said the old woman, hobbling to the cupboard; 'and there's little here, and little' – diving down into her pocket, and jingling a few halfpence on the table – 'little here. Have you any money, Alice, deary?'

The covetous, sharp, eager face with which she asked the question and looked on, as her daughter took out of her bosom the little gift she had so lately received, told almost as much of the history of this parent and child as the child herself had told in words.

'Is that all?' said the mother.

'I have no more. I should not have this, but for charity.'

'But for charity, eh, deary?' said the old woman, bending greedily over the table to look at the money, which she appeared distrustful of her daughter's still retaining in her hand, and gazing on. 'Humph! six and six is twelve, and six eighteen – so – we must make the most of it. I'll go buy something to eat and drink.'

With greater alacrity than might have been expected in one of her appearance – for age and misery seemed to have made her as decrepit as ugly – she began to occupy her trembling hands in tying an old bonnet on her head, and folding a torn shawl about herself; still eyeing the money in her daughter's hand, with the same sharp desire.

'What joy is to come to us of this marriage, mother?' asked the daughter. 'You have not told me that.'

'The joy,' she replied, attiring herself, with fumbling fingers, 'of no love at all, and much pride and hate, my deary. The joy of confusion and strife among 'em, proud as they are, and of danger – danger, Alice!'

'What danger?'

'*I* have seen what I have seen. *I* know what I know!' chuckled the mother. 'Let some look to it. Let some be upon their guard. My gal may keep good company yet!'

Then, seeing that in the wondering earnestness with which her daughter regarded her, her hand involuntarily closed upon the money, the old woman made more speed to secure it, and hurriedly added, 'but I'll go buy something; I'll go buy something.'

As she stood with her hand stretched out before her daughter, her daughter, glancing again at the money, put it to her lips before parting with it.

'What, Ally! Do you kiss it?' chuckled the old woman. 'That's like me – I often do. Oh, it's so good to us!' squeezing her own tarnished halfpence up to her bag of a throat, 'so good to us in everything but not coming in heaps!'

'I kiss it, mother,' said the daughter, 'or I did then – I don't know that I ever did before – for the giver's sake.'

'The giver, eh, deary?' retorted the old woman, whose dimmed eyes glistened as she took it. 'Aye! I'll kiss it for the giver's sake, too, when the giver can make it go farther. But I'll go spend it, deary. I'll be back directly.'

'You seem to say you know a great deal, mother,' said the daughter, following her to the door with her eyes. 'You have grown very wise since we parted.'

'Know!' croaked the old woman, coming back a step or two, 'I know more than you think. I know more than *he* thinks, deary, as I'll tell you by and bye. I know all about him.'

The daughter smiled incredulously.

'I know of his brother, Alice,' said the old woman, stretching out her neck with a leer of malice absolutely frightful, 'who might have been where you have been – for stealing money – and who lives with his sister, over yonder, by the north road out of London.'

'Where?'

'By the north road out of London, deary. You shall see the house if you like. It an't much to boast of, genteel as his own is. No, no, no,' cried the old woman, shaking her head and laughing; for her daughter had started up, 'not now; it's too far off; it's by the milestone, where the stones are heaped; – to-morrow, deary, if it's fine, and you are in the humour. But I'll go spend—'

'Stop!' and the daughter flung herself upon her, with her former passion raging like a fire. 'The sister is a fair-faced Devil, with brown hair?'

The old woman, amazed and terrified, nodded her head.

'I see the shadow of him in her face! It's a red house standing by itself. Before the door there is a small green porch.'

Again the old woman nodded.

'In which I sat to-day! Give me back the money.'

'Alice! Deary!'

'Give me back the money, or you'll be hurt.'

She forced it from the old woman's hand as she spoke, and utterly indifferent to her complainings and entreaties, threw on the garments she had taken off, and hurried out, with headlong speed.

The mother followed, limping after her as she could, and expostulating with no more effect upon her than upon the wind and rain and darkness that encompassed them. Obdurate and fierce in her own purpose, and indifferent to all besides, the daughter defied the weather and the distance, as if she had known no travel or fatigue, and made for the house where she had been relieved. After some quarter of an hour's walking, the old woman, spent and out of breath, ventured to hold by her skirts; but she ventured no more, and they travelled on in silence through the wet and gloom. If the mother now and then uttered a word of complaint, she stifled it lest her daughter should break away from her and leave her behind; and the daughter was dumb.

It was within an hour or so of midnight, when they left the regular streets behind them, and entered on the deeper gloom of that neutral ground where the house was situated. The town lay in the distance, lurid and lowering; the bleak wind howled over the open space; all around was black, wild, desolate.

'This is a fit place for me!' said the daughter, stopping to look back. 'I thought so, when I was here before, to-day.'

'Alice, my deary,' cried the mother, pulling her gently by the skirt. 'Alice!'

'What now, mother?'

'Don't give the money back, my darling; please don't. We can't afford it. We want supper, deary. Money is money, whoever gives it. Say what you will, but keep the money.'

'See there!' was all the daughter's answer. 'That is the house I mean. Is that it?'

The old woman nodded in the affirmative; and a few more paces brought them to the threshold. There was the light of fire and candle in the room where Alice had sat to dry her clothes; and on her knocking at the door, John Carker appeared from that room.

He was surprised to see such visitors at such an hour, and asked Alice what she wanted.

'I want your sister,' she said. 'The woman who gave me money to-day.'

At the sound of her raised voice, Harriet came out.

'Oh!' said Alice. 'You are here! Do you remember me?'

'Yes,' she answered, wondering.

The face that had humbled itself before her, looked on her now with such invincible hatred and defiance; and the hand that had gently touched her arm, was clenched with such a show of evil purpose, as if it would gladly strangle her; that she drew close to her brother for protection.

'That I could speak with you, and not know you! That I could come near you, and not feel what blood was running in your veins, by the tingling of my own!' said Alice, with a menacing gesture.

'What do you mean? What have I done?'

'Done!' returned the other. 'You have sat me by your fire; you have given me food and money; you have bestowed your compassion on me! You! whose name I spit upon!'

The old woman, with a malevolence that made her ugliness quite awful, shook her withered hand at the brother and sister in confirmation of her daughter, but plucked her by the skirts again, nevertheless, imploring her to keep the money.

'If I dropped a tear upon your hand, may it wither it up! If I spoke a gentle word in your hearing, may it deafen you! If I touched you with my lips, may the touch be poison to you! A curse upon this roof that gave me shelter! Sorrow and shame upon your head! Ruin upon all belonging to you!'

As she said the words, she threw the money down upon the ground, and spurned it with her foot.

'I tread it in the dust: I wouldn't take it if it paved my way to Heaven! I would the bleeding foot that brought me here today, had rotted off, before it led me to your house!'

Harriet, pale and trembling, restrained her brother, and suffered her to go on uninterrupted.

'It was well that I should be pitied and forgiven by you, or any one of your name, in the first hour of my return! It was well that you should act the kind good lady to me! I'll thank you when I die; I'll pray for you, and all your race, you may be sure!'

With a fierce action of her hand, as if she sprinkled hatred on the ground, and with it devoted those who were standing there to destruction, she looked up once at the black sky, and strode out into the wild night.

The mother, who had plucked at her skirts again and again in vain, and had eyed the money lying on the threshold with an absorbing greed that seemed to concentrate her faculties upon it, would have prowled about, until the house was dark, and then groped in the mire on the chance of repossessing herself of it. But the daughter drew her away, and they set forth, straight, on their return to their dwelling; the old woman whimpering and bemoaning their loss upon the road, and fretfully bewailing, as openly as she dared, the undutiful conduct of her handsome girl in depriving her of a supper, on the very first night of their reunion.

Supperless to bed she went, saving for a few coarse fragments; and those she sat mumbling and munching over a scrap of fire, long after her undutiful daughter lay asleep.

Were this miserable mother, and this miserable daughter, only the reduction to their lowest grade, of certain social vices sometimes prevailing higher up? In this round world of many circles within circles, do we make a weary journey from the high grade to the low, to find at last that they lie close together, that the two extremes

The rejected alms

touch, and that our journey's end is but our starting-place? Allowing for great difference of stuff and texture, was the pattern of this woof repeated among gentle blood at all?

Say, Edith Dombey! And Cleopatra, best of mothers, let us have your testimony!

CHAPTER 35

The Happy Pair

The dark blot on the street is gone. Mr Dombey's mansion, if it be a gap among the other houses any longer, is only so because it is not to be vied with in its brightness, and haughtily casts them off. The saying is, that home is home, be it never so homely. If it hold good in the opposite contingency, and home is home be it never so stately, what an altar to the Household Gods[1] is raised up here!

Lights are sparkling in the windows this evening, and the ruddy glow of fires is warm and bright upon the hangings and soft carpets, and the dinner waits to be served, and the dinner-table is handsomely set forth, though only for four persons, and the sideboard is cumbrous with plate. It is the first time that the house has been arranged for occupation since its late changes, and the happy pair are looked for every minute.

Only second to the wedding morning, in the interest and expectation it engenders among the household, is this evening of the coming home. Mrs Perch is in the kitchen taking tea; and has made the tour of the establishment, and priced the silks and damasks by the yard, and exhausted every interjection in the dictionary and out of it expressive of admiration and wonder. The upholsterer's foreman, who has left his hat, with a pocket-handkerchief in it, both smelling strongly of varnish, under a chair in the hall, lurks about the house, gazing upwards at the cornices, and downward at the carpets, and occasionally, in a silent transport of enjoyment, taking a rule out of his pocket, and skirmishingly measuring expensive objects, with unutterable feelings. Cook is in high spirits, and says give *her* a place where there's plenty of company (as she'll bet you sixpence there will be now), for she is of a lively disposition, and she always was from a child, and she don't mind who knows it; which sentiment elicits from the breast of Mrs Perch a responsive murmur of support and approbation. All the housemaid hopes is, happiness for 'em – but marriage is a lottery, and the more she thinks about it, the more she feels the independence and the safety of a single life. Mr Towlinson is saturnine and grim, and says that's his opinion too, and give him War besides, and down with the French – for this young man has a general impression that every foreigner is a Frenchman, and must be by the laws of nature.

At each new sound of wheels, they all stop, whatever they are saying, and listen; and more than once there is a general starting up and a cry of 'Here they are!' But here they are not yet; and Cook begins to mourn over the dinner, which has been put back twice, and the upholsterer's foreman still goes lurking about the rooms, undisturbed in his blissful reverie!

Florence is ready to receive her father and her new mama. Whether the emotions that are throbbing in her breast originate in pleasure or in pain, she hardly knows. But the fluttering heart sends added colour to her cheeks, and brightness to her eyes; and they say downstairs, drawing their heads together – for they always speak softly when they speak of her – how beautiful Miss Florence looks to-night, and what a sweet young lady she has grown, poor dear! A pause succeeds; and then Cook, feeling, as president, that her sentiments are waited for, wonders whether – and there stops. The housemaid wonders too, and so does Mrs Perch, who has the happy social faculty of always wondering when other people wonder, without being at all particular what she wonders at. Mr Towlinson, who now descries an opportunity of bringing down the spirits of the ladies to his own level, says wait and see; he wishes some people were well out of this. Cook leads a sigh then, and a murmur of 'Ah, it's a strange world, it is indeed!' and when it has gone round the table, adds persuasively, 'but Miss Florence can't well be the worse for any change, Tom.' Mr Towlinson's rejoinder, pregnant with frightful meaning, is 'Oh, can't she though!' and sensible that a mere man can scarcely be more prophetic, or improve upon that, he holds his peace.

Mrs Skewton, prepared to meet her darling daughter and dear son-in-law with open arms, is appropriately attired for that purpose in a very youthful costume, with short sleeves. At present, however, her ripe charms are blooming in the shade of her own apartments, whence she has not emerged since she took possession of them a few hours ago, and where she is fast growing fretful, on account of the postponement of dinner. The maid who ought to be a skeleton, but is in truth a buxom damsel, is, on the other hand, in a most amiable state: considering her quarterly stipend much safer than heretofore, and foreseeing a great improvement in her board and lodging.

Where are the happy pair, for whom this brave home is waiting? Do steam, tide, wind, and horses, all abate their speed, to linger on such happiness? Does the swarm of loves and graces hovering about them retard their progress by its numbers? Are there so many flowers in their happy path, that they can scarcely move along, without entanglement in thornless roses, and sweetest briar?

They are here at last! The noise of wheels is heard, grows louder, and a carriage drives up to the door! A thundering knock from the obnoxious foreigner anticipates the rush of Mr Towlinson and party to open it; and Mr Dombey and his bride alight, and walk in arm in arm.

'My sweetest Edith!' cries an agitated voice upon the stairs. 'My dearest Dombey!' and the short sleeves wreath themselves about the happy couple in turn, and embrace them.

Florence had come down to the hall too, but did not advance: reserving her timid welcome until these nearer and dearer transports should subside. But the eyes of Edith sought her out, upon the threshold; and dismissing her sensitive parent with a slight kiss on the cheek, she hurried on to Florence and embraced her.

'How do you do, Florence?' said Mr Dombey, putting out his hand.

As Florence, trembling, raised it to her lips, she met his glance. The look was cold and distant enough, but it stirred her heart to think that she observed in it something more of interest than he had ever shown before. It even expressed a kind of faint surprise, and not a disagreeable surprise, at sight of her. She dared not raise her eyes to his any more; but she felt that he looked at her once again, and not less favourably. Oh what a thrill of joy shot through her, awakened by even this intangible and baseless confirmation of her hope that she would learn to win him, through her new and beautiful mama!

'You will not be long dressing, Mrs Dombey, I presume?' said Mr Dombey.

'I shall be ready immediately.'

'Let them send up dinner in a quarter of an hour.'

With that Mr Dombey stalked away to his own dressing-room, and Mrs Dombey went upstairs to hers. Mrs Skewton and Florence repaired to the drawing-room, where that excellent mother considered it incumbent on her to shed a few irrepressible tears, supposed to be forced from her by her daughter's felicity; and which she was still drying, very gingerly, with a laced corner of her pocket-handkerchief, when her son-in-law appeared.

'And how, my dearest Dombey, did you find that delightfullest of cities, Paris?' she asked, subduing her emotion.

'It was cold,' returned Mr Dombey.

'Gay as ever,' said Mrs Skewton, 'of course.'

'Not particularly. I thought it dull,' said Mr Dombey.

'Fie, my dearest Dombey!' archly; 'dull!'

'It made that impression upon me, madam,' said Mr Dombey, with grave politeness. 'I believe Mrs Dombey found it dull too. She mentioned once or twice that she thought it so.'

'Why, you naughty girl!' cried Mrs Skewton, rallying her dear child, who now entered, 'what dreadfully heretical things have you been saying about Paris?'

Edith raised her eyebrows with an air of weariness; and passing the folding-doors which were thrown open to display the suite of rooms in their new and handsome garniture, and barely glancing at them as she passed, sat down by Florence.

'My dear Dombey,' said Mrs Skewton, 'how charmingly these people have carried out every idea that we hinted. They have made a perfect palace of the house, positively.'

'It is handsome,' said Mr Dombey, looking round. 'I directed that no expense should be spared; and all that money could do, has been done, I believe.'

'And what can it not do, dear Dombey?' observed Cleopatra.

'It is powerful, madam,' said Mr Dombey.

He looked in his solemn way towards his wife, but not a word said she.

'I hope, Mrs Dombey,' addressing her after a moment's silence, with especial distinctness; 'that these alterations meet with your approval?'

'They are as handsome as they can be,' she returned, with haughty carelessness. 'They should be so, of course. And I suppose they are.'

An expression of scorn was habitual to the proud face, and seemed inseparable from it; but the contempt with which it received any appeal to admiration, respect, or consideration on the ground of his riches, no matter how slight or ordinary in itself, was a new and different expression, unequalled in intensity by any other of which it was capable. Whether Mr Dombey, wrapped in his own greatness, was at all aware of this, or no, there had not been wanting opportunities already for his complete enlightenment; and at that moment it might have been effected by the one glance of the dark eye that lighted on him, after it had rapidly and scornfully surveyed the theme of his self-glorification. He might have read in that one glance that nothing that his wealth could do, though it were increased ten thousandfold, could win him for its own sake, one look of softened recognition from the defiant woman, linked to him, but arrayed with her whole soul against him. He might have read in that one glance that even for its sordid and mercenary influence upon herself, she spurned it, while she claimed its utmost power as her right, her bargain – as the base and worthless recompense for which she had become his wife. He might have read in it that, ever baring her own head for the lightning of her own contempt and pride to strike, the most innocent allusion to the power of his riches degraded her anew, sunk her deeper in her own respect, and made the blight and waste within her more complete.

But dinner was announced, and Mr Dombey led down Cleopatra; Edith and his daughter following. Sweeping past the gold and silver demonstration on the sideboard as if it were heaped-up dirt, and deigning to bestow no look upon the elegancies around her, she took her place at his board for the first time, and sat, like a statue, at the feast.

Mr Dombey, being a good deal in the statue way himself, was well enough pleased to see his handsome wife immovable and proud and cold. Her deportment being always elegant and graceful, this as a general behaviour was agreeable and congenial to him. Presiding, therefore, with his accustomed dignity, and not at all reflecting on his wife by any warmth or hilarity of his own, he performed his share of the honours of the table with a cool satisfaction; and the installation dinner,[2] though not regarded downstairs as a great success, or very promising beginning, passed off, above, in a sufficiently polite, genteel, and frosty manner.

Soon after tea, Mrs Skewton, who affected to be quite overcome and worn out by her emotions of happiness, arising in the contemplation of her dear child united to the man of her heart, but who, there is reason to suppose, found this family party somewhat dull, as she yawned for one hour continually behind her fan, retired to bed. Edith, also, silently withdrew and came back no more. Thus, it happened that Florence, who had been upstairs to have some conversation with Diogenes, returning to the drawing-room with her little work-basket, found no one there but her father, who was walking to and fro, in dreary magnificence.

'I beg your pardon. Shall I go away, papa?' said Florence faintly, hesitating at the door.

'No,' returned Mr Dombey, looking round over his shoulder; 'you can come and go here, Florence, as you please. This is not my private room.'

Florence entered, and sat down at a distant little table with her work: finding herself for the first time in her life – for the very first time within her memory from her infancy to that hour – alone with her father, as his companion. She, his natural companion, his only child, who in her lonely life and grief had known the suffering of a breaking heart; who, in her rejected love, had never breathed his name to God at night, but with a tearful blessing, heavier on him than a curse; who had prayed to die young, so she might only die in his arms; who had, all through, repaid the agony of slight and coldness, and dislike, with patient unexacting love, excusing him, and pleading for him, like his better angel!

She trembled, and her eyes were dim. His figure seemed to grow in height and bulk before her as he paced the room: now it was all blurred and indistinct; now clear again, and plain; and now she seemed to think that this had happened, just the same, a multitude of years ago. She yearned towards him, and yet shrunk from his approach. Unnatural emotion in a child, innocent of wrong! Unnatural the hand that had directed the sharp plough, which furrowed up her gentle nature for the sowing of its seeds!

Bent upon not distressing or offending him by her distress, Florence controlled herself, and sat quietly at her work. After a few more turns across and across the room, he left off pacing it; and withdrawing into a shadowy corner at some distance, where there was an easy chair, covered his head with a handkerchief, and composed himself to sleep.

It was enough for Florence to sit there watching him; turning her eyes towards his chair from time to time; watching him with her thoughts, when her face was intent upon her work; and sorrowfully glad to think that he *could* sleep, while she was there, and that he was not made restless by her strange and long-forbidden presence.

What would have been her thoughts if she had known that he was steadily regarding her; that the veil upon his face, by accident or by design, was so adjusted that his sight was free, and that it never wandered from her face an instant! That when she looked towards him, in the obscure dark corner, her speaking eyes, more earnest and pathetic in their voiceless speech than all the orators of all the world, and impeaching him more nearly in their mute address, met his, and did not know it! That when she bent her head again over her work, he drew his breath more easily, but with the same attention looked upon her still – upon her white brow and her falling hair, and busy hands; and once attracted, seemed to have no power to turn his eyes away!

And what were his thoughts meanwhile? With what emotions did he prolong the attentive gaze covertly directed on his unknown daughter? Was there reproach to him in the quiet figure and the mild eyes? Had he begun to feel her disregarded claims, and did they touch him home at last, and waken him to some sense of his cruel injustice?

There are yielding moments in the lives of the sternest and harshest men, though such men often keep their secret well. The sight of her in her beauty, almost changed into a woman without his knowledge, may have struck out some such moments even in his life of pride. Some passing thought that he had had a happy home within his reach – had had a household spirit bending at his feet – had overlooked it in his stiff-necked sullen arrogance, and wandered away and lost himself, may have engendered them. Some simple eloquence distinctly heard, though only uttered in her eyes, unconscious that he read them, as 'By the death-beds I have tended, by the childhood I have suffered, by our meeting in this dreary house at midnight, by the cry wrung from me in the anguish of my heart, oh, father, turn to me and seek a refuge in my love before it is too late!' may have arrested them. Meaner and lower thoughts, as that his dead boy was now superseded by new ties, and he could forgive the having been supplanted in his affection, may have occasioned them. The mere association of her as an ornament with all the ornament and pomp about him, may have been sufficient. But as he looked, he softened to her, more and more. As he looked, she became blended with the child he had loved, and he could hardly separate the two. As he looked, he saw her for an instant by a clearer and a brighter light, not bending over that child's pillow as his rival – monstrous thought – but as the spirit of his home, and in the action tending himself no less, as he sat once more with his bowed-down head upon his hand at the foot of the little bed. He felt inclined to speak to her, and call her to him. The words 'Florence, come here!' were rising to his lips – but slowly and with difficulty, they were so very strange – when they were checked and stifled by a footstep on the stair.

It was his wife's. She had exchanged her dinner dress for a loose robe, and unbound her hair, which fell freely about her neck. But this was not the change in her that startled him.

'Florence, dear,' she said, 'I have been looking for you everywhere.'

As she sat down by the side of Florence, she stooped and kissed her hand. He hardly knew his wife. She was so changed. It was not merely that her smile was new to him – though that he had never seen; but her manner, the tone of her voice, the light of her eyes, the interest, and confidence, and winning wish to please, expressed in all – this was not Edith.

'Softly, dear mama. Papa is asleep.'

It was Edith now. She looked towards the corner where he was, and he knew that face and manner very well.

'I scarcely thought you could be here, Florence.'

Again, how altered and how softened, in an instant!

'I left here early,' pursued Edith, 'purposely to sit upstairs and talk with you. But, going to your room, I found my bird was flown, and I have been waiting there ever since, expecting its return.'

If it had been a bird, indeed, she could not have taken it more tenderly and gently to her breast, than she did Florence.

'Come, dear!'

'Papa will not expect to find me, I suppose, when he wakes,' hesitated Florence.

'Do you think he will, Florence?' said Edith, looking full upon her.

Florence drooped her head, and rose, and put up her work-basket. Edith drew her hand through her arm, and they went out of the room like sisters. Her very step was different and new to him, Mr Dombey thought, as his eyes followed her to the door.

He sat in his shadowy corner so long, that the church clocks struck the hour three times before he moved that night. All that while his face was still intent upon the spot where Florence had been seated. The room grew darker, as the candles waned and went out; but a darkness gathered on his face, exceeding any that the night could cast, and rested there.

Florence and Edith, seated before the fire in the remote room where little Paul had died, talked together for a long time. Diogenes, who was of the party, had at first objected to the admission of Edith, and, even in deference to his mistress's wish, had only permitted it under growling protest. But, emerging by little and little from the ante-room, whither he had retired in dudgeon, he soon appeared to comprehend, that with the most amiable inten-tions he had made one of those mistakes which will occasionally arise in the best-regulated[3] dogs' minds; as a friendly apology for which he stuck himself up on end between the two, in a very hot place in front of the fire, and sat panting at it, with his tongue out, and a most imbecile expression of countenance, listening to the conversation.

It turned, at first, on Florence's books and favourite pursuits, and on the manner in which she had beguiled the interval since the marriage. The last theme opened up to her a subject which lay very near her heart, and she said, with the tears starting to her eyes:

'Oh, mama! I have had a great sorrow since that day.'

'You a great sorrow, Florence!'

'Yes. Poor Walter is drowned.'

Florence spread her hands before her face, and wept with all her heart. Many as were the secret tears which Walter's fate had cost her, they flowed yet, when she thought or spoke of him.

'But tell me, dear,' said Edith, soothing her. 'Who was Walter? What was he to you?'

'He was my brother, mama. After dear Paul died, we said we would be brother and sister. I had known him a long time – from a little child. He knew Paul, who liked him very much; Paul said, almost at the last, "Take care of Walter, dear papa! I was fond of him!" Walter had been brought in to see him, and was there then – in this room.'

'And *did* he take care of Walter?' inquired Edith, sternly.

'Papa? He appointed him to go abroad. He was drowned in shipwreck on his voyage,' said Florence, sobbing.

'Does he know that he is dead?' asked Edith.

'I cannot tell, mama. I have no means of knowing. Dear mama!' cried Florence, clinging to her as for help, and hiding her face upon her bosom, 'I know that you have seen—'

'Stay! Stop, Florence.' Edith turned so pale, and spoke so earnestly, that Florence did not need her restraining hand upon her lips. 'Tell me all about Walter first; let me understand this history all through.'

Florence related it, and everything belonging to it, even down to the friendship of Mr Toots, of whom she could hardly speak in her distress without a tearful smile, although she was deeply grateful to him. When she had concluded her account, to the whole of which Edith, holding her hand, listened with close attention, and when a silence had succeeded, Edith said:

'What is it that you know I have seen, Florence?'

'That I am not,' said Florence, with the same mute appeal, and the same quick concealment of her face as before, 'that I am not a favourite child, mama. I never have been. I have never known how to be. I have missed the way, and had no one to show it to me. Oh, let me learn from you how to become dearer to papa. Teach me! you, who can so well!' and clinging closer to her, with some broken fervent words of gratitude and endearment, Florence, relieved of her sad secret, wept long, but not as painfully as of yore, within the encircling arms of her new mother.

Pale even to her lips, and with a face that strove for composure until its proud beauty was as fixed as death, Edith looked down upon the weeping girl, and once kissed her. Then gradually disengaging herself, and putting Florence away, she said, stately, and quiet as a marble image, and in a voice that deepened as she spoke, but had no other token of emotion in it:

'Florence, you do not know me! Heaven forbid that you should learn from me!'

'Not learn from you?' repeated Florence, in surprise.

'That I should teach you how to love, or be loved, Heaven forbid!' said Edith. 'If you could teach me, that were better; but it is too late. You are dear to me, Florence. I did not think that anything could ever be so dear to me, as you are in this little time.'

She saw that Florence would have spoken here, so checked her with her hand, and went on.

'I will be your true friend always. I will cherish you, as much, if not as well as any one in this world could. You may trust in me – I know it and I say it, dear – with the whole confidence even of your pure heart. There are hosts of women whom he might have married, better and truer in all other respects than I am, Florence; but there is not one who could come here, his wife, whose heart could beat with greater truth to you than mine does.'

'I know it, dear mama!' cried Florence. 'From that first most happy day I have known it.'

'Most happy day!' Edith seemed to repeat the words involuntarily, and went on. 'Though the merit is not mine, for I thought little of you until I saw you, let the undeserved reward be mine in your trust and love. And in this – in this, Florence; on the first night of my taking up my abode here; I am led on as it is best I should be, to say it for the first and last time.'

Florence, without knowing why, felt almost afraid to hear her proceed, but kept her eyes riveted on the beautiful face so fixed upon her own.

'Never seek to find in me,' said Edith, laying her hand upon her breast, 'what is not here. Never if you can help it, Florence, fall off from me because it is *not* here. Little by little you will know me better, and the time will come when you will know me, as I know myself. Then, be as lenient to me as you can, and do not turn to bitterness the only sweet remembrance I shall have.'

The tears that were visible in her eyes as she kept them fixed on Florence, showed that the composed face was but as a handsome mask; but she preserved it, and continued:

'I *have* seen what you say, and know how true it is. But believe me – you will soon, if you cannot now – there is no one on this earth less qualified to set it right or help you, Florence, than I. Never ask me why, or speak to me about it or of my husband, more. There should be, so far, a division, and a silence between us two, like the grave itself.'

She sat for some time silent; Florence scarcely venturing to breathe meanwhile, as dim and imperfect shadows of the truth, and all its daily consequences, chased each other through her terrified, yet incredulous imagination. Almost as soon as she had ceased to speak, Edith's face began to subside from its set composure to that quieter and more relenting aspect, which it usually wore when she and Florence were alone together. She shaded it, after this change, with her hands; and when she arose, and with an affectionate embrace bade Florence good night, went quickly, and without looking round.

But when Florence was in bed, and the room was dark except for the glow of the fire, Edith returned, and saying that she could not sleep, and that her dressing-room was lonely, drew a chair upon the hearth, and watched the embers as they died away. Florence watched them too from her bed, until they, and the noble figure before them, crowned with its flowing hair, and in its thoughtful eyes reflecting back their light, became confused and indistinct, and finally were lost in slumber.

In her sleep, however, Florence could not lose an undefined impression of what had so recently passed. It formed the subject of her dreams, and haunted her; now in one shape, now in another; but always oppressively; and with a sense of fear. She dreamed of seeking her father in wildernesses, of following his track up fearful heights, and down into deep mines and caverns; of being charged with something that would release him from extraordinary suffering – she knew not what, or why – yet never being able to attain the goal and set him free. Then she saw him dead, upon that very bed, and in that very room, and knew that he had never loved her to the last, and fell upon his cold breast, passionately weeping. Then a prospect opened, and a river flowed, and a plaintive voice she knew, cried, 'It is running on, Floy! It has never stopped! You are moving with it!' And she saw him at a distance stretching out his arms towards her, while a figure such as Walter's used to be, stood near him, awfully serene and still. In every vision, Edith came and went, sometimes to her joy, sometimes to her sorrow, until they were alone upon the brink of a dark grave, and Edith pointing down, she looked and saw – what! – another Edith lying at the bottom.

In the terror of this dream, she cried out and awoke, she thought. A soft voice seemed to whisper in her ear, 'Florence, dear Florence, it is nothing but a dream!' and stretching out her arms, she returned the caress of her new mama, who then went out at the door in the light of the grey morning. In a moment, Florence sat up wondering whether this had really taken place or not; but she was only certain that it was grey morning indeed, and that the blackened ashes of the fire were on the hearth, and that she was alone.

So passed the night on which the happy pair came home.

CHAPTER 36

Housewarming

Many succeeding days passed in like manner; except that there were numerous visits received and paid, and that Mrs Skewton held little levees in her own apartments, at which Major Bagstock was a frequent attendant, and that Florence encountered no second look from her father, although she saw him every day. Nor had she much communication in words with her new mama, who was imperious and proud to all the house but her – Florence could not but observe that – and who, although she always sent for her or went to her when she came home from visiting, and would always go into her room at night, before retiring to rest, however late the hour, and never lost an opportunity of being with her, was often her silent and thoughtful companion for a long time together.

Florence, who had hoped for so much from this marriage, could not help sometimes comparing the bright house with the faded dreary place out of which it had arisen, and wondering when, in any shape, it would begin to be a home; for that it was no home then, for any one, though everything went on luxuriously and regularly, she had always a secret misgiving. Many an hour of sorrowful reflection by day and night, and many a tear of blighted hope, Florence bestowed upon the assurance her new mama had given her so strongly, that there was no one on the earth more powerless than herself to teach her how to win her father's heart. And soon Florence began to think – resolved to think would be the truer phrase – that as no one knew so well, how hopeless of being subdued or changed her father's coldness to her was, so she had given her this warning, and forbidden the subject in very compassion. Unselfish here, as in her every act and fancy, Florence preferred to bear the pain of this new wound, rather than encourage any faint foreshadowings of the truth as it concerned her father; tender of him, even in her wandering thoughts. As for his home, she hoped it would become a better one, when its state of novelty and transition should be over; and for herself, thought little and lamented less.

If none of the new family were particularly at home in private, it was resolved that Mrs Dombey at least should be at home in public, without delay. A series of entertainments in celebration of the late nuptials, and in cultivation of society, were arranged, chiefly by Mr Dombey and Mrs Skewton; and it was settled that the festive proceedings should commence by Mrs Dombey's being at home upon a certain evening, and by Mr and Mrs Dombey's requesting the honour of the company of a great many incongruous people to dinner on the same day.

Accordingly, Mr Dombey produced a list of sundry eastern magnates who were to be bidden to this feast on his behalf; to which Mrs Skewton, acting for her dearest child, who was haughtily careless on the subject, subjoined a western list, comprising Cousin Feenix, not yet returned to Baden-Baden, greatly to the detriment of his personal estate; and a variety of moths of various degrees and ages, who had, at various times, fluttered round the light of her fair daughter, or herself, without any lasting injury to their wings. Florence was enrolled as a member of the dinner-party, by Edith's command – elicited by a moment's doubt and hesitation on the part of Mrs Skewton; and Florence, with a wondering heart, and with a quick instinctive sense of everything that grated on her father in the least, took her silent share in the proceedings of the day.

The proceedings commenced by Mr Dombey, in a cravat of extraordinary height and stiffness, walking restlessly about the drawing-room until the hour appointed for dinner; punctual to which, an East India Director, of immense wealth, in a waistcoat apparently constructed in serviceable deal by some plain carpenter, but really engendered in the tailor's art, and composed of the material called nankeen, arrived and was received by Mr Dombey alone. The next stage of the proceedings was Mr Dombey's sending his compliments to Mrs Dombey, with a correct statement of the time; and the next, the East India Director's falling prostrate, in a conventional point of view, and as Mr Dombey was not the man to pick him up, staring at the fire until rescue appeared in the person of Mrs Skewton; whom the director, as a pleasant start in life for the evening, mistook for Mrs Dombey, and greeted with enthusiasm.

The next arrival was a Bank Director, reputed to be able to buy up anything – human Nature generally, if he should take it in his head to influence the money market in that direction – but who was a wonderfully modest-spoken man, almost boastfully so, and mentioned his 'little place' at Kingston-upon-Thames, and its just being barely equal to giving Dombey a bed and a chop, if he would come and visit it. Ladies, he said, it was not for a man who lived in his quiet way to take upon himself to invite – but if Mrs Skewton and her daughter, Mrs Dombey, should ever find themselves in that direction, and would do him the honour to look at a little bit of a shrubbery they would find there, and a poor little flower-bed or so, and a humble apology for a pinery, and two or three little attempts of that sort without any pretension, they would distinguish him very much. Carrying out his character, this gentleman was very plainly dressed, in a wisp of cambric for a neckcloth, big shoes, a coat that was too loose for him, and a pair of trousers that were too spare; and mention being made of the Opera by Mrs Skewton, he said he very seldom went there for he couldn't afford it. It seemed greatly to delight and exhilarate him to say so: and he beamed on his audience afterwards, with his hands in his pockets, and excessive satisfaction twinkling in his eyes.

Now Mrs Dombey appeared, beautiful and proud, and as disdainful and defiant of them all as if the bridal wreath upon her head had been a garland of steel spikes put on to force concession from her which she would die sooner than yield. With her was Florence. When they entered together, the shadow of the night of the return again darkened Mr Dombey's face. But unobserved: for Florence did not venture to raise her eyes to his, and Edith's indifference was too supreme to take the least heed of him.

The arrivals quickly became numerous. More directors, chairmen of public companies, elderly ladies carrying burdens on their heads for full dress, Cousin Feenix, Major Bagstock, friends of Mrs Skewton, with the same bright bloom on their complexion, and very precious necklaces on very withered necks. Among these, a young lady of sixty-five, remarkably coolly dressed as to her back and shoulders, who spoke with an engaging lisp, and whose eyelids wouldn't keep up well, without a great deal of trouble on her part, and whose manners had that indefinable charm which so frequently attaches to the giddiness of youth. As the greater part of Mr Dombey's list were disposed to be taciturn, and the greater part of Mrs Dombey's list were disposed to be talkative, and there was no sympathy between them, Mrs Dombey's list, by magnetic agreement, entered into a bond of union against Mr Dombey's list, who, wandering about the rooms in a desolate manner, or seeking refuge in corners, entangled themselves with company coming in, and became barricaded behind sofas, and had doors opened smartly from without against their heads, and underwent every sort of discomfiture.

When dinner was announced, Mr Dombey took down an old lady like a crimson velvet pincushion stuffed with bank notes, who might have been the identical old lady of Threadneedle Street,[1] she was so rich, and looked so unaccommodating; Cousin Feenix took down Mrs Dombey; Major Bagstock took down Mrs Skewton; the young thing with the shoulders was bestowed, as an extinguisher, upon the East India Director; and the remaining ladies were left on view in the drawing-room by the remaining gentlemen, until a forlorn hope volunteered to conduct them downstairs, and those brave spirits with their captives blocked up the dining-room door, shutting out seven mild men in the stony-hearted hall. When all the rest were got in and were seated, one of these mild men still appeared, in smiling confusion, totally destitute and unprovided for, and escorted by the butler, made the complete circuit of the table twice before his chair could be found, which it finally was, on Mrs Dombey's left hand; after which the mild man never held up his head again.

Now, the spacious dining-room, with the company seated round the glittering table, busy with their glittering spoons, and knives and forks, and plates, might have been taken for a grown-up exposition of Tom Tiddler's ground,[2] where children pick up gold and silver. Mr Dombey, as Tiddler, looked his character to admiration, and the long plateau of precious metal frosted, separating him from Mrs Dombey, whereon frosted Cupids offered scentless flowers to each of them, was allegorical to see.

Cousin Feenix was in great force, and looked astonishingly young. But he was sometimes thoughtless in his good humour – his memory occasionally wandering like his legs – and on this occasion caused the company to shudder. It happened thus. The young lady with the back, who regarded Cousin Feenix with sentiments of tenderness, had entrapped the East India Director into leading her to the chair next him; in return for which good office, she immediately abandoned the Director, who, being shaded on the other side by a gloomy black velvet hat surmounting a bony and speechless female with a fan, yielded to a depression of spirits and withdrew into himself. Cousin Feenix and the young lady were very lively and humorous, and the young lady laughed so much at something Cousin Feenix related to her, that Major Bagstock begged leave to inquire on behalf of Mrs Skewton (they were sitting opposite, a little lower down), whether that might not be considered public property.

'Why, upon my life,' said Cousin Feenix, 'there's nothing in it; it really is not worth repeating: in point of fact, it's merely an anecdote of Jack Adams. I dare say my friend Dombey;' for the general attention was concentrated on Cousin Feenix; 'may remember Jack Adams, Jack Adams, not Joe; that was his brother. Jack – little Jack – man with a cast in his eye, and slight impediment in his speech – man who sat for somebody's borough.[3] We used to call him in my parliamentary time W. P. Adams, in consequence of his being Warming Pan[4] for a young fellow who was in his minority. Perhaps my friend Dombey may have known the man?'

Mr Dombey, who was as likely to have known Guy Fawkes, replied in the negative. But one of the seven mild men unexpectedly leaped into distinction, by saying *he* had known him, and adding – 'always wore Hessian boots!'

'Exactly,' said Cousin Feenix, bending forward to see the mild man, and smile encouragement at him down the table. 'That was Jack. Joe wore—'

'Tops!'[5] cried the mild man, rising in public estimation every instant.

'*Of* course,' said Cousin Feenix, 'you were intimate with 'em?'

'I knew them both,' said the mild man. With whom Mr Dombey immediately took wine.

'Devilish good fellow, Jack!' said Cousin Feenix, again bending forward, and smiling.

'Excellent,' returned the mild man, becoming bold on his success. 'One of the best fellows I ever knew.'

'No doubt you have heard the story?' said Cousin Feenix.

'I shall know,' replied the bold mild man, 'when I have heard your Ludship tell it.' With that, he leaned back in his chair and smiled at the ceiling, as knowing it by heart and being already tickled.

'In point of fact, it's nothing of a story in itself,' said Cousin Feenix, addressing the table with a smile, and a gay shake of his head, 'and not worth a word of preface. But it's illustrative of the neatness of Jack's humour. The fact is, that Jack was invited down to a marriage – which I think took place in Barkshire?'

'Shropshire,' said the bold mild man, finding himself appealed to.

'Was it? Well! In point of fact it might have been in any shire,' said Cousin Feenix. 'So my friend being invited down to this marriage in Anyshire,' with a pleasant sense of the readiness of this joke, 'goes. Just as some of us, having had the honour of being invited to the marriage of my lovely and accomplished relative with my friend Dombey, didn't require to be asked twice, and were devilish glad to be present on so interesting an occasion. – Goes – Jack goes. Now, this marriage was, in point of fact, the marriage of an uncommonly fine girl with a man for whom she didn't care a button, but whom she accepted on account of his property, which was immense. When Jack returned to town, after the nuptials, a man he knew, meeting him in the lobby of the House of Commons, says, "Well, Jack, how are the ill-matched couple?" "Ill-matched," says Jack. "Not at all. It's a perfectly fair and equal transaction. *She* is regularly[6] bought, and you may take your oath *he* is as regularly sold!"'[7]

In his full enjoyment of this culminating point of his story, the shudder, which had gone all round the table like an electric spark, struck Cousin Feenix, and he stopped. Not a smile occasioned by the only general topic of conversation broached that day, appeared on any face. A profound silence ensued; and the wretched mild man, who had been as innocent of any real foreknowledge of the story as the child unborn, had the exquisite misery of reading in every eye that he was regarded as the prime mover of the mischief.

Mr Dombey's face was not a changeful one, and being cast in its mould of state that day, showed little other apprehension of the story, if any, than that which he expressed when he said solemnly, amidst the silence, that it was 'Very good.' There was a rapid glance from Edith towards Florence, but otherwise she remained, externally, impassive and unconscious.

Through the various stages of rich meats and wines, continual gold and silver, dainties of earth, air, fire, and water, heaped-up fruits, and that unnecessary article in Mr Dombey's banquets – ice

– the dinner slowly made its way: the later stages being achieved to the sonorous music of incessant double knocks,[8] announcing the arrival of visitors, whose portion of the feast was limited to the smell thereof. When Mrs Dombey rose, it was a sight to see her lord, with stiff throat and erect head, hold the door open for the withdrawal of the ladies; and to see how she swept past him with his daughter on her arm.

Mr Dombey was a grave sight, behind the decanters, in a state of dignity; and the East India Director was a forlorn sight near the unoccupied end of the table, in a state of solitude; and the Major was a military sight, relating stories of the Duke of York to six of the seven mild men (the ambitious one was utterly quenched); and the Bank Director was a lowly sight, making a plan of his little attempt at a pinery, with dessert-knives, for a group of admirers; and Cousin Feenix was a thoughtful sight, as he smoothed his long wristbands and stealthily adjusted his wig. But all these sights were of short duration, being speedily broken up by coffee, and the desertion of the room.

There was a throng in the state-rooms upstairs, increasing every minute; but still Mr Dombey's list of visitors appeared to have some native impossibility of amalgamation with Mrs Dombey's list, and no one could have doubted which was which. The single exception to this rule perhaps was Mr Carker, who now smiled among the company, and who, as he stood in the circle that was gathered about Mrs Dombey – watchful of her, of them, his chief, Cleopatra and the Major, Florence, and everything around – appeared at ease with both divisions of guests, and not marked as exclusively belonging to either.

Florence had a dread of him, which made his presence in the room a nightmare to her. She could not avoid the recollection of it, for her eyes were drawn towards him every now and then, by an attraction of dislike and distrust that she could not resist. Yet her thoughts were busy with other things; for as she sat apart – not unadmired or unsought, but in the gentleness of her quiet spirit – she felt how little part her father had in what was going on, and saw, with pain, how ill at ease he seemed to be, and how little regarded he was as he lingered about near the door, for those visitors whom he wished to distinguish with particular attention, and took them up to introduce them to his wife, who received them with proud coldness, but showed no interest or wish to please, and never, after the bare ceremony of reception, in consultation of his wishes, or in welcome of his friends, opened her lips. It was not the

Mrs Dombey at home

less perplexing or painful to Florence, that she who acted thus, treated her so kindly and with such loving consideration, that it almost seemed an ungrateful return on her part even to know of what was passing before her eyes.

Happy Florence would have been, might she have ventured to bear her father company, by so much as a look: and happy Florence was, in little suspecting the main cause of his uneasiness. But afraid of seeming to know that he was placed at any disadvantage, lest he should be resentful of that knowledge; and divided between her impulse towards him, and her grateful affection for Edith; she scarcely dared to raise her eyes towards either. Anxious and unhappy for them both, the thought stole on her through the crowd, that it might have been better for them if this noise of tongues and tread of feet had never come there, – if the old dulness and decay had never been replaced by novelty and splendour, – if the neglected child had found no friend in Edith, but had lived her solitary life, unpitied and forgotten.

Mrs Chick had some such thoughts too, but they were not so quietly developed in her mind. This good matron had been outraged in the first instance by not receiving an invitation to dinner. That blow partially recovered, she had gone to a vast expense to make such a figure before Mrs Dombey at home, as should dazzle the senses of that lady, and heap mortification, mountains high, on the head of Mrs Skewton.

'But I am made,' said Mrs Chick to Mr Chick, 'of no more account than Florence! Who takes the smallest notice of me? No one!'

'No one, my dear,' assented Mr Chick, who was seated by the side of Mrs Chick against the wall, and could console himself, even there, by softly whistling.

'Does it at all appear as if I was wanted here?' exclaimed Mrs Chick, with flashing eyes.

'No, my dear, I don't think it does,' said Mr Chick.

'Paul's mad!' said Mrs Chick.

Mr Chick whistled.

'Unless you are a monster, which I sometimes think you are,' said Mrs Chick with candour, 'don't sit there humming tunes. How any one with the most distant feelings of a man, can see that mother-in-law of Paul's, dressed as she is, going on like that, with Major Bagstock, for whom, among other precious things, we are indebted to your Lucretia Tox—'

'*My* Lucretia Tox, my dear!' said Mr Chick, astounded.

'Yes,' retorted Mrs Chick, with great severity, '*your* Lucretia Tox – I say how anybody can see that mother-in-law of Paul's, and that haughty wife of Paul's, and these indecent old frights with their backs and shoulders, and in short this at home generally, and hum—,' on which word Mrs Chick laid a scornful emphasis that made Mr Chick start, 'is, I thank Heaven, a mystery to me!'

Mr Chick screwed his mouth into a form irreconcilable with humming or whistling, and looked very contemplative.

'But I hope I know what is due to myself,' said Mrs Chick, swelling with indignation, 'though Paul has forgotten what is due to me. I am not going to sit here, a member of this family, to be taken no notice of. I am not the dirt under Mrs Dombey's feet, yet – not quite yet,' said Mrs Chick, as if she expected to become so, about the day after to-morrow. 'And I shall go. I will not say (whatever I may think) that this affair has been got up solely to degrade and insult me. I shall merely go. I shall not be missed!'

Mrs Chick rose erect with these words, and took the arm of Mr Chick, who escorted her from the room, after half an hour's shady sojourn there. And it is due to her penetration to observe that she certainly was not missed at all.

But she was not the only indignant guest; for Mr Dombey's list (still constantly in difficulties) were, as a body, indignant with Mrs Dombey's list, for looking at them through eye-glasses, and audibly wondering who all those people were, while Mrs Dombey's list complained of weariness, and the young thing with the shoulders, deprived of the attentions of that gay youth Cousin Feenix (who went away from the dinner-table), confidentially alleged to thirty or forty friends that she was bored to death. All the old ladies with the burdens on their heads, had greater or less cause of complaint against Mrs Dombey; and the Directors and Chairmen coincided in thinking that if Dombey must marry, he had better have married somebody nearer his own age, not quite so handsome, and a little better off. The general opinion among this class of gentlemen was, that it was a weak thing in Dombey, and he'd live to repent it. Hardly anybody there, except the mild men, stayed, or went away without considering himself or herself neglected and aggrieved by Mr Dombey or Mrs Dombey; and the speechless female in the black velvet hat was found to have been stricken mute, because the lady in the crimson velvet had been handed down before her. The nature even of the mild men got corrupted, either from their curdling it with too much lemonade, or from the general inoculation that prevailed; and they made sarcastic jokes to one another, and whispered disparagement on stairs and in bye-places. The general dissatisfaction and discomfort so diffused itself, that the assembled footmen in the hall were as well acquainted with it as the company above. Nay, the very linkmen[9] outside got hold of it, and compared the party to a funeral out of mourning, with none of the company remembered in the will.

At last, the guests were all gone, and the linkmen, too; and the street, crowded so long with carriages, was clear; and the dying lights showed no one in the rooms, but Mr Dombey and Mr Carker, who were talking together apart, and Mrs Dombey and her mother: the former seated on an ottoman; the latter reclining in the Cleopatra attitude, awaiting the arrival of her maid. Mr Dombey having finished his communication to Carker, the latter advanced obsequiously to take leave.

'I trust,' he said, 'that the fatigues of this delightful evening will not inconvenience Mrs Dombey to-morrow.'

'Mrs Dombey,' said Mr Dombey, advancing, 'has sufficiently spared herself fatigue, to relieve you from any anxiety of that kind. I regret to say, Mrs Dombey, that I could have wished you had fatigued yourself a little more on this occasion.'

She looked at him with a supercilious glance, that it seemed not worth her while to protract, and turned away her eyes without speaking.

'I am sorry, madam,' said Mr Dombey, 'that you should not have thought it your duty—'

She looked at him again.

'Your duty, madam,' pursued Mr Dombey, 'to have received my friends with a little more deference. Some of those whom you have been pleased to slight to-night in a very marked manner, Mrs Dombey, confer a distinction upon you, I must tell you, in any visit they pay you.'

'Do you know that there is some one here?' she returned, now looking at him steadily.

'No! Carker! I beg that you do not. I insist that you do not,' cried Mr Dombey, stopping that noiseless gentleman in his withdrawal. 'Mr Carker, madam, as you know, possesses my confidence. He is as well acquainted as myself with the subject on which I speak. I beg to tell you, for your information, Mrs Dombey, that I consider these wealthy and important persons confer a distinction upon *me*:' and Mr Dombey drew himself up, as having now rendered them of the highest possible importance.

'I ask you,' she repeated, bending her disdainful, steady gaze upon him, 'do you know that there is some one here, Sir?'

'I must entreat,' said Mr Carker, stepping forward, 'I must beg, I must demand, to be released. Slight and unimportant as this difference is—'

Mrs Skewton, who had been intent upon her daughter's face, took him up here.

'My sweetest Edith,' she said, 'and my dearest Dombey; our excellent friend Mr Carker, for so I am sure I ought to mention him—'

Mr Carker murmured, 'Too much honour.'

'—has used the very words that were in my mind, and that I have been dying, these ages, for an opportunity of introducing. Slight and unimportant! My sweetest Edith, and my dearest Dombey, do we not know that any difference between you two – No, Flowers; not now.'

Flowers was the maid, who, finding gentlemen present, retreated with precipitation.

'That any difference between you two,' resumed Mrs Skewton, 'with the Heart you possess in common, and the excessively charming bond of feeling that there is between you, *must* be slight and unimportant? What words could better define the fact? None. Therefore I am glad to take this slight occasion – this trifling occasion, that is so replete with Nature, and your individual characters, and all that – so truly calculated to bring the tears into a parent's eyes – to say that I attach no importance to them in the least, except as developing these minor elements of Soul; and that, unlike most mamas-in-law (that odious phrase, dear Dombey!) as they have been represented to me to exist in this I fear too artificial world, I never shall attempt to interpose between you, at such a time, and never can much regret, after all, such little flashes of the torch of What's-his-name – not Cupid but the other delightful creature.'

There was a sharpness in the good mother's glance at both her children as she spoke, that may have been expressive of a direct and well-considered purpose hidden between these rambling words. That purpose, providently to detach herself in the beginning from all the clankings of their chain that were to come, and to shelter herself with the fiction of her innocent belief in their mutual affection, and their adaptation to each other.

'I have pointed out to Mrs Dombey,' said Mr Dombey, in his most stately manner, 'that in her conduct thus early in our married life, to which I object, and which, I request, may be corrected. Carker,' with a nod of dismissal, 'good night to you!'

Mr Carker bowed to the imperious form of the Bride, whose sparkling eye was fixed upon her husband; and stopping at Cleopatra's couch on his way out, raised to his lips the hand she graciously extended to him, in lowly and admiring homage.

If his handsome wife had reproached him, or even changed countenance, or broken the silence in which she remained, by one word, now that they were alone (for Cleopatra made off with all speed), Mr Dombey would have been equal to some assertion of his case against her. But the intense, unutterable, withering scorn, with which, after looking upon him, she dropped her eyes as if he were too worthless and indifferent to her to be challenged with a syllable – the ineffable disdain and haughtiness in which she sat before him – the cold inflexible resolve with which her every feature seemed to bear him down, and put him by – these, he had no resource against; and he left her, with her whole overbearing beauty concentrated on despising him.

Was he coward enough to watch her, an hour afterwards, on the old well staircase,[10] where he had once seen Florence in the moonlight, toiling up with Paul? Or was he in the dark by accident, when, looking up, he saw her coming, with a light, from the room where Florence lay, and marked again the face so changed, which *he* could not subdue?

But it could never alter as his own did. It never, in its utmost pride and passion, knew the shadow that had fallen on his, in the dark corner, on the night of the return; and often since; and which deepened on it now as he looked up.

CHAPTER 37

More Warnings than One

Florence, Edith, and Mrs Skewton were together next day, and the carriage was waiting at the door to take them out. For Cleopatra had her galley again now, and Withers, no longer the wan, stood upright in a pigeon-breasted jacket and military trousers, behind her wheel-less chair at dinner-time, and butted no more. The hair of Withers was radiant with pomatum,[1] in these days of down,[2] and he wore kid gloves and smelt of the water of Cologne.

They were assembled in Cleopatra's room. The Serpent of old Nile[3] (not to mention her disrespectfully) was reposing on her sofa, sipping her morning chocolate at three o'clock in the afternoon, and Flowers the Maid was fastening on her youthful cuffs and frills, and performing a kind of private coronation ceremony on her, with a peach-coloured velvet bonnet; the artificial roses in which nodded to uncommon advantage, as the palsy trifled with them, like a breeze.

'I think I am a little nervous this morning, Flowers,' said Mrs Skewton. 'My hand quite shakes.'

'You were the life of the party last night, ma'am, you know,' returned Flowers, 'and you suffer for it, to-day, you see.'

Edith, who had beckoned Florence to the window, and was looking out, with her back turned on the toilet of her esteemed mother, suddenly withdrew from it, as if it had lightened.

'My darling child,' cried Cleopatra, languidly, '*you* are not nervous? Don't tell me, my dear Edith, that you, so enviably self-possessed, are beginning to be a martyr[4] too, like your unfortunately constituted mother! Withers, some one at the door.'

'Card, ma'am,' said Withers, taking it towards Mrs Dombey.

'I am going out,' she said without looking at it.

'My dear love,' drawled Mrs Skewton, 'how very odd to send that message without seeing the name! Bring it here, Withers. Dear me, my love; Mr Carker, too! That very sensible person!'

'I am going out,' repeated Edith, in so imperious a tone that Withers, going to the door, imperiously informed the servant who was waiting, 'Mrs Dombey is going out. Get along with you,' and shut it on him.

But the servant came back after a short absence, and whispered to Withers again, who once more, and not very willingly, presented himself before Mrs Dombey.

'If you please, ma'am, Mr Carker sends his respectful compliments and begs you would spare him one minute, if you could – for business, ma'am, if you please.'

'Really, my love,' said Mrs Skewton in her mildest manner, for her daughter's face was threatening; 'if you would allow me to offer a word, I should recommend—'

'Show him this way,' said Edith. As Withers disappeared to execute the command, she added, frowning on her mother, 'As he comes at your recommendation, let him come to your room.'

'May I – shall I go away?' asked Florence, hurriedly.

Edith nodded yes, but on her way to the door Florence met the

visitor coming in. With the same disagreeable mixture of familiarity
and forbearance with which he had first addressed her, he addressed
her now in his softest manner – hoped she was quite well – needed
not to ask, with such looks to anticipate the answer – had scarcely
had the honour to know her, last night, she was so greatly changed
– and held the door open for her to pass out; with a secret sense of
power in her shrinking from him, that all the deference and
politeness of his manner could not quite conceal.

He then bowed himself for a moment over Mrs Skewton's
condescending hand, and lastly bowed to Edith. Coldly returning
his salute without looking at him, and neither seating herself nor
inviting him to be seated, she waited for him to speak.

Entrenched in her pride and power, and with all the obduracy of
her spirit summoned about her, still her old conviction that she and
her mother had been known by this man in their worst colours,
from their first acquaintance; that every degradation she had
suffered in her own eyes was as plain to him as to herself; that he
read her life as though it were a vile book, and fluttered the leaves
before her in slight looks and tones of voice which no one else
could detect; weakened and undermined her. Proudly as she
opposed herself to him, with her commanding face exacting his
humility, her disdainful lip repulsing him, her bosom angry at his
intrusion, and the dark lashes of her eyes sullenly veiling their light,
that no ray of it might shine upon him – and submissively as he
stood before her, with an entreating injured manner, but with
complete submission to her will – she knew, in her own soul, that
the cases were reversed, and that the triumph and superiority were
his, and that he knew it full well.

'I have presumed,' said Mr Carker, 'to solicit an interview, and I
have ventured to describe it as being one of business, because—'

'Perhaps you are charged by Mr Dombey with some message of
reproof,' said Edith. 'You possess Mr Dombey's confidence in such
an unusual degree, Sir, that you would scarcely surprise me if that
were your business.'

'I have no message to the lady who sheds a lustre upon his name,'
said Mr Carker. 'But I entreat that lady, on my own behalf, to be
just to a very humble claimant for justice at her hands – a mere
dependant of Mr Dombey's – which is a position of humility; and
to reflect upon my perfect helplessness last night, and the impossibility of my avoiding the share that was forced upon me in a very
painful occasion.'

'My dearest Edith,' hinted Cleopatra in a low voice, as she held her eye-glass aside, 'really very charming of Mr What's-his-name. And full of heart!'

'For I do,' said Mr Carker, appealing to Mrs Skewton with a look of grateful deference, – 'I do venture to call it a painful occasion, though merely because it was so to me, who had the misfortune to be present. So slight a difference, as between the principals – between those who love each other with disinterested devotion, and would make any sacrifice of self, in such a cause – is nothing. As Mrs Skewton herself expressed with so much truth and feeling last night, it is nothing.'

Edith could not look at him, but she said after a few moments, 'And your business, Sir—'

'Edith, my pet,' said Mrs Skewton, 'all this time Mr Carker is standing! My dear Mr Carker, take a seat, I beg.'

He offered no reply to the mother, but fixed his eyes on the proud daughter, as though he would only be bidden by her, and was resolved to be bidden by her. Edith, in spite of herself, sat down, and slightly motioned with her hand to him to be seated too. No action could be colder, haughtier, more insolent in its air of supremacy and disrespect, but she had struggled against even that concession ineffectually, and it was wrested from her. That was enough! Mr Carker sat down.

'May I be allowed, madam,' said Carker, turning his white teeth on Mrs Skewton like a light – 'a lady of your excellent sense and quick feeling will give me credit, for good reason, I am sure – to address what I have to say, to Mrs Dombey, and to leave her to impart it to you who are her best and dearest friend – next to Mr Dombey?'

Mrs Skewton would have retired, but Edith stopped her. Edith would have stopped him too, and indignantly ordered him to speak openly or not at all, but that he said, in a low voice – 'Miss Florence – the young lady who has just left the room—'

Edith suffered him to proceed. She looked at him now. As he bent forward, to be nearer, with the utmost show of delicacy and respect, and with his teeth persuasively arrayed, in a self-depreciating smile, she felt as if she could have struck him dead.

'Miss Florence's position,' he began, 'has been an unfortunate one. I have a difficulty in alluding to it to you, whose attachment to her father is naturally watchful and jealous of every word that applies to him.' Always distinct and soft in speech, no language could describe the extent of his distinctness and softness, when he said these words, or came to any others of a similar import. 'But, as one who is devoted to Mr Dombey in his different way, and whose life is passed in admiration of Mr Dombey's character, may I say, without offence to your tenderness as a wife, that Miss Florence has unhappily been neglected – by her father? May I say by her father?'

Edith replied, 'I know it.'

'You know it!' said Mr Carker, with a great appearance of relief. 'It removes a mountain from my breast. May I hope you know how the neglect originated; in what an amiable phase of Mr Dombey's pride – character, I mean?'

'You may pass that by, Sir,' she returned, 'and come the sooner to the end of what you have to say.'

'Indeed, I am sensible, madam,' replied Carker, – 'trust me, I am deeply sensible, that Mr Dombey can require no justification in anything to you. But, kindly judge of my breast by your own, and you will forgive my interest in him, if in its excess, it goes at all astray.'

What a stab to her proud heart, to sit there, face to face with him, and have him tendering her false oath at the altar again and again for her acceptance, and pressing it upon her like the dregs of a sickening cup she could not own her loathing of, or turn away from! How shame, remorse, and passion raged within her, when, upright and majestic in her beauty before him she knew that in her spirit she was down at his feet!

'Miss Florence,' said Carker, 'left to the care – if one may call it care – of servants and mercenary people, in every way her inferiors, necessarily wanted some guide and compass in her younger days, and, naturally, for want of them, has been indiscreet, and has in some degree forgotten her station. There was some folly about one Walter, a common lad, who is fortunately dead now: and some very undesirable association, I regret to say, with certain coasting sailors, of anything but good repute, and a runaway old bankrupt.'

'I have heard the circumstances, Sir,' said Edith, flashing her disdainful glance upon him, 'and I know that you pervert them. You may not know it. I hope so.'

'Pardon me,' said Mr Carker, 'I believe that nobody knows them so well as I. Your generous and ardent nature, madam – the same nature which is so nobly imperative in vindication of your beloved and honoured husband, and which has blessed him as even his merits deserve – I must respect, defer to, bow before. But, as regards the circumstances, which is indeed the business I presumed to solicit your attention to, I can have no doubt, since, in the execution of my trust as Mr Dombey's confidential – I presume to say – friend, I have fully ascertained them. In my execution of that trust; in my deep concern, which you can so well understand, for everything relating to him, intensified, if you will (for I fear I labour under your displeasure), by the lower motive of desire to prove my diligence, and make myself the more acceptable; I have long pursued these circumstances by myself and trustworthy instruments, and have innumerable and most minute proofs.'

She raised her eyes no higher than his mouth, but she saw the means of mischief vaunted in every tooth it contained.

'Pardon me, madam,' he continued, 'if in my perplexity, I presume to take counsel with you, and to consult your pleasure. I think I have observed that you are greatly interested in Miss Florence?'

What was there in her he had not observed, and did not know? Humbled and yet maddened by the thought, in every new present-ment of it, however faint, she pressed her teeth upon her quivering lip to force composure on it, and distinctly inclined her head in reply.

'This interest, madam – so touching an evidence of everything associated with Mr Dombey being dear to you – induces me to pause before I make him acquainted with these circumstances, which, as yet, he does not know. It so far shakes me, if I may make the confession, in my allegiance, that on the intimation of the least desire to that effect from you, I would suppress them.'

Edith raised her head quickly, and starting back, bent her dark glance upon him. He met it with his blandest and most deferential smile, and went on.

'You say that as I describe them, they are perverted. I fear not – I fear not: but let us assume that they are. The uneasiness I have for some time felt on the subject, arises in this: that the mere circum-stance of such association often repeated, on the part of Miss Florence, however innocently and confidingly, would be conclusive with Mr Dombey, already predisposed against her, and would lead him to take some step (I know he has occasionally contemplated it) of separation and alienation of her from his home. Madam, bear with me, and remember my intercourse with Mr Dombey, and my knowledge of him, and my reverence for him, almost from child-hood, when I say that if he has a fault, it is a lofty stubbornness, rooted in that noble pride and sense of power which belong to him, and which we must all defer to; which is not assailable like the obstinacy of other characters; and which grows upon itself from day to day, and year to year.'

She bent her glance upon him still; but, look as steadfast as she would, her haughty nostrils dilated, and her breath came somewhat deeper, and her lip would slightly curl, as he described that in his patron to which they must all bow down. He saw it; and though his expression did not change, she knew he saw it.

'Even so slight an incident as last night's,' he said, 'if I might refer to it once more, would serve to illustrate my meaning, better than a greater one. Dombey and Son know neither time, nor place, nor season, but bear them all down. But I rejoice in its occurrence, for it has opened the way for me to approach Mrs Dombey with this subject to-day, even if it has entailed upon me the penalty of her temporary displeasure. Madam, in the midst of my uneasiness and apprehension on this subject, I was summoned by Mr Dombey to Leamington. There I saw you. There I could not help knowing what relation you would shortly occupy towards him – to his enduring happiness and yours. There I resolved to await the time of your establishment at home here, and to do as I have now done. I have, at heart, no fear that I shall be wanting in my duty to Mr Dombey, if I bury what I know in your breast; for where there is but one heart and mind between two persons – as in such a marriage – one almost represents the other. I can acquit my conscience therefore, almost equally, by confidence, on such a theme, in you or him. For the reasons I have mentioned I would select you. May I aspire to the distinction of believing that my confidence is accepted, and that I am relieved from my responsibility?'

He long remembered the look she gave him – who could see it, and forget it? – and the struggle that ensued within her. At last she said:

'I accept it, Sir. You will please to consider this matter at an end, and that it goes no farther.'

He bowed low, and rose. She rose too, and he took leave with all humility. But Withers, meeting him on the stairs, stood amazed at the beauty of his teeth, and at his brilliant smile; and as he rode away upon his white-legged horse, the people took him for a dentist, such was the dazzling show he made. The people took *her*, when she rode out in her carriage presently, for a great lady, as happy as she was rich and fine. But they had not seen her, just before, in her own room with no one by; and they had not heard her utterance of the three words, 'Oh Florence, Florence!'

Mrs Skewton, reposing on her sofa, and sipping her chocolate, had heard nothing but the low word business, for which she had a mortal aversion, insomuch that she had long banished it from her vocabulary, and had gone nigh, in a charming manner and with an immense amount of heart, to say nothing of soul, to ruin divers milliners and others in consequence. Therefore Mrs Skewton asked no questions, and showed no curiosity. Indeed, the peach-velvet bonnet gave her sufficient occupation out of doors; for being perched on the back of her head, and the day being rather windy, it was frantic to escape from Mrs Skewton's company, and would be coaxed into no sort of compromise. When the carriage was closed, and the wind shut out, the palsy played among the artificial roses again like an almshouse-full of superannuated zephyrs;[5] and altogether Mrs Skewton had enough to do, and got on but indifferently.

She got on no better towards night; for when Mrs Dombey, in her dressing-room, had been dressed and waiting for her half an hour, and Mr Dombey, in the drawing-room, had paraded himself into a state of solemn fretfulness (they were all three going out to dinner), Flowers the Maid appeared with a pale face to Mrs Dombey, saying:

'If you please, ma'am, I beg your pardon, but I can't do nothing with missis!'

'What do you mean?' asked Edith.

'Well, ma'am,' replied the frightened maid, 'I hardly know. She's making faces!'

Edith hurried with her to her mother's room. Cleopatra was arrayed in full dress, with the diamonds, short sleeves, rouge, curls, teeth, and other juvenility all complete; but Paralysis was not to be deceived, had known her for the object of its errand, and had struck her at her glass, where she lay like a horrible doll that had tumbled down.

They took her to pieces in very shame, and put the little of her that was real on a bed. Doctors were sent for, and soon came. Powerful remedies were resorted to; opinions given that she would rally from this shock, but would not survive another; and there she lay speechless, and staring at the ceiling for days; sometimes making inarticulate sounds in answer to such questions as did she know who were present, and the like: sometimes giving no reply either by sign or gesture, or in her unwinking eyes.

At length she began to recover consciousness, and in some degree the power of motion, though not yet of speech. One day the use of her right hand returned; and showing it to her maid who was in attendance on her, and appearing very uneasy in her mind, she made signs for a pencil and some paper. This the maid immediately provided, thinking she was going to make a will, or write some last request; and Mrs Dombey being from home, the maid awaited the result with solemn feelings.

After much painful scrawling and erasing, and putting in of wrong characters, which seemed to tumble out of the pencil of their own accord, the old woman produced this document:

'Rose-coloured curtains.'

The maid being perfectly transfixed, and with tolerable reason, Cleopatra amended the manuscript by adding two words more, when it stood thus:

'Rose-coloured curtains for doctors.'

The maid now perceived remotely that she wished these articles to be provided for the better presentation of her complexion to the faculty; and as those in the house who knew her best, had no doubt of the correctness of this opinion, which she was soon able to establish for herself, the rose-coloured curtains were added to her bed, and she mended with increased rapidity from that hour. She was soon able to sit up, in curls and a laced cap and night-gown, and to have a little artificial bloom dropped into the hollow caverns of her cheeks.

It was a tremendous sight to see this old woman in her finery leering and mincing at Death, and playing off her youthful tricks upon him as if he had been the Major; but an alteration in her mind that ensued on the paralytic stroke was fraught with as much matter for reflection, and was quite as ghastly.

Whether the weakening of her intellect made her more cunning and false than before, or whether it confused her between what she had assumed to be and what she really had been, or whether it had awakened any glimmering of remorse, which could neither struggle into light nor get back into total darkness, or whether, in the jumble of her faculties, a combination of these effects had been shaken up, which is perhaps the more likely supposition, the result was this: – That she became hugely exacting in respect of Edith's affection and gratitude and attention to her; highly laudatory of herself as a most inestimable parent: and very jealous of having any rival in Edith's regard. Further, in place of remembering that compact made between them for an avoidance of the subject, she constantly alluded to her daughter's marriage as a proof of her being an incomparable mother; and all this, with the weakness and peevishness of such a state, always serving for a sarcastic commentary on her levity and youthfulness.

'Where is Mrs Dombey?' she would say to her maid.

'Gone out, ma'am.'

'Gone out! Does she go out to shun her mama, Flowers?'

'La bless you, no, ma'am. Mrs Dombey has only gone out for a ride with Miss Florence.'

'Miss Florence. Who's Miss Florence? Don't tell me about Miss Florence. What's Miss Florence to her, compared to me?'

The apposite display of the diamonds, or the peach-velvet bonnet (she sat in the bonnet to receive visitors, weeks before she could stir out of doors), or the dressing of her up in some gaud[6] or other, usually stopped the tears that began to flow hereabouts; and she would remain in a complacent state until Edith came to see her; when, at a glance of the proud face, she would relapse again.

'Well, I am sure, Edith!' she would cry, shaking her head.

'What is the matter, mother?'

'Matter! I really don't know what *is* the matter. The world is coming to such an artificial and ungrateful state, that I begin to think there's no Heart – or anything of that sort – left in it, positively. Withers is more a child to me than you are. He attends to me much more than my own daughter. I almost wish I did not look so young – and all that kind of thing – and then perhaps I should be more considered.'

'What would you have, mother?'

'Oh, a great deal, Edith,' impatiently.

'Is there anything you want that you have not? It is your own fault if there be.'

'My own fault!' beginning to whimper. 'The parent I have been to you, Edith: making you a companion from your cradle! And when you neglect me, and have no more natural affection for me than if I was a stranger – not a twentieth part of the affection that you have for Florence – but I am only your mother, and should corrupt *her* in a day! – you reproach me with its being my own fault.'

'Mother, mother, I reproach you with nothing. Why will you always dwell on this?'

'Isn't it natural that I should dwell on this, when I am all affection and sensitiveness, and am wounded in the cruellest way, whenever you look at me?'

'I do not mean to wound you, mother. Have you no remembrance of what has been said between us? Let the Past rest.'

'Yes, rest! And let gratitude to me rest; and let affection for me rest; and let *me* rest in my out-of-the-way room, with no society and no attention, while you find new relations to make much of, who have no earthly claim upon you! Good gracious, Edith, do you know what an elegant establishment you are at the head of?'

'Yes. Hush!'

'And that gentlemanly creature, Dombey? Do you know that you are married to him, Edith, and that you have a settlement, and a position, and a carriage, and I don't know what?'

'Indeed, I know it, mother; well.'

'As you would have had with that delightful good soul – what did they call him? – Granger – if he hadn't died. And who have you to thank for all this, Edith?'

'You, mother; you.'

'Then put your arms round my neck, and kiss me; and show me, Edith, that you know there never was a better mama than I have been to you. And don't let me become a perfect fright with teasing and wearing myself at your ingratitude, or when I'm out again in society no soul will know me, not even that hateful animal, the Major.'

But, sometimes, when Edith went nearer to her, and bending down her stately head, put her cold cheek to hers, the mother would draw back as if she were afraid of her, and would fall into a fit of trembling, and cry out that there was a wandering in her wits. And sometimes she would entreat her, with humility, to sit down on the chair beside her bed, and would look at her (as she sat there brooding) with a face that even the rose-coloured curtains could not make otherwise than seared and wild.

The rose-coloured curtains blushed, in course of time, on Cleopatra's bodily recovery, and on her dress – more juvenile than ever to repair the ravages of illness – and on the rouge, and on the teeth, and on the curls, and on the diamonds, and the short sleeves, and the whole wardrobe of the doll that had tumbled down before the mirror. They blushed, too, now and then, upon an indistinctness in her speech which she turned off with a girlish giggle, and on an occasional failing in her memory, that had no rule in it, but came and went fantastically, as if in mockery of her fantastic self.

But they never blushed upon a change in the new manner of her thought and speech towards her daughter. And though that daughter often came within their influence, they never blushed upon her loveliness irradiated by a smile, or softened by the light of filial love, in its stern beauty.

CHAPTER 38

Miss Tox improves an Old Acquaintance

The forlorn Miss Tox, abandoned by her friend Louisa Chick, and bereft of Mr Dombey's countenance – for no delicate pair of wedding cards,[1] united by a silver thread, graced the chimney-glass in Princess's Place, or the harpsichord, or any of those little posts of display which Lucretia reserved for holiday occupation – became depressed in her spirits, and suffered much from melancholy. For a time the Bird Waltz was unheard in Princess's Place, the plants were neglected, and dust collected on the miniature of Miss Tox's ancestor with the powdered head and pigtail.

Miss Tox, however, was not of an age or of a disposition long to abandon herself to unavailing regrets. Only two notes of the harpsichord were dumb from disuse when the Bird Waltz again warbled and trilled in the crooked drawing-room: only one slip of geranium fell a victim to imperfect nursing, before she was gardening at her green baskets again, regularly every morning; the powdered-headed ancestor had not been under a cloud for more than six weeks, when Miss Tox breathed on his benignant visage, and polished him up with a piece of wash-leather.

Still, Miss Tox was lonely, and at a loss. Her attachments, however ludicrously shown, were real and strong; and she was, as she expressed it, 'deeply hurt by the unmerited contumely she had met with from Louisa.' But there was no such thing as anger in Miss Tox's composition. If she had ambled on through life, in her soft-spoken way, without any opinions, she had, at least, got so far without any harsh passions. The mere sight of Louisa Chick in the street one day at a considerable distance, so overpowered her milky nature,[2] that she was fain to seek immediate refuge in a pastry-cook's, and there, in a musty little back room usually devoted to the consumption of soups, and pervaded by an ox-tail atmosphere, relieve her feelings by weeping plentifully.

Against Mr Dombey Miss Tox hardly felt that she had any reason of complaint. Her sense of that gentleman's magnificence was such, that once removed from him, she felt as if her distance always had been immeasurable, and as if he had greatly condescended in tolerating her at all. No wife could be too handsome, or too stately for him, according to Miss Tox's sincere opinion. It was perfectly natural that in looking for one, he should look high. Miss Tox with tears laid down this proposition, and fully admitted it, twenty times a day. She never recalled the lofty manner in which Mr Dombey had made her subservient to his convenience and caprices, and had graciously permitted her to be one of the nurses of his little son. She only thought, in her own words, 'that she had passed a great many happy hours in that house, which she must ever remember with gratification, and that she could never cease to regard Mr Dombey as one of the most impressive and dignified of men.'

Cut off, however, from the implacable Louisa, and being shy of the Major (whom she viewed with some distrust now), Miss Tox found it very irksome to know nothing of what was going on in Mr Dombey's establishment. And as she really had got into the habit of considering Dombey and Son as the pivot on which the world in general turned, she resolved, rather than be ignorant of intelligence which so strongly interested her, to cultivate her old acquaintance, Mrs Richards, who she knew, since her last memorable appearance before Mr Dombey, was in the habit of sometimes holding communication with his servants. Perhaps Miss Tox, in seeking out the Toodle family, had the tender motive hidden in her breast of having somebody to whom she could talk about Mr Dombey, no matter how humble that somebody might be.

At all events, towards the Toodle habitation Miss Tox directed her steps one evening, what time⁴ Mr Toodle, cindery and swart, was refreshing himself with tea, in the bosom of his family. Mr Toodle had only three stages of existence. He was either taking refreshment in the bosom just mentioned, or he was tearing through the country at from twenty-five to fifty miles an hour, or he was sleeping after his fatigues. He was always in a whirlwind or a calm, and a peaceable, contented, easy-going man Mr Toodle was in either state, who seemed to have made over all his own inheritance of fuming and fretting to the engines with which he was connected, which panted, and gasped, and chafed, and wore themselves out, in a most unsparing manner, while Mr Toodle led a mild and equable life.

'Polly, my gal,' said Mr Toodle, with a young Toodle on each knee, and two more making tea for him, and plenty more scattered about – Mr Toodle was never out of children, but always kept a good supply on hand – 'you an't seen our Biler lately, have you?'

'No,' replied Polly, 'but he's almost certain to look in to-night. It's his right evening, and he's very regular.'

'I suppose,' said Mr Toodle, relishing his meal infinitely, 'as our Biler is a doin' now about as well as a boy *can* do, eh, Polly?'

'Oh! he's a doing beautiful!' responded Polly.

'He an't got to be at all secret-like – has he, Polly?' inquired Mr Toodle.

'No!' said Mrs Toodle, plumply.

'I'm glad he an't got to be at all secret-like, Polly,' observed Mr Toodle in his slow and measured way, and shovelling in his bread and butter with a clasp knife, as if he were stoking himself, 'because that don't look well; do it, Polly?'

'Why, of course it don't, father. How can you ask!'

'You see, my boys and gals,' said Mr Toodle, looking round upon his family, 'wotever you're up to in a honest way, it's my opinion as you can't do better than be open. If you find yourselves in cuttings or in tunnels, don't you play no secret games. Keep your whistles going, and let's know where you are.'

The rising Toodles set up a shrill murmur, expressive of their resolution to profit by the paternal advice.

'But what makes you say this along of Rob, father?' asked his wife, anxiously.

'Polly, old 'ooman,' said Mr Toodle, 'I don't know as I said it partickler along o' Rob, I'm sure. I starts light with Rob only; I comes to a branch; I takes on what I finds there, and a whole train of ideas gets coupled on to him, afore I knows where I am, or where they comes from. What a Junction a man's thoughts is,' said Mr Toodle, 'to-be-sure!'

This profound reflection Mr Toodle washed down with a pint mug of tea, and proceeded to solidify with a great weight of bread and butter; charging his young daughters meanwhile, to keep plenty of hot water in the pot, as he was uncommon dry and should take the indefinite quantity of 'a sight of⁴ mugs,' before his thirst was appeased.

In satisfying himself, however, Mr Toodle was not regardless of the younger branches about him, who, although they had made their own evening repast, were on the look-out for irregular morsels, as possessing a relish. These he distributed now and then to the expectant circle, by holding out great wedges of bread and butter, to be bitten at by the family in lawful succession, and by serving out small doses of tea in like manner with a spoon; which snacks had such a relish in the mouths of these young Toodles, that, after partaking of the same, they performed private dances of ecstasy among themselves, and stood on one leg apiece, and hopped, and indulged in other saltatory tokens of gladness. These vents for their excitement found, they gradually closed about Mr Toodle again, and eyed him hard as he got through more bread and butter and tea; affecting, however, to have no further expectations of their own in reference to those viands, but to be conversing on foreign subjects, and whispering confidentially.

Mr Toodle, in the midst of this family group, and setting an awful example to his children in the way of appetite, was conveying the two young Toodles on his knees to Birmingham by special engine, and was contemplating the rest over a barrier of bread and butter, when Rob the Grinder, in his sou'wester hat and mourning slops, presented himself, and was received with a general rush of brothers and sisters.

'Well, mother!' said Rob, dutifully kissing her; 'how are you, mother?'

'There's my boy!' cried Polly, giving him a hug and a pat on the back. 'Secret! Bless you, father, not he!'

This was intended for Mr Toodle's private edification, but Rob the Grinder, whose withers were not unwrung,[5] caught the words as they were spoken.

'What! father's been a saying something more again me, has he?' cried the injured innocent. 'Oh, what a hard thing it is that when a cove has once gone a little wrong, a cove's own father should be always a throwing it in his face behind his back! It's enough,' cried Rob, resorting to his coat-cuff in anguish of spirit, 'to make a cove go and do something out of spite!'

'My poor boy!' cried Polly, 'father didn't mean anything.'

'If father didn't mean anything,' blubbered the injured Grinder, 'why did he go and say anything, mother? Nobody thinks half so bad of me as my own father does. What a unnatural thing! I wish somebody'd take and chop my head off. Father wouldn't mind doing it, I believe, and I'd much rather he did that than t'other.'

At these desperate words all the young Toodles shrieked; a pathetic effect, which the Grinder improved by ironically adjuring them not to cry for him, for they ought to hate him, they ought, if they was good boys and girls; and this so touched the youngest Toodle but one, who was easily moved, that it touched him not only in his spirit but in his wind too; making him so purple that Mr Toodle in consternation carried him out to the water-butt, and would have put him under the tap, but for his being recovered by the sight of that instrument.

Matters having reached this point, Mr Toodle explained, and the virtuous feelings of his son being thereby calmed, they shook hands, and harmony reigned again.

'Will you do as I do, Biler, my boy?' inquired his father, returning to his tea with new strength.

'No, thank'ee, father. Master and I had tea together.'

'And how *is* master, Rob?' said Polly.

'Well, I don't know, mother; not much to boast on. There ain't no bis'ness done, you see. He don't know anything about it, the Cap'en don't. There was a man come into the shop this very day, and says, "I want a so-and-so," he says – some hard name or another. "A which?" says the Cap'en. "A so-and-so," says the man. "Brother," says the Cap'en, "will you take a observation round the shop?" "Well," says the man, "I've done it." "Do you see wot you want?" says the Cap'en. "No, I don't," says the man. "Do you know it when you *do* see it?" says the Cap'en. "No, I don't," says the man. "Why, then I tell you wot, my lad," says the Cap'en, "you'd better go back and ask wot it's like, outside, for no more don't I!"'

'That ain't the way to make money, though, is it?' said Polly.

'Money, mother! He'll never make money. He has such ways as I never see. He ain't a bad master though, I'll say that for him. But that ain't much to me, for I don't think I shall stop with him long.'

'Not stop in your place, Rob!' cried his mother; while Mr Toodle opened his eyes.

'Not in that place, p'raps,' returned the Grinder, with a wink. 'I shouldn't wonder – friends at court[6] you know – but never *you* mind, mother, just now; I'm all right, that's all.'

The indisputable proof afforded in these hints, and in the Grinder's mysterious manner, of his not being subject to that failing which Mr Toodle had, by implication, attributed to him, might have led to a renewal of his wrongs, and of the sensation in the family, but for the opportune arrival of another visitor, who, to Polly's great surprise, appeared at the door, smiling patronage and friendship on all there.

'How do you do, Mrs Richards?' said Miss Tox. 'I have come to see you. May I come in?'

The cheery face of Mrs Richards shone with a hospitable reply, and Miss Tox, accepting the proffered chair, and gracefully recognising Mr Toodle on her way to it, untied her bonnet strings, and said that in the first place she must beg the dear children, one and all, to come and kiss her.

The ill-starred youngest Toodle but one, who would appear, from the frequency of his domestic troubles, to have been born under an unlucky planet, was prevented from performing his part

Miss Tox pays a visit to the Toodle Family

in this general salutation by having fixed the sou'wester hat (with which he had been previously trifling) deep on his head, hind side before, and being unable to get it off again; which accident presenting to his terrified imagination a dismal picture of his passing the rest of his days in darkness, and in hopeless seclusion from his friends and family, caused him to struggle with great violence, and to utter suffocating cries. Being released, his face was discovered to be very hot, and red, and damp; and Miss Tox took him on her lap, much exhausted.

'You have almost forgotten me, Sir, I dare say,' said Miss Tox to Mr Toodle.

'No, ma'am, no,' said Toodle. 'But we've all on us got a little older since then.'

'And how do you find yourself, Sir?' inquired Miss Tox, blandly.

'Hearty, ma'am, thank'ee,' replied Toodle. 'How do *you* find *yourself*, ma'am? Do the rheumaticks keep off pretty well, ma'am? We must all expect to grow into 'em, as we gets on.'

'Thank you,' said Miss Tox. 'I have not felt any inconvenience from that disorder yet.'

'You're wery fortunate, ma'am,' returned Mr Toodle. 'Many people at your time of life, ma'am, is martyrs to it. There was my mother—' But catching his wife's eye here, Mr Toodle judiciously buried the rest in another mug of tea.

'You never mean to say, Mrs Richards,' cried Miss Tox, looking at Rob, 'that that is your—'

'Eldest, ma'am,' said Polly. 'Yes, indeed, it is. That's the little fellow, ma'am, that was the innocent cause of so much.'

'This here, ma'am,' said Toodle, 'is him with the short legs – and they was,' said Mr Toodle, with a touch of poetry in his tone, 'unusual short for leathers[7] – as Mr Dombey made a Grinder on.'

The recollection almost overpowered Miss Tox. The subject of it had a peculiar interest for her directly. She asked him to shake hands, and congratulated his mother on his frank, ingenuous face. Rob, overhearing her, called up a look, to justify the eulogium, but it was hardly the right look.

'And now, Mrs Richards,' said Miss Tox, – 'and you too, Sir,' addressing Toodle – 'I'll tell you, plainly and truly, what I have come here for. You may be aware, Mrs Richards – and, possibly, you may be aware too, Sir – that a little distance has interposed itself between me and some of my friends, and that where I used to visit a good deal, I do not visit now.'

Polly, who, with a woman's tact, understood this at once,

expressed as much in a little look. Mr Toodle, who had not the faintest idea of what Miss Tox was talking about, expressed that also, in a stare.

'Of course,' said Miss Tox, 'how our little coolness has arisen is of no moment, and does not require to be discussed. It is sufficient for me to say, that I have the greatest possible respect for, and interest in, Mr Dombey;' Miss Tox's voice faltered; 'and everything that relates to him.'

Mr Toodle, enlightened, shook his head, and said he had heerd it said, and, for his own part, he did think, as Mr Dombey was a difficult subject.

'Pray don't say so, Sir, if you please,' returned Miss Tox. 'Let me entreat you not to say so, Sir, either now, or at any future time. Such observations cannot but be very painful to me; and to a gentleman, whose mind is constituted as, I am quite sure, yours is, can afford no permanent satisfaction.'

Mr Toodle, who had not entertained the least doubt of offering a remark that would be received with acquiescence, was greatly confounded.

'All that I wish to say, Mrs Richards,' resumed Miss Tox, – 'and I address myself to you too, Sir, – is this. That any intelligence of the proceedings of the family, of the welfare of the family, of the health of the family, that reaches you, will be always most acceptable to me. That I shall be always very glad to chat with Mrs Richards about the family, and about old times. And as Mrs Richards and I never had the least difference (though I could wish now that we had been better acquainted, but I have no one but myself to blame for that), I hope she will not object to our being very good friends now, and to my coming backwards and forwards here, when I like, without being a stranger. Now, I really hope, Mrs Richards,' said Miss Tox, earnestly, 'that you will take this, as I mean it, like a good-humoured creature, as you always were.'

Polly was gratified, and showed it. Mr Toodle didn't know whether he was gratified or not, and preserved a stolid calmness.

'You see, Mrs Richards,' said Miss Tox – 'and I hope you see too, Sir – there are many little ways in which I can be slightly useful to you, if you will make no stranger of me; and in which I shall be delighted to be so. For instance, I can teach your children something. I shall bring a few little books, if you'll allow me, and some work, and of an evening now and then, they'll learn – dear me, they'll learn a great deal, I trust, and be a credit to their teacher.'

Mr Toodle, who had a great respect for learning, jerked his head approvingly at his wife, and moistened his hands with dawning satisfaction.

'Then, not being a stranger, I shall be in nobody's way,' said Miss Tox, 'and everything will go on just as if I were not here. Mrs Richards will do her mending, or her ironing, or her nursing, whatever it is, without minding me: and you'll smoke your pipe, too, if you're so disposed, Sir, won't you?'

'Thank'ee, mum,' said Mr Toodle. 'Yes; I'll take my bit of backer.'[8]

'Very good of you to say so, Sir,' rejoined Miss Tox, 'and I really do assure you now, unfeignedly, that it will be a great comfort to me, and that whatever good I may be fortunate enough to do the children, you will more than pay back to me, if you'll enter into this little bargain comfortably, and easily, and good-naturedly, without another word about it.'

The bargain was ratified on the spot; and Miss Tox found herself so much at home already, that without delay she instituted a preliminary examination of the children all round – which Mr Toodle much admired – and booked their ages, names, and acquirements, on a piece of paper. This ceremony, and a little attendant gossip prolonged the time until after their usual hour of going to bed, and detained Miss Tox at the Toodle fireside until it was too late for her to walk home alone. The gallant Grinder, however, being still there, politely offered to attend her to her own door; and as it was something to Miss Tox to be seen home by a youth whom Mr Dombey had first inducted into those manly garments which are rarely mentioned[9] by name, she very readily accepted the proposal.

After shaking hands with Mr Toodle and Polly, and kissing all the children, Miss Tox left the house, therefore, with unlimited popularity, and carrying away with her so light a heart that it might have given Mrs Chick offence if that good lady could have weighed it.

Rob the Grinder, in his modesty, would have walked behind, but Miss Tox desired him to keep beside her, for conversational purposes; and, as she afterwards expressed it to his mother, 'drew him out' upon the road.

He drew out so bright, and clear, and shining, that Miss Tox was charmed with him. The more Miss Tox drew him out, the finer he came – like wire. There never was a better or more promising youth – a more affectionate, steady, prudent, sober, honest, meek, candid young man – than Rob drew out that night.

'I am quite glad,' said Miss Tox, arrived at her own door, 'to know you. I hope you'll consider me your friend, and that you'll come and see me as often as you like. Do you keep a money-box?'

'Yes, ma'am,' returned Rob; 'I'm saving up against I've got enough to put in the Bank, ma'am.'

'Very laudable indeed,' said Miss Tox. 'I'm glad to hear it. Put this half-crown into it, if you please.'

'Oh thank you, ma'am,' replied Rob, 'but really I couldn't think of depriving you.'

'I commend your independent spirit,' said Miss Tox, 'but it's no deprivation, I assure you. I shall be offended if you don't take it, as a mark of my good-will. Good night, Robin.'

'Good night, ma'am,' said Rob, 'and thank you!'

Who ran sniggering off to get change, and tossed it away with a pieman.[10] But they never taught honour at the Grinders' School, where the system that prevailed was particularly strong in the engendering of hypocrisy. Insomuch, that many of the friends and masters of past Grinders said, if this were what came of education for the common people, let us have none. Some more rational said, let us have a better one. But the governing powers of the Grinders' Company were always ready for *them*, by picking out a few boys who had turned out well, in spite of the system, and roundly asserting that they could have only turned out well because of it. Which settled the business of those objectors out of hand, and established the glory of the Grinders' Institution.

CHAPTER 39

Further Adventures of Captain Edward Cuttle, Mariner

Time, sure of foot and strong of will, had so pressed onward, that the year enjoined by the old Instrument-maker, as the term during which his friend should refrain from opening the sealed packet accompanying the letter he had left for him, was now nearly expired, and Captain Cuttle began to look at it, of an evening, with feelings of mystery and uneasiness.

The Captain, in his honour, would as soon have thought of opening the parcel one hour before the expiration of the term, as he would have thought of opening himself, to study his own anatomy.

He merely brought it out, at a certain stage of his first evening pipe, laid it on the table, and sat gazing at the outside of it, through the smoke, in silent gravity, for two or three hours at a spell. Sometimes, when he had contemplated it thus for a pretty long while, the Captain would hitch his chair, by degrees, farther and farther off, as if to get beyond the range of its fascination; but if this were his design, he never succeeded: for even when he was brought up by the parlour wall, the packet still attracted him; or if his eyes, in thoughtful wandering, roved to the ceiling or the fire, its image immediately followed, and posted itself conspicuously among the coals, or took up an advantageous position on the whitewash.

In respect of Heart's Delight, the Captain's parental regard and admiration knew no change. But since his last interview with Mr Carker, Captain Cuttle had come to entertain doubts whether his former intervention in behalf of that young lady and his dear boy Wal'r, had proved altogether so favourable as he could have wished, and as he at the time believed. The Captain was troubled with a serious misgiving that he had done more harm than good, in short; and in his remorse and modesty he made the best atonement he could think of, by putting himself out of the way of doing any harm to any one, and, as it were, throwing himself overboard for a dangerous person.

Self-buried, therefore, among the instruments, the Captain never went near Mr Dombey's house, or reported himself in any way to Florence or Miss Nipper. He even severed himself from Mr Perch, on the occasion of his next visit, by dryly informing that gentleman, that he thanked him for his company, but had cut himself adrift from all such acquaintance, as he didn't know what magazine he mightn't blow up,[1] without meaning of it. In this self-imposed retirement, the Captain passed whole days and weeks without interchanging a word with any one but Rob the Grinder, whom he esteemed as a pattern of disinterested attachment and fidelity. In this retirement, the Captain, gazing at the packet of an evening, would sit smoking, and thinking of Florence and poor Walter, until they both seemed to his homely fancy to be dead, and to have passed away into eternal youth, the beautiful and innocent children of his first remembrance.

The Captain did not, however, in his musings, neglect his own improvement, or the mental culture of Rob the Grinder. That young man was generally required to read out of some book to the Captain, for one hour, every evening; and as the Captain implicitly believed that all books were true, he accumulated, by this means,

many remarkable facts. On Sunday nights, the Captain always read
for himself, before going to bed, a certain Divine Sermon once
delivered on a Mount;[2] and although he was accustomed to quote
the text, without book, after his own manner, he appeared to read
it with as reverent an understanding of its heavenly spirit, as if he
had got it all by heart in Greek, and had been able to write any
number of fierce theological disquisitions on its every phrase.

Rob the Grinder, whose reverence for the inspired writings under
the admirable system of the Grinders' School, had been developed
by a perpetual bruising of his intellectual shins against all the proper
names of all the tribes of Judah,[3] and by the monotonous repetition
of hard verses, especially by way of punishment, and by the
parading of him at six years old in leather breeches, three times a
Sunday, very high up, in a very hot church, with a great organ
buzzing against his drowsy head, like an exceedingly busy bee –
Rob the Grinder made a mighty show of being edified when the
Captain ceased to read, and generally yawned and nodded while
the reading was in progress. The latter fact being never so much as
suspected by the good Captain.

Captain Cuttle, also, as a man of business, took to keeping books.
In these he entered observations on the weather, and on the currents
of the waggons and other vehicles: which he observed, in that
quarter, to set westward in the morning and during the greater part
of the day, and eastward towards the evening. Two or three
stragglers appearing in one week, who 'spoke him' – so the Captain
entered it – on the subject of spectacles, and who, without positively
purchasing, said they would look in again, the Captain decided that
the business was improving, and made an entry in the day-book to
that effect: the wind then blowing (which he first recorded) pretty
fresh, west and by north; having changed in the night.

One of the Captain's chief difficulties was Mr Toots, who called
frequently, and who without saying much seemed to have an idea
that the little back parlour was an eligible room to chuckle in, as he
would sit and avail himself of its accommodations in that regard by
the half-hour together, without at all advancing in intimacy with
the Captain. The Captain, rendered cautious by his late experience,
was unable quite to satisfy his mind whether Mr Toots was the
mild subject he appeared to be, or was a profoundly artful and
dissimulating hypocrite. His frequent reference to Miss Dombey
was suspicious; but the Captain had a secret kindness for Mr
Toots's apparent reliance on him, and forbore to decide against him
for the present; merely eyeing him, with a sagacity not to be

described, whenever he approached the subject that was nearest to his heart.

'Captain Gills,' blurted out Mr Toots, one day all at once, as his manner was, 'do you think you could think favourably of that proposition of mine, and give me the pleasure of your acquaintance?'

'Why, I tell you what it is, my lad,' replied the Captain, who had at length concluded on a course of action; 'I've been turning that there over.'

'Captain Gills, it's very kind of you,' retorted Mr Toots. 'I'm much obliged to you. Upon my word and honour, Captain Gills, it would be a charity to give me the pleasure of your acquaintance. It really would.'

'You see, brother,' argued the Captain slowly, 'I don't know you.'

'But you never *can* know me, Captain Gills,' replied Mr Toots, steadfast to his point, 'if you don't give me the pleasure of your acquaintance.'

The Captain seemed struck by the originality and power of this remark, and looked at Mr Toots as if he thought there was a great deal more in him than he had expected.

'Well said, my lad,' observed the Captain, nodding his head thoughtfully; 'and true. Now look'ee here: You've made some observations to me, which gives me to understand as you admire a certain sweet creetur. Hey?'

'Captain Gills,' said Mr Toots, gesticulating violently with the hand in which he held his hat, 'Admiration is not the word. Upon my honour, you have no conception what my feelings are. If I could be dyed black, and made Miss Dombey's slave I should consider it a compliment. If, at the sacrifice of all my property, I could get transmigrated into Miss Dombey's dog – I – I really think I should never leave off wagging my tail. I should be so perfectly happy, Captain Gills!'

Mr Toots said it with watery eyes, and pressed his hat against his bosom with deep emotion.

'My lad,' returned the Captain, moved to compassion, 'if you're in arnest—'

'Captain Gills,' cried Mr Toots, 'I'm in such a state of mind, and am so dreadfully in earnest, that if I could swear to it upon a hot piece of iron, or a live coal, or melted lead, or burning sealing-wax, or anything of that sort, I should be glad to hurt myself, as a relief to my feelings.' And Mr Toots looked hurriedly about the room, as

if for some sufficiently painful means of accomplishing his dread
purpose.

The Captain pushed his glazed hat back upon his head, stroked
his face down with his heavy hand – making his nose more mottled
in the process – and planting himself before Mr Toots, and hooking
him by the lapel of his coat, addressed him in these words, while
Mr Toots looked up into his face, with much attention and some
wonder.

'If you're in arnest, you see, my lad,' said the Captain, 'you're a
object of clemency, and clemency is the brightest jewel in the crown
of a Briton's head, for which you'll overhaul the constitution as laid
down in Rule Britannia, and, when found, *that* is the charter as
them garden angels[4] was a singing of, so many times over. Stand
by! This here proposal o' you'rn takes me a little aback. And why?
Because I holds my own only, you understand, in these here waters,
and haven't got no consort, and may be don't wish for none.
Steady! You hailed me first, along of a certain young lady, as you
was chartered by. Now if you and me is to keep one another's
company at all, that there young creetur's name must never be
named nor referred to. I don't know what harm mayn't have been
done by naming of it too free, afore now, and thereby I brings up
short. D'ye make me out pretty clear, brother?'

'Well, you'll excuse me, Captain Gills,' replied Mr Toots, 'if I
don't quite follow you sometimes. But upon my word I – it's a hard
thing, Captain Gills, not to be able to mention Miss Dombey. I
really have got such a dreadful load here!' – Mr Toots pathetically
touched his shirt-front with both hands – 'that I feel night and day,
exactly as if somebody was sitting upon me.'

'Them,' said the Captain, 'is the terms I offer. If they're hard
upon you, brother, as mayhap they are, give 'em a wide berth, sheer
off, and part company cheerily!'

'Captain Gills,' returned Mr Toots, 'I hardly know how it is, but
after what you told me when I came here, for the first time, I – I
feel that I'd rather think about Miss Dombey in your society than
talk about her in almost anybody else's. Therefore, Captain Gills, if
you'll give me the pleasure of your acquaintance, I shall be very
happy to accept it on your own conditions. I wish to be honourable,
Captain Gills,' said Mr Toots, holding back his extended hand for
a moment, 'and therefore I am obliged to say that I *can not* help
thinking about Miss Dombey. It's impossible for me to make a
promise not to think about her.'

'My lad,' said the Captain, whose opinion of Mr Toots was much improved by this candid avowal, 'a man's thoughts is like the winds, and nobody can't answer for 'em for certain, any length of time together. Is it a treaty as to words?'

'As to words, Captain Gills,' returned Mr Toots, 'I think I can bind myself.'

Mr Toots gave Captain Cuttle his hand upon it, then and there; and the Captain with a pleasant and gracious show of condescension, bestowed his acquaintance upon him formally. Mr Toots seemed much relieved and gladdened by the acquisition, and chuckled rapturously during the remainder of his visit. The Captain, for his part, was not ill pleased to occupy that position of patronage, and was exceedingly well satisfied by his own prudence and foresight.

But rich as Captain Cuttle was in the latter quality, he received a surprise that same evening from a no less ingenuous and simple youth, than Rob the Grinder. That artless lad, drinking tea at the same table, and bending meekly over his cup and saucer, having taken sidelong observations of his master for some time, who was reading the newspaper with great difficulty, but much dignity, through his glasses, broke silence by saying—

'Oh! I beg your pardon, Captain, but you mayn't be in want of any pigeons, may you, Sir?'

'No, my lad,' replied the Captain.

'Because I was wishing to dispose of mine, Captain,' said Rob.

'Aye, aye?' cried the Captain, lifting up his bushy eyebrows a little.

'Yes; I'm going, Captain, if you please,' said Rob.

'Going? Where are you going?' asked the Captain, looking round at him over the glasses.

'What? didn't you know that I was going to leave you, Captain?' asked Rob, with a sneaking smile.

The Captain put down the paper, took off his spectacles, and brought his eyes to bear on the deserter.

'Oh yes, Captain, I am going to give you warning. I thought you'd have known that beforehand, perhaps,' said Rob, rubbing his hands, and getting up. 'If you could be so good as provide yourself soon, Captain, it would be a great convenience to me. You couldn't provide yourself by to-morrow morning, I am afraid, Captain: could you, do you think?'

'And you're a going to desert your colours, are you, my lad?' said the Captain, after a long examination of his face.

'Oh, it's very hard upon a cove, Captain,' cried the tender Rob, injured and indignant in a moment, 'that he can't give lawful warning, without being frowned at in that way, and called a deserter. You haven't any right to call a poor cove names, Captain. It ain't because I'm a servant and you're a master, that you're to go and libel me. What wrong have I done? Come, Captain, let me know what my crime is, will you?'

The stricken Grinder wept, and put his coat-cuff in his eye.

'Come, Captain,' cried the injured youth, 'give my crime a name! What have I been and done? Have I stolen any of the property? Have I set the house a-fire? If I have, why don't you give me in charge, and try it? But to take away the character of a lad that's been a good servant to you, because he can't afford to stand in his own light for your good, what a injury it is, and what a bad return for faithful service! This is the way young coves is spiled and drove wrong. I wonder at you, Captain, I do.'

All of which the Grinder howled forth in a lachrymose whine, and backing carefully towards the door.

'And so you've got another berth, have you, my lad?' said the Captain, eyeing him intently.

'Yes, Captain, since you put it in that shape, I *have* got another berth,' cried Rob, backing more and more; 'a better berth than I've got here, and one where I don't so much as want your good word, Captain, which is fort'nate for me, after all the dirt you've throw'd at me, because I'm poor, and can't afford to stand in my own light for your good. Yes, I *have* got another berth; and if it wasn't for leaving you unprovided, Captain, I'd go to it now, sooner than I'd take them names from you, because I'm poor, and can't afford to stand in my own light for your good. Why do you reproach me for being poor, and not standing in my own light for your good, Captain? How can you so demean yourself?'

'Look ye here, my boy,' replied the peaceful Captain. 'Don't you pay out no more of them words.'

'Well, then, don't you pay in no more of your words, Captain,' retorted the roused innocent, getting louder in his whine, and backing into the shop. 'I'd sooner you took my blood than my character.'

'Because,' pursued the Captain calmly, 'you have heerd, may be, of such a thing as a rope's end.'

'Oh, have I though, Captain?' cried the taunting Grinder. 'No I haven't. I never heerd of any such a article!'

'Well,' said the Captain, 'it's my belief as you'll know more about it pretty soon, if you don't keep a bright lookout. I can read your signals, my lad. You may go.'

'Oh! I may go at once, may I, Captain?' cried Rob, exulting in his success. 'But mind! *I* never asked to go at once, Captain. You are not to take away my character again, because you send me off of your own accord. And you're not to stop any of my wages, Captain!'

His employer settled the last point by producing the tin canister and telling the Grinder's money out in full upon the table. Rob, snivelling and sobbing, and grievously wounded in his feelings, took up the pieces one by one, with a sob and a snivel for each, and tied them up separately in knots in his pocket-handkerchief; then he ascended to the roof of the house and filled his hat and pockets with pigeons; then, came down to his bed under the counter and made up his bundle, snivelling and sobbing louder as if he were cut to the heart by old associations; then he whined, 'Good night, Captain. I leave you without malice!' and then, going out upon the door-step, pulled the little Midshipman's nose as a parting indignity, and went away down the street grinning triumph.

The Captain, left to himself, resumed his perusal of the news as if nothing unusual or unexpected had taken place, and went reading on with the greatest assiduity. But never a word did Captain Cuttle understand, though he read a vast number, for Rob the Grinder was scampering up one column and down another all through the newspaper.

It is doubtful whether the worthy Captain had ever felt himself quite abandoned until now; but now, old Sol Gills, Walter, and Heart's Delight were lost to him indeed, and now Mr Carker deceived and jeered him cruelly. They were all represented in the false Rob, to whom he had held forth many a time on the recollections that were warm within him; he had believed in the false Rob, and had been glad to believe in him; he had made a companion of him as the last of the old ship's company; he had taken the command of the little Midshipman with him at his right hand; he had meant to do his duty by him, and had felt almost as kindly towards the boy as if they had been shipwrecked and cast upon a desert place together. And now, that the false Rob had brought distrust, treachery, and meanness into the very parlour, which was a kind of sacred place, Captain Cuttle felt as if the parlour might have gone down next, and not surprised him much by its sinking, or given him any very great concern.

Therefore Captain Cuttle read the newspaper with profound

attention and no comprehension, and therefore Captain Cuttle said nothing whatever about Rob to himself, or admitted to himself that he was thinking about him, or would recognise in the most distant manner that Rob had anything to do with his feeling as lonely as Robinson Crusoe.

In the same composed, business-like way, the Captain stepped over to Leadenhall Market in the dusk, and affected an arrangement with a private watchman on duty there, to come and put up and take down the shutters⁵ of the Wooden Midshipman every night and morning. He then called in at the eating-house to diminish by one half the daily rations theretofore supplied to the Midshipman, and at the public-house to stop the traitor's beer. 'My young man,' said the Captain, in explanation to the young lady at the bar, 'my young man having bettered himself, Miss.' Lastly, the Captain resolved to take possession of the bed under the counter, and to turn in there o' nights instead of up stairs, as sole guardian of the property.

From this bed Captain Cuttle daily rose thenceforth, and clapped on his glazed hat at six o'clock in the morning, with the solitary air of Crusoe finishing his toilet with his goat-skin cap; and although his fears of a visitation from the savage tribe, MacStinger, were somewhat cooled, as similar apprehensions on the part of that lone mariner used to be by the lapse of a long interval without any symptoms of the cannibals, he still observed a regular routine of defensive operations, and never encountered a bonnet without previous survey from his castle of retreat. In the meantime (during which he received no call from Mr Toots, who wrote to say he was out of town) his own voice began to have a strange sound in his ears; and he acquired such habits of profound meditation from much polishing and stowing away of the stock, and from much sitting behind the counter reading, or looking out of window, that the red rim made on his forehead by the hard glazed hat, sometimes arched again with excess of reflection.

The year being now expired, Captain Cuttle deemed it expedient to open the packet; but as he had always designed doing this in the presence of Rob the Grinder, who had brought it to him, and as he had an idea that it would be regular and ship-shape to open it in the presence of somebody, he was sadly put to it for want of a witness. In this difficulty, he hailed one day with unusual delight the announcement in the Shipping Intelligence of the arrival of the Cautious Clara, Captain John Bunsby, from a coasting voyage; and to that philosopher immediately dispatched a letter by post, enjoining inviolable secrecy as to his place of residence, and requesting to be favoured with an early visit, in the evening season.

Bunsby, who was one of those sages who act upon conviction, took some days to get the conviction thoroughly into his mind, that he had received a letter to this effect. But when he had grappled with the fact, and mastered it, he promptly sent his boy with the message, 'He's a coming to-night.' Who being instructed to deliver those words and disappear, fulfilled his mission like a tarry spirit, charged with a mysterious warning.

The Captain, well pleased to receive it, made preparation of pipes and rum and water, and awaited his visitor in the back parlour. At the hour of eight, a deep lowing, as of a nautical Bull, outside the shop-door, succeeded by the knocking of a stick on the panel, announced to the listening ear of Captain Cuttle, that Bunsby was alongside: whom he instantly admitted, shaggy and loose, and with his stolid mahogany visage, as usual, appearing to have no consciousness of anything before it, but to be attentively observing something that was taking place in quite another part of the world.

'Bunsby,' said the Captain, grasping him by the hand, 'what cheer, my lad, what cheer?'

'Shipmet,' replied the voice within Bunsby, unaccompanied by any sign on the part of the Commander himself, 'hearty, hearty.'

'Bunsby!' said the Captain, rendering irrepressible homage to his genius, 'here you are! a man as can give an opinion as is brighter than di'monds – and give me the lad with the tarry trousers[6] as shines to me like di'monds bright, for which you'll overhaul the Stanfell's Budget,[7] and when found make a note. Here you are, a man as gave an opinion in this here very place, that has come true, every letter on it,' which the Captain sincerely believed.

'Aye, aye?' growled Bunsby.

'Every letter,' said the Captain.

'For why?' growled Bunsby, looking at his friend for the first time. 'Which way? If so, why not? Therefore.' With these oracular words – they seemed almost to make the Captain giddy; they launched him upon such a sea of speculation and conjecture – the sage submitted to be helped off with his pilot-coat, and accompanied his friend into the back parlour, where his hand presently alighted on the rum-bottle, from which he brewed a stiff glass of grog; and presently afterwards on a pipe, which he filled, lighted, and began to smoke.

Captain Cuttle, imitating his visitor in the matter of these particulars, though the rapt and imperturbable manner of the great

Commander was far above his powers, sat in the opposite corner of the fireside, observing him respectfully, and as if he waited for some encouragement or expression of curiosity on Bunsby's part which should lead him to his own affairs. But as the mahogany philosopher gave no evidence of being sentient of anything but warmth and tobacco, except once, when taking his pipe from his lips to make room for his glass, he incidentally remarked with exceeding gruffness, that his name was Jack Bunsby – a declaration that presented but small opening for conversation – the Captain bespeaking his attention in a short complimentary exordium, narrated the whole history of Uncle Sol's departure, with the change it had produced in his own life and fortunes; and concluded by placing the packet on the table.

After a long pause, Mr Bunsby nodded his head.

'Open?' said the Captain.

Bunsby nodded again.

The Captain accordingly broke the seal, and disclosed to view two folded papers, of which he severally read the endorsements, thus: 'Last Will and Testament of Solomon Gills.' 'Letter for Ned Cuttle.'

Bunsby, with his eye on the coast of Greenland, seemed to listen for the contents. The Captain therefore hemmed to clear his throat, and read the letter aloud.

'"My dear Ned Cuttle. When I left home for the West Indies"—'

Here the Captain stopped, and looked hard at Bunsby, who looked fixedly at the coast of Greenland.

—'"in forlorn search of intelligence of my dear boy, I knew that if you were acquainted with my design, you would thwart it, or accompany me; and therefore I kept it secret. If you ever read this letter, Ned, I am likely to be dead. You will easily forgive an old friend's folly then, and will feel for the restlessness and uncertainty in which he wandered away on such a wild voyage. So no more of that. I have little hope that my poor boy will ever read these words, or gladden your eyes with the sight of his frank face any more." No, no; no more,' said Captain Cuttle, sorrowfully meditating; 'no more. There he lays, all his days—'[8]

Mr Bunsby, who had a musical ear, suddenly bellowed, 'In the Bays of Biscay, O!' which so affected the good Captain, as an appropriate tribute to departed worth, that he shook him by the hand in acknowledgment, and was fain to wipe his eyes.

'Well, well!' said the Captain with a sigh, as the Lament of Bunsby ceased to ring and vibrate in the skylight. 'Affliction sore,

long time he bore,' and let us overhaul the wollume, and there find
it.'

'Physicians,' observed Bunsby, 'was in vain.'

'Aye, aye, to be sure,' said the Captain, 'what's the good o' *them*
in two or three hundred fathoms o' water!' Then returning to the
letter, he read on: – '"But if he should be by, when it is opened;"'
the Captain involuntarily looked round, and shook his head; '"or
should know of it at any other time;"' the Captain shook his head
again; '"my blessing on him! In case the accompanying paper is not
legally written, it matters very little, for there is no one interested
but you and he, and my plain wish is, that if he is living he should
have what little there may be, and if (as I fear) otherwise, that you
should have it, Ned. You will respect my wish, I know. God bless
you for it, and for all your friendliness besides, to SOLOMON
GILLS." Bunsby!' said the Captain, appealing to him solemnly,
'what do you make of this? There you sit, a man as has had his
head broke from infancy up'ards, and has got a new opinion into it
at every seam as has been opened. Now, what do you make o' this?'

'If so be,' returned Bunsby, with unusual promptitude, 'as he's
dead, my opinion is he won't come back no more. If so be as he's
alive, my opinion is he will. Do I say he will? No. Why not? Because
the bearings of this obserwation lays in the application on it.'

'Bunsby!' said Captain Cuttle, who would seem to have estimated
the value of his distinguished friend's opinions in proportion to the
immensity of the difficulty he experienced in making anything out
of them; 'Bunsby,' said the Captain, quite confounded by admiration, 'you carry a weight of mind easy, as would swamp one of my
tonnage soon. But in regard o' this here will, I don't mean to take
no steps towards the property – Lord forbid! – except to keep it for
a more rightful owner; and I hope yet as the rightful owner, Sol
Gills, is living and 'll come back, strange as it is that he ain't
forwarded no dispatches. Now, what is your opinion, Bunsby, as to
stowing of these here papers away again, and marking outside as
they was opened, such a day, in the presence of John Bunsby and
Ed'ard Cuttle?'

Bunsby, descrying no objection, on the coast of Greenland or
elsewhere, to this proposal, it was carried into execution; and that
great man, bringing his eye into the present for a moment, affixed
his sign-manual[10] to the cover, totally abstaining, with characteristic
modesty, from the use of capital letters. Captain Cuttle, having
attached his own left-handed signature, and locked up the packet in
the iron safe, entreated his guest to mix another glass and smoke

another pipe; and doing the like himself, fell a musing over the fire on the possible fortunes of the poor old Instrument-maker.

And now a surprise occurred, so overwhelming and terrific that Captain Cuttle, unsupported by the presence of Bunsby, must have sunk beneath it, and been a lost man from that fatal hour.

How the Captain, even in the satisfaction of admitting such a guest, could have only shut the door, and not locked it, of which negligence he was undoubtedly guilty, is one of those questions that must for ever remain mere points of speculation, or vague charges against destiny. But by that unlocked door, at this quiet moment, did the fell MacStinger dash into the parlour, bringing Alexander MacStinger in her parental arms, and confusion and vengeance (not to mention Juliana MacStinger, and the sweet child's brother, Charles MacStinger, popularly known about the scenes of his youthful sports, as Chowley) in her train. She came so swiftly and so silently, like a rushing air from the neighbourhood of the East India Docks, that Captain Cuttle found himself in the very act of sitting looking at her, before the calm face with which he had been meditating, changed to one of horror and dismay.

But the moment Captain Cuttle understood the full extent of his misfortune, self-preservation dictated an attempt at flight. Darting at the little door which opened from the parlour on the steep little range of cellar-steps, the Captain made a rush, head-foremost, at the latter, like a man indifferent to bruises and contusions, who only sought to hide himself in the bowels of the earth. In this gallant effort he would probably have succeeded, but for the affectionate dispositions of Juliana and Chowley, who pinning him by the legs – one of those dear children holding on to each – claimed him as their friend, with lamentable cries. In the meantime, Mrs MacStinger, who never entered upon any action of importance without previously inverting Alexander MacStinger, to bring him within the range of a brisk battery of slaps, and then sitting him down to cool as the reader first beheld him, performed that solemn rite, as if on this occasion it were a sacrifice to the Furies;[11] and having deposited the victim on the floor, made at the Captain with a strength of purpose that appeared to threaten scratches to the interposing Bunsby.

The cries of the two elder MacStingers, and the wailing of young Alexander, who may be said to have passed a piebald childhood, forasmuch as he was black in the face during one half of that fairy period of existence, combined to make this visitation the more awful. But when silence reigned again, and the Captain, in a violent

The Midshipman is boarded by the enemy

perspiration, stood meekly looking at Mrs MacStinger, its terrors
were at their height.

'Oh, Cap'en Cuttle, Cap'en Cuttle!' said Mrs MacStinger, making
her chin rigid, and shaking it in unison with what, but for the
weakness of her sex, might be described as her fist. 'Oh, Cap'en
Cuttle, Cap'en Cuttle, do you dare to look me in the face, and not
be struck down in the herth!'

The Captain, who looked anything but daring, feebly muttered
'Stand by!'

'Oh I was a weak and trusting Fool when I took you under *my*
roof, Cap'en Cuttle, I was!' cried Mrs MacStinger. 'To think of the
benefits I've showered on that man, and the way in which I brought
my children up to love and *h*onour him as if he was a father to 'em,
when there an't a 'ousekeeper, no nor a lodger in our street, don't
know that I lost money by that man, and by his guzzlings and his
muzzlings' – Mrs MacStinger used the last word for the joint sake
of alliteration and aggravation, rather than for the expression of
any idea – 'and when they cried out one and all, shame upon him
for putting upon an industrious woman, up early and late for the
good of her young family, and keeping her poor place so clean that
a individual might have ate his dinner, yes, and his tea too, if he
was so disposed, off any one of the floors or stairs, in spite of all his
guzzlings *and* his muzzlings, such was the care and pains bestowed
upon him!'

Mrs MacStinger stopped to fetch her breath; and her face flushed
with triumph in this second happy introduction of Captain Cuttle's
muzzlings.

'And he runs awa-a-a-y!' cried Mrs MacStinger, with a lengthen-
ing out of the last syllable that made the unfortunate Captain regard
himself as the meanest of men; 'and keeps away a twelvemonth!
From a woman! Sitch is his conscience! He hasn't the courage to
meet her hi-i-i-igh;'[12] long syllable again; 'but steals away, like a
felion. Why, if that baby of mine,' said Mrs MacStinger, with
sudden rapidity, 'was to offer to go and steal away, I'd do my duty
as a mother by him, till he was covered with wales!'[13]

The young Alexander, interpreting this into a positive promise,
to be shortly redeemed, tumbled over with fear and grief, and lay
upon the floor, exhibiting the soles of his shoes and making such a
deafening outcry, that Mrs MacStinger found it necessary to take
him up in her arms, where she quieted him, ever and anon, as he
broke out again, by a shake that seemed enough to loosen his teeth.

'A pretty sort of a man is Cap'en Cuttle,' said Mrs MacStinger, with a sharp stress on the first syllable of the Captain's name, 'to take on for – and to lose sleep for – and to faint along of – and to think dead forsooth – and to go up and down the blessed town like a madwoman, asking questions after! Oh, a pretty sort of a man! Ha ha ha ha! He's worth all that trouble and distress of mind, and much more. *That's* nothing, bless you! Ha ha ha ha! Cap'en Cuttle,' said Mrs MacStinger, with severe reaction in her voice and manner, 'I wish to know if you're a-coming home?'

The frightened Captain looked into his hat, as if he saw nothing for it but to put it on, and give himself up.

'Cap'en Cuttle,' repeated Mrs MacStinger, in the same determined manner, 'I wish to know if you're a-coming home, Sir?'

The Captain seemed quite ready to go, but faintly suggested something to the effect of 'not making so much noise about it.'

'Aye, aye, aye,' said Bunsby, in a soothing voice. 'Awast, my lass, awast!'

'And who may YOU be, if you please!' retorted Mrs MacStinger, with chaste loftiness. 'Did you ever lodge at Number Nine, Brig Place, Sir? My memory may be bad, but not with me, I think. There was a Mrs Jollson lived at Number Nine before me, and perhaps you're mistaking me for her. That is my only ways of accounting for your familiarity, Sir.'

'Come, come, my lass, awast, awast!' said Bunsby.

Captain Cuttle could hardly believe it, even of this great man, though he saw it done with his waking eyes; but Bunsby, advancing boldly, put his shaggy blue arm round Mrs MacStinger, and so softened her by his magic way of doing it, and by these few words – he said no more – that she melted into tears, after looking upon him for a few moments, and observed that a child might conquer her now, she was so low in her courage.

Speechless and utterly amazed, the Captain saw him gradually persuade this inexorable woman into the shop, return for rum and water and a candle, take them to her, and pacify her without appearing to utter one word. Presently he looked in with his pilot-coat on, and said, 'Cuttle, I'm a-going to act as convoy home'; and Captain Cuttle, more to his confusion than if he had been put in irons himself, for safe transport to Brig Place, saw the family pacifically filing off, with Mrs MacStinger at their head. He had scarcely time to take down his canister, and stealthily convey some money into the hands of Juliana MacStinger, his former favourite, and Chowley, who had the claim upon him that he was naturally of a maritime build, before the Midshipman was abandoned by them all; and Bunsby whispering that he'd carry on smart, and hail Ned Cuttle again before he went aboard, shut the door upon himself, as the last member of the party.

Some uneasy ideas that he must be walking in his sleep, or that he had been troubled with phantoms, and not a family of flesh and blood, beset the Captain at first, when he went back to the little parlour, and found himself alone. Illimitable faith in, and immeasurable admiration of, the Commander of the Cautious Clara, succeeded, and threw the Captain into a wondering trance.

Still, as time wore on, and Bunsby failed to reappear, the Captain began to entertain uncomfortable doubts of another kind. Whether Bunsby had been artfully decoyed to Brig Place and was there detained in safe custody as hostage for his friend; in which case it would become the Captain, as a man of honour, to release him, by the sacrifice of his own liberty. Whether he had been attacked and defeated by Mrs MacStinger, and was ashamed to show himself after his discomfiture. Whether Mrs MacStinger, thinking better of it, in the uncertainty of her temper, had turned back to board the Midshipman again, and Bunsby, pretending to conduct her by a short cut, was endeavouring to lose the family amid the wilds and savage places of the City. Above all, what it would behove him, Captain Cuttle, to do, in case of his hearing no more, either of the MacStingers or of Bunsby, which, in these wonderful and unforeseen conjunctions of events, might possibly happen.

He debated all this until he was tired; and still no Bunsby. He made up his bed under the counter, all ready for turning in! and still no Bunsby. At length, when the Captain had given him up, for that night at least, and had begun to undress, the sound of approaching wheels was heard, and, stopping at the door, was succeeded by Bunsby's hail.

The Captain trembled to think that Mrs MacStinger was not to be got rid of, and had been brought back in a coach.

But no. Bunsby was accompanied by nothing but a large box, which he hauled into the shop with his own hands, and as soon as he had hauled in, sat upon. Captain Cuttle knew it for the chest he had left at Mrs MacStinger's house, and looking, candle in hand, at Bunsby more attentively, believed that he was three sheets in the wind, or, in plain words, drunk. It was difficult, however, to be sure of this; the Commander having no trace of expression in his face when sober.

'Cuttle,' said the Commander, getting off the chest, and opening the lid, 'are these here your traps?'[14]

Captain Cuttle looked in and identified his property.

'Done pretty taut and trim, hey, shipmet?' said Bunsby.

The grateful and bewildered Captain grasped him by the hand, and was launching into a reply expressive of his astonished feelings, when Bunsby disengaged himself by a jerk of his wrist, and seemed to make an effort to wink with his revolving eye, the only effect of which attempt, in his condition, was nearly to overbalance him. He then abruptly opened the door, and shot away to rejoin the Cautious Clara with all speed – supposed to be his invariable custom, whenever he considered he had made a point.

As it was not his humour to be often sought, Captain Cuttle decided not to go or send to him next day, or until he should make his gracious pleasure known in such wise, or failing that, until some little time should have elapsed. The Captain, therefore, renewed his solitary life next morning, and thought profoundly, many mornings, noons, and nights, of old Sol Gills, and Bunsby's sentiments concerning him, and the hopes there were of his return. Much of such thinking strengthened Captain Cuttle's hopes; and he humoured them and himself by watching for the Instrument-maker at the door as he ventured to do now, in his strange liberty – and setting his chair in its place, and arranging the little parlour as it used to be, in case he should come home unexpectedly. He likewise, in his thoughtfulness, took down a certain little miniature of Walter as a schoolboy, from its accustomed nail, lest it should shock the old man on his return. The Captain had his presentiments, too, sometimes, that he would come on such a day; and one particular Sunday, even ordered a double allowance of dinner, he was so sanguine. But come, old Solomon did not; and still the neighbours noticed how the seafaring man in the glazed hat, stood at the shop-door of an evening, looking up and down the street.

CHAPTER 40

Domestic Relations

It was not in the nature of things that a man of Mr Dombey's mood, opposed to such a spirit as he had raised against himself, should be softened in the imperious asperity of his temper; or that the cold hard armour of pride in which he lived encased, should be made more flexible by constant collision with haughty scorn and defiance. It is the curse of such a nature – it is a main part of the heavy retribution on itself it bears within itself – that while deference and concession swell its evil qualities, and are the food it grows upon, resistance and a questioning of its exacting claims, foster it too, no less. The evil that is in it finds equally its means of growth and propagation in opposites. It draws support and life from sweets and bitters; bowed down before, or unacknowledged, it still enslaves the breast in which it has its throne; and, worshipped or rejected, is as hard a master as the Devil in dark fables.

Towards his first wife, Mr Dombey, in his cold and lofty arrogance, had borne himself like the removed Being he almost conceived himself to be. He had been 'Mr Dombey' with her when she first saw him, and he was 'Mr Dombey' when she died. He had asserted his greatness during their whole married life, and she had meekly recognised it. He had kept his distant seat of state on the top of his throne, and she her humble station on its lowest step; and much good it had done him, so to live in solitary bondage to his one idea! He had imagined that the proud character of his second wife would have been added to his own – would have merged into it, and exalted his greatness. He had pictured himself haughtier than ever, with Edith's haughtiness subservient to his. He had never entertained the possibility of its arraying itself against him. And now, when he found it rising in his path at every step and turn of his daily life, fixing its cold, defiant, and contemptuous face upon him, this pride of his, instead of withering, or hanging down its head beneath the shock, put forth new shoots, became more concentrated and intense, more gloomy, sullen, irksome, and unyielding, than it had ever been before.

Who wears such armour, too, bears with him ever another heavy retribution. It is of proof against conciliation, love, and confidence! against all gentle sympathy from without, all trust, all tenderness, all soft emotion; but to deep stabs in the self-love, it is as vulnerable as the bare breast to steel; and such tormenting festers rankle there, as follow on no other wounds, no, though dealt with the mailed hand of Pride itself, on weaker pride, disarmed and thrown down.

Such wounds were his. He felt them sharply, in the solitude of his old rooms; whither he now began often to retire again, and pass long solitary hours. It seemed his fate to be ever proud and powerful; ever humbled and powerless where he would be most strong. Who seemed fated to work out that doom?

Who? Who was it who could win his wife as she had won his boy? Who was it who had shown him that new victory, as he sat in the dark corner? Who was it whose least word did what his utmost means could not? Who was it who, unaided by his love, regard or notice, thrived and grew beautiful when those so aided died? Who could it be, but the same child at whom he had often glanced uneasily in her motherless infancy, with a kind of dread, lest he might come to hate her; and of whom his foreboding was fulfilled, for he DID hate her in his heart?

Yes, and he would have it hatred, and he made it hatred, though some sparkles of the light in which she had appeared before him on the memorable night of his return home with his Bride, occasionally hung about her still. He knew now that she was beautiful; he did not dispute that she was graceful and winning, and that in the bright dawn of her womanhood she had come upon him, a surprise. But he turned even this against her. In his sullen and unwholesome brooding, the unhappy man, with a dull perception of his alienation from all hearts, and a vague yearning for what he had all his life repelled, made a distorted picture of his rights and wrongs, and justified himself with it against her. The worthier she promised to be of him, the greater claim he was disposed to ante-date upon her duty and submission. When had she ever shown him duty and submission? Did she grace his life – or Edith's? Had her attractions been manifested first to him – or Edith? Why, he and she had never been, from her birth, like father and child! They had always been estranged. She had crossed him every way and everywhere. She was leagued against him now. Her very beauty softened natures that were obdurate to him, and insulted him with an unnatural triumph.

It may have been that in all this there were mutterings of an awakened feeling in his breast, however selfishly aroused by his position of disadvantage, in comparison with what she might have made his life. But he silenced the distant thunder with the rolling of his sea of pride. He would bear nothing but his pride. And in his pride, a heap of inconsistency, and misery, and self-inflicted torment, he hated her.

To the moody, stubborn, sullen demon, that possessed him, his wife opposed her different pride in its full force. They never could have led a happy life together; but nothing could have made it more unhappy, than the wilful and determined warfare of such elements. His pride was set upon maintaining his magnificent supremacy, and forcing recognition of it from her. She would have been racked to death, and turned but her haughty glance of calm inflexible disdain upon him, to the last. Such recognition from Edith! He little knew through what a storm and struggle she had been driven onward to the crowning honour of his hand. He little knew how much she thought she had conceded, when she suffered him to call her wife.

Mr Dombey was resolved to show her that he was supreme. There must be no will but his. Proud he desired that she should be, but she must be proud for, not against him. As he sat alone, hardening, he would often hear her go out and come home, treading the round of London life with no more heed of his liking or disliking, pleasure or displeasure, than if he had been her groom. Her cold supreme indifference – his own unquestioned attribute usurped – stung him more than any other kind of treatment could have done; and he determined to bend her to his magnificent and stately will.

He had been long communing with these thoughts, when one night he sought her in her own apartment, after he had heard her return home late. She was alone, in her brilliant dress, and had but that moment come from her mother's room. Her face was melancholy and pensive, when he came upon her; but it marked him at the door; for, glancing at the mirror before it, he saw immediately, as in a picture-frame, the knitted brow, and darkened beauty that he knew so well.

'Mrs Dombey,' he said, entering, 'I must beg leave to have a few words with you.'

'To-morrow,' she replied.

'There is no time like the present, madam,' he returned. 'You mistake your position. I am used to choose my own times; not to have them chosen for me. I think you scarcely understand who and what I am, Mrs Dombey.'

'I think,' she answered, 'that I understand you very well.'

She looked upon him as she said so, and folding her white arms sparkling with gold and gems, upon her swelling breast, turned away her eyes.

If she had been less handsome, and less stately in her cold composure, she might not have had the power of impressing him with the sense of disadvantage that penetrated through his utmost pride. But she had the power, and he felt it keenly. He glanced round the room: saw how the splendid means of personal adornment, and the luxuries of dress, were scattered here and there, and disregarded; not in mere caprice and carelessness (or so he thought), but in a steadfast haughty disregard of costly things: and felt it more and more. Chaplets of flowers, plumes of feathers, jewels, laces, silks and satins; look where he would, he saw riches, despised, poured out, and made of no account. The very diamonds – a marriage gift – that rose and fell impatiently upon her bosom, seemed to pant to break the chain that clasped them round her neck, and roll down on the floor where she might tread upon them.

He felt his disadvantage, and he showed it. Solemn and strange among this wealth of colour and voluptuous glitter, strange and constrained towards its haughty mistress, whose repellent beauty it repeated, and presented all around him, as in so many fragments of a mirror, he was conscious of embarrassment and awkwardness. Nothing that ministered to her disdainful self-possession could fail to gall him. Galled and irritated with himself, he sat down, and went on in no improved humour:

'Mrs Dombey, it is very necessary that there should be some understanding arrived at between us. Your conduct does not please me, madam.'

She merely glanced at him again, and again averted her eyes; but she might have spoken for an hour, and expressed less.

'I repeat, Mrs Dombey, does not please me. I have already taken occasion to request that it may be corrected. I now insist upon it.'

'You chose a fitting occasion for your first remonstrance, Sir, and you adopt a fitting manner, and a fitting word for your second. *You* insist! To *me!*'

'Madam,' said Mr Dombey, with his most offensive air of state, 'I have made you my wife. You bear my name. You are associated with my position and my reputation. I will not say that the world in general may be disposed to think you honoured by that association; but I will say that I am accustomed to "insist," to my connexions and dependents.'

'Which may you be pleased to consider me?' she asked.

'Possibly I may think that my wife should partake – or does partake, and cannot help herself – of both characters, Mrs Dombey.'

She bent her eyes upon him steadily, and set her trembling lips. He saw her bosom throb, and saw her face flush and turn white. All this he could know, and did: but he could not know that one word was whispering in the deep recesses of her heart, to keep her quiet; and that the word was Florence.

Blind idiot, rushing to a precipice! He thought she stood in awe of *him!*

'You are too expensive, madam,' said Mr Dombey. 'You are extravagant. You waste a great deal of money – or what would be a great deal in the pockets of most gentlemen – in cultivating a kind of society that is useless to me, and, indeed, that upon the whole is disagreeable to me. I have to insist upon a total change in all these respects. I know that in the novelty of possessing a tithe of such means as Fortune has placed at your disposal, ladies are apt to run into a sudden extreme. There has been more than enough of that extreme. I beg that Mrs Granger's very different experiences may now come to the instruction of Mrs Dombey.'

Still the fixed look, the trembling lips, the throbbing breast, the face now crimson and now white; and still the deep whisper Florence, Florence, speaking to her in the beating of her heart.

His insolence of self-importance dilated as he saw this alteration in her. Swollen no less by her scorn of him, and his so recent feeling of disadvantage, than by her present submission (as he took it to be), it became too mighty for his breast, and burst all bounds. Why, who could long resist his lofty will and pleasure! He had resolved to conquer her, and look here!

'You will further please, madam,' said Mr Dombey, in a tone of sovereign command, 'to understand distinctly, that I am to be deferred to and obeyed. That I must have a positive show and confession of deference before the world, madam. I am used to this. I require it as my right. In short I will have it. I consider it no unreasonable return for the worldly advancement that has befallen you; and I believe nobody will be surprised, either at its being required from you, or at your making it. – To Me – To Me!' he added, with emphasis.

No word from her. No change in her. Her eyes upon him.

'I have learnt from your mother, Mrs Dombey,' said Mr Dombey, with magisterial importance, 'what no doubt you know, namely, that Brighton is recommended for her health. Mr Carker has been so good—'

She changed suddenly. Her face and bosom glowed as if the red light of an angry sunset had been flung upon them. Not unobservant of the change, and putting his own interpretation upon it, Mr Dombey resumed:

'Mr Carker has been so good as to go down and secure a house there, for a time. On the return of the establishment to London, I shall take such steps for its better management as I consider necessary. One of these will be the engagement at Brighton (if it is to be effected), of a very respectable reduced person there, a Mrs Pipchin, formerly employed in a situation of trust in my family, to act as housekeeper. An establishment like this, presided over but nominally, Mrs Dombey, requires a competent head.'

She had changed her attitude before he arrived at these words, and now sat – still looking at him fixedly – turning a bracelet round and round upon her arm; not winding it about with a light, womanly touch, but pressing and dragging it over the smooth skin, until the white limb showed a bar of red.

'I observed,' said Mr Dombey – 'and this concludes what I deem it necessary to say to you at present, Mrs Dombey – I observed a moment ago, madam, that my allusion to Mr Carker was received in a peculiar manner. On the occasion of my happening to point out to you, before that confidential agent, the objection I had to your mode of receiving my visitors, you were pleased to object to his presence. You will have to get the better of that objection, madam, and to accustom yourself to it very probably on many similar occasions; unless you adopt the remedy which is in your own hands, of giving me no cause of complaint. Mr Carker,' said Mr Dombey, who, after the emotion he had just seen, set great store by this means of reducing his proud wife, and who was perhaps sufficiently willing to exhibit his power to that gentleman in a new and triumphant aspect, 'Mr Carker being in my confidence, Mrs Dombey, may very well be in yours to such an extent. I hope, Mrs Dombey,' he continued, after a few moments, during which, in his increasing haughtiness, he had improved on his idea, 'I may not find it necessary ever to intrust Mr Carker with any message of objection or remonstrance to you; but as it would be derogatory to my position and reputation to be frequently holding trivial disputes with a lady upon whom I have conferred the highest distinction that it is in my power to bestow, I shall not scruple to avail myself of his services if I see occasion.'

'And now,' he thought, rising in his moral magnificence, and rising a stiffer and more impenetrable man than ever, 'she knows me and my resolution.'

The hand that had so pressed the bracelet was laid heavily upon her breast, but she looked at him still, with an unaltered face, and said in a low voice:

'Wait! For God's sake! I must speak to you.'

Why did she not, and what was the inward struggle that rendered her incapable of doing so, for minutes, while, in the strong constraint she put upon her face, it was as fixed as any statue's – looking upon him with neither yielding nor unyielding, liking nor hatred, pride nor humility: nothing but a searching gaze?

'Did I ever tempt you to seek my hand? Did I ever use any art to win you? Was I ever more conciliating to you when you pursued me, than I have been since our marriage? Was I ever other to you than I am?'

'It is wholly unnecessary, madam,' said Mr Dombey, 'to enter upon such discussions.'

'Did you think I loved you? Did you know I did not? Did you ever care, Man! for my heart, or propose to yourself to win the worthless thing? Was there any poor pretence of any in our bargain? Upon your side, or on mine?'

'These questions,' said Mr Dombey, 'are all wide of the purpose, madam.'

She moved between him and the door to prevent his going away, and drawing her majestic figure to its height, looked steadily upon him still.

'You answer each of them. You answer me before I speak, I see. How can you help it; you who know the miserable truth as well as I? Now, tell me. If I loved you to devotion, could I do more than render up my whole will and being to you, as you have just demanded? If my heart were pure and all untried, and you its idol, could you ask more; could you have more?'

'Possibly not, madam,' he returned coolly.

'You know how different I am. You see me looking on you now, and you can read the warmth of passion for you that is breathing in my face.' Not a curl of the proud lip, not a flash of the dark eye, nothing but the same intent and searching look, accompanied these words. 'You know my general history. You have spoken of my mother. Do you think you can degrade, or bend or break, *me* to submission and obedience?'

Mr Dombey smiled, as he might have smiled at an inquiry whether he thought he could raise ten thousand pounds.

'If there is anything unusual here,' she said, with a slight motion of her hand before her brow, which did not for a moment flinch from its immovable, and otherwise expressionless gaze, 'as I know there are unusual feelings here,' raising the hand she pressed upon her bosom, and heavily returning it, 'consider that there is no common meaning in the appeal I am going to make you. Yes, for I am going;' she said it as in prompt reply to something in his face; 'to appeal to you.'

Mr Dombey, with a slightly condescending bend of his chin that rustled and crackled his stiff cravat, sat down on a sofa that was near him, to hear the appeal.

'If you can believe that I am of such a nature now,' – he fancied he saw tears glistening in her eyes, and he thought, complacently, that he had forced them from her, though none fell on her cheek, and she regarded him as steadily as ever, – 'as would make what I now say almost incredible to myself, said to any man who had become my husband, but, above all, said to you, you may, perhaps, attach the greater weight to it. In the dark end to which we are tending, and may come, we shall not involve ourselves alone (that might not be much) but others.'

Others! He knew at whom that word pointed, and frowned heavily.

'I speak to you for the sake of others. Also your own sake; and for mine. Since our marriage, you have been arrogant to me; and I have repaid you in kind. You have shown to me and every one around us, every day and hour, that you think I am graced and distinguished by your alliance. I do not think so, and have shown that too. It seems you do not understand, or (so far as your power can go) intend that each of us shall take a separate course; and you expect from me instead, a homage you will never have.'

Although her face was still the same, there was emphatic confirmation of this 'Never' in the very breath she drew.

'I feel no tenderness towards you; that you know. You would care nothing for it, if I did or could. I know as well that you feel none towards me. But we are linked together; and in the knot that ties us, as I have said, others are bound up. We must both die; we are both connected with the dead already, each by a little child. Let us forbear.'

Mr Dombey took a long respiration, as if he would have said, Oh! was *this* all!

'There is no wealth,' she went on, turning paler as she watched him, while her eyes grew yet more lustrous in their earnestness, 'that could buy these words of me, and the meaning that belongs to them. Once cast away as idle breath, no wealth or power can bring them back. I mean them; I have weighed them; and I will be true to what I undertake. If you will promise to forbear on your part, I will promise to forbear on mine. We are a most unhappy pair, in whom, from different causes, every sentiment that blesses marriage, or justifies it, is rooted out; but in the course of time, some friendship, or some fitness for each other, may arise between us. I will try to hope so, if you will make the endeavour too; and I will look forward to a better and a happier use of age than I have made of youth or prime.'

Throughout she had spoken in a low plain voice, that neither rose nor fell; ceasing, she dropped the hand with which she had enforced herself to be so passionless and distinct, but not the eyes with which she had so steadily observed him.

'Madam,' said Mr Dombey, with his utmost dignity, 'I cannot entertain any proposal of this extraordinary nature.'

She looked at him yet, without the least change.

'I cannot,' said Mr Dombey, rising as he spoke, 'consent to temporise or treat with you, Mrs Dombey, upon a subject as to which you are in possession of my opinions and expectations. I have stated my *ultimatum*, madam, and have only to request your very serious attention to it.'

To see the face change to its old expression, deepened in intensity! To see the eyes droop as from some mean and odious object! To see the lighting of the haughty brow! To see scorn, anger, indignation, and abhorrence starting into sight, and the pale blank earnestness vanish like a mist! He could not choose but look, although he looked to his dismay.

'Go, Sir!' she said, pointing with an imperious hand towards the door. 'Our first and last confidence is at an end. Nothing can make us stranger to each other than we are henceforth.'

'I shall take my rightful course, madam,' said Mr Dombey, 'undeterred, you may be sure, by any general declamation.'

She turned her back upon him, and, without replying, sat down before her glass.

'I place my reliance on your improved sense of duty and more correct feeling, and better reflection, madam,' said Mr Dombey.

She answered not one word. He saw no more expression of any heed of him, in the mirror, than if he had been an unseen spider on the wall, or beetle on the floor, or rather, than if he had been the one or other, seen and crushed when she last turned from him, and forgotten among the ignominious and dead vermin of the ground.

He looked back, as he went out of the door, upon the well-lighted and luxurious room, the beautiful and glittering objects everywhere displayed, the shape of Edith in its rich dress seated before her glass, and the face of Edith as the glass presented it to him; and betook himself to his old chamber of cogitation, carrying away with him a vivid picture in his mind of all these things, and a rambling and unaccountable speculation (such as sometimes comes into a man's head) how they would all look when he saw them next.

For the rest, Mr Dombey was very taciturn, and very dignified, and very confident of carrying out his purpose; and remained so.

He did not design accompanying the family to Brighton; but he graciously informed Cleopatra at breakfast, on the morning of departure, which arrived a day or two afterwards, that he might be expected down, soon. There was no time to be lost in getting Cleopatra to any place recommended as being salutary; for, indeed, she seemed upon the wane, and turning of the earth, earthy.

Without having undergone any decided second attack of her malady, the old woman seemed to have crawled backward in her recovery from the first. She was more lean and shrunken, more uncertain in her imbecility, and made stranger confusions in her mind and memory. Among other symptoms of this last affliction, she fell into the habit of confounding the names of her two sons-in-law, the living and the deceased; and in general called Mr Dombey, either 'Grangeby,' or 'Domber,' or indifferently, both.

But she was youthful, very youthful still; and in her youthfulness appeared at breakfast, before going away, in a new bonnet made express, and a travelling robe that was embroidered and braided like an old baby's. It was not easy to put her into a fly-away bonnet[1] now, or to keep the bonnet in its place on the back of her poor nodding head, when it was got on. In this instance, it had not only the extraneous effect of being always on one side, but of being perpetually tapped on the crown by Flowers the maid, who attended in the background during breakfast to perform that duty.

'Now, my dearest Grangeby,' said Mrs Skewton, 'you must positively prom,' she cut some of her words short, and cut out others altogether, 'come down very soon.'

'I said just now, madam,' returned Mr Dombey, loudly and laboriously, 'that I am coming in a day or two.'

'Bless you, Domber!'

Here the Major, who was come to take leave of the ladies, and who was staring through his apoplectic eyes at Mrs Skewton's face, with the disinterested composure of an immortal being, said:

'Begad, ma'am, you don't ask old Joe to come!'

'Sterious wretch, who's he?' lisped Cleopatra. But a tap on the bonnet from Flowers seeming to jog her memory, she added, 'Oh! You mean yourself, you naughty creature!'

'Devilish queer, Sir,' whispered the Major to Mr Dombey. 'Bad case. Never *did* wrap up enough;' the Major being buttoned to the chin. 'Why, who should J. B. mean by Joe, but old Joe Bagstock – Joseph – your slave – Joe, ma'am? Here! Here's the man! Here are the Bagstock bellows, ma'am!' cried the Major, striking himself a sounding blow on the chest.

'My dearest Edith – Grangeby – it's most trordinry thing,' said Cleopatra, pettishly, 'the Major—'

'Bagstock! J. B.!' cried the Major, seeing that she faltered for his name.

'Well, it don't matter,' said Cleopatra. 'Edith, my love, you know I never could remember names – what was it? oh! – most trordinry thing that so many people want to come down to see me. I'm not going for long. I'm coming back. Surely they can wait, till I come back!'

Cleopatra looked all round the table as she said it, and appeared very uneasy.

'I won't have visitors – really don't want visitors,' she said; 'little repose – and all that sort of thing – is what I quire. No odious brutes must proach me till I've shaken off this numbness,' and in a grisly resumption of her coquettish ways, she made a dab at the Major with her fan, but overset Mr Dombey's breakfast cup instead, which was in quite a different direction.

Then she called for Withers, and charged him to see particularly that word was left about some trivial alterations in her room, which must be all made before she came back, and which must be set about immediately, as there was no saying how soon she might come back; for she had a great many engagements, and all sorts of people to call upon. Withers received these directions with becoming deference, and gave his guarantee for their execution, but when he withdrew a pace or two behind her, it appeared as if he couldn't help looking strangely at the Major, who couldn't help looking strangely at Mr Dombey, who couldn't help looking strangely at Cleopatra, who couldn't help nodding her bonnet over one eye, and rattling her knife and fork upon her plate in using them, as if she were playing castanets.

Edith alone never lifted her eyes to any face at the table, and never seemed dismayed by anything her mother said or did. She listened to her disjointed talk, or at least, turned her head towards her when addressed; replied in a few low words when necessary; and sometimes stopped her when she was rambling, or brought her thoughts back with a monosyllable, to the point from which they had strayed. The mother, however unsteady in other things, was constant in this – that she was always observant of her. She would look at the beautiful face, in its marble stillness and severity, now with a kind of fearful admiration; now in a giggling foolish effort to move it to a smile; now with capricious tears and jealous shakings of her head, as imagining herself neglected by it; always with an attraction towards it, that never fluctuated like her other ideas, but had constant possession of her. From Edith she would sometimes look at Florence, and back again at Edith, in a manner that was wild enough; and sometimes she would try to look elsewhere, as if to escape from her daughter's face; but back to it she seemed forced to come, although it never sought hers unless sought, or troubled her with one single glance.

The breakfast concluded, Mrs Skewton, affecting to lean girlishly upon the Major's arm, but heavily supported on the other side by Flowers, the maid, and propped up behind by Withers the page, was conducted to the carriage, which was to take her, Florence, and Edith to Brighton.

'And is Joseph absolutely banished?' said the Major, thrusting in his purple face over the steps. 'Damme, ma'am, is Cleopatra so hard-hearted as to forbid her faithful Antony Bagstock to approach the presence?'

'Go along!' said Cleopatra, 'I can't bear you. You shall see me when I come back, if you are very good.'

'Tell Joseph, he may live in hope, ma'am,' said the Major; 'or he'll die in despair.'

Cleopatra shuddered, and leaned back. 'Edith, my dear,' she said. 'Tell him—'

'What?'

'Such dreadful words,' said Cleopatra. 'He uses such dreadful words!'

Edith signed to him to retire, gave the word to go on, and left the objectionable major to Mr Dombey. To whom he returned, whistling.

'I'll tell you what, Sir,' said the Major, with his hands behind him, and his legs very wide asunder, 'a fair friend of ours has removed to Queer Street.'[2]

'What do you mean, Major?' inquired Mr Dombey.

'I mean to say, Dombey,' returned the Major, 'that you'll soon be an orphan-in-law.'

Mr Dombey appeared to relish this waggish description of himself so very little, that the Major wound up with the horse's cough, as an expression of gravity.

'Damme, Sir,' said the Major, 'there is no use in disguising a fact. Joe is blunt, Sir. That's his nature. If you take old Josh at all, you take him as you find him; and a de-vilish rusty, old rasper, of a close-toothed, J. B. file, you *do* find him. Dombey,' said the Major, 'your wife's mother is on the move, Sir.'

'I fear,' returned Mr Dombey, with much philosophy, 'that Mrs Skewton is shaken.'

'Shaken, Dombey!' said the Major. 'Smashed!'

'Change, however,' pursued Mr Dombey, 'and attention may do much yet.'

'Don't believe it, Sir,' returned the Major. 'Damme, Sir, she never wrapped up enough. If a man don't wrap up,' said the Major, taking in another button of his buff waistcoat, 'he has nothing to fall back upon. But some people *will* die. They *will* do it. Damme, they *will*. They're obstinate. I tell you what, Dombey, it may not be ornamental; it may not be refined; it may be rough and tough; but a little of the genuine old English Bagstock stamina, Sir, would do all the good in the world to the human breed.'

After imparting this precious piece of information, the Major, who was certainly true blue, whatever other endowments he may have possessed or wanted, coming within the 'genuine old English' classification, which has never been exactly ascertained, took his lobster-eyes and his apoplexy to the club, and choked there all day.

Cleopatra, at one time fretful, at another self-complacent, sometimes awake, sometimes asleep, and at all times juvenile, reached Brighton the same night, fell to pieces as usual, and was put away in bed; where a gloomy fancy might have pictured a more potent skeleton than the maid, who should have been one, watching at the rose-coloured curtains, which were carried down to shed their bloom upon her.

It was settled in high council of medical authority that she should take a carriage airing every day, and that it was important she should get out every day, and walk if she could. Edith was ready to attend her – always ready to attend her, with the same mechanical attention and immovable beauty – and they drove out alone; for Edith had an uneasiness in the presence of Florence, now that her mother was worse, and told Florence, with a kiss, that she would rather they two went alone.

Mrs Skewton, on one particular day, was in the irresolute, exacting, jealous temper that had developed itself on her recovery from her first attack. After sitting silent in the carriage watching Edith for some time, she took her hand and kissed it passionately. The hand was neither given nor withdrawn, but simply yielded to her raising of it, and being released, dropped down again, almost as if it were insensible. At this she began to whimper and moan, and say what a mother she had been, and how she was forgotten! This she continued to do at capricious intervals, even when they had alighted: when she herself was halting along with the joint support of Withers and a stick, and Edith was walking by her side, and the carriage slowly following at a little distance.

It was a bleak, lowering, windy day, and they were out upon the Downs with nothing but a bare sweep of land between them and the sky. The mother, with a querulous satisfaction in the monotony of her complaint, was still repeating it in a low voice from time to time, and the proud form of her daughter moved beside her slowly, when there came advancing over a dark ridge before them, two other figures, which in the distance, were so like an exaggerated imitation of their own, that Edith stopped.

Almost as she stopped, the two figures stopped; and that one which to Edith's thinking was like a distorted shadow of her mother, spoke to the other, earnestly, and with a pointing hand towards them. That one seemed inclined to turn back, but the other, in which Edith recognised enough that was like herself to strike her with an unusual feeling, not quite free from fear, came on; and then they came on together.

The greater part of this observation, she made while walking towards them, for her stoppage had been momentary. Nearer observation showed her that they were poorly dressed, as wanderers about the country; that the younger woman carried knitted work or some such goods for sale; and that the old one toiled on empty-handed.

And yet, however far removed she was in dress, in dignity, in beauty, Edith could not but compare the younger woman with herself, still. It may have been that she saw upon her face some traces which she knew were lingering in her own soul, if not yet written on that index; but, as the woman came on, returning her gaze, fixing her shining eyes upon her, undoubtedly presenting something of her own air and stature, and appearing to reciprocate her own thoughts, she felt a chill creep over her, as if the day were darkening, and the wind were colder.

They had now come up. The old woman holding out her hand importunately, stopped to beg of Mrs Skewton. The younger one stopped too, and she and Edith looked in one another's eyes.

'What is it that you have to sell?' said Edith.

'Only this,' returned the woman, holding out her wares, without looking at them. 'I sold myself long ago.'

'My lady, don't believe her,' croaked the old woman to Mrs Skewton; 'don't believe what she says. She loves to talk like that. She's my handsome and undutiful daughter. She gives me nothing but reproaches, my lady, for all I have done for her. Look at her

A chance meeting

now, my lady, how she turns upon her poor old mother with her looks.'

As Mrs Skewton drew her purse out with a trembling hand, and eagerly fumbled for some money, which the other old woman greedily watched for – their heads all but touching, in their hurry and decrepitude – Edith interposed:

'I have seen you,' addressing the old woman, 'before.'

'Yes, my lady,' with a curtsey. 'Down in Warwickshire. The morning among the trees. When you wouldn't give me nothing. But the gentleman, *he* give me something! Oh, bless him, bless him!' mumbled the old woman, holding up her skinny hand, and grinning frightfully at her daughter.

'It's of no use attempting to stay me, Edith!' said Mrs Skewton, angrily anticipating an objection from her. 'You know nothing about it. I won't be dissuaded. I am sure this is an excellent woman, and a good mother.'

'Yes, my lady, yes,' chattered the old woman, holding out her avaricious hand. 'Thankee, my lady. Lord bless you, my lady. Sixpence more, my pretty lady, as a good mother yourself.'

'And treated undutifully enough, too, my good old creature, sometimes, I assure you,' said Mrs Skewton, whimpering. 'There! Shake hands with me. You're a very good old creature – full of what's-his-name – and all that. You're all affection and et cetera, an't you?'

'Oh, yes, my lady!'

'Yes, I'm sure you are; and so's that gentlemanly creature Grangeby. I must really shake hands with you again. And now you can go, you know; and I hope,' addressing the daughter, 'that you'll show more gratitude, and natural what's-its-name, and all the rest of it – but I never *did* remember names – for there never was a better mother than the good old creature's been to you. Come, Edith!'

As the ruin of Cleopatra tottered off whimpering, and wiping its eyes with a gingerly remembrance of rouge in their neighbourhood, the old woman hobbled another way, mumbling and counting her money. Not one word more, nor one other gesture, had been exchanged between Edith and the younger woman, but neither had removed her eyes from the other for a moment. They had remained confronted until now, when Edith, as awakening from a dream, passed slowly on.

'You're a handsome woman,' muttered her shadow, looking after her; 'but good looks won't save us. And you're a proud woman;

but pride won't save us. We had need to know each other when we meet again!'

CHAPTER 41

New Voices in the Waves

All is going on as it was wont. The waves are hoarse with repetition of their mystery; the dust lies piled upon the shore; the sea-birds soar and hover; the winds and clouds go forth upon their trackless flight; the white arms beckon, in the moonlight, to the invisible country far away.

With a tender melancholy pleasure, Florence finds herself again on the old ground so sadly trodden, yet so happily, and thinks of him in the quiet place, where he and she have many and many a time conversed together, with the water welling up about his couch. And now, as she sits pensive there, she hears in the wild low murmur of the sea, his little story told again, his very words repeated; and finds that all her life and hopes, and griefs, since – in the solitary house, and in the pageant it has changed to – have a portion in the burden of the marvellous song.

And gentle Mr Toots, who wanders at a distance, looking wistfully towards the figure that he dotes upon, and has followed there, but cannot in his delicacy disturb at such a time, likewise hears the requiem of little Dombey on the waters, rising and falling in the lulls of their eternal madrigal in praise of Florence. Yes! and he faintly understands, poor Mr Toots, that they are saying something of a time when he was sensible of being brighter and not addle-brained; and the tears rising in his eyes when he fears that he is dull and stupid now, and good for little but to be laughed at, diminish his satisfaction in their soothing reminder that he is relieved from present responsibility to the Chicken, by the absence of that game head of poultry in the country, training (at Toots's cost) for his great mill[1] with the Larkey Boy.

But Mr Toots takes courage, when they whisper a kind thought to him; and by slow degrees and with many indecisive stoppages on the way, approaches Florence. Stammering and blushing, Mr Toots affects amazement when he comes near her, and says (having followed close on the carriage in which she travelled, every inch of the way from London, loving even to be choked by the dust of its wheels) that he never was so surprised in all his life.

'And you've brought Diogenes, too, Miss Dombey!' says Mr Toots, thrilled through and through by the touch of the small hand so pleasantly and frankly given him.

No doubt Diogenes is there, and no doubt Mr Toots has reason to observe him, for he comes straightway at Mr Toots's legs, and tumbles over himself in the desperation with which he makes at him, like a very dog of Montargis.[2] But he is checked by his sweet mistress.

'Down, Di, down. Don't you remember who first made us friends, Di? For shame!'

Oh! Well may Di lay his loving cheek against her hand, and run off, and run back, and run round her, barking, and run headlong at anybody coming by, to show his devotion. Mr Toots would run headlong at anybody, too. A military gentleman goes past, and Mr Toots would like nothing better than to run at him, full tilt.

'Diogenes is quite in his native air, isn't he, Miss Dombey?' says Mr Toots.

Florence assents, with a grateful smile.

'Miss Dombey,' says Mr Toots, 'beg your pardon, but if you would like to walk to Blimber's, I – I'm going there.'

Florence puts her arm in that of Mr Toots without a word, and they walk away together, with Diogenes going on before. Mr Toots's legs shake under him; and though he is splendidly dressed, he feels misfits, and sees wrinkles, in the masterpieces of Burgess and Co., and wishes he had put on that brightest pair of boots.

Doctor Blimber's house, outside, has as scholastic and studious an air as ever: and up there is the window where she used to look for the pale face, and where the pale face brightened when it saw her, and the wasted little hand waved kisses as she passed. The door is opened by the same weak-eyed young man, whose imbecility of grin at sight of Mr Toots is feebleness of character personified. They are shown into the Doctor's study, where blind Homer and Minerva give them audience as of yore, to the sober ticking of the great clock in the hall; and where the globes stand still in their accustomed places, as if the world were stationary too, and nothing in it ever perished in obedience to the universal law, that, while it keeps it on the roll, calls everything to earth.

And here is Doctor Blimber, with his learned legs; and here is Mrs Blimber, with her sky-blue cap; and here is Cornelia, with her sandy little row of curls, and her bright spectacles, still working like a sexton in the graves of languages. Here is the table upon which he sat forlorn and strange, the 'new boy' of the school; and hither comes the distant cooing of the old boys, at their old lives in the old room on the old principle!

'Toots,' says Doctor Blimber, 'I am very glad to see you, Toots.'

Mr Toots chuckles in reply.

'Also to see you, Toots, in such good company,' says Doctor Blimber.

Mr Toots, with a scarlet visage, explains that he has met Miss Dombey by accident, and that Miss Dombey wishing, like himself, to see the old place, they have come together.

'You will like,' says Doctor Blimber, 'to step among our young friends, Miss Dombey, no doubt. All fellow-students of yours, Toots, once. I think we have no new disciples in our little portico, my dear,' says Doctor Blimber to Cornelia, 'since Mr Toots left us.'

'Except Bitherstone,' returns Cornelia.

'Aye, truly,' says the Doctor. 'Bitherstone is new to Mr Toots.'

New to Florence, too, almost; for, in the schoolroom, Bitherstone – no longer Master Bitherstone of Mrs Pipchin's – shows in collars and a neckcloth, and wears a watch. But Bitherstone, born beneath some Bengal star of ill-omen, is extremely inky; and his Lexicon has got so dropsical[3] from constant reference, that it won't shut, and yawns as if it really could not bear to be so bothered. So does Bitherstone its master, forced at Doctor Blimber's highest pressure; but in the yawn of Bitherstone there is malice and snarl, and he has been heard to say that he wishes he could catch 'old Blimber' in India. He'd precious soon find himself carried up the country by a few of his (Bitherstone's) Coolies, and handed over to the Thugs;[4] he can tell him that.

Briggs is still grinding in the mill of knowledge; and Tozer, too; and Johnson, too; and all the rest; the older pupils being principally engaged in forgetting, with prodigious labour, everything they knew when they were younger. All are as polite and as pale as ever; and among them, Mr Feeder, B.A., with his bony hand and bristly head, is still hard at it: with his Herodotus[5] stop on just at present, and his other barrels on a shelf behind him.

A mighty sensation is created, even among these grave young gentlemen, by a visit from the emancipated Toots; who is regarded with a kind of awe, as one who has passed the Rubicon,[6] and is pledged never to come back, and concerning the cut of whose clothes, and fashion of whose jewellery, whispers go about, behind hands; the bilious Bitherstone, who is not of Mr Toots's time, affecting to despise the latter to the smaller boys, and saying he knows better, and that he should like to see him coming that sort of thing in Bengal, where his mother has got an emerald belonging to him that was taken out of the footstool of a Rajah. Come now![7]

Bewildering emotions are awakened also by the sight of Florence, with whom every young gentleman immediately falls in love, again: except, as aforesaid, the bilious Bitherstone, who declines to do so, out of contradiction. Black jealousies of Mr Toots arise, and Briggs is of opinion that he an't so very old after all. But this disparaging insinuation is speedily made nought by Mr Toots saying aloud to Mr Feeder, B.A., 'How are you, Feeder?' and asking him to come and dine with him to-day at the Bedford; in right of which feats he might set up as Old Parr,[8] if he chose, unquestioned.

There is much shaking of hands, and much bowing, and a great desire on the part of each young gentleman to take Toots down in Miss Dombey's good graces; and then, Mr Toots having bestowed a chuckle on his old desk, Florence and he withdraw with Mrs Blimber and Cornelia; and Doctor Blimber is heard to observe behind them as he comes out last, and shuts the door, 'Gentlemen, we will now resume our studies.' For that and little else is what the Doctor hears the sea say, or has heard it saying all his life.

Florence then steals away and goes upstairs to the old bedroom with Mrs Blimber and Cornelia; Mr Toots, who feels that neither he nor anybody else is wanted there, stands talking to the Doctor at the study-door, or rather hearing the Doctor talk to him, and wondering how he ever thought the study a great sanctuary, and the Doctor, with his round turned legs like a clerical pianoforte, an awful[9] man. Florence soon comes down and takes leave; Mr Toots takes leave; and Diogenes who has been worrying the weak-eyed young man pitilessly all the time, shoots out at the door, and barks a glad defiance down the cliff; while 'Melia, and another of the Doctor's female domestics, look out of an upper window, laughing 'at that there Toots,' and saying of Miss Dombey, 'But really though, now – ain't she like her brother, only prettier?'

Mr Toots, who saw when Florence came down that there were tears upon her face, is desperately anxious and uneasy and at first fears that he did wrong in proposing the visit. But he is soon relieved by her saying she is very glad to have been there again, and by her talking quite cheerfully about it all, as they walked on by the sea. What with the voices there, and her sweet voice, when they come near Mr Dombey's house, and Mr Toots must leave her, he is so enslaved that he has not a scrap of free-will left; when she gives him her hand at parting, he cannot let it go.

'Miss Dombey, I beg your pardon,' says Mr Toots, in a sad fluster, 'but if you would allow me to – to—'

The smiling and unconscious look of Florence brings him to a dead stop.

'If you would allow me to – if you would not consider it a liberty, Miss Dombey, if I was to – without any encouragement at all, if I was to hope, you know,' says Mr Toots.

Florence looks at him inquiringly.

'Miss Dombey,' says Mr Toots, who feels that he is in for it now, 'I really am in that state of adoration of you that I don't know what to do with myself. I am the most deplorable wretch. If it wasn't at the corner of the Square at present, I should go down on my knees, and beg and entreat of you, without any encouragement at all, just to let me hope that I may – may think it possible that you—'

'Oh, if you please, don't!' cries Florence, for the moment quite alarmed and distressed. 'Oh, pray don't, Mr Toots. Stop, if you please. Don't say any more. As a kindness and a favour to me, don't.'

Mr Toots is dreadfully abashed, and his mouth opens.

'You have been so good to me,' says Florence, 'I am so grateful to you, I have such reason to like you for being a kind friend to me, and I do like you so much;' and there the ingenuous face smiles upon him with the pleasantest look of honesty in the world; 'that I am sure you are only going to say good-bye!'

'Certainly, Miss Dombey,' says Mr Toots, 'I – I – that's exactly what I mean. It's of no consequence.'

'Good-bye!' cries Florence.

'Good-bye, Miss Dombey!' stammers Mr Toots. 'I hope you won't think anything about it. It's – it's of no consequence, thank you. It's not of the least consequence in the world.'

Poor Mr Toots goes home to his Hotel in a state of desperation, locks himself into his bedroom, flings himself upon his bed, and lies there for a long time; as if it were of the greatest consequence, nevertheless. But Mr Feeder, B.A., is coming to dinner, which happens well for Mr Toots, or there is no knowing when he might get up again. Mr Toots is obliged to get up to receive him, and to give him hospitable entertainment.

And the generous influence of that social virtue, hospitality (to make no mention of wine and good cheer), opens Mr Toots's heart, and warms him to conversation. He does not tell Mr Feeder, B.A., what passed at the corner of the Square; but when Mr Feeder asks him 'When it is to come off?' Mr Toots replies, 'that there are certain subjects – ' which brings Mr Feeder down a peg or two immediately. Mr Toots adds, that he don't know what right Blimber had to notice his being in Miss Dombey's company, and that if he thought he meant impudence by it, he'd have him out,[10] Doctor or no Doctor; but he supposes it's only his ignorance. Mr Feeder says he has no doubt of it.

Mr Feeder, however, as an intimate friend, is not excluded from the subject. Mr Toots merely requires that it should be mentioned mysteriously, and with feeling. After a few glasses of wine, he gives Miss Dombey's health, observing, 'Feeder, you have no idea of the sentiments with which I propose that toast.' Mr Feeder replies, 'Oh, yes, I have, my dear Toots; and greatly they redound to your honour, old boy.' Mr Feeder is then agitated by friendship, and shakes hands; and says, if ever Toots wants a brother, he knows where to find him, either by post or parcel. Mr Feeder likewise says, that if he may advise, he would recommend Mr Toots to learn the guitar, or, at least the flute; for women like music, when you are paying your addresses to 'em, and he has found the advantage of it himself.

This brings Mr Feeder, B.A., to the confession that he has his eye upon Cornelia Blimber. He informs Mr Toots that he don't object to spectacles, and that if the Doctor were to do the handsome thing and give up the business, why, there they are – provided for. He says it's his opinion that when a man has made a handsome sum by his business, he is bound to give it up; and that Cornelia would be an assistance in it which any man might be proud of. Mr Toots replies by launching wildly out into Miss Dombey's praises, and by insinuations that sometimes he thinks he should like to blow his brains out. Mr Feeder strongly urges that it would be a rash attempt, and shows him, as a reconcilement to existence, Cornelia's portrait, spectacles and all.

Thus these quiet spirits pass the evening; and when it has yielded place to night, Mr Toots walks home with Mr Feeder, and parts with him at Doctor Blimber's door. But Mr Feeder only goes up the steps, and when Mr Toots is gone, comes down again, to stroll upon the beach alone, and think about his prospects. Mr Feeder plainly hears the waves informing him, as he loiters along, that Doctor Blimber will give up the business; and he feels a soft romantic pleasure in looking at the outside of the house, and thinking that the Doctor will first paint it, and put it into thorough repair.

Mr Toots is likewise roaming up and down, outside the casket that contains his jewel; and in a deplorable condition of mind, and not unsuspected by the police, gazes at a window where he sees a light, and which he has no doubt is Florence's. But it is not, for that is Mrs Skewton's room; and while Florence, sleeping in another chamber, dreams lovingly, in the midst of the old scenes, and their old associations live again, the figure which in grim reality is substituted for the patient boy's on the same theatre, once more to connect it – but how differently! – with decay and death, is stretched there, wakeful and complaining. Ugly and haggard it lies upon its bed of unrest; and by it, in the terror of her unimpassioned loveliness – for it *has* terror in the sufferer's failing eyes – sits Edith. What do the waves say, in the stillness of the night, to them?

'Edith, what is that stone arm raised to strike me? Don't you see it?'

'There is nothing, mother, but your fancy.'

'But my fancy! Everything is my fancy. Look! Is it possible that you don't see it?'

'Indeed, mother, there is nothing. Should I sit unmoved, if there were any such thing there?'

'Unmoved?' looking wildly at her – 'it's gone now – and why are you so unmoved? That is not my fancy, Edith. It turns me cold to see you sitting at my side.'

'I am sorry, mother.'

'Sorry! You seem always sorry. But it is not for me!'

With that, she cries; and tossing her restless head from side to side upon her pillow, runs on about neglect, and the mother she has been, and the mother the good old creature was, whom they met, and the cold return the daughters of such mothers make. In the midst of her incoherence, she stops, looks at her daughter, cries out that her wits are going, and hides her face upon the bed.

Edith, in compassion, bends over her and speaks to her. The sick old woman clutches her round the neck, and says, with a look of horror,

'Edith! we are going home soon; going back. You mean that I shall go home again?'

'Yes, mother, yes.'

'And what he said – what's-his-name, I never could remember names – Major – that dreadful word, when we came away – it's not true? Edith!' with a shriek and a stare, 'it's not *that* that is the matter with me.'

Night after night, the lights burn in the window, and the figure lies upon the bed, and Edith sits beside it, and the restless waves are calling to them both the whole night long. Night after night, the waves are hoarse with repetition of their mystery; the dust lies piled upon the shore; the sea-birds soar and hover; the winds and clouds are on their trackless flight; the white arms beckon, in the moonlight, to the invisible country far away.

And still the sick old woman looks into the corner, where the stone arm – part of a figure of some tomb, she says – is raised to strike her. At last it falls; and then a dumb old woman lies upon the bed, and she is crooked and shrunk up, and half of her is dead.

Such is the figure, painted and patched for the sun to mock, that is drawn slowly through the crowd from day to day; looking, as it goes, for the good old creature who was such a mother, and making mouths as it peers among the crowd in vain. Such is the figure that is often wheeled down to the margin of the sea, and stationed there; but on which no wind can blow freshness, and for which the murmur of the ocean has no soothing word. She lies and listens to it by the hour; but its speech is dark and gloomy to her, and a dread is on her face, and when her eyes wander over the expanse, they see but a broad stretch of desolation between earth and heaven.

Florence she seldom sees, and when she does, is angry with and mows at. Edith is beside her always, and keeps Florence away; and Florence, in her bed at night, trembles at the thought of death in such a shape, and often wakes and listens, thinking it has come. No one attends on her but Edith. It is better that few eyes should see her; and her daughter watches alone by the bedside.

A shadow even on that shadowed face, a sharpening even of the sharpened features, and a thickening of the veil before the eyes into a pall that shuts out the dim world, is come. Her wandering hands upon the coverlet join feebly palm to palm, and move towards her daughter; and a voice not like hers, not like any voice that speaks our mortal language – says, 'For I nursed you!'

Edith, without a tear, kneels down to bring her voice closer to the sinking head, and answers:

'Mother, can you hear me?'

Staring wide, she tries to nod in answer.

'Can you recollect the night before I married?'

The head is motionless, but it expresses somehow that she does.

'I told you then that I forgave your part in it, and prayed God to forgive my own. I told you that the past was at an end between us. I say so now, again. Kiss me, mother.'

Edith touches the white lips, and for a moment all is still. A moment afterwards, her mother, with her girlish laugh, and the skeleton of the Cleopatra manner, rises in her bed.

Draw the rose-coloured curtains. There is something else upon its flight besides the wind and clouds. Draw the rose-coloured curtains close!

Intelligence of the event is sent to Mr Dombey in town, who waits upon Cousin Feenix (not yet able to make up his mind for Baden-Baden), who has just received it too. A good-natured creature like Cousin Feenix is the very man for a marriage or a funeral, and his position in the family renders it right that he should be consulted.

'Dombey,' said Cousin Feenix, 'upon my soul, I am very much shocked to see you on such a melancholy occasion. My poor aunt! She was a devilish lively woman.'

Mr Dombey replies, 'Very much so.'

'And made up,' says Cousin Feenix, 'really young, you know, considering. I am sure, on the day of your marriage, I thought she was good for another twenty years. In point of fact, I said so to a man at Brooks's – little Billy Joper – you know him, no doubt – man with a glass in his eye?'

Mr Dombey bows a negative. 'In reference to the obsequies,' he hints, 'whether there is any suggestion—'

'Well, upon my life,' says Cousin Feenix, stroking his chin, which he has just enough of hand below his wristbands to do; 'I really don't know. There's a Mausoleum down at my place, in the park, but I'm afraid it's in bad repair, and, in point of fact, in a devil of a state. But for being a little out at elbows, I should have had it put to rights; but I believe the people come and make pic-nic parties there inside the iron railings.'

Mr Dombey is clear that this won't do.

'There's an uncommon good church in the village,' says Cousin Feenix, thoughtfully; 'pure specimen of the Anglo-Norman style, and admirably well sketched too by Lady Jane Finchbury – woman with tight stays – but they've spoilt it with whitewash, I understand, and it's a long journey.'

'Perhaps Brighton itself,' Mr Dombey suggests.

'Upon my honour, Dombey, I don't think we could do better,' says Cousin Feenix. 'It's on the spot, you see, and a very cheerful place.'

'And when,' hints Mr Dombey, 'would it be convenient?'

'I shall make a point,' says Cousin Feenix, 'of pledging myself for any day you think best. I shall have great pleasure (melancholy pleasure, of course) in following my poor aunt to the confines of the – in point of fact, to the grave,' says Cousin Feenix, failing in the other turn of speech.

'Would Monday do for leaving town?' says Mr Dombey.

'Monday would suit me to perfection,' replies Cousin Feenix. Therefore Mr Dombey arranges to take Cousin Feenix down on that day, and presently takes his leave, attended to the stairs by Cousin Feenix, who says, at parting, 'I'm really excessively sorry, Dombey, that you should have so much trouble about it;' to which Mr Dombey answers, 'Not at all.'

At the appointed time, Cousin Feenix and Mr Dombey meet, and go down to Brighton, and representing, in their two selves, all the other mourners for the deceased lady's loss, attend her remains to their place of rest. Cousin Feenix, sitting in the mourning-coach, recognises innumerable acquaintances on the road, but takes no other notice of them, in decorum, than checking them off aloud, as they go by, for Mr Dombey's information, as 'Tom Johnson. Man with cork leg from White's.[11] What, are *you* here, Tommy? Foley on a blood mare.[12] The Smalder girls' – and so forth. At the ceremony Cousin Feenix is depressed, observing that these are the occasions to make a man think, in point of fact, that he is getting shaky; and his eyes are really moistened, when it is over. But he soon recovers; and so do the rest of Mrs Skewton's relatives and friends, of whom the Major continually tells the club that she never did wrap up enough, while the young lady with the back, who has so much trouble with her eyelids, says, with a little scream, that she must have been enormously old, and that she died of all kinds of horrors, and you mustn't mention it.

So Edith's mother lies unmentioned of her dear friends, who are deaf to the waves that are hoarse with repetition of their mystery, and blind to the dust that is piled upon the shore, and to the white arms that are beckoning, in the moonlight, to the invisible country far away. But all goes on, as it was wont, upon the margin of the unknown sea; and Edith standing there alone, and listening to its waves, has dank weed cast up at her feet, to strew her path in life withal.

CHAPTER 42

Confidential and Accidental

Attired no more in Captain Cuttle's sable slops and sou'wester hat, but dressed in a substantial suit of brown livery, which, while it affected to be a very sober and demure livery indeed, was really as self-satisfied and confident a one as tailor need desire to make, Rob the Grinder, thus transformed as to his outer man, and all regardless within of the Captain and the Midshipman, except when he devoted a few minutes of his leisure time to crowing over those inseparable worthies, and recalling, with much applauding music from that brazen instrument, his conscience, the triumphant manner in which he had disembarrassed himself of their company, now served his patron, Mr Carker. Inmate of Mr Carker's house, and serving about his person, Rob kept his round eyes on the white teeth with fear and trembling, and felt that he had need to open them wider than ever.

He could not have quaked more, through his whole being, before the teeth, though he had come into the service of some powerful enchanter, and they had been his strongest spell. The boy had a sense of power and authority in this patron of his that engrossed his whole attention and exacted his most implicit submission and obedience. He hardly considered himself safe in thinking about him when he was absent, lest he should feel himself immediately taken by the throat again, as on the morning when he first became bound to him, and should see every one of the teeth finding him out, and taxing him with every fancy of his mind. Face to face with him, Rob had no more doubt that Mr Carker read his secret thoughts, or that he could read them by the least exertion of his will if he were so inclined, than he had that Mr Carker saw him when he looked at him. The ascendency was so complete, and held him in such enthralment, that, hardly daring to think at all, but with his mind filled with a constantly dilating impression of his patron's irresistible command over him, and power of doing anything with him, he would stand watching his pleasure, and trying to anticipate his orders, in a state of mental suspension, as to all other things.

Rob had not informed himself perhaps – in his then state of mind it would have been an act of no common temerity to inquire – whether he yielded so completely to this influence in any part, because he had floating suspicions of his patron's being a master of certain treacherous arts in which he had himself been a poor scholar at the Grinders' School. But certainly Rob admired him, as well as feared him. Mr Carker, perhaps, was better acquainted with the sources of his power, which lost nothing by his management of it.

On the very night when he left the Captain's service, Rob, after disposing of his pigeons, and even making a bad bargain in his hurry, had gone straight down to Mr Carker's house and hotly presented himself before his new master with a glowing face that seemed to expect commendation.

'What, scapegrace!' said Mr Carker, glancing at his bundle. 'Have you left your situation and come to me?'

'Oh if you please, Sir,' faltered Rob, 'you said, you know, when I come here last—'

'*I* said,' returned Mr Carker, 'what did I say?'

'If you please, Sir, you didn't say nothing at all, Sir,' returned Rob, warned by the manner of this inquiry, and very much disconcerted.

His patron looked at him with a wide display of gums, and shaking his forefinger, observed:

'You'll come to an evil end, my vagabond friend, I foresee. There's ruin in store for you.'

'Oh if you please, don't, Sir!' cried Rob, with his legs trembling under him. 'I'm sure, Sir, I only want to work for you, Sir, and to wait upon you, Sir, and to do faithful whatever I'm bid, Sir.'

'You had better do faithfully whatever you are bid,' returned his patron, 'if you have anything to do with me.'

'Yes, I know that, Sir,' pleaded the submissive Rob; 'I'm sure of that, Sir. If you'll only be so good as try me, Sir! And if ever you find me out, Sir, doing anything against your wishes, I give you leave to kill me.'

'You dog!' said Mr Carker, leaning back in his chair, and smiling at him serenely. 'That's nothing to what I'd do to you if you tried to deceive me.'

'Yes, Sir,' replied the abject Grinder, 'I'm sure you would be down upon me dreadful, Sir. I wouldn't attempt for to go and do it, Sir, not if I was bribed with golden guineas.'

Thoroughly checked in his expectations of commendation, the crestfallen Grinder stood looking at his patron, and vainly endeavouring not to look at him, with the uneasiness which a cur will often manifest in a similar situation.

'So you have left your old service, and come here to ask me to take you into mine, eh?' said Mr Carker.

'Yes, if you please, Sir,' returned Rob, who, in doing so, had acted on his patron's own instructions, but dared not justify himself by the least insinuation to that effect.

'Well!' said Mr Carker. 'You know me, boy?'

'Please, Sir, yes, Sir,' returned Rob, fumbling with his hat, and still fixed by Mr Carker's eye, and fruitlessly endeavouring to unfix himself.

Mr Carker nodded. 'Take care, then!'

Rob expressed in a number of short bows his lively understanding of this caution, and was bowing himself back to the door, greatly relieved by the prospect of getting on the outside of it, when his patron stopped him.

'Halloa!' he cried, calling him roughly back. 'You have been – shut that door.'

Rob obeyed as if his life had depended on his alacrity.

'You have been used to eaves-dropping. Do you know what that means?'

'Listening, Sir?' Rob hazarded, after some embarrassed reflection.

His patron nodded. 'And watching, and so forth.'

'I wouldn't do such a thing here, Sir,' answered Rob; 'upon my word and honour, I wouldn't, Sir, I wish I may die if I would, Sir, for anything that could be promised to me. I should consider it is as much as all the world was worth, to offer to do such a thing, unless I was ordered, Sir.'

'You had better not. You have been used, too, to babbling and tattling,' said his patron with perfect coolness. 'Beware of that here, or you're a lost rascal,' and he smiled again, and again cautioned him with his forefinger.

The Grinder's breath came short and thick with consternation. He tried to protest the purity of his intentions, but could only stare at the smiling gentleman in a stupor of submission, with which the smiling gentleman seemed well enough satisfied, for he ordered him downstairs, after observing him for some moments in silence, and gave him to understand that he was retained in his employment.

This was the manner of Rob the Grinder's engagement by Mr Carker, and his awe-stricken devotion to that gentleman had strengthened and increased, if possible, with every minute of his service.

It was a service of some months' duration, when early one morning, Rob opened the garden gate to Mr Dombey, who was come to breakfast with his master, by appointment. At the same moment his master himself came hurrying forth to receive the distinguished guest, and give him welcome with all his teeth. 'I never thought,' said Carker, when he had assisted him to alight from his horse, 'to see you here, I'm sure. This is an extraordinary day in my calendar. No occasion is very special to a man like you, who may do anything; but to a man like me, the case is widely different.'

'You have a tasteful place here, Carker,' said Mr Dombey, condescending to stop upon the lawn, to look about him.

'You can afford to say so,' returned Carker. 'Thank you.'

'Indeed,' said Mr Dombey, in his lofty patronage, 'any one might say so. As far as it goes, it is a very commodious and well-arranged place – quite elegant.'

'As far as it goes, truly,' returned Carker, with an air of disparagement. 'It wants that qualification. Well! we have said enough about it; and though you can afford to praise it, I thank you none the less. Will you walk in?'

Mr Dombey, entering the house, noticed, as he had reason to do, the complete arrangement of the rooms, and the numerous contrivances for comfort and effect that abounded there. Mr Carker, in his ostentation of humility, received this notice with a deferential smile, and said he understood its delicate meaning, and appreciated it, but in truth the cottage was good enough for one in his position – better, perhaps, than such a man should occupy, poor as it was.

'But perhaps to you, who are so far removed, it really does look better than it is,' he said, with his false mouth distended to its fullest stretch. 'Just as monarchs imagine attractions in the lives of beggars.'

He directed a sharp glance and a sharp smile at Mr Dombey as he spoke, and a sharper glance, and a sharper smile yet, when Mr Dombey, drawing himself up before the fire, in the attitude so often copied by his second in command, looked round at the pictures on the walls. Cursorily as his cold eye wandered over them, Carker's keen glance accompanied his, and kept pace with his, marking exactly where it went, and what it saw. As it rested on one picture in particular, Carker hardly seemed to breathe, his sidelong scrutiny was so catlike and vigilant, but the eye of his great chief passed from that, as from the others, and appeared no more impressed by it than by the rest.

Carker looked at it – it was the picture that resembled Edith – as if it were a living thing; and with a wicked, silent laugh upon his face, that seemed in part addressed to it, though it was all derisive of the great man standing so unconscious beside him. Breakfast was soon set upon the table; and, inviting Mr Dombey to a chair which had its back towards this picture, he took his own seat opposite to it as usual.

Mr Dombey was even graver than it was his custom to be, and quite silent. The parrot, swinging in the gilded hoop within her gaudy cage, attempted in vain to attract notice, for Carker was too observant of his visitor to heed her; and the visitor, abstracted in meditation, looked fixedly, not to say sullenly, over his stiff neckcloth, without raising his eyes from the table-cloth. As to Rob, who was in attendance, all his faculties and energies were so locked up in observation of his master, that he scarcely ventured to give shelter to the thought that the visitor was the great gentleman before whom he had been carried as a certificate of the family health, in his childhood, and to whom he had been indebted for his leather smalls.

'Allow me,' said Carker suddenly, 'to ask how Mrs Dombey is?'

He leaned forward obsequiously, as he made the inquiry, with his chin resting on his hand; and at the same time his eyes went up to the picture, as if he said to it, 'Now, see, how I will lead him on!'

Mr Dombey reddened as he answered:

'Mrs Dombey is quite well. You remind me, Carker, of some conversation that I wish to have with you.'

'Robin, you can leave us,' said his master, at whose mild tones Robin started and disappeared, with his eyes fixed on his patron to the last. 'You don't remember that boy, of course?' he added, when the immeshed Grinder was gone.

'No,' said Mr Dombey, with magnificent indifference.

'Not likely that a man like you would. Hardly possible,' murmured Carker. 'But he is one of that family from whom you took a nurse. Perhaps you may remember having generously charged yourself with his education?'

'Is it that boy?' said Mr Dombey, with a frown. 'He does little credit to his education, I believe.'

'Why, he is a young rip, I am afraid,' returned Carker, with a shrug. 'He bears that character. But the truth is, I took him into my service because, being able to get no other employment, he conceived (had been taught at home, I dare say) that he had some sort of claim upon you, and was constantly trying to dog your heels with his petition. And although my defined and recognised connexion with your affairs is merely of a business character, still I have that spontaneous interest in everything belonging to you, that—'

He stopped again, as if to discover whether he had led Mr

Dombey far enough yet. And again, with his chin resting on his hand, he leered at the picture.

'Carker,' said Mr Dombey, 'I am sensible that you do not limit your—'

'Service,' suggested his smiling entertainer.

'No; I prefer to say your regard,' observed Mr Dombey; very sensible, as he said so, that he was paying him a handsome and flattering compliment, 'to our mere business relations. Your consideration for my feelings, hopes, and disappointments, in the little instance you have just now mentioned, is an example in point. I am obliged to you, Carker.'

Mr Carker bent his head slowly, and very softly rubbed his hands, as if he were afraid by any action to disturb the current of Mr Dombey's confidence.

'Your allusion to it is opportune,' said Mr Dombey, after a little hesitation; 'for it prepares the way to what I was beginning to say to you, and reminds me that that involves no absolutely new relations between us, although it may involve more personal confidence on my part than I have hitherto—'

'Distinguished me with,' suggested Carker, bending his head again: 'I will not say to you how honoured I am; for a man like you well knows how much honour he has in his power to bestow at pleasure.'

'Mrs Dombey and myself,' said Mr Dombey, passing this compliment with august self-denial, 'are not quite agreed upon some points. We do not appear to understand each other yet. Mrs Dombey has something to learn.'

'Mrs Dombey is distinguished by many rare attractions; and has been accustomed, no doubt, to receive much adulation,' said the smooth, sleek watcher of his slightest look and tone. 'But where there is affection, duty, and respect, any little mistakes engendered by such causes are soon set right.'

Mr Dombey's thoughts instinctively flew back to the face that had looked at him in his wife's dressing-room, when an imperious hand was stretched towards the door; and remembering the affection, duty, and respect, expressed in it, he felt the blood rush to his own face quite as plainly as the watchful eyes upon him saw it there.

'Mrs Dombey and myself,' he went on to say, 'had some discussion, before Mrs Skewton's death, upon the causes of my dissatisfaction; of which you will have formed a general understanding from having been a witness of what passed between Mrs

Dombey and myself on the evening when you were at our – at my house.'

'When I so much regretted being present,' said the smiling Carker. 'Proud as a man in my position necessarily must be of your familiar notice – though I give you no credit for it; you may do anything you please without losing caste – and honoured as I was by an early presentation to Mrs Dombey, before she was made eminent by bearing your name, I almost regretted that night, I assure you, that I had been the object of such especial good fortune.'

That any man could, under any possible circumstances, regret the being distinguished by his condescension and patronage, was a moral phenomenon which Mr Dombey could not comprehend. He therefore responded, with a considerable accession of dignity. 'Indeed! And why, Carker?'

'I fear,' returned the confidential agent, 'that Mrs Dombey, never very much disposed to regard me with favourable interest – one in my position could not expect that, from a lady naturally proud, and whose pride becomes her so well – may not easily forgive my innocent part in that conversation. Your displeasure is no light matter, you must remember; and to be visited with it before a third party—'

'Carker,' said Mr Dombey, arrogantly; 'I presume that *I* am the first consideration?'

'Oh! Can there be a doubt about it?' replied the other, with the impatience of a man admitting a notorious and incontrovertible fact.

'Mrs Dombey becomes a secondary consideration, when we are both in question, I imagine,' said Mr Dombey. 'Is that so?'

'Is it so?' returned Carker. 'Do you know better than any one, that you have no need to ask?'

'Then I hope, Carker,' said Mr Dombey, 'that your regret in the acquisition of Mrs Dombey's displeasure, may be almost counter-balanced by your satisfaction in retaining *my* confidence and good opinion.'

'I have the misfortune, I find,' returned Carker, 'to have incurred that displeasure. Mrs Dombey has expressed it to you?'

'Mrs Dombey has expressed various opinions,' said Mr Dombey, with majestic coldness and indifference, 'in which I do not partici-pate, and which I am not inclined to discuss, or to recall. I made Mrs Dombey acquainted, some time since, as I have already told you, with certain points of domestic deference and submission on which I felt it necessary to insist. I failed to convince Mrs Dombey of the expediency of her immediately altering her conduct in those respects, with a view to her own peace and welfare, and my dignity; and I informed Mrs Dombey that if I should find it necessary to object or remonstrate again, I should express my opinion to her through yourself, my confidential agent.'

Blended with the look that Carker bent upon him, was a devilish look at the picture over his head, that struck upon it like a flash of lightning.

'Now, Carker,' said Mr Dombey, 'I do not hesitate to say to you that I *will* carry my point. I am not to be trifled with. Mrs Dombey must understand that my will is law, and that I cannot allow of one exception to the whole rule of my life. You will have the goodness to undertake this charge, which, coming from me, is not unacceptable to you, I hope, whatever regret you may politely profess – for which I am obliged to you on behalf of Mrs Dombey; and you will have the goodness, I am persuaded, to discharge it as exactly as any other commission.'

'You know,' said Mr Carker, 'that you have only to command me.'

'I know,' said Mr Dombey, with a majestic indication of assent, 'that I have only to command you. It is necessary that I should proceed in this. Mrs Dombey is a lady undoubtedly highly qualified, in many respects, to—'

'To do credit even to your choice,' suggested Carker, with a fawning show of teeth.

'Yes; if you please to adopt that form of words,' said Mr Dombey, in his tone of state; 'and at present I do not conceive that Mrs Dombey does that credit to it, to which it is entitled. There is a principle of opposition in Mrs Dombey that must be eradicated; that must be overcome: Mrs Dombey does not appear to understand,' said Mr Dombey, forcibly, 'that the idea of opposition to Me is monstrous and absurd.'

'We, in the City, know you better,' replied Carker, with a smile from ear to ear.

'You know me better,' said Mr Dombey. 'I hope so. Though, indeed, I am bound to do Mrs Dombey the justice of saying, however inconsistent it may seem with her subsequent conduct (which remains unchanged), that on my expressing my disapprobation and determination to her, with some severity, on the occasion to which I have referred, my admonition appeared to produce a very powerful effect.' Mr Dombey delivered himself of those words with most portentous stateliness. 'I wish you to have the goodness, then, to inform Mrs Dombey, Carker, from me, that I must recall our former conversation to her remembrance, in some surprise that it had not yet had its effect. That I must insist upon her regulating her conduct by the injunctions laid upon her in that conversation. That I am not satisfied with her conduct. That I am greatly dissatisfied with it. And that I shall be under the very disagreeable necessity of making you the bearer of yet more unwelcome and explicit communications, if she has not the good sense and the proper feeling to adapt herself to my wishes, as the first Mrs Dombey did, and, I believe I may add, as any other lady in her place would.'

'The first Mrs Dombey lived very happily,' said Carker.

'The first Mrs Dombey had great good sense,' said Mr Dombey, in a gentlemanly toleration of the dead, 'and very correct feeling.'

'Is Miss Dombey like her mother, do you think?' said Carker.

Swiftly and darkly, Mr Dombey's face changed. His confidential agent eyed it keenly.

'I have approached a painful subject,' he said, in a soft regretful tone of voice, irreconcilable with his eager eye. 'Pray forgive me. I forget these chains of association in the interest I have. Pray forgive me.'

But for all he said, his eager eye scanned Mr Dombey's downcast face none the less closely; and then it shot a strange triumphant look at the picture, as appealing to it to bear witness how he led him on again, and what was coming.

'Carker,' said Mr Dombey, looking here and there upon the table, and speaking in a somewhat altered and more hurried voice, and with a paler lip, 'there is no occasion for apology. You mistake. The association is with the matter in hand, and not with any recollection, as you suppose. I do not approve of Mrs Dombey's behaviour towards my daughter.'

'Pardon me,' said Mr Carker, 'I don't quite understand.'

'Understand then,' returned Mr Dombey, 'that you may make that – that you *will* make that, if you please – matter of direct objection from me to Mrs Dombey. You will please to tell her that her show of devotion for my daughter is disagreeable to me. It is likely to be noticed. It is likely to induce people to contrast Mrs Dombey in her relation towards my daughter, with Mrs Dombey in her relation towards myself. You will have the goodness to let Mrs Dombey know, plainly, that I object to it; and that I expect her to defer, immediately, to my objection. Mrs Dombey may be in earnest, or she may be pursuing a whim, or she may be opposing

Mr Dombey and his 'confidential agent'

me; but I object to it in any case, and in every case. If Mrs Dombey is in earnest, so much the less reluctant should she be to desist; for she will not serve my daughter by any such display. If my wife has any superfluous gentleness and duty over and above her proper submission to me, she may bestow them where she pleases, perhaps; but I will have submission first! – Carker,' said Mr Dombey, checking the unusual emotion with which he had spoken, and falling into a tone more like that in which he was accustomed to assert his greatness, 'you will have the goodness not to omit or slur this point, but to consider it a very important part of your instructions.'

Mr Carker bowed his head, and rising from the table, and standing thoughtfully before the fire, with his hand to his smooth chin, looked down at Mr Dombey with the evil slyness of some monkish carving, half human and half brute; or like a leering face on an old water-spout. Mr Dombey, recovering his composure by degrees, or cooling his emotion in his sense of having taken a high position, sat gradually stiffening again, and looking at the parrot as she swung to and fro, in her great wedding ring.

'I beg your pardon,' said Carker, after a silence, suddenly resuming his chair, and drawing it opposite to Mr Dombey's, 'but let me understand. Mrs Dombey is aware of the probability of your making me the organ of your displeasure?'

'Yes,' replied Mr Dombey. 'I have said so.'

'Yes,' rejoined Carker, quickly; 'but why?'

'Why!' Mr Dombey repeated, not without hesitation. 'Because I told her.'

'Aye,' replied Carker. 'But why did you tell her? You see,' he continued with a smile, and softly laying his velvet hand, as a cat might have laid its sheathed claws, on Mr Dombey's arm; 'if I perfectly understand what is in your mind, I am so much more likely to be useful, and to have the happiness of being effectually employed. I think I *do* understand. I have not the honour of Mrs Dombey's good opinion. In my position, I have no reason to expect it; but I take the fact to be, that I have not got it?'

'Possibly not,' said Mr Dombey.

'Consequently,' pursued Carker, 'your making these communications to Mrs Dombey through me, is sure to be particularly unpalatable to that lady?'

'It appears to me,' said Mr Dombey, with haughty reserve, and yet with some embarrassment, 'that Mrs Dombey's views upon the subject form no part of it as it presents itself to you and me, Carker. But it may be so.'

'And – pardon me – do I misconceive you,' said Carker, 'when I think you descry in this, a likely means of humbling Mrs Dombey's pride – I use the word as expressive of a quality which, kept within due bounds, adorns and graces a lady so distinguished for her beauty and accomplishments – and, not to say of punishing her, but of reducing her to the submission you so naturally and justly require?'

'I am not accustomed, Carker, as you know,' said Mr Dombey, 'to give such close reasons for any course of conduct I think proper to adopt, but I will gainsay nothing of this. If you have any objection to found upon it, that is indeed another thing, and the mere statement that you have one will be sufficient. But I have not supposed, I confess, that any confidence I could entrust to you, would be likely to degrade you—'

'Oh! *I* degraded!' exclaimed Carker. 'In *your* service!'

'—or to place you,' pursued Mr Dombey, 'in a false position.'

'*I* in a false position!' exclaimed Carker. 'I shall be proud – delighted – to execute your trust. I could have wished, I own, to have given the lady at whose feet I would lay my humble duty and devotion – for is she not your wife! – no new cause of dislike; but a wish from you is, of course, paramount to every other consideration on earth. Besides, when Mrs Dombey is converted from these little errors of judgment, incidental, I would presume to say, to the novelty of her situation, I shall hope that she will perceive in the slight part I take, only a grain – my removed and different sphere gives room for little more – of the respect for you, and sacrifice of all considerations to you, of which it will be her pleasure and privilege to garner up a great store every day.'

Mr Dombey seemed, at the moment, again to see her with her hand stretched out towards the door, and again to hear through the mild speech of his confidential agent an echo of the words, 'Nothing can make us stranger to each other than we are henceforth!' But he shook off the fancy, and did not shake in his resolution, and said, 'Certainly, no doubt.'

'There is nothing more,' quoth Carker, drawing his chair back to its old place – for they had taken little breakfast as yet – and pausing for an answer before he sat down.

'Nothing,' said Mr Dombey, 'but this. You will be good enough to observe, Carker, that no message to Mrs Dombey with which you are or may be charged, admits of reply. You will be good enough to bring me no reply. Mrs Dombey is informed that it does not become me to temporise or treat upon any matter that is at issue between us, and that what I say is final.'

Mr Carker signified his understanding of these credentials, and they fell to breakfast with what appetite they might. The Grinder also, in due time, reappeared, keeping his eyes upon his master without a moment's respite, and passing the time in a reverie of worshipful terror. Breakfast concluded, Mr Dombey's horse was ordered out again, and Mr Carker mounting his own, they rode off for the City together.

Mr Carker was in capital spirits, and talked much. Mr Dombey received his conversation with the sovereign air of a man who had a right to be talked to, and occasionally condescended to throw in a few words to carry on the conversation. So they rode on characteristically enough. But Mr Dombey, in his dignity, rode with very long stirrups, and a very loose rein, and very rarely deigned to look down to see where his horse went. In consequence of which it happened that Mr Dombey's horse, while going at a round trot, stumbled on some loose stones, threw him, rolled over him, and lashing out with his iron-shod feet, in his struggles to get up, kicked him.

Mr Carker, quick of eye, steady of hand, and a good horseman, was afoot, and had the struggling animal upon his legs and by the bridle, in a moment. Otherwise that morning's confidence would have been Mr Dombey's last. Yet even with the flush and hurry of this action red upon him, he bent over his prostrate chief with every tooth disclosed, and muttered as he stooped down, 'I have given good cause of offence to Mrs Dombey *now*, if she knew it!'

Mr Dombey being insensible, and bleeding from the head and face, was carried by certain menders of the road, under Carker's direction, to the nearest public-house, which was not far off, and where he was soon attended by divers surgeons, who arrived in quick succession from all parts, and who seemed to come by some mysterious instinct, as vultures are said to gather about a camel who dies in the desert. After being at some pains to restore him to consciousness, these gentlemen examined into the nature of his injuries. One surgeon who lived hard by was strong for a compound fracture of the leg, which was the landlord's opinion also; but two surgeons who lived at a distance, and were only in that neighbourhood by accident, combated this opinion so disinterestedly, that it was decided at last that the patient, though severely cut and bruised, had broken no bones but a lesser rib or so, and might be carefully taken home before night. His injuries being dressed and bandaged, which was a long operation, and he at length left to repose, Mr Carker mounted his horse again, and rode away to carry the intelligence home.

Crafty and cruel as his face was at the best of times, though it was a sufficiently fair face as to form and regularity of feature, it was at its worst when he set forth on this errand; animated by the craft and cruelty of thoughts within him, suggestions of remote possibility rather than of design or plot, that made him ride as if he hunted men and women. Drawing rein at length, and slackening in his speed, as he came into the more public roads, he checked his white-legged horse into picking his way along as usual, and hid himself beneath his sleek, hushed, crouched manner, and his ivory smile, as he best could.

He rode direct to Mr Dombey's house, alighted at the door, and begged to see Mrs Dombey on an affair of importance. The servant who showed him to Mr Dombey's own room, soon returned to say that it was not Mrs Dombey's hour for receiving visitors, and that he begged pardon for not having mentioned it before.

Mr Carker, who was quite prepared for a cold reception, wrote upon a card that he must take the liberty of pressing for an interview, and that he would not be so bold as to do so, *for the second time* (this he underlined), if he were not equally sure of the occasion being sufficient for his justification. After a trifling delay, Mrs Dombey's maid appeared, and conducted him to a morning room upstairs, where Edith and Florence were together.

He had never thought Edith half so beautiful before. Much as he admired the graces of her face and form, and freshly as they dwelt within his sensual remembrance, he had never thought her half so beautiful.

Her glance fell haughtily upon him in the doorway; but he looked at Florence – though only in the act of bending his head, as he came in – with some irrepressible expression of the new power he held; and it was his triumph to see the glance droop and falter, and to see that Edith half rose up to receive him.

He was very sorry, he was deeply grieved; he couldn't say with what unwillingness he came to prepare her for the intelligence of a very slight accident. He entreated Mrs Dombey to compose herself. Upon his sacred word of honour, there was no cause of alarm. But Mr Dombey—

Florence uttered a sudden cry. He did not look at her, but at

Edith. Edith composed and reassured her. *She* uttered no cry of distress. No, no.

Mr Dombey had met with an accident in riding. His horse had slipped, and he had been thrown.

Florence wildly exclaimed that he was badly hurt; that he was killed!

No. Upon his honour, Mr Dombey, though stunned at first, was soon recovered, and though certainly hurt was in no kind of danger. If this were not the truth, he, the distressed intruder, never could have had the courage to present himself before Mrs Dombey. It was the truth indeed, he solemnly assured her.

All this he said as if he were answering Edith, and not Florence, and with his eyes and his smile fastened on Edith.

He then went on to tell her where Mr Dombey was lying, and to request that a carriage might be placed at his disposal to bring him home.

'Mama,' faltered Florence in tears, 'if I might venture to go!'

Mr Carker, having his eyes on Edith when he heard these words, gave her a secret look and slightly shook his head. He saw how she battled with herself before she answered him with her handsome eyes, but he wrested the answer from her – he showed her that he would have it, or that he would speak and cut Florence to the heart – and she gave it to him. As he had looked at the picture in the morning, so he looked at her afterwards, when she turned her eyes away.

'I am directed to request,' he said, 'that the new housekeeper – Mrs Pipchin, I think, is the name—'

Nothing escaped him. He saw in an instant, that she was another slight of Mr Dombey's on his wife.

'—may be informed that Mr Dombey wishes to have his bed prepared in his own apartments downstairs, as he prefers those rooms to any other. I shall return to Mr Dombey almost immediately. That every possible attention has been paid to his comfort, and that he is the object of every possible solicitude, I need not assure you, Madam. Let me again say, there is no cause for the least alarm. Even you may be quite at ease, believe me.'

He bowed himself out, with his extremest show of deference and conciliation; and having returned to Mr Dombey's room, and there arranged for a carriage being sent after him to the City, mounted his horse again, and rode slowly thither. He was very thoughtful as he went along, and very thoughtful there, and very thoughtful in the carriage on his way back to the place where Mr Dombey had

been left. It was only when sitting by that gentleman's couch that
he was quite himself again, and conscious of his teeth.

About the time of twilight, Mr Dombey, grievously afflicted with
aches and pains, was helped into his carriage, and propped with
cloaks and pillows on one side of it, while his confidential agent
bore him company upon the other. As he was not to be shaken,
they moved at little more than a foot pace; and hence it was quite
dark when he was brought home. Mrs Pipchin, bitter and grim, and
not oblivious of the Peruvian mines, as the establishment in general
had good reason to know, received him at the door, and freshened
the domestics with several little sprinklings of wordy vinegar, while
they assisted in conveying him to his room. Mr Carker remained in
attendance until he was safe in bed, and then, as he declined to
receive any female visitor, but the excellent Ogress who presided
over his household, waited on Mrs Dombey once more, with his
report on her lord's condition.

He again found Edith alone with Florence, and he again
addressed the whole of his soothing speech to Edith, as if she were
a prey to the liveliest and most affectionate anxieties. So earnest he
was in his respectful sympathy, that on taking leave, he ventured –
with one more glance towards Florence at the moment – to take her
hand, and bending over it, to touch it with his lips.

Edith did not withdraw the hand, nor did she strike his fair face
with it, despite the flush upon her cheek, the bright light in her eyes,
and the dilation of her whole form. But when she was alone in her
own room, she struck it on the marble chimney-shelf, so that, at
one blow, it was bruised, and bled; and held it from her, near the
shining fire, as if she could have thrust it in and burned it.

Far into the night she sat alone, by the sinking blaze, in dark and
threatening beauty, watching the murky shadows looming on the
wall, as if her thoughts were tangible, and cast them there. Whatever
shapes of outrage and affront, and black foreshadowings of things
that might happen, flickered, indistinct and giant-like, before her,
one resented figure marshalled them against her. And that figure
was her husband.

CHAPTER 43

The Watches of the Night

Florence, long since awakened from her dream, mournfully observed the estrangement between her father and Edith, and saw it widen more and more, and knew that there was greater bitterness between them every day. Each day's added knowledge deepened the shade upon her love and hope, roused up the old sorrow that had slumbered for a little time, and made it even heavier to bear than it had been before.

It had been hard – how hard may none but Florence ever know! – to have the natural affection of a true and earnest nature turned to agony; and slight, or stern repulse, substituted for the tenderest protection and the dearest care. It had been hard to feel in her deep heart what she had felt, and never know the happiness of one touch of response. But it was much more hard to be compelled to doubt either her father or Edith, so affectionate and dear to her, and to think of her love for each of them, by turns, with fear, distrust, and wonder.

Yet Florence now began to do so; and the doing of it was a task imposed upon her by the very purity of her soul, as one she could not fly from. She saw her father cold and obdurate to Edith, as to her; hard, inflexible, unyielding. Could it be, she asked herself with starting tears, that her own dear mother had been made unhappy by such treatment, and had pined away and died? Then she would think how proud and stately Edith was to every one but her, with what disdain she treated him, how distantly she kept apart from him, and what she had said on the night when she came home; and quickly it would come on Florence, almost as a crime, that she loved one who was set in opposition to her father, and that her father knowing of it, must think of her in his solitary room as the unnatural child who added this wrong to the old fault, so much wept for, of never having won his fatherly affection from her birth. The next kind word from Edith, the next kind glance, would shake these thoughts again, and make them seem like black ingratitude; for who but she had cheered the drooping heart of Florence, so lonely and so hurt, and been its best of comforters! Thus, with her gentle nature yearning to them both, feeling the misery of both, and whispering doubts of her own duty to both, Florence in her wider and expanded love, and by the side of Edith, endured more than when she had hoarded up her undivided secret in the mournful house, and her beautiful mama had never dawned upon it.

One exquisite unhappiness that would have far outweighed this, Florence was spared. She never had the least suspicion that Edith by her tenderness for her widened the separation from her father, or gave him new cause of dislike. If Florence had conceived the possibility of such an effect being wrought by such a cause, what grief she would have felt, what sacrifice she would have tried to make, poor loving girl, how fast and sure her quiet passage might have been beneath it to the presence of that higher Father who does not reject his children's love, or spurn their tried and broken hearts, Heaven knows! But it was otherwise, and that was well.

No word was ever spoken between Florence and Edith now, on these subjects. Edith had said there ought to be between them, in that wise, a division and a silence like the grave itself: and Florence felt that she was right.

In this state of affairs her father was brought home suffering and disabled: and gloomily retired to his own rooms, where he was tended by servants, not approached by Edith, and had no friend or companion but Mr Carker, who withdrew near midnight.

'And nice company *he* is, Miss Floy,' said Susan Nipper. 'Oh, he's a precious piece of goods! If ever he wants a character[1] don't let him come to me whatever he does, that's all I tell him.'

'Dear Susan,' urged Florence, 'don't!'

'Oh, it's very well to say "don't" Miss Floy,' returned the Nipper, much exasperated; 'but raly begging your pardon we're coming to such passes that it turns all the blood in a person's body into pins and needles, with their pints all ways. Don't mistake me, Miss Floy, I don't mean nothing again your ma-in-law who has always treated me as a lady should though she is rather high I must say not that I have any right to object to that particular, but when we come to Mrs Pipchinses and having them put over us and keeping guard at your pa's door like crocodiles (only make us thankful that they lay no eggs!) we are a growing too outrageous!'

'Papa thinks well of Mrs Pipchin, Susan,' returned Florence, 'and has a right to choose his housekeeper, you know. Pray don't!'

'Well Miss Floy,' returned the Nipper, 'when you say don't, I never do I hope but Mrs Pipchin acts like early gooseberries upon me Miss, and nothing less.'

Susan was unusually emphatic and destitute of punctuation in her discourse on this night, which was the night of Mr Dombey's being brought home, because, having been sent downstairs by

Florence to inquire after him, she had been obliged to deliver her message to her mortal enemy Mrs Pipchin; who, without carrying it in to Mr Dombey, had taken upon herself to return what Miss Nipper called a huffish answer, on her own responsibility. This, Susan Nipper construed into presumption on the part of that exemplary sufferer by the Peruvian mines, and a deed of disparagement upon her young lady, that was not to be forgiven; and so far her emphatic state was special. But she had been in a condition of greatly increased suspicion and distrust, ever since the marriage; for, like most persons of her quality of mind, who form a strong and sincere attachment to one in the different station which Florence occupied, Susan was very jealous, and her jealousy naturally attached to Edith, who divided her old empire, and came between them. Proud and glad as Susan Nipper truly was, that her young mistress should be advanced towards her proper place in the scene of her old neglect, and that she should have her father's handsome wife for her companion and protectress, she could not relinquish any part of her own dominion to the handsome wife, without a grudge and a vague feeling of ill-will, for which she did not fail to find a disinterested justification in her sharp perception of the pride and passion of the lady's character. From the background to which she had necessarily retired somewhat, since the marriage, Miss Nipper looked on, therefore, at domestic affairs in general, with a resolute conviction that no good would come of Mrs Dombey: always being very careful to publish on all possible occasions, that she had nothing to say against her.

'Susan,' said Florence, who was sitting thoughtfully at her table, 'it is very late. I shall want nothing more to-night.'

'Ah, Miss Floy!' returned the Nipper, 'I'm sure I often wish for them old times when I sat up with you hours later than this and fell asleep through being tired out when you was as broad awake as spectacles, but you've ma's-in-law to come and sit with you now Miss Floy and I'm thankful for it I'm sure. I've not a word to say against 'em.'

'I shall not forget who was my old companion when I had none, Susan,' returned Florence, gently, 'never.' And looking up, she put her arm round the neck of her humble friend, drew her face down to hers, and bidding her good night, kissed it; which so mollified Miss Nipper, that she fell a sobbing.

'Now my dear Miss Floy,' said Susan, 'let me go downstairs again and see how your pa is, I know you're wretched about him, do let me go downstairs again and knock at his door my own self.'

'No,' said Florence, 'go to bed. We shall hear more in the morning. I will inquire myself in the morning. Mama has been down, I dare say;' Florence blushed, for she had no such hope; 'or is there now, perhaps. Good night!'

Susan was too much softened to express her private opinion on the probability of Mrs Dombey's being in attendance on her husband; and silently withdrew. Florence left alone, soon hid her head upon her hands as she had often done in other days, and did not restrain the tears from coursing down her face. The misery of this domestic discord and unhappiness; the withered hope she cherished now, if hope it could be called, of ever being taken to her father's heart; her doubts and fears between the two; the yearning of her innocent breast to both; the heavy disappointment and regret of such an end as this, to what had been a vision of bright hope and promise to her; all crowded on her mind and made her tears flow fast. Her mother and her brother dead, her father unmoved towards her, Edith opposed to him and casting him away, but loving her, and loved by her, it seemed as if her affection could never prosper, rest where it would. That weak thought was soon hushed, but the thoughts in which it had arisen were too true and strong to be dismissed with it; and they made the night desolate.

Among such reflections there rose up, as there had risen up all day, the image of her father, wounded and in pain, alone in his own room, untended by those who should be nearest to him, and passing the tardy hours in lonely suffering. A frightened thought which made her start and clasp her hands – though it was not a new one in her mind – that he might die, and never see her or pronounce her name, thrilled her whole frame. In her agitation she thought, and trembled while she thought, of once more stealing downstairs, and venturing to his door.

She listened at her own. The house was quiet, and all the lights were out. It was a long, long time, she thought, since she used to make her nightly pilgrimages to his door! It was a long, long time, she tried to think, since she had entered his room at midnight, and he had led her back to the stair-foot!

With the same child's heart within her, as of old: even with the child's sweet timid eyes and clustering hair: Florence, as strange to her father in her early maiden bloom, as in her nursery time, crept down the staircase listening as she went, and drew near to his room. No one was stirring in the house. The door was partly open to admit air; and all was so still within, that she could hear the burning of the fire, and count the ticking of the clock that stood upon the chimneypiece.

She looked in. In that room, the housekeeper wrapped in a blanket was fast asleep in an easy chair before the fire. The doors between it and the next were partly closed, and a screen was drawn before them; but there was a light there, and it shone upon the cornice of his bed. All was so very still that she could hear from his breathing that he was asleep. This gave her courage to pass round the screen, and look into his chamber.

It was as great a start to come upon his sleeping face as if she had not expected to see it. Florence stood arrested on the spot, and if he had awakened then, must have remained there.

There was a cut upon his forehead, and they had been wetting his hair, which lay bedabbled and entangled on the pillow. One of his arms, resting outside the bed, was bandaged up, and he was very white. But it was not this, that after the first quick glance, and first assurance of his sleeping quietly, held Florence rooted to the ground. It was something very different from this, and more than this, that made him look so solemn in her eyes.

She had never seen his face in all her life, but there had been upon it – or she fancied so – some disturbing consciousness of her. She had never seen his face in all her life, but hope had sunk within her, and her timid glance had drooped before its stern, unloving, and repelling harshness. As she looked upon it now, she saw it, for the first time, free from the cloud that had darkened her childhood. Calm, tranquil night was reigning in its stead. He might have gone to sleep, for anything she saw there, blessing her.

Awake, unkind father! Awake, now, sullen man! The time is flitting by; the hour is coming with an angry tread. Awake!

There was no change upon his face; and as she watched it, awfully, its motionless repose recalled the faces that were gone. So they looked, so would he; so she, his weeping child, who should say when! so all the world of love and hatred and indifference around them! When that time should come, it would not be the heavier to him, for this that she was going to do; and it might fall something lighter upon her.

She stole close to the bed, and drawing in her breath bent down, and softly kissed him on the face, and laid her own for one brief moment by its side, and put the arm, with which she dared not touch him, round about him on the pillow.

Awake, doomed man, while she is near. The time is flitting by;

the hour is coming with an angry tread; its foot is in the house. Awake!

In her mind, she prayed to God to bless her father, and to soften him towards her, if it might be so; and if not, to forgive him if he was wrong, and pardon her the prayer which almost seemed impiety. And doing so, and looking back at him with blinded eyes, and stealing timidly away, passed out of his room, and crossed the other, and was gone.

He may sleep on now. He may sleep on while he may. But let him look for that slight figure when he wakes, and find it near him when the hour is come!

Sad and grieving was the heart of Florence, as she crept upstairs. The quiet house had grown more dismal since she came down. The sleep she had been looking on, in the dead of night, had the solemnity to her of death and life in one. The secrecy and silence of her own proceeding made the night secret, silent, and oppressive. She felt unwilling, almost unable, to go on to her own chamber; and turning into the drawing-rooms, where the clouded moon was shining through the blinds, looked out into the empty streets.

The wind was blowing drearily. The lamps looked pale, and shook as if they were cold. There was a distant glimmer of something that was not quite darkness, rather than of light, in the sky; and foreboding night was shivering and restless, as the dying are who make a troubled end. Florence remembered how, as a watcher, by a sick-bed, she had noted this bleak time, and felt its influence, as if in some hidden natural antipathy to it; and now it was very, very gloomy.

Her mama had not come to her room that night, which was one cause of her having sat late out of her bed. In her general uneasiness, no less than in her ardent longing to have somebody to speak to, and to break the spell of gloom and silence, Florence directed her steps towards the chamber where she slept.

The door was not fastened within, and yielded smoothly to her hesitating hand. She was surprised to find a bright light burning; still more surprised, on looking in, to see that her mama, but partially undressed, was sitting near the ashes of the fire, which had crumbled and dropped away. Her eyes were intently bent upon the air; and in their light, and in her face, and in her form, and in the grasp with which she held the elbows of her chair as if about to start up, Florence saw such fierce emotion that it terrified her.

'Mama!' she cried, 'what is the matter?'

Edith started; looking at her with such a strange dread in her face, that Florence was more frightened than before.

'Mama!' said Florence, hurriedly advancing. 'Dear mama! what is the matter?'

'I have not been well,' said Edith, shaking, and still looking at her in the same strange way. 'I have had bad dreams, my love.'

'And not yet been to bed, mama?'

'No,' she returned. 'Half-waking dreams.'

Her features gradually softened; and suffering Florence to come close to her, within her embrace, she said in a tender manner, 'But what does my bird do here? What does my bird do here?'

'I have been uneasy, mama, in not seeing you to-night, and in not knowing how papa was; and I—'

Florence stopped there, and said no more.

'Is it late?' asked Edith, fondly putting back the curls that mingled with her own dark hair, and strayed upon her face.

'Very late. Near day.'

'Near day!' she repeated in surprise.

'Dear mama, what have you done to your hand?' said Florence.

Edith drew it suddenly away, and, for a moment, looked at her with the same strange dread (there was a sort of wild avoidance in it) as before; but she presently said, 'Nothing, nothing. A blow.' And then she said, 'My Florence!' and then her bosom heaved, and she was weeping passionately.

'Mama!' said Florence. 'Oh mama, what can I do, what should I do, to make us happier? Is there anything?'

'Nothing,' she replied.

'Are you sure of that? Can it never be? If I speak now of what is in my thoughts, in spite of what we have agreed,' said Florence, 'you will not blame me, will you?'

'It is useless,' she replied, 'useless. I have told you, dear, that I have had bad dreams. Nothing can change them, or prevent their coming back.'

'I do not understand,' said Florence, gazing on her agitated face, which seemed to darken as she looked.

'I have dreamed,' said Edith in a low voice, 'of a pride that is all powerless for good, all powerful for evil; of a pride that has been galled and goaded, through many shameful years, and has never recoiled except upon itself; a pride that has debased its owner with the consciousness of deep humiliation, and never helped its owner boldly to resent it or avoid it, or to say, "This shall not be!"; a pride that, rightly guided, might have led perhaps to better things, but which, misdirected and perverted, like all else belonging to the same possessor, has been self-contempt, mere hardihood, and ruin.'

She neither looked nor spoke to Florence now, but went on as if she were alone.

'I have dreamed,' she said, 'of such indifference and callousness, arising from this self-contempt; this wretched, inefficient, miserable pride; that it has gone on with listless steps even to the altar, yielding to the old, familiar, beckoning finger, – oh mother, oh mother! – while it spurned it; and willing to be hateful to itself for once and for all, rather than to be stung daily in some new form. Mean, poor thing!'

And now with gathering and darkening emotion, she looked as she had looked when Florence entered.

'And I have dreamed,' she said, 'that in a first late effort to achieve a purpose, it has been trodden on, and trodden down by a base foot, but turns and looks upon him. I have dreamed that it is wounded, hunted, set upon by dogs, but that it stands at bay, and will not yield; no, that it cannot if it would; but that it is urged on to hate him, rise against him, and defy him!'

Her clenched hand tightened on the trembling arm she had in hers, and as she looked down on the alarmed and wondering face, her own subsided. 'Oh Florence!' she said, 'I think I have been nearly mad to-night!' and humbled her proud head upon her neck, and wept again.

'Don't leave me! be near me! I have no hope but in you!' These words she said a score of times.

Soon she grew calmer, and was full of pity for the tears of Florence, and for her waking at such untimely hours. And the day now dawning, Edith folded her in her arms and laid her down upon her bed, and, not lying down herself, sat by her, and bade her try to sleep.

'For you are weary, dearest, and unhappy, and should rest.'

'I am indeed unhappy, dear mama, to-night,' said Florence. 'But you are weary and unhappy, too.'

'Not when you lie asleep so near me, sweet.'

They kissed each other, and Florence, worn out, gradually fell into a gentle slumber; but as her eyes closed on the face beside her, it was so sad to think upon the face downstairs, that her hand drew closer to Edith for some comfort; yet, even in the act, it faltered, lest it should be deserting him. So, in her sleep, she tried to reconcile the two together, and to show them that she loved them both, but could not do it, and her waking grief was part of her dreams.

Edith, sitting by, looked down at the dark eyelashes lying wet on the flushed cheeks, and looked with gentleness and pity, for she knew the truth. But no sleep hung upon her own eyes. As the day came on she still sat watching and waking, with the placid hand in hers, and sometimes whispered, as she looked at the hushed face, 'Be near me, Florence, I have no hope but in you!'

CHAPTER 44

A Separation

With the day, though not so early as the sun, uprose Miss Susan Nipper. There was a heaviness in this young maiden's exceedingly sharp black eyes, that abated somewhat of their sparkling, and suggested – which was not their usual character – the possibility of their being sometimes shut. There was likewise a swollen look about them, as if they had been crying over-night. But the Nipper, so far from being cast down, was singularly brisk and bold, and all her energies appeared to be braced up for some great feat. This was noticeable even in her dress, which was much more tight and trim than usual; and in occasional twitches of her head as she went about the house, which were mightily expressive of determination.

In a word, she had formed a determination, and an aspiring one: it being nothing less than this – to penetrate to Mr Dombey's presence, and have speech of that gentleman alone. 'I have often said I would,' she remarked, in a threatening manner, to herself, that morning, with many twitches of her head, 'and now I *will!*'

Spurring herself on to the accomplishment of this desperate design, with a sharpness that was peculiar to herself, Susan Nipper haunted the hall and staircase during the whole forenoon, without finding a favourable opportunity for the assault. Not at all baffled by this discomfiture, which indeed had a stimulating effect, and put her on her mettle, she diminished nothing of her vigilance; and at last discovered, towards evening, that her sworn foe Mrs Pipchin, under pretence of having sat up all night, was dozing in her own room, and that Mr Dombey was lying on his sofa, unattended.

With a twitch – not of her head merely, this time, but of her whole self – the Nipper went on tiptoe to Mr Dombey's door, and knocked. 'Come in!' said Mr Dombey. Susan encouraged herself with a final twitch, and went in.

Mr Dombey, who was eyeing the fire, gave an amazed look at his visitor, and raised himself a little on his arm. The Nipper dropped a curtsey.

'What do you want?' said Mr Dombey.

'If you please, Sir, I wish to speak to you,' said Susan.

Mr Dombey moved his lips as if he were repeating the words, but he seemed so lost in astonishment at the presumption of the young woman as to be incapable of giving them utterance.

'I have been in your service, Sir,' said Susan Nipper, with her usual rapidity, 'now twelve year a waiting on Miss Floy my own young lady who couldn't speak plain when I first come here and I was old in this house when Mrs Richards was new, I may not be Meethosalem,[1] but I am not a child in arms.'

Mr Dombey, raised upon his arm and looking at her, offered no comment on this preparatory statement of facts.

'There never was a dearer or a blesseder young lady than is my young lady, Sir,' said Susan, 'and I ought to know a great deal better than some for I have seen her in her grief and I have seen her in her joy (there's not been much of it) and I have seen her with her brother and I have seen her in her loneliness and some have never seen her, and I say to some and all – I do!' and here the black-eyed shook her head, and slightly stamped her foot; 'that she's the blessedest and dearest angel is Miss Floy that ever drew the breath of life, the more that I was torn to pieces Sir the more I'd say it though I may not be a Fox's Martyr.'[2]

Mr Dombey turned yet paler than his fall had made him, with indignation and astonishment; and kept his eyes upon the speaker as if he accused them, and his ears too, of playing him false.

'No one could be anything but true and faithful to Miss Floy, Sir,' pursued Susan, 'and I take no merit for my service of twelve year, for I love her – yes, I say to some and all I do!' – and here the black-eyed shook her head again, and slightly stamped her foot again, and checked a sob; 'but true and faithful service gives me right to speak I hope, and speak I must and will now, right or wrong.'

'What do you mean, woman?' said Mr Dombey, glaring at her. 'How do you dare?'

'What I mean, Sir, is to speak respectful and without offence, but out, and how I dare I know not but I do!' said Susan. 'Oh! you don't know my young lady Sir you don't indeed, you'd never know so little of her, if you did.'

Mr Dombey, in a fury, put his hand out for the bell-rope but there was no bell-rope on that side of the fire, and he could not rise and cross to the other without assistance. The quick eye of the Nipper detected his helplessness immediately, and now, as she afterwards observed, she felt she had got him.

'Miss Floy,' said Susan Nipper, 'is the most devoted and most patient and most dutiful and beautiful of daughters, there an't no gentleman, no Sir, though as great and rich as all the greatest and richest of England put together, but might be proud of her and would and ought. If he knew her value right he'd rather lose his greatness and his fortune piece by piece and beg his way in rags from door to door, I say to some and all, he would!' cried Susan Nipper, bursting into tears, 'than bring the sorrow on her tender heart that I have seen it suffer in this house!'

'Woman,' cried Mr Dombey, 'leave the room.'

'Begging your pardon, not even if I am to leave the situation, Sir,' replied the steadfast Nipper, 'in which I have been so many years and seen so much – although I hope you'd never have the heart to send me from Miss Floy for such a cause – will I go now till I have said the rest, I may not be a Indian widow[3] Sir and I am not and I would not so become but if I once made up my mind to burn myself alive, I'd do it! And I've made my mind up to go on.'

Which was rendered no less clear by the expression of Susan Nipper's countenance, than by her words.

'There an't a person in your service, Sir,' pursued the black-eyed, 'that has always stood more in awe of you than me and you may think how true it is when I make so bold as say that I have hundreds and hundreds of times thought of speaking to you and never been able to make my mind up to it till last night, but last night decided of me.'

Mr Dombey, in a paroxysm of rage, made another grasp at the bell-rope that was not there, and, in its absence, pulled his hair rather than nothing.

'I have seen,' said Susan Nipper, 'Miss Floy strive and strive when nothing but a child so sweet and patient that the best of women might have copied from her, I've seen her sitting nights together half the night through to help her delicate brother with his learning, I've seen her helping him and watching him at other times – some well know when – I've seen her, with no encouragement and no help, grow up to be a lady, thank God! that is the grace and pride of every company she goes in, and I've always seen her cruelly neglected and keenly feeling of it – I say to some and all, I have! – and never said one word, but ordering one's self lowly and reverently towards one's betters, is not to be a worshipper of graven images,[4] and I will and must speak!'

'Is there anybody there?' cried Mr Dombey, calling out. 'Where are the men? where are the women? Is there no one there?'

'I left my dear young lady out of bed late last night,' said Susan, nothing checked, 'and I knew why, for you was ill Sir and she didn't know how ill and that was enough to make her wretched as I saw it did. I may not be a Peacock; but I have my eyes – and I sat up a little in my own room thinking she might be lonesome and might want me, and I saw her steal downstairs and come to this door as if it was a guilty thing to look at her own pa, and then steal back again and go into them lonely drawing-rooms, a crying so, that I could hardly bear to hear it. I *can not* bear to hear it,' said Susan Nipper, wiping her black eyes, and fixing them undauntingly on Mr Dombey's infuriated face. 'It's not the first time I have heard it, not by many and many a time you don't know your own daughter, Sir, you don't know what you're doing, Sir, I say to some and all,' cried Susan Nipper, in a final burst, 'that it's a sinful shame!'

'Why, hoity toity!' cried the voice of Mrs Pipchin, as the black bombazeen garments of that fair Peruvian Miner swept into the room 'What's this, indeed?'

Susan favoured Mrs Pipchin with a look she had invented expressly for her when they first became acquainted, and resigned the reply to Mr Dombey.

'What's this?' repeated Mr Dombey, almost foaming. 'What's this, madam? You who are at the head of this household, and bound to keep it in order, have reason to inquire. Do you know this woman?'

'I know very little good of her, Sir,' croaked Mrs Pipchin. 'How dare you come here, you hussy? Go along with you!'

But the inflexible Nipper, merely honouring Mrs Pipchin with another look, remained.

'Do you call it managing this establishment, madam,' said Mr Dombey, 'to leave a person like this at liberty to come and talk to *me!* A gentleman – in his own house – in his own room – assailed with the impertinences of women-servants!'

'Well, Sir,' returned Mrs Pipchin, with vengeance in her hard grey eye, 'I exceedingly deplore it; nothing can be more irregular; nothing can be more out of all bounds and reason; but I regret to say, Sir, that this young woman is quite beyond control. She has been spoiled by Miss Dombey, and is amenable to nobody. You know you're not,' said Mrs Pipchin, sharply, and shaking her head at Susan Nipper. 'For shame, you hussy! Go along with you!'

'If you find people in my service who are not to be controlled, Mrs Pipchin,' said Mr Dombey, turning back towards the fire, 'you know what to do with them, I presume. You know what you are here for? Take her away!'

'Sir, I know what to do,' retorted Mrs Pipchin, 'and of course shall do it. Susan Nipper,' snapping her up particularly short, 'a month's warning from this hour.'

'Oh indeed!' cried Susan, loftily.

'Yes,' returned Mrs Pipchin, 'and don't smile at me, you minx, or I'll know the reason why! Go along with you this minute!'

'I intend to go this minute, you may rely upon it,' said the voluble Nipper. 'I have been in this house waiting on my young lady a dozen year and I won't stop in it one hour under notice from a person owning to the name of Pipchin, trust me, Mrs P.'

'A good riddance of bad rubbish!' said that wrathful old lady. 'Get along with you, or I'll have you carried out!'

'My comfort is,' said Susan, looking back at Mr Dombey, 'that I have told a piece of truth this day which ought to have been told long before and can't be told too often or too plain and that no amount of Pipchinses – I hope the number of 'em mayn't be great' (here Mrs Pipchin uttered a very sharp 'Go along with you!' and Miss Nipper repeated the look) 'can unsay what I have said, though they gave a whole year full of warnings beginning at ten o'clock in the forenoon and never leaving off till twelve at night and died of the exhaustion which would be a Jubilee!'[5]

With these words, Miss Nipper preceded her foe out of the room; and walking upstairs to her own apartments in great state, to the choking exasperation of the ireful Pipchin, sat down among her boxes and began to cry.

From this soft mood she was soon aroused, with a very wholesome and refreshing effect, by the voice of Mrs Pipchin outside the door.

'Does that bold-faced slut,' said the fell Pipchin, 'intend to take her warning, or does she not?'

Miss Nipper replied from within that the person described did not inhabit that part of the house, but that her name was Pipchin, and she was to be found in the housekeeper's room.

'You saucy baggage!' retorted Mrs Pipchin, rattling at the handle of the door. 'Go along with you this minute. Pack up your things directly! How dare you talk in this way to a gentlewoman who has seen better days?'

To which Miss Nipper rejoined from her castle, that she pitied the better days that had seen Mrs Pipchin; and that for her part she considered the worst days in the year to be about that lady's mark, except that they were much too good for her.

'But you needn't trouble yourself to make a noise at my door,' said Susan Nipper, 'nor to contaminate the key-hole with your eye, I'm packing up and going you may take your affidavit.'[6]

The Dowager expressed her lively satisfaction at this intelligence, and with some general opinions upon young hussies as a race, and especially upon their demerits after being spoiled by Miss Dombey, withdrew to prepare the Nipper's wages. Susan then bestirred herself to get her trunks in order, that she might take an immediate and dignified departure; sobbing heartily all the time, as she thought of Florence.

The object of her regret was not long in coming to her, for the news soon spread over the house that Susan Nipper had had a disturbance with Mrs Pipchin, and that they had both appealed to Mr Dombey, and that there had been an unprecedented piece of work in Mr Dombey's room, and that Susan was going. The latter part of this confused rumour, Florence found to be so correct, that Susan had locked the last trunk and was sitting upon it with her bonnet on, when she came into her room.

'Susan!' cried Florence. 'Going to leave me! You!'

'Oh for goodness gracious sake, Miss Floy,' said Susan, sobbing, 'don't speak a word to me or I shall demean myself before them Pi-i-ipchinses, and I wouldn't have 'em see me cry Miss Floy for worlds!'

'Susan!' said Florence. 'My dear girl, my old friend! What shall I do without you! Can you bear to go away so?'

'No-n-o-o, my darling dear Miss Floy, I can't indeed,' sobbed Susan. 'But it can't be helped, I've done my duty Miss, I have indeed. It's no fault of mine. I am quite resi-igned. I couldn't stay my month or I could never leave you then my darling and I must at last as well as at first, don't speak to me Miss Floy, for though I'm pretty firm I'm not a marble doorpost, my own dear.'

'What is it? Why is it?' said Florence. 'Won't you tell me?' For Susan was shaking her head.

'No-n-no, my darling,' returned Susan. 'Don't ask me, for I mustn't, and whatever you do don't put in a word for me to stop, for it couldn't be and you'd only wrong yourself, and so God bless you my own precious and forgive me any harm I have done, or any temper I have showed in all these many years!'

With which entreaty, very heartily delivered, Susan hugged her mistress in her arms.

'My darling there's a many that may come to serve you and be glad to serve you and who'll serve you well and true,' said Susan, 'but there can't be one who'll serve you so affectionate as me or love you half as dearly, that's my comfort. Go-oodbye, sweet Miss Floy!'

'Where will you go, Susan?' asked her weeping mistress.

'I've got a brother down in the country Miss – a farmer in Essex,' said the heart-broken Nipper, 'that keeps ever so many co-o-ows and pigs and I shall go down there by the coach and sto-op with him, and don't mind me, for I've got money in the Savings' Banks my dear, and needn't take another service just yet, which I couldn't, couldn't, couldn't do, my heart's own mistress!' Susan finished with a burst of sorrow, which was opportunely broken by the voice of Mrs Pipchin talking downstairs; on hearing which, she dried her red and swollen eyes, and made a melancholy feint of calling jauntily to Mr Towlinson to fetch a cab and carry down her boxes.

Florence, pale and hurried and distressed, but withheld from useless interference even here, by her dread of causing any new division between her father and his wife (whose stern, indignant face had been a warning to her a few moments since), and by her apprehension of being in some way unconsciously connected already with the dismissal of her old servant and friend, followed, weeping, downstairs to Edith's dressing-room, whither Susan betook herself to make her parting curtsey.

'Now, here's the cab, and here's the boxes, get along with you, do!' said Mrs Pipchin, presenting herself at the same moment. 'I beg your pardon, ma'am, but Mr Dombey's orders are imperative.'

Edith, sitting under the hands of her maid – she was going out to dinner – preserved her haughty face, and took not the least notice.

'There's your money,' said Mrs Pipchin, who in pursuance of her system, and in recollection of the mines, was accustomed to rout the servants about, as she had routed her young Brighton boarders; to the everlasting acidulation of Master Bitherstone, 'and the sooner this house sees your back the better.'

Susan had no spirits even for the look that belonged to Mrs Pipchin by right; so she dropped her curtsey to Mrs Dombey (who inclined her head without one word, and whose eye avoided every one but Florence), and gave one last parting hug to her young

Florence parts from a very old friend

mistress, and received her parting embrace in return. Poor Susan's face at this crisis, in the intensity of her feelings and the determined suffocation of her sobs, lest one should become audible and be a triumph to Mrs Pipchin, presented a series of the most extraordinary physiognomical phenomena ever witnessed.

'I beg your pardon, Miss, I'm sure,' said Towlinson, outside the door with the boxes, addressing Florence, 'but Mr Toots is in the drawing-room, and sends his compliments, and begs to know how Diogenes and Master is.'

Quick as thought, Florence glided out and hastened downstairs, where Mr Toots, in the most splendid vestments, was breathing very hard with doubt and agitation on the subject of her coming.

'Oh, how de do, Miss Dombey,' said Mr Toots, 'God bless my soul!'

This last ejaculation was occasioned by Mr Toots's deep concern at the distress he saw in Florence's face; which caused him to stop short in a fit of chuckles, and become an image of despair.

'Dear Mr Toots,' said Florence, 'you are so friendly to me, and so honest, that I am sure I may ask a favour of you.'

'Miss Dombey,' returned Mr Toots, 'if you'll only name one, you'll – you'll give me an appetite. To which,' said Mr Toots, with some sentiment, 'I have long been a stranger.'

'Susan, who is an old friend of mine, the oldest friend I have,' said Florence, 'is about to leave here suddenly, and quite alone, poor girl. She is going home, a little way into the country. Might I ask you to take care of her until she is in the coach?'

'Miss Dombey,' returned Mr Toots, 'you really do me an honour and a kindness. This proof of your confidence, after the manner in which I was Beast enough to conduct myself at Brighton—'

'Yes,' said Florence, hurriedly – 'no – don't think of that. Then would you have the kindness to – to go? and to be ready to meet her when she comes out? Thank you a thousand times! You ease my mind so much. She doesn't seem so desolate. You cannot think how grateful I feel to you, or what a good friend I am sure you are!' And Florence in her earnestness thanked him again and again; and Mr Toots, in *his* earnestness, hurried away – but backwards, that he might lose no glimpse of her.

Florence had not the courage to go out, when she saw poor Susan in the hall, with Mrs Pipchin driving her forth, and Diogenes jumping about her, and terrifying Mrs Pipchin to the last degree by making snaps at her bombazeen skirts, and howling with anguish at the sound of her voice – for the good duenna was the dearest and most cherished aversion of his breast. But she saw Susan shake hands with the servants all round, and turn once to look at her old home; and she saw Diogenes bound out after the cab, and want to follow it, and testify an impossibility of conviction that he had no longer any property in the fare; and the door was shut, and the hurry over, and her tears flowed fast for the loss of an old friend, whom no one could replace. No one. No one.

Mr Toots, like the leal[7] and trusty soul he was, stopped the cabriolet in a twinkling, and told Susan Nipper of his commission, at which she cried more than before.

'Upon my soul and body!' said Mr Toots, taking his seat beside her, 'I feel for you. Upon my word and honour I think you can hardly know your own feelings better than I imagine them. I can conceive nothing more dreadful than to have to leave Miss Dombey.'

Susan abandoned herself to her grief now, and it really was touching to see her.

'I say,' said Mr Toots, 'now, don't! at least I mean now do, you know!'

'Do what, Mr Toots?' cried Susan.

'Why, come home to my place, and have some dinner before you start,' said Mr Toots. 'My cook's a most respectable woman – one of the most motherly people I ever saw – and she'll be delighted to make you comfortable. Her son,' said Mr Toots, as an additional recommendation, 'was educated in the Blue-coat School,[8] and blown up in a powder-mill.'[9]

Susan accepting this kind offer, Mr Toots conducted her to his dwelling, where they were received by the Matron in question who fully justified his character of her, and by the Chicken, who at first supposed, on seeing a lady in the vehicle, that Mr Dombey had been doubled up, agreeably to his old recommendation, and Miss Dombey abducted. This gentleman awakened in Miss Nipper some considerable astonishment, for, having been defeated by the Larkey Boy, his visage was in a state of such great dilapidation, as to be hardly presentable in society with comfort to the beholders. The Chicken himself attributed this punishment to his having had the misfortune to get into Chancery early in the proceedings, when he was severely fibbed by the Larkey one, and heavily grassed. But it appeared from the published records of that great contest that the Larkey Boy had had it all his own way from the beginning, and that the Chicken had been tapped, and bunged, and had received pepper, and had been made groggy, and had come up piping, and had endured a complication of similar strange inconveniences, until he had been gone into and finished.[10]

After a good repast, and much hospitality, Susan set out for the coach-office in another cabriolet, with Mr Toots inside, as before, and the Chicken on the box, who, whatever distinction he conferred on the little party by the moral weight and heroism of his character, was scarcely ornamental to it, physically speaking, on account of his plasters; which were numerous. But the Chicken had registered a vow, in secret, that he would never leave Mr Toots (who was secretly pining to get rid of him), for any less consideration than the good-will and fixtures of a public-house; and being ambitious to go into that line, and drink himself to death as soon as possible, he felt it his cue to make his company unacceptable.

The night-coach by which Susan was to go, was on the point of departure. Mr Toots having put her inside, lingered by the window, irresolutely, until the driver was about to mount; when, standing on the step, and putting in a face that by the light of the lamp was anxious and confused, he said abruptly:

'I say, Susan! Miss Dombey, you know—'

'Yes, Sir.'

'Do you think she could – you know – eh?'

'I beg your pardon, Mr Toots,' said Susan, 'but I don't hear you.'

'Do you think she could be brought, you know – not exactly at once, but in time – in a long time – to – to love me, you know? There!' said poor Mr Toots.

'Oh dear no!' returned Susan, shaking her head. 'I should say, never. Ne–ver!'

'Thank'ee!' said Mr Toots. 'It's of no consequence. Good night. It's of no consequence, thank'ee!'

CHAPTER 45

The Trusty Agent

Edith went out alone that day, and returned home early. It was but a few minutes after ten o'clock, when her carriage rolled along the street in which she lived.

There was the same enforced composure on her face, that there had been when she was dressing; and the wreath upon her head encircled the same cold and steady brow. But it would have been better to have seen its leaves and flowers reft into fragments by her passionate hand, or rendered shapeless by the fitful searches of a throbbing and bewildered brain for any resting-place, than adorning such tranquillity. So obdurate, so unapproachable, so unrelenting, one would have thought that nothing could soften such a woman's nature, and that everything in life had hardened it.

Arrived at her own door, she was alighting, when some one coming quietly from the hall, and standing bareheaded, offered her his arm. The servant being thrust aside, she had no choice but to touch it; and she then knew whose arm it was.

'How is your patient, Sir?' she said, with a curled lip.

'He is better,' returned Carker. 'He is doing very well. I have left him for the night.'

She bent her head, and was passing up the staircase, when he followed and said, speaking at the bottom:

'Madam! May I beg the favour of a minute's audience?'

She stopped and turned her eyes back. 'It is an unreasonable time, Sir, and I am fatigued. Is your business urgent?'

'It is very urgent,' returned Carker. 'As I am so fortunate as to have met you, let me press my petition.'

She looked down for a moment at his glistening mouth; and he looked up at her, standing above him in her stately dress, and thought, again, how beautiful she was.

'Where is Miss Dombey?' she asked the servant, aloud.

'In the morning room, ma'am.'

'Show the way there!' Turning her eyes again on the attentive gentleman at the bottom of the stairs, and informing him with a slight motion of her head, that he was at liberty to follow, she passed on.

'I beg your pardon! Madam! Mrs Dombey!' cried the soft and nimble Carker at her side in a moment. 'May I be permitted to entreat that Miss Dombey is not present?'

She confronted him, with a quick look, but with the same self-possession and steadiness.

'I would spare Miss Dombey,' said Carker, in a low voice, 'the knowledge of what I have to say. At least, Madam, I would leave it to you to decide whether she shall know of it or not. I owe that to you. It is my bounden duty to you. After our former interview, it would be monstrous in me if I did otherwise.'

She slowly withdrew her eyes from his face, and turning to the servant, said, 'Some other room.' He led the way to a drawing-room, which he speedily lighted up and then left them. While he remained, not a word was spoken. Edith enthroned herself upon a couch by the fire; and Mr Carker, with his hat in his hand and his eyes bent upon the carpet, stood before her, at some little distance.

'Before I hear you, Sir,' said Edith, when the door was closed, 'I wish you to hear me.'

'To be addressed by Mrs Dombey,' he returned, 'even in accents of unmerited reproach, is an honour I so greatly esteem, that although I were not her servant in all things, I should defer to such a wish, most readily.'

'If you are charged by the man whom you have just now left, Sir;' Mr Carker raised his eyes, as if he were going to counterfeit surprise, but she met them, and stopped him, if such were his intention; 'with any message to me, do not attempt to deliver it, for I will not receive it. I need scarcely ask you if you are come on such an errand. I have expected you some time.'

'It is my misfortune,' he replied, 'to be here, wholly against my will, for such a purpose. Allow me to say that I am here for two purposes. That is one.'

'That one, Sir,' she returned, 'is ended. Or, if you return to it—'

'Can Mrs Dombey believe,' said Carker, coming nearer, 'that I would return to it in the face of her prohibition? Is it possible that Mrs Dombey, having no regard to my unfortunate position, is so determined to consider me inseparable from my instructor as to do me great and wilful injustice?'

'Sir,' returned Edith, bending her dark gaze full upon him, and speaking with a rising passion that inflated her proud nostril and her swelling neck, and stirred the delicate white down upon a robe she wore, thrown loosely over shoulders that could bear its snowy neighbourhood. 'Why do you present yourself to me, as you have done, and speak to me of love and duty to my husband, and pretend to think that I am happily married, and that I honour him? How dare you venture so to affront me, when you know – *I* do not know better, Sir: I have seen it in your every glance, and heard it in your every word – that in place of affection between us there is aversion and contempt, and that I despise him hardly less than I despise myself for being his! Injustice! If I had done justice to the torment you have made me feel, and to my sense of the insult you have put upon me, I should have slain you!'

She had asked him why he did this. Had she not been blinded by her pride and wrath, and self-humiliation, – which she was, fiercely as she bent her gaze upon him, – she would have seen the answer in his face. To bring her to this declaration.

She saw it not, and cared not whether it was there or no. She saw only the indignities and struggles she had undergone, and had to undergo, and was writhing under them. As she sat looking fixedly at them, rather than at him, she plucked the feathers from a pinion of some rare and beautiful bird, which hung from her wrist by a golden thread, to serve her as a fan, and rained them on the ground.

He did not shrink beneath her gaze, but stood, until such outward signs of her anger as had escaped her control subsided, with the air of a man who had his sufficient reply in reserve and would presently deliver it. And he then spoke, looking straight into her kindling eyes.

'Madam,' he said, 'I know, and knew before to-day, that I have found no favour with you; and I knew why. Yes. I knew why. You have spoken so openly to me; I am so relieved by the possession of your confidence—'

'Confidence!' she repeated, with disdain.

He passed it over.

'—that I will make no pretence of concealment. I *did* see from the first, that there was no affection on your part for Mr Dombey – how could it possibly exist between such different subjects? And I *have* seen, since, that stronger feelings than indifference have been engendered in your breast – how could that possibly be otherwise, either, circumstanced as you have been? But was it for me to presume to avow this knowledge to you in so many words?'

'Was it for you, Sir,' she replied, 'to feign that other belief, and audaciously to thrust it on me day by day?'

'Madam, it was,' he eagerly retorted. 'If I had done less, if I had done anything but that, I should not be speaking to you thus; and I foresaw – who could better foresee, for who has had greater experience of Mr Dombey than myself? – that unless your character should prove to be as yielding and obedient as that of his first submissive lady, which I did not believe—'

A haughty smile gave him reason to observe that he might repeat this.

'I say, which I did not believe, – the time was likely to come, when such an understanding as we have now arrived at, would be serviceable.'

'Serviceable to whom, Sir?' she demanded scornfully.

'To you. I will not add to myself, as warning me to refrain even from that limited commendation of Mr Dombey, in which I can honestly indulge, in order that I may not have the misfortune of saying anything distasteful to one whose aversion and contempt,' with great expression, 'are so keen.'

'Is it honest in you, Sir,' said Edith, 'to confess to your "limited commendation," and to speak in that tone of disparagement, even of him: being his chief counsellor and flatterer!'

'Counsellor, – yes,' said Carker. 'Flatterer, – no. A little reservation I fear I must confess to. But our interest and convenience commonly oblige many of us to make professions that we cannot feel. We have partnerships of interest and convenience, friendships of interest and convenience, dealings of interest and convenience, marriages of interest and convenience, every day.'

She bit her blood-red lip; but without wavering in the dark, stern watch she kept upon him.

'Madam,' said Mr Carker, sitting down in a chair that was near her, with an air of the most profound and most considerate respect, 'why should I hesitate now, being altogether devoted to your service, to speak plainly? It was natural that a lady, endowed as you are, should think it feasible to change her husband's character in some respects, and mould him to a better form.'

'It was not natural to *me*, Sir,' she rejoined. 'I had never any expectation or intention of that kind.'

The proud undaunted face showed him it was resolute to wear no mask he offered, but was set upon a reckless disclosure of itself, indifferent to any aspect in which it might present itself to such as he.

'At least it was natural,' he resumed, 'that you should deem it quite possible to live with Mr Dombey as his wife, at once without submitting to him, and without coming into such violent collision with him. But, madam, you did not know Mr Dombey (as you have since ascertained), when you thought that. You did not know how exacting and how proud he is, or how he is, if I may say so, the slave of his own greatness, and goes yoked to his own triumphal car like a beast of burden with no idea on earth but that it is behind him and is to be drawn on, over everything and through everything.'

His teeth gleamed through his malicious relish of this conceit, as he went on talking:

'Mr Dombey is really capable of no more true consideration for you, madam, than for me. The comparison is an extreme one; I intend it to be so; but quite just. Mr Dombey, in the plenitude of his power, asked me – I had it from his own lips yesterday morning – to be his go-between to you, because he knows I am not agreeable to you, and because he intends that I shall be a punishment for your contumacy; and besides that, because he really does consider, that I, his paid servant, am an ambassador whom it is derogatory to the dignity – not of the lady to whom I have the happiness of speaking; she has no existence in his mind – but of his wife, a part of himself, to receive. You may imagine how regardless of me, how obtuse to the possibility of my having any individual sentiment or opinion he is, when he tells me, openly, that I am so employed. You know how perfectly indifferent to your feelings he is, when he threatens you with such a messenger. As you, of course, have not forgotten that he did.'

She watched him still attentively. But he watched her too; and he saw that this indication of a knowledge on his part, of something that had passed between herself and her husband, rankled and smarted in her haughty breast, like a poisoned arrow.

'I do not recall all this to widen the breach between yourself and Mr Dombey, madam – Heaven forbid! what would it profit me? – but as an example of the hopelessness of impressing Mr Dombey with a sense that anybody is to be considered when he is in question. We who are about him, have, in our various positions, done our part, I dare say, to confirm him in his way of thinking; but if we had not done so, others would – or they would not have been about him; and it has always been from the beginning, the very staple of his life. Mr Dombey has had to deal, in short, with none but submissive and dependent persons, who have bowed the knee, and bent the neck, before him. He has never known what it is to have angry pride and strong resentment opposed to him.'

'But he will know it now!' she seemed to say; though her lips did not part, nor her eyes falter. He saw the soft down tremble once again, and he saw her lay the plumage of the beautiful bird against her bosom for a moment; and he unfolded one more ring of the coil into which he had gathered himself.

'Mr Dombey, though a most honourable gentleman,' he said, 'is so prone to pervert even facts to his own view, when he is at all opposed, in consequence of the warp in his mind, that he – can I give a better instance than this! – he sincerely believes (you will excuse the folly of what I am about to say; it not being mine) that his severe expression of opinion to his present wife, on a certain special occasion she may remember, before the lamented death of Mrs Skewton, produced a withering effect, and for the moment quite subdued her!'

Edith laughed. How harshly and unmusically need not be described. It is enough that he was glad to hear her.

'Madam,' he resumed, 'I have done with this. Your own opinions are so strong, and, I am persuaded, so unalterable,' he repeated those words slowly and with great emphasis, 'that I am almost afraid to incur your displeasure anew, when I say that in spite of these defects and my full knowledge of them, I have become habituated to Mr Dombey, and esteem him. But when I say so, it is not, believe me, for the mere sake of vaunting a feeling that is so utterly at variance with your own, and for which you can have no sympathy' – oh how distinct and plain and emphasized this was! – 'but to give you an assurance of the zeal with which, in this unhappy matter, I am yours, and the indignation with which I regard the part I am required to fill!'

She sat as if she were afraid to take her eyes from his face.

And now to unwind the last ring of the coil!

'It is growing late,' said Carker, after a pause, 'and you are, as you said, fatigued. But the second object of this interview, I must not forget. I must recommend you, I must entreat you in the most earnest manner, for sufficient reasons that I have, to be cautious in your demonstrations of regard for Miss Dombey.'

'Cautious! What do you mean?'

'To be careful how you exhibit too much affection for that young lady.'

'Too much affection, Sir!' said Edith, knitting her broad brow and rising. 'Who judges my affection, or measures it out? You?'

'It is not I who do so.' He was, or feigned to be, perplexed.

'Who then?'

'Can you not guess who then?'

'I do not choose to guess,' she answered.

'Madam,' he said after a little hesitation; meantime they had been, and still were, regarding each other as before; 'I am in a difficulty here. You have told me you will receive no message, and you have forbidden me to return to that subject; but the two subjects are so closely entwined, I find, that unless you will accept this vague caution from one who has now the honour to possess your confidence, though the way to it has been through your displeasure, I must violate the injunction you have laid upon me.'

'You know that you are free to do so, Sir,' said Edith. 'Do it.'

So pale, so trembling, so impassioned! He had not miscalculated the effect then!

'His instructions were,' he said, in a low voice, 'that I should inform you that your demeanour towards Miss Dombey is not agreeable to him. That it suggests comparisons to him which are not favourable to himself. That he desires it may be wholly changed; and that if you are in earnest, he is confident it will be; for your continued show of affection will not benefit its object.'

'That is a threat,' she said.

'That is a threat,' he answered, in his voiceless manner of assent: adding aloud, 'but not directed against *you*.'

Proud, erect, and dignified, as she stood confronting him; and looking through him as she did, with her full bright flashing eye; and smiling, as she was, with scorn and bitterness; she sunk as if the ground had dropped beneath her, and in an instant would have fallen on the floor, but that he caught her in his arms. As instantaneously she threw him off, the moment that he touched her, and, drawing back, confronted him again, immovable, with her hand stretched out.

'Please to leave me. Say no more to-night.'

'I feel the urgency of this,' said Mr Carker, 'because it is impossible to say what unforeseen consequence might arise, or how soon, from your being unacquainted with his state of mind. I understand Miss Dombey is concerned, now, at the dismissal of her old servant, which is likely to have been a minor consequence in itself. You don't blame me for requesting that Miss Dombey might not be present. May I hope so?'

'I do not. Please to leave me, Sir.'

'I knew that your regard for the young lady, which is very sincere and strong, I am well persuaded, would render it a great unhappiness to you, ever to be a prey to the reflection that you had injured her position and ruined her future hopes,' said Carker hurriedly, but eagerly.

'No more to-night. Leave me, if you please.'

'I shall be here constantly in my attendance upon him, and in the transaction of business matters. You will allow me to see you again, and to consult what should be done, and learn your wishes?'

She motioned him towards the door.

'I cannot even decide whether to tell him I have spoken to you yet; or to lead him to suppose that I have deferred doing so, for want of opportunity, or for any other reason. It will be necessary that you should enable me to consult with you very soon.'

'At any time but now,' she answered.

'You will understand, when I wish to see you, that Miss Dombey is not to be present; and that I seek an interview as one who has the happiness to possess your confidence, and who comes to render you every assistance in his power, and, perhaps, on many occasions, to ward off evil from her?'

Looking at him still with the same apparent dread of releasing him for a moment from the influence of her steady gaze, whatever that might be, she answered, 'Yes!' and once more bade him go.

He bowed, as if in compliance; but turning back, when he had nearly reached the door, said:

'I am forgiven, and have explained my fault. May I – for Miss Dombey's sake, and for my own – take your hand before I go?'

She gave him the gloved hand she had maimed last night. He took it in one of his, and kissed it, and withdrew. And when he had closed the door, he waved the hand with which he had taken hers, and thrust it in his breast.

CHAPTER 46

Recognizant and Reflective

Among sundry minor alterations in Mr Carker's life and habits that began to take place at this time, none was more remarkable than the extraordinary diligence with which he applied himself to business, and the closeness with which he investigated every detail that the affairs of the House laid open to him. Always active and penetrating in such matters, his lynx-eyed vigilance now increased twenty-fold. Not only did his weary watch keep pace with every present point that every day presented to him in some new form, but in the midst of these engrossing occupations he found leisure – that is, he made it – to review the past transactions of the Firm, and his share in them, during a long series of years. Frequently when the clerks were all gone, the offices dark and empty, and all similar places of business shut up, Mr Carker, with the whole anatomy of the iron room laid bare before him, would explore the mysteries of books and papers, with the patient progress of a man who was dissecting the minutest nerves and fibres of his subject. Perch, the messenger, who usually remained on these occasions, to entertain himself with the perusal of the Price Current by the light of one candle, or to doze over the fire in the outer office, at the imminent risk every moment of diving head foremost into the coal-box, could not withhold the tributes of his admiration from this zealous conduct, although it much contracted his domestic enjoyments; and again, and again, expatiated to Mrs Perch (now nursing twins) on the industry and acuteness of their managing gentleman in the City.

The same increased and sharp attention that Mr Carker bestowed on the business of the House, he applied to his own personal affairs. Though not a partner in the concern – a distinction hitherto reserved solely to inheritors of the great name of Dombey – he was in the receipt of some per centage on its dealings; and, participating in all its facilities for the employment of money to advantage, was considered, by the minnows among the tritons of the East,[1] a rich man. It began to be said, among these shrewd observers, that Jem Carker, of Dombey's, was looking about him to see what he was worth; and that he was calling in his money at a good time, like the long-headed[2] fellow he was; and bets were even offered on the Stock Exchange that Jem was going to marry a rich widow.

Yet these cares did not in the least interfere with Mr Carker's watching of his chief, or with his cleanness, neatness, sleekness, or any cat-like quality he possessed. It was not so much that there was a change in him, in reference to any of his habits, as that the whole man was intensified. Everything that had been observable in him before, was observable now, but with a greater amount of concentration. He did each single thing, as if he did nothing else – a pretty certain indication in a man of that range of ability and purpose, that he is doing something which sharpens and keeps alive his keenest powers.

The only decided alteration in him was, that as he rode to and fro along the streets, he would fall into deep fits of musing, like that in which he had come away from Mr Dombey's house, on the morning of that gentleman's disaster. At such times, he would keep clear of the obstacles in his way, mechanically; and would appear to see and hear nothing until arrival at his destination, or some sudden chance or effort roused him.

Walking his white-legged horse thus, to the counting-house of Dombey and Son one day, he was as unconscious of the observation of two pairs of women's eyes, as of the fascinated orbs of Rob the Grinder, who, in waiting a street's length from the appointed place, as a demonstration of punctuality, vainly touched and retouched his hat to attract attention, and trotted along on foot, by his master's side, prepared to hold his stirrup when he should alight.

'See where he goes!' cried one of these two women, an old creature, who stretched out her shrivelled arm to point him out to

Abstraction and Recognition

her companion, a young woman, who stood close beside her, withdrawn like herself into a gateway.

Mrs Brown's daughter looked out, at this bidding on the part of Mrs Brown; and there were wrath and vengeance in her face.

'I never thought to look at him again,' she said, in a low voice; 'but it's well I should, perhaps. I see. I see!'

'Not changed!' said the old woman, with a look of eager malice.

'*He* changed!' returned the other. 'What for? What has *he* suffered? There is change enough for twenty in me. Isn't that enough?'

'See where he goes!' muttered the old woman, watching her daughter with her red eyes; 'so easy and so trim, a-horseback, while we are in the mud—'

'And of it,' said her daughter impatiently. 'We are mud, underneath his horse's feet. What should we be?'

In the intentness with which she looked after him again, she made a hasty gesture with her hand when the old woman began to reply, as if her view could be obstructed by mere sound. Her mother watching her, and not him, remained silent; until her kindling glance subsided, and she drew a long breath, as if in relief of his being gone.

'Deary!' said the old woman then. 'Alice! Handsome gal! Ally!' She gently shook her sleeve to arouse her attention. 'Will you let him go like that, when you can wring money from him? Why, it's a wickedness, my daughter.'

'Haven't I told you, that I will not have money from him?' she returned. 'And don't you yet believe me? Did I take his sister's money? Would I touch a penny, if I knew it, that had gone through his white hands – unless it was, indeed, that I could poison it, and send it back to him? Peace, mother, and come away.'

'And him so rich?' murmured the old woman. 'And us so poor!'

'Poor is not being able to pay him any of the harm we owe him,' returned her daughter. 'Let him give me that sort of riches, and I'll take them from him, and use them. Come away. It's no good looking at his horse. Come away, mother!'

But the old woman, for whom the spectacle of Rob the Grinder returning down the street, leading the riderless horse, appeared to have some extraneous interest that it did not possess in itself, surveyed that young man with the utmost earnestness; and seeming to have whatever doubts she entertained, resolved as he drew nearer, glanced at her daughter with heightened eyes and with her finger on her lip, and emerging from the gateway at the moment of his passing, touched him on the shoulder.

'Why, where's my sprightly Rob been, all this time!' she said, as he turned round.

The sprightly Rob, whose sprightliness was very much diminished by the salutation, looked exceedingly dismayed, and said, with the water rising in his eyes:

'Oh! why can't you leave a poor cove alone, Misses Brown, when he's getting an honest livelihood and conducting himself respectable? What do you come and deprive a cove of his character for, by talking to him in the streets, when he's taking his master's horse to a honest stable – a horse you'd go and sell for cats' and dogs' meat if you had *your* way! Why, I thought,' said the Grinder, producing his concluding remark as if it were the climax of all his injuries, 'that you was dead long ago!'

'This is the way,' cried the old woman, appealing to her daughter, 'that he talks to me, who knew him weeks and months together, my deary, and have stood his friend many and many a time among the pigeon-fancying tramps and bird-catchers.'

'Let the birds be, will you, Misses Brown?' retorted Rob, in a tone of the acutest anguish. 'I think a cove had better have to do with lions than them little creeturs, for they're always flying back in your face when you least expect it. Well, how d'ye do and what do you want?' These polite inquiries the Grinder uttered, as it were under protest, and with great exasperation and vindictiveness.

'Hark how he speaks to an old friend, my deary!' said Mrs Brown, again appealing to her daughter. 'But there's some of his old friends not so patient as me. If I was to tell some that he knows, and has sported and cheated with, where to find him—'

'Will you hold your tongue, Misses Brown?' interrupted the miserable Grinder, glancing quickly round, as though he expected to see his master's teeth shining at his elbow. 'What do you take a pleasure in ruining a cove for? At your time of life too! when you ought to be thinking of a variety of things!'

'What a gallant horse!' said the old woman, patting the animal's neck.

'Let him alone, will you, Misses Brown?' cried Rob, pushing away her hand. 'You're enough to drive a penitent cove mad!'

'Why, what hurt do I do him, child?' returned the old woman.

'Hurt?' said Rob. 'He's got a master that would find it out if he was touched with a straw.' And he blew upon the place where the old woman's hand had rested for a moment, and smoothed it gently with his finger, as if he seriously believed what he said.

The old woman looking back to mumble and mouth at her daughter, who followed, kept close to Rob's heels as he walked on with the bridle in his hand; and pursued the conversation.

'A good place, Rob, eh?' said she. 'You're in luck, my child.'

'Oh don't talk about luck, Misses Brown,' returned the wretched Grinder, facing round and stopping. 'If you'd never come, or if you'd go away, then indeed a cove might be considered tolerably lucky. Can't you go along, Misses Brown, and not foller me!' blubbered Rob, with sudden defiance. 'If the young woman's a friend of yours, why don't she take you away, instead of letting you make yourself so disgraceful!'

'What!' croaked the old woman, putting her face close to his, with a malevolent grin upon it that puckered up the loose skin down in her very throat. 'Do you deny your old chum! Have you lurked to my house fifty times, and slept sound in a corner when you had no other bed but the paving-stones, and do you talk to *me* like this! Have I bought and sold with you, and helped you in my way of business, schoolboy, sneak, and what not, and do you tell *me* to go along! Could I raise a crowd of old company about you to-morrow morning, that would follow you to ruin like copies of your own shadow, and do you turn on *me* with your bold looks! I'll go. Come, Alice.'

'Stop, Misses Brown!' cried the distracted Grinder. 'What are you doing of? Don't put yourself in a passion! Don't let her go, if you please. I haven't meant any offence. I said "how d'ye do," at first, didn't I? But you wouldn't answer. How *do* you do? Besides,' said Rob piteously, 'look here! How can a cove stand talking in the street with his master's prad[3] a wanting to be took to be rubbed down, and his master up to every individge thing that happens!'

The old woman made a show of being partially appeased, but shook her head, and mouthed and muttered still.

'Come along to the stables, and have a glass of something that's good for you, Misses Brown, can't you?' said Rob, 'instead of going on, like that, which is no good to you, nor anybody else. Come along with her, will you be so kind?' said Rob. 'I'm sure I'm delighted to see her, if it wasn't for the horse!'

With this apology, Rob turned away, a rueful picture of despair, and walked his charge down a bye-street. The old woman, mouthing at her daughter, followed close upon him. The daughter followed.

Turning into a silent little square or court-yard that had a great church tower rising above it, and a packer's warehouse, and a bottle-maker's warehouse, for its places of business, Rob the Grinder delivered the white-legged horse to the hostler of a quaint stable at the corner; and inviting Mrs Brown and her daughter to seat themselves upon a stone bench at the gate of that establishment, soon reappeared from a neighbouring public-house with a pewter measure and a glass.

'Here's master – Mr Carker, child!' said the old woman, slowly, as her sentiment before drinking. 'Lord bless him!'

'Why, I didn't tell you who he was?' observed Rob, with staring eyes.

'We know him by sight,' said Mrs Brown, whose working mouth and nodding head stopped for the moment, in the fixedness of her attention. 'We saw him pass this morning, afore he got off his horse; when you were ready to take it.'

'Aye, aye,' returned Rob, appearing to wish that his readiness had carried him to any other place. – 'What's the matter with her? Won't she drink?'

This inquiry had reference to Alice, who, folded in her cloak, sat a little apart profoundly inattentive to his offer of the replenished glass.

The old woman shook her head. 'Don't mind her,' she said; 'she's a strange creetur, if you know'd her, Rob. But Mr Carker—'

'Hush!' said Rob, glancing cautiously up at the packer's, and at the bottle-maker's, as if, from any one of the tiers of warehouses, Mr Carker might be looking down. 'Softly.'

'Why, he ain't here!' cried Mrs Brown.

'I don't know that,' muttered Rob, whose glance even wandered to the church tower, as if he might be there, with a supernatural power of hearing.

'Good master?' inquired Mrs Brown.

Rob nodded; and added, in a low voice, 'precious sharp.'

'Lives out of town, don't he, lovey?' said the old woman.

'When he's at home,' returned Rob; 'but we don't live at home just now.'

'Where then?' asked the old woman.

'Lodgings; up near Mr Dombey's,' returned Rob.

The younger woman fixed her eyes so searchingly upon him, and so suddenly, that Rob was quite confounded, and offered the glass again, but with no more effect upon her than before.

'Mr Dombey – you and I used to talk about him, sometimes, you know,' said Rob to Mrs Brown. 'You used to get me to talk about him.'

The old woman nodded.

'Well, Mr Dombey, he's had a fall from his horse,' said Rob, unwillingly; 'and my master has to be up there, more than usual, either with him, or Mrs Dombey, or some of 'em; and so we've come to town.'

'Are they good friends, lovey?' asked the old woman.

'Who?' retorted Rob.

'He and she?'

'What, Mr and Mrs Dombey?' said Rob. 'How should I know!'

'Not them – Master and Mrs Dombey, chick,' replied the old woman, coaxingly.

'I don't know,' said Rob, looking round him again. 'I suppose so. How curious you are, Misses Brown! Least said, soonest mended.'

'Why, there's no harm in it!' exclaimed the old woman, with a laugh, and a clap of her hands. 'Sprightly Rob has grown tame since he has been well off! There's no harm in it.'

'No, there's no harm in it, I know,' returned Rob, with the same distrustful glance at the packer's and the bottle-maker's, and the church; 'but blabbing,[4] if it's only about the number of buttons on my master's coat, won't do. I tell you it won't do with him. A cove had better drown himself. He says so. I shouldn't have so much as told you what his name was, if you hadn't known it. Talk about somebody else.'

As Rob took another cautious survey of the yard, the old woman made a secret motion to her daughter. It was momentary, but the daughter, with a slight look of intelligence, withdrew her eyes from the boy's face, and sat folded in her cloak as before.

'Rob, lovey!' said the old woman, beckoning him to the other end of the bench. 'You were always a pet and favourite of mine. Now, weren't you? Don't you know you were?'

'Yes, Misses Brown,' replied the Grinder, with a very bad grace.

'And you could leave me!' said the old woman, flinging her arms about his neck. 'You could go away, and grow almost out of knowledge, and never come to tell your poor old friend how fortunate you were, proud lad! Oho, Oho!'

'Oh here's a dreadful go for a cove that's got a master wide awake in the neighbourhood!' exclaimed the wretched Grinder. 'To be howled over like this here!'

'Won't you come and see me, Robby?' cried Mrs Brown. 'Oho, won't you ever come and see me?'

'Yes, I tell you! Yes, I will!' returned the Grinder.

'That's my own Rob! That's my lovey!' said Mrs Brown, drying the tears upon her shrivelled face, and giving him a tender squeeze. 'At the old place, Rob?'

'Yes,' replied the Grinder.

'Soon, Robby dear?' cried Mrs Brown; 'and often?'

'Yes. Yes. Yes,' replied Rob. 'I will indeed, upon my soul and body.'

'And then,' said Mrs Brown, with her arms uplifted towards the sky, and her head thrown back and shaking, 'if he's true to his word, I'll never come a-near him, though I know where he is, and never breathe a syllable about him! Never!'

This ejaculation seemed a drop of comfort to the miserable Grinder, who shook Mrs Brown by the hand upon it, and implored her with tears in his eyes to leave a cove and not destroy his prospects. Mrs Brown, with another fond embrace, assented; but in the act of following her daughter, turned back, with her finger stealthily raised, and asked in a hoarse whisper for some money.

'A shilling, dear!' she said, with her eager avaricious face, 'or sixpence! For old acquaintance sake. I'm so poor. And my handsome gal' – looking over her shoulder – 'she's my gal, Rob – half starves me.'

But as the reluctant Grinder put it in her hand, her daughter, coming quietly back, caught the hand in hers, and twisted out the coin.

'What,' she said, 'mother! always money! money from the first, and to the last. Do you mind so little what I said but now? Here. Take it!'

The old woman uttered a moan as the money was restored, but without in any other way opposing its restoration, hobbled at her daughter's side out of the yard, and along the bye-street upon which it opened. The astonished and dismayed Rob staring after them, saw that they stopped, and fell to earnest conversation very soon; and more than once observed a darkly threatening action of the younger woman's hand (obviously having reference to some one of whom they spoke), and a crooning feeble imitation of it on the part of Mrs Brown, that made him earnestly hope he might not be the subject of their discourse.

With the present consolation that they were gone, and with the prospective comfort that Mrs Brown could not live for ever, and was not likely to live long to trouble him, the Grinder, not otherwise regretting his misdeeds than as they were attended with such disagreeable incidental consequences, composed his ruffled features to a more serene expression by thinking of the admirable manner in which he had disposed of Captain Cuttle (a reflection that seldom failed to put him in a flow of spirits), and went to the Dombey Counting House to receive his master's orders.

There his master, so subtle and vigilant of eye, that Rob quaked before him, more than half expecting to be taxed with Mrs Brown, gave him the usual morning's box of papers for Mr Dombey, and a note for Mrs Dombey: merely nodding his head as an enjoinder to be careful, and to use dispatch[5] – a mysterious admonition, fraught in the Grinder's imagination with dismal warnings and threats; and more powerful with him than any words.

Alone again, in his own room, Mr Carker applied himself to work, and worked all day. He saw many visitors; overlooked a number of documents; went in and out, to and from, sundry places of mercantile resort; and indulged in no more abstraction until the day's business was done. But, when the usual clearance of papers from his table was made at last, he fell into his thoughtful mood once more.

He was standing in his accustomed place and attitude, with his eyes intently fixed upon the ground, when his brother entered to bring back some letters that had been taken out in the course of the day. He put them quietly on the table, and was going immediately, when Mr Carker the Manager, whose eyes had rested on him, on his entrance, as if they had all this time had him for the subject of their contemplation, instead of the office-floor, said:

'Well, John Carker, and what brings *you* here?'

His brother pointed to the letters, and was again withdrawing.

'I wonder,' said the Manager, 'that you can come and go, without inquiring how our master is.'

'We had word this morning in the counting-house, that Mr Dombey was doing well,' replied his brother.

'You are such a meek fellow,' said the Manager, with a smile, ' – but you have grown so, in the course of years – that if any harm came to him, you'd be miserable, I dare swear now.'

'I should be truly sorry, James,' returned the other.

'He would be sorry!' said the Manager, pointing at him, as if there were some other person present to whom he was appealing. 'He would be truly sorry! This brother of mine! This junior of the place, this slighted piece of lumber, pushed aside with his face to the wall, like a rotten picture, and left so, for Heaven knows how many years: *he's* all gratitude and respect, and devotion too, he would have me believe!'

'I would have you believe nothing, James,' returned the other. 'Be as just to me as you would to any other man below you. You ask a question, and I answer it.'

'And have you nothing, Spaniel,'[6] said the Manager, with unusual irascibility, 'to complain of in him? No proud treatment to resent, no insolence, no foolery of state, no exaction of any sort! What the devil! are you man or mouse?'

'It would be strange if any two persons could be together for so many years, especially as superior and inferior, without each having something to complain of in the other – as he thought, at all events,' replied John Carker. 'But apart from my history here—'

'His history here!' exclaimed the Manager. 'Why, there it is. The very fact that makes him an extreme case, puts him out of the whole chapter! Well?'

'Apart from that, which, as you hint, gives me a reason to be thankful that I alone (happily for all the rest) possess, surely there is no one in the House who would not say and feel at least as much. You do not think that anybody here would be indifferent to a mischance or misfortune happening to the head of the House, or anything than truly sorry for it?'

'You have good reason to be bound to him too!' said the Manager contemptuously. 'Why, don't you believe that you are kept here, as a cheap example, and a famous instance of the clemency of Dombey and Son, redounding to the credit of the illustrious House?'

'No,' replied his brother, mildly, 'I have long believed that I am kept here for more kind and disinterested reasons.'

'But you were going,' said the Manager, with the snarl of a tiger-cat, 'to recite some Christian precept, I observed.'

'Nay, James,' returned the other, 'though the tie of brotherhood between us has been long broken and thrown away—'

'Who broke it, good Sir?' said the Manager.

'I, by my misconduct. I do not charge it upon you.'

The Manager replied, with that mute action of his bristling mouth, 'Oh, you don't charge it upon me!' and bade him go on.

'I say, though there is not that tie between us, do not, I entreat, assail me with unnecessary taunts, or misinterpret what I say, or would say. I was only going to suggest to you that it would be a mistake to suppose that it is only you, who have been selected here, above all others, for advancement, confidence and distinction (selected, in the beginning, I know, for your great ability and trustfulness), and who communicate more freely with Mr Dombey than any one, and stand, it may be said, on equal terms with him, and have been favoured and enriched by him – that it would be a mistake to suppose that it is only you who are tender of his welfare and reputation. There is no one in the House, from yourself down to the lowest, I sincerely believe, who does not participate in that feeling.'

'You lie!' said the Manager, red with sudden anger. 'You're a hypocrite, John Carker, and you lie.'

'James!' cried the other, flushing in his turn. 'What do you mean by these insulting words? Why do you so basely use them to me, unprovoked?'

'I tell you,' said the Manager, 'that your hypocrisy and meekness – that all the hypocrisy and meekness of this place – is not worth *that* to me,' snapping his thumb and finger, 'and that I see through it as if it were air! There is not a man employed here, standing between myself and the lowest in place (of whom you are very considerate, and with reason, for he is not far off), who wouldn't be glad at heart to see his master humbled: who does not hate him, secretly: who does not wish him evil rather than good: and who would not turn upon him, if he had the power and boldness. The nearer to his favour, the nearer to his insolence; the closer to him, the farther from him. That's the creed here!'

'I don't know,' said his brother, whose roused feelings had soon yielded to surprise, 'who may have abused your ear with such representations; or why you have chosen to try me, rather than another. But that you have been trying me, and tampering with me, I am now sure. You have a different manner and a different aspect from any that I ever saw in you. I will only say to you, once more, you are deceived.'

'I know I am,' said the Manager. 'I have told you so.'

'Not by me,' returned his brother. 'By your informant, if you have one. If not, by your own thoughts and suspicions.'

'I have no suspicions,' said the Manager. 'Mine are certainties. You pusillanimous, abject, cringing dogs! All making the same show, all canting the same story, all whining the same professions, all harbouring the same transparent secret.'

His brother withdrew, without saying more, and shut the door as he concluded. Mr Carker the Manager drew a chair close before the fire, and fell to beating the coals softly with the poker.

'The faint-hearted, fawning knaves,' he muttered, with his two shining rows of teeth laid bare. 'There's not one among them, who wouldn't feign to be so shocked and outraged – ! Bah! There's not one among them, but if he had at once the power, and the wit and daring to use it, would scatter Dombey's pride and lay it low, as ruthlessly as I rake out these ashes.'

As he broke them up and strewed them in the grate, he looked on with a thoughtful smile at what he was doing. 'Without the same queen beckoner too!' he added presently; 'and there is pride there, not to be forgotten – witness our own acquaintance!' With that he fell into a deeper reverie, and sat pondering over the blackening grate, until he rose up like a man who had been absorbed in a book, and looking round him he took his hat and gloves, went to where his horse was waiting, mounted, and rode away through the lighted streets, for it was evening.

He rode near Mr Dombey's house; and falling into a walk as he approached it, looked up at the windows. The window where he had once seen Florence sitting with her dog, attracted his attention first, though there was no light in it; but he smiled as he carried his eyes up the tall front of the house, and seemed to leave that object superciliously behind.

'Time was,' he said, 'when it was well to watch even your rising little star, and know in what quarter there were clouds to shadow you if needful. But a planet has arisen, and you are lost in its light.'

He turned the white-legged horse round the street corner, and sought one shining window from among those at the back of the house. Associated with it was a certain stately presence, a gloved hand, the remembrance how the feathers of a beautiful bird's wing had been showered down upon the floor, and how the light white down upon a robe had stirred and rustled, as in the rising of a distant storm. These were the things he carried with him as he turned away again, and rode through the darkening and deserted Parks at a quick rate.

In fatal truth, these were associated with a woman, a proud woman, who hated him, but who by slow and sure degrees had been led on by his craft, and her pride and resentment, to endure his company, and little by little to receive him as one who had the privilege to talk to her of her own defiant disregard of her own husband, and her abandonment of high consideration for herself. They were associated with a woman who hated him deeply, and who knew him, and who mistrusted him because she knew him, and because he knew her; but who fed her fierce resentment by suffering him to draw nearer and yet nearer to her every day, in spite of the hate she cherished for him. In spite of it! For that very

reason; since in i
pierce, though she
tion, whose faintest
seen again, would ha

Did the phantom of
to the reality, and obvi

Yes. He saw her in l
company with her pride,
her beauty; with nothing
saw her sometimes haughty
down among his horse's fee
saw her as she was, witho
dangerous way that she was go

And when his ride was over, ,and
into the light of her bright room   ..pected the
soothing smile, he saw her yet ⸱   ⸱ger in his own for
mystery of the gloved hand, and he
that suspicion. Upon the dangerous   ⸱ she was going, he was
still; and not a footprint did she ma⸱ upon it, but he set his own
there, straight.

CHAPTER 47

The Thunderbolt

The barrier between Mr Dombey and his wife was not weakened
by time. Ill-assorted couple, unhappy in themselves and in each
other, bound together by no tie but the manacle that joined their
fettered hands, and straining that so harshly, in their shrinking
asunder, that it wore and chafed to the bone, Time, consoler of
affliction and softener of anger, could do nothing to help them.
Their pride, however different in kind and object, was equal in
degree; and, in their flinty opposition, struck out fire between them
which might smoulder or might blaze, as circumstances were, but
burned up everything within their mutual reach, and made their
marriage way a road of ashes.

Let us be just to him: In the monstrous delusion of his life,
swelling with every grain of sand that shifted in its glass, he urged
her on, he little thought to what, or considered how; but still his
feeling towards her, such as it was, remained as at first. She had the

...tting herself in opposition to the
...nce, and to the acknowledgment of
...it, and so far it was necessary to correct
...herwise he still considered her, in his cold
...e of doing honour, if she would, to his choice
...reflecting credit on his proprietorship.

..., with all her might of passionate and proud resentment,
...dark glance from day to day, and hour to hour – from that
...in her own chamber, when she had sat gazing at the shadows
on the wall, to the deeper night fast coming – upon one figure
directing a crowd of humiliations and exasperations against her;
and that figure, still her husband's.

Was Mr Dombey's master-vice, that ruled him so inexorably, an
unnatural characteristic? It might be worth while, sometimes, to
inquire what Nature is, and how men work to change her, and
whether, in the enforced distortions so produced, it is not natural
to be unnatural. Coop any son or daughter of our mighty mother
within narrow range, and bind the prisoner to one idea, and foster
it by servile worship of it on the part of the few timid or designing
people standing round, and what is Nature to the willing captive
who has never risen up upon the wings of a free mind – drooping
and useless soon – to see her in her comprehensive truth!

Alas! are there so few things in the world, about us, most
unnatural, and yet most natural in being so? Hear the magistrate or
judge admonish the unnatural outcasts of society; unnatural in
brutal habits, unnatural in want of decency, unnatural in losing and
confounding all distinctions between good and evil; unnatural in
ignorance, in vice, in recklessness, in contumacy, in mind, in looks,
in everything. But follow the good clergyman or doctor, who, with
his life imperilled at every breath he draws, goes down into their
dens, lying within the echoes of our carriage wheels and daily tread
upon the pavement stones. Look round upon the world of odious
sights – millions of immortal creatures have no other world on
earth – at the lightest mention of which humanity revolts, and
dainty delicacy living in the next street, stops her ears, and lisps 'I
don't believe it!' Breathe the polluted air, foul with every impurity
that is poisonous to health and life; and have every sense, conferred
upon our race for its delight and happiness, offended, sickened and
disgusted, and made a channel by which misery and death alone
can enter. Vainly attempt to think of any simple plant, or flower, or
wholesome weed, that, set in this fœtid bed, could have its natural
growth, or put its little leaves off to the sun as GOD designed it.

And then, calling up some ghastly child, with stunted form and wicked face, hold forth on its unnatural sinfulness, and lament its being, so early, far away from Heaven – but think a little of its having been conceived, and born and bred, in Hell!

Those who study the physical sciences, and bring them to bear upon the health of Man, tell us that if the noxious particles that rise from vitiated air were palpable to the sight, we should see them lowering in a dense black cloud above such haunts, and rolling slowly on to corrupt the better portions of a town. But if the moral pestilence that rises with them, and in the eternal laws of outraged Nature, is inseparable from them, could be made discernible too, how terrible the revelation! Then should we see depravity, impiety, drunkenness, theft, murder, and a long train of nameless sins against the natural affections and repulsions of mankind overhanging the devoted spots, and creeping on, to blight the innocent and spread contagion among the pure. Then should we see how the same poisoned fountains that flow into our hospitals and lazar-houses,[1] inundate the jails, and make the convict-ships swim deep, and roll across the seas, and over-run vast continents with crime. Then should we stand appalled to know, that where we generate disease to strike our children down and entail itself on unborn generations, there also we breed, by the same certain process, infancy that knows no innocence, youth without modesty or shame, maturity that is mature in nothing but in suffering and guilt, blasted old age that is a scandal on the form we bear. Unnatural humanity! When we shall gather grapes from thorns, and figs from thistles;[2] when fields of grain shall spring up from the offal in the bye-ways of our wicked cities, and roses bloom in the fat churchyards that they cherish; then we may look for natural humanity and find it growing from such seed.

Oh for a good spirit who would take the house-tops off, with a more potent and benignant hand than the lame demon in the tale, and show a Christian people what dark shapes issue from amidst their homes, to swell the retinue of the Destroying Angel as he moves forth among them! For only one night's view of the pale phantoms rising from the scenes of our too-long neglect; and from the thick and sullen air where Vice and Fever propagate together, raining the tremendous social retributions which are ever pouring down, and ever coming thicker! Bright and blest the morning that should rise on such a night; for men, delayed no more by stumbling-blocks of their own making, which are but specks of dust upon the path between them and eternity, would then apply themselves, like creatures of one common origin, owing one duty to the Father of one family, and tending to one common end, to make the world a better place!

Not the less bright and blest would that day be for rousing some who never have looked out upon the world of human life around them, to a knowledge of their own relation to it, and for making them acquainted with a perversion of nature in their own contracted sympathies and estimates; as great, and yet as natural in its development when once begun, as the lowest degradation known.

But no such day had ever dawned on Mr Dombey, or his wife; and the course of each was taken.

Through six months that ensued upon his accident, they held the same relations one towards the other. A marble rock could not have stood more obdurately in his way than she; and no chilled spring, lying uncheered by any ray of light in the depths of a deep cave, could be more sullen or more cold than he.

The hope that had fluttered within her when the promise of her new home dawned, was quite gone from the heart of Florence now. That home was nearly two years old; and even the patient trust that was in her, could not survive the daily blight of such experience. If she had any lingering fancy in the nature of hope left, that Edith and her father might be happier together, in some distant time, she had none, now, that her father would ever love her. The little interval in which she had imagined that she saw some small relenting in him, was forgotten in the long remembrance of his coldness since and before, or only remembered as a sorrowful delusion.

Florence loved him still, but, by degrees, had come to love him rather as some dear one who had been, or who might have been, than as the hard reality before her eyes. Something of the softened sadness with which she loved the memory of little Paul, or of her mother, seemed to enter now into her thoughts of him, and to make them, as it were, a dear remembrance. Whether it was that he was dead to her, and that partly for this reason, partly for his share in those old objects of her affection, and partly for the long association of him with hopes that were withered and tendernesses he had frozen, she could not have told; but the father whom she loved began to be a vague and dreamy idea to her: hardly more substantially connected with her real life, than the image she would sometimes conjure up, of her dear brother yet alive, and growing to be a man, who would protect and cherish her.

The change, if it may be called one, had stolen on her like the change from childhood to womanhood, and had come with it. Florence was almost seventeen, when, in her lonely musings, she was conscious of these thoughts.

She was often alone now, for the old association between her and her mama was greatly changed. At the time of her father's accident, and when he was lying in his room downstairs, Florence had first observed that Edith avoided her. Wounded and shocked, and yet unable to reconcile this with her affection when they did meet, she sought her in her own room at night, once more.

'Mama,' said Florence, stealing softly to her side, 'have I offended you?'

Edith answered 'No.'

'I must have done something,' said Florence. 'Tell me what it is. You have changed your manner to me, dear mama. I cannot say how instantly I feel the least change; for I love you with my whole heart.'

'As I do you,' said Edith. 'Ah, Florence, believe me never more than now!'

'Why do you go away from me so often, and keep away?' asked Florence. 'And why do you sometimes look so strangely on me, dear mama? You do so, do you not?'

Edith signified assent with her dark eyes.

'Why?' returned Florence imploringly. 'Tell me why, that I may know how to please you better; and tell me this shall not be so any more.'

'My Florence,' answered Edith, taking the hand that embraced her neck, and looking into the eyes that looked into hers so lovingly, as Florence knelt upon the ground before her; 'why it is, I cannot tell you. It is neither for me to say, nor you to hear; but that it is, and that it must be, I know. Should I do it if I did not?'

'Are *we* to be estranged, mama?' asked Florence, gazing at her like one frightened.

Edith's silent lips formed 'Yes.'

Florence looked at her with increasing fear and wonder, until she could see her no more through the blinding tears that ran down her face.

'Florence! my life!' said Edith, hurriedly, 'listen to me. I cannot bear to see this grief. Be calmer. You see that I am composed, and is it nothing to me?'

She resumed her steady voice and manner as she said the latter words, and added presently:

'Not wholly estranged. Partially: and only that, in appearance,

Florence, for in my own breast I am still the same to you, and ever will be. But what I do is not done for myself.'

'Is it for me, mama?' asked Florence.

'It is enough,' said Edith, after a pause, 'to know what it is; why, matters little. Dear Florence, it is better – it is necessary – it must be – that our association should be less frequent. The confidence there has been between us must be broken off.'

'When?' cried Florence. 'Oh, mama, when?'

'Now,' said Edith.

'For all time to come?' asked Florence.

'I do not say that,' answered Edith. 'I do not know that. Nor will I say that companionship between us is, at the best, an ill-assorted and unholy union, of which I might have known no good could come. My way here has been through paths that you will never tread, and my way henceforth may lie – God knows – I do not see it—'

Her voice died away into silence; and she sat, looking at Florence, and almost shrinking from her, with the same strange dread and wild avoidance that Florence had noticed once before. The same dark pride and rage succeeded, sweeping over her form and features like an angry chord across the strings of a wild harp. But no softness or humility ensued on that. She did not lay her head down now, and weep, and say that she had no hope but in Florence. She held it up as if she were a beautiful Medusa,[3] looking on him, face to face, to strike him dead. Yes, and she would have done it, if she had had the charm.

'Mama,' said Florence, anxiously, 'there is a change in you, in more than what you say to me, which alarms me. Let me stay with you a little.'

'No,' said Edith, 'no, dearest. I am best left alone now and I do best to keep apart from you, of all else. Ask me no questions, but believe that what I am when I seem fickle or capricious to you, I am not of my own will, or for myself. Believe, though we are stranger to each other than we have been, that I am unchanged to you within. Forgive me for having ever darkened your dark home – I am a shadow on it, I know well – and let us never speak of this again.'

'Mama,' sobbed Florence, 'we are not to part?'

'We do this that we may not part,' said Edith. 'Ask no more. Go, Florence! My love and my remorse go with you!'

She embraced her, and dismissed her; and as Florence passed out of her room, Edith looked on the retiring figure, as if her good angel went out in that form, and left her to the haughty and indignant passions that now claimed her for their own, and set their seal upon her brow.

From that hour, Florence and she were, as they had been, no more. For days together, they would seldom meet, except at table, and when Mr Dombey was present. Then Edith, imperious, inflexible, and silent, never looked at her. Whenever Mr Carker was of the party, as he often was, during the progress of Mr Dombey's recovery, and afterwards, Edith held herself more removed from her, and was more distant towards her, than at other times. Yet she and Florence never encountered, when there was no one by, but she would embrace her as affectionately as of old, though not with the same relenting of her proud aspect; and often, when she had been out late, she would steal up to Florence's room, as she had been used to do, in the dark, and whisper 'Good Night,' on her pillow. When unconscious, in her slumber, of such visits, Florence would sometimes awake, as from a dream of those words, softly spoken, and would seem to feel the touch of lips upon her face. But less and less often as the months went on.

And now the void in Florence's own heart began again, indeed, to make a solitude around her. As the image of the father whom she loved had insensibly become a mere abstraction, so Edith, following the fate of all the rest about whom her affections had entwined themselves, was fleeting, fading, growing paler in the distance, every day. Little by little, she receded from Florence, like the retiring ghost of what she had been; little by little, the chasm between them widened and seemed deeper; little by little, all the power of earnestness and tenderness she had shown, was frozen up in the bold, angry hardihood with which she stood, upon the brink of a deep precipice unseen by Florence, daring to look down.

There was but one consideration to set against the heavy loss of Edith, and though it was slight comfort to her burdened heart, she tried to think it some relief. No longer divided between her affection and duty to the two, Florence could love both and do no injustice to either. As shadows of her fond imagination, she could give them equal place in her own bosom, and wrong them with no doubts.

So she tried to do. At times, and often too, wondering speculations on the cause of this change in Edith would obtrude themselves upon her mind and frighten her; but in the calm of its abandonment once more to silent grief and loneliness, it was not a curious mind. Florence had only to remember that her star of promise was clouded in the general gloom that hung upon the house, and to weep and be resigned.

Thus living, in a dream wherein the overflowing love of her young heart expended itself on airy forms, and in a real world where she had experienced little but the rolling back of that strong tide upon itself, Florence grew to be seventeen. Timid and retiring as her solitary life had made her, it had not embittered her sweet temper, or her earnest nature. A child in innocent simplicity; a woman in her modest self-reliance, and her deep intensity of feeling; both child and woman seemed at once expressed in her fair face and fragile delicacy of shape, and gracefully to mingle there; – as if the spring should be unwilling to depart when summer came, and sought to blend the earlier beauties of the flowers with their bloom. But in her thrilling voice, in her calm eyes, sometimes in a strange ethereal light that seemed to rest upon her head, and always in a certain pensive air upon her beauty, there was an expression, such as had been seen in the dead boy; and the council in the Servants' Hall whispered so among themselves, and shook their heads, and ate and drank the more, in a closer bond of good-fellowship.

This observant body had plenty to say of Mr and Mrs Dombey, and of Mr Carker, who appeared to be a mediator between them, and who came and went as if he were trying to make peace, but never could. They all deplored the uncomfortable state of affairs, and all agreed that Mrs Pipchin (whose unpopularity was not to be surpassed) had some hand in it; but, upon the whole, it was agreeable to have so good a subject for a rallying point, and they made a great deal of it, and enjoyed themselves very much.

The general visitors who came to the house, and those among whom Mr and Mrs Dombey visited, thought it a pretty equal match, as to haughtiness, at all events, and thought nothing more about it. The young lady with the back did not appear for some time after Mrs Skewton's death; observing to some particular friends, with her usual engaging little scream, that she couldn't separate the family from a notion of tombstones, and horrors of that sort; but when she did come, she saw nothing wrong, except Mr Dombey's wearing a bunch of gold seals to his watch, which shocked her very much, as an exploded superstition. This youthful fascinator considered a daughter-in-law objectionable in principle; otherwise, she had nothing to say against Florence, but that she sadly wanted 'style' – which might mean back, perhaps. Many, who only came to the house on state occasions, hardly knew who Florence was, and said, going home, 'Indeed, was *that* Miss

Dombey, in the corner? Very pretty, but a little delicate and thoughtful in appearance!'

None the less so, certainly, for her life of the last six months, Florence took her seat at the dinner-table, on the day before the second anniversary of her father's marriage to Edith (Mrs Skewton had been lying stricken with paralysis when the first came round), with an uneasiness, amounting to dread. She had no other warrant for it, than the occasion, the expression of her father's face, in the hasty glance she caught of it, and the presence of Mr Carker, which, always unpleasant to her, was more so on this day, than she had ever felt it before.

Edith was richly dressed, for she and Mr Dombey were engaged in the evening to some large assembly, and the dinner-hour that day was late. She did not appear until they were seated at table, when Mr Carker rose and led her to her chair. Beautiful and lustrous as she was, there was that in her face and air which seemed to separate her hopelessly from Florence, and from every one, for ever more. And yet, for an instant, Florence saw a beam of kindness in her eyes, when they were turned on her, that made the distance to which she had withdrawn herself, a greater cause of sorrow and regret than ever.

There was very little said at dinner. Florence heard her father speak to Mr Carker sometimes on business matters, and heard him softly reply, but she paid little attention to what they said, and only wished the dinner at an end. When the dessert was placed upon the table, and they were left alone, with no servant in attendance, Mr Dombey, who had been several times clearing his throat in a manner that augured no good, said:

'Mrs Dombey, you know, I suppose, that I have instructed the housekeeper that there will be some company to dinner here to-morrow.'

'I do not dine at home,' she answered.

'Not a large party,' pursued Mr Dombey, with an indifferent assumption of not having heard her; 'merely some twelve or fourteen. My sister, Major Bagstock, and some others whom you know but slightly.'

'I do not dine at home,' she repeated.

'However doubtful reason I may have, Mrs Dombey,' said Mr Dombey, still going majestically on, as if she had not spoken, 'to hold the occasion in very pleasant remembrance just now, there are appearances in these things which must be maintained before the world. If you have no respect for yourself, Mrs Dombey—'

'I have none,' she said.

'Madam,' cried Mr Dombey, striking his hand upon the table, 'hear me if you please. I say, if you have no respect for yourself—'

'And *I* say I have none,' she answered.

He looked at her; but the face she showed him in return would not have changed, if death itself had looked.

'Carker,' said Mr Dombey, turning more quietly to that gentleman, 'as you have been my medium of communication with Mrs Dombey on former occasions, and as I choose to preserve the decencies of life, so far as I am individually concerned, I will trouble you to have the goodness to inform Mrs Dombey that if she has no respect for herself, I have some respect for *myself*, and therefore insist on my arrangements for to-morrow.'

'Tell your sovereign master, Sir,' said Edith, 'that I will take leave to speak to him on this subject by-and-bye, and that I will speak to him alone.'

'Mr Carker, madam,' said her husband, 'being in possession of the reason which obliges me to refuse you that privilege, shall be absolved from the delivery of any such message.' He saw her eyes move, while he spoke, and followed them with his own.

'Your daughter is present, Sir,' said Edith.

'My daughter will remain present,' said Mr Dombey.

Florence, who had risen, sat down again, hiding her face in her hands, and trembling.

'My daughter, madam'—began Mr Dombey.

But Edith stopped him, in a voice which, although not raised in the least, was so clear, emphatic, and distinct, that it might have been heard in a whirlwind.

'I tell you I will speak to you alone,' she said. 'If you are not mad, heed what I say.'

'I have authority to speak to you, madam,' returned her husband, 'when and where I please; and it is my pleasure to speak here and now.'

She rose up as if to leave the room; but sat down again, and looking at him with all outward composure, said, in the same voice:

'You shall!'

'I must tell you first, that there is a threatening appearance in your manner, madam,' said Mr Dombey, 'which does not become you.'

She laughed. The shaken diamonds in her hair started and trembled. There are fables of precious stones that would turn pale, their wearer being in danger. Had these been such, their imprisoned rays of light would have taken flight that moment, and they would have been as dull as lead.

Carker listened, with his eyes cast down.

'As to my daughter, madam,' said Mr Dombey, resuming the thread of his discourse, 'it is by no means inconsistent with her duty to me, that she should know what conduct to avoid. At present you are a very strong example to her of this kind, and I hope she may profit by it.'

'I would not stop you now,' returned his wife, immovable in eye, and voice, and attitude; 'I would not rise and go away, and save you the utterance of one word, if the room were burning.'

Mr Dombey moved his head, as if in a sarcastic acknowledgment of the attention, and resumed. But not with so much self-possession as before; for Edith's quick uneasiness in reference to Florence, and Edith's indifference to him and his censure, chafed and galled him like a stiffening wound.

'Mrs Dombey,' said he, 'it may not be inconsistent with my daughter's improvement to know how very much to be lamented, and how necessary to be corrected, a stubborn disposition is, especially when it is indulged in – unthankfully indulged in, I will add – after the gratification of ambition and interest. Both of which, I believe, had some share in inducing you to occupy your present station at this board.'

'No! I would not rise, and go away, and save you the utterance of one word,' she repeated, exactly as before, 'if the room were burning.'

'It may be natural enough, Mrs Dombey,' he pursued, 'that you should be uneasy in the presence of any auditors of these disagreeable truths; though why' – he could not hide his real feelings here, or keep his eyes from glancing gloomily at Florence – 'why any one can give them greater force and point than myself, whom they so nearly concern, I do not pretend to understand. It may be natural enough that you should object to hear, in anybody's presence, that there is a rebellious principle within you which you cannot curb too soon; which you must curb, Mrs Dombey; and which, I regret to say, I remember to have seen manifested – with some doubt and displeasure, on more than one occasion before our marriage – towards your deceased mother. But you have the remedy in your own hands. I by no means forgot, when I began, that my daughter was present, Mrs Dombey. I beg *you* will not forget, to-morrow, that there are several persons present; and that, with some regard to appearances, you will receive your company in a becoming manner.'

'So it is not enough,' said Edith, 'that you know what has passed between yourself and me; it is not enough that you can look here,' pointing to Carker, who still listened, with his eyes cast down, 'and be reminded of the affronts you have put upon me; it is not enough that you can look here,' pointing to Florence with a hand that slightly trembled for the first and only time, 'and think of what you have done, and of the ingenious agony, daily, hourly, constant, you have made me feel in doing it; it is not enough that this day, of all others in the year, is memorable to me for a struggle (well-deserved, but not conceivable by such as you) in which I wish I had died! You add to all this, do you, the last crowning meanness of making *her* a witness of the depth to which I have fallen; when you know that you have made me sacrifice to her peace, the only gentle feeling and interest of my life, when you know that for her sake, I would now if I could – but I *can not*, my soul recoils from you too much – submit myself wholly to your will and be the meekest vassal that you have!'

This was not the way to minister to Mr Dombey's greatness. The old feeling was roused by what she said, into a stronger and fiercer existence than it had ever been. Again, his neglected child, at this rough passage of his life, put forth by even this rebellious woman, as powerful where he was powerless, and everything where he was nothing!

He turned on Florence, as if it were she who had spoken, and bade her leave the room. Florence with her covered face obeyed, trembling and weeping as she went.

'I understand, madam,' said Mr Dombey, with an angry flush of triumph, 'the spirit of opposition that turned your affections in that channel, but they have been met, Mrs Dombey; they have been met, and turned back!'

'The worse for you!' she answered, with her voice and manner still unchanged. 'Aye!' for he turned sharply when she said so, 'what is the worse for me, is twenty million times the worse for you. Heed that, if you heed nothing else.'

The arch of diamonds spanning her dark hair, flashed and glittered like a starry bridge. There was no warning in them, or they would have turned as dull and dim as tarnished honour. Carker still sat and listened, with his eyes cast down.

'Mrs Dombey,' said Mr Dombey, resuming as much as he could

of his arrogant composure, 'you will not conciliate me, or turn me from my purpose, by this course of conduct.'

'It is the only true, although it is a faint expression of what is within me,' she replied. 'But if I thought it would conciliate you, I would repress it, if it were repressible by any human effort. I will do nothing that you ask.'

'I am not accustomed to ask, Mrs Dombey,' he observed; 'I direct.'

'I will hold no place in your house to-morrow, or on any recurrence of to-morrow. I will be exhibited to no one, as the refractory slave you purchased, such a time. If I kept my marriage-day, I would keep it as a day of shame. Self-respect! appearances before the world! what are these to me? You have done all you can to make them nothing to me, and they *are* nothing.'

'Carker,' said Mr Dombey, speaking with knitted brows, and after a moment's consideration, 'Mrs Dombey is so forgetful of herself and me in all this, and places me in a position so unsuited to my character, that I must bring this state of matters to a close.'

'Release me, then,' said Edith, immovable in voice, in look, and bearing, as she had been throughout, 'from the chain by which I am bound. Let me go.'

'Madam?' exclaimed Mr Dombey.

'Loose me. Set me free!'

'Madam?' he repeated, 'Mrs Dombey?'

'Tell him,' said Edith, addressing her proud face to Carker, 'that I wish for a separation between us. That there had better be one. That I recommend it to him. Tell him it may take place on his own terms – his wealth is nothing to me – but that it cannot be too soon.'

'Good Heaven, Mrs Dombey!' said her husband, with supreme amazement, 'do you imagine it possible that I could ever listen to such a proposition? Do you know who I am, madam? Do you know what I represent? Did you ever hear of Dombey and Son? People to say that Mr Dombey – Mr Dombey! – was separated from his wife! Common people to talk of Mr Dombey and his domestic affairs! Do you seriously think, Mrs Dombey, that I would permit my name to be handed about in such connexion? Pooh, pooh, madam! Fie for shame! You're absurd.' Mr Dombey absolutely laughed.

But not as she did. She had better have been dead than laugh as she did, in reply, with her intent look fixed upon him. He had better have been dead, than sitting there, in his magnificence, to hear her.

'No, Mrs Dombey,' he resumed. 'No, madam. There is no possibility of separation between you and me, and therefore I the more advise you to be awakened to a sense of duty. And, Carker, as I was about to say to you—'

Mr Carker, who had sat and listened all this time, now raised his eyes, in which there was a bright unusual light.

'—As I was about to say to you,' resumed Mr Dombey, 'I must beg you, now that matters have come to this, to inform Mrs Dombey, that it is not the rule of my life to allow myself to be thwarted by anybody – anybody, Carker – or to suffer anybody to be paraded as a stronger motive for obedience in those who owe obedience to me than I am myself. The mention that has been made of my daughter, and the use that is made of my daughter, in opposition to me, are unnatural. Whether my daughter is in actual concert with Mrs Dombey, I do not know, and do not care; but after what Mrs Dombey has said to-day, and my daughter has heard to-day, I beg you to make known to Mrs Dombey, that if she continues to make this house the scene of contention it has become, I shall consider my daughter responsible in some degree, on that lady's own avowal, and shall visit her with my severe displeasure. Mrs Dombey has asked "whether it is not enough," that she had done this and that. You will please to answer no, it is not enough.'

'A moment!' cried Carker, interposing, 'permit me! painful as my position is, at the best, and unusually painful in seeming to entertain a different opinion from you,' addressing Mr Dombey, 'I must ask, had you not better reconsider the question of a separation? I know how incompatible it appears with your high public position, and I know how determined you are when you give Mrs Dombey to understand' – the light in his eyes fell upon her as he separated his words each from each, with the distinctness of so many bells – 'that nothing but death can ever part you. Nothing else. But when you consider that Mrs Dombey, by living in this house, and making it as you have said, a scene of contention, not only has her part in that contention, but compromises Miss Dombey every day (for I know how determined you are), will you not relieve her from a continual irritation of spirit, and a continual sense of being unjust to another, almost intolerable? Does this not seem like – I do not say it is – sacrificing Mrs Dombey to the preservation of your pre-eminent and unassailable position?'

Again the light in his eyes fell upon her, as she stood looking at her husband: now with an extraordinary and awful smile upon her face.

'Carker,' returned Mr Dombey, with a supercilious frown, and in a tone that was intended to be final, 'you mistake your position in offering advice to me on such a point, and you mistake me (I am surprised to find) in the character of your advice. I have no more to say.'

'Perhaps,' said Carker, with an unusual and indefinable taunt in his air, '*you* mistook my position, when you honoured me with the negotiations in which I have been engaged here' – with a motion of his hand towards Mrs Dombey.

'Not at all, Sir, not at all,' returned the other haughtily. 'You were employed—'

'Being an inferior person, for the humiliation of Mrs Dombey. I forgot. Oh, yes, it was expressly understood!' said Carker. 'I beg your pardon!'

As he bent his head to Mr Dombey, with an air of deference that accorded ill with his words, though they were humbly spoken, he moved it round towards her, and kept his watching eyes that way.

She had better have turned hideous and dropped dead, than have stood up with such a smile upon her face, in such a fallen spirit's majesty of scorn and beauty. She lifted her hand to the tiara of bright jewels radiant on her head, and, plucking it off with a force that dragged and strained her rich black hair with heedless cruelty, and brought it tumbling wildly on her shoulders, cast the gems upon the ground. From each arm, she unclasped a diamond bracelet, flung it down, and trod upon the glittering heap. Without a word, without a shadow on the fire of her bright eye, without abatement of her awful smile, she looked on Mr Dombey to the last, in moving to the door; and left him.

Florence had heard enough before quitting the room, to know that Edith loved her yet; that she had suffered for her sake; and that she had kept her sacrifices quiet, lest they should trouble her peace. She did not want to speak to her of this – she could not, remembering to whom she was opposed – but she wished, in one silent and affectionate embrace, to assure her that she felt it all, and thanked her.

Her father went out alone that evening, and Florence issuing from her own chamber soon afterwards, went about the house in search of Edith, but unavailingly. She was in her own rooms, where Florence had long ceased to go, and did not dare to venture now, lest she should unconsciously engender new trouble. Still Florence, hoping to meet her before going to bed, changed from room to room, and wandered through the house so splendid and so dreary, without remaining anywhere.

She was crossing a gallery of communication that opened at some little distance on the staircase, and was only lighted on great occasions, when she saw, through the opening, which was an arch, the figure of a man coming down some few stairs opposite. Instinctively apprehensive of her father, whom she supposed it was, she stopped, in the dark, gazing through the arch into the light. But it was Mr Carker coming down alone, and looking over the railing into the hall. No bell was rung to announce his departure, and no servant was in attendance. He went down quietly, opened the door for himself, glided out, and shut it softly after him.

Her invincible repugnance to this man, and perhaps the stealthy act of watching any one, which, even under such innocent circumstances, is in a manner guilty and oppressive, made Florence shake from head to foot. Her blood seemed to run cold. As soon as she could – for at first she felt an insurmountable dread of moving – she went quickly to her own room and locked her door; but even then, shut in with her dog beside her, felt a chill sensation of horror, as if there were danger brooding somewhere near her.

It invaded her dreams and disturbed the whole night. Rising in the morning, unrefreshed, and with a heavy recollection of the domestic unhappiness of the preceding day, she sought Edith again in all the rooms, and did so, from time to time, all the morning. But she remained in her own chamber, and Florence saw nothing of her. Learning, however, that the projected dinner at home was put off, Florence thought it likely that she would go out in the evening to fulfil the engagement she had spoken of; and resolved to try and meet her, then, upon the staircase.

When the evening had set in, she heard, from the room in which she sat on purpose, a footstep on the stairs that she thought to be Edith's. Hurrying out, and up towards her room, Florence met her immediately, coming down alone.

What was Florence's affright and wonder when, at sight of her, with her tearful face, and outstretched arms, Edith recoiled and shrieked!

'Don't come near me!' she cried. 'Keep away! Let me go by!'

'Mama!' said Florence.

'Don't call me by that name! Don't speak to me! Don't look at me! – Florence!' shrinking back, as Florence moved a step towards her, 'don't touch me!'

As Florence stood transfixed before the haggard face and staring

Florence and Edith on the staircase

eyes, she noted, as in a dream, that Edith spread her hands over them, and shuddering through all her form, and crouching down against the wall, crawled by her like some lower animal, sprang up, and fled away.

Florence dropped upon the stairs in a swoon; and was found there by Mrs Pipchin, she supposed. She knew nothing more, until she found herself lying on her own bed, with Mrs Pipchin and some servants standing round her.

'Where is mama?' was her first question.

'Gone out to dinner,' said Mrs Pipchin.

'And papa?'

'Mr Dombey is in his own room, Miss Dombey,' said Mrs Pipchin, 'and the best thing you can do, is to take off your things and go to bed this minute.' This was the sagacious woman's remedy for all complaints, particularly lowness of spirits, and inability to sleep; for which offences, many young victims in the days of the Brighton Castle had been committed to bed at ten o'clock in the morning.

Without promising obedience, but on the plea of desiring to be very quiet, Florence disengaged herself, as soon as she could, from the ministration of Mrs Pipchin and her attendants. Left alone, she thought of what had happened on the staircase, at first in doubt of its reality; then with tears; then with an indescribable and terrible alarm, like that she had felt the night before.

She determined not to go to bed until Edith returned, and if she could not speak to her, at least to be sure that she was safe at home. What indistinct and shadowy dread moved Florence to this resolution, she did not know and did not dare to think. She only knew that until Edith came back, there was no repose for her aching head or throbbing heart.

The evening deepened into night: midnight came; no Edith.

Florence could not read, or rest a moment. She paced her own room, opened the door and paced the staircase-gallery outside, looked out of window on the night, listened to the wind blowing and the rain falling, sat down and watched the faces in the fire, got up and watched the moon flying like a storm-driven ship through the sea of clouds.

All the house was gone to bed, except two servants who were waiting the return of their mistress, down stairs.

One o'clock. The carriages that rumbled in the distance, turned away, or stopped short, or went past; the silence gradually deepened, and was more and more rarely broken, save by a rush of wind or sweep of rain. Two o'clock. No Edith!

Florence, more agitated, paced her room, and paced the gallery outside; and looked out at the night, blurred and wavy with the raindrops on the glass, and the tears in her own eyes; and looked up at the hurry in the sky, so different from the repose below, and yet so tranquil and solitary. Three o'clock! There was a terror in every ash that dropped out of the fire. No Edith yet.

More and more agitated, Florence paced her room, and paced the gallery, and looked out at the moon with a new fancy of her likeness to a pale fugitive hurrying away and hiding her guilty face. Four struck! Five! No Edith yet.

But now there was some cautious stir in the house; and Florence found that Mrs Pipchin had been awakened by one of those who sat up, had risen and had gone down to her father's door. Stealing lower down the stairs, and observing what passed, she saw her father come out in his morning gown, and start when he was told his wife had not come home. He dispatched a messenger to the stables to inquire whether the coachman was there; and while the man was gone, dressed himself very hurriedly.

The man came back, in great haste, bringing the coachman with him, who said he had been at home and in bed since ten o'clock. He had driven his mistress to her old house in Brook Street, where she had been met by Mr Carker—

Florence stood upon the very spot where she had seen him coming down. Again she shivered with the nameless terror of that sight, and had hardly steadiness enough to hear and understand what followed.

—Who had told him, the man went on to say, that his mistress would not want the carriage to go home in; and had dismissed him.

She saw her father turn white in the face, and heard him ask in a quick, trembling voice for Mrs Dombey's maid. The whole house was roused; for she was there, in a moment, very pale too, and speaking incoherently.

She said she had dressed her mistress early – full two hours before she went out – and had been told, as she often was, that she would not be wanted at night. She had just come from her mistress's rooms, but—

'But what! what was it?' Florence heard her father demand like a madman.

'But the inner-dressing room was locked, and the key gone.'

Her father seized a candle that was flaming on the ground – some one had put it down there, and forgotten it – and came running upstairs with such fury, that Florence, in her fear, had hardly time to fly before him. She heard him striking in the door as she ran on, with her hands widely spread, and her hair streaming, and her face like a distracted person's, back to her own room.

When the door yielded, and he rushed in, what did he see there? No one knew. But thrown down in a costly mass upon the ground, was every ornament she had had, since she had been his wife: every dress she had worn; and everything she had possessed. This was the room in which he had seen, in yonder mirror, the proud face discard him. This was the room in which he had wondered, idly, how these things would look when he should see them next.

Heaping them back into the drawers, and locking them up in a rage of haste, he saw some papers on the table. The deed of settlement he had executed on their marriage, and a letter. He read that she was gone. He read that he was dishonoured. He read that she had fled, upon her shameful wedding-day, with the man whom he had chosen for her humiliation; and he tore out of the room, and out of the house, with a frantic idea of finding her yet, at the place to which she had been taken, and beating all trace of beauty out of the triumphant face with his bare hand.

Florence, not knowing what she did, put on a shawl and bonnet, in a dream of running through the streets until she found Edith, and then clasping her in her arms, to save and bring her back. But when she hurried out upon the staircase, and saw the frightened servants going up and down with lights, and whispering together, and falling away from her father as he passed down, she awoke to a sense of her own powerlessness; and hiding in one of the great rooms that had been made gorgeous for *this*, felt as if her heart would burst with grief.

Compassion for her father was the first distinct emotion that made head against the flood of sorrow which overwhelmed her. Her constant nature turned to him in his distress, as fervently and faithfully, as if, in his prosperity, he had been the embodiment of that idea which had gradually become so faint and dim. Although she did not know, otherwise than through the suggestions of a shapeless fear, the full extent of his calamity, he stood before her wronged and deserted; and again her yearning love impelled her to his side.

He was not long away: for Florence was yet weeping in the great room and nourishing these thoughts, when she heard him come back. He ordered the servants to set about their ordinary occupations, and went into his own apartment, where he trod so heavily that she could hear him walking up and down from end to end.

Yielding at once to the impulse of her affection, timid at all other times, but bold in its truth to him in his adversity, and undaunted by past repulse, Florence, dressed as she was, hurried downstairs. As she set her light foot in the hall, he came out of his room. She hastened towards him unchecked, with her arms stretched out, and crying 'Oh dear, dear papa!' as if she would have clasped him round the neck.

And so she would have done. But in his frenzy, he lifted up his cruel arm, and struck her, crosswise, with that heaviness, that she tottered on the marble floor; and as he dealt the blow, he told her what Edith was, and bade her follow her, since they had always been in league.

She did not sink down at his feet; she did not shut out the sight of him with her trembling hands; she did not weep; she did not utter one word of reproach. But she looked at him, and a cry of desolation issued from her heart. For as she looked, she saw him murdering that fond idea to which she had held in spite of him. She saw his cruelty, neglect, and hatred dominant above it, and stamping it down. She saw she had no father upon earth, and ran out, orphaned, from his house.

Ran out of his house. A moment, and her hand was on the lock, the cry was on her lips, his face was there, made paler by the yellow candles hastily put down and guttering away, and by the daylight coming in above the door. Another moment, and the close darkness of the shut-up house (forgotten to be opened, though it was long since day) yielded to the unexpected glare and freedom of the morning; and Florence, with her head bent down to hide her agony of tears, was in the streets.

CHAPTER 48

The Flight of Florence

In the wildness of her sorrow, shame, and terror, the forlorn girl hurried through the sunshine of a bright morning, as if it were the darkness of a winter night. Wringing her hands and weeping bitterly, insensible to everything but the deep wound in her breast, stunned by the loss of all she loved, left like the sole survivor on a lonely shore from the wreck of a great vessel, she fled without a thought, without a hope, without a purpose, but to fly somewhere – anywhere.

The cheerful vista of the long street, burnished by the morning light, the sight of the blue sky and airy clouds, the vigorous freshness of the day, so flushed and rosy in its conquest of the night, awakened no responsive feelings in her so hurt bosom. Somewhere, anywhere, to hide her head! somewhere, anywhere, for refuge, never more to look upon the place from which she fled!

But there were people going to and fro; there were opening shops, and servants at the doors of houses; there was the rising clash and roar of the day's struggle. Florence saw surprise and curiosity in the faces flitting past her; saw long shadows coming back upon the pavement; and heard voices that were strange to her asking her where she went, and what the matter was; and though these frightened her the more at first, and made her hurry on the faster, they did her the good service of recalling her in some degree to herself, and reminding her of the necessity of greater composure.

Where to go? Still somewhere, anywhere! still going on; but where! She thought of the only other time she had been lost in the wild wilderness of London – though not lost as now – and went that way. To the home of Walter's uncle.

Checking her sobs, and drying her swollen eyes, and endeavouring to calm the agitation of her manner, so as to avoid attracting notice, Florence, resolving to keep to the more quiet streets as long as she could, was going on more quietly herself, when a familiar little shadow darted past upon the sunny pavement, stopped short, wheeled about, came close to her, made off again, bounded round and round her, and Diogenes, panting for breath, and yet making the street ring with his glad bark, was at her feet.

'Oh, Di! oh, dear, true, faithful Di, how did you come here? How could I ever leave you, Di, who would never leave me?'

Florence bent down on the pavement, and laid his rough, old, loving, foolish head against her breast, and they got up together, and went on together; Di more off the ground than on it, endeavouring to kiss his mistress flying, tumbling over and getting up again without the least concern, dashing at big dogs in a jocose defiance of his species, terrifying with touches of his nose young housemaids who were cleaning doorsteps, and continually stopping, in the midst of a thousand extravagances, to look back at Florence, and bark until all the dogs within hearing answered, and all the dogs who could come out, came out to stare at him.

With this last adherent, Florence hurried away in the advancing morning, and the strengthening sunshine, to the City. The roar soon grew more loud, the passengers more numerous, the shops more busy, until she was carried onward in a stream of life setting that way, and flowing, indifferently, past marts and mansions, prisons, churches, market-places, wealth, poverty, good, and evil, like the broad river side by side with it, awakened from its dreams of rushes, willows, and green moss, and rolling on, turbid and troubled, among the works and cares of men, to the deep sea.

At length the quarters of the little Midshipman arose in view. Nearer yet, and the little Midshipman himself was seen upon his post, intent as ever on his observations. Nearer yet, and the door stood open, inviting her to enter. Florence, who had again quickened her pace, as she approached the end of her journey, ran across the road (closely followed by Diogenes, whom the bustle had somewhat confused), ran in, and sank upon the threshold of the well-remembered little parlour.

The Captain, in his glazed hat, was standing over the fire, making his morning's cocoa, with that elegant trifle, his watch, upon the chimneypiece, for easy reference during the progress of the cookery. Hearing a footstep and the rustle of a dress, the Captain turned with a palpitating remembrance of the dreadful Mrs MacStinger, at the instant when Florence made a motion with her hand towards him, reeled, and fell upon the floor.

The Captain, pale as Florence, pale in the very knobs upon his face, raised her like a baby, and laid her on the same old sofa upon which she had slumbered long ago.

'It's Heart's Delight!' said the Captain, looking intently in her face. 'It's the sweet creetur grow'd a woman!'

Captain Cuttle was so respectful of her, and had such a reverence for her, in this new character, that he would not have held her in his arms, while she was unconscious, for a thousand pounds.

'My Heart's Delight!' said the Captain, withdrawing to a little distance, with the greatest alarm and sympathy depicted on his countenance. 'If you can hail Ned Cuttle with a finger, do it!'

But Florence did not stir.

'My Heart's Delight!' said the trembling Captain. 'For the sake of Wal'r drownded in the briny deep, turn to, and histe up something or another, if able.'

Finding her insensible to this impressive adjuration also, Captain Cuttle snatched from his breakfast-table a basin of cold water, and sprinkled some upon her face. Yielding to the urgency of the case, the Captain then, using his immense hand with extraordinary gentleness, relieved her of her bonnet, moistened her lips and forehead, put back her hair, covered her feet with his own coat which he pulled off for the purpose, patted her hand – so small in his, that he was struck with wonder when he touched it – and seeing that her eyelids quivered, and that her lips began to move, continued these restorative applications with a better heart.

'Cheerily,' said the Captain. 'Cheerily! Stand by, my pretty one, stand by! There! You're better now. Steady's the word, and steady it is. Keep her so! Drink a little drop o' this here,' said the Captain. 'There you are! What cheer,[1] now, my pretty, what cheer now?'

At this stage of her recovery, Captain Cuttle, with an imperfect association of a Watch with a Physician's treatment of a patient, took his own down from the mantel-shelf, and holding it out on his hook, and taking Florence's hand in his, looked steadily from one to the other, as expecting the dial to do something.

'What cheer, my pretty?' said the Captain. 'What cheer now? You've done her some good, my lad, I believe,' said the Captain, under his breath, and throwing an approving glance upon his watch. 'Put you back half-an-hour every morning, and about another quarter towards the afternoon, and you're a watch as can be ekalled by few and excelled by none. What cheer, my lady lass?'

'Captain Cuttle! Is it you?' exclaimed Florence, raising herself a little.

'Yes, yes, my lady lass,' said the Captain, hastily deciding in his own mind upon the superior elegance of that form of address, as the most courtly he could think of.

'Is Walter's uncle here?' asked Florence.

'Here, pretty?' returned the Captain. 'He an't been here this many a long day. He an't been heerd on, since he sheered off arter poor Wal'r. But,' said the Captain, as a quotation, 'Though lost to sight, to memory dear,[2] and England, Home, and Beauty!'[3]

'Do you live here?' asked Florence.

'Yes, my lady lass,' returned the Captain.

'Oh, Captain Cuttle!' cried Florence, putting her hands together, and speaking wildly. 'Save me! keep me here! Let no one know where I am! I'll tell you what has happened by-and-by, when I can. I have no one in the world to go to. Do not send me away!'

'Send *you* away, my lady lass!' exclaimed the Captain. 'You, my Heart's Delight! Stay a bit! We'll put up this here dead-light,[4] and take a double turn on the key!'

With these words, the Captain, using his one hand and his hook with the greatest dexterity, got out the shutter of the door, put it up, made it all fast, and locked the door itself.

When he came back to the side of Florence, she took his hand, and kissed it. The helplessness of the action, the appeal it made to him, the confidence it expressed, the unspeakable sorrow in her face, the pain of mind she had too plainly suffered, and was suffering then, his knowledge of her past history, her present lonely, worn, and unprotected appearance, all so rushed upon the good Captain together, that he fairly overflowed with compassion and gentleness.

'My lady lass,' said the Captain, polishing the bridge of his nose with his arm until it shone like burnished copper, 'don't you say a word to Ed'ard Cuttle, until such times as you finds yourself a riding smooth and easy; which won't be to-day, nor yet to-morrow. And as to giving of you up, or reporting where you are, yes verily, and by God's help, so I won't,[5] Church catechism, make a note on!'

This the Captain said, reference and all, in one breath, and with much solemnity; taking off his hat at 'yes verily,' and putting it on again, when he had quite concluded.

Florence could do but one thing more to thank him, and to show him how she trusted in him; and she did it. Clinging to this rough creature as the last asylum of her bleeding heart, she laid her head upon his honest shoulder, and clasped him round his neck, and would have kneeled down to bless him, but that he divined her purpose, and held her up like a true man.

'Steady!' said the Captain. 'Steady! You're too weak to stand, you see, my pretty, and must lie down here again. There, there!' To see the Captain lift her on the sofa, and cover her with his coat, would have been worth a hundred state sights. 'And now,' said the Captain, 'you must take some breakfast, lady lass, and the dog shall have some too. And arter that you shall go aloft to old Sol Gills's room, and fall asleep there, like a angel.'

Captain Cuttle patted Diogenes when he made allusion to him, and Diogenes met that overture graciously, half-way. During the administration of the restoratives he had clearly been in two minds whether to fly at the Captain or to offer him his friendship; and he had expressed that conflict of feeling by alternate waggings of his tail, and displays of his teeth, with now and then a growl or so. But by this time his doubts were all removed. It was plain that he considered the Captain one of the most amiable of men, and a man whom it was an honour to a dog to know.

In evidence of these convictions, Diogenes attended on the

Captain while he made some tea and toast, and showed a lively interest in his housekeeping. But it was in vain for the kind Captain to make such preparations for Florence, who sorely tried to do some honour to them, but could touch nothing, and could only weep and weep again.

'Well, well!' said the compassionate Captain, 'arter turning in, my Heart's Delight, you'll get more way upon you. Now, I'll serve out your allowance, my lad.' To Diogenes. 'And you shall keep guard on your mistress aloft.'

Diogenes, however, although he had been eyeing his intended breakfast with a watering mouth and glistening eyes, instead of falling to, ravenously, when it was put before him, pricked up his ears, darted to the shop-door, and barked there furiously: burrowing with his head at the bottom, as if he were bent on mining his way out.

'Can there be anybody there!' asked Florence, in alarm.

'No, my lady lass,' returned the Captain. 'Who'd stay there, without making any noise! Keep up a good heart, pretty. It's only people going by.'

But for all that, Diogenes barked and barked, and burrowed and burrowed, with pertinacious fury; and whenever he stopped to listen, appeared to receive some new conviction into his mind, for he set to, barking and burrowing again, a dozen times. Even when he was persuaded to return to his breakfast, he came jogging back to it, with a very doubtful air; and was off again, in another paroxysm, before touching a morsel.

'If there should be some one listening and watching,' whispered Florence. 'Some one who saw me come – who followed me, perhaps.'

'It an't the young woman, lady lass, is it?' said the Captain, taken with a bright idea.

'Susan?' said Florence, shaking her head. 'Ah no! Susan has been gone from me a long time.'

'Not deserted, I hope?' said the Captain. 'Don't say that that there young woman's run, my pretty!'

'Oh, no, no!' cried Florence. 'She is one of the truest hearts in the world!'

The Captain was greatly relieved by this reply, and expressed his satisfaction by taking off his hard glazed hat, and dabbing his head all over with his handkerchief, rolled up like a ball, observing several times, with infinite complacency, and with a beaming countenance, that he know'd it.

'So you're quiet now, are you, brother?' said the Captain to Diogenes. 'There warn't nobody there, my lady lass, bless you!'

Diogenes was not so sure of that. The door still had an attraction for him at intervals; and he went snuffing about it, and growling to himself, unable to forget the subject. This incident, coupled with the Captain's observation of Florence's fatigue and faintness, decided him to prepare Sol Gills's chamber as a place of retirement for her immediately. He therefore hastily betook himself to the top of the house, and made the best arrangement of it that his imagination and his means suggested.

It was very clean already; and the Captain being an orderly man, and accustomed to make things ship-shape, converted the bed into a couch, by covering it all over with a clean white drapery. By a similar contrivance, the Captain converted the little dressing-table into a species of altar, on which he set forth two silver teaspoons, a flower-pot, a telescope, his celebrated watch, a pocket-comb, and a song-book, as a small collection of rarities, that made a choice appearance. Having darkened the window, and straightened the pieces of carpet on the floor, the Captain surveyed these preparations with great delight, and descended to the little parlour again, to bring Florence to her bower.

Nothing would induce the Captain to believe that it was possible for Florence to walk upstairs. If he could have got the idea into his head, he would have considered it an outrageous breach of hospitality to allow her to do so. Florence was too weak to dispute the point, and the Captain carried her up out of hand, laid her down, and covered her with a great watch-coat.[6]

'My lady lass!' said the Captain, 'you're as safe here as if you was at the top of St Paul's Cathedral, with the ladder cast off. Sleep is what you want, afore all other things, and may you be able to show yourself smart with that there balsam for the still small woice of a wownded mind![7] When there's anything you want, my Heart's Delight, as this here humble house or town can offer, pass the word to Ed'ard Cuttle, as'll stand off and on outside that door, and that there man will wibrate with joy.' The Captain concluded by kissing the hand that Florence stretched out to him, with the chivalry of any old knight-errant, and walking on tip-toe out of the room.

Descending to the little parlour, Captain Cuttle, after holding a hasty council with himself, decided to open the shop-door for a few minutes, and satisfy himself that now, at all events, there was no one loitering about it. Accordingly he set it open, and stood upon the threshold, keeping a bright look-out, and sweeping the whole street with his spectacles.

'How de do, Captain Gills?' said a voice beside him. The Captain, looking down, found that he had been boarded by Mr Toots while sweeping the horizon.

'How are you, my lad?' replied the Captain.

'Well, I'm pretty well, thank'ee, Captain Gills,' said Mr Toots. 'You know I'm never quite what I could wish to be, now. I don't expect that I ever shall be any more.'

Mr Toots never approached any nearer than this to the great theme of his life, when in conversation with Captain Cuttle, on account of the agreement between them.

'Captain Gills,' said Mr Toots, 'if I could have the pleasure of a word with you, it's – it's rather particular.'

'Why, you see, my lad,' replied the Captain, leading the way into the parlour, 'I an't what you may call exactly free this morning; and therefore if you can clap on[8] a bit, I should take it kindly.'

'Certainly, Captain Gills,' replied Mr Toots, who seldom had any notion of the Captain's meaning. 'To clap on, is exactly what I could wish to do. Naturally.'

'If so be, my lad,' returned the Captain, 'do it!'

The Captain was so impressed by the possession of his tremendous secret – by the fact of Miss Dombey being at that moment under his roof, while the innocent and unconscious Toots sat opposite to him – that a perspiration broke out on his forehead, and he found it impossible while slowly drying the same, glazed hat in hand, to keep his eyes off Mr Toots's face. Mr Toots, who himself appeared to have some secret reasons for being in a nervous state, was so unspeakably disconcerted by the Captain's stare, that after looking at him vacantly for some time in silence, and shifting uneasily on his chair, he said:

'I beg your pardon, Captain Gills, but you don't happen to see anything particular in me, do you?'

'No, my lad,' returned the Captain. 'No.'

'Because you know,' said Mr Toots with a chuckle, 'I KNOW I'm wasting away. You needn't at all mind alluding to that. I – I should like it. Burgess and Co. have altered my measure, I'm in that state of thinness. It's a gratification to me. I – I'm glad of it. I – I'd a great deal rather go into a decline, if I could. I'm a mere brute you know, grazing upon the surface of the earth, Captain Gills.'

The more Mr Toots went on in this way, the more the Captain was weighed down by his secret, and stared at him. What with this cause of uneasiness, and his desire to get rid of Mr Toots, the Captain was in such a scared and strange condition, indeed, that if he had been in conversation with a ghost, he could hardly have evinced greater discomposure.

'But I was going to say, Captain Gills,' said Mr Toots. 'Happening to be this way early this morning – to tell you the truth, I was coming to breakfast with you. As to sleep, you know, I never sleep now. I might be a Watchman, except that I don't get any pay, and he's got nothing on his mind.'

'Carry on, my lad!' said the Captain, in an admonitory voice.

'Certainly, Captain Gills,' said Mr Toots. 'Perfectly true! Happening to be this way early this morning (an hour or so ago), and finding the door shut—'

'What! were *you* waiting there, brother?' demanded the Captain.

'Not at all, Captain Gills,' returned Mr Toots. 'I didn't stop a moment. I thought you were out. But the person said – by the bye you *don't* keep a dog, *do* you, Captain Gills?'

The Captain shook his head.

'To be sure,' said Mr Toots, 'that's exactly what I said. I knew you didn't. There *is* a dog, Captain Gills, connected with – but excuse me. That's forbidden ground.'

The Captain stared at Mr Toots until he seemed to swell to twice his natural size; and again the perspiration broke out on the Captain's forehead, when he thought of Diogenes taking it into his head to come down and make a third in the parlour.

'The person said,' continued Mr Toots, 'that he had heard a dog barking in the shop: which I knew couldn't be, and I told him so. But he was as positive as if he had seen the dog.'

'What person, my lad?' inquired the Captain.

'Why, you see there it is, Captain Gills,' said Mr Toots, with a perceptible increase in the nervousness of his manner. 'It's not for me to say what may have taken place, or what may not have taken place. Indeed, I don't know. I get mixed up with all sorts of things that I don't quite understand, and I think there's something rather weak in my – in my head, in short.'

The Captain nodded his own, as a mark of assent.

'But the person said, as we were walking away,' continued Mr Toots, 'that you knew what, under existing circumstances, *might* occur – he said "might," very strongly – and that if you were requested to prepare yourself, you would, no doubt, come prepared.'

'Person, my lad!' the Captain repeated.

'I don't know what person, I'm sure, Captain Gills,' replied Mr Toots, 'I haven't the least idea. But coming to the door, I found him waiting there, and he said was I coming back again, and I said yes; and he said did I know you, and I said yes, I had the pleasure of your acquaintance – you had given me the pleasure of your acquaintance, after some persuasion; and he said, if that was the case, would I say to you what I *have* said, about existing circumstances and coming prepared, and as soon as ever I saw you, would I ask you to step round the corner, if it was only for one minute, on most important business, to Mr Brogley's the Broker's. Now, I tell you what, Captain Gills – whatever it is, I am convinced it's very important; and if you like to step round, now, I'll wait here till you come back.'

The Captain, divided between his fear of compromising Florence in some way by not going, and his horror of leaving Mr Toots in possession of the house with a chance of finding out the secret, was a spectacle of mental disturbance that even Mr Toots could not be blind to. But that young gentleman, considering his nautical friend as merely in a state of preparation for the interview he was going to have, was quite satisfied, and did not review his own discreet conduct without chuckles.

At length the Captain decided, as the lesser of two evils, to run round to Brogley's the Broker's: previously locking the door that communicated with the upper part of the house, and putting the key in his pocket. 'If so be,' said the Captain to Mr Toots, with not a little shame and hesitation, 'as you'll excuse my doing of it, brother.'

'Captain Gills,' returned Mr Toots, 'whatever you do, is satisfactory to me.'

The Captain thanked him heartily, and promising to come back in less than five minutes, went out in quest of the person who had intrusted Mr Toots with this mysterious message. Poor Mr Toots, left to himself, lay down upon the sofa, little thinking who had reclined there last, and, gazing up at the skylight and resigning himself to visions of Miss Dombey, lost all heed of time and place.

It was as well that he did so; for although the Captain was not gone long, he was gone much longer than he had proposed. When he came back, he was very pale indeed, and greatly agitated, and even looked as if he had been shedding tears. He seemed to have lost the faculty of speech, until he had been to the cupboard and taken a dram of rum from the case-bottle,⁹ when he fetched a deep breath, and sat down in a chair with his hand before his face.

'Captain Gills,' said Toots, kindly, 'I hope and trust there's nothing wrong?'

'Thank'ee, my lad, not a bit,' said the Captain. 'Quite contrary.'

'You have the appearance of being overcome, Captain Gills,' observed Mr Toots.

'Why, my lad, I *am* took aback,' the Captain admitted. 'I am.'

'Is there anything I can do, Captain Gills?' inquired Mr Toots. 'If there is, make use of me.'

The Captain removed his hand from his face, looked at him with a remarkable expression of pity and tenderness, and took him by the hand and shook it hard.

'No, thank'ee,' said the Captain. 'Nothing. Only I'll take it as a favour if you'll part company for the present. I believe, brother,' wringing his hand again, 'that, after Wal'r, and on a different model, you're as good a lad as ever stepped.'

'Upon my word and honour, Captain Gills,' returned Mr Toots, giving the Captain's hand a preliminary slap before shaking it again, 'it's delightful to me to possess your good opinion. Thank'ee.'

'And bear a hand and cheer up,' said the Captain, patting him on the back. 'What! There's more than one sweet creetur in the world!'

'Not to me, Captain Gills,' replied Mr Toots gravely. 'Not to me, I assure you. The state of my feelings towards Miss Dombey is of that unspeakable description, that my heart is a desert island, and she lives in it alone. I'm getting more used up[10] every day, and I'm proud to be so. If you could see my legs when I take my boots off, you'd form some idea of what unrequited affection is. I have been prescribed bark,[11] but I don't take it, for I don't wish to have any tone whatever given to my constitution. I'd rather not. This, however, is forbidden ground. Captain Gills, good-bye!'

Captain Cuttle cordially reciprocating the warmth of Mr Toots's farewell, locked the door behind him, and shaking his head with the same remarkable expression of pity and tenderness as he had regarded him with before, went up to see if Florence wanted him.

There was an entire change in the Captain's face as he went upstairs. He wiped his eyes with his handkerchief, and he polished the bridge of his nose with his sleeve as he had done already that morning, but his face was absolutely changed. Now, he might have been thought supremely happy; now, he might have been thought sad; but the kind of gravity that sat upon his features was quite new to them and was as great an improvement to them as if they had undergone some sublimating process.

He knocked softly, with his hook, at Florence's door, twice or thrice; but, receiving no answer, ventured first to peep in, and then to enter: emboldened to take the latter step, perhaps, by the familiar recognition of Diogenes, who, stretched upon the ground by the side of her couch, wagged his tail, and winked his eyes at the Captain, without being at the trouble of getting up.

She was sleeping heavily, and moaning in her sleep; and Captain Cuttle, with a perfect awe of her youth and beauty, and her sorrow, raised her head, and adjusted the coat that covered her, where it had fallen off, and darkened the window a little more that she might sleep on, and crept out again, and took his post of watch upon the stairs. All this, with a touch and tread as light as Florence's own.

Long may it remain in this mixed world a point not easy of decision, which is the more beautiful evidence of the Almighty's goodness – the delicate fingers that are formed for sensitiveness and sympathy of touch, and made to minister to pain and grief or the rough hard Captain Cuttle hand, that the heart teaches, guides, and softens in a moment!

Florence slept upon her couch, forgetful of her homelessness and orphanage, and Captain Cuttle watched upon the stairs. A louder sob or moan than usual, brought him sometimes to her door; but by degrees she slept more peacefully and the Captain's watch was undisturbed.

CHAPTER 49

The Midshipman makes a Discovery

It was long before Florence awoke. The day was in its prime, the day was in its wane, and still, uneasy in mind and body, she slept on; unconscious of her strange bed, of the noise and turmoil in the street, and of the light that shone outside the shaded window. Perfect unconsciousness of what had happened in the home that existed no more, even the deep slumber of exhaustion could not produce. Some undefined and mournful recollection of it, dozing uneasily but never sleeping, pervaded all her rest. A dull sorrow, like a half-lulled sense of pain, was always present to her; and her pale cheek was oftener wet with tears than the honest Captain, softly putting in his head from time to time at the half-closed door, could have desired to see it.

The sun was getting low in the west, and, glancing out of a red mist, pierced with its rays opposite loop-holes and pieces of fret-work in the spires of city churches, as if with golden arrows that struck through and through them – and far away athwart the river and its flat banks, it was gleaming like a path of fire – and out at sea it was irradiating sails of ships – and, looked towards, from quiet churchyards, upon hill-tops in the country, it was steeping distant prospects in a flush and glow that seemed to mingle earth and sky together in one glorious suffusion – when Florence, opening her heavy eyes, lay at first, looking without interest or recognition at the unfamiliar walls around her, and listening in the same regardless manner to the noises in the street. But presently she started up upon her couch, gazed round with a surprised and vacant look, and recollected all.

'My pretty,' said the Captain, knocking at the door, 'what cheer?'

'Dear friend,' cried Florence, hurrying to him, 'is it you?'

The Captain felt so much pride in the name, and was so pleased by the gleam of pleasure in her face, when she saw him, that he kissed his hook, by way of reply, in speechless gratification.

'What cheer, bright di'mond?' said the Captain.

'I have surely slept very long,' returned Florence. 'When did I come here? Yesterday?'

'This here blessed day, my lady lass,' replied the Captain.

'Has there been no night? Is it still day?' asked Florence.

'Getting on for evening now, my pretty,' said the Captain, drawing back the curtain of the window. 'See!'

Florence, with her hand upon the Captain's arm, so sorrowful and timid, and the Captain with his rough face and burly figure, so quietly protective of her, stood in the rosy light of the bright evening sky, without saying a word. However strange the form of speech into which he might have fashioned the feeling, if he had had to give it utterance, the Captain felt, as sensibly as the most eloquent of men could have done, that there was something in the tranquil time and in its softened beauty that would make the wounded heart of Florence overflow; and that it was better that such tears should have their way. So not a word spake Captain Cuttle. But when he felt his arm clasped closer, and when he felt the lonely head come nearer to it, and lay itself against his homely coarse blue sleeves, he pressed it gently with his rugged hand, and understood it, and was understood.

'Better now, my pretty!' said the Captain. 'Cheerily, cheerily; I'll go down below, and get some dinner ready. Will you come down

of your own self, arterwards, pretty, or shall Ed'ard Cuttle come
and fetch you?'

As Florence assured him that she was quite able to walk downstairs, the Captain, though evidently doubtful of his own hospitality
in permitting it, left her to do so, and immediately set about roasting
a fowl at the fire in the little parlour. To achieve his cookery with
the greater skill, he pulled off his coat, tucked up his wristbands,
and put on his glazed hat, without which assistant he never applied
himself to any nice or difficult undertaking.

After cooling her aching head and burning face in the fresh water
which the Captain's care had provided for her while she slept,
Florence went to the little mirror to bind up her disordered hair.
Then she knew – in a moment, for she shunned it instantly – that
on her breast there was the darkening mark of an angry hand.

Her tears burst forth afresh at the sight; she was ashamed and
afraid of it; but it moved her to no anger against him. Homeless
and fatherless, she forgave him everything; hardly thought that she
had need to forgive him, or that she did; but she fled from the idea
of him as she had fled from the reality, and he was utterly gone and
lost. There was no such Being in the world.

What to do, or where to live, Florence – poor, inexperienced girl!
– could not yet consider. She had indistinct dreams of finding, a
long way off, some little sisters to instruct, who would be gentle
with her, and to whom, under some feigned name, she might attach
herself, and who would grow up in their happy home, and marry,
and be good to their old governess, and perhaps intrust her, in time,
with the education of their own daughters. And she thought how
strange and sorrowful it would be, thus to become a grey-haired
woman, carrying her secret to the grave, when Florence Dombey
was forgotten. But it was all dim and clouded to her now. She only
knew that she had no Father upon earth, and she said so, many
times, with her suppliant head hidden from all, but her Father who
was in Heaven.

Her little stock of money amounted to but a few guineas.[1] With
a part of this, it would be necessary to buy some clothes, for she
had none but those she wore. She was too desolate to think how
soon her money would be gone – too much a child in worldly
matters to be greatly troubled on that score yet, even if her other
trouble had been less. She tried to calm her thoughts and stay her
tears; to quiet the hurry in her throbbing head, and bring herself to
believe that what had happened were but the events of a few hours

ago, instead of weeks or months, as they appeared; and went down to her kind protector.

The Captain had spread the cloth with great care, and was making some egg-sauce in a little saucepan: basting the fowl from time to time during the process with a strong interest, as it turned and browned on a string before the fire. Having propped Florence up with cushions on the sofa, which was already wheeled into a warm corner for her greater comfort, the Captain pursued his cooking with extraordinary skill, making hot gravy in a second little saucepan, boiling a handful of potatoes in a third, never forgetting the egg-sauce in the first, and making an impartial round of basting and stirring with the most useful of spoons every minute. Besides these cares, the Captain had to keep his eye on a diminutive frying-pan, in which some sausages were hissing and bubbling in a most musical manner, and there was never such a radiant cook as the Captain looked, in the height and heat of these functions: it being impossible to say whether his face or his glazed hat shone the brighter.

The dinner being at length quite ready, Captain Cuttle dished and served it up, with no less dexterity than he had cooked it. He then dressed for dinner, by taking off his glazed hat and putting on his coat. That done, he wheeled the table close against Florence on the sofa, said grace, unscrewed his hook, screwed his fork into its place, and did the honours of the table.

'My lady lass,' said the Captain, 'cheer up, and try to eat a deal.[2] Stand by, my deary! Liver wing[3] it is. Sarse it is. Sassage it is. And potato!' all which the Captain ranged symmetrically on a plate, and pouring hot gravy on the whole with the useful spoon, set before his cherished guest.

'The whole row o' dead lights is up, for'ard,[4] lady lass,' observed the Captain, encouragingly, 'and everythink is made snug. Try and pick a bit, my pretty. If Wal'r was here—'

'Ah! If I had him for my brother now!' cried Florence.

'Don't! don't take on, my pretty!' said the Captain, 'awast[5] to obleege me! He *was* your nat'ral born friend like, warn't he, Pet?'

Florence had no words to answer with. She only said, 'Oh, dear, dear Paul! oh, Walter!'

'The wery planks she walked on,' murmured the Captain, looking at her drooping face, 'was as high esteemed by Wal'r, as the water brooks is by the hart which never rejices![6] I see him now, the wery day as he was rated on them Dombey books, a speaking of her with his face a glistening with doo – leastways with his modest sentiments

– like a new blowed rose, at dinner. Well, well! If our poor Wal'r was here, my lady lass – or if he could be – for he's drownded, an't he?'

Florence shook her head.

'Yes, yes; drownded,' said the Captain, soothingly; 'as I was saying, if he could be here he'd beg and pray of you, my precious, to pick a leetle bit, with a look-out for your own sweet health. Whereby, hold your own, my lady lass, as if it was for Wal'r's sake, and lay your pretty head to the wind.'

Florence essayed to eat a morsel, for the Captain's pleasure. The Captain, meanwhile, who seemed to have quite forgotten his own dinner, laid down his knife and fork, and drew his chair to the sofa.

'Wal'r was a trim lad, warn't he, precious?' said the Captain, after sitting for some time silently rubbing his chin, with his eyes fixed upon her, 'and a brave lad, and a good lad?'

Florence tearfully assented.

'And he's drownded, Beauty, an't he?' said the Captain, in a soothing voice.

Florence could not but assent again.

'He was older than you, my lady lass,' pursued the Captain, 'but you was like two children together, at first; warn't you?'

Florence answered 'Yes.'

'And Wal'r's drownded,' said the Captain. 'An't he?'

The repetition of this inquiry was a curious source of consolation, but it seemed to be one to Captain Cuttle, for he came back to it again and again. Florence, fain to push from her her untasted dinner, and to lie back on her sofa, gave him her hand, feeling that she had disappointed him, though truly wishing to have pleased him after all his trouble, but he held it in his own (which shook as he held it), and appearing to have quite forgotten all about the dinner and her want of appetite, went on growling at intervals, in a ruminating tone of sympathy, 'Poor Wal'r. Aye, aye! Drownded. An't he?' And always waited for her answer, in which the great point of these singular reflections appeared to consist.

The fowl and sausages were cold, and the gravy and the egg-sauce stagnant, before the Captain remembered that they were on the board, and fell to with the assistance of Diogenes, whose united efforts quickly dispatched the banquet. The Captain's delight and wonder at the quiet housewifery of Florence in assisting to clear the table, arrange the parlour, and sweep up the hearth – only to be equalled by the fervency of his protest when she began to assist him – were gradually raised to that degree, that at last he could not choose but do nothing himself, and stand looking at her as if she were some Fairy, daintily performing these offices for him; the red rim on his forehead glowing again, in his unspeakable admiration.

But when Florence, taking down his pipe from the mantel-shelf, gave it into his hand, and entreated him to smoke it, the good Captain was so bewildered by her attention that he held it as if he had never held a pipe in all his life. Likewise, when Florence, looking into the little cupboard, took out the case-bottle and mixed a perfect glass of grog for him, unasked, and set it at his elbow, his ruddy nose turned pale, he felt himself so graced and honoured. When he had filled his pipe in an absolute reverie of satisfaction, Florence lighted it for him – the Captain having no power to object, or to prevent her – and resuming her place on the old sofa, looked at him with a smile so loving and so grateful, a smile that showed him so plainly how her forlorn heart turned to him, as her face did, through grief, that the smoke of the pipe got into the Captain's throat and made him cough, and got into the Captain's eyes, and made them blink and water.

The manner in which the Captain tried to make believe that the cause of these effects lay hidden in the pipe itself, and the way in which he looked into the bowl for it, and not finding it there, pretended to blow it out of the stem, was wonderfully pleasant. The pipe soon getting into better condition, he fell into that state of repose becoming a good smoker; but sat with his eyes fixed on Florence, and, with a beaming placidity not to be described, and stopping every now and then to discharge a little cloud from his lips, slowly puffed it forth, as if it were a scroll coming out of his mouth, bearing the legend 'Poor Wal'r, aye, aye. Drownded, an't he?' after which he would resume his smoking with infinite gentleness.

Unlike as they were externally – and there could scarcely be a more decided contrast than between Florence in her delicate youth and beauty, and Captain Cuttle with his knobby face, his great broad weather-beaten person, and his gruff voice – in simple innocence of the world's ways and the world's perplexities and dangers, they were nearly on a level. No child could have surpassed Captain Cuttle in inexperience of everything but wind and weather; in simplicity, credulity, and generous trustfulness. Faith, hope, and charity, shared his whole nature among them. An odd sort of romance, perfectly unimaginative, yet perfectly unreal, and subject to no considerations of worldly prudence or practicability, was the only partner they had in his character. As the Captain sat, and smoked, and looked at Florence, God knows what impossible pictures, in which she was the principal figure, presented themselves to his mind. Equally vague and uncertain, though not so sanguine, were her own thoughts of the life before her; and even as her tears made prismatic colours in the light she gazed at, so, through her new and heavy grief, she already saw a rainbow faintly shining in the far-off sky. A wandering princess and a good monster in a story-book might have sat by the fireside, and talked as Captain Cuttle and poor Florence thought – and not have looked very much unlike them.

The Captain was not troubled with the faintest idea of any difficulty in retaining Florence, or of any responsibility thereby incurred. Having put up the shutters and locked the door, he was quite satisfied on this head. If she had been a Ward in Chancery,[7] it would have made no difference at all to Captain Cuttle. He was the last man in the world to be troubled by any such considerations.

So the Captain smoked his pipe very comfortably, and Florence and he meditated after their own manner. When the pipe was out, they had some tea; and then Florence entreated him to take her to some neighbouring shop, where she could buy the few necessaries she immediately wanted. It being quite dark, the Captain consented; peeping carefully out first, as he had been wont to do in his time of hiding from Mrs MacStinger; and arming himself with his large stick, in case of an appeal to arms being rendered necessary by any unforeseen circumstance.

The pride Captain Cuttle had, in giving his arm to Florence, and escorting her some two or three hundred yards, keeping a bright look-out all the time, and attracting the attention of every one who passed them, by his great vigilance and numerous precautions, was extreme. Arrived at the shop, the Captain felt it a point of delicacy to retire during the making of the purchases, as they were to consist of wearing apparel; but he previously deposited his tin canister on the counter, and informing the young lady of the establishment that it contained fourteen pound two, requested her, in case that amount of property should not be sufficient to defray the expenses of his niece's little outfit – at the word 'niece,' he bestowed a most significant look on Florence, accompanied with pantomime, expressive of sagacity and mystery – to have the goodness to 'sing out,' and he would make up the difference from his pocket. Casually consulting his big watch, as a deep means of dazzling the establishment, and impressing it with a sense of property, the Captain then kissed his hook to his niece, and retired outside the window, where it was a choice sight to see his great face looking in from time to time, among the silks and ribbons, with an obvious misgiving that Florence had been spirited away by a back door.

'Dear Captain Cuttle,' said Florence, when she came out with a parcel, the size of which greatly disappointed the Captain, who had expected to see a porter following with a bale of goods, 'I don't want this money, indeed. I have not spent any of it. I have money of my own.'

'My lady lass,' returned the baffled Captain, looking straight down the street before them, 'take care on it for me, will you be so good, till such time as I ask ye for it?'

'May I put it back in its usual place,' said Florence, 'and keep it there?'

The Captain was not at all gratified by this proposal, but he answered, 'Aye, aye, put it anywheres, my lady lass, so long as you know where to find it again. It an't o' no use to *me*,' said the Captain. 'I wonder I haven't chucked it away afore now.'

The Captain was quite disheartened for the moment, but he revived at the first touch of Florence's arm, and they returned with the same precautions as they had come, the Captain opening the door of the little Midshipman's berth, and diving in, with a suddenness which his great practice only could have taught him. During Florence's slumber in the morning, he had engaged the daughter of an elderly lady, who usually sat under a blue umbrella in Leadenhall Market, selling poultry, to come and put her room in order, and render her any little services she required; and this damsel now appearing, Florence found everything about her as convenient and orderly, if not as handsome, as in the terrible dream she had once called Home.

When they were alone again, the Captain insisted on her eating a slice of dry toast, and drinking a glass of spiced negus (which he made to perfection); and, encouraging her with every kind word and inconsequential quotation he could possibly think of, led her upstairs to her bedroom. But he too had something on his mind, and was not easy in his manner.

'Good-night, dear heart,' said Captain Cuttle to her at her chamber-door.

Florence raised her lips to his face, and kissed him.

At any other time the Captain would have been overbalanced by such a token of her affection and gratitude; but now, although he was very sensible of it, he looked in her face with even more uneasiness than he had testified before, and seemed unwilling to leave her.

'Poor Wal'r!' said the Captain.

'Poor, poor Walter!' sighed Florence.

'Drownded, an't he?' said the Captain.

Florence shook her head, and sighed.

'Good night, my lady lass!' said Captain Cuttle, putting out his hand.

'God bless you, dear, kind friend!'

But the Captain lingered still.

'Is anything the matter, dear Captain Cuttle?' said Florence, easily alarmed in her then state of mind. 'Have you anything to tell me?'

'To tell you, lady lass!' replied the Captain, meeting her eyes in confusion. 'No, no; what should I have to tell you, pretty! You don't expect as I've got anything good to tell you, sure?'

'No!' said Florence, shaking her head.

The Captain looked at her wistfully, and repeated 'No,' – still lingering, and still showing embarrassment.

'Poor Wal'r!' said the Captain. 'My Wal'r, as I used to call you! Old Sol Gills's nevy! Welcome to all as knowed you, as the flowers in May! Where are you got to, brave boy? Drownded, an't he?'

Concluding his apostrophe with this abrupt appeal to Florence, the Captain bade her good night, and descended the stairs, while Florence remained at the top, holding the candle out to light him down. He was lost in the obscurity, and, judging from the sound of his receding footsteps, was in the act of turning into the little parlour, when his head and shoulders unexpectedly emerged again, as from the deep, apparently for no other purpose than to repeat, 'Drownded, an't he, pretty?' For when he had said that in a tone of tender condolence, he disappeared.

Florence was very sorry that she should unwittingly, though naturally, have awakened these associations in the mind of her protector, by taking refuge there; and sitting down before the little table where the Captain had arranged the telescope and song-book, and those other rarities, thought of Walter, and of all that was connected with him in the past, until she could have almost wished to lie down on her bed and fade away. But in her lonely yearning to the dead whom she had loved, no thought of home – no possibility of going back – no presentation of it as yet existing, or as sheltering her father – once entered her thoughts. She had seen the murder done. In the last lingering natural aspect in which she had cherished him through so much, he had been torn out of her heart, defaced, and slain. The thought of it was so appalling to her, that she covered her eyes, and shrunk trembling from the least remembrance of the deed, or of the cruel hand that did it. If her fond heart could have held his image after that, it must have broken; but it could not; and the void was filled with a wild dread that fled from all confronting with its shattered fragments – with such a dread as could have risen out of nothing but the depths of such a love, so wronged.

She dared not look into the glass; for the sight of the darkening mark upon her bosom made her afraid of herself, as if she bore about her something wicked. She covered it up, with a hasty, faltering hand, and in the dark; and laid her weary head down, weeping.

The Captain did not go to bed for a long time. He walked to and fro in the shop and in the little parlour, for a full hour, and, appearing to have composed himself by that exercise, sat down with a grave and thoughtful face, and read out of a Prayer-book the forms of prayer appointed to be used at sea. These were not easily disposed of; the good Captain being a mighty slow, gruff reader, and frequently stopping at a hard word to give himself such encouragement as 'Now, my lad! With a will!' or, 'Steady, Ed'ard Cuttle, steady!' which had a great effect in helping him out of any difficulty. Moreover, his spectacles greatly interfered with his powers of vision. But notwithstanding these drawbacks, the Captain, being heartily in earnest, read the service to the very last line, and with genuine feeling too; and approving of it very much when he had done, turned in under the counter (but not before he had been upstairs, and listened at Florence's door), with a serene breast, and most benevolent visage.

The Captain turned out several times in the course of the night, to assure himself that his charge was resting quietly; and once, at daybreak, found that she was awake; for she called to know if it were he, on hearing footsteps near her door.

'Yes, my lady lass,' replied the Captain, in a growling whisper. 'Are you all right, di'mond?'

Florence thanked him, and said 'Yes.'

The Captain could not lose so favourable an opportunity of applying his mouth to the keyhole, and calling through it, like a hoarse breeze, 'Poor Wal'r! Drownded, an't he?' After which he withdrew, and turning in again, slept till seven o'clock.

Nor was he free from his uneasy and embarrassed manner all

that day; though Florence, being busy with her needle in the little parlour, was more calm and tranquil than she had been on the day preceding. Almost always when she raised her eyes from her work, she observed the Captain looking at her, and thoughtfully stroking his chin; and he so often hitched his arm-chair close to her, as if he were going to say something very confidential, and hitched it away again, as not being able to make up his mind how to begin, that in the course of the day he cruised completely round the parlour in that frail bark, and more than once went ashore against the wainscot[3] or the closet door, in a very distressed condition.

It was not until the twilight that Captain Cuttle, fairly dropping anchor, at last, by the side of Florence, began to talk at all connectedly. But when the light of the fire was shining on the walls and ceiling of the little room, and on the tea-board and the cups and saucers that were ranged upon the table, and on her calm face turned towards the flame, and reflecting it in the tears that filled her eyes, the Captain broke a long silence thus:

'You never was at sea, my own?'

'No,' replied Florence.

'Aye,' said the Captain, reverentially; 'it's a almighty element. There's a wonders in the deep, my pretty. Think on it when the winds is roaring and the waves is rowling. Think on it when the stormy nights is so pitch dark,' said the Captain, solemnly holding up his hook, 'as you can't see your hand afore you, excepting when the wiwid lightning reweals the same; and when you drive, drive, drive, through the storm and dark, as if you was a driving, head on, to the world without end, evermore, amen, and when found making a note of. Them's the times, my beauty, when a man may say to his messmate (previously a overhauling of the wollume), "A stiff nor'wester's blowing, Bill;[9] hark, don't you hear it roar now! Lord help 'em, how I pitys all unhappy folks ashore now!"' Which quotation, as particularly applicable to the terrors of the ocean, the Captain delivered in a most impressive manner, concluding with a sonorous 'Stand by!'

'Were *you* ever in a dreadful storm?' asked Florence.

'Why aye, my lady lass, I've seen my share of bad weather,' said the Captain, tremulously wiping his head, 'and I've had my share of knocking about; but – but it an't of myself as I was a meaning to speak. Our dear boy,' drawing closer to her, 'Wal'r, darling, as was drownded.'

The Captain spoke in such a trembling voice, and looked at

Florence with a face so pale and agitated, that she clung to his hand in affright.

'Your face is changed,' said Florence. 'You are altered in a moment. What is it? Dear Captain Cuttle, it turns me cold to see you!'

'What! Lady lass,' returned the Captain, supporting her with his hand, 'don't be took aback. No, no! All's well, all's well, my dear. As I was a saying – Wal'r – he's – he's drownded. An't he?'

Florence looked at him intently; her colour came and went; and she laid her hand upon her breast.

'There's perils and dangers on the deep, my beauty,' said the Captain; 'and over many a brave ship, and many and many a bould heart, the secret waters has closed up, and never told no tales. But there's escapes upon the deep, too, and sometimes one man out of a score, – ah! maybe out of a hundred, pretty, – has been saved by the mercy of God, and come home after being given over for dead, and told of all hands lost. I – I know a story, Heart's Delight,' stammered the Captain, 'o' this natur, as was told to me once; and being on this here tack, and you and me sitting alone by the fire, maybe you'd like to hear me tell it. Would you, deary?'

Florence, trembling with an agitation which she could not control or understand, involuntarily followed his glance, which went behind her into the shop, where a lamp was burning. The instant that she turned her head, the Captain sprung out of his chair, and interposed his hand.

'There's nothing there, my beauty,' said the Captain. 'Don't look there.'

'Why not?' asked Florence.

The Captain murmured something about its being dull that way, and about the fire being cheerful. He drew the door ajar, which had been standing open until now, and resumed his seat. Florence followed him with her eyes, and looked intently in his face.

'The story was about a ship, my lady lass,' began the Captain, 'as sailed out of the Port of London, with a fair wind and in fair weather, bound for – don't be took aback, my lady lass, she was only out'ard bound, pretty, only out'ard bound!'

The expression on Florence's face alarmed the Captain, who was himself very hot and flurried, and showed scarcely less agitation than she did.

'Shall I go on, Beauty?' said the Captain.

'Yes, yes, pray!' cried Florence.

The Captain made a gulp as if to get down something that was sticking in his throat, and nervously proceeded:

'That there unfort'nate ship met with such foul weather, out at sea, as don't blow once in twenty year, my darling. There was hurricanes ashore as tore up forests and blowed down towns, and there was gales at sea in them latitudes, as not the stoutest wessel ever launched could live in. Day arter day that there unfortunate ship behaved noble, I'm told, and did her duty brave, my pretty, but at one blow a'most her bulwarks was stove in, her masts and rudder carried away, her best men swept overboard, and she left to the mercy of the storm as had no mercy but blowed harder and harder yet, while the waves dashed over her, and beat her in, and every time they come a thundering at her, broke her like a shell. Every black spot in every mountain of water that rolled away was a bit o' the ship's life or a living man, and so she went to pieces, Beauty, and no grass will never grow upon the graves of them as manned that ship.'

'They were not all lost!' cried Florence. 'Some were saved! – Was one?'

'Aboard o' that there unfort'nate wessel,' said the Captain, rising from his chair, and clenching his hand with prodigious energy and exultation, 'was a lad, a gallant lad – as I've heerd tell – that had loved, when he was a boy, to read and talk about brave actions in shipwrecks – I've heerd him! I've heerd him! – and he remembered of 'em in his hour of need; for when the stoutest hearts and oldest hands was hove down, he was firm and cheery. It warn't the want of objects to like and love ashore that gave him courage, it was his nat'ral mind. I've seen it in his face, when he was no more than a child – aye, many a time! – and when I thought it nothing but his good looks, bless him!'

'And was he saved!' cried Florence. 'Was he saved!'

'That brave lad,' said the Captain, – 'look at me, pretty! Don't look round—'

Florence had hardly power to repeat, 'Why not?'

'Because there's nothing there, my deary,' said the Captain. 'Don't be took aback, pretty creetur! Don't, for the sake of Wal'r, as was dear to all on us! That there lad,' said the Captain, 'arter working with the best, and standing by the faint-hearted, and never making no complaint nor sign of fear, and keeping up a spirit in all hands that made 'em honour him as if he'd been a admiral – that lad, along with the second-mate and one seaman, was left, of all the

beatin' hearts that went aboard that ship, the only living creeturs –
lashed to a fragment of the wreck, and driftin' on the stormy sea.'

'Were they saved?' cried Florence.

'Days and nights they drifted on them endless waters,' said the
Captain, 'until at last – No! Don't look that way, pretty! – a sail
bore down upon 'em, and they was, by the Lord's mercy, took
aboard: two living and one dead.'

'Which of them was dead?' cried Florence.

'Not the lad I speak on,' said the Captain.

'Thank God! oh thank God!'

'Amen!' returned the Captain hurriedly. 'Don't be took aback! A
minute more, my lady lass! with a good heart! – aboard that ship,
they went a long voyage, right away across the chart (for there
warn't no touching nowhere,[10] and on that voyage the seaman as
was picked up with him died. But he was spared, and—'

The Captain, without knowing what he did, had cut a slice of
bread from the loaf, and put it on his hook (which was his usual
toasting fork), on which he now held it to the fire; looking behind
Florence with great emotion in his face, and suffering the bread to
blaze and burn like fuel.

'Was spared,' repeated Florence, 'and—?'

'And come home in that ship,' said the captain, still looking in
the same direction, 'and – don't be frightened, pretty – and landed;
and one morning come cautiously to his own door to take a
obserwation, knowing that his friends would think him drownded,
when he sheered off at the unexpected—'

'At the unexpected barking of a dog?' cried Florence, quickly.

'Yes,' roared the Captain. 'Steady, darling! courage! Don't look
round yet. See there! upon the wall!'

There was the shadow of a man upon the wall close to her. She
started up, looked round, and with a piercing cry, saw Walter Gay
behind her!

She had no thought of him but as a brother, a brother rescued
from the grave; a shipwrecked brother saved and at her side; and
rushed into his arms. In all the world, he seemed to be her hope,
her comfort, refuge, natural protector. 'Take care of Walter, I was
fond of Walter!' The dear remembrance of the plaintive voice that
said so, rushed upon her soul, like music in the night. 'Oh welcome
home, dear Walter! Welcome to this stricken breast!' She felt the
words, although she could not utter them, and held him in her pure
embrace.

Captain Cuttle, in a fit of delirium, attempted to wipe his head

The Shadow in the little parlour

with the blackened toast upon his hook: and finding it an uncongenial substance for the purpose, put it into the crown of his glazed hat, put the glazed hat on with some difficulty, essayed to sing a verse of Lovely Peg, broke down at the first word, and retired into the shop, whence he presently came back, express, with a face all flushed and besmeared, and the starch completely taken out of his shirt-collar, to say these words:

'Wal'r, my lad, here is a little bit of property as I should wish to make over, jintly!'

The Captain hastily produced the big watch, the tea-spoons, the sugar-tongs, and the canister, and laying them on the table, swept them with his great hand into Walter's hat; but in handing that singular strong box to Walter, he was so overcome again, that he was fain to make another retreat into the shop, and absent himself for a longer space of time than on his first retirement.

But Walter sought him out, and brought him back; and then the Captain's great apprehension was, that Florence would suffer from this new shock. He felt it so earnestly, that he turned quite rational, and positively interdicted any further allusion to Walter's adventures for some days to come. Captain Cuttle then became sufficiently composed to relieve himself of the toast in his hat, and to take his place at the tea-board; but finding Walter's grasp upon his shoulder, on one side, and Florence whispering her tearful congratulations on the other, the Captain suddenly bolted again, and was missing for a good ten minutes.

But never in all his life had the Captain's face so shone and glistened, as when, at last, he sat stationary at the tea-board, looking from Florence to Walter, and from Walter to Florence. Nor was this effect produced or at all heightened by the immense quantity of polishing he had administered to his face with his coat-sleeve during the last half-hour. It was solely the effect of his internal emotions. There was a glory and delight within the Captain that spread itself over his whole visage, and made a perfect illumination there.

The pride with which the Captain looked upon the bronzed cheek and the courageous eyes of his recovered boy; with which he saw the generous fervour of his youth, and all its frank and hopeful qualities, shining once more, in the fresh, wholesome manner, and the ardent face, would have kindled something of this light in his countenance. The admiration and sympathy with which he turned his eyes on Florence, whose beauty, grace, and innocence could have won no truer or more zealous champion than himself, would

have had an equal influence upon him. But the fulness of the glow
he shed around him could only have been engendered in his
contemplation of the two together, and in all the fancies springing
out of that association, that came sparkling and beaming into his
head, and danced about it.

How they talked of poor old Uncle Sol, and dwelt on every little
circumstance relating to his disappearance; how their joy was
moderated by the old man's absence and by the misfortunes of
Florence; how they released Diogenes, whom the Captain had
decoyed upstairs some time before, lest he should bark again; the
Captain, though he was in one continual flutter, and made many
more short plunges into the shop, fully comprehended. But he no
more dreamed that Walter looked on Florence, as it were, from a
new and far-off place; that while his eyes often sought the lovely
face, they seldom met its open glance of sisterly affection, but
withdrew themselves when hers were raised towards him; than he
believed that it was Walter's ghost who sat beside him. He saw
them there together in their youth and beauty, and he knew the
story of their younger days, and he had no inch of room beneath
his great blue waistcoat for anything save admiration of such a pair,
and gratitude for their being reunited.

They sat thus, until it grew late. The Captain would have been
content to sit so for a week. But Walter rose, to take leave for the
night.

'Going, Walter!' said Florence. 'Where?'

'He slings his hammock for the present, lady lass,' said Captain
Cuttle, 'round at Brogley's. Within hail, Heart's Delight.'

'I am the cause of your going away, Walter,' said Florence. 'There
is a houseless sister in your place.'

'Dear Miss Dombey,' replied Walter, hesitating – 'if it is not too
bold to call you so! –'

'– Walter!' she exclaimed, surprised.

'If anything could make me happier in being allowed to see and
speak to you, would it not be the discovery that I had any means
on earth of doing you a moment's service! Where would I not go,
what would I not do for your sake?'

She smiled, and called him brother.

'You are so changed,' said Walter –

'I changed!' she interrupted.

'To me,' said Walter, softly, as if he were thinking aloud,
'changed to me. I left you such a child, and find you – oh! something
so different –'

'But your sister, Walter. You have not forgotten what we promised to each other when we parted?'

'Forgotten!' But he said no more.

'And if you had – if suffering and danger had driven it from your thoughts – which it has not – you would remember it now, Walter, when you find me poor and abandoned, with no home but this, and no friends but the two who hear me speak!'

'I would! Heaven knows I would!' said Walter.

'Oh, Walter,' exclaimed Florence, through her sobs and tears. 'Dear brother! Show me some way through the world – some humble path that I may take alone, and labour in, and sometimes think of you as one who will protect and care for me as for a sister! Oh, help me, Walter, for I need help so much!'

'Miss Dombey! Florence! I would die to help you. But your friends are proud and rich. Your father—'

'No, no! Walter!' She shrieked, and put her hands up to her head, in an attitude of terror that transfixed him where he stood. 'Don't say that word!'

He never, from that hour, forgot the voice and look with which she stopped him at the name. He felt that if he were to live a hundred years, he never could forget it.

Somewhere – anywhere – but never home! All past, all gone, all lost and broken up! The whole history of her untold slight and suffering was in the cry and look; and he felt he never could forget it, and he never did.

She laid her gentle face upon the Captain's shoulder and related how and why she had fled. If every sorrowing tear she shed in doing so, had been a curse upon the head of him she never named or blamed, it would have been better for him, Walter thought, with awe, than to be renounced out of such a strength and might of love.

'There, precious!' said the Captain, when she ceased; and deep attention the Captain had paid to her while she spoke; listening, with his glazed hat all awry and his mouth wide open. 'Awast, awast, my eyes! Wal'r, dear lad, sheer off for to-night, and leave the pretty one to me!'

Walter took her hand in both of his, and put it to his lips, and kissed it. He knew now that she was, indeed, a homeless wandering fugitive; but, richer to him so, than in all the wealth and pride of her right station, she seemed farther off than even on the height that had made him giddy in his boyish dreams.

Captain Cuttle, perplexed by no such meditations, guarded Florence to her room, and watched at intervals upon the charmed ground outside her door – for such it truly was to him – until he felt sufficiently easy in his mind about her, to turn in under the counter. On abandoning his watch for that purpose, he could not help calling once, rapturously, through the keyhole, 'Drownded. An't he, pretty?' – or, when he got downstairs, making another trial at that verse of Lovely Peg. But it stuck in his throat somehow, and he could make nothing of it; so he went to bed, and dreamed that old Sol Gills was married to Mrs MacStinger, and kept prisoner by that lady in a secret chamber on a short allowance of victuals.

CHAPTER 50

Mr Toots's Complaint

There was an empty room above-stairs at the Wooden Midshipman's, which, in days of yore, had been Walter's bedroom. Walter, rousing up the Captain betimes in the morning, proposed that they should carry thither such furniture out of the little parlour as would grace it best, so that Florence might take possession of it when she rose. As nothing could be more agreeable to Captain Cuttle than making himself very red and short of breath in such a cause, he turned to (as he himself said) with a will; and in a couple of hours, this garret was transformed into a species of land-cabin, adorned with the choicest movables out of the parlour, inclusive even of the Tartar frigate, which the Captain hung up over the chimneypiece with such extreme delight, that he could do nothing for half-an-hour afterwards but walk backward from it, lost in admiration.

The Captain could be induced by no persuasion of Walter's to wind up the big watch, or to take back the canister, or to touch the sugar-tongs and teaspoons. 'No, no, my lad,' was the Captain's invariable reply to any solicitation of the kind, 'I've made that there little property over, jintly.' These words he repeated with great unction and gravity, evidently believing that they had the virtue of an Act of Parliament, and that unless he committed himself by some new admission of ownership, no flaw could be found in such a form of conveyance.

It was an advantage of the new arrangement, that besides the greater seclusion it afforded Florence, it admitted of the Midshipman being restored to his usual post of observation, and also of the shop shutters being taken down. The latter ceremony, however little importance the unconscious Captain attached to it, was not wholly superfluous; for, on the previous day, so much excitement had been occasioned in the neighbourhood, by the shutters remaining unopened, that the Instrument-maker's house had been honoured with an unusual share of public observation, and had been intently stared at from the opposite side of the way, by groups of hungry gazers, at any time between sunrise and sunset. The idlers and vagabonds had been particularly interested in the Captain's fate; constantly grovelling in the mud to apply their eyes to the cellar-grating, under the shop-window, and delighting their imaginations with the fancy that they could see a piece of his coat as he hung in a corner; though this settlement of him was stoutly disputed by an opposite faction, who were of opinion that he lay murdered with a hammer, on the stairs. It was not without exciting some discontent, therefore, that the subject of these rumours was seen early in the morning standing at his shop-door as hale and hearty as if nothing had happened; and the beadle of that quarter, a man of an ambitious character, who had expected to have the distinction of being present at the breaking open of the door, and of giving evidence in full uniform before the coroner, went so far as to say to an opposite neighbour, that the chap in the glazed hat had better not try it on there – without more particularly mentioning what – and further, that he, the Beadle, would keep his eye upon him.

'Captain Cuttle,' said Walter, musing, when they stood resting from their labours at the shop-door, looking down the old familiar street; it being still early in the morning; 'nothing at all of Uncle Sol, in all that time!'

'Nothing at all, my lad,' replied the Captain, shaking his head.

'Gone in search of me, dear, kind old man,' said Walter: 'yet never write to you! But why not? He says, in effect, in this packet that you gave me,' taking the paper from his pocket, which had been opened in the presence of the enlightened Bunsby, 'that if you never hear from him before opening it, you may believe him dead. Heaven forbid! But you would have heard *of* him, even if he *were* dead! Some one would have written, surely, by his desire, if he could not; and have said, "on such a day, there died in my house," or "under my care," or so forth, "Mr Solomon Gills of London, who left this last remembrance and this last request to you."'

The Captain, who had never climbed to such a clear height of probability before, was greatly impressed by the wide prospect it opened, and answered, with a thoughtful shake of his head, 'Well said, my lad, very well said.'

'I have been thinking of this, or, at least,' said Walter, colouring, 'I have been thinking of one thing and another, all through a sleepless night, and I cannot believe, Captain Cuttle, but that my Uncle Sol (Lord bless him!) is alive, and will return. I don't so much wonder at his going away, because, leaving out of consideration that spice of the marvellous which was always in his character, and his great affection for me, before which every other consideration of his life became nothing, as no one ought to know so well as I who had the best of fathers in him,' – Walter's voice was indistinct and husky here, and he looked away, along the street, – 'leaving that out of consideration, I say, I have often read and heard of people who, having some near and dear relative, who was supposed to be shipwrecked at sea, have gone down to live on that part of the sea-shore where any tidings of the missing ship might be expected to arrive, though only an hour or two sooner than elsewhere, or have even gone upon her track to the place whither she was bound, as if their going would create intelligence. I think I should do such a thing myself, as soon as another, or sooner than many, perhaps. But why my uncle shouldn't write to you, when he so clearly intended to do so, or how he should die abroad, and you not know it through some other hand, I cannot make out.'

Captain Cuttle observed, with a shake of his head, that Jack Bunsby himself hadn't made it out, and that he was a man as could give a pretty taut opinion too.

'If my uncle had been a heedless young man, likely to be entrapped by jovial company to some drinking-place, where he was to be got rid of for the sake of what money he might have about him,' said Walter; 'or if he had been a reckless sailor, going ashore with two or three months' pay in his pocket, I could understand his disappearing, and leaving no trace behind. But, being what he was – and is, I hope – I can't believe it.'

'Wal'r, my lad,' inquired the Captain, wistfully eyeing him as he pondered and pondered, 'what do you make of it, then?'

'Captain Cuttle,' returned Walter, 'I don't know what to make of it. I suppose he never *has* written! There is no doubt about that?'

'If so be as Sol Gills wrote, my lad,' replied the Captain, argumentatively, 'where's his dispatch?'

'Say that he intrusted it to some private hand,' suggested Walter, 'and that it has been forgotten, or carelessly thrown aside, or lost. Even that is more probable to me, than the other event. In short, I not only cannot bear to contemplate that other event, Captain Cuttle, but I can't, and won't.'

'Hope, you see, Wal'r,' said the Captain, sagely, 'Hope. It's that as animates you. Hope is a buoy, for which you overhaul your Little Warbler, sentimental diwision,[1] but Lord, my lad, like any other buoy, it only floats; it can't be steered nowhere. Along with the figure-head of Hope,' said the Captain, 'there's a anchor; but what's the good of my having a anchor, if I can't find no bottom to let it go in?'

Captain Cuttle said this rather in his character of a sagacious citizen and householder, bound to impart a morsel from his stores of wisdom to an inexperienced youth, than in his own proper person. Indeed, his face was quite luminous as he spoke, with new hope, caught from Walter; and he appropriately concluded by slapping him on the back; and saying, with enthusiasm, 'Hooroar, my lad! Indiwidually, I'm o' your opinion.'

Walter, with his cheerful laugh, returned the salutation, and said:

'Only one word more about my uncle at present, Captain Cuttle. I suppose it is impossible that he can have written in the ordinary course – by mail packet, or ship letter, you understand—'

'Aye, aye, my lad,' said the Captain approvingly.

'—And that you have missed the letter anyhow?'

'Why, Wal'r,' said the Captain, turning his eyes upon him with a faint approach to a severe expression, 'an't I been on the look-out for any tidings of that man o' science, old Sol Gills, your uncle, day and night, ever since I lost him? An't my heart been heavy and watchful always, along of him and you? Sleeping and waking, an't I been upon my post, and wouldn't I scorn to quit it while this here Midshipman held together!'

'Yes, Captain Cuttle,' replied Walter, grasping his hand, 'I know you would, and I know how faithful and earnest all you say and feel is. I am sure of it. You don't doubt that I am as sure of it as I am that my foot is again upon this doorstep, or that I again have hold of this true hand. Do you?'

'No, no, Wal'r,' returned the Captain, with his beaming face.

'I'll hazard no more conjectures,' said Walter, fervently shaking the hard hand of the Captain, who shook his with no less good-will. 'All I will add is, Heaven forbid that I should touch my uncle's possessions, Captain Cuttle! Everything that he left here, shall remain in the care of the truest of stewards and kindest of men – and if his name is not Cuttle, he has no name! Now, best of friends, about – Miss Dombey.'

There was a change in Walter's manner, as he came to these two words; and when he uttered them, all his confidence and cheerfulness appeared to have deserted him.

'I thought, before Miss Dombey stopped me when I spoke of her father last night,' said Walter, ' – you remember how?'

The Captain well remembered, and shook his head.

'I thought,' said Walter, 'before that, that we had but one hard duty to perform, and that it was, to prevail upon her to communicate with her friends, and to return home.'

The Captain muttered a feeble 'Awast!' or a 'Stand by!' or something or other, equally pertinent to the occasion; but it was rendered so extremely feeble by the total discomfiture with which he received this announcement, that what it was, is mere matter of conjecture.

'But,' said Walter, 'that is over. I think so no longer. I would sooner be put back again upon that piece of wreck, on which I have so often floated, since my preservation, in my dreams, and there left to drift, and drive, and die!'

'Hooroar, my lad!' exclaimed the Captain, in a burst of uncontrollable satisfaction. 'Hooroar! hooroar! hooroar!'

'To think that she, so young, so good, and beautiful,' said Walter, 'so delicately brought up, and born to such a different fortune, should strive with the rough world! But we have seen the gulf that cuts off all behind her, though no one but herself can know how deep it is; and there is no return.'

Captain Cuttle, without quite understanding this, greatly approved of it, and observed, in a tone of strong corroboration, that the wind was quite abaft.[2]

'She ought not to be alone here; ought she, Captain Cuttle?' said Walter, anxiously.

'Well, my lad,' replied the Captain, after a little sagacious consideration. 'I don't know. You being here to keep her company, you see, and you two being jintly—'

'Dear Captain Cuttle!' remonstrated Walter. 'I being here! Miss Dombey, in her guileless innocent heart, regards me as her adopted brother; but what would the guile and guilt of *my* heart be, if I pretended to believe that I had any right to approach her, familiarly, in that character – if I pretended to forget that I am bound, in honour, not to do it?'

'Wal'r, my lad,' hinted the Captain, with some revival of his discomfiture, 'an't there no other character as—'

'Oh!' returned Walter, 'would you have me die in her esteem – in such esteem as hers – and put a veil between myself and her angel's face for ever, by taking advantage of her being here for refuge, so trusting and so unprotected, to endeavour to exalt myself into her lover? What do I say? There is no one in the world who would be more opposed to me if I could do so, than you.'

'Wal'r, my lad,' said the Captain, drooping more and more, 'prowiding as there is any just cause or impediment why two persons should not be jined together in the house of bondage,[3] for which you'll overhaul the place and make a note, I hope I should declare it as promised and wowed in the banns. So there an't no other character; an't there, my lad?'

Walter briskly waved his hand in the negative.

'Well, my lad,' growled the Captain slowly, 'I won't deny but what I find myself wery much down by the head, along o' this here, or but what I've gone clean about.[4] But as to Lady-lass, Wal'r, mind you, wot's respect and duty to her is respect and duty in my articles, howsumiver disapinting; and therefore I follows in your wake, my lad, and feel as you are, no doubt, acting up to yourself. And there an't *no* other character, an't there?' said the Captain, musing over the ruins of his fallen castle with a very despondent face.

'Now, Captain Cuttle,' said Walter, starting a fresh point with a gayer air, to cheer the Captain up – but nothing could do that; he was too much concerned – 'I think we should exert ourselves to find some one who would be a proper attendant for Miss Dombey while she remains here, and who may be trusted. None of her relations may. It's clear Miss Dombey feels that they are all subservient to her father. What has become of Susan?'

'The young woman?' returned the Captain. 'It's my belief as she was sent away again the will of Heart's Delight. I made a signal for her when Lady-lass first come, and she rated of her wery high, and said she had been gone a long time.'

'Then,' said Walter, 'do you ask Miss Dombey where she's gone, and we'll try to find her. The morning's getting on, and Miss Dombey will soon be rising. You are her best friend. Wait for her upstairs, and leave me to take care of all down here.'

The Captain, very crestfallen indeed, echoed the sigh with which Walter said this, and complied. Florence was delighted with her new room, anxious to see Walter, and overjoyed at the prospect of greeting her old friend Susan. But Florence could not say where Susan was gone, except that it was in Essex, and no one could say, she remembered, unless it were Mr Toots.

With this information the melancholy Captain returned to Walter, and gave him to understand that Mr Toots was the young gentleman whom he had encountered on the door-step, and that he was a friend of his, and that he was a young gentleman of property, and that he hopelessly adored Miss Dombey. The Captain also related how the intelligence of Walter's supposed fate had first made him acquainted with Mr Toots, and how there was solemn treaty and compact between them, that Mr Toots should be mute upon the subject of his love.

The question then was, whether Florence could trust Mr Toots; and Florence saying, with a smile, 'Oh, yes, with her whole heart!' it became important to find out where Mr Toots lived. This Florence didn't know, and the Captain had forgotten; and the Captain was telling Walter, in the little parlour, that Mr Toots was sure to be there soon, when in came Mr Toots himself.

'Captain Gills,' said Mr Toots, rushing into the parlour without any ceremony, 'I'm in a state of mind bordering on distraction!'

Mr Toots had discharged those words, as from a mortar,[5] before he observed Walter, whom he recognised with what may be described as a chuckle of misery.

'You'll excuse me, Sir,' said Mr Toots, holding his forehead, 'but I'm at present in that state that my brain is going, if not gone, and anything approaching to politeness in an individual so situated would be a hollow mockery. Captain Gills, I beg to request the favour of a private interview.'

'Why, Brother,' returned the Captain, taking him by the hand, 'you are the man as we was on the look-out for.'

'Oh, Captain Gills,' said Mr Toots, 'what a look-out that must be, of which I am the object! I haven't dared to shave, I'm in that rash state. I haven't had my clothes brushed. My hair is matted together. I told the Chicken that if he offered to clean my boots, I'd stretch him a corpse before me!'

All these indications of a disordered mind were verified in Mr Toots's appearance, which was wild and savage.

'See here, Brother,' said the Captain. 'This here's old Sol Gills's nevy Wal'r. Him as was supposed to have perished at sea.'

Mr Toots took his hand from his forehead, and stared at Walter.

'Good gracious me!' stammered Mr Toots. 'What a complication of misery! How-de-do? I – I – I'm afraid you must have got very wet. Captain Gills, will you allow me a word in the shop?'

He took the Captain by the coat, and going out with him whispered:

'That then, Captain Gills, is the party you spoke of, when you said that he and Miss Dombey were made for one another?'

'Why, aye, my lad,' replied the disconsolate Captain; 'I was of that mind once.'

'And at this time!' exclaimed Mr Toots, with his hand to his forehead again. 'Of all others! – a hated rival! At least, he an't a hated rival,' said Mr Toots, stopping short, on second thoughts, and taking away his hand; 'what should I hate him for? No. If my affection has been truly disinterested, Captain Gills, let me prove it now!'

Mr Toots shot back abruptly into the parlour, and said, wringing Walter by the hand:

'How-de-do? I hope you didn't take any cold. I – I shall be very glad if you'll give me the pleasure of your acquaintance. I wish you many happy returns of the day. Upon my word and honour,' said Mr Toots, warming as he became better acquainted with Walter's face and figure, 'I'm very glad to see you!'

'Thank you, heartily,' said Walter. 'I couldn't desire a more genuine and genial welcome.'

'Couldn't you, though?' said Mr Toots, still shaking his hand. 'It's very kind of you. I'm much obliged to you. How-de-do? I hope you left everybody quite well over the – that is, upon the – I mean wherever you came from last, you know.'

All these good wishes, and better intentions, Walter responded to manfully.

'Captain Gills,' said Mr Toots, 'I should wish to be strictly honourable; but I trust I may be allowed now, to allude to a certain subject that—'

'Aye, aye, my lad,' returned the Captain. 'Freely, freely.'

'Then, Captain Gills,' said Mr Toots, 'and Lieutenant Walters, are you aware that the most dreadful circumstances have been happening at Mr Dombey's house, and that Miss Dombey herself has left her father, who, in my opinion,' said Mr Toots, with great excitement, 'is a Brute, that it would be a flattery to call a – a marble monument, or a bird of prey, and that she is not to be found, and has gone no one knows where?'

'May I ask how you heard this?' inquired Walter.

'Lieutenant Walters,' said Mr Toots, who had arrived at that appellation by a process peculiar to himself; probably by jumbling up his Christian name with the seafaring profession, and supposing some relationship between him and the Captain, which would extend, as a matter of course, to their titles; 'Lieutenant Walters, I can have no objection to make a straightforward reply. The fact is, that feeling extremely interested in everything that relates to Miss

Dombey – not for any selfish reason, Lieutenant Walters, for I am well aware that the most agreeable thing I could do for all parties would be to put an end to my existence, which can only be regarded as an inconvenience – I have been in the habit of bestowing a trifle now and then upon a footman; a most respectable young man, of the name of Towlinson, who has lived in the family some time; and Towlinson informed me, yesterday evening, that this was the state of things. Since which, Captain Gills – and Lieutenant Walters – I have been perfectly frantic, and have been lying down on the sofa all night, the Ruin you behold.'

'Mr Toots,' said Walter, 'I am happy to be able to relieve your mind. Pray calm yourself. Miss Dombey is safe and well.'

'Sir!' cried Mr Toots, starting from his chair and shaking hands with him anew, 'the relief is so excessive, and unspeakable, that if you were to tell me now that Miss Dombey was married even, I could smile. Yes, Captain Gills,' said Mr Toots, appealing to him, 'upon my soul and body, I really think, whatever I might do to myself immediately afterwards, that I could smile, I am so relieved.'

'It will be a greater relief and delight still, to such a generous mind as yours,' said Walter, not at all slow in returning his greeting, 'to find that you can render service to Miss Dombey. Captain Cuttle, will you have the kindness to take Mr Toots upstairs?'

The Captain beckoned to Mr Toots, who followed him with a bewildered countenance, and, ascending to the top of the house, was introduced, without a word of preparation from his conductor, into Florence's new retreat.

Poor Mr Toots's amazement and pleasure at sight of her were such, that they could find a vent in nothing but extravagance. He ran up to her, seized her hand, kissed it, dropped it, seized it again, fell upon one knee, shed tears, chuckled, and was quite regardless of his danger of being pinned by Diogenes, who, inspired by the belief that there was something hostile to his mistress in these demonstrations, worked round and round him, as if only undecided at what particular point to go in for the assault, but quite resolved to do him a fearful mischief.

'Oh Di, you bad, forgetful dog! Dear Mr Toots, I am so rejoiced to see you!'

'Thankee,' said Mr Toots, 'I am pretty well, I'm much obliged to you, Miss Dombey. I hope all the family are the same.'

Mr Toots said this without the least notion of what he was talking about, and sat down on a chair, staring at Florence with the liveliest contention of delight and despair going on in his face that any face could exhibit.

'Captain Gills and Lieutenant Walters have mentioned, Miss Dombey,' gasped Mr Toots, 'that I can do you some service. If I could by any means wash out the remembrance of that day at Brighton, when I conducted myself – much more like a Parricide than a person of independent property,' said Mr Toots, with severe self-accusation, 'I should sink into the silent tomb[6] with a gleam of joy.'

'Pray, Mr Toots,' said Florence, 'do not wish me to forget anything in our acquaintance. I never can, believe me. You have been far too kind and good to me always.'

'Miss Dombey,' returned Mr Toots, 'your consideration for my feelings is a part of your angelic character. Thank you a thousand times. It's of no consequence at all.'

'What we thought of asking you,' said Florence, 'is, whether you remember where Susan, whom you were so kind as to accompany to the coach-office when she left me, is to be found.'

'Why I do not certainly, Miss Dombey,' said Mr Toots, after a little consideration, 'remember the exact name of the place that was on the coach; and I do recollect that she said she was not going to stop there, but was going farther on. But, Miss Dombey, if your object is to find her, and to have her here, myself and the Chicken will produce her with every dispatch that devotion on my part, and great intelligence on the Chicken's, can insure.'

Mr Toots was so manifestly delighted and revived by the prospect of being useful, and the disinterested sincerity of his devotion was so unquestionable, that it would have been cruel to refuse him. Florence, with an instinctive delicacy, forbore to urge the least obstacle, though she did not forbear to overpower him with thanks; and Mr Toots proudly took the commission upon himself for immediate execution.

'Miss Dombey,' said Mr Toots, touching her proffered hand, with a pang of hopeless love visibly shooting through him, and flashing out in his face, 'Good-bye! Allow me to take the liberty of saying, that your misfortunes make me perfectly wretched, and that you may trust me, next to Captain Gills himself. I am quite aware, Miss Dombey, of my own deficiencies – they're not of the least consequence, thank you – but I am entirely to be relied upon, I do assure you, Miss Dombey.'

With that Mr Toots came out of the room, again accompanied by the Captain, who, standing at a little distance, holding his hat under his arm and arranging his scattered locks with his hook, had been a not uninterested witness of what passed. And when the door closed behind them, the light of Mr Toots's life was darkly clouded again.

'Captain Gills,' said that gentleman, stopping near the bottom of the stairs, and turning round, 'to tell you the truth, I am not in a frame of mind at the present moment, in which I could see Lieutenant Walters with that entirely friendly feeling towards him that I should wish to harbour in my breast. We cannot always command our feelings, Captain Gills, and I should take it as a particular favour if you'd let me out at the private door.'

'Brother,' returned the Captain, 'you shall shape your own course. Wotever course you take, is plain and seaman-like, I'm wery sure.'

'Captain Gills,' said Mr Toots, 'you're extremely kind. Your good opinion is a consolation to me. There is one thing,' said Mr Toots, standing in the passage, behind the half-opened door, 'that I hope you'll bear in mind, Captain Gills, and that I should wish Lieutenant Walters to be made acquainted with. I have quite come into my property now, you know, and – and I don't know what to do with it. If I could be at all useful in a pecuniary point of view, I should glide into the silent tomb with ease and smoothness.'

Mr Toots said no more, but slipped out quietly and shut the door upon himself, to cut the Captain off from any reply.

Florence thought of this good creature, long after he had left her, with mingled emotions of pain and pleasure. He was so honest and warm-hearted, that to see him again and be assured of his truth to her in her distress, was a joy and comfort beyond all price; but for that very reason, it was so affecting to think that she caused him a moment's unhappiness, or ruffled, by a breath, the harmless current of his life, that her eyes filled with tears, and her bosom overflowed with pity. Captain Cuttle, in his different way, thought much of Mr Toots too; and so did Walter; and when the evening came, and they were all sitting together in Florence's new room, Walter praised him in a most impassioned manner, and told Florence what he had said on leaving the house, with every graceful setting-off in the way of comment and appreciation that his own honesty and sympathy could surround it with.

Mr Toots did not return upon the next day, or the next, or for several days; and in the meanwhile Florence, without any new alarm, lived like a quiet bird in a cage, at the top of the old Instrument-maker's house. But Florence drooped and hung her head more and more plainly, as the days went on: and the expression that had been seen in the face of the dead child, was often turned to the sky from her high window, as if it sought his angel out, on the bright shore of which he had spoken: lying on his little bed.

Florence had been weak and delicate of late, and the agitation she had undergone was not without its influences on her health. But it was no bodily illness that affected her now. She was distressed in mind; and the cause of her distress was Walter.

Interested in her, anxious for her, proud and glad to serve her, and showing all this with the enthusiasm and ardour of his character, Florence saw that he avoided her. All the long day through, he seldom approached her room. If she asked for him, he came, again for the moment as earnest and as bright as she remembered him when she was a lost child in the staring streets; but he soon became constrained – her quick affection was too watchful not to know it – and uneasy, and soon left her. Unsought, he never came, all day, between the morning and the night. When the evening closed in, he was always there, and that was her happiest time, for then she half believed that the old Walter of her childhood was not changed. But, even then, some trivial word, look, or circumstance would show her that there was an indefinable division between them which could not be passed.

And she could not but see that these revealings of a great alteration in Walter manifested themselves in despite of his utmost efforts to hide them. In his consideration for her, she thought, and in the earnestness of his desire to spare her any wound from his kind hand, he resorted to innumerable little artifices and disguises. So much the more did Florence feel the greatness of the alteration in him; so much the oftener did she weep at this estrangement of her brother.

The good Captain – her untiring, tender, ever zealous friend – saw it, too, Florence thought, and it pained him. He was less cheerful and hopeful than he had been at first, and would steal looks at her and Walter, by turns, when they were all three together of an evening, with quite a sad face.

Florence resolved, at last, to speak to Walter. She believed she knew now what the cause of his estrangement was, and she thought it would be a relief to her full heart, and would set him more at ease, if she told him she had found it out, and quite submitted to it, and did not reproach him.

It was on a certain Sunday afternoon, that Florence took this resolution. The faithful Captain, in an amazing shirt-collar, was sitting by her, reading with his spectacles on, and she asked him where Walter was.

'I think he's down below, my lady lass,' returned the Captain.

'I should like to speak to him,' said Florence, rising hurriedly as if to go downstairs.

'I'll rouse him up here, Beauty,' said the Captain, 'in a trice.'

Thereupon the Captain, with much alacrity, shouldered his book – for he made it a point of duty to read none but very large books on a Sunday, as having a more staid appearance: and had bargained, years ago, for a prodigious volume at a book-stall, five lines of which utterly confounded him at any time, insomuch that he had not yet ascertained of what subject it treated – and withdrew. Walter soon appeared.

'Captain Cuttle tells me, Miss Dombey,' he eagerly began on coming in – but stopped when he saw her face.

'You are not so well to-day. You look distressed. You have been weeping.'

He spoke so kindly, and with such a fervent tremor in his voice, that the tears gushed into her eyes at the sound of his words.

'Walter,' said Florence, gently, 'I am not quite well, and I have been weeping. I want to speak to you.'

He sat down opposite to her, looking at her beautiful and innocent face: and his own turned pale, and his lips trembled.

'You said, upon the night when I knew that you were saved – and oh! dear Walter, what I felt that night, and what I hoped!' –

He put his trembling hand upon the table between them, and sat looking at her.

' – that I was changed. I was surprised to hear you say so, but I understand, now, that I am. Don't be angry with me, Walter. I was too much overjoyed to think of it, then.'

She seemed a child to him again. It was the ingenuous, confiding, loving child he saw and heard. Not the dear woman, at whose feet he would have laid the riches of the earth.

'You remember the last time I saw you, Walter, before you went away?'

He put his hand into his breast, and took out a little purse.

'I have always worn it round my neck! If I had gone down in the deep, it would have been with me at the bottom of the sea.'

'And you will wear it still, Walter, for my old sake?'

'Until I die!'

She laid her hand on his, as fearlessly and simply, as if not a day had intervened since she gave him the little token of remembrance.

'I am glad of that. I shall be always glad to think so, Walter. Do you recollect that a thought of this change seemed to come into our minds at the same time that evening, when we were talking together?'

'No!' he answered, in a wondering tone.

'Yes, Walter. I had been the means of injuring your hopes and prospects even then. I feared to think so, then, but I know it now. If you were able, then, in your generosity, to hide from me that you knew it too, you cannot do so now, although you try as generously as before. You *do*. I thank you for it, Walter, deeply, truly; but you cannot succeed. You have suffered too much in your own hardships, and in those of your dearest relation, quite to overlook the innocent cause of all the peril and affliction that has befallen you. You cannot quite forget me in that character, and we can be brother and sister no longer. But, dear Walter, do not think that I complain of you in this. I might have known it – ought to have known it – but forgot it in my joy. All I hope is that you may think of me less irksomely when this feeling is no more a secret one; and all I ask is, Walter, in the name of the poor child who was your sister once, that you will not struggle with yourself, and pain yourself, for my sake, now that I know all!'

Walter had looked upon her while she said this, with a face so full of wonder and amazement, that it had room for nothing else. Now he caught up the hand that touched his, so entreatingly, and held it between his own.

'Oh, Miss Dombey,' he said, 'is it possible that while I have been suffering so much, in striving with my sense of what is due to you, and must be rendered to you, I have made you suffer what your words disclose to me? Never, never, before Heaven, have I thought of you but as the single, bright, pure, blessed recollection of my boyhood and my youth. Never have I from the first, and never shall I to the last, regard your part in my life, but as something sacred, never to be lightly thought of, never to be esteemed enough, never, until death, to be forgotten. Again to see you look, and hear you speak, as you did on that night when we parted, is happiness to me that there are no words to utter; and to be loved and trusted as your brother, is the next great gift I could receive and prize!'

'Walter,' said Florence, looking at him earnestly, but with a changing face, 'what is that which is due to me, and must be rendered to me, at the sacrifice of all this?'

'Respect,' said Walter, in a low tone. 'Reverence.'

The colour dawned in her face, and she timidly and thoughtfully withdrew her hand; still looking at him with unabated earnestness.

'I have not a brother's right,' said Walter. 'I have not a brother's claim. I left a child. I find a woman.'

The colour overspread her face. She made a gesture as if of entreaty that he would say no more, and her face dropped upon her hands.

They were both silent for a time; she weeping.

'I owe it to a heart so trusting, pure, and good,' said Walter, 'even to tear myself from it, though I rend my own. How dare I say it is my sister's!'

She was weeping still.

'If you had been happy; surrounded as you should be by loving and admiring friends, and by all that makes the station you were born to enviable,' said Walter; 'and if you had called me brother, then, in your affectionate remembrance of the past, I could have answered to the name from my distant place, with no inward assurance that I wronged your spotless truth by doing so. But here – and now!' –

'Oh thank you, thank you, Walter! Forgive my having wronged you so much. I had no one to advise me. I am quite alone.'

'Florence!' said Walter, passionately. 'I am hurried on to say, what I thought, but a few moments ago, nothing could have forced from my lips. If I had been prosperous; if I had any means or hope of being one day able to restore you to a station near your own; I would have told you that there was one name you might bestow upon me – a right above all others, to protect and cherish you – that I was worthy of in nothing but the love and honour that I bore you, and in my whole heart being yours. I would have told you that it was the only claim that you could give me to defend and guard you, which I dare accept and dare assert; but that if I had that right, I would regard it as a trust so precious and so priceless, that the undivided truth and fervour of my life would poorly acknowledge its worth.'

The head was still bent down, the tears still falling, and the bosom swelling with its sobs.

'Dear Florence! Dearest Florence! whom I called so in my thoughts before I could consider how presumptuous and wild it was. One last time let me call you by your own dear name, and touch this gentle hand in token of your sisterly forgetfulness of what I have said.'

She raised her head, and spoke to him with such a solemn sweetness in her eyes; with such a calm, bright, placid smile shining on him through her tears; with such a low, soft tremble in her frame and voice; that the innermost chords of his heart were touched, and his sight was dim as he listened.

'No, Walter, I cannot forget it. I would not forget it, for the world. Are you – are you very poor?'

'I am but a wanderer,' said Walter, 'making voyages to live across the sea. That is my calling now.'

'Are you soon going away again, Walter?'

'Very soon.'

She sat looking at him for a moment; then timidly put her trembling hand in his.

'If you will take me for your wife, Walter, I will love you dearly. If you will let me go with you, Walter, I will go to the world's end without fear. I can give up nothing for you – I have nothing to resign, and no one to forsake; but all my love and life shall be devoted to you, and with my last breath I will breathe your name to God if I have sense and memory left.'

He caught her to his heart, and laid her cheek against his own, and now, no more repulsed, no more forlorn, she wept indeed, upon the breast of her dear lover.

Blessed Sunday Bells, ringing so tranquilly in their entranced and happy ears! Blessed Sunday peace and quiet, harmonising with the calmness in their souls, and making holy air around them! Blessed twilight stealing on, and shading her so soothingly and gravely, as she falls asleep, like a hushed child, upon the bosom she has clung to!

Oh load of love and trustfulness that lies so lightly there! Aye, look down at the closed eyes, Walter, with a proudly tender gaze; for in all the wide wide world they seek but thee now – only thee!

The Captain remained in the little parlour until it was quite dark. He took the chair on which Walter had been sitting, and looked up at the skylight, until the day, by little and little, faded away, and the stars peeped out. He lighted a candle, lighted a pipe, smoked it out, and wondered what on earth was going on upstairs, and why they didn't call him to tea.

Florence came to his side while he was in the height of his wonderment.

'Aye! lady lass!' cried the Captain. 'Why, you and Wal'r have had a long spell o' talk, my beauty.'

Florence put her little hand round one of the great buttons of his coat, and said, looking down into his face:

'Dear Captain, I want to tell you something, if you please.'

The Captain raised his head pretty smartly, to hear what it was. Catching by this means a more distinct view of Florence, he pushed back his chair, and himself with it as far as they could go.

'What! Heart's Delight!' cried the Captain, suddenly elated. 'Is it that?'

'Yes!' said Florence, eagerly.

'Wal'r! Husband! THAT?' roared the Captain, tossing up his glazed hat into the skylight.

'Yes!' cried Florence, laughing and crying together.

The Captain immediately hugged her; and then, picking up the glazed hat and putting it on, drew her arm through his, and conducted her upstairs again; where he felt that the great joke of his life was now to be made.

'What, Wal'r my lad!' said the Captain, looking in at the door, with his face like an amiable warming-pan. 'So there ain't NO other character, ain't there?'

He had like to have suffocated himself with this pleasantry, which he repeated at least forty times during tea; polishing his radiant face with the sleeve of his coat, and dabbing his head all over with his pocket-handkerchief, in the intervals. But he was not without a graver source of enjoyment to fall back upon, when so disposed, for he was repeatedly heard to say in an under tone, as he looked with ineffable delight at Walter and Florence:

'Ed'ard Cuttle, my lad, you never shaped a better course in your life, than when you made that there little property over, jintly!'

CHAPTER 51

Mr Dombey and the World

What is the proud man doing, while the days go by? Does he ever think of his daughter, or wonder where she is gone? Does he suppose she has come home, and is leading her old life in the weary house? No one can answer for him. He has never uttered her name, since. His household dread him too much to approach a subject on which he is resolutely dumb; and the only person who dares question him, he silences immediately.

'My dear Paul!' murmurs his sister, sidling into the room, on the day of Florence's departure, 'your wife! that upstart woman! Is it possible that what I hear confusedly, is true, and that this is her return for your unparalleled devotion to her; extending, I am sure, even to the sacrifice of your own relations, to her caprices and haughtiness? My poor brother!'

With this speech, feelingly reminiscent of her not having been asked to dinner on the day of the first party, Mrs Chick makes great use of her pocket-handkerchief, and falls on Mr Dombey's neck. But Mr Dombey frigidly lifts her off, and hands her to a chair.

'I thank you, Louisa,' he says, 'for this mark of your affection; but desire that our conversation may refer to any other subject. When I bewail my fate, Louisa, or express myself as being in want of consolation, you can offer it, if you will have the goodness.'

'My dear Paul,' rejoins his sister, with her handkerchief to her face, and shaking her head, 'I know your great spirit, and will say no more upon a theme so painful and revolting;' on the heads of which two adjectives, Mrs Chick visits scathing indignation; 'but pray let me ask you – though I dread to hear something that will shock and distress me – that unfortunate child Florence—'

'Louisa!' says her brother, sternly, 'silence. Not another word of this!'

Mrs Chick can only shake her head, and use her handkerchief, and moan over degenerate Dombeys, who are no Dombeys. But whether Florence has been inculpated in the flight of Edith, or has followed her, or has done too much, or too little, or anything, or nothing, she has not the least idea.

He goes on, without deviation, keeping his thoughts and feelings close within his own breast, and imparting them to no one. He makes no search for his daughter. He may think that she is with his sister, or that she is under his own roof. He may think of her constantly, or he may never think about her. It is all one for any sign he makes.

But this is sure; he does *not* think that he has lost her. He has no suspicion of the truth. He has lived too long shut up in his towering supremacy, seeing her, a patient gentle creature, in the path below it, to have any fear of that. Shaken as he is by his disgrace, he is not yet humbled to the level earth. The root is broad and deep, and in the course of years its fibres have spread out and gathered nourishment from everything around it. The tree is struck, but not down.

Though he hide the world within him from the world without – which he believes has but one purpose for the time, and that, to watch him eagerly wherever he goes – he cannot hide those rebel traces of it, which escape in hollow eyes and cheeks, a haggard forehead, and a moody, brooding air. Impenetrable as before, he is still an altered man: and, proud as ever, he is humbled, or those marks would not be there.

The world. What the world thinks of him, how it looks at him, what it sees in him, and what it says – this is the haunting demon of his mind. It is everywhere where he is; and, worse than that, it is everywhere where he is not. It comes out with him among his servants, and yet he leaves it whispering behind; he sees it pointing after him in the street; it is waiting for him in his counting-house; it leers over the shoulders of rich men among the merchants; it goes beckoning and babbling among the crowd; it always anticipates him, in every place; and is always busiest, he knows, when he has gone away. When he is shut up in his room at night, it is in his house, outside it, audible in footsteps on the pavement, visible in print upon the table, steaming to and fro on railroads and in ships: restless and busy everywhere, with nothing else but him.

It is not a phantom of his imagination. It is as active in other people's minds as in his. Witness Cousin Feenix, who comes from Baden Baden, purposely to talk to him. Witness Major Bagstock, who accompanies Cousin Feenix on that friendly mission.

Mr Dombey receives them with his usual dignity, and stands erect, in his old attitude, before the fire. He feels that the world is looking at him out of their eyes. That it is in the stare of the pictures. That Mr Pitt,[1] upon the bookcase, represents it. That there are eyes in its own map, hanging on the wall.

'An unusually cold spring,' says Mr Dombey – to deceive the world.

'Damme, Sir,' says the Major, in the warmth of friendship, 'Joseph Bagstock is a bad hand at a counterfeit. If you want to hold your friends off, Dombey, and to give them the cold shoulder, J. B. is not the man for your purpose. Joe is rough and tough, Sir; blunt, Sir, blunt, is Joe. His Royal Highness the late Duke of York did me the honour to say, deservedly or undeservedly – never mind that – "If there is a man in the service on whom I can depend for coming to the point, that man is Joe – Joe Bagstock."'

Mr Dombey intimates his acquiescence.

'Now, Dombey,' says the Major, 'I am a man of the world. Our friend Feenix – if I may presume to—'

'Honoured, I am sure,' says Cousin Feenix.

'—is,' proceeds the Major, with a wag of his head, 'also a man of

Mr Dombey and the World

the world, Dombey. *You* are a man of the world. Now, when three men of the world meet together, and are friends – as I believe'– again appealing to Cousin Feenix.

'I am sure,' says Cousin Feenix, 'most friendly.'

'–and are friends,' resumes the Major, 'Old Joe's opinion is (J. may be wrong), that the opinion of the world on any particular subject, is very easily got at.'

'Undoubtedly,' says Cousin Feenix. 'In point of fact, it's quite a self-evident sort of thing. I am extremely anxious, Major, that my friend Dombey should hear me express my very great astonishment and regret, that my lovely and accomplished relative, who was possessed of every qualification to make a man happy, should have so far forgotten what was due – to in point of fact, to the world – as to commit herself in such a very extraordinary manner. I have been in a devilish state of depression ever since; and said indeed to Long Saxby last night – man of six foot ten, with whom my friend Dombey is probably acquainted – that it had upset me in a confounded way, and made me bilious. It induces a man to reflect, this kind of fatal catastrophe,' says Cousin Feenix, 'that events do occur in quite a providential manner; for if my Aunt had been living at the time, I think the effect upon a devilish lively woman like herself, would have been prostration, and that she would have fallen, in point of fact, a victim.'

'Now, Dombey!–' says the Major, resuming his discourse with great energy.

'I beg your pardon,' interposes Cousin Feenix. 'Allow me another word. My friend Dombey will permit me to say, that if any circumstance could have added to the most infernal state of pain in which I find myself on this occasion, it would be the natural amazement of the world at my lovely and accomplished relative (as I must still beg leave to call her) being supposed to have so committed herself with a person – man with white teeth. in point of fact – of very inferior station to her husband. But while I must, rather peremptorily, request my friend Dombey not to criminate[2] my lovely and accomplished relative until her criminality is perfectly established, I beg to assure my friend Dombey that the family I represent, and which is now almost extinct (devilish sad reflection for a man), will interpose no obstacle in his way, and will be happy to assent to any honourable course of proceeding, with a view to the future, that he may point out. I trust my friend Dombey will give me credit for the intentions by which I am animated in this very melancholy affair, and – a – in point of fact, I am not aware that I need trouble my friend Dombey with any further observations.'

Mr Dombey bows, without raising his eyes, and is silent.

'Now, Dombey,' says the Major, 'our friend Feenix having, with an amount of eloquence that Old Joe B. has never heard surpassed – no, by the Lord, Sir! never!' – says the Major, very blue, indeed, and grasping his cane in the middle – 'stated the case as regards the lady, I shall presume upon our friendship, Dombey, to offer a word on another aspect of it. Sir,' says the Major, with the horse's cough, 'the world in these things has opinions, which must be satisfied.'

'I know it,' rejoins Mr Dombey.

'Of course you know it, Dombey,' says the Major. 'Damme, Sir, I know you know it. A man of your calibre is not likely to be ignorant of it.'

'I hope not,' replies Mr Dombey.

'Dombey!' says the Major, 'you will guess the rest. I speak out – prematurely, perhaps – because the Bagstock breed have always spoken out. Little, Sir, have they ever got by doing it; but it's in the Bagstock blood. A shot is to be taken at this man. You have J. B. at your elbow. He claims the name of friend. God bless you!'

'Major,' returns Mr Dombey, 'I am obliged. I shall put myself in your hands when the time comes. The time not being come, I have forborne to speak to you.'

'Where is the fellow, Dombey?' inquires the Major, after gasping and looking at him, for a minute.

'I don't know.'

'Any intelligence of him?' asks the Major.

'Yes.'

'Dombey, I am rejoiced to hear it,' says the Major. 'I congratulate you.'

'You will excuse – even you, Major,' replies Mr Dombey, 'my entering into any further detail at present. The intelligence is of a singular kind, and singularly obtained. It may turn out to be valueless; it may turn out to be true; I cannot say at present. My explanation must stop here.'

Although this is but a dry reply to the Major's purple enthusiasm, the Major receives it graciously, and is delighted to think that the world has such a fair prospect of soon receiving its due. Cousin Feenix is then presented with his meed of acknowledgment by the husband of his lovely and accomplished relative, and Cousin Feenix and Major Bagstock retire, leaving that husband to the world again, and to ponder at leisure on their representation of its state of mind concerning his affairs, and on its just and reasonable expectations.

But who sits in the housekeeper's room, shedding tears, and talking to Mrs Pipchin in a low tone, with uplifted hands? It is a lady with her face concealed in a very close black bonnet, which appears not to belong to her. It is Miss Tox, who has borrowed this disguise from her servant, and comes from Princess's Place, thus secretly, to revive her old acquaintance with Mrs Pipchin, in order to get certain information of the state of Mr Dombey.

'How does he bear it, my dear creature?' asks Miss Tox.

'Well,' says Mrs Pipchin, in her snappish way, 'he's pretty much as usual.'

'Externally,' suggests Miss Tox. 'But what he feels within!'

Mrs Pipchin's hard grey eye looks doubtful as she answers, in three distinct jerks, 'Ah! Perhaps. I suppose so.'

'To tell you my mind, Lucretia,' says Mrs Pipchin; she still calls Miss Tox Lucretia, on account of having made her first experiments in the child-quelling line of business on that lady, when an unfortunate and weazen[3] little girl of tender years; 'to tell you my mind, Lucretia, I think it's a good riddance. I don't want any of your brazen faces here, myself!'

'Brazen indeed! Well may you say brazen, Mrs Pipchin!' returns Miss Tox. 'To leave him! Such a noble figure of a man!' And here Miss Tox is overcome.

'I don't know about noble, I'm sure,' observes Mrs Pipchin, irascibly rubbing her nose. 'But I know this – that when people meet with trials, they must bear 'em. Hoity, toity! I have had enough to bear myself, in my time! What a fuss there is! She's gone and well got rid of. Nobody wants her back, I should think!'

This hint of the Peruvian Mines, causes Miss Tox to rise to go away; when Mrs Pipchin rings the bell for Towlinson to show her out. Mr Towlinson, not having seen Miss Tox for ages, grins, and hopes she's well; observing that he didn't know her at first, in that bonnet.

'Pretty well, Towlinson, I thank you,' says Miss Tox. 'I beg you'll have the goodness, when you happen to see me here, not to mention it. My visits are merely to Mrs Pipchin.'

'Very good, Miss,' says Towlinson.

'Shocking circumstances occur, Towlinson,' says Miss Tox.

'Very much so indeed, Miss,' rejoins Towlinson.

'I hope, Towlinson,' says Miss Tox, who, in her instruction of the Toodle family, has acquired an admonitorial tone, and a habit of improving passing occasions, 'that what has happened here, will be a warning to you, Towlinson.'

'Thank you, Miss, I'm sure,' says Towlinson.

He appears to be falling into a consideration of the manner in which this warning ought to operate in his particular case, when the vinegary Mrs Pipchin, suddenly stirring him up with a 'What are you doing? Why don't you show the lady to the door?' he ushers Miss Tox forth. As she passes Mr Dombey's room, she shrinks into the inmost depths of the black bonnet, and walks on tip-toe; and there is not another atom in the world which haunts him so, that feels such sorrow and solicitude about him, as Miss Tox takes out under the black bonnet into the street, and tries to carry home shadowed from the newly-lighted lamps.

But Miss Tox is not a part of Mr Dombey's world. She comes back every evening at dusk; adding clogs and an umbrella to the bonnet on wet nights; and bears the grins of Towlinson, and the huffs and rebuffs of Mrs Pipchin, and all to ask how he does, and how he bears his misfortune: but she has nothing to do with Mr Dombey's world. Exacting and harassing as ever, it goes on without her; and she, a by no means bright or particular star,[4] moves in her little orbit in the corner of another system, and knows it quite well, and comes, and cries, and goes away, and is satisfied. Verily Miss Tox is easier of satisfaction than the world that troubles Mr Dombey so much!

At the Counting House, the clerks discuss the great disaster in all its lights and shades, but chiefly wonder who will get Mr Carker's place. They are generally of opinion that it will be shorn of some of its emoluments, and made uncomfortable by newly-devised checks and restrictions; and those who are beyond all hope of it, are quite sure they would rather not have it, and don't at all envy the person for whom it may prove to be reserved. Nothing like the prevailing sensation has existed in the Counting House since Mr Dombey's little son died; but all such excitements there take a social, not to say a jovial turn, and lead to the cultivation of good fellowship. A reconciliation is established on this propitious occasion between the acknowledged wit of the Counting House and an aspiring rival, with whom he has been at deadly feud for months; and a little dinner being proposed, in commemoration of their happily restored amity, takes place at a neighbouring tavern; the wit in the chair; the rival acting as Vice-President. The orations following the removal of the cloth[5] are opened by the Chair, who says, Gentlemen, he can't disguise from himself that this is not a time for private dissensions. Recent occurrences to which he need not more particularly allude, but which have not been altogether without notice in some Sunday Papers,[6] and in a daily paper[7] which he need not name (here every other member of the company names it in an audible murmur), have caused him to reflect; and he feels that for him and Robinson to have any personal differences at such a moment, would be for ever to deny that good feeling in the general cause, for which he has reason to think and hope that the gentlemen in Dombey's House have always been distinguished. Robinson replies to this like a man and a brother; and one gentleman who has been in the office three years, under continual notice to quit on account of lapses in his arithmetic, appears in a perfectly new light, suddenly bursting out with a thrilling speech, in which he says, May their respected chief never again know the desolation which has fallen on his hearth! and says a great variety of things, beginning with 'May he never again,' which are received with thunders of applause. In short, a most delightful evening is passed, only interrupted by a difference between two juniors, who, quarrelling about the probable amount of Mr Carker's late receipts per annum, defy each other with decanters, and are taken out greatly excited. Soda water is in general request at the office next day, and most of the party deem the bill an imposition.

As to Perch, the messenger, he is in a fair way of being ruined for life. He finds himself again constantly in bars of public-houses, being treated and lying dreadfully. It appears that he met everybody concerned in the late transaction, everywhere, and said to them, 'Sir,' or 'Madam,' as the case was, 'why do you look so pale?' at which each shuddered from head to foot, and said, 'Oh, Perch!' and ran away. Either the consciousness of these enormities, or the reaction consequent on liquor, reduces Mr Perch to an extreme state of low spirits at that hour of the evening when he usually seeks consolation in the society of Mrs Perch at Ball's Pond;[8] and Mrs Perch frets a good deal, for she fears his confidence in woman is shaken now, and that he half expects on coming home at night to find her gone off with some Viscount.

Mr Dombey's servants are becoming, at the same time, quite dissipated, and unfit for other service. They have hot suppers every night, and 'talk it over' with smoking drinks upon the board. Mr Towlinson is always maudlin after half-past ten, and frequently begs to know whether he didn't say that no good would ever come of living in a corner house? They whisper about Miss Florence, and wonder where she is; but agree that if Mr Dombey don't know,

Mrs Dombey does. This brings them to the latter, of whom Cook says, She had a stately way though, hadn't she? But she was too high! They all agree that she was too high, and Mr Towlinson's old flame, the housemaid (who is very virtuous), entreats that you will never talk to her any more about people who hold their heads up, as if the ground wasn't good enough for 'em.

Everything that is said and done about it, except by Mr Dombey, is done in chorus. Mr Dombey and the world are alone together.

CHAPTER 52

Secret Intelligence

Good Mrs Brown and her daughter Alice kept silent company together, in their own dwelling. It was early in the evening, and late in the spring. But a few days had elapsed since Mr Dombey had told Major Bagstock of his singular intelligence, singularly obtained, which might turn out to be valueless, and might turn out to be true; and the world was not satisfied yet.

The mother and daughter sat for a long time without interchanging a word: almost without motion. The old woman's face was shrewdly anxious and expectant; that of her daughter was expectant too, but in a less sharp degree, and sometimes it darkened, as if with gathering disappointment and incredulity. The old woman, without heeding these changes in its expression, though her eyes were often turned towards it, sat mumbling and munching, and listening confidently.

Their abode, though poor and miserable, was not so utterly wretched as in the days when only Good Mrs Brown inhabited it. Some few attempts at cleanliness and order were manifest, though made in a reckless, gipsy way, that might have connected them, at a glance, with the younger woman. The shades of evening thickened and deepened as the two kept silence, until the blackened walls were nearly lost in the prevailing gloom.

Then Alice broke the silence which had lasted so long, and said:

'You may give him up, mother. He'll not come here.'

'Death give him up!' returned the old woman, impatiently. 'He *will* come here.'

'We shall see,' said Alice.

'We shall see *him*,' returned her mother.

'And doomsday,' said the daughter.

'You think I'm in my second childhood, I know!' croaked the old woman. 'That's the respect and duty that I get from my own gal, but I'm wiser than you take me for. He'll come. T'other day when I touched his coat in the street, he looked round as if I was a toad. But Lord, to see him when I said their names, and asked him if he'd like to find out where they was!'

'Was it so angry?' asked her daughter, roused to interest in a moment.

'Angry? ask if it was bloody. That's more like the word. Angry? Ha, ha! To call that only angry!' said the old woman, hobbling to the cupboard, and lighting a candle, which displayed the workings of her mouth to ugly advantage, as she brought it to the table. 'I might as well call your face only angry, when you think or talk about 'em.'

It was something different from that, truly, as she sat as still as a crouched tigress, with her kindling eyes.

'Hark!' said the old woman, triumphantly. 'I hear a step coming. It's not the tread of any one that lives about here, or comes this way often. We don't walk like that. We should grow proud on such neighbours! Do you hear him?'

'I believe you are right, mother,' replied Alice, in a low voice. 'Peace! open the door.'

As she drew herself within her shawl, and gathered it about her, the old woman complied; and peering out, and beckoning, gave admission to Mr Dombey, who stopped when he had set his foot within the door, and looked distrustfully around.

'It's a poor place for a great gentleman like your worship,' said the old woman, curtseying and chattering. 'I told you so, but there's no harm in it.'

'Who is that?' asked Mr Dombey, looking at her companion.

'That's my handsome daughter,' said the old woman. 'Your worship won't mind her. She knows all about it.'

A shadow fell upon his face not less expressive than if he had groaned aloud, 'Who does not know all about it!' but he looked at her steadily, and she, without any acknowledgment of his presence, looked at him. The shadow on his face was darker when he turned his glance away from her; and even then it wandered back again, furtively, as if he were haunted by her bold eyes, and some remembrance they inspired.

'Woman,' said Mr Dombey to the old witch who was chuckling and leering close at his elbow, and who, when he turned to address her, pointed stealthily at her daughter, and rubbed her hands, and pointed again, 'Woman! I believe that I am weak and forgetful of my station in coming here, but you know why I come, and what you offered when you stopped me in the street the other day. What is it that you have to tell me concerning what I want to know; and how does it happen that I can find voluntary intelligence in a hovel like this,' with a disdainful glance about him, 'when I have exerted my power and means to obtain it in vain? I do not think,' he said, after a moment's pause, during which he had observed her, sternly, 'that you are so audacious as to mean to trifle with me, or endeavour to impose upon me. But if you have that purpose, you had better stop on the threshold of your scheme. My humour is not a trifling one, and my acknowledgment will be severe.'

'Oh a proud, hard gentleman!' chuckled the old woman, shaking her head, and rubbing her shrivelled hands, 'oh hard, hard, hard! But your worship shall see with your own eyes and hear with your own ears; not with ours – and if your worship's put upon their track, you won't mind paying something for it, will you, honourable deary?'

'Money,' returned Mr Dombey, apparently relieved, and reassured by this inquiry, 'will bring about unlikely things, I know. It may turn even means as unexpected and unpromising as these, to account. Yes. For any reliable information I receive, I will pay. But I must have the information first, and judge for myself of its value.'

'Do you know nothing more powerful than money?' asked the younger woman, without rising, or altering her attitude.

'Not here, I should imagine,' said Mr Dombey.

'You should know of something that is more powerful elsewhere, as I judge,' she returned. 'Do you know nothing of a woman's anger?'

'You have a saucy tongue, Jade,' said Mr Dombey.

'Not usually,' she answered, without any show of emotion: 'I speak to you now, that you may understand us better, and rely more on us. A woman's anger is pretty much the same here, as in your fine house. I am angry. I have been so, many years. I have as good cause for my anger as you have for yours, and its object is the same man.'

He started, in spite of himself, and looked at her with astonishment.

'Yes,' she said, with a kind of laugh. 'Wide as the distance may seem between us, it is so. How it is so, is no matter; that is my story, and I keep my story to myself. I would bring you and him

together, because I have a rage against him. My mother there, is
avaricious and poor; and she would sell any tidings she could glean,
or anything, or anybody, for money. It is fair enough, perhaps, that
you should pay her some, if she can help you to what you want to
know. But that is not my motive. I have told you what mine is, and
it would be as strong and all-sufficient with me if you haggled and
bargained with her for a sixpence. I have done. My saucy tongue
says no more, if you wait here till sunrise to-morrow.'

The old woman, who had shown great uneasiness during this
speech, which had a tendency to depreciate her expected gains,
pulled Mr Dombey softly by the sleeve, and whispered to him not
to mind her. He glanced at them both, by turns, with a haggard
look, and said, in a deeper voice than was usual with him:

'Go on – what do you know?'

'Oh, not so fast, your worship! we must wait for some one,'
answered the old woman. 'It's to be got from some one else –
wormed out – screwed and twisted from him.'

'What do you mean?' said Mr Dombey.

'Patience,' she croaked, laying her hand, like a claw, upon his
arm. 'Patience. I'll get at it. I know I can! If he was to hold it back
from me,' said Good Mrs Brown, crooking her ten fingers, 'I'd tear
it out of him!'

Mr Dombey followed her with his eyes as she hobbled to the
door, and looked out again: and then his glance sought her
daughter; but she remained impassive, silent, and regardless of him.

'Do you tell me, woman,' he said, when the bent figure of Mrs
Brown came back, shaking its head and chattering to itself, 'that
there is another person expected here?'

'Yes!' said the old woman, looking up into his face, and nodding.

'From whom you are to exact the intelligence that is to be useful
to me?'

'Yes,' said the old woman, nodding again.

'A stranger?'

'Chut!'[1] said the old woman, with a shrill laugh. 'What signifies![2]
Well, well; no. No stranger to your worship. But he won't see you.
He'd be afraid of you, and wouldn't talk. You'll stand behind that
door, and judge him for yourself. We don't ask to be believed on
trust. What! Your worship doubts the room behind the door? Oh
the suspicion of you rich gentlefolks! Look at it, then.'

Her sharp eye had detected an involuntary expression of this
feeling on his part, which was not unreasonable under the circumstances. In satisfaction of it she now took the candle to the door she

spoke of. Mr Dombey looked in; assured himself that it was an empty, crazy[3] room, and signed to her to put the light back in its place.

'How long,' he asked, 'before this person comes?'

'Not long,' she answered. 'Would your worship sit down for a few odd minutes?'

He made no answer; but began pacing the room with an irresolute air, as if he were undecided whether to remain or depart, and as if he had some quarrel with himself for being there at all. But soon his tread grew slower and heavier, and his face more sternly thoughtful: as the object with which he had come, fixed itself in his mind, and dilated there again.

While he thus walked up and down with his eyes on the ground, Mrs Brown, in the chair from which she had risen to receive him, sat listening anew. The monotony of his step, or the uncertainty of age, made her so slow of hearing, that a footfall without had sounded in her daughter's ears for some moments, and she had looked up hastily to warn her mother of its approach, before the old woman was roused by it. But then she started from her seat, and whispering 'Here he is!' hurried her visitor to his place of observation, and put a bottle and glass upon the table, with such alacrity as to be ready to fling her arms round the neck of Rob the Grinder on his appearance at the door.

'And here's my bonny boy,' cried Mrs Brown, 'at last! – oho, oho! You're like my own son, Robby!'

'Oh! Misses Brown!' remonstrated the Grinder. 'Don't! Can't you be fond of a cove without squeedging and throttling of him? Take care of the birdcage in my hand, will you?'

'Thinks of a birdcage, afore me!' cried the old woman, apostrophizing the ceiling. 'Me that feels more than a mother for him!'

'Well, I'm sure I'm very much obliged to you, Misses Brown,' said the unfortunate youth, greatly aggravated; 'but you're so jealous of a cove. I'm very fond of you myself, and all that, of course; but I don't smother you, do I, Misses Brown?'

He looked and spoke as if he would have been far from objecting to do so, however, on a favourable occasion.

'And to talk about birdcages, too!' whimpered the Grinder. 'As if that was a crime! Why, look'ee here! Do you know who this belongs to?'

'To Master, dear?' said the old woman with a grin.

'Ah!' replied the Grinder, lifting a large cage tied up in a wrapper, on the table, and untying it with his teeth and hands. 'It's our parrot, this is.'

'Mr Carker's parrot, Rob?'

'Will you hold your tongue, Misses Brown?' returned the goaded Grinder. 'What do you go naming names for? I'm blest,' said Rob, pulling his hair with both hands in the exasperation of his feelings, 'if she an't enough to make a cove run wild!'

'What! Do you snub me, thankless boy!' cried the old woman, with ready vehemence.

'Good gracious, Misses Brown, no!' returned the Grinder, with tears in his eyes. 'Was there ever such a—! Don't I dote on you, Misses Brown?'

'Do you, sweet Rob? Do you truly, chickabiddy?' With that, Mrs Brown held him in her fond embrace once more; and did not release him until he had made several violent and ineffectual struggles with his legs, and his hair was standing on end all over his head.

'Oh!' returned the Grinder, 'what a thing it is to be perfectly pitched into with affection like this here. I wish she was— How have you been, Misses Brown?'

'Ah! Not here since this night week!' said the old woman, contemplating him with a look of reproach.

'Good gracious, Misses Brown,' returned the Grinder, 'I said to-night's a week,[4] that I'd come to-night, didn't I? And here I am. How you do go on! I wish you'd be a little rational, Misses Brown. I'm hoarse with saying things in my defence, and my very face is shiny with being hugged.' He rubbed it hard with his sleeve, as if to remove the tender polish in question.

'Drink a little drop to comfort you, my Robin,' said the old woman, filling the glass from the bottle and giving it to him.

'Thank'ee, Misses Brown,' returned the Grinder. 'Here's your health. And long may you – et ceterer.' Which to judge from the expression of his face, did not include any very choice blessings. 'And here's *her* health,' said the Grinder, glancing at Alice, who sat with her eyes fixed, as it seemed to him, on the wall behind him, but in reality on Mr Dombey's face at the door, 'and wishing her the same and many of 'em!'

He drained the glass to these two sentiments, and set it down.

'Well, I say, Misses Brown!' he proceeded. 'To go on a little rational now. You're a judge of birds, and up to their ways, as I know to my cost.'

'Cost!' repeated Mrs Brown.

Secret intelligence

'Satisfaction, I mean,' returned the Grinder. 'How you do take up a cove, Misses Brown! You've put it all out of my head again.'

'Judge of birds, Robby,' suggested the old woman.

'Ah!' said the Grinder. 'Well, I've got to take care of this parrot – certain things being sold, and a certain establishment broke up – and as I don't want no notice took at present, I wish you'd attend to her for a week or so, and give her board and lodging, will you? If I *must* come backwards and forwards,' mused the Grinder with a dejected face, 'I may as well have something to come for.'

'Something to come for?' screamed the old woman.

'Besides you, I mean, Misses Brown,' returned the craven Rob. 'Not that I want any inducement but yourself, Misses Brown, I'm sure. Don't begin again, for goodness' sake.'

'He don't care for me! He don't care for me, as I care for him!' cried Mrs Brown, lifting up her skinny hands. 'But I'll take care of his bird.'

'Take good care of it too, you know, Mrs Brown,' said Rob, shaking his head. 'If you was so much as to stroke its feathers once the wrong way, I believe it would be found out.'

'Ah, so sharp as that, Rob?' said Mrs Brown, quickly.

'Sharp, Misses Brown!' repeated Rob. 'But this is not to be talked about.'

Checking himself abruptly, and not without a fearful glance across the room, Rob filled the glass again, and having slowly emptied it, shook his head, and began to draw his fingers across and across the wires of the parrot's cage by way of a diversion from the dangerous theme that had just been broached.

The old woman eyed him slily, and hitching her chair nearer his, and looking in at the parrot, who came down from the gilded dome at her call, said:

'Out of place now, Robby?'

'Never *you* mind, Misses Brown,' returned the Grinder, shortly.

'Board wages,[5] perhaps, Rob?' said Mrs Brown.

'Pretty Polly!' said the Grinder.

The old woman darted a glance at him that might have warned him to consider his ears in danger, but it was his turn to look in at the parrot now, and however expressive his imagination may have made her angry scowl, it was unseen by his bodily eyes.

'I wonder Master didn't take you with him, Rob,' said the old woman, in a wheedling voice, but with increased malignity of aspect.

Rob was so absorbed in contemplation of the parrot, and in trolling his forefinger on the wires, that he made no answer.

The old woman had her clutch within a hair's breadth of his shock of hair as it stooped over the table; but she restrained her fingers, and said, in a voice that choked with its efforts to be coaxing:

'Robby, my child.'

'Well, Misses Brown,' returned the Grinder.

'I say I wonder Master didn't take you with him, dear.'

'Never *you* mind, Misses Brown,' returned the Grinder.

Mrs Brown instantly directed the clutch of her right hand at his hair, and the clutch of her left hand at his throat, and held on to the object of her fond affection with such extraordinary fury, that his face began to blacken in a moment.

'Misses Brown!' exclaimed the Grinder, 'let go, will you? What are you doing of? Help, young woman! Misses Brow—Brow—!'

The young woman, however, equally unmoved by his direct appeal to her, and by his inarticulate utterance, remained quite neutral, until, after struggling with his assailant into a corner, Rob disengaged himself, and stood there panting and fenced in by his own elbows, while the old woman, panting too, and stamping with rage and eagerness, appeared to be collecting her energies for another swoop upon him. At this crisis Alice interposed her voice, but not in the Grinder's favour, by saying, 'Well done, mother. Tear him to pieces!'

'What, young woman!' blubbered Rob, 'are you against me too? What have I been and done? What am I to be tore to pieces for, I should like to know? Why do you take and choke a cove who has never done you any harm, neither of you? Call yourselves females, too!' said the frightened and afflicted Grinder, with his coat-cuff at his eye. 'I'm surprised at you! Where's your feminine tenderness?'

'You thankless dog!' gasped Mrs Brown. 'You impudent insulting dog!'

'What have I been and done to go and give you offence, Misses Brown?' retorted the fearful Rob. 'You was very much attached to me a minute ago.'

'To cut me off with his short answers and his sulky words,' said the old woman. 'Me! Because I happen to be curious to have a little bit of gossip about Master and the lady, to dare to play at fast and loose with me! But I'll talk to you no more, my lad. Now go!'

'I'm sure, Misses Brown,' returned the abject Grinder, 'I never insiniwated that I wished to go. Don't talk like that, Misses Brown, if you please.'

'I won't talk at all,' said Mrs Brown, with an action of her crooked fingers that made him shrink into half his natural compass in the corner. 'Not another word with him shall pass my lips. He's an ungrateful hound. I cast him off! Now let him go! And I'll slip those after him that shall talk too much; that won't be shook away; that'll hang to him like leeches, and slink arter him like foxes. What! He knows 'em. He knows his old games and his old ways. If he's forgotten 'em, they'll soon remind him. Now let him go, and see how he'll do Master's business, and keep Master's secrets, with such company always following him up and down. Ha, ha, ha! He'll find 'em a different sort from you and me, Ally; close as he is with you and me. Now let him go, now let him go!'

The old woman, to the unspeakable dismay of the Grinder, walked her twisted figure round and round, in a ring of some four feet in diameter, constantly repeating these words, and shaking her fist above her head, and working her mouth about.

'Misses Brown,' pleaded Rob, coming a little out of his corner, 'I'm sure you wouldn't injure a cove, on second thoughts and in cold blood, would you?'

'Don't talk to me,' said Mrs Brown, still wrathfully pursuing her circle. 'Now let him go, now let him go!'

'Misses Brown,' urged the tormented Grinder. 'I didn't mean to – Oh, what a thing it is for a cove to get into such a line as this! – I was only careful of talking, Misses Brown, because I always am, on account of his being up to everything; but I might have known it wouldn't have gone any further. I'm sure I'm quite agreeable,' with a wretched face, 'for any little bit of gossip, Misses Brown. Don't go on like this, if you please. Oh, couldn't you have the goodness to put in a word for a miserable cove, here?' said the Grinder, appealing in desperation to the daughter.

'Come, mother, you hear what he says,' she interposed, in her stern voice, and with an impatient action of her head; 'try him once more, and if you fall out with him again, ruin him if you like, and have done with him.'

Mrs Brown, moved as it seemed by this very tender exhortation, presently began to howl; and softening by degrees, took the apologetic Grinder to her arms, who embraced her with a face of unutterable woe, and like a victim as he was, resumed his former seat, close by the side of his venerable friend, whom he suffered, not without much constrained sweetness of countenance, combating

very expressive physiognomical revelations of an opposite character, to draw his arm through hers, and keep it there.

'And how's Master, deary dear?' said Mrs Brown, when, sitting
in this amicable posture, they had pledged each other.

'Hush! If you'd be so good, Misses Brown, as to speak a little
lower,' Rob implored. 'Why, he's pretty well, thank'ee, I suppose.'

'You're not out of place, Robby?' said Mrs Brown in a wheedling
tone.

'Why, I'm not exactly out of place, nor in,' faltered Rob. 'I – I'm
still in pay, Misses Brown.'

'And nothing to do, Rob?'

'Nothing particular to do just now, Misses Brown, but to – keep
my eyes open,' said the Grinder, rolling them in a forlorn way.

'Master abroad, Rob?'

'Oh, for goodness' sake, Misses Brown, couldn't you gossip with
a cove about anything else?' cried the Grinder, in a burst of despair.

The impetuous Mrs Brown rising directly, the tortured Grinder
detained her, stammering 'Ye-es, Misses Brown, I believe he's
abroad. What's she staring at?' he added, in allusion to the
daughter, whose eyes were fixed upon the face that now again
looked out behind him.

'Don't mind her, lad,' said the old woman, holding him closer to
prevent his turning round. 'It's her way – her way. Tell me, Rob.
Did you ever see the lady, deary?'

'Oh, Misses Brown, what lady?' cried the Grinder in a tone of
piteous supplication.

'What lady?' she retorted. 'The lady; Mrs Dombey.'

'Yes, I believe I see her once,' replied Rob.

'The night she went away, Robby, eh?' said the old woman in his
ear, and taking note of every change in his face. 'Aha! I know it
was that night.'

'Well, if you know it was that night, you know, Misses Brown,'
replied Rob, 'it's no use putting pinchers into a cove to make him
say so.'

'Where did they go that night, Rob? Straight away? How did
they go? Where did you see her? Did she laugh? Did she cry? Tell
me all about it,' cried the old hag, holding him closer yet, patting
the hand that was drawn through her arm against her other hand,
and searching every line in his face with her bleared eyes. 'Come!
Begin! I want to be told all about it. What, Rob, boy! You and me
can keep a secret together, eh? We've done so before now. Where
did they go first, Rob?'

The wretched Grinder made a gasp, and a pause.

'Are you dumb?' said the old woman, angrily.

'Lord, Misses Brown, no! You expect a cove to be a flash of lightning. I wish I *was* the electric fluency,' muttered the bewildered Grinder. 'I'd have a shock at somebody, that would settle their business.'

'What do you say?' asked the old woman, with a grin.

'I'm wishing my love to you, Misses Brown,' returned the false Rob, seeking consolation in the glass. 'Where did they go to first, was it? Him and her, do you mean?'

'Ah!' said the old woman, eagerly. 'Them two.'

'Why, they didn't go nowhere – not together, I mean,' answered Rob.

The old woman looked at him, as though she had a strong impulse upon her to make another clutch at his head and throat, but was restrained by a certain dogged mystery in his face.

'That was the art of it,' said the reluctant Grinder; 'that's the way nobody saw 'em go, or has been able to say how they did go. They went different ways, I tell you, Misses Brown.'

'Ay, ay, ay! To meet at an appointed place,' chuckled the old woman, after a moment's silent and keen scrutiny of his face.

'Why, if they weren't a going to meet somewhere, I suppose they might as well have stayed at home, mightn't they, Misses Brown?' returned the unwilling Grinder.

'Well, Rob? Well?' said the old woman, drawing his arm yet tighter through her own, as if, in her eagerness, she were afraid of his slipping away.

'What, haven't we talked enough yet, Misses Brown?' returned the Grinder, who, between his sense of injury, his sense of liquor, and his sense of being on the rack, had become so lachrymose, that at almost every answer he scooped his coat-cuff into one or other of his eyes, and uttered an unavailing whine or remonstrance. 'Did she laugh that night, was it? Didn't you ask if she laughed, Misses Brown?'

'Or cried?' added the old woman, nodding assent.

'Neither,' said the Grinder. 'She kept as steady when she and me – oh, I see you *will* have it out of me, Misses Brown! But take your solemn oath now, that you'll never tell anybody.'

This Mrs Brown very readily did: being naturally Jesuitical;[6] and having no other intention in the matter than that her concealed visitor should hear for himself.

'She kept as steady, then, when she and me went down to

Southampton,' said the Grinder, 'as a image. In the morning she was just the same, Misses Brown. And when she went away in the packet[7] before daylight, by herself – me pretending to be her servant, and seeing her safe aboard – she was just the same. *Now*, are you contented, Misses Brown?'

'No, Rob. Not yet,' answered Mrs Brown, decisively.

'Oh, here's a woman for you!' cried the unfortunate Rob, in an outburst of feeble lamentation over his own helplessness 'What did you wish to know next, Misses Brown?'

'What became of Master? Where did he go?' she inquired, still holding him tight, and looking close into his face, with her sharp eyes.

'Upon my soul, I don't know, Misses Brown,' answered Rob. 'Upon my soul I don't know what he did, nor where he went, nor anything about him. I only know what he said to me as a caution to hold my tongue, when we parted; and I tell you this, Misses Brown, as a friend, that sooner than ever repeat a word of what we're saying now, you had better take and shoot yourself, or shut yourself up in this house, and set it a-fire, for there's nothing he wouldn't do, to be revenged upon you. You don't know him half as well as I do, Misses Brown. You're never safe from him, I tell you.'

'Haven't I taken an oath,' retorted the old woman, 'and won't I keep it?'

'Well, I'm sure I hope you will, Misses Brown,' returned Rob, somewhat doubtfully, and not without a latent threatening in his manner. 'For your own sake quite as much as mine.'

He looked at her as he gave her this friendly caution, and emphasized it with a nodding of his head; but finding it uncomfortable to encounter the yellow face with its grotesque action, and the ferret eyes with their keen old wintry gaze, so close to his own, he looked down uneasily and sat shuffling in his chair, as if he were trying to bring himself to a sullen declaration that he would answer no more questions. The old woman, still holding him as before, took this opportunity of raising the forefinger of her right hand in the air, as a stealthy signal to the concealed observer to give particular attention to what was about to follow.

'Rob,' she said, in her most coaxing tone.

'Good gracious, Misses Brown, what's the matter now?' returned the exasperated Grinder.

'Rob! where did the lady and Master appoint to meet?'

Rob shuffled more and more, and looked up and looked down,

and bit his thumb, and dried it on his waistcoat, and finally said, eyeing his tormentor askant, 'How should *I* know, Misses Brown?'

The old woman held up her finger again, as before, and replying, 'Come, lad! It's no use leading me to that, and there leaving me. I want to know' – waited for his answer.

Rob, after a discomfited pause, suddenly broke out with, 'How can I pronounce the names of foreign places, Mrs Brown? What an unreasonable woman you are!'

'But you have heard it said, Robby,' she retorted firmly, 'and you know what it sounded like. Come!'

'I never heard it said, Misses Brown,' returned the Grinder.

'Then,' retorted the old woman quickly, 'you have seen it written, and you can spell it.'

Rob, with a petulant exclamation between laughing and crying – for he was penetrated with some admiration of Mrs Brown's cunning, even through this persecution – after some reluctant fumbling in his waistcoat pocket, produced from it a little piece of chalk. The old woman's eyes sparkled when she saw it between his thumb and finger, and hastily clearing a space on the deal table, that he might write the word there, she once more made her signal with a shaking hand.

'Now I tell you beforehand what it is, Misses Brown,' said Rob, 'it's no use asking me anything else. I won't answer anything else; I can't. How long it was to be before they met, or whose plan it was that they was to go away alone, I don't know no more than you do. I don't know any more about it. If I was to tell you how I found out this word, you'd believe that. Shall I tell you, Misses Brown?'

'Yes, Rob.'

'Well then, Misses Brown. The way – now you won't ask any more, you know?' said Rob, turning his eyes, which were now fast getting drowsy and stupid, upon her.

'Not another word,' said Mrs Brown.

'Well then, the way was this. When a certain person left the lady with me, he put a piece of paper with a direction written on it in the lady's hand, saying it was in case she should forget. She wasn't afraid of forgetting, for she tore it up as soon as his back was turned, and when I put up the carriage steps, I shook out one of the pieces – she sprinkled the rest out of the window, I suppose, for there was none there afterwards, though I looked for 'em. There was only one word on it, and that was this, if you must and will know. But remember! You're upon your oath, Misses Brown.'

Mrs Brown knew that, she said. Rob, having nothing more to say, began to chalk, slowly and laboriously, on the table.

'"D,"' the old woman read aloud, when he had formed the letter.

'Will you hold your tongue, Misses Brown?' he exclaimed, covering it with his hand, and turning impatiently upon her. 'I won't have it read out. Be quiet, will you!'

'Then write large, Rob,' she returned, repeating her secret signal; 'for my eyes are not good, even at print.'

Muttering to himself, and returning to his work with an ill will, Rob went on with the word. As he bent his head down, the person for whose information he so unconsciously laboured, moved from the door behind him to within a short stride of his shoulder, and looked eagerly towards the creeping track of his hand upon the table. At the same time, Alice, from her opposite chair, watched it narrowly as it shaped the letters, and repeated each one on her lips as he made it, without articulating it aloud. At the end of every letter her eyes and Mr Dombey's met, as if each of them sought to be confirmed by the other; and thus they both spelt D. I. J. O. N.

'There!' said the Grinder, moistening the palm of his hand hastily, to obliterate the word; and not content with smearing it out, rubbing and planing all trace of it away with his coat-sleeve, until the very colour of the chalk was gone from the table. 'Now, I hope you're contented, Misses Brown!'

The old woman, in token of her being so, released his arm and patted his back; and the Grinder, overcome with mortification, cross-examination, and liquor, folded his arms on the table, laid his head upon them, and fell asleep.

Not until he had been heavily asleep some time, and was snoring roundly, did the old woman turn towards the door, where Mr Dombey stood concealed, and beckon him to come through the room, and pass out. Even then, she hovered over Rob, ready to blind him with her hands, or strike his head down if he should raise it while the secret step was crossing to the door. But though her glance took sharp cognizance of the sleeper, it was sharp too for the waking man; and when he touched her hand with his, and in spite of all his caution, made a chinking, golden sound, it was as bright and greedy as a raven's.

The daughter's dark gaze followed him to the door, and noted well how pale he was, and how his hurried tread indicated that the least delay was an insupportable restraint upon him, and how he was burning to be active and away. As he closed the door behind him, she looked round at her mother. The old woman trotted to her; opened her hand to show what was within; and, tightly closing it again in her jealousy and avarice, whispered:

'What will he do, Ally?'

'Mischief,' said the daughter.

'Murder?' asked the old woman.

'He's a madman, in his wounded pride, and may do that, for anything we can say, or he either.'

Her glance was brighter than her mother's, and the fire that shone in it was fiercer; but her face was colourless, even to her lips.

They said no more, but sat apart; the mother communing with her money; the daughter with her thoughts; the glance of each, shining in the gloom of the feebly lighted room. Rob slept and snored. The disregarded parrot only was in action. It twisted and pulled at the wires of its cage, with its crooked beak, and crawled up to the dome, and along its roof like a fly, and down again head foremost, and shook, and bit, and rattled at every slender bar, as if it knew its master's danger, and was wild to force a passage out, and fly away to warn him of it.

CHAPTER 53

More Intelligence

There were two of the traitor's own blood – his renounced brother and sister – on whom the weight of his guilt rested almost more heavily, at this time, than on the man whom he had so deeply injured. Prying and tormenting as the world was, it did Mr Dombey the service of nerving him to pursuit and revenge. It roused his passion, stung his pride, twisted the one idea of his life into a new shape, and made some gratification of his wrath, the object into which his whole intellectual existence resolved itself. All the stubbornness and implacability of his nature, all its hard impenetrable quality, all its gloom and moroseness, all its exaggerated sense of personal importance, all its jealous disposition to resent the least flaw in the ample recognition of his importance by others, set this way like many streams united into one, and bore him on upon their tide. The most impetuously passionate and violently impulsive of mankind would have been a milder enemy to encounter than the sullen Mr Dombey wrought to this. A wild beast would have been easier turned or soothed than the grave gentleman without a wrinkle in his starched cravat.

But the very intensity of his purpose became almost a substitute for action in it. While he was yet uninformed of the traitor's retreat, it served to divert his mind from his own calamity, and to entertain it with another prospect. The brother and sister of his false favourite had no such relief; everything in their history, past and present, gave his delinquency a more afflicting meaning to them.

The sister may have sometimes sadly thought that if she had remained with him, the companion and friend she had been once, he might have escaped the crime into which he had fallen. If she ever thought so, it was still without regret for what she had done, without the least doubt of her duty, without any pricing or enhancing of her self-devotion. But when this possibility presented itself to the erring and repentant brother, as it sometimes did, it smote upon his heart with such a keen, reproachful touch as he could hardly bear. No idea of retort upon his cruel brother came into his mind. New accusation of himself, fresh inward lamentings over his own unworthiness, and the ruin in which it was at once his consolation and his self-reproach that he did not stand alone, were the sole kind of reflections to which the discovery gave rise in him.

It was on the very same day whose evening set upon the last chapter, and when Mr Dombey's world was busiest with the elopement of his wife, that the window of the room in which the brother and sister sat at their early breakfast, was darkened by the unexpected shadow of a man coming to the little porch: which man was Perch the Messenger.

'I've stepped over from Ball's Pond at a early hour,' said Mr Perch, confidentially looking in at the room door, and stopping on the mat to wipe his shoes all round, which had no mud upon them, 'agreeable to my instructions last night. They was, to be sure and bring a note to you, Mr Carker, before you went out in the morning. I should have been here a good hour and a half ago,' said Mr Perch, meekly, 'but for the state of health of Mrs P., who I thought I should have lost in the night, I do assure you, five distinct times.'

'Is your wife so ill?' asked Harriet.

'Why, you see,' said Mr Perch, first turning round to shut the door carefully, 'she takes what has happened in our House so much to heart, Miss. Her nerves is so very delicate, you see, and soon unstrung. Not but what the strongest nerves had good need to be shook, I'm sure. You feel it very much yourself, no doubts.'

Harriet repressed a sigh, and glanced at her brother.

'I'm sure I feel it myself, in my humble way,' Mr Perch went on to say, with a shake of his head, 'in a manner I couldn't have believed if I hadn't been called upon to undergo. It has almost the effect of drink upon me. I literally feels every morning as if I had been taking more than was good for me overnight.'

Mr Perch's appearance corroborated this recital of his symptoms. There was an air of feverish lassitude about it, that seemed referable to drams; and, which, in fact, might no doubt have been traced to those numerous discoveries of himself in the bars of public-houses, being treated and questioned, which he was in the daily habit of making.

'Therefore I can judge,' said Mr Perch, shaking his head again, and speaking in a silvery murmur, 'of the feelings of such as is at all peculiarly sitiwated in this most painful rewelation.'

Here Mr Perch waited to be confided in; and receiving no confidence, coughed behind his hand. This leading to nothing, he coughed behind his hat; and that leading to nothing, he put his hat on the ground and sought in his breast pocket for the letter.

'If I rightly recollect, there was no answer,' said Mr Perch, with an affable smile; 'but perhaps you'll be so good as cast your eye over it, sir.'

John Carker broke the seal, which was Mr Dombey's, and possessing himself of the contents, which were very brief, replied, 'No. No answer is expected.'

'Then I shall wish you good morning, Miss,' said Perch, taking a step toward the door, 'and hoping, I'm sure, that you'll not permit yourself to be more reduced in mind than you can help, by the late painful rewelation. The Papers,' said Mr Perch, taking two steps back again, and comprehensively addressing both the brother and sister in a whisper of increased mystery, 'is more eager for news of it than you'd suppose possible. One of the Sunday ones, in a blue cloak and a white hat, that had previously offered for to bribe me – need I say with what success? – was dodging about our court last night as late as twenty minutes after eight o'clock. I see him myself, with his eye at the counting-house keyhole, which being patent is impervious. Another one,' said Mr Perch, 'with military frogs,[1] is in the parlour of the King's Arms all the blessed day. I happened, last week, to let a little obserwation fall there, and next morning, which was Sunday, I see it worked up in print, in a most surprising manner.'

Mr Perch resorted to his breast pocket, as if to produce the paragraph, but receiving no encouragement, pulled out his beaver gloves, picked up his hat, and took his leave; and before it was high noon, Mr Perch had related to several select audiences at the King's Arms and elsewhere, how Miss Carker, bursting into tears, had caught him by both hands, and said, 'Oh! dear dear Perch, the sight of you is all the comfort I have left!' and how Mr John Carker had said, in an awful voice, 'Perch, I disown him. Never let me hear him mentioned as a brother more!'

'Dear John,' said Harriet, when they were left alone, and had remained silent for some few moments. 'There are bad tidings in that letter.'

'Yes. But nothing unexpected,' he replied. 'I saw the writer yesterday.'

'The writer?'

'Mr Dombey. He passed twice through the counting-house while I was there. I had been able to avoid him before, but of course could not hope to do that long. I know how natural it was that he should regard my presence as something offensive; I felt it must be so, myself.'

'He did not say so?'

'No; he said nothing: but I saw that his glance rested on me for a moment, and I was prepared for what would happen – for what *has* happened. I am dismissed!'

She looked as little shocked and as hopeful as she could, but it was distressing news, for many reasons.

'"I need not tell you,"' said John Carker, reading the letter, '"why your name would henceforth have an unnatural sound, in however remote a connexion with mine, or why the daily sight of any one who bears it, would be unendurable to me. I have to notify the cessation of all engagements between us, from this date, and to request that no renewal of any communication with me, or my establishment, be ever attempted by you." – Enclosed is an equivalent in money to a generously long notice, and this is my discharge. Heaven knows, Harriet, it is a lenient and considerate one, when we remember all!'

'If it be lenient and considerate to punish you at all, John, for the misdeed of another,' she replied gently, 'yes.'

'We have been an ill-omened race to him,' said John Carker. 'He has reason to shrink from the sound of our name, and to think that there is something cursed and wicked in our blood. I should almost think it too, Harriet, but for you.'

'Brother, don't speak like this. If you have any special reason, as you say you have, and think you have – though I say, No! – to love me, spare me the hearing of such wild mad words!'

He covered his face with both his hands; but soon permitted her, coming near him, to take one in her own.

'After so many years, this parting is a melancholy thing, I know,' said his sister, 'and the cause of it is dreadful to us both. We have to live, too, and must look about us for the means. Well, well! We can do so, undismayed. It is our pride, not our trouble, to strive, John, and to strive together!'

A smile played on her lips, as she kissed his cheek, and entreated him to be of good cheer.

'Oh, dearest sister! Tied, of your own noble will, to a ruined man! whose reputation is blighted; who has no friend himself, and has driven every friend of yours away!'

'John!' she laid her hand hastily upon his lips, 'for my sake! In remembrance of our long companionship!' He was silent. 'Now let me tell you, dear,' quietly sitting by his side, 'I have, as you have, expected this; and when I have been thinking of it, and fearing that it would happen, and preparing myself for it, as well as I could, I have resolved to tell you, if it should be so, that I have kept a secret from you, and that we *have* a friend.'

'What's our friend's name, Harriet?' he answered with a sorrowful smile.

'Indeed, I don't know, but he once made a very earnest protestation to me of his friendship and his wish to serve us: and to this day I believe him.'

'Harriet!' exclaimed her wondering brother, 'where does this friend live?'

'Neither do I know that,' she returned. 'But he knows us both, and our history – all our little history, John. That is the reason why, at his own suggestion, I have kept the secret of his coming here from you, lest his acquaintance with it should distress you.'

'Here! Has he been here, Harriet?'

'Here, in this room. Once.'

'What kind of man?'

'Not young. "Grey-headed," as he said, "and fast growing greyer." But generous, and frank, and good, I am sure.'

'And only seen once, Harriet?'

'In this room only once,' said his sister, with the slightest and most transient glow upon her cheek; 'but when here, he entreated me to suffer him to see me once a week as he passed by, in token of our being well, and continuing to need nothing at his hands. For I told him, when he proffered us any service he could render – which was the object of his visit – that we needed nothing.'

'And once a week—'

'Once every week since then, and always on the same day, and at the same hour, he has gone past; always on foot; always going in the same direction – towards London; and never pausing longer than to bow to me, and wave his hand cheerfully, as a kind guardian might. He made that promise when he proposed these curious interviews, and has kept it so faithfully and pleasantly, that if I ever felt any trifling uneasiness about them in the beginning (which I don't think I did, John; his manner was so plain and true) it very soon vanished, and left me quite glad when the day was coming. Last Monday – the first since this terrible event – he did not go by; and I have wondered whether his absence can have been in any way connected with what has happened.'

'How?' inquired her brother.

'I don't know how. I have only speculated on the coincidence; I have not tried to account for it. I feel sure he will return. When he does, dear John, let me tell him that I have at last spoken to you, and let me bring you together. He will certainly help us to a new livelihood. His entreaty was that he might do something to smooth my life and yours; and I gave him my promise that if we ever wanted a friend, I would remember him. Then his name was to be no secret.'

'Harriet,' said her brother, who had listened with close attention, 'describe this gentleman to me. I surely ought to know one who knows me so well.'

His sister painted, as vividly as she could, the features, stature, and dress of her visitor; but John Carker, either from having no knowledge of the original, or from some fault in her description, or from some abstraction of his thoughts as he walked to and fro, pondering, could not recognise the portrait she presented to him.

However, it was agreed between them that he should see the original when he next appeared. This concluded, the sister applied herself, with a less anxious breast, to her domestic occupations; and the grey-haired man, late Junior of Dombey's, devoted the first day of his unwonted liberty to working in the garden.

It was quite late at night, and the brother was reading aloud while the sister plied her needle, when they were interrupted by a knocking at the door. In the atmosphere of vague anxiety and dread that lowered about them in connexion with their fugitive brother, this sound, unusual there, became almost alarming. The brother going to the door, the sister sat and listened timidly. Some one spoke to him, and he replied and seemed surprised; and after a few words, the two approached together.

'Harriet,' said her brother, lighting in their late visitor, and speaking in a low voice, 'Mr Morfin – the gentleman so long in Dombey's House with James.'

His sister started back, as if a ghost had entered. In the doorway stood the unknown friend, with the dark hair sprinkled with grey, the ruddy face, the broad clear brow, and hazel eyes, whose secret she had kept so long!

'John!' she said, half-breathless. 'It is the gentleman I told you of, to-day!'

'The gentleman, Miss Harriet,' said the visitor, coming in – for he had stopped a moment in the doorway – 'is greatly relieved to hear you say that: he has been devising ways and means, all the way here, of explaining himself, and has been satisfied with none. Mr John, I am not quite a stranger here. You were stricken with astonishment when you saw me at your door just now. I observe you are more astonished at present. Well! That's reasonable enough under existing circumstances. If we were not such creatures of habit as we are, we shouldn't have reason to be astonished half so often.'

By this time, he had greeted Harriet with that agreeable mingling of cordiality and respect which she recollected so well, and had sat down near her, pulled off his gloves, and thrown them into his hat upon the table.

'There's nothing astonishing,' he said, 'in my having conceived a desire to see your sister, Mr John, or in my having gratified it in my own way. As to the regularity of my visits since (which she may have mentioned to you), there is nothing extraordinary in that. They soon grew into a habit; and we are creatures of habit – creatures of habit!'

Putting his hands into his pockets, and leaning back in his chair, he looked at the brother and sister as if it were interesting to him to see them together; and went on to say, with a kind of irritable thoughtfulness: 'It's this same habit that confirms some of us, who are capable of better things, in Lucifer's own pride and stubbornness – that confirms and deepens others of us in villany – more of us in indifference – that hardens us from day to day, according to the temper of our clay, like images, and leaves us as susceptible as images to new impressions and convictions. You shall judge of its influence on me, John. For more years than I need name, I had my small, and exactly defined share, in the management of Dombey's

House, and saw your brother (who has proved himself a scoundrel! Your sister will forgive my being obliged to mention it) extending and extending his influence, until the business and its owner were his football; and saw you toiling at your obscure desk every day; and was quite content to be as little troubled as I might be, out of my own strip of duty, and to let everything about me go on, day by day, unquestioned, like a great machine – that was its habit and mine – and to take it all for granted, and consider it all right. My Wednesday nights came regularly round, our quartette parties came regularly off, my violoncello was in good tune, and there was nothing wrong in my world – or if anything not much – or little or much, it was no affair of mine.'

'I can answer for your being more respected and beloved during all that time than anybody in the House, Sir,' said John Carker.

'Pooh! Good-natured and easy enough, I dare say,' returned the other, 'a habit I had. It suited the Manager; it suited the man he managed: it suited me best of all. I did what was allotted to me to do, made no court to either of them and was glad to occupy a station in which none was required. So I should have gone on till now, but that my room had a thin wall. You can tell your sister that it was divided from the Manager's room by a wainscot partition.'

'They were adjoining rooms; had been one, perhaps, originally; and were separated, as Mr Morfin says,' said her brother, looking back to him for the resumption of his explanation.

'I have whistled, hummed tunes, gone accurately through the whole of Beethoven's Sonata in B,[2] to let him know that I was within hearing,' said Mr Morfin; 'but he never heeded me. It happened seldom enough that I was within hearing of anything of a private nature, certainly. But when I was, and couldn't otherwise avoid knowing something of it, I walked out. I walked out once, John, during a conversation between two brothers, to which, in the beginning, young Walter Gay was a party. But I overheard some of it before I left the room. You remember it sufficiently, perhaps, to tell your sister what its nature was?'

'It referred, Harriet,' said her brother in a low voice, 'to the past, and to our relative positions in the House.'

'Its matter was not new to me, but was presented in a new aspect. It shook me in my habit – the habit of nine-tenths of the world – of believing that all was right about me, because I was used to it,' said their visitor; 'and induced me to recall the history of the two brothers, and to ponder on it. I think it was almost the first time in my life when I fell into this train of reflection – how will many things that are familiar, and quite matters of course to us now, look when we come to see them from that new and distant point of view which we must all take up, one day or other? I was something less good-natured, as the phrase goes, after that morning, less easy and complacent altogether.'

He sat for a minute or so, drumming with one hand on the table; and resumed in a hurry, as if he were anxious to get rid of his confession.

'Before I knew what to do, or whether I could do anything, there was a second conversation between the same two brothers, in which their sister was mentioned. I had no scruples of conscience in suffering all the waifs and strays of that conversation to float to me as freely as they would. I considered them mine by right. After that, I came here to see the sister for myself. The first time I stopped at the garden gate, I made a pretext of inquiring into the character of a poor neighbour; but I wandered out of that tract, and I think Miss Harriet mistrusted me. The second time I asked leave to come in; came in; and said what I wished to say. Your sister showed me reasons which I dared not dispute, for receiving no assistance from me then, but I established a means of communication between us, which remained unbroken until within these few days, when I was prevented, by important matters that have lately devolved upon me, from maintaining them.'

'How little I have suspected this,' said John Carker, 'when I have seen you every day, Sir! If Harriet could have guessed your name—'

'Why, to tell you the truth, John,' interposed the visitor, 'I kept it to myself for two reasons. I don't know that the first might have been binding alone; but one has no business to take credit for good intentions, and I made up my mind, at all events, not to disclose myself until I should be able to do you some real service or other. My second reason was, that I always hoped there might be some lingering possibility of your brother's relenting towards you both; and in that case, I felt that where there was the chance of a man of his suspicious, watchful character, discovering that you had been secretly befriended by me, there was the chance of a new and fatal cause of division. I resolved, to be sure, at the risk of turning his displeasure against myself – which would have been no matter – to watch my opportunity of serving you with the head of the House; but the distractions of death, courtship, marriage, and domestic unhappiness, have left us no head but your brother for this long,

long time. And it would have been better for us,' said the visitor, dropping his voice, 'to have been a lifeless trunk.'

He seemed conscious that these latter words had escaped him against his will, and stretching out a hand to the brother, and a hand to the sister, continued:

'All I could desire to say, and more, I have now said. All I mean goes beyond words, as I hope you understand and believe. The time has come, John – though most unfortunately and unhappily come – when I may help you without interfering with that redeeming struggle, which has lasted through so many years; since you were discharged from it to-day by no act of your own. It is late; I need say no more to-night. You will guard the treasure you have here, without advice or reminder from me.'

With these words he rose to go.

'But go you first, John,' he said good-humouredly, 'with a light, without saying what you want to say, whatever that may be;' John Carker's heart was full, and he would have relieved it in speech, if he could; 'and let me have a word with your sister. We have talked alone before, and in this room too; though it looks more natural with you here.'

Following him out with his eyes, he turned kindly to Harriet, and said in a lower voice, and with an altered and graver manner:

'You wish to ask me something of the man whose sister it is your misfortune to be.'

'I dread to ask,' said Harriet.

'You have looked so earnestly at me more than once,' rejoined the visitor, 'that I think I can divine your question. Has he taken money? Is that it?'

'Yes.'

'He has not.'

'I thank Heaven!' said Harriet. 'For the sake of John.'

'That he has abused his trust in many ways,' said Mr Morfin; 'that he has oftener dealt and speculated to advantage for himself, than for the House he represented; that he has led the House on, to prodigious ventures, often resulting in enormous losses; that he has always pampered the vanity and ambition of his employer, when it was his duty to have held them in check, and shown, as it was in his power to do, to what they tended here or there; will not, perhaps, surprise you now. Undertakings have been entered on, to swell the reputation of the house for vast resources, and to exhibit it in magnificent contrast to other merchants' houses, of which it requires a steady head to contemplate the possibly – a few disastrous changes of affairs might render them the probably – ruinous consequences. In the midst of the many transactions of the House, in most parts of the world: a great labyrinth of which only he has held the clue: he has had the opportunity, and he seems to have used it, of keeping the various results afloat, when ascertained, and substituting estimates and generalities for facts. But latterly – you follow me, Miss Harriet?'

'Perfectly, perfectly,' she answered, with her frightened face fixed on his. 'Pray tell me all the worst at once.'

'Latterly, he appears to have devoted the greatest pains to making these results so plain and clear, that reference to the private books enables one to grasp them, numerous and varying as they are, with extraordinary ease. As if he had resolved to show his employer at one broad view what has been brought upon him by ministration to his ruling passion! That it has been his constant practice to minister to that passion basely, and to flatter it corruptly, is indubitable. In that, his criminality, as it is connected with the affairs of the House, chiefly consists.'

'One other word before you leave me, dear Sir,' said Harriet. 'There is no danger in all this?'

'How danger?' he returned, with a little hesitation.

'To the credit of the House?'

'I cannot help answering you plainly, and trusting you completely,' said Mr Morfin, after a moment's survey of her face.

'You may. Indeed you may!'

'I am sure I may. Danger to the House's credit? No; none. There may be difficulty, greater or less difficulty, but no danger, unless – unless, indeed – the head of the House, unable to bring his mind to the reduction of its enterprises, and positively refusing to believe that it is, or can be, in any position but the position in which he has always represented it to himself, should urge it beyond its strength. Then it would totter.'

'But there is no apprehension of that?' said Harriet.

'There shall be no half-confidence,' he replied, shaking her hand, 'between us. Mr Dombey is unapproachable by any one, and his state of mind is haughty, rash, unreasonable, and ungovernable, now. But he is disturbed and agitated now beyond all common bounds, and it may pass. You now know all, both worst and best. No more to-night, and good night!'

With that he kissed her hand, and, passing out to the door where her brother stood awaiting his coming, put him cheerfully aside when he essayed to speak; told him that, as they would see each other soon and often, he might speak at another time, if he would, but there was no leisure for it then; and went away at a round pace, in order that no word of gratitude might follow him.

The brother and sister sat conversing by the fireside, until it was almost day; made sleepless by this glimpse of the new world that opened before them, and feeling like two people shipwrecked long ago, upon a solitary coast, to whom a ship had come at last, when they were old in resignation, and had lost all thought of any other home. But another and different kind of disquietude kept them waking too. The darkness out of which this light had broken on them gathered around; and the shadow of their guilty brother was in the house where his foot had never trod.

Nor was it to be driven out, nor did it fade before the sun. Next morning it was there; at noon; at night. Darkest and most distinct at night, as is now to be told.

John Carker had gone out, in pursuance of a letter of appointment from their friend, and Harriet was left in the house alone. She had been alone some hours. A dull, grave evening, and a deepening twilight, were not favourable to the removal of the oppression on her spirits. The idea of this brother, long unseen and unknown, flitted about her in frightful shapes. He was dead, dying, calling to her, staring at her, frowning on her. The pictures in her mind were so obtrusive and exact that, as the twilight deepened, she dreaded to raise her head and look at the dark corners of the room, lest his wraith, the offspring of her excited imagination, should be waiting there, to startle her. Once she had such a fancy of his being in the next room, hiding – though she knew quite well what a distempered fancy it was, and had no belief in it – that she forced herself to go there, for her own conviction. But in vain. The room resumed its shadowy terrors, the moment she left it; and she had no more power to divest herself of these vague impressions of dread, than if they had been stone giants, rooted in the solid earth.

It was almost dark, and she was sitting near the window, with her head upon her hand, looking down, when, sensible of a sudden increase in the gloom of the apartment, she raised her eyes, and uttered an involuntary cry. Close to the glass, a pale scared face gazed in; vacantly, for an instant, as searching for an object; then the eyes rested on herself, and lighted up.

'Let me in! Let me in! I want to speak to you!' and the hand rattled on the glass.

She recognised immediately the woman with the long dark hair, to whom she had given warmth, food, and shelter, one wet night.

Naturally afraid of her, remembering her violent behaviour, Harriet, retreating a little from the window, stood undecided and alarmed.

'Let me in! Let me speak to you! I am thankful – quiet – humble – anything you like. But let me speak to you.'

The vehement manner of the entreaty, the earnest expression of the face, the trembling of the two hands that were raised imploringly, a certain dread and terror in the voice akin to her own condition at the moment, prevailed with Harriet. She hastened to the door and opened it.

'May I come in, or shall I speak here?' said the woman, catching at her hand.

'What is it that you want? What is it that you have to say?'

'Not much, but let me say it out, or I shall never say it. I am tempted now to go away. There seem to be hands dragging me from the door. Let me come in, if you can trust me for this once!'

Her energy again prevailed, and they passed into the firelight of the little kitchen, where she had before sat, and ate, and dried her clothes.

'Sit there,' said Alice, kneeling down beside her, 'and look at me. You remember me?'

'I do.'

'You remember what I told you I had been, and where I came from, ragged and lame, with the fierce wind and weather beating on my head?'

'Yes.'

'You know how I came back that night, and threw your money in the dirt, and cursed you and your race. Now, see me here, upon my knees. Am I less earnest now, than I was then?'

'If what you ask,' said Harriet, gently, 'is forgiveness—'

'But it's not!' returned the other, with a proud, fierce look. 'What I ask is to be believed. Now you shall judge if I am worthy of belief, both as I was, and as I am.'

Still upon her knees, and with her eyes upon the fire, and the fire shining on her ruined beauty and her wild black hair, one long tress of which she pulled over her shoulder, and wound about her hand, and thoughtfully bit and tore while speaking, she went on:

'When I was young and pretty, and this,' plucking contemptuously at the hair she held, 'was only handled delicately, and couldn't be admired enough, my mother, who had not been very mindful of me as a child, found out my merits, and was fond of me, and proud of me. She was covetous and poor, and thought to make a sort of property of me. No great lady ever thought that of a daughter yet, I'm sure, or acted as if she did – it's never done, we all know – and that shows that the only instances of mothers bringing up their daughters wrong, and evil coming of it, are among such miserable folks as us.'

Looking at the fire, as if she were forgetful, for the moment, of having any auditor, she continued in a dreamy way, as she wound the long tress of hair tight round and round her hand.

'What came of that, I needn't say. Wretched marriages don't come of such things, in our degree; only wretchedness and ruin. Wretchedness and ruin came on me – came on me.'

Raising her eyes swiftly from their moody gaze upon the fire, to Harriet's face, she said:

'I am wasting time, and there is none to spare; yet if I hadn't thought of all, I shouldn't be here now. Wretchedness and ruin came on me, I say. I was made a short-lived toy, and flung aside more cruelly and carelessly than even such things are. By whose hand do you think?'

'Why do you ask me?' said Harriet.

'Why do you tremble?' rejoined Alice, with an eager look. 'His usage made a Devil of me. I sunk in wretchedness and ruin, lower and lower yet. I was concerned in a robbery – in every part of it but the gains – and was found out, and sent to be tried, without a friend, without a penny. Though I was but a girl, I would have gone to Death, sooner than ask him for a word, if a word of his could have saved me. I would! To any death that could have been invented. But my mother, covetous always, sent to him in my name, told the true story of my case, and humbly prayed and petitioned for a small last gift – for not so many pounds as I have fingers on this hand. Who was it, do you think, who snapped his fingers at me in my misery, lying, as he believed, at his feet, and left me without even this poor sign of remembrance; well satisfied that I should be sent abroad, beyond the reach of further trouble to him, and should die, and rot there? Who was this, do you think?'

'Why do you ask me?' repeated Harriet.

'Why do you tremble?' said Alice, laying her hand upon her arm, and looking in her face, 'but that the answer is on your lips! It was your brother James.'

Harriet trembled more and more, but did not avert her eyes from the eager look that rested on them.

'When I knew you were his sister – which was on that night – I came back, weary and lame, to spurn your gift. I felt that night as

if I could have travelled, weary and lame, over the whole world, to
stab him, if I could have found him in a lonely place with no one
near. Do you believe that I was earnest in all that?'

'I do! Good Heaven, why are you come again?'

'Since then,' said Alice, with the same grasp of her arm, and the
same look in her face, 'I have seen him! I have followed him with
my eyes, in the broad day. If any spark of my resentment slumbered
in my bosom, it sprung into a blaze when my eyes rested on him.
You know he has wronged a proud man, and made him his deadly
enemy. What if I had given information of him to that man?'

'Information!' repeated Harriet.

'What if I had found out one who knew your brother's secret;
who knew the manner of his flight; who knew where he and the
companion of his flight were gone? What if I had made him utter
all his knowledge, word by word, before his enemy, concealed to
hear it? What if I had sat by at the time, looking into this enemy's
face, and seeing it change till it was scarcely human? What if I had
seen him rush away, mad, in pursuit? What if I knew, now, that he
was on his road, more fiend than man, and must, in so many hours,
come up with him?'

'Remove your hand!' said Harriet, recoiling. 'Go away! Your
touch is dreadful to me!'

'I have done this,' pursued the other, with her eager look,
regardless of the interruption. 'Do I speak and look as if I really
had? Do you believe what I am saying?'

'I fear I must. Let my arm go!'

'Not yet. A moment more. You can think what my revengeful
purpose must have been, to last so long, and urge me to do this?'

'Dreadful!' said Harriet.

'Then when you see me now,' said Alice hoarsely, 'here again,
kneeling quietly on the ground, with my touch upon your arm, with
my eyes upon your face, you may believe that there is no common
earnestness in what I say, and that no common struggle has been
battling in my breast. I am ashamed to speak the words, but I
relent. I despise myself; I have fought with myself all day, and all
last night; but I relent towards him without reason, and wish to
repair what I have done, if it is possible. I wouldn't have them come
together while his pursuer is so blind and headlong. If you had seen
him as he went out last night, you would know the danger better.'

'How shall it be prevented? What can I do?' cried Harriet.

'All night long,' pursued the other, hurriedly, 'I had dreams of him – and yet I didn't sleep – in his blood. All day, I have had him near me.'

'What can I do?' cried Harriet, shuddering at these words.

'If there is any one who'll write, or send, or go to him, let them lose no time. He is at Dijon. Do you know the name, and where it is?'

'Yes.'

'Warn him that the man he has made his enemy is in a frenzy, and that he doesn't know him if he makes light of his approach. Tell him that he is on the road! – I know he is! – and hurrying on. Urge him to get away while there is time – if there *is* time – and not to meet him yet. A month or so will make years of difference. Let them not encounter, through me. Anywhere but there! Any time but now! Let his foe follow him, and find him for himself, but not through me! There is enough upon my head without.'

The fire ceased to be reflected in her jet black hair, uplifted face, and eager eyes; her hand was gone from Harriet's arm; and the place where she had been was empty.

CHAPTER 54

The Fugitives

The time, an hour short of midnight; the place, a French apartment, comprising some half-dozen rooms; – a dull cold hall or corridor, a dining-room, a drawing-room, a bedchamber, and an inner drawing-room, or boudoir, smaller and more retired than the rest. All these shut in by one large pair of doors on the main staircase, but each room provided with two or three pairs of doors of its own, establishing several means of communication with the remaining portion of the apartment, or with certain small passages within the wall, leading, as is not unusual in such houses, to some back stairs with an obscure outlet below. The whole situated on the first floor of so large an Hotel, that it did not absorb one entire row of windows upon one side of the square court-yard in the centre, upon which the whole four sides of the mansion looked.

An air of splendour, sufficiently faded to be melancholy, and sufficiently dazzling to clog and embarrass the details of life with a show of state, reigned in these rooms. The walls and ceilings were gilded and painted; the floors were waxed and polished; crimson drapery hung in festoons from window, door, and mirror; candelabra, gnarled and intertwisted, like the branches of trees, or horns of animals, stuck out from the panels of the wall. But in the daytime, when the lattice-blinds (now closely shut) were opened, and the light let in, traces were discernible among this finery, of wear and tear and dust, of sun and damp and smoke, and lengthened intervals of want of use and habitation, when such shows and toys of life seem sensitive like life, and waste as men shut up in prison do. Even night, and clusters of burning candles, could not wholly efface them, though the general glitter threw them in the shade.

The glitter of bright tapers, and their reflection in looking-glasses, scraps of gilding and gay colours, were confined, on this night, to one room – that smaller room within the rest, just now enumerated. Seen from the hall, where a lamp was feebly burning, through the dark perspective of open doors, it looked as shining and precious as a gem. In the heart of its radiance sat a beautiful woman – Edith.

She was alone. The same defiant, scornful woman still. The cheek a little worn, the eye a little larger in appearance, and more lustrous, but the haughty bearing just the same. No shame upon her brow; no late repentance bending her disdainful neck. Imperious and stately yet, and yet regardless of herself and of all else, she sat with her dark eyes cast down, waiting for some one.

No book, no work, no occupation of any kind but her own thought, beguiled the tardy time. Some purpose, strong enough to fill up any pause, possessed her. With her lips pressed together, and quivering if for a moment she released them from her control; with her nostril inflated; her hands clasped in one another; and her purpose swelling in her breast; she sat, and waited.

At the sound of a key in the outer door, and a footstep in the hall, she started up, and cried, 'Who's that?' The answer was in French, and two men came in with jingling trays, to make preparation for supper.

'Who had bade them to do so?' she asked.

'Monsieur had commanded it, when it was his pleasure to take the apartment. Monsieur had said, when he stayed there for an hour, *en route*, and left the letter for Madame – Madame had received it surely?'

'Yes.'

'A thousand pardons! The sudden apprehension that it might have been forgotten had struck him;' a bald man, with a large beard from a neighbouring *restaurant*: 'with despair! Monsieur had said that supper was to be ready at that hour: also that he had forewarned Madame of the commands he had given, in his letter. Monsieur had done the Golden Head the honour to request that the supper should be choice and delicate. Monsieur would find that his confidence in the Golden Head was not misplaced.'

Edith said no more, but looked on thoughtfully while they prepared the table for two persons, and set the wine upon it. She arose before they had finished, and taking a lamp, passed into the bedchamber and into the drawing-room, where she hurriedly but narrowly examined all the doors; particularly one in the former room that opened on the passage in the wall. From this she took the key, and put it on the outer side. She then came back.

The men – the second of whom was a dark, bilious subject, in a jacket, close shaved, and with a black head of hair close cropped – had completed their preparation of the table, and were standing looking at it. He who had spoken before, inquired whether Madame thought it would be long before Monsieur arrived?

'She couldn't say. It was all one.'

'Pardon! There was the supper! It should be eaten on the instant. Monsieur (who spoke French like an Angel – or a Frenchman – it was all the same) had spoken with great emphasis of his punctuality. But the English nation had so grand a genius for punctuality. Ah! what noise! Great Heaven, here was Monsieur. Behold him!'

In effect, Monsieur, admitted by the other of the two, came, with his gleaming teeth, through the dark rooms, like a mouth; and arriving in that sanctuary of light and colour, a figure at full length, embraced Madame, and addressed her in the French tongue as his charming wife.

'My God! Madame is going to faint. Madame is overcome with joy!' The bald man with the beard observed it, and cried out.

Madame had only shrunk and shivered. Before the words were spoken, she was standing with her hand upon the velvet back of a great chair; her figure drawn up to its full height, and her face immovable.

'François has flown over to the Golden Head for supper. He flies on these occasions like an angel or a bird. The baggage of Monsieur is in his room. All is arranged. The supper will be here this moment.' These facts the bald man notified with bows and smiles, and presently the supper came.

The hot dishes were on a chafing-dish;[1] the cold already set forth, with the change of service on a sideboard. Monsieur was satisfied with this arrangement. The supper table being small, it pleased him very well. Let them set the chafing-dish upon the floor, and go. He would remove the dishes with his own hands.

'Pardon!' said the bald man, politely. 'It was impossible!'

Monsieur was of another opinion. He required no further attendance that night.

'But Madame—' the bald man hinted.

'Madame,' replied Monsieur, 'had her own maid. It was enough.'

'A million pardons! No! Madame had no maid!'

'I came here alone,' said Edith. 'It was my choice to do so. I am well used to travelling; I want no attendance. They need send nobody to me.'

Monsieur accordingly, persevering in his first proposed impossibility, proceeded to follow the two attendants to the outer door, and secure it after them for the night. The bald man turning round to bow, as he went out, observed that Madame still stood with her hand upon the velvet back of the great chair, and that her face was quite regardless of him, though she was looking straight before her.

As the sound of Carker's fastening the door resounded through the intermediate rooms, and seemed to come hushed and stifled into that last distant one, the sound of the Cathedral clock striking twelve mingled with it, in Edith's ears. She heard him pause, as if he heard it too and listened; and then come back towards her, laying a long train of footsteps through the silence, and shutting all the doors behind him as he came along. Her hand, for a moment, left the velvet chair to bring a knife within her reach upon the table; then she stood as she had stood before.

'How strange to come here by yourself, my love!' he said as he entered.

'What?' she returned.

Her tone was so harsh; the quick turn of her head so fierce; her attitude so repellent; and her frown so black; that he stood, with the lamp in his hand, looking at her, as if she had struck him motionless.

'I say,' he at length repeated, putting down the lamp, and smiling his most courtly smile, 'how strange to come here alone! It was unnecessary caution surely, and might have defeated itself. You were to have engaged an attendant at Havre or Rouen, and have had abundance of time for the purpose, though you had been the most capricious and difficult (as you are the most beautiful, my love) of women.'

Her eyes gleamed strangely on him, but she stood with her hand resting on the chair, and said not a word.

'I have never,' resumed Carker, 'seen you look so handsome, as you do to-night. Even the picture I have carried in my mind during this cruel probation, and which I have contemplated night and day, is exceeded by the reality.'

Not a word. Not a look. Her eyes completely hidden by their drooping lashes, but her head held up.

'Hard, unrelenting terms they were!' said Carker, with a smile, 'but they are all fulfilled and passed, and make the present more delicious and more safe. Sicily shall be the place of our retreat. In the idlest and easiest part of the world, my soul, we'll both seek compensation for old slavery.'

He was coming gaily towards her, when, in an instant, she caught the knife up from the table, and started one pace back.

'Stand still!' she said, 'or I shall murder you!'

The sudden change in her, the towering fury and intense abhorrence sparkling in her eyes and lighting up her brow, made him stop as if a fire had stopped him.

'Stand still!' she said, 'come no nearer me, upon your life!'

They both stood looking at each other. Rage and astonishment were in his face, but he controlled them, and said lightly,

'Come, come! Tush, we are alone, and out of everybody's sight and hearing. Do you think to frighten me with these tricks of virtue?'

'Do you think to frighten *me*,' she answered fiercely, 'from any purpose that I have, and any course I am resolved upon, by reminding me of the solitude of this place, and there being no help near? Me, who am here alone, designedly? If I feared you, should I not have avoided you? If I feared you, should I be here, in the dead of night, telling you to your face what I am going to tell?'

'And what is that,' he said, 'you handsome shrew? Handsomer so, than any other woman in her best humour?'

'I tell you nothing,' she returned, 'until you go back to that chair – except this, once again – Don't come near me! Not a step nearer. I tell you, if you do, as Heaven sees us, I shall murder you!'

'Do you mistake me for your husband?' he retorted, with a grin.

Disdaining to reply, she stretched her arm out, pointing to the chair. He bit his lip, frowned, laughed, and sat down in it, with a baffled, irresolute, impatient air, he was unable to conceal; and biting his nail nervously, and looking at her sideways, with bitter discomfiture, even while he feigned to be amused by her caprice.

She put the knife down upon the table, and touching her bosom with her hand, said:

'I have something lying here that is no love trinket; and sooner than endure your touch once more, I would use it on you – and you know it, while I speak – with less reluctance than I would on any other creeping thing that lives.'

He affected to laugh jestingly, and entreated her to act her play out quickly, for the supper was growing cold. But the secret look with which he regarded her, was more sullen and lowering, and he struck his foot once upon the floor with a muttered oath.

'How many times,' said Edith, bending her darkest glance upon him, 'has your bold knavery assailed me with outrage and insult? How many times in your smooth manner, and mocking words and looks, have I been twitted with my courtship and my marriage? How many times have you laid bare my wound of love for that sweet, injured girl, and lacerated it? How often have you fanned the fire on which, for two years, I have writhed; and tempted me to take a desperate revenge, when it has most tortured me?'

'I have no doubt, ma'am,' he replied, 'that you have kept a good account, and that it's pretty accurate. Come, Edith. To your husband, poor wretch, this was well enough—'

'Why, if,' she said, surveying him with a haughty contempt and disgust, that he shrunk under, let him brave it as he would, 'if all my other reasons for despising him could have been blown away like feathers, his having you for his counsellor and favourite, would have almost been enough to hold their place.'

'Is that a reason why you have run away with me?' he asked her, tauntingly.

'Yes, and why we are face to face for the last time. Wretch! We meet to-night, and part to-night. For not one moment after I have ceased to speak, will I stay here!'

He turned upon her with his ugliest look, and gripped the table with his hand; but neither rose, nor otherwise answered or threatened her.

'I am a woman,' she said, confronting him steadfastly, 'who from her very childhood has been shamed and steeled. I have been offered and rejected, put up and appraised, until my very soul has sickened. I have not had an accomplishment or grace that might have been a resource to me, but it has been paraded and vended to enhance my value, as if the common crier had called it through the streets. My poor, proud friends, have looked on and approved; and every tie between us has been deadened in my breast. There is not one of them for whom I care, as I could care for a pet dog. I stand alone in the world, remembering well what a hollow world it has been to me, and what a hollow part of it I have been myself. You know this, and you know that my fame with it is worthless to me.'

'Yes; I imagined that,' he said.

'And calculated on it,' she rejoined, 'and so pursued me. Grown too indifferent for any opposition but indifference, to the daily working of the hands that had moulded me to this; and knowing that my marriage would at least prevent their hawking of me up and down; I suffered myself to be sold as infamously as any woman with a halter round her neck is sold in any market-place. You know that.'

'Yes,' he said, showing all his teeth. 'I know that.'

'And calculated on it,' she rejoined once more, 'and so pursued me. From my marriage day, I found myself exposed to such new shame – to such solicitation and pursuit (expressed as clearly as if it had been written in the coarsest words, and thrust into my hand at every turn) from one mean villain, that I felt as if I had never known humiliation till that time. This shame my husband fixed upon me; hemmed me round with, himself; steeped me in, with his own hands, and of his own act, repeated hundreds of times. And thus – forced by the two from every point of rest I had – forced by the two to yield up the last retreat of love and gentleness within me, or to be a new misfortune on its innocent object – driven from each to each, and beset by one when I escaped the other – my anger rose almost to distraction against both. I do not know against which it rose higher – the master or the man!'

He watched her closely, as she stood before him in the very triumph of her indignant beauty. She was resolute, he saw; undauntable; with no more fear of him than of a worm.

'What should I say of honour or of chastity to you!' she went on. 'What meaning would it have to you; what meaning would it have from me! But if I tell you that the lightest touch of your hand makes my blood cold with antipathy; that from the hour when I first saw and hated you, to now, when my instinctive repugnance is enhanced by every minute's knowledge of you I have since had, you have been a loathsome creature to me which has not its like on earth; how then?'

He answered with a faint laugh, 'Aye! How then, my queen?'

'On that night, when, emboldened by the scene you had assisted at, you dared come to my room and speak to me,' she said, 'What passed?'

He shrugged his shoulders, and laughed again.

'What passed?' she said.

Mr Carker in his hour of triumph

'Your memory is so distinct,' he returned, 'that I have no doubt you can recall it.'

'I can,' she said. 'Hear it! Proposing then, this flight – not this flight, but the flight you thought it – you told me that in the having given you that meeting, and leaving you to be discovered there, if you so thought fit; and in the having suffered you to be alone with me many times before, – and having made the opportunities, you said, – and in the having openly avowed to you that I had no feeling for my husband but aversion, and no care for myself – I was lost; I had given you the power to traduce my name; and I lived, in virtuous reputation, at the pleasure of your breath.'

'All stratagems in love—' he interrupted, smiling. 'The old adage—'[2]

'On that night,' said Edith, 'and then the struggle that I long had had with something that was not respect for my good fame – that was I know not what – perhaps the clinging to that last retreat – was ended. On that night, and then, I turned from everything but passion and resentment. I struck a blow that laid your lofty master in the dust, and set you there, before me, looking at me now, and knowing what I mean.'

He sprung up from his chair with a great oath. She put her hand into her bosom, and not a finger trembled, not a hair upon her head was stirred. He stood still: she too: the table and chair between them.

'When I forget that this man put his lips to mine that night, and held me in his arms as he has done again to-night,' said Edith, pointing at him; 'when I forget the taint of his kiss upon my cheek – the cheek that Florence would have laid her guiltless face against – when I forget my meeting with her, while that taint was hot upon me, and in what a flood the knowledge rushed upon me when I saw her, that in releasing her from the persecution I had caused by my love, I brought a shame and degradation on her name through mine, and in all time to come should be the solitary figure representing in her mind her first avoidance of a guilty creature – then, Husband, from whom I stand divorced henceforth, I will forget these last two years, and undo what I have done, and undeceive you!'

Her flashing eyes, uplifted for a moment, lighted again on Carker, and she held some letters out in her left hand.

'See these!' she said, contemptuously. 'You have addressed these to me in the false name you go by; one here, some elsewhere on my road. The seals are unbroken. Take them back!'

She crunched them in her hand, and tossed them to his feet. And as she looked upon him now, a smile was on her face.

'We meet and part to-night,' she said. 'You have fallen on Sicilian days and sensual rest, too soon. You might have cajoled, and fawned, and played your traitor's part, a little longer, and grown richer. You purchase your voluptuous retirement dear!'

'Edith!' he retorted, menacing her with his hand. 'Sit down! Have done with this! What devil possesses you?'

'Their name is Legion,'[3] she replied, uprearing her proud form as if she would have crushed him; 'you and your master have raised them in a fruitful house, and they shall tear you both. False to him, false to his innocent child, false every way and everywhere, go forth and boast of me, and gnash your teeth for once to know that you are lying!'

He stood before her muttering and menacing, and scowling round as if for something that would help him to conquer her; but with the same indomitable spirit she opposed him, without faltering.

'In every vaunt you make,' she said, 'I have my triumph. I single out in you the meanest man I know, the parasite and tool of the proud tyrant, that his wound may go the deeper and may rankle more. Boast, and revenge me on him! You know how you came here to-night; you know how you stand cowering there; you see yourself in colours quite as despicable, if not as odious, as those in which I see you. Boast then, and revenge me on yourself.'

The foam was on his lips; the wet stood on his forehead. If she would have faltered once for only one half-moment, he would have pinioned her; but she was as firm as rock, and her searching eyes never left him.

'We don't part so,' he said. 'Do you think I am drivelling, to let you go in your mad temper?'

'Do you think,' she answered, 'that I am to be stayed?'

'I'll try, my dear,' he said with a ferocious gesture of his head.

'God's mercy on you, if you try by coming near me!' she replied.

'And what,' he said, 'if there are none of these same boasts and vaunts on my part? What if I were to turn too? Come!' and his teeth fairly shone again. 'We must make a treaty of this, or I may take some unexpected course. Sit down, sit down!'

'Too late!' she cried, with eyes that seemed to sparkle fire. 'I have thrown my fame and good name to the winds! I have resolved to bear the shame that will attach to me – resolved to know that it attaches falsely – that you know it too – and that he does not, never can, and never shall. I'll die, and make no sign. For this I am here alone with you, at the dead of night. For this I have met you here, in a false name, as your wife. For this, I have been seen here by those men, and left here. Nothing can save you now.'

He would have sold his soul to root her, in her beauty, to the floor, and make her arms drop at her sides, and have her at his mercy. But he could not look at her, and not be afraid of her. He saw a strength within her that was resistless. He saw that she was desperate, and that her unquenchable hatred of him would stop at nothing. His eyes followed the hand that was put with such rugged uncongenial purpose into her white bosom, and he thought that if it struck at him, and failed, it would strike there, just as soon.

He did not venture, therefore, to advance towards her: but the door by which he had entered was behind him, and he stepped back to lock it.

'Lastly, take my warning! Look to yourself!' she said, and smiled again. 'You have been betrayed, as all betrayers are. It has been made known that you are in this place, or were to be, or have been. If I live, I saw my husband in a carriage in the street to-night!'

'Strumpet; it's false!' cried Carker.

At the moment, the bell rang loudly in the hall. He turned white, as she held her hand up like an enchantress, at whose invocation the sound had come.

'Hark! do you hear it?'

He set his back against the door; for he saw a change in her, and fancied she was coming on to pass him. But, in a moment she was gone through the opposite doors communicating with the bedchamber, and they shut upon her.

Once turned, once changed in her inflexible unyielding look, he felt that he could cope with her. He thought a sudden terror, occasioned by this night-alarm, had subdued her; not the less readily, for her overwrought condition. Throwing open the doors, he followed, almost instantly.

But the room was dark; and as she made no answer to his call, he was fain to go back for the lamp. He held it up, and looked round everywhere, expecting to see her crouching in some corner; but the room was empty. So into the drawing-room and dining-room he went, in succession, with the uncertain steps of a man in a strange place; looking fearfully about, and prying behind screens and couches; but she was not there. No, nor in the hall, which was so bare that he could see that, at a glance.

All this time, the ringing at the bell was constantly renewed; and those without were beating at the door. He put his lamp down at a distance, and going near it, listened. There were several voices talking together: at least two of them in English; and though the door was thick, and there was great confusion, he knew one of these too well to doubt whose voice it was.

He took up his lamp again, and came back quickly through all the rooms, stopping as he quitted each, and looking round for her, with the light raised above his head. He was standing thus in the bedchamber, when the door, leading to the little passage in the wall, caught his eye. He went to it, and found it fastened on the other side; but she had dropped a veil in going through, and shut it in the door.

All this time the people on the stairs were ringing at the bell, and knocking with their hands and feet.

He was not a coward: but these sounds; what had gone before; the strangeness of the place, which had confused him, even in his return from the hall; the frustration of his scheme (for, strange to say, he would have been much bolder, if they had succeeded); the unseasonable time; the recollection of having no one near to whom he could appeal for any friendly office; above all, the sudden sense, which made even his heart beat like lead, that the man whose confidence he had outraged and whom he had so treacherously deceived, was there to recognise and challenge him with his mask plucked off his face; struck a panic through him. He tried the door in which the veil was shut, but couldn't force it. He opened one of the windows, and looked down through the lattice of the blind, into the court-yard; but it was a high leap, and the stones were pitiless.

The ringing and knocking still continuing – his panic too – he went back to the door in the bedchamber, and with some new efforts, each more stubborn than the last, wrenched it open. Seeing the little staircase not far off, and feeling the night-air coming up, he stole back for his hat and coat, made the door as secure after him as he could, crept down lamp in hand, extinguished it on seeing the street, and having put it in a corner, went out where the stars were shining.

CHAPTER 55

Rob the Grinder loses his Place

The porter at the iron gate which shut the court-yard from the street, had left the little wicket[1] of his house open, and was gone away; no doubt to mingle in the distant noise at the door of the great staircase. Lifting the latch softly, Carker crept out, and shutting the jangling gate after him with as little noise as possible, hurried off.

In the fever of his mortification and unavailing rage, the panic that had seized upon him mastered him completely. It rose to such a height that he would have blindly encountered almost any risk, rather than meet the man of whom, two hours ago, he had been utterly regardless. His fierce arrival, which he had never expected; the sound of his voice; their having been so near a meeting, face to face; he would have braved out this, after the first momentary shock of alarm, and would have put as bold a front upon his guilt as any villain. But the springing of his mine upon himself, seemed to have rent and shivered all his hardihood and self-reliance. Spurned like any reptile; entrapped and mocked; turned upon, and trodden down by the proud woman whose mind he had slowly poisoned, as he thought, until she had sunk into the mere creature of his pleasure; undeceived in his deceit, and with his fox's hide stripped off, he sneaked away, abashed, degraded, and afraid.

Some other terror came upon him quite removed from this of being pursued, suddenly, like an electric shock, as he was creeping through the streets. Some visionary terror, unintelligible and inexplicable, associated with a trembling of the ground, – a rush and sweep of something through the air, like Death upon the wing. He shrunk, as if to let the thing go by. It was not gone, it never had been there, yet what a startling horror it had left behind.

He raised his wicked face, so full of trouble, to the night sky, where the stars, so full of peace, were shining on him as they had been when he first stole out into the air; and stopped to think what he should do. The dread of being hunted in a strange remote place, where the laws might not protect him – the novelty of the feeling that it *was* strange and remote, originating in his being left alone so suddenly amid the ruins of his plans – his greater dread of seeking refuge now, in Italy or in Sicily, where men might be hired to assassinate him, he thought, at any dark street corner – the waywardness of guilt and fear – perhaps some sympathy of action with the turning back of all his schemes – impelled him to turn back too, and go to England.

'I am safer there, in any case. If I should not decide,' he thought, 'to give this fool a meeting, I am less likely to be traced there, than abroad here, now. And if I should (this cursed fit being over), at least I shall not be alone, without a soul to speak to, or advise with, or stand by me. I shall not be run in upon and worried like a rat.'

He muttered Edith's name, and clenched his hand. As he crept along, in the shadow of the massive buildings, he set his teeth, and muttered dreadful imprecations on her head, and looked from side to side, as if in search of her. Thus, he stole on to the gate of an inn-yard. The people were a-bed; but his ringing at the bell soon produced a man with a lantern, in company with whom he was presently in a dim coach-house, bargaining for the hire of an old phaeton,[2] to Paris.

The bargain was a short one; and the horses were soon sent for. Leaving word that the carriage was to follow him when they came, he stole away again, beyond the town, past the old ramparts, out on the open road, which seemed to glide away along the dark plain, like a stream.

Whither did it flow? What was the end of it? As he paused, with some such suggestion within him, looking over the gloomy flat where the slender trees marked out the way, again that flight of Death came rushing up, again went on, impetuous and resistless, again was nothing but a horror in his mind, dark as the scene and undefined as its remotest verge.

There was no wind; there was no passing shadow on the deep shade of the night; there was no noise. The city lay behind him, lighted here and there, and starry worlds were hidden by the masonry of spire and roof that hardly made out any shapes against the sky. Dark and lonely distance lay around him everywhere, and the clocks were faintly striking two.

He went forward for what appeared a long time, and a long way; often stopping to listen. At last the ringing of horses' bells greeted his anxious ears. Now softer, and now louder, now inaudible, now ringing very slowly over bad ground, now brisk and merry, it came on; until with a loud shouting and lashing, a shadowy postillion muffled to the eyes, checked his four struggling horses at his side.

'Who goes there! Monsieur?'

'Yes.'

'Monsieur has walked a long way in the dark midnight.'

'No matter. Every one to his taste. Were there any other horses ordered at the Post-house?'[3]

'A thousand devils! – and pardons! other horses? at this hour? No.'

'Listen, my friend. I am much hurried. Let me see how fast we can travel! The faster, the more money there will be to drink. Off we go then! Quick!'

'Halloa! whoop! Halloa! Hi!' Away, at a gallop, over the black landscape, scattering the dust and dirt like spray!

The clatter and commotion echoed to the hurry and discordance of the fugitive's ideas. Nothing clear without, and nothing clear within. Objects flitting past, merging into one another, dimly descried, confusedly lost sight of, gone! Beyond the changing scraps of fence and cottage immediately upon the road, a lowering waste. Beyond the shifting images that rose up in his mind and vanished as they showed themselves, a black expanse of dread and rage and baffled villany. Occasionally, a sigh of mountain air came from the distant Jura, fading along the plain. Sometimes that rush which was so furious and horrible, again came sweeping through his fancy, passed away, and left a chill upon his blood.

The lamps, gleaming on the medley of horses' heads, jumbled with the shadowy driver, and the fluttering of his cloak, made a thousand indistinct shapes, answering to his thoughts. Shadows of familiar people, stooping at their desks and books, in their remembered attitudes; strange apparitions of the man whom he was flying from, or of Edith; repetitions in the ringing bells and rolling wheels, of words that had been spoken; confusions of time and place, making last night a month ago, a month ago last night – home now distant beyond hope, now instantly accessible; commotion, discord, hurry, darkness, and confusion in his mind, and all around him. – Hallo! Hi! away at a gallop over the black landscape; dust and dirt flying like spray, the smoking horses snorting and plunging as if each of them were ridden by a demon, away in a frantic triumph on the dark road – whither?

Again the nameless shock comes speeding up, and as it passes, the bells ring in his ears 'whither?' The wheels roar in his ears 'whither?' All the noise and rattle shapes itself into that cry. The lights and shadows dance upon the horses' heads like imps. No stopping now: no slackening! On, on! Away with him upon the dark road wildly!

He could not think to any purpose. He could not separate one subject of reflection from another, sufficiently to dwell upon it, by

On the dark road

itself, for a minute at a time. The clash of his project for the gaining of a voluptuous compensation for past restraint; the overthrow of his treachery to one who had been true and generous to him, but whose least proud word and look he had treasured up, at interest, for years – for false and subtle men will always secretly despise and dislike the object upon which they fawn, and always resent the payment and receipt of homage that they know to be worthless; these were the themes uppermost in his mind. A lurking rage against the woman who had so entrapped him and avenged herself was always there; crude and misshapen schemes of retaliation upon her, floated in his brain; but nothing was distinct. A hurry and contradiction pervaded all his thoughts. Even while he was so busy with this fevered, ineffectual thinking, his one constant idea was, that he would postpone reflection until some indefinite time.

Then, the old days before the second marriage rose up in his remembrance. He thought how jealous he had been of the boy, how jealous he had been of the girl, how artfully he had kept intruders at a distance, and drawn a circle round his dupe that none but himself should cross; and then he thought, had he done all this to be flying now, like a scared thief, from only the poor dupe?

He could have laid hands upon himself for his cowardice, but it was the very shadow of his defeat, and could not be separated from it. To have his confidence in his own knavery so shattered at a blow – to be within his own knowledge such a miserable tool – was like being paralysed. With an impotent ferocity he raged at Edith, and hated Mr Dombey and hated himself, but still he fled, and could do nothing else.

Again and again he listened for the sound of wheels behind. Again and again his fancy heard it, coming on louder and louder. At last he was so persuaded of this, that he cried out, 'Stop!' preferring even the loss of ground to such uncertainty.

The word soon brought carriage, horses, driver, all in a heap together, across the road.

'The devil!' cried the driver, looking over his shoulder, 'what's the matter?'

'Hark? What's that?'

'What?'

'That noise?'

'Ah Heaven, be quiet, cursed brigand!' to a horse who shook his bells. 'What noise?'

'Behind. Is it not another carriage at a gallop? There! what's that?'

'Miscreant with a pig's head, stand still!' to another horse, who bit another, who frightened the other two, who plunged and backed. 'There is nothing coming.'

'Nothing.'

'No, nothing but the day yonder.'

'You are right, I think. I hear nothing now, indeed. Go on!'

The entangled equipage, half hidden in the reeking cloud from the horses, goes on slowly at first, for the driver, checked unnecessarily in his progress, sulkily takes out a pocket-knife, and puts a new lash to his whip. Then 'Hallo, whoop! Hallo, hi!' Away once more, savagely.

And now the stars faded, and the day glimmered, and standing in the carriage, looking back, he could discern the track by which he had come, and see that there was no traveller within view, on all the heavy expanse. And soon it was broad day, and the sun began to shine on corn-fields and vineyards; and solitary labourers, risen from little temporary huts by heaps of stone upon the road, were, here and there, at work repairing the highway, or eating bread. By and by, there were peasants going to their daily labour, or to market, or lounging at the doors of poor cottages, gazing idly at him as he passed. And then there was a postyard, ankle-deep in mud, with steaming dunghills and vast outhouses half ruined; and looking on this dainty prospect, an immense, old, shadeless, glaring, stone chateau, with half its windows blinded, and green damp crawling lazily over it, from the balustraded terrace to the taper tips of the extinguishers upon the turrets.

Gathered up moodily in a corner of the carriage, and only intent on going fast – except when he stood up, for a mile together, and looked back; which he would do whenever there was a piece of open country – he went on, still postponing thought indefinitely, and still always tormented with thinking to no purpose.

Shame, disappointment, and discomfiture gnawed at his heart; a constant apprehension of being overtaken, or met – for he was groundlessly afraid even of travellers, who came towards him by the way he was going – oppressed him heavily. The same intolerable awe and dread that had come upon him in the night, returned unweakened in the day. The monotonous ringing of the bells and tramping of the horses; the monotony of his anxiety, and useless rage; the monotonous wheel of fear, regret, and passion, he kept turning round and round; made the journey like a vision, in which nothing was quite real but his own torment.

It was a vision of long roads; that stretched away to an horizon, always receding and never gained; of ill-paved towns, up hill and down, where faces came to dark doors and ill-glazed windows, and where rows of mud-bespattered cows and oxen were tied up for sale in the long narrow streets, butting and lowing, and receiving blows on their blunt heads from bludgeons that might have beaten them in; of bridges, crosses, churches, postyards, new horses being put in against their wills, and the horses of the last stage reeking, panting, and laying their drooping heads together dolefully at stable doors; of little cemeteries with black crosses settled sideways in the graves, and withered wreaths upon them dropping away; again of long, long roads, dragging themselves out, up hill and down, to the treacherous horizon.

Of morning, noon, and sunset; night, and the rising of an early moon. Of long roads temporarily left behind, and a rough pavement reached; of battering and clattering over it; and looking up, among house-roofs, at a great church-tower; of getting out and eating hastily, and drinking draughts of wine that had no cheering influence; of coming forth afoot, among a host of beggars – blind men with quivering eyelids, led by old women holding candles to their faces; idiot girls; the lame, the epileptic, and the palsied – of passing through the clamour, and looking from his seat at the upturned countenances and outstretched hands, with a hurried dread of recognising some pursuer pressing forward – of galloping away again, upon the long, long road, gathered up, dull and stunned, in his corner, or rising to see where the moon shone faintly on a patch of the same endless road miles away, or looking back to see who followed.

Of never sleeping, but sometimes dozing with unclosed eyes, and springing up with a start, and a reply aloud to an imaginary voice. Of cursing himself for being there, for having fled, for having let her go, for not having confronted and defied him. Of having a deadly quarrel with the whole world, but chiefly with himself. Of blighting everything with his black mood as he was carried on and away.

It was a fevered vision of things past and present all confounded together; of his life and journey blended into one. Of being madly hurried somewhere, whither he must go. Of old scenes starting up among the novelties through which he travelled. Of musing and brooding over what was past and distant, and seeming to take no notice of the actual objects he encountered, but with a wearisome exhausting consciousness of being bewildered by them, and having their images all crowded in his hot brain after they were gone.

A vision of change upon change, and still the same monotony of bells and wheels, and horses' feet, and no rest. Of town and country, postyards, horses, drivers, hill and valley, light and darkness, road and pavement, height and hollow, wet weather and dry, and still the same monotony of bells and wheels, and horses' feet, and no rest. A vision of tending on at last, towards the distant capital, by busier roads, and sweeping round, by old cathedrals, and dashing through small towns and villages, less thinly scattered on the road than formerly, and sitting shrouded in his corner, with his cloak up to his face, as people passing by looked at him.

Of rolling on and on, always postponing thought, and always racked with thinking; of being unable to reckon up the hours he had been upon the road, or to comprehend the points of time and place in his journey. Of being parched and giddy, and half mad. Of pressing on, in spite of all, as if he could not stop, and coming into Paris, where the turbid river held its swift course undisturbed, between two brawling streams of life and motion.

A troubled vision, then, of bridges, quays, interminable streets; of wine-shops, water-carriers, great crowds of people, soldiers, coaches, military drums, arcades. Of the monotony of bells and wheels and horses' feet being at length lost in the universal din and uproar. Of the gradual subsidence of that noise as he passed out in another carriage by a different barrier from that by which he had entered. Of the restoration, as he travelled on towards the sea-coast, of the monotony of bells and wheels, and horses' feet, and no rest.

Of sunset once again, and nightfall. Of long roads again, and dead of night, and feeble lights in windows by the road-side; and still the old monotony of bells and wheels, and horses' feet, and no rest. Of dawn, and daybreak, and the rising of the sun. Of toiling slowly up a hill, and feeling on its top the fresh sea-breeze; and seeing the morning light upon the edges of the distant waves. Of coming down into a harbour when the tide was at its full, and seeing fishing-boats float on, and glad women and children waiting for them. Of nets and seamen's clothes spread out to dry upon the shore; of busy sailors, and their voices high among ships' masts and rigging; of the buoyancy and brightness of the water, and the universal sparkling.

Of receding from the coast, and looking back upon it from the deck when it was a haze upon the water, with here and there a little opening of bright land where the Sun struck. Of the swell, and flash, and murmur of the calm sea. Of another grey line on the ocean, on the vessel's track, fast growing clearer and higher. Of cliffs and buildings, and a windmill, and a church, becoming more and more visible upon it. Of steaming on at last into smooth water, and mooring to a pier whence groups of people looked down, greeting friends on board. Of disembarking, passing among them quickly, shunning every one; and of being at last again in England.

He had thought, in his dream, of going down into a remote country-place he knew, and lying quiet there, while he secretly informed himself of what transpired, and determined how to act. Still in the same stunned condition, he remembered a certain station on the railway,[4] where he would have to branch off to his place of destination, and where there was a quiet Inn. Here, he indistinctly resolved to tarry and rest.

With this purpose he slunk into a railway carriage as quickly as he could, and lying there wrapped in his cloak as if he were asleep, was soon borne far away from the sea, and deep into the inland green. Arrived at his destination he looked out, and surveyed it carefully. He was not mistaken in his impression of the place. It was a retired spot, on the borders of a little wood. Only one house, newly-built or altered for the purpose, stood there, surrounded by its neat garden; the small town that was nearest, was some miles away. Here he alighted then; and going straight into the tavern, unobserved by any one, secured two rooms upstairs communicating with each other, sufficiently retired.

His object was to rest, and recover the command of himself, and the balance of his mind. Imbecile discomfiture and rage – so that, as he walked about his room, he ground his teeth – had complete possession of him. His thoughts, not to be stopped or directed, still wandered where they would, and dragged him after them. He was stupefied, and he was wearied to death.

But, as if there were a curse upon him that he should never rest again, his drowsy senses would not lose their consciousness. He had no more influence with them in this regard, than if they had been another man's. It was not that they forced him to take note of present sounds and objects, but that they would not be diverted from the whole hurried vision of his journey. It was constantly before him all at once. She stood there, with her dark disdainful eyes again upon him; and he was riding on nevertheless, through town and country, light and darkness, wet weather and dry, over road and pavement, hill and valley, height and hollow, jaded and scared by the monotony of bells and wheels, and horses' feet, and no rest.

'What day is this?' he asked of the waiter, who was making preparations for his dinner.

'Day, Sir?'

'Is it Wednesday?'

'Wednesday, Sir? No, Sir. Thursday, Sir.'

'I forgot. How goes the time? My watch is unwound.'

'Wants a few minutes to five o'clock, Sir. Been travelling a long time, Sir, perhaps?'

'Yes.'

'By rail, Sir?'

'Yes.'

'Very confusing, Sir. Not much in the habit of travelling by rail myself, Sir, but gentlemen frequently say so.'

'Do many gentlemen come here?'

'Pretty well, Sir, in general. Nobody here at present. Rather slack just now, Sir. Everything *is* slack, Sir.'

He made no answer; but had risen into a sitting posture on the sofa where he had been lying, and leaned forward with an arm on each knee, staring at the ground. He could not master his own attention for a minute together. It rushed away where it would, but it never, for an instant, lost itself in sleep.

He drank a quantity of wine after dinner, in vain. No such artificial means would bring sleep to his eyes. His thoughts, more incoherent, dragged him more unmercifully after them – as if a wretch, condemned to such expiation, were drawn at the heels of wild horses. No oblivion, and no rest.

How long he sat, drinking and brooding, and being dragged in imagination hither and thither, no one could have told less correctly than he. But he knew that he had been sitting a long time by candle-light, when he started up and listened, in a sudden terror.

For now, indeed, it was no fancy. The ground shook, the house rattled, the fierce impetuous rush was in the air! He felt it come up, and go darting by; and even when he had hurried to the window, and saw what it was, he stood, shrinking from it, as if it were not safe to look.

A curse upon the fiery devil, thundering along so smoothly, tracked through the distant valley by a glare of light and lurid smoke, and gone! He felt as if he had been plucked out of its path, and saved from being torn asunder. It made him shrink and shudder even now, when its faintest hum was hushed, and when the lines of iron road he could trace in the moonlight, running to a point, were as empty and as silent as a desert.

Unable to rest, and irresistibly attracted – or he thought so – to this road, he went out and lounged on the brink of it, marking the way the train had gone, by the yet smoking cinders that were lying in its track. After a lounge of some half hour in the direction by which it had disappeared, he turned and walked the other way – still keeping to the brink of the road – past the inn garden, and a long way down; looking curiously at the bridges, signals, lamps, and wondering when another Devil would come by.

A trembling of the ground, and quick vibration in his ears; a distant shriek; a dull light advancing, quickly changed to two red eyes, and a fierce fire, dropping glowing coals; an irresistible bearing on of a great roaring and dilating mass; a high wind, and a rattle – another come and gone, and he holding to a gate, as if to save himself!

He waited for another, and for another. He walked back to his former point, and back again to that, and still, through the wearisome vision of his journey, looked for these approaching monsters. He loitered about the station, waiting until one should stay to call there; and when one did, and was detached for water, he stood parallel with it, watching its heavy wheels and brazen front, and thinking what a cruel power and might it had. Ugh! To see the great wheels slowly turning, and to think of being run down and crushed!

Disordered with wine and want of rest – that want which nothing, although he was so weary, would appease – these ideas and objects assumed a diseased importance in his thoughts. When he went back to his room, which was not until near midnight, they still haunted him, and he sat listening for the coming of another.

So in his bed, whither he repaired with no hope of sleep. He still lay listening; and when he felt the trembling and vibration, got up and went to the window, to watch (as he could from its position) the dull light changing to the two red eyes, and the fierce fire dropping glowing coals, and the rush of the giant as it fled past, and the track of glare and smoke along the valley. Then he would glance in the direction by which he intended to depart at sunrise, as there was no rest for him there; and would lie down again, to be troubled by the vision of his journey, and the old monotony of bells and wheels and horses' feet, until another came. This lasted all night. So far from resuming the mastery of himself, he seemed, if possible, to lose it more and more, as the night crept on. When the dawn appeared, he was still tormented with thinking, still postponing thought until he should be in a better state; the past, present, and future, all floated confusedly before him, and he had lost all power of looking steadily at any one of them.

'At what time,' he asked the man who had waited on him overnight, now entering with a candle, 'do I leave here, did you say?'

'About a quarter after four, Sir. Express comes through at four, Sir. – It don't stop.'

He passed his hand across his throbbing head, and looked at his watch. Nearly half-past three.

'Nobody going with you, Sir, probably,' observed the man. 'Two gentlemen here, Sir, but they're waiting for the train to London.'

'I thought you said there was nobody here,' said Carker, turning upon him with the ghost of his old smile, when he was angry or suspicious.

'Not then, Sir. Two gentlemen came in the night by the short train that stops here, Sir. Warm water, Sir?'

'No; and take away the candle. There's day enough for me.'

Having thrown himself upon the bed, half-dressed, he was at the window as the man left the room. The cold light of morning had succeeded to night, and there was already, in the sky, the red suffusion of the coming sun. He bathed his head and face with water – there was no cooling influence in it for him – hurriedly put on his clothes, paid what he owed, and went out.

The air struck chill and comfortless, as it breathed upon him. There was a heavy dew; and, hot as he was, it made him shiver. After a glance at the place where he had walked last night, and at the signal-lights burning feebly in the morning, and bereft of their significance, he turned to where the sun was rising, and beheld it, in its glory, as it broke upon the scene.

So awful, so transcendent in its beauty, so divinely solemn. As he cast his faded eyes upon it, where it rose, tranquil and serene, unmoved by all the wrong and wickedness on which its beams had shone since the beginning of the world, who shall say that some weak sense of virtue upon Earth, and its reward in Heaven, did not manifest itself, even to him? If ever he remembered sister or brother with a touch of tenderness and remorse, who shall say it was not then?

He needed some such touch then. Death was on him. He was marked off from the living world and going down into his grave.

He paid the money for his journey to the country-place he had thought of; and was walking to and fro, alone, looking along the lines of iron, across the valley in one direction, and towards a dark bridge near at hand in the other; when, turning in his walk, where it was bounded by one end of the wooden stage on which he paced up and down, he saw the man from whom he had fled, emerging from the door by which he himself had entered there. And their eyes met.

In the quick unsteadiness of the surprise, he staggered, and slipped on to the road below him. But recovering his feet immediately, he stepped back a pace or two upon that road, to interpose some wider space between them, and looked at his pursuer, breathing short and quick.

He heard a shout – another – saw the face change from its vindictive passion to a faint sickness and terror – felt the earth tremble – knew in a moment that the rush was come – uttered a shriek – looked round – saw the red eyes, bleared and dim, in the daylight, close upon him – was beaten down, caught up, and whirled away upon a jagged mill, that spun him round and round, and struck him limb from limb, and licked his stream of life up with its fiery heat, and cast his mutilated fragments in the air.

When the traveller, who had been recognised, recovered from a swoon, he saw them bringing from a distance something covered, that lay heavy and still, upon a board, between four men, and saw that others drove some dogs away that sniffed upon the road, and soaked his blood up, with a train of ashes.

CHAPTER 56

Several People Delighted, and the Game Chicken Disgusted

The Midshipman was all alive. Mr Toots and Susan had arrived at last. Susan had run upstairs like a young woman bereft of her senses, and Mr Toots and the Chicken had gone into the parlour.

'Oh my own pretty darling sweet Miss Floy!' cried the Nipper, running into Florence's room, 'to think that it should come to this and I should find you here my own dear dove with nobody to wait upon you and no home to call your own but never never will I go away again Miss Floy for though I may not gather moss I'm not a rolling stone[1] nor is my heart a stone or else it wouldn't bust as it is busting now oh dear oh dear!'

Pouring out these words, without the faintest indication of a stop, of any sort, Miss Nipper, on her knees beside her mistress, hugged her close.

'Oh love!' cried Susan, 'I know all that's past I know it all my tender pet and I'm a choking give me air!'

'Susan, dear good Susan!' said Florence.

'Oh bless her! I that was her little maid when she was a little child! and is she really, really truly going to be married?' exclaimed Susan, in a burst of pain and pleasure, pride and grief, and Heaven knows how many other conflicting feelings.

'Who told you so?' said Florence.

'Oh gracious me! that innocentest creetur Toots,' returned Susan hysterically. 'I knew he must be right my dear because he took on so.[2] He's the devotedest and innocentest infant! And is my darling,' pursued Susan, with another close embrace and burst of tears, 'really really going to be married!'

The mixture of compassion, pleasure, tenderness, protection, and regret with which the Nipper constantly recurred to this subject, and at every such recurrence, raised her head to look in the young face and kiss it, and then laid her head again upon her mistress's shoulder, caressing her and sobbing, was as womanly and good a thing, in its way, as ever was seen in the world.

'There, there!' said the soothing voice of Florence presently. 'Now you're quite yourself, dear Susan!'

Miss Nipper, sitting down upon the floor, at her mistress's feet, laughing and sobbing, holding her pocket-handkerchief to her eyes with one hand, and patting Diogenes with the other as he licked her face, confessed to being more composed and laughed and cried a little more in proof of it.

'I – I – I never did see such a creetur as that Toots,' said Susan, 'in all my born days never!'

'So kind,' suggested Florence.

'And so comic!' Susan sobbed. 'The way he's been going on inside with me with that disrespectable Chicken on the box!'

'About what, Susan?' inquired Florence timidly.

'Oh about Lieutenant Walters, and Captain Gills, and you my dear Miss Floy, and the silent tomb,' said Susan.

'The silent tomb!' repeated Florence.

'He says,' here Susan burst into a violent hysterical laugh, 'that he'll go down into it now immediately and quite comfortable, but bless your heart my dear Miss Floy he won't, he's a great deal too happy in seeing other people happy for that, he may not be a Solomon,'[3] pursued the Nipper, with her usual volubility, 'nor do I say he is but this I do say a less selfish human creature human nature never knew!'

Miss Nipper being still hysterical, laughed immoderately after making this energetic declaration, and then informed Florence that he was waiting below to see her; which would be a rich repayment for the trouble he had had in his late expedition.

Florence entreated Susan to beg of Mr Toots as a favour that she might have the pleasure of thanking him for his kindness; and Susan, in a few moments, produced that young gentleman, still very much dishevelled in appearance, and stammering exceedingly.

'Miss Dombey,' said Mr Toots. 'To be again permitted to – to – gaze – at least, not to gaze, but – I don't exactly know what I was going to say, but it's of no consequence.'

'I have to thank you so often,' returned Florence, giving him both her hands, with all her innocent gratitude beaming in her face, 'that I have no words left, and don't know how to do it.'

'Miss Dombey,' said Mr Toots, in an awful[4] voice, 'if it was possible that you could, consistently with your angelic nature, Curse me, you would – if I may be allowed to say so – floor me infinitely less, than by these undeserved expressions of kindness. Their effect upon me – is – but,' said Mr Toots, abruptly, 'this is a digression, and's of no consequence at all.'

As there seemed to be no means of replying to this, but by thanking him again, Florence thanked him again.

'I could wish,' said Mr Toots, 'to take this opportunity, Miss Dombey, if I might, of entering into a word of explanation. I should have had the pleasure of – of returning with Susan at an earlier period; but, in the first place, we didn't know the name of the relation to whose house she had gone, and, in the second, as she had left that relation's and gone to another at a distance, I think that scarcely anything short of the sagacity of the Chicken, would have found her out in the time.'

Florence was sure of it.

'This, however,' said Mr Toots, 'is not the point. The company of Susan has been, I assure you, Miss Dombey, a consolation and satisfaction to me, in my state of mind, more easily conceived than described. The journey has been its own reward. That, however, still, is not the point. Miss Dombey, I have before observed that I know I am not what is considered a quick person. I am perfectly aware of that. I don't think anybody could be better acquainted with his own – if it was not too strong an expression, I should say with the thickness of his own head – than myself. But, Miss

Dombey, I do, notwithstanding, perceive the state of – of things – with Lieutenant Walters. Whatever agony that state of things may have caused me (which is of no consequence at all), I am bound to say, that Lieutenant Walters is a person who appears to be worthy of the blessing that has fallen on his – on his brow. May he wear it long, and appreciate it, as a very different, and very unworthy individual, that it is of no consequence to name, would have done! That, however, still, is not the point. Miss Dombey, Captain Gills is a friend of mine; and during the interval that is now elapsing, I believe it would afford Captain Gills pleasure to see me occasionally coming backwards and forwards here. It would afford me pleasure so to come. But I cannot forget that I once committed myself, fatally, at the corner of the Square at Brighton; and if my presence will be, in the least degree, unpleasant to you, I only ask you to name it to me now, and assure you that I shall perfectly understand you. I shall not consider it at all unkind, and shall only be too delighted and happy to be honoured with your confidence.'

'Mr Toots,' returned Florence, 'if you, who are so old and true a friend of mine, were to stay away from this house now, you would make me very unhappy. It can never, never, give me any feeling but pleasure to see you.'

'Miss Dombey,' said Mr Toots, taking out his pocket-handker-chief, 'if I shed a tear, it is a tear of joy. It is of no consequence, and I am very much obliged to you. I may be allowed to remark, after what you have so kindly said, that it is not my intention to neglect my person any longer.'

Florence received this intimation with the prettiest expression of perplexity possible.

'I mean,' said Mr Toots, 'that I shall consider it my duty as a fellow-creature generally, until I am claimed by the silent tomb, to make the best of myself, and to – to have my boots as brightly polished, as – as circumstances will admit of. This is the last time, Miss Dombey, of my intruding any observation of a private and personal nature. I thank you very much indeed. If I am not, in a general way, as sensible as my friends could wish me to be, or as I could wish myself, I really am, upon my word and honour, particularly sensible of what is considerate and kind. I feel,' said Mr Toots, in an impassioned tone, 'as if I could express my feelings, at the present moment, in a most remarkable manner, if – if – I could only get a start.'

Appearing not to get it, after waiting a minute or two to see if it would come, Mr Toots took a hasty leave, and went below to seek the Captain, whom he found in the shop.

'Captain Gills,' said Mr Toots, 'what is now to take place between us, takes place under the sacred seal of confidence. It is the sequel, Captain Gills, of what has taken place between myself and Miss Dombey, upstairs.'

'Alow and aloft, eh, my lad?' murmured the Captain.

'Exactly so, Captain Gills,' said Mr Toots, whose fervour of acquiescence was greatly heightened by his entire ignorance of the Captain's meaning. 'Miss Dombey, I believe, Captain Gills, is to be shortly united to Lieutenant Walters?'

'Why, aye, my lad. We're all shipmets here, – Wal'r and sweetheart will be jined together in the house of bondage, as soon as the askings[5] is over,' whispered Captain Cuttle, in his ear.

'The askings, Captain Gills!' repeated Mr Toots.

'In the church, down yonder,' said the Captain, pointing his thumb over his shoulder.

'Oh! Yes!' returned Mr Toots.

'And then,' said the Captain, in his hoarse whisper, and tapping Mr Toots on the chest with the back of his hand, and falling from him with a look of infinite admiration, 'what follers? That there pretty creetur, as delicately brought up as a foreign bird, goes away upon the roaring main with Wal'r on a woyage to China!'

'Lord, Captain Gills!' said Mr Toots.

'Aye!' nodded the Captain. 'The ship as took him up, when he was wrecked in the hurricane that had drove her clean out of her course, was a China trader, and Wal'r made the woyage and got into favour, aboard and ashore – being as smart and good a lad as ever stepped – and so, the supercargo[6] dying at Canton, he got made (having acted as clerk afore), and now he's supercargo aboard another ship, same owners. And so, you see,' repeated the Captain, thoughtfully, 'the pretty creetur goes away upon the roaring main with Wal'r, on a woyage to China.'

Mr Toots and Captain Cuttle heaved a sigh in concert.

'What then?' said the Captain. 'She loves him true. He loves her true. Them as should have loved and tended of her, treated of her like the beasts as perish.[7] When she, cast out of home, come here to me, and dropped upon them planks, her wownded heart was broke. I know it. I, Ed'ard Cuttle, see it. There's nowt but true, kind, steady love, as can ever piece it up again. If so be I didn't know that, and didn't know as Wal'r was her true love, brother, and she his, I'd have these here blue arms and legs chopped off, afore I'd let her go. But I *do* know it, and what then? Why, then, I say, Heaven go with 'em both, and so it will! Amen!'

'Captain Gills,' said Mr Toots, 'let me have the pleasure of shaking hands. You've a way of saying things, that gives me an agreeable warmth, all up my back. *I* say Amen. You are aware, Captain Gills, that I, too, have adored Miss Dombey.'

'Cheer up!' said the Captain, laying his hand on Mr Toots's shoulder. 'Stand by, boy!'

'It is my intention, Captain Gills,' returned the spirited Mr Toots, '*to* cheer up. Also to stand by, as much as possible. When the silent tomb shall yawn, Captain Gills, I shall be ready for burial; not before. But not being certain, just at present, of my power over myself, what I wish to say to you, and what I shall take it as a particular favour if you will mention to Lieutenant Walters, is as follows.'

'Is as follers,' echoed the Captain. 'Steady!'

'Miss Dombey being so inexpressibly kind,' continued Mr Toots with watery eyes, 'as to say that my presence is the reverse of disagreeable to her, and you and everybody here being no less forbearing and tolerant towards one who – who certainly,' said Mr Toots, with momentary dejection, '*would* appear to have been born by mistake, I shall come backwards and forwards of an evening, during the short time we can all be together. But what I ask is this. If, at any moment, I find that I cannot endure the contemplation of Lieutenant Walters's bliss, and should rush out, I hope, Captain Gills, that you and he will both consider it as my misfortune and not my fault, or the want of inward conflict. That you'll feel convinced I bear no malice to any living creature – least of all to Lieutenant Walters himself – and that you'll casually remark that I have gone out for a walk, or probably to see what o'clock it is by the Royal Exchange. Captain Gills, if you could enter into this arrangement, and could answer for Lieutenant Walters, it would be a relief to my feelings that I should think cheap at the sacrifice of a considerable portion of my property.'

'My lad,' returned the Captain, 'say no more. There ain't a colour you can run up,[8] as won't be made out, and answered to, by Wal'r and self.'

'Captain Gills,' said Mr Toots, 'my mind is greatly relieved. I wish to preserve the good opinion of all here. I – I – mean well, upon my honour, however badly I may show it. You know,' said Mr Toots, 'it's exactly as if Burgess and Co. wished to oblige a customer with a most extraordinary pair of trousers, and *could not* cut out what they had in their minds.'

With this apposite illustration, of which he seemed a little proud, Mr Toots gave Captain Cuttle his blessing and departed.

The honest Captain, with his Heart's Delight in the house, and Susan tending her, was a beaming and a happy man. As the days flew by, he grew more beaming and more happy, every day. After some conferences with Susan (for whose wisdom the Captain had a profound respect, and whose valiant precipitation of herself on Mrs MacStinger he could never forget), he proposed to Florence that the daughter of the elderly lady who usually sat under the blue umbrella in Leadenhall Market, should, for prudential reasons and consider-ations of privacy, be superseded in the temporary discharge of the household duties, by some one who was not unknown to them, and in whom they could safely confide. Susan, being present, then named, in furtherance of a suggestion she had previously offered to the Captain, Mrs Richards. Florence brightened at the name. And Susan, setting off that very afternoon to the Toodle domicile, to sound Mrs Richards, returned in triumph the same evening, accom-panied by the identical rosy-cheeked apple-faced Polly, whose demonstrations, when brought into Florence's presence, were hardly less affectionate than those of Susan Nipper herself.

This piece of generalship accomplished; from which the Captain derived uncommon satisfaction, as he did, indeed, from everything else that was done, whatever it happened to be; Florence had next to prepare Susan for their approaching separation. This was a much more difficult task, as Miss Nipper was of a resolute disposition, and had fully made up her mind that she had come back never to be parted from her old mistress any more.

'As to wages dear Miss Floy,' she said, 'you wouldn't hint and wrong me so as think of naming them, for I've put money by and wouldn't sell my love and duty at a time like this even if the Savings' Banks and me were total strangers or the Banks were broke to pieces, but you've never been without me darling from the time your poor dear ma was took away, and though I'm nothing to be boasted of you're used to me and oh my own dear mistress through so many years don't think of going anywhere without me, for it mustn't and can't be!'

'Dear Susan, I am going on a long, long voyage.'

'Well Miss Floy, and what of that? the more you'll want me. Lengths of voyages ain't an object in my eyes, thank God!' said the impetuous Susan Nipper.

'But Susan, I am going with Walter, and I would go with Walter anywhere – everywhere! Walter is poor, and I am very poor, and I must learn, now, both to help myself, and help him.'

'Dear Miss Floy! cried Susan, bursting out afresh, and shaking her head violently, 'it's nothing new to you to help yourself and others too and be the patientest and truest of noble hearts, but let me talk to Mr Walter Gay and settle it with him, for suffer you to go away across the world alone I cannot, and I won't.'

'Alone, Susan?' returned Florence. 'Alone? and Walter taking me with him!' Ah, what a bright, amazed, enraptured smile was on her face!— He should have seen it. 'I am sure you will not speak to Walter if I ask you not,' she added tenderly; 'and pray don't, dear.'

Susan sobbed, 'Why not, Miss Floy?'

'Because,' said Florence, 'I am going to be his wife, to give him up my whole heart, and to live with him and die with him. He might think, if you said to him what you have said to me, that I am afraid of what is before me, or that you have some cause to be afraid for me. Why, Susan, dear, I love him!'

Miss Nipper was so much affected by the quiet fervour of these words, and the simple, heartfelt, all-pervading earnestness expressed in them, and making the speaker's face more beautiful and pure than ever, that she could only cling to her again, crying Was her little mistress really, really going to be married, and pitying, caressing, and protecting her, as she had done before.

But the Nipper, though susceptible of womanly weaknesses, was almost as capable of putting constraint upon herself as of attacking the redoubtable MacStinger. From that time, she never returned to the subject, but was always cheerful, active, bustling, and hopeful. She did, indeed, inform Mr Toots privately, that she was only 'keeping up' for the time, and that when it was all over, and Miss Dombey was gone, she might be expected to become a spectacle distressful; and Mr Toots did also express that it was his case too, and that they would mingle their tears together; but she never otherwise indulged her private feelings in the presence of Florence or within the precincts of the Midshipman.

Limited and plain as Florence's wardrobe was – what a contrast to that prepared for the last marriage in which she had taken part! – there was a good deal to do in getting it ready, and Susan Nipper worked away at her side, all day, with the concentrated zeal of fifty sempstresses. The wonderful contributions Captain Cuttle would have made to this branch of the outfit, if he had been permitted – as pink parasols, tinted silk stockings, blue shoes, and other articles no less necessary on shipboard – would occupy some space in the recital. He was induced, however, by various fraudulent representations, to limit his contributions to a workbox and dressing-case, of each of which he purchased the very largest specimen that could be got for money. For ten days or a fortnight afterwards, he generally sat, during the greater part of the day, gazing at these boxes; divided between extreme admiration of them, and dejected misgivings that they were not gorgeous enough, and frequently diving out into the street to purchase some wild article that he deemed necessary to their completeness. But his master-stroke was, the bearing of them both off, suddenly, one morning, and getting the two words FLORENCE GAY engraved upon a brass heart inlaid over the lid of each. After this, he smoked four pipes successively in the little parlour by himself, and was discovered chuckling, at the expiration of as many hours.

Walter was busy and away all day, but came there every morning early to see Florence, and always passed the evening with her. Florence never left her high rooms but to steal downstairs to wait for him when it was his time to come, or, sheltered by his proud, encircling arm, to bear him company to the door again, and sometimes peep into the street. In the twilight they were always together. Oh blessed time! Oh wandering heart at rest! Oh deep, exhaustless, mighty well of love, in which so much was sunk!

The cruel mark was on her bosom yet. It rose against her father with the breath she drew, it lay between her and her lover when he pressed her to his heart. But she forgot it. In the beating of that heart for her, and in the beating of her own for him, all harsher music was unheard, all stern unloving hearts forgotten. Fragile and delicate she was, but with a might of love within her that could, and did, create a world to fly to, and to rest in, out of his one image.

How often did the great house, and the old days, come before her in the twilight time, when she was sheltered by the arm, so proud, so fond, and, creeping closer to him, shrunk within it at the recollection! How often, from remembering the night when she went down to that room and met the never-to-be-forgotten look, did she raise her eyes to those that watched her with such loving earnestness, and weep with happiness in such a refuge! The more she clung to it, the more the dear dead child was in her thoughts: but as if the last time she had seen her father, had been when he was sleeping and she kissed his face, she always left him so, and never, in her fancy, passed that hour.

'Walter, dear,' said Florence, one evening, when it was almost dark. 'Do you know what I have been thinking to-day?'

'Thinking how the time is flying on, and how soon we shall be upon the sea, sweet Florence?'

'I don't mean that, Walter, though I think of that too. I have been thinking what a charge I am to you.'

'A precious, sacred charge, dear heart! Why I think that sometimes.'

'You are laughing, Walter. I know that's much more in your thoughts than mine. But I mean a cost.'

'A cost, my own?'

'In money, dear. All these preparations that Susan and I are so busy with – I have been able to purchase very little for myself. You were poor before. But how much poorer I shall make you, Walter!'

'And how much richer, Florence'

Florence laughed, and shook her head.

'Besides,' said Walter, 'long ago – before I went to sea – I had a little purse presented to me, dearest, which had money in it.'

'Ah!' returned Florence, laughing sorrowfully, 'very little! Very little, Walter! But, you must not think,' and here she laid her light hand on his shoulder, and looked into his face, 'that I regret to be this burden on you. No, dear love, I am glad of it. I am happy in it. I wouldn't have it otherwise for all the world!'

'Nor I, indeed, dear Florence.'

'Aye! but, Walter, you can never feel it as I do. I am so proud of you! It makes my heart swell with such delight to know that those who speak of you must say you married a poor disowned girl, who had taken shelter here; who had no other home, no other friends; who had nothing – nothing! Oh, Walter, if I could have brought you millions, I never could have been so happy for your sake, as I am!'

'And you, dear Florence? are you nothing?' he returned.

'No, nothing, Walter. Nothing but your wife.' The light hand stole about his neck, and the voice came nearer – nearer. 'I am nothing any more, that is not you. I have no earthly hope any more, that is not you. I have nothing dear to me any more that is not you.'

Oh! well might Mr Toots leave the little company that evening, and twice go out to correct his watch by the Royal Exchange, and once to keep an appointment with a banker which he suddenly remembered, and once to take a little turn to Aldgate Pump and back!

But before he went up on these expeditions, or indeed before he came, and before lights were brought, Walter said:

'Florence, love, the lading of our ship is nearly finished, and probably on the very day of our marriage she will drop down the river. Shall we go away that morning, and stay in Kent until we go on board at Gravesend within a week?'

'If you please, Walter. I shall be happy anywhere. But—'

'Yes, my life?'

'You know,' said Florence, 'that we shall have no marriage party, and that nobody will distinguish us by our dress from other people. As we leave the same day, will you – will you take me somewhere that morning, Walter – early – before we go to church?'

Walter seemed to understand her, as so true a lover so truly loved should, and confirmed his ready promise with a kiss – with more than one perhaps, or two or three, or five or six; and in the grave, peaceful evening, Florence was very happy.

Then into the quiet room came Susan Nipper and the candles: shortly afterwards, the tea, the Captain, and the excursive Mr Toots, who, as above mentioned, was frequently on the move afterwards, and passed but a restless evening. This, however, was not his habit: for he generally got on very well, by dint of playing at cribbage with the Captain under the advice and guidance of Miss Nipper, and distracting his mind with the calculations incidental to the game; which he found to be a very effectual means of utterly confounding himself.

The Captain's visage on these occasions presented one of the finest examples of combination and succession of expression ever observed. His instinctive delicacy and his chivalrous feeling towards Florence, taught him that it was not a time for any boisterous jollity, or violent display of satisfaction. Certain floating reminiscences of Lovely Peg, on the other hand, were constantly struggling for a vent, and urging the Captain to commit himself by some irreparable demonstration. Anon, his admiration of Florence and Walter – well-matched, truly, and full of grace and interest in their youth, and love, and good looks, as they sat apart – would take such complete possession of him, that he would lay down his cards, and beam upon them, dabbing his head all over with his pocket-handkerchief; until warned, perhaps, by the sudden rushing forth of Mr Toots, that he had unconsciously been very instrumental, indeed, in making that gentleman miserable. This reflection would make the Captain profoundly melancholy, until the return of Mr Toots; when he would fall to his cards again, with many side winks and nods, and polite waves of his hook at Miss Nipper, importing that he wasn't going to do so any more. The state that ensued on this, was, perhaps, his best; for then, endeavouring to discharge all expression from his face, he would sit, staring round the room, with all these expressions conveyed into it at once, and each wrestling with the other. Delighted admiration of Florence and Walter always overthrew the rest, and remained victorious and undisguised, unless Mr Toots made another rush into the air, and then the Captain would sit, like a remorseful culprit, until he came back again, occasionally calling upon himself, in a low reproachful voice, to 'Stand by!' or growling some remonstrance to 'Ed'ard Cuttle, my lad,' on the want of caution observable in his behaviour.

One of Mr Toots's hardest trials, however, was of his own seeking. On the approach of the Sunday which was to witness the last of those askings in church of which the Captain had spoken, Mr Toots thus stated his feelings to Susan Nipper.

'Susan,' said Mr Toots, 'I am drawn towards the building. The words which cut me off from Miss Dombey for ever, will strike upon my ears like a knell you know, but upon my word and honour, I feel that I must hear them. Therefore,' said Mr Toots, 'will you accompany me to-morrow, to the sacred edifice?'

Miss Nipper expressed her readiness to do so, if that would be any satisfaction to Mr Toots, but besought him to abandon his idea of going.

'Susan,' returned Mr Toots, with much solemnity, 'before my whiskers began to be observed by anybody but myself, I adored Miss Dombey. While yet a victim to the thraldom of Blimber, I adored Miss Dombey. When I could no longer be kept out of my property, in a legal point of view, and – and accordingly came into it – I adored Miss Dombey. The banns which consign her to Lieutenant Walters, and me to – to Gloom, you know,' said Mr Toots, after hesitating for a strong expression, 'may be dreadful, *will* be dreadful; but I feel that I should wish to hear them spoken. I feel that I should wish to know that the ground was certainly cut from under me, and that I hadn't a hope to cherish, or a – or a leg, in short, to – to go upon.'

Susan Nipper could only commiserate Mr Toots's unfortunate condition, and agree, under these circumstances, to accompany him; which she did next morning.

The church Walter had chosen for the purpose, was a mouldy old church in a yard, hemmed in by a labyrinth of back streets and courts, with a little burying-ground round it, and itself buried in a kind of vault, formed by the neighbouring houses, and paved with echoing stones. It was a great dim, shabby pile, with high old oaken pews, among which about a score of people lost themselves every Sunday; while the clergyman's voice drowsily resounded through the emptiness, and the organ rumbled and rolled as if the church had got the colic, for want of a congregation to keep the wind and damp out. But so far was this city church from languishing for the company of other churches, that spires were clustered round it, as the masts of shipping cluster on the river. It would have been hard to count them from its steeple-top, they were so many. In almost every yard and blind-place near, there was a church. The confusion of bells when Susan and Mr Toots betook themselves towards it on the Sunday morning, was deafening. There were twenty churches close together, clamouring for people to come in.

The two stray sheep in question were penned by a beadle in a commodious pew, and, being early, sat for some time counting the congregation, listening to the disappointed bell high up in the tower, or looking at a shabby little old man in the porch behind the screen, who was ringing the same, like the Bull in Cock Robin,[9] with his foot in a stirrup. Mr Toots, after a lengthened survey of the large books on the reading-desk whispered Miss Nipper that he wondered where the banns were kept, but that young lady merely shook her head and frowned; repelling for the time all approaches of a temporal nature.

Mr Toots, however, appearing unable to keep his thoughts from the banns, was evidently looking out for them during the whole preliminary portion of the service. As the time for reading them approached, the poor young gentleman manifested great anxiety and trepidation, which was not diminished by the unexpected apparition of the Captain in the front row of the gallery. When the clerk handed up a list to the clergyman, Mr Toots, being then seated, held on by the seat of the pew; but when the names of Walter Gay and Florence Dombey were read aloud as being in the third and last stage of that association, he was so entirely conquered by his feelings as to rush from the church without his hat, followed by the beadle and pew-opener, and two gentlemen of the medical profession, who happened to be present; of whom the first-named presently returned for that article, informing Miss Nipper in a whisper that she was not to make herself uneasy about the gentleman, as the gentleman said his indisposition was of no consequence.

Miss Nipper, feeling that the eyes of that integral portion of

Europe which lost itself weekly among the high-backed pews, were upon her, would have been sufficiently embarrassed by this incident, though it had terminated here; the more so, as the Captain in the front row of the gallery, was in a state of unmitigated consciousness which could hardly fail to express to the congregation that he had some mysterious connexion with it. But the extreme restlessness of Mr Toots painfully increased and protracted the delicacy of her situation. That young gentleman, incapable, in his state of mind, of remaining alone in the churchyard, a prey to solitary meditation, and also desirous, no doubt, of testifying his respect for the offices he had in some measure interrupted, suddenly returned – not coming back to the pew, but stationing himself on a free seat in the aisle, between two elderly females who were in the habit of receiving their portion of a weekly dole of bread then set forth on a shelf in the porch. In this conjunction Mr Toots remained, greatly disturbing the congregation, who felt it impossible to avoid looking at him, until his feelings overcame him again, when he departed silently and suddenly. Not venturing to trust himself in the church any more, and yet wishing to have some social participation in what was going on there, Mr Toots was, after this, seen from time to time, looking in, with a lorn[10] aspect, at one or other of the windows; and as there were several windows accessible to him from without, and as his restlessness was very great, it not only became difficult to conceive at which window he would appear next, but likewise became necessary, as it were, for the whole congregation to speculate upon the chances of the different windows, during the comparative leisure afforded them by the sermon. Mr Toots's movements in the churchyard were so eccentric, that he seemed generally to defeat all calculation, and to appear, like the conjurer's figure, where he was least expected; and the effect of these mysterious presentations was much increased by its being difficult to him to see in, and easy to everybody else to see out: which occasioned his remaining, every time, longer than might have been expected, with his face close to the glass, until he all at once became aware that all eyes were upon him, and vanished.

These proceedings on the part of Mr Toots, and the strong individual consciousness of them that was exhibited by the Captain, rendered Miss Nipper's position so responsible a one that she was mightily relieved by the conclusion of the service; and was hardly so affable to Mr Toots as usual, when he informed her and the Captain, on the way back, that now he was sure he had no hope, you know, he felt more comfortable – at least not exactly more comfortable, but more comfortably and completely miserable.

Swiftly now, indeed, the time flew by until it was the evening before the day appointed for the marriage. They were all assembled in the upper room at the Midshipman's, and had no fear of interruption; for there were no lodgers in the house now, and the Midshipman had it all to himself. They were grave and quiet in the prospect of to-morrow, but moderately cheerful too. Florence, with Walter close beside her, was finishing a little piece of work intended as a parting gift to the Captain. The Captain was playing cribbage with Mr Toots. Mr Toots was taking counsel as to his hand, of Susan Nipper. Miss Nipper was giving it, with all due secrecy and circumspection. Diogenes was listening, and occasionally breaking out into a gruff half-smothered fragment of a bark, of which he afterwards seemed half-ashamed, as if he doubted having any reason for it.

'Steady, steady!' said the Captain to Diogenes, 'what's amiss with you? You don't seem easy in your mind to-night, my boy!'

Diogenes wagged his tail, but pricked up his ears immediately afterwards, and gave utterance to another fragment of a bark; for which he apologised to the Captain, by again wagging his tail.

'It's my opinion, Di,' said the Captain, looking thoughtfully at his cards, and stroking his chin with his hook, 'as you have your doubts of Mrs Richards; but if you're the animal I take you to be, you'll think better o' that; for her looks is her commission. Now, Brother:' to Mr Toots: 'if so be as you're ready, heave ahead.'

The Captain spoke with all composure and attention to the game, but suddenly his cards dropped out of his hand, his mouth and eyes opened wide, his legs drew themselves up and stuck out in front of his chair, and he sat staring at the door with blank amazement. Looking round upon the company, and seeing that none of them observed him or the cause of his astonishment, the Captain recovered himself with a great gasp, struck the table a tremendous blow, cried in a stentorian roar, 'Sol Gills ahoy!' and tumbled into the arms of a weather-beaten pea-coat that had come with Polly into the room.

In another moment, Walter was in the arms of the weather-beaten pea-coat. In another moment, Florence was in the arms of the weather-beaten pea-coat. In another moment, Captain Cuttle had embraced Mrs Richards, and Miss Nipper, and was violently shaking hands with Mr Toots, exclaiming, as he waved his hook above his head, 'Hooroar, my lad, hooroar!' To which Mr Toots,

An arrival

wholly at a loss to account for these proceedings, replied with great politeness, 'Certainly, Captain Gills, whatever you think proper!'

The weather-beaten pea-coat, and a no less weather-beaten cap and comforter belonging to it, turned from the Captain and from Florence back to Walter and sounds came from the weather-beaten pea-coat, cap, and comforter, as of an old man sobbing underneath them; while the shaggy sleeves clasped Walter tight. During this pause, there was an universal silence, and the Captain polished his nose with great diligence. But when the pea-coat, cap, and comforter lifted themselves up again, Florence gently moved towards them; and she and Walter taking them off, disclosed the old Instrument-maker, a little thinner and more careworn than of old, in his old Welsh wig and his old coffee-coloured coat and basket buttons, with his old infallible chronometer ticking away in his pocket.

'Chock full o' science,' said the radiant Captain, 'as ever he was! Sol Gills, Sol Gills, what have you been up to, for this many a long day, my ould boy?'

'I'm half blind, Ned,' said the old man, 'and almost deaf and dumb with joy.'

'His wery woice,' said the Captain, looking round with an exultation to which even his face could hardly render justice – 'his wery woice as chock full o' science as ever it was! Sol Gills, lay to, my lad, upon your own wines and fig-trees,[11] like a taut ould patriark as you are, and overhaul them there adwentures o' yourn, in your own formilior woice. 'Tis *the* woice,' said the Captain, impressively, and announcing a quotation with his hook, 'of the sluggard,[12] I heerd him complain, you have woke me too soon, I must slumber again. Scatter his ene-mies, and make 'em fall!'

The Captain sat down with the air of a man who had happily expressed the feeling of everybody present, and immediately rose again to present Mr Toots, who was much disconcerted by the arrival of anybody, appearing to prefer a claim to the name of Gills.

'Although,' stammered Mr Toots, 'I had not the pleasure of your acquaintance, Sir, before you were – you were –'

'Lost to sight, to memory dear,' suggested the Captain, in a low voice.

'Exactly so, Captain Gills!' assented Mr Toots. 'Although I had not the pleasure of your acquaintance, Mr – Mr Sols,' said Toots, hitting on that name in the inspiration of a bright idea, 'before that happened, I have the greatest pleasure, I assure you, in – you know, in knowing you. I hope,' said Mr Toots, 'that you're as well as can be expected.'

With these courteous words, Mr Toots sat down blushing and chuckling.

The old Instrument-maker, seated in a corner between Walter and Florence, and nodding at Polly, who was looking on, all smiles and delight, answered the Captain thus:

'Ned Cuttle, my dear boy, although I have heard something of the changes of events here, from my pleasant friend there – what a pleasant face she has to be sure, to welcome a wanderer home!' said the old man, breaking off, and rubbing his hands in his old dreamy way.

'Hear him!' cried the Captain gravely. ''Tis woman as seduces[13] all mankind. For which,' aside to Mr Toots, 'you'll overhaul your Adam and Eve, brother.'

'I shall make a point of doing so, Captain Gills,' said Mr Toots.

'Although I have heard something of the changes of events, from her,' resumed the Instrument-maker, taking his old spectacles from his pocket, and putting them on his forehead in his old manner, 'they are so great and unexpected, and I am so overpowered by the sight of my dear boy, and by the,' – glancing at the downcast eyes of Florence, and not attempting to finish the sentence – 'that I – I can't say much to-night. But my dear Ned Cuttle, why didn't you write?'

The astonishment depicted in the Captain's features positively frightened Mr Toots, whose eyes were quite fixed by it, so that he could not withdraw them from his face.

'Write!' echoed the Captain. 'Write, Sol Gills?'

'Aye,' said the old man, 'either to Barbados, or Jamaica, or Demerara. That was what I asked.'

'What you asked, Sol Gills?' repeated the Captain.

'Aye,' said the old man. 'Don't you know, Ned? Sure you have not forgotten? Every time I wrote to you.'

The Captain took off his glazed hat, hung it on his hook, and smoothing his hair from behind with his hand, sat gazing at the group around him: a perfect image of wondering resignation.

'You don't appear to understand me, Ned!' observed old Sol.

'Sol Gills,' returned the Captain, after staring at him and the rest for a long time, without speaking, 'I'm gone about and adrift. Pay out a word or two respecting them adwenturs, will you! Can't I bring up, nohows? Nohows?' said the Captain, ruminating, and staring all round.

'You know, Ned,' said Sol Gills, 'why I left here. Did you open my packet, Ned?'

'Why, aye, aye,' said the Captain. 'To be sure, I opened the packet.'

'And read it?' said the old man.

'And read it,' answered the Captain, eyeing him attentively and proceeding to quote it from memory. '"My dear Ned Cuttle, when I left home for the West Indies in forlorn search of intelligence of my dear—" There he sits! There's Wal'r!' said the Captain, as if he were relieved by getting hold of anything that was real and indisputable.

'Well, Ned. Now attend a moment!' said the old man. 'When I wrote first – that was from Barbados – I said that though you would receive that letter long before the year was out, I should be glad if you would open the packet, as it explained the reason of my going away. Very good, Ned. When I wrote the second, third, and perhaps the fourth times – that was from Jamaica – I said I was in just the same state, couldn't rest, and couldn't come away from that part of the world, without knowing that my boy was lost or saved. When I wrote next – that, I think, was from Demerara, wasn't it?'

'That he thinks was from Demerara, warn't it!' said the Captain, looking hopelessly round.

'—I said,' proceeded old Sol, 'that still there was no certain information got yet. That I found many captains and others, in that part of the world, who had known me for years and who assisted me with a passage here and there, and for whom I was able, now and then, to do a little in return, in my own craft. That every one was sorry for me, and seemed to take a sort of interest in my wanderings; and that I began to think it would be my fate to cruise about in search of tidings of my boy until I died.'

'Began to think as how he was a scientific flying Dutchman!' said the Captain, as before, and with great seriousness.

'But when the news come one day, Ned, – that was to Barbados, after I got back there, – that a China trader home'ard bound had been spoke, that had my boy aboard, then, Ned, I took passage in the next ship and came home; arrived at home to-night to find it true, thank God!' said the old man, devoutly.

The Captain, after bowing his head with great reverence, stared all round the circle, beginning with Mr Toots, and ending with the Instrument-maker; then gravely said:

'Sol Gills! The observation as I'm a-going to make is calc'lated to blow every stitch of sail as you can carry, clean out of the bolt-ropes,[14] and bring you on your beam ends with a lurch. Not one of them letters was ever delivered to Ed'ard Cuttle. Not one o' them letters,' repeated the Captain, to make his declaration the more solemn and impressive, 'was ever delivered unto Ed'ard Cuttle, Mariner, of England, as lives at home at ease, and doth improve each shining hour!'[15]

'And posted by my own hand! And directed by my own hand, Number nine Brig Place!' exclaimed old Sol.

The colour all went out of the Captain's face, and all came back again in a glow.

'What do you mean, Sol Gills, my friend, by Number nine Brig Place?' inquired the Captain.

'Mean? Your lodgings, Ned,' returned the old man. 'Mrs What's-her-name! I shall forget my own name next, but I am behind the present time – I always was, you recollect – and very much confused. Mrs—'

'Sol Gills!' said the Captain, as if he were putting the most improbable case in the world, 'it ain't the name of MacStinger as you're a trying to remember?'

'Of course it is!' exclaimed the Instrument-maker. 'To be sure Ned. Mrs MacStinger!'

Captain Cuttle, whose eyes were now as wide open as they could be, and the knobs upon whose face were perfectly luminous, gave a long shrill whistle of a most melancholy sound, and stood gazing at everybody in a state of speechlessness.

'Overhaul that there again, Sol Gills, will you be so kind?' he said at last.

'All these letters,' returned Uncle Sol, beating time with the forefinger of his right hand upon the palm of his left, with a steadiness and distinctness that might have done honour, even to the infallible chronometer in his pocket, 'I posted with my own hand, and directed with my own hand, to Captain Cuttle, at Mrs MacStinger's, Number nine Brig Place.'

The Captain took his glazed hat off his hook, looked into it, put it on, and sat down.

'Why, friends all,' said the Captain, staring round in the last state of discomfiture, 'I cut and run from there!'

'And no one knew where you were gone, Captain Cuttle?' cried Walter hastily.

'Bless your heart, Wal'r,' said the Captain, shaking his head, 'she'd never have allowed o' my coming to take charge o' this here property. Nothing could be done but cut and run. Lord love you,

Wal'r!' said the Captain, 'you've only seen her in a calm! But see her when her angry passions rise[16] – and make a note on!'

'*I'd* give it her!' remarked the Nipper, softly.

'Would you, do you think, my dear?' returned the Captain with feeble admiration. 'Well, my dear, it does you credit. But there ain't no wild animal I wouldn't sooner face myself. I only got my chest away by means of a friend as nobody's a match for. It was no good sending any letter there. *She* wouldn't take in any letter, bless you,' said the Captain, 'under them circumstances! Why, you could hardly make it worth a man's while to be the postman!'

'Then it's pretty clear, Captain Cuttle, that all of us, and you and Uncle Sol especially,' said Walter, 'may thank Mrs MacStinger for no small anxiety.'

The general obligation in this wise to the determined relict of the late Mr MacStinger, was so apparent, that the Captain did not contest the point; but being in some measure ashamed of his position, though nobody dwelt upon the subject, and Walter especially avoided it, remembering the last conversation he and the Captain had held together respecting it, he remained under a cloud for nearly five minutes – an extraordinary period for him – when that sun, his face, broke out once more, shining on all beholders with extraordinary brilliancy; and he fell into a fit of shaking hands with everybody over and over again.

At an early hour, but not before Uncle Sol and Walter had questioned each other at some length about their voyages and dangers, they all, except Walter, vacated Florence's room, and went down to the parlour. Here they were soon afterwards joined by Walter, who told them Florence was a little sorrowful and heavy-hearted, and had gone to bed. Though they could not have disturbed her with their voices down there, they all spoke in a whisper after this: and each, in his different way, felt very lovingly and gently towards Walter's fair young bride: and a long explanation there was of everything relating to her, for the satisfaction of Uncle Sol; and very sensible Mr Toots was of the delicacy with which Walter made his name and services important, and his presence necessary to their little council.

'Mr Toots,' said Walter, on parting with him at the house door, 'we shall see each other to-morrow morning?'

'Lieutenant Walters,' returned Mr Toots, grasping his hand fervently, 'I shall certainly be present.'

'This is the last night we shall meet for a long time – the last night we may ever meet,' said Walter. 'Such a noble heart as yours, must feel, I think, when another heart is bound to it. I hope you know that I am very grateful to you?'

'Walters,' replied Mr Toots, quite touched, 'I should be glad to feel that you had reason to be so.'

'Florence,' said Walter, 'on this last night of her bearing her own name, has made me promise – it was only just now, when you left us together – that I would tell you – with her dear love—'

Mr Toots laid his hand upon the doorpost, and his eyes upon his hand.

'—with her dear love,' said Walter, 'that she can never have a friend whom she will value above you. That the recollection of your true consideration for her always, can never be forgotten by her. That she remembers you in her prayers to-night, and hopes that you will think of her when she is far away. Shall I say anything for you?'

'Say, Walters,' replied Mr Toots indistinctly, 'that I shall think of her every day, but never without feeling happy to know that she is married to the man she loves, and who loves her. Say, if you please, that I am sure her husband deserves her – even her! – and that I am glad of her choice.'

Mr Toots got more distinct as he came to these last words, and raising his eyes from the doorpost, said them stoutly. He then shook Walter's hand again with a fervour that Walter was not slow to return, and started homeward.

Mr Toots was accompanied by the Chicken, whom he had of late brought with him every evening, and left in the shop, with an idea that unforeseen circumstances might arise from without, in which the prowess of that distinguished character would be of service to the Midshipman. The Chicken did not appear to be in a particularly good humour on this occasion. Either the gas-lamps were treacherous, or he cocked his eye in a hideous manner, and likewise distorted his nose, when Mr Toots, crossing the road, looked back over his shoulder at the room where Florence slept. On the road home, he was more demonstrative of aggressive intentions against the other foot-passengers, than comported with a professor of the peaceful art of self-defence. Arrived at home, instead of leaving Mr Toots in his apartments when he had escorted him thither, he remained before him weighing his white hat in both hands by the brim, and twitching his head and nose (both of which had been many times broken, and but indifferently repaired), with an air of decided disrespect.

His patron being much engaged with his own thoughts, did not observe this for some time, nor indeed until the Chicken, determined not to be overlooked, had made divers clicking sounds with his tongue and teeth, to attract attention.

'Now, master,' said the Chicken, doggedly, when he, at length, caught Mr Toots's eye, 'I want to know whether this here gammon[17] is to finish it, or whether you're a going in to win?'

'Chicken,' returned Mr Toots, 'explain yourself.'

'Why then, here's all about it, Master,' said the Chicken. 'I ain't a cove to chuck a word away. Here's wot it is. Are any on 'em to be doubled up?'

When the Chicken put this question he dropped his hat, made a dodge and a feint with his left hand, hit a supposed enemy a violent blow with his right, shook his head smartly, and recovered himself.

'Come, Master,' said the Chicken. 'Is it to be gammon or pluck?[18] Which?'

'Chicken,' returned Mr Toots, 'your expressions are coarse, and your meaning is obscure.'

'Why, then, I tell you what, Master,' said the Chicken. 'This is where it is. It's mean.'

'What is mean, Chicken?' asked Mr Toots.

'*It* is,' said the Chicken, with a frightful corrugation of his broken nose. 'There! Now, Master! Wot! When you could go and blow on[19] this here match to the stiff 'un;' by which depreciatory appellation it has been since supposed that the Game One intended to signify Mr Dombey; 'and when you could knock the winner and all the kit of 'em dead out o' wind and time, are you going to give in? To *give in?*' said the Chicken, with contemptuous emphasis. 'Wy, it's mean!'

'Chicken,' said Mr Toots, severely, 'you're a perfect Vulture! Your sentiments are atrocious.'

'My sentiments is Game and Fancy, Master,' returned the Chicken. 'That's wot my sentiments is. I can't abear a meanness. I'm afore the public, I'm to be heerd on at the bar of the Little Helephant, and no Gov'ner o' mine mustn't go and do what's mean. Wy, it's mean,' said the Chicken, with increased expression. 'That's where it is. It's mean.'

'Chicken,' said Mr Toots, 'you disgust me.'

'Master,' returned the Chicken, putting on his hat, 'there's a pair on us, then. Come! Here's a offer! You've spoke to me more than once't or twice't about the public line. Never mind! Give me a fi'typunnote to-morrow, and let me go.'

'Chicken,' returned Mr Toots, 'after the odious sentiments you have expressed, I shall be glad to part on such terms.'

'Done then,' said the Chicken. 'It's a bargain. This here conduct of yourn won't suit *my* book, Master. Wy, it's mean,' said the Chicken; who seemed equally unable to get beyond that point, and to stop short of it. 'That's where it is; it's mean!'

So Mr Toots and the Chicken agreed to part on this incompatibility of moral perception; and Mr Toots lying down to sleep, dreamed happily of Florence, who had thought of him as her friend upon the last night of her maiden life, and who had sent him her dear love.

CHAPTER 57

Another Wedding

Mr Sownds the beadle, and Mrs Miff the pew-opener, are early at their posts in the fine church where Mr Dombey was married. A yellow-faced old gentleman from India, is going to take unto himself a young wife this morning, and six carriages full of company are expected, and Mrs Miff has been informed that the yellow-faced old gentleman could pave the road to church with diamonds and hardly miss them. The nuptial benediction is to be a superior one, proceeding from a very reverend, a dean, and the lady is to be given away, as an extraordinary present, by somebody who comes express from the Horse Guards.

Mrs Miff is more intolerant of common people this morning, than she generally is; and she has always strong opinions on that subject, for it is associated with free sittings.[1] Mrs Miff is not a student of political economy (she thinks the science is connected with dissenters; 'Baptists or Wesleyans, or some o' them,' she says), but she can never understand what business your common folks have to be married.[2] 'Drat 'em,' says Mrs Miff, 'you read the same things over 'em, and instead of sovereigns get sixpences!'

Mr Sownds the beadle is more liberal than Mrs Miff – but then he is not a pew-opener. 'It must be done, ma'am,' he says. 'We must marry 'em. We must have our national schools[3] to walk at the head of, and we must have our standing armies. We must marry 'em, ma'am,' says Mr Sownds, 'and keep the country going.'

Mr Sownds is sitting on the steps and Mrs Miff is dusting in the church, when a young couple, plainly dressed, come in. The mortified bonnet of Mrs Miff is sharply turned towards them, for she espies in this early visit indications of a runaway match. But they don't want to be married – 'Only,' says the gentleman, 'to walk round the church.' And as he slips a genteel compliment into the palm of Mrs Miff, her vinegary face relaxes, and her mortified bonnet and her spare dry figure dip and crackle.

Mrs Miff resumes her dusting and plumps up her cushions – for the yellow-faced old gentleman is reported to have tender knees – but keeps her glazed, pew-opening eye on the young couple who are walking round the church. 'Ahem,' coughs Mrs Miff, whose cough is drier than the hay in any hassock in her charge, 'you'll come to us one of these mornings, my dears, unless I'm much mistaken!'

They are looking at a tablet on the wall, erected to the memory of some one dead. They are a long way off from Mrs Miff, but Mrs Miff can see with half an eye how she is leaning on his arm, and how his head is bent down over her. 'Well, well,' says Mrs Miff, 'you might do worse. For you're a tidy pair!'

There is nothing personal in Mrs Miff's remark. She merely speaks of stock-in-trade. She is hardly more curious in couples than in coffins. She is such a spare, straight, dry old lady – such a pew of a woman – that you should find as many individual sympathies in a chip. Mr Sownds, now, who is fleshy, and has scarlet in his coat, is of a different temperament. He says, as they stand upon the steps watching the young couple away, that she has a pretty figure, hasn't she, and as well as he could see (for she held her head down coming out), an uncommon pretty face. 'Altogether, Mrs Miff,' says Mr Sownds with a relish, 'she is what you may call a rosebud.'

Mrs Miff assents with a spare nod of her mortified bonnet; but approves of this so little, that she inwardly resolves she wouldn't be the wife of Mr Sownds for any money he could give her, Beadle as he is.

And what are the young couple saying as they leave the church, and go out at the gate?

'Dear Walter, thank you! I can go away, now, happy.'

'And when we come back, Florence, we will come and see his grave again.'

Florence lifts her eyes, so bright with tears, to his kind face; and clasps her disengaged hand on that other modest little hand which clasps his arm.

'It is very early, Walter, and the streets are almost empty yet. Let us walk.'

'But you will be so tired, my love.'

'Oh no! I was very tired the first time that we ever walked together, but I shall not be so to-day.'

And thus – not much changed – she, as innocent and earnest-hearted – he, as frank, as hopeful, and more proud of her – Florence and Walter, on their bridal morning, walk through the streets together.

Not even in that childish walk of long ago, were they so far removed from all the world about them as to-day. The childish feet of long ago, did not tread such enchanted ground as theirs do now. The confidence and love of children may be given many times, and will spring up in many places; but the woman's heart of Florence, with its undivided treasure, can be yielded only once, and under slight or change, can only droop and die.

They take the streets that are the quietest, and do not go near that in which her old home stands. It is a fair, warm summer morning, and the sun shines on them, as they walk towards the darkening mist that overspreads the City. Riches are uncovering in shops; jewels, gold, and silver flash in the goldsmith's sunny windows; and great houses cast a stately shade upon them as they pass. But through the light, and through the shade, they go on lovingly together, lost to everything around; thinking of no other riches, and no prouder home, than they have now in one another.

Gradually they come into the darker, narrower streets, where the sun, now yellow, and now red, is seen through the mist, only at street corners, and in small open spaces where there is a tree, or one of the innumerable churches, or a paved way and a flight of steps, or a curious little patch of garden, or a burying-ground, where the few tombs and tombstones are almost black. Lovingly and trustfully, through all the narrow yards and alleys and the shady streets, Florence goes, clinging to his arm, to be his wife.

Her heart beats quicker now, for Walter tells her that their church is very near. They pass a few great stacks of warehouses, with waggons at the doors, and busy carmen[4] stopping up the way – but Florence does not see or hear them – and then the air is quiet, and the day is darkened, and she is trembling in a church which has a strange smell like a cellar.

The shabby little old man, ringer of the disappointed bell, is standing in the porch, and has put his hat in the font – for he is quite at home there, being sexton. He ushers them into an old brown, panelled, dusty vestry, like a corner-cupboard with the shelves taken out; where the wormy registers diffuse a smell like faded snuff, which has set the tearful Nipper sneezing.

Youthful, and how beautiful, the young bride looks, in this old dusty place, with no kindred object near her but her husband. There is a dusty old clerk, who keeps a sort of evaporated news shop underneath an archway opposite, behind a perfect fortification of posts. There is a dusty old pew-opener who only keeps herself, and finds that quite enough to do. There is a dusty old beadle (these are Mr Toots's beadle and pew-opener of last Sunday), who has something to do with a Worshipful Company who have got a Hall[5] in the next yard, with a stained-glass window in it that no mortal ever saw. There are dusty wooden ledges and cornices poked in and out over the altar, and over the screen and round the gallery, and over the inscription about what the Master and Wardens of the Worshipful Company did in one thousand six hundred and ninety-four. There are dusty old sounding-boards[6] over the pulpit and reading-desk, looking like lids to be let down on the officiating ministers in case of their giving offence. There is every possible provision for the accommodation of dust, except in the church-yard, where the facilities in that respect are very limited.

The Captain, Uncle Sol, and Mr Toots are come; the clergyman is putting on his surplice in the vestry, while the clerk walks round him, blowing the dust off it; and the bride and bridegroom stand before the altar. There is no bridesmaid, unless Susan Nipper is one; and no better father than Captain Cuttle. A man with a wooden leg, chewing a faint apple and carrying a blue bag in his hand, looks in to see what is going on; but finding it nothing entertaining, stumps off again, and pegs his way among the echoes out of doors.

No gracious ray of light is seen to fall on Florence, kneeling at the altar with her timid head bowed down. The morning luminary is built out,[7] and don't shine there. There is a meagre tree outside, where the sparrows are chirping a little; and there is a blackbird in an eyelet-hole of sun in a dyer's garret, over against the window, who whistles loudly whilst the service is performing; and there is the man with the wooden leg stumping away. The amens of the dusty clerk appear, like Macbeth's,[8] to stick in his throat a little; but Captain Cuttle helps him out, and does it with so much goodwill that he interpolates three entirely new responses of that word, never introduced into the service before.

They are married, and have signed their names in one of the old sneezy registers, and the clergyman's surplice is restored to the dust, and the clergyman is gone home. In a dark corner of the dark church, Florence has turned to Susan Nipper, and is weeping in her arms. Mr Toots's eyes are red. The Captain lubricates his nose.

Uncle Sol has pulled down his spectacles from his forehead, and walked out to the door.

'God bless you, Susan; dearest Susan! If you ever can bear witness to the love I have for Walter, and the reason that I have to love him, do it for his sake. Good-bye! Good-bye!'

They have thought it better not to go back to the Midshipman, but to part so; a coach is waiting for them, near at hand.

Miss Nipper cannot speak; she only sobs and chokes, and hugs her mistress. Mr Toots advances, urges her to cheer up, and takes charge of her. Florence gives him her hand – gives him, in the fulness of her heart, her lips – kisses Uncle Sol, and Captain Cuttle, and is borne away by her young husband.

But Susan cannot bear that Florence should go away with a mournful recollection of her. She had meant to be so different, that she reproaches herself bitterly. Intent on making one last effort to redeem her character, she breaks from Mr Toots and runs away to find the coach, and show a parting smile. The Captain, divining her object, sets off after her; for he feels it his duty also to dismiss them with a cheer, if possible. Uncle Sol and Mr Toots are left behind together, outside the church, to wait for them.

The coach is gone, but the street is steep, and narrow, and blocked up, and Susan can see it at a stand-still in the distance, she is sure. Captain Cuttle follows her as she flies down the hill, and waves his glazed hat as a general signal, which may attract the right coach and which may not.

Susan outstrips the Captain, and comes up with it. She looks in at the window, sees Walter, with the gentle face beside him, and claps her hands and screams:

'Miss Floy, my darling! look at me! We are all so happy now, dear! One more good-bye, my precious, one more!'

How Susan does it, she don't know, but she reaches to the window, kisses her, and has her arms about her neck, in a moment.

'We are all so – so happy now, my dear Miss Floy!' says Susan, with a suspicious catching in her breath. 'You, you won't be angry with me now. Now *will* you?'

'Angry, Susan!'

'No, no; I am sure you won't. I say you won't, my pet, my dearest!' exclaims Susan; 'and here's the Captain too – your friend the Captain, you know – to say good-bye once more!'

'Hooroar, my Heart's Delight!' vociferates the Captain, with a countenance of strong emotion. 'Hooroar, Wal'r my lad. Hooroar! Hooroar!'

What with the young husband at one window, and the young wife at the other; the Captain hanging on at this door, and Susan Nipper holding fast by that; the coach obliged to go on whether it will or no, and all the other carts and coaches turbulent because it hesitates; there never was so much confusion on four wheels. But Susan Nipper gallantly maintains her point. She keeps a smiling face upon her mistress, smiling through her tears, until the last. Even when she is left behind, the Captain continues to appear and disappear at the door, crying 'Hooroar, my lad! Hooroar, my Heart's Delight!' with his shirt-collar in a violent state of agitation, until it is hopeless to attempt to keep up with the coach any longer. Finally, when the coach is gone, Susan Nipper, being rejoined by the Captain, falls into a state of insensibility, and is taken into a baker's shop to recover.

Uncle Sol and Mr Toots wait patiently in the churchyard, sitting on the coping-stone of the railings, until Captain Cuttle and Susan come back. Neither being at all desirous to speak, or to be spoken to, they are excellent company, and quite satisfied. When they all arrive again at the little Midshipman, and sit down to breakfast, nobody can touch a morsel. Captain Cuttle makes a feint of being voracious about toast, but gives it up as a swindle. Mr Toots says, after breakfast, he will come back in the evening; and goes wandering about the town all day, with a vague sensation upon him as if he hadn't been to bed for a fortnight.

There is a strange charm in the house, and in the room, in which they have been used to be together, and out of which so much is gone. It aggravates, and yet it soothes, the sorrow of the separation. Mr Toots tells Susan Nipper when he comes at night, that he hasn't been so wretched all day long, and yet he likes it. He confides in Susan Nipper, being alone with her, and tells her what his feelings were when she gave him that candid opinion as to the probability of Miss Dombey's ever loving him. In the vein of confidence engendered by these common recollections, and their tears, Mr Toots proposes that they shall go out together, and buy something for supper. Miss Nipper assenting, they buy a good many little things; and, with the aid of Mrs Richards, set the supper out quite showily before the Captain and old Sol came home.

The Captain and old Sol have been on board the ship, and have established Di there, and have seen the chests put aboard. They have much to tell about the popularity of Walter, and the comforts he will have about him, and the quiet way in which it seems he has been working early and late, to make his cabin what the Captain calls 'a picter,' to surprise his little wife. 'A admiral's cabin, mind you,' says the Captain, 'ain't more trim.'

But one of the Captain's chief delights is, that he knows the big watch, and the sugar-tongs, and tea-spoons, are on board: and again and again he murmurs to himself, 'Ed'ard Cuttle, my lad, you never shaped a better course in your life than when you made that there little property over jintly. *You* see how the land bore, Ed'ard,' says the Captain, 'and it does you credit, my lad.'

The old Instrument-maker is more distraught and misty than he used to be, and takes the marriage and the parting very much to heart. But he is greatly comforted by having his old ally, Ned Cuttle, at his side; and he sits down to supper with a grateful and contented face.

'My boy has been preserved and thrives,' says old Sol Gills, rubbing his hands. 'What right have I to be otherwise than thankful and happy!'

The Captain, who has not yet taken his seat at the table, but who has been fidgeting about for some time, and now stands hesitating in his place, looks doubtfully at Mr Gills, and says:

'Sol! There's the last bottle of the old Madeira down below. Would you wish to have it up to-night, my boy, and drink to Wal'r and his wife?'

The Instrument-maker, looking wistfully at the Captain, puts his hand into the breast-pocket of his coffee-coloured coat, brings forth his pocket-book, and takes a letter out.

'To Mr Dombey,' says the old man. 'From Walter. To be sent in three weeks' time. I'll read it.'

' "Sir. I am married to your daughter. She is gone with me upon a distant voyage. To be devoted to her is to have no claim on her or you, but God knows that I am.

' "Why, loving her beyond all earthly things, I have yet, without remorse, united her to the uncertainties and dangers of my life, I will not say to you. You know why, and you are her father.

' "Do not reproach her. She has never reproached you.

' "I do not think or hope that you will ever forgive me. There is nothing I expect less. But if an hour should come when it will comfort you to believe that Florence has some one ever near her, the great charge of whose life is to cancel her remembrance of past sorrow, I solemnly assure you, you may, in that hour, rest in that belief." '

Solomon puts back the letter carefully in his pocket-book and puts back his pocket-book in his coat.

'We won't drink the last bottle of the old Madeira yet, Ned,' says the old man thoughtfully. 'Not yet.'

'Not yet,' assents the Captain. 'No. Not yet.'

Susan and Mr Toots are of the same opinion. After a silence they all sit down to supper, and drink to the young husband and wife in something else; and the last bottle of the old Madeira still remains among its dust and cobwebs, undisturbed

A few days have elapsed, and a stately ship is out at sea, spreading its white wings to the favouring wind.

Upon the deck, image to the roughest man on board of something that is graceful, beautiful, and harmless – something that it is good and pleasant to have there, and that should make the voyage prosperous – is Florence. It is night, and she and Walter sit alone, watching the solemn path of light upon the sea between them and the moon.

At length she cannot see it plainly, for the tears that fill her eyes; and then she lays her head down on his breast, and puts her arms round his neck, saying, 'Oh Walter, dearest love, I am so happy!'

Her husband holds her to his heart, and they are very quiet, and the stately ship goes on serenely.

'As I hear the sea,' says Florence, 'and sit watching it, it brings so many days into my mind. It makes me think so much—'

'Of Paul, my love. I know it does.'

Of Paul and Walter. And the voices in the waves are always whispering to Florence, in their ceaseless murmuring, of love – of love, eternal and illimitable, not bounded by the confines of this world, or by the end of time, but ranging still, beyond the sea, beyond the sky, to the invisible country far away!

CHAPTER 58

After a Lapse

The sea had ebbed and flowed, through a whole year. Through a whole year, the winds and clouds had come and gone; the ceaseless work of Time had been performed, in storm and sunshine. Through a whole year, the tides of human chance and change had set in their allotted courses. Through a whole year, the famous House of Dombey and Son had fought a fight for life, against cross accidents, doubtful rumours, unsuccessful ventures, unpropitious times, and most of all, against the infatuation of its head, who would not contract its enterprises by a hair's breadth; and would not listen to a word of warning that the ship he strained so hard against the storm, was weak, and could not bear it.

The year was out, and the great House was down.

One summer afternoon; a year, wanting some odd days, after the marriage in the City church; there was a buzz and whisper upon 'Change[1] of a great failure. A certain cold proud man, well known there, was not there, nor was he represented there. Next day it was noised abroad that Dombey and Son had stopped, and next night there was a List of Bankrupts published, headed by that name.

The world was very busy now, in sooth, and had a deal to say. It was an innocently credulous and a much ill-used world. It was a world in which there was no other sort of bankruptcy whatever. There were no conspicuous people in it, trading far and wide on rotten banks of religion, patriotism, virtue, honour. There was no amount worth mentioning of mere paper in circulation, on which anybody lived pretty handsomely, promising to pay great sums of goodness with no effects. There were no shortcomings anywhere, in anything but money. The world was very angry indeed; and the people especially, who, in a worse world, might have been supposed to be bankrupt traders themselves in shows and pretences, were observed to be mightily indignant.

Here was a new inducement to dissipation, presented to that sport of circumstances, Mr Perch the Messenger! It was apparently the fate of Mr Perch to be always waking up, and finding himself famous. He had but yesterday, as one might say, subsided into private life from the celebrity of the elopement and the events that followed it; and now he was made a more important man than ever, by the bankruptcy. Gliding from his bracket in the outer office where he now sat, watching the strange faces of accountants and others, who quickly superseded nearly all the old clerks, Mr Perch had but to show himself in the court outside, or, at farthest, in the bar of the King's Arms, to be asked a multitude of questions, almost certain to include that interesting question, what would he take to drink? Then would Mr Perch descant upon the hours of acute uneasiness he and Mrs Perch had suffered out at Ball's Pond, when they first suspected 'things was going wrong.' Then would Mr Perch relate to gaping listeners, in a low voice, as if the corpse of the deceased House were lying unburied in the next room, how Mrs Perch had first come to surmise that things *was* going wrong by hearing him (Perch) moaning in his sleep, 'twelve and ninepence in the pound, twelve and ninepence in the pound!' Which act of somnambulism he supposed to have originated in the impression made upon him by the change in Mr Dombey's face. Then would he inform them how he had once said, 'Might I make so bold as ask, Sir, are you unhappy in your mind?' and how Mr Dombey had replied, 'My faithful Perch – but no, it cannot be!' and with that had struck his hand upon his forehead and said, 'Leave me, Perch!' Then, in short, would Mr Perch, a victim to his position, tell all manner of lies; affecting himself to tears by those that were of a moving nature, and really believing that the inventions of yesterday had, on repetition, a sort of truth about them to-day.

Mr Perch always closed these conferences by meekly remarking, That, of course, whatever his suspicions might have been (as if he had ever had any!) it wasn't for *him* to betray his trust, was it? Which sentiment (there never being any creditors present) was received as doing great honour to his feelings. Thus, he generally brought away a soothed conscience and left an agreeable impression behind him, when he returned to his bracket: again to sit watching the strange faces of the accountants and others, making so free with the great mysteries, the Books; or now and then to go on tiptoe into Mr Dombey's empty room, and stir the fire; or to take an airing at the door, and have a little more doleful chat with any straggler whom he knew; or to propitiate, with various small attentions, the head accountant: from whom Mr Perch had expectations of a messengership in a Fire Office, when the affairs of the House should be wound up.

To Major Bagstock, the bankruptcy was quite a calamity. The Major was not a sympathetic character – his attention being wholly concentrated on J. B. – nor was he a man subject to lively emotions, except in the physical regards of gasping and choking. But he had so paraded his friend Dombey at the club; had so flourished him at the heads of the members in general, and so put them down by continual assertion of his riches; that the club, being but human, was delighted to retort upon the Major, by asking him, with a show of great concern, whether this tremendous smash had been at all expected, and how his friend Dombey bore it. To such questions, the Major, waxing very purple, would reply that it was a bad world, Sir, altogether; that Joey knew a thing or two, but had been done, Sir, done like an infant; that if you had foretold this, Sir, to J. Bagstock, when he went abroad with Dombey and was chasing that vagabond up and down France, J. Bagstock would have pooh-

pooh'd you – would have pooh-pooh'ed you, Sir, by the Lord! That Joe had been deceived, Sir, taken in, hoodwinked, blindfolded, but was broad awake again and staring; insomuch, Sir, that if Joe's father were to rise up from the grave to-morrow, he wouldn't trust the old blade with a penny piece, but would tell him that his son Josh was too old a soldier to be done again, Sir. That he was a suspicious, crabbed, cranky, used-up, J. B. infidel, Sir; and that if it were consistent with the dignity of a rough and tough old Major, of the old school, who had had the honour of being personally known to, and commended by, their late Royal Highnesses the Dukes of Kent and York, to retire to a tub and live in it, by Gad! Sir, he'd have a tub in Pall Mall to-morrow, to show his contempt for mankind![2]

Of all this, and many variations of the same tune, the Major would deliver himself with so many apoplectic symptoms, such rollings of his head, and such violent growls of ill usage and resentment, that the younger members of the club surmised he had invested money in his friend Dombey's House, and lost it; though the older soldiers and deeper dogs, who knew Joe better, wouldn't hear of such a thing. The unfortunate Native, expressing no opinion, suffered dreadfully; not merely in his moral feelings, which were regularly fusilladed by the Major every hour in the day, and riddled through and through, but in his sensitiveness to bodily knocks and bumps, which was kept continually on the stretch. For six entire weeks after the bankruptcy, this miserable foreigner lived in a rainy season of boot-jacks and brushes.

Mrs Chick had three ideas upon the subject of the terrible reverse. The first was that she could not understand it. The second, that her brother had not made an effort. The third, that if she had been invited to dinner on the day of that first party, it never would have happened; and that she had said so, at the time.

Nobody's opinion stayed the misfortune, lightened it, or made it heavier. It was understood that the affairs of the House were to be wound up as they best could be; that Mr Dombey freely resigned everything he had, and asked for no favour from any one. That any resumption of the business was out of the question, as he would listen to no friendly negotiation having that compromise in view; that he had relinquished every post of trust or distinction he had held, as a man respected among merchants; that he was dying, according to some; that he was going melancholy mad, according to others; that he was a broken man, according to all.

The clerks dispersed after holding a little dinner of condolence among themselves, which was enlivened by comic singing, and went off admirably. Some took places abroad, and some engaged in other Houses at home; some looked up relations in the country, for whom they suddenly remembered they had a particular affection; and some advertised for employment in the newspapers. Mr Perch alone remained of all the late establishment, sitting on his bracket looking at the accountants, or starting off it, to propitiate the head accountant, who was to get him into the Fire Office. The Counting House soon got to be dirty and neglected. The principal slipper and dogs' collar seller, at the corner of the court, would have doubted the propriety of throwing up his forefinger to the brim of his hat, any more, if Mr Dombey had appeared there now; and the ticket porter, with his hands under his white apron, moralised good sound morality about ambition, which (he observed) was not, in his opinion, made to rhyme to perdition, for nothing.

Mr Morfin, the hazel-eyed bachelor, with the hair and whiskers sprinkled with grey, was perhaps the only person within the atmosphere of the House – its head, of course, excepted – who was heartily and deeply affected by the disaster that had befallen it. He had treated Mr Dombey with due respect and deference through many years, but he had never disguised his natural character, or meanly truckled to him, or pampered his master passion for the advancement of his own purposes. He had, therefore, no self-disrespect to avenge; no long-tightened springs to release with a quick recoil. He worked early and late to unravel whatever was complicated or difficult in the records of the transactions of the House; was always in attendance to explain whatever required explanation; sat in his old room sometimes very late at night, studying points by his mastery of which he could spare Mr Dombey the pain of being personally referred to; and then would go home to Islington,[3] and calm his mind by producing the most dismal and forlorn sounds out of his violoncello before going to bed.

He was solacing himself with this melodious grumbler one evening, and, having been much dispirited by the proceedings of the day, was scraping consolation out of its deepest notes, when his landlady (who was fortunately deaf, and had no other consciousness of these performances than a sensation of something rumbling in her bones) announced a lady.

'In mourning,' she said.

The violoncello stopped immediately; and the performer, laying it on the sofa with great tenderness and care, made a sign that the lady was to come in. He followed directly, and met Harriet Carker on the stair.

'Alone!' he said, 'and John here this morning! Is there anything the matter, my dear? But no,' he added, 'your face tells quite another story.'

'I am afraid it is a selfish revelation that you see there, then,' she answered.

'It is a very pleasant one,' said he; 'and, if selfish, a novelty too, worth seeing in you. But I don't believe that.'

He had placed a chair for her by this time, and sat down opposite; the violoncello lying snugly on the sofa between them.

'You will not be surprised at my coming alone, or at John's not having told you I was coming,' said Harriet; 'and you *will* believe that, when I tell you why I have come. May I do so now?'

'You can do nothing better.'

'You were not busy?'

He pointed to the violoncello lying on the sofa, and said, 'I have been, all day. Here's my witness. I have been confiding all my cares to it. I wish I had none but my own to tell.'

'Is the House at an end?' said Harriet, earnestly.

'Completely at an end.'

'Will it never be resumed?'

'Never.'

The bright expression of her face was not overshadowed as her lips silently repeated the word. He seemed to observe this with some little involuntary surprise: and said again:

'Never. You remember what I told you. It has been, all along, impossible to convince him; impossible to reason with him; sometimes, impossible even to approach him. The worst has happened; and the House has fallen, never to be built up any more.'

'And Mr Dombey, is he personally ruined?'

'Ruined.'

'Will he have no private fortune left? Nothing?'

A certain eagerness in her voice, and something that was almost joyful in her look, seemed to surprise him more and more; to disappoint him too, and jar discordantly against his own emotions. He drummed with the fingers of one hand on the table, looking wistfully at her, and shaking his head, said, after a pause:

'The extent of Mr Dombey's resources is not accurately within my knowledge; but though they are doubtless very large, his obligations are enormous. He is a gentleman of high honour and integrity. Any man in his position could, and many a man in his position would, have saved himself, by making terms which would have very slightly, almost insensibly, increased the losses of those who had had dealings with him, and left him a remnant to live upon. But he is resolved on payment to the last farthing of his means. His own words are, that they will clear, or nearly clear, the House, and that no one can lose much. Ah, Miss Harriet, it would do us no harm to remember oftener than we do, that vices are sometimes only virtues carried to excess! His pride shows well in this.'

She heard him with little or no change in her expression, and with a divided attention that showed her to be busy with something in her own mind. When he was silent, she asked him hurriedly:

'Have you seen him lately?'

'No one sees him. When this crisis of his affairs renders it necessary for him to come out of his house, he comes out for the occasion, and again goes home, and shuts himself up, and will see no one. He has written me a letter, acknowledging our past connexion in higher terms than it deserved, and parting from me. I am delicate of obtruding myself upon him now, never having had much intercourse with him in better times; but I have tried to do so. I have written, gone there, entreated. Quite in vain.'

He watched her, as in the hope that she would testify some greater concern than she had yet shown; and spoke gravely and feelingly, as if to impress her the more; but there was no change in her.

'Well, well, Miss Harriet,' he said, with a disappointed air, 'this is not to the purpose. You have not come here to hear this. Some other and pleasanter theme is in your mind. Let it be in mine, too, and we shall talk upon more equal terms. Come!'

'No, it is the same theme,' returned Harriet, with frank and quick surprise. 'Is it not likely that it should be? Is it not natural that John and I should have been thinking and speaking very much of late of these great changes? Mr Dombey, whom he served so many years – you know upon what terms – reduced, as you describe; and we quite rich!'

Good, true face, as that face of hers was, and pleasant as it had been to him, Mr Morfin, the hazel-eyed bachelor, since the first time he had ever looked upon it, it pleased him less at that moment, lighted with a ray of exultation, than it had ever pleased him before.

'I need not remind you,' said Harriet, casting down her eyes upon her black dress, 'through what means our circumstances changed.

You have not forgotten that our brother James, upon that dreadful day, left no will, no relations but ourselves.'

The face was pleasanter to him now, though it was pale and melancholy, than it had been a moment since. He seemed to breathe more cheerily.

'You know,' she said, 'our history, the history of both my brothers, in connexion with the unfortunate, unhappy gentleman, of whom you have spoken so truly. You know how few our wants are – John's and mine – and what little use we have for money, after the life we have led together for so many years; and now that he is earning an income that is ample for us, through your kindness. You are not unprepared to hear what favour I have come to ask of you?'

'I hardly know. I was, a minute ago. Now, I think, I am not.'

'Of my dead brother I say nothing. If the dead know what we do – but you understand me. Of my living brother I could say much: but what need I say more, than that this act of duty, in which I have come to ask your indispensable assistance, is his own, and that he cannot rest until it is performed!'

She raised her eyes again; and the light of exultation in her face began to appear beautiful, in the observant eyes that watched her.

'Dear Sir,' she went on to say, 'it must be done very quietly and secretly. Your experience and knowledge will point out a way of doing it. Mr Dombey may, perhaps, be led to believe that it is something saved, unexpectedly, from the wreck of his fortunes; or that it is a voluntary tribute to his honourable and upright character, from some of those with whom he has had great dealings; or that it is some old lost debt repaid. There must be many ways of doing it. I know you will choose the best. The favour I have come to ask is, that you will do it for us in your own kind, generous, considerate manner. That you will never speak of it to John, whose chief happiness in this act of restitution is to do it secretly, unknown, and unapproved of: that only a very small part of the inheritance may be reserved to us, until Mr Dombey shall have possessed the interest of the rest for the remainder of his life; that you will keep our secret, faithfully – but that I am sure you will; and that, from this time, it may seldom be whispered, even between you and me, but may live in my thoughts only as a new reason for thankfulness to Heaven, and joy and pride in my brother.'

Such a look of exultation there may be on Angels' faces, when the one repentant sinner enters Heaven, among ninety-nine just men. It was not dimmed or tarnished by the joyful tears that filled her eyes, but was the brighter for them.

'My dear Harriet,' said Mr Morfin, after a silence, 'I was not prepared for this. Do I understand you that you wish to make your own part in the inheritance available for your good purpose, as well as John's?'

'Oh, yes,' she returned. 'When we have shared everything together for so long a time, and have had no care, hope, or purpose apart, could I bear to be excluded from my share in this? May I not urge a claim to be my brother's partner and companion to the last?'

'Heaven forbid that I should dispute it!' he replied.

'We may rely on your friendly help?' she said. 'I knew we might!'

'I should be a worse man than, – than I hope I am, or would willingly believe myself, if I could not give you that assurance from my heart and soul. You may, implicitly. Upon my honour, I will keep your secret. And if it should be found that Mr Dombey is so reduced as I fear he will be, acting on a determination that there seem to be no means of influencing, I will assist you to accomplish the design, on which you and John are jointly resolved.'

She gave him her hand, and thanked him with a cordial, happy face.

'Harriet,' he said, detaining it in his. 'To speak to you of the worth of any sacrifice that you can make now – above all, of any sacrifice of mere money – would be idle and presumptuous. To put before you any appeal to reconsider your purpose or to set narrow limits to it, would be, I feel, not less so. I have no right to mar the great end of a great history, by any obtrusion of my own weak self. I have every right to bend my head before what you confide to me, satisfied that it comes from a higher and better source of inspiration than my poor worldly knowledge. I will say only this: I am your faithful steward; and I would rather be so, and your chosen friend, than I would be anybody in the world, except yourself.'

She thanked him again, cordially, and wished him good night.

'Are you going home?' he said. 'Let me go with you.'

'Not to-night. I am not going home now; I have a visit to make alone. Will you come to-morrow?'

'Well, well,' said he, 'I'll come to-morrow. In the meantime, I'll think of this, and how we can best proceed. And perhaps *you'll* think of it, dear Harriet, and – and – think of me a little in connexion with it.'

He handed her down to a coach she had in waiting at the door; and if his landlady had not been deaf, she would have heard him muttering as he went back upstairs, when the coach had driven off, that we were creatures of habit, and it was a sorrowful habit to be an old bachelor.

The violoncello lying on the sofa between the two chairs, he took it up, without putting away the vacant chair, and sat droning on it, and slowly shaking his head at the vacant chair, for a long, long time. The expression he communicated to the instrument at first, though monstrously pathetic and bland, was nothing to the expression he communicated to his own face, and bestowed upon the empty chair: which was so sincere, that he was obliged to have recourse to Captain Cuttle's remedy more than once, and to rub his face with his sleeve. By degrees, however, the violoncello, in unison with his own frame of mind, glided melodiously into the Harmonious Blacksmith,[4] which he played over and over again, until his ruddy and serene face gleamed like true metal on the anvil of a veritable blacksmith. In fine, the violoncello and the empty chair were the companions of his bachelorhood until nearly midnight; and when he took his supper, the violoncello set up on end in the sofa corner, big with the latent harmony of a whole foundry full of harmonious blacksmiths, seemed to ogle the empty chair out of its crooked eyes, with unutterable intelligence.

When Harriet left the house, the driver of her hired coach, taking a course that was evidently no new one to him, went in and out by bye-ways, through that part of the suburbs, until he arrived at some open ground, where there were a few quiet little old houses standing among gardens. At the garden-gate of one of these he stopped, and Harriet alighted.

Her gentle ringing at the bell was responded to by a dolorous-looking woman, of light complexion, with raised eyebrows, and head drooping on one side, who curtseyed at sight of her, and conducted her across the garden to the house.

'How is your patient, nurse, to-night?' said Harriet.

'In a poor way, Miss, I'm afraid. Oh how she do remind me, sometimes, of my uncle's Betsey Jane!' returned the woman of the light complexion, in a sort of doleful rapture.

'In what respect?' asked Harriet.

'Miss, in all respects,' replied the other, 'except that she's grown up, and Betsey Jane, when at death's door, was but a child.'

'But you have told me she recovered,' observed Harriet mildly; 'so there is the more reason for hope, Mrs Wickam.'

'Ah, Miss, hope is an excellent thing for such as has the spirits to bear it!' said Mrs Wickam, shaking her head. 'My own spirits is not equal to it, but I don't owe it any grudge. I envys them that is so blest!'

'You should try to be more cheerful,' remarked Harriet.

'Thank you, Miss, I'm sure,' said Mrs Wickam grimly. 'If I was so inclined, the loneliness of this situation – you'll excuse my speaking so free – would put it out of my power in four and twenty hours; but I an't at all. I'd rather not. The little spirits that I ever had, I was bereaved of at Brighton some few years ago, and I think I feel myself the better for it.'

In truth, this was the very Mrs Wickam who had superseded Mrs Richards as the nurse of little Paul, and who considered herself to have gained the loss in question, under the roof of the amiable Pipchin. The excellent and thoughtful old system, hallowed by long prescription, which has usually picked out from the rest of mankind the most dreary and uncomfortable people that could possibly be laid hold of, to act as instructors of youth, finger-posts to the virtues, matrons, monitors, attendants on sick beds, and the like, had established Mrs Wickam in very good business as a nurse, and had led to her serious qualities being particularly commended by an admiring and numerous connexion.

Mrs Wickam, with her eyebrows elevated, and her head on one side, lighted the way upstairs to a clean, neat chamber, opening on another chamber dimly lighted, where there was a bed. In the first room, an old woman sat mechanically staring out at the open window, on the darkness. In the second, stretched upon the bed, lay the shadow of a figure that had spurned the wind and rain, one wintry night; hardly to be recognised now, but by the long black hair that showed so very black against the colourless face, and all the white things about it.

Oh, the strong eyes, and the weak frame! The eyes that turned so eagerly and brightly to the door when Harriet came in; the feeble head that could not raise itself, and moved so slowly round upon its pillow!

'Alice!' said the visitor's mild voice, 'am I late to-night?'

'You always seem late, but are always early.'

Harriet had sat down by the bedside now, and put her hand upon the thin hand lying there.

'You are better?'

Mrs Wickam, standing at the foot of the bed, like a disconsolate spectre, most decidedly and forcibly shook her head to negative this position.

'It matters very little!' said Alice, with a faint smile. 'Better or worse to-day, is but a day's difference – perhaps not so much.

Mrs Wickam, as a serious character, expressed her approval with a groan; and having made some cold dabs at the bottom of the bedclothes, as feeling for the patient's feet and expecting to find them stony, went clinking among the medicine bottles on the table, as who should say, 'while we *are* here, let us repeat the mixture as before.'

'No,' said Alice, whispering to her visitor, 'evil courses, and remorse, travel, want, and weather, storm within, and storm without, have worn my life away. It will not last much longer.'

She drew the hand up as she spoke, and laid her face against it.

'I lie here, sometimes, thinking I should like to live until I had had a little time to show you how grateful I could be! It is a weakness, and soon passes. Better for you as it is. Better for me!'

How different her hold upon the hand, from what it had been when she took it by the fireside on the bleak winter evening! Scorn, rage, defiance, recklessness, look here! This is the end.

Mrs Wickam having clinked sufficiently among the bottles, now produced the mixture. Mrs Wickam looked hard at her patient in the act of drinking, screwed her mouth up tight, her eyebrows also, and shook her head, expressing that tortures shouldn't make her say it was a hopeless case. Mrs Wickam then sprinkled a little cooling-stuff about the room, with the air of a female grave-digger, who was strewing ashes on ashes, dust on dust – for she was a serious character – and withdrew to partake of certain funeral baked meats[5] downstairs.

'How long is it,' asked Alice, 'since I went to you and told you what I had done, and when you were advised it was too late for any one to follow?'

'It is a year and more,' said Harriet.

'A year and more,' said Alice, thoughtfully intent upon her face. 'Months upon months since you brought me here!'

Harriet answered 'Yes.'

'Brought me here, by force of gentleness and kindness. Me!' said Alice, shrinking with her face behind the hand, 'and made me human by woman's looks and words, and angel's deeds!'

Harriet bending over her, composed and soothed her. By and bye, Alice lying as before, with the hand against her face, asked to have her mother called.

Harriet called to her more than once, but the old woman was so absorbed looking out at the open window on the darkness, that she did not hear. It was not until Harriet went to her and touched her, that she rose up, and came.

'Mother,' said Alice, taking the hand again, and fixing her lustrous eyes lovingly upon her visitor, while she merely addressed a motion of her finger to the old woman, 'tell her what you know.'

'To-night, my deary?'

'Aye, mother,' answered Alice, faintly and solemnly, 'to-night!'

The old woman, whose wits appeared disordered by alarm, remorse, or grief, came creeping along the side of the bed, opposite to that on which Harriet sat; and kneeling down, so as to bring her withered face upon a level with the coverlet, and stretching out her hand, so as to touch her daughter's arm, began:

'My handsome gal—'

Heaven, what a cry was that, with which she stopped there, gazing at the poor form lying on the bed!

'Changed, long ago, mother! Withered, long ago,' said Alice, without looking at her. 'Don't grieve for that now.'

'—My daughter,' faltered the old woman, 'my gal who'll soon get better, and shame 'em all with her good looks.'

Alice smiled mournfully at Harriet, and fondled her hand a little closer, but said nothing.

'Who'll soon get better, I say,' repeated the old woman, menacing the vacant air with her shrivelled fist, 'and who'll shame 'em all with her good looks – she will. I say she will! she shall!' – as if she were in passionate contention with some unseen opponent at the bedside, who contradicted her – 'my daughter has been turned away from, and cast out, but she could boast relationship to proud folks too, if she chose. Ah! To proud folks! There's relationship without your clergy and your wedding rings – they may make it, but they can't break it – and my daughter's well related. Show me Mrs Dombey, and I'll show you my Alice's first cousin.'

Harriet glanced from the old woman to the lustrous eyes intent upon her face, and derived corroboration from them.

'What!' cried the old woman, her nodding head bridling with a ghastly vanity. 'Though I am old and ugly now, – much older by life and habit than years though, – I was once as young as any. Ah! as pretty, too, as many! I was a fresh country wench in my time, darling,' stretching out her arm to Harriet, across the bed, 'and looked it, too. Down in my country, Mrs Dombey's father and his brother were the gayest gentlemen and the best-liked that came a visiting from London – they have long been dead, though! Lord,

Lord, this long while! The brother, who was my Ally's father, longest of the two.'

She raised her head a little, and peered at her daughter's face; as if from the remembrance of her own youth, she had flown to the remembrance of her child's. Then, suddenly, she laid her face down on the bed, and shut her head up in her hands and arms.

'They were as like,' said the old woman, without looking up, 'as you could see two brothers, so near an age – there wasn't much more than a year between them, as I recollect – and if you could have seen my gal, as I have seen her once, side by side with the other's daughter, you'd have seen, for all the difference of dress and life, that they were like each other. Oh! is the likeness gone, and is it my gal – only my gal – that's to change so!'

'We shall all change, mother, in our turn,' said Alice.

'Turn!' cried the old woman, 'but why not hers as soon as my gal's! The mother must have changed – she looked as old as me, and full as wrinkled through her paint – but *she* was handsome. What have *I* done, I, what have *I* done worse than her, that only my gal is to lie there fading!'

With another of those wild cries, she went running out into the room from which she had come; but immediately, in her uncertain mood, returned, and creeping up to Harriet, said:

'That's what Alice bade me tell you, deary. That's all. I found it out when I began to ask who she was, and all about her, away in Warwickshire there, one summer-time. Such relations was no good to me, then. They wouldn't have owned me, and had nothing to give me. I should have asked 'em, maybe, for a little money, afterwards, if it hadn't been for my Alice; she'd a'most have killed me, if I had, I think. She was as proud as t'other in her way,' said the old woman, touching the face of her daughter fearfully, and withdrawing her hand, 'for all she's so quiet now; but she'll shame 'em with her good looks yet. Ha, ha! *She'll* shame 'em, will my handsome daughter!'

Her laugh, as she retreated, was worse than her cry; worse than the burst of imbecile lamentation in which it ended; worse than the doting air with which she sat down in her old seat, and stared out at the darkness.

The eyes of Alice had all this time been fixed on Harriet, whose hand she had never released. She said now:

'I have felt, lying here, that I should like you to know this. It might explain, I have thought, something that used to help to harden me. I had heard so much, in my wrong-doing, of my neglected duty, that I took up with the belief that duty had not been done to me, and that as the seed was sown, the harvest grew. I somehow made it out that when ladies had bad homes and mothers, they went wrong in their way, too; but that their way was not so foul a one as mine, and they had need to bless God for it. That is all past. It is like a dream, now, which I cannot quite remember or understand. It has been more and more like a dream, every day, since you began to sit here, and to read to me. I only tell it you, as I can recollect it. Will you read to me a little more?'

Harriet was withdrawing her hand to open the book, when Alice detained it for a moment.

'You will not forget my mother? I forgive her, if I have any cause. I know that she forgives me, and is sorry in her heart. You will not forget her?'

'Never, Alice!'

'A moment yet. Lay my head so, dear, that as you read I may see the words in your kind face.'

Harriet complied and read – read the eternal book for all the weary and the heavy-laden; for all the wretched, fallen, and neglected on this earth – read the blessed history, in which the blind lame palsied beggar, the criminal, the woman stained with shame, the shunned of all our dainty clay, has each a portion, that no human pride, indifference, or sophistry, through all the ages that this world shall last, can take away, or by the thousandth atom of a grain reduce – read the ministry of Him who, through the round of human life, and all its hopes and griefs, from birth to death, from infancy to age, had sweet compassion for, and interest in, its every scene and stage, its every suffering and sorrow.[6]

'I shall come,' said Harriet, when she shut the book, 'very early in the morning.'

The lustrous eyes, yet fixed upon her face, closed for a moment, then opened; and Alice kissed and blest her.

The same eyes followed her to the door; and in their light, and on the tranquil face, there was a smile when it was closed.

They never turned away. She laid her hand upon her breast, murmuring the sacred name that had been read to her; and life passed from her face, like light removed.

Nothing lay there, any longer, but the ruin of the mortal house on which the rain had beaten, and the black hair that had fluttered in the wintry wind.

CHAPTER 59

Retribution

Changes have come again upon the great house in the long dull street, once the scene of Florence's childhood and loneliness. It is a great house still, proof against wind and weather, without breaches in the roof, or shattered windows, or dilapidated walls; but it is a ruin none the less, and the rats fly from it.

Mr Towlinson and company are, at first, incredulous in respect of the shapeless rumours that they hear. Cook says our people's credit ain't so easy shook as that comes to, thank God; and Mr Towlinson expects to hear it reported that the Bank of England's a-going to break, or the jewels in the Tower[1] to be sold up. But, next come the Gazette,[2] and Mr Perch: and Mr Perch brings Mrs Perch to talk it over in the kitchen, and to spend a pleasant evening.

As soon as there is no doubt about it, Mr Towlinson's main anxiety is that the failure should be a good round one – not less than a hundred thousand pound. Mr Perch don't think himself that a hundred thousand pound will nearly cover it. The women, led by Mrs Perch and Cook, often repeat 'a hun-dred thou-sand pound!' with awful satisfaction – as if handling the words were like handling the money; and the housemaid, who has her eye on Mr Towlinson, wishes she had only a hundredth part of the sum to bestow on the man of her choice. Mr Towlinson, still mindful of his old wrong, opines that a foreigner would hardly know what to do with so much money, unless he spent it on his whiskers; which bitter sarcasm causes the housemaid to withdraw in tears.

But not to remain long absent; for Cook, who has the reputation of being extremely good-hearted, says, whatever they do, let 'em stand by one another now, Towlinson, for there's no telling how soon they may be divided. They have been in that house (says Cook) through a funeral, a wedding, and a running-away; and let it not be said that they couldn't agree among themselves at such a time as the present. Mrs Perch is immensely affected by this moving address, and openly remarks that Cook is an angel. Mr Towlinson replies to Cook, far be it from him to stand in the way of that good feeling which he could wish to see; and adjourning in quest of the housemaid, and presently returning with that young lady on his arm, informs the kitchen that foreigners is only his fun, and that him and Anne have now resolved to take one another for better for worse, and to settle in Oxford Market in the general greengrocery and herb and leech line,[3] where your kind favours is particular requested. This announcement is received with acclamation; and Mrs Perch, projecting her soul into futurity, says, 'girls,' in Cook's ear, in a solemn whisper.

Misfortune in the family without feasting, in these lower regions, couldn't be. Therefore Cook tosses up a hot dish or two for supper, and Mr Towlinson compounds a lobster salad to be devoted to the same hospitable purpose. Even Mrs Pipchin, agitated by the occasion, rings her bell, and sends down word that she requests to have that little bit of sweetbread that was left, warmed up for her supper, and sent to her on a tray with about a quarter of a tumbler-full of mulled sherry; for she feels poorly.

There is a little talk about Mr Dombey, but very little. It is chiefly speculation as to how long he has known that this was going to happen. Cook says shrewdly, 'Oh a long time, bless you! Take your oath of that.' And reference being made to Mr Perch, he confirms her view of the case. Somebody wonders what he'll do, and whether he'll go out in any situation. Mr Towlinson thinks not, and hints at a refuge in one of them genteel almshouses of the better kind. 'Ah, where he'll have his little garden, you know,' says Cook plaintively, 'and bring up sweet peas in the spring.' 'Exactly so,' says Mr Towlinson, 'and be one of the Brethren of something or another.' 'We are all brethren,' says Mrs Perch, in a pause of her drink. 'Except the sisters,' says Mr Perch. 'How are the mighty fallen!'[4] remarks Cook. 'Pride shall have a fall,[5] and it always was and will be so!' observes the housemaid.

It is wonderful how good they feel, in making these reflections; and what a Christian unanimity they are sensible of, in bearing the common shock with resignation. There is only one interruption to this excellent state of mind, which is occasioned by a young kitchen-maid of inferior rank – in black stockings – who, having sat with her mouth open for a long time, unexpectedly discharges from it words to this effect, 'Suppose the wages shouldn't be paid!' The company sit for a moment speechless; but Cook recovering first, turns upon the young woman, and requests to know how she dares insult the family, whose bread she eats, by such a dishonest supposition, and whether she thinks that anybody, with a scrap of honour left, could deprive poor servants of their pittance? 'Because if *that* is your religious feelings, Mary Daws,' says Cook warmly, 'I don't know where you mean to go to.'

Mr Towlinson don't know either; nor anybody; and the young

kitchen-maid, appearing not to know exactly, herself, and scouted by the general voice, is covered with confusion, as with a garment.[6]

After a few days, strange people begin to call at the house, and to make appointments with one another in the dining-room, as if they lived there. Especially, there is a gentleman, of a Mosaic Arabian[7] cast of countenance, with a very massive watch-guard, who whistles in the drawing-room, and, while he is waiting for the other gentleman, who always has pen and ink in his pocket, asks Mr Towlinson (by the easy name of 'Old Cock,') if he happens to know what the figure of them crimson and gold hangings might have been, when new bought. The callers and appointments in the dining-room become more numerous every day, and every gentleman seems to have pen and ink in his pocket, and to have some occasion to use it. At last it is said that there is going to be a Sale; and then more people arrive, with pen and ink in their pockets, commanding a detachment of men with carpet caps, who immediately begin to pull up the carpets, and knock the furniture about, and to print off thousands of impressions of their shoes upon the hall and staircase.

The council down stairs are in full conclave all this time, and, having nothing to do, perform perfect feats of eating. At length, they are one day summoned in a body to Mrs Pipchin's room, and thus addressed by the fair Peruvian:

'Your master's in difficulties,' says Mrs Pipchin, tartly. 'You know that, I suppose?'

Mr Towlinson, as spokesman, admits a general knowledge of the fact.

'And you're all on the look-out for yourselves, I warrant you,' says Mrs Pipchin, shaking her head at them.

A shrill voice from the rear exclaims, 'No more than yourself!'

'That's your opinion, Mrs Impudence, is it?' says the ireful Pipchin, looking with a fiery eye over the intermediate heads.

'Yes, Mrs Pipchin, it is,' replies Cook, advancing. 'And what then, pray?'

'Why, then you may go as soon as you like,' says Mrs Pipchin. 'The sooner the better; and I hope I shall never see your face again.'

With this the doughty Pipchin produces a canvas bag; and tells her wages out to that day, and a month beyond it: and clutches the money tight until a receipt for the same is duly signed, to the last up-stroke; when she grudgingly lets it go. This form of proceeding Mrs Pipchin repeats with every member of the household, until all are paid.

'Now those that choose can go about their business,' says Mrs Pipchin, 'and those that choose can stay here on board wages for a week or so, and make themselves useful. Except,' says the inflammable Pipchin, 'that slut of a cook, who'll go immediately.'

'That,' says Cook, 'she certainly will! I wish you good day, Mrs Pipchin, and sincerely wish I could compliment you on the sweetness of your appearance!'

'Get along with you,' says Mrs Pipchin, stamping her foot.

Cook sails off with an air of beneficent dignity, highly exasperating to Mrs Pipchin, and is shortly joined below stairs by the rest of the confederation.

Mr Towlinson then says that, in the first place, he would beg to propose a little snack of something to eat; and over that snack would desire to offer a suggestion which he thinks will meet the position in which they find themselves. The refreshment being produced, and very heartily partaken of, Mr Towlinson's suggestion is, in effect, that Cook is going, and that if we are not true to ourselves, nobody will be true to us. That they have lived in that house a long time, and exerted themselves very much to be sociable together. (At this, Cook says, with emotion, 'Hear, hear!' and Mrs Perch, who is there again, and full to the throat, sheds tears.) And that he thinks, at the present time, the feeling ought to be 'Go one, go all!' The housemaid is much affected by this generous sentiment, and warmly seconds it. Cook says she feels it's right, and only hopes it's not done as a compliment to her, but from a sense of duty. Mr Towlinson replies, from a sense of duty; and that now he is driven to express his opinions, he will openly say, that he does not think it over-respectable to remain in a house where Sales and such-like are carrying forwards. The housemaid is sure of it; and relates, in confirmation, that a strange man, in a carpet cap, offered this very morning to kiss her on the stairs. Hereupon, Mr Towlinson is starting from his chair, to seek and 'smash' the offender; when he is laid hold on by the ladies, who beseech him to calm himself, and to reflect that it is easier and wiser to leave the scene of such indecencies at once. Mrs Perch, presenting the case in a new light, even shows that delicacy towards Mr Dombey, shut up in his own rooms, imperatively demands precipitate retreat. 'For what,' says the good woman, 'must his feelings be, if he was to come upon any of the poor servants that he once deceived into thinking him immensely rich!' Cook is so struck by this moral consideration that Mrs Perch improves it with several pious axioms, original and selected. It becomes a clear case that they must all go. Boxes are packed, cabs fetched, and at dusk that evening there is not one member of the party left.

The house stands, large and weather-proof, in the long dull street; but it is a ruin, and the rats fly from it.

The men in the carpet caps go on tumbling the furniture about; and the gentlemen with the pens and ink make out inventories of it, and sit upon pieces of furniture never made to be sat upon, and eat bread and cheese from the public-house on other pieces of furniture never made to be eaten on, and seem to have a delight in appropriating precious articles to strange uses. Chaotic combinations of furniture also take place. Mattresses and bedding appear in the dining-room; the glass and china get into the conservatory; the great dinner service is set out in heaps on the long divan in the large drawing-room; and the stair-wires, made into fasces,[8] decorate the marble chimneypieces. Finally, a rug, with a printed bill upon it, is hung out from the balcony; and a similar appendage graces either side of the hall door.

Then, all day long, there is a routine of mouldy gigs and chaise-carts in the street; and herds of shabby vampires, Jew and Christian, over-run the house, sounding the plate-glass mirrors with their knuckles, striking discordant octaves on the Grand Piano, drawing wet forefingers over the pictures, breathing on the blades of the best dinner-knives, punching the squabs of chairs and sofas with their dirty fists, touzling the feather beds, opening and shutting all the drawers, balancing the silver spoons and forks, looking into the very threads of the drapery and linen, and disparaging everything. There is not a secret place in the whole house. Fluffy and snuffy strangers stare into the kitchen-range as curiously as into the attic clothes-press. Stout men with napless hats on, look out of the bedroom windows, and cut jokes with friends in the street. Quiet, calculating spirits withdraw into the dressing-rooms with catalogues, and make marginal notes thereon, with stumps of pencils. Two brokers invade the very fire-escape, and take a panoramic survey of the neighbourhood from the top of the house. The swarm and buzz, and going up and down, endure for days. The Capital Modern Household Furniture, etc., is on view.

Then there is a palisade of tables made in the best drawing-room; and on the capital, french-polished, extending, telescopic range of Spanish mahogany dining-tables with turned legs, the pulpit of the Auctioneer is erected; and the herds of shabby vampires, Jew and Christian, the strangers fluffy and snuffy, and the stout men with the napless hats, congregate about it and sit upon everything within reach, mantel-pieces included, and begin to bid. Hot, humming, and dusty are the rooms all day; and – high above the heat, hum, and dust – the head and shoulders, voice and hammer, of the Auctioneer, are ever at work. The men in the carpet caps get flustered and vicious with tumbling the Lots about, and still the Lots are going, going, gone; still coming on. Sometimes there is joking and a general roar. This lasts all day and three days following. The Capital Modern Household Furniture, etc., is on sale.

Then the mouldy gigs and chaise-carts reappear; and with them come spring-vans[9] and waggons, and an army of porters with knots.[10] All day long, the men with carpet caps are screwing at screw-drivers and bed-winches, or staggering by the dozen together on the staircase under heavy burdens, or up-heaving perfect rocks of Spanish mahogany, best rosewood, or plate-glass, into the gigs and chaise-carts, vans and waggons. All sorts of vehicles of burden are in attendance, from a tilted waggon to a wheelbarrow. Poor Paul's little bedstead is carried off in a donkey-tandem. For nearly a whole week, the Capital Modern Household Furniture, etc., is in course of removal.

At last it is all gone. Nothing is left about the house but scattered leaves of catalogues, littered scraps of straw and hay, and a battery of pewter pots behind the hall-door. The men with the carpet caps gather up their screw-drivers and bed-winches into bags, shoulder them, and walk off. One of the pen-and-ink gentlemen goes over the house as a last attention; sticking up bills in the windows respecting the lease of this desirable family mansion, and shutting the shutters. At length he follows the men with the carpet caps. None of the invaders remain. The house is a ruin, and the rats fly from it.

Mrs Pipchin's apartments, together with those locked rooms on the ground-floor where the window-blinds are drawn down close, have been spared the general devastation. Mrs Pipchin has remained austere and stony during the proceedings in her own room; or has occasionally looked in at the sale to see what the goods are fetching, and to bid for one particular easy chair. Mrs Pipchin has been the highest bidder for the easy chair, and sits upon her property when Mrs Chick comes to see her.

'How is my brother, Mrs Pipchin?' says Mrs Chick

'I don't know any more than the deuce,' says Mrs Pipchin. 'He never does me the honour to speak to me. He has his meat and drink put in the next room to his own; and what he takes, he comes out and takes when there's nobody there. It's no use asking me. I know no more about him than the man in the south who burnt his mouth by eating cold plum porridge.'[11]

This the acrimonious Pipchin says with a flounce.

'But good gracious me!' cries Mrs Chick blandly. 'How long is this to last! If my brother will not make an effort, Mrs Pipchin, what is to become of him? I am sure I should have thought he had seen enough of the consequences of *not* making an effort, by this time, to be warned against that fatal error.'

'Hoity toity!' says Mrs Pipchin, rubbing her nose. 'There's a great fuss, I think, about it. It an't so wonderful a case. People have had misfortunes before now, and been obliged to part with their furniture. I'm sure *I* have!'

'My brother,' pursues Mrs Chick profoundly, 'is so peculiar – so strange a man. He is the most peculiar man *I* ever saw. Would any one believe that when he received news of the marriage and emigration of that unnatural child – it's a comfort to me, now, to remember that I always said there was something extraordinary about that child; but nobody minds me – would anybody believe, I say, that he should then turn round upon me and say he had supposed, from my manner, that she had come to my house? Why, my gracious! And would anybody believe that when I merely say to him, "Paul, I may be very foolish, and I have no doubt I am, but I cannot understand how your affairs can have got into this state," he should actually fly at me, and request that I will come to see him no more until he asks me! Why, my goodness!'

'Ah!' says Mrs Pipchin. 'It's a pity he hadn't a little more to do with mines. They'd have tried his temper for him.'

'And what,' resumes Mrs Chick, quite regardless of Mrs Pipchin's observations, 'is it to end in? That's what I want to know. What does my brother mean to do? He must do something. It's of no use remaining shut up in his own rooms. Business won't come to him. No. He must go to it. Then why don't he go! He knows where to go, I suppose, having been a man of business all his life. Very good. Then why not go there?'

Mrs Chick, after forging this powerful chain of reasoning, remains silent for a minute to admire it.

'Besides,' says the discreet lady, with an argumentative air, 'who ever heard of such obstinacy as his staying shut up here through all these dreadful disagreeables? It's not as if there was no place for him to go to. Of course he could have come to our house. He knows he is at home there, I suppose? Mr Chick has perfectly bored about it, and I said with my own lips, "Why surely, Paul, you don't imagine that because your affairs have got into this state, you are the less at home to such near relatives as ourselves? You don't imagine that we are like the rest of the world?" But no; here he stays all through, and here he is. Why, good gracious me, suppose the house was to be let! What would he do then? He couldn't remain here then. If he attempted to do so, there would be an ejectment, an action for Doe,[12] and all sorts of things; and then he *must* go. Then why not go at first instead of at last? And that brings me back to what I said just now, and I naturally ask what is to be the end of it?'

'I know what's to be the end of it, as far as *I* am concerned,' replies Mrs Pipchin, 'and that's enough for me. I'm going to take *myself* off in a jiffy.'

'In a which, Mrs Pipchin,' says Mrs Chick.

'In a jiffy,' retorts Mrs Pipchin sharply.

'Ah, well! really I can't blame you, Mrs Pipchin,' says Mrs Chick, with frankness.

'It would be pretty much the same to me, if you could,' replies the sardonic Pipchin. 'At any rate I'm going. I can't stop here. I should be dead in a week. I had to cook my own pork chop yesterday, and I'm not used to it. My constitution will be giving way next. Besides, I had a very fair connexion at Brighton when I came here – little Pankey's folks alone were worth a good eighty pounds a-year to me – and I can't afford to throw it away. I've written to my niece, and she expects me by this time.'

'Have you spoken to my brother? 'inquires Mrs Chick.

'Oh, yes, it's very easy to say speak to him,' retorts Mrs Pipchin. 'How is it done? I called out to him yesterday, that I was no use here, and that he had better let me send for Mrs Richards. He grunted something or other that meant yes, and I sent! Grunt indeed! If he had been Mr Pipchin, he'd have had some reason to grunt. Yah! I've no patience with it!'

Here this exemplary female, who has pumped up so much fortitude and virtue from the depths of the Peruvian mines, rises from her cushioned property to see Mrs Chick to the door. Mrs Chick, deploring to the last the peculiar character of her brother, noiselessly retires, much occupied with her own sagacity and clearness of head.

In the dusk of the evening Mr Toodle, being off duty, arrives with Polly and a box, and leaves them, with a sounding kiss, in the hall of the empty house, the retired character of which affects Mr Toodle's spirits strongly.

'I tell you what, Polly, my dear,' says Mr Toodle, 'being now an ingein-driver, and well to do in the world, I shouldn't allow of your coming here, to be made dull-like, if it warn't for favours past. But favours past, Polly, is never to be forgot. To them which is in adversity, besides, your face is a cord'l.[13] So let's have another kiss on it, my dear. You wish no better than to do a right act, I know; and my views is, that it's right and dutiful to do this. Good night, Polly!'

Mrs Pipchin by this time looms dark in her black bombazeen skirts, black bonnet, and shawl; and has her personal property packed up; and has her chair (late a favourite chair of Mr Dombey's and the dead bargain of the sale) ready near the street door; and is only waiting for a fly-van,[14] going to-night to Brighton on private service, which is to call for her, by private contract, and convey her home.

Presently it comes. Mrs Pipchin's wardrobe being handed in and stowed away, Mrs Pipchin's chair is next handed in, and placed in a convenient corner among certain trusses of hay; it being the intention of the amiable woman to occupy the chair during her journey. Mrs Pipchin herself is next handed in, and grimly takes her seat. There is a snaky gleam in her hard grey eye, as of anticipated rounds of buttered toast, relays of hot chops, worryings and quellings of young children, sharp snappings at poor Berry, and all the other delights of her Ogress's castle. Mrs Pipchin almost laughs as the fly-van drives off, and she composes her black bombazeen skirts, and settles herself among the cushions of her easy chair.

The house is such a ruin that the rats have fled, and there is not one left.

But Polly, though alone in the deserted mansion – for there is no companionship in the shut-up rooms in which its late master hides his head – is not alone long. It is night; and she is sitting at work in the housekeeper's room, trying to forget what a lonely house it is, and what a history belongs to it; when there is a knock at the hall door, as loud sounding as any knock can be, striking into such an empty place. Opening it, she returns across the echoing hall, accompanied by a female figure in a close black bonnet. It is Miss Tox, and Miss Tox's eyes are red.

'Oh, Polly,' says Miss Tox, 'when I looked in to have a little lesson with the children just now, I got the message that you left for me; and as soon as I could recover my spirits at all, I came on after you. Is there no one here but you?'

'Ah! not a soul,' says Polly.

'Have you seen him?' whispers Miss Tox.

'Bless you,' returns Polly, 'no; he has not been seen this many a day. They tell me he never leaves his room.'

'Is he said to be ill?' inquires Miss Tox.

'No, ma'am, not that I know of,' returns Polly, 'except in his mind. He must be very bad there, poor gentleman!'

Miss Tox's sympathy is such that she can scarcely speak. She is no chicken, but she has not grown tough with age and celibacy. Her heart is very tender, her compassion very genuine, her homage very real. Beneath the locket with the fishy eye in it, Miss Tox bears better qualities than many a less whimsical outside; such qualities as will outlive, by many courses of the sun, the best outsides and brightest husks that fall in the harvest of the great reaper.[15]

It is long before Miss Tox goes away, and before Polly, with a candle flaring on the blank stairs, looks after her, for company, down the street, and feels unwilling to go back into the dreary house, and jar its emptiness with the heavy fastenings of the door, and glide away to bed. But all this Polly does; and in the morning sets in one of those darkened rooms such matters as she has been advised to prepare, and then retires and enters them no more until next morning at the same hour. There are bells there, but they never ring; and though she can sometimes hear a footfall going to and fro, it never comes out.

Miss Tox returns early in the day. It then begins to be Miss Tox's occupation to prepare little dainties – or what are such to her – to be carried into these rooms next morning. She derives so much satisfaction from the pursuit, that she enters on it regularly from that time; and brings daily in her little basket, various choice condiments selected from the scanty stores of the deceased owner of the powdered head and pigtail. She likewise brings, in sheets of curl-paper, morsels of cold meats, tongues of sheep, halves of fowls, for her own dinner; and sharing these collations with Polly, passes the greater part of her time in the ruined house that the rats have fled from: hiding, in a fright at every sound, stealing in and out like a criminal; only desiring to be true to the fallen object of her admiration, unknown to him, unknown to all the world but one poor simple woman.

The Major knows it; but no one is the wiser for that, though the Major is much the merrier. The Major, in a fit of curiosity, has charged the Native to watch the house sometimes, and find out what becomes of Dombey. The Native has reported Miss Tox's fidelity, and the Major has nearly choked himself dead with laughter. He is permanently bluer from that hour, and constantly wheezes to himself, his lobster eyes starting out of his head, 'Damme, Sir, the woman's a born idiot!'

And the ruined man. How does he pass the hours, alone?

'Let him remember it in that room, years to come!' He did remember it. It was heavy on his mind now; heavier than all the rest.

'Let him remember it in that room, years to come! The rain that falls upon the roof, the wind that mourns outside the door, may have foreknowledge in their melancholy sound. Let him remember it in that room, years to come!'

He did remember it. In the miserable night he thought of it; in the dreary day, the wretched dawn, the ghostly, memory-haunted twilight. He did remember it. In agony, in sorrow, in remorse, in despair! 'Papa! Papa! Speak to me, dear papa!' He heard the words again, and saw the face. He saw it fall upon the trembling hands, and heard the one prolonged low cry go upward.

He was fallen, never to be raised up any more. For the night of his worldly ruin there was no to-morrow's sun; for the stain of his domestic shame there was no purification; nothing, thank Heaven, could bring his dead child back to life. But that which he might have made so different in all the Past – which might have made the Past itself so different, though this he hardly thought of now – that which was his own work, that which he could so easily have wrought into a blessing, and had set himself so steadily for years to form into a curse: that was the sharp grief of his soul.

Oh! He did remember it! The rain that fell upon the roof, the wind that mourned outside the door that night, had had foreknowledge in their melancholy sound. He knew, now, what he had done. He knew, now, that he had called down that upon his head, which bowed it lower than the heaviest stroke of fortune. He knew, now, what it was to be rejected and deserted; now, when every loving blossom he had withered in his innocent daughter's heart was snowing down in ashes on him.

He thought of her, as she had been that night when he and his bride came home. He thought of her as she had been, in all the home-events of the abandoned House. He thought, now, that of all around him, she alone had never changed. His boy had faded into dust, his proud wife had sunk into a polluted creature, his flatterer and friend had been transformed into the worst of villains, his riches had melted away, the very walls that sheltered him looked on him as a stranger; she alone had turned the same mild gentle look upon him always. Yes, to the latest and the last. She had never changed to him – nor had he ever changed to her – and she was lost.

As, one by one, they fell away from his mind – his baby-hope, his wife, his friend, his fortune – oh how the mist, through which he had seen her, cleared, and showed him her true self! Oh, how much better than this that he had loved her as he had his boy, and lost her as he had his boy, and laid them in their early grave together!

In his pride – for he was proud yet – he let the world go from him freely. As it fell away, he shook it off. Whether he imagined its face as expressing pity for him, or indifference to him, he shunned it alike. It was in the same degree to be avoided, in either aspect. He had no idea of any one companion in his misery, but the one he had driven away. What he would have said to her, or what consolation submitted to receive from her, he never pictured to himself. But he always knew she would have been true to him, if he had suffered her. He always knew she would have loved him better now than at any other time: he was as certain that it was in her nature, as he was that there was a sky above him; and he sat thinking so, in his loneliness, from hour to hour. Day after day uttered this speech; night after night showed him this knowledge.

It began, beyond all doubt (however slowly it advanced for some time), in the receipt of her young husband's letter, and the certainty that she was gone. And yet – so proud he was in his ruin, or so reminiscent of her, only as something that might have been his, but was lost beyond redemption – that if he could have heard her voice in an adjoining room, he would not have gone to her. If he could have seen her in the street, and she had done no more than look at him as she had been used to look, he would have passed on with his old cold unforgiving face, and not addressed her, or relaxed it, though his heart should have broken soon afterwards. However turbulent his thoughts, or harsh his anger had been, at first, concerning her marriage, or her husband, that was all past now. He chiefly thought of what might have been, and what was not. What was, was all summed up in this: that she was lost, and he bowed down with sorrow and remorse.

And now he felt that he had had two children born to him in that house, and that between him and the bare wide empty walls there was a tie, mournful, but hard to rend asunder, connected with a double childhood, and a double loss. He had thought to leave the house – knowing he must go, not knowing whither – upon the evening of the day on which this feeling first struck root in his breast; but he resolved to stay another night, and in the night to ramble through the rooms once more.

He came out of his solitude when it was the dead of night, and with a candle in his hand went softly up the stairs. Of all the footmarks there, making them as common as the common street, there was not one, he thought, but had seemed at the time to set itself upon his brain while he had kept close, listening. He looked at their number, and their hurry, and contention – foot treading foot out, and upward track and downward jostling one another – and thought, with absolute dread and wonder how much he must have suffered during that trial, and what a changed man he had cause to be. He thought, besides, oh was there, somewhere in the world, a light footstep that might have worn out in a moment half those marks! – and bent his head, and wept as he went up.

He almost saw it, going on before. He stopped, looking up towards the skylight; and a figure, childish itself, but carrying a child, and singing as it went, seemed to be there again. Anon, it was the same figure, alone, stopping for an instant, with suspended breath; the bright hair clustering loosely round its tearful face; and looking back at him.

He wandered through the rooms: lately so luxurious; now so bare and dismal and so changed, apparently, even in their shape and size. The press of footsteps was as thick here; and the same consideration of the suffering he had had, perplexed and terrified him. He began to fear that all this intricacy in his brain would drive him mad; and that his thoughts already lost coherence as the footprints did, and were pieced on to one another, with the same trackless involutions, and varieties of indistinct shapes.

He did not so much as know in which of these rooms she had lived, when she was alone. He was glad to leave them, and go wandering higher up. Abundance of associations were here, connected with his false wife, his false friend and servant, his false grounds of pride; but he put them all by now, and only recalled miserably, weakly, fondly, his two children.

Everywhere, the footsteps! They had had no respect for the old room high up, where the little bed had been; he could hardly find a clear space there, to throw himself down, on the floor, against the wall, poor broken man, and let his tears flow as they would. He had shed so many tears here, long ago, that he was less ashamed of his weakness in this place than in any other – perhaps, with that consciousness, had made excuses to himself for coming here. Here, with stooping shoulders, and his chin dropped on his breast, he had come. Here, thrown upon the bare boards, in the dead of night, he wept, alone – a proud man, even then; who, if a kind hand could have been stretched out, or a kind face could have looked in, would have risen up, and turned away, and gone down to his cell.

When the day broke he was shut up in his rooms again. He had meant to go away to-day, but clung to this tie in the house as the last and only thing left to him. He would go to-morrow. To-morrow came. He would go to-morrow. Every night, within the knowledge of no human creature, he came forth, and wandered through the despoiled house like a ghost. Many a morning when the day broke, his altered face, drooping behind the closed blind in his window imperfectly transparent to the light as yet, pondered on the loss of his two children. It was one child no more. He reunited them in his thoughts, and they were never asunder. Oh, that he could have united them in his past love, and in death, and that one had not been so much worse than dead!

Strong mental agitation and disturbance was no novelty to him, even before his late sufferings. It never is, to obstinate and sullen natures; for they struggle hard to be such. Ground, long under-mined, will often fall down in a moment; what was undermined here in so many ways, weakened, and crumbled, little by little, more and more, as the hand moved on the dial.

At last he began to think he need not go at all. He might yet give up what his creditors had spared him (that they had not spared him more, was his own act), and only sever the tie between him and the ruined house, by severing that other link—

It was then that his footfall was audible in the late housekeeper's room, as he walked to and fro; but not audible in its true meaning, or it would have had an appalling sound.

The world was very busy and restless about him. He became aware of that again. It was whispering and babbling. It was never quiet. This, and the intricacy and complication of the footsteps, harassed him to death. Objects began to take a bleared and russet colour in his eyes. Dombey and Son was no more – his children no more. This must be thought of, well, to-morrow.

He thought of it to-morrow; and sitting thinking in his chair, saw in the glass, from time to time, this picture:

A spectral, haggard, wasted likeness of himself, brooded and brooded over the empty fireplace. Now it lifted up its head, examining the lines and hollows in its face; now hung it down again, and brooded afresh. Now it rose and walked about; now passed into the next room, and came back with something from the dressing-table in its breast. Now, it was looking at the bottom of the door, and thinking.

– Hush! what?

It was thinking that if blood were to trickle that way, and to leak out into the hall, it must be a long time going so far. It would move so stealthily and slowly, creeping on, with here a lazy little pool, and there a start, and then another little pool, that a desperately wounded man could only be discovered through its means, either dead or dying. When it had thought of this a long while, it got up again, and walked to and fro with its hand in its breast. He glanced at it occasionally, very curious to watch its motions, and he marked how wicked and murderous that hand looked.

Now it was thinking again! What was it thinking?

Whether they would tread in the blood when it crept so far, and carry it about the house among those many prints of feet, or even out into the street.

It sat down, with its eyes upon the empty fireplace, and as it lost itself in thought there shone into the room a gleam of light; a ray of sun. It was quite unmindful, and sat thinking. Suddenly it rose, with a terrible face, and that guilty hand grasping what was in its breast. Then it was arrested by a cry – a wild, loud, piercing, loving, rapturous cry – and he only saw his own reflection in the glass, and at his knees, his daughter!

Yes. His daughter! Look at her Look here! Down upon the ground, clinging to him, calling to him, folding her hands, praying to him.

'Papa! Dearest papa! Pardon me, forgive me! I have come back to ask forgiveness on my knees. I never can be happy more, without it!'

Unchanged still. Of all the world, unchanged. Raising the same face to his, as on that miserable night. Asking *his* forgiveness!

'Dear papa, oh don't look strangely on me! I never meant to leave you. I never thought of it, before or afterwards. I was frightened when I went away, and could not think. Papa, dear, I am changed. I am penitent. I know my fault. I know my duty better now. Papa, don't cast me off, or I shall die!'

He tottered to his chair. He felt her draw his arms about her neck; he felt her put her own round his; he felt her kisses on his

'Let him remember it in that room, years to come!'

face; he felt her wet cheek laid against his own; he felt – oh, how deeply! – all that he had done.

Upon the breast that he had bruised, against the heart that he had almost broken, she laid his face, now covered with his hands, and said, sobbing:

'Papa, love, I am a mother. I have a child who will soon call Walter by the name by which I call you. When it was born, and when I knew how much I loved it, I knew what I had done in leaving you. Forgive me, dear papa! oh say God bless me, and my little child!'

He would have said it, if he could. He would have raised his hands and besought her for pardon, but she caught them in her own, and put them down, hurriedly.

'My little child was born at sea, papa. I prayed to God (and so did Walter for me) to spare me, that I might come home. The moment I could land, I came back to you. Never let us be parted any more, papa!'

His head, now grey, was encircled by her arm; and he groaned to think that never, never, had it rested so before.

'You will come home with me, papa, and see my baby. A boy, papa. His name is Paul. I think – I hope – he's like—'

Her tears stopped her.

'Dear papa, for the sake of my child, for the sake of the name we have given him, for my sake, pardon Walter. He is so kind and so tender to me. I am so happy with him. It was not his fault that we were married. It was mine. I loved him so much.'

She clung closer to him, more endearing and more earnest.

'He is the darling of my heart, papa. I would die for him. He will love and honour you as I will. We will teach our little child to love and honour you; and we will tell him, when he can understand, that you had a son of that name once, and that he died, and you were very sorry; but that he is gone to Heaven, where we all hope to see him when our time for resting comes. Kiss me, papa, as a promise that you will be reconciled to Walter – to my dearest husband – to the father of the little child who taught me to come back, papa. Who taught me to come back!'

As she clung closer to him, in another burst of tears, he kissed her on her lips, and, lifting up his eyes, said, 'Oh my God, forgive me, for I need it very much!'

With that he dropped his head again, lamenting over and caressing her, and there was not a sound in all the house for a long,

long time; they remaining clasped in one another's arms, in the glorious sunshine that had crept in with Florence.

He dressed himself for going out, with a docile submission to her entreaty; and walking with a feeble gait, and looking back, with a tremble, at the room in which he had been so long shut up, and where he had seen the picture in the glass, passed out with her into the hall. Florence, hardly glancing round her, lest she should remind him freshly of their last parting – for their feet were on the very stones where he had struck her in his madness – and keeping close to him, with her eyes upon his face, and his arm about her, led him out to a coach that was waiting at the door, and carried him away.

Then, Miss Tox and Polly came out of their concealment, and exulted tearfully. And then they packed his clothes, and books, and so forth, with great care; and consigned them in due course to certain persons sent by Florence in the evening, to fetch them. And then they took a last cup of tea in the lonely house.

'And so, Dombey and Son, as I observed upon a certain sad occasion,'[16] said Miss Tox, winding up a host of recollections, 'is indeed a daughter, Polly, after all.'

'And a good one!' exclaimed Polly.

'You are right,' said Miss Tox; 'and it's a credit to you, Polly, that you were always her friend when she was a little child. You were her friend long before I was, Polly,' said Miss Tox; 'and you're a good creature. Robin!'

Miss Tox addressed herself to a bullet-headed young man, who appeared to be in but indifferent circumstances, and in depressed spirits, and who was sitting in a remote corner. Rising, he disclosed to view the form and features of the Grinder.

'Robin,' said Miss Tox, 'I have just observed to your mother, as you may have heard, that she is a good creature.'

'And so she is, Miss,' quoth the Grinder, with some feeling.

'Very well, Robin,' said Miss Tox, 'I am glad to hear you say so. Now, Robin, as I am going to give you a trial, at your urgent request, as my domestic, with a view to your restoration to respectability, I will take this impressive occasion of remarking that I hope you will never forget that you have, and have always had, a good mother, and that you will endeavour so to conduct yourself as to be a comfort to her.'

'Upon my soul I will, Miss,' returned the Grinder. 'I have come through a good deal, and my intentions is now as straightfor'ard, Miss, as a cove's—'

'I must get you to break yourself of that word, Robin, if you please,' interposed Miss Tox, politely.

'If you please, Miss, as a chap's—'

'Thankee, Robin, no,' returned Miss Tox. 'I should prefer individual.'

'As a indiwiddle's,' said the Grinder.

'Much better,' remarked Miss Tox, complacently; 'infinitely more expressive!'

'—can be,' pursued Rob. 'If I hadn't been and got made a Grinder on, Miss and mother, which was a most unfortunate circumstance for a young co— indiwiddle.'

'Very good indeed,' observed Miss Tox, approvingly.

'—and if I hadn't been led away by birds, and then fallen into a bad service,' said the Grinder, 'I hope I might have done better. But it's never too late for a—'

'Indi—' suggested Miss Tox.

'—widdle,' said the Grinder, 'to mend; and I hope to mend, Miss, with your kind trial; and wishing, mother, my love to father, and brothers and sisters, and saying of it.'

'I am very glad indeed to hear it,' observed Miss Tox. 'Will you take a little bread and butter, and a cup of tea, before we go, Robin?'

'Thankee, Miss,' returned the Grinder; who immediately began to use his own personal grinders in a most remarkable manner, as if he had been on very short allowance for a considerable period.

Miss Tox, being in good time, bonneted and shawled, and Polly too, Rob hugged his mother, and followed his new mistress away; so much to the hopeful admiration of Polly, that something in her eyes made luminous rings round the gas-lamps as she looked after him. Polly then put out her light, locked the house-door, delivered the key at an agent's hard by, and went home as fast as she could go; rejoicing in the shrill delight that her unexpected arrival would occasion there. The great house, dumb as to all that had been suffered in it, and the changes it had witnessed, stood frowning like a dark mute on the street; baulking any nearer inquiries with the staring announcement that the lease of this desirable Family Mansion was to be disposed of.

CHAPTER 60

Chiefly Matrimonial

The grand half-yearly festival holden by Doctor and Mrs Blimber, on which occasion they requested the pleasure of the company of every young gentleman pursuing his studies in that genteel establishment, at an early party, when the hour was half-past seven o'clock, and when the object was quadrilles, had duly taken place, about this time; and the young gentlemen, with no unbecoming demonstrations of levity, had betaken themselves, in a state of scholastic repletion, to their own homes. Mr Skettles had repaired abroad, permanently to grace the establishment of his father Sir Barnet Skettles, whose popular manners had obtained him a diplomatic appointment, the honours of which were discharged by himself and Lady Skettles, to the satisfaction even of their own countrymen and countrywomen: which was considered almost miraculous. Mr Tozer, now a young man of lofty stature, in Wellington boots,[1] was so extremely full of antiquity as to be nearly on a par with a genuine ancient Roman in his knowledge of English: a triumph that affected his good parents with the tenderest emotions, and caused the father and mother of Mr Briggs (whose learning, like ill-arranged luggage, was so tightly packed that he couldn't get at anything he wanted) to hide their diminished heads. The fruit laboriously gathered from the tree of knowledge by this latter young gentleman, in fact, had been subjected to so much pressure, that it had become a kind of intellectual Norfolk Biffin,[2] and had nothing of its original form or flavour remaining. Master Bitherstone now, on whom the forcing system had the happier and not uncommon effect of leaving no impression whatever, when the forcing apparatus ceased to work, was in a much more comfortable plight; and being then on shipboard, bound for Bengal, found himself forgetting, with such admirable rapidity, that it was doubtful whether his declensions of noun-substantives would hold out to the end of the voyage.

When Doctor Blimber, in pursuance of the usual course, would have said to the young gentlemen, on the morning of the party, 'Gentlemen, we will resume our studies on the twenty-fifth of next month,' he departed from the usual course, and said, 'Gentlemen, when our friend Cincinnatus[3] retired to his farm, he did not present to the senate any Roman whom he sought to nominate as his successor. But there is a Roman here,' said Doctor Blimber, laying his hand on the shoulder of Mr Feeder, B.A., *'adolescens imprimis*

gravis et doctus,[4] gentlemen, whom I, a retiring Cincinnatus, wish
to present to *my* little senate, as their future Dictator. Gentlemen,
we will resume our studies on the twenty-fifth of next month, under
the auspices of Mr Feeder, B.A.' At this (which Doctor Blimber had
previously called upon all the parents, and urbanely explained), the
young gentlemen cheered; and Mr Tozer, on behalf of the rest,
instantly presented the Doctor with a silver inkstand, in a speech
containing very little of the mother-tongue, but fifteen quotations
from the Latin, and seven from the Greek, which moved the younger
of the young gentlemen to discontent and envy: they remarking,
'Oh, ah! It was all very well for old Tozer, but they didn't subscribe
money for old Tozer to show off with, they supposed; did they?
What business was it of old Tozer's more than anybody else's? It
wasn't *his* inkstand. Why couldn't he leave the boys' property
alone?' and murmuring other expressions of their dissatisfaction,
which seemed to find a greater relief in calling him old Tozer, than
in any other available vent.

Not a word had been said to the young gentlemen, nor a hint
dropped, of anything like a contemplated marriage between Mr
Feeder, B.A., and the fair Cornelia Blimber. Doctor Blimber,
especially, seemed to take pains to look as if nothing would surprise
him more; but it was perfectly well known to all the young
gentlemen nevertheless, and when they departed for the society of
their relations and friends, they took leave of Mr Feeder with awe.

Mr Feeder's most romantic visions were fulfilled. The Doctor had
determined to paint the house outside, and put it in thorough repair;
and to give up the business, and to give up Cornelia. The painting
and repairing began upon the very day of the young gentlemen's
departure, and now behold! the wedding morning was come, and
Cornelia, in a new pair of spectacles, was waiting to be led to the
hymeneal altar.

The Doctor with his learned legs, and Mrs Blimber in a lilac
bonnet, and Mr Feeder, B.A., with his long knuckles and his bristly
head of hair, and Mr Feeder's brother, the Reverend Alfred Feeder,
M.A., who was to perform the ceremony, were all assembled in the
drawing-room, and Cornelia with her orange-flowers and bridesmaids had just come down, and looked, as of old, a little squeezed
in appearance, but very charming, when the door opened, and the
weak-eyed young man, in a loud voice, made the following
proclamation:

MR AND MRS TOOTS!

Upon which there entered Mr Toots, grown extremely stout, and on his arm a lady very handsomely and becomingly dressed, with very bright black eyes.

'Mrs Blimber,' said Mr Toots, 'allow me to present my wife.'

Mrs Blimber was delighted to receive her. Mrs Blimber was a little condescending, but extremely kind.

'And as you've known me for a long time, you know,' said Mr Toots, 'let me assure you that she is one of the most remarkable women that ever lived.'

'My dear!' remonstrated Mrs Toots.

'Upon my word and honour she is,' said Mr Toots. 'I – I assure you, Mrs Blimber, she's a most extraordinary woman.'

Mrs Toots laughed merrily, and Mrs Blimber led her to Cornelia. Mr Toots having paid his respects in that direction, and having saluted his old preceptor, who said, in allusion to his conjugal state, 'Well, Toots, well, Toots! So you are one of us, are you, Toots?' – retired with Mr Feeder, B.A., into a window.

Mr Feeder, B.A., being in great spirits, made a spar at Mr Toots, and tapped him skilfully with the back of his hand on the breast-bone.

'Well, old Buck!' said Mr Feeder with a laugh. 'Well! Here we are! Taken in and done for. Eh?'

'Feeder,' returned Mr Toots. 'I give you joy. If you're as – as – as perfectly blissful in a matrimonial life, as I am myself, you'll have nothing to desire.'

'I don't forget *my* old friends, you see,' said Mr Feeder. 'I ask 'em to *my* wedding, Toots.'

'Feeder,' replied Mr Toots gravely, 'the fact is, that there were several circumstances which prevented me from communicating with you until after my marriage had been solemnised. In the first place, I had made a perfect Brute of myself to you, on the subject of Miss Dombey; and I felt that if you were asked to any wedding of mine, you would naturally expect that it was *with* Miss Dombey, which involved explanations, that upon my word and honour, at that crisis, would have knocked me completely over. In the second place, our wedding was strictly private; there being nobody present but one friend of myself and Mrs Toots's, who is a Captain in – I don't exactly know in what,' said Mr Toots, 'but it's of no consequence. I hope, Feeder, that in writing a statement of what had occurred before Mrs Toots and myself went abroad upon our foreign tour, I fully discharged the offices of friendship.'

'Toots, my boy,' said Mr Feeder, shaking his hands, 'I was joking.'

'And now, Feeder,' said Mr Toots, 'I should be glad to know what you think of my union.'

'Capital!' returned Mr Feeder.

'You think it's capital, do you, Feeder?' said Mr Toots solemnly. 'Then how capital must it be to Me! For *you* can never know what an extraordinary woman that is.'

Mr Feeder was willing to take it for granted. But Mr Toots shook his head, and wouldn't hear of that being possible.

'You see,' said Mr Toots, 'what *I* wanted in a wife was – in short, was sense. Money, Feeder, I had. Sense I – I had not, particularly.'

Mr Feeder murmured, 'Oh, yes, you had, Toots!' But Mr Toots said:

'No, Feeder, I had *not*. Why should I disguise it? I had *not*. I knew that sense was There,' said Mr Toots, stretching out his hand towards his wife, 'in perfect heaps. I had no relation to object or be offended, on the score of station;[5] for I had no relation. I have never had anybody belonging to me but my guardian, and him, Feeder, I have always considered as a Pirate and a Corsair. Therefore, you know it was not likely,' said Mr Toots, 'that I should take *his* opinion.'

'No,' said Mr Feeder.

'Accordingly,' resumed Mr Toots, 'I acted on my own. Bright was the day on which I did so! Feeder! Nobody but myself can tell what the capacity of that woman's mind is. If ever the Rights of Women,[6] and all that kind of thing, are properly attended to, it will be through her powerful intellect. – Susan, my dear!' said Mr Toots, looking abruptly out of the window-curtains, 'pray do not exert yourself!'

'My dear,' said Mrs Toots, 'I was only talking.'

'But, my love,' said Mr Toots, 'pray do not exert yourself. You really must be careful. Do not, my dear Susan, exert yourself. She's so easily excited,' said Mr Toots, apart to Mrs Blimber, 'and then she forgets the medical man altogether.'

Mrs Blimber was impressing on Mrs Toots the necessity of caution, when Mr Feeder, B.A., offered her his arm, and led her down to the carriages that were in waiting to go to church. Doctor Blimber escorted Mrs Toots. Mr Toots escorted the fair bride, around whose lambent spectacles two gauzy little bridesmaids fluttered like moths. Mr Feeder's brother, Mr Alfred Feeder, M.A., had already gone on, in advance, to assume his official functions.

The ceremony was performed in an admirable manner. Cornelia, with her crisp little curls, 'went in,'[7] as the Chicken might have said, with great composure; and Doctor Blimber gave her away, like a man who had quite made up his mind to it. The gauzy little bridesmaids appeared to suffer most. Mrs Blimber was affected, but gently so; and told the Reverend Mr Alfred Feeder, M.A., on the way home, that if she could only have seen Cicero in his retirement at Tusculum, she would not have had a wish, now, ungratified.

There was a breakfast afterwards, limited to the same small party; at which the spirits of Mr Feeder, B.A., were tremendous, and so communicated themselves to Mrs Toots that Mr Toots was several times heard to observe, across the table, 'My dear Susan, *don't* exert yourself!' The best of it was, that Mr Toots felt it incumbent on him to make a speech; and in spite of a whole code of telegraphic dissuasions from Mrs Toots, appeared on his legs for the first time in his life.

'I really,' said Mr Toots, 'in this house, where whatever was done to me in the way of – of any mental confusion sometimes – which is of no consequence and I impute to nobody – I was always treated like one of Doctor Blimber's family, and had a desk to myself for a considerable period – can – not – allow my friend Feeder to be—'

Mrs Toots suggested 'married.'

'It may not be inappropriate to the occasion, or altogether uninteresting,' said Mr Toots with a delightful face, 'to observe that my wife is a most extraordinary woman, and would do this much better than myself – allow my friend Feeder to be married – especially to—'

Mrs Toots suggested 'to Miss Blimber.'

'To Mrs Feeder, my love!' said Mr Toots, in a subdued tone of private discussion: '"whom God hath joined," you know, "let no man" – don't you know? I cannot allow my friend Feeder to be married – especially to Mrs Feeder – without proposing their – their – Toasts; and may,' said Mr Toots, fixing his eyes on his wife, as if for inspiration in a high flight, 'may the torch of Hymen[8] be the beacon of joy, and may the flowers we have this day strewed in their path, be the – the banishers of – of gloom!'

Doctor Blimber, who had a taste for metaphor, was pleased with this, and said, 'Very good, Toots! Very well said, indeed, Toots!' and nodded his head and patted his hands. Mr Feeder made in reply, a comic speech chequered with sentiment. Mr Alfred Feeder, M.A., was afterwards very happy on Doctor and Mrs Blimber; Mr Feeder, B.A., scarcely less so, on the gauzy little bridesmaids. Doctor Blimber then, in a sonorous voice, delivered a few thoughts in the pastoral style, relative to the rushes among which it was the intention of himself and Mrs Blimber to dwell, and the bee that would hum around their cot. Shortly after which, as the Doctor's eyes were twinkling in a remarkable manner, and his son-in-law had already observed that time was made for slaves, and had inquired whether Mrs Toots sang, the discreet Mrs Blimber dissolved the sitting, and sent Cornelia away, very cool and comfortable, in a post-chaise, with the man of her heart.

Mr and Mrs Toots withdrew to the Bedford (Mrs Toots had been there before in old times, under her maiden name of Nipper), and there found a letter, which it took Mr Toots such an enormous time to read, that Mrs Toots was frightened.

'My dear Susan,' said Mr Toots, 'fright is worse than exertion. Pray be calm!'

'Who is it from?' asked Mrs Toots.

'Why, my love,' said Mr Toots, 'it's from Captain Gills. Do not excite yourself. Walters and Miss Dombey are expected home!'

'My dear,' said Mrs Toots, raising herself quickly from the sofa, very pale, 'don't try to deceive me, for it's no use, they're come home – I see it plainly in your face!'

'She's a most extraordinary woman!' exclaimed Mr Toots, in rapturous admiration. 'You're perfectly right, my love, they have come home. Miss Dombey has seen her father, and they are reconciled!'

'Reconciled!' cried Mrs Toots, clapping her hands.

'My dear,' said Mr Toots, 'pray do not exert yourself. Do remember the medical man! Captain Gills says – at least he don't say, but I imagine, from what I can make out, he means – that Miss Dombey has brought her unfortunate father away from his old house, to one where she and Walters are living; that he is lying very ill there – supposed to be dying; and that she attends upon him night and day.'

Mrs Toots began to cry quite bitterly.

'My dearest Susan,' replied Mr Toots, 'do, do, if you possibly can, remember the medical man! If you can't, it's of no consequence – but do endeavour to!'

His wife, with her old manner suddenly restored, so pathetically entreated him to take her to her precious pet, her little mistress, her own darling, and the like, that Mr Toots, whose sympathy and admiration were of the strongest kind, consented from his very heart of hearts; and they agreed to depart immediately, and present themselves in answer to the Captain's letter.

Now some hidden sympathies of things, or some coincidences,

had that day brought the Captain himself (toward whom Mr and Mrs Toots were soon journeying) into the flowery train of wedlock; not as a principal, but as an accessory. It happened accidentally, and thus:

The Captain, having seen Florence and her baby for a moment, to his unbounded content, and having had a long talk with Walter, turned out for a walk; feeling it necessary to have some solitary meditation on the changes of human affairs, and to shake his glazed hat profoundly over the fall of Mr Dombey, for whom the generosity and simplicity of his nature were awakened in a lively manner. The Captain would have been very low, indeed, on the unhappy gentleman's account, but for the recollection of the baby; which afforded him such intense satisfaction whenever it arose, that he laughed aloud as he went along the street, and, indeed, more than once, in a sudden impulse of joy, threw up his glazed hat and caught it again; much to the amazement of the spectators. The rapid alternations of light and shade to which these two conflicting subjects of reflection exposed the Captain, were so very trying to his spirits, that he felt a long walk necessary to his composure; and as there is a great deal in the influence of harmonious associations, he chose, for the scene of his walk, his old neighbourhood, down among the mast, oar, and block makers, ship-biscuit bakers, coal-whippers, pitch-kettles, sailors, canals, docks, swing-bridges, and other soothing objects.

These peaceful scenes, and particularly the region of Limehouse Hole⁹ and thereabouts, were so influential in calming the Captain, that he walked on with restored tranquillity, and was, in fact, regaling himself, under his breath, with the ballad of Lovely Peg, when, on turning a corner, he was suddenly transfixed and rendered speechless by a triumphant procession that he beheld advancing towards him.

This awful demonstration was headed by that determined woman, Mrs MacStinger, who, preserving a countenance of inexorable resolution, and wearing conspicuously attached to her obdurate bosom a stupendous watch and appendages, which the Captain recognised at a glance as the property of Bunsby, conducted under her arm no other than that sagacious mariner; he, with the distraught and melancholy visage of a captive borne into a foreign land, meekly resigning himself to her will. Behind them appeared the young MacStingers, in a body, exulting. Behind them, two ladies of a terrible and steadfast aspect, leading between them a short gentleman in a tall hat, who likewise exulted. In the wake,

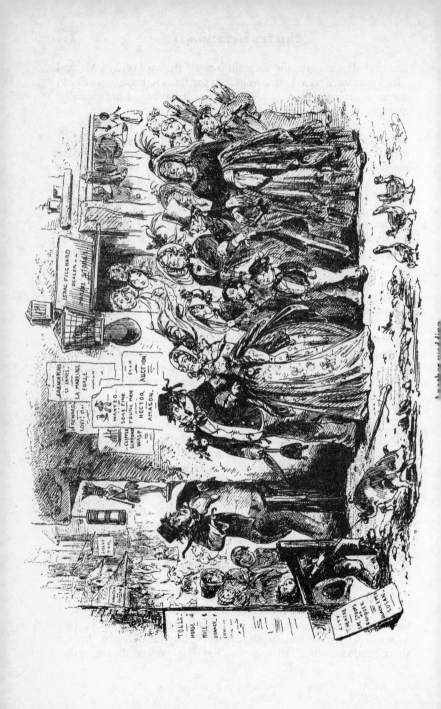

Another wedding

appeared Bunsby's boy, bearing umbrellas. The whole were in good marching order; and a dreadful smartness that pervaded the party would have sufficiently announced, if the intrepid countenances of the ladies had been wanting, that it was a procession of sacrifice, and that the victim was Bunsby.

The first impulse of the Captain was to run away. This also appeared to be the first impulse of Bunsby, hopeless as its execution must have proved. But a cry of recognition proceeding from the party, and Alexander MacStinger running up to the Captain with open arms, the Captain struck.

'Well, Cap'en Cuttle!' said Mrs MacStinger. 'This is indeed a meeting! I bear no malice now. Cap'en Cuttle – you needn't fear that I'm going to cast any reflections. I hope to go to the altar in another spirit.' Here Mrs MacStinger paused, and drawing herself up, and inflating her bosom with a long breath, said, in allusion to the victim, 'My 'usband, Cap'en Cuttle!'

The abject Bunsby looked neither to the right nor to the left, nor at his bride, nor at his friend, but straight before him at nothing. The Captain putting out his hand, Bunsby put out his; but, in answer to the Captain's greeting, spake no word.

'Cap'en Cuttle,' said Mrs MacStinger, 'if you would wish to heal up past animosities, and to see the last of your friend, my 'usband, as a single person, we should be 'appy of your company to chapel. Here is a lady here,' said Mrs MacStinger, turning round to the more intrepid of the two, 'my bridesmaid, that will be glad of your protection, Cap'en Cuttle.'

The short gentleman in the tall hat, who it appeared was the husband of the other lady, and who evidently exulted at the reduction of a fellow-creature to his own condition, gave place at this, and resigned the lady to Captain Cuttle. The lady immediately seized him, and, observing that there was no time to lose, gave the word, in a strong voice, to advance.

The Captain's concern for his friend, not unmingled, at first, with some concern for himself – for a shadowy terror that he might be married by violence, possessed him, until his knowledge of the service came to his relief, and remembering the legal obligation of saying, 'I will,' he felt himself personally safe so long as he resolved, if asked any question, distinctly to reply 'I won't' – threw him into a profuse perspiration; and rendered him, for a time, insensible to the movements of the procession, of which he now formed a feature, and to the conversation of his fair companion. But as he became less agitated, he learnt from this lady that she was the widow of a Mr Bokum, who had held an employment in the Custom House; that she was the dearest friend of Mrs MacStinger, whom she considered a pattern for her sex; that she had often heard of the Captain, and now hoped he had repented of his past life; that she trusted Mr Bunsby knew what a blessing he had gained, but that she feared men seldom did know what such blessings were, until they had lost them; with more to the same purpose.

All this time, the Captain could not but observe that Mrs Bokum kept her eyes steadily on the bridegroom, and that whenever they came near a court or other narrow turning which appeared favourable for flight, she was on the alert to cut him off if he attempted to escape. The other lady, too, as well as her husband, the short gentleman with the tall hat, were plainly on guard, according to a preconcerted plan; and the wretched man was so secured by Mrs MacStinger, that any effort at self-preservation by flight was rendered futile. This indeed, was apparent to the mere populace, who expressed their perception of the fact by jeers and cries; to all of which, the dread MacStinger was inflexibly indifferent, while Bunsby himself appeared in a state of unconsciousness.

The Captain made many attempts to accost the philosopher, if only in a monosyllable or a signal; but always failed, in consequence of the vigilance of the guard, and the difficulty, at all times peculiar to Bunsby's constitution, of having his attention aroused by any outward and visible sign whatever. Thus they approached the chapel, a neat whitewashed edifice, recently engaged by the Reverend Melchisedech Howler, who had consented, on very urgent solicitation, to give the world another two years of existence, but had informed his followers that, then, it must positively go.

While the Reverend Melchisedech was offering up some extemporary orisons, the Captain found an opportunity of growling in the bridegroom's ear:

'What cheer, my lad, what cheer?'

To which Bunsby replied, with a forgetfulness of the Reverend Melchisedech, which nothing but his desperate circumstances could have excused:

'D–d bad.'

'Jack Bunsby,' whispered the Captain, 'do you do this here o' your own free will?'

Mr Bunsby answered 'No.'

'Why do you do it, then, my lad?' inquired the Captain, not unnaturally.

Bunsby, still looking, and always looking with an immovable countenance, at the opposite side of the world, made no reply.

'Why not sheer off?' said the Captain.

'Eh?' whispered Bunsby, with a momentary gleam of hope.

'Sheer off,' said the Captain.

'Where's the good?' retorted the forlorn sage. 'She'd capter me agen.'

'Try!' replied the Captain. 'Cheer up! Come! Now's your time. Sheer off, Jack Bunsby!'

Jack Bunsby, however, instead of profiting by the advice, said in a doleful whisper:

'It all began in that there chest o'yourn. Why did I ever conwoy her into port that night?'

'My lad,' faltered the Captain, 'I thought as you had come over her; not as she had come over you. A man as has got such opinions as you have!'

Mr Bunsby merely uttered a suppressed groan.

'Come!' said the Captain, nudging him with his elbow, 'now's your time! Sheer off! I'll cover your retreat. The time's a flying. Bunsby! It's for liberty. Will you once?'

Bunsby was immovable.

'Bunsby!' whispered the Captain, 'will you twice?'

Bunsby wouldn't twice.

'Bunsby!' urged the Captain, 'it's for liberty; will you three times? Now or never!'

Bunsby didn't then, and didn't ever; for Mrs MacStinger immediately afterwards married him.

One of the most frightful circumstances of the ceremony to the Captain, was the deadly interest exhibited therein by Juliana MacStinger; and the fatal concentration of her faculties, with which that promising child, already the image of her parent, observed the whole proceedings. The Captain saw in this a succession of mantraps stretching out infinitely; a series of ages of oppression and coercion, through which the seafaring line was doomed. It was a more memorable sight than the unflinching steadiness of Mrs Bokum and the other lady, the exultation of the short gentleman in the tall hat, or even the fell inflexibility of Mrs MacStinger. The Master MacStingers understood little of what was going on, and cared less; being chiefly engaged, during the ceremony, in treading on one another's half-boots;[10] but the contrast afforded by those wretched infants only set off and adorned the precocious woman in

Juliana. Another year or two, the Captain thought, and to lodge where that child was, would be destruction.

The ceremony was concluded by a general spring of the young family on Mr Bunsby, whom they hailed by the endearing name of father, and from whom they solicited halfpence. These gushes of affection over, the procession was about to issue forth again, when it was delayed for some little time by an unexpected transport on the part of Alexander MacStinger. That dear child, it seemed, connecting a chapel with tombstones, when it was entered for any purpose apart from the ordinary religious exercises, could not be persuaded but that his mother was now to be decently interred, and lost to him for ever. In the anguish of this conviction, he screamed with astonishing force, and turned black in the face. However touching these marks of a tender disposition were to his mother, it was not in the character of that remarkable woman to permit her recognition of them to degenerate into weakness. Therefore, after vainly endeavouring to convince his reason by shakes, pokes, bawlings-out, and similar applications to his head, she led him into the air, and tried another method; which was manifested to the marriage party by a quick succession of sharp sounds, resembling applause, and subsequently, by their seeing Alexander in contact with the coolest paving-stone in the court, greatly flushed, and loudly lamenting.

The procession being then in a condition to form itself once more, and repair to Brig Place, where a marriage feast was in readiness, returned as it had come; not without the receipt, by Bunsby, of many humorous congratulations from the populace on his recently-acquired happiness. The Captain accompanied it as far as the house-door, but, being made uneasy by the gentler manner of Mrs Bokum, who, now that she was relieved from her engrossing duty – for the watchfulness and alacrity of the ladies sensibly diminished when the bridegroom was safely married – had greater leisure to show an interest in his behalf, there left it and the captive; faintly pleading an appointment, and promising to return presently. The Captain had another cause for uneasiness, in remorsefully reflecting that he had been the first means of Bunsby's entrapment, though certainly without intending it, and through his unbounded faith in the resources of that philosopher.

To go back to old Sol Gills at the Wooden Midshipman's, and not first go round to ask how Mr Dombey fared – albeit the house where he lay was out of London, and away on the borders of a fresh heath – was quite out of the Captain's course. So he got a lift when he was tired, and made out the journey gaily.

The blinds were pulled down, and the house so quiet, that the Captain was almost afraid to knock; but listening at the door, he heard low voices within, very near it, and knocking softly, was admitted by Mr Toots. Mr Toots and his wife had, in fact, just arrived there; having been at the Midshipman's to seek him, and having there obtained the address.

They were not so recently arrived, but that Mrs Toots had caught the baby from somebody, taken it in her arms, and sat down on the stairs, hugging and fondling it. Florence was stooping down beside her; and no one could have said which Mrs Toots was hugging and fondling most, the mother or the child, or which was the tenderer, Florence of Mrs Toots, or Mrs Toots of her, or both of the baby; it was such a little group of love and agitation.

'And is your pa very ill, my darling dear Miss Floy?' asked Susan.

'He is very, very ill,' said Florence. 'But, Susan, dear, you must not speak to me as you used to speak. And what's this?' said Florence, touching her clothes, in amazement. 'Your old dress, dear? Your old cap, curls, and all?'

Susan burst into tears, and showered kisses on the little hand that had touched her so wonderingly.

'My dear Miss Dombey,' said Mr Toots, stepping forward, 'I'll explain. She's the most extraordinary woman. There are not many to equal her! She has always said – she said before we were married, and has said to this day – that whenever you came home, she'd come to you in no dress but the dress she used to serve you in, for fear she might seem strange to you, and you might like her less. I admire the dress myself,' said Mr Toots, 'of all things. I adore her in it! My dear Miss Dombey, she'll be your maid again, your nurse, all that she ever was, and more. There's no change in her. But, Susan, my dear,' said Mr Toots, who had spoken with great feeling and high admiration, 'all I ask is, that you'll remember the medical man, and not exert yourself too much.'

CHAPTER 61

Relenting

Florence had need of help. Her father's need of it was sore, and made the aid of her old friend invaluable. Death stood at his pillow. A shade, already, of what he had been, shattered in mind, and perilously sick in body, he laid his weary head down on the bed his daughter's hands prepared for him, and had never raised it since.

She was always with him. He knew her, generally; though, in the wandering of his brain, he often confused the circumstances under which he spoke to her. Thus he would address her, sometimes, as if his boy were newly dead; and would tell her, that although he had said nothing of her ministering at the little bedside, yet he had seen it – he had seen it; and then would hide his face and sob, and put out his worn hand. Sometimes he would ask her for herself. 'Where is Florence?' 'I am here, papa, I am here.' 'I don't know her!' he would cry. 'We have been parted so long, that I don't know her!' and then a staring dread would be upon him, until she could soothe his perturbation; and recall the tears she tried so hard, at other times, to dry.

He rambled through the scenes of his old pursuits – through many where Florence lost him as she listened – sometimes for hours. He would repeat that childish question, 'What is money?' and ponder on it, and think about it, and reason with himself, more or less connectedly, for a good answer; as if it had never been proposed to him until that moment. He would go on with a musing repetition of the title of his old firm twenty thousand times, and at every one of them, would turn his head upon his pillow. He would count his children – one – two – stop, and go back, and begin again in the same way.

But this was when his mind was in its most distracted state. In all the other phases of its illness, and in those to which it was most constant, it always turned on Florence. What he would oftenest do was this: he would recall that night he had so recently remembered, the night on which she came down to his room, and would imagine that his heart smote him, and that he went out after her, and up the stairs to seek her. Then, confounding that time with the later days of the many footsteps, he would be amazed at their number, and begin to count them as he followed her. Here, of a sudden, was a bloody footstep going on among the others; and after it there began to be, at intervals, doors standing open, through which certain terrible pictures were seen, in mirrors, of haggard men, concealing something in their breasts. Still, among the many footsteps and the bloody footsteps here and there, was the step of Florence. Still she was going on before. Still the restless mind went, following and counting, ever farther, ever higher, as to the summit of a mighty tower that it took years to climb.

One day he inquired if that were not Susan who had spoken a long while ago.

Florence said 'Yes, dear papa;' and asked him would he like to see her?

He said 'very much.' And Susan, with no little trepidation, showed herself at his bedside.

It seemed a great relief to him. He begged her not to go; to understand that he forgave her what she had said; and that she was to stay. Florence and he were very different now, he said, and very happy. Let her look at this! He meant his drawing the gentle head down to the pillow, and laying it beside him.

He remained like this for days and weeks. At length, lying, the faint feeble semblance of a man, upon his bed, and speaking in a voice so low that they could only hear him by listening very near to his lips, he became quiet. It was dimly pleasant to him now, to lie there, with the window open, looking out at the summer sky and the trees: and, in the evening, at the sunset. To watch the shadows of the clouds and leaves, and seem to feel a sympathy with shadows. It was natural that he should. To him, life and the world were nothing else.

He began to show now that he thought of Florence's fatigue: and often taxed his weakness to whisper to her, 'Go and walk, my dearest, in the sweet air. Go to your good husband!' One time when Walter was in his room, he beckoned him to come near, and to stoop down; and pressing his hand, whispered an assurance to him that he knew he could trust him with his child when he was dead.

It chanced one evening, towards sunset, when Florence and Walter were sitting in his room together, as he liked to see them, that Florence, having her baby in her arms, began in a low voice to sing to the little fellow, and sang the old tune she had so often sung to the dead child. He could not bear it at the time; he held up his trembling hand, imploring her to stop; but next day he asked her to repeat it, and to do so often of an evening: which she did. He listening, with his face turned away.

Florence was sitting on a certain time by his window, with her work-basket between her and her old attendant, who was still her faithful companion. He had fallen into a doze. It was a beautiful evening, with two hours of light to come yet; but the tranquillity and quiet made Florence very thoughtful. She was lost to everything for the moment, but the occasion when the so altered figure on the bed had first presented her to her beautiful mama; when a touch from Walter leaning on the back of her chair, made her start.

'My dear,' said Walter, 'there is some one downstairs who wishes to speak to you.'

She fancied Walter looked grave, and asked him if anything had happened.

'No, no, my love!' said Walter. 'I have seen the gentleman myself, and spoken with him. Nothing has happened. Will you come?'

Florence put her arm through his; and confiding her father to the black-eyed Mrs Toots, who sat as brisk and smart at her work as black-eyed woman could, accompanied her husband downstairs. In the pleasant little parlour opening on the garden sat a gentleman, who rose to advance towards her when she came in, but turned off, by reason of some peculiarity in his legs, and was only stopped by the table.

Florence then remembered Cousin Feenix, whom she had not at first recognised in the shade of the leaves. Cousin Feenix took her hand, and congratulated her upon her marriage.

'I could have wished, I am sure,' said Cousin Feenix, sitting down as Florence sat, 'to have had an earlier opportunity of offering my congratulations; but, in point of fact, so many painful occurrences have happened, treading, as a man may say, on one another's heels,' that I have been in a devil of a state myself, and perfectly unfit for every description of society. The only description of society I have kept, has been my own; and it certainly is anything but flattering to a man's good opinion of his own resources, to know that, in point of fact, he has the capacity of boring himself to a perfectly unlimited extent.'

Florence divined, from some indefinable constraint and anxiety in this gentleman's manner – which was always a gentleman's, in spite of the harmless little eccentricities that attached to it – and from Walter's manner no less, that something more immediately tending to some object was to follow this.

'I have been mentioning to my friend Mr Gay, if I may be allowed to have the honour of calling him so,' said Cousin Feenix, 'that I am rejoiced to hear that my friend Dombey is very decidedly mending. I trust my friend Dombey will not allow his mind to be too much preyed upon, by any mere loss of fortune. I cannot say that I have ever experienced any very great loss of fortune myself: never having had, in point of fact, any great amount of fortune to lose. But as much as I could lose, I have lost; and I don't find that I particularly care about it. I know my friend Dombey to be a devilish honourable man; and it's calculated to console my friend Dombey very much, to know, that this is the universal sentiment. Even Tommy Screwzer, – a man of an extremely bilious habit, with whom my friend Gay is probably acquainted – cannot say a syllable in disputation of the fact.'

Florence felt, more than ever, that there was something to come; and looked earnestly for it. So earnestly, that Cousin Feenix answered, as if she had spoken.

'The fact is,' said Cousin Feenix, 'that my friend Gay and myself have been discussing the propriety of entreating a favour at your hands; and that I have the consent of my friend Gay – who has met me in an exceedingly kind and open manner, for which I am very much indebted to him – to solicit it. I am sensible that so amiable a lady as the lovely and accomplished daughter of my friend Dombey, will not require much urging; but I am happy to know, that I am supported by my friend Gay's influence and approval. As in my parliamentary time, when a man had a motion to make of any sort – which happened seldom in those days, for we were kept very tight in hand,[2] the leaders on both sides being regular Martinets,[3] which was a devilish good thing for the rank and file, like myself, and prevented our exposing ourselves continually, as a great many of us had a feverish anxiety to do – as, in my parliamentary time, I was about to say, when a man had leave to let off any little private pop-gun, it was always considered a great point for him to say that he had the happiness of believing that his sentiments were not without an echo in the breast of Mr Pitt, the pilot, in point of fact, who had weathered the storm.[4] Upon which, a devilish large number of fellows immediately cheered, and put him in spirits. Though the fact is, that these fellows, being under orders to cheer most excessively whenever Mr Pitt's name was mentioned, became so proficient that it always woke 'em. And they were so entirely innocent of what was going on, otherwise, that it used to be commonly said by Conversation Brown – four-bottle man[5] at the Treasury Board, with whom the father of my friend Gay was probably acquainted, for it was before my friend Gay's time – that if a man had risen in his place, and said that he regretted to inform the house that there was an Honourable Member in the last stage of convulsions in the Lobby, and that the Honourable Member's name was Pitt, the approbation would have been vociferous.'

This postponement of the point, put Florence in a flutter; and she looked from Cousin Feenix to Walter, in increasing agitation.

'My love,' said Walter, 'there is nothing the matter.'

'There is nothing the matter, upon my honour,' said Cousin Feenix; 'and I am deeply distressed at being the means of causing you a moment's uneasiness. I beg to assure you that there is nothing the matter. The favour that I have to ask is simply – but it really does seem so exceeding singular, that I should be in the last degree obliged to my friend Gay if he would have the goodness to break the – in point of fact, the ice,' said Cousin Feenix.

Walter thus appealed to, and appealed to no less in the look that Florence turned towards him, said:

'My dearest, it is no more than this. That you will ride to London with this gentleman, whom you know.'

'And my friend Gay, also – I beg your pardon!' interrupted Cousin Feenix.

'–And with me – and make a visit somewhere.'

'To whom?' asked Florence, looking from one to the other.

'If I might entreat,' said Cousin Feenix, 'that you would not press for an answer to that question, I would venture to take the liberty of making the request.'

'Do you know, Walter?'

'Yes.'

'And think it right?'

'Yes. Only because I am sure that you would too. Though there may be reasons I very well understand, which make it better that nothing more should be said beforehand.'

'If papa is still asleep, or can spare me if he is awake, I will go immediately,' said Florence. And rising quietly, and glancing at them with a look that was a little alarmed but perfectly confiding, left the room.

When she came back, ready to bear them company, they were talking together, gravely, at the window; and Florence could not but wonder what the topic was, that had made them so well acquainted in so short a time. She did not wonder at the look of pride and love with which her husband broke off as she entered; for she never saw him, but that rested on her.

'I will leave,' said Cousin Feenix, 'a card for my friend Dombey, sincerely trusting that he will pick up health and strength with every returning hour. And I hope my friend Dombey will do me the favour to consider me a man who has a devilish warm admiration of his character, as, in point of fact, a British merchant and a devilish upright gentleman. My place in the country is in a most confounded state of dilapidation, but if my friend Dombey should require a change of air, and would take up his quarters there, he would find it a remarkably healthy spot – as it need be, for it's amazingly dull. If my friend Dombey suffers from bodily weakness, and would allow me to recommend what has frequently done myself good, as a man who has been extremely queer at times, and who lived pretty freely in the days when men lived very freely, I should say, let it be in point of fact the yolk of an egg, beat up with sugar and nutmeg, in a glass of sherry, and taken in the morning with a slice of dry toast. Jackson, who kept the boxing-rooms in Bond Street[6] – man of very superior qualifications, with whose reputation my friend Gay is no doubt acquainted – used to mention that in training for the ring they substituted rum for sherry. I should recommend sherry in this case, on account of my friend Dombey being in an invalided condition; which might occasion rum to fly – in point of fact to his head – and throw him into a devil of a state.'

Of all this, Cousin Feenix delivered himself with an obviously nervous and discomposed air. Then, giving his arm to Florence, and putting the strongest possible constraint upon his wilful legs, which seemed determined to go out into the garden, he led her to the door, and handed her into a carriage that was ready for her reception.

Walter entered after him, and they drove away.

Their ride was six or eight miles long. When they drove through certain dull and stately streets, lying westward in London, it was growing dusk. Florence had, by this time, put her hand in Walter's; and was looking very earnestly, and with increasing agitation, into every new street into which they turned.

When the carriage stopped, at last, before that house in Brook Street, where her father's unhappy marriage had been celebrated, Florence said, 'Walter, what is this? Who is here?' Walter cheering her, and not replying, she glanced up at the house-front, and saw that all the windows were shut, as if it were uninhabited. Cousin Feenix had by this time alighted, and was offering his hand.

'Are you not coming, Walter?'

'No, I will remain here. Don't tremble! there is nothing to fear, dearest Florence.'

'I know that, Walter, with you so near. I am sure of that, but—'

The door was softly opened, without any knock, and Cousin

Feenix led her out of the summer evening air into the close dull house. More sombre and brown than ever, it seemed to have been shut up from the wedding-day, and to have hoarded darkness and sadness ever since.

Florence ascended the dusky staircase, trembling; and stopped, with her conductor, at the drawing-room door. He opened it, without speaking, and signed an entreaty to her to advance into the inner room, while he remained there. Florence, after hesitating an instant, complied.

Sitting by the window at a table, where she seemed to have been writing or drawing, was a lady, whose head, turned away towards the dying light, was resting on her hand. Florence advancing, doubtfully, all at once stood still, as if she had lost the power of motion. The lady turned her head.

'Great Heaven!' she said, 'what is this?'

'No, no!' cried Florence, shrinking back as she rose up, and putting out her hands to keep her off. 'Mama!'

They stood looking at each other. Passion and pride had worn it, but it was the face of Edith, and beautiful and stately yet. It was the face of Florence, and through all the terrified avoidance it expressed, there was pity in it, sorrow, a grateful tender memory. On each face, wonder and fear were painted vividly; each so still and silent, looking at the other over the black gulf of the irrevocable past.

Florence was the first to change. Bursting into tears, she said from her full heart, 'Oh, mama, mama! why do we meet like this? Why were you ever kind to me when there was no one else, that we should meet like this?'

Edith stood before her, dumb and motionless. Her eyes were fixed upon her face.

'I dare not think of that,' said Florence, 'I am come from papa's sick bed. We are never asunder now; we never shall be, any more. If you would have me ask his pardon, I will do it, mama. I am almost sure he will grant it now, if I ask him. May Heaven grant it to you, too, and comfort you!'

She answered not a word.

'Walter – I am married to him, and we have a son,' said Florence, timidly – 'is at the door, and has brought me here. I will tell him that you are repentant; that you are changed,' said Florence, looking mournfully upon her; 'and he will speak to papa with me, I know. Is there anything but this that I can do?'

Edith, breaking her silence, without moving eye or limb, answered slowly:

'The stain upon your name, upon your husband's, on your child's. Will that ever be forgiven, Florence?'

'Will it ever be, mama? It is! Freely, freely, both by Walter and by me. If that is any consolation to you, there is nothing that you may believe more certainly. You do not – you do not,' faltered Florence, 'speak of papa; but I am sure you wish that I should ask him for his forgiveness. I am sure you do.'

She answered not a word.

'I will!' said Florence. 'I will bring it you, if you will let me; and then, perhaps, we may take leave of each other more like what we used to be to one another. I have not,' said Florence very gently, and drawing nearer to her, 'I have not shrunk back from you, mama, because I fear you, or because I dread to be disgraced by you. I only wish to do my duty to papa. I am very dear to him, and he is very dear to me. But I never can forget that you were very good to me. Oh, pray to Heaven,' cried Florence, falling on her bosom, 'pray to Heaven, mama, to forgive you all this sin and shame, and to forgive me if I cannot help doing this (if it is wrong), when I remember what you used to be!'

Edith, as if she fell beneath her touch, sunk down on her knees, and caught her round the neck.

'Florence!' she cried. 'My better angel! Before I am mad again, before my stubbornness comes back and strikes me dumb, believe me, upon my soul I am innocent.'

'Mama!'

'Guilty of much! Guilty of that which sets a waste between us evermore. Guilty of what must separate me, through the whole remainder of my life, from purity and innocence – from you, of all the earth. Guilty of a blind and passionate resentment, of which I do not, cannot, will not, even now, repent; but not guilty with that dead man. Before God!'

Upon her knees upon the ground, she held up both her hands, and swore it.

'Florence!' she said, 'purest and best of natures, – whom I love – who might have changed me long ago, and did for a time work some change even in the woman that I am, – believe me, I am innocent of that; and once more, on my desolate heart, let me lay this dear head, for the last time!'

She was moved and weeping. Had she been oftener thus in older days, she had been happier now.

'There is nothing else in all the world,' she said, 'that would have wrung denial from me. No love, no hatred, no hope, no threat. I said that I would die, and make no sign. I could have done so, and I would, if we had never met, Florence.'

'I trust,' said Cousin Feenix, ambling in at the door, and speaking, half in the room, and half out of it, 'that my lovely and accomplished relative will excuse my having, by a little stratagem, effected this meeting. I cannot say that I was, at first, wholly incredulous as to the possibility of my lovely and accomplished relative having, very unfortunately, committed herself with the deceased person with white teeth; because, in point of fact, one does see, in this world – which is remarkable for devilish strange arrangements, and for being decidedly the most unintelligible thing within a man's experience – very odd conjunctions of that sort. But as I mentioned to my friend Dombey, I could not admit the criminality of my lovely and accomplished relative until it was perfectly established. And feeling, when the deceased person was, in point of fact, destroyed in a devilish horrible manner, that her position was a very painful one – and feeling besides that our family had been a little to blame in not paying more attention to her, and that we are a careless family – and also that my aunt, though a devilish lively woman, had perhaps not been the very best of mothers – I took the liberty of seeking her in France, and offering her such protection as a man very much out at elbows could offer. Upon which occasion, my lovely and accomplished relative did me the honour to express that she believed I was, in my way, a devilish good sort of fellow; and that therefore she put herself under my protection. Which in point of fact I understood to be a kind thing on the part of my lovely and accomplished relative, as I am getting extremely shaky, and have derived great comfort from her solicitude.'

Edith, who had taken Florence to a sofa, made a gesture with her hand as if she would have begged him to say no more.

'My lovely and accomplished relative,' resumed Cousin Feenix, still ambling about at the door, 'will excuse me, if, for her satisfaction, and my own, and that of my friend Dombey, whose lovely and accomplished daughter we so much admire, I complete the thread of my observations. She will remember that, from the first, she and I have never alluded to the subject of her elopement. My impression, certainly, has always been, that there was a mystery in the affair which she could explain if so inclined. But my lovely and accomplished relative being a devilish resolute woman, I knew that she was not, in point of fact, to be trifled with, and therefore did not involve myself in any discussions. But observing lately, that her accessible point did appear to be a very strong description of tenderness for the daughter of my friend Dombey, it occurred to me that if I could bring about a meeting, unexpected on both sides, it might lead to beneficial results. Therefore, we being in London, in the present private way, before going to the south of Italy, there to establish ourselves, in point of fact, until we go to our long homes, which is a devilish disagreeable reflection for a man, I applied myself to the discovery of the residence of my friend Gay – handsome man of an uncommon frank disposition, who is probably known to my lovely and accomplished relative – and had the happiness of bringing his amiable wife to the present place. And now,' said Cousin Feenix, with a real and genuine earnestness shining through the levity of his manner and his slipshod speech, 'I do conjure my relative, not to stop half way, but to set right, as far as she can, whatever she has done wrong – not for the honour of her family, not for her own fame, not for any of those consider-ations which unfortunate circumstances have induced her to regard as hollow, and in point of fact, as approaching to humbug – but because it *is* wrong, and not right.'

Cousin Feenix's legs consented to take him away after this; and leaving them alone together, he shut the door.

Edith remained silent for some minutes, with Florence sitting close beside her. Then she took from her bosom a sealed paper.

'I debated with myself a long time,' she said in a low voice, 'whether to write this at all, in case of dying suddenly or by accident, and feeling the want of it upon me. I have deliberated, ever since, when and how to destroy it. Take it, Florence. The truth is written in it.'

'Is it for papa?' asked Florence.

'It is for whom you will,' she answered. 'It is given to you, and is obtained by you. He never could have had it otherwise.'

Again they sat silent, in the deepening darkness.

'Mama,' said Florence, 'he has lost his fortune; he has been at the point of death, he may not recover, even now. Is there any word that I shall say to him from you?'

'Did you tell me,' asked Edith, 'that you were very dear to him?'

'Yes!' said Florence, in a thrilling[7] voice.

'Tell him I am sorry that we ever met.'

'No more?' said Florence after a pause.

'Tell him, if he asks, that I do not repent of what I have done – not yet – for if it were to do again to-morrow, I should do it. But if he is a changed man—'

She stopped. There was something in the silent touch of Florence's hand that stopped her.

'—But that being a changed man, he knows, now, it would never be. Tell him I wish it never had been.'

'May I say,' said Florence, 'that you grieved to hear of the afflictions he has suffered?'

'Not,' she replied, 'if they have taught him that his daughter is very dear to him. He will not grieve for them himself, one day, if they have brought that lesson, Florence.'

'You wish well to him, and would have him happy. I am sure you would!' said Florence. 'Oh! let me be able, if I have the occasion at some future time, to say so?'

Edith sat with her dark eyes gazing steadfastly before her, and did not reply until Florence had repeated her entreaty; when she drew her hand within her arm, and said, with the same thoughtful gaze upon the night outside:

'Tell him that if, in his own present, he can find any reason to compassionate my past, I sent word that I asked him to do so. Tell him that if, in his own present, he can find a reason to think less bitterly of me, I asked him to do so. Tell him, that, dead as we are to one another, never more to meet on this side of eternity, he knows there is one feeling in common between us now, that there never was before.'

Her sternness seemed to yield, and there were tears in her dark eyes.

'I trust myself to that,' she said, 'for his better thoughts of me, and mine of him. When he loves his Florence most, he will hate me least. When he is most proud and happy in her and her children, he will be most repentant of his own part in the dark vision of our married life. At that time, I will be repentant too – let him know it then – and think that when I thought so much of all the causes that had made me what I was, I needed to have allowed more for the causes that had made him what he was. I will try, then, to forgive him his share of blame. Let him try to forgive me mine!'

'Oh mama!' said Florence. 'How it lightens my heart, even in such a meeting and parting, to hear this!'

'Strange words in my own ears,' said Edith, 'and foreign to the sound of my own voice! But even if I had been the wretched creature I have given him occasion to believe me, I think I could have said them still, hearing that you and he were very dear to one another. Let him, when you are dearest, ever feel that he is most forbearing in his thoughts of me – that I am most forbearing in my thoughts of him! Those are the last words I send him! Now, good-bye, my life!'

She clasped her in her arms, and seemed to pour out all her woman's soul of love and tenderness at once.

'This kiss for your child! These kisses for a blessing on your head! My own dear Florence, my sweet girl, farewell!'

'To meet again!' cried Florence.

'Never again! Never again! When you leave me in this dark room, think that you have left me in the grave. Remember only that I was once, and that I loved you!'

And Florence left her, seeing her face no more, but accompanied by her embraces and caresses to the last.

Cousin Feenix met her at the door, and took her down to Walter in the dingy dining-room: upon whose shoulder she laid her head weeping.

'I am devilish sorry,' said Cousin Feenix, lifting his wristbands to his eyes in the simplest manner possible, and without the least concealment, 'that the lovely and accomplished daughter of my friend Dombey and amiable wife of my friend Gay, should have had her sensitive nature so very much distressed and cut up by the interview which is just concluded. But I hope and trust I have acted for the best, and that my honourable friend Dombey will find his mind relieved by the disclosures which have taken place. I exceedingly lament that my friend Dombey should have got himself, in point of fact, into a devil's own state of conglomeration by an alliance with our family; but am strongly of opinion that if it hadn't been for the infernal scoundrel Barker – man with white teeth – everything would have gone on pretty smoothly. In regard to my relative who does me the honour to have formed an uncommonly good opinion of myself, I can assure the amiable wife of my friend Gay, that she may rely on my being, in point of fact, a father to her. And in regard to the changes of human life, and the extraordinary manner in which we are perpetually conducting ourselves, all I can say is, with my friend Shakespeare – man who wasn't for an age but for all time,[8] and with whom my friend Gay is no doubt acquainted – that it's like the shadow of a dream.'[9]

CHAPTER 62

Final

A bottle that has been long excluded from the light of day, and is hoary with dust and cobwebs, has been brought into the sunshine; and the golden wine within it sheds a lustre on the table.

It is the last bottle of the old Madeira.

'You are quite right, Mr Gills,' says Mr Dombey. 'This is a very rare and most delicious wine.'

The Captain, who is of the party, beams with joy. There is a very halo of delight round his glowing forehead.

'We always promised ourselves, Sir,' observes Mr Gills, 'Ned and myself, I mean—'

Mr Dombey nods at the Captain, who shines more and more with speechless gratification.

'—that we should drink this, one day or other, to Walter safe at home: though such a home we never thought of. If you don't object to our old whim, Sir, let us devote this first glass to Walter and his wife.'

'To Walter and his wife!' says Mr Dombey. 'Florence, my child' – and turns to kiss her.

'To Walter and his wife!' says Mr Toots.

'To Wal'r and his wife!' exclaims the Captain. 'Hooroar!' and the Captain exhibiting a strong desire to clink his glass against some other glass, Mr Dombey, with a ready hand, holds out his. The others follow; and there is a blithe and merry ringing, as of a little peal of marriage bells.

Other buried wine grows older, as the old Madeira did in its time; and dust and cobwebs thicken on the bottles.

Mr Dombey is a white-haired gentleman, whose face bears heavy marks of care and suffering; but they are traces of a storm that has passed on for ever, and left a clear evening in its track.

Ambitious projects trouble him no more. His only pride is in his daughter and her husband. He has a silent, thoughtful, quiet manner, and is always with his daughter. Miss Tox is not unfrequently of the family party, and is quite devoted to it, and a great favourite. Her admiration of her once stately patron is, and has been ever since the morning of her shock in Princess's Place, platonic, but not weakened in the least.

Nothing has drifted to him from the wreck of his fortunes, but a certain annual sum that comes he knows not how, with an earnest entreaty that he will not seek to discover, and with the assurance that it is a debt, and an act of reparation. He has consulted with his old clerk about this, who is clear it may be honourably accepted, and has no doubt it arises out of some forgotten transaction in the times of the old House.

That hazel-eyed bachelor, a bachelor no more, is married now, and to the sister of the grey-haired Junior. He visits his old chief sometimes, but seldom. There is a reason in the grey-haired Junior's history, and yet a stronger reason in his name, why he should keep retired from his old employer; and as he lives with his sister and her husband, they participate in that retirement. Walter sees them sometimes – Florence too – and the pleasant house resounds with profound duets arranged for the Piano-Forte and Violoncello, and with the labours of Harmonious Blacksmiths.[1]

And how goes the Wooden Midshipman in these changed days? Why, here he still is, right leg foremost, hard at work upon the hackney coaches, and more on the alert than ever, being newly painted from his cocked hat to his buckled shoes; and up above him, in golden characters, these names shine refulgent, GILLS AND CUTTLE.

Not another stroke of business does the Midshipman achieve beyond his usual easy trade. But they do say, in a circuit of some half-mile round the blue umbrella in Leadenhall Market, that some of Mr Gills's old investments are coming out wonderfully well; and that instead of being behind the time in those respects, as he supposed, he was, in truth, a little before it, and had to wait the fulness of the time and the design. The whisper is that Mr Gills's money has begun to turn itself, and that it is turning itself over and over pretty briskly. Certain it is that standing at his shop-door, in his coffee-coloured suit, with his chronometer in his pocket, and his spectacles on his forehead, he don't appear to break his heart at customers not coming, but looks very jovial and contented, though full as misty as of yore.

As to his partner, Captain Cuttle, there is a fiction of a business in the Captain's mind which is better than any reality. The Captain is as satisfied of the Midshipman's importance to the commerce and navigation of the country, as he could possibly be, if no ship left the Port of London without the Midshipman's assistance. His delight in his own name over the door, is inexhaustible. He crosses the street, twenty times a day, to look at it from the other side of the way; and invariably says, on these occasions, 'Ed'ard Cuttle, my lad, if your mother could ha' know'd as you would ever be a man o' science, the good old creetur would ha' been took aback indeed!'

But here is Mr Toots descending on the Midshipman with violent rapidity, and Mr Toots's face is very red as he bursts into the little parlour.

'Captain Gills,' says Mr Toots, 'and Mr Sols, I am happy to inform you that Mrs Toots has had an increase to her family.'

'And it does her credit!' cried the Captain.

'I give you joy, Mr Toots!' says old Sol.

'Thank'ee,' chuckles Mr Toots, 'I'm very much obliged to you. I knew that you'd be glad to hear, and so I came down myself. We're positively getting on, you know. There's Florence, and Susan, and now here's another little stranger.'

'A female stranger?' inquires the Captain.

'Yes, Captain Gills,' says Mr Toots, 'and I'm glad of it. The oftener we can repeat that most extraordinary woman, my opinion is, the better!'

'Stand by!' says the Captain, turning to the old case-bottle with no throat – for it is evening, and the Midshipman's usual moderate provision of pipes and glasses is on the board. 'Here's to her, and may she have ever so many more!'

'Thank'ee, Captain Gills,' says the delighted Mr Toots. 'I echo the sentiment. If you'll allow me, as my so doing cannot be unpleasant to anybody, under the circumstances, I think I'll take a pipe.'

Mr Toots begins to smoke, accordingly, and in the openness of his heart is very loquacious.

'Of all the remarkable instances that that delightful woman has given of her excellent sense, Captain Gills and Mr Sols,' said Toots, 'I think none is more remarkable than the perfection with which she has understood my devotion to Miss Dombey.'

Both his auditors assent.

'Because you know,' says Mr Toots, '*I* have never changed my sentiments towards Miss Dombey. They are the same as ever. She is the same bright vision to me, at present, that she was before I made Walters's acquaintance. When Mrs Toots and myself first began to talk of – in short, of the tender passion, you know, Captain Gills.'

'Aye, aye, my lad,' says the Captain, 'as makes us all slue[2] round – for which you'll overhaul the book—'

'I shall certainly do so, Captain Gills,' says Mr Toots, with great earnestness; 'when we first began to mention such subjects, I explained that I was what you may call a Blighted Flower, you know.'

The Captain approves of this figure greatly; and murmurs that no flower as blows, is like the rose.

'But Lord bless me,' pursues Mr Toots, 'she was as entirely conscious of the state of my feelings as I was myself. There was nothing I could tell *her*. She was the only person who could have stood between me and the silent Tomb, and she did it, in a manner to command my everlasting admiration. She knows that there's nobody in the world I look up to, as I do to Miss Dombey. She knows that there's nothing on earth I wouldn't do for Miss Dombey. She knows that I consider Miss Dombey the most beautiful, the most amiable, the most angelic of her sex. What is her observation upon that? The perfection of sense. "My dear, you're right. *I* think so too."'

'And so do I!' says the Captain.

'So do I,' says Sol Gills.

'Then,' resumes Mr Toots, after some contemplative pulling at his pipe, during which his visage has expressed the most contented reflection, 'what an observant woman my wife is! What sagacity she possesses! What remarks she makes! It was only last night, when we were sitting in the enjoyment of connubial bliss – which, upon my word and honour, is a feeble term to express my feelings in the society of my wife – that she said how remarkable it was to consider the present position of our friend Walters. "Here," observes my wife, "he is, released from sea-going, after that first long voyage with his young bride" – as you know he was, Mr Sols.'

'Quite true,' says the old Instrument-maker, rubbing his hands.

'"Here he is," says my wife, "released from that, immediately appointed by the same establishment to a post of great trust and confidence at home; showing himself again worthy; mounting up the ladder with the greatest expedition; beloved by everybody; assisted by his uncle at the very best possible time of his fortunes" – which I think is the case, Mr Sols? My wife is always correct.'

'Why yes, yes – some of our lost ships, freighted with gold, have come home, truly,' returns old Sol, laughing. 'Small craft, Mr Toots, but serviceable to my boy!'

'Exactly so,' says Mr Toots. 'You'll never find my wife wrong. "Here he is," says that most remarkable woman, "so situated, – and what follows? What follows?" observed Mrs Toots. Now pray remark, Captain Gills, and Mr Sols, the depth of my wife's penetration. "Why that, under the very eye of Mr Dombey, there is a foundation going on, upon which a – an Edifice;" that was Mrs Toots's word,' says Mr Toots exultingly, '"is gradually rising, perhaps to equal, perhaps excel, that of which he was once the head, and the small beginnings of which (a common fault, but a bad one, Mrs Toots said) escaped his memory. Thus," said my wife, "from his daughter, after all, another Dombey and Son will ascend" – no "rise"; that was Mrs Toots's word – "triumphant."'

Mr Toots, with the assistance of his pipe – which he is extremely glad to devote to oratorical purposes, as its proper use affects him with a very uncomfortable sensation – does such grand justice to this prophetic sentence of his wife's, that the Captain, throwing away his glazed hat in a state of the greatest excitement, cries:

'Sol Gills, you man of science and my ould pardner, what did I tell Wal'r to overhaul on that there night when he first took to business? Was it this here quotation, "Turn again Whittington, Lord Mayor of London, and when you are old you will never depart from it?"[3] Was it them words, Sol Gills?'

'It certainly was, Ned,' replied the old Instrument-maker. 'I remember well.'

'Then I tell you what,' says the Captain, leaning back in his chair, and composing his chest for a prodigious roar. 'I'll give you Lovely Peg right through; and stand by, both on you, for the chorus!'

Buried wine grows older, as the old Madeira did, in its time; and dust and cobwebs thicken on the bottles.

Autumn days are shining, and on the sea-beach there are often a young lady and a white-haired gentleman. With them, or near them, are two children: boy and girl. And an old dog is generally in their company.[4]

The white-haired gentleman walks with the little boy, talks with him, helps him in his play, attends upon him, watches him, as if he were the object of his life. If he be thoughtful, the white-haired gentleman is thoughtful too; and sometimes when the child is sitting by his side, and looks up in his face, asking him questions, he takes the tiny hand in his, and holding it, forgets to answer. Then the child says:

'What, grandpapa! Am I so like my poor little uncle again?'

'Yes, Paul. But he was weak, and you are very strong.'

'Oh yes, I am very strong.'

'And he lay on a little bed beside the sea, and you can run about.'

And so they range away again, busily, for the white-haired

gentleman likes best to see the child free and stirring; and as they go about together, the story of the bond between them goes about, and follows them.

But no one, except Florence, knows the measure of the white-haired gentleman's affection for the girl. That story never goes about. The child herself almost wonders at a certain secrecy he keeps in it. He hoards her in his heart. He cannot bear to see a cloud upon her face. He cannot bear to see her sit apart. He fancies that she feels a slight, when there is none. He steals away to look at her, in her sleep. It pleases him to have her come, and wake him in the morning. He is fondest of her and most loving to her, when there is no creature by. The child says then, sometimes:

'Dear grandpapa, why do you cry when you kiss me?'

He only answers, 'Little Florence! Little Florence!' and smooths away the curls that shade her earnest eyes.[5]

THE END

NOTES

I have made use of information from some of the notes by 'T. Kent Brumleigh' (T. W. Hill), published in *The Dickensian* 38 and 39 (1942–3) and from *The Dickens Index* (1988), ed. N. Bentley, M. Slater and N. Burgis. I would also like to acknowledge the help of Dr David Brown, Professor Norman Page, Mrs Mary Witt and Dr Richard Witt in answering several specific queries.

DEDICATION

1. (xxxix) **THE MARCHIONESS OF NORMANBY**: Maria, daughter of Thomas Henry Lidell, 1st Baron Ravensworth, who married Constantine Henry Phipps, 1st Marquis of Normanby, in 1816. Dickens met them frequently during the writing of *DS*, in 1846–7 in Paris, where the Marquis was British Ambassador.

PREFACE OF 1848

1. (xli) **a sorrow ... on which this fiction turns**: Because of the original serial publication, Dickens was already well aware of the profound impact made on his audience by the death of Little Paul in Chapter 16 (first issued in the fifth monthly number in January 1847); see epigraph to Dickens and His Critics, p. 891.

PREFACE OF 1858

1. (xli) **no violent ... change**: Dickens is here responding to criticism like that of John Eagles in *Blackwood's Magazine* LXIV (October 1848, pp. 468–9): 'The entire change of character in Dombey is out of all nature – it is impossible.' In 1846, Dickens had been forced to cut Chapters 1 to 3 severely, having 'overwritten' the first monthly number. In the cancelled portions, Mr Dombey's inner struggle is more clearly spelt out.

2. (xlii) **the lake of Geneva ... France**: The novel was begun in Lausanne, Switzerland, at the end of June 1846, continued in Paris from November 1846, and concluded in London in February and March 1848.

CHAPTER 1

1. (6) **puffed:** bragged about.

2. (6) **muffled ... like the knocker:** In cases of illness, the front-door knocker was swathed in wrappings to protect the invalid from noise.

3. (6) **Sir Hubert Stanley:** 'Approbation from Sir Hubert Stanley is praise indeed!' is a catchphrase from Thomas Morton's comedy *A Cure for the Heartache* (1797).

4. (9) **speculation:** sight; cf *Macbeth*, Act III, Sc.4 (of Banquo's ghost): 'thou hast no speculation in those eyes/That thou dost glare withal . . .'

5. (10) **spasmodic:** convulsive.

6. (10) **A pecuniary Duke of York:** Frederick Augustus (1763–1827), second son of George III and the original 'Grand Old Duke of York' of the nursery rhyme. He was Commander-in-Chief of the Army 1798–1809. His commemorative Column in the Mall was completed in 1833, and he was a powerful figure in popular memory well into the 1840s. There is also the possibility of irony here in that the Duke was well known for his debts and for selling and allowing his mistresses to sell commissions in the army.

CHAPTER 2

1. (12) **mantua-makers:** dress-makers, here fitting the family with mourning garments. A mantua was originally a loose-fitting ladies' gown.

2. (13) **A cobbler there was:** first line of a popular eighteenth-century song: 'A cobbler there was and he lived in a stall/Which served him for parlour, for kitchen for hall . . .'

3. (13) **college hornpipe:** now better known as the Sailor's Hornpipe.

4. (13) **deuce:** Devil.

5. (16) **Queen Charlotte's Royal Married Females:** the 'lying-in' hospital on the Marylebone Road in London, which, as well as being a maternity hospital, encouraged its poorer clients to gain employment as 'wet-nurses', breast-feeding the babies of the well-to-do.

6. (18) **he was all abroad:** He was completely lost.

7. (20) **Mostly underground ... railroads when they comes into full play:** Assuming the story to end in the year of publication (1848), then Mr Toodle's fortunes were tied to the beginning of the railway boom in the 1830s. Like many others, he had left the mines to take advantage of these new opportunities for manual workers.

8. (20) **Hind:** labourer, serf.

9. (21) **invested ... as if it were an Order:** The baby is handed over with as much solemnity as if he were an 'order', an award presented by the Monarch at a Royal Investiture.

10. (21) **suppressing:** Mr Toodle's version of the polite form of acceptance, 'Since you are so pressing'.

11. (21) **porter:** cheap beer, supposedly helpful in maintaining breast-feeding. It was made by Meux and Co. in the eighteenth century and was very popular with heavy workers like porters, hence the name.

12. (22) **Biler:** i.e. 'boiler', the source of a steam engine's power. In a cancelled passage, Dickens has Mr Toodle say that the steam engine has been 'as good as a godfather to him'.

13. (22) **hackney-coach:** horse-drawn carriage for hire.

14. (22) **preferred to ride behind among the spikes:** Dickens neatly conflates the old and the new here. Mr Toodle takes the footman's position at the back of the coach, since it reminds him of his usual place as fireman at the back of the steam locomotive. A row of spikes adorned the rear axle of hackney-coaches to stop children from stealing rides.

CHAPTER 3

1. (23) **between Portland Place and Bryanstone Square:** This area of London, south of Regent's Park, was a favourite for businessmen in the 1830s; see, for example, Humphry House, *The Dickens World* (1941), p. 146. It was also where Dickens himself lived (in Devonshire Terrace) between 1839 and 1851.

2. (23) **water-carts:** barrels or tanks on wheels, carrying water, which were designed so that water escaped through a number of small holes in their sides as they were wheeled along. They were used to reduce dust on the streets.

3. (23) **the man ... Dutch clock:** The itinerant watch-and-clock-mender would announce his presence in the street in this way. Dutch clocks were particular attractions as they often contained mechanical figures which moved when the hour was struck. 'Dutch' is probably a corruption of 'Deutsch', the clock's origin being not Holland but Germany.

4. (23) **Punch's shows:** Punch and Judy shows, traditional stories acted out with glove puppets, were extremely popular (and still survive).

5. (23) **organs . . . white mice . . . porcupine:** Street entertainments were many and various and included curiosities exhibited for money by enterprising urchins. A *Morning Chronicle* article of the period explains that 'boys pay their master for whatever curiosity they may take with them to exhibit. . . . For a Porcupine (very rare) 2s a day; For a box of white mice 1.6d a day; For an organ with figures waltzing 3s 5d a day' (quoted by Mary A. Macey in *The Dickensian* 46, summer 1950, p. 97).

6. (23) **lamplighter:** The use of gas for street lighting began in the 1820s. The lamplighter used a pole with a small oil lamp in the head with which he reached up and turned on the gas tap of each street lamp-post.

7. (24) **holland:** a type of heavy linen material.

8. (24) **straw:** i.e. to muffle the sound of horses' hooves and carriages – customary practice in cases of illness.

9. (24) **hot-pressed paper . . . Russia leather:** A valet would press the morning newspaper for his master to make it easier to read; **vellum:** high-quality writing paper; **morocco, Russia leather:** named after the places which supplied leather for expensive book-bindings.

10. (26) **pennywinkles:** periwinkles, a popular type of shellfish (now simply 'winkles').

11. (27) **permanency . . . temporary:** i.e. the servants' jobs attached to each child – but also an ironic foreshadowing of Paul's early death.

12. (27) **a Tartar:** These Mongolian warriors were proverbial for their cruelty. Slang for a tyrannical, bad-tempered person.

13. (28) **the young idea:** echoes Thomson's line about teaching: 'Delightful task! to rear the tender thought/To teach the young idea to shoot' (*The Seasons*, Spring, l. 1152).

14. (28) **Chaney:** i.e. China.

15. (33) **address:** i.e. style, attack.

16. (34) **stays:** whalebone corsets, worn even by young girls like Susan to improve the appearance of the figure.

17. (34) **a excellent party-wall:** a reference to the expression 'to go to the wall', meaning here to be defeated or pushed aside by Polly.

CHAPTER 4

1. (34) **City of London . . . Bow Bells:** from the business centre to Cheapside – thought of as the emotional heart of the City: a true Cockney has to be born 'within sound of Bow Bells'.

2. (34) **Gog and Magog:** 14-foot statues of two legendary giants which were erected in the Guildhall in 1708, replacing those destroyed in the Great Fire in 1666. The characters are mentioned in the Biblical Book of Revelation as symbolising the enemies of the Kingdom of God.

3. (34) **East India House:** trading company set up at the height of British imperial expansion. The building stood in Leadenhall Street at the west corner of Lime Street until 1862.

4. (34) **little timber midshipmen:** symbols for ships' instrument-makers' shops, just as barbers' poles still are for barbers' shops. A midshipman was the rank in the Royal Navy between naval cadet and lowest commissioned officer.

5. (34) **that midshipman:** This effigy has been identified as one outside No. 157 Leadenhall Street (now in the Dickens House Museum, London).

6. (35) **Welsh wig:** old-fashioned worsted cap.

7. (36) **inexpressibles:** breeches, trousers.

8. (36) **nankeen:** hard-wearing yellow cotton material.

9. (37) **'Hurrah for the admiral!':** chorus of a popular sea shanty of the time.

10. (38) **Lord Mayor ... Common Council, and Livery:** The Lord Mayor's procession still takes place in London every November. (This chapter's events happen on 'an autumn afternoon'.) The traditions associated with the Lord Mayor go back to the Middle Ages. The Common Council manages the affairs of the City of London, and the Livery companies, descended from the medieval trade guilds, still have considerable power in social and charitable work. Their name comes from the individual dress or livery of their members.

11. (40) **sovereign:** gold coin worth £1 or twenty shillings (100 new pence).

12. (40) **Mile-End Turnpike:** i.e. the toll-gate on the Mile End Road just east of the junction of Cambridge Heath Road and Mile End Road – exactly a mile from Aldgate. (This toll-gate was removed in 1864.)

13. (40) **Robinson Crusoe's Island:** Daniel Defoe's *Robinson Crusoe* (1719), about a shipwrecked sailor, was one of Dickens's favourite childhood books.

14. (41) **yards:** i.e. yard-arms: horizontal masts on sailing ships from which wrongdoers were hung.

15. (43) **privateers-man:** sailor on an armed private vessel; i.e. a mercenary.

16. (43) **Love! Honour! And Obey!:** actually from the wedding service in the Anglican Book of Common Prayer rather than the Catechism: an early example of Captain Cuttle's propensity to confuse quotations. The Catechism was a series of questions and answers aimed at inculcating the Christian religion, which children were forced to learn by heart.

17. (43) **young Norval's ... store:** quotation from a popular play, *Douglas* (1756), by John Home, in which the hero is reared as a shepherd's son: 'My name is Norval: on the Grampian Hills/My father feeds his flocks; a frugal swain/Whose constant care is to increase his store . . .'

18. (44) **grog:** rum and water, traditional sailors' rations.

19. (44) **Richard Whittington:** The true story of Dick Whittington (d. 1423) inspired many generations of ambitious young men: having come to London in a vain attempt to make his fortune, the boy was about to leave the city in despair when the city bells rang out, as if they were saying, 'Turn again Whittington, Lord Mayor of London!' He returned, resumed his efforts, eventually married his employer's daughter and became Lord Mayor.

20. (44) **never depart from it:** Proverbs 22:6: 'Train up a child in the way he should go, and when he is old he will never depart from it.'

CHAPTER 5

1. (46) **physic:** medicine.

2. (47) **nailed her colours to the mast:** declared her position irrevocably. Colours (flags) so fixed on a ship cannot be lowered to signal defeat or surrender.

3. (48) **the other sponsors:** It is still customary in the Church of England for a baby boy to be given two godfathers and one godmother, and a girl one godfather and two godmothers. The godparents act as 'sponsors', presenting the child to God at the Christening.

4. (51) **cabriolet:** two-wheeled one-horse chaise with a large hood.

5. (52) **Griffins:** monsters in Greek mythology, half-eagle, half-lion.

6. (52) **mulotter:** i.e. mulatto, half-breed slave in the West Indies.

7. (53) **Mr Pitt ... celestial origin:** William Pitt (1759–1806), Prime

Minister; his colleague George Canning had called him a 'Heaven-born minister'.

8. (53) **enchanted Moor:** a reference to *The Arabian Nights*, another of Dickens's favourite childhood books. However, the Moor in the story of Aladdin is not 'enchanted': he himself is the enchanter who plots to kill Aladdin and gain the 'unattainable treasure', the magic lamp.

9. (54) **lighter mourning:** The Victorian custom was to move by prescribed stages from 'deep mourning' immediately after a bereavement to progressively lighter clothes after the lapse of weeks or months.

10. (56) **beadle:** a parish official employed in this case to look after the upkeep of a church.

11. (57) **Babylonian:** sumptuous (beadles wore gold lace), ostentatiously grand.

12. (57) **into my grave?:** *Hamlet*, Act II, Sc. 2.

13. (57) **free seats:** Separate box pews were paid for by the family who occupied them; 'free seating' was for the poorest members of the congregation.

14. (57) **pew-opener:** someone paid to look after the box pews of the wealthy, locking and unlocking them as needed.

15. (58) **grampus:** a species of whale which spouts water as it moves; used, therefore, of a person given to puffing and blowing.

16. (58) **Gunpowder Plot:** a service giving thanks for the failure of the conspiracy by Guy Fawkes and others to blow up the Houses of Parliament in 1605. It was not removed from the Anglican Prayer Book until 1859.

17. (58) **its history:** The first baptism was of Christ Himself by John the Baptist. John (unlike Mr Dombey) was humble, declaring that he was not worthy to baptise his Master (Matthew 3:13-17).

18. (59) **sexton:** gravedigger.

19. (61) **Charitable Grinders:** Charitable Schools were an important feature of mid-Victorian education, but generally provided an inadequate schooling, 'grinding' their pupils down with rote learning; the children, in their distinctive uniforms, were never allowed to forget their inferior position.

20. (61) **small-clothes:** knee breeches.

21. (61) **Dead March in Saul:** Handel was a favourite composer of the

Victorians, who produced imposing settings of his eighteenth-century oratorios. *Saul* was composed in 1739.

22. (62) **'With a hey ho chevy!':** from the chorus of a hunting song, 'Old Towler' by William Shield (1748–1829): 'With a hey ho chevy,/Hark forward, hark forward,/Tantivy.'

CHAPTER 6

1. (63) **Tony Lumpkin:** see Oliver Goldsmith's *She Stoops to Conquer* (1773), Act I, Sc. 1.

2. (63) **Staggs's Gardens:** a fictional area based on Camden Town, north London.

3. (64) **the ... Railroad:** see Chapter 2, n. 7. Presumably this is the London–Birmingham line, begun in London in 1834 and opened in 1838. In Chapter 20, set in the early 1840s, Mr Dombey and the Major depart for Leamington from the London terminus of this line, at Euston.

4. (65) **Mr Staggs:** A 'stag' was slang for someone who bought shares (particularly, in the 1840s, railway shares) with the intention of making a quick profit.

5. (66) **Banbury Cross:** The nursery rhyme 'Ride a Cock Horse to Banbury Cross' involves bouncing the baby on the knee in time to the words.

6. (67) **at score:** at full speed; hence, **go off at score:** fire up, lose her temper.

7. (68) **chandler's shop:** a general dealer's, nowadays a grocer's.

8. (75) **jockey:** lad, lackey. Walter distances himself from this slightly contemptuous term by replying, 'I'm in Dombey's House. . . .'

9. (76) **Whittington:** see Chapter 4, n. 19.

CHAPTER 7

1. (84) **Princess's Place:** This has been identified as Devonshire Place Mews, close to Devonshire Terrace; see Chapter 3, n. 1, and the article by Gwen Major in *The Dickensian* 62, Spring 1966, pp. 122–4.

2. (84) **Macbeth's banners:** 'Hang out our banners on the outer walls: the cry is still they come' (*Macbeth*, Act V, Sc. 5).

3. (87) **Copenhagen and Bird Waltzes ... own copying:** two popular and easy pieces of piano music, *The Copenhagen Waltz* by Matthias von

Holst (1814) and *The Bird Waltz* by François Panormo (1818). It was usual, before copyright laws developed, to copy such pieces into one's own music book.

4. (87) **froze its young blood:** see *Hamlet*, Act I, Sc. 5.

5. (88) **cockade:** i.e. the 'puckered cap' referred to in the following paragraph.

CHAPTER 8

1. (89) **thrush:** both a songbird and the name of a throat infection common in babyhood.

2. (89) **chickens:** i.e. chickenpox.

3. (90) **Some philosophers:** Jeremy Bentham (1748–1832) and the Utilitarians propounded the thesis that all human action is ultimately motivated by self-interest.

4. (91) **Beings in the Fairy tales:** i.e. changelings: disguised fairies who were substituted for stolen children.

5. (95) **Momus:** Greek God of ridicule; hence, here, a jokey, cheerful character.

6. (96) **Mrs Pipchin:** When he was twelve, Dickens was sent to stay with a Mrs Roylance in Camden Town, while his father was in the debtors' prison: 'I ... was handed over as a lodger to a reduced old lady ... who took children in to board, and had once done so at Brighton; and who, with a few alterations and embellishments, unconsciously began to sit for Mrs Pipchin in *Dombey* when she took in me [*sic*]' (Forster, *Life*, Book 1, Chapter 2).

7. (97) **Peruvian Mines:** In 1824, the Republic of Peru was founded after a rebellion against Spain. England had supported that rebellion and English investors were therefore given favourable terms for heavy investment in enterprises like the silver mines. Mr Pipchin, like many other such investors, presumably gambled on an increase in the value of his shares, a mistake which brought about his financial ruin.

8. (98) **bombazeen:** a dress material, half-silk, half-wool, usually black and associated with the lighter period of mourning, after the dark crepe period was over.

9. (98) **cupping-glasses:** cup-shaped vessels used by surgeons for bleeding patients. They adhered to the skin by suction.

10. (100) **Cock Lane Ghost:** a celebrated haunting in 1762, in West Smithfield, London, which turned out to be a fake.

11. (101) **a pedigree from Genesis:** a passage from the first book in the Bible which includes many lengthy genealogies.

12. (101) **a lion, or a bear:** The moralising children's stories of the day included one identified by Kathleen Tillotson (*The Dickensian* 79, 1983, pp. 31–4) from Daniel Fenning's *Universal Spelling Book* (first published 1756) about two brothers, good Tommy and naughty Harry. As a result of his misdeeds, Harry is eventually shipwrecked on a desolate shore, where he becomes 'A Prey to Wild Beasts'. The woodcut illustration shows him being eaten by a lion.

13. (101) **Falstaff's assailants:** *Henry IV Part 1*, Act II, Sc. 4. Falstaff exaggerated his own heroism by saying that he had been attacked by eleven 'men in buckram' when in fact there had been only two.

14. (103) **notes of admiration:** i.e. exclamation marks.

15. (103) **gashliness:** ghastliness.

16. (105) **biles:** boils.

CHAPTER 9

1. (109) **a ballad:** Popular songs were printed on single sheets and sold widely. Many were on nautical themes.

2. (109) **coal-whipper:** workman who operated the pulley to unload coal from a coal barge.

3. (109) **'lovely Peg':** Dickens seems here to be parodying a typical ballad plot, though 'lovely Peg' does occur in a verse from Charles Dibdin's 'The Saturday Night at Sea' (1789), from which Captain Cuttle borrows 'Heart's-delight'; see Chapter 23, n. 16.

4. (109) **collier:** coal barge. Newcastle-upon-Tyne was famous for its export of coal.

5. (109) **non-Dominical:** i.e. not an official Christian festival.

6. (110) **all the colours of the dolphin:** The legend is that the dolphin changes colour when dying. The allusion is to the naval tradition (abandoned in 1865) of ranking all admirals, below the rank of Admiral of the Fleet, by dividing them into the red, white and blue squadrons.

7. (110) **Post-Captain:** a full captain, in charge of a ship containing twenty or more guns.

8. (113) **Bishopsgate Street Without:** i.e. a London street originally outside the city walls.

9. (113) **sworn broker and appraiser:** receiver and assessor of goods to be sold to relieve bankruptcy.

10. (114) **Caius Marius:** Roman consul (155–86 BC), forced to flee to Carthage, where he compared its ruins to the collapse of his own hopes.

11. (115) **stranded leviathan:** a sea-monster (Job 41:1) or whale – occasionally beached on the shore.

12. (115) **slopsellers ... Guernsey shirts, sou'wester hats:** dealers in cheap clothing, including sailors' close-knitted blue woollen tunics and waterproof hats with a flap to cover the neck.

13. (115) **chips:** i.e. wood-chippings.

14. (116) **block making:** Blocks were solid pieces of wood used in various ways about a ship, e.g. fixed under the keel or as stabilisers in transporting the ship.

15. (116) **oak ... hearts:** see David Garrick's song, popularly misquoted: 'Heart of Oak are our Ships, Heart of Oak are our Men' (1759).

16. (117) **Englishwoman's house ... her castle:** adapted from the proverbial 'An Englishman's home is his castle.' An Englishman was thought of as unassailable in his own home because no bailiff had the right to break down the door to arrest him or seize his goods.

17. (118) **atomies:** diminutive beings.

18. (118) **walk the same all the days of your life:** from the Catechism; see Chapter 4, n. 16. This is part of the answer to the third question, on the vows for the child by its godparents at baptism, which ends: 'that I should keep God's holy will and commandments and walk in the same all the days of my life'.

CHAPTER 10

1. (123) **Yellow Jack:** yellow fever.

2. (124) **give Joey B. the go-by:** i.e. give him up, drop his acquaintance.

3. (124) **the Duke of York:** see Chapter 1, n. 6.

4. (125) **ours:** i.e. our regiment.

5. (125) **public school:** Thirty-five public (i.e. private) schools were built

between 1830 and 1870 and were the best path to social advancement for the children of an aspiring middle-class businessman.

6. (125) **Sandhurst:** still the top military college in England. British public schools in the nineteenth century took a pride in brutal traditions which supposedly developed stoicism in later life.

7. (130) **prannum:** per annum, yearly.

8. (130) **one flowing ... with milk and honey:** Exodus 3:8. The phrase used in the Bible to describe the Land of Promise, Captain Cuttle uses here to describe a 'lad of promise'.

CHAPTER 11

1. (134) **sweetbreads:** delicacy made from the pancreas of an animal.

2. (139) **cherub ... much too long:** from the popular song, 'Poor Jack' by Charles Dibdin (1745–1814): 'There's a sweet little cherub that sits up aloft/To keep watch for the life of poor Jack.'

3. (140) **posed a boy:** i.e. asked a boy a difficult question.

4. (140) **Cicero:** Roman orator (106–43 BC).

5. (141) **Curtius:** the legendary hero of Republican Rome, Marcus Curtius. A great chasm opened in the city which would not close, it was said, until Rome's prize possession was thrown into it. Curtius leapt on horseback into the abyss, which immediately closed over him.

6. (141) **turnspits:** lowly servants who turned the roasting meat in great households.

7. (142) **Homer:** the greatest Greek poet, author of the *Iliad* and the *Odyssey*.

8. (142) **Minerva:** Roman goddess of wisdom.

9. (144) **Parnassus:** Mount Parnassus, home of the Muses and thus of the Arts.

10. (144) **Virgil ... Cicero:** the standard Classics used in nineteenth-century schools.

11. (144) **Tusculum:** a city fifteen miles north-west of Rome, where Cicero had his villa.

12. (144) **Davy-lamp:** miners' safety lamp, invented by Sir Humphrey Davy in 1815.

13. (145) **Portico:** the painted porch at Athens, where philosophers met and taught; thus a figurative reference to a school.

14. (145) **the drowsy god:** in Classical mythology Morpheus, god of sleep; his 'dominions' are the dormitories.

CHAPTER 12

1. (149) **his Virgil stop:** The 'stops' or draw-knobs of a church organ enable it to play a variety of tunes in different modes.

2. (150) **knocked up:** exhausted.

3. (151) **Miller ... Jest Book:** Joe Miller (1684–1738), the comedian. His *Jests* were published in 1739 and by the 1840s had come to mean old jokes.

4. (152) **elephant and castle:** elephants in wartime bore soldiers on their backs in a fortified structure called a 'castle'.

5. (153) **come to a period:** i.e. reach a full stop.

6. (153) **Vitellius:** Roman emperor for a few months in 69 AD, who, according to Suetonius, was famed for his gluttony.

7. (154) **sounds:** airbladders.

8. (154) **Titus ... Nero ... Heliogabalus:** Roman emperors known for luxurious living.

9. (157) **dreadful note of preparation:** *Henry V*, Act IV, chorus, 14.

10. (159) **twenty Romuluses ... Taurus a bull: Romulus and Remus:** legendary brothers who founded Rome; **hic, haec, hoc:** Latin masculine, feminine and neuter forms of the demonstrative adjective 'this'; **troy weight:** the system of weights used in weighing precious metals and gems; **ancient Briton:** one of the early inhabitants of the British Isles, before the Anglo-Saxon invasions of the fifth and sixth centuries; **Taurus a bull:** part of an early lesson in Latin vocabulary.

11. (159) **Guy Faux ... Bogle:** Guy Fawkes, the best known of the Gunpowder plotters, had given his name to the stuffed 'guys' burnt to commemorate the event every November. A Bogle is a scarecrow, also stuffed with straw. See Chapter 5, n. 16.

12. (160) **Sabbaths:** The Jewish Sabbath or Holy Day is Saturday while for the Christian it is Sunday.

13. (160) **threw away the scabbard:** drew the sword from its sheath and discarded the latter, i.e. declared open war.

14. (164) **the Arabian story:** 'The Fisherman and the Jinni' from the *Arabian Nights*, in which smoke from a casket turns into a genie.

15. (165) **Preventive:** i.e. Customs officers whose job was to prevent smuggling.

CHAPTER 13

1. (169) **ticket-porter:** a London street-porter licensed by the City Corporation. He wore his licence as a badge on his arm and could be hired to carry messages or parcels.

2. (167) **hung the newspaper to air:** see Chapter 3, n. 9. A gentleman's valet would dry the morning newspaper, still damp with printing ink, before the fire before presenting it to him.

3. (167) **Caliph Haroun Alraschid:** Caliph of Bagdad (763–809), who appears in many of the *Arabian Nights* stories (see Chapter 5, n. 8) as a figure of enormous power. There are many references in this chapter to *The Arabian Nights*, e.g. the Grand Vizier, the Sultan and the Eastern form of address, 'You are the light of my eyes.' All contribute to the impression of Dombey's power.

4. (168) **mussulman:** a Muslim, thought of as shaving the hair for religious reasons.

5. (169) **gained a stave:** climbed a rung.

6. (171) **post-letters:** i.e. letters that had come long-distance rather than being delivered by hand.

CHAPTER 14

1. (180) *Verbum personale . . . simillima cygno:* exercise from a Latin primer: 'A personal verb . . . like a swan.' The last phrase comes from the sixth Satire of Juvenal, l. 165: '*Rara avis in terris nigroque simillima cygno*' ('As rare a bird in the world as a black swan.')

2. (180) **Walker:** John Walker 1732–1807, the eighteenth-century lexicographer, who compiled two dictionaries.

3. (183) **porter . . . table-beer:** i.e. added the beer drunk by adults to the watered-down version given to children; see Chapter 2, n. 11.

4. (183) **mysteries of London . . . Peckham:** a reference to the hugely popular *Mysteries of London* by G. W. M. Reynolds, which was being published in weekly penny numbers at the same time as *Dombey and Son*. Peckham was at that time a remote and extremely respectable suburb.

5. (183) **slashing:** (*slang*) dashing.

6. (184) **Quadrilles:** dances usually performed by four couples.

7. (186) **Apothecary:** a cross between a modern chemist and a doctor, who could deal with minor ailments.

8. (188) **Curfew Bell:** from the Anglo-Norman 'coevrefu', cover fire: a bell rung at dusk in medieval times warning townspeople to extinguish lights and fires for safety during the night.

9. (188) **King Alfred's idea:** Alfred the Great (849–901) was noted for his scientific as well as his political skills.

10. (189) **in fine:** in short.

11. (190) **pointing upward:** Popular sentimental paintings of Christ, like those of Sir Joshua Reynolds in the late eighteenth century, often presented him thus.

12. (190) **resumption:** revision.

13. (191) **great-coat:** overcoat.

14. (191) **play-bill:** sheet advertising theatrical performances, printed on thin paper and therefore ideal for making rollers to curl the hair.

15. (192) **pumped:** wearing smart dancing shoes or 'pumps'.

16. (193) **catch the Speaker's eye ... touch up the Radicals:** make telling points against the Radicals once he got the Speaker's permission to address the House.

17. (196) **D:** Damn.

18. (196) **custard-cups of negus:** large breakfast-cups of wine and hot water, sweetened with spice and lemon.

19. (196) **Had I a heart ... You:** R. B. Sheridan, *The Duenna* (1775), Act I, Sc. 5.

20. (198) **Diogenes:** The Greek Stoic philosopher (402?–323 BC) was referred to as 'Diogenes the Cynic'; 'cynic' literally means 'like a dog'.

21. (200) **young Chesterfields:** Lord Chesterfield (1694–1773), in his *Letters ... to his Son* (1774), advised him always to keep control of his emotions.

CHAPTER 15

1. (202) **beat up ... quarters:** to strike cover, as when rousing or 'beating up' game in hunting; therefore, to visit unexpectedly, disturb.

2. (202) **the general enemy:** i.e. Satan.

3. (203) **puncheons:** large casks for beer. The Reverend Howler has been found drunk after making holes in beer casks and drinking the beer through them.

4. (205) **Ranting persuasion:** sect of Primitive Methodists noted for their emotional preaching.

5. (205) **Proverbs of Solomon:** the Biblical Solomon was famous for his wisdom; however, this is from a less exalted source, a popular song beginning 'From the first dawn of reason...' already quoted by Dickens in *The Old Curiosity Shop*, Chapter 56.

6. (206) **for the port of Barbados:** chorus of a popular sea shanty.

7. (207) **the buoy at the Nore:** a lightship on the Thames Estuary sandbank, midway between the Essex and Kent coasts, roughly forty-eight miles below London Bridge.

8. (210) **ankle-jacks:** boots reaching between ankle and knee.

9. (213) **There was no such place as Staggs's Gardens:** see Chapter 6, ns 2 and 3. Many poorer London neighbourhoods were indeed demolished in the 1840s during the rapid expansion of the railways.

10. (214) **railway time:** As a result of the coming of the railways, time was standardised over the whole country in the 1840s.

11. (214) **whilom:** once upon a time, formerly.

12. (214) **electric telegraph:** installed along railway lines in 1842 (patented in 1837 by Wheatstone and Cooke).

13. (214) **not a rood of English ground:** from Wordsworth's 1844 sonnet 'On the Projected Kendal and Windermere Railway': 'Is then no nook of English ground secure...?'

CHAPTER 16

1. (221) **to the ocean!:** The first printed version of the novel continued: '"Dear me, dear me! To think," said Miss Tox, bursting out afresh that night, as if her heart were broken, "that Dombey and Son should be a Daughter after all!"' Omitted from the Cheap Edition (1858) onwards, this is needed, however, to make sense of Miss Tox's later remark (see p. 811).

CHAPTER 17

1. (227) **cheer:** chair.

2. (227) **clipper:** a fast sailing ship, i.e. ahead of the rest.

3. (227) **down by the head:** prow low in the water, i.e. overloaded.

4. (227) **wore round a bit:** resumed his course, recovered.

5. (229) **your business, and your buzzums:** dedication to Francis Bacon's *Essays* (1625): 'My essays ... come home, to men's business, and bosoms.'

6. (231) **Wal'r ... poet of that name:** Mr Perch is obviously thinking of Edmund Waller (1606–87), the Royalist poet.

7. (232) **Roman matron:** i.e. noted for moral rectitude. The best-known example of the Roman matron is Volumnia in Shakespeare's *Coriolanus*.

CHAPTER 18

1. (233) **fillet:** scarf.

2. (233) **worsted drawers:** trousers of a coarse material.

3. (234) **statuary:** a sculptor; here, a monumental mason.

4. (235) **Amendment:** i.e. moral improvement.

5. (235) **Oxford Market:** meat, fish and vegetable market in London's West End, near Oxford Street (demolished 1876).

6. (239) **sacred fire ... brightened and unhurt:** the tongues of fire which came to the disciples on Whitsunday as a token of Christ's resurrection and of the continuing power of the Holy Spirit in their lives (Acts 2:1–4).

7. (242) **oyster:** proverbially shut up in itself, like a clam.

8. (244) **cabriolet:** see Chapter 5, n. 4.

9. (244) **as ridiculous a dog ... summer's day:** see *A Midsummer Night's Dream*, Act 1, Sc. 2: 'a proper man as one shall see in a summer's day.'

10. (245) **Diogenes the man ... :** Plutarch records that Diogenes the philosopher (see Chapter 14, n. 20) was asked by Alexander the Great

if he needed anything; he replied, 'Yes, that you stand out of my sun a little.'

CHAPTER 19

1. (251) **Archimedes ... Syracuse:** Archimedes (c. 287–212 BC), Greek mathematician, was killed by an enemy soldier when his native city, Syracuse, was captured by the Roman general Marcellus. He had been so intent on working at his mathematical diagrams in the sand that he had not realised the danger.

2. (260) **train up a fig-tree ... shade on it:** Proverbs 22:6: 'Train up a child ...' (see Chapter 4, n. 20) is here combined with Micah 4:4: 'every man under his vine and under his fig tree'.

3. (262) **watermen:** the boatmen who plied for hire on the Thames.

4. (262) **Cyclops:** one of the race of one-eyed giants in Greek mythology.

5. (262) **caboose:** small cabin fitted up for cooking.

CHAPTER 20

1. (264) **Devil a bit!:** Certainly not!

2. (264) **K.C.B.:** Knight Commander of the Bath. Appointment to this prestigious Order of Knights is in the gift of the Sovereign. 'Bath' refers to the ceremony of bathing, as a sign of purity, which accompanied the inauguration of a knight until 1661.

3. (266) **devilled:** grilled with hot condiments.

4. (266) **Duke of York ... levee:** see Chapter 1, n. 6; **levee:** originally a morning assembly in pre-Revolutionary France. In nineteenth-century Britain, the Sovereign held levees at St James's Palace, usually in the afternoon.

5. (269) **Seltzer water:** effervescent mineral water, named after a village in Germany.

6. (269) **rumble:** the back of a carriage, provided with seats for servants or space for luggage.

7. (269) **Titan:** in Greek mythology, one of the powerful offspring of Uranus and Gaea (Heaven and Earth), who unsuccessfully rebelled against the Olympian gods. Dickens is here confusing them with the giants who hurled rocks and trees at the gods.

8. (269) **During the bustle of preparation at the railway:** It is probable that Mr Dombey's own carriage was hoisted on to a railway train carriage and pulled behind the other coaches. 'Carriage' can still mean both a horse-drawn vehicle and a railway train compartment. See the debate in *The Dickensian* 28 (1932), p. 205, and 29 (1933), p. 25. It was shortly after this period that the practice was discontinued, as the increasing speed of the trains made it dangerous.

9. (270) **stokin' of you down:** i.e. acting as engine stoker on the outward journey.

10. (270) **rubs on:** struggles on.

11. (271) **quondam:** erstwhile, former.

12. (271) **jobbed into:** i.e. hired by corrupt influence (as in 'a put-up job').

13. (272) **crape:** black material worn during mourning.

14. (276) **like a giant refreshed:** Psalms 78:66.

15. (276) **Pump-room:** the place in a spa town where the mineral water is dispensed for drinking – which is therefore a centre for meeting people.

CHAPTER 21

1. (277) **tight stock:** high collar.

2. (280) **barouche:** a four-wheeled carriage used for pleasure outings.

3. (280) **Cleopatra ... her galley:** see *Antony and Cleopatra*, Act II, Sc. 2, where the proverbially beautiful Queen of Egypt is described aboard her state barge, or galley.

4. (280) **bucks:** fashionable men-about-town in the Regency period.

5. (280) **Arcadian:** simple shepherd/shepherdess dwelling in the idealised countryside of Pastoral poetry.

6. (281) **celebrated bull:** 'A bull in a china shop' is a proverbial description of someone who wrecks his surroundings.

7. (281) **cauliflower nosegay:** huge posy of flowers as a buttonhole.

8. (282) **jointure:** property held jointly by husband and wife, which, after the husband's death, becomes a provision for the widow.

9.   (284)   **closet:** separate cubicle within main room.

10.   (284)   **Sisyphus:** a figure in Greek legend who was punished in Hades by having to push uphill every day a heavy stone, which would roll downhill again every night.

11.   (284)   **age could not wither:** 'age cannot wither her, nor custom stale her infinite variety' *Antony and Cleopatra*, Act II, Sc.2.

12.   (285)   **hand-screen:** fan.

13.   (287)   **to prove them all:** to test them all out.

14.   (287)   **picquet:** card game for two, with points scored for various combinations of cards.

15.   (287)   **undeveloped recollections . . . existence:** vague paraphrase of Wordsworth's 'Immortality Ode', the source of much of Mrs Skewton's once-fashionable Romanticism.

16.   (287)   **to put a period to my life:** i.e. to end it (period = full stop); see Chapter 12, n. 5.

CHAPTER 22

1.   (289)   **crooked dial-plate:** i.e. the usually flat surface of a sundial, which told the time by means of the shadow cast by the arm in the centre.

2.   (291)   **taking part with you:** i.e. taking your side.

3.   (293)   **in wants of a sitiwation:** in need of a job.

4.   (293)   **take my affidavit:** take my oath, i.e. bear witness against him.

5.   (294)   **Cain:** i.e. an outcast. In the Bible story, Cain killed his brother Abel (Genesis 2).

6.   (295)   **bird-catching and walking-matching:** two of the many street occupations of the period: trapping wild birds for the cage-bird market and (presumably) taking part in gambling associated with walking contests.

7.   (295)   **cove:** (*sl.*) man.

8.   (295)   **velveteen:** cheap cotton material which looks like velvet.

9.   (295)   **gorget:** collar.

10. (295) **There's hempseed sown for *you*:** i.e. you're heading for the gallows! Hemp was used to make the hangman's rope.

11. (299) **prodigal son:** Luke 15:12–24.

12. (299) **Mr Ketch:** i.e. the public hangman. Jack Ketch, who filled the role in the 1690s, had become a proverbial figure.

13. (303) **Apollo ... Pantheon:** the sun-god in the Temple dedicated to the gods.

14. (303) **on which the sun never sets:** The phrase was first recorded in *Blackwood's Magazine*, 20 April 1829, and became a proverbial description for the British Empire.

CHAPTER 23

1. (308) **Gorgon-like:** in Greek mythology the Gorgons were three female monsters whose look could turn people to stone.

2. (308) **piping organ:** a barrel organ decorated with moving figures – one of the many ingenious street entertainments of the time; see Chapter 3, n. 5.

3. (311) **down-stairs:** i.e. the servants' quarters; the family live upstairs.

4. (312) **avocations:** business.

5. (313) **a plea in bar:** i.e. a plea against (barring, preventing) the notion that the Skettles are acting simply out of kindness.

6. (314) **Amazon:** in Classical mythology, a female warrior.

7. (314) **camel ... dromedary:** both known for their capacity to bear heavy loads. 'The straw that breaks the camel's back' is the event which finally cracks such endurance, the 'last straw'.

8. (315) **conscience-stricken pigeons:** the (still popular) hobby of pigeon-racing involves the transportation of specially bred birds many miles from their home loft. They are then released to race home. Rob's aim was to distract them from the purpose of their journey, catch and resell them.

9. (316) **transport:** ecstasy, excitement.

10. (317) **knocked up by the policeman:** The developing police force, founded by Sir Robert Peel in 1829, would patrol the city streets

at night and, if requested, would wake citizens who needed to rise early for work.

11. (317) **pattens:** wooden or metal overshoes used in wet weather or for domestic cleaning.

12. (318) **cast pearls before swine:** waste precious things on the unworthy (Matthew 7:6).

13. (319) **potboy:** boy employed by tavern to carry beer or food to outside customers.

14. (319) **Flying Dutchman's family:** from the sixteenth-century legend of Van Der Decken, a Dutch sailor who was condemned to sail the seas for all eternity.

15. (319) **Triton:** in Greek mythology a seagod, half-human, half-fish, attendant on Neptune.

16. (320) **Heart's-delight:** from Charles Dibdin's song, 'The Saturday Night at Sea' (1789): '"I'll give", I cried, "my charming Nan,/ Trim, handsome, neat and tight:/What joy so fine a ship to man –/She is my heart's delight."' See Chapter 9, n. 3.

17. (320) **out'ard and visible sign . . . grasp:** 'an outward and visible sign of an inward and spiritual grace': from the Catechism (see Chapter 4, n. 16). This is the answer to the question, 'What meanest thou by this word Sacrament?'

18. (320) **hearts of oak:** see Chapter 9, n. 15.

19. (320) **buzzums:** human breasts (bosoms).

20. (320) **bringing it up with a round turn:** This, to Captain Cuttle, ties up the argument for Walter's survival. A round turn is a sailor's knot.

21. (320) **until death do us part . . . stormy winds do blow, do blow, do blow:** a splicing of the Marriage Service, from the Anglican Book of Common Prayer, and 'Ye Mariners of England!' by Thomas Campbell (1777–1844).

22. (321) **swabbing of these here planks . . . stopped my liberty:** The Captain uses nautical terminology. He means the washing of the floor and his consequent confinement to his room (as a sailor might be refused permission to go ashore).

23. (321) **full ... and round:** i.e. she changes direction unexpectedly.

24. (322) **fire-ship:** an empty ship set on fire and sent to cause havoc among the enemy.

25. (322) **coach-box:** on the high seat with the driver.

26. (323) **tier:** row of ships anchored in the same place.

27. (323) **standing rigging:** those sections of the sailropes which could not be lowered when the ship was at anchor.

28. (323) **curing:** i.e. drying, as were the various items of meat and fish.

29. (323) **oakum:** rough fibre made by unwinding rope.

30. (323) **succedaneum:** substitute.

31. (324) **science ... knows no law:** misremembered from the proverbs, 'Necessity is the Mother of Invention' and 'Necessity knows no law'.

32. (324) **wear:** i.e. veer, change course.

33. (327) **auditory:** the listeners.

34. (328) **Sen' George's Channel ... the Downs ... The Goodwins:** St George's Channel lies between the coasts of Ireland and Wales. This reference must, however, be to a smaller channel off the eastern coast of Kent, part of the English Channel. The Downs is a safe anchorage in the English Channel, between Deal and the treacherous sandbanks of the Goodwin Sands.

35. (328) **leads:** i.e. the roof (made of leaded tiles).

36. (328) **roads:** i.e. roadsteads, safe anchorage for shipping.

37. (329) **take you in tow:** pull you along, keep you company.

38. (330) **weigh anchor:** pull up the anchor, set off.

CHAPTER 24

1. (331) **Ptolemy the Great:** (*c.* 367–282 BC), one of Alexander the Great's generals, who founded the Ptolemaic Dynasty in Egypt.

2. (331) **so killed a brace of birds:** to kill two birds with one stone; to achieve two aims at once.

3. (331) **Jericho:** walled city destroyed by Joshua (Joshua 6). The phrase 'to go to Jericho' means to get lost.

4. (331) **Terence:** Publius Terentius (*c.* 185-159 BC), Roman dramatist whose actual words were: 'I am a man; nothing human is (properly) indifferent to me.'

5. (336) **heap of fiery coals:** to heap coals of fire on someone's head; to build up a heavy load of guilt upon someone's conscience.

6. (337) **shelving:** sloping.

7. (337) **caulk:** stop up the seams, first with oakum, then with hot tar, to prevent leaking.

8. (341) **passing over her grave:** The superstition is that an unexpected shiver is caused by someone walking over the place where you will one day be buried.

CHAPTER 25

1. (343) **Flowed:** i.e. flown (as in 'the bird has flown').

2. (343) **will ... and Testament:** a single document prepared for use in the event of death.

3. (344) **Keep her free ... ride easy:** steer a course away from obstacles, i.e. avoid committing yourself.

4. (347) **hand-bills:** printed sheets containing details of missing persons and of bodies found.

5. (347) **roadstead:** see Chapter 23, n. 36.

6. (349) **It's a breather!:** i.e. It makes me out of breath!

7. (350) **quotations of the Funds:** stocks and shares whose prices are 'quoted' (listed) in the press.

CHAPTER 26

1. (351) **Colossus:** someone who dominates all around him – from the gigantic statue at Rhodes, one of the Seven Wonders of the ancient world.

2. (353) **Lloyd's:** Lloyd's of London, official keeper of all British shipping records.

3. (354) **straddled:** strutted, swaggered.

4. (357) **garnered up her heart:** treasured up her affections; *Othello* Act IV, Sc. 2: 'there, where I have garnered up my heart'.

5. (359) **Cleopatra ... Antony:** see Chapter 21, n. 3.

6. (359) **as proud ... as Lucifer:** The rebel archangel was too proud to submit to God and was flung from Heaven.

7. (360) **quite a form:** only a formality.

8. (361) **plumed himself:** prided himself.

9. (361) **fatigue duty:** extra military duty, outside a soldier's normal work.

10. (363) **gay dogs:** fashionable men-about-town.

11. (365) **plied his light artillery:** attacked him with light-hearted humour.

12. (365) **his bear dancing:** Dancing bears were still popular features of nineteenth-century street entertainment.

CHAPTER 27

1. (368) **Death's Head:** skull.

2. (369) **munching ... in vain:** *Macbeth*, Act I, Sc. 3: 'A sailor's wife had chestnuts in her lap, and munch'd and munch'd and munch'd ...'

3. (369) **familiar:** the companion of a witch, often a cat.

4. (370) **Beldamite:** contemptuous term for an ugly old woman.

5. (370) **carried it hollow:** triumphed easily.

6. (371) **cross one's arms ... prophet!:** a parody of the Islamic incantation, 'There is no God but Allah and Mohammed is his prophet.'

7. (372) **admirable Carker:** a tribute to his varied accomplishments: the 'Admirable Crichton', James Crichton (1560–85?), was a soldier, athlete, scholar, poet and linguist.

8. (373) **the sword wears out:** from Byron's poem, 'We'll go no more a-roving': 'For the sword wears out its sheath/And the heart wears out the breast ...'

9. (373) **dagger of lath:** the stage weapon used by the Vice in Morality Plays; hence, an imitation weapon.

10. (375) **Queen Bess:** Elizabeth I (1533–1603).

11. (375) **Harry the Eighth:** Elizabeth's father, Henry VIII (1491–1547), famous, of course, not for benevolence, but for the savage treatment of his six wives, two of whom were beheaded.

12. (375) **livery:** servant's uniform, therefore a sign of servitude.

13. (376) **crow's nest:** look-out room at the top of the castle.

14. (378) **haunted ruins of Kenilworth:** a glance at Sir Walter Scott; the ruined late-medieval castle in Warwickshire was the setting for Scott's novel, *Kenilworth* (1821), based on the tradition that Amy Robsart, wife of the Earl of Leicester, was murdered there during the reign of Elizabeth I.

15. (380) **dart and hour-glass:** the conventional objects associated with Death in seventeenth-century paintings.

CHAPTER 28

1. (383) **little Pitchers:** 'little pitchers have big ears', i.e. young listeners understand more than they should of adult conversation. (Pitcher handles were often shaped like two ears.)

2. (386) **quite a deal:** Visiting cards, showing the name and address of the visitor and left behind after a social call, are here deliberately confused with playing cards, which have to be 'dealt' in order to win a game.

3. (386) **six-oared cutter:** large racing boat for three rowers.

CHAPTER 29

1. (394) **rasped:** with a rough crusty surface.

2. (395) **Legends:** i.e. advertising posters.

3. (395) **the worthy gentlemen ... stickle ... miserable:** stickle: stand up for. Dickens was deeply committed to the movement for sanitary reform, which resulted from the cholera epidemics of the mid-century. Sir Edwin Chadwick's Report of 1842 demanding drastic public action was still being strongly contested by conservatives, who felt that it involved an infringement of traditional liberties.

4. (396) **chimney-glass:** mirror hanging over the fireplace.

5. (400) **Mephistophelean:** devilish, scheming, after the devil in *Faust* who plots successfully to win Faust's soul.

6. (402) **smelling-bottle:** filled with ammonia as a restorative after fainting.

7. (402) **the murdered king ... sorrow:** *Hamlet*, Act III, Sc 1. Hamlet's father's ghost reportedly looked 'more in sorrow than in anger'.

8. (403) **The scales ... have fallen from my sight:** St Paul was blinded on the road to Damascus and his sight was restored only when he 'saw the light' and became a Christian: 'And immediately the scales fell from his eyes' (Acts 9:18). Mrs Chick confuses these scales on the eyes with weighing machines used in shops.

9. (403) **like a serpent:** the serpent wound itself into the confidence of Eve in the Garden of Eden (Genesis 3).

10. (406) **fawner and toad-eater:** two terms for a sycophant or flatterer.

CHAPTER 30

1. (411) **dressing in the City:** i.e. dressing for dinner at his office in town without coming home first.

2. (413) **organ of veneration:** the bump on the head said to indicate that quality. Phrenology was very popular among the mid-Victorians. The belief was that the structure of the cranium decided which qualities were more prominent in one individual than in another.

3. (413) **absence:** i.e. absentmindedness.

4. (414) **hatchments:** funereal-looking pictures; originally, the coat of arms of a nobleman displayed outside his home after his death.

5. (414) **mutes:** people hired to attend funerals, professional mourners.

6. (417) **malice aforethought:** legal term for a premeditated crime.

7. (417) **Bashaw:** high-ranking Turkish officer who would expect absolute obedience (Pasha).

8. (420) **prophet's rod:** Aaron's rod struck water from the rock (Numbers 10:11).

CHAPTER 31

1. (422) **free seats:** see Chapter 5, n. 13. Middle-class church-goers in the Church of England paid for their family pews and Mrs Miff

received commission. She was not therefore in favour of the idea of extending the number of free pews for the use of the very poor, as the Evangelical churches did.

2. (422)   **spanker:** fine figure of a woman.

3. (422)   **Bonaparte:** Napoleon, Emperor of the French 1804–15.

4. (423)   **marrow-bones and cleavers:** traditional street music played on bones and on butchers' knives.

5. (423)   **Battle-bridge:** area of London named after a battle there between Boadicea and the Romans. The name had been officially changed in 1830 to its present name, King's Cross, but the old name persisted for many years.

6. (423)   **traitor tradesman:** All the local street entertainers want to serenade the wedding party. Dickens's original readers would, like him, have regarded them as public nuisances, to be bribed to stay away if possible.

7. (425)   **take open order:** set up military formation in which individuals are three or more yards apart; hence, be more distant.

8. (425)   **stand on forms:** stick to formalities.

9. (425)   **warm:** emotional.

10. (425)   **late Duke of Kent:** younger brother of the Duke of York (see chapter 1, n. 6) and father of Queen Victoria.

11. (426)   **up-to-snuff:** not easily fooled.

12. (426)   **cocked hat:** official beadle's uniform.

13. (426)   **chairs in the vestry:** The bridegroom and his party arrive at a wedding first and have the option of waiting out of sight of the congregation, in the vestry.

14. (426)   **double him up:** i.e. by punching him in the stomach.

15. (427)   **Baden-Baden:** fashionable German spa.

16. (433)   **in another place:** The 'other Place' is the conventional term used in the House of Commons for the House of Lords.

17. (433)   **a sadder and wiser man:** the last lines of Coleridge's

'Ancient Mariner' (1798) – also about a wedding guest: 'A sadder and a wiser man/He rose the morrow morn.'

18. (433)   **drugs:** i.e. 'drugs on the market', unsaleable items.

19. (434)   **saw:** saying.

20. (434)   **boning:** (*slang*) stealing.

21. (435)   **scouted:** scornfully rejected.

22. (435)   **heel-taps:** dregs left at the bottom (heel) of a glass.

23. (436)   **Long's:** fashionable hotel at 16 New Bond Street in the West End of London; in 1815 Scott met Byron there for the last time.

CHAPTER 32

1. (437)   **the wind ... nailed there:** i.e. that favourable winds are liable to change and to blow the weathercock round. (A weathercock is a wooden or metal shape which spins to show the direction of the wind.)

2. (438)   **stand off and on:** This chapter is strewn with nautical expressions. **Stand by:** be at the ready; **sheer off:** move quickly away; **stand off and on:** return at regular intervals.

3. (438)   **horse-road:** i.e. the main thoroughfare, dangerously full of horse-drawn traffic.

4. (442)   **drain of nothing short:** a 'short' drink, i.e. spirits.

5. (442)   **Cap'en Cuttle ... Job:** actually a children's motto often inscribed in school books. The Book of Job is perhaps the least likely Biblical source.

6. (448)   **broadside to you broach ... head foremost!:** (*naut.*) **broadside:** sideways on; **broach to:** veer suddenly, i.e. turn sideways suddenly and capsize.

7. (451)   **skirts:** i.e. of his frockcoat.

8. (452)   **out of soundings:** not too deep to be fathomed.

9. (454)   **when night comes on a hurricane ... rowling:** These lines cannot be traced in Dr Watts (see next note). They are more likely to be from a contemporary sea shanty.

10. (454) **Doctor Watts:** Isaac Watts (1674–1748), author of *Hymns* (1707) and *Divine Songs* (hymns for children) (1715).

CHAPTER 33

1. (455) **Norwood:** prosperous suburb in south-east London.

2. (455) **Juno:** queen of the Roman gods, wife of Jupiter.

3. (455) **Potiphar's Wife:** After trying in vain to seduce Joseph, she had him imprisoned on a false accusation of attempted rape (Genesis 29).

4. (457) **stuffs:** material, cloth.

5. (458) **not heroic to their valets:** proverbial expression first recorded in a letter of Mme Cornuel, French society hostess (1605–94): 'No man is a hero to his valet.'

6. (465) **I have been where convicts go:** i.e. I have been sent away to Australia. The sentence of transportation to Botany Bay was current until 1840.

CHAPTER 34

1. (470) **mowing:** grimacing.

CHAPTER 35

1. (479) **Household Gods:** from the Roman Lares and Penates, the Gods of hearth and home, in whose honour small domestic altars were set up.

2. (483) **installation dinner:** the ceremonial first meal of a married couple in their own house on their return from honeymoon.

3. (486) **will occasionally arise in the best-regulated ... :** proverbial; first recorded in *Blackwood's Magazine* (August 1834), in an article by Christopher North (John Wilson).

CHAPTER 36

1. (493) **old lady of Threadneedle Street:** (*coll.*) the Bank of England. Threadneedle Street in the City of London (see Chapter 4, n. 1), runs from the Mansion House into Bishopsgate, the financial centre of the City.

2. (493) **Tom Tiddler's ground:** children's game in which the child chosen to be 'Tom Tiddler' tries to prevent the other children from picking up his imaginary gold and silver coins.

3. (494) **sat for somebody's borough:** Until the Reform Act of 1832, there were many such 'pocket boroughs' where the Member of Parliament was chosen by the local landowner.

4. (494) **Warming Pan:** keeping the seat 'warm' for someone more important until they are of age to take it over.

5. (494) **Tops!:** i.e. topboots, high riding boots.

6. (495) **regularly:** absolutely, completely.

7. (495) **sold:** cheated, deceived.

8. (496) **double knocks:** knocks on the street door announcing the arrival of 'carriage company'.

9. (500) **linkmen:** men paid to carry torches (links) to light people home through the unlit parts of the city.

10. (502) **old well staircase:** the central opening space from roof to basement of a winding or spiral staircase.

CHAPTER 37

1. (502) **pomatum:** scented ointment for dressing the hair.

2. (502) **days of down:** times of luxury (from 'down' meaning soft feathers, as in pillows).

3. (503) **Serpent of old Nile:** see *Antony and Cleopatra*, Act I, Sc. 5.

4. (503) **martyr:** i.e. to nerves.

5. (509) **zephyrs:** spirits of the West Wind, warm breezes (from Greek mythology).

6. (511) **gaud:** jewellery.

CHAPTER 38

1. (513) **wedding cards:** left by a newly married couple when they went visiting.

2. (513) **milky nature:** see *Macbeth*, Act I, Sc. 5: 'Yet do I fear thy nature;/It is too full o' th' milk of human kindness.'

3. (514) **what time:** *quo tempore* (epic style), at the time when.

4. (515) **a sight of:** a great many.

5. (516) **withers ... not unwrung:** *Hamlet*, Act III, Sc. 2. Someone

with a guilty conscience will smart, like a whipped horse, at a chance remark.

6. (517) **friends at court:** proverbial expression for influential friends in high places.

7. (519) **leathers:** leather breeches (the Grinders' uniform).

8. (521) **backer:** tobacco (more usually 'baccy').

9. (521) **garments which are rarely mentioned:** i.e. trousers (otherwise known as unmentionables or inexpressibles; see Chapter 4, n. 7).

10. (522) **tossed it away with a pieman:** To 'toss the pieman' was a popular gamble involving tossing a coin; if the pieman won the toss, he kept the money without offering a pie; if he lost, a pie had to be handed over for nothing (see Henry Mayhew, *London Labour and the London Poor*, vol. 1, 1861).

CHAPTER 39

1. (523) **magazine ... blow up:** i.e. what trouble he might cause. **Magazine:** powder keg.

2. (524) **a certain Divine Sermon ... Mount:** The Sermon on the Mount (Matthew 5:3).

3. (524) **proper names of all the tribes of Judah:** i.e. the genealogies of the Old Testament rather than the spirit of love of the New; see Chapter 8, n. 11.

4. (526) **clemency ... garden angels:** 'Clemency is the standing policy of constitutional government' (Henry Hallam); India was often referred to as 'the jewel in the crown' of the British Empire; the first verse of 'Rule Britannia' contains the lines: 'This was the charter, the charter of the Land,/And guardian angels sang this strain.'

5. (530) **shutters:** heavy wooden ones to protect business premises – too much for the one-handed Captain to do himself.

6. (531) **give me the lad with the tarry trousers:** from an old Essex folksong: 'My mother wants me to wed with a tailor/And not give me my heart's delight:/But give me the man with the tarry trousers,/That shine to me like diamonds bright.'

7. (531) **Stanfell's Budget:** A budget was a songbook. This is prob-

ably a private joke referring to Dickens's friend, Clarkson Stanfield, who had been a sailor before becoming a marine painter.

8. (532) **There he lays, all his days:** adapted from 'The Bay of Biscay', tune by J. Davy (1765–1824), words by A. Cherry.

9. (533) **Affliction sore ... bore:** a favourite epitaph on nineteenth-century tombstones: 'Affliction sore long time I bore,/Physicians were in vain;/Till death did seize and God did please/To ease me of my pain.'

10. (533) **sign-manual:** signature.

11. (534) **Furies:** ancient Greek goddesses who exacted vengeance for acts of family impiety, particularly (as in Aeschylus' *Eumenides*) harm done to a mother.

12. (536) **hi-i-i-igh:** i.e. eye.

13. (536) **wales:** weals (caused by beating).

14. (538) **traps:** trappings, property.

CHAPTER 40

1. (549) **fly-away bonnet:** i.e. loose, with streaming ribbons – a youthful style.

2. (551) **removed to Queer Street:** is on her way out (the phrase is used both of madness and of illness generally).

CHAPTER 41

1. (556) **mill:** fight.

2. (557) **dog of Montargis:** from the popular melodrama *The Dog of Montargis, or The Forest of Bondy* (1814) by W. Barrymore, adapted from *Le Chien de Montargis* by René-Charles Pixérécourt (1773–1844). The dog identifies and attacks his master's murderer.

3. (538) **dropsical:** collapsed.

4. (558) **Thugs:** Indian assassins who strangled their victims; originally worshippers of the god Kali.

5. (558) **Herodotus:** (c. 485–c. 424 BC), Ancient Greek historian.

6. (558) **passed the Rubicon:** taken an irrevocable step. Julius Caesar crossed this river in 49 BC, thus invading Pompey's territory and effectively declaring war.

7. (559)   **Come now!:** So there!

8. (559)   **Old Parr:** Thomas Parr (1483?–1635) lived, apparently, to be 152, though the date of his birth was unproven.

9. (559)   **awful:** i.e. awe-inspiring.

10. (561)   **have him out:** challenge him to a duel.

11. (565)   **White's:** exclusive gentleman's club in St James's Street, in the West End of London, founded in the late seventeenth century and a noted Tory stronghold.

12. (565)   **blood mare:** thoroughbred.

CHAPTER 43

1. (583)   **wants a character:** needs a character reference.

CHAPTER 44

1. (591)   **Meethosalem:** someone of great age. Methuselah, at 969, is the oldest person in the Bible (Genesis 5:27).

2. (591)   **Fox's Martyr:** The *Book of Martyrs* (1563) by John Fox (1516–87) was a lurid and popular account of the deaths of Protestant martyrs.

3. (592)   **Indian widow:** According to the Indian custom of suttee, a widow was required to throw herself upon the funeral pyre of her husband. The British abolished the practice in India in 1829.

4. (593)   **graven images:** The second of the Ten Commandments (Exodus 20:1) is 'Thou shalt not make unto thee any graven image . . .'

5. (594)   **Jubilee:** cause for celebration.

6. (595)   **take your affidavit:** take your oath, be certain of.

7. (599)   **leal:** loyal.

8. (599)   **Blue-coat School:** London's Christ's Hospital School, a charity school but greatly superior to the Charitable Grinders.

9. (599)   **powder-mill:** place for the manufacture of gunpowder.

10. (600)   **get into Chancery . . . finished:** get into chancery: had his head gripped under his opponent's arm; **fibbed:** beaten; **grassed:** knocked down; **tapped:** hit on the nose; **bunged:** had his eyes closed up; **pepper:** heavy punishment; **gone into:** laid into.

CHAPTER 46

1. (609) **minnows among the tritons of the East:** small fry among the great – a reversal of *Coriolanus*, Act III, Sc. 1: '... Hear you this Triton of the minnows?/Mark you his absolute shall?'; **triton:** (Greek mythology) sea-god, son of Poseidon and Amphitrite, who makes the roaring of the ocean by blowing through a shell; **of the East:** Job 1: 'greatest of all the men in the east'.

2. (609) **long-headed:** perspicacious, showing foresight.

3. (613) **prad:** horse (probably linked to German '*pferd*').

4. (615) **blabbing:** (*slang*) telling tales.

5. (617) **use dispatch:** make haste.

6. (618) **Spaniel:** dog proverbial for fawning on its master.

CHAPTER 47

1. (623) **lazar-houses:** hospitals for lepers, or more generally for all infectious diseases.

2. (623) **gather grapes from thorns, and figs from thistles:** Matthew 7:16.

3. (626) **Medusa:** in Greek mythology, a female monster with snakes for hair whose look can strike men dead.

CHAPTER 48

1. (644) **What cheer ... ?:** how are you?

2. (644) **Though lost to sight, to memory dear:** first line of a song by George Linley (1798–1865).

3. (644) **England, Home, and Beauty:** from 'The Death of Nelson' (1811), words by S. J. Arnold, music by J. Braham.

4. (644) **dead-light:** i.e. the shutter.

5. (644) **yes, verily ... so I won't:** the conclusion of the Catechism (see Chapter 4, n. 16), when the child makes promises of Christian behaviour. The original version ends with 'so I will'.

6. (647) **watch-coat:** thick, heavy coat worn in bad weather by seamen and watchmen.

7. (647) **balsam ... wownded mind!:** 'Sleep ... balm of hurt minds':
Macbeth, Act II, Sc. 2; the 'still, small voice': Kings 19:11.

8. (648) **clap on:** hurry up.

9. (650) **case-bottle:** hip flask, bottle protected by leather or wick-
erwork cover.

10. (651) **used up:** wasted away.

11. (651) **bark:** probably Jesuit bark, from which quinine is also
produced. Ground into a powder, this was used to soothe fever.

CHAPTER 49

1. (654) **guineas:** The guinea (twenty-one shillings) was succeeded
by the sovereign (£1) in 1817, but the word was still loosely used in the
1840s to mean money generally.

2. (655) **a deal:** sufficient.

3. (655) **Liver wing:** the choice right wing of the fowl, which has the
liver tucked under it.

4. (655) **The whole row ... for'ard:** all the shutters are up in front
of the house.

5. (655) **awast:** i.e. avast – (*naut.*) stop.

6. (655) **as the water brooks ... never rejices:** Psalm 42:1: 'as the
hart panteth after the water brooks . . .', elided with the proverb, 'It's a
poor heart that never rejoices.'

7. (658) **Ward in Chancery:** a young person whose official guardian
until they come of age is the Chancery Court; see *Bleak House*, Chapter
2.

8. (662) **wainscot:** skirting board panelled with wood.

9. (662) **A stiff nor'-wester's blowing, Bill:** from 'The Sailor's Consolation' by William Pitt (of Malta) (*d.* 1840): 'A strong nor'wester's
blowing, Bill,/Hark, don't you hear it roar now?/Lord help me, how I
pities all/Unhappy folks ashore now.'

10. (665) **there warn't no touching nowhere:** There was no port to
put into.

CHAPTER 50

1. (673) **Little Warbler, sentimental diwision:** There were several early nineteenth-century poetry and song miscellanies which included the word 'Warbler'. One published in 1816 by 'a lover of children' was called *The Little Warbler of the Cottage, and her dog Constant*. The 'sentimental diwision' is Dickens's joke.

2. (674) **wind . . . abaft:** favourable wind from behind.

3. (675) **two persons . . . house of bondage:** an amalgam of the Marriage Service and Exodus 20:1, in which Egypt is referred to as the 'house of bondage' for the Israelites.

4. (675) **gone clean about:** turned back from his intended plan.

5. (676) **mortar:** artillery piece designed for firing shells.

6. (679) **the silent tomb:** from Wordsworth's 'Surprised by Joy': 'Surprised by joy – impatient as the wind/I turned to share the transport – Oh! with whom/But thee, deep buried in the silent tomb.'

CHAPTER 51

1. (688) **Mr Pitt:** William Pitt the Younger, Prime Minister 1783–1801 and 1804–6; see Chapter 5, n. 7.

2. (690) **criminate:** incriminate.

3. (692) **weazen:** shrunken, small.

4. (693) **bright or particular star:** see *All's Well That Ends Well*, Act 1, Sc. 1.

5. (693) **removal of the cloth:** The tablecloth laid for meals was customarily removed before speeches began.

6. (694) **Sunday Papers:** The founding of *Lloyd's Weekly Newspaper* (1842) and *The News of the World* (1843) marked the beginning of popular journalism as we know it today. Dickens is almost certainly referring to the latter. By dint of bribery and 'snooping' it acquired a reputation as a popular scandal sheet, which built up its circulation from 17,500 in January 1845 to 30,000 by December 1845.

7. (694) **a daily paper:** This could possibly be *The Times*, but more likely the *Morning Post*, which was the source of 'fashionable intelligence', information on the activities of the upper classes.

8. (694) **Ball's Pond:** village near Islington, north London.

CHAPTER 52

1. (698) **Chut!:** exclamation of impatience, cf. 'Tut!'

2. (698) **What signifies!:** What does it matter?

3. (699) **crazy:** derelict, falling to pieces.

4. (700) **to-night's a week:** a week ago tonight.

5. (702) **Board wages:** His master is still paying for his board and lodgings.

6. (706) **Jesuitical:** i.e. prepared to justify herself ingeniously by keeping the exact letter of the oath.

7. (707) **packet:** mail boat, carrying postal packages between two ports.

CHAPTER 53

1. (712) **frogs:** ornamental fastenings on the front of a soldier's coat.

2. (717) **Beethoven's Sonata in B:** There is no such piece for 'cello in Beethoven's works; see also Chapter 58, n. 4, and Chapter 62, n. 1.

CHAPTER 54

1. (727) **chafing-dish:** vessel holding burning charcoal, to keep food warm during a meal.

2. (733) **All stratagems ... the old adage:** i.e. 'all's fair in love and war'.

3. (734) **Their name is Legion:** from the parable of the Gadarene swine, Mark 5:9.

CHAPTER 55

1. (737) **wicket:** small gate.

2. (738) **phaeton:** light four-wheeled open carriage.

3. (739) **Post-house:** rest house where carriage horses ('post-horses') were changed.

4. (745) **a certain station on the railway:** The description would fit Paddock Wood in Kent; see *The Dickensian* 34, 1938, p. 123.

CHAPTER 56

1. (749) **gather moss ... rolling stone**: from 'a rolling stone gathers no moss': someone always on the move will not acquire wealth (OED).

2. (750) **took on so**: was so upset.

3. (750) **Solomon**: King of Israel (c. 962–922 BC), proverbial for his wisdom.

4. (751) **awful**: i.e. impressive, serious; see Chapter 41, n. 9.

5. (753) **the askings**: i.e. the banns, the announcement of the marriage which has to be read in church for three consecutive weeks before the ceremony, to allow for any objections to be raised.

6. (753) **supercargo**: superintendent of cargo.

7. (753) **beasts that perish**: Psalms 49:10.

8. (754) **a colour you can run up**: a flag that you can raise, i.e. a signal you can give.

9. (761) **the Bull in Cock Robin**: from the nursery rhyme, 'Who killed Cock Robin?': 'Who tolled the bell?/I, said the Bull,/Because I can pull,/I tolled the bell.'

10. (762) **lorn**: forlorn.

11. (765) **own wines and fig-trees**: i.e. vines. Micah 4:4: 'They shall sit every man under his vine and under his fig-tree.'

12. (765) **'Tis *the* woice ... of the sluggard**: from 'The Sluggard' by Isaac Watts (see Chapter 32, n. 10). For once an accurate quotation, although Captain Cuttle immediately adds to it a line from the National Anthem: 'Scatter his enemies/And make them fall.'

13. (766) **'Tis woman as seduces**: from the *Beggar's Opera* (1728) by John Gay. Captain Cuttle links this to the story of the temptation of Eve by the serpent in Genesis 3; it was Eve who persuaded Adam to eat of the forbidden fruit.

14. (767) **blow every stitch ... out of the bolt-ropes**: bolt-ropes held the canvas sails in place.

15. (768) **Mariner, of England ... improve each shining hour**: see Chapter 23, n. 21. Thomas Campbell's 'Ye Mariners of England!' includes the lines, 'Ye gentlemen of England/That live at home at

ease . . .', and Isaac Watts's *Divine Songs* (1715), 'Against Idleness and Mischief': 'How doth the little busy bee/Improve each shining hour,/ and gather honey all the day/From every opening flower!'

16. (769) **angry passions rise:** see previous note and Chapter 32, n. 10. Isaac Watts, *Divine Songs*, 'Against Quarrelling': But, children, you should never let/Such angry passions rise;/Your little hands were never made/To tear each other's eyes.'

17. (771) **gammon:** nonsense.

18. (771) **pluck:** courage.

19. (771) **blow on:** reveal, disclose.

CHAPTER 57

1. (772) **free sittings:** see Chapter 5, n. 13, and Chapter 31, n. 1.

2. (772) **political economy . . . common folks have to be married:** an attack on the sort of Utilitarian thinking which valued statistics at the expense of the individual and therefore saw the reduction in numbers of the poor in simple mathematical terms. The extreme example of such a theorist is T. R. Malthus (1766–1834).

3. (772) **national schools:** The National Society for Promoting the Education of the Poor in the Principles of the Established Church was set up in 1809; by 1831, there were 13,000 National Schools.

4. (774) **carmen:** carters, carriers.

5. (775) **Worshipful Company . . . Hall:** one of the London City Companies, based on the medieval trade guilds, and the official building where its business is transacted.

6. (775) **sounding-boards:** wooden panels to improve the acoustics.

7. (775) **morning luminary . . . built out:** i.e. the sun's rays are kept out by the surrounding buildings.

8. (775) **The amens . . . Macbeth's:** see *Macbeth*, Act II, Sc. 2.

CHAPTER 58

1. (780) **upon 'Change:** at the Royal Exchange in the City of London, a trading centre for merchants.

2. (782) **contempt for mankind:** The Cynic philosopher Diogenes

(see Chapter 14, n. 20) is reported by Seneca to have lived in a tub to show his contempt for human society.

3. (783) **Islington:** area of north London.

4. (788) **Harmonious Blacksmith:** This is in fact a piece by Handel (1720) for the harpsichord, not the 'cello; see also Chapter 53, n. 2.

5. (790) **funeral baked meats:** see *Hamlet*, Act 1, Sc. 2.

6. (793) **the blessed history . . . suffering and sorrow:** While writing *Dombey and Son*, Dickens was preparing his *Life of Our Lord* for his own children. This recounts in simple language the New Testament stories of Christ's Ministry mentioned here.

CHAPTER 59

1. (794) **jewels in the Tower:** the Crown Jewels, kept in the Tower of London.

2. (794) **Gazette:** official weekly publication of business news including bankruptcies.

3. (795) **herb and leech line:** Greengrocers often sold dried herbs, and leeches in bottles; the latter were used for medicinal purposes, being applied to the skin to produce painless bleeding.

4. (795) **How are the mighty fallen!:** II Samuel 1:19.

5. (795) **Pride shall have a fall:** 'Pride goeth before destruction, and an haughty spirit before a fall' (Proverbs 16:18).

6. (796) **covered with confusion, as with a garment:** Psalms 104:3.

7. (796) **Mosaic Arabian:** i.e. Jewish. From Disraeli's *Coningsby* (1844), Book IV, Chapter 10.

8. (798) **fasces:** bundles of rods carried in front of Roman dignitaries for the punishment of offenders.

9. (799) **spring-vans:** small vehicles with spring suspension.

10. (799) **porters with knots:** Market porters, when carrying heavy burdens, wore a thick pad, or 'knot', on their shoulders, so called because it was often made of twisted rope.

11. (800) **the man in the south . . . plum porridge:** from the nursery rhyme about 'The man in the moon': 'He went by the south/And burnt his mouth/With supping cold pease porridge.'

12. (801) **Doe:** John Doe was the invented name used to indicate the plaintiff in actions to eject illegal occupiers.

13. (802) **cord'l:** a cordial, i.e. a tonic.

14. (802) **fly-van:** small, one-horse-drawn covered vehicle.

15. (803) **great reaper:** i.e. Death.

16. (811) **a certain sad occasion:** a reference to the cancelled final sentence of Chapter 16; see Chapter 16, n. 1.

CHAPTER 60

1. (813) **Wellington boots:** fashionable high boots named after the Duke of Wellington (1769–1852).

2. (813) **Norfolk Biffin:** cooking apple baked slowly and pressed into shape – a good analogy for Dr Blimber's teaching methods.

3. (813) **Cincinnatus:** Roman hero who was summoned from his home in 458 BC to lead his country to victory and who then returned to his farm.

4. (814) *adolescens imprimis gravis et doctus:* 'a young man of outstanding dignity and learning'. Apparently composed by Dr Blimber, as no source has been found.

5. (816) **on the score of station:** on the issue of Susan's lowly position in society.

6. (816) **Rights of Women:** Mary Wollstonecraft's *Vindication of the Rights of Women* was published in 1792; however, the main impetus towards Women's Rights in the Victorian period was still to come, from the work of such pioneers as Frances Cobbe, J. S. Mill and Harriet Taylor in the 1850s and 1860s.

7. (816) **'went in':** boxing term for going into the ring, beginning the attack.

8. (817) **Hymen:** god of marriage in Classical mythology.

9. (819) **Limehouse Hole:** in Stepney, the place where the Thames was joined by the Limehouse Cut to the River Lea.

10. (823) **half-boots:** boots reaching halfway up to the knee.

CHAPTER 61

1. (828) **painful occurrences ... treading on one another's heels:** reminiscent of *Hamlet*, Act IV, Sc. 5.

2. (829) **kept very tight in hand:** i.e. well under control (from horse-riding, cf. 'on a tight rein').

3. (829) **Martinets:** military or naval officers who were sticklers for discipline – from General Martinet, drillmaster for Louis XIV.

4. (829) **Mr Pitt ... storm:** William Pitt the Younger (see Chapter 5, n. 7), applauded in Cousin Feenix's time as 'the pilot who weathered the storm' for having led England against Napoleon.

5. (829) **four-bottle man:** Excessive drinking, particularly of port, was common and probably contributed to the prevalence of gout.

6. (831) **boxing-rooms in Bond Street:** professional boxers (like the Game Chicken) taught 'the noble art of self-defence' to the aristocracy in the fashionable part of the City.

7. (835) **thrilling:** quivering, trembling.

8. (837) **for an age ... for all time:** from Ben Jonson's sonnet 'To the Memory of ... Shakespeare' (1623): 'He was not of an age, but for all time.'

9. (837) **shadow of a dream:** see *Hamlet*, Act II, Sc. 2.

CHAPTER 62

1. (839) **Harmonious Blacksmiths:** see Chapter 58, n. 4.

2. (840) **slue:** slew, swing; thus Captain Cuttle inadvertently reverses the meaning of ''Tis love that makes the world go round'.

3. (842) **never depart from it:** see Chapter 4, n. 20.

4. (842) **And an old dog ... their company:** Dickens originally forgot to include Diogenes in his happy ending; he wrote urgently to Forster asking him to add these words at proof stage.

5. (843) **... earnest eyes:** two extra paragraphs were cancelled by Dickens at the proof stage of the book:

> The voices in the waves speak low to him of Florence, day and night –
> plainest when he, his blooming daughter, and her husband, walk
> beside them in the evening, or sit at an open window, listening to their
> roar. They speak to him of Florence and his altered heart; of Florence

and their ceaseless murmuring to her of the love, eternal and illimitable, extending still, beyond the sea, beyond the sky, to the invisible country far away.

Never from the mighty sea may voices rise too late, to come between us and the unseen region on the other shore! Better, far better, that they whispered of that region in our childish ears, and the swift river hurried us away! [See Introduction, p. xxxiii]

APPENDIX

Dickens's plans for *Dombey and Son*, in a letter written to John Forster from Lausanne, Switzerland, which reached Forster on 25 July 1846 (Forster, *Life*, Book VI, Chapter 2; Pilgrim IV, 589–90, 593):

I will now go on to give you an outline of my immediate intentions in reference to *Dombey*. I design to show Mr D. with that one idea of the Son taking firmer and firmer possession of him, and swelling and bloating his pride to a prodigious extent. As the boy begins to grow up, I shall show him quite impatient for his getting on, and urging his masters to set him great tasks, and the like. But the natural affection of the boy will turn towards the despised sister; and I purpose showing her learning all sorts of things, of her own application and determination, to assist him in his lessons: and helping him always. When the boy is about ten years old (in the fourth number), he will be taken ill, and will die; and when he is ill, and when he is dying, I mean to make him turn always for refuge to the sister still, and keep the stern affection of the father at a distance. So Mr Dombey – for all his greatness, and for all his devotion to the child – will find himself at arms' length from him even then; and will see that his love and confidence are all bestowed upon his sister, whom Mr Dombey has used – and so has the boy himself too, for that matter – as a mere convenience and handle to him. The death of the boy is a death-blow, of course, to all the father's schemes and cherished hopes; and 'Dombey and Son,' as Miss Tox will say at the end of the number, 'is a Daughter after all.' ... From that time, I purpose changing his feeling of indifference and uneasiness towards his daughter into a positive hatred. For he will always remember how the boy had his arm round her neck when he was dying, and whispered to her, and would take things only from her hand, and never thought of him. ... At the same time I shall change *her* feeling toward *him* for one of a greater desire to love him, and to be loved by him; engendered in her compassion for his loss, and her love for the dead boy whom, in his way, he loved so well too. So I mean to carry the story on, through all the branches and off-shoots and meanderings that come up; and through the decay and downfall of the house, and the bankruptcy of Dombey, and all the rest of it; when his only staff and treasure, and his unknown Good Genius always, will be this rejected daughter, who will come out better than any son at last, and whose love for him, when discovered and understood, will be his bitterest reproach. For the struggle with himself, which goes on in all such obstinate natures, will have ended then; and the sense of his injustice, which you may be sure has never quitted him, will have at last a gentler office than that of only making him more harshly unjust. . . . I rely very much on Susan Nipper grown up, and acting partly as Florence's maid, and partly as a kind of companion to her, for a strong character throughout the book. I also rely on the Toodles, and on Polly, who, like everybody else, will be found by Mr Dombey to have gone over to his daughter and become attached to her. This is what cooks call 'the stock of the soup.' All kinds of things will be added to it, of course.

. . . About the boy, who appears in the last chapter of the first number, I think it would be a good thing to disappoint all the expectations that chapter seems to raise of his happy connection with the story and the heroine, and to show him gradually and naturally trailing away, from that love of adventure and boyish light-heartedness, into negligence, idleness, dissipation, dishonesty, and ruin. To show, in short, that common, every-day, miserable declension of which we know so much in our ordinary life; to exhibit something of the philosophy of it, in great temptations and an easy nature; and to show how the good turns into bad, by degrees. If I kept some little notion of Florence always at the bottom of it, I think it might be made very powerful and very useful. What do you think? Do you think it may be done, without making people angry? I could bring out Solomon Gills and Captain Cuttle well, through such a history; and I descry, anyway, an opportunity for good scenes between Captain Cuttle and Miss Tox. This question of the boy is very important. . . . Let me hear all you think about it. Hear! I wish I could.

DICKENS AND HIS CRITICS

> Oh, my dear, dear Dickens! what a No. 5 you have now given us! I have so cried and sobbed over it last night, and again this morning; and felt my heart purified by those tears, and blessed and loved you for making me shed them; and I never can bless or love you enough. Since the divine Nelly was found dead on her humble couch, beneath the snow and the ivy, there has been nothing like the actual dying of that sweet Paul, in the summer sunshine of that lofty room. And the long vista that leads us so gently and sadly, and yet so gracefully and winningly, to the plain consummation! [quoted in Philip Collins, *Dickens: The Critical Heritage* (1971), p. 217]

Lord Jeffrey's letter to Dickens in January 1847 is perhaps the best-known critical comment on *Dombey and Son*. Paul's death at the end of the fifth number 'flung a nation into mourning' (comment quoted by Forster in 1848, Collins, *ibid.*, p. 232). Sales of the book had from the beginning passed expectations. 'The *Dombey* sale is BRILLIANT!' wrote Dickens to Forster after the first number (Pilgrim IV, 631), and by the third and fourth numbers the print-run was 32,000 copies. The relatively small sale of *Martin Chuzzlewit* seemed not to have harmed but indeed to have primed expectations for the next book and the two-year wait may also have contributed to its immediate success. Yet a later portion of Jeffrey's letter suggests another side to the coin: 'But after reaching this climax in the fifth number, what are you to do with the fifteen that are to follow?'

Dombey was much praised for its contemporaneity, for its treatment of the railway boom and for the highly topical figure of Dombey, the merchant adventurer. However, this assumption that there was bound to be a 'falling off' after the death of Paul in No. 5 was widespread (though, as Robert L. Patten has shown in *Charles Dickens and His Publishers* [1978], p. 188, contrary to critical tradition there seems to have been no real drop in sales, which, after a dip in the middle numbers, actually grew to 33,000 for the final number). Interestingly, the other major issue discussed was that of sentimentality. Several influential Victorians displayed a healthy scepticism to set against Jeffrey's lachrymosity. Coventry Patmore of all people found his taste satiated and dared to go against the popular acclamation. In an anonymous review in the *North British Review* of 1847, he confessed: 'We might, indeed, were we so minded, find some flaws in the beautiful sentimentalism of Paul's deathbed scene . . . some little mawkishness of feeling . . . but we forbear.' Maclise found Florence 'insipid' (Pilgrim IV, 599n.). Henry Hallam in a letter to Mrs Brookfield (1847) observed acidly: 'Everybody is pretending that the death of Paul Dombey is the most beautiful thing ever written. Milnes, Thackeray . . . all in tears. I am so hardened as to be unable to look on it in any light but pure business' (quoted in R. C. Churchill, *Bibliography of Dickensian Criticism* [1975], pp. 183–4).

The number plan for the first number and the long letter to Forster (printed in the Appendix on p. 889) acquit Dickens beyond doubt of such accusations of cynical opportunism. Paul was 'born to die' as part of the larger strategy of the novel's original conception. However, *The Man in the Moon*, a rival to *Punch*, set up an 'Inquest on the late Master Paul Dombey' in which Dickens was accused of having killed Paul off with an attack of 'Don't-know-what-to-do-with-him-phobia' (March 1847). A solemn funeral was described, including a Requiem sung by a chorus of Circulating Library Keepers:

> Thou art gone from our counter,
> Thou are lost to our pocket
> Thou has fallen, brief meteor,
> Like spark of a rocket.
> New numbers appearing
> Fresh interest may borrow,
> But we go on 'Oh dearing,
> For Paul there's no morrow!'
> [quoted in Collins, *op. cit.*, pp. 218–19]

Parker's *London Magazine* (1848) went further:

When Mr Dickens began writing, the semi-pathetic was admirable, because original – it has ceased to be so; we are more inclined to laugh at than with it. The book is moreover full to overflowing of waves whispering and wandering; of dark rivers rolling to the sea; of winds, and golden ripples, and such like matters, which are sometimes very pretty, generally very untrue, and here become, at all events, excessively stale. [quoted in Collins, *op. cit.*, p. 213]

George H. Ford has shown (in *Dickens and His Readers* [1955]) that Victorian sentimentality always had influential critics among Victorian readers. On the other side, of course, there were encomiums aplenty. Perhaps the most impressive, because spontaneous, was from Thackeray. His *Vanity Fair* had just started serialisation when the *Dombey* fifth number appeared, and it is at this time that the two authors begin to be compared, although the relative sales of the two novels put the 'rivalry' into perspective, *Dombey*'s 33,000 dwarfing Thackeray's 5,000 per number. Thackeray's response to Paul's death is recorded in an anecdote which speaks volumes for both writers:

Putting No. 5 of Dombey and Son in his pocket, he hastened down to Mr Punch's printing-office, and entering the editor's room ... where he dashed it on the table with startling vehemence, and exclaimed, 'There's no writing against such power as this – one has no chance! Read that chapter describing young Paul's death: it is unsurpassed – it is stupendous!' [George Hodder, quoted in Collins, *op. cit.*, p. 219]

Reactions like Thackeray's and Jeffrey's were registered by Macaulay, who wept over Florence's plight as if his heart would break (Alan Shelston, *Dombey and Son and Little Dorrit* [1985], p. 32), and by many others, but beneath the outpouring of emotion, the subtlety of Dicken's achievement with Paul was often missed. His letter to Forster reveals that his plan was to describe events entirely from the child's point of view, rather than treating the child, as he had done with Nell, as simple emotional object. When the Paul chapters escape censure for sentimentality, therefore, it is most convincingly on the grounds of their humour and specificity of observation. Edward Fitzgerald, who loathed the unremittingly sentimental *Battle of Life* which Dickens wrote while in the midst of writing *Dombey*, much admired the particularity of the Blimber scenes: 'The boy who talks Greek in his sleep seems to me terrible as Macbeth,' he observed wryly (quoted in Shelston, *ibid.*, p. 34). The *Westminster Review* (April 1847) declared: 'No other writer can approach Dickens in a perfect analysis of the mind of children ... the reflections of little Dombey upon all that is passing about him at Doctor Blimber's, is a study for moralists and metaphysicians ... [Chapter 16's] merit lies in the minutiae and truthfulness of its details' (quoted in Collins, *op. cit.*, pp. 225–6). Charles Kent, whom

Dickens himself thought one of his most sympathetic readers, looked back on the whole novel after its completion and felt its summit had been reached in Chapter 16: 'If there were nothing worthy of admiration in *Dombey and Son* beyond the passage descriptive of the death of Little Paul, it would from that solitary passage have been worthy of a distinguished place among the classic books of our national literature' (*The Sun*, 13 April 1848, quoted in Collins, *op. cit.*, p. 229).

The second part of the novel from the outset attracted stronger criticism – though Wilkie Collins's assessment is more savage than most: 'The latter half of *Dombey* no intelligent person can read without astonishment at the badness of it' (quoted in Churchill, *op. cit.*, p. 80). Harrison Ainsworth found 'the last *Dombeys* infernally bad' (Pilgrim V, 267n.). Jeffrey, on the other hand, ever partisan, was prepared to find subtlety even in the descriptions of Edith: they contain, he says, 'all the lofty and terrible elements of tragedy . . . bringing before us the appalling struggles of a proud, scornful and repentant spirit' (quoted in Churchill, *op. cit.*, p. 75). It was he who persuaded Dickens to change his mind over the elopement because, said Dickens, 'he won't believe (positively refuses) that Edith is Carker's mistress' (Pilgrim V, 211). This leaves the scene in Dijon with implausible motivation and open even more to accusations of crude melodrama.

The other area of dissatisfaction was Mr Dombey's final conversion: 'The entire change of character of Dombey is out of all nature – it is impossible,' fumed the *Blackwood's Magazine* reviewer in October 1848 (quoted in Collins, *op. cit.*, p. 231). Hippolyte Taine, writing in 1859, also took a sceptical view: Dombey, he says, 'becomes the best of fathers and spoils a fine novel' (quoted in Shelston, *op. cit.*, p. 35). Forster has explained how carefully Dickens prepared for the eventual conversion in the first number, and how he was forced to cancel important passages because of overwriting. The later Prefaces to the novels give a good indication of what were the critical issues when they were written, and when Dickens was writing the 1858 Preface it was to this question of Mr Dombey's plausibility that he returned. He could by 1858 assume the success of Paul, and indeed he ends with a sentimental evocation of the death of 'my little friend'. However, popular misunderstanding of Dombey still irritates him:

> The two commonest mistakes in judgement . . . are, the confounding of shyness with arrogance . . . and the not understanding that an obstinate nature exists in a perpetual struggle with itself.

> Mr Dombey undergoes no violent internal change, either in this
> book or in life. A sense of his injustice is with him all along.

Dickens's own assessment of the novel on its completion is
judicious: 'I have a strong belief that, if any of my books are read
years hence, *Dombey* will be remembered as among the best of
them' (Forster, *op. cit.*, Book VI, Chapter 4). Certainly this novel
marked the consolidation both of Dickens's financial position and
of his reputation, which was by now an international one. 'Your
Dombey continues to inspire with enthusiasm the whole of the
literary St Petersburg,' wrote a Russian correspondent, much to his
gratification and amusement (Forster, *ibid.*). The novel rapidly
became part of popular culture. A ballad by Glover and Carpenter
(1850), *What Are the Wild Waves Saying*, returned to the favourite
theme of Paul and Florence and was extremely popular. (F. R.
Leavis remembered hearing it sung during his Edwardian childhood.) The scene by the sea at Brighton was painted and exhibited
by Charles Nicholls, as was 'Florence in Captain Cuttle's Parlour'
by William Maw Egley. Captain Cuttle became the eponymous
hero of a play produced in New York in 1850, written by John
Brougham, one of several contemporary stage adaptations of the
novel. Others included *Heart's Delight* by Andrew Halliday and a
production in Manchester in 1861 in which Henry Irving played
Mr Dombey. (See Malcolm Morley, *The Dickensian* 48 [1952],
pp. 128–33.)

Later critics sniped increasingly at the sentimental and melodramatic parts of the story and by 1882 A. A. Ward could comment that
Dombey and Son had, 'perhaps, been more criticised than any other
[of Dickens's novels]', while also recognising that it 'is one of his
most ambitious endeavours' (quoted in Shelston, *op. cit.*, p. 44).
George Gissing (1900) and A. C. Swinburne (1902) were particularly scathing. Gissing gives a useful insight into the shift in
contemporary taste: 'It has become the fashion to sneer at Dickens's
pathos, and the death of Little Paul is commonly mentioned as an
example of intolerable mawkishness' (reprinted in *The Immortal
Dickens* [1925], p. 148). He himself defends the treatment of Paul,
making the point (picked up again by Stephen Leacock in 1933)
that 'England sadly needed awakening to her responsibilities in the
matter of childhood'. He also develops the increasingly popular line
that it is in his good grotesques and in their 'sacred simplicity' that
Dickens is strongest. However, the general feeling is that the
humour is more muted than in the earlier works, which leaves little

for this generation of critics to admire. The novel also seems, to this next generation, unacceptably Victorian. George Santayana (1921) sees *Dombey and Son* as failing because of Dickens's need to conform to Victorian proprieties. Thus Walter does not go to the bad and Edith does not become Carker's mistress (*The Dickens Critics*, eds G. Ford and L. Lane [1970], p. 139). George Saintsbury (1916) and G. K. Chesterton (1907) are the first to see *Dombey* as a transitional novel and to pick up what was to become a staple of mid-twentieth-century criticism, Dickens's new interest at this point in his career in structure and planning. *Dombey and Son*, says Saintsbury, was Dickens's 'first attempt at painting actual modern society' and 'marks a very important transition in the handling of scene and personage' (quoted in Churchill, *op. cit.*, p. 76). Chesterton sees the break as even more marked: 'Before *Dombey and Son* even his pathos had been really frivolous. After *Dombey and Son* even his absurdity was intentional and grave.' He contrasts the novel with *Nicholas Nickleby*: the humour in the latter is episodic, about nothing but itself, whilst that in *Dombey and Son* is organised; thus Squeers exists for his own sake, whereas Blimber is 'a very good foil to Paul'. However, there are losses. Like the other turn-of-the-century critics, Chesterton actually prefers the excesses of the early novels and finds a loss of invention, even in such a popular figure as Captain Cuttle: *Dombey*, he feels, 'shows an advance in art and unity' though it 'does not show an advance in genius and creation' (Introduction to the Everyman Edition [1907]; reprinted in Shelston, *op. cit.*, pp. 55–7).

Since the 1940s, as Dickens's critical reputation has grown, *Dombey* has attracted huge attention and prompted some excellent critical writing. Mid-century criticism tended to ignore or take for granted the earlier major 'weaknesses' (Paul and sentimentality, Edith and melodrama) and to look instead at what now seemed important strengths – the novel's treatment of contemporary society and its larger organisation. Thus Humphry House in *The Dickens World* (1941) sets the novel firmly in context with a vivid description of the Railway Age. He notes Dickens's fascination with change and tries to explain the narrator's attitude to the demolition of Staggs's Gardens: 'the *process* [of change] truly fascinated Dickens, the *achievement* merely wins sober moral approval' (p. 150). Kathleen Tillotson in *Novels of the 1840s* (1954) is not interested in Chestertonian episodic exuberance but develops instead the idea of 'an advance in art and unity':

> *Dombey and Son* stands out from among Dickens's novels as the
> earliest example of responsible and careful planning; it has unity not
> only of action, but of design and feeling. It is also the first in which a
> pervasive uneasiness about contemporary society takes the place of an
> intermittent concern with specific social wrongs. [p. 157]

She is forced to recognise the diversity of the novel, but does so with
reluctance: 'the presence of different modes in a narrative is something we must accept in his novels, as in poetic drama' (p. 175).

In *Dickens at Work* (1957), John Butt and Kathleen Tillotson
turn their attention to the number plans and continue the mid-
century re-evaluation of Dickens as a conscious artist rather than,
as the early twentieth century had seen him, a spontaneous entertainer of genius. They examine the process of writing in detail and
reveal the shaping of the whole design. They make particular play
with Dickens's self-adjuration for No. 6: 'Great point of the No. to
throw the interest of Paul, at once on Florence.' Florence's centrality
to the design is discussed and Butt and Tillotson end with another
assertion of, and commendation of, the unity of the whole: 'It is
with the two Florences that Dickens ends; mindful in valediction of
his main design' (p. 113).

Steven Marcus in *From Pickwick to Dombey* (1965) confirms the
latter novel as inaugurating a new phase in Dickens's work: 'The
prose of *Martin Chuzzlewit* was all bugles and trumpets. The prose
of *Dombey and Son* is by contrast subdued ... it speaks to us in
one character, the voice of one man who understands that he is
saying something very seriously.' Unlike Butt and Tillotson with
their stress on unity, however, Marcus positively celebrates Dickens's ambivalence, both about society and about himself:

> In *Dombey and Son* we see how deeply divided Dickens has become.
> On the one hand he is affirming the changing world symbolised by the
> railroad, and on the other condemning the society which produced it.
> That society has in every way grown more uncongenial to the life of
> feeling and moral decency. More than ever before, these two orders of
> value – in effect they constitute two worlds – are for Dickens
> incompatible. His insight into the nature of society and the people
> who represented it was outstripping and working at cross-purposes to
> his beliefs more relentlessly than they had ever done before. The
> unevenness, incompleteness, unsureness of touch, and even morbidity
> we feel throughout the story of Florence give the principal evidence of
> this.... Having a woman for one of his central characters (as he was

to have in two of his three next novels) seems to me in this novel to have been Dickens's unconscious strategy for prolonging one of his fundamental and by now forlorn beliefs: the possibility of the life without will, the life of simplicity and of exclusively affectionate feeling. That Dickens's own life contradicted this idea in almost every way can only confirm in us a sense of how deep and critical was his need to hold on to it, how profoundly at odds with himself he had become. Part of Dickens's genius was to see that society had suffered similar contradictions. [pp. 355–6]

The Leavises' *Dickens the Novelist* (1970) officially announced Dickens's critical rehabilitation from the academic contempt into which he had fallen earlier in the century. The title of their opening chapter, developed from F. R. Leavis's essay in *The Sewanee Review* (1962), gives particular promotion to *Dombey*: 'The First Major Novel: *Dombey and Son*'. They devote much effort in this chapter to separating the acceptable from the unacceptable – with a strenuousness which recalls Dickens's own effortful separation of evil from good – and seek, in short, to identify what they call 'the strong half of the book' (p. 13). In this they include the presentation of Paul, which is complex and shows 'an intense concern for the real'. Here Dickens 'isn't tempted to sentimentalise' (p. 14). Like Tillotson and Marcus, they struggle with the contradictions within the novel and as part of the rehabilitation process confront directly the issue of high and popular culture, finding, as it were, a compatibilist solution: Dickens's 'distinctive genius was the ability to respond freely and expansively to the inspirations of popular taste, popular tradition and the market, and, in doing so, to evolve for himself (and for the world) a high intellectual art' (p. 27). They admit reluctantly, however, the power of those debased popular art forms, sentimental drama and melodrama, and continue the move away from the notion of unity:

> Contemplating the diverse and disparate elements brought together into a specious unity in *Dombey and Son* (specious, because to be just to Dickens one must insist that the strength represented by the early treatment of the theme of money-pride and the conventional nullity of the treatment of pride and scruple in Edith remain at odds), one asks how the confident show of unity is achieved, and is perhaps inclined to reply that it is done through the dominant resonance on the moral side of the sentimental and the melodramatic – with which so much of the humour and comedy consort quite happily. [p. 27]

In this same Centennial year, Raymond Williams also tackled the relationship between high and popular culture in Dickens's work and in particular in *Dombey*: he glories in Dickens's populism, accepts his diversity and challenges anyone ever again to read him as if he were a sort of failed George Eliot. He also sees him as a novelist supremely able to explore industrial society and its effect on the individual:

> There is a kind of moral analysis in which society is a background against which the drama of personal virtues and vices is enacted. There is another kind – increasingly important in the development of nineteenth-century literature – in which society is the creator of virtues and vices.... The source of the strength of *Dombey and Son* is its juxtaposition of the most primary relationship – the family and the house – with the social forms of family and house in a city determined by a trading civilisation.... [In describing the destruction and rebuilding of Staggs's Gardens] Dickens is responding to the real contradiction – the power for life or death; for disintegration, order and false order – of the new social and economic forces of his time. His concern, always, is to keep human recognition and human kindness alive, through these unprecedented strains, and within this unrecognisably altered landscape.... [Introduction to the Penguin Edition of *Dombey and Son* (1970), pp. 16, 28–9, 34]

John Lucas in an essay in *Tradition and Tolerance in Nineteenth-Century Fiction* (ed. David Howard *et al.*, 1966) also deals with *Dombey*'s links with the contemporary world and stresses the central role of change in the novel and the ambivalence of Dickens's attitude to it: *should* Staggs's Gardens have been destroyed by the railway? It 'is and is not representative of something valuable'. The fact that the Wooden Midshipman is presented as a last refuge against the new England shows just how pessimistic is Dickens's vision of the emergent society. Lucas suggests that Dickens's 'failure of nerve about industrialisation' contributes to the much greater failure of *Hard Times* six years later (p. 108). However, in his later study, *The Melancholy Man* (1970), Lucas's work reflects the huge shift in critical taste from the middle to the later twentieth century, from a preoccupation with artistic success or failure to an interest in openness and plurality. He now reads Walter's triumph as 'a final gesture of open-mindedness, a refusal to settle for an apocalyptic vision', and an attempt to suggest 'a ceaseless process of change, decay and renewal' (p. 165).

Biographical insights went on being fruitfully developed, after

Edmund Wilson's ground-breaking essay 'The Two Scrooges' (1944), in particular by Michael Slater in *Dickens and Women* (1983). He sees the development of Dickens's art in the 1840s as being directly related to his deepening interest in female values:

> ... however little Dickens's basic beliefs about and attitudes towards women had changed, it seems clear that by 1846, the year in which he began writing *Dombey* ... Dickens's imagination was more deeply engaged with women, their nature and their social role, than it had been since creating Nancy. [p. 245]

Peter Ackroyd, in his vivid and unabashedly personal *Dickens* (1990) and in his *Introduction to Dickens* (1990), also asserts that *Dombey* must be read in terms of Dickens's own development: it 'has the closest connection with the immediate circumstances of Dickens's life'. He stresses too the religious theme: *Dombey and Son* is 'illuminated by what can only be described as a religious spirit ... at its centre are grace and redemption' (*Introduction*, p. 112). 'The novel has a sense of the numinous, is more profoundly touched by the sense of last things than any of Dickens's previous novels' (*Dickens*, p. 526).

In Victorian iconography, women and religion combine in the figure of the Angel in the House – a figure strongly reminiscent of Florence. Late-twentieth-century critics have therefore, in attempting to understand the novel's power, slowly turned their attention to the figure of the (critically as well as paternally) neglected daughter. The process began with Hillis Miller's *Charles Dickens: The World of His Novels* in 1958. 'The central problem of *Dombey and Son*,' he declared, 'a problem faced by all the characters, is how to break through the barriers separating one from the world and from other people' (p. 146). Dickens's answer seems, says Miller, to be 'unintellectualised feeling' – seen metaphorically as the ocean and containing 'an authentic religious motif ... an apprehension of a transcendent spirit ... human feeling, an undifferentiated current of sympathy ... flowing out ... to bathe all those around in a warm glow of love' (p. 149). Miller ends his chapter on *Dombey* with the figure of Florence and quotes the description of her love for Walter: 'Fragile and delicate she was, with a might of love within her that could, and did, create a world to fly to, and rest in. ...'

Other critics have been less eager to see Florence as a quasi-religious figure. In a quixotic 1970 essay in *The Inimitable Dickens: A Reading of the Novels*, A. E. Dyson declared open season for

Florence-baiting, taking her to task for selfishness: 'Her feeling that she is deprived of love is not strictly justified . . . she is resolutely self-centred and driven by need' (p. 114). He compares her unfavourably with Nell and Little Dorrit and suggests that she is moved too far towards allegory to be successful, so that the novel becomes a 'direct confrontation between cold materialism and Christian love' (p. 117). He is, however, one of the earliest critics to find the character genuinely interesting – 'a fascinating portrayal of a neglected child' (p. 118). Alexander Welsh, in the fine but misleadingly titled *The City in Dickens* (1971), develops further the notion of Florence as a figure of ambivalent power, an 'angel of death', and comments: 'it is the special office of young women to watch over the dying' (pp. 184–5). This anti-Florence line had been pioneered in 1962 by Julian Moynahan (in *Dickens and the Twentieth Century*, eds John Gross and Gabriel Pearson) in a justly famous, and very funny, essay, 'Dealings with the Firm of Dombey and Son: Firmness versus Wetness'. In a Dickensian tour-de-force, Moynahan presents a beleaguered Mr Dombey pursued through the novel's pages by his terrifyingly powerful daughter, who is determined to drown him in tears:

> . . . for Dombey . . . the sharing of love seems a death by water. To be saved from his own stoniness he must leap from the bank and dissolve his proud self in his daughter's tears. . . . After attempted suicide he passes into the arms of Florence. She teaches him to weep. On the last page of the book he is alone with the new Florence. She asks him, 'Dear grandpapa, why do you cry when you kiss me?' He evades this sensible question, but we can answer it for him. He has been reborn from the damp pillow of his invalidism into a new career of sentiment. Father and daughter are finally alike, with a genius for weeping.

Moynahan realises that he is in danger of being 'barred from the pages of *The Dickensian* for life' for this subversive reading. Much more dangerous to his survival in the 1990s, though, is surely his characterisation of gender roles: Dombey's 'is a tensely masculine world, a society of heads without hearts. Florence's sphere of influence is a slackly feminine one, consisting in a society of hearts without heads.'

Interestingly enough, when feminist and psychoanalytic critics turned to *Dombey and Son* from the 1970s onwards, beginning with Kate Millett in *Sexual Politics* (1970), they tended to amplify Moynahan's Dombey-like arguments rather than to contradict them. The big difference was that, instead of treating the 'Firmness–

Wetness' theme with his dismissive (or self-defensive?) irony, feminist critics have stressed its seriousness. What fascinates them about *Dombey and Son* is Dickens's acute presentation of the crippling effects – in both social and personal terms – of a rigid male/female divide. Nina Auerbach discusses the way in which the 'separate spheres' philosophy of the Victorians operates in the novel. Mr Dombey's 'ethos is at one with his inveterate phallicism ... [in the mid-Victorian world] the female [is] defective because she is out of time with the basic masculine rhythms of the cosmos' (*Dickens Studies Annual* 5 [1976], p. 100). Helene Moglen (*Victorian Studies* 35, 2, Winter 1992) discusses the damage done in the Dombey world by 'the radical disjunction between the demands of masculine society and the needs of the hidden feminine self' (p. 162). Dian Sadoff (*Monsters of Affection: Dickens, Eliot and Bronte on Fatherhood*, 1982) applies the insights of psychoanalysis to the work and transmutes Florence from religious icon to incestuous temptress: 'the figure of the daughter draws to herself the father and lover ... and also redeems the desire that calls this incestuous structure into being' (p. 17). Psychoanalysis of Florence yields increasingly alarming results. Richard Currie (*Dickens Studies Annual* 21 [1992], pp. 113–29) finds her to be full of 'murderous rage'. Less contentiously, Patricia Ingham in *Dickens, Women and Language* (University of Toronto, 1992) argues that Dickens's treatment of women reveals deep contradictions. She sees Dickens's 'idealised' women as actually subversive: 'it is the elaborately "ideal" figures who undermine the very social structure that they are supposed to sustain' (p. 16). She applies linguistic analysis to the stereotypical female figures to reveal the source of their power and suggests, as many recent writers have done, that the relationship between Florence and her father is presented, in the structure and language of the novel, as that of girl and lover. Displacement, in the Freudian sense, thus becomes the source of the narrative's power.

Terry Eagleton, in his Introduction to Steven Connor's volume on Dickens in the *Rereading Literature* series (1985), attempts to set Dickens criticism in perspective. There are two major camps, he says: one sees the novels as 'windows onto the world' and represses their fictionality; the other sees them as 'structures of symbolic meaning'. Connor's reading, says Eagleton, 'breaks decisively with both these perspectives'. It charts 'less ... the actual development of Dickens's fiction than a cumulative movement of contemporary critical approaches to it' (p. v). Thus the fiction is read not for its own sake, but to illuminate theory. The trend had actually begun with Susan R. Horton's *Interpreting Interpreting: Interpreting Dickens's Dombey* (1979), which, she explains, is not so much about the novel itself as about 'how all novels come to mean'. It is in fact an exploration of hermeneutics and of Reader-Response criticism and makes much use of Foucault and of Stanley Fish. 'Does *Dombey and Son* make sense, or do I, as reader, make sense of it, as Stanley Fish suggests?' (p. 15) In the process of illuminating theory, however, there are some perceptive readings of the novel, particularly of Chapter 1, in which the reader's alternating responses to the comedy and the tragedy are scrupulously charted and in which the conclusions, as opposed to the terminology, are strangely similar to Leavis's: both show how it is in the tension between these conflicting responses that the power of the chapter lies.

Similarly linking the traditional and the theoretical is Steven Connor's nicely sceptical structuralist reading of *Dombey*, first using Greimas's narratological methods and then using structuralist linguistics in a discussion of the alternation of metaphor and metonymy in the novel. Connor's conclusion is that 'the reconciliation of openness and closure considered as a theme in the book is achieved by a reconciliation in the signifying surface of the book of the open mode of metonymy with the closed modes of metaphor' (p. 55).

Since 1848, *Dombey and Son* has proved eminently 'rereadable' both in the literal and in the theoretical sense: each generation of critics and ordinary readers has produced its own version of the novel – from Jeffrey's ecstasy of tears to Connor's hermeneutic sequences. This would suggest, in Frank Kermode's words, that the book has the 'surplus of signifier' which makes it a classic on any terms. When sentiment was highly valued, *Dombey* reduced its readers to tears; when attention shifted to 'unity of feeling', *Dombey* was found to be focused and highly unified; now that pluralism and diversity are sought, these qualities are found in the novel too. What was once read as Dickens's discontent with newly industrialised capitalist society is now read as his discontent with aggressive masculinity (including, of course, his own). Having survived being read for its sentiment, melodrama, humour, symbolism, religious feeling, unity and plurality by sociologists, structuralists, psychoanalysts, feminists and post-structuralists, *Dombey and Son* emerges triumphant as a work of continuing power and increasing relevance. It seems destined for ever greater attention and even higher valuation in an age which sees, in Dickens's story of Mr Dombey and his daughter, a preoccupation strangely close to its own, with the complex divide between masculinity and femininity.

SUGGESTIONS FOR FURTHER READING

John Forster's *Life of Charles Dickens* (3 vols, 1872–4) remains the classic, indispensable biography; the most recent edition is the two-volume Everyman Edition, ed. A. H. Hoppé (1969). The standard modern biography is Edgar Johnson's *Charles Dickens: His Tragedy and Triumph* (2 vols, 1952), but two more recent ones are also valuable: Fred Kaplan's *Dickens: A Biography* (1988) and Peter Ackroyd's remarkable *Dickens* (1990). Dickens's letters were first collected in three volumes of the limited Nonesuch Edition of Dickens's works (ed. Walter Dexter, 1938). These are being superseded by the magnificent Clarendon Press *Pilgrim Edition of the Letters of Charles Dickens*, ed. M. House, G. Storey, K. Tillotson *et al.* (1965–in progress). The latest volume to appear, vol. 8 (1995), covers the years 1856–8. Vols 4 (1844) and 5 (1847–9) are especially valuable for the study of the genesis, writing, publication and reception of *Dombey and Son*. A Garland Bibliography of *Dombey and Son*, edited by Leon Litvak and under the General Editorship of Duane DeVries, is currently in preparation.

Besides the studies mentioned in Note on the Text (p. xxxvii) and in Dickens and His Critics (pp. 891–903) above, the following are of particular interest to readers of *Dombey and Son*:

Philip Collins, *Charles Dickens: The Public Readings* (1975): details the stages by which 'The Story of Little Dombey' took shape and points out that it was 'his private reading of the opening number of *Dombey and Son* . . . that first suggested to Dickens the notion of giving public readings for pay'.

Philip Collins, *Dickens and Education* (1963): sets the Blimber scenes in their historical and social context.

Peter Coveney, *The Image of Childhood* (1967; originally published 1957 as *Poor Monkey*): looks at Dickens's representation of childhood in the light of Romanticism and its influence on Victorian ideas.

Ian Duncan, *Modern Romance and the Transformations of the Novel*

(1992): describes *Dombey* as a 'revolutionary narrative', but shows also Dickens's distrust of 'collective transformation'. Some new and telling comparisons with Sir Walter Scott.

Barbara Hardy, *The Moral Art of Charles Dickens* (1970): an early recognition, in a chapter on 'The Change of Heart', that Edith is a 'morally complex' character.

Frank McCrombie, 'Sexual Repression in *Dombey and Son*', *The Dickensian* 88 (1992), pp. 25–38: an uncompromisingly Freudian reading.

Valerie Purton, 'The Rape of the Sentimental Heroine' in *ARIEL* (January 1985): discusses Florence in relation to Wilkie Collins's heroines.

Harry Stone, *Dickens and the Invisible World* (1979): a close analysis of the 'new fairytale method' Dickens adopts in *Dombey and Son*.

Harvey Peter Sucksmith, *The Narrative Art of Charles Dickens* (1970): deals thoroughly with the difficult issue of Dickens's sentimentality and contains a useful discussion of Mrs Dombey's death.

Alexander Welsh, *From Copyright to Copperfield* (1987): argues for Dickens's close identification with Mr Dombey and explores *Dombey*'s links with *King Lear*.

Angus Wilson, 'Dickens on Children and Childhood' in *Dickens 1970*, ed. Michael Slater (1970): praises Little Paul as 'one of the most brilliantly drawn children in fiction' and sets him in the context of other Dickens children and of Victorian attitudes to childhood.

Louise Yelin, 'Strategies for Survival: Florence and Edith in *Dombey and Son*', *Victorian Studies* 22 (1979), pp. 297–319: sees Edith as representing a defiant feminist response to a society which circumscribes women as (in Dombey's phrase) mere 'connexions and dependants'.

Lynda Zwingler, 'The Fear of the Father: Dombey and Daughter', *Nineteenth-Century Fiction* 39 (1985), pp. 420–40: approaches the relationship between Mr Dombey and Florence through current critical theories.

TEXT SUMMARY

Chapter 1
Mr Dombey's wife dies with their little daughter Florence in her arms after giving birth to his son and heir.

Chapter 2
Miss Tox finds a wet-nurse for baby Paul.

Chapter 3
Polly Toodle discovers that Florence is neglected by her father and befriends her.

Chapter 4
Walter Gay returns home to his uncle, Sol Gills, after his first day's work for Dombey and Son. Captain Cuttle is introduced.

Chapter 5
Paul is christened. Mr Dombey has enrolled Polly's eldest son into the Charitable Grinders.

Chapter 6
During Polly's secret visit to her family, Florence is kidnapped by Good Mrs Brown and is rescued and returned home by Walter. Polly is dismissed.

Chapter 7
Miss Tox neglects her old suitor, Major Bagstock, for the Dombey family. The Major plots revenge.

Chapter 8
Paul is sent with Florence to stay at Mrs Pipchin's establishment in Brighton.

Chapter 9
Sol Gills faces bankruptcy; Captain Cuttle plans to enlist Mr Dombey's help.

Chapter 10
Major Bagstock pursues Mr Dombey to Brighton to cultivate his acquaintance. Mr Dombey pays off Sol Gills's debts in order to show Paul the power of money.

Chapter 11
Paul becomes a pupil at Dr Blimber's Academy in Brighton.

Chapter 12
Paul struggles with the forcing system of education, helped at weekends by Florence. He is befriended by Mr Toots.

Chapter 13
Mr Dombey appoints Walter to a post in the West Indies. Mr Carker the Manager upbraids his disgraced brother John, who still works for the Firm in a junior capacity.

Chapter 14
Paul sinks into a decline, but rallies to enjoy the end-of-year celebrations at Dr Blimber's before being taken home.

Chapter 15
Walter consults Captain Cuttle about his future and later helps Susan Nipper to find Polly Toodle and bring her to Paul's bedside.

Chapter 16
Paul dies, after talking of being reunited with his mother in 'the invisible country far away'.

Chapter 17
Walter breaks the news of his imminent departure to Uncle Sol. Captain Cuttle unwittingly increases Carker's enmity towards Walter by exulting in the idea of a 'romance' between him and Florence.

Chapter 18
Paul's funeral. Mr Toots brings Diogenes, the Blimbers' dog, as a present to Florence. Florence approaches her father, but is rebuffed.

Chapter 19
Walter is visited by Florence and Susan, and then by John Carker, before he embarks for Barbados.

Chapter 20
Mr Dombey and Major Bagstock travel by train to Leamington for a holiday. Mr Toodle is their stoker and Mr Dombey is offended by his wearing mourning for Paul.

Chapter 21
Mr Dombey makes the acquaintance, through the Major, of Mrs Skewton and her widowed daughter, Edith.

Chapter 22

John Carker tries in vain to interest his brother in their sister Harriet's health. Mr Dombey has written to withdraw Walter from the *Son and Heir* voyage, but it is too late. Carker terrorises Rob the Grinder and billets him on Sol Gills. Mr Toots attempts to visit Florence and is attacked by Diogenes when stealing a kiss from Susan.

Chapter 23

Florence lives alone in the empty house. She visits the Wooden Midshipman for news of Walter. Captain Cuttle is appealed to and brings Jack Bunsby to pronounce on the likely fate of the *Son and Heir*.

Chapter 24

Florence goes to stay at the Skettles' home and is made uneasy there by a visit from Carker.

Chapter 25

Sol Gills vanishes. Captain Cuttle escapes from Mrs MacStinger's and sets up home at the Wooden Midshipman.

Chapter 26

Mr Dombey's interest in Edith is encouraged by the Major and Mrs Skewton. Carker visits them and works to harden Mr Dombey's heart against Florence and Walter.

Chapter 27

Mr Dombey and his party explore Warwick Castle. He prepares to ask for Edith's hand in marriage. Edith reproaches her mother for her mercenary upbringing.

Chapter 28

Florence, who has been much visited at the Skettles' by Mr Toots, returns home and is introduced to Mrs Skewton and Edith, who is to be her 'new Mama'.

Chapter 29

Mrs Chick breaks with Miss Tox, affecting to be astonished at the discovery of the latter's presumption in aspiring to marry Mr Dombey.

Chapter 30

Edith's fondness for Florence grows. Mr Dombey too softens somewhat towards her. Edith protects Florence from Mrs Skewton's clutches.

Chapter 31

Edith and Mr Dombey are married. Good Mrs Brown is in the crowd. Cousin Feenix makes a wedding speech.

Chapter 32

Mr Toots brings news to Captain Cuttle of the loss of the *Son and Heir*. The Captain visits Mr Carker and discovers his true nature.

Chapter 33

Mr Carker's luxurious but decadent Norwood home is contrasted with that of his brother and sister in North London. Harriet Carker is visited by a kind but mysterious stranger, and then by a 'fallen woman', newly returned from the colonies, to whom she gives some money.

Chapter 34

The woman is revealed as Alice Marwood, daughter of Good Mrs Brown. They are bitter enemies of Mr Carker, who years ago seduced and betrayed Alice. They return the money to Harriet and vent their hatred of the Carker family.

Chapter 35

Mr Dombey and Edith return from their honeymoon. Mr Dombey continues to soften towards Florence until he sees Edith's attachment to her, when his jealousy returns.

Chapter 36

At the grand Housewarming Party, Edith displeases Mr Dombey by making no effort to propitiate his influential guests and he reprimands her in front of Carker.

Chapter 37

Mr Carker uses Edith's love of Florence to form an intimacy with her despite her intense dislike of him.

Chapter 38

Miss Tox in her loneliness takes up with the Toodle family. Rob is becoming more secretive about his work for Mr Carker.

Chapter 39

Captain Cuttle finally, after much demurring, 'bestows his acquaintance' on Mr Toots. Rob abandons the Wooden Midshipman. Mrs MacStinger attempts to reclaim Captain Cuttle, but he is rescued by Bunsby.

Chapter 40

Mr Dombey confronts Edith and she defies him. Edith and her mother travel to Brighton for the latter's health and there encounter Good Mrs Brown and Alice.

Chapter 41

Mr Toots takes Florence to revisit Dr Blimber's. Mrs Skewton dies.

Chapter 42
Mr Dombey employs Carker to 'humble' Edith. In particular, she is to give up her affection for Florence. Mr Dombey has a riding accident.

Chapter 43
Florence creeps to her injured father's room and kisses him while he sleeps. She is disturbed by Edith's passionate despair; Edith says she has no hope but in Florence.

Chapter 44
Susan Nipper at long last confronts the injured Mr Dombey with his neglect of Florence and is summarily dismissed. Mr Toots helps her.

Chapter 45
Carker executes his commission from Mr Dombey to Edith, who realises she must give up Florence.

Chapter 46
Carker plans his desertion of the firm. He is himself spied on by Good Mrs Brown and Alice, via the unsuspecting Rob the Grinder.

Chapter 47
After another confrontation with Mr Dombey, Edith elopes, apparently with Carker. Mr Dombey strikes Florence, who flees from the house.

Chapter 48
Florence finds sanctuary at the Wooden Midshipman. A stranger arranges to meet Captain Cuttle.

Chapter 49
The stranger proves to be Walter, the only survivor of the wreck of the *Son and Heir*.

Chapter 50
Mr Toots is sent in search of Susan Nipper. Walter and Florence declare their love for each other.

Chapter 51
'The world' enjoys the scandal of Edith's elopement.

Chapter 52
Mr Dombey learns, through Good Mrs Brown's interrogation of Rob the Grinder, that Edith and Carker are to meet at Dijon.

Chapter 53
John Carker is dismissed from Dombey and Son because of his hated name. Mr Morfin the Undermanager, Harriet Carker's unknown visitor, pledges

his help. Alice visits Harriet to warn her that Mr Dombey is in pursuit of her brother.

Chapter 54
Edith meets Carker as arranged at Dijon, but only to declare her hatred of him before vanishing from his life. Mr Dombey arrives in pursuit and Carker flees.

Chapter 55
Carker reaches England. At a country railway station he panics when Mr Dombey appears in pursuit, and dies under a train.

Chapter 56
Susan is reunited with Florence. Florence and Walter prepare to be married before going abroad. Mr Toots and Susan go to church to hear the banns being read. Sol Gills returns from the West Indies. Mr Toots and the Game Chicken separate.

Chapter 57
Florence and Walter visit the church where Paul is buried before going on to their wedding. They set sail for China.

Chapter 58
A year has passed. The firm of Dombey and Son has failed. Harriet Carker plans with Mr Morfin to help Mr Dombey financially. She visits the dying Alice and learns from Mrs Brown that Alice and Edith are full cousins. Alice dies.

Chapter 59
Mr Dombey's servants are paid off and the contents of his house auctioned. Only Miss Tox and Polly care for him. On the verge of suicide he is saved by the return of Florence and the two are finally reunited. Florence has a child, born at sea.

Chapter 60
Dr Blimber is handing his school on to Mr Feeder, who is to marry Cornelia Blimber. Susan Nipper is now married to Mr Toots and is pregnant. Captain Cuttle encounters Bunsby being marched to the altar by Mrs MacStinger.

Chapter 61
Having been close to death, Mr Dombey begins to recover under Florence's care. Florence and Edith meet for the last time before Edith leaves to live abroad under the protection of Cousin Feenix.

Chapter 62

The last bottle of the old Madeira is finally opened after Mr Dombey's recovery. Years pass. Mr Morfin and Harriet are married. Sol Gills prospers. The final scene shows Mr Dombey and Florence on the beach with the new little Paul and a new and much beloved little Florence.